D0147258

FORD MADOX FORD

FORD MADOX FORD

A DUAL LIFE

VOLUME I
THE WORLD BEFORE THE WAR

You have a period of muddle, a few of the brightest lads
have a vague idea that something is a bit wrong, and no one
quite knows the answer. As a matter of fact Madox Ford
knew the answer but no one believed him . . .

> (Ezra Pound, 'Harold Monro', *Polite Essays*)

He knew how to invent the truth.

> (Walter Lowenfels, 'The End was Ugly')

Max Saunders

Oxford   New York

OXFORD UNIVERSITY PRESS

1996

Oxford University Press, Walton Street, Oxford OX2 6DP
Oxford New York
Athens Auckland Bangkok Bombay
Calcutta Cape Town Dar es Salaam Delhi
Florence Hong Kong Istanbul Karachi
Kuala Lumpur Madras Madrid Melbourne
Mexico City Nairobi Paris Singapore
Taipei Tokyo Toronto
and associated companies in
Berlin Ibadan

Oxford is a trade mark of Oxford University Press

British Library Cataloguing in Publication Data
Data available

Library of Congress Cataloging in Publication Data
Saunders, Max.
Ford Maddox Ford: a dual life / Max Saunders.
p.   cm.
Includes bibliographical references and index.
1. Ford, Ford Madox, 1873–1939—Biography
2. Authors, English—20th century—Biography.
3. Editors—Great Britain—Biography.
4. Critics—Great Britain—Biography.
I. Title. PR6011.053Z83 1996 823′.912—dc20 95–13548
ISBN 0–19–211789–0

1 3 5 7 9 10 8 6 4 2

Typeset by Pure Tech India Ltd., Pondicherry
Printed in Great Britain
on acid-free paper by
Biddles Ltd.
Guildford and King's Lynn

PREFACE

I desire a little to be remembered as a living man.

(Ford, 'Preface' to *On Heaven*)

Ford Madox Ford wrote some of the best English prose of the twentieth century, mastering and metamorphosing all its major forms: the novel, the memoir, literary criticism, travel writing, even historical and cultural discourse. He was also an innovative and influential poet, as well as the century's greatest literary editor. His energies of creativity and encouragement changed the course of English and American literature. He sustained two of the most constructive literary debates of the era. Joseph Conrad collaborated with him intermittently over ten years, and Ford's memoir, *Joseph Conrad*, remains a milestone in the history of fiction-criticism. The novel techniques they elaborated enabled Ford to write his pre-war masterpiece, *The Good Soldier*, the most powerful portrayal of upper-middle-class Edwardian England, and a work of such brilliance that, according to Rebecca West (who was only slightly exaggerating), it 'set the pattern for perhaps half the novels which have been written since'.[1] His admirers include novelists as diverse as Sinclair Lewis, Sherwood Anderson, Jean Rhys, Graham Greene, V. S. Pritchett, John Hawkes, Alison Lurie, Gore Vidal, William Gass, and Malcolm Bradbury. Anthony Burgess called him 'the greatest British novelist of the century'. Between 1908 and 1912 Ford transformed Ezra Pound's verse as he had earlier transformed his own prose, from medieval and Elizabethan pastiche to a modern idiom, charged by the energies of the vernacular. It was often Ford's critical ideas—such as that 'poetry should be as well written as prose', and that descriptions of objects could express emotional attitudes—for which Pound became the vigorous propagandist. As Donald Davie suspects, Ford's poetics made an impression on the young T. S. Eliot. Pound called Ford 'the man who did the *work* for English writing', and thought that through his (Pound's) mediation Ford also influenced Yeats's later, more conversational style. Poets who have confessed to an admiration for Ford's writing include Allen Tate, W. H. Auden, Robert Lowell, Basil Bunting, and William Carlos Williams.[2]

The period of literary modernism is 'the Ford Era' as much as it is Pound's, T. S. Eliot's, or Joyce's. Ford was at the centre of the three most innovative groups of writers this century. His friends Henry James, Stephen Crane, and Conrad formed what he imagined another friend, H. G. Wells, calling 'a ring of foreign conspirators plotting against British letters'. All these men lived near Rye, where Ford conspired with them about the plotting of novels. Later, in Edwardian London he gathered the best writers together to contribute to his *English Review*, in which he published D. H. Lawrence, Wyndham Lewis, and Pound for the first time in London, next to James, Bennett, Wells, and Hardy. He was associated with the avant-garde groups of Vorticists and Imagists, and he wrote for the Suffragettes. After the Great War, in which he served, and was shell-shocked, Ford moved to Paris. There he founded the *transatlantic review*, bringing together the work of Joyce, Gertrude Stein, Jean Rhys, and Ernest Hemingway. During this second burst of creative engagement, he wrote his post-war masterpiece, the series of four novels now known collectively as *Parade's End*, increasingly recognized as the best English fiction about the war, even as 'the greatest war novel ever written by an Englishman'.[3]

These are his essential claims on our attention. Yet until the 1960s he suffered a scandalous neglect, and most of his seventy-nine books remained out of print. There are personal reasons for this. He was a singular, compellingly unusual person. He infuriated and exasperated as many of those who knew him as he inspired with fierce admiration and loyalty. His writing, too, provokes comparably mixed responses. Many of the writers he knew felt compelled to write about this unassimilable personality, to name and describe him in bizarre ways (which his own writing often anticipated)—as being like a 'friendly walrus', Falstaff, an 'overgrown duckling', an 'animated adenoid', 'Humpty-Dumpty'. He figures not just in literary memoirs, but as Fordian characters in novels by Conrad, May Sinclair, Richard Aldington, Hemingway, Rhys, Wells, and many others—perhaps even Henry James. His private life was at times messy, and messily public. He was an unforgettable raconteur, incapable of telling a story without improving it. His freedom with fact made enemies of friends he wrote about, and earned him a reputation as a liar. This turned into a self-fulfilling travesty, causing many of his true claims to be disbelieved, even when opposed by witnesses no more reliable, or equally adept at fabulation—Conrad and his wife, Violet Hunt, Wells, Rhys, or Hemingway. The accusation of lying has bedevilled Ford's defenders too, who often tangle themselves in tortuous arguments claiming that all fictions are lies, so Ford's lies are simply fictions. His has been a rare case of a biographical smoke-screen obscuring the nature of a creative achievement. It is only now, half-a-century after his death, when most of the personal animosities have burned themselves out, that it becomes possible to gauge and judge: to see, for example, that his outrageousness has more to do with humorous role-playing than vanity or vice; to see the full range of his playful roles, and to see how his self-dramatization in life is reciprocal with his explorations of role-playing in prose, partaking of the same virtues of wry self-awareness. Ford now appears as one of the most fascinating, complex, and entertaining personalities of his age.[4]

Besides personal idiosyncrasies and accidents, there are literary reasons for his uncertain status. He lacked the prudence of James and Eliot; the self-righteousness of Pound; or Joyce's conviction of his own genius. He did not calculate his literary career; need drove him to write pot-boilers. Though he never wrote a lifeless sentence, much of his work is uneven, and he is only occasionally great. He is a transitional figure—a central transforming force of early English modernism. His technical virtuosity puts his work at odds with representative Edwardian performances, yet his experiments in sentiment, romance, reminiscence, and the historical novel look slightly dated beside the ferocious impersonality of Eliot or

Lewis. When literary modernism was defined by examples of authoritarian, male-orientated figures, Ford appeared too diffuse and diverse a writer to count as more than a marginal figure. His apparently relaxed verse looks dated besides Pound's similar experiments in derivation and imitation. *The Good Soldier* seemed out of date when *A Portrait of the Artist as a Young Man* appeared the following year; the first volume of *Parade's End* looks old-fashioned beside *Ulysses*, which preceded it by two years. Yet now Ford's influence on other writers—Conrad, Pound, Lawrence—has become more visible, and his example has proved to be one younger writers could profit from, whereas the techniques of 'The Waste Land', *Finnegans Wake*, or the *Cantos* could be mimicked but scarcely developed. Ford did not go to university, and his virtues are not academic ones. He became a casualty of the academic guardianship of literature: his works are too readable to need the industries of explicators and annotators; a man of extraordinary critical sensibility and penetration, his reminiscences and criticisms are embarrassing to those whose first criterion is scholarly accuracy. But it is mainly by scholars and students that he has recently been read. It has taken more than fifty years for his qualities to come into focus. The difficulty of 'placing' him has led to even his best work being placed outside most canons. As modernism has been reinvestigated, his differences from the 'canonical' authors have become reasons for reading him, and comparing, rather than ignoring him. Indeed, his emphases on fiction, on memory, and on sexuality are helping to redefine modernism.

The *work* of Ford criticism and biography was done first by David Harvey, whose pioneering bibliography charted the magnitude of Ford's creativity; and by Arthur Mizener, who began the exacting task of establishing what facts and dates of Ford's life can be known with any certainty, and of offering critical introductions to many of the little-known novels. Before their books, Ford's biography was riddled with ignorance. Anyone who has studied the primary sources will know how much detective work done by these scholars unobtrusively supports each page of this book. However, the discovery of new material, and three decades of scholarship and interpretation have done much to modify their versions of Ford and his relations with others. In particular, Richard M. Ludwig's edition of Ford's letters has been supplemented by Sondra Stang, who published sixty new letters in her *Reader*, and, with Karen Cochran, produced an annotated edition of Ford's correspondence with Stella Bowen. The fine criticism of Samuel Hynes, Sondra Stang, and Ann Snitow has helped to deepen our understanding of his art. Other studies that have most significantly broadened the biography are: Robert Green's *Ford Madox Ford: Prose and Politics*, which detailed the social and political context which the predominantly formalist studies of the 1960s tended to filter out; *Pound/Ford*, edited by Brita Lindberg-Seyersted, which demonstrated the centrality of their 'literary friendship' to the history of early modernism; *The Return of the Good Soldier: Ford Madox Ford and Violet Hunt's 1917 Diary*, edited by Robert and Marie Secor; the magnificent *Collected Letters of Joseph Conrad*, still being edited by Frederick Karl and Laurence Davies, which is clearing a wilderness of error in the dating and sequence of the correspondence; and

Thomas Moser's *The Life in the Fiction of Ford Madox Ford*. Moser's discovery of Olive Garnett's diary has provided one of the most significant new documents, which I follow him in using extensively. His psycho-biography also broke ground in analysing Ford's mental breakdown, and relating his agoraphobia to his aesthetics. Stang's collection, *The Presence of Ford Madox Ford*, gathered together valuable new reminiscences. Alan Judd's novelistic biography gave a sympathetic portrait of Ford; but his dependence on secondary sources led him to reduplicate Mizener's errors. These are the main developments; there is also a plethora of recent work which includes new information about Ford, particularly in bio-graphies of his contacts—Conrad, Lawrence, Rhys, Caroline Gordon, Katherine Anne Porter—as well as the published correspondence of these and other writers, notably Ezra Pound.[5]

Most importantly, new writings have been discovered. Cornell University bought the manuscripts that had been owned by Ford's daughters, Katharine Lamb and Julia Loewe. These collections included many pieces Harvey had not seen: a wealth of Ford's earliest writings, an unpublished novel among them; his musical compositions; essays, including two important pieces on the First World War; his partial French translation of *The Good Soldier*; many unpublished short stories. A cache of almost sixty letters, cards, and telegrams, and ten poems, all to Elizabeth Cheatham—a lover unknown to previous biographers—appeared when her grandson wrote to Alan Judd. Ford's final partner, Janice Biala, has very kindly let me see some of her letters from Ford, also unavailable to earlier scholars. Cornell acquired a lost batch of Violet Hunt's papers in 1990. Finally, I have discovered over thirty previously unrecorded periodical pieces, including Ford's first reminiscential essay and some revealing short stories.

This study discusses all the new material, offering a new synthesis of critical and biographical research. Our sense of Ford has been restricted by the stereotype of the 'Tory gentleman'. Here the aim has been to bring out the complex relationships between his ideas of art, politics, sexuality, psychology, and the reader.

ACKNOWLEDGEMENTS

It would have been impossible to write this book without the generous co-oper-ation of the person who knew Ford best in his last decade, Janice Biala. Her patience and candour in answering letters and being interviewed have been exemplary. I am particularly grateful for her permission to quote freely from Ford's published and unpublished work, which has enabled me to let Ford's *esprit* and expressiveness manifest itself in his own words; in his books and mauscripts, but also in his marvellous letters, many previously unpublished.

Many others offered help and encouragement. I should like to thank: Chris-topher Ricks for suggesting I should write Ford's biography; Ford's great-nephew, the Hon. Oliver Soskice, for letting me see his family memorabilia, and for his enthusiasm for the project; Alan Judd, for his Fordian absence of rivalry towards a fellow Ford biographer; Dido Davies, for years of sympathetic conversation about (amongst other things) literary biography; Barry Johnson, for sharing his impeccable knowledge of Olive Garnett and her circle; Wil Sanders, for his formidable example as a critic and teacher, and for his conviction of why and how Ford matters; Robert Hampson, for reading the typescript and making scrupulous suggestions; Carole Angier, for detailed help on Jean Rhys. Sondra Stang was generous with her immense knowledge of Ford's works; I am very sorry she did not live to see how much my work owes to her. I am also very grateful to Caradoc King, for being a skilful agent, and to Will Harris, for a summer's conscientious research assistance.

The British Academy generously awarded me two grants to visit Cornell. I am also grateful to the Master and Fellows of Selwyn College, Cambridge, for financial and moral support during the early stages of the project, and to the Department of English Language and Literature, King's College London, for allowing me leave and research assistance to complete it, and for not doubting its existence.

The following contributed information or welcome help and advice: Jane Abraham, Hugh Anson-Cartwright, Doreen Batchelor, Claire Daunton, Oliver Davies, Philip Davis, Mike Dooley, Herbert Eaton, Jennifer Fitzgerald, Dr Oliver Flint, Richard Garnett, H. Joachim Gerke, James Gindin, Tom Goldwasser, Robert Gomme, Joy Grant, Sue Gray, David Dow Harvey, Sara Haslam, Eric Homberger, Peter Howard of Serendipity Books, Dr Anton Wilhelm Hüffer, Peter Hutchinson, Lawrence Iles, Alexander R. James, George Jefferson, Frede-rick Karl, Sir Frank Kermode, John Lamb, Mark Samuels Lasner, Clive Lewis, Walton Litz, Alison Lurie, Maynard Mack, Lady Mander, Neville Masterman, Jeremy Maule, Ann Lee Michell, Arthur and Rosemary Mizener, Julian Nangle, Teresa Newman, Lucy O'Conor, Ian Patterson, Adrian Poole, Eric Quayle, Sally Sanderlin, Robert and Marie Secor, Paul Skinner, Richard Stang, Oliver Stonor, Lady Stow Hill, Tony Tanner, Nancy Tennant, Michael Tilby, Nora Tomlinson,

David Trotter, Bruce A. White, Caroline White, Mrs William A. P. White, Joe Wiesenfarth, Sir John Winnifrith, Joan Winterkorn.

The largest collection of Ford's manuscripts and letters is in the Olin Library, Cornell University. I am grateful to two of its librarians, Donald D. Eddy and Mark Dimunation, for permission to read and quote from the material and to their friendly and professional staff for making my visits so enjoyable, particularly James Tyler, Lucy B. Burgess, Janet Carruthers, and Lynne Farrington, for their apparently tireless efforts and courtesy; and also Denise R. Barbaret, Katie Bevington, Nick Halmi, and Lois Fischler. Princeton University Library and the Beinecke Rare Book and Manuscript Library of Yale University hold the other major collections. I am grateful to the librarians of both for copying material for me, and allowing me to quote from it.

I am grateful to the following libraries and institutions for their help, and, in most cases, for permission to quote from their holdings or reproduce illustrations: BBC Written Archives Centre; Hulton Picture Library (BBC); University Library, University of Birmingham; Bodleian Library, Oxford; British Library; British Library Newspaper Library, Colindale; British Library of Political and Economic Science; Brotherton Collection, Leeds University Library; State University of New York at Buffalo; Calderdale District Archives, Halifax; University Library, Cambridge; Canterbury, The King's School; Case Western Reserve University, Cleveland, Ohio; University of Chicago, Joseph Regenstein Library; Columbia University; Library of Congress; Constable & Co. Ltd.; Dartmouth College Library; Delaware Art Museum; Dorset County Museum; East Sussex County Record Office, Lewes; University of Edinburgh Library; Essex Record Office; General Registers Office; Giessen Stadtarchiv; Glasgow University Library; the Houghton Library, Harvard University; House of Lords Record Office; Huntington; University of Illinois at Urbana-Champaign; Indiana University Library; Institute of Historical Research; Kenneth Spencer Research Library, University of Kansas; King's College Library, Cambridge; Mairies de Paris; Manchester City Art Gallery; Convent of the Holy Child, Mayfield, East Sussex; Museum of Broadcasting, New York; NBC; University of Nevada, Reno; Northwestern University Library; the Henry W. and Albert A. Berg Collection, New York Public Library; Octopus Publishing Group Library; Olivet College; Oxford University Press, New York; The English Centre of International PEN; Van Pelt Library, University of Pennsylvania; Public Record Office; University of Reading Library; Royal Commission on Historical Manuscripts; Rutgers University Libraries; National Library of Scotland; Southend Central Library; University of Sussex Library; Office of Population Censuses and Surveys, General Register Office, St Catharine's House; Harry Ransom Humanities Research Centre, University of Texas; Theatre Museum, London; Tower Hamlets Health Authority; University Library, UCLA; The Jean and Alexander Heard Library, Vanderbilt University; University of Victoria, British Columbia; Washington University, St Louis; Witt Library, Courtauld Institute of Art.

I should like to thank: Caroline White for permission to quote from Olive Garnett's diary, and from Ann Lee Michell's annotated typescript selection from it; Richard Garnett, for permission to quote from family papers and reproduce photographs; and the Trustees of the Joseph Conrad Estate, for permission to quote from Conrad's unpublished letters.

Earlier versions of parts of this book have appeared in *Agenda* and the introduction to the Everyman's Library edition of *The Good Soldier*. I am grateful to the editor and publisher respectively for permission to incorporate the revised version here.

For permission to quote I should also like to thank the following publishers: Bartletts Press, for excerpts from *Tea and Anarchy!* and *Olive & Stepniak*, ed. Barry Johnson; John Calder (Publishers) Ltd., for excerpts from Wyndham Lewis's *Blasting and Bombardiering*; Cambridge University Press, for excerpts from the *Collected Letters of Joseph Conrad*, ed. Frederick R. Karl and Laurence Davies, and *The Letters of D. H. Lawrence*, ed. James T. Boulton; Jonathan Cape Ltd., for excerpts from 'Daniel Chaucer', *The New Humpty-Dumpty*, Ford's *The Good Soldier*, Ford and Hunt's *Zeppelin Nights*, and Arthur Mizener's *The Saddest Story*; Chapman & Hall Ltd., for excerpts from Ford's *Ancient Lights*; Chatto & Windus, for excerpts from David Garnett's *The Golden Echo*; Constable & Co. Ltd., for excerpts from Douglas Goldring's *South Lodge*; Gerald Duckworth & Co. Ltd., for excerpts from Ford's *Joseph Conrad*; Faber & Faber (Publishers) Ltd., for excerpts from *Pound/Ford: The Story of a Literary Friendship*, ed. Brita Lindberg-Seyersted; Victor Gollancz Ltd., for excerpts from Ford's *Return to Yesterday*; William Heinemann Ltd., for excerpts from Ford's *The Good Soldier*; Princeton University Press, for excerpts from *Letters of Ford Madox Ford*, ed. Richard M. Ludwig; Martin Secker & Warburg Ltd., for excerpts from Ford's *Henry James* and Samuel Hynes's *The Edwardian Turn of Mind*.

To Alfred and Diana Cohen

CONTENTS

LIST OF ILLUSTRATIONS

FORD'S PATERNAL LINE

Johann Hermann Hüffer 1784–1855 = (1) 1812 Amalia Hosius 1789–1825

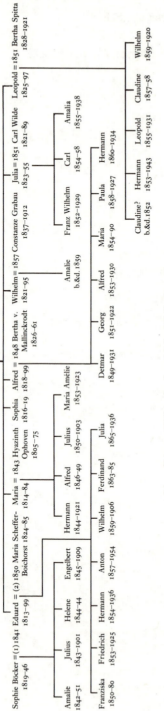

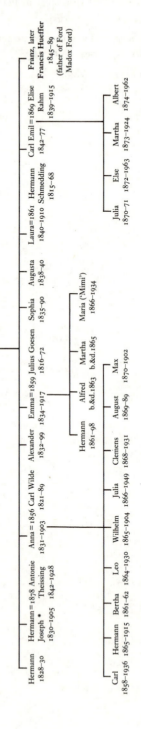

Johann Hermann Hüffer 1784–1855 = (2) 1827 Julia Kaufmann 1809–70

Franz, later Francis Hueffer 1845–89 (father of Ford Madox Ford)

This drawing is designed to show all Ford's paternal uncles, cousins, and aunts. It is derived from 'Die Hüffer', in Wilhelm Schulte, *Westfälische Köpfe* (Munster: Verlag Aschendorff, 1963), which gives further information about the cousins' marriages and descendants.

* This was the uncle Hermann who was a professor in History at Bonn.
Ford's paternal grandfather had 17 children by two wives. His youngest child, Franz Hüffer, born when he was 61, became the father of Ford Hueffer, who changed his name to Ford Madox Ford.

The year of marriage is given after the '=' sign

FORD'S MATERNAL LINE AND DESCENDANTS

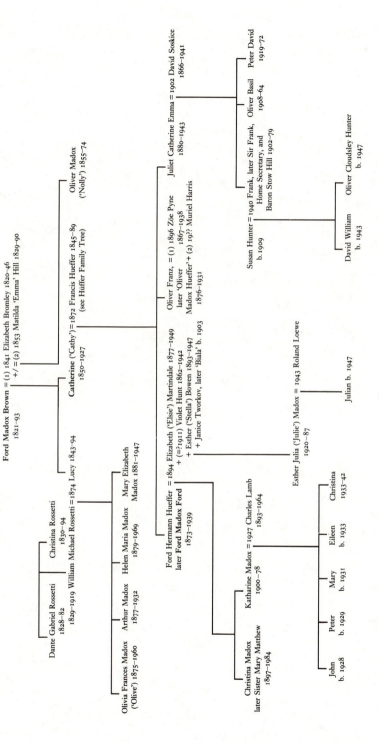

Notes: the year of marriage is given after the '=' sign
the sign '+' is used to indicate unmarried couples living together

INTRODUCTION

In the realm of fiction we find the plurality of lives we need.

(Freud, 'Thoughts for the Times on War and Death')

Ford Madox Ford was born in June 1919, aged 45. The birth was a rebirth, as the dual re-christening suggests. Ford Madox Hueffer—who had already partly anglicized his name from Ford Hermann Hueffer by deed poll in July 1915, although he had been writing as Ford Madox Hueffer since 1900—finally changed his name to Ford Madox Ford by another deed poll on 4 June 1919; and on 24 June; and on 28 June. The first two dates mark the beginning and end of the legal process: the deed poll is dated 4 June, and it was 'Enrolled in the Central Office of the Supreme Court of Judicature' on the 24th. But what about the 28th? Why did he write to at least three friends giving that as the date of the transformation? Why did he want to transform the chronology as well as the dramatis persona?

Ford's biography is inseparable from such questions. Reviewing a *Life and Letters* of Joseph Conrad he wrote: 'The Poet—and particularly the poor devil so harried as was Conrad—must have escape from the world, anodynes, and drugs of which the lay public has neither need or knowledge. One of these is to *Poetiser un peu*—to romance a little when he talks of himself. Then that romance becomes part of himself and is the true truth.'[1] This is characteristic in the way it reflects upon Ford's own self, without being any less true of the other (as Conrad's biographers keep discovering). Most of his writing is obliquely, but inescapably, autobiographical. Like his own criticism, it poses a quality of 'personality' as the transcendent origin of the works of literature, which is expressed by those works. The writing always looks searchingly beyond itself, towards the personality of the artist. Such 'personality' is a biographical quality, though it may not be capturable by the biographical quantities of names and dates, by the category of factual, archival 'truth' which Ford opposes to 'the true truth', the artist's romance of the self. He understood how he too would 'romance a little when he talks of himself'; and he understood the complementary truth that the romance became a part of himself. For example, he was pleased to accept the—probably fictional—Ruthenian ancestors he said Conrad 'rooted out' for him. 'I prefer to think that one of my great grandfathers came from Poland in the ranks of Poniatowski's legion', said Ford: 'Certainly I should prefer to consider that what Slav blood I had was Polish rather than Russian in origin [. . .] Poles seem more romantic than Russians.'[2] Such preferences pose a crucial problem for Ford's biography. How far should one point reprovingly at his inaccuracies, as Arthur Mizener relentlessly did? Ford's wish for Ruthenian ancestry may not tell us anything factual about his genealogy, but it does tell us much about his imagination: about his desire to reinvent himself and history; and about his intellectual kinship with the Polish romancer Conrad. Ford's biography must be doubly responsible: responsive to both the factual and the fictive; to what the fictions express, not just what they repress; and to how the given facts get doubled by their literary transmutations: to how the romanced selves became a part of—but did not simply depart from—the former self; to how the reproduced 'Ford' both is and is not the same as the original Ford.

Changing names made it harder to confuse Ford with his brother, also a writer, Oliver Madox Hueffer. But it sowed as much confusion as it cleared. The two Hueffers were not one, but were Ford Madox Hueffer and Ford Madox Ford two? A change of name in mid-career is a dangerous decision for a writer, whose sales depend on the familiarity of his name. There were, however, other reasons why Ford wanted to distance himself from his 'Hueffer' self. In 1909 he had left his wife for the novelist Violet Hunt, and he and Hunt claimed to be married. When in 1912 a newspaper glossed Violet as 'Mrs Ford Madox Hueffer', Elsie Hueffer sued. By 1919 Ford was estranged from Hunt and had begun a new relationship, with the Australian painter Stella Bowen. With two women already claiming to be Ford's wife, Stella could not become another Mrs Hueffer. The desire for respectability was satisfied by Ford—once again working faction into fiction—introducing Stella as 'Mrs Ford'.[3]

Although Ford's change of name may register the wish, or the need, to escape, it also recognizes the impossibility of escaping, revisiting as it does its origin, and re-creating the self in its own image. If we say that in turning from Hueffer to Ford he was proclaiming that he was not his father's man, but now his own, we should also note that the second 'Ford' is not self-regarding, but a sign of love and allegiance to his maternal grandfather, Ford Madox Brown. (The 'Madox' was also a name assumed by Ford, which he began to add to his given name 'Ford Hermann Hueffer', first as the initial 'M.', then as a middle name, in his earliest publications.)[4]

These are personal reasons, but also ones which touch on his public identity: nationality, celebrity, publicity, artistic heritage, religion, even marital status. The very act of naming or renaming publishes the private. Even in such an apparently un-literary activity as changing his name, he is revealed as the complete writer, rewriting his own identity. He may have been thinking of (Józef Teodor) Konrad Korzeniowski's metamorphosis into Joseph Conrad; he certainly thought of pseudonymity and writing as connected, telling a story of how Conrad first thought of becoming a writer when he saw on a station bookstall a row of books in Edward Garnett's Pseudonym Library.[5] Other names might have answered to most of the needs. But, as in his greatest writing, Ford mastered his predicament, fixing on a curiously double name which also reflects one of his most pervasive and profound senses of his own life: the sense of being a dual person, what he described as *homo duplex*.

It is an idea which informs much in his life and work: the difference between his various selves, especially between his pre-war and post-war incarnations; the similarities he found between himself and others. But it particularly stands for the writer as someone who is, precisely, both a life and its works: a private person who makes his living, and earns his life in literature, as a public 'personality'. 'Ford Madox Ford' is a self-created character, someone inviting (while challenging and resisting) public scrutiny, anticipating analyses of his motives. But instead of being the role-playing of a flamboyant poseur, it is a character which expresses the duality of the literary life. The memorable doubleness of name juxtaposes, as literary biography must, the 'true truth' of the personality enshrined in the *œuvre* with the archival truths about the artist's person to which that personality cannot be reduced.

It is possible that the official confirmation of the deed poll arrived on 28 June; but there is a more powerful reason why he wanted the story of Ford Madox Ford to begin on this date: it was the day the Treaty of Versailles was signed. He had served in the army for three-and-a-half years, had been in the Battle of the Somme, and was now recuperating from shell-shock and from lung-damage brought on by pneumonia and possibly also poison gas. All his post-war writings treat the war as he had (in 1911) described the Boer War: as 'a chasm separating the new world from the old', 'the end of everything'.[6] The title *Parade's End* which Ford chose for his tetralogy of novels about the Great War stands for the fracture in English Society which both precipitated and was revealed by the war. 'Parade'—the ceremony and convention of imperial pomp—is no longer credible. It is no longer even effective at papering over the cracks it was meant to prevent. Ford also saw the war as making a decisive break in his own life. He wrote of having taken his 'formal farewell' of literature in a way which intimates that he did not expect to be returning.[7]

When he did, he had come through experiences that were like death, including a mental breakdown in which he could not remember his own name (an experience that perhaps suggested the idea of changing it). So in his first published post-war book he plays 'an insubstantial ghost, revisiting the light of a moon I had purposed never to see again'. *Thus to Revisit* (1921) takes its title from *Hamlet*:

> What may this mean,
> That thou, dead corpse, again in complete steel,
> Revisitst thus the glimpses of the moon [. . .][8]

He habitually renames the war 'Armageddon', which recognizes its destructiveness, as well as its effect of turning survivors into their own ghosts. But it also indicates that the Judgement is past; that fear of Hell, together with the hellish torments of war, are over; that the survivors have been reprieved.[9] Ford's reminiscences of this period in *It Was the Nightingale* recount his post-war life as a new beginning. The beginning of the book images Ford's release from army service as a rebirth: 'Naked came I from my mother's womb. On that day I was nearly as denuded of possessions.' It is an example of Ford's bringing to bear upon the facts of history what Ernst Cassirer called the 'mythic consciousness', which 'does not see human personality as something fixed and unchanging, but conceives every *phase* of a man's life as a new personality, a new self; and this metamorphosis is first of all made manifest in the changes which his name undergoes'.[10] This mythic view of self-transformation is a vital part of Ford's literary personality; though it is always complemented by his search for the continuities of selfhood. His acts of autobiography are myths of the self, but also recuperations of past selves. *No Enemy*, for example, the first substantial prose work Ford was able to complete after the war, is subtitled 'A Tale of Re-Construction'. He sounds the full symbolic range of the term. Like most of his post-war writing, *No Enemy* explores an interrelated variety of reconstructive projects: how to rehabilitate the damaged, shell-shocked individual psyche; how to repair the physical damage to bodies, buildings, landscapes, nations; how to reconstitute the social order; and how to find the 'new form', a new technique of construction, for prose.

The beginning of his new life coincides with the new life of the post-war world, which Ford described as 'being reborn' on Armistice Day. He too felt at peace, with himself and the world, after a long and enervating period of being harried by entanglements and scandal (both domestic and literary). Thus the shifting of the deed poll date allies the private and the public. 'I wanted my change of name to take effect exactly on the day when the peace terms were signed and the world was to begin again.'[11] It is characteristic of his desire to improve upon fact. If these 'improvements' can seem self-aggrandizing—especially when nervous strain drives him into self-exculpation, or feelings of persecution—they are morally innocuous. He sometimes felt it necessary to tell Americans that he had been to a 'great public school', occasionally substituting Eton or Westminster for University College School (which his audiences would probably not have heard of). Such white lies were not intended as facts, but rather to give the impression of someone representative of, and authoritative about, the ruling classes. His claim—probably false—to have married Violet Hunt should probably be seen as another white lie: a fabrication meant to make life easier. In fact it made things much worse. Such fictions violated the English taboos about class and sex, and consolidated the impression of a liar with that of a cad, causing lasting damage to his literary reputation.[12] His transformations of reality forgo the truth of a lawyer or historian, to bring out what for him was always the truer truth; the symbolic truth: that he did know English upper-class society from the inside; that he and Hunt did live as man and wife; or, in the case of his change of name, that after the death-trauma of the Somme, a man could be reborn. He wrote a youthful essay called 'Creative History and the Historic Sense'.[13] His change of name shows him re-creating the history of his self, but in terms of what he called *A History of Our Own Times*. As in his fiction, he needed to change himself in order to find himself.

It is emblematic of the way his writing changes his life; the way his romances become a part of himself. He lived a life among stories. His friends consistently testify to how time spent with Ford was time spent being entertained with Fordian anecdotes. He kept retelling his favourite ones throughout his life, although they were never the same twice. Like a jazz musician improvising around a standard tune, he would highlight, embellish, and often transform those tales which had been most formative. There is nothing surprising about that. Folk-tales, too, need random mutations in order to evolve and survive. What is curious about Ford's stories is how they alter details about real people as well as imaginary details. He seems not to recognize a meaningful distinction between fact and fiction, or when he acknowledges that there might be such a distinction, it is to dismiss it as pedantic. He offers as an aesthetic principle what, according to the conventional separation between memoir and fiction, has often been construed as irresponsibility. He called the principle 'impressionism', defining it—pre-emp-tively—in his first volume of reminiscences, *Ancient Lights* (1911): 'This book, in short, is full of inaccuracies as to facts, but its accuracy as to impressions is absolute [. . .] I don't really deal in facts, I have for facts a most profound contempt. I try to give you what I see to be the spirit of an age, of a town, of a movement. This can not be done with facts' (pp. xv–xvi). The language here reveals the paradox: 'I don't *really* deal in facts.' But he does deal in 'unreal' facts: statements which have the logical form of facts, but not their relation to a verifiable objective reality. All fiction needs to look as though it *could* correspond to the world, though it need not. But the paradox of fiction's pseudo-factuality is particularly heightened in Ford's case because his method depends so heavily on the appearance of factual precision. His successes are made possible by their scrupulous accumulation of particularities. Whether he describes a medieval castle, the court of Henry VIII, an Edwardian country house, or a dugout in the trenches, the authenticity and power of illusion is sustained by strategic and telling details.

To call this method 'impressionism' can be misleading, since instead of the glows and hazes of Impressionist painting, Ford's surfaces scintillate with the glints of hard edges, dazzling clarities. What his writing does have in common with the painting of Monet or Renoir is the concentration on the act of perception. Consciousness is his subject, rather than the objects of that conscious-ness. Literary impressionism is thus concerned with how facts make an impression on the mind, how objects impress themselves upon the subject.

The objection to the method is that it is inconceivable that impressions can be divorced entirely from the facts that produced them. When, as often happens, Ford chooses to exaggerate details—and the exaggeration is usually evident, and carried off with relish—the effects he gets can be humorously vivid. When he describes his childhood as spent being intimidated by the 'Middle Victorian, tumultuously bearded Great', we do not have to believe—the overstatement oppresses us into *dis*believing—that everybody he met as a child was either 'Great' or 'tumultuously bearded', in order to get a memorable impression of how a small boy could be daunted by the towering and energetic personalities who befriended his father and his grandfather.[14]

But his rewriting of anecdotes can go so far that one becomes sceptical of the authenticity of the impression given, if it could be given by such divergent circumstances. Reviewing Thomas Hardy's volume of stories, *A Changed Man*, in 1913, Ford wrote for the first time about an episode that recurs through his later reminiscences. At a house-party given by 'a hospitable but militant atheist of the 1880 type' (the later versions identify him as Edward Clodd, and the house as at Aldeburgh), Ford is astonished by a confession Hardy made. In the later versions Hardy's 'shy avowal' is that he is a practising Anglican.[15] But the first version has Hardy announcing 'from the shadows that he believed in ghosts'; and then proceeding to tell a gruesome ghost tale:

I don't know how many of us believed in ghosts till that moment, but I will bet that every one of us, whilst that tale was telling—the tale of the midwife carried off through the darkness to Littlecote, of the throwing of the newborn child into the fire, of the woman's cutting the little piece from the bed-curtains, by means of which she afterwards identified the place—I will bet anything you like that every one of us—including our host—for the time being believed in the ghost of Wild Darrell![16]

Both confessions are of a belief in the supernatural, of course; but the difference between belief in God and belief in ghosts matters for a writer like Hardy; and the first is (philosophically) much more surprising than the second. We can grant that Ford's surprise at the avowal is what motivates his telling and retelling, and even that the fact of the emotion is perhaps more important than the facts which produced it. But we might still wonder whether the same kind of surprise would be produced by both confessions. Is it then a case in which to change the facts is to change the entire impression? So at least the argument could run if we did not also have a third variation, written in Ford's obituary notice for Hardy. Here, the mystery is cleared up: Hardy first confessed his Anglicanism, then later told the ghost story, at the same party.[17] This version brings out more clearly than the others why it was that seeing Hardy as a changed man made Ford feel a changed man himself. It is that relationship between belief and story-telling which so fascinated him: the dual paradox whereby Hardy, the Anglican who in his novels appears a sceptic, can, through telling a story, transform his sceptical listeners into momentary believers. It was because of this that it was 'the most memorable tale-telling' Ford ever attended.

One of the friends who later turned on Ford for the way he told memorable but changed tales about his own life was Archibald Marshall, who had worked for the firm Alston Rivers, one of Ford's publishers from 1905 to 1907. Marshall quotes Ford's impressions of this period from *Return to Yesterday*, adding exasperatedly:

Has there ever before been anything quite like this in a book of personal reminiscences—detailed accounts of actual events, with names mentioned, every statement in which is either deliberately untrue or inaccurate? You must not go to Hueffer, he warns you in his preface, for 'factual accuracies'. Well, no, you wouldn't. But the accuracy of his impressions, which he does invite you to go to him for, is not more trustworthy. You are told that something which never happened at all was one of the most disagreeable episodes in which he has ever been concerned, and facts are invented to give it colour. There is no truth to be found anywhere.[18]

The stories about Hardy show—as do the rather trivial details Marshall fixes on, such as Ford's misremembering of the names and activities of publishers a quarter-of-a-century earlier—how what Ford generally does is something much less drastic than fabricating entire episodes; instead, he selects and modifies aspects, sometimes emphasizing one and sometimes another, to bring out the multiple significances of a situation. He had too full and vivid a life not to confuse some of its dates and circumstances. Marshall had personal reasons for his attack. A disappointed author, he came to believe that Ford's help and influence had been what prevented him from writing saleable books. *Return to Yesterday* rankled, not only because by 1931 Ford had been selling better than ever before, but because Marshall felt its mention of him to be a denigration. Ford said that he agreed to Northcliffe's request that he should help Marshall edit the *Daily Mail* Books Supplement, adding: 'It meant that I could pretty well set the pace of that periodical myself.' Marshall's pique is evident, when he asks: 'He doesn't rate me very high, does he?'[19] His denial of the truth of Ford's *impressions* is not cogent, because he does not grasp what Ford meant by impressions. Nevertheless, Ford's disregard for fact remains at the centre of the controversy surrounding his life and reputation. Even though scholars have vindicated Ford's truthfulness in many of the crucial instances, his reputation for lying has persisted.

Lies need to be judged according to their use, and Ford did not lie in order to make money, cheat, steal, libel, propagandize, or kill. Edward Shanks, an acquaintance who said that in his lifetime there had been 'no more remarkable character in the whole world of English Literature' than Ford, thought that though sometimes Ford would lie 'for definite ends', or sometimes as 'the romantic liar who lies for self-magnification or simply for fun', it was his habit of being untruthful 'for no discoverable reason' that seemed 'incalculable, baffling, and even sometimes frightening'. Rebecca West thought that way with truth was something quite other than lying: 'Liars see facts as they are and transform them into fantasies, but in Ford's case facts changed to fantasies in the very instant of their impact on his senses.'[20] The fantasies themselves changed over time. His differing versions of the same memories are usually written far apart in time and place: even if he had wanted to, it would have often been difficult for him to locate earlier versions. But the important point is that he tried never to tell the same story in quite the same way. He never had the compulsive liar's tricks of denying that he had said whatever he was being accused of having said, or of accusing someone else of having said it. He stood by his words, by his impressions, frankly avowing their dual relation to fact—their superimposing fictional portrayals upon the portrayals of actual persons, as a historical novelist fictionalizes the factual past. Where a historian or psychologist might find no 'discoverable reason' for Ford's reimaginations, a critic can find literary reasons: that Ford wanted to tell ever new, ever better stories.

Controversies incite single-minded polemic; and though it is a travesty to call Ford a liar, an unequivocal rebuttal would miss a fundamental quality of his art, and of his literary personality. The fact that he risked the charge is revealing. If the vehemence of most of the attacks made on him seems far in excess of any provocation, one must concede that his contemporaries did find him variously provocative. This is in turn something that his writing has been accused of falsifying. His own comment has a disingenuous glint: 'My life through I seem to have been mixed up in terrific rows with people who appeared singularly touchy. This is probably my own fault. I suppose I've always rather liked teasing public characters and public characters must dislike being teased more than I imagined they did.'[21] It presents magnanimity ('probably my own fault') and humour ('teasing public characters') in such a way as to suggest that it could not possibly be Ford's fault if offence were taken where none was meant. Arthur Mizener, glossing this passage, wrote of 'the extent to which Ford's fanciful impression of events governed his conception of reality. The cause of his difficulties remained incomprehensible to him [. . .] Thus it was that Ford stirred up the enmities that seemed to him so undeserved.' To argue that Ford improved the stories of his life to flatter and justify himself, but could not see how provocative this could be, is to cast him as doubly obtuse: as blind to the effects of his narrations as to their causes. This is, to say the least, implausible about a writer who was a lifelong champion of 'conscious artistry'. When he writes, 'I am a perfectly self-conscious writer; I know exactly how I get my effects, as far as those effects go', is it possible that he could be so conscious of himself *as* a writer without being as conscious of himself as a man—of the effects he produced in life as well as in literature?[22] Of course such protestations might be smoke-screens designed to keep repressed knowledge out of conscious view. However, Ford's best writing confronts any such tendency towards self-justification or self-deceit in the portrait of Christopher Tietjens in *Parade's End*, for example, which charts with great sensitivity and imagination exactly why it is that Tietjens provokes his persecutors or as here, where there is more than a hint of teasing the reader with a *faux-naïveté* that is certain to provoke the kind of row Ford is disavowing. Ford knew—and his novels make it clear he knew—that his rows also sprang from sources other than teasing: from his sexual and financial embarrassments; from misunderstandings in business and in friendship; from pain, anguish, and humiliation. He knows that his readers may know this too—especially since they were likely to include the very people with whom he had had the rows. He also knew that 'public characters' have their private sensitivities, and that it is hard to tease one without vexing the other.

These issues have necessitated some rethinking of what a properly 'critical biography' of Ford would be. Biographical criticism will try to explain the fiction in terms of the life. Because one gets arresting glimpses of Ford's personal experiences beneath the veils of fiction, and because most of his writing incites and resists biographical curiosity, it is always tempting us to speculate about the kind of *man* who is veiling himself in his writing. At times his fictions even provided the raw material for his life—causing acquaintances to call him 'a self-invented character', a figure who might have stepped out of one of his own books. On the other hand, he is an eloquent champion of the artist's need of privacy. And whereas the critical orthodoxy of the 1950s and 1960s forbade such speculations, arguing that art should achieve autonomy from its sources, which renders statements about an artist's intentions fallacious, Ford had a more challenging—and more intelligent—view of the way intentions, or personality, can be expressed in the work. His imaginative prose embodies his untold stories.

Despite the claim that biographical criticism 'uses fiction to explain life, life to explain fiction', it has none the less ultimately been more committed to the latter.[23] Such approaches use Ford's writing to support an account of his life—a life which, because of his reticences, is unusually irrecoverable as documented history. But the main emphasis is to 'explain' the fiction by means of this 'life'; to ground it on biography, and thus give it biographical rather than artistic or critical significance. The writing is repeatedly treated as a symptom of mental distress, sexual involvement, parental anxiety. Up to a point this approach can be valuable, telling us much about how it is that certain characters and events come to be in the works (and often, to recur in them). But it can also be severely limiting, particularly when it fails to distinguish between subject-matter and technical treatment; between the given experiences that artists bring to their work, and the works of art they make out of their experiences.

Both Mizener and Moser recognize that the imagination which produced some of the century's indispensable prose is inextricable from the imagination that used constantly to re-imagine its own past, and to heighten reminiscences into tall stories. Yet their methods tend to belittle the writing, by seeing it ultimately as neurotic distortion rather than conscious elaboration and transformation of reality. Ford (they argue) cannot bear his problems and his lack of recognition, so he fantasizes better versions of his life and self. Subjected to this reading, the art is of interest in so far as it can be shown to interpret the life; but the interpretation it offers is of a man too irresponsible, self-obsessed, and limited to merit serious attention. Even Ford's uneven works are more valuable, and more subtle, than his biographers have made them sound. If one listens closely enough, Ford's prose tells another story: the story of an imaginative life, rather than of a fatuously imaginary one. His characteristic effects exploit our sense of their duality, of a felt discrepancy between what we read and what we know (or suspect); and this produces a particularly engaging dual effect in the reader.

Ford's life can only be understood by doing justice to the stories within which he lived and moved. Because we read literary biographies to discover more about an *author*, the *œuvre* should be where a truly *critical* biography begins and ends. Ford's sixty-five full years spent at centres of creative activity in Europe and America generated vast amounts of other kinds of evidence, and of course this must be taken into account. But the most important events in his life are his creations, and these should not be subordinated as footnotes to the less significant story of where he sat down each day to write his pages, and how much he was paid for them. Ford's own criticism is alive with subtle suggestions of how what is most personal and individual in a writer is often at odds with, or shielded by, a public persona. He wrote eloquently about how the study of writers' minds is inextricable from a study of their styles, and demonstrated a sane wariness about how their art might reveal more than their apparently artless self-revelations. His own memoirs give a truthful picture of his mind exercising its transforming and formalizing power on the past. He was committed to the belief that 'the real lives of men are enshrined in their products', and argued forcefully that the stern Victorian monster, the 'official biography' (come back to haunt us as the baggy monster of 'definitive' biography), was more likely to sound the death-knell of its subject than to render the real life. 'But then comes the Official Biography . . . and the poor man dies', he wrote, 'no man being willing to read an author's books when he can read salacious, moral, or merely imbecile details about the Great Man's . . . say, affection for his doggie-doggies.' Ford himself is too massive and paradoxical a figure to succumb so quietly—he has already survived five-and-a-half biographies—but he is in danger of ossification.[24] A belletristic caricature of him walks, like the living dead, through a host of literary reminiscences, rehearsing, with stultifying regularity, the same anecdotes and foibles.

'Ford was incapable of simplicities', wrote one disciple. His attitude to biography is characteristic of his capable grasp of the complexity of any situation. While mistrustful of biography's tendency to distract attention from an artist's works, he constantly used biographical material and approaches, though always with a sense of what they could reveal about art. When he wrote that 'almost all writers would prefer to be remembered by their imaginations rather than by their records', he is clearly generalizing from an autobiographical insight—and one which touches on the central question of literary biography, of why someone becomes a writer.[25] His first—and almost his only—book of non-fiction was itself an 'official biography', *Ford Madox Brown: A Record of his Life and Work*, written as an act of devotion to his grandfather, and published when its author was only 22. What he detested about Victorian 'official biography' was the whitewashing of lives into moral examples. Yet he always used biography, in his lifelong writing about other writers and artists, with wit and penetration. One of his American characters says of taciturn and obliquely allusive Englishmen: 'You had to know their life story before you could understand them.' One could take this as the motto for some of his best *Portraits from Life*, in which a biographical anecdote illuminates an author's work: as when Hardy confides that he is a practising Anglican, or Wells lectures Ford on 'the theory of protective colouring in birds' while relating 'the whole of his biography'—his 'official biography'—for Ford to retell to others in order to cast some 'protective colouring' over Wells's exploits.[26] These are both fine instances of the inextricability of imaginations and records; and of Ford's subtle sense of how writers' self-revelations shade off into self-protections: how, though their autobiographies be fictions, their fictions are their truest autobiographies. Ford's greatest demonstration of this is his *Joseph*

Conrad, subtitled 'A Personal Remembrance', in memory not only of the man, but of Conrad's own reminiscences (partly dictated to Ford), *A Personal Record*. It is the best elaboration of how the real—the significant—lives of writers are enshrined in their products. What he wrote later about his intimate collaborator is doubly true—as true of himself as of Conrad: 'The novel was, in fact, his religion, his country, his unchanging home and his only real means of communication with his fellow beings. So that really to know Conrad you had to read all his books and then to fuse the innumerable Conrads that are in all of them into what used to be called a composite photograph.'[27]

Ford wrote to Galsworthy: 'When one reads a book one is always wondering what kind of man the writer is—as writer be it said.' But to put it that way is to raise the very question you then erase: the question of what kind of *man* the writer is. The point that Ford's criticism makes with originality and tact is that the kind of *man* a writer is is a *writer*, and it is impossible to understand one without the other: 'to know the really extraordinarily Promethean quality of Conrad's mind'— and Ford's—'you had to realize that he was always acting a part [. . .] He had to make his desperate sorties into the wearisome and disreputable pursuit of weaving innumerable lies.' The uncertainty there about whether the role-playing and lying are characteristics of Conrad as man or as writer is to the point. Douglas Goldring's sympathetic account of Ford suggests how Ford was recognizing in Conrad what he knew in himself: 'In his presentation of himself [. . .] he gave a protean performance which enabled him to hide under a multiplicity of romantic disguises.'[28]

My aims are to wonder at the kind of man Ford is as a writer; to ask how he became that writer; to investigate what happened *while* he was writing, as well as while he wasn't; to consider the implications for biography of Janice Biala's comment that 'His true private life and the one far more difficult to write . . . is his inner life, the one that produced the books, not the gossip'; and to attempt something like a composite portrait of Ford as revealed in his books. Ford's example suggests a new approach to literary biography's perpetual problem of how to tell the two stories (the life, the work) in one narrative. Eliot's influential post-Romantic attempt to separate the two created an unease about the form of literary biography. If it is true that 'the more perfect the artist, the more completely separate in him will be the man who suffers and the mind which creates', then the story of the man who suffered is either largely irrelevant to his creativity, or reveals the imperfections of his art.[29] It was a salutary corrective in 1919, when aesthetics was obscured by the suffering of war. But Ford's case shows how an artist's objective presentation of his suffering is not the same as a 'separation' from it. Like all artists, he was not always perfect. But he is the kind of artist who places his own experiences at the centre of his work, and whose best work is intimately connected with his private suffering. Like Eliot and Conrad, he gave some of the most compelling renderings of nervous breakdown. His Flaubertian advocacy of the author's self-effacement is often—like Eliot's theory of impersonality—a necessary fiction rather than an accurate description of what he achieved: a device to preserve the artist's sanity re-entering the whirlpool.

This critical biography is based on Ford's perception that a writer's life is (as he says of Conrad's 'passion' for the New Form for the novel) 'a dual affair'. The life enshrined in the writing, the quality of mind manifested in the art, both are and are not the same as the life lived by the man, the mind prized by his friends. Violet Hunt, who lived and worked with Ford during ten fraught years, called him 'an author unfortunately doubled with a man'.[30] But his own writings celebrate rather than lament the combination; and his own comments on the 'dual personality', the *homo duplex* that a writer must be, emphasize 'duality' rather than 'doubleness': a complexly integrated sensibility, rather than a mind divided or multiple. One persistent and tantalizing duality of his writing is that an intensely private man, as reticent about his childhood or his relations with women as is his great character Christopher Tietjens, none the less produced voluminous reminiscences, touching on painful personal episodes such as his nervous breakdown. This is a 'dual life' not only because it tells the two stories, but also because it tries to do justice to Ford's presentation of his own complex dualities.

It is a study of what Ford called 'literary personality'—the quality for which, like Conrad, he most valued art.[31] The cynic might object that artists should not be allowed to be remembered by their imaginations instead of their records; that Ford's art-long fictionalizing of his life is a case of the imagination working to erase the life's record. According to this view, 'literary personality' is a cosmetic fiction. Yet Ford's 'literary personality' is extraordinarily sensitive to its own dualities; it reveals as much as it conceals; in its overlappings with, and transformations of the facts of his life, it is more truly expressive of the whole man than any other surviving testimony—inevitably fragmentary and partial— could ever be. Crucial facts and dates still elude his biographers. There can hardly be a few major figures of this century whose marital status remains as uncertain as Ford's (we do not know whether he and Hunt actually underwent some form of marriage ceremony, however illegal). The records that have survived are far from representative. Perhaps there are no letters between Ford and one of his closest friends, Arthur Marwood, because the two men saw each other too often for letters to be necessary. Or perhaps Marwood or his family destroyed them? Few letters can be found from Ford to Conrad. (Did Conrad or his wife destroy them?) Those from Conrad to Ford are mostly in the shorthand of a man who knows he can speak more fully at their next meeting. Very few letters to Ford from his first (and only legal) wife have survived. On the other hand, since publishers and agents keep better records than many friends and lovers, Ford's querulous, dismayed letters, in which he emphasized the role of important-but-neglected writer, tended distortingly to dominate Mizener's biography. Given the tenuousness of the record in vital areas, a conventional biography would be a more than usually fictitious recreation. This is a critical biography, not a novel. It is written in the belief that a writer's life can only be judged through a critical appreciation of the writing, and that previous biographies of Ford have been limited by their misunderstandings of the nature of his art; in particular, of the ways in which he thought about literature as an expression of personality. It is an attempt to understand how his writing works, rather than to patronize him with a rival, inferior fiction.

Ford conceived of 'literary personality' as an effect of transcendence—his favourite image for it is of a reader becoming aware of a disembodied smile smiling out from the page. The notion expresses a wish for literary immortality: the smile is an image of how the author's soul lives in the work, transfiguring the words. But rather than being a transcendental fantasy emptied of lived content, it is a fiction profoundly expressive of the gaps between the facts and the fabrications. His prose, that is, is a mastery rather than an evasion of the actual circumstances of his life. But when literary biography is at the mercy of circumstantial evidence, it pictures the artist at the mercy of life. Ford wrote compellingly of the predicaments of characters overwhelmed by complex circum-stance, and his own life was often complicated enough to make him feel so. But the effectiveness of his art tells another story.

The essential Ford has escaped while his biographers have been arguing about the 'originals' for characters, and other fictionalizing of facts. But, as William Empson wrote, 'discoveries of language and feeling made from a personal situation may develop themselves so that they can be applied to quite different dramatic situations'. The life of an artist's mind is at least as concerned with the imagining of these different, fictionalized situations, as with the original personal contexts. Ford's biographers and critics have sometimes tried to place him in a double-bind, complaining when he doesn't change the original situations enough (when similar character-types recur in the novels), and complaining when he changes them too much (when he 'improves' upon facts). To ask what his transformations express, rather than what the fiction may express about his original, personal predicaments, is a matter of attending to art before attending to its psychological origins. For, as T. S. Eliot argued, what art primarily expresses is itself: 'If poetry is a form of "communication", yet that which is to be communicated is the poem itself, and only incidentally the experience and the thought that have gone into it.'[32] Ford thought prose too was expressive in this fundamentally symbolist way. I have tried to discuss him in some of his own critical language, to see what his concepts of 'personality', 'vicarious experience', sympathy, reading, composite photography, agoraphobia, and duality can tell us about his life in writing.

Looking at the kind of man Ford was *as a writer* means giving closer attention to his writing than is customary in literary biography, quoting to bring out how his best expression is his own creation. This is because the life of his imagination is recorded not only in the themes and ideas which his work takes up, but in the *way* he rearranges and reconstructs them: in the style, the texture of language, the handling of narrative, authorial presence, and control. In a writer so preoccupied with literary form, formal choices become as expressive as choices of material. His letters, too, are inimitably expressive. I have quoted from them liberally, so that his unique ironic self-pity and humour can speak for themselves, revealing a person of greater humanity and creativity than has been recognized.

He was not a thinker or a theorist, but an impressionist and a novelist. So the concern here with social history, with politics, with Ford's literary criticism, is to bring out the quality of his mind, and the modes in which he approached these matters. These were before all, aesthetic modes: that is, his thinking was dominated by ideas of literary technique, composition, rendering, and expression, even when he was confronting subjects other than literature.

Ford's brilliant story-telling has been neglected in the attempt to present him as a damaged, deranged psyche (a view only made possible by his brilliant stories of damage and derangement). What is needed now is not more paraphrasing of the old, familiar fables, but an investigation of some of the less familiar material, together with a closer look at one of the most curious features of his work: his tendency to retell and re-imagine the same stories. He described Conrad's quest for Form as a 'for ever unsatisfied longing of his life'. Because it is inexhaustible, narrative is always dual: its satisfactions of completeness can only suspend, not satisfy, the longing for certainty, for the complete understanding of mysteries. Ford called his recursive method of narration 'the exhaustion of aspects'. What he wrote of Provençal history is equally true of the structures of his novels and reminiscences: 'To get any pattern at all out of these confusions it is necessary to go through them several times from different angles.' Think of Dowell or Tietjens going back and forth over their lives. The significance of a life, or an episode from a life, can be as inexhaustible as the meaning of a novel. Ford needed to go through his own memories several times from different angles. Rather than considering the significance of his rewritings, and the implications of the changes he made, criticism has tended to be opportunistic about which version is used. We still lack a systematic charting of these multiple narrations, let alone a detailed study. Where appropriate in my text I have discussed different versions of some stories.[33]

Ford's impressionism followed Conrad's dictum that the writer's task is 'before all, to make you *see*'. This visionary role makes literature revisionary: it makes us see again, see anew. Ford revised his impressions because his impressions revised his life. One of his great subjects is how literature makes up our world, and unmakes and remakes it. Poets, he writes, 'modify for you the aspect of the world and of your relation to your world'.[34]

This aspect of Ford's work anticipates modern critical developments. In an era when criticism sought for undissociated sensibility in its writers, Ford appeared as dangerously un-moored to fact, fantastic, uncertain, self-contradictory, incoherent. These qualities make him all the more instructive in an age more alert to the construction of subjectivity, sceptical of objectivity, of the very notion of a 'fact', and preoccupied with the elusiveness of 'meaning'. Paul Delany has written well of the 'extreme and inescapable textuality' of Ford's relationship with Jean Rhys: an affair which now reads as if based on *The Good Soldier*, and about which all four participants later wrote.[35] Ford's style everywhere suggests an awareness of the *written* and of how, as Wilbur Sanders has said, a character like Ashburnham 'changes in the telling'. *The Good Soldier* is one of the great deconstructive novels in the language; *Parade's End* is one of the great *re-*constructive ones. Both are alive with a sense of how literature, textuality, affects life; and both are alive with a sense of their own irrepressible fictionality.[36]

Rather than being a quality he displays unawares, Ford's provocativeness is a technique that he cultivated. Why? Fashions of biographical style have changed, of course. Faced with a problem such as Ford's habit of fabrication, a post-Freudian critic will want to explain, not to reprove. Both outrage and admiration have been present throughout, and it would be unwise to try to extricate them. Instead, one could see the divided responses as issuing from a dual quality in the writing, seeking a dual response within each particular reader; a response which would answer to Ford's sense of his own duality.

All of his writing could be characterized in this way. Reinventing history produces division, whether in his memoirs or his historical fiction. We laugh at an anecdote while we are doubting its improbable symmetry; or we allow ourselves to be fictively persuaded by the archaeological reconstruction of period detail while knowing either that what we are reading is only a fiction (as in a medieval romance like *The Young Lovell*), or, even if it is based on fact (like *The Fifth Queen* trilogy), that it did not quite happen in this way. Fordian romance in general works like this: the extreme and the incredible can excite, but one thing they excite is disbelief. The very romance elements which proclaim that all's right with the world—heroic actions, extraordinary or supernatural adventures, happy endings—are also the elements that insist that it is not quite our world. Even Ford's style could be said to achieve comparable effects in miniature. Despite his advocacy of the 'unobtrusive' in prose—W. H. Hudson was his exemplar here—his own writing often operates with what Keats said poetry needs: 'a fine excess'. It has a brilliance which could be said to obstruct its own insights. Ford had a genius for exaggeration. This is not just a matter of statistics. Questions of characterization, plotting, description, conversation all get exaggerated. For example, Ford's portrayal of Americans has frequently been criticized by Americans for inaccuracy and stereotyping. But it is in America in particular that *Parade's End* has been so successful, whereas there is still much scepticism from English critics about its portrayal of Englishness. It was not only public characters that Ford teased, but the character of his reading publics.

What is the origin of his desire for the dual response? One curious fact which needs to be accounted for—and which militates against seeing it as a purely Fordian idiosyncrasy—is that Ford's brother Oliver shared many of these characteristics: he was also an excellent raconteur, though equally unreliable factually. He too became a prolific writer. The Preface to his book *A Vagabond in New York* shows that he too shared Ford's ingrained tendency to provoke a dual response in his readers, delighting in a created uncertainty about—in the title of another of his books—*Where Truth Lies*: 'At the time when some of these sketches were appearing in the pages of *Truth* I received a letter from an earnest-minded reader, enquiring whether they were supposed to be "remotely founded on fact," or were merely "the imaginative efforts of a common or garden liar." ' [37] His own life was as beset with financial and sexual scandal as Ford's. He seemed to share Ford's genius for creating confusion and exasperation in equal measure with entertainment. How did both the Hueffer boys acquire these traits?

I

FAMILY

The marriage of Ford's parents in September 1872—the wedding portraits were painted by Lawrence Alma-Tadema—was a union of contrasts. Ford conceives himself as embodying the complementary qualities of Francis Hueffer and Catherine Madox Brown:

My father [. . .] represents for me the Just Man! [. . .] He was enormous in stature, had a great red beard and rather a high voice. He comes back to me most frequently as standing back on his heels and visibly growing larger and larger . . . My mother, who was incurably romantic and unreasonable with the unreason that was proper to the femininity of pre-Suffrage days, comes back to me as saying:

'Frank, isn't it just that Fordie should give his rabbit to his brother?' My brother having accidentally stepped on his own rabbit and killed it, my mother considered that I as the eldest should show an example of magnanimity by giving him mine.

So my father, as large as Rhadamanthus and much more terrible, says: 'No, my dear, it is not *just* that Fordie should give his rabbit to his brother, but if you wish it he must obey your orders as a matter of filial piety. . . .' And then the dread, slow: 'Fordie . . . give your . . . rabbit . . . to your . . . brother. . . . *Et plus vite que ça!*' He was fond of throwing in a French phrase.

I don't know who was more dissatisfied with that judgement, I or my mother. But that is no doubt what justice is for.

Analysing, as I sometimes do, my heredity I suppose I got from my mother—who got it from her father—my faculty for running up against oddnesses . . . and for taking geese for swans. From my father I must have acquired my passion for Provence, for good cooking—and possibly for New York.[1]

Francis Hueffer was not (according to W. M. Rossetti) particularly tall. But the father grows into God the Father in Ford's memory: in this case a God of justice, impartially and remorselessly delivering the moral law—though with palpably *unjust* results. Even while he had been courting Cathy Madox Brown he became angry if her mind wandered during his discourses on Latin, or if anyone disagreed with him. 'It is great fun to watch you getting more and more excited', she teased him, 'until you end by rushing up and down the room brandishing the first stick or thing that comes in your way'. Another quality Francis Hueffer shares both with God and with the God-like author advocated by Ford's literary ancestor Flaubert is that of absence: 'I never knew my father well. He died whilst I was still a child and, as I was sent to a boarding school at the age of eight and he, during the summer holidays, was usually at Bayreuth, I have hardly any memories of him. I remember a few stories that he used to tell me in rare moments when he must have felt the urge to shape my infant mind.'[2] Ford was 15 when his father died. Although 'still a child', he was none the less quite an old child to have so few memories of him. What is significant in the growth of the novelist is how the few memories he does record of his father are not memories of the man, but of his stories. Once again we see the curious extent to which Ford conceives of his life as existing within narrative. Narratives shape his life, as his father's stories were intended to shape his mind.

The Hüffers were a large, prosperous, Catholic family based in Münster. Ford's great-great-grandfather, Christoph, became a law professor at the University of Münster, and married the daughter of Anton Wilhelm Aschendorff, a publisher, bookseller, and university printer. The firm also owned the *Westfälische Zeitung*. When Aschendorff died, their eldest son, Ford's grandfather, Johann Hermann Hüffer, took over the family business. The Verlag Aschendorff is still run by the Münster Hüffers. Johann Hermann married twice and had seventeen children, three of whom died in childhood. Franz—Ford's father—was the youngest, born in 1845 when his father was 61. From an early age Ford was aware of belonging to a large, cosmopolitan clan, spread across Europe and the Atlantic. This made him, as Richard Aldington said, a 'good European', not just because he was dually English and German, but because the Catholic tradition on his German side encouraged a belief in a common Western culture 'existing above and beyond national rivalries'; which was also Francis Hueffer's conception of music, literature, and philosophy, and Madox Brown's of painting. His uncle Wilhelm lived in Rome, where he was known as 'Barone Hüffer' (a fictional title that Ford and Oliver would both later claim to inherit). He handed his tobacco-importing business over to his brother Leopold, who Ford said had a plantation in Virginia, and with whom he stayed in Paris and on the Riviera. Ford was to feel equally at home—and equally in exile—all over Europe and America; their cultures were his legacy. Franz was a free-thinker: an agnostic, and enthusiast for the avant-garde. Ford said he was 'the bad boy of the family', which—together with the imminent Franco-Prussian conflict—may have led him to emigrate to England in 1869. He too made changes to his name, appearing variously as Franz Carl Christoph Johannes Hüffer, and Franz Xavier Hüffer, before Anglicizing himself to Francis Hueffer. He was a proud, learned man, who could also be kindly and ironic. When asked why he wore his long beard, he said: 'It makes me look venerable!'[3]

The other most important recollection of his father also bears oddly on Ford's vocation. In this case it is the father and (maternal) grandfather, the painter Ford Madox Brown, who are contrasted:

My father's last words to me were: 'Fordie, whatever you do, never write a book.' Indeed, so little idea had I of meddling with the arts that, although to me a writer was a very wonderful person, I prepared myself very strenuously for the Indian Civil Service. This was a real grief to my grandfather, and I think he was exceedingly overjoyed when the doctors refused to pass me for that service on the ground that I had an enlarged liver. And when then I seriously proposed to go into an office, his wrath became tempestuous.

Tearing off his nightcap [. . .] he flung it to the other end of the room.

'God damn and blast my soul!' he exclaimed [. . .] 'I tell you, I will turn you straight out of my house if you go in for any kind of commercial life.' So that my fate was settled for me.[4]

It was not just that Madox Brown settled his fate by foreclosing the commercial life. For the juxtaposition of the fateful decrees from the two father figures establishes a double-bind: Ford must 'never write a book', must not think of 'meddling with the arts'. Yet his parents, grandfather, and Pre-Raphaelite relations and connections convinced him—and it was a conviction that shaped the subsequent triumphs as well as many of the excesses of his life—that if he were to be above their contempt or indifference he must become a genius of some artistic kind. The fact that these are given as Francis Hueffer's last words, and that (together with Madox Brown's outburst) they prescribe Ford's 'fate', suggests how Ford's graphomania, his compulsive writing of books, invokes the idea of death. It is as if agreeing not to write might be his last word too: he convinces himself he is not in mortal danger (despite the doctors' words) by not letting his father have his last words, but letting his grandfather's voice outsound his father's.

A fine example of the humane self-awareness of Ford's autobiography, this juxtaposition registers how much of Ford's authorship is, at a deep level, answering those voices of authority: trying to convince the father, whom he never could now convince, that he was worthy to write a book; trying to convince the grandfather that he had fulfilled his hopes, and become a genius. Ford's lifelong hostility to academies owes most to Madox Brown's paranoiac mistrust of the Royal Academy; but it also relates to his ambivalences about paternal Germany; to his dislike of Germanic philological scholarship, which he conceived to be antipathetic to the art it studied. Francis Hueffer's position is ambiguous in this respect. Ford tells stories of his father's brushes with university authorities, to show that his own prejudices are congenital. (He told a similar story that his grandfather had only become a painter because his father, Ford Brown, a purser in the navy, had quarrelled with his former captain, Commodore Coffin, thus scuppering the naval career of midshipman Ford Madox Brown.) It was, said Ford, his father's prodigious memory that got him expelled from Berlin University. Overhearing the university rector reading through the speech he was to deliver the next day when conferring a degree on a Russian prince, he memorized it, and delivered it word for word himself just before the rector was due to speak. Ford too prided himself on his memory, and its ability to get him into trouble. Francis Hueffer was himself an exile—a self-imposed one—from Germany, as Ford was from England when he wrote about these things. Hueffer composed music and wrote libretti; Ford would compose both music and words for his songs and song-dramas. Ford's blue eyes and 'brilliant yellow hair' were Hüffer traits; mentally, too, he was very much his father's son. Both men were gifted, versatile critics of all the arts. Both founded 'intellectually serious, financially disastrous magazines': Francis Hueffer started the *New Quarterly* to boost Schopenhauer, and the *Musical World* to champion Wagner. His avant-garde activities had set him at odds with the German artistic establishment. And yet in England he became the music critic for *The Times* in 1879, someone very much *of* the established English artistic circles. In writing the kind of books he did, Ford was both reiterating and contradicting his father: disobeying his injunction never to write, but often writing criticism which also championed the new; writing books which are so far from what Hueffer meant by a book that they almost elude his edict; yet in precisely this quality—their impressionist disregard for scholarship—they are written against much of what he stood for. Ford remembered his father as 'a man of encyclopaedic knowledge'; and indeed he contributed to the *Encyclopaedia Britannica*. Encyclopaedic knowledge was something Ford admired: it is the way he defines the genius of Tietjens, the hero of *Parade's End*; and it was something he emulated in his own air of omniscient authority. But it was also something he parodied; an air he put on, in his reminiscential impressions of facts. Ford's dual attitude to fact and imagination can itself be recognized in his father, who was a polymath rather than a pedant. He wrote the *Britannica* entry for Boccaccio. That conjunction of authority and fabulation was one Ford was continually to reinvent.[5]

Francis Hueffer made his fiancée worry that she was too 'stupid' for him; and he created the same anxiety in Ford. He 'habitually' called him 'the patient but extremely stupid donkey'—a phrase he had remembered from a child's spelling book. It was a remark that haunted Ford all his life, and was to influence his behaviour and his writing. He would complain of feeling dull or stupid after bouts of writing. He exemplified a passivity in the face of personal attacks, refusing to strike back in public, to the point of either sainthood or stupidity. He even provoked the attacks for the gratification of suffering them. His grievances can be glimpsed, often years afterwards, transformed into fictional variations on his feelings of victimization and betrayal. His ethics are at one with his aesthetics here: he advocates writing in which the passive consciousness receives impressions from a world of suffering. 'Patience' is thus fundamental to the literary approach he called 'impressionism', which he opposed to the self-display and discursive analysis of his consciously 'clever' contemporaries like Wells and Shaw. Fordian impressionism is a complex and evolving notion, but at one level it is always answering Francis Hueffer's cutting comment, by trying to redeem 'patience' and 'stupidity' as the cardinal aesthetic virtues. The phrase also prefigures the tonal duality of most of Ford's writing. The donkey's patience (about suffering? toil? appetite?) make it an object of pathos; its stupidity (obstinacy? acceptance of ill-treatment? silence?) make it potentially ridiculous. Many of Ford's characters, like Edward Ashburnham or Mark Tietjens, evoke pity and laughter simultaneously. Ironic pathos is Ford's quintessential mode. It is something unique in literature (though it owes much to Sterne and to Flaubert); and when it comes off—as it

does particularly in *The Good Soldier*, *Parade's End*, and in Ford's autobiographical books—it is magnificent.[6]

If Ford's father represented 'the Just Man', his mother represented the unjust
woman, 'incurably romantic and unreasonable'. She was a gifted painter, in the
manner of Madox Brown, and also a talented pianist. His sister Juliet portrayed
her as very pretty—she too had bright blue eyes—and, like her father, a fighter
against injustice: 'timid on her own account', but afraid of nothing when
protecting someone weaker than herself. 'She didn't much like being contradicted
because, she said, "I never insist upon anything unless I'm *positively certain*".'
She was to be very loyal to Ford when he needed her protection. And he said
they had a 'telepathic' *rapport*. But his published memories of her turn on his
feeling that Oliver was her favourite son. As with her intervention over the rabbit,
she may have meant to champion the underdog; but if it was always the smaller
brother who is the underdog, her concern probably felt like rejection to Ford. His
tops, catapult, and stuffed squirrel all went the way of that rabbit, he said. Francis
Hueffer, 'respecting the rights of primogeniture', used to give Ford sixpence
a week pocket-money, and Oliver, who was two years younger, fourpence-
halfpenny. But their mother used to insist on Ford equalizing the sums. Ford
would repeatedly become involved with strong-minded women, and feel obliged
to do what they wanted even when he thought it irrational or unjust. He also had
a gift for getting involved with two of them at a time. It is tempting here to see
him unconsciously trying to turn the tables on the mother's love for two boys,
pre-empting the feeling of betrayal he dreaded by falling in love with the next
woman before the last fell out of love with him.[7]

An episode Ford recorded as his first memory is curiously expressive about his
childhood fears, and their possible source in his feelings about his mother:

The earliest thing that I can remember is this, and the odd thing is that, as I
remember it, I seem to be looking at myself from outside. I see myself a very tiny
child in a long blue pinafore looking into the breeding-box of some Barbary ring-doves
that my grandmother kept in the window of the huge studio in Fitzroy Square [. . .]
I perceive greyish and almost shapeless objects with, upon them, little speckles, like
the very short spines of hedgehogs, and I stand with the first surprise of my life and
with the first wonder of my life. I ask myself: can these be doves?—these unrecognizable, panting morsels of flesh. And then, very soon, my grandmother comes in and is
angry. She tells me that if the mother dove is disturbed she will eat her young. This
I believe is quite incorrect. Nevertheless I know quite well that for many days
afterwards I thought I had destroyed life and that I was exceedingly sinful.[8]

Thomas Moser gives an ingenious Freudian reading of this memory as standing
for 'the male child's earliest enlightenment as to the mysterious, terrifyingly *not*
phallic nature of the female sex organ'; and he relates the grandmother's anger at
the 'very tiny child' to the mother-dove's violence towards its young. 'To little
boys, such knowledge is utterly forbidden, the punishment annihilation.' Ford
uses the clause 'I seem to be looking at myself from outside' as a caption for
Madox Brown's painting of him as William Tell's son, holding up the two halves

of the apple divided by his father's arrow. ('In short,' says Moser, 'father will castrate him and mother will devour him.') Moser also argues that this connects human sexuality with knowledge in general. In *Ancient Lights*'s dedication to his own children Ford connects the memory of the baby doves with his father's calling him stupid. He characteristically presents himself as wondering perplexedly at the world, and being terrified by 'the incomprehensible explosion of murderous feelings in gigantic persons'. What needs adding is that, besides trying to understand where his feeling of sinfulness in the face of the Great came from, the interest for Ford of his earliest memory is also that it seems formative of an aesthetic attitude: it is not just that 'wonder' and 'surprise' are qualities that—like Henry James—he valued in art, and privileged in his own writing. It is that the duality of perspective—seeing himself from outside while describing his deepest interiority—is fundamental to his impressionism, which seeks verbal correlatives that can objectify subjective impressions.[9]

Ford's most explicit account of his brother Oliver is—characteristically—an elegy, written in 1933, two years after his death. The sympathy it evinces makes it strange that he did not write more about such a waywardly flamboyant character. He said that he saw little of Oliver 'except in his more coruscating moments'. But there is a hint of another possible reason: besides Ford's tact in not discussing him during his lifetime, it is evident that he felt overshadowed by the younger brother whom many felt to be the more gifted, attractive, and witty of the two boys:

My brother's character and temperament must much have resembled my own. He had inherited from my mother and my grandfather a little more of their romantic tendency to take geese for swans—though Heaven knows I too have enough of that. And I got from my father enough of a passion for justness in expression and judgement to rob me of the chance of his undoubted brilliance. So that in conversation, I am really rather inarticulate, whereas when it came to what is called back-chat he was the most amazing performer that I have ever heard, not excluding Mr. H. G. Wells. But what was singular, was that whenever we were together alone and silent, when one of us broke the silence it was to say exactly what the other had been about to bring out.[10]

A 'passion for justness in expression': the phrase shows Ford connecting the *justice* of his father ('the Just Man') with his own passion for the *mot juste*: justness in expression. His feeling of being (over)shadowed by his brother is also perhaps a source of his fascination with doubles.

Ford was born at 5 Fair Lawn Villas, Merton, Surrey. On the day of his birth, 17 December 1873, Dante Gabriel Rossetti prophesied that he would bring 'glory to whichever of his two countries he may choose to adopt and that the other will have to mourn the eclipse of a leading luminary'. The first of the several combinations of names he was to bear signalled his national duality: Ford (for his grandfather) Hermann (for his Hüffer uncle) Hueffer (Anglicized German). There was another cause for mourning in the family within the year, however, when Madox Brown's only son, Oliver (named after Cromwell, and 'Nolly' for short), died of blood-poisoning. The blow left the Madox Browns 'quite alone in the world', said Ford later. Both their daughters had left home: Cathy, when she married Francis Hueffer, and Lucy, when on 31 March 1874 she had married William Michael Rossetti, the brother of Dante Gabriel and Christina. The Hueffers went to stay with the Browns at Fitzroy Square to console them. It must have been Ford's first lesson in mortality and grief.[11]

Another of the earliest surviving records of him comes in a letter from Ford Madox Brown to Cathy Hueffer, suggesting how importantly Brown's grandchildren were to assuage his sense of loss: 'we are very glad indeed to have Fordie—He is very good always & very amusing & we are just going with him & Miss Blind to see Hengler's Circus'. Mathilde Blind was a poetess whom the Madox Browns had virtually adopted. The 2-year-old Ford had become 'very fond of Miss Blind': 'the other day at dinner after asking him if he liked this thing & that & what else he liked he told her he liked *Bind* & then he added that he liked Granma too—& he goes up to Miss Blind & wakes her out of a doze with "Bind what's a cock".' Her reaction isn't known, but she got her revenge later, quizzing a 16-year-old Ford about synonyms when she was correcting her proofs. With her 'Medusa head' she frightened him out of his life, he said, and reduced him 'to a miserable muteness'; whereupon she took up his father's refrain: ' "Fordie," she would say with an awful scrutiny, "your grandfather says you are a genius, but I have never been able to discover in you any signs but those of your being as stupid as a donkey".'[12]

Between the births of their other two children, Oliver Franz (later Oliver Madox: 9 January 1876) and Juliet (known as 'Poppy': 28 November 1880), the Hueffers moved to 72 Elsham Road in Holland Park. They also took the two boys to visit the Hüffer relations in Europe. The tour was to map out the places Ford would love best in the world: 'London, Paris, the Rhine, Alsace-Lorraine, the Midi.' Half-a-century later he could still remember his father roaring at him for imitating the breakfast-table manners of his *oncle de l'Amerique*, Leopold, who he had seen in Paris breaking an egg on the edge of a glass. After hurling the egg and the glass overboard from their Rhine steamer, Francis Hueffer explained that: 'no one who expected to grow into an English gentleman could do anything else with his breakfast egg than delicately to slice off its top with a knife and extract the contents with a tea-spoon.' Curious that Ford's obsessive fascination with 'Englishness' and the ideal of the 'gentleman' should have been instilled by his German intellectual father. Though it may account for the way he always describes the social codes as if seen from outside as well as inside (there's a slight strangeness in the precision of that description: '*extract* the *contents* with a tea-spoon').[13]

All three Hueffer children adored Madox Brown and all three later used 'Madox' as a middle name, though it doesn't appear on their birth certificates. 'A possibly too stern father of the old school,' wrote Ford, 'he was as a grandfather extravagantly indulgent.' His son Nolly had been only 19 when he died, but his talent had been prodigious. At 13 he had painted a picture which W. M. Rossetti

said had attracted 'considerable attention' when it was exhibited. By 17 he had
begun his first novel. Rossetti said: 'Barring Chatterton the precosity of his
intellectual development appears almost unparalleled in the history of literature.'
Ford's sister Juliet said Madox Brown 'had never forgotten him for a moment
since his death'.[14] By urging his grandchildren to become artists, Madox Brown
hoped they would fulfil the promise his son's tragic death had broken. It was
Oliver Hueffer—named in piety after Oliver Madox Brown—who appeared the
one most likely to manage the metamorphosis into swan:

Under my grandfather's reign, after my father's death, Oliver went through a great
series of coruscating avatars. My grandfather had to have geniuses for his
grandchildren. Of an evening he would go through our names in turn, beginning with
the young Rossettis:
    'Olive's a genius, Arthur's a genius, Helen's certainly a genius.' Then he would
begin with my mother's children: 'Juliet's a perfect genius; Fordie is too perhaps. But
as for Oliver, I can't make out whether he's a genius or mad. . . . I think he's both!'
    That was high praise. That all his grandchildren should be mere geniuses was a
commonplace to him. But that the gods should vouchsafe to him a mad genius—that
was almost beyond his most private hopes! . . .
    So, with his aid, my brother [. . .] ran through the careers of Man About Town,
Army Officer, Actor, Stockbroker, Painter, Author and, under the auspices of the
father of one of his fiancées, that of valise manufacturer!
    My grandfather, with his square white beard and his long white hair cut square,
exactly resembled the King of Hearts in a pack of cards [. . .]
    One morning a week the early hours would be pierced by his imprecations. He
would send for my brother, who would look more than usually cherubic. He would
fling his nightcap across the room and shout:
    'God damn and blast you, Oliver, what have you done with my watch and chain
and spectacles?'
    Oliver would say, with an air of ingenuousness:
    'Well, you see, Granpa, I had to have a couple of quid for debts of honour, and I
knew you would not want me not to have them whilst I did not want to wake you.
So I took them down to Attenborough's. But here are the pawn tickets.'
    I think my grandfather was, in secret, rather proud of these exploits.[15]

This is some of Ford's finest comedy. He transforms the commonplace cliché
about his 'grandfather's reign' by pointing up the reverse succession (his
grandfather reigned after his father's death); and he turns it into a lovingly
exaggerated portrait of the 'King of Hearts' performing a litany of his dynasty of
geniuses. Ford recognizes the danger of devaluing 'that terrible word "genius" '
by over-valuing the commonplace; but the passage is anything but reproving of
the king of art's ambitions.[16] Ford is clearly as proud of his grandfather's influence
as the grandfather was of Oliver's panache.
    Ford's consolation, he said, was that the one thing he could excel Oliver in was
in growing a moustache. He also said he could always knock him down, though
he seldom wanted to. Once, however, he pushed Oliver out of a second-floor
window, though miraculously 'he didn't even have a bruise to show'. Two further

traits can be haruspicated out of Ford's childhood experience of sibling rivalry. 'From my earliest days I was taught—by my father, my mother, and [Oliver] himself—to regard him as the sparkling jewel of the family, whilst I was its ugly duckling.' First, Ford managed almost completely to repress any resentment towards either his parents or his siblings. He did this by feigning indifference to what others felt about him; and when later on he was feeling most vulnerable, this claim to be absolutely indifferent to what people should do to him, or say about him and his books, would be wrung from him. As a youth he ascribed this stance to a discipleship of 'Berlioz's system of "Absolute Indifferentism in Universal Matter" '; and he opposes it to the danger of being 'overcome by a passion'. It is hard not to feel that he borrowed the romantic attitude to defend himself against his own passions of unrequited love. These terms of passion and indifference (or aloofness) are again cardinal for his art: both as subject (Ashburnham's passions, and passion's indifference to the havoc it can wreak) and as technique (in which the author is at once passionately involved in the characters' pathos, and ironically detached from it). He was later to write: 'before you can approach any work of art and expect to derive anything from it you must realise that you are a matter of profound indifference to everything.' His writing is profoundly concerned with altruism and renunciation—again both as subjects to be explored, and as authorial attitudes towards human predicaments. That his altruism may have its roots in his denial of rivalry, envy, and resentment doesn't make it an ignoble plant. He cultivated it to extraordinary heights, performing to the letter Madox Brown's exacting code, which also enjoined renunciation:

Fordie, never refuse to help a lame dog over a stile. Never lend money: always give it. When you give money to a man that is down, tell him that it is to help him get up; tell him that when he is up he should pass on the money you have given him to any other poor devil that is down. Beggar yourself rather than refuse assistance to any one whose genius you think shows promise of being greater than your own.[17]

Ford was rare among artists in almost never expressing envy of others' talents. Any stirrings of animosity he transmuted into generosity. This process is itself implicated in his fictional imagination, founded as it is on the idea of 'sympathetic insight' into others (seeing them from the inside as well as the outside). For, as Melanie Klein showed, empathy can be cultivated as a means of overcoming antagonism.[18]

Secondly, this altruism, bound up as it is with the idea of genius, expresses Ford's hope for his own genius. Like his grandfather, Ford took all his geese for swans (though an amazing number of his literary ducklings *became* swans). This is partly because, having been told he was the ugly duckling, he hoped to metamorphose into a swan himself, and tended to treat others as he wanted to be treated by them. He too 'went through a great series of coruscating avatars', regularly reinventing himself with rare imaginative fertility every few years. This was not just a symptom of genius; it was a visible demonstration of it. The magical self-transformations in Ford's endlessly altering stories about himself were his way of showing himself metamorphosing from ugly duckling to swan. He knew that much of his writing was a *tour de force*, and would try to check the tendency to self-display by advocating a style of self-effacement. But where his work sometimes seems over-written, obtrusively virtuoso, one can hear him needing to live up to the hopes of his grandfather's circle. Brown's expectations were probably a more powerful spur to Ford's creativity than was sibling rivalry and had an effect on Oliver too; for, after all, Oliver was the favourite son, so shouldn't have shared Ford's sense of injustice and indifference. Yet in his irresponsibility and fabulation he was a more exaggerated version of Ford.

Ford idealized Madox Brown, saying he was 'the best man I ever knew' (paraphrasing what Brown's friend Gabriel Rossetti said of him), and that his studios were 'the glamorous places' of his youth. In Freud's 'family romances' children fantasize about having grander parents than their actual ones. In Ford's case the family romance was actual: his grandfather had usurped Francis Hueffer as his male parent. If he later found it remarkable how little he could remember of his real father, it wasn't just because Francis Hueffer had spent his summers at Bayreuth; it was because Ford's memory had reshaped his past, substituting Brown for Hueffer. His first book, *The Brown Owl*, can be read (as Thomas Moser has shown) as Ford's 'private family allegory'. It was written to amuse Juliet, who was only 8 when their father died, and begins with the death of the Princess's father, and the consoling appearance of the Owl ('it seemed as if the Owl had become a companion to her that would take the place of her father'). As the Brown Owl, so the wise and protective Madox Brown. Though Ford felt their grandfather too was more impressed by Oliver, he had no doubt of Madox Brown's love for him, and felt more filial towards him than towards his father. His crucial earliest memories place him in Madox Brown's house. The opening of *Ancient Lights* makes the point inescapably, describing the Fitzroy Square house, and saying: 'it was in this house [. . .] that my eyes first opened, if not to the light of day, at least to any visual impression that has not since been effaced.' Though he does it with a characteristically dual juxtaposition of the fictional and the real. For in fact he opens not with his own account of Madox Brown's house, but a description from a novel: Thackeray's *The Newcomes*, in which Colonel Newcome takes number 120 Fitzroy Square. It was, said Ford, in *Colonel Newcome*'s house that his eyes first opened. Madox Brown opened his eyes to visual impressions; Ford's impressionism in words thus pays perpetual homage to the painter. But by transforming 37 Fitzroy Square into Colonel Newcome's 120, Ford is implying that his life with Madox Brown was the making of him as an artist in another way: it brought him up in the house of fiction. His impressionist autobiographies all start in similar ways, charting the coming into consciousness of Ford as writer. *Return to Yesterday* opens with his 'oldest literary recollection' (reading Kipling aged 18—years later than the childhood reading he often recollected, but significant there because his own first book had just been published, so it was his first literary recollection as a literary man). *Thus to Revisit* had also begun with this period of his young authorship, defined there as the first stirrings of 'the Writer's conscious literary life', as he began to read, and then to meet, Conrad, James, Crane, and Hudson. And *It Was the Nightingale* opens with his first consciousness of rebirth after the war, and literary rebirth after the gestation of *Parade's End*.[19]

Ford also thought his grandfather had lived an exemplary artist's life. Madox Brown came from a family of innovators. His own grandfather, Dr John Brown, was the physician who invented the 'Brunonian system' of medicine, according to which diseases were caused by either an excess or lack of excitement, and should be treated by debilitating drugs or stimulants. This anti-lancet heterodoxy, and his 'unconciliatory manner', set him at odds with the Edinburgh Faculty. But Madox Brown was proud to say that John Brown was invited by Frederick the Great to settle in Berlin (he refused); and that Napoleon had been a passionate advocate of the Brunonian system. Madox Brown, though not a great artist, was himself 'a kind of pioneer': 'He had had to initiate a Movement that certainly did something to make "modern painting" possible.' Ford's words of 1903 would later become true of himself, as his own poetry and fiction and criticism helped to make English literary modernism possible. His grandfather had been seen as the father of the Pre-Raphaelites; not quite *of* them, despite being Rossetti's closest friend. Ford himself would become the father of modernism, without quite being *of* the movement. Brown's habit of painting his family and friends into his pictures— Ford, Oliver, and Juliet all appear in his Manchester Town Hall frescos—showed Ford ways of turning familiar material into something quite other. His historical compositions, with their glare and bustle and audacious scale, were a model for Ford's historical fiction and reminiscence. Above all, it was Madox Brown's dedication to *work* that most impressed Ford, and many of Ford's friends were to be impressed by the same quality in him. He thought Brown's painting called *Work* his most important, both for the eleven years' work the painter had put into it, and for the way it allegorized the artist's labour. Many of Ford's characteristics can be traced back to his grandfather, especially those that got Ford labelled unreliable: his belief that 'the artist *must* live with enjoyment'; his high-handedness with patrons (both were careless of their 'careers' to the point of self-destruction). Brown showed Ford how to be a serious artist without becoming a pompously respectable and minatory Great Figure.[20]

Madox Brown's attitude was formative too. When Ford wrote of the 'tremendous Victorians who always aroused rage in me—and in whom I always aroused rage', he was following in his grandfather's footsteps. Brown was a fighter, but one who fought institutions rather than individuals. 'He hated all Academicians, all Cabinet Ministers, all Officials, all Tories, all Whigs and the *Times* newspaper. Yet whenever he came into contact with any individual connected with those obnoxious institutions he would begin by finding redeeming points in him and ended by proclaiming the man "a genius".' So Ford hated most literary academies or politicians, and the *Times Literary Supplement*. And so he valued in art the 'gift of sympathy' and freedom from envy for which he thought his grandfather deserved to be remembered. What Ford said of Madox Brown became true of himself: 'to any one whom he suspected of patronising him he was capable of being hastily and singularly disagreeable.' Both men had a knack for professional self-destruction, wrecking their successes by biting the hands that paid them. Once he had finished his Manchester murals, some of the members of the corporation were outspokenly contemptuous of the work. 'They proposed', said Ford, 'to paint out his frescoes and use the wall-spaces for advertising the products of the city.' Ford was outraged, and wrote what is possibly his first published work after *The Brown Owl* denouncing the Burghers in a letter to the *Manchester Guardian*. He later felt that they were responsible for worrying Madox Brown to death; and this paranoid paradigm of the unrecognized genius persecuted—perhaps to death—by philistine businessmen was to be a powerful force in Ford's own management—and mismanagement—of his life.[21]

'God damn and blast'! Ford found that explosion into indulgent rage deeply characteristic of his grandfather. Ford remembered him shouting at him as he was about to light the 'gas-daylight apparatus' Brown had invented for his studio: 'God damn and blast it, Fordie, do you want to blow us all to hell. That gas pipe leaks.' His real motive, said Ford, was to avoid the indignity of having one of his paintings 'blessed' by the President of the Royal Academy, who was then visiting. In *Ancient Lights* he bursts out with the phrase when W. M. Rossetti kept knocking over the fire-irons. Rossetti objected that Brown had not used 'any such violent or profane language'. He may have had a better memory than Ford of this particular conversation. But Ford's story—apart from catching so funnily Rossetti's embarrassment and Brown's exasperation—is impressionistically true to the spirit of Brown's talk. Olive Garnett's scrupulous diary records his spirited swearing, when he read one of her stories admiringly and wondered 'Who the devil had written it'. Madox Brown's dual response to the eccentricities and outrageousnesses which he surely encouraged in his grandchildren is another example of the Fordian truth which is often alien to the encyclopaedic accuracy of a William Rossetti. Part of that truth resides in the dual response the outburst causes in its reader: the justness of the grandparental indignation intempered by the intemperance of his expression likely to *épater les bourgeois*—including the bourgeois son-in-law. Recalling his multiplicity of political personalities at this time, Ford later wrote of how he consciously aimed at humorous irritation: 'To irritate my relatives, who advocated advanced thought, I dimly remember that I professed myself a Tory. Amongst the bourgeoisie whom it was my inherited duty to *épater* I passed for a dangerous anarchist. In general speech, manner and appearance, I must have resembled a socialist of the Morris group. I don't know what I was: I don't know what I am.'[22]

The anarchical-socialist-Tory combination is itself something Ford saw in his grandfather, who 'In his passion and in emotions' was 'a hard-swearing, old-fashioned Tory: his reasoning, however, and circumstances made him a revolutionary of the romantic type. I am not sure, even, that towards his latter years he would not have called himself an Anarchist, and have damned your eyes if you had faintly doubted this obviously extravagant assertion.' Such a paradox was a compelling strategy for a Victorian medievalizer who felt the way to progress beyond industrialized alienation was to reassert the values of pre-industrial society. Thus Ruskin, too, could enjoy the irony in proclaiming himself 'a violent Tory of the old school' as well as 'a Communist of the old school'.[23] Ford not only reduplicated Madox Brown's dual politics, but also his conversational manner. One reason he seemed more at ease with himself from his fifties on is that he was approaching the age of which he had prematurely assumed the manner. He described to Olive Garnett the 'childlike old age of Madox Brown', 'the last state the perfect one in which man through failing power renounces': Ford could never renounce renunciation; he used fictional narrators and characters whose age (like John Kemp's in *Romance*) or failing powers elicit a tone of renunciation. He may have sounded like a William Morris socialist in speech and manner, but his biography of his grandfather gives a poignant sketch of the man he most wanted to sound like. And though this youthful work (published in 1896, *aetat.* 22) impersonates the measure and balance of the Victorian academic reviews, Ford gives a good impression of his own manner of speech, and a good description of his later, more fluent and more impressionist prose:

His conversation was marvellously entertaining, and his conversational mannerisms naïve and charming. His range of subjects was almost unbounded, and his faculty of throwing his whole mind into the subject under consideration and of enunciating original views most unusual. His speech was always distinct and noticeably slow, as if he desired to attach great importance to all his utterances.

Violet Hunt said that her mother thought Ford sounded like his grandfather. The *Times Literary Supplement*'s obituarist described Ford's 'undertone of irony that gave life to his conversation, into which he threw a weary utterance as if the action of speech was tiresome to him'. The surviving radio broadcasts of his voice bear out the 'irony' and the 'weary utterance', though the effect is to combine Madox Brown's stress with a note of omniscient sadness.[24]

Madox Brown was a narrative as well as a stylistic influence. It is not just that he too contributed to Ford's house of fiction, but his practice of modifying his 'lavish and picturesque' anecdotes is also one which his grandson 'inherited'—as he was later to inherit Brown's gout. Juliet recalled: 'My grandfather told stories so well that some people said he did it better than anybody else in London, and you never got tired of them because they were a little different each time.' William Rossetti too thought him 'a good narrator', though he admired the opposite virtue: that Brown could 'tell you the story of a novel with great precision and at ample length'. Ford relates a story about a poet, a descendant of the Pre-Raphaelites, who, while reading at the breakfast table, would mark his place in his friend's valuable books with a slice of bacon, and he adds: 'the habit of anecdote, incisive however wanting in veracity, is still remaining to the surviving connections of this Old Circle'. If the anonymous poet wasn't him, the kind of anecdotalist he describes exactly was. Ford improves his own stories (as well as some of Brown's), then, out of a multiple piety. He is continuing the line of spirited insouciance.

Madox Brown told him to read Charles Waterton, the naturalist and travel writer, 'a splendid liar'. Ford's own fictional splendours also pay homage to his adored grandfather as a sympathetic presence; summoning him up, as it were, as an ideal reader. For the dual response he seeks in his readers is precisely Madox Brown's to his family: the admiring curse—'God damn and blast you!' His technical emphasis on 'how great writers *get their effects*' is well known. The conscious craftsmanship is vital, but not an end in itself. It is always directed towards a reader, and intended to produce a precise emotional response. The combination Ford strives for can be a particularly emotive one, like all love-hate double-binds.[25]

Sartre, whose father died before the son could know him, describes how the loss made him a child of liberty: 'Eût-il vécu, mon père se fut couché sur moi de tout son long et m'eût écrasé.' Lacking such parental superimposition, Sartre agrees with a psychoanalyst's verdict: 'je n'ai pas de Sur-moi.' In his case too, the father was succeeded by an indulgent and God-like grandfather. But despite the similarities, Ford's knowledge of his father makes a difference. There is a sense that his performances can be less constrained than they might have otherwise been, thanks to the absence of paternal authority to define and punish transgressions. It is also possible that Ford's literary determination to produce lively responses is intensified by his loss of the father. It is not just that the dead parent frustrates his need for recognition and love, but that his father's judgement on him is now irrevocable. Oliver was the favourite son, the fledgling genius; and nothing Ford could do would be able to change this, or convince his father that he too was as worthy of love or approval. One can therefore see in his pursuit of the dual response, not only the craving for a response as such, but also a reflection of his paternal bind: the desire for recognition, combined with the realization that it will be frustrated.[26]

2

CHILDHOOD

By the mid-1880s the Hueffers had moved again, to 90 Brook Green in nearby Hammersmith. Two things impressed Ford most when he remembered his early childhood. First, stories. Those of his nurse, Mrs Atterbury, who had 'come into contact with more murders and deaths by violence than any person' he knew (before the war) were particularly vivid; in consequence, said Ford, 'my childhood was haunted by imaginary horrors and was most miserable'. The stories of the Pre-Raphaelites fascinated him. He retells some of the best of Madox Brown's in *Ancient Lights*, such as Brown's visit to Wales with an impoverished painter. They arrived at a watering-place at two in the morning, and, unable to rouse anyone at the inn, Brown's companion used his palette-knife to open the window of a lodging house. The two men slept in the drawing-room and slipped out the next morning. Madox Brown's own housemaid, Charlotte Kirby, was another source of stories. 'I do not know how many of my details of the lives of the great of the early eighties do not come to me from listening, unobserved, to Charlotte's conversations with my mother in the great linen room of the Fitzroy Square house.' Charlotte told him how she had got the cabman to help carry Swinburne upstairs to sober up in the bath. (It was characteristic of Ford's impressionability to well-told stories that he later described the episode as if he had himself overheard her exchange with the cabman.)[1]

Swinburne seemed one of the more congenial of the great figures, perhaps because of Charlotte's admiration for him, or for his kindness to Ford. Ford said the poet found him one misty day on Wimbledon Common, 'intensely distressed because my dog Dido had gone into one of the ponds and would not come out . . . So Mr. Swinburne wrote me a series of little jingles about the adventures of that faithful hound, and used to deliver them furtively as if he were slipping me little parcels of candy.' Otherwise, the Pre-Raphaelite great seemed as 'terrible and forbidding' to the young Ford as any of the spectres summoned up by Nurse Atterbury's grisly reminiscences. Fear was the other most important component of his childhood memories. 'To me life was simply not worth living because of the existence of Carlyle, of Mr. Ruskin, of Mr. Holman Hunt, of Mr. Browning, or of the gentleman [Sir Joseph Paxton] who built the Crystal Palace', he said. 'These people were perpetually held up to me as standing upon unattainable heights, and at the same time I was perpetually being told that if I could not attain to these heights I might just as well not cumber the earth. What was there left for me? Nothing. Simply nothing.' Hence, he implies, his art's preoccupation with god-like beings, who fail to live up to their impossibly demanding ethical ideals. Hence too, his impossibly demanding aesthetical ideal of self-effacement. 'I always considered myself to be the most obscure of obscure persons—a very small, a very sinful, a very stupid child.' 'I had been too much hammered by the Pre-Raphaelites. So that my troubled mind took refuge in an almost passionate desire for self-effacement.' From the safe distance of hindsight, Ford could write with magnanimous mockery of the hot-house atmosphere of Pre-Raphaelite intrigue, in which threats and abusive letters were often relayed via Brown: 'Swinburne would write: "Dear Brown, if P—— says that I said that Gabriel was in the habit of . . ., P—— lies." ' But the sense of intimidation never completely left him: 'ever since he had been a tiny child—he had, he said, been so much a creature of dreads [. . .] The dreads of original sin, of poverty, of bankruptcy, of incredible shyness, of insults, misunderstandings, of disease, of death, of succumbing to blackmailers, forgers, brain-troubles, punishments, undeserved ingratitudes, betrayals'. The catalogue reads like an abstract of Pre-Raphaelite social life; but Ford would re-enact all these dreads throughout his life, and become one of the greatest writers about fear. His cousin, Helen Rossetti, perhaps identified another source of his childhood terrors in his father's disciplining, when she recalled how her visits to the Hueffers were made unpleasant by 'old Franz's bullying of the boys'—something Ford characteristically never complained of.[2]

Ford is first glimpsed as a stylist aged 6. Madox Brown had been spending the spring and summer of 1879 and 1880 in Manchester, where he had begun work on his great project of painting historical frescos and canvases for the Town Hall. 'I hope you are not cross with me', he wrote to Ford when he eventually found time to reply to what appears to have been his first letter—or perhaps his first piece of writing with a pen: 'both your Grand-ma & I were glad to have your first note. The style of it was much to our taste, but we thought the scrap on which it was *wrote too* small for such a first work in pen-boy-ship: your ma will I hope tell you what that is'—and he signed himself 'your gran-pa me, Ford Mad-Ox Brown'.[3]

Ford was pleased to remember that the first public act of his writer's life—he called it 'the earliest incident of my chequered and adventurous career'—was to offer a chair to Turgenev, who had been brought by his physical double, his translator Ralston, to visit Madox Brown's studio, probably on the morning of 22 October 1881. Characteristically, he didn't so much remember the episode as remember being told it, since he said Turgenev told his mother who then told him—'imitating Turgenev's imitation of my squeaky voice'. The Russian made an impression that was to remain Ford's example of impressionism—and of how the Impressionist author's personality should be expressed by his books: 'I was conscious simply of a singular, compassionate smile that still seems to me to look up out of the pages of his books when—as I constantly do, and always with a sense of amazement—I re-read them.' Turgenev seemed tall and was bearded, and might have been expected to inspire Ford's awe: 'When one is suddenly introduced to such immensenesses one—or at least *I* do—gulps in one's breath in awe and, for the moment, believes that one is being visited by some supernatural manifestation.' Yet Turgenev's compassion for 'anything that was very young, small, and helpless' meant that Ford didn't feel that 'touch of the fear of the death that visits one when one sees Gods'. He didn't just emulate Turgenev in his own writings, but he would re-read him when he was depressed—perhaps precisely because his personality still felt like an antidote to intimidation, and could relieve Ford's childhood feelings of guilt and mortality.[4]

In the autumn of 1881 Madox Brown moved to Manchester to complete his Town Hall paintings. Ford, now aged 7, was sent to a boarding school in Folkestone run by a German couple from Frankfurt, Elizabeth and Alfred Praetorius, who were friends of Madox Brown. Ford remembered Mrs Praetorius as 'a very great educationalist', the favourite pupil of Friedrich Froebel, whose ideas for kindergartens which let the child's mind grow freely and spontaneously were beginning to revolutionize educational theory. He said he learned everything he ever learned at school from Elizabeth Praetorius. But he also learned one of his most enduring literary lessons from her husband, who told him: 'Schreib wie du sprichst' (Write as you speak). Ford, and Oliver too, who joined him at Pretoria House, received a truly cosmopolitan education, rather than the more conventional form of schooling which narrows the social definition of the individual. The conversation in French one day, and German the next, soon made Ford fluently trilingual. Like his father, he too is fond of throwing in a French phrase. But doubly fond, since it also makes him like his grandfather: '[Madox Brown] had been born and educated and lived in France until comparatively well on in life. He spoke always with a slightly un-English accent, and supplied missing words and phrases in his conversation with French expressions, a little old-fashioned because he dated from the days of Brummel in Calais.'[5]

Ford remained grateful to a Scottish usher at Pretoria House, who 'was probably responsible for the immense amount of reading in all sorts of languages that this writer got through before the age of twelve':

David Watson, M.A., of St. Andrews University, used to spend every spare moment of his day and whole Sundays on end with this writer standing beside him at his pulpit and construing for him every imaginable kind of book from the *Artaxerxes* of Madame de Scudéry and *Les Enfants de Capitaine Grant* by Jules Verne, to ode after ode of Tibullus, Fouqué's *Undine*, all of the *Inferno*, the greater part of *Lazarillo de Tormes* and *Don Quixote* in the original [. . .] In addition, Mr. Watson had this writer translate for him orally into French *The Two Admirals*, *The Deerslayer*, and *The Last of the Mohicans*—which made this writer appreciate what a magnificent prose writer Cooper was.

The young boy was struck by the look of Watson's head: 'he had the largest and reddest ears that can ever have been affixed to a human head.' He was also struck by Watson himself, in a bizarre episode in which the usher jabbed a sharp pencil into Ford's hand, and broke off the lead. In the published account Ford doesn't explain the incident; he said he was then teaching Watson French, so perhaps the precocity of the pupil had infuriated his supposed teacher. In *The March of Literature* he blesses him ('may his soul be being read to by whole choirs of little Anglican angels'—the phrasing of which might suggest that the attack was a piece of religious persecution). But the episode could stand as an emblem of how Ford felt his intimates, collaborators, masters, or protégés would ultimately betray him, turning on him with an inexplicable violence. An unpublished version offers another possible explanation. The usher, he said, insisted he read Lockhart's life of Walter Scott. Ford refused 'with grim obstinacy'. It was after one such refusal that Watson dug the pencil into him. 'Thus', says Ford, 'I may well consider myself to have been one of the first martyrs of the crusade against the Serious Book.'[6]

His voracious reading of fiction carried on through the holidays. He said he had read *Lorna Doone* thirteen times by his thirteenth birthday, and that his uncle William Rossetti gave him a volume called *The Novelists and Romanciers Library*, which included *Captain Singleton*, *The Mysteries of Udolpho*, and Sue's *Mystères de Paris*. Ford said it had been the childhood delight of Christina and Gabriel Rossetti as well, and that it had been given to them by Louis Napoleon: '(Napoleon III had, as he obviously would have, his uses for the Literature of Escape).' Ford's memories of his engrossed reading in that book suggest how it helped to form the novelist and romancier he became. In an unfinished manuscript, *True Love & a G.C.M.*, the Fordian protagonist Gabriel Morton is sent to visit the man he was named after, D. G. Rossetti, who gives him a volume called *Novelists' and Romancists' Library*, with over twenty, mainly picaresque, tales. As Ford must often have done, Gabriel Morton recalls the 'extraordinary first experiences' of his childhood reading:

He had been used to reading far into the twilights, close to windows so as to catch upon his book the last rays of the declining day; and then he had been engrossed. He would be so engrossed that no sounds from the encircling world and no voices were able to make him move. He had read in *Ivanhoe*, in *The Scalphunters*, in *Percival Keene*, in *Lorna Doone*, in *Copperfield*—reading coiled up in a window seat as a dog sleeps. If you had touched him then he would have complained inarticulately as a sleeping dog complains. It had been something rapt, like that. He had read also Waterton's *Wanderings in South America*; Bates on the Amazon; the *Life of a Scottish Naturalist*.[7]

'[T]here is no reading like that of a boy in the long dusks', wrote Ford: 'it is the deepest abandonment of the soul that we know on this earth.' Reading became his mode of 'gazing beyond': a visionary self-oblivion that seemed the sign of the highest art, as well as an escape from family conflicts. He would hide in the coal-hole, so as to read 'the adventures of Jack Harkaway, of Turpin the Highwayman, of Sitting Bull and of a thousand heroes' without his father knowing. In the 'great and mysterious garden' at Brook Green they dug a pond in the 'discouraged lawn' for the duck, Ike, 'who liked claret better than water'.

The water only stayed in the pond for long enough to let their pet jackdaw, Jack, take a bath. But the children romanced about the mound of earth displaced from the pond. They planted Jerusalem artichokes on it, creating 'a forest as black and mysterious as the one in which Nicolette met the woodcutters'. Ford would always be fascinated by the mystery of growing things; and he would continue to name his beasts, and to project his life of imagination on to his material surroundings.[8]

He said that since a boy he had thought Samuel Smiles's *Life of a Scotch Naturalist* 'the most beautiful book in the world'; and he also came to admire the naturalists Gilbert White and W. H. Hudson. Ford's earliest surviving letter shows him as the young naturalist at Pretoria House, telling his grandfather: 'We went on to the rocks yesterday & they were dotted over with sea anemones. We saw a lizard & I caught it & let it go after & then Harri & I lifted a stone up & we saw a snake which seemed to wake up in a strang[e] manner & then went lazily into some grass.'[9]

Some of the holidays were spent at seaside resorts such as Bournemouth or Hythe. The Hueffers and the W. M. Rossettis would take lodging-houses side by side. Then, said Ford, 'we were delivered over to the full educational fury of our aunt'. There was 'a long standing feud' between the half-sisters Cathy Hueffer and Lucy Rossetti. The Rossetti cousins were 'horrible monsters of precocity'. 'Olive wrote a Greek play at the age of something like five', said Ford, and as if it were not enough to have the young Rossettis perpetually being held up to them as 'marvels of genius', Ford had to act in 'cousin Olive's infernal Greek play' about Theseus and the Minotaur:

I was drilled, a lanky boy of twelve or so, to wander round and round the back drawing-room of Endsleigh Gardens, imbecilely flapping my naked arms before an audience singularly distinguished who were seated in the front room [. . .] it was my unhappy fate to wander round in the garb of a captive before an audience that consisted of Pre-Raphaelite poets, ambassadors of foreign powers, editors, poets laureate, and Heaven knows what. Such formidable beings at least did they appear to my childish imagination. From time to time the rather high voice of my father would exclaim from the gloomy depths of the auditorium, 'Speak up, Fordie!'

The only words he had to declaim were a Greek lamentation; it was his cousin Arthur, half his height, who played Theseus, striding about with a big sword, addressing 'perorations in the Tennysonian "o" and "a" style'. But Ford tried, of course. As with all the childhood memories he wrote about, this does more than evoke pity for the defenceless, overwhelmed child-self (held captive before his exacting figures of authority). It also explores the sources of his creativity, wondering if his need to write were not a response to that paternal edict to 'Speak up, Fordie!'[10]

The revenge of the Hueffer children was to lead their 'unsuspecting cousins into dangerous situations from which they only emerged by breaking limbs':

I bagged my cousin Arthur with one collar-bone, broken on a boat slide in my company, whilst my younger sister brought down her cousin Mary with a broken elbow fractured in a stone hall. Olive Rossetti, I also remember with gratification, cut her head open at a party given my Miss Mary Robinson because she wanted to follow me down some dangerous steps and fell on to a flower-pot [. . .] my cousins in the full glory of their genius were never really all of them together quite out of the bone-setter's hands.

When 7-year-old Helen Rossetti stayed with the Hueffers, however, she only remembered being jeered at (Ford asked her whether she was for Oxford or Cambridge, meaning the boat race, but she didn't understand and said 'Rome'). She remembered Ford, then about 12, as 'a very agreeable boy'. Theodore Watts-Dunton, Swinburne's friend, was also taken with young Ford a few years later: 'What a nice and intelligent lad he seems', he told Madox Brown.[11]

Another of his most vivid childhood memories is of Franz Liszt, whom Ford saw entering St James's Hall to listen to a concert. Ford had been taken by his father's assistant, Mr Rudall, who was always absent-minded, and on this occasion, finding that they were sitting just behind the royal seats, he had realized that he had forgotten to put his tie on, and so left to find another. The excited rustle in the audience suddenly burst into applause as Liszt entered, followed by the prince and princess of Wales. But Liszt's showman's modesty made him unwilling to sit in the central one of the three gilt chairs. He made what Ford called 'a little pantomime of humility', and lifted Ford out of his seat, choosing to sit there instead. What happened next depends on which of Ford's versions of the story you consider. In 1903 he said Liszt sat down with Ford upon his knee; though it is possible that this version combines the episode with the memory of sitting on Turgenev's knee. In 1911 he remembered being left standing, 'the very small lonely child with the long golden curls, underneath all those eyes and stupefied by the immense sounds of applause'. Someone—probably the princess of Wales—eventually gets Liszt into the appointed seat; and in the later version the princess then sits down in Ford's seat to stop Liszt returning to it, but graciously takes young Ford on *her* knee, 'as if she realized my littleness and my loneliness'. As with most of Ford's retold stories, the variants aren't irreconcilable (he might, after all, have sat on both illustrious knees). But what comes across in both is the powerful sense of the young boy 'stupefied' (transfixed as the stupid donkey he dreaded being) by the gaze of the awesome adults. There is an intimation of the agoraphobia from which he would later suffer in his comment that 'It was like being in a whirlpool'. He remembered 'a shudder of apprehension, of dread, and perhaps also of pride' at his proximity to this living legend. The musical setting, the being abandoned, and the feeling of being at the mercy of the adults' perplexing attention, all suggest how the episode reworks feelings about his home life, with the princess figuring in another 'family romance', acting as the ideal mother Ford felt he lacked. But the combination of his shudder and his pride suggest how the story also emblematizes his choice—if his training for genius allows one to call it a choice—of an artist's life. If Liszt's magisterial presence induced that 'touch of the fear of the death that visits one when one sees Gods'— and if, sitting in the seat that was reserved for Francis Hueffer as *Times* critic, and acting as the kindly father Ford felt he lacked, Liszt may also have summoned a frisson of the dread Ford felt before his father—then Liszt also exemplified how the artist can overcome the fear of mortality through fame, and become as loved and celebrated as royalty. Liszt was in London for his seventy-fifth birthday Jubilee tour in the spring of 1886, when he was received by Queen Victoria. He died later that year.[12]

In 'Nice People', the hitherto undiscovered anonymous essay in which he first told this story about Liszt, Ford juxtaposes people he had encountered with 'personal magnetism'. They are all either artists, or people prone to visionary states or with heightened sympathetic insight into their fellow mortals. One was a concert singer:

I used to hear her singing in the drawing-room and to listen outside the door, almost trembling with delight. She was very tall, very graceful, and very quiet, with grey eyes and lips that were always half smiling. When she sang her eyelids fluttered a little, and it was as if she were smiling at something at a great distance. Her voice was pure, like spring water, and tender and moving and wonderfully penetrating.

Staying outside the door spared Ford from the terribly penetrating gaze of less sympathetic adults, before whom he felt desperately shy in his ostentatious Pre-Raphaelite uniform of 'a suit of greenish-yellow corduroy velveteen with gold buttons, and two stockings of which the one was red and the other green'. 'These garments were the curse of my young existence', he wrote, 'and the joy of every street boy who saw me.' Like the concert singer, Liszt's eyes had 'something of that quality of gazing beyond'. The 'Nice People' didn't just offer relief from the frightening gaze of condemnation; they exemplified the kind of art into which they were initiating him, so that he could stand 'gazing beyond' the door, recapturing the vision of the smiling face he couldn't see.[13]

The other pupils at Pretoria house were children of the enlightened upper-middle class: 'they were omnivorous readers, they were delightful conversational-ists, they had fine manners, they were enthusiastic sportsmen.' Oliver was an absent-minded sportsman, starting off for the football field in his bedroom slippers. Ford was awkward at games, though Goldring said he had become captain of the school cricket team. There were also a few girl pupils at the school, who had come with the Praetoriuses from their previous school, one in the West End for girls. One of these girls was Elsie Martindale, who suffered from a tubercular knee, and required extra care. She soon became Ford's girlfriend. They would play chess together in the evenings, and she was nicknamed 'the captain's wife'. A decade later they were to marry in earnest. She was the daughter of Dr William Martindale, an analytical chemist whose *Extra Pharmacopoeia* remains a standard work. Ford shared a room with the son of a water-colourist called Beavis, and another Scottish usher, Robert Skinner, who had joined the school in 1888. Skinner said Ford used to waken him by munching Huntley and Palmer biscuits; and that 'he loved stories about Scotsmen (Aberdeen was unknown in those pre-historic times)'. Skinner found himself in a new world in the south-east, and was impressed by the worldly Hueffer boys, and their stories of 'Uncle William' Rossetti, and their bated breath when they spoke of Madox Brown. When the boys walked to the cricket field, or to the Downs on Sundays, Ford, who was the tallest pupil, would walk beside Skinner, who recalled his 'falsetto voice', long yellow hair, and red cheeks. At the beginning of the Christmas vacation Ford went with him to the docks to see him off on the boat back to Aberdeen. His sharp schoolboy wit survives in a Christmas card he sent Skinner: 'May the times be propitious to you! May your revels last as long as the Parnell Commission, though the cost be not so heavy!'[14]

'Ford quite a young man now—height 5 foot 11', reported Uncle William to his wife Lucy. 'Says he is well enough; nor did I observe anything definitely amiss'— which suggests there may have been something, or at least that the family feared there might have been, and had been fostering a hypochondriac vigilance. Ford later said his mother had impressed on him that he had 'a weak heart, an enlarged liver, a tendency towards tuberculosis, hereditary gout, and throat troubles'. 'His voice has altered,' noted Rossetti: 'I think only what takes place with all youths of his age.' He was 15. Later that January of 1889 it was Francis Hueffer who became ill, developed erysipelas, fainted, regained consciousness, had a second fainting fit, and on the 19th suddenly died, aged only 43. Everyone had thought him merely hypochondriacal. But 'the heart was wrong', according to William Rossetti, who was fetched by Ford and arrived at Brook Green to find the Madox Browns already there, and the whole family 'wonderfully composed and reasonable' under the devastating circumstances. He was struck by their 'stoical demeanour', but nevertheless saw 'terrible affliction' in Cathy's face. Ford's life and his art was to remain haunted by the fallibilities of the heart. Hueffer had had to live by his writings, and left almost nothing: the house, on which about £300 of the mortgage remained to be paid and a life-insurance policy for £2,000, though that too had been used as security for a loan of £250. Madox Brown's pride made him resent any suggestion that he could not support his family. Juliet said that 'Once a gentleman came to the house to bring my mother some money from the Queen, because my father had died too young for her to have a pension and she was very poor.' But Brown flew into a rage, and refused to let her accept, saying to the man: 'Tell Her Majesty my daughter is not a beggar.' The family and trustees met to decide whether Cathy Hueffer could go on living at Brook Green. Her health broke down after her husband's death. Ford and Oliver went to live with Madox Brown, who had returned to London and now lived at 1 St Edmund's Terrace, Regent's Park, two doors away from his old friend and neighbour Dr Richard Garnett of the British Museum. Juliet was sent to live with her Rossetti uncle and aunt and their extraordinary children.[15]

There was also the question of the boys' expensive education. Uncle William thought that Ford 'ought now to regard his schooling as finished', as he had had to himself at the same age. There were six Hüffer brothers and four sisters still living, but offers of help were slow to materialize. When Ford's bachelor uncle Alexis came over for the funeral, William Rossetti tried to interest him in providing for both his nephews, but he replied that he would prefer to help Oliver alone due to his 'more Huefferian type of face'. Eventually Uncle Wilhelm in Rome offered to pay for the boys' education provided that it was in a Catholic institution in Germany. He was not accepted, perhaps due to Madox Brown's opposition.[16]

Ford left Pretoria House and was in London during the spring, following his uncle's advice and example: 'Ford Hueffer came round to me from Brown's', noted Rossetti, 'bringing a letter which he proposes to send to the Civil Service Commissioners, asking when the next examination for Boy Clerkships would be held; as he thinks (and I consider it a reasonable idea) of competing at such an examination.' A month later he reported, 'Ford is attending, for 3 months, a Civil Service College in Chancery Lane'. He didn't become a civil servant, of course—Brown's opposition to his grandson becoming any kind of 'cursed clerk' may have been overwhelming. But that he made the attempt tells us three things about him. He was taking his responsibilities seriously; he knew from the inside what a clerical existence would mean; and a career in public service was a real possibility. So that the clerk-figures who dominate his early unpublished fiction are not expressions of an aesthete's condescension; his rendering of what he called 'the English public official class' was not a self-aggrandizing fantasy about power his artist's life denied him. Rather, these things were visions of what his life had almost been. However, three months later he was at school again, this time as a day-boy in London at University College School, where Oliver joined him later.[17]

The school was then in Gower Street, which Ford called 'surely the longest, the grayest and the most cruel of all London streets'. He said that 'very properly all education except the teaching of Latin verse and the reading of Plutarch was treated as a joke' at the school. It was in the dim, shadowy schoolrooms, 'with inkstains on the desk and bars before the windows', that he made his 'first acquaintance with the suns of Avignon', when the French class read Alphonse Daudet. Once again, reading meant escape and prestige: his languages were good enough for him to be placed in a class with older boys, one of whom Ford recalled twisting his arm because he wouldn't indicate 'the more salacious passages of *Tom Jones*'. One schoolmate, Charles Kinross, was a closer friend of Oliver's—who was now known as 'the Baron'— but was in Ford's French class when Ford was asked a question. 'Ford, a tall, golden-haired lad (both brothers had this attractive "chevelure"), rose to answer, and began in his rather Max Beerbohmish accent to discourse when, without warning, he fell full length over his desk in a dead faint. Water was brought whilst the other boys for once went silent before "Froggy". Ford, with the help of the master, soon came round and merely explained that he didn't frequently do that kind of thing.'[18] A *dead* faint? There is some evidence that Ford's feelings towards figures of authority at school were in turmoil following his father's death after a fainting fit. He intended to become a composer, and said that he was permitted to leave the school in the afternoons to attend concerts. But his German master ('Mr. P——') disapproved, and set for

translation the sentence 'Whilst I was idling away my time at a concert, the rest
of my classmates were diligently engaged in study of the German language.' The
German master could all too easily be associated with the German father.
Certainly Ford's account of what happened next makes the connection, and gives
an early example of his strategy of 'indifferentism', by which he subsumes his
personal anger into an artistic crusade:

Proceeding mechanically with the translation—for I paid no particular attention to
Mr. P——, because my father, in his reasonable tones, had always taught me that
schoolmasters were men of inferior intelligence to whom personally we should pay
little attention, though the rules for which they stood must be exactly observed—I
had got as far as *Indem ich faulenzte* . . . when it suddenly occurred to me that Mr.
P—— in setting this sentence to the class was aiming a direct insult not only at myself,
but at Beethoven, Bach, Mozart, Wagner and Robert Franz. An extraordinary and
now inexplicable fury overcame me [. . .] I rose in my seat propelled by an irresistible
force, and I addressed Mr. P—— with words the most insulting and the most
contemptuous. I pointed out that music was the most divine of all arts, that German
was a language fit only for horses; that German literature contained nothing that any
sensible person could want to read except the works of Schopenhauer, who was an
anglomaniac, and in any case was much better read in an English translation.[19]

In one way the attack on German culture exempts Francis Hueffer, a Schopenhauerian and another Anglomaniac. Yet it is aimed at him in another, since he
had seemed the schoolmaster when he *taught* Ford about schoolmasters; and it
was his injunction to respect the rules that Ford was now transgressing (though
he said that with 'some idea of respect for discipline', he had kept his speech in
German, which his classmates didn't understand). Mr. P—— threw an inkpot at
him, hitting him on the shoulder and ruining his 'second-best coat and waistcoat'.
Here the story resonates curiously. Though the master would 'throw an inkpot at
a boy who had made an exasperating mistranslation', he had never hit anybody
before. Ford implies that it was for this reason he later apologized profusely to
the master (as if to say that injuring Ford must have been the most upsetting
aspect). The master apologizes 'almost more profusely'; they make it up, walk
home together, and Ford has 'the greatest difficulty in preventing his buying
[him] a new suit of clothes'. But soon afterwards the headmaster summons him
to tell him he had 'better not return to the school'. The explanation Ford said he
gave was that there was a rule that 'no boy engaged in business could be permitted
to remain', which Ford had broken by publishing a book and getting paid for it.
'Mr. K—— was exceedingly nice and sympathetic, and he remarked that in his
day my uncle Oliver Madox Brown had had the reputation of being the laziest
boy at that establishment, whilst I had amply carried on that splendid tradition.'
After twenty years Ford's memory played him false here, since his first book
wasn't published until at least ten months after he had left school. Yet the point
of this story is to explain how 'music or the enthusiasm for music' put an end to
his education, stopped him from going to university, but ultimately led to his
becoming a writer instead of a composer. Backdating his authorship does this

more economically, suggesting that his writing career had already begun—which it had. He wants to illustrate how the established ethos is hostile to the arts: the master jeers at music, the rules discriminate against writers. Anyway, he disavows the headmaster's reason, saying that a schoolfriend later told him how he had reported the incident in the German class to the headmaster, and said that Ford's 'powers of invective were so considerable' that he would 'gravely menace the authority of any master'. Gravely indeed, since Ford says Mr. P—— was taken to task by the headmaster 'to such effect that the poor man resigned from the school and shortly afterwards died in Alsace-Lorraine'. Ford's emphasis on the inexplicability of his outburst, and his comment that he 'thought really no more of the incident', suggest that the cause remained repressed. He ends the story of Mr. P—— with an enigmatic coda: 'from that day to this and never before, can I remember having addressed a cutting speech to any living soul except once to a German waiter in the refreshment-room of Frankfort Hauptbanhof'. Enigmatic, because what Ford doesn't say here (though, as we shall see, he does elsewhere, when he omits to mention the 'cutting speech') is that the waiter committed suicide hours later. In both cases German-speakers die as a result of Ford's cutting speeches. It is hard to avoid the inference that, as with his dead faint in the French lesson, Ford was acting out the trauma of his father's death, for which (so the stories of Mr. P—— and the waiter intimate) he felt guilty. This works by what psychoanalysis calls an 'omnipotence fantasy'. Children inevitably have feelings of anger towards their parents, which they are taught to repress. If a child wishes a parent dead, and then the parent dies, the child may believe—unconsciously—that the wish became fact. This can produce coexisting feelings of power and guilt; and both feelings are bound up with Ford's conception of writing. His fiction explores power, creating or recreating the lives of kings, gods, demigods, potentates, the governing classes. It is also a *manifestation of* power. The pen is 'mightier than the sword' for him: he was always preoccupied with what Conrad called 'the power of the written word', both to 'revive the splendid ghosts' of the past (and thus make reparation for the death words had seemed to cause), and to provoke the punishment their outburst demanded. We don't, of course, know whether Ford ever said he wished his father dead, let alone whether he ever thought it. His sense of 'original sin' before paternal Great Victorians pre-dated Francis Hueffer's death, so that death alone cannot account for the way Ford's writing is haunted by guilt, the vertiginous fear of judgement from above, and a morbidity and suicidal longing that led him into nervous breakdown. But it was after his father's death that these traits became apparent, and that he became a writer.[20]

1889–1892

Ford left school for good before his seventeenth birthday. He said he took the 'entrance examination of one of the British royal institutions for education in music', but that although his grasp of musical theory was good enough, the principal bore a grudge that Francis Hueffer had 'domineered over that institution', and after a heated argument threatened to give Ford 'a hot time of it'. He turns the story to wry effect, saying that 'musical passion' had worked them both up to such a 'pitch of emotion' that he feared music might be an 'unbalancing' career. Anyway, his friends, enthusiastic about their own musical ambitions, were discouraging about his: 'This might be evidence that all musicians were hopelessly self-centred, or it might be evidence that my music was no good at all. I dare say both were true.' Either way, he decided (in an appealingly candid clause recognizing that musicians have no monopoly on self-centredness) that music was 'no career for a person craving the sympathy of enthusiasm and the contagious encouragement of applause. Possibly had I lived in Germany it would have been different.' The irony here is that he chose instead the solitary occupation of writing, in which the audience's response is so much less evident. The implicit contrast here between the virtuoso demanding applause (whether Lisztian genius or egoistic charlatan) and the self-effacing creator was one Ford knew from his family contacts—in the contrast between histrionic Gabriel Rossetti and quiet, resigned Christina. He dramatized it in an early story, 'The Old Conflict', in which the ostensible moral is that true art triumphs over vulgar display in the long term; but Ford was evidently also exploring the dual aspects of his own artistic personality. Mizener said that Ford's life during the early 1890s 'appears idle, and in a way it was'. It is true that he didn't try again to get a job. Madox Brown would have blasted him out of the house. It was never in doubt that he should be a genius of some kind: but should he paint, write music, poetry, fiction, criticism? He was trying them all. His musical ambitions were not taken particularly seriously by his biographers until the rediscovery in 1980 of about eighty pages of unpublished music written between 1894 and 1905; but it is now clear that he was a gifted composer, writing pieces for voice and piano, in the manners of Schubert, Liszt, Franck, Wagner, Fauré, and Sir Arthur Sullivan. A fine essay by Sondra Stang and Carl Smith argues for the importance of music and musical ideas throughout Ford's writing. They distinguish between his 'technical resources, which were limited, and his musical ideas, which were never unimaginative or meager. With little or no systematic instruction, Ford went rather far [. . .] The music he left is ambitious, full of character, and often eloquent':

Like his father, Ford tended to set fairly regular metric verse to repeated rhythmic patterns; both father and son employed a parlor-music vocabulary which was not marked by rhythmic contrast or rhythmic subtlety. But Ford was far bolder than his father, and the single greatest influence on Francis Hueffer—the music of Richard Wagner, 'the Music of the Future'—proved a much more liberating influence on the son, who was less afraid of failure in his melodic, accompanimental, and, above all, harmonic allegiance to Wagner.

His early work adheres to the troubadour ideal of the inseparability of words and music, and most of his early poems were written as songs. His first volume of verse, *The Questions at the Well* (1893), was subtitled: *With Sundry Other Verses for Notes of Music*. Stang and Smith noted his knowledge—gained before the era of recording—of a wide variety of European music over four centuries, adding that he apparently found the dominant Victorian musical culture provincial. He was also making an effort to understand the history of European music, and its relationship to the other arts, as can be seen from a timetable he drew up of musical and literary events taking place between 1878 and 1888.[1]

In October 1891 he became a published author. Madox Brown drew two illustrations for *The Brown Owl*, and persuaded Edward Garnett to get T. Fisher Unwin (for whom he worked as a reader) to publish it. 'I had written it to amuse my sister Juliet', said Ford: 'it was about Princesses and Princes and magicians and such twaddle.' He had written her a story, 'Princess Goldenhair', for Christmas 1889; and his second book, another fairy-tale, *The Feather*, was dedicated 'To Juliet'. She was the first of the sympathetic female listeners he would continue to seek, and his writing would continue to conjure. As Mizener said, Ford always loved children, and understood their love of the magical intertwined with the familial and the mundane. The success of the book 'made Ford an author'.[2]

His political education was undertaken by the young Garnetts and Rossettis. Richard Garnett—always an example to Ford of fabulous erudition—was made keeper of printed books at the British Museum in February 1890, and in June his family moved into one of the official residences on the east of the front courtyard. The W. M. Rossettis took over their house at 3 St Edmund's Terrace, and Cathy Hueffer and her three children were soon all living with Madox Brown, two doors away. Ford would work in the Reading Room at the museum, but eventually he would need to go outside to smoke:

Mr. Edward Garnett would drift along with his peculiar lounging stride of the slow bowler and, taking me by the elbow, would lead me to the Vienna Cafe, where in those days met all the youthful intelligentsia, and would lecture me on the Social Revolution. Or, if it was Thursday, I would go to Mrs. Garnett's tea behind the windows that you can see at the end of the East Wing. And there Mr. Gosse would trumpet the latest news from literary Scandinavia; and Mr. Sidney Colvin, keeper of prints, would drop in from next door, and tell us how, in the latest letter from poor dear Robert Louis, that exiled invalid would talk minutely about his health in Samoa; and Samuel Butler would relate the latest fluctuations in the four per cents. And I would be kept in a corner by Mr. Robert Garnett, who would tell me the latest eccentricities of his extraordinarily eccentric clients; or by Miss Olive Garnett, who wrote some very admirable stories about St. Petersburg and would tell me that I ought to become a Nihilist.[3]

He said the Garnetts' hospitality was 'as boundless as it was beneficent', and that his parents had courted in their drawing-room. It is from Olive Garnett's detailed diaries—wonderful documents, written from the heart of British Imperial culture, about her revolutionary and bohemian friends—that we get the most intimate portrait of Ford in the early 1890s. She was very fond of both the Hueffer boys; even slightly in love with them. Oliver took a patronizing line with her, and said he was afraid she would become a socialist or a nihilist, so he would go with her 'to listen to the Russian ravings' by the nihilist exiles Felix Volkhovsky and Sergey Stepniak. Volkhovsky had been made permanently deaf after a gruelling six-and-a-half years of solitary confinement in the St Petersburg's Peter-Paul Fortress, where he had been imprisoned three times without trial. He had escaped after eleven years of exile in Siberia, where his youngest daughter died and his wife committed suicide. Stepniak (whose real name was Kravchinsky, but whose alias means 'man of the Steppes') had been an active revolutionary propagandist. His eloquence was irresistible: he is said to have been 'the only man who ever succeeded in reducing Bernard Shaw to silence'. The Garnetts were impressed by his intellectual integrity, and found him quiet and gentle. They did not yet know how the news that one of his circle had been executed for armed resistance to the police had so roused him that he had ambushed the St Petersburg chief of police, General Mezentsev, and stabbed him to death. He had escaped, and came to London to edit *Free Russia*, for which Volkhovsky also wrote. Ford remembered Stepniak as 'huge, flat-featured, with small, fiery black eyes and an enormous dark beard. He was always serious. He once came to sit for my grandfather but could not sit still for long enough.' The 'Friends of Russian Freedom' (founded by Stepniak) were so many that there weren't enough seats at the meeting Oliver went to with Olive, but he got her one 'by industriously kicking a man in front of him'. William Morris 'sprang up & dashed into English Socialism', saying 'it was all very well to free Russia but were we not slaves ourselves'.[4]

Ford's Rossetti cousins too could lecture on the social revolution. Juliet left a vivid impression of the Rossetti household at this time: 'I had four cousins, who, though they were young, were social reformers. Mary was seven; Helen was nine; Arthur was about fourteen; and Olive was fifteen at least. I was eight, and I became a social reformer too. We were anarchists.' There was a printing press in the basement, on which they printed an anarchist paper called *The Torch*, mostly written by Olive and Arthur, but with occasionally an article by 'a real outside social reformer'. Ford said it published the first lines he ever wrote, the poem

'The Wind's Quest', which is, as he said, 'not very Anarchist in coloration', though it is quintessential young Ford in its romantic association of love, unrest, and (implied) death:

> 'Oh, where shall I find rest?'
> Sighed the Wind from the west,
>   'I've sought in vain o'er dale and down,
>   Through tangled woodland, tarn and town
> But found no rest.'
>
> 'Rest thou ne'er shalt find . . .'
> Answered Love to the Wind;
>   'For thou and I, and the great grey sea
>   May never rest till Eternity
> Its end shall find.'

The Torch was sold in Hyde Park on Sundays, and at railway stations. 'I think it must have been interesting and uncommon', she said, 'because whenever anybody bought a copy they would first stand some time staring at the cover, and as soon as they got to the title of the first article they would to an absolute certainty (we knew because we used to watch) turn round suddenly and stare after us.' Ford also told a story about another of the press's 'literary curiosities', a pamphlet by George Bernard Shaw entitled *Why I am an Anarchist*. Later, when he had become a socialist, and was addressing a meeting in Hyde Park and announced his title as 'The Foolishness of Anarchism', 'childish voices arose on the silence', repeating: 'Buy *Why I am an Anarchist* by the Lecturer. *Why I am an Anarchist* by the Lecturer. One penny'.[5]

Edward Garnett's wife Constance was also meeting the Russian émigrés through Volkhovsky and in particular Stepniak, with whom she fell 'more than a little' in love—as did Olivé. Stepniak encouraged Constance to learn Russian; her famous translations began appearing in 1894 with Goncharov, Tolstoy, and Turgenev. Ford was to say: 'For me Turgenev is the greatest of all writers and Mrs. Garnett's rendering of his Russian into English is the most flawless and limpid of carryings across from one country to another of a literary masterpiece.' As was usual with him, his admiration for her work—and for Turgenev's—was inseparable from his admiration for the personality of the writer. He recalled how when she appeared at the museum she 'would look in and beam absently with her blue eyes through her spectacles for a minute or two, and it all became much nicer'. He said later she was one of the women he had liked best all his life ('I mean as one likes men'); and he confessed that he 'popped her as heroine' into a novel. Stepniak introduced them to the philosophic anarchist Prince Peter Kropotkin, whom David Garnett remembered radiating benevolence and perpetual excitement as he 'walked about the room gesticulating with a forgotten cup of cold tea in one hand'. Through the Garnetts and Rossettis Ford learned much of the melodramatic world of the revolutionaries. He said he had been at meetings with August Vaillant, who was executed for throwing a bomb into the French Chamber of Deputies in December 1893. Ford was able to provide Conrad with the plot of *The Secret Agent* (on the first page we hear that Mr Verloc's shop-window displays 'a few apparently old copies of obscure newspapers, badly printed, with titles like the *Torch*, the *Gong*—rousing titles') and useful background information for *Under Western Eyes*.[6]

Ford cast himself as a gloomy Schopenhauerian in response to the revolutionary fervour of his friends. In another of his earliest surviving letters he characterized his own philosophy to Olive (she was still 'Dear Miss Garnett' at this stage) as of the 'pessim-agnostic, don't care-a-hang type', and threatened to start a rival publication to *The Torch*, the *Extinguisher: A Journal of International Pessimism*, with 'Patron: His Supreme Holiness / The Czar of All Russia / Official Editor: His Serenity the Prince of Darkness'. He drew up a mock front-page. The contents would include a 'slashing review' of a piece Olive had sent him to read; and articles on the prospect of Universal War, Universal Famine, and Universal Extinction. He joked about how his pessimism made it impossible to publish until he could be certain of failure—a sentiment which looks back to his father's magazines, as it anticipates his own editorial career. One can hear a similar seriousness being mastered through mockery in the journal's 'Statement of Principles: Let us eat, drink & sleep, for tomorrow WE DIE'. Pessimists shouldn't be merry. Olive was the only Garnett who could forgive Ford for his affectionate satire. But when she invited the four Rossetti children to tea to meet Volkhovsky and talk about 'Anarchism, Russian, & revolutionary affairs generally', she gave strict instructions that no uninvited guests were to be admitted, and noted with relief that her and her father's literary friends, including Ford—who had brought his first novel for Edward to read—had been 'successfully intercepted'. 'For my part he would have been a welcome guest', she wrote, 'but I suppose the Rossettis would have thought I had arranged it, & would have been terribly disgusted.' 'I wish the Rossettis had even some *small* sense of humour', she noted later. Ford's large sense of humour manifested itself by inventing imaginary works of fiction mocking anarchism. He assured her that 'he was preparing a most crushing allegory to hurl' at her. When she told him that she had just finished her novel (yes, she too was writing), he said he was continuing what he called 'his Anarchist Messiah': 'That the Duke, the young lady & the Messiah were all to be burned together at the end'. When, on 6 March, she visited Kropotkin and his wife, Olive contrasted their belief in 'the power of the moral sense' with 'Ford & his pessimism'. He was rapidly becoming an intimate of the Garnett family by then. Two days later her mother went to Madox Brown's for a viewing of his latest Manchester picture of 'Bridgewater Canal'—the one greeted with such opprobrium in Manchester. Olive heard how Ford was amused by people commenting on the frame if they didn't know what to think of the picture: 'He it appears stood like an iceberg in the middle of the room & behaved with great ceremony.' Mrs Garnett asked Madox Brown about his plans for the next cartoon. 'I see no reason why I should not begin,' he told her, 'but my grandson Ford says that I must

design a frontispiece for his novel, & that he can't wait.' Three days after that
Ford visited them after dinner to play chess with Dr Garnett, and entertained
them with his adventures, and his precocious habit of omniscience:

He said that he was in an omnibus in correct Sunday attire & some evident socialists
taking him for a swell made remarks on his appearance. He turned to them & said 'I
have prophetic foresight. I know who you are & where you are going. You are going
to a Socialist meeting at Kelmscott House.' It was so, the tables were turned. Papa
asked him about his music & he said 'I am writing a pot-boiler which I want
Antoinette Stirling to sing; if she will, I should get some thousands of pounds.' This
may be a Huefferism but it is delightful any way.[7]

There had been strife between the Madox Browns and Hueffers at Christmas.
William Rossetti thought it was due to Brown having 'been very forbearing with
the two youths, who were by no means so dutiful or deferential as they might or
should have been'. It may have been then that Ford had his 'skirmish in the
never-dying religious warfare that goes on between youth and age', leaving his
grandfather speechless with an arrogant display of his superior knowledge of
Provençal history. 'I do not think that there is much of my life that I would care
to change if I could', he said later, 'but that at least is a memory I should be glad
to be rid of.' In his fiction and his life he was—even from his youth—to identify
with the old being mercilessly attacked by the young, as if trying to exorcize that
shameful memory.[8]

   In January 1892 the Hueffers decamped back to the house at Brook Green. Ford
went for a walking tour in Sussex by himself in March. He called on Olive one
evening after dinner when he got back, and told her he had walked 120 miles:

One night he walked on the [railway] line for about five miles, it was very dark & he
had to avoid the mud by stepping from sleeper to sleeper. On reaching the station,
the station master asked how he had come & he said on the line whereupon a village
policeman who was by, arrested him(?) & suggested that they should go off together.
'But how far is it?' 'Fourteen miles.' 'Don't you think it would be rather inconvenient
to go all that way now?' The policeman seemed to fall in with this idea on his own
account, & the matter ended by the stationmaster's pointing out that Ford's nearest
way to Rye was on along the line. He also had an adventure with a tramp. When he
got to Rye he found another policeman who offered him his bed as he was on night
duty, & gave him breakfast in the morning, as he didn't want any himself, & then
refused remuneration. 'Do you know whose cottage you are in?' 'Yours.' 'Ah yes, but
do you know Fletcher?' 'The prize-fighter?' 'No the poet.' So he had been sleeping
under Fletcher's roof as well.

It is another early instance of his tendency to populate his surroundings with
literary ghosts. Olive recorded a long conversation they had that evening, in which
Ford's intellectual curiosity flashes through questions of philosophy, religion,
sexuality, and art. It shows him a remarkably self-aware 18-year-old, who was not
only beginning to grasp the contradictions and dualities of his nature, but was
beginning to find paradoxical ways of expressing them that would disturb his

audience with his candour about complexities which his contemporaries were still trained to deny.

To Olive he represented 'unreliability, inaccuracy &—genius'; though, as Moser says, she saw this was only one side of a Fordian paradox, since she also found him 'ultra-respectable and steady going':

We went into the dining-room, where we had a long & uninterrupted argument, just for the pleasure of thinking & talking, & exchanging impressions, with never the possibility of agreeing or convincing—But still delightful enough besides, a voyage of discovery into an intelligent being's mind, seasoned with laughter, is intoxicating always. I was however shocked when Ford admitted that as a relief from the gospel of perfect indifference to everything, he sought refuge in bigoted pietism in the Brompton Oratory, not that he thought that Catholicism was rational, outside its circle, but that it satisfied his sensual religious needs, he found poetry in it, etc.

In fact he started the paradox theory saying that in the mean lies torpor, in extremes madness; he balanced the two parts of his nature one against the other. Atheistic indifference on the one hand, bigoted pietism on the other. To my well ordered & I think carefully trained little rational mind, such confession seemed to reveal an abyss at my feet . . .

I was as much surprised when Ford also declared that the only thing really interesting & unfathomable was love, not the higher kind, but the lower kind. 'Helen of Troy the everlasting symbol.' Men to become beasts etc . . .

Ford has developed the argument to the point of 'paradox', anarchy & despotism, the one to relieve the other, atheism & bigoted pietism. His conscience does not reproach him for conceit or selfishness, nor would it for any crime; What is crime? But this way lies madness.

Could his 'excellent spirits' have had anything to do with having visited Elsie Martindale at Folkestone? He was certainly courting Elsie seriously by 23 July 1892, when he wrote a florid diary-type account of a day out with the Martindales by Taplow lock (on the Thames near Slough).[9]

Garnett's diary reveals a very different aspect of Ford to the one that rather intimidated his sister. Juliet remembered him as 'a fair, clever young man, rather scornful, with smooth pink cheeks and a medium-sized hook nose like my grandfather's, a high, intellectual forehead, and quiet, absent-looking blue eyes that seemed as if they were always pondering over something'. Like the 'Nice People' he later described, he had already the visionary habit of 'gazing beyond'. 'I was rather nervous with him,' she said, 'because he was very critical and thought that nearly every one was stupid and not worth disagreeing with. But he was very kind and liked to take me out to tea.' In June he called on the Garnetts in an astonishing 'outer and inner garb of the greatest ceremony' before going abroad for several months. 'He has been studying the Neo-platonists, beginning a 3 volume novel, expects the *Feather* to be out shortly, has been playing tennis, writing till 4 in the morning & then going out for a walk in the streets of London.' He also showed her the letter he had written to the *Manchester Guardian* defending Madox Brown's frescos. She found it 'thoroughly Brown, Hueffer &

Ford, its combined daring & cleverness almost took my breath away & it seems to have shaken up the Manchester folk a bit since they replied saying that so far was it from being true that they did not care for babies, that they had actually founded several societies for prevention of cruelty to Children'. By now relations were restored with Madox Brown. When he and Cathy Hueffer called on William Rossetti, Ford joined them there. They seemed 'cordial', noted Rossetti, 'and gave no evidence of a "fantasia Huefferica" '. Ford had often tried to impress on Olive that 'studying human nature & laughing at everyone is his greatest delight'. It is a side of his mind that was to produce anarchic satirical novels; but it is one that also sparkles in more sombre settings, flashing out in illuminating comic moments even in *The Fifth Queen* or *The Good Soldier*, where his comic imagination is felt in the rendering itself. 'I must say that his lordly air is caviare to me,' wrote Garnett, 'it delights me hugely, it is so absolutely unblushingly put on.' Throughout his life some would resent his patronizing manner; but she could appreciate it as an entertaining pose. 'I said that he might repent sitting up so late one day, that health was the most precious possession & so forth—the usual platitudes. "We were speaking of Goethe, I think" he said when I paused.' Such hauteur was one of the comic routines sketched with such freshness in her diary:

He caught a man trying to steal his watch. 'I did not prosecute him—ah, too much trouble.' [. . .] Edward came out of the B. M. at last, bowed low with mock ceremony & then hit him in the chest after which they proceeded to business. The Hueffer imagination is most refreshing. It had never occurred to me that a torch light procession over the Museum roofs was an ordinary & agreeable amusement for the residents at night [. . .] Oh dear I wonder if one would get very much bored if all ones [*sic*] friends were original people.[10]

Ford later said he had spent three winters in Paris and two summers in Germany before he was 20. Cathy Hueffer thought he should establish contact with the wealthy German relatives. He later recalled a voyage on a Rhine boat to Wiesbaden with his American uncle (Leopold), during which they had to telegraph the Vatican in order to resolve a disagreement about whether eels were 'canonically edible during Lent and on fast days'. He stayed with his uncle Hermann, who was a professor of history and canon law at Bonn, and said he studied history under him. (Certainly his wartime propaganda books reveal an impressive knowledge of German history and culture.) His uncle was 'the type of the absent-minded professor'. Once Ford was walking with him in the public gardens, he said, and a lady passed them and smiled. 'That is a very attractive woman,' said Hermann, 'I should like to make her acquaintance.' It was his wife, Antonie, who had been a prima donna and was said to have sung 'before all the crowned heads of Europe'. Ford's stories of these travels were written forty years later, with a high degree of vivid, picaresque romancing. Here too he mixed with emancipated youth, and was reading Nietzsche, as well as 'the pornographic books of young Germany' that he said the authors had asked him to read in proofs. When he said 'as far as Germany meant anything for me at all it meant so much more the romantic tales of Wilhelm Hauff's "Wirtshaus in Spessart," the romantic stories, told to each other, by travellers sheltering in the inn, in fear of robbers', he may have been warning us that he had re-imagined his experiences of Germany through such romantic fabulation. His stories that he had fought a duel in Bonn with a student who trod on the tail of his dog, and that he fought another in Paris soon after ('over a celebrated professional beauty'), should probably be taken as impressions of the 'patriarchal and archaic' nature of *fin de siècle* European student life and literature, rather than chronicles of what his own life was like. On the other hand, he may well have seen Bismarck, and met the Emperor William II (who had indeed studied at Bonn, where Ford said he was one of Hermann's pupils, and would visit his university acquaintances when passing through Bonn).[11]

He stayed at Bad Soden 'under the care of a quite atheist and strongly Nietzschean Lutheran clergyman' who acted as his tutor. They visited Frankfurt to see an electrical exhibition (not the world's first, as Ford thought: there had been one in Munich in 1883) , and went on a 'reading-party' to 'Hauff's own Wirtschaft' in the Spessart woods. The rural community could not have been a greater contrast to the industrial town, and he thought it 'an earthly paradise', enchanted by the blowing of horns, pan pipes, and whistles, by the 'swine, goat and sheep herds and the goose girl, summoning their respective beasts'. The inn had another literary past: it was 'reputed to have been the home of an alchemist', whose books and papers were gradually being used to light fires with. Ford tried to buy them, but was told they were the property of the community and so couldn't be sold. He said he stole two seventeenth-century volumes: 'I presented the treatise on the squaring of the circle to the British Museum. That on the nature of the Blessed Virgin I fear I have lost.' As always, Ford needed to turn landscape into literature: superimpose his different kinds of reading (Nietzsche, Hauff, alchemy, theology) on the surroundings, and populate his itinerary with figures from literary history. He also recalled 'a Russian-Polish Nihilist studentess called Magdalena Schabrowsky', who made a romantic impression: 'As became a Russian conspiratress she wore on her raven locks a sealskin toque and on her tall person a sealskin jacket.' She was ten years older than Ford, but filled his soul 'with heroic resolves and all the bliss of calf love'.[12]

In the autumn he was back in London, and sent Elsie a ring for her sixteenth birthday on 3 October. He wrote to explain to her mother that he hoped she would allow Elsie to accept it: 'You must have observed that, for a very long time, I have been fond, and more than fond of her':

Of course I am well aware that we are both of us too young for you to sanction anything like a definite engagement between us, & indeed, unreasonable as I am, I can see for my self that it would be wrong for me to wish to fetter her in any way [. . .] If, however you should consider the matter entirely out of the question I beseech you to say as much & I will resign myself never to trouble you or her again.

His feelings about the Martindales may account for his talking to Edward and Constance Garnett 'in a most despondent manner of the utter corruption of the

English Middle Classes'. He knew that the Martindales would want a financially more eligible fiancé for Elsie, so he tried to assure them: 'my prospects in life are fairly good & I do not think you would deem me over boastful were I to say that I have been more successful than many boys of my age—& there seems to be no particular reason why I should not continue to succeed.' To prove the point he had two books published that month: his second fairy story, *The Feather*, with a frontispiece by Madox Brown, and his first novel, *The Shifting of the Fire*, published in the Independent Novel Series by T. Fisher Unwin.[13]

The Feather is a more rambling work than *The Brown Owl*, though it too has the charm of Ford's quirky hilarity. Alison Lurie has suggested that the independent-minded Princess Ernalie has Elsie's brown hair and hazel eyes. In which case, her father's comic indignation might read as a witty re-working of what Ford feared from Dr Martindale, as well as an attempt to make light of envy towards possible rivals; 'You don't mean to say that you're in love with one another? Now I call that too bad. Here have I promised you to three dukes, and you've gone and fallen in love with a Prince. Now I shall have no end of a nuisance with them.' When Ernalie 'energetically' refuses to marry the dukes, Ford even jokes about the subject that was to energize most of his fiction: polygamy: 'I don't want you to marry *them*,' the King replies, 'one's quite enough at a time', and then he softens when she cries, and ponders: 'I'm afraid the only thing to do will be to have all their heads cut off. That'll keep them quiet, at any rate.' The story is also interesting for the way it exemplifies another quintessential Fordian concern. The feather of the title is its main magic device. When Ernalie finds it, 'she found rolled round the quill end of it a small piece of paper on which was written: "Guard well the feather, for whoso toucheth his hair therewith— though he be but feather-brained—shall be invisible, yet shall he see all".' The feather is presented as pen (quill) and paper; it confers not just invisibility but power, transforming even a stupid donkey into a god-like figure, invisible but omniscient. It is Ford's earliest exploration of the magic of writing to re-invent his life.[14]

Conrad said the best that can be said of *The Shifting of the Fire* when he read it soon after he had met Ford:

I have read it several times looking for your 'inside' in that book; the first impression being that there is a considerable 'inside' in you. The book is delightfully young [. . .] Felicitous phrasing is plentiful and with that the writing is wonderfully level. There is certainly crudeness in the presentation of the idea [. . .] The analysis however if not crafty is true and every fact is significant. That's indubitable. Nevertheless it is apparent only on reflection. And that's *the* fault. Why exactly it is so I am of course unable to say [. . .] I feel that the effects are partly lost [. . .] No doubt the general cause is (O! happy man) youth—inexperience [. . .] What is mostly obvious is the talent of the writer and that I have the sense to recognise.[15]

It is a remarkable performance for an 18-year-old, which shows how, even in its earliest productions, Ford's fiction reflects upon and spins fantasies out of his own experiences. The Fordian hero, a wealthy young chemist, Clement Hollebone, is of foreign descent which he traces back to Holbein. He is engaged to Edith Rylands, but—the first of a series of Fordian protagonists to be susceptible to multiple passions—he is also attracted to her room-mate Julia, and then to a young American cousin Kate. This, together with Edith's jealousy of Julia, might be evidence that as early as 1892 Ford was aware that Elsie's sister, Mary, had conceived a passion for him, and that he was not indifferent to it. The Martindales' horror of this possibility is thought to have been one of their objections to a marriage between Ford and Elsie, compounded by their fear for Mary's mental state. It is one of the many ways in which this strange novel seems uncannily to predict some of the events of Ford's life during the next decade. Its investigation of the 'higher' and 'lower' kinds of love deepens when, after Clem loses his fortune, Edith marries a rich old monomaniac libertine, Kasker-Ryves, so that she will be able to inherit his money and marry Clem. It is thus also Ford's first study of altruistic renunciation—of the kind he had already offered when he told Elsie's parents he would resign himself to forgoing her if they decreed it. The plot becomes even more adolescently absurd—though again in a way that foreshadows much that is best in Ford's later writing. Clem conveniently but ironically inherits a second fortune. As a birthday present he had given Edith a bottle of a new poison he has developed. When Kasker-Ryves dies, he is convinced she has poisoned him. Yet by this time his passion for her is so overwhelming he marries her anyway. The story ends happily, with an ingenious but entirely implausible psychological twist, as she realizes that this was the acid test of his love: 'You thought I had committed a murder, and *yet* you married me!' The title denotes the fire shifting in the grate, which Clem notices at decisive moments in his life. But, as Thomas Moser says, it connotes passion, which impels people as it consumes them. As he says, the novel deals with the complications caused by Clem's and Edith's misconceived self-sacrifices; but, like *The Good Soldier*, it also 'dramatizes the destructiveness of passion and shows human beings murderously preying upon one another'. The book's seriousness persuaded Ford's Rossetti cousins to take him more seriously: 'the tone in which they speak of the author is distinctly more genial,' noted Olive Garnett, 'as if they had discovered that he was human after all, & not a monster of worldliness.'[16]

Moser gives an ingenious reading of the novel in terms of Ford's preoccupation with Dante Gabriel Rossetti, and argues that in 'a recurrent, highly charged, grotesque scene, depicting a powerful Kasker-Ryves, an inert Edith, and a terrorized, fascinated young man, Ford comes close to dramatizing his sexual anxieties'. When Clem and Edith find Kasker-Ryves dead, she 'flung her arms round the neck of the motionless corpse and fell to the ground with it', while Clem remains 'in paralysed amazement surveying the living and the dead, lying together on the floor. In his strained state of mind he had hard work to keep from laughing at the grotesque figure of the corpse as it lay, stiff and unnatural like an artist's lay figure, across Edith.' Moser says that even in death 'the old man remains a potent Rossetti'. But the dead father-figure frozen in a *liebestod* embrace with Clem's love brings together two haunting fathers: Francis Hueffer, whose death prostrated Ford's mother, and Dr Martindale, whose protective jealousy of Elsie (the novel implies) was disturbingly sexual. Clem's tonal duality— appalled, but struggling to suppress a laugh—confirms the suggestion that Ford had repressed a wish that his father should die. In Clem's transfixed moment Ford is again exploring the sources of his art, which re-enacts the death of the father-figure before the spectator paralysed with guilt ('I have made her do it', says Clem), and simultaneously offers relief from that guilt, since Clem's paralysis is also the 'gazing beyond' of aesthetic rapture.[17]

Ford dedicated the novel—the first proof of his commitment to the artist's life—to his grandfather. He inscribed a copy for him too: 'Ford Madox Brown E^{sqre} | from his affectionate Grandson | the Author'. Not just the author of this particular book, but Brown's 'grandson the author', something his other potential geniuses of grandchildren had not yet become. Reviewers were often to comment on his way of describing himself as 'the writer' in his reminiscences, in a way which seems at once modestly to efface his personal identity while emphasizing his literary personality. His inscription shows how much it meant for Ford to be able to think (and write) of himself as 'the author', even in 1892. He began to do the sorts of things authors do, such as writing an obituary for the Poet Laureate, Tennyson, when he died on 6 October 1892.[18]

In November 1892 Ford was back on the continent. He stayed in Paris with 'American relatives who belonged to the rich Anglo-American Catholic circle that solidly ornamented in those days the French capital', but who lived in terror of the French equivalent of the very anarchists with whom Ford had been mixing in London. Uncle Leopold and his family from Virginia were living near the Arc de Triomphe. Ford later recalled 'winter after winter spent in an immensely luxurious, gilded and absolutely tranquil *appartement* of a millionaire's house'. When they took him to the opera:

my eldest cousin used to sit in the back of the box reading the libretto with attention—ahead of what was happening on the stage. Just before anything at all *risqué* was about to happen he would warn my uncle who would stand up with great solemnity and draw the curtains of the box so that my cousins' wives should not be scandalised. I remember that we thus saw practically nothing of Massenet's MANON with Sybil [*sic*] Sanderson in the title role.

The Hüffer relations, said Ford, 'made very strong and ultimately successful efforts towards my conversion'. He used to slip out every morning to the English Church of St Joseph's in Avenue Hoche to receive 'instruction'. One of his cousins, a 40-year-old American banker with an air of extreme gravity, took him there first, and made Ford's first impression of the Passionist fathers memorable by releasing a small clockwork duckling on the floor as Ford went in. The 'delighted burst of laughter' from the fathers impressed Ford with their 'simplicity and unworldliness', and ensured that they too became classed as 'Nice People'. Ford remembered one in particular whose 'ancient face wore precisely the smile that was always upon the Abbé Liszt's'. Mizener thought Ford's religious views were 'essentially a by-product of his social and political views rather than a religious attitude'. Certainly Ford's conversations with Olive Garnett show that part of the appeal of his Catholicism was in the way it provoked the rationalist friends he was defining himself against. But his social and political views were no more firmly grounded than his religious attitude. 'I don't know how deep my Tory-Papistry of those days went,' he confessed, 'but I know that my manifestations of that spirit of lost causes gained a good deal in what we used to call cockiness from the fact that my cousins [. . .] made my life rather a burden with their militant atheism and anarchism.' He was untroubled by theology and dogma. He admired the response of 'old Father Peter' when he said he couldn't compass the idea of the Third Person of the Trinity: 'He, being old and wise and having the interests of the Church cannily at heart, replied: "Calm yourself, my son; that is matter for theologians. Believe as much as you can"—since when I have never given a personal thought to matters theological.' However, whereas Mizener was right to say that most of the time he was 'scarcely Catholic in either feeling or conduct', Ford's own account of his conversion intimates that the Church ministered to greater needs than ingratiating rich relations or colourful posing. The naïve laughter of the familial priests remained his first impression 'when thinking of that tremendous organism "Rome," whose roots sink so deep down into the weaknesses, the terrors, the childish heart of man that is afraid in the dark'. His childhood dreads, and feelings of original sin had been exacerbated by his father's death. He could believe in the Father and the Son ('the one vengeful, the other infinitely forgiving'); the Church offered to redeem the figure of the vengeful father into the loving fathers who could welcome him with joy and forgive his inadequacies. On 7 November he was received into the Church. Immediately after his baptism he went to see Father Peter, whose 'eyes shone at the netting of this one more soul'. He clasped Ford's hands, kissed him on the cheek, slapped him gently on the shoulder, and exclaimed: 'Now you're a b——y Papist!'[19]

4

1893: ART AND ELEGY

As soon as a fact is *narrated* no longer with a view to acting directly on reality but intransitively, that is to say, finally outside of any function other than that of the very practice of the symbol itself, this disconnection occurs, the voice loses its origin, the author enters into his own death, writing begins.

(Roland Barthes, 'The Death of the Author')

At the end of the year Ford was back in London, living with his mother at 90 Brook Green. In January 1893 his mother told Olive Garnett he would write after dinner until two or three in the morning, and come down at midday 'reading really "dry" books & going on with music quietly'. Oliver too was writing— 'comic' stories. Garnett said he was 'spending his time in getting his own way', and was 'much sought after'. He had 'solemnly' told his mother he was engaged—perhaps not wanting to be upstaged by Ford. Even Juliet, now 12 and suffering from rheumatism, was 'betraying a tendency to write': 'the whole world seems to be "writing" ', wrote Olive.[1]

Ford's love-letters to Elsie written over the next eighteen months reveal the more earnest side of his romantic pessimism: 'it is the unforeseen that always comes about,' he told her, 'so let us at least foresee disasters & contrive beforehand what steps we may take if the worst cometh—This is the philosophy of Ford the son of Francis, the son of Wilhelm, the son of Eduard u.s.w. whoso followeth in its footsteps shall walk aright.' He was preparing her to confront her parents' opposition, which was becoming stronger: 'it is not impossible that very well minded people will conceive it their duty to separate you & me—and so render it more difficult for the Will to bring us together—but only difficult—not *impossible*.' By March 1893 he had told Madox Brown that they were engaged. 'Mrs. Hueffer likes Miss Martindale who is seventeen only, pretty, musical & delicate', wrote Olive Garnett. But she added that Cathy Hueffer was worried about Ford's heart: 'he is not at all well & taking his grandfather's advice has gone to Salisbury to walk about there. Oliver has gone with him to look after him.' Madox Brown was worried too when he heard that not only Ford's father but two of his uncles had 'died suddenly from heart disease'. 'Ford won't see a doctor,' recorded Olive, 'he says that he knows all about himself, his heart *is* weak.' *The Shifting of the Fire* had already sounded the pun on 'heart' that echoes so disturbingly through *The Good Soldier*. When people asked Kasker-Ryves's doctor

whether there was 'anything wrong with his heart', 'the great physician quite
understood society's innuendo'. Juliet Soskice said that because so many people
Cathy Hueffer loved had died, 'she always seemed to be afraid that other people
were going to die'. She doubtless conveyed the fear to Ford. This helps to account
for the extreme morbidity of most of his earlier and much of his later work. Yet
Olive Garnett's comment suggests that it was also his mother who encouraged the
connection (already implicit in his Passionist religion) between sexuality, suffering, and death. He announces his desire for Elsie; his mother worries about his
heart.[2]

He took Elsie to one of the Garnetts' 'at homes', where Olive found her 'a
charming girl, exceedingly pretty & not merely so, but she has a soul in her face';
and she noticed especially 'the light in her eyes. At times she smiled in their
depths as at a secret happiness. She has too, charming manners & neither conceit
nor shyness.' Ford 'looked proud of her, as well he might'. Olive 'was of course
rather on the look out for signs of ill health in Ford', and noted that 'his hands
have a very dangerous look' (she didn't say how), but thought that 'otherwise he
seemed well'; though it was the frail Elsie who 'looked the more robust of the
two'.[3]

The Martindales liked Ford 'very much', said Olive, and permitted Elsie to see
him; but they were uneasy from the start about the idea of him as a son-in-law.
Mizener said that not only were they suspicious of his advanced ideas, 'especially
about sex; they also suspected him of wanting to marry Elsie for her money'.
Martindale had a prosperous pharmaceutical business in New Cavendish Street.
He was also mayor of Winchelsea, where they had a second house. They were the
kind of conservative, *arriviste* middle-class people that both Ford's (and Madox
Brown's) Toryism and radicalism would have made him look down on.
Mrs Martindale drank—a habit she had formed when 'an overworked country
nurse in Ireland' before her marriage, and which (as Mizener also said) 'encouraged the young people's belief in their own superior good sense'. By May it had
become necessary for Ford Madox Brown to call on the Martindales and discuss
whether they would allow Ford to go on seeing their daughter. They said that
although they weren't trying to separate them, they were worried about the health
of Elsie's elder sister Mary, and proposed to send her to Bad Soden in Elsie's care
for the cure. This gave Ford the opportunity to lecture Elsie on renunciation: 'if
it will be so much for Mary's good that she should go away—would it not be well
if we should sacrifice ourselves.—It would be very bitter—but self-sacrifice is the
greatest of all virtues [. . .] for dearest, we must remember that we are Christians,
you & I,— & if our creeds differ in small matters from those of others—the great
virtue of it remains—that we should give our lives for other people.' However,
the Martindales did not reveal the main reason for their opposition. 'From
childhood Mary had been of such an excitable temper that her parents feared for
her sanity. Now they had discovered that she cherished a passion for Ford and
they were terrified of the effect on her of any special intimacy between Ford
and her younger sister.' If (as *The Shifting of the Fire* might indicate) Ford had

given Mary any encouragement, he didn't now: 'I am glad there are prospects of Mary's amelioration,' he told Elsie. 'If they could only chip off a little of her spite at the same time, it would not inconvenience her very much.—But perhaps they would fear lest the edge of their instruments should be turned.' Elsie was later to say that if she had known of this reason, she would probably have obeyed her parents. But because they didn't tell her, first they seemed 'incapable of deciding anything'; then when they showed their opposition it must have seemed intolerably bourgeois, and only hardened the lovers' resolve. Olive Garnett heard (from the Hueffers) that the Martindales would 'not allow that it is a formal engagement till she is stronger'. To Ford it seemed as if they were exploiting Elsie's health as a pretext for procrastination, and as a means of dominating her. He wrote that 'this insensate cruelty, which wounds merely to give the inflictor the gratifying sense of power over some-one weaker, is to me utterly abhorrent'. He advised Elsie to be 'quite coldly polite' to her mother: 'It was a maxim of Johnson's that if one argues with a man one lowers oneself to his level.'[4]

When Olive Garnett encountered the Martindale sisters in Regent's Park, 'dressed in an art shade of bright green velvet in the aesthetic style, with capes to match their dresses & green hats', she said Elsie looked 'very handsome', but produced quite a different impression from the last time she had seen her. The strain was beginning to tell: 'her face wore an utterly bored, indifferent, & rather tired, perhaps a little cross expression. She was pale too, & so was her sister who was more grown up & less striking in appearance.' Olive smiled at Elsie, who didn't recognize her. 'I cannot reconcile the red velvet Elsie with the green velvet Elsie at all', she wrote. It was a shrewd perception of a hardness underneath the feminine grace.[5]

Ford began to imagine suicides again. '[S]ometimes a fearful panic seizes me—a dread of the unknown,' he wrote to Elsie, '& then I think we must be buried in each other's arms dear—for we must & shall die together. Would it not be the greatest of all bliss for us to lie in each other's arms with nothing to look at from our bed of the stream of death, save the bubbles that pass overhead.' In his first volume of verse, *The Questions at the Well*, published in the summer of 1893 under the pseudonym 'Fenil Haig' and dedicated to Elsie, the title-poem imagines a suicide pact between lovers who hurl themselves down a deep well and fall eternally. In 'Hope in the Park' a lover contemplates suicide, described curiously as 'His bride—the Hope of Rest in Death'. He translated Rückert's 'Du bist die Ruh'—'You are rest'—a phrase which he often addressed to Elsie. The association between sexuality and death is ancient, of course, but Ford was to remake it into something quite his own. 'The most attractive of his various ideas was the one which prompted him to make away with himself ', he had written in *The Shifting of the Fire*. 'There is a sort of jingo glamour about suicide that captivates shallow thinkers or people that brood too much. It was, however, mainly indigestion with Hollebone.' The joke is more bitter than it might look: Ford himself would complain of 'dyspepsia' when most depressed and these writings show him to have experienced suicidal depressions even before his marriage to Elsie. But he understood the meretricious self-indulgence and self-pity of suicidal brooding. Even at his most morbid and sombre his characteristic tonal duality seeks the relief of irony and facetiousness. One can hear him trying to keep his spirits up in his letters. He would sign himself 'Fraud M. Hueffer' to Edward Garnett, or to his fellow punster Walter Jerrold. Relations with the Martindales became more serious. They still refused to sanction the engagement. When they did invite Ford to call on them he wondered, in a letter to Elsie, whether he should reply by saying that he 'should be delighted to accept kind inv. on condition that I am treated on the occasion as the affianced husband of Elsie'. But six weeks later Mrs Martindale had said she would rather see Elsie dead than married to Ford, whom she had called an 'impostor'. 'Your mother is a most dangerous woman', he told Elsie.[6]

He was also depressed because of Oliver's antics. Madox Brown had to pay off £200 of his debts 'for use of horses Dog Carts &c'. Olive Garnett said that Brown was complaining: 'Oliver has no conscience, he laughs when I speak seriously to him. The only thing that has the least effect is to say "Well Oliver, whatever you do, remember that you are a gentleman, your father was a gentleman, don't do anything dishonourable".' Ford may well have heard something of this: he was often to remind himself that he was a gentleman, and sometimes would remind his acquaintances. When there was another financial crisis that summer, Oliver tried to get his grandfather to lend him money 'to carry out some unexplained scheme with his uncle William Rossetti, the most practical man imaginable and the last one anybody would expect to involve himself in a scheme of Oliver's'. The family then tried to persuade Oliver to go to Africa, but he replied scornfully that 'it would cost 200£ for the outfit alone'. 'No one understands him, no one knows whether he will be hanged, or become a great person', wrote Olive Garnett, who added understandingly: 'I think of Peer Gynt, & keep a certain image of him undefiled in my heart.' (She had been struck by the audacity and charm with which he had asked her for her photograph, even though four-and-a-half-years her junior.) 'O. is gradually ruining the V[enerable] P[arent],' Ford told Elsie gloomily, 'so that unless something turns up he will probably be sold up—& so things will go from bad to worse.' Ford was 'as poor as ever', as Olive found out from his mother. Seventeen-year-old Oliver was scarcely a good advertisement for Hueffer reliability and responsibility, and the Martindales would look even less favourably on the grandson of a bankrupt. '[T]he thing is coming nearer and nearer & he will take no steps to stop it himself— he is too good natured or obstinate.' Ford was himself to prove too good natured or obstinate to avoid his own financial catastrophes; indeed, he was often to invite them so as to venerate his grandparent. 'There is I fear a crash coming sooner or later—& then—the deluge—& although I can generally shut my eyes in the face of approaching evil & wait quietly— just of late I have had too much of that & I am getting nervous. Mrs H. too, is becoming exceedingly queer with all the worry—so I don't know what is to come'; but, 'I had a most affectionate letter from Mrs M. this morning

& so I suppose in that quarter things may fairly be considered made up. But compensatory things are breaking out elsewhere.' Again he offered to renounce Elsie. He suspected her family of trying to interest her in more suitable matches. There was a 'Eustace W' he said was 'so much in love' with her; and then an 'extremely handsome friend'. 'I think I had better become jealous', said Ford bitter-sweetly: 'It is quite a tragic affair.' He wrote her a letter which contemplated renunciation, while ending with his familiar rhythmic refrain pledging eternal love:

—And my dear, dear baby, it would be better for you if you could—bring yourself to love someone else.

　If you could I would give you up—but you know what that would mean for me.—You see, dear, things are going from bad to worse with us here, & what makes it all the more bitter is that it is through no fault of our own [. . .]

　So if you do meet any nice young man—the W's will look out for that—& if he is quite well off & handsome & stupid—so that you can keep him quite under your thumb in the future— why, dear, just give me up, you will give up a lot of trouble & a lot of heartburning.—It will be a little longer for me to wait for you [until they would meet after death?] & perhaps it will all be a little less bitter when I can think that I am not dragging you to misery.

　You see dear, I love you so very much & it is like that we are working out—& you must not put the idea aside for the sake of mere sentiment—because it is not the plot of a novel—not even of the poor old 'Shifting'.

　You are so clever & have a great future before you—or would have if you could work at your ease, without a thought of bread & butter—& it is a crime against humanity in me if I drag you down into a soul-wearing struggle that saps both body & mind.— And, afterwards—there is a long, long time to come afterwards & may be then we shall see everything aright. And this alone endures: that I love you, love you, love, love, love, love, love you, more, more, more, more, ever, ever, ever more than ever.— As for me—I can wait. 'Man that is born of woman is of few years & full of trouble.'

Even as he says his plan of renunciation is 'not the plot of a novel', one sees how the novelist's imagination broods on and hatches the plots and thoughts of a life. It *was*, approximately, to become the plot of one of his most intensely renunciatory novels, *A Call*, sixteen years later. Olive Garnett said that 'Ford speaks to everybody as if he were their great grandfather'. Talking of his youthful first novel as the 'poor old "Shifting"' was indicative of a trait of pitying himself by projecting himself into the future, into old age. Why did he do this throughout his life (and in much of his fiction: think of the aged narrator of *Romance*, the exhausted narrator of *The Good Soldier*)? This letter gives one answer: it enables him to distance himself from the emotional stress of the present. Imagining himself as his own grandfather resigns him to the present necessity of resignation (as he had always felt he had to renounce what he treasured, from his rabbit onwards), and enables him to imagine a time when he will be free of the parental injunction to renounce.[7]

Mrs Hueffer's way of trying to avert the crash was to take Ford on a second trip to Germany for three weeks in the summer of 1893, to visit more Hüffer relations in Paderborn and Münster. But he was feeling no better when he got back. 'Exactly why I feel so bad I cannot say but somehow Devonshire Street is so hopelessly depressing to me—& the constant keeping up of idiotic small talk tires me out [. . .]', he told Elsie: 'In the meantime M^r· M. is getting into a nasty state of mind—& M^{rs}· will spare no possible means of making you pose as a rebellious child—before him.' In the hope of larger talk he went to meet 'the great Le Gallienne—you see, he is a great, great man & it is as well to conciliate him'. But even 'all these wonderful great men [. . .] contrived to make a wonderful deal of small talk among them'. A greater poet than his fellow-Rhymer, Richard Le Gallienne was struck by *The Questions at the Well*: 'one of the few new books of promise which come to a reviewer in a season; nor is the promise the less evident because one does not quite know what it promises [. . .] he is yet but little of an artist, for art is before all other things the finding and cleaving to one's own [. . .] There is a right lyrical vehemence in most of his shorter verses.' A sensitive and prophetic response. The reviewer? W. B. Yeats.[8]

The crash came that autumn. Madox Brown had been ill for about a year. One day he got down into his painting chair and tried to pick up his brushes, but dropped them:

He pulled off his glasses and looked attentively at his right hand; the short sturdy fingers moved only imperceptibly. He looked at them for a long time, reflecting. Then he shrugged his shoulders, fitted the palette on to his right thumb, and began to paint with his left hand. I was looking on at the time, but it was not till afterwards that I realised exactly what it meant, he did it so silently and so naturally. Six months later he had finished half the picture. He said: 'I'm always glad when a thing is half done. It feels like going home.' [H]e sat for some time talking about Rossetti's personal waywardnesses; his last words were: 'But Gabriel was a *genius*,' and then he went up to bed and never came down again alive.[9]

The Hueffers came to St Edmund's Terrace, and were in the house when he died on 6 October 1893. They were devastated. Both Ford and Juliet felt they would never forget him, and his death, as long as they lived. In fact Brown's last words in his conversation about Rossetti were not his last words. He was in bed for several days, talking with vivacity, and then trying to dictate to Ford the sketch of his life on which Ford based his biography. In that book Ford says that his 'last quite coherent words must, I think, have been uttered whilst advising some alterations to a work of Miss Blind's, or perhaps in taking leave of Mrs. Rossetti, who was on the point of departure for the Riviera'. (Lucy Rossetti, his elder daughter, died there the following April.) Even in this account Ford elides Brown's gruesome last days of incoherence. Juliet had a terrifying experience when she slipped past the nurse. Brown woke up and said to her: 'I'm sorry, I don't know you.' When she called him 'Grandpapa' he remembered his 'little pigeon' again for a moment. Then he began to confuse her with her mother, as his memory dragged him back to the death of his beloved son Oliver. It wasn't that Ford wanted to rewrite history in talking of his grandfather's death. His official biography, published three years later, is too scrupulous for that. But, as he says in it, he could not bear to write in too personal a way about him: 'when I come to write of Madox Brown as a man, my debt of gratitude to him is so great, the thought of him as he was so constantly present in my mind, that did I allow myself to praise him at all my emotion must carry me too far for sober print.' Though some of the book drags—it is, as Ford concedes, 'documentary', 'a simple chronicle'—its ending is extremely moving, as only then does he reveal his kinship with the subject, and the act of self-suppression that has kept the writing so subdued. It was to become a characteristic Fordian twist. Dowell, in *The Good Soldier*, could be speaking for him when he says: 'Forgive my writing of these monstrous things in this frivolous manner. If I did not I should break down and cry.' It mattered to Ford to leave the impression that his grandfather's last words had been a celebration of an artist-friend; and it mattered to him to think that the last word of those 'last words' was that terrible but compelling word which epitomized Ford's own Pre-Raphaelite inheritance: genius. The physical symbol of this inheritance was Rossetti's Inverness cape, which had 'descended' to Madox Brown when Rossetti died, and which now descended to Ford. 'I wore it with feelings of immense pride', he said, 'as if it had been—and indeed was it not?—the mantle of a prophet.' He soon tried to express his grief in writing. 'The painter of "*Work*" is no more', he began, and stressed, 'his message was "Work"'. In his first published reminiscence of his grandfather, written ten years later, Ford describes the eyes of Brown's portrait looking at him 'with an inexpressibly sad, inexpressibly disillusioned resignation, and as if with the last irony of a closing life'. Ten years after that, he was to begin recapturing the emotional appeal in that combination of sadness, disillusion, and resignation in his 'saddest story', *The Good Soldier*.[10]

Madox Brown's death produced a *rapprochement* with the Martindales, who allowed Elsie to accompany Ford to Birchington-on-Sea to look at Brown's monument for Rossetti's grave. Then Ford tried to distract himself by going off on another walking tour, this time to Somerset. His hand was still troubling him—he complained of gout in it, and told Elsie 'I shall give up smoking & see if that does any good'. 'I go hoping to come back stronger & better calculated to fight the battles that are before us', he told her. 'Sometimes, when thinking of you, a great wave of feeling for the hopelessness of your life comes over me & I feel perhaps even worse than you do about it.' But it didn't help. 'Here I am back home again [. . .] I feel so out of sorts & hostile to all the world [. . .].' He continued educating Elsie in his letters, perhaps following Madox Brown's example, who had educated his own child-bride Emma Hill before marrying her. He decided, 'it is time we set about enunciating our creed—that is the philosophic religious light by which we view the World'; he thought they should, 'assimilate & evolve a belief that shall be the mainspring of our lives & of our Love'.

The tendency of modern thought, with which we have chimed in, has been to get rid of, or ridicule the old dogmatic theology. Indeed, looking at the matter calmly, it seems ridiculous to have any thought of belief in the farrago of nonsense that has passed for revealed religion. At the same time it is useless to ignore the craving for religious belief that is in one. There was a time for both of us when we were more or less deeply religious, when mechanical prayers & sounding words moved us deeply. Indeed who has not been moved by it & rightly.

He never lost that susceptibility to be deeply moved by sounding words. His exchanges with the Garnetts or with Elsie are woolly with adolescent pretentious-ness. But they were his equivalent of undergraduate exploratory talks, in which he was beginning (in Yeats's phrase) to find and cleave to his own. He continued this letter to Elsie by sounding like something between a sermon—'Let us think of the Godhead'—and a lecture on the Platonic thought he had been studying. But this soon develops into an idea which, though its slightly deranged expression bears the impress of his grief for Madox Brown, is none the less profoundly suggestive of what attracted him to the novel:

Whether the individual soul remains individual or whether it be merged into the great centre of life as the potter might return a clay form & re-knead it into the mass of clay from which beforehand he took it, that too we cannot know.

Perhaps we shall each of us become God, each of us merge all the other souls into his own in the realm where Time & Space are unknown & non-existent. That too we do not know, we cannot say.[11]

That tension between omniscience and limitation was to energize much of his prose, especially in his presentation of a god like Mr Apollo, a demigod like Napoleon, or the god-like moments of his heroes like Christopher Tietjens. That idea of merging other souls into your own could be read as an oblique, mystical way of talking about the novel's possibilities of entering into other consciousnesses through the act of sympathetic imagination. Similarly, what he did soon find he could say about God merged romantic love with romantic aesthetics, submerging dogmatic theology in the process: 'I have two feelings,' he told Elsie charac-teristically; 'first you are my friend because to you alone I can talk with a feeling of perfect ease & your ideas alone fit mine, & in the rapture of your kisses & the thrill of your hand touch I know that you are my love. And, in the beauty of your being, you are my God, since in beauty alone is the true God manifest.'[12]

He became impatient: 'our philosophy is not progressing with the rapidity to have been expected of, or hoped from, it', he wrote to Elsie a month later, and asked her, 'would you care to have any more of the Fairy Tale? I am getting ahead with it pretty rapidly.' This was his third, last, and best full-length fairy story, *The Queen Who Flew*, published the following year with a frontispiece by Burne-Jones. It is an odd mixture of fantasy and satire, which shows the influence of his politically active friends. The young queen who magically acquires the power of flight—perhaps an image of Ford's desire to escape from his depres-sions—discovers that she has been kept ignorant of the economic realities of her realm, which is torn by oppression and revolution. She hears a voice (of God?) 'like a great rushing of wind' telling her to go back down and help humanity. She arrives in 'the land of the Happy Folk', a sort of Anarchist Utopia which manages without a ruler. She falls in love with a blind ploughman, and sacrifices her power of flight in order to cure his sight. If the story negotiates Ford's politics, it also obliquely contemplates his art, which would continue to ponder the relationship between flights of fantasy and the attempt 'to make you *see*'.[13]

The combination of escapism and politics might reflect an episode that figures in one of Ford's favourite anecdotes. The Manchester socialist Charles Rowley, who had been a friend of Madox Brown's and knew the Garnetts and Rossettis, invited Ford to a dinner at the Holborn Restaurant—'a haunt of everything that was middle-class and Free Masonic'. Rowley, said Ford, 'was anxious to improve my morals'—by 'converting me to advanced opinions'. The dinner was to introduce the labour leaders Tom Mann and Ben Tillett, organizers of the 1889 London Dock Strike (which was 'instrumental in unionizing unskilled British laborers') to 'the most distinguished of the Communist-Anarchists of that day'—Prince Kropotkin. The management was terrified by the presence of so many 'notorious promoters of disorder'. They got on well for most of the meal, as long as the discussion 'remained on general lines'. But when they moved on to remedies, it became 'one of those discussions in which each says the same thing over and over again, without in the least penetrating to the other's mind'. Mann and Tillett banged the table and demanded destruction: 'We must be rid of tyrants!' Rowley tried to quieten them. Kropotkin 'would go on trying to get a hearing for his gentle voice', arguing that their 'doctrines of extermination' were falsely Darwinist, and urging instead: 'Mutual aid. You see it in all Nature'; 'We must build the hearts of men. We must establish a kingdom of God'. 'Kropotkin's quietism acted like a bomb at the table', said Ford—the bomb that the waiters probably feared he was carrying. It 'seemed to drive the others mad'.[14]

The words 'trying to get a hearing' echo an unpublished poem, 'At the Fairing', which contains the lines:

> Like poor Dan Robin, thankful for your crumb
> While bigger birds sing mortal loud & swearing
> If the wind lulls I try to get a hearing.[15]

Ford always associated this image with what he aimed at in his writing: an ideal of quiet conversation. His identification with Kropotkin becomes even clearer when he describes attending an anarchist meeting in the outhouse beside William Morris's Kelmscott House in Hammersmith. Ford would take Elsie: 'we used to meet to hasten on the Social Revolution and to reconstruct a lovely world', he wrote with the irony of hindsight. But when he went without her one day he heard a lecture on 'The Foolishness of Anarchism', 'and there was an audience as unfair as any Tory pot-house meeting: 'all socialists about 200 strong, pitching into [. . .] just four Anarchists and even they (the A's) took the wrong side, or boggled about the dynamitards. I did my best and decried any kind of force, physical or moral—but it weren't no good—I got howled down by the entire audience, inclusive of the four Anarchists.'[16]

'Tory-Papist Anarchism was clearly not for Kelmscott House', said Mizener, who saw Ford's action simply as 'a boldly dramatic assertion'. But the significance is less to do with the views, than the effect Ford wanted to produce. It is a quintessential Fordian situation, in which he advocates quietism in such a way as to be treated as an *agent provocateur*. It demonstrates the point he later made out of it: 'I think I must have been on the side of the anarchists, because the socialists were unreasonably aggressive.' But it could also stand as an emblem of his subsequent career, whether as writer, lover, soldier, or editor. He relished scenarios in which (in life or in fiction) he could be the poor robin overwhelmed by elements and by the larger, louder, birds—whom he would invariably, if not always quite consciously, provoke into abuse. He continued to outrage both the conventionally conservative and the conventionally religious (like the Martindales), just as here he was able to alienate everyone: both the anarchists and the socialists (as he did the young Rossettis and Garnetts).[17]

His dinner with Kropotkin and the socialists was important in other ways. It is offered as an example of how his political contacts reinforced the anxieties of his childhood: they 'impressed me with the sense of my unworthiness', he wrote. Kropotkin appeared both as an example of humane integrity, and as the proof that it was a lost cause. But he also had a lesson for Ford as a writer. As they waited sheltering from the rain later in the evening, Kropotkin asked Ford what he was doing and he told him about his fairy stories. Kropotkin, who was himself a real prince as well as a character of fairy-tale benevolence, said tactfully 'that he hoped the fairy tale was not about Princes and Princesses—or at least that I would write one that would be about simple and ordinary people'. 'I must begin now to proclaim the beauty of the humble and of the impotent,' Ford recalled; 'I have been trying to do so ever since.' Though he added that this too had been a lost cause: 'And I did write a third book inculcating these doctrines; it sold nothing at all, and for a fourth I was never able even to find a publisher.'[18]

For all his attempts to philosophize about mortality, Ford's state of mind became more morbid at the end of 1893. He began complaining sardonically of 'the vagaries of God Almighty who is a plaging beast in his way'. 'If we could only take our Fate into our own hands & drag it round.—But there is the stupid creature called God Almighty who sits grinning & says in dreary platitudes: "Wait, wait, all things in the fitness of time". How can one reconcile oneself to it when talent is wasting & Death stalking over the land.' The author of 'The Wind's Quest' heard in the voice of the wind a sardonic God stalking through the city: 'It always seems to me when I hear the voice of the wind in London, as if God had wandered out of the free country, where one may hear him & see him and having got here by mistake is saying: "Damn my eyes, but this is a queer place. I wonder if I've got any influence here." But a creature called M^rs G[rundy—the epitome of middle-class respectability] kicked him out long ago & reigns in his stead.' This fiction of the estranged God of wind seemed to Ford 'the only thing about that is what it professes to be, in Babylon—otherwise there is nothing real'. What mostly made him feel unreal was the thought of his own death stalking him. He began to write more frequently of suicide. 'I would like to cut my throat but then my poor beard is so young it would be a shame to spoil it', he told Elsie. 'When it has grown longer it will be tired of life poor brave thing—you see we are poor brave things or else we shouldn't go on living knowing as much as we do.'[19]

It was probably at this time that he wrote a bizarre letter to be sent to Elsie after he was dead. The imagination of his own death was a powerful lifelong impulse of his art. His literary personality inherited it from his aunt by marriage, Christina Rossetti, whose poems about expiring, like 'When I am dead my dearest', and 'Passing away, saith the World, passing away', were to inspire Ford. But in the wake of so many deaths in his family his writing has an obsessive, restless anguish, a need to stress the morbid to try to work through his morbid distress. The letter is striking both for what it says about Elsie's presence in his early work, and for the way he explains it by saying he can express in art what it would be dishonourable actually to say to her; but also for its significant connecting of love, death, and writing:

At the moment of writing a fearful storm is raging without and the sight of the fearful flashes of lightning reiterated & reiterated unceasingly, must of necessity turn one's thoughts towards that which awaits us at the end of Life—and the thought of Death—as indeed the thought of anything seriously affecting myself, must of necessity turn my thoughts towards you in whom my life and soul are wrapped [. . .] if you do love me even a very little it may please you to know that I love you with my whole heart and that all my thoughts are towards you—when I have written and whatever I have written has been written with a view to perpetuating your memory to all time if it be in my power, & written merely to ease my breast of what it would not be honourable in me to tell you [. . .] for the type of woman, great, calm, sweet & chivalrously self-sacrificing that I have portrayed, is but the vain striving (that I am capable of) to express what you are and what you seem to me [. . .]
The storm is passing over, the flashes of lightning are more distant and the moon is already hanging thin & watery in a star bejewelled cloudless corner of the sky
 —& I—I am dead—dead—dead—for you are reading this letter, oh it says so little but it means more than tongue can utter or pen refrain from writing.—And you, what are you doing?—I know. I can see you—for I am dead [. . .] Farewell for ever for oh, my love—*I am dead.* Can you send a sigh to me whose life has been one long sigh?[20]

That frisson from willing the writing to create him a ghostly presence after death was to animate much of his work. The desire is implicit in his autobiographical writing, in which he casts himself as his own ghost revisiting his past, in order that the book might preserve his spirit in the future. It is all too macabrely obvious in the fragment he wrote in collaboration with Conrad (but which was based on a story of Ford's own), *The Nature of a Crime*, which is written in exactly this form of a letter to the narrator's lover, to be read after his suicide. But most of all, it can be felt in Ford's strong impulse to elegize others:

'whatever I have written has been written with a view to perpetuating your memory.'

The double shadow cast by the premature deaths of Oliver Madox Brown and then Francis Hueffer made the family morbid. Ford said Madox Brown was 'deeply impressed' by the 'series of deaths' that marked his last years. Brown kept all his son's paintings, and the books he had liked to read, in a locked room next to his own. It was known as 'Oliver's [or Nolly's] room'. 'He had the key in his pocket, and he used to go in all alone and touch the things and look at them', said Juliet. 'Sometimes he took my hand and let me go in with him.' Ford's mother's and grandfather's fears for his health gave him an unusually pressing sense that his own death was imminent; sometimes, even, that it had already—if symbolic-ally—occurred. The deaths of Emma Madox Brown in 1890, of Madox Brown himself in 1893, then of his daughter (Cathy Hueffer's half-sister) Lucy Rossetti and of Christina Rossetti in 1894 made him even more possessed by death—or more aware of his predisposition to morbidity, which he saw in some of his earliest childhood memories. For the frontispiece of *Ancient Lights* he chose a photograph of Brown's house at 37 Fitzroy Square, with a great funeral urn perched on a corbel over the front door. 'I can remember vividly, as a very small boy, shuddering as I stood upon the door-step at the thought that the great stone urn [. . .] might fall upon me and crush me entirely out of existence', said Ford. 'Such a possible happening, I remember, was a frequent subject of discussion among Madox Brown's friends.' 'Of course the mental processes of a young child may have an immense effect upon his subsequent fate', he wrote:

I am perfectly aware that the most important, the most far-reaching, the most agonising event of my life happened when I was about nine. I was probably a muddle-headed, absent-minded child, given to long reveries in which I was unconscious of the actions of my hands. At any rate, one night in bed, in the pitch pitch darkness only known to children, I found myself sucking the end of a burnt match. I found myself doing it—I had no idea where it had come from. But at once I remembered that phosphorus was a poison; at once the most ghastly fears possessed me; I began to scream; I screamed for ages and ages, in a blackness that was palpable and stifling, as if I had been beneath a thin soft curtain. (I dare say it was not half a minute before a servant came—but it was my whole life!)[21]

From an early age he made the connection between reverie, art and death. 'For myself,' he wrote in 1928, 'from my earliest childhood I was brought up to believe that humanity divided itself into two classes—those who were creative artists and those who were merely the stuff to fill graveyards. In that belief I tranquilly abide.' Consistently rather than 'tranquilly', however. The idea of 'the stuff to fill graveyards' resounds through his work with an eerie fascination and abhorrence. Witness this description from *The Inheritors* (1901): 'everywhere, faces of panic-stricken little people of no more account than the dead in graveyards, just the material to make graveyards, nothing more.' An artist, on the other hand, is someone who 'added to the thought and emotions of mankind, and he alone—had any divine right to existence'. Here too Ford was adding to something he had originally heard from Madox Brown, who said, 'to wield authority in the house, one must have been the "author", the "auctor," or adder to it of at least one stone during its building'.[22]

Also from an early age he had decided his own life should be the stuff to fill books. It is surprising how early he begins to write his memoirs. Although he largely effaces himself from his biography of his grandfather, soon afterwards he began publishing articles with a substantial content of reminiscence. Quite apart from the ways in which his life gets preserved in his novels, his habit of reminiscential anecdote is well established by 1903. In that year he published the essay with the uninspiring title 'Nice People'. That blandness is very much to the point, however, since the essay consists of Ford wondering about the significance of a series of his cherished memories; wondering what transforms a sequence of impressions into a coherent personality or a unified work of art. When he writes that 'dwelling on facts leads at best to death', one sees what impelled him to define his 'memories' and 'impressions' against 'fact'. (When he described one of his books as 'full of inaccuracies as to facts, but its accuracy as to impressions is absolute', he was asserting the impression as a record of living consciousness.) Fordian impressionism is dual, elicited by death, but founded on a denial of the fact of death. One of the things he valued about Madox Brown was his anecdotes which could 'revive the splendid ghosts of Pre-Raphaelites', a feat Ford repeated by reviving his grandfather's splendid ghost in his own memoirs. His writing has a dual relation to his own death, both anticipating it, and anticipating his survival as a literary personality: 'when I really analyse my thoughts, I find I am writing all the while with an eye to posterity [...] I find myself still thinking that I am writing for an entirely unprofitable immortality.'[23]

His predominant mode is thus not only retrospective—revisiting the past, returning to yesterday, re-illuminating the 'Ancient' figures of his childhood memories—it is also elegiac. It is loss which spurs his creativity. A death precipitates a remembrance, as with his brother Oliver, or even more magnificent-ly in the tribute to Conrad which he managed to complete within five months of his friend's death: *Joseph Conrad: A Personal Remembrance* (1924). His best novels—*The Fifth Queen, The Good Soldier,* or *Parade's End*—could all be subtitled 'The Last of England', the title of Madox Brown's fictionalized portrait of himself and his wife leaving by ship. This sense of the passing of an era chimes with the prevalent Edwardian feeling that change was accelerating, that England was changing hands (as both Ashburnham's and Tietjens' estates are occupied by Americans), and later that the Edwardian Garden Party had been devastated by the war, in which a whole generation was thought of as lost. Or the elegiac reference can be more personal, such as when it is the prospect of forgetting which incites him to perpetuate in prose a memory, a personality, an experience, or a phase. This is the explicit rationale for the writing of history and memoirs too: 'I discovered that I had grown up only when I discovered quite suddenly that I was forgetting my own childhood [...] these impressions are beginning to grow a little dim. So I have tried to rescue them now before they go out of my mind altogether. And whilst trying to rescue them, I have tried to compare them with my impressions of the world as it is at the present day.'[24]

That last sentence captures the double positioning of Fordian elegy: not just a wish to relive the past, but to superimpose it upon the present. (The phrase 'go out of my mind altogether' obliquely intimates the maddening feeling of mortality, and the fear of madness, that impels the wish.) *Ancient Lights and Certain New Reflections: Being the Memories of a Young Man*: the title-page presents the duality. Is the Ford of 1911 (*aetat.* 37) the young man; or is he remembering being a young man? The latter possibility again suggests his concern with the way experience is saturated by memory, by narrative. For he is not just remembering being younger, but also remembering (re-remembering?) the memories he then had: memories of a young man's memories. The syntax is characteristically ambiguous. By juxtaposing past and present, ancient and new, it queries how separable they are. The 'Ancient Lights' stand for the leading lights of Pre-Raphaelism and aestheticism who are the subjects of most of the chapters. They haunt his memory with the *auctoritas* of the Ancients. But one construction of the syntax gives us, 'Ancient Lights (and certain new reflections), being the memories'. It is not just that Ford is reflecting on those Ancient Lights who are his (artistic as well as familial) ancestors. The 'Ancient Lights' also *are* the memories—incandescent childhood traces, opposed to the more muted present 'reflections' upon them.

An 'ancient light' is a window whose light is legally protected from obstruction by new buildings. The Victorian figures are admirable and illuminating monuments; but they also inhibit present creativity. In this sense the title hints at the anxieties of influence. The book's dedication to Ford's two daughters says he began it with the idea 'of analysing for your benefit what my heredity had to bestow upon you' (p. vii); which he does by pondering what his had bestowed upon him. But besides transmitting riches, heredity makes us mere 'reflections' of the illustrious, fainter imitations or impressions of our originals. These senses are glimpsed but not indulged. (So too with the touching sense that the book being dedicated to his daughters is itself a modest legacy from a *jeune homme pauvre*.)

The more positive implications of the title come from the idea—central to all Ford's reminiscence—that recounting your memories is an essential act of self-recognition: that the subjects of his portraits are his formative acquaintances, and that in looking at them he can see himself reflected there, as in a window. It is another image of duality, and one which anticipates Ford's 1914 definition of 'impressionist' writing:

I suppose that Impressionism exists to render those queer effects of real life that are like so many views seen through bright glass—through glass so bright that whilst you perceive through it a landscape or a backyard, you are aware that, on its surface, it reflects a face of a person behind you. For the whole of life is really like that; we are almost always in one place with our minds somewhere quite other.[25]

The mental doubleness, split between here and 'somewhere quite other', corresponds not only to the visual duality (the face reflected *in* the glass), but also to the temporal superimposition. Ford as reminiscer is almost always in one time with his mind some*when* quite other. He recalls the line from Shakespeare's *Richard II*—'O! call back yesterday, bid time return'—and with an ingenious turn makes yesterday sound like a place to which one can 'return'; as if it were as easy as returning to the words of an earlier author. (Dowell says 'the world is full of places to which I want to return'. His narrative is similarly full of *moments* to which he keeps obsessively coming back.)

The movement of Ford's reminiscence is then not to go back in time, but to summon the past back to the present:

I do not think that I would care to live my life over again—I have had days that I would not again face for a good deal—but I would give very much of what I possess to be able, having still such causes for satisfaction as I now have in life, to be able to live once more some of those old evenings in [Madox Brown's] studio.

I would give a great deal to have some of the things, some of the people, some of the atmosphere of those days—to have them now. But nothing in the world would make me go back to those days if I must sacrifice what now I have.[26]

Ostensibly the possessions he prizes here are not personal ones, but social advantages. The book is weighing the glamour but injustice of the past against the civilized blandness of the present. What he is reluctant to sacrifice is social progress. But there is also a psychological component, for if he were to relive his past what he would lose would be precisely the memories he so cherishes. Thomas Moser, describing Ford's dedicatory poem in *Romance*, gives a perceptive account of his 'characteristic longing to leap out of the present so that he can look back at it':

> If we could have remembrance now
> And see, as in the days to come
> We shall, what's venturous in these hours [. . .][27]

'Remembrance now' could be taken as Ford's literary motto. Again there is the ring of Shakespearean archaism (as in 'I summon up remembrance of things past'). But it is also a suggestively funereal and respectful term ('If we could have the memory now' would have been a vastly inferior line). It captures the elegiac impulse of his memoirs. 'If we could have remembrance now' also craves that 'we' will be remembered. If the elegy is for the dead, it is also for the past self, each seen reflected in the other. It is this dual movement that makes Ford's reveries about escaping from the present (whether to the past or the future) more than mere escapism; they are also attempts to understand the present: 'My business in life, in short, is to attempt to discover, and to try to let you see, where we stand.'[28]

For a self reflected in its writing—a literary personality—reminiscence is a paradoxical activity, because the act of recalling the past, trying to see it and understand it, necessarily has an effect on the self being expressed. Fordian impressionism is an extreme case of memory's transformation of the self, since in writing and rewriting his memories Ford effects transformations upon them too. Dowell, the narrator of *The Good Soldier*, also locked into a habit of returning to his memories to re-describe them, imagines his readers asking a question that Ford the reminiscer and historian might well have imagined his readers asking: 'You may well ask why I write. And yet my reasons are quite many. For it is not unusual in human beings who have witnessed the sack of a city or the falling to pieces of a people to desire to set down what they have witnessed for the benefit of unknown heirs or of generations infinitely remote; or, if you please, just to get the sight out of their heads' (p. 9). If you please? If the unknown heirs, the readers, are pleased; if the writer's witness makes the readers *see*; then the writer can get the disturbing sight out of his head. This is not, exactly, to say that Dowell writes to forget (his 'if you please' virtually disavows the whole idea anyway). But it does bring out the dual motive of autobiography: to remember, and to be remembered; but also to liberate oneself from the pressures of the past. The compulsive reminiscer is at the mercy of his memories. Ford the reminiscential impressionist seeks to master his memories by transforming them into impressions, literary artefacts under authorial control.

When, in his last decade, Ford turned to writing history, he remained an impressionist. *A History of Our Own Times* was planned to cover the period of his whole life. It is a history of his own time because the history that most matters to him is the history contemporary with his own memory. The first chapter begins with an idea that charged his best prose: the question of subjectivity and impersonality; of private and public; of particular and general; of the individual and destiny, or great social forces and movements:

in spite of the fact that, never in the history of man has the individual been less able to direct the destinies of peoples, still we must consider that our own times are our own property in a sense that nothing else is or can be, for our own times are made up of the most intimate and most inviolable portion of a man—of his memories. Great movements go on, passionate popular ideals are consummated or found vain, the faces of whole regions of the earth may change, dynasties may disappear, laureates may sound across this world and then be no more listened to—but for us these immense movements are alive and our own because of minute contacts with immense happenings. (p. 15)

Memories may be unreliable, but they are inviolable in the sense that they cannot be altered at will. History is only alive and our own in so far as it can be animated by memory, which gives the history of our selves back to us. To say memories are 'the most intimate and the most inviolable portion of a man' is partly a joke: not what you thought were the most private parts. However, it is also to hint that they cannot be violated by fact, or history, or refutation. Ford often writes as if he feels his memory under threat—perhaps from the same forces that have changed the remembered past, or perhaps from the death which will ultimately violate unwritten memories. A 'History of Our Own Times' is something of a paradox, since we do not normally think of our own times as the past. Like all Ford's writing, it is, amongst other things, an attempt to write his own memorial.

1894: PERPETRATING MATRIMONY

Ford had disappeared from the lives of friends like Olive Garnett and Walter Jerrold after Madox Brown's death. Olive next saw him after she sent tickets for Stepniak's lecture on 'The Russian Drama' at the Opera Comique Theatre on 14 January 1894. He came with Elsie, and they 'looked as if they had enjoyed themselves'. On the 28th she saw them again at a lecture by Volkhovsky on his escape from Siberia: 'Ford is letting his hair grow long', she noted: 'the intermediate process [. . .] is very ugly. But his face was beaming. I think that dignity & sweetness are Elsie's characteristics.'[1]

The crash with Elsie's parents came this year. After Ford visited her one day he said he felt 'rather cowardly' at having left her 'in the jaws of death': 'It is wretched to think that at this moment you are surrounded by the sound of hymns or something almost as dismal if possible.' His anger at the Martindales was turning into contempt. 'The mayoral interview this afternoon was a mere nothing', he told Elsie on St Valentine's Day; he imagined Elsie 'being tortured by an ignorant woman'. The Martindales agreed to let Elsie's brother take her, Mary, Ford, and some friends to the theatre on 24 February. But when Elsie came down in an old cloak, her mother objected, and told her to change it for the new one they had bought her (and which, said Dr Martindale, Elsie had herself chosen). But this must have been the one Ford had seen her wearing in November, and had said, 'it gave me quite a shock—to see how appallingly smart you can look,—I only hope never to see it again'. An angry someone—almost certainly Dr Martindale—wrote on this letter: '*She* would not wear it after *this*.' It wasn't just that Ford's bohemianism was beginning to *épater* the bourgeois doctor. Elsie's father was furious that someone else was exercising the control that he insisted was his right. Elsie refused to change her cloak, and was supported by Ford, 'who said he had quite as much to do with my daughter's dressing as my wife had', wrote Martindale. 'I resented this interference with my household and angry words passed between the said Ford Herman [*sic*] Madox Hueffer my wife and myself on the subject.' The resentments simmered for a week. Martindale then went to speak to Cathy Hueffer. Whatever he hoped to achieve, he left Ford just as perplexed:

he does not seem to have effected anything or to have made up his mind to do anything so there it all rests.

It does not very much matter either way what these folks say or do because as I get to feel more & more we can always cut our throats and have it over.

I will give you Berlioz's last words wh are powerful & suggestive: 'When I see the way in which certain people look on love, & what they seek in artistic creation, I am involuntarily reminded of hogs rooting & grunting for truffles amongst the loveliest flowers & under the grandest trees' which is singularly appropriate [. . .]

So now I am about to set out youwards and after having considered the matter from every side and thought out a hundred irresistible points of attack in the battle that must come with the unfortunate mayor.[2]

But on the same day Dr Martindale saw red. While 'remonstrating with her for her disobedience', he asked Elsie how she could ask for the blessing of God if she behaved in this way. 'Her answer was that she did not want the blessing of God. She further said that there was no need to obey her father and mother when she could think for herself and in reply to further questions from me said that it might be right to steal as all property ought to be in common.' He told her she had no right to think. And, thinking that, he could only think that it was Ford's 'baneful influence' which had 'corrupted' his daughter; so, on the following day, he forbade him to come to their house. Ford became Ford Madox Hamlet:

So my own old baby let us try to wait a little patiently—at worst there's a garter—or a second story [sic.] window—or your hair, your soft hair—that too would be like kisses—indeed I have kissed it often enough.

A long, soft pang & then a long sweet rest.

You know, as well as I do, how much I am against self-slaying—but better that than let your mind fail beneath hopeless tyranny[.]

And then one should at least be for ever together[.] But this is all merely night-writing—the morning will find us both perhaps more ready to fight against outrageous fortune [. . .]

It did. He defied the mayoral edict and called on the evening of the 5th. He wasn't admitted, but he waited outside until Elsie could slip out. The Martindales 'were unable to overtake them'.[3]

Dr Martindale probably hoped to catch Elsie with Ford at Brook Green. But he noted later: 'Mrs. H.[ueffer] acted a *lie* to me on night of 5th.' Presumably she said they weren't there, or that she didn't know where they were. At eleven that night Ford came back to Devonshire Street to tell Martindale that he would return Elsie 'if she was not interfered with but not otherwise'. He brought a letter from her: 'Dear Daddy, As you have chosen to use force against me to-day & to lock me in I shall take effectual steps to prevent such a thing occurring again. Unless you give Ford an absolute promise that I shall be unmolested—I shall not return to the house of my own will. your affectionate daughter *Elsie*'. 'I was very angry with [Ford] on this occasion and shook him', said Martindale. 'I was most anxious that my daughter should be restored to my house and I temporised and eventually he brought her to my house at twenty minutes to one o'clock in the morning of the following day.' As Ford's earlier reference to torture and the invocation of Berlioz suggests, he was now casting himself as the Romantic liberator from oppression. He wrote to Elsie:

You may be certain that I shall leave no stone unturned and flinch before no threats in the giving you your liberty. Of course the Mayoress is capable of legal proceedings—(she is capable of many things) but I am by no means afraid of that.

Our own capabilities are by no means inconsiderable now that the time has come [. . .] so be confident my own old baby & give in to nothing.

For obvious reasons this is no safe vehicle for definite plans but only for general encouragement.

Only this is certain that you are mine & I am yours chance what can.

M^rs. H. by-the-bye has nobly come to the rescue &, unless more agreeably engaged, to-night I shall go and rouse W. M. R.[ossetti] & a few more great guns and to Shaen Roscoe & Co., just to see how far one can act within the law—but as you well know, my own dear baby no law presents any fears to me [. . .]

At the last M^rs. H. however, queer she may have been in the past, will not turn you out if you come here—& after that the fight must begin.[4]

The cautious William Rossetti was prevailed upon to discuss the affair with Dr Martindale. They 'interchanged views with some frankness' on the 8th. Later that day Rossetti wrote a sensible letter to him attempting to make peace. He pointed out that in three years' time the 'young people' would be able to do what they liked. It was just a matter of agreeing to a *modus vivendi* until then. He suggested that Martindale should ask Ford to write expressing regret 'for having caused dissension & commotion in the family', and to promise to try to avoid causing any more. Then, after a month's cooling-off period, a limited number of visits, letters, and outings could be allowed. He tactfully refrained from getting drawn into an argument about Elsie's political views which had so disturbed her father, except to intimate stoically what he knew all too well from his own children: 'if she does entertain those opinions, no power on earth will prevent her entertaining them.' Martindale had to admit that Rossetti's advice was 'reasonable', and he relayed it to Ford. But his anger made him unreasonably (though perhaps not unsurprisingly for the times) confuse the legal, medical, and sexual; and it made him anything but conciliatory:

Considering the state of Elsie's health, after again consulting a medical friend, she is quite unfit to marry till she is of age. Till then she will be in my care. In the meantime you must apply yourself more diligently to work & to your studies (if such you consider your work) and prove to me that you possess more *true manliness* than you have exhibited during the last 12 months—that you can *get your own living* & *support a delicate wife* in *comfort* or you shall *never* marry Elsie with my consent. If you write to me as Mr Rossetti suggests, the details of your times of visiting shall have my careful consideration.[5]

Ford reacted as hotly to such attempts to crush as would anybody else; but the sneer at his 'manliness'—a virtue defined in terms so middle-class as to exclude art and learning—together with the sneer at his writing could scarcely have been better calculated to infuriate him. Certainly the idea that art might be irreconcilably at odds with manliness or gentlemanliness would perplex much of his writing. Nevertheless, he stalled for time, while trying to find out more about the law, and questioned what Martindale was actually proposing. The mayor became curt and threatening, writing to him not as 'Dear Ford', but simply beginning 'Ford H. M. Hueffer': 'My letter is plain enough. It gave you the conditions of a *modus vivendi* as suggested by Mr Rossetti to whom I refer you. Do you accept it or not? In my present frame of mind you had better keep out of my way.' Ford tried to reclaim the moral high ground. He said there was one thing to settle first: 'You have been pleased to apply the term "infamous liar" to my mother' (because she had covered up for him on the night of the 5th?). He assumed indifference, and drew himself up to Martindale's patriarchal stature, saying he was 'speaking quite apart from the personal view of the matter but merely as the head of this house'. He wondered whether Martindale's idea of 'true manliness' was to drag a poor bereaved woman into the argument. Martindale backed down, and he gave his terms for the *modus vivendi*. He had earlier given what Rossetti called a 'qualified sanction' to Ford's and Elsie's idea that they were engaged. But now he wrote of 'the terms on which the friendship can be resumed'. He was determined to monitor everything that passed between the lovers. There could only be two meetings per week, with another Martindale or appointed deputy present; Ford had to undertake not to meet Elsie out of doors, 'nor hover about the house in which she is living'; a few days earlier, Martindale had demanded that Ford should only send letters to Elsie through him at his work address. Now he was forbidden to write her letters altogether—only postcards excusing his absence were to be allowed, which Martindale would of course be able to read. Ford had forty-eight hours to accept, 'failing which the acquaintance must cease'. In other words, he wanted to end Ford's influence by stopping them talking politics, religion, or love.[6]

Ford counselled Elsie to keep her spirits up, 'for something shall be done'. If not, there was always suicide: 'a short shrift and a few feet of rope always getatable. I have waited 10 years for you my dear old baby and it will go hard before after all that waiting it would be necessary to puncture one's jugular.' The next day he 'quietly negatived' the ultimatum. Ford wrote to Elsie to tell her, heading his letter 'My own dear baby, I love you', and saying: 'This should be a letter of Farewell—(so it shall be, for you will fare the better by being the more mine) [...] & so we open a new chapter—see I have written the heading up above as its first words.' All the participants were talking as if they were living in a romantic novel. Ford suggested that if they couldn't communicate any other way she should 'formulate proposals' and he would 'answer them by the passing method *once* yes, *twice* no'. He evidently intended to continue hovering about in Devonshire Street. He told her that every day at nine she should 'withdraw from any company & give your thoughts absolutely & entirely to me for half an hour & I will do the same'. It was a romantic idea that was never to lose its appeal for him—that lovers could achieve happiness, even a mystical form of union, through an act of will. 'Tonight is a wild & wet night,' he told her, 'it is the last night of the old time before us (perhaps it was a rather bourgeois, stupid old time) but it was a dear old time—so give him a kiss & let him go. Something truer & better lies before us.'[7]

Elsie too found her father's terms intolerable. She planned to run away to a sympathetic aunt in Carlisle, where she imagined she would be given greater freedom. But Robert Garnett, who had become Ford's and her enthusiastic ally, had a better idea, arranging for his relative Mrs William Garnett, who lived at Clifton, to shelter Elsie. When on 16 March Dr Martindale sent his daughters to Winchelsea to get Elsie away from Ford, he played into the hands of his opponents. They had to change trains at Ashford where, instead of continuing to Winchelsea, Elsie crossed the platform and boarded the up train from Dover, back to London, from where she went to Bristol. The rest of the day was telegrams and anger. Just after one o'clock Mary telegraphed to her father: 'Elsie has gone from Ashford Beware Dover Train Mary.' Perhaps she was told to stay there in case Elsie returned, since she sent another message less than two hours later: 'Elsie not turned up look out at London stations Mary.' Mizener says Dr Martindale didn't trust Mary's judgement; indeed, he probably didn't trust Mary, and suspected she was a conspirator. He got Edward Elgar to check, who duly wired from Ashford at 3.14: 'One daughter here other not here Elgar'. Martindale rushed to St Edmund's Terrace, and to Brook Green but Elsie wasn't there. He got his solicitor to call on William Rossetti, who later wrote to him at nine that evening that Mrs Hueffer had just telegraphed him to say that Ford had not been out of the house all day, and so couldn't have abducted Elsie. It isn't known what—if anything—passed between Ford and Martindale. The latter was still searching London stations that evening, and sent a telegram to the Praetoriuses at Folkestone. The next day he checked with friends at Winchelsea, and went to Ashford to talk to the station-master and the police. He found no clues, so he hired detectives to find her, and got the police to watch St Edmund's Terrace—where Ford had taken Elsie the first time she ran away. The young Rossettis were amused 'that people at such opposite poles as they & the Hueffers are should both be under police supervision'; and Olive Rossetti entertained Olive Garnett with an account of the two sets of detectives watching numbers 1 and 3 St Edmund's Terrace. 'They have enough to do in following the inmates of No. 3 about & must spend quite a lot on omnibus fares etc.', Olive Rossetti told her.[8]

When Olive Garnett got home on 17 March she was told that Ford 'had rushed in & wanted Robert on business immediately'. But Robert was dining with the Harradens. (Beatrice Harraden was a novelist friend of the Garnetts.) 'Ford took a hansom & pursued him.' Just after he had left Oliver arrived, pursuing Ford. He didn't need much persuasion to stay to dinner though, said Olive. 'How my heart beat!' when she heard it was him, she wrote. Oliver, who was now thinking of a theatrical career, evidently didn't like being in Ford's limelight—the sibling rivalry cut both ways. The story he told Olive after dinner reads like an attempt to outdo Ford's adventures walking in Kent:

About a month ago he was on a visit to people in Folkestone, & went out hunting a good deal. One day, wishing to show off he rode at a hedge & as he does not ride very well, the horse remained one side while he shot off to the other. After this for some reason or other he decided to return home but no[t] wishing to telegraph for money he took the train to Ashford where he was landed with 1/6. It was late besides; he enquired how far to London, was told 30 miles & thought he could do it. So he spent his 1/6 on a meal & set off. On the way he felt so tired that he sat in a ditch & went to sleep. It rained & when he awoke he was wet through. He pushed on to Sidcup: 12 miles from London Bridge, & as he felt quite done up went into the police station. A friendly policeman let him steam by the fire and gave him a cup of tea.

He went on again thinking he could hold out till he got to London Bridge & thinking with rapture of the seats there. But the agony of the walk was awful, his boots were full of water and weighed as if they had pounds of lead in them, his feet were raw & he had no sensation in his legs.

At last he reached the bridge, sat down, & became unconscious immediately. It was about 3.30 a.m. on Sunday morning. By & bye a policeman awakened him, said, 'Come, young fellar, move on'. 'I can't move on' said Oliver. 'Haven't you got no money then?' 'Twopence' 'Haven't you got no friends?' 'All over London, but I can't get to them.' He told his story and the policeman called a cab, lifted him in & sent him home.

He was awfully afraid that there wouldn't be any money in the house to pay the cabman when he was conscious of anything. At about half past six he got to Brook Green and knocked Ford up, who fortunately had half a sovereign & who put him to bed. After that he was very ill indeed. One doctor said he was in a consumption, another that he had a weak heart and a third, congestion of the lungs & all that he wouldn't recover [. . .]

He looks very weak in spite of his height, breadth [Oliver was 'enormously fat'] and high colour, and was very gentle and ready to be amused.

He says that having tried most things and failed, it now remains to become an actor.[9]

When he had left, Robert returned and told Olive what had been happening while she had been dining with Oliver. As he was on top of an omnibus on his way to the Harradens, a hansom in pursuit pulled up alongside, and Ford jumped out and rushed up the steps of the bus. 'I am in great trouble, can you give me ten minutes?' he asked Robert. 'He then paid the bus driver & the cabman, who together with everyone else were very much astonished.' The Martindales had threatened to prosecute Ford, who 'seemed to think that he might even be arrested, & was afraid that all this state of things might seriously affect Elsie's health'. Robert consulted a barrister friend, who thought Ford had a good case, and that 'by their extraordinary behaviour Mr and Mrs Martindale have put themselves in the wrong'. We don't know what that 'extraordinary behaviour' was. Given their anxiety over Elsie's health they would have been unlikely to beat her. The force they used against her was more probably to keep her locked in her room. Olive thought 'Elsie seems to have acted in a most determined manner for her age'. Ford was 'very excited', and seemed to think that 'the whole of London is talking about the affair, & that it will be in the papers next week'. He was particularly sensitive about this because Mrs Belcher, the one-legged needlewoman whose husband helped the Rossettis print *The Torch*, had said that Arthur Rossetti had been alluded to in the *Echo* as the 'head of a band of Anarchists, & the maker of nitro-glycerine for bombs'. A month before, on 15 February, Martial Bourdin had blown himself to pieces in the park near the Royal Observatory at Greenwich. (This was the incident on which, with Ford's suggestions, Conrad was to base *The Secret Agent*.) The police suspected young Arthur (then only 12 or 13, but an amateur chemist) of complicity. The Martindales were anxious enough about Ford's radicalism; this was the last sort of publicity he needed now. Olive had doubted the story when Oliver told it, and said she couldn't find anything about it in the *Echo*. But Ford confirmed it, saying that he had himself found 'a lot of explosive powders scattered on the study mantelpiece', and remonstrated, 'as Mr. Rossetti was in the habit of peering about with lighted spills'—as if his uncle shared his gift for avoiding getting blasted into the next world.[10]

On the evening of 18 March Ford and Robert took a train from Paddington, in order to see Elsie and come back the following day. The Garnetts were in turmoil too. Edward had a nervous collapse and was given two months off work. Olive was told that Lucy Rossetti had died. William Rossetti left for San Remo as soon as he got the telegram saying 'Mother passed away come'; but as soon as he had left another telegram arrived saying 'Better'. She was kept alive for a little longer with cocaine injections. Robert said he felt 'as if he were acting in one of Meredith's novels' in helping Ford and Elsie, '& as if Ford were his grandfather come to life again as a young man'. Only Elsie was able to keep 'calm as a mill-pond'. Ford and Olive were both intoxicated with the excitement. When he dined with her on the 20th, she wrote in her diary: 'I think I never enjoyed a dinner so much before':

Ford sat next me & we talked to ourselves the whole time & there were a good many long drawn out courses. My idea was to make the time pass pleasantly for Ford, as he has so much trouble before him, & I succeeded, I know.

It seemed to be tacitly agreed upon that we were real friends, & meant to take and enjoy just for the moment what we found good in one another [. . .] I had never found Ford so delightful, so good, the ideal so near and conversation so enthralling.

I shall never forget that dinner.

We talked of pictures, Mr Rowley, the Rossettis, the sale [of Madox Brown's possessions] at no. 1 [St Edmund's Terrace], Stepniak's Russian drama lecture, F[elix] V[olkhovsky]. the sort of people we like, Edward & Connie [. . .] Music as it is to a composer & connoisseur, and to an outsider and—women—in general and exceptions. Character.[11]

After he had left, Robert told her the full story of 'their adventures' of the last few days: 'A more romantic, interesting story I never heard.' She couldn't say quite the same for the manuscript Ford had given her to read, an otherwise entirely unknown work called 'The Wooing in the Wind', for which he planned to use the 'Fenil Haig' pseudonym again. Olive gave an illuminating account of it:

The hero is a grave, pale faced, small slight young man, who has been educated by the Jesuits at Geneva, has written a learned work 'on the Future of the Church' & having come into his property has come to his guardian, an English banker living in London, to see something of the world before settling down to found a religious house on his estates. The banker, Mr Meltime, a prosperous self made creature, has a son, Tom & a daughter Ethel; the former a light hearted go as you please boy, the latter a serious minded, good girl with quiet ways & a face like a madonna. The hero Arthur Dean falls in love with her, & tries to convert her to Catholicism, but she is full of broad social, & radical ideas. Also, she is in love with Mr Hurstledean, a lover whom she has persuaded to marry his mistress Frances Orre. The idea of her sacrifice fascinates Arthur Dean but he is refused by her & goes to his estates, where the Hurstledeans live. The husband & wife are living most unhappily together, he becomes the former's friend & is attracted by the wife, an unpleasant young woman with a more unpleasant mother. There is gossip in the village etc. & at last the Hurstledeans' house is accidentally set on fire, Hurstledean rescued by Arthur is badly burned & becomes blind & Frances eventually dies. Whereupon Ethel arrives, marries Hurstledean, & Arthur devotes himself entirely to his religion. The plot is worked out with insufficient detail, the characters do not give one sufficiently clear ideas as to their nature, only general ideas. Parts are poor, & inexperience of the world crops up here & there to the book's disadvantage. *But* the descriptions are very good, the fire, the baby grasping at the moonlight etc., excellent. There is go, & nothing strikingly bad. It might be worked up with a good deal of trouble into something good, but it wants ever so much development. It is not nearly so good as the 'Shifting of the Fire' or Edward says 'as the new novel['], but it makes one, curiously enough, have a more kindly feeling for the author.[12]

Few are likely to regret the loss of this youthful, melodramatic fantasy. But its tensions between the ascetic and the worldly, Catholicism and radicalism, desire and renunciation, tell us much about the issues that mattered to the young Ford, and would continue to perplex the older man. That hero, fated to reduplicate the act of renunciation that so impressed him in another, is quintessentially Fordian: dual renunciations are at the heart of *A Call*, *The Good Soldier*, and *Parade's End*.

Shaen Roscoe then told Martindale's solicitors that Elsie was quite safe with 'a respectable lady' who was a client of theirs. But they also revealed that Ford knew her address. Martindale demanded to be told. His solicitors said he would not 'insist upon her immediate return to home providing he finds her in proper care and provided also that your client in the meantime, while she is allowed to remain away from home undertakes not to communicate with her either verbally or by letter'. He was, as he was soon to say, determined 'to sever all connection between my said daughter and the said Ford Herman [*sic*.] Madox Hueffer'. His further request that Elsie should not be warned when he was given her address probably made Ford doubt his sincerity about not forcing Elsie to return, so Shaen Roscoe refused to disclose the address. Ford undertook not to see Elsie, but wouldn't agree not to write. Meanwhile Elsie wrote to her father (through the solicitors):

Dear Daddy

Just a line to let you know of my existence and comfort—I am well treated and cared for here—so you need have no fear for me on that account. I do not mean to return to you until you arrange something definite regarding the continuance of my old acquaintance with Ford. I had written you a note to let you know of my disappearance on Friday but I found no convenient opportunity to leave it for you. I think I need not say any more. So I am

Your daughter

Elsie[13]

She was offering her father a chance to make reasonable concessions, in the hope that she could return home and see Ford again. But Martindale was already irate enough; when he broke open the box in which she had kept Ford's letters he became even more so. The comments about the mayor and mayoress strengthened his conviction that it had been Ford who was manipulating his daughter. Like many parents, he couldn't believe that his child could disagree with him of her own free will. He already knew of Elsie's views; in order to strengthen his legal case he exaggerated his surprise, though he may have been genuinely shocked by Ford's comments about suicide pacts: 'I am intensely shocked to discover from the said letters that the said Ford Herman [*sic*.] Madox Hueffer is an Anarchist frequenting places to which Anarchists resort a scoffer at all religion and that he has systematically incited my said daughter Elsie to disobey and defy her parents and has several times suggested suicide to her.' He was in no mood to back down.[14]

He had threatened to get Elsie made a Ward of Court in the hope that a judge would order her home on account of her age, and that he could stop the couple getting married. (He presumably anticipated that the judge would take a dim view of Elsie's socialism and Ford's disdain for law, and would uphold paternal authority.) The 'resourceful' Robert Garnett realized that there would be no quick solution, so over the Easter weekend he took Elsie from Bristol to Gloucester, to stay with the Garnetts' retired nurse Chapple, who was staying there with her sister. Chapple at first thought Robert had eloped with Elsie. After the explanations, he spent Sunday the 25th walking about Robin Hood's Hill, getting to know Elsie: 'He says she is most attractive,' wrote Olive, 'sketches, sings beautifully when she has any voice, is full of fun, walks well & looks so lovely that the people in the street turn round to look at her.' He also thought her 'hard, extravagant, very youthful, changeable, loving only Ford, & him to distraction'. She was thought to be writing a novel.[15]

Elsie was made a Ward of Court on 11 April. Mizener said Robert Garnett began pressing her and Ford to marry at once for fear of scandal. But presumably it was also because, unmarried, Elsie would be subject to court orders, and he didn't want them breaking the law. But Elsie didn't want to estrange her father completely; and it says something for their ability to rise above youthful extravagance that they were prepared to wait until they were of age, and Ford could support them. He spent a week in Gloucester at the end of April, 'tramping

& driving all round the neighbourhood with Elsie'. Robert Garnett told Olive he thought Martindale had consulted a friend who advised him not to prosecute Ford. After the waiting game had gone on for six weeks Elsie wrote to her father to reiterate her conditions:

Dear Daddy,

I imagine you have not realised my firm determination not to return to you, a determination which increases daily.

This, I suppose, surprises you—but if it were possible for you to view the matter slightly from my point of view—I do not doubt but that it would lead you to seeing that I was perfectly justified in leaving your house.

Perhaps you still do not understand my reasons for so doing.

They are—Mother's continual intemperance & the weak, unhealthy condition of Mary's mind, (which, I may tell you, was the main cause of her illness last year.)

You may deny the existence of either—the former, of course, was evident to all, & of the latter, I, who am as well acquainted with Mary as anyone, can assure you I am not mistaken.

No doubt you will still insist in thinking it is my duty to remain with such companions—but I, as you know, think differently.

I repeat that my leaving was quite uninspired by Ford—except that the usual misery of my life became insupportable without him to give me occasional happiness.

If you can propose any arrangement which will be at all bearable to me—I am quite ready to consider it—as I have no wish to utterly estrange myself from you.

I am, as you already know, very well & happy in my present condition, but I think it only right to say that unless you send me word that you intend to make some such arrangement, as you can understand we consider there remains no alternative but an early marriage.

I am

your affectionate daughter

Elsie[16]

Martindale's only response was to continue his legal proceedings, effectively forcing Elsie and Ford to choose between marriage or surrender. On 1 June his application came before Mr Justice North in the Chancery Division. The judge 'made an order restraining all communication between the young lady' and Ford, whom he summoned to court on the 6th. He duly appeared, 'arrayed in Oliver[']s best clothes, frock coat, grey trousers top hat etc.', and having been to a barber's 'whence he emerged with short hair & shining like a bridegroom'. Robert and several other Garnetts went to hear, as did Oliver. Elsie, veiled, looked outwardly calm, but leant back to avoid being seen, and kept grabbing Olive Garnett's arm to ask who had come in. The judge decided to hear the case in private, so the parties filed behind his chair into his private room for half an hour. Ford produced an affidavit swearing that 'he did not know, and had no reason to believe, that the young lady was a ward of Court'. The judge said this was false, since Ford had written to acknowledge the letter from Martindale's solicitors on 18 March saying Elsie had already been made a ward. Yet, as the judge also pointed out, it had been false to say on 18 March that Elsie had already been made a ward: that was when the proceedings had begun. Robert Garnett must have explained this to Ford, since his firm's letter to Martindale's solicitors was very careful to say that as soon as Ford was made aware of any court order he would 'comply with it absolutely'—which would mean not seeing Elsie. Ford's counsel then made the surprise announcement: the lovers were already married. There was 'no longer any Miss Martindale to protect. That lady became Mrs. Madox Hueffer some three weeks ago.'[17]

When Ford and Elsie had heard that she had finally been made a ward of court, and when they had feared a court order was imminent, they had gone to a register office in Gloucester on 17 May 1894. Ford told the registrar Elsie was over 21 and he was 24, and they were married, with Chapple as a witness. They went to Exmoor for a honeymoon, visiting Lynton and Brendon, and found a house by Selworthy Green they planned to take for a year from Sir Thomas Acland. The area may have appealed to Ford as the setting of *Lorna Doone*, in which John Ridd rescues his childhood sweetheart Lorna from her kidnappers—the same Doones who killed his father when he was 12. Ford came back to London for the sale of Madox Brown's possessions at the end of May. It made £1,067, said Olive Garnett (who went). She thought it 'a cruel horrible thing'; Mrs Hueffer was ill at Brook Green, and Ford was 'quiet'. The Garnetts even bought some of the furniture: the George IV sofa, originally made for the Brighton Pavilion, was installed in the museum residence. Ford said the sale had a 'note of tragedy' for him 'in the breaking up of a home that had seemed so romantic—that still after so many years seems to me so romantic'—but that it also had about it 'something extremely comic', in the way that 'with the coming of the auctioneer's man it all fell to pieces so extraordinarily'. After the sale he went back to Devonshire 'to finish the honeymoon'. The telegram from Robert Garnett about the court had to be brought on horseback. They immediately took a coach to Minehead, and telegraphed for their fares to London. Olive Garnett said they were 'penniless', and that they would have to live at Brook Green with Ford's mother.[18]

When the judge heard of the marriage he had to adjourn the proceedings until the certificate was produced. Mr Martindale just cast one swift glance at Elsie as they came out of the judge's room: he was 'apparently furious', said Olive Garnett. Ford looked 'pink & white & limp', she said. He had 'been obliged to take brandy beforehand'. After they had left, Shaen Roscoe sent a copy of the certificate to the judge, who became angry and said he had been deceived when he saw that the ages given on it didn't tally with those on the affidavits—though he confirmed that the marriage was still valid even though the couple had lied about their ages. He refused to suspend the order restricting intercourse, so Robert Garnett thought Ford and Elsie ought to separate until the case was heard again the following Saturday, 9 June. She stayed with the Garnetts, while he stayed at Brook Green. He went to the Times Office to place an announcement of the marriage, and to the National Liberal Club, where he found his journalist friend George Perris. He persuaded Perris to let him write a paragraph for the

Star about the hearing which he hoped would puff *The Queen Who Flew*, published about a week before the wedding:

A POET'S LOVE AFFAIR.
A Chancery Court Chapter of 'The Queen who Flew.'

In Chancery Court Nr. 2 to-day a rarely romantic story was unrolled before Mr. Justice North, who sat in private to hear the action innocently set down as '*In re* Martindale.' The action was one to forbid a Miss Martindale, said to be a ward in chancery, from perpetrating matrimony, the danger arising in connexion with the attentions of a young poet and novelist who has already achieved a certain measure of distinction by 'The Shifting of the Fire' and other of his books—to wit, Mr. Ford H. Madox Hueffer [. . .].[19]

Ford spent the evening at the Garnetts, talking over the whole affair with Olive and Edward 'as if it were someone else's novel', and becoming 'gleeful with the aid of some thimblefuls of sloe gin'. On the Friday Olive went with 'the infant'—as they were now calling Elsie—to the Chancery Court to 'get an idea of Mr. Justice North's characteristics'. They went back 'by Oxford Street for the pleasure of seeing the Queen who Flew in the shop windows'. But the waiting was 'horrible', Elsie and Robert marching 'up & down the room like animals in a cage'. She expected to be sent back home to her parents. The hearing was again in private, but Olive heard afterwards from Robert that the Martindale affidavits seemed frivolous, with their detailed accounts of 'the cloak affair' and the Burne-Jones illustration for *The Queen who Flew* as 'grave charges against Ford's character'. 'What have I to do with this person's publications?' asked the judge, now getting cross with both parties. He said that the newspaper reports of his previous hearing were contempt of court, and that if it happened again he would prosecute. But he quashed the order restricting intercourse, and said he would take no further action, though Ford had 'laid himself open to criminal proceedings under more than one head'; 'it was open to prosecute for perjury but he rather seemed to intimate that the whole affair had better be allowed to drop'. Ford and Elsie went to report to his mother at Brook Green, and to William Rossetti, who was in bed with gout. Then they spent a 'very jubilant evening' at the Garnetts, Ford playing and Elsie singing 'Twist me a Crown of Windflowers' and Tennyson's 'Ring out the old, ring in the new', the latter at least in Ford's setting. Elsie sang 'magnificently', said Olive, and afterwards 'Ford talked enthusiastically of literary plans'. Longman had asked him to write the biography of Madox Brown.[20]

Dr Martindale refused to admit defeat, and tried to have Ford—and Perris and the printers and publishers of the four papers which had carried the story—committed for contempt of court. Olive Garnett thought that if the judge found in Ford's favour then Martindale would prosecute him for perjury. There were more hearings in June. Olive went on the 22nd, and noted that when Martindale was mentioned 'the judge said he would take the more important cases first'. Ford's defence was that the motion was being made in Elsie's name, but that because she

was now a married woman no one had the right to make a motion in her name
to which she did not consent. Judgement was reserved. The *Star*'s report of this
hearing was followed by an account of a tragic case which reveals much about the
times, and the pressures which had forced Ford and Elsie into such an early
marriage. A married baker with three children had been having an affair with a
domestic servant, unmarried, but also with three children. They had been
'keeping company for some months', but had then been 'mobbed' by their
neighbours. The couple had made a suicide pact, tying their waists together with
handkerchiefs and drowning in a canal near Stockport.[21]

Elsie accompanied the Hueffers and Olive Garnett to see Oliver acting in a play
given in aid of the Royal Free Hospital. He 'looked flushed & shy & stooped',
said Olive, who felt 'complicated' sensations during the performance. She
couldn't understand why someone so theatrical in everyday life couldn't act.
While they were waiting for the judgement Ford and Elsie started looking for a
house around Hythe: they had had to give up the idea of the house in Exmoor.
Brook Green was too small for them all, especially as it was now crammed with
furniture of Madox Brown's. They found a little semi-detached stucco house at
Bonnington, looming out of the Romney Marsh mists. It was called Blomfield
Villa, was by a spot called 'Hog Turd Green', and was the first of Ford's many
houses to have little in the way of sanitation: there were no drains, and the
drinking water had to be brought from a mile away. It was damp, because built
over a stream. There was a well nearby into which Ford would lower their boots
on a string to clean them, drying them afterwards in front of a fire. When Oliver
went down to visit them later in the summer he told Olive of 'cheese & muddy
boots on the dining room table', and said he had caught a cold sleeping near a
broken window, but none the less had 'a jolly time'. He had gone down 'to see if
it were true that Elsie smoked shag in a cutty pipe, & found that she & Ford did
so constantly on their walks, & were known as the Frenchies. Their society was
that of the vicar & his pretty daughter.' Ford resigned from the 'Cemented
Bricks'—the literary society of which Jerrold and Perris were founder-members.[22]

Mr. Justice North delivered his judgement on 9 August. Olive Garnett said he
'lectured everyone'. But he was ultimately lenient. He didn't believe contempt of
court was intended—though he complained of the 'vulgarity and bad taste' of
making publicity out of the hearing. What contempt there was lay not in revealing
the marriage, but reporting what he had decided should be heard in private. He
didn't think the contempt was a serious one, though he also reprimanded the line
of defence taken by Ford's counsel, 'the boldness of which cannot be appreciated
by anyone who has not heard it', and adding that if the respondents 'had really
done what their counsel asserted their right to do with impunity, I should
certainly have committed every one of them'. As it was, he thought it just that
Ford and *the Star* should pay the costs for the motion against them. (Olive
Garnett wondered what Ford would pay his with, not having any money.) He
dismissed the other motions (against Perris and the other papers) as 'puerile',
'vexatious', and 'an abuse of the process of the Court'. Martindale had to pay the

costs for all of them, as well as for himself. When Ford heard the judgement he wrote to apologize to Perris: 'I do not feel quite fit to look an honest man in the face after having been the cause of so much worry to you'; and he invited Perris to come and stay, assuring him he would not be expected to clean his boots 'as other people must.—The Ward & I will do one apiece in memory of the trouble we have given you.'[23]

1894–1898: THE LIFE OF THE COUNTRY

Ford was later to say that he had 'buried' himself in the country. After a decade he had a severe nervous breakdown, and fell out of love with Elsie. Then his life on the Romney Marsh felt like lost years, when he had been out of the swim of London literary life, and he had wanted to forget them. Olive Garnett's contemporary account gives a different picture of adventure and animation in their early marriage. Yet there was a truth—of a Fordian, impressionistic kind, but characteristically profound—in his saying: 'my grandfather being dead, I suddenly reacted': 'I did not know then, but I know now that my brain was singing to me: "Under the bright and starry sky Dig my grave and let me lie." Only I wanted to have some tussles with the "good brown earth" before that hill-top should receive me.'[1]

The good *brown*? Ford's escape to the countryside was connected in his mind with his grandfather in another way. It was during the summer of 1894 that he began working on his biography. Olive Garnett thought that William Rossetti became angry with him because he'd sent Ford material for the life under the impression that Ford had a contract, then discovered he hadn't. But Ford denied the rift, saying that his uncle was 'most cordial and kind', but was 'in an almost hysterical condition owing to his sister's state': Christina was terminally ill with cancer. Ford told Edward Garnett that Rossetti had 'always been a *brick*—bound round with official red tape'. Garnett gave valuable critical advice, talking to Ford 'brilliantly, & gradually evolved something practical out of the vagueness'. Both Bell and Longmans expressed an interest that autumn, so Ford and Elsie came up to London for a few days. Olive was impressed by the dress Elsie had made from green furniture serge.[2]

They asked Olive to stay with them, and she went down on 17 November with Edward (who was to help Ford go through Madox Brown's correspondence) and Elsie; Ford was still seeing publishers in London and missed the train. Edward had to climb in through a bedroom window because Ford had the key:

Elsie lit the fire & Ford arrived. Welcome to Blomfield. It had evidently been left in a hurry [. . .] We sat round fire behind entrenchment of mattresses airing, holding sheets and blankets to the blaze & talking poetry [. . .] Made up bed among the apples for Edward, & I found another just as Oliver had left it,—a nest—with books, matches & cigarettes & cigarette ends handy, cycling maps & cycling gear, Vaseline & Elliman's embrocation strewn round. I did not trust the sheets so slept between blankets, put on a flannel shirt of Ford's or Oliver's over my night gown, & piled on top several old jackets, Ford's great coat and Elsie's green cloak. Slept like a dormouse.

Sunday 18th. One has to pass through Ford & Elsie's room to get downstairs so they get up first. This is late in the day [. . .] At about three o'clock we started across the wonderful marsh for Dymchurch [. . .] mud, dykes, sunset, mist effect, berries, ruin black silhouette, willows, peewhits. As we neared the coast we heard the waves breaking & saw dotted lights. Whistlerish effect. Through the village, & then we sat on a beach facing the sea, & drank loveliness.[3]

They tried to find descriptions for the 'mingling of backward fall of wave with oncoming rush,—in poetry—in music'; then they walked back in the starlight. The next day Ford explained Oliver's 'genius' and 'character' to them, '& fitted the bits of the puzzle together'. On the 20th they continued to draw up plans for the life of Madox Brown for Edward to present to Longmans. At three o'clock they set off on the seven- or eight-mile walk to Ashford. Olive remembered having the best 'at one' talk with Ford she had ever had—he defended *The Shifting of the Fire* against her criticisms, and they discussed Morris, the 'bad influence of Rossetti & Burne Jones', 'Idealism. Teutonic sentimentalism. Simple life. Reaction. Truth not beauty. Realism. Daudet. Minnesingers. Wagner. Shelley.' Edward caught the train to London; the others caught the one back to Smeeth. At supper they were still talking: this time about 'Carlyle's letters. F.M.B.'s mother & father. Discussion art v. science. Feeling v. intellect', recorded Olive. The following day she had a long discussion with Ford on some of the other topics that would be central to his art: 'Law v. Sympathy, Anarchism, Sacrifice etc. On building a house. Sticking to ideals. Elsie attacks Ford & he defends his position. Families': 'Elsie gave me her "Mrs. Larkins" story to read. Unconsciousness necessary to production of work of art. Analysis v. synthesis. Morality. Retire to scullery & wash up. I lie awake so contented & happy, thinking how much I love the two sleeping below & that there are good people in the world after all.' She was managing to live up to the ideal she had formulated in her best philosophical schoolgirl manner that spring: 'I have only one idea to love, love, love, overwhelmingly everyone & everything, & to sacrifice myself in some way. In fact I feel that if I can't, I shall *burst*.' They woke her up in the morning by playing the William Morris piano (lent by W. M. Rossetti), and Ford shouted up: 'It is a quarter past two, Olive.' She was sad to leave on the 25th, but knew they had no money for entertaining. 'As it was, they have only 1/- with which to pay the sweep if he came on Tuesday. They proposed to lie in bed & afterwards to write saying they "had heard that he had come & would he come again." '[4]

Cathy Hueffer stayed with them over Christmas. Elsie hoped the country would 'do her good, for she is worried & sad at losing Miss Christina Rossetti'. Elsie was herself worried and sad at not being able to see her own parents, so on Christmas Day she made a gesture of peace and goodwill, writing to her father: 'Dear Daddy, My affection for you is sincere &, in spite of everything will be lasting & it will be to me a real cause of grief if the gulf between us cannot be bridged over.' She asked him not to let the year end without this having been done. He told her she had proved herself 'an undutiful wilful, & ungrateful child', and that he certainly couldn't accept a reconciliation. He even accused Ford of telling her what to write. She tried again in the New Year, saying: 'I think you would be pleased with us if you could resolve to be so generous as to forgive me & to forgive Ford for being so brave (if so wrong & foolish) as to marry me.' And she added a postscript: 'As you seem to think it is Ford & not I who write he shall [not] even see this letter.' But the reconciliation was not to come until the following Christmas, eighteen months after the marriage. Elsie was pregnant by early 1895. She was 'enormous' by February, but then became unwell and miscarried. Olive found her 'depressed' when Elsie came to lunch in May.[5]

Longmans accepted the proposal for *Ford Madox Brown* in February, offering Ford £50 advance, £50 on publication, and royalties of twopence in the shilling ($16\frac{2}{3}$ per cent) on the sales. This was a godsend—£50 was the amount Mrs Hueffer was giving them to last a whole year on. She had promised them £4 per week, but Oliver's debts and the exiguousness of Madox Brown's legacy meant she couldn't afford so much. According to Lloyd George in 1909, a working-class family needed £3 per week for reasonable food, clothing, and shelter. Now Ford and Elsie had almost exactly that—until her father's solicitors started pressuring them to pay the court costs of £30 in the spring. Ford wrote to Edward Garnett: 'Thanks for all you've done—I don't know why you do it. If I were F.M.B., I should imagine some R.A. [Royal Academician] had been getting at you & you were mixed up in a horrible conspiracy to get my work—as it is I can only say to quote him again—"The whole thing's a mystery to me." ' Most biographers will—or should—recognize that temptation to identify with the subject, though in Ford's case it was his book's cause rather than its result. He worked hard on the book through the winter, and told Edward he hoped 'to be able to touch some of Longman's gold to be able to get up to London' to interview friends of Brown's: 'till then I'm rather stuck in the mud—but one gets used to that here.' But where gold was concerned, Ford was no Midas. Money didn't last long in his hands. He characteristically lost nine shillings and sixpence through a hole in his pocket as he walked about in London when they got there in February. William Rossetti, whose sister Christina had died on 29 December, offered them some of her furniture. They were probably staying with Cathy Hueffer, who had now moved with Oliver to Linden Gardens, and had just finished a portrait begun by Madox Brown of Elsie wearing a conspicuous wedding ring ('a regular Madox Brown', said Olive Garnett when she saw it, adding that the family called it 'portrait of a wedding ring'). They visited the Garnetts, and heard a lecture by Morris. On 19 March they left for Manchester, to stay with Charles Rowley, and collect material about Brown's life there; to see Madox Brown pictures in private collections in Newcastle; and to visit Elsie's aunt in Carlisle. They were back in London at the end of March and went back to Bonnington on 2 April; but Olive saw them again in June, when they came up 'to buy or hire a double tricycle'.

They looked very well, and joked about how 'it seemed as if a plague spot was on their cottage since no one would visit them'.[6]

Olive also recorded Oliver's story this year. Not having succeeded as an actor in plays, he was determined to write them. When he finished one, his mother got angry: 'For now that you have written this play', she said, 'I see that you are not a fool as I thought you were, & I consider that you have been wasting your time, all these years.' He asked her for five pounds. With which, he said, he would leave the house and never come back. She refused. 'As for control over the boy, she said she had none & never had any.' 'Meanwhile', he told Olive, 'my name is posted at the clubs for not paying my subscriptions. Last night [. . .] I wrote half of another play. I shall try to finish it tonight, if not I shall throw it away. I don't dream of wasting more than two nights over a play.' Despite this animated posing, Olive thought him 'in a dismal state of mind', and said she believed he suffered from 'periodic fits of melancholia'. In February he heard that someone was calling him the most 'accomplished liar he knew', and saying that he had made 'an awful fool of himself over a girl'. He became very ill, took to his bed, and had to be nursed by his mother. In April he told Olive about his courtship of 'the fair Alicia', saying 'I have not the energy to make love now.' Olive thought his doubts 'as to whether he would make a good husband' did him honour. She exhorted him to become 'a real realist', which meant 'not to deceive anyone, especially a girl, any more'. His reply shows what Ford meant when he said Oliver was an exaggerated version of himself. He 'protested that he only lived to enjoy the excitement of getting out of scrapes, that a prosperous existence wouldn't suit him & that his pleasure lay in producing impressions on people'. She replied with the 'platitudinal reflection' that 'One cannot live by impressions alone', and chaffed him: 'isn't our platonic flirtation a little slow?' By September he had produced an impression on Zoe Pyne, a violinist, daughter of a musician, and sister of an organist Madox Brown had known in Manchester. He became engaged to her, much to Olive's surprise, since he had omitted to mention it when they met. He had also been given a job at the Lyceum at a guinea a week 'for doing nothing effectively'. In fact he was Tybalt's understudy in a production of *Romeo and Juliet*, as well as being a lord who just had to say 'I know not, Sir.' He created his next scrape from which to escape by getting newspapers to misreport that ' "M[r.] Ford M. Hueffer who recently" . . . etc etc is going to take the part of Tybalt etc. This clever young fellow & so on.' The Martindales were furious again, and Ford was indignant. Oliver then burst into the Garnetts' house with 'You know I'm not Tybalt!', and said he didn't know who had been spreading the rumours. He later confessed. The actor who had taken him under his wing, Ian Robertson, told him 'he did worse every night'; partly because he acted the part differently every night; and partly because he made a face in Mercutio's death scene, which caused another actor to laugh, for which he was told he would be sacked until Oliver confessed yet again.[7]

Juliet too was beginning to show signs of Huefferian creativity (she too would compose, write, sing, and translate). Oliver wrote her some verse 'On the occasion

of my sister gaining 6 prizes' which recalls his telling of tall stories, and touches
on the family fascination with truth and untruth:

> It really alas! does not matter at all
>   If I'm truthful or not unto you
> For though *sometimes* believed when I *don't* tell the Truth
>   I am *never* believed when I *do!*[8]

Ford asked Edward Garnett for criticisms of the manuscript of *Ford Madox
Brown*, but he got more than he may have bargained for. Garnett found it
'German-cumbrous-slovenly-vague, will generalise about things of which he
knows nothing etc—'. He was a formidable publisher's reader, a sharp critic and
discoverer of new talent, and had already been working for T. Fisher Unwin for
several years. Yet he was deeply frustrated. His 'large critical sense only inhibited
him' in his own writing, which he found 'a constant struggle'. Doubtless Ford's
book profited from his comments; but they were not made without envy of the
creative fluency of a man six years his junior, who also knew much more than he
did about painting, about literature, and about Madox Brown. Edward was
sexually frustrated as well, his marriage to Constance having become 'virtually
celibate' due to a gynaecological injury. His son, the writer David Garnett,
recalled that he was apt to be 'irritable and neurotic and became easily exasperated
with his wife and child'. Olive Garnett recorded a curious episode while they were
staying at Bonnington. 'Edward amused us incessantly, his mock reverence for
Elsie's masculine powers & treating Ford like a well meaning baby. "Are you
awake?" stroking his hair patting him on the back etc.' Constance described him
as 'just a bundle of paradoxes whom *no one* can possibly understand'. Douglas
Goldring was told that Edward had 'a sort of instinctive *physical* antipathy to
Ford'. If true, the reason he gives for not understanding it is probably its
explanation: Garnett 'was quite remarkably ugly while Ford, with his fresh
complexion, tall lean figure, and blond hair and moustache was, if not good-looking, at all events in appearance reasonably attractive, especially to women'. The
facility with which he captivated the Martindale sisters and Olive Garnett must
have been further grounds for envy.[9]

When Olive went to stay on 16 November 1895, Ford met her on the platform
at Ashford, where he had just seen off her sister Lucy. He seemed 'a substantial,
fair, smiling apparition in new grey suit'. Elsie appeared with their two dogs,
Cromwell and Le Gallienne, and she and Olive walked to Aldington to buy
provisions. Back at Blomfield Villa, she 'was soon admiring the Christina Rossetti
furniture, at each piece of which she "wrote all her poems", as F. playfully put
it', and the Broadwood upright piano, which Ford played after supper. Two days
later they decided to 'make an expedition' to Froghole, where Edward and
Constance were living in a rat-infested cottage while their new house, the Cearne,
was being built. It was the first house designed by their smock-wearing, Fabian
architect-friend Harrison Cowlishaw, who was engaged to Lucy Garnett, and it
was to be built along William Morris rustic medieval lines. 'It was a lovely day,

summer again, so hot and balmy—St. Martin's summer, Ford said, carrying his famous Rossettian coat.' At Ashford Elsie got alarmed when she lost Ford and Olive. When she found them at the station she said she had 'thought you two had gone off in the train & left me'. It was the first of several signs of nervous tension in the marriage, and possibly of jealousy. As Olive commented: 'This brings back that day here when she escaped from her sister Mary & began for Ford & herself their present life.' They had a starlight ramble over the building site, 'the lantern held now to a window a rafter, or a chimney-nook, or a loose plank'. There were no stairs yet, so they sat on top of a ladder and 'saw the stars shining serenely in the sky roof'. Olive shared a room with Elsie in a nearby cottage, and heard her talking in her sleep: 'The roof is coming down, I can't hold it up any longer.' Moser argues that the roofless Cearne became the image for 'Elsie's weary sense of responsibility for the marriage, her recollection of its complicated history, and her anxiety as to its permanence'. How long would Ford's writing keep a roof over their heads? At the time of their marriage he had told her: 'You must not expect me to be always faithful to you.' After the breach with her family, then her miscarriage, it must have been the last thing she needed to think of.[10]

The next day Ford came down 'sleepily', having 'read to read himself asleep as his custom is far into the night'. They took the train to Tunbridge Wells, and from there decided to walk the thirty-five miles back to Bonnington. It took two days, limping for blisters. 'Played spelling word game & capping verses. Mrs. Madox Brown and D. G. Rossetti good at that & so we beguiled the way—with acid drops for me, pipe for Ford, & lemon for Elsie.' They broke the journey at Tenterden, staying at an inn. 'Next day was bright, we inspected the church and hobbled on our way' back to Bonnington. Not surprisingly, Olive 'felt disinclined to walk' the following day. She sat working on a translation of the life of a Russian friend, Madame Bervi, while Elsie played the piano. The parson's daughter called, to ask Elsie (whom she had heard singing as she had walked past the house) to perform at a concert she was organizing in the next village of Bilsington to pay for new church lamps. After supper Ford played while Elsie read Olive's translation. When Olive mentioned a note Stepniak had added to the manuscript offering a psychological explanation, Ford's mood suddenly swung to vindictive outrage. Olive and her Russian friends became the targets of his outburst:

This set Ford off. He threw back his head & in his slowest & most tempered tones inveighed bitterly against Stepniak, myself & my family 'You are all alike[;] the simplest, most sacred indisputable altruism is twisted & turned by you to suit your own worldly convenience. Give up all & follow Christ. Could anything be plainer. Fomin does here in this story & here Stepniak puts in his own wretched, philistine, bourgeois note to *explain* forsooth, to explain it away, & you agree, you would publish it.' Fomin was right, you are wrong, etc. etc.

'I thought Stepniak was such a wonderful person,' said Elsie, & Ford said some rude, damning things, if they were true 'To die for the truth, what is finer, truer, higher? According to me [Fomin] erred only in one thing, when giving himself up to the police prompted by physical pain; had he let himself starve he would have been perfect.' Logical, I replied, not perfect, only perfectly logical, as it is not given to human nature, even to Fomin to be, Fomin who is while still a young man leading a useless existence, supported by the very authorities of whom he disapproves.

We argued on, Ford lucidly, logically; I lamely, confusedly, yet clinging clinging to some idea I knew was implanted in me & in Stepniak.

How can I describe my feelings, my wounds! Ford's brutality certainly had moved me, even to tears [. . .] I could not say good-night to Ford or Elsie, so hurt was I, & lay long awake scarcely able to think, praying for intellectual light, & relying only on the tenderness that Stepniak would have given me, to heal the wounds that Ford had so coldly dealt me.[11]

Ford kept to himself until dinner the next day; the atmosphere was tense, with Olive 'almost crying aloud with pain, & dismay' now and then. She felt Ford had 'suddenly got thousands of miles away, he seemed cold & shrunken'. Elsie was 'no help' either, because 'she is a reflection of Ford intellectually, & cold in herself'. 'I hated Ford then I suppose & was glad when he went off in the rain [. . .] I didn't want to hate Ford.' He brought back a pair of scissors with which she and Elsie 'set to work & unpicked Madox Brown's fur sack, which he sat painting in', and with which Elsie was going to line a new cloak. Olive had 'choked down' her feelings. Later, 'sitting round the parlour fire we got almost gay again though still subdued'. She soon forgave him: 'I knew at the time even when most wounded, he was only expressing according to his nature, what was in his mind, & I believe *he* believed what I overheard him saying to Elsie [. . .]—"it's for her moral good".' 'My serenity was no doubt partly restored by a fling at Ford', she said. He had been rereading *The Shifting of the Fire* and said 'I think it is one of the most vulgar books I have ever read. But it is a bit of life.' Olive then told him what she thought of it, which can't have been much. Elsie, 'who was almost in tears, said that the same vulgarity appeared in the Brown Owl'. But Ford took the criticism better, attributing the 'vulgarity' to his 'having been brought up among ultra-refined people, & afterwards revelling in what he imagined to be nearer real life'. It could stand as an abstract of his best novels' plots, in which the hero discovers the vulgarity and squalor underlying the lives of the ultra-refined. Ford called Olive 'with vigour' the next morning, 'so the breach was healed' before she left. That evening they amused themselves drawing pictures for the others to guess their subject. (Ford drew 27, West Hill Highgate, Mathilde Blind, and the suicide of Hedda Gabler.)[12]

What is it that this outburst expresses about Ford's nature? His defensiveness suggests that Stepniak's attempt to explain altruism struck at some of his deepest feelings. It was Madox Brown who particularly represented the altruist for Ford, so he may have felt (unconsciously?) an implicit attack on his grandfather. Altruism mattered so deeply to Ford—it is at the heart of his fiction and his conception of religion, and it seems here to stand for all that distinguishes Brown and his descendants from the rational, progressive Garnetts. As Moser says, Ford may have wondered 'whether he himself could be faithful to Madox Brown's high ideals'. As he also argues, the scene suggests that Ford had powerful anxieties about the psychological sources of his own altruism: 'Perhaps he unconsciously wondered whether his commitment to altruism masked an ultimately irresistible tendency toward self-indulgence.' He was certainly pondering his own nature, and what it might owe to his family. Before Olive left Ford expatiated to her, as he had before, on 'the Hueffer characteristics. The only family in the world. Respectability, selfishness, clannishness, the Hueffer sniff, religion etc.' Stepniak may himself have been disturbing to Ford: the gentle altruism that he ought to have admired, but which could issue in assassination. He was the kind of character associated in fiction with Dostoevsky and Conrad, but which Ford tended to avoid in his own work. There may also have been an element of jealousy in his reaction. He must have known, or guessed, by now that Olive was in love with Stepniak. His assassination of Stepniak's character may have reflected his hurt that he had been replaced by the Russian in Olive's admiration. This episode is important, too, for being the first known sign since his marriage of his nervous strain, which was to cast a shadow over most of the rest of his life. [13]

Towards the end of the year Mrs Martindale sent Elsie 'a packet containing her childhood's treasures, clothes & violin', and a reconciliation began. Elsie replied with a 'kind' letter, and in December Dr Martindale was making the not very promising effort to say 'I cannot forget the past but I will endeavour to do so', though he added: 'Christmas coming round gives us an opportunity of being reconciled & I trust that we may be so.' Ford and Elsie were invited to spend Christmas at Winchelsea. Ford had proved that he could support Elsie for eighteen months without asking for assistance, so her father's fear that he was after his money may have been allayed. 'Ford is in a "whirl" ', noted Olive. 'So here ends the romance.'[14]

Ford liked to imagine that it was at Bonnington that Caesar had landed in Britain, bringing Mediterranean civilization to the harsh north. In the chapter on the Romney Marsh in *The Cinque Ports*—the book he wrote after living in the area for five years—he even found an authority to support him, arguing from the details of the landscape given in Caesar's *De Bello Gallico*. In a slightly later book he said he liked this countryside

better than any other I have known before or since, and indeed, with its deep folds of the hills, its little jewel-green, dark and misty fields between tangled coppices, with its small cottages, its aged farms and its high and deep woods covering the ground like a mantle further than the eye could reach from any height; with its good, nourishing, greasy mud, its high hedgerows and its spreading neglected small orchards, it remains for me my particular heart of the country.[15]

It is a mystical romantic *fin de siècle* landscape as he describes it. But it was, as he said, above all for the local people that he loved it. Other scenes found their place in his heart: London, the Rhineland and the Spessart, West Sussex, Paris, New York, and especially Provence. But he never forgot the peasant women and men he befriended at Bonnington. Foremost was Meary Walker, of whom he said,

'I think I cared for her more than for any friend I have made before or since'. He recalled their meeting when he offered to 'carry her burdens' as they were walking along the same path. The phrase is significant, evoking not just her parcels, but the cares of a life of long toil. She replied: 'Why, thank ye, mister. I'll do as much for you when ye come to be my age.' She was almost 70. In a sense she did, and sooner than she thought, for the memory of her wry resilience became Ford's cherished example of fortitude and endurance when he felt overburdened. 'A hard life—a life so hard and so grinding that to an onlooker like myself it seemed something heroic and romantic—had left not a touch of bitterness in her.' He called her 'the wisest and upon the whole the most estimable human being that I ever knew at all well'. He began writing his elegies for her as soon as she had become the stuff to fill graveyards. But the fact of his admiration for Meary, in so many ways the antithesis of the refined, cosmopolitan artist that Ford was becoming, proves his lack of snobbery or élitism.[16]

Her 'one unfailing form of words', for which Ford always honoured her, was 'Ah keep all on gooing!'—'And that was at once her philosophy and her reason for existence', he said. Those words came back to him whenever he felt his struggle to find new forms of words was failing, and he needed a reason for his own existence. In the Bonnington peasants he discovered a world into which middle-class morality and religion had failed to permeate. When Meary ran away with a gypsy from the house where she had been in service since the age of 14 (and in which the housemaids all slept in one room, telling folk legends into the night), they had a wandering existence, living together unmarried for years. She once said to Ford about a bible, 'I don't believe it can be real old, because it's got the New Testament in it'. When Walker, her husband, was dying of gangrene she broke her leg and was taken to hospital against her will:

One night, driven beyond endurance by the want of news of Walker and of her sitting hen she escaped from the hospital window and crawled on her hands and knees the whole seven miles from the hospital to her home. She found when she arrived in the dawn that Walker was in his coffin. The chickens however were a healthy brood. Her admiration for Walker, the weak and lazy artist in basket making never decreased. She treasured his best baskets to the end of her life as you and I might treasure Rembrandts. Once, ten years after, she sat for a whole day on his grave. The old sexton, growing confused with years, had made a mistake and was going to inter another man's wife on top of Walker. Meary stopped that.[17]

Then there was the emotional and mendacious Meary Spratt, who, when begging, 'would scream and howl and yell in the highest of keys, pulling her gnarled, rheumatic fingers into repulsive shapes and screaming like a locomotive to show how much they pained her'. Ford said that when she was 73 she had married Mr Spratford, who was 82, and between them they had thirty-one children, and lived 'in a little brick cottage not much larger than a dog kennel'. Spratford looked like 'a Biblical patriarch', but was 'extremely dishonest and had three times been to prison for robbing poor old women'. Meary Walker and

Meary Spratt were regular visitors at Ford and Elsie's house. Olive Garnet met them there in 1895. There were also the village idiot 'Shaking Ben who had been ruined by the bad gels of Rye', and 'Ragged Ass Wilson', so called because of 'the frailty of his nether garments', and who was 'singularly handsome, dark with a little beard like Shakespeare's and that poet's eyes'. Ford said he was the 'most faithful soul' he had ever known, and that he never saw him not working—another way in which he was like an artist. And there was Grocer Rayner at Aldington Corner, who was stone deaf, 'So he read. He read Henry James, Joseph Conrad, Stephen Crane [. . .] When Crane and Conrad came into his shop one day Rayner's emotion was so great that he was ill for some time.'[18]

Ezra Pound admired Ford's 'peasant biographies' as 'specimens of Impressionist mode at its best', and said that there was 'nothing that more registers the fact of our day' than the portraits Ford later published as *Women & Men*. Ford said he was once given directions in a strange countryside: 'You go down the lane till you come to the place where Farmer Banks's old barn used to stand when he kept six cows in it.' He argued that we all need 'some cloud of human ghosts to people' our landscapes: 'few can dispense with the invisible presence of the dead.' Meary Walker and her neighbours were the ghosts with which he populated his remembered landscapes of the Romney Marsh. 'We see our country-side through this veil, and the trees, the hillocks, and the smithies seem to speak to us with human voices.' He personifies the landscape in a more curious way, not just seeing it through people, but seeing it *as* a person. 'One gets, if one be at all sensitive, odd little shocks and emotions in the fields', he wrote, and described how one dusk he was digging potatoes, and when he thrust his hand into the earth found it flesh-warm. 'After all the heat seemed to have departed from the world it was like suddenly coming into contact with a living being. I am, perhaps, over-fanciful, but to me it has always seemed like finding the breast of a woman—as if Nature herself had taken a body and the heat of life.' In a haunting monologue he presented a more sinister version of this anthropomorphic fancy:

> I wonder why we toiled upon the earth
> From sunrise until sunset, dug and delved,
> Crook-backed, cramp-fingered, making little marks
> On the unmoving bosom of the hills,
> And nothing came of it. And other men
> In the same places dug and delved and ended
> As we have done; and other men just there
> Shall do the self-same things until the end.
> I wonder why we did it. . . . Underneath
> The grass that fed my sheep, I often thought
> Something lay hidden, some sinister thing
> Lay looking up at us as if it looked
> Upwards thro' quiet waters; that it saw
> Us futile toilers scratching little lines

And doing nothing. And maybe it smiled
Because it knew that we must come to this. . . .'[19]

Early in 1896 the Hueffers acquired a grandfather clock, and inside it pasted sheets of paper recording their guests. Ford was always gregarious, needing the rhythm of escape into his work and escape from it. He was a generous and entertaining host. Harry Cowlishaw visited in the spring with Lucy Garnett. Robert Garnett and his wife Martha were there in August, followed by Harri Martindale and two other friends. 'Oliver, Baron von Hüffer-Schaumbirg' visited on the 24th, followed by Elsie's parents and Mary three days later. Dr Martindale was distressed by the dampness, and encouraged them to move. So when they cycled past an attractive red-brick and tiled farmhouse on the Pilgrim's Way near Postling and found it was available, they rented it. There were five good-sized bedrooms, and downstairs a drawing-room 'with a beam across the middle of the low ceiling', a dining-room, and a long kitchen with a running spring just outside the door. There was an immense thatched tithe-barn next door, though it later burned down. It was only a couple of miles from Sandling Junction. They moved into Pent Farm on 15 October 1896, and duly inscribed the date on the piece of paper pasted inside their grandfather clock that would serve as a guest-book. The Pent was to be their home for two years. Then they handed it over to the Conrads, when it became the Hueffers' second home until the Conrads left in 1907. 'We are just under the most magnificent sheep-downs', Ford told Walter Jerrold, when inviting him to be their first guest, as he had been at Bonnington: 'we've got room for a small army and welcomes for a large one (this is the old country gentleman style up to wh. we are trying to live.—It is rather difficult. We have only just moved in—last Thursday—and have managed to keep it up so far however.' He told him to bring his cycle, as it was 'glorious country for that sport. You push up a hill—jump on, ride down—push up and so on for miles and miles.'[20]

At the end of the month *Ford Madox Brown* was published. Mizener said Ford 'was evidently determined to achieve the pompous tone of the official Victorian biography', and it is true that the book lacks the humour and animation of his reminiscences of the Pre-Raphaelites in *Ancient Lights*. It is as if it needs to verge on parody of earnest official-biographese in order to suppress any hint of facetiousness. But the reviews were extraordinarily encouraging about a book finished soon after its author was 22. *The Times* called it 'in every way an admirable biography', and said it was written 'with fullness of knowledge'—'Considering the youth of the author, it exhibits a discretion and soundness of judgement which are really remarkable.' The *Dial* called it 'easily one of the most entertaining of recent artists' biographies'. The *Magazine of Art* found it 'well-informed and brightly written'—'In this admirable volume the literary and artistic sections are well balanced; and each in its own way could hardly be bettered [. . .] a commendable memorial to a distinguished man.' In December Ford went to Manchester and Liverpool to arrange the loan of Brown's pictures from public collections for an exhibition he was helping to organize at the Grafton

Galleries in January 1897. 'We are always miserable when we are separated', Elsie confided to Olive Garnett. She was expecting a baby the following summer. She took to her bed. Then their small servant, Annie, took to hers, so Mary came to help. Ford told Jerrold it was 'no kind of a joke' having the whole house on their hands. But he was invigorated by the prospect of a child. 'We are both tremendously pleased, of course', Elsie told Olive, 'in fact F has got almost well since he has had this to look forward to.' Christina (after her great aunt) Margaret Madox Hueffer was born on the afternoon of 3 July 1897. Whatever was wrong with Ford, he was only *almost* well. Soon after the birth he had to take a cycling trip in Surrey to rest his 'nerves', travelling along the Hog's Back, and visiting Gilbert White's Selborne.[21]

One of the rich Hüffer uncles had died, and left his nephews and nieces over £3,000 each. In order to keep up his old country gentleman style Ford said, 'I added golf to my occupations.' He said a cousin, George Wilkes, had just opened a links at Hythe, and that it was there that he played with two future Liberal cabinet ministers, Dr Macnamara, president of the National Union of Teachers in 1896, an MP in 1900, and Lloyd George's Minister for Education in 1920; and C. F. G. Masterman, Ford's contemporary, an MP from 1906 to 1914, and briefly a member of Asquith's cabinet. Masterman was to become one of his closest friends years later. He also befriended the Portuguese Consul-General, 'Señor Don Jaime Batalha Reis', 'whose lovely daughter Celeste sat unconsciously for Seraphina', the heroine of the story about pirates he wrote at about this time, and which—after a long collaboration with Conrad—would eventually become *Romance*. 'Batalha Reis was a bearded person with the most extravagant gestures I have ever met', said Ford, 'and I am afraid he sat for Tomas Castro in the same book.' He got on well with Ford's peasant friends, and once, 'when he put on his preposterous Portuguese diplomatic uniform to please Mrs. Walker, he created a sensation in Bonnington that that village can never have got over'. Thanks to his legacy, Ford was also able to take a small apartment at the top of an eighteenth-century house in John Street, Bloomsbury, which he shared with Cowlishaw for £15 a year each.[22]

He was writing poems, and articles of art criticism. But what was lacking was the creative stimulus of London and the Garnetts. In January 1898 he stayed with Olive while reviewing the Rossetti and Millais exhibitions at the Royal Academy and the New Gallery. According to Goldring, Elsie found the Pent 'lonely and depressing'. And later Ford too remembered this as 'the most depressing period of a life not lacking in depressing periods'. So in March 1898 they moved to Limpsfield, letting the farmhouse to the artist and illustrator Walter Crane, a disciple of William Morris. (They returned to find that he had painted a crane on the front door, and numbers on all the doors; and that his family had surprised the locals by taking their baths on the lawn.) They lived at Limpsfield for a year, in Grace's Cottage, named after Constance's sister, Grace Black, who had married a man called Human, who became head of a technical college in Colombo before their cottage was completed. 'It will be very nice for us to have such pleasant neighbours so near', wrote Constance Garnett to her father. 'It is a most beautiful little cottage and will just suit them.' Grace's Cottage was another Cowlishaw design, built two fields away from the Cearne. When Edward Garnett brought Stephen Crane across, to meet Ford and plant a rose tree by the cottage, Crane thought the still-unfinished medieval-style building was a 'bully baronial relic', said Ford. He found Crane 'the most beautiful spirit I have ever known'. 'He was small, frail, energetic, at times virulent. He was full of phantasies and fanaticisms. He would fly at and deny every statement before it was out of your mouth.' Ford recalled Crane thinking he was a verbose Pre-Raphaelite poet, and shouting at him about how he ruined all his verse by dragging in words to fill up the metre, and making digressions for the sake of rhyme: 'he had never seen a word of mine.' It was not only Crane's aptitude with a spade that impressed Ford, but also his knack of swatting flies with the bead-sight of his revolver. Crane became one of the writers Ford most admired—especially for stories such as 'The Open Boat', and his masterpiece, *The Red Badge of Courage*, which he was to emulate in his own war novels. He was a near-contemporary of Ford's—just two years older. His histrionic bravado impressed Ford too: 'I have known him change his apparent personality half a dozen times in the course of an afternoon', he commented, suggesting one way the American may have seemed his own alter-ego. He was dying of consumption when Ford knew him, and his death at the age of 28 made him figure as a powerful alter-ego in another way in Ford's imagination, as the writer, taken advantage of by his entourage, and struggling in pathos under the shadow of death: 'Poor, frail Steevie [. . .] writing incessantly—like a spider that gave its entrails to nourish a wilderness of parasites. For, with his pen that moved so slowly in microscopic black trails over the immense sheets of paper that he affected, he had to support all that wilderness. That was the thought I could not bear.'[23]

The Garnetts had chosen the site for the Cearne because it was near the colony of Fabians and friends living near the Chart Woods east of Oxted. They included Henry Salt, who had resigned his job as a master at Eton 'in protest against working with "cannibals in cap and gown," deciding to devote his life to vegetarian and humanitarian causes, and opting for the Simple Life on a hundred pounds a year'; Sydney Olivier, who had been Colonial Secretary in British Honduras; and Edward Pease, who founded the Fabian Society in 1883, and became its Secretary. Ford later said: 'A mistaken search for high thinking took me to Limpsfield.' He developed an antipathy to the contradictions and eccentricities of this group of radical commuters:

Limpsfield was the extra-urban headquarters of the Fabian Society [. . .] there meetings sanctioning the marriages of members—in the case of the Committee usually with wealthy American women—were held. Mr. Shaw's marriage was there sanctioned. Other meetings defined the beliefs, rules of conduct and other private details of the lives of the members. To-day [1931] the Fabian Society is an integral part of the British Government. It was not then. Its members then wore beards, queer, useful or homespun clothes and boots and talked Gas and Water Socialism. They were the Advanced.[24]

He was later to write scathing hilarious satires of the Garnetts' circle in *The Simple Life Limited* and (to a lesser extent) in *The Panel*. They left him with a deep mistrust of 'reformers'. Up to 1898 Ford and Elsie were very much of this world—he even had the beard then. And he would continue to advocate literary, political, and economic reforms. But his memoirs and novels testify to his dual attitude, showing how he also felt the outsider and critic. David Garnett gave a novelistic impression of their life at Grace's Cottage—though his testimony needs to be taken with caution, since he was only 5 at the time, and though he remained fond of Ford, his comment that the 'young Garnetts were inclined to regard the Hueffer boys as half egregious asses and half charlatans' shows the distortion produced by later animosity. (Olive Garnett's diary shows that she thought Ford half-charlatan and half-genius.)

Ford was at this period playing at being a farmer and an expert on agriculture, so he wore a smock frock and gaiters. The only sign of the farm was that he kept ducks. There was no pond for them, so Ford sank a hipbath in the ground and the ducks stood in a queue, waiting their turn to swim in it. These birds were named after my mother and my aunts. When Ford dug in the garden [. . .] the ducks stood round him in a semi-circle, waiting to gobble up earthworms. 'Lucy is so very greedy,' Ford would pronounce in a sorrowful drawl, 'she always manages to eat some of Connie's share.' 'Katie was such a clumsy thing, she broke one of my tomato frames. Really I could *not* feel fond of her, so we had her roast on Sunday. Rather tough.' It was a simple way of teasing, but effective. My aunts would repeat such remarks to each other, but their laughter was not without a trace of indignation.[25]

Garnett's own teasing is simple but effective here. Ford was not a farmer; but *The Cinque Ports* and *The Heart of the Country* show that his expertise about agriculture was not fictional. The references to tomato-frames and digging in the garden show that there was more to his small-producer role than playing with the animals.

David recalled Elsie as 'tall, high-breasted and dark, with a bold eye and a rich, high colour, like a ripe nectarine':

She dressed in richly coloured garments of the William Morris style and wore earrings and a great amber necklace, and I, at the age of five, was at once greatly attracted to her. Without undue hesitation I proposed marriage, and when Elsie pointed out that Ford was an obstacle, I said cheerfully that it would be a good thing if he died soon. Although Ford was at once informed of my intention of superseding him, he bore no rancour and was a most charming entertainer of my youth. He would suddenly squat and then bound after me like a gigantic frog. He could twitch one ear without moving the other—a dreadful but fascinating accomplishment. He would also tell me stories, just as he told everyone else stories—but I do not think I ever believed that anything he said was true.[26]

It was probably during this year at Limpsfield that Ford met David Soskice. He was a Russian Jew, another of the political exiles attracted by Constance Garnett to the spot that Edward was later to call 'Dostoevsky Corner', 'on account of the eccentricity of its inhabitants'. Soskice had spent three years in St Petersburg prisons without trial. He came to England with his wife and son, but 'Madame Soskice did not care for English cottages', and took her son back to Paris, where she studied medicine. 'David Soskice was a squarely built man, with a curly black beard, a square forehead and the simplest ideas of right and wrong which he put into practice with little regard for the consequences', said David Garnett. 'For instance, he believed that Dreyfus was innocent and he believed one should tell the truth in all circumstances—a much more doubtful proposition.' Garnett said he had 'a literal mind and no imagination'. He was an irresistible target for Ford's teasing. His education of Soskice by imparting parodic agricultural information became 'an enduring Garnett legend'. D. H. Lawrence, who didn't meet Ford until ten years later, must have heard the story from them, and in the 1920s was still reproducing their impersonations of Ford. 'Yaws, yaws . . . rye . . . rye is one of our—ah—lawgest crops.' He also tried to convince Soskice that the most profitable crop was 'a very tall cabbage, the stalks of which supplied the walking-out canes for soldiers in the British Army'. It is not surprising that Soskice never warmed to Ford. But two years later he met and fell in love with Juliet Hueffer, whom David Garnett described as 'a ravishingly beautiful blonde, a good deal like an idealised child's doll', and with 'a great capacity for enjoying life, and a rich sense of humour'. Soskice divorced his wife (who was by then living with a fellow medical student, and didn't contest the divorce), and they married in 1902. Juliet learned Russian, became 'one of Constance's more valuable collaborators', and later an accomplished translator (in her own right) of Kryshanovskaya and Nekrasov. She also became 'a Wagnerian contralto of great ability and heard at Covent Garden'.[27]

Back in 1894 Edward Garnett had descended on Bonnington, 'bringing with him a great basket of manuscripts that had been submitted to his firm'. 'We were all dressed more or less mediaevally, after the manner of true disciples of socialism of the William Morris school', recalled Ford. 'We were drinking, I think, mead out of cups made of bullock's horn.' Garnett threw Ford a manuscript. 'I think that then I had the rarest literary pleasure of my existence. It was to come into contact with a spirit of romance, of adventure, of distant lands, and with an English that was new, magic, and unsurpassed.' It was *Almayer's Folly*, Conrad's first novel. Ford had just missed Conrad in the spring of 1898, when he had been staying with the Garnetts, and had left the same day the Hueffers arrived at Grace's Cottage. But that autumn—probably in the first week of September—Garnett brought the Polish ex-mariner to meet Ford. It was to prove the crucial event in both men's literary lives.[28]

7

MEETING CONRAD

Ford's reminiscence of that meeting at Grace's Cottage is vivid and bristling:

Conrad came round the corner of the house. I was doing something at the open fireplace in the house-end. He was in advance of Mr. Garnett, who had gone inside, I suppose, to find me. Conrad stood looking at the view. His hands were in the pockets of his reefer-coat, the thumbs sticking out. His black torpedo beard pointed at the horizon. He placed a monocle in his eye. Then he caught sight of me.
I was very untidy in my working clothes. He started back a little. I said 'I'm Hueffer.' He had taken me for the gardener.
His whole being melted together in enormous politeness. His spine inclined forward; he extended both hands to take mine. He said:
'My dear faller. . . . Delighted. . . . *Ench . . . anté*.' He added: '*What* conditions to work in. . . . Your admirable cottage. . . . Your adorable view. . . . '
It was symbolic that the first remark he should make to me should be about conditions in which to work. Poor fellow! Work was at once his passion and his agony, and no one, till the very end of his life, had much worse conditions. On the last time I saw him, a few weeks before his death, he said to me:
'You see, I have at last now got a real study of my own. I can work here uninterrupted.'[1]

This first impression of Conrad, from Ford's reminiscences a third of a century later, does exactly what Ford (in his book on Conrad) said first impressions should do in a novel. It 'gets in' a strong image of its subject which persists (like a radiance on the retina) throughout any subsequent revisions and developments. Conrad is pre-eminently the visualizer, seeing for himself so that he can make others see. He takes his bearings as he takes in the view. There is a navigational precision in the image of him pointing his beard, like an instrument of orientation, at the horizon; then using his monocle as a captain would use a telescope. In the first paragraph of *Joseph Conrad*, Ford gives a comparable first impression of him as artistic observer: 'He entered a room with his head held high, rather stiffly and with a haughty manner, moving his head once semi-circularly. In this one movement he had expressed to himself the room and its contents; his haughtiness was due to his determination to master that room, not to dominate its occupants, his chief passion being the realisation of aspects to himself.'[2]
The symbolism that Ford makes explicit in the later memory—that Conrad's first speech should be of work, foreshadowing the passionate agonizing over writing that would occupy them jointly during their collaborations over the next

ten years—is symbolic for Ford as well as for Conrad. In it, Ford is realizing to himself aspects of their long, intense friendship. It suggests how in Conrad he had found a figure who could replace Madox Brown, 'the painter of "Work" ', as his artistic 'Master'. Ford was 24, and 'very late in maturing', as he said later; Conrad was 41. Their complex mutual dependencies make it trivial to talk of father and child substitutes. But Ford knew that Conrad, like Madox Brown and Henry James (and later Arthur Marwood), had become exemplary and formative. By 1898 Ford had published an impressive amount for someone of his age, but a minute fraction of his ultimate *œuvre*: three fairy stories, a volume of poetry, some essays of art-criticism, the substantial biography of his grandfather, and one adolescent novel. Through his association with Conrad, and through Conrad's example, he learned how to *work* with the kind of dedication that made him an important writer.[3]

There is a further way in which Ford's impression of their first meeting is symbolic. It can be glimpsed in the irony that, for all his visionary concentration, Conrad mistakes Ford for the gardener. Ford recalls the mistake not to score a point against the writer he admired fervently and the man he faithfully loved. Rather, what the incident expresses is his uneasy feeling that Conrad had indeed mistaken him throughout their relationship, and had conceived of him as the inferior, menial partner. After Conrad's death there were several attacks on Ford's account of the partnership in his memoir, *Joseph Conrad*. Conrad's wife Jessie, who had never liked him, led the assault in her campaign of 'hoofing out Hueffer'. Ford's claims to intimacy with Conrad outraged Conradians, just as his claims to intimacy with James outraged Jamesians. It was a reaction he foresaw. As he explained in a cancelled passage from the manuscript of *Joseph Conrad*, the view that Conrad 'chose to live on terms of extreme intimacy with a parasitic person' was as damaging to Conrad's reputation as it was to Ford's: 'if he chose to consult that person as to the most private details of his personal life and—what is still more important—as to the form and the very wording of his books,—if he chose for this intimacy a person of a parasitic type, he was less upright a man than might reasonably be supposed. . . . And less of a psychologist.' Ford felt that jealous critics and partners couldn't appreciate how his 'literary friendship' with Conrad had been 'for its lack of jealousy a very beautiful thing'. Yet his language also intimates the anxieties which he was suppressing out of respect for Conrad's memory: an 'extreme intimacy' also existed between the Dowells and the Ashburnhams in *The Good Soldier*.[4]

From Ford's work published by 1898 it would not have been possible to guess what kind of writer he would later become. But enough unpublished stories have survived from the previous decade to show how he was gradually, uncertainly, discovering that his greatest gift was for fiction. Only two of the following seven works were mentioned in Harvey's bibliography, and none has received any critical attention before. Yet they give the best sense of Ford's intellectual and literary development before he embarked on 'Seraphina', and then collaboration with Conrad to turn it into the novel *Romance*.

'Elspeth', a contemporary love story written in Ford's entertainingly arch fairy-tale manner, none the less contains haunting, disturbing material anticipating some of his most effective subjects. Edward Gore, a young poet, leaves London to visit Hythe. He spots a girl suddenly illuminated in a church, and says impulsively, 'I shall marry her.' When he meets her, together with her outcast fisherman father, he finds her strange, lively, bookish. After some intimate, literary conversation with her he promises her father that he will marry her 'in spite of everything and everybody, in spite of whatever happens' (p. 34). But rumours that he is engaged to a society lady have reached the newspapers, as Gore discovers on his way to meet Elspeth again. He lays down to rest on a beach, and experiences a strange 'death-dream', in which Elspeth emerges from the sea like a dead Venus Anadyomene. He wakes to find things have taken a more macabre turn. Elspeth and her father have both drowned, and Gore finds two letters from her: one saying that she had seen her father murder a blackmailer and then kill himself; the other saying that she had read about Gore's engagement to Lady Betty. He decides to marry Betty, and to try to forget Elspeth. But during the marriage service he faints, and wakes to find himself back on the original beach. His earlier waking up to find the corpses had thus been part of the dream; and yet the dream was eerily prophetic, since Elspeth's father is indeed actually dying. After his death Gore and Elspeth do marry, but the happy ending does not resolve the dark mysteries. 'In spite of' *what* does the marriage take place? If the dream was accurate about the father's death (though not about Elspeth's), should we believe in the blackmail (or is that image suggested in the dream by the father's mysterious manner)? Or is Gore's rumoured engagement the impediment? The associations here of passion with death, haunting visions, disturbing secrets, and with figures of artists and outcasts are ones which reverberate throughout all of Ford's later fiction. The dream-plot prefigures the structure of *Ladies Whose Bright Eyes* (1911), and the hero entangled with two women figures in all his major novels. Though Elspeth sounds like Elsie in more than just name, the manuscript is dated May 1891, so the dream of a dead father is more likely to recall Francis Hueffer's death two years earlier than wishfully to imagine the death of Elsie Martindale's father. Their courtship did not begin in earnest until a year later— she was only 14 in 1891—and thus the story precedes Dr Martindale's attempts to stop their marriage by nearly two years.

Another manuscript, incomplete and untitled, concerns the experiences of another bookish figure, Bodurdoe, 'a reading man'. He also encounters a mysterious and captivating girl, falls in love, and has a vision of her. When she wants to go to rescue a drowning man, he offers to go instead. But this drowning also turns out to have been a dream vision, since he is woken at this point by his friend Gunter, with a wet sponge. Yet here too the dream of drowning acquires an aura of prophecy, when he finds out that the girl was orphaned in a shipwreck about fifteen years before.[5] The narrative manner is slightly stilted, but the story is amusing and suspenseful. The recurrence of that conjunction of literature, sexuality, visions, and death suggests more than just the stock-in-trade of uncanny romances. There is a creative disturbance here, a sense of the power of fantasy both to mobilize and to minister to desires and anxieties. Ford was drafting more fiction than anything else in the 1890s; the only substantial exception being the biography of Madox Brown. The pressure under which he began these tentative but compelling stories suggests that it was the fictive and the fantastic which best answered his creative needs.

Ford's intentions in the stories of this period are clarified in a set of five pieces entitled 'Idylls and Ideals, being five Prose Idylls'. This work also survives in a fragmentary manuscript, and dates from 1893–4. In the preface Ford explains that the stories are 'conceived and narrated in an Idyllo-Idealistic frame of mind, as distinguished from the present day Realistic mode'. Though not written in the 'present day Realistic mode' of Hardy, Meredith or Gissing, these pieces are entirely of their time, the time of Victorian Medievalism, of the 'Celtic Twilight', of the revival of interest in spiritualism and the supernatural. Only two of the stories can be made out from the leaves that survive. One, 'An Idyll of the Spessart-wald', is a charming romanticized folk-tale about a young poetic story-telling youth, [Jo]Hannes, whom the peasant community think mad, and his love for Rickchen (short for Fredericka), who, like many of Ford's later characters, does not 'know what it means'. She tells him, 'even I do not see that things are beautiful until thou sayest they are—and then— they seem to change suddenly—and yet be the same' (p. 18). It is an early attempt to relate art to a common humanity, rather than to the *literati* and the academies, as Madox Brown had done in his masterpiece *Work*, and as Ford later did in his English trilogy—and especially in *The Heart of the Country*. Ford is working out his feelings about his national identity as well as his artistic one. If he is the German story-teller within the tale, he is also a translated German, the Englishman telling us the story of the story-teller. It is an early exploration of how a life inventing fictions can be a life on the edge of insanity. The other surviving story, 'The Idyllic Courtship of Coytmore', is much slighter, but also foreshadows some of the later preoccupations. It is a comedy of manners, told in an intimate, smoking-room tone: 'Do you happen to know Coytmore?—Not? Well [. . .].' Coytmore, who is indecisive and aesthetic, falls in love with not one but two girls, the twins Lydia and Lucy Waters. Coytmore proposes, but he does not know which sister he has proposed to. Just as the story looks as if it might turn into something interesting, it collapses as the narrator displays a pose of suave indifference, having himself forgotten which sister it was. Its silly suavity tries to make light of the troubling subject of desire and polygamy (possibly suggested by his relationship to the Martindale sisters). Like 'Elspeth', it is a comic version of the 'Tale of Two Passions' that would return in tragic form in *A Call* and *The Good Soldier*; and it is an early version of the 'double' motif that predominated in his late fiction.

'The Land of Song: a phantasy' blends fairy-tale and parody. A boat beaches dramatically on a coast where it is the custom not to speak without singing. Harfager, a giant Viking, and his friend Conrad (the naming is coincidental: the story was finished by 1894, four years before meeting Joseph Conrad) rescue a princess, Elaine, who would be queen had she not been bewitched and imprisoned by her evil double, Eleine. We are in a world in which unjustly imprisoned princesses escape with the help of ropes made from their own hair; and in which the hero falls in love with the princess, while his friend is bewitched by her evil and sexual usurper. Yet even the stock devices of such tales are tonally unstable. The hair-rope idea becomes a parody of the class-system, for in this land class is signified by length of hair. The romance in the idea of a land of song sits uncomfortably with the way the plot parodies the magical world of Wagnerian song-drama, also populated by superhuman Nordics, and in which no one speaks without singing. When he was 17 Ford began an essay entitled 'Wagner Educationally Considered'. He can't have thought of Wagner without thinking of his father, who had written two books on him. 'The essay, as far as it goes before it breaks off, is an act of filial piety', wrote Sondra Stang and Carl Smith. But the facetious title-page, inventing the pseudonym 'Hermann Ritter, Royal Proffessor and Granducal Kammervirtuoso at Würzburg', is a sign of Ford's familiar tonal duality. The fact that the proposed book *does* break off might also be a sign of Ford's ambivalence. Though much of his own early music is Wagnerian, he was later to write (in the first of his wartime propaganda books), 'I am considerably out of sympathy with Wagner's music and intensely dislike his operatic conventions'. The tonal uncertainties of *The Land of Song* can thus perhaps be explained as an attempt to reconcile filial piety with strongly divergent aesthetic instincts which, only five or six years after his father's death, it would have been hard for the young Ford to voice.[6]

The longest unpublished manuscript from these years is 'The Last Sowing', a romance partly based on Madox Brown's elopement with Emma Hill, the daughter of a Herefordshire farmer. A confidential clerk, Willie Bevan, gets engaged to Gladys, the daughter of his employer, Mr Bush. He doesn't really love her, but is given to fantasizing about 'the new life he was going to lead' for her sake. He is thus one of Ford's first fictional self-transformers (excluding the characters in the fairy-tales). Bevan takes a holiday staying at a farmhouse, and soon becomes enamoured of the farmer's daughter, Bessy Scargill. It's a light-weight tale, less intelligent than *The Shifting of the Fire*, and the style is awkward, pompous, and coy. Yet it is again striking how many of what were to be Ford's central preoccupations are already developed: class; sexual desire (of a polygamous kind), deceit, and guilt; the contrast between city and country; fear of paternal anger; insanity. Bevan tells himself he 'mustn't do any flirting' while on holiday. And when he is joined by the provocative and sophisticated journalist, Joaynes— an atheist, aesthete, and socialist—he is appalled by the way he, despite loving his wife, advocates free love. Yet Bevan himself is meanwhile already flirting with Bessy, having come to feel that 'talking to a girl is always more or less like a flirtation'. There is a strange encounter at an inn with a 'private mad-doctor' and a patient he never lets out of his sight. Bevan appears to let his own conscious, social self out of his sight as he makes advances toward Bessy as in a dream, putting his arm around her 'as if he were irresponsible for his actions'. Guilt follows rapidly. First there is a thunderclap after they kiss; this violent outburst is echoed by Bessy's father's rage; then Bevan encounters his fiancée's father, Mr Bush; though it turns out that he is in the area because he too is having an affair. The title first suggests that the flirtation with Bessy is Bevan's last opportunity to sow wild oats before marrying Gladys; but cliché takes an unexpected turn as unpremeditated impulses incur troubling consequences, as sown oats take root and grow. Like Edward Ashburnham in *The Good Soldier*, Bevan begins making declarations to Bessie that seem beyond his conscious control: 'hardly knowing what he was about he heard himself pouring out words of love with more passion than one would have awaited in a mere ball room flirtation.' He proposes to Bessy as well; but her father, who she says hates him, refuses. Bessy, who shows much of Elsie (Eliza*beth*) Martindale's determination, takes control. She suggests they elope, since she is under-age, and Bevan, who is easily swayed, agrees. Her powers of organization make him feel 'emasculated'. Like most of Ford's protagonists, Bevan finds himself moving among mysteries: 'What the deuce does it all mean?', he wonders. His predicament becomes more and more entangled. He can't bear to tell Bessie the truth about Gladys, but feels that one of them must be 'undeceived'. An improbably convenient solution is offered when Mr Bush, on the day before Bevan is due to marry Bessy, offers to make him a partner in his firm if only he'll give up Gladys. (Bush has just been divorced by his wife for his adultery.) But Bessy is horrified at the idea: 'If I thought you could be selfish or deceitful, it would break my heart', she tells Bevan, making it all the harder for him to confess his dilemma to her. Yet eventually he does, and she doesn't appear to mind. This time the romance resolution is achieved thanks to Joaynes' diplomacy, who has reconciled Mr Scargill to the idea of Bevan as a son-in-law (as Dr Martindale had eventually been placated?). After a happy reunion at the wedding breakfast, they go to live with him on the farm, Bevan having given up his city career, as Ford and Elsie had left London in 1894.[7]

The other most substantial unpublished manuscript dating from the period just before the meeting with Conrad is 'A Romance of the Times Before Us'. The temporal ambiguity in the title is of the essence. The story is not the historical fiction it might sound: ostensibly the 'Times Before Us' are the times *ahead* of us, not the times that preceded us. Telling of a German invasion, Ford is poised between the vogues for invasion novels in the 1870s and 1880s following the Franco-Prussian War and the Channel Tunnel scare, and in the Edwardian decade, when fears about Prussian militarism resurfaced.[8]

Ford's historical imagination can be seen subtly at work here, in ways which anticipate not only his novels of past or of contemporary history, but also the dual temporal perspectives of reminiscence, in which the experiences at the time are contrasted with a nostalgic retrospective view. This contrast is at the heart of *Romance* and *The Good Soldier*. But there is something even more intriguing happening in 'A Romance of the Times Before Us', and this is an exploration of how our sense of the past shapes our understanding of the present. In a climactic scene the heroine, Dorothy, undertakes a dangerous ride to save her grandmother and a sympathetic wounded German soldier from being burnt by the peasant mob. The adventure makes her feel more *real*, more alive, than before; and yet the feeling is expressed in terms of literature. She feels she is living one of the historical romances she has read about:

The feeling that lives depended upon her ride[,] that murder and conflagrations and the rough things of the world were abroad in the land filled her mind with the exalting sensation of being for the first time a part of the more real world. It was much as if she had been reading one of those old Elizabethan tragedies of blood in wh. Shag bag and Black Will the murderers figured.[9]

Ford then quotes Browning's poem of another exhilarating ride, 'How They Brought the Good News from Ghent to Aix'. It is an early instance of his turning a self-consciousness about a literary genre—'do people ever actually behave like this?'—into a presentation of the literariness of experience—of how our understanding of the world, and our acting in it, get informed by what we read and imagine. As so often, Ford was pondering what he called the 'trick of imagining things' he had had since childhood, whereby 'those things would be more real to me than the things that surrounded me'; wondering about the reality of literature, of the experience of reading and the act of writing.[10]

Imagining a war between England and Germany, Ford again explores his own conflicting national identity. There is also a description of a Jew who has set up in the country 'to play the old English gentleman' (p. 10). Ford was often thought Jewish because of his German surname; he had certainly begun consciously to play the squire: 'I was in the mood to be an English country gentleman and, for the time being, I was', he said later. The story approaches national duality from a further perspective. Dorothy's mentor is a German professor, whose intermittent accent is treated as a matter for humour, but whose mind is seen as an example for the non-doctrinaire novelist: 'I am shust a humple sicker afder Drooth [. . .] When you take one side of the question I take the other to see what the back as well as the face of Truth is like—But really I have no feelings at all.'[11]

Ford's fascination with indifference, with English self-suppression, is a prime trait of his literary personality. His writing expresses his passions, while achieving aloofness from them. The professor is contrasted with a German who does have feelings—the wounded soldier Herzog, who has fallen in love with Dorothy. He too is a man of dual perspectives: 'that wonderful double-mindedness which is the property of the Teuton—allowed him to reason on the other side of the matter and that quite calmly after a paroxysm of adoration.'[12] Yet Ford's attitude to this Teutonic duality is heavily ironic. What is 'wonderful' is that even after a paroxysm of adoration Herzog swings back to *bürgerlich* pragmatism, worrying whether Dorothy is 'marriageable' or not. It is largely this unromantic attitude that leads her to reject his proposal at the end. The ambivalence here is important for Ford's development. The plot of failed courtship and war between nations shows a failure to reconcile the English and the German; and yet the story does bring both together, reconciling them in the material of art if not in the outcome of plot.

Although there is some attempt to 'justify' the uprising, by providing the chief rabble-rouser, Hoppy Shumekker, with a motive of vengeance—he was lamed in prison— the story's sympathies are all with the upper-middle class heroine and her family. The writing bespeaks a feeling of class isolation in the country (among the 'rough things of the world'?), before Ford got to know the local peasants at Bonnington. Nevertheless, the professor observes a double-mindedness in Dorothy's political sympathies which we can recognize throughout Ford's life and writing: 'You are very benevolent—pud your het is chust a little touched with a migssdure of ideas—at one moment you are a sozialissd & at another an Individualissd' (p. 10). Also under scrutiny are the motives of that benevolence, and this too was to become one of Ford's great themes, notably in *The Benefactor*, *A Call*, *Mr. Fleight*, *The Good Soldier*, and *Parade's End*. When, in the 'Envoi', Dorothy is left bewildered by world's recalcitrance to good intentions, she says, 'I have tried so hard to make people love me and to make them better and yet—and yet [. . .].' The professor replies: 'but every kind deed one does in the world—everything that makes one liked is bribery.' The possibility that virtuous actions might all be founded upon self-love, or at least that altruism might be inextricably bound up with vanity, was more than an intellectual paradox for the young Ford. It is an idea he was constantly to worry at from all sides. The story suggests that Ford's 'indifferentism' answered to this anxiety that interest might be self-interest.

Lastly, there is a manuscript of a story called 'A Mother', which deserves mention for the way it anticipates the project that would engross Ford during the first five years of his collaboration with Conrad. In 1895 he wrote to Edward Garnett, 'I am thinking of writing a novel all about smugglers.' This was assumed to be the first reference to 'Seraphina', the story that Ford and Conrad would rewrite as *Romance*. But that novel is about pirates rather than smugglers. 'A Mother' is the work about smugglers that Ford eventually wrote. A long story rather than a novel, it tells of one of the gangs living in Aldington and Bonnington in 1815 that he had heard about from the villagers. The protagonist, Elgar Swaffer, is a precursor of later Fordian neurasthenic heroes: 'The women he was deadly afraid of [. . .] they paralysed him.' The story accounts for this paralysis in terms of the triangle of maternal versus sexual love (in a way which suggests that Cathy Hueffer's ambivalence towards Elsie had a more profound effect on Ford than was discernible at the time). The mother realizes that she can no longer 'sit and see her son tear his mind to bits', so she relents and sends for the woman, Lydia, without whom Elgar cannot go on. The piece ends: 'It was part of her sufferings that she must risk ruin to protect this girl that she despised—& that this girl must be called in to give a [son things?] that she could not give—That is what it is to have a child.' It is powerful fathers rather than mothers that dominate Ford's fiction, but two mothers do stand out: that of Augustus Greville (perhaps a spoof of Oliver Hueffer?) in *The English Girl*, whose flightiness appears the result of his being mercilessly manipulated by the mother he needs to escape from; and Valentine Wannop's mother, whose presence overshadows Tietjens' relationship with Valentine in *Parade's End*.[13]

With hindsight, Ford's unpublished early work can be seen to anticipate his subsequent writing. But it is beset by problems of conception, depth, and tone. He was becoming more and more engaged in creating fiction, but he was having difficulty in getting it to 'gel', in realizing, completing, and publishing it. The same is true of the best story he had written by the time he met Conrad, 'Seraphina'. Either Ford or Edward Garnett must have told Conrad about this story, and about Ford's impasse. For Conrad wrote to Ford (now briefly back at the Pent) suggesting that they should use it as a basis for a collaborative novel. Ford tells the story that Conrad told to him: that because of his difficulties with English style—English was his third language—he had consulted various literary figures of the day, and that W. E. Henley had suggested Ford as a collaborator.[14]

In telling and retelling this story, Ford lays himself open to the charge of vanity. It is such anecdotes that particularly brought down that charge upon his memoir of Conrad. But, although it is true that there is flattery in the telling, it is much more a question of Conrad's flattery of Ford than of Ford's flattery of himself. Of course it might be argued that to show a man of Conrad's stature flattering you is to present yourself as worthy of someone like Conrad's respect. But this is only an objection to Ford's writing if you have already decided that he is not worthy of your respect. One of the ways he shows himself worthy is in his fine capturing of the dual impression of pleasure and slight unease and uncertainty that Conrad's obsequiousness could produce. Conrad, said Ford,

stated succinctly and carefully that he had said to Henley—Henley had published the *Nigger of the Narcissus* in his Review—'Look here. I write with such difficulty: my intimate, automatic less expressed thoughts are in Polish; when I express myself with care I do it in French. When I write I think in French and then translate the words of my thoughts into English. This is an impossible process for one desiring to make a living by writing in the English language. . . .' And Henley, according to Conrad on that evening, had said: 'Why don't you ask H. to collaborate with you. He is the finest stylist in the English language of to-day. . . .' The writer, it should be remembered, though by ten or fifteen years his junior of Conrad was by some years his senior at any rate as a published author, and was rather the more successful of the two as far as sales went.

Henley obviously had said nothing of the sort. Indeed, as the writer has elsewhere related, on the occasion of a verbal duel that he had later with Henley that violent-mouthed personality remarked to him: 'Who the Hell are you? I never even heard your name!' or words to that effect. It probably does not very much matter. What had no doubt happened was that Conrad had mentioned the writer's name to Henley and Henley had answered: 'I daresay he'll do as well as anyone else.' No, it probably does not matter, except as a light on the character and methods of Joseph Conrad, and as to his ability to get his own way. . . .'[15]

Certainly Ford would *like* to be thought of as 'the finest stylist in the English language of today', and his reiteration of the comment he does not believe Henley could have said expresses the desire. If this is vanity, though, it is a vanity from which few authors are exempt. The candour with which Ford lets such wishes play across his prose is one of the features that makes him a better autobiographer than he is usually thought to be. The point is that Conrad was using courteous hyperbole in order 'to get his own way', and thought that it would encourage Ford to believe in his evolving gifts if he thought someone else believed in them. Ford recognizes that the story is not true, and he spells out why it cannot have been. He probably did not quite believe it even at the time, even as the flattery was working on him. Conrad says that when he expresses himself 'with care' it is in French, yet Ford records him stating his decision 'succinctly and carefully'—and in English. He knows Conrad's English style is better than Conrad pretends. But the whole treatment of Conrad's dual-dealing is exemplary in its sympathetic comprehension. There is not a hint that Conrad lied, or misled; just a vivid account of a kindred spirit, someone who, like Ford himself, might exaggerate or elaborate a fact to produce an effect; in short, a fellow impressionist. In a later version of the story Ford writes that 'Conrad liked to please as much as Henley liked to knock the nonsense out of you'. What he said about Henley's speaking voice is illuminating both about how Ford relished the hint of exaggeration in his own words, and about how much harder this is to achieve with the written word: 'You had the man before you, you were much better able to appreciate from his tone of voice where he exaggerated and where he meant you to know that he exaggerated.'[16] What he conveys in each telling is that double effect of being pleased *and* having the nonsense knocked out of him. It is a double effect obtained not only by juxtaposing Conrad's caution with Henley's explosion; for Conrad's speech alone produces it, as Ford is both pleased and also incredulous. He needs our incredulity—'Henley *can't* have said that: how can Ford think we'll believe *that*?', and so on—to convey the mixture of his own response.

Ford's explanation of what probably happened is borne out by Conrad's letter to Henley of 18 October 1898. This makes it clear that Conrad had consulted Henley on the collaboration, the suggestion for which probably came from Edward Garnett. Henley's response has not survived, but it evidently voiced an anxiety that the proposed collaboration might be injurious to Ford's career. Henley, who had himself collaborated with Robert Louis Stevenson, understood the perils. Conrad wrote back in terms which reveal much about his motives for entering into such an improbable venture:

The line of your argument has surprised me. R.L.S.—Dumas—these are big names and I assure You it had never occurred to me they could be pronounced in connection with my plan to work with Hueffer [. . .] When talking with Hueffer my first thought was that the man there who couldn't find a publisher had some good stuff to use and that if we worked it up together my name, probably, would get a publisher for it. On the other hand I thought that working with him would keep under the particular devil that spoils my work for me as quick as I turn it out (that's why I work so slow and break my word to publishers), and that the material being of the kind that appeals to my imagination and the man being an honest workman we could turn out something tolerable—perhaps; and if not he would be no worse off than before. It struck me the expression he cared for was in verse; he has the faculty; I have not; I reasoned that partnership in prose would not affect any chances he may have to attain distinction— of the real kind—in verse. It seemed to me that a man capable of the higher form could not care much for the lower. These considerations encouraged me in my idea. It never entered my head that I could be dangerous to Hueffer in the way you point out. The affair had a material rather than an artistic aspect for me. It would give—I reflected—more time to Hueffer for tinkering at his verses; for digging hammering, chiselling or whatever process by which that mysterious thing—a poem—is shaped out of that barren thing—inspiration. As for myself I meant to keep the right to descend into my own private little hell—whenever the spirit moved me to do that foolish thing—and produce alone from time to time—verbiage no doubt—my own—therefore very dear.[17]

As in Ford's anecdote, Conrad is magnificently eloquent about his inability to express. It is also striking how, even before the collaboration had been arranged, Conrad is expressing a profound ambivalence about the worth of the project (which might at best produce 'something tolerable') and about his partner (who is merely an 'honest workman', someone 'tinkering at his verses'). Nevertheless, what determines him to approach Ford is the fact that he too has hit a creative impasse, and hopes that the collaboration will pull him out. It is here that the idea of an 'honest workman' is something admirable rather than belittling.

At this date Conrad appears to be undecided about collaborating: 'If I do speak at all I shall recite to him faithfully the substance of your letter—that is if he does not kick me out before we get so far.' But he had already spoken to Ford, who, far from kicking him out, had sublet him the Pent 'awfully cheap'. He found Ford 'an exceedingly decent chap', and said: 'Besides the whole place is full of rubbishy relics of Browns and Rossettis.' These relics included Madox Brown's death-masks of Rossetti and Oliver Cromwell. Conrad left Stanford-le-Hope on 26 October. The Hueffers had returned to Grace's cottage at Limpsfield, after taking a brief cycling holiday in the South of France. By 28 October they had spoken again, for he wrote to Galsworthy that the arrangements for collaboration were now complete. 'Ford is full of the scheme of collaboration with Conrad', wrote Olive Garnett in her diary for November. Strangely, Conrad had not yet seen the story he was to help rewrite. It was soon after 17 November that Ford read 'Seraphina' to him at the Pent. Even Conrad was not pessimistic enough to foresee that it would be five years before it would be published as *Romance*.[18]

Literary collaboration is unusual enough to appear foolhardy; collaborating to write novels, with scarcely any precedents besides the Goncourts, might seem insane. Why did they do it? Ford recognized in Conrad's writing the strengths that his own immature manuscripts lacked. He liked later to give the impression that he was the more successful figure of the two in 1898, which is an exaggeration, though he had published six books to Conrad's four superior ones.

Part of the point of the exaggeration was to show that Conrad approached 'this rather aloof and patronising [. . .] English gentleman-farmer', as Ford travestied himself, because, as it took a psychologist of Conrad's insight to appreciate, Ford was 'the sort of man who would be ready [to]—and who would—devote his life to the sort of poet that Conrad felt himself to be'. Ford deleted this passage from the manuscript of his study of Conrad, though it probably tells us more about the dynamics of the relationship than does their forlorn hope that 'Seraphina' could be turned into something popular. Certainly, the language of devoting his life to another indicates how the emotional needs underwrote the literary ones. Conrad had recently quarrelled with and lost his old friend Adolf Krieger. Ford still sought a fatherly, or grandfatherly, presence, to fill the void left by the death of Madox Brown.[19]

'Seraphina' was based very closely on an essay from Dickens's *All the Year Round* called 'Cuban Pirates: A True Narrative', recounting the adventures of Aaron Smith, tried for piracy in 1823. 'The story told by him in the dock', wrote Ford, 'was sufficiently that of *Romance*.' His memories of that formative reading form one of the great moments of *Joseph Conrad*:

The writer has seldom seen such suffering as was gone through by Conrad during the reading of that first draft of *Romance*. Conrad had expected a drama of Cuban pirates, immense and gloomy, like *Salammbo*, with a reddish illumination, passing as it were upon a distant stage. . . . For the first chapter or two—those passing at the Pent Farm—he was silent. Then he became—silent. For he seemed to have about him a capacity for as it were degrees of intensity of his silence [. . . .]

The writer sat in the grandfather's chair, his back to the window, beside the fireplace, reading, his manuscript held up to the light: Conrad sat forward on a rush-bottomed armchair listening intently. (For how many years did the writer and Conrad not sit like that!)[20]

Thus far the scene reads as a display of egotism. Secure in his aesthetic inheritance (Madox Brown's chair), he has secured the rapt attention of one of the greatest writers of his day; and not just once, but for many years. But the craft of the book is to show Ford's vanity being tickled, so as to make it that much more effective when Conrad's response knocks the nonsense out of him and his unachieved, slight story:

We began that reading after lunch of a shortish day; the lamps were brought in along with the tea. During that interval Conrad showed nervous and depressed; sunk in on himself and hardly answering questions. Conrad being then almost a stranger, this was the writer's first experience of to what Conrad's depression over an artistic problem could amount [. . .]

Conrad began to groan. . . . It was by then fairly apparent to the writer that Conrad disapproved of the treatment of the adventures of John Kemp; at any rate in Cuba; and the writer had a sufficient sense already of Conrad's temperament to be disinclined to ask whether his guest were ill. He feels now the sense of as it were dumb obstinacy with which he read on into those now vocal shadows in the fireside warmth. . . . The interruptions grew in length of ejaculation. They became: 'O! O! . . . O God, my dear Hueffer. . . .' And towards the end: 'O God, my dear *faller*, how is it possible. . . .' The writer finished with the statement that, as it was June the nightingale sang a trifle hoarsely. This zoological observation, in spite of the cadence, gave the final touch to Conrad's dejection. The writer's voice having stopped he exclaimed: 'What? What? What's that?' When he heard that that was the end he groaned and said: 'Good *God*!'—for the last time. There are writers—French writers—who can keep the final revelation of a whole long novel back until the last three words. For this he had hoped. (pp. 23–4)

Ford explains how that sentence about the nightingale was written as 'an exact pastiche' of a cadence of Flaubert's, and how 'Every sentence had a dying fall and every paragraph faded out'. He had wanted to capture the tone of 'a very old man, looking back upon that day of his romance'. The original version of 'Seraphina' does indeed have this hoarse, understated quality. Ford did not have access to the typescript when he wrote *Joseph Conrad* a quarter of a century later, so he slightly reinvented the ending. There is a nightingale near the end, but it is not in the last sentence, nor in that particular sentence. What he originally had was: 'suddenly from behind us rang out the voice of a nightingale.' The point of the reinvented version is that Ford had missed the point of his subject. He was so lost in the stylistic trees that he could not see the formal woods. The lost opportunities in his treatment of the story leave Conrad unimpressed with its tricks of language:

Before dinner, then, Conrad listened to the writer's apologia with a certain frigid deference. Of course if that was the way of it, no doubt. . . . But why choose such a subject? . . . A man of sixty-two. . . . Yes, yes, of course. . . . He remained however shut up in the depth of his disappointment and still more in his reprobation of the criminal who could take hold of such a theme and not, gripping it by the throat, extract from it every drop of blood and glamour. . . .[21]

Ford always said that of the two collaborators he was the more preoccupied with style; seeking 'a limpidity of expression that should make prose seem like the sound of some one talking in rather a low voice into the ear of a person that he liked'. Whereas Conrad was the more concerned about 'a new form for the novel'; Ford praised his 'infinitely greater hold over the architectonics of the novel'. This is borne out by a letter of Conrad's written to him in the middle of the work on *Romance*. Ford has evidently consulted him on a matter of plot or phrasing— probably about whether John Kemp and Seraphina should be married:

As to *married*. I say: go on by all means. I shall bring the pages with me (if I can come) and then offer certain minor remarks. The value of creative work of any kind is in the *whole* of it. Till that is seen no judgment is possible. Questions of phrasing and such like—*technique*—may be discussed upon a fragmentary examination; but phrasing, expression—*technique* in short has importance only when the Conception of the whole has a significance of its own apart from the details that go to make it up—if it (the Conception) is imaginative, distinct and has an independent life of its own—as apart from the 'life' of the style.

My love to you all[22]

One of the ways in which *Joseph Conrad* is a tribute to its subject is that in it Ford works his memories of the man who taught him most about writing into a 'novel' (as he provocatively designated the book) of the kind that Conrad had taught him to write—or rather, that the collaboration taught him to write. The whole mode of the book is that developed in *Romance*; one which Conrad had used for 'Youth', and would develop in *Heart of Darkness* and *Lord Jim*, and with which Ford too would find his most effective voice in *The Good Soldier*: the first-person narrator recalling the entanglements of his past experiences and inexperiences. Ford makes explicit the fact that *Joseph Conrad* is written in this mode: '["Seraphina"] was the narrative of a very old man, looking back upon that day of his romance—as to-day this narrator looks back. You are getting the real first draft of *Romance* now. This is how in truth it comes out according to the technical scheme then laid down by us two.' Ford was 50 when he wrote this elegiac book. Though not a 'very old man', his frank nostalgia imbues his friend with 'every drop of blood and glamour'. If Conrad comes out with a slightly melodramatic, stagy air, this is because for Ford he was more than intensely literary: he was literature. 'Conrad was Conrad because he was his books. It was not that he made literature: he was literature, the literature of the Elizabethan Gentleman Adventurer' (p. 25). Writing a book bearing Conrad's name, Ford enshrines him as still more literature. It is fascinating how he gives him a voice which is totally convincing even in its slight exaggeratedness—friends of Conrad such as Edward Garnett testified to how Ford had caught Conrad's mannerisms— and yet it is also the voice of Ford's narrator of 'Seraphina': hoarse, each utterance ending with a dying fall of suspension dots.[23] The overall effect of *Joseph Conrad* is not like that; it is at once a more moving, playful, vigorous, and inventive affair than 'Seraphina'. But it is a tribute to Conrad's influence on Ford that he could now find the right context for an authentic aspect of his voice, by imagining Conrad speaking and listening.

The final reason why that first reading was so important to Ford was that it established an imaginative rapport which affected everything else he wrote. Though Conrad's agonized groans hardly bespeak imaginative sympathy, he did decide to collaborate on the story, and that pattern of reading or thinking aloud to each other became the dominant one in both their creative lives for the next five years. It also became the dominant one within Ford's writing. His doctrine of impressionism implicitly attaches immense importance to the impression made on the reader. Sometimes this becomes explicit, as when Dowell in *The Good Soldier* imagines a rather similar situation to the one in *Joseph Conrad*, of himself talking to a 'silent listener' sitting at the hearth-side. As Ford wrote as late as 1930, 'we had got so used to reading our own works aloud to each other that we finally wrote for the purpose of reading aloud the one to the other'.[24]

Before Christmas Ford was visiting the Pent again. The collaborators' spirits were high. Conrad sent Elsie a copy of Robert Cunninghame Graham's *Mogreb-el-Acksa*, saying: 'In the intervals of concocting with your husband circumstantial untruths for sale we looked into this truthful book.' On 22 December the collaborators paid a call on H. G. Wells, living five miles away at Sandgate, to tell him of their plans: 'As we stood on the doorstep of Mr. Wells's villa . . . behold, the electric bell-push, all of itself went in and the bell sounded. . . . Conrad exclaimed: "Tiens! . . . The Invisible Man!" and burst into incredible and incredulous laughter. In the midst of it the door opened before grave faces. . . .' Galsworthy too relished Conrad's 'almost ferocious enjoyment of the absurd'. 'Writing seemed to dry or sardonise his humour', whereas in conversation his sense of fun would 'leap up in the midst of gloom or worry, and take charge with a shout'. It was with that duality of angst and anarchic *esprit* that Ford always remembered Conrad.[25]

Wells's invisibility had also caused them to miss him on the road that day, since he was out at the time, paying a call on the Pent. The lease on Grace's cottage expired on 25 March 1899, and Ford, Elsie, and Christina returned to the Pent to stay while looking for a house nearby. There was confusion. 'Ford not certain whether he had taken a cottage at Ham Street or near the Knoll', recorded Olive Garnett, adding: 'All are excited & delighted at moving.' When she called on Fanny Stepniak she heard more about their high spirits. Fanny was in 'full flow of pleasure of society of the Hueffers—the Rossetti genius & strange old charm'. On 30 March they moved into Stocks Hill, a coastguard's cottage perched under Aldington Knoll. Ford later said that Wells eventually called there to warn him that collaboration would probably ruin Conrad's 'delicate Oriental style', and that, referring to the 'virulent controversy that was then raging between Henley and Mrs. Stevenson' he warned Ford he would probably regret the step all his life.[26]

He never did regret it, despite its devastating personal and professional costs. Conrad, on the other hand, appears already to have been regretting the arrangement, or bridling at his need of something like it, even before the work had begun in earnest. Writing to Edward Garnett the day after the Hueffers left to move into Stocks Hill, he described himself as 'overwhelmed and utterly flattened'. Such depression was the aftermath of one of his most relentlessly caustic and self-mistrusting works, *Heart of Darkness*. He had written earlier to Galsworthy that 'The finishing of *H of D* took a lot out of me'. He describes himself as a hollow man, whose work seems hollow, condemned to a hollow fate:

The more I write the less substance do I see in my work. The scales are falling off my eyes. It is tolerably awful. And I face it, I face it but the fright is growing on me. My fortitude is shaken by the view of the monster. It does not move; its eyes are baleful; it is as still as death itself—and it will devour me. Its stare has eaten into my soul already deep, deep. I am alone with it in a chasm with perpendicular sides of black basalt. Never were sides so perpendicular and smooth, and high.[27]

This was Conrad's state of mind when he and Ford began to re-work 'Seraphina'. It is possible that it was during the Hueffers' stay in March that he had discussed the proofs of *Heart of Darkness*. Ford recalled this episode in 1935, in his last series of reminiscences: 'We must have argued over it for three whole days, going from time to time over the beginning and the body of the story, but always at the back of the mind considering that last paragraph and returning to it to suggest one or another minute change in wording or in punctuation.'[28] For Ford it was an exciting foretaste of what collaboration would be like: a lesson in how the quest for the *mot juste* was something more serious, more demanding, than an imitation of French cadences. But in Conrad there are the first signs of a hypocritical attitude towards Ford that was to underlie their entire relationship. After this first taste of what a close relationship with Ford would be like, he wrote in the same letter to Garnett: 'Why didn't you come? I expected you and fate has sent Hueffer. Let this be written on my tombstone.' It is as if, rather than offering a rescue from his psychological prison of basalt, the projected collaboration appears as a deadly fate, serving only to entomb him.

8

1899–1900: COLLABORATION

The first phase of the collaboration established the pattern of the two families' lives over the next five years: protracted stays and frayed nerves; animated discussions between the collaborators, going on long into the night after the wives and children had gone to bed; frenetic bursts of writing and reading-out and rewriting, interspersed with bursts of work on the books of their own that both authors kept writing throughout the partnership. However, little progress was made on the rewriting of 'Seraphina'. Instead, the first fruits of the collaboration were the more independent works. The arrangement had indeed kept under the particular devil Conrad felt spoiled his work; but not quite in the way he had imagined. Rather than facilitating creation, the act of collaborating, with its inevitable tangle of split aims and cross-purposes, tended to exacerbate the agonies of writing. Ford described Conrad as 'eternally clamourous' of moral support; and, as is evident from a novel like *The Good Soldier*, he too needed just as much 'assurance of [his] own worthiness' himself. The collaboration provided this mutual support; it provided what Frederick Karl calls 'the dependency pattern that seems intrinsic to Conrad's way of working and surviving' (though Ford would later surround himself with younger disciples, he needed them to confirm his status as *maître*, involving himself in improving their work, rather than involving them in his own writing). Yet its advantages were offset by the added difficulties it introduced: difficulties of artistic uncertainty, financial dependence, family strains, and, not least, the fact that when the writing went badly the time of two people was being wasted, so that despite Conrad's assurance to Henley that failure in prose would not affect Ford's career, in fact each man could feel guilty about distracting the other from more important work. As Karl says, the 'intense love–hate relationships' between the two couples are reflected in the 'four-square coterie' of *The Good Soldier*.[1]

Against the background of collaboration, however, the creativity of both men found new impetus. Before meeting Ford, Conrad had published *Almayer's Folly*, *An Outcast of the Islands*, *The Nigger of the 'Narcissus'*, and *Tales of Unrest*. He had written 'Youth', the first of the Marlow stories, and he had begun *Lord Jim*. But the bulk of his greatest fiction—the completed *Lord Jim*, *Heart of Darkness*, *Nostromo*, and *The Secret Agent*—was written while collaborating with Ford.[2]

While Conrad worked on *Heart of Darkness* and *Lord Jim*, Ford contemplated a historical novel on Oliver Cromwell, and began a book of impressionistic local history—*The Cinque Ports*. It was illustrated by William Hyde, 'a mysterious and, with his black beard and his secret process, a ferocious, gipsy-like figure'. 'My wife & I intend to ride over to Brede shortly', Ford wrote to Stephen Crane, who was now living in a Tudor manor house there.

I am writing a foul & filthy book about the Cinque Ports & have to pervade the district a good deal. Would you resent our looking you up? I wish particularly to hear the stories you have gathered about Brede Place. I have had to invent so much about Rye and Winchelsea that my imaginative powers are strained & need rest. I don't intend to cold bloodedly fall back upon yours—but in the contemplation of another man's inventive gymnastics I trust to be spurred to further flights.[3]

As in all Ford's writings about places and histories, it was the stories about them rather than the facts that most interested him; and he is engagingly candid about his fiction. Mizener quotes the earnest preface dedicated to Robert Garnett, in which Ford explains how Garnett's 'desire for accuracy' finally triumphed over Ford's desire to write 'a piece of literature pure and simple'. Mizener takes the claim that everything in the book can be supported by 'the work of a chronicler as nearly as possible contemporaneous with the event asserted' as serious, a 'concern for accuracy' the later, impressionistic Ford would have greatly scorned. But Ford told Olive Garnett *The Cinque Ports* was a 'colossal' joke. Like Conrad, he relished concocting circumstantial untruths for sale. This letter to Crane is also revealing about how the collaboration was helping the collaborators even in their own work, by spurring each to further flights through the contemplation of the other's inventive gymnastics. Finally, the letter gives an idea of Ford's tone—the tone that made Crane say of him: 'You must not be offended by Mr. Hueffer's manner. He patronizes Mr. James. He patronizes Mr. Conrad. Of course, he patronizes me and he will patronize Almighty God when they meet but God will get used to it, for Hueffer is all right.' 'And the words are my greatest pride after so many years', added Ford.[4]

By the summer Ford had given up the Cromwell idea, and began a novel concerned with modern politics, *The Inheritors*. It is a curious hybrid work, mingling a political *roman à clef* with a Wellsean science-fiction fantasy of futuristic invasion. (The technician of the time-shift must have been interested in *The Time Machine* of 1895: what is a retrospective narration, but a machine for travelling through time?) The 'Inheritors' are a breed of cold, materialist, individualist characters from the 'Fourth Dimension' who, lacking respect for human feeling and history, will inevitably usurp the power of the humane but ineffectual élite. Conrad was soon collaborating on *The Inheritors* too. Indeed, he may even have contributed the scientific notion it is based upon. In the few months before meeting Ford, Conrad's work on *The Rescue* was floundering, and he sought the help of his friend Robert Bontine Cunninghame Graham, the Scottish writer, horseman, and traveller, in trying to find a command at sea. Soon after meeting Ford, he travelled to Glasgow for interviews, and while there was entertained by Graham's friend and surgeon Dr John MacIntyre. MacIntyre had one of the first X-ray machines in his home, and demonstrated it by revealing the ribs of one of the guests as a party-piece. Conrad was excited by the machine and the discussion it generated: 'X rays, talk about *the* secret of the Universe, and the nonexistence of, so called, matter', he wrote to Edward Garnett, explaining (or was he parodying?) how 'the secret of the universe is in the existence of horizontal waves whose varied vibrations are at the bottom of all states of consciousness'. Cedric Watts conjectures very plausibly that it was Conrad's relaying these ideas to Ford that suggested the idea of a science-fiction collaboration, and points out how the Fourth Dimensionist woman first reveals her powers to the narrator by making 'the solid world dissolve like a mirage before his eyes'. For a Fordian impressionist, the solid world is *perceived* as dissolved, like a mirage. The philosophical ideas may have appealed to the writers less for their topicality and pot-boiling potential, and more for the way they could be investigated as figures for the phenomenon of art. Conrad continued to Garnett: 'there is nothing in the world to prevent the simultaneous existence of vertical waves. Therefore it follows that two universes may exist in the same place and in the same time—and not only two universes but an infinity of different universes—if by universe we mean a set of states of consciousness.'5 Which is not only a diagram of the basis of *The Inheritors*. It is also an image for literary dualities: for collaboration (including the collaboration that is the relationship between writers and their readers); and most importantly, for the duality of the artist, whose suffering self must be doubled with the unsentimental observer. The Fordian artist doesn't need X-rays to reveal people's skeletons, but a second sight into their minds and beings.

In August 1899 Olive Garnett visited the Kentish coast. Her diary gives vivid glimpses of how the Hueffers and Garnetts were working and relaxing:

Wednesday 9th.
Penshurst 12.45. arr. Smeeth 2.17. Elsie & Xtina met me. When we got to Stock's Hall the door was wide open & Edward & Carl Heath were inside getting tea [...]
Thurs. 10th.
Elsie Xtina & I drove in [Grocer] Rayner's pony trap, on trial to Dymchurch. Met Mrs. H[ueffer]. & Juliet on the road. Went to the Ship & got bathing dresses & put pony up. Bathed out of a boat with Edward who was teaching Elsie to swim. Dinner at the City of London. Sat on the beach in the afternoon, tea at City of London & drove home in the evening [...]
Sat. 12th.
[...] Bathed [...] Elsie & I had a fright, got out of our depths & screamed [...] Tea at Mrs. Hueffer's. Sat up till 12 P.M. with type writer [...]
Sunday 13th.
[...] F. & E. played chess. Elsie sang from 'Tristan und Isolde', 'Lohengrin', Cornélius, Willow, willow [...]
Tuesday 15th.
[...] Juliet came. Walked to Smeeth with Ford: told me plot of London novel. 'An old man, breaking up etc'. They decided not to go to Germany [...]
Wednesday 23rd.
Went to B[ritish]. M[useum]. With Ford & Papa [Dr Richard Garnett, the Keeper of

Printed Books there] who got me a ticket for the Reading Room [. . .] Copied for Ford all day for the part about Sandwich [. . .] Ford wrote a letter to Longmans 1: for permission to use title of 'Cinque Ports' 2. suggestion to bring out guinea edition of Life of Brown. Tea at Express Dairy. 'I haven't got any friends but you and the Cowlishaws.'[6]

By 6 October Ford had written enough of *The Inheritors* to try it out on Conrad: he drove over to the Pent 'with the manuscript of the opening chapters of the novel rather shyly in his pocket'. But, according to Elsie's diary, Conrad was 'upset' with the novel—whether with the kind of novel it was, or with the quality of Ford's draft, or merely with the fact that Ford was working on something other than 'Seraphina' is not clear. Conrad was sinking into a depression, telling Cunninghame Graham that he had 'lost all sense of reality', and later that his 'malaria, bronchitis and gout' were 'in reality a breakdown' (or a breakdown in reality). Once again he was prepared to get involved in a collaboration with Ford about which he had doubts from the outset. As with 'Seraphina', the suggestion of collaborating had come from Conrad, though Ford's impression in *Joseph Conrad* makes the decision to collaborate on *The Inheritors* as well something of a collaborative decision.[7] Clearly Ford had wanted to involve Conrad in the work, at least to the extent of hearing it read out, and being its first critic. After hearing a few pages, however, Conrad gave Ford the impression that he wanted to become involved in the writing of this story as well: 'already the writer knew that either he was in for another collaboration or that he would hand over the manuscript altogether' (p. 133).

Ford shows Conrad surprised by what his collaborator has been quietly producing: 'he was exclaiming: "But what is this? What the devil is this? [so far it could be a Conradian exclamation of gloom, as occasioned by 'Seraphina'; but:] It is très, très, très chic! It is *épatant*. That's magnificent" ' (pp. 132–3). And Conrad does appear to have been genuinely surprised—partly because he realized he had been underestimating his collaborator. A letter to Ford written a month later measures Conrad's sense of how rapidly Ford was developing. It also reveals some of the domestic strain that the collaboration was causing. As the projects multiplied, Elsie was beginning to feel that Ford's time spent away from home was likely to be time wasted. 'My dear Ford,' Conrad was soon trying to reassure him:

Your letter distressed me a little by the signs of nervous irritation and its exasperated tone. I can quite enter into your feelings. I am sorry your wife seems to think I've induced you to waste your time. I had no idea you had any profitable work to do—for otherwise effort after expression is not wasted even if it is not paid for. What you have written now is infinitely nearer to actuality, to life to reality than anything (in prose) you've written before. It is nearer 'creation' than the *Shifting of the Fire*. That much for the substance. I do not want to repeat here how highly I think of the purely literary side of your work. You know my opinion.

But beautiful lines do not make a drawing nor splashes of beautiful colour a picture. Out of discussion there may come conception however. For discussion I am ready, willing and even anxious. If I had influence enough with the publishers I would make them publish the book in your name alone—because the *work* is all yours—I've shared only a little of your worry. Well—you worry very much—and so do I—over my own stuff. I sweat and worry, and I have no illusions about it. I stick to it with death for the brightest prospect—for there may be even a more sordid end to my endeavours— some abject ruin material or physical for me—and almost inevitably some ghastly form of poverty for those I love. Voilà. Am I on a bed of roses?

Whether I am worth anything to you or not it is for you to determine. The proposal certainly came from me under a false impression of my power for work. I am much weaker than I thought I was but this does not affect you fundamentally. Heinemann (and McClure too I fancy) are waiting for our joint book and I am not going to draw back if You will only consent to sweat long enough. I am not going to make any sort of difficulty about it—I shall take the money if you make a point of that. I am not going to stick at that trifle.

Do come when you like. Bring only one (or at most two) chapters at a time and we shall have it out over each separately. Don't you good people think hardly of me. I've been—I am!—animated by the best intentions. I shall always be![8]

The tone of this is difficult to gauge without Ford's letter (which has not survived). Conrad's attempted reassurance is undermined by his defensiveness in the face of Ford's and Elsie's exasperation. Though he says he is animated by the best intentions, his way of saying it raises the very doubt it is ostensibly aimed at quelling—the doubt that his intentions might have changed: 'I've been—I am!' There are other ominous hints: Conrad's refusal actually to state the high opinion of Ford he says he has, combined with his making it clear that his opinion cannot have been that high ('I had no idea you had any profitable work to do'). Even his comment about not having enough influence with publishers to get them to publish the book under Ford's name alone, despite its scrupulousness about not wanting to seem to hijack a work in which his role was minor, suggests a desire to dissociate himself from the project he had suggested. John Batchelor's comment that the collaboration 'seems to have met a need in each man to deny responsibility for his own work' rings truer of Conrad's part in it than of Ford's. Frederick Karl is more precise, saying that Conrad 'needed Ford's presence and support for personal reasons and yet disdained the collaboration for professional reasons'.[9]

Ford sent the completed manuscript of *The Inheritors* to Heinemann on 16 March 1900. It was accepted by both Heinemann and the New York publisher McClure, Phillips, who both thought it should also be serialized. When Conrad wrote to Edward Garnett, who was now working for Heinemann, he evidently wanted to distance himself from the book. Mizener says he used a sardonic tone to amuse Garnett, but it is worse than that, casting severe doubts on the honesty of his intentions towards Ford:

All my bits of luck come through you! You must be—indeed—as Jess says—the best of men. I consider the accept^{ce} of the *Inh:*^{ors} a distinct bit of luck. Jove! What a lark!

I set myself to look upon the thing as a sort of skit upon the political (?!) novel, fools of the Morley Roberts sort do write. This in my heart of hearts. And poor *H* was dead in earnest! Oh Lord. How he worked! There is not a chapter I haven't made him write twice—most of them three times over.

This is collaboration if you like! Joking apart the expenditure of nervous fluid was immense. There were moments when I cursed the day I was born and dared not look up at the light of day I had to live through with this thing on my mind. H has been as patient as no angel had ever been. I've been fiendish. I've been rude to him; if I've not called him names I've *implied* in my remarks and in the course of our discussions the most opprobrious epithets. He wouldn't recognize them. 'Pon my word it was touching. And there's no doubt that in the course of that agony I have been ready to weep more than once. Yet not for him. Not for him.

You'll have to burn this letter—but I shall say no more. Some day we shall meet and then—!¹⁰

Mizener argued that Conrad's motives for entering into collaboration 'almost certainly did not include personal affection'; that Conrad felt Ford could be useful, and thought all that was needed was 'a decorous pretense of friendship'. This is probably right, though it's hard to believe Conrad didn't develop an affection for Ford after a decade of intimate literary involvement. There is a (less decorous) pretence of friendship in this letter to Garnett too, flattering him that he was the closer friend. It is characteristic of Conrad's concealment and mistrust of his feelings, and his 'misleading habit of taking the attitude he thought his correspondent would like'. Instead of burning the letter Garnett kept it, and when he published it in 1928 Ford felt deeply betrayed by both men as he had to confront public evidence of Conrad's ambivalence towards him. And yet he sensed this ambivalence much earlier, as is clear from *Joseph Conrad* itself. For, right at the heart of the book which chronicles the most intimate phases of their relationship, he sounds a devastatingly frank note of isolation: 'It is that that makes life the queer, solitary thing that it is. You may live with another for years and years in a condition of the closest daily intimacy and never know what, at the bottom of the heart, goes on in your companion. Not really.'¹¹

There were good reasons why he should have felt this about Conrad. It is Ford's great topic: that the heart of another is a dark forest. It is also his most Conradian. And to say that he sounds here like Dowell, the narrator of *The Good Soldier*, is only to say that his fictional presentations of moral isolation and bewilderment were in part shaped by his perplexing experiences of working with Conrad. Reading Conrad's letters to Ford, it is impossible not to believe that his ambivalence was evident even at the time. There is barely a line that is not double-edged, and at least one edge cuts into his younger colleague. His professions of affection are frequently so theatrical that they verge on parody, perhaps contempt; his praise for Ford's writing is so floridly ironic that it verges on sarcasm. Garnett may have meant to put an end to what he saw as Ford's exaggerated claims of friendship in *Joseph Conrad*; he felt strongly enough about the book to give it two ambivalent reviews in 1924. There is a hint of envy in them, and it may have motivated the publication of the letter too—an act which smacks more of trying to displace Ford from Conrad's friendship rather than to respect Conrad's wishes or to consolidate his reputation. For it is, as Conrad recognizes, a fiendish letter—a product of his mentally disturbed state—especially given that the major phase of collaboration lay ahead. Conrad tended to imply that the recipients of his letters were his only true friends; probably, like Ford with Olive Garnett, he said as much in conversation. In thinking about Conrad, as he did throughout the rest of his life, Ford had to reconcile his own experience of Conrad's friendship with the very different versions retailed by Garnett, Jessie Conrad, and the Conradians. [12]

Even before he found out about this letter, Ford had realized that his Conrad might not be the same as everyone else's. Reviewing the first biography about him, Jean-Aubry's *Joseph Conrad: Life and Letters*, he distinguished between 'true truth—and truth':

Which was Conrad? The bothered, battered person who wrote innumerable, woeful, tearful, timid letters that are here connected by a string of properly non-committal prose, or the amazing being that I remember? With a spoken word or two he could create a whole world and give to himself the aspect of a returned Sir Francis Drake emerging from the territory of the Anthropophagi and the darkness of the Land of Fire.[13]

Literary biography can all too easily become a less romantic territory of Anthropophagi, in which one collaborator indeed appears to be 'eating up' the other in the way Henley had feared. Ford felt that 'there is no great man that is not belittled and rendered common by his biographer', citing the example of Samuel Butler, who appeared in one biography as 'sound, mean, mercenary, hypochondriac, selfish, lying and, in the end, monstrous', whereas 'Butler is infinitely greater than the shivering and fearful wretch that [the biographer] presents us with'. The creative energies of *The Good Soldier* are exercised by exactly this biographical question: how to give what Dowell calls an 'all-round impression' of a person who can appear in radically different guises. For role-players such as Conrad and Ford, writers who often lived their way into their fictional worlds, experimenting with tones and attitudes, one man's true impression will be another's exaggeration, or misprision.[14]

Ford had always recognized Conrad's agile, volatile multiplicity. And, despite what Conrad wrote about Ford's not hearing the implications and innuendoes of his criticisms, he evidently was receptive to Conrad's doubts about him, and his worth. Reading Conrad's letters to him, it is inconceivable that he would not be aware of their double-edge. For example, Conrad had introduced the Hueffers to his aunt, Marguerite Poradowska, when she visited in 1900, and later sent her a copy of *The Inheritors*. When Mme Poradowska replied, Conrad sent Ford a page of her letter. Ostensibly the purpose was to cheer Ford up, who was perhaps dismayed at the unappreciative reception of the novel, and probably dispirited about working on 'Seraphina'. But Conrad's language bristles with ironies:

Very pleased to hear of ex^{llt} review in the rotten Telegraph. This indeed is fame. Gals[wor]^{thy}, here for a day (yesterday), has sung the praise of your art, as shown in the Inh^{tors}. He is really and truly struck. So is Mme Poradowska from whom I just had a letter this afternoon. Her general disquisition on You is remarkable by the force and justness of outside observation—so clever as to amount almost to the reading of character. I have had a greatly enhanced opinion of the excellent woman since she—French!—has been so fascinated by Your verse and impressed by Your personality. In comparison with her insight—(shallow if you like)—James's 'Un jeune homme modeste' has an effect of farcical blindness.[15]

Ford was touched that James should describe him to Conrad as '*votre ami, le jeune homme modeste*', and he repeats the story in his reminiscences. He did not think that he was merely modest. In *New York Essays* he juxtaposes the comment with Crane's letter about his patronizing manner. But with James, 'the Master', he became a shy, 'rather silent person who walked so often beside him on the Rye Road'. It is this aspect of Ford's relationship with his other Master that Conrad's story captures. But there is something excessive, almost hysterical, in Conrad's description of its 'effect of farcical blindness'. If either Conrad or James had attributed 'farcical blindness' to Ford, the remark would be taken to signify contempt for his imagination. Whereas Ford knew that Conrad's nervous bristling did not compromise his affections and admirations, and he later magnificently defended Conrad against the belittling effect of biography which attaches too much importance to the barely premeditated hectic fragments of a relationship which survive as letters. On the other hand, his reminiscences of James's high ironic banter and Conrad's sardonic irony are disturbed by his glimpses that he was taken seriously as a writer by neither of the two writers he took most seriously.[16]

Katharine Mary Madox Hueffer, Elsie's and Ford's second daughter, was born on 16 April 1900. Juliet (who, together with Cathy Hueffer, was staying with them) wrote that 'Ford quite lost his head when Elsie's troubles began, and rushed up and down outside her room, nearly mad'. Jessie Conrad reported their disappointment at not having a son.[17] Ford had now finished *The Cinque Ports* and towards the end of May his second volume of verse, *Poems for Pictures*, was published. He had found a rhythm of productive work, as had Conrad. *Lord Jim* had expanded from a story into a novel, but Conrad was still in a buoyant mood, giving himself a characteristically unrealistic deadline. Then Crane's fatal lung haemorrhages began. Conrad had rapidly become intimate with Crane, who has been described as searching for a father-figure (he had been orphaned from an early age). In May Conrad went to Dover to see him off to a German health resort. He died there in June. Like Ford, Crane was a younger writer whom Conrad could involve in his dependency patterns; someone who would behave filially while also offering example or advice. After Crane's illness and death Conrad turned once again to Ford. In mid–July the Hueffers went to Bruges. The plan was for the Conrads to follow when *Lord Jim* was completed, so that the collaborators could work on 'Seraphina', refreshed by a change of scene. Ford had asked Olive Garnett to accompany them 'as a sort of support for Elsie', but she did not go.[18]

Conrad was not ready to leave until 20 July, by which time his son Borys was ill. Ford and Elsie had been staying at the depressing English Pension, and encountering anti-British hostility in Bruges due to the Boer War. This was ironic, since Ford said that he was 'as hot a pro-Boer as any one well could be' (though he 'came very near to crying with joy' when Mafeking was relieved in May 1900), and that he was once 'chased for three-quarters of a mile along New Oxford Street by a howling mob of patriots' for 'wishing solely that South Africa might be returned to its real owners, the natives'. But it was characteristic of him to take up a position in a dispute which enabled him to be attacked by both sides. For Conrad, irritated by overwork, exasperated by 'the train, the boat, the mislaid trunks, the ticket-collectors and the whole dreary waste of foreigners', and 'overburdened by the weight of a large-small boy, not very well', who needed carrying, the Pension was the last straw:

At the first sight of the first placard on the first landing, surrounded by long teeth that peeped from the gloom of corridors Conrad stiffened, like a sudden corpse. WATER MUST NOT BE DRAWN FROM THIS TAP BETWEEN THE HOURS OF ELEVEN AND TEN MORNING OR EVENING. GUESTS WILL BE STRICTLY SILENT ON THE STAIRS. A FINE OF ONE FRANC TWENTY-FIVE WILL BE ENACTED FOR EVERY FIVE MINUTES LATE AT MEALS.[19]

They moved at once to Knocke-sur-Mer, where Borys developed dysentery. Writing had to give way to nursing. Conrad developed gout. 'Elsie Hueffer helped a bit but poor H. did not get much collaboration out of me this tide', Conrad wrote to Galsworthy. Jessie Conrad, whose resentment of Ford's involvement with her husband rarely abated, was forced to acknowledge Ford's support: 'At this crisis I have nothing but praise for F.M.H. He earned my gratitude and appreciation by the manner he showed his practical sympathy. He was always at hand to shift my small invalid, fetch the doctor or help with the nursing.' The Conrads had returned (presumably with the Hueffers) on 18 August, and Ford came over to stay at the Pent until the middle of September to make up for time lost in Belgium. By 19 September Conrad's familiar sardonic scorn of the collaboration was again surfacing. He wrote to Galsworthy: 'I am drooping still. Working at Seraphina. Bosh! Horrors!' After another bout in October, Conrad said that after Ford left he felt 'half dead and crawled into bed for two days'.[20]

One powerful reason for thinking that Conrad's doubts must have been transmitted to Ford is that even this autumn, almost a year before 'Seraphina' was ready to submit to publishers, Ford was experiencing severe doubts about himself. He had written two books, *The Inheritors* and *The Cinque Ports*, which were much more accomplished than anything he had written before—even if Conrad's assistance with *The Inheritors* had undermined Ford's confidence in its conception. But, as the collaboration on 'Seraphina' began to seem more like a depressing burden than a profitable diversion, Ford began to feel a disparity between the talent he was newly discovering in himself, and the progress he was not making with it. On 3 November 1900 he wrote an important, unpublished letter to Olive Garnett about her volume of short stories. She mentioned it in her diary, with the comment: 'A long letter from Ford, which being unwell, upset me.' It is indeed a disturbing piece of writing, demonstrating a power, only touched upon in the narratorial voice of *The Inheritors*, to project a disturbed personality. It is a candid, expressive record of some of Ford's early feelings about women, about writing, about creative envy, and the desire for recognition:

My Dear Olive,

Excuse my writing to you by machine but Elsie has just carried off the Pen of the House & there is no other. I want to write to you about the 'Petersburg Tales.' I say boldly & with a candour of self-abasement, that I approached them with a spirit of much scepticism. One is bound to, I don't know why, or perhaps I do. One has a small, very small, circle of people to whom one concedes the right to do anything: write, paint or ride a bicycle. When it comes to writing I suppose I admit three o[r] four living, & a few more dead, souls who count, who have the right to write or to exist or to have existed.

Again I hate all Russians with a bitter, temperamental shuddering (I except Kropotkin) I can't bear them, I don't want to know that they exist & I would much rather they did not. I expect too when everything is said & done, I hate you too & gibe at you (or should if gibing were part of my limited expression) just as you gibe at me. Then too I don't believe that any woman CAN write. I say all this to explain what I want to say about what you have WRITTEN.

I waltzed round the confounded book: opened it: sneered at the middle paragraph on page 3, put it down, picked it up & so on. Then I read 'The Secret of the Universe,' plunging into it as one plunges into the cold, cold sea. I sneered at 'bury Barry' & recognised the plot; thought what I would have made of the idea. I had at the end of reading it the dawn of a sort of feeling that the 'Jacobean' opening, the plot, the idea did not count, and that there was nothing that did. Then I read 'The Case of Vetrova' & detested it.

I was very tired at the time, I could not remember the damned Russian names, I did not want to be introduced to all those people in that steaming atmosphere. I said: 'Oh, this is all loathsome nonsense & Olive is weak & sentimental & Great-Moral-Purpose-y'. So I put the book away for a long time. Then I took it over to the Pent.

In the train I read 'Roukoff' again & was alarmed. I said: [']This is the Real Thing but that young person (Yes, I said Young Person) has no right to get hold of the Real Thing in Techniques.' So the train stopped at the station. I got out & walked to the Pent. In the evening I gave the book to Conrad. I said: 'No' Here read this in bed. I don't think it[']s up to much but read 'Roukoff.' He opened it at page 3 & read aloud 'With what startling life her figure rose before me. . . . A tide of compassion for all human creatures. . . . etc' and he jeered. I said 'Well, I don't say the book's anything, but you know my dear chap, I would not have brought it you if I did not think it had a chance of being SOMETHING. Read the 'Secret' & 'Roukoff.' I was a little confirmed in my idea that there WAS something in it by that time. I lay upstairs in the silence of the house at four in the morning, reading another book; I heard Conrad laughing— through two doors & a passage. I wondered if the labours of collaboration had been too much for his brain. As a matter of fact he was reading 'Roukoff' & laughing, not at, but with you. In the morning he damned me severely for not having told him that the thing was a masterpiece 'Dans Ma Note.' It had he said upset him, because he said he couldn't have done it better dans se [*sic.: ce* or *sa?*] note. I don't go that length because Conrad is Conrad & I [have] not yet been able to bring myself to want to sit at your feet; I am compounded of envies & things & am pretty tired of having to say to people: 'You are five cuts above me.' But that is what I think of 'Roukoff' 'The Secret of the Universe'—though, bless you, I would not say it to you or anyone for many many pounds.

Is it an impertinence for an obscure minor poet to write these things to you[?] I don't think it will be absolutely distasteful to you, because although you, in your character of artist, don't care what I think it must still be pleasant to you to trample on anyone so conceited, argumentative, shoddy & stupid as I: and in your capacity as woman (You write like a man) it must be pleasant to you to trample on a person of the persuasion that no woman can write.

The merits of 'Roukoff' are very great. It stands on its own legs, it walks, it gets there. I can find no fault with mannerisms in the writing, but it is WRITTEN. I dislike the characters but they live & the carpet has its figure. 'The Secret of the Universe' is to me more get-at-able, I suppose because it is laid to take place in England, it pleases me better tho' I don't think it is as good. As for 'Out of It', I do not understand it but take it on trust because, on the strength of the others you have the right to do what you like. As for 'The Case of Vetrova' it affects me with extreme aversion—but that is the measure of its merit I being I & Petersburg what you choose to represent it. The fact of the matter is—you have temperament & you express it, you have the gift of presenting things & you present them, you have a pen & you use it & a sardonic humour &, by Jove, you use that too.

Therefore, my dear chap, you LIVE for me & there are so many many, many with great names & tiny names & no names at all, that don't for me, even exist. I introduce many me's and I's into this not because I am really hyperbolically egotist but because I want you to see what effect you have produced on a person who tries to do something with the tools you use. It may do you good to see that, & I would like to do you good—for the sake of your good work. You don't of course write for a public of me's, you defer to a public of you's. But just as a fisherman making for a certain port finds his way by landmarks that are not that port so you may be a little helped by seeing me stuck up, like a tree, a ruined castle, a church spire or a pig-stye on some part of the coast, near or far from the haven you have desired.

You are many degrees above me in things that I would like to do: there are some things I can do that you can't, but I think it is the duty of one person struggling through bogs & mire to give a friendly hail to another going in the same direction, even though she be walking on firmer ground. These friendly hails don't come too often, can't in the nature of the case. For that reason I sink that sense of humour that is the fear of being thought ridiculous, write to you unasked at the risk of being thought a fool & return to my muddy ways. And remember, O thou, that if I seem be-plastered with mire, grotesque, plunging deeper in & getting always further from the real road, I remain your friend & well-wisher,
Ford M. H.

[PS in longhand:]

Don't tell anyone else what I say of Conrad, though you can tell all the world that I would give my M.S. [manuscripts] to wipe your boots on if you wanted them. I wanted to let you know that he really did admire your work even at the expense of his own & being subject to fits of acute depression—(ALWAYS in such fits) said what he did.[21]

This is an early instance of a habit of mind and writing that profoundly influences Ford's art: a tendency to extrapolate from nuances of feeling, and work them up into an objective presentation that cuts a figure for the reader, that produces an effect. It is a habit that has misled his critics and biographers into mistaking his elaboration and exaggeration of emotions—his seizing upon half-glimpsed responses for their artistic potential—for a simple transcription of the emotions themselves. Ford did not hate Olive; he did not really hate Russians either: he often said Turgenev's *Sportsman's Sketches* was his favourite book. It was partly that he was assuming a Conradian prejudice. He was also just being particularly—unusually—candid about his feelings of gloom at the life of St Petersburg captured by Olive Garnett, and of envy at her skill in capturing it: feelings that more conventional friends would have immediately repressed. The intention was to create a convincing portrait of someone—based on himself—reading her stories; and to testify to her achievement by showing how her writing could overcome even the deepest prejudice and antipathy. Despite the letter's intensity of raw response, it is also carefully crafted. The way Ford calls Olive 'my dear chap', using the same masculine slang he had used to Conrad; the way the opening detail about Elsie carrying off the pen is recapitulated by his telling Olive: 'you have a pen & you use it'; the way he does say—and twice—the very thing he says he would not want to, that Olive is 'above' him; and the way he caricatures his own reaction ('I waltzed') in order to *make her see* the *effect* she has produced—all this shows a sophisticated technical awareness of the effect he intends to produce on Olive. One must read the letter in its context of the familiar bantering friendship and correspondence Ford and Olive had kept up since the early 1890s. Their 'gibing' was deeply affectionate. He would tease her as being a 'Superior Person', a descendant of the intimidating Great Moral Beings that had overshadowed his childhood. So the 'self-abasement' here is at least partly mock, and the image of Ford as 'really hyperbolically egotist' is part of the shared joke, since Olive would tease him for his omniscient, theatrical manner.[22]

The letter is more than a joke, of course; and it is not surprising that it had a more upsetting effect than that of a 'friendly hail'. To be told that she had 'upset' both Ford and Conrad with her writing was for Olive an ambivalent tribute. Ford presents both men as gripped by the throat as they read her, though the impression of violence and disturbance was probably less encouraging to Olive than Ford meant it to be. For the situation touches upon too many sensitive areas of Ford's mind, leading him to trespass beyond the established bounds of their friendship. To tell a woman in 1900 that she wrote 'like a man' might have been less offensive than it would be now; but Olive's response suggests that it was none the less dismaying to be told that it was unfeminine to write well. The notion of her acceptance into the male club of conscious artists is also very much of its time; though here too Ford exaggerates his prejudice to enhance Olive's achievement. He did not actually think that 'no woman can write' (one only has to remember his lifelong admiration for the verse of Sappho or Christina Rossetti, and his later championing of many women writers). But he is saying more than that her writing would convert anyone who thought women could not write. He suggests that he is emasculated by women writers; he pictures himself in a world where the women have the pens, and he is abased and trampled upon. Elsie was again writing fiction.[23]

Finally, the letter also touches on Ford's anxieties about the collaboration. He wrote soon afterwards to Olive that 'Conrad has a considerable influence on me; I a considerable influence on him, whether for good or ill in either case there is no knowing. The collaborative work is quite different from either of our personal works, but it takes a sufficiently decided line of its own [. . .] Paradoxical as it may sound our temperaments are extraordinarily similar, we speak as nearly in each other's language as it is possible for two inhabitants of this Babel to do.' He presents the criticism of Garnett's stories as itself a collaborative exercise; he gives Conrad's response as if to validate his own. More striking still is the way that Ford's manner of responding to Garnett's prose approaches Conrad's reactions to his. When Ford read out an early draft of *The Benefactor*, he wrote to Elsie: 'I have just finished reading "George" to Joseph who says, naturally, that it's a masterpiece & then pulls it to pieces from start to finish.'[24] Ford does the reverse with *Petersburg Tales*, first postulating distaste, then showing the writing triumphing over it. But the unsettling duality of hyperbolic praise and devastating criticism sounds very close to Conrad's reactions, as dramatized in *Joseph Conrad*: the desperate, contemptuous groaning over 'Seraphina', the mixture of praise and exasperation over *The Inheritors*. One way Ford coped with Conrad's critical double-bind was to translate the relationship, and play Conrad to a younger 'collaborator', Olive, who had previously sent Ford the manuscript of some of the tales for comments. He may even have realized that that was what Conrad was doing: for Edward Garnett made *him* rewrite, and one way of working out the frustration was to play Garnett's role to Ford, transferring the anxiety to him. It would have been an economical means of working off such frustrations, since Olive had witnessed Edward's humiliating comments about Ford's life of Madox Brown. As the collaboration was maturing him as a writer, he could assume a superior tone with those 'Superior Persons', the Garnetts.[25]

The long letter of 3 November voices anxiety about the collaboration having become bogged down, and about whether 'the labours of collaboration had been too much' for either writer's brain; it shows that Ford was by now familiar with the extent of Conrad's creative depressions; and it also worries that Ford's own career may have lost its bearings, and be 'struggling through bogs & mire'. And yet the depressive stance may itself be imitative of Conrad, or at least indicative of how Conrad's gloom over the collaboration affected his collaborator. But by the time of the subsequent letter, Ford, back at Stock's Hill (which had now been gentrified, in name at least, as 'Stock's Hall'), wrote to invite Olive to stay. He reassures her that he hadn't meant her writing was 'ugly'; and this time his praise is less ambivalent. Though there was still a tone of despair mixed with the social banter—'We w^d be glad (Elsie says "I always thought O. was *rather* nice") if you w^d pay a visit to this abode of desolation where there seem to be 1,000 kids & the greater part of the mud of this world'—yet the picture of their life suggests a degree of fulfilment and contentment. After warning Olive not to idealize it, saying 'it is no better & no worse than any other life', he details it:

Xtina Margaret wants the Pen to write with, in a few minutes I shall shave, afterwards make the tea, afterwards brush the pony down, afterwards go to the shop for the papers, afterwards sup, afterwards go to the farm, afterwards read 'Roukoff' to Elsie, afterwards write out a song & afterwards go to bed with a book of Anatole France's. That is life—&, la vie, voyez vous, n'est jamais si bonne ni si mauvaise que l'on ne croit. . . .[26]

During this period the Hueffers often met H. G. Wells and his wife (Amy Catherine, but usually known as 'Jane'). Ford later wrote: 'The two women I have always liked best all my life—I mean as one likes men—were—and are! Connie [Constance Garnett] and Jane Wells.' Wells was becoming another of Ford's most important literary friends, someone he would work into his fiction, and return to in his reminiscences. It was his discussions with Ford that helped shape Wells's sense of the difference between his own journalistic and discursive fiction and that of the impressionist and formalist moderns like James, Conrad, and Ford himself: 'and what an omniscient man he is too!', Wells marvelled. He pictured Ford: 'with distraught blue eyes, laying his hands on heads and shoulders, the Only Uncle of the Gifted young, talking in a languid, plangent tenor, now boasting about trivialities, and now making familiar criticisms (which are invariably ill-received), and occasionally quite absent-mindedly producing splendid poetry.' Wells remembered the charades and dumb-shows played by his family and guests at Spade House in Sandgate: 'Ford Madox Hueffer was the sole croupier at a green table in a marvellous Monte Carlo scene and Jane was a gambling duchess of entirely reckless habits.' Like Mr Hoopdriver in Wells's *The Wheels of Chance*, the Hueffers and the Wellses had bicycles—though the Wellses' were kept in better repair. Meanwhile, Conrad and Ford had begun collaborating more effectively on 'Seraphina'. Conrad later recalled that the collaboration had begun in December 1900.[27]

9

1901: 'A SINGULAR MOSAIC'

Stock's Hall was not only primitive; it was too small for a family with two children. In January 1901 Dr Martindale offered to buy Ford and Elsie a house in Winchelsea. He got them 'The Bungalow'—despite its name, a charming two-storey clapboard, shuttered house, which Ford said had been built in 1782 for General Prescott, the first governor-general of Canada—and on 10 April they moved in. The house was near to the Martindales' own house, Glebe Cottage, making it an unfortunate choice, because Mary was living there with her parents. Their earlier fears for the effects on her of Elsie's marriage to Ford now proved justified, though in a way they had probably not foreseen. Some time between 1901 and 1903 Ford and Mary appear to have had an affair. Given the taboos involved, it is not surprising that there is no written evidence for the relationship. Arthur Mizener, who discovered it, cites no sources, but is most likely to have heard the details from Katharine Hueffer Lamb (the younger of Ford's and Elsie's children), who also discussed it with Thomas Moser, saying that she 'believed, but was not certain, that the beginning of the affair was in 1903'. Now that all of Ford's children are dead, we are unlikely to learn more than is contained in Mizener's speculative, novelistic sketch:

Mary Martindale was a tall girl with red-gold hair. After Ford and Elsie's marriage, she had become engaged to a young Frenchman, but she soon broke with him. Her feelings about Ford seemed to have been intensified by jealousy of the position marriage to him had given her younger sister [. . .] Mary had a vivacity that was in marked contrast to Elsie's seriousness. How well Ford understood that this vivacity was the comparatively controlled expression of an hysterical nature it is not easy to say, but it appealed to him strongly at this moment, when marriage was beginning to be more a routine than a romance [. . .]

It was inevitably an affair of snatched moments and clandestine encounters, of the cryptic telegram, the hansom cab, and the hotel. In their different ways they must both have found these conditions romantically exciting [. . .]

Elsie eventually found out about this affair, through one of those accidents that sounds as if it had been invented by Pinero, the mistaken delivery to her of a revealing telegram from Ford to Mary. But they managed to keep their relation secret for some time and continued to see each other—no doubt almost as a matter of principle—even after Elsie found out about them.[1]

Ford certainly found Mary attractive. If it is not possible to establish precise dates, it is none the less possible to see the affair looming much earlier. Even as early as *The Shifting of the Fire*, published in October 1892, after Ford had begun seriously to court Elsie, there are hints of quasi-incestuous sexual treachery: the hero, Clem Hollebone, is attracted both to his fiancée's best friend and room-mate, Julia, and to a lively American cousin. Moser notes that Julia's feeling for Clem reflects Mary's for Ford—in which case Ford must have registered the possibility of such an illicit affair even before his marriage. More significantly, in *The Inheritors*, which Ford had completed more than a year before the move to Winchelsea, the narrator, Etchingham Granger, has fallen in love with the Fourth Dimensionist lady, whose name is never mentioned (as if needing to be suppressed?), but who lives with him as his sister. The note of hopeless estrangement at the close—'It was impossible to understand that I was never to see her again, never to hear her voice, after this'—perhaps suggests that Ford was preoccupied with Mary long before 1901, but that their desire had not been consummated. Granger is also Ford's first fictional agoraphobic, indicating that Ford's own agoraphobia (which Moser interprets persuasively as being precipitated by guilt over this affair) had begun well before his 1904 breakdown. He wrote a suggestive poem—'An Imitation' (of Catullus and his Renaissance imitators) and dedicated it 'To M.M.' in 1900:

> Come, my Sylvia, let us rove
> To that secret silent grove
> Where the painted birds agree
> To tune their throats for you and me.

We don't know whether the affair was eventually consummated. But there is evidence of Elsie's jealousy. 'It was said by one: "I will say this for Ford, he really liked Elsie's sister, and Elsie determined to cut her out. By God, she got what she asked for!" '[2]

At Winchelsea Ford renewed his acquaintanceship with Henry James. They had met on 14 September 1896, when James asked him to lunch. Olive and Edward Garnett had heard that Ford would be visiting the Martindales in Winchelsea, and persuaded him to write to James, who was spending August and September at the Old Vicarage in Rye, to ask if he could call. James was 'their cynosure', said Ford, who claimed he had not then read anything by the man he (like Conrad) would later come reverently to call 'the Master'. It was probably true: he said the Garnetts' admiration made him 'stubbornly determined' to avoid James. But his 'resistance broke down eventually' when a novelist friend, Lucy (Mrs W.K.) Clifford, also asked him to go and call on James, saying she was worried about his health. Ford found the bearded, 53-year-old James 'the most masterful man I have ever met'. He was 'composed and magisterial [. . .] in the manner of a police magistrate, civil but determined to receive true answers to his questions'. Ford wasn't able to 'gather anything about the state of his eyes', probably because 'the whole meal was one long questionnaire': 'He demanded particulars as to my age, means of support, establishment, occupations, tastes in books, food, music, painting, scenery, politics. He sat sideways to me across the corner of the dining table, letting drop question after question. The answers he received with no show at all of either satisfaction or reproof.'[3]

Then, as he recalled Stephen Crane accusing him of writing Pre-Raphaelite poems Crane hadn't read, Ford recalled James launching into 'a singularly vivid display of dislike for the persons rather than the works of my family's circle'—not Madox Brown or Francis Hueffer, for whom he expressed 'a perhaps feigned deference' because they were 'at least staid and sober men'. Rossetti, Swinburne, Morris, and Hunt, though, 'he regarded with a sort of shuddering indignation'. Ford explained the antipathy to Rossetti by saying that the painter-poet received James in his studio wearing 'the garment in which he painted', which James mistook for a dressing-gown. 'For Mr. James the wearing of a dressing-gown implied a moral obloquy that might end who knows where', he said, and elaborated the joke with a parody of Jamesian elaboration, saying that on this basis James deduced that Rossetti was 'disgusting in his habits, never took baths, and was insupportably lecherous'. He ends his account of this first meeting with James's story about Ford's uncle, William Rossetti, whom 'Mr. James considered to be an unbelievable bore'. The story is about how Rossetti even managed to make the story of how 'he had seen George Eliot proposed to by Herbert Spencer on the leads of the terrace at Somerset House' sound boring, in his 'querulous official' voice and 'Secretary to the Inland Revenue' manner, which James mimicked. ' "Is that," Mr. James concluded, "the way to tell *that* story?".' That (excepting a brief coda) is how Ford concludes his story of James's story of Rossetti's story (about another story-teller). The *effect* of the story, like many of Ford's reminiscences of his encounters with the bearded great, is to present Ford as the victim of unwarranted attack, sensitized to the character of his attacker, which could also reveal to Ford characteristics of himself. Worrying later that he had portrayed James as too waspish in *Return to Yesterday* he mused:

I will not say that loveableness was the predominating feature of the Old Man: he was too intent on his own particular aims to be lavishly sentimental over surrounding humanity [. . .] For some protective reason or other, just as Shelley used to call himself the Atheist, he loved to appear in the character of a sort of Mr. Pickwick— with the rather superficial benevolences, and the mannerisms of which he was perfectly aware. But below that protective mask was undoubtedly a plane of nervous cruelty. I have heard him be—to simple and quite unpretentious people—more diabolically blighting than it was quite decent for a man to be—for he was always an artist in expression.[4]

So Ford protected himself with the characters of the Socialist or the Tory, or the characters of his novels. And so he, too, was perfectly aware of his own mannerisms. His later reminiscences are eloquent about his own dislikes. He couldn't afford to be lavishly sentimental either, and understood how his expression as an artist might also be projected from a plane of nervous cruelty. Seeing these things in James enables him to see them in himself, and vice versa. His noticing of James noticing, his mimicking of James mimicking, his telling of

James's story-telling, are at once homage to and liberation from James's mastery. His reminiscences of his Master are as searchingly interrogative as that first lunch.

There were other contacts between the two men over the next five years. Ford sent tickets for the Madox Brown exhibition he helped organize in January 1897, and James courteously promised to go. At the end of the year he sent him an essay he had written on the artist William Hyde, who was to illustrate *The Cinque Ports*. Ford's accompanying letter hasn't survived, but it probably asked whether James could recommend Hyde to other authors, or consider using his illustrations for his own work. Again James was polite, saying he had just taken a lease on Lamb House, 'a charming old house at Rye', and adding, 'I hope to see you there'. He offered to do what he could for Hyde, though he was firm about not wanting his own writing illustrated: 'I like so my prose, such as it is, to stand by itself, that I almost dread a good illustrator more than a bad one.' In July 1899 James thanked Ford for sending him a copy of Edward Garnett's review of *The Awkward Age*. James said it was a 'very responsive' review, and it gave him 'great pleasure' and greatly touched him, though he added: 'There is a figure in the carpet of *The A. A.* which I think Mr. G. hasn't quite made out—but I am none the less yours & his most truly.' Ford gave the letter to Garnett, who showed it to Olive. He must have been delighted that their cynosure thought they didn't quite understand him. When Constance Garnett came to stay at Aldington Knoll, bringing her young son David, they were 'driven over to Brede Place in a hired wagonette to see Stephen Crane and his wife and were accompanied by Henry James riding a bicycle'. David thought that it was at about this time that Olive and Elsie went to tea at Lamb house, and Elsie announced that Ford had just finished *The Inheritors* in collaboration with Conrad. 'To me this is like a bad dream which one relates at breakfast!', Olive recalled James saying: 'Their traditions and their gifts are so dissimilar. Collaboration between them is to me inconceivable.' What James knew about Ford's gift at this stage was almost certainly only his second volume of verse, *Poems for Pictures*, published at the end of May 1900, and dedicated to Edward Garnett. 'I take it very kindly that you have sent me your so curious & interesting book of verses, with so friendly a letter', wrote James, '& I thank you on both heads':

I think your doubt about the verses misplaced & unjustified—all those that I have yet read seeming to me to hold their own very firmly indeed. Those I have read—& re-read—are the little rustic lays—several of which I think admirable: terribly natural & true & 'right', drawn from the real wretchedness of things. The poetry of the cold and the damp & the mud & the nearness to earth—this is a chord you touch in a way that makes me wonder if there isn't still more for you to get from it. But doubtless it is only feasible &, so to speak, bearable when it *comes*, & it mustn't, for one's philosophy, come too often! May your genuine note find handsome recognition. Shall you not again pass, soon, this way? I shall be very glad to see you, & I am yours very truly

Henry James.[5]

The two men met soon after the Hueffers had moved to Winchelsea, and the subject came up of Ford's next book, *The Cinque Ports*, published on 29 October

1900. It is a large volume, beautifully illustrated and presented, and was published in an edition of only 525 copies. This meant it sold for three guineas, whereas Ford's other early books (apart from *Ford Madox Brown* at two guineas) sold for between two and six shillings. James probably joked about not being able to afford it, whereupon Ford wrote to say a presentation copy was on its way. James's reply displays the ambivalence that coloured all his dealings with Ford. As in the case of Conrad, some sharp remarks in surviving letters have misled scholars into assuming that James simply disliked Ford, and that therefore Ford's writings about his friendship with James were the product of wishful thinking. We do not know what James had said to Ford, but his tact and solicitude bespeak an anxiety that an inadvertent joke might have hurt him:

My dear F. M. Hueffer,
    I am overwhelmed by your letter, touched by your sympathy, and almost appalled by your munificence:—in the light, that is, of my fear that my crude pleasantries, my reckless and accidental levity on the subject of your brave Book may have seemed (while you evidently sought, or awaited, but a pretext for kindness) to put a kind of pressure on you in respect to my deprived state. I thank you none the less cordially, but I feel embarrassed and confused; as if I were really inhuman to consent to receive from you an offering of such value [. . .] For the rest I respond very gratefully to the charming things you tell me in relation to your so friendly acquaintance with things of mine. I'm delighted, this sentiment and this history—which you so happily express— exist for you; and only a little alarmed—or a little depressed—as always—when my earlier perpetrations come back to me as loved or esteemed objects. I seem to see them, in that character, shrink and shrivel, rock, dangerously, in the kindly blast, and threaten to collapse altogether. I am always moved to say 'Wait'—but I suppose I ought really to be thankful about anything that helps you to wait! Meantime, too, I can't but feel that at Winchelsea you and your wife are beautifully placed for doing so. I fall again to stoking my furnace as I think of you there, and to trying to produce some approach to the right metal. This is one of the reasons why I am glad you have come.[6]

James had realized that there was more to the *jeune homme modeste* than had met his eye. Ford's later claim to 'almost daily colloquies with Mr. James, which extended over a number of years' is an exaggeration. But his repeated claim to intimacy appears more reasonable than it has been thought in the light of the frequent meetings recorded by Olive Garnett and others. And even when exaggerating his intimacy, Ford's purpose is a more complex one than mere self-aggrandizement by association, since he records what must have been for him the most frustrating aspect of their friendship: 'I do not think that, till the end of his days, he regarded me as a serious writer.' As Mizener said, James 'clearly enjoyed Ford's company and often during the next few years sought him out'.[7]

The Inheritors was published in June 1901 as a collaboration. It was Ford's second published novel, coming out nine years after *The Shifting of the Fire*. He did most of the writing himself, though he discussed it extensively with Conrad, whose role, he said, was 'to give each scene a final tap'.[8] What Ford was trying to achieve in the book was, as in 'Seraphina', primarily a tone of voice. But whereas in later works such as *The Good Soldier*, or his reminiscences, a masterly control of tone enables the prose to achieve a variety of effects, in *The Inheritors* he was still experimenting. His reminiscences about the conception of the novel provide another comic high-point of *Joseph Conrad*:

We both desired to get into situations, at any rate when anyone was speaking, the sort of indefiniteness that is characteristic of all human conversations, and particularly of English conversations that are almost always conducted entirely by means of allusions and unfinished sentences. If you listen to two English communicating by means of words, for you can hardly call it conversing, you will find that their speeches are little more than this: A. says: 'What sort of a fellow is . . . *you* know!' B. replies: 'Oh, he's a sort of a . . . ' and A. exclaims: 'Ah, I always thought so. . . .' This is caused partly by sheer lack of vocabulary, partly by dislike for uttering any definite statement at all [. . .]

　　The writer used to try to get that effect by almost directly rendering speeches that, practically, never ended so that the original draft of the *Inheritors* consisted of a series of vague scenes in which nothing definite was ever said. These scenes melted one into the other until the whole book, in the end, came to be nothing but a series of the very vaguest hints. The writer hoped by this means to get an effect of a sort of silverpoint: a delicacy. No doubt he succeeded. But the strain of reading him must have been intolerable.

In the examples Ford gives, Conrad's 'final tap' makes the difference between unintelligible vagueness and intelligible detail. Conrad wrote ' "Baron Halder-schrodt has *committed suicide*," which the writer [Ford] for greater delicacy had rendered: "Baron Halderschrodt has . . . " '. Ford's comic treatment of this apprentice work brings out its failure; he had sought to emulate *Heart of Darkness*, but *The Inheritors* takes on political actualities without actualizing them. Granger's political and moral impotence parallels his sexual ineffectuality (which anticipates Dowell's; as does his baffled narration): 'I wanted to make love to her—oh, immensely,' he says, 'but I was never in the mood.' But in Ford's preoccupation with tone, even these subjects all but disappear. Writing a book about insubstantiality is a risky gamble. It took a further experiment, *A Call*, before, in *The Good Soldier*, he was to achieve mastery over the expressiveness of blankness: the turning of indeterminacy into a scintillating rendering of entirely enigmatic and possibly vacuous personalities. There is justice in Moser's description of *The Inheritors* as a 'neurotic portrait of a neurotic hero'.[9]

　　The *Times* review was typical in its qualified response, finding that the book 'leaves the bewildered student with the impression that it is a very clever book, and that he is a very stupid person for not seeing what it is all about'; that it was 'a kind of moral nightmare [. . .] an experiment, and, though unsuccessful in its aim, is full of intelligence astray'. The more favourable notices tended to assume that the book owed most to Conrad. The *New York Times* Saturday reviewer did not even mention Ford, and this drew forth Conrad's only public reply to a review.[10]

There is an element of chivalry in his wanting Ford to get the recognition he deserved. Jessie Conrad (who had already begun to begrudge Conrad's intimacy with the Hueffers) said Conrad 'was ready at all times, in those early days, to take up the cudgels in defence of his collaborator'. But Conrad also omits to mention Ford's name; and, despite his honourable pre-emptive assertions to the contrary, his emphasis on Ford's contribution does have the effect of distancing himself from a book that he realized was a commercial, if not an aesthetic, failure. He was disingenuous about the latter, not saying that it was not, but only that it need not confess itself one: 'Doubtless a novel that wants explaining is a bad novel: but this is only an extravagant story—and it is an experiment. An experiment may bear a certain amount of explanation without confessing itself a failure.' His emphasis on the experimental nature of the book betrays his sense of its lack of achievement:

The book is emphatically an experiment in collaboration; but only the first paragraph of the review mentions 'the authors' in the plural—afterwards it seems as if Mr. Conrad alone were credited with the qualities of style and conception detected by the friendly glance of the critic. The elder of the authors is well aware how much of these generously estimated qualities [too generously estimated?] the book owes to the younger collaborator. Without disclaiming his own share of the praise or evading the blame, the older man is conscious that his scruples in the matter of treatment, however sincere in themselves, may have stood in the way of a very individual talent deferring to him more out of friendship, perhaps, than from conviction; that they may have robbed the book of much freshness and of many flashes of that 'private vision' (as our critic calls them) which would have made the story more actual and more convincing.

Anxious to deny that the novel had been intended as a satire against 'some of the most cherished traditions' of his adopted country, Conrad argues that: 'It is rather directed at the self-seeking, at the falsehood that had been (to quote the book) "hiding under the words that for ages had spurred men to noble deeds, to self-sacrifice, and to heroism." And apart from this view, to direct one's little satire at the tradition and the achievements of a race would have been an imbecile futility—something like making a face at the great pyramid.' After the rift with Ford, Conrad said the book had no importance in his *œuvre*. While it is true that the published book could not be mistaken for one of Conrad's, it would be misleading to suggest that the activity of collaborating over it had no significance for Conrad's writing, and for the development of his ideas about art. The letter ends with a magnificent statement of joint purpose which, in its applicability to the major work of both authors, testifies to Ford's remark about their similar temperaments. Only Conrad could have written it; yet it could be taken as a set of convictions underlying everything either man wrote—and also as an eloquent demonstration that the work of both writers is as relevant to Britain towards the end of the twentieth century as it was towards the beginning:

The extravagance of its form [the book was subtitled: 'An Extravagant Story'] is meant to point out forcibly the materialistic exaggeration of individualism, whose unscrupulous efficiency it is the temper of the time to worship.

It points it out simply—and no more, because the business of a work striving to be art is not to teach or to prophesy (as we have been charged, on this side, with attempting,) nor yet to renounce a definite conclusion [. . .] in the sphere of an art dealing with a subject matter whose origin and end are alike unknown there is no possible conclusion. The only indisputable truth of life is our ignorance [. . .] Egoism, which is the moving force of the world, and altruism, which is its morality, these two contradictory instincts of which one is so plain and the other so mysterious, cannot serve us unless in the incomprehensible alliance of their irreconcilable antagonism. Each alone would be fatal to our ambition. For, in the hour of undivided triumph, one would make our inheritance too arid to be worth having and the other too sorrowful to own.

Fiction, at the point of development at which it has arrived, demands from the writer a spirit of scrupulous abnegation. The only legitimate basis of creative work lies in the courageous recognition of all the irreconcilable antagonisms that make our life so enigmatic, so burdensome, so dangerous—so full of hope. They exist! And this is the only fundamental truth of fiction. Its recognition must be critical in its nature, inasmuch that in its character it may be joyous, it may be sad; it may be angry with revolt, or submissive in resignation. The mood does not matter. It is only the writer's self-forgetful fidelity to his sensations that matters. But, whatever light he flashes on it, the fundamental truth remains, and it is only in its name that the barren struggle of contradictions assumes the dignity of moral strife going on ceaselessly to a mysterious end—with our consciousness powerless but concerned sitting enthroned like a melancholy parody of eternal wisdom above the dust of the contest.[11]

Like all Ford's unachieved exploratory works, *The Inheritors* attempts something very elusive and difficult: the kind of dual tone Conrad suggests. We are to view Granger's experiences as a tragedy of loss and futility, a struggle of irresolvable conflicts; and yet we are also to hear it as parody—parody both of Granger's embattled predicament, and of the conventional modes of presenting such predicaments as hopeless loves, science-fiction invasions, and political novels, novels of ideas. ' "Ideas," she said', the novel begins, ' "Oh, as for ideas—".' So much for *ideas*, says Ford: what we need is an art above philosophy, above propaganda. Ford wrote to Olive Garnett, between the writing and the publication of the book, that, 'qua Artist—you ought to be above all the characters [. . .] Your greatness lies in your being above *all* the philosophies'. What criticism of the book there has been has attended thoroughly to the political context, to the identifying of the public and private figures behind the characters. Ford later said the book was to be 'a political work, rather allegorically backing Mr. Balfour in the then Government; the villain was to be Joseph Chamberlain who had made the [Boer] War. The sub-villain was to be Leopold II, King of the Belgians, the foul—and incidentally lecherous—beast who had created the Congo Free State in order to grease the wheels of his harems with the blood of murdered negroes.' It was conceived as 'an allegorico-realist romance: it showed the superseding of previous generations and codes by the merciless young who are always alien and without remorse'. Ford's grasp of domestic politics made the satiric portraits effective. Balfour appears (with inadvertent historical irony) as 'Churchill', Chamberlain as 'Gurnard', Leopold as 'the Duc de Mersch', and Northcliffe as 'Fox'. The artistic and literary world is represented by the neglected painter Jenkins (Madox Brown), Polehampton (Fisher Unwin), Lea (Edward Garnett), and Callan (who combines characteristics of James and Hall Caine, but was also taken to represent R. S. Crockett, the Scottish kailyard novelist). What Ford didn't know enough about was colonialism, which is where his collaborator could have been of most use. But the dilatoriness of Conrad's involvement is shown not just by the way he let pass Ford's confusion over whether the book's equivalent of the Belgian Congo—'Greenland'—was populated by Eskimos or Africans. It is also evident in the book's vagueness about the political fraud on which the plot turns, 'a dynastic revolution somewhere, a revolution that was to cause a slump all over the world, and that had been engineered in our Salon'. As Robert Green has argued,

A political novel must be articulate about the mechanics of fraud and jobbery [. . .] to have functioned effectively, the Greenland scheme should have been established with the same centrality and resonance as the 'silver' of *Nostromo* or *Heart of Darkness'* 'ivory'. However, as the novel develops, we can see that Ford was less interested in the public effects of Granger's treachery than in the psychology of the traitor.[12]

Ford, that is, wanted to write something different from a *roman à clef* about politics. The chief interest lies in the attempt to go beyond these things, to sustain a tone of Olympian irony felt to be under threat from 'the temper of the time'. The difficulty of the exercise is to distance the narrator from the authors, since Granger's own moral superiority to the world of political machinations is precisely what brings about his despair, because it renders him ineffectual against the worldly manipulations of the other-worldly Dimensionists. How can the authors maintain their similar detachment from a degrading and degraded world, without also alienating themselves from it, and appearing as ineffectual as their protagonist? Aesthetics blur with economics here, since the sceptical artist must live a dual life, negotiating the antagonism of market forces with aesthetic convictions: there are at least two ways for a writer to be ineffectual—to sell out, or not to sell. Conrad and Ford evolved to face this antagonism a dual tone of pathos and irony, a tone which enacts a mastery over the world it abjures; a tone which, at the very point where a reader begins to feel the novel is itself a symptom of the moral disease it purports to diagnose, can turn around and claim that you have mistaken for empathy what is in fact parody.

Despite the grand manner of Conrad's letter, there is an unmistakable undertow hinting that his criticism is part of the farce of everyone taking seriously what was in fact a joke. Certainly the (parodic?) tone of high seriousness is at odds with the dismissive comment to Edward Garnett that, whereas he looked upon the novel as a skit on political novels, 'poor *H* was dead in earnest'. Yet it does introduce the notion of 'melancholy parody'—surely the best description of what *The Inheritors* is—into the public discussion of the novel. There is evidence that

Conrad had either misunderstood Ford's attitude towards the book, or was being disingenuous about it to Garnett. In July 1901 (before Conrad's letter to the *New York Times Saturday Review*), Ford had written to Olive Garnett replying to her remarks on the novel. She had not liked it, and evidently wrote (rather as Ford wrote to her about her stories) with comments about how it might have been done otherwise. Ford's answer proves that he was not merely 'in earnest', and brings out his own sense of the novel's dual tone. More importantly, it shows how a similar conception of tonal duality lay at the heart of the re-imagining of 'Seraphina', which at about the same time was being sent, incomplete, to William Blackwood in the hope that he would accept it for serialization in *Blackwood's Magazine*. 'Respected Person,' he wrote, invoking his habitual mockery of the Garnetts as 'Superior Persons':

Your excellently penetrative letter flitted very prettily round a—let us say—'A might have been.'

You see, the Dimensionist Idea might have been approached differently—but il faut etre de la fatalite de sa race; de son temperament, de son age & so on. If we had made the lady a mere genius the novel would have been one of intrigue—but we were intent on reducing the N.[ovel?] of I.[deas?] AD ABSURDAM—on making fun of & waltzing round it—just as you delicately make fun of a waltz and its result. And anyhow it is not a serious work. Wait! And keep your lamp full of oil.

You say: 'see them (Inheritors) all through our Pictian history'.—Just so—does this not justify the existence of the midge—the day-fly—of a thing? [. . .] *Seraphina* will be better & the next better still. With regard to *Seraphina*, as it happens, you will find the moral in a scrap of verse scribbled on p. 4 of this letter [. . .] *Seraphina* is to be called not 'S' but *Romance*—isn't that a gem of a title; & the last words are 'And, looking back, there is Romance.' And before that come smugglers, & Admirals, & Dons & Pirates, & Seraphine & Newgate &, in the last chapter (or rather the last words of the last chapter because the mental harrowing goes on up to the last forty lines) REAL JAM & KISSES.

And the hero looks back—he did'nt like any of it when he was going through it & snaps & sneers & bites on his human contemporaries,—looks back & says . . . . . 'There is Romance.'

So there is, is'nt there?[13]

Telling Olive to 'Wait!', he repeats James's word to him, impersonating his other great master in order to become masterful towards another writer.

Throughout the summer of 1901 work on *Romance* had intensified. Conrad came to stay at Winchelsea for a fortnight in mid-May and a week in June. He had also borrowed £100 from Ford. Robert Garnett, Ford's solicitor, had tried to make Ford get some security for the loan. Ford resisted what Madox Brown's teaching would have made him see as philistine, bourgeois niggardliness. But eventually the melodramatic—if the only possible—solution was that Conrad turned over to Ford his life-insurance policy. Writing to thank Ford 'for staving off the impending annihilation', Conrad turned to two of the more favourable reviews of *The Inheritors*, saying 'I feel more and more like a thief of Your cleverness'. He may also have felt more and more a thief of Ford's money. He was not only living in Ford's old house, the Pent, but also frequently enjoying his and Elsie's hospitality in the new one. Earlier in the year he had approached his new agent, J. B. Pinker, on Ford's behalf about selling Madox Brown's correspondence.[14] It is possible that *Nostromo*, the work he launched into immediately after *Romance*, was being shaped by aspects of the collaboration: *Nostromo*, the story about the man whose incorruptible reputation seems compromised when some of the silver he was entrusted to save goes missing—used by the (Fordian) Decoud for weights with which to annihilate himself by drowning. There is, in the dealings over the insurance policy, a sense that Conrad is entrusting his *life* as well as his reputation to Ford: by saving him from annihilation, Ford somehow becomes responsible for his life. Conrad's desire not to claim too great a share of Ford's success is honourable. Yet his excessive disclaimer has yet again the effect of distancing himself from Ford's work. In Conrad's novels after *Romance*—*Nostromo*, *The Secret Agent*, and *Under Western Eyes*—there is a persistent questioning of what it takes to corrupt someone's reputation: how much money will buy their name, their words, their actions. By bringing together money and collaboration, Conrad could be saying that if Ford wants his name (which, as Conrad had written to Henley, might help him sell his books), then he would have to pay for it.

The incomplete typescript of *Romance* was sent to Blackwood in early July, and Ford then worked on his projected biography of Henry VIII.[15] But on 15 August Blackwood took the wind out of the collaborators' sails by rejecting *Romance*. David Meldrum, Blackwood's adviser, thought the problem was that 'it is Hueffer's story and Conrad's telling; and that the dramatic intensity, while there, appears a little forced'. (In fact, though Ford may already have learned much about Conrad's manner of telling, relatively little of the version sent to Blackwood was actually written by Conrad. So Meldrum's impression of 'Conrad's telling' testifies to the success of the collaboration rather than its failure.) It took Conrad nearly three months to be able to discuss his reaction with Blackwood. He wrote to him ten days after receiving the circumlocutory letter of rejection. But he makes no mention of *Romance*. His comments on another author are nevertheless obliquely eloquent about his dismay: 'Now a book of that sort *is* the man—the man disclosed absolutely; and the contact of such a genuine personality is like an invigorating bath for one's mind jaded by infinite effort after literary expression, wearied by all the unreality's of a writing life, discouraged by a sunless, starless sort of mental solitude, having lost its reckoning in a grey sea of words, words.' By 7 November he was able to say: 'I will admit the rejection of *Seraphina* had shaken the confidence with which I looked upon that work. So, as one can not turn back till the furrow is ploughed to the end, I took it in hand; and whether I've finally spoiled a big lot of paper or made some sort of tale I can't say.'[16]

The result of the rejection was, then, that Conrad, who had till then left most of the writing to Ford, became much more closely and creatively involved. He felt that the Part he had held back from Blackwood (the third in the typescript, third and fourth in the book) needed to 'be given hard *reality*', and he told Ford 'I shall do the thing myself of course but I would want to speak to you about it'. Moser suggests that he mistrusted Ford, 'had a lurking fear of Ford's mental instability'. If he did have any such fear this early, it is inextricable from his fear for his own stability, and ability to achieve 'hard *reality*'. Ford's mental disturbances had scarcely begun to show. Conrad rewrote this section virtually single-handed. As Ford recognized, this 'matchless Fourth Part' is the most successful section of the book. The other Parts are what Ford called 'a singular mosaic of passages written alternately by one or other of the collaborators'.[17] It was their most thoroughly collaborative work. On the same day that he wrote to Blackwood about his shaken confidence, Conrad also wrote to J. B. Pinker about how his burst of work had gone some way towards restoring it: 'I've at last finished *S*. I've put remarkable guts into that story.' He explained how he thought Pinker might handle it:

You may describe and introduce the book (if You do such things in that way) as a Straight romantic narrative of adventure where the hero is a Kent youth of good birth, the heroine a Spanish girl, the scene in England, Jamaica, Cuba, and on the sea—the personages involved besides Hero and Heroine smugglers, planters, sailors and authentic pirates—the last of the West Indian pirates; the whole story being founded on a fact carefully looked up in contemporary press and report of trial in Eng.—but by us brought about Romantically—the Romantic feeling being the basis of the book which is *not* a boy's story [. . .]
    It is rather the old thing (if you like) done in a way that is new only through the artistic care of the execution. The aim being to present the scenes and events and people *strictly realistically* in a glamour of *Romance*. The hero goes (accidentally so to speak) to seek Romance and finds it—a thing rather hard and difficult to live through. The time about 1823 is just far enough to bear the glamour of the past and near enough to enable us to dispense with elaborate explanations. In fact it is a serious attempt at *interesting, animated Romance*, with no more psychology than comes naturally into the action.

Mizener's fine description of Conrad's 'double game of staying uninvolved with the subject and deeply involved with the composition of the work' captures the book's central problem. The subject wasn't really Ford's either (as his story of Richard Garnett suggesting it to him conveys); and he too had a sometimes dangerous attraction to subjects which offered the possibility of such a double game. Conrad also wanted to boost his agent's confidence in the work. 'You may take my word for it that it is a piece of literature of which we are neither of us at all ashamed', he said. Not only was Pinker about to be given *Romance* to place with a publisher, but Conrad was about to ask him for a loan: he was becoming increasingly indebted to his agent as well as to Ford.[18]
    Pinker now became Ford's agent as well, and was to become as important in his life as in Conrad's. He was a Scotsman, who started his agency in 1896 after working as assistant editor on the successful literary magazine *Black and White*, which printed stories by Hardy, Stevenson, James, and Violet Hunt. Like Ford,

Pinker was prepared to back innovative writers through their unprofitable phases. He also represented Wells, Crane, Bennett, Lawrence (for a time), and Joyce, who mentions him in *Ulysses*. He wasn't the first literary agent. A. P. Watt had represented authors (including Francis Hueffer) since the 1870s, and he was followed by Curtis Brown. But Pinker has been called an 'intermediary of genius', and 'the greatest agent of his time'. Frank Swinnerton, another of his authors, described him as a 'clean-shaven grey haired sphinx with a protrusive under-lip, who drove four-in-hand, spoke distinctly in a hoarse voice that was almost a whisper, shook hands shoulder-high, laughed without moving, knew the monetary secrets of authors and the weaknesses of publishers, terrified some of these last and was refused admittance by others'. The authors respected his acumen and tenacity. Even one who was severing their connection wrote: 'I know of no one of less tact than yourself', but added, 'or greater probity'. Ford said they had 'mysterious and obscure rows', and that he never understood what they were about. 'I suppose he was sensitive and I patronising', suggested Ford, perhaps hinting at how the converse was also true, since nothing aroused his Madox Brownian emotions like feeling he was being patronized by anyone not an artist.[19]

Olive Garnett visited Winchelsea for a fortnight in November, arriving on the same train as Henry James's new cook. James was at the station, and said, 'I have come to meet my doom.' Olive had met James briefly in London, but they evidently didn't speak at Winchelsea. She had already fallen in well with the general preoccupation with the person they called (with an irony that did not efface their awe) 'the Great Man', and she solemnly recorded two dreams about him in her diary. Most of her visit revolved around the question of whether or not she would meet him again. When Elsie took her to visit Conrad, who began despondently, despairing of his work and fantasizing about going back to sea, she began to perceive the underlying tensions between the collaborators. Olive's presence seems to have cheered Conrad up, but Elsie's comment that he had been in 'a good mood' speaks volumes of bad ones. Excited that Ford had been walking with him the day she went to the Conrads, Olive finally did meet James—in the chemist's: 'H.J. asked me if I had known Madox Brown & what he was like; & he also talked of the – – – abysmal vulgarity of the British public', coming down the street with them as far as the toy-shop. As Olive left on 25 November, Ford and Elsie were waiting at Ashford station to meet Galsworthy, the next in a steady succession of visitors.[20]

Conversation at the Hueffers had been as lively as ever; but Olive records 'Great talk about Ford's work. Depression.' There was a great amount of his work to talk about: one reason for his depression was 'E[dward]'s criticism of his Rossetti Life'. Somehow, between bouts of *Romance* and of 'The Life and Times of Henry VIII', Ford had managed to draft *Rossetti: A Critical Study of his Art*. It was not published until June 1902, when it appeared in Duckworth's Popular Library of Art series, organized by Edward Garnett. The book 'remains one of the most arresting assessments of this enigmatic practitioner of the arts of painting and poetry', writes Joseph Kestner. Given Ford's sentimental attachment to the Pre-Raphaelites, it is the critical balance of his monograph that is perhaps its most striking feature (though his scepticism about Rossetti's achievement confirms his picture of Madox Brown as the major force in the movement). 'Rossetti's work is almost always a matter of re-reflected personal influences', wrote Ford. He praised Rossetti's poem 'Jenny' (in terms which foreshadow the aims of books like *The Good Soldier* and *Parade's End*) because 'the writer neither shudders with the citizen at the prostitute, nor falls to the other and obvious extreme of railing at the society that keeps her beyond the pale'. In such instances, Rossetti could exemplify 'the sympathetic insight and the conscious aloofness that, to the creator in the Arts, is the one quality essential for permanence'. In part, his own sympathy is enabled by the fact that Rossetti was one of his own personal influences, one of many that are 're-reflected' in Ford's study. Another is Conrad, whose conscious aloofness he echoes in a comment to Garnett answering more criticisms about the manuscript: 'Rossetti undoubtedly did *fail*—the point is whether his failure was or was not *ignoble*'. Ford sees Rossetti's failure as the defect of his qualities: he 'was an Amateur, because he never really mastered the theory of either of his arts'. Here Ford recognizes the kind of artist he might have been had not his collaboration with Conrad involved its gruelling mastery of the art of fiction. *Rossetti* is Ford's first sustained and mature engagement with the theory of art. Though some of its terms now seem dated (such as the privileging of 'charm'), it is striking how most of his central critical ideas—'sympathy', 'surprise', 'atmosphere', 'personality', 'sentimentalism', vision—were firmly established by his twenty-eighth year. Ford's reflection on Rossetti's failure shows his own predicament re-reflected in another way. In the idea that 'Rossetti was beguiled by his friendships'—that his true gift was for direct representation, but that 'the real trouble was that other people did not want him to develop this side of his individuality'—one can hear Ford wondering whether his involvement with Conrad and Garnett might not be obstructing his development in his other art, poetry; whether it might not be equally true of him that in subjugating his own career to Conrad's he was, as he thought Rossetti, 'in all things a better friend to others than to himself'. The depth of his 'sympathetic identification' with Rossetti was partly due to his sense that they were both dual natures as artists, and partly due to his depression, linked to Conrad's, that *Romance* would be a dual failure: commercial as well as artistic.[21]

There was still much revising and integrating to be done before *Romance* could be adventured again, and both collaborators began to develop psychosomatic illnesses as a result. The work intensified throughout December, but then during a party for his birthday on 17 December Ford swallowed a chicken-bone. Mizener wryly calls it 'a signal victory in the competition over which of them suffered more from illness and nerves'. It was also a profoundly disturbing experience. Conrad, who came to Winchelsea for a fortnight over Christmas and the New Year, told Pinker that Ford didn't get rid of the bone until Boxing Day, and was 'as limp as a rag afterwards and totally unable to work. Then he developed a swollen face, a mild abscess in the cheek'. The episode not only prostrated him until the New Year, but haunted him long afterwards. He saw it as the starting-point of a run of bad luck, writing to his mother: 'It is exactly a year since I swallowed (or rather didn't swallow) that chicken bone & since then things have gone in a most vicious string.' The story became part of the family mythology, suitably transformed. Helen Rossetti Angeli was told 'that he'd swallowed a fish bone, and that it had affected him, that it had made him ill, and that afterwards he had had this nervous breakdown'. But she was too shrewd to swallow the story, adding: 'He didn't, apparently, get on with his wife.'[22]

He always had a morbid fascination with contemplating his own death, whether by suicide (which figures in the fiction from *The Shifting of the Fire* right up to *The Rash Act* (1933) and *Henry for Hugh* (1934)), by treachery (John Kemp at the hands of pirates in *Romance*; Tietjens unjustly sent into the Front Line in a war in which civilians betray the military), or punishment (Kemp living in the shadow of the gallows). Accidents bring home the fragility of human life; they can cause one to take stock of what has been achieved, and make one wonder what forces might militate against future achievement—especially if they occur on birthdays, when one is particularly conscious of ageing. The chicken-bone need not actually have nearly killed Ford for him to feel that he had nearly died. He was on the point of collapse from the strain of the collaboration, and the accident became a metaphor for his stress as much as a cause of it (perhaps a metaphor for the way he would be punished for physical appetites); an alibi for the recuperation he needed anyway.

Perhaps realizing that he had made Ford sweat too much over the rewriting, Conrad took over, and the roles of the collaborators were effectively reversed. '*Seraphina* seems to hang about me like a curse', cursed Conrad. Ford, staying at the Pent in January 1902, complained to Elsie, 'Conrad apparently wants me to sit around and look pleasant'. He recalled taking pot-shots at rats with a writerly sounding rifle, the Flobert. A 'great old grey rat' collapsed after Ford shot at it from 'an incredible distance', and this 'immense feat of marksmanship' passed into collaborative legend. 'Ah, but you should have seen Ford's shot at the rat! . . .', he records Conrad as saying when 'anyone talked of shooting'. If it sounds like boasting, it is of the Fordian self-mocking kind: for he was sure, he says, that 'the rat was dying of old age before it was fired at, the bullet never reaching it'.[23]

The next in the string of disasters following Ford's twenty-eighth birthday was the death, on 2 February 1902, of Elsie's father. The abruptness and mystery of his death are Conradian. The death certificate reads: 'Syncope | Poisoning by Prussic Acid | Suicide | Unsound Mind.' The only other clues to what happened come again from Olive Garnett. She was told the cause was 'Melancholia': 'Ford hopes to take Elsie to Paris directly. Mr. M. wrote "thank Ford" at the end of his letter.' Moser concedes that this might be 'bitterly sardonic', though he does not elaborate; then he opts for a reading of the words as 'affectionate', 'in the light of Ford's tenderness to sufferers and previous helpfulness to his father-in-law'.[24] But 'thanking' someone in your suicide note is at best an equivocal act. The

Martindales had long ago buried their anger over Elsie's elopement, and accepted Ford as their son-in-law. The only new development that could have produced such disastrous results is surely Ford's affair with Mary, which, had it begun and been discovered by this time, would have seemed even to a less stolid and less public a figure than Dr Martindale unspeakably to have blighted his family and his life.

As with the chicken-bone, what Ford thought Dr Martindale had meant was as important (to a study of his work and life) as what he had actually meant. Suicide, whatever its motives, is often hushed up; so the fact that this one was need not prove that its motives were unspeakable. But when Ford sent some funeral verses and a wreath 'From his daughter and grandchildren', was he excluding himself—and possibly Mary too, since Elsie was not Martindale's only daughter—as if to acknowledge that he was for ever banished from Martindale's sympathy? This is to read the occasion through *The Good Soldier*, and to read the harrowing vision of judgement in that novel, culminating in despair, suicide, and madness, as drawing on Ford's guilt over his own sexual entanglements.[25]

Ford was evidently deeply shocked by the suicide. His fiction shows him worrying about his possible responsibility for it, and trying to understand what would drive a man to such a violently negative act. This is particularly evident in *The Benefactor*, in which the Fordian altruistic hero, George Moffat, feels that he has to renounce the woman he loves, Clara Brede, not only because he is married (though separated from his wife), but because he feels responsible for the insanity of her clergyman father. The book was not published until 1905, by which time Ford had rewritten it several times. But he had been working hard on it through 1901.[26]

In the haunting image of the mad Revd. Brede (who himself haunts Ford's later fiction, walking again as the mad Revd. Duchemin in *Some Do Not . . .*), a man who is described as if he were dead, Ford was exploring the fictional potential to express and try to assuage his grief and guilt over Dr Martindale:

The black and tremendous figure of her father had risen before George's eyes once more. The man was dead, the man was more than dead; but his memory remained. This thing [their affair] would never vex his troubled spirit. But his memory was in their hands, and George seemed to hear men's voices say, 'Oh, Brede. He's in a lunatic asylum, and his daughter ran away with a married man.' That contempt would fall on the memory of this man that they had both loved, and both impelled to his ruin [. . .] it would be a final and despicable treachery.

Ford never lost this sense of the power of father-figures to rise, as if from the dead, and overwhelm someone on the verge of sexual involvement. (Did Martindale's death render Ford impotent?)[27] The suicide of Dr Martindale probably tapped his feelings about the death of his own overshadowing father, whose name would be betrayed were a Hueffer to become the centre of a scandal. These feelings returned during the Great War, when Ford's quasi-marriage with Violet Hunt was also breaking down; then they issued in 'True Love & a G.C.M.'

(1918–19), an unfinished novel in which overpowering memories of a dead father are associated with an immobilized rapture of sexual longing; and in *The Marsden Case* (1923), a novel about a son driven to imitate in exact detail a father's suicide, and about how (the suicide attempt mercifully failing) the father's good name can be restored.

Ford took Elsie for a trip to Germany after the funeral, but plunged immediately back into collaboration. At the beginning of March he went to stay at the Pent. His letters to Elsie show how lonely she felt, and how much she needed Ford's companionship to disperse her grief. For the third time, *Romance* appeared to be finished (though it was to need cutting before Pinker could try to get it serialized). Conrad told Galsworthy of his relief: 'Seraphina is finished and gone out of the house she has haunted for this year past.' But he needed Ford's company. In the middle of March he took his family for a 'little holiday' with the Hueffers. And after a month of separation, he too began to complain of loneliness: 'These interrupted relations must be taken up again [. . .] I miss collaboration in the most ridiculous manner. I hope you don't intend dropping me altogether [. . .] I don't know how it is but with the end of Seraphina everything in the world seemed to come to an end [. . .] How rotten everything is!' Ford too was depressed. 'Your letters have been touching in their suggestion of your mental state', Conrad told him, and expressed his 'impatience to see you and to see, hear, taste, absorb your George'—Ford's new novel, *The Benefactor*—though Conrad's way of expressing his interest in his collaborator's own work was typically ambivalent:

I say anxious, frankly, because not distrusting you in the least, I have from personal experience a rooted mistrust towards our work—yours and mine—which is under the patronage of a Devil. For indeed unless beguiled by a malicious fiend what man would undertake it? What creature would be mad enough to take upon itself the task of a creator? It is a thing unlawful. Une chose néfaste, carrying with it its own punishment of toil, unceasing doubt and deception.

In Conrad's self-mistrust lay the seeds of his eventual vindictive anger towards Ford. When the madness that seemed inseparable from 'the task of a creator' struck him again, it was Ford whom he attacked as the embodiment of transgressive megalomania. Hence the later reproofs that Ford exaggerated their intimacy. But in fact he played down Conrad's statements to Cathy Hueffer (in words he probably knew): that 'there is between Ford and me a bond of genuine friendship'; that 'In the close intercourse of our common toil I've learned to appreciate his exceptional artistic gifts, his great intelligence, his many solid qualities. Indeed I count myself very fortunate in that friendship'. In their obsessive quality, their dramatization of (art's) passion and agony, Conrad's letters to Ford often read like a melancholy parody of a romance. By dividing his life between Elsie and Conrad, Ford had created for himself a double-bind. During the Edwardian decade his work became more involved with the literary life of London, and it became harder to reconcile with his family life.[28]

1902–1903

... if you read Conrad sentence by sentence with minute care you will
see that each sentence is a mosaic of little crepitations of surprise and that
practically every paragraph contains its little jolt.

(Ford, introduction to Conrad's *The Sisters*)

In the 'Author's Note' for the 1924 Collected Edition of *Tales of Unrest*, Conrad's reminiscence suggests an allegory of his collaboration with Ford. Conrad muses on the continuity of style between *An Outcast of the Islands* and his story 'The Lagoon': 'there has been no change of pen, figuratively speaking.' This was literally true too: 'It was the same pen: a common steel pen':

I thought the pen had been a good pen and that it had done enough for me, and so, with the idea of keeping it for a sort of memento on which I could look later with tender eyes [like Ford, Conrad too wanted to 'have remembrance now'], I put it into my waistcoat pocket. Afterwards it used to turn up in all sorts of place[s ...] till at last it found permanent rest in a large wooden bowl containing some loose keys, bits of sealing-wax, bits of string, small broken chains, a few buttons, and similar minute wreckage that washes out of a man's life into such receptacles. I would catch sight of it from time to time with a distinct feeling of satisfaction till, one day, I perceived with horror that there were two old pens in there. How the other pen found its way into the bowl instead of the fireplace or the wastepaper basket I can't imagine, but there the two were, lying side by side, both encrusted with ink and completely undistinguishable from each other. It was very distressing, but being determined not to share my sentiment between two pens or run the risk of sentimentalising over a mere stranger, I threw them both out of the window into a flower-bed—which strikes me now as a poetical grave for the remnants of one's past.[1]

As he tells the story of that pen, the literal, which had only just materialized from the haze of the figurative, dissolves back into figure. If the gesture of throwing the pens out of the window strikes him as 'poetical', isn't the rest of the story comparably figurative? Not just for the way that 'minute wreckage [...] washes out of a man's life into such receptacles' as his books, through such receptacles as his pens. But also for the way Conrad's horror at the doubling of pens combines a fear that writing might tap unconscious aspects of personality which threaten his self-possession, with a fear of the loss of his individuality in the doubling of pens which is literary collaboration. With one pen one knows where one is: one's style is unified. With two, there is the possibility of misprision.

The same anxiety about doubling is visible in his story 'The Secret Sharer', which has also been read as, on one level, an allegory about the collaboration. In 1905 Conrad was still able to tell Wells that Ford was 'a life-long habit of which I am not ashamed because he is a much better fellow than the world gives him credit for'. By the time he wrote the note on *Tales of Unrest* Conrad wanted to wash the wreckage of their friendship out of his life, and throw the memory of their collaboration out of the window. (As we shall see, discussions about republishing their collaborations later filled Conrad with a comparable horror.)[2]

Collaboration is a double jeopardy, since both writers risk being held responsible for the other's failures as well as for their own. But it was not just the fear that readers might think he had written Ford's words, or that they might not be able to tell the authors' styles apart, that upset Conrad. It was the very sympathy that had drawn them together in the first place—their literary pantheon, their dedication to technical expertise, their need for recognition, for sympathy, for support—that also made them seem so disturbingly alike, as men and as writers. Ford was not exaggerating when he said they 'worked together during many years with absolute one-ness of purpose and absolute absence of rivalry'. Both felt alien despite long familiarity with England and the English. Both were preoccupied with doubleness, double perspectives, doubled protagonists. The Conrad who had presented Kurtz as at once a great man and a ghoulish maniac, or whose Lord Jim is ambiguously heroic in his moral cowardice, recognized a kindred spirit in Ford's preoccupation with moral ambiguity and paradox. Collaboration answered to both men's sense of themselves as already double. 'Homo duplex has in my case more than one meaning', wrote Conrad. It was an expression Ford repeated. After writing about Conrad, Wells, Bennett, and himself, he said, 'Mr. Bennett, in short, like all the rest of us is homo duplex: he has a talent that kicks up a devil of a row in the world, and he has a real genius, which is a much quieter affair.' (It is characteristic of Ford to appear to claim genius for himself too, while leaving us unsure whether 'all the rest of us' are that group of writers, all writers, or every human being. Characteristic, too, to use such uncertainties as a smoke-screen under which to smuggle in one of the best descriptions of his own genius, which precisely provokes a devil of a row in order to operate more subtly and subliminally.) Zdzisław Najder's biography discriminates between the two men's psychological complexities. Although Conrad was 'himself of mercurial and unstable disposition, he did not celebrate his changeability the way Ford did', he argues. 'Although he too had fits of mythomania, his myths were not, like Ford's, an expansion of his own various incarnations, of the many visions of his own possibilities; they were efforts to integrate, retrospectively, his life into a cohesive whole.' But since people are subject to conflicting impulses, abrupt mood-changes, unrecognizable phases, why should variety not be celebrated? It is partly the combination of pathos and celebration that distinguishes Ford's writing.[3]

None of the three books published as collaborations are important achievements, though *Romance* is of great interest as an experiment (how else could one imagine a cross between Flaubert and Stevenson?), even if the experiment failed. It also presents an intriguing puzzle for critics determined to attribute every utterance to a single originating author. But the real significance of the collaboration lies in the way it affected the lives, and shaped the works, of the two writers. What had each gained from their involvement? Gerard Tetley (who worked briefly as Ford's secretary in 1906, when the collaborators were still intimate) said that Wells 'always said that Hueffer did a great deal to "English" Conrad'. Ford's memoir of Conrad provoked denunciations of his motives, explained Tetley, but after his death 'there has been a greater tendency to believe that Hueffer gave to Conrad a stability, through patience, and what seemed to be the strongest sort of sympathy and adulation'. Frederick Karl corroborates this, arguing that Conrad 'could not work effectively unless he were close to break-down'. Here too there was a temperamental affinity, though Ford's best work was to come immediately after his greatest distresses. Conradians, starting with Jessie Conrad, were scandalized by Ford's claim to be involved with books that Conrad published under his own name. 'Over many of the books [. . .] we laboured together for so many years,' wrote Ford, 'for I should say that not merely over *Romance*, but over *Nostromo*, *The Rescue* or "The End of the Tether," I laboured at least as hard as over any book of my own of these days.' These claims are all true. Indeed, Ford modestly omits here any mention of his help with Conrad's memoirs, *The Mirror of the Sea* and *A Personal Record*; or with the dramatization of 'Tomorrow' as *One Day More*; and of his telling Conrad the stories that provided the plots for 'Amy Foster' and *The Secret Agent*. Ford may not have wanted to recognize the extent to which Conrad's impressions of him washed into his books. It would have been as unflattering to him as it would have been immodest for him to see himself in Lord Jim, Martin Decoud, the Secret Sharer, Peter Ivanovitch in *Under Western Eyes*, or de Barral in *Chance*. His own accounts of the collaboration are a striking combination of pride in the association, and modesty about his role: 'I do not mean to claim any special creative part in these works, but in such matters as providing good working conditions, trying passages from dictation, suggesting words, listening to reading and the endless supplying of the moral support [. . .] I certainly bothered more over Conrad's work than over my own.' Conrad never dedicated a book to him (but got Ford's *The Fifth Queen* dedicated to himself). True to Madox Brown's injunction, Ford beggared himself for the sake of the man whose genius he knew to be greater than his own. 'And in what does greatness in a writer or in another take its rise if not in his power of attraction—of exacting sacrifices from other human beings!'[4]

The question of technical influence has been as controversial. Conradians have felt that Ford's claim that the two men evolved together the techniques he catalogues in *Joseph Conrad* is belied by the technical sophistication of Conrad's pre-collaborative work. J. J. Martin complicates the argument, introducing Edward Garnett as a third term, and showing that Ford's emphases on 'inevitability', 'complexity', verisimilitude, and even the 'time-shift' are anticipated in

Garnett's 1898 essay on Turgenev. Martin finds it 'odd' that Ford's discussion of Conrad didn't attribute their theoretical ideas to Garnett:

Regardless of whether or not Ford got his ideas directly from Garnett or through Conrad, there can be no question but that most of the important principles of technique which he claimed Conrad and he worked out together were advocated by Garnett before the famous partnership came into being. Although this does not preclude the possibility that Ford's enthusiastic reception of these ideas helped Conrad to develop them further, it is obvious it was Conrad who brought most of the technical inspiration to the partnership.[5]

The problem here is that the fact that Garnett was the first to *publish* a discussion of the principles is scarcely proof that he thought of them alone, or was the first to think of them. Martin's partisanship leads him to suppress the fact that Ford knew Garnett long before Conrad did, and had been discussing literature (including his own fiction) with him for at least seven years. Garnett was writing the Turgenev essay while the Hueffers were neighbours in Grace's Cottage, and the month after he introduced Conrad and Ford. His assault on impressionist writers as giving 'amazingly clever pictures of life', but which in general 'do not reveal more than the actual thinking and acting that men betray to one another', probably has Conrad, Ford, and James in mind. With such a close coterie, attempts to prove 'influence' are a falsification of the dynamics of mutual inspiration in sustained discussion. Once we grant that Ford influenced Garnett as much as he was influenced by him, then it is anything but 'obvious' that it was Conrad who 'brought most of the technical inspiration to the partnership'. Edward Crankshaw, by contrast, thought that Conrad's *practice* had gained immensely from Ford's sharing his convictions about technique. 'This', he explained, 'is not to suggest that Conrad's technical dexterity is due bodily to Ford [. . .] But he is in the earlier books still muddled in the application of his ideas; the whole first person convention in "The Nigger of the Narcissus" is several times misused [. . .] the signs point to the collaboration as the turning point, and to all the talk it must have involved, talk which sharpens nebulous ideas as nothing else can.'[6]

What the collaboration did for Ford is clearer. It satisfied 'his desire, a driving need, to ally himself with the chief literary forces of the day', James, Wells, Crane, and now Conrad. It probably gave him a 'feeling of superior worldliness' to help Conrad manage his affairs. But most importantly, working with Conrad gave him 'a settled purpose in life', and taught him how to turn his talent into great fiction. 'But most of all I owe him that strong faith', he said, 'that in our day and hour the writing of novels is the only pursuit worth while for a proper man.' He admired Conrad as the 'politician of the impasse', and learned from him (as a man as well as a writer) how to create compelling, morally ambiguous situations and characters. There's little doubt of Edith's fundamental innocence in *The Shifting of the Fire*, even though the plot needs the *frisson* of suspecting her of murder. But with Carlos Riego and Tomas Castro in *Romance*, the authors keep us wondering about their true motivations. Before he met Conrad, Ford knew that what he wrote of his precocious uncle, Oliver Madox Brown, was true of himself too: 'His mind teemed with pictures. His novels are a succession of splendidly painted scenes.' Ford never lost this visual power—a form of sustained homage to his grandfather's vivid compositions. The risk of his impressionism was always that the succession of scenes would appear inconsequential. This was the problem with 'Seraphina'. And, as Raymond Brebach has shown, Conrad's revision of Part Four of *Romance* became an example to Ford both of an artist's engagement with his writing, and of the 'precision and directness of narration' that he temperamentally avoided. The young Ford had been in danger of becoming an aesthete. Fordian 'indifference to fact' (that he ascribed to the protagonist of *An English Girl*) was the link between his 'indifferentism' and his 'impressionism'. But it was, he said, 'impossible to be indifferent to Conrad': 'if you do not dislike him, you must love him.' Like Madox Brown, Conrad gave Ford a model of the artist as romantic raconteur:

tell his adventures how he might, C's motive was not self-glorification. He had in the end too much contempt for his fellow human beings to care much how he stood in their eyes—unless it was a matter of the sale of his books. But he had the conviction that if he was in the society of a human being it was his duty to please his society—the writer has heard him give by far the most embroidered accounts of his personal adventures to quite the least important of his companions [. . .] And it is to be remembered that C's circumstances in those days were so unfortunately gloomy—or gloomily monotonous that somehow *Romance* must be brought into them so that the highly coloured accounts of early adventures in Marseilles served nobly for romance to colour his life at the Pent [rather?] than to make himself seem marvellous in the eyes of others. Some such colour he must have or he must have died.

Collaboration taught Ford the value of art as communication; the importance of imagining his readers as well as his impressions. Without the clarity and narrative drive learned with Conrad, he would never have been able to write *The Fifth Queen*, *The Good Soldier*, or *Parade's End*. He said, 'if I know anything of how to write almost the whole of that knowledge was acquired then'. As Sondra Stang wrote: 'Their relationship became one of the central facts of Ford's consciousness as a novelist.' Finally, the collaboration also contributed to Ford's imminent nervous breakdown.[7]

Ford's next stroke of ill luck in the spring of 1902 was to discover a *doppelgänger.* The professional historian A. F. Pollard was just about to bring out his own biography of Henry VIII. Ford's publishers cried off. Pollard's *Henry VIII* came out in June, and Ford reviewed it a year later in an essay called 'Creative History & the Historic Sense'. In *Return to Yesterday* Ford wrote that it was Dr Richard Garnett who suggested that he should turn the fruits of his researches into novels. 'I didn't want to write novels—and particularly not historical novels', said Ford, still feeling sharply after thirty years the depressions over *Romance*. 'It put me off for six months', he told his mother. He did, of course, eventually re-imagine his 'life' of Henry as the trilogy of historical romances, *The Fifth Queen*, but he wasn't able to begin for another three years. Yet even in the *Rossetti* study he anticipated his change of direction, in discussing 'the type of creative realism attempting to apply poetic interpretation to history'. Again, as a statement of his aesthetic principles, this is central. He would always be deeply intrigued by questions of history, and he had always been drawn to romance.[8]

He became exasperated with McClure, the American publisher of *Romance*. This was partly because McClure was behind with royalty statements for *The Inheritors*; and, as Conrad (who owed money to McClure as well) said, it looked as if he had pawned Ford's part of the work to the firm as well as his own. Since the work was mostly Ford's, this might well have rankled. But the reason is more likely to be that Ford got wind of McClure's desire to publish *Romance* as by Conrad alone.[9]

In the summer Ford's nervous exhaustion began developing symptoms. He was ill 'with the tummy', he told his mother, a sign that his dyspepsia was becoming more serious. Elsie was ill. 'But the children continue to flourish & make unbearable noises.' There had been 'plenty trouble with the servants', he explained (they had a nurse and a new cook):

Bessy turned out not only no better, but very much worse, than she ought to have been. Then we had an interregnum of an Early Victorian Treasure, owning to 57.—But she could remember the birth of George III. She was a good cook but was too weak to cook more than one chop per day; she ate 4 lb. of meat for every meal; she was deaf & blind & in consequence broke everything in the kitchen without knowing she had broken it. Consequently she was indignant when we remonstrated. However, she was strictly virtuous.

He had, none the less, managed to finish a draft of his new novel, *The Benefactor*.[10]

Oliver reappeared in Ford's life in 1902. He had married Zoë Pyne in 1897. In 1899 he had asked Ford to lend him £500 to go into the tobacco business, but in 1901 he had been to America, and returned 'full of literary projects'. Now he was in financial trouble again, and visited Ford to ask for help, and money. Ford wrote to Wells to enlist his help: 'I have a brother who having failed in every blessed thing that can be failed in wants to become a journalist. He hasn't, I sh^d. say, the merest inkling of what's required.' Ford told his mother, 'it's been a fearful nuisance to me'. But it became worse, when Zoë 'got so perfectly outrageous in abuse of me to my unfortunate face' that he had to forbid her to continue writing to him. 'I certainly hadn't done anything to deserve it', he said. But his telling his mother 'they've bled me so considerably & abused me so shamelessly at the same time', while *still* arranging to supply them with more money anonymously through their mother, shows him thriving on ingratitude and victimization, and provoking the abuse of his beneficiaries. This may have been unconscious while Ford was doing it, but he recognizes the trait in his fictional *alter egos*, the benefactors George Moffat or Christopher Tietjens.[11]

Then, on 23 June, an oil-lamp exploded at the Pent, damaging the table William Morris had designed for Madox Brown, and destroying the manuscript

Conrad had been working on, the second part of 'The End of the Tether'. 'The
fire ran in streams and Jess and I threw blankets and danced around on them',
he told Ford: 'my head swam; it seemed to me the earth was turning backwards.' Elsie was sunk in a mood of self-reproach (perhaps fearing she was
losing her husband, and blaming herself). She was ill; Christina had measles. But
Conrad was writing to a deadline for *Blackwood's Magazine*. Ford hired a
two-room cottage for Conrad opposite the Bungalow, and the collaboration
was on again. Until the middle of July they worked to reconstruct the lost
story, after which Ford needed to escape, taking a holiday alone in the West
Country. Now the tournament in ill-health and hypochondria was being
waged between Ford and Elsie. Back in June he had written to his mother that
he despaired of Elsie ever getting well again.[12] His fears were borne out:
Elsie's illness remained undefined at this stage, but over the next few years she
suffered from a tubercular kidney, which was not correctly diagnosed until 1908.
Until Ford unequivocally left her in 1909 she became more and more of an
invalid.

Their marriage had gone seriously wrong, and the tone of Ford's letters to Elsie
from the West Country indicates that she was estranged from him as much as she
was mourning her father. Ford was severely depressed himself, writing, 'I expect
you're tired of my letters—as of me', and, 'I feel at times more hopelessly
solitary—an[d] on so many grounds—than its possible to express, but I keep all
on going'. Elsie had followed Conrad's advice, and picked up her own writing
after her father's death. She finished 'Novel No. I', *Margaret Hever*, while Ford
was away, and sent it to Conrad for advice.[13] Perhaps she thought that she would
have to become a novelist (or another collaborator) if she were to keep her
husband at home. *Margaret Hever* was not published until 1909, when she was
losing Ford for good. She published some essays in his *English Review* at the same
time, but her literary career ended with her relationship with Ford, and her other
novel, 'Ellen Slingsby', remains unpublished. Ford's reaction to her writing was
ambivalent: 'congratulations!', he wrote, adding: 'Just as I'm feeling, with greater
and greater certitude that I shall never write anything more, that I don't want to
& don't in the least mean to try, you take up the running in this astonishing
way.—And, because you're such a much less ineffectual person than I, I haven't
the least doubt you'll succeed one way or the other.—All Joy!' It was only at his
lowest points, and after his most extreme creative exhaustions, that he would say
he'd never write again (he said he felt it after finishing *The Good Soldier*; and after
the First World War). Saying he'd stop writing was virtually saying he'd stop
living, since writing is 'an endless business of course,' as he told Elsie, 'but then
so is life—and if occupation fills up life, passes it away, that's always so much to
the good'. This depression, as his comment suggests, was involved with Elsie's
changed feelings towards him. In the same letter he writes: 'This is quite
extravagantly lovely country; if you haven't changed in this particular as in others
then it would delight your heart.' There is more in this than what you would
write to someone devastated by grief: he felt she had ceased to love him, and it

was always that doubting of his own worth that caused him to feel his world was crumbling, leaving him solitary.[14]

Ford's stoic phrase 'I keep all on going' echoes the weathered and enduring Meary Walker, who used to say 'that we can't all have everything and that the only thing to do is to "keep all on gooing"'. Ford has often been accused of indulging in self-pity, both as a man and a writer.[15] But he seems to me to be a great writer *of* pity: someone who could sympathize easily and powerfully, yet who was well aware of the dangers of excessive pity to effective writing. As with almost every aspect of literary technique, his comments on this topic are deeply paradoxical. In describing Galsworthy as 'that temperament of infinite pity and charity', he argues that Galsworthy's dedication to moral causes damages his work, allowing sentimentality to prevail over observation. And yet not only is his own account of Galsworthy a feeling tribute to one of the most humane and sympathetic of writers, but he even calls him 'Poor Jack'. By letting irony play over the nickname, he manages not to pity Galsworthy in the sense that he might justly resent; but his criticism is instinct with a pity for the loss to literature due to such talented writing being spoiled. Thus Ford can argue that novelists should be pitiless, but also that sympathy is the basis of art.[16] It is in *The Good Soldier* that he achieves the most compelling oscillations of pity and irony in words like 'poor'. And in his reminiscential writing he is able to create similar effects about himself: there is always a glimpse of irony that enables us to see that rather than listening to someone feeling sorry for themselves, we are watching a technical master produce the effect of the pitiful. Ford's advocacy of pitilessness presumably stems from feeling he needed to control his tendency to feel pathos. There is always the feeling in his writing about others' suffering—whether they are fictional or real characters—that his pity for them is at the same time pity for himself. But that is simply an honest presentation of a disconcerting truth about human sentiment, since much of our feeling for others involves an imagination of what it would be like for ourselves to suffer as they do. What is particularly interesting about his writing on Kentish countrywomen is the way it becomes a triumph over self-pity. When he feels he cannot go on, he remembers Meary Walker and he keeps all on going. His moving, beautifully simple renderings of her appearance, her hovel, her biography, fend off the temptation to see his own struggle against poverty and depression as something heroic and romantic. Before castigating him for self-pity, critics should recognize the candour with which he presents both the tendency to feel self-pity, and the way his generous sympathy for the suffering of others draws him out of his own depression.

Like Conrad, Ford was imaginatively drawn towards situations arousing both pathos and irony. Circumstances of victimization, desperation, moral and social isolation, of the misconstruction of a character's motives, appealed to his temperament and drew forth his most powerful writing. He would recall the only epigram he heard Oscar Wilde deliver—that he would not attend the dinner of a literary club because he would be 'like a poor lion in a den of savage Daniels'—and he even used it to joke about his own situation while lecturing to a female audience at University College, London.[17] The combination of pathos and paradox was irresistible, particularly since it expresses several of Ford's firmest beliefs about art and doubts about his literary standing: about how he is valued and how treated by the literary establishment. Instead of being lionized, the solitary, noble beast is savaged—by 'Daniels': prophets, those trying to impose their moral purposes and political propaganda upon the disinterested artist.

The fictional techniques Ford evolved with Conrad are themselves expressions of the temperament of a poor lion in a den of savage Daniels. Ford argued that a novel should be the history of an 'affair', a circumscribed series of episodes concerning a group of people: what, in the subtitle to *The Benefactor*, he called 'A Tale of a Small Circle'. In the affairs of a group of intimates, tragedy implies treachery: friends have become savage betrayers. Ford's cherished technical idea of *progression d'effet*—that a narrative should gather momentum, as each word adds to the cumulative effect of the whole, and as each incident contributes to the inevitable outcome—is peculiarly suited to stories in which a small circle closes around a beleaguered individual in a deadly net of circumstance. Inevitability is the primary aim of those techniques that flare in *The Good Soldier*. 'Justification'—the inclusion of enough of the background history of the affair to show that its result is pre-determined; the time-shift, which jumps forwards to tell you in advance the end towards which the entire plot is working, and which again produces the effect that events are overshadowed by their inevitable conclusion; the *coup de canon* ending, so admired in Maupassant, in which the closing words of a story strike the reader like a lightning-bolt, casting new light on what has gone before—and which carries the implication of a '*coup de grâce*', a tragic death towards which the story has progressed: all these things build a sense of inevitable destiny.[18]

This is not to say that Ford was a fatalist; rather, that he felt fiction was not effective unless it created an effect of the complexity and contingency of an actual life. And, combined with his rigorous sense of how to produce such effects, his was always a master performer's sense that what was being produced was above all an *effect*, an illusion of inevitable destiny. It is Wilde who again becomes Ford's touchstone in his reminiscences for this dual sense of art's power and its play. Wilde, who eventually—inevitably—became the poor lion savaged by the self-righteous Daniels of late-Victorian morality, appears in an attitude of extreme self-pity:

There came a dramatic moment in the lawyer's office. Wilde began to lament his wasted life. He uttered a tremendous diatribe about his great talents thrown away, his brilliant genius dragged in the mud, his early and glorious aspirations come to nothing. He became almost epic. Then he covered his face and wept. His whole body was shaken by his sobs. Humphreys [his solicitor] was extremely moved. He tried to find consolations.

Wilde took his hands down from his face. He winked at Humphreys and exclaimed triumphantly:

'Got you then, old fellow.'[19]

The 'dramatic moment' turns out to be a moment of high drama indeed, and the great talents, far from having been thrown away, are being used in the very act of lamenting their waste. Ford does not leave his paragraph ending on a note of comic dissolving of difficulties. Wilde adds that he will certainly not go to Paris to escape arrest, as his lawyer has been urging. Ford ends with a dying fall: 'He was arrested that evening.' Ford's own fiction tends to mobilize both the comedy and the pathos in a more ambiguous relationship; as here, when he overlayers with pathos Wilde's own comic subversion of the pathetic. Yet there is always the *possibility* of that authorial wink; the possibility that, even at moments of the highest pathos, the writer is saying 'Got you then'; or at least, in the act of dramatizing his feelings, he is achieving a form of objectivity, as Wilde does in his anecdote, exorcizing shame by exaggerating it into sham.

One such example of Ford, in his own person, achieving a distance from his feelings of self-pity through a cathartic expression of them, is given by David Garnett (the son of Edward and Constance). In 1908 or 1909, after Ford had been visiting the Cearne, Garnett walked with him to Westerham station:

He had been cheerful at tea, but in Squerries Park a mood of melancholy stole over him, and he sang me one melancholy song after another, some French, some German, ending with the Westmoreland folksong *Poor Old Horse*. Ford's voice was not bad, his ear was good, and the expression he put into the words of the horse's cruel master was pathetic in the extreme. . . . [Then] in the most unhappy voice Ford broke in to say something like this: 'I am that poor old horse, David. . . . The world is cruel to the old, David. It is very cruel to me . . . once I was a brilliant young poet, a famous writer . . . now I am no more use to anyone and they kick me, now they have got me down. . . . Poor old horse. . . .' I was in tears and, seeing this, Ford was also; then brushed his tears aside for a moment to look at his watch and make sure that he was not late for his train.[20]

There is no doubt that Ford felt he had been 'got down' at the time; but that does not preclude a touch of showmanship. Garnett was recollecting the episode some forty-five years later; he admits he cannot remember the exact words, and his recollection of the song is questionable (in the version printed by Edward Thomas at the end of his *The Heart of England*, there is nothing explicitly cruel about the master, who just 'frowns upon' the horse, saying 'Poor old horse'). David was always more sympathetic to Ford than was his more supercilious father. He said his parents seemed 'heartless' when he told them the story, and were just 'frankly amused' by it. 'I think the emotional display was because he was genuinely moved by the song he had been singing and improvised a suitable part to play—in fact, he dramatised a fleeting but sincere emotion', Garnett explained. Yet even he adopted the patronizing ploy Ford's performances provoked, contrasting what Ford led him to believe with his own 'fact'—a purely speculative doubt that Ford was really 'in despair, and wanted my mother's advice at a critical turning-point in his life'. He was wrong, since, as we shall see, this was the most critical turning-point of Ford's life, when he made his decisive break with Elsie, and lost contact with his children, and his closest friends, including

Conrad. Garnett was responding to Ford's pathos, though observant enough to notice the surprising self-composure beneath the breaking down. ('I have never known anyone else behave in such a way,' he added, 'but I can imagine Dickens doing so.') If Ford had winked at him, he probably would have noticed that too. Ford was not trying to trick him, or play a joke on him in the way that Wilde was having some fun with his earnest lawyer. But one gets the impression that Ford's identification with the poor old horse, and his impassioned expression of melancholy, had a strongly therapeutic value. The masterly *use* of pathos is Ford's method of controlling self-pity. Rather than viewing him as locked into a mode of self-indulgent mawkishness, one must admire the agility with which he can use words to escape from the grip of self-pity.

His letter to his mother explaining how they had had 'a most disastrous year' in 1902 is a case in point. He had 'hardly made £100 in all', he explained. But among the catalogue of illnesses and misfortunes comes the comic version of the misunderstood artist. Daisy the nurse revealed that she ('& the rest of the village') thought the Hueffers were Mohammedans because they never went to church. 'Elsie never allows currants to be put into anything & Daisy said she had been told that that was part of our Religion.' Even the Meary Walker refrain, which Ford repeats here too, summons up her good humour as well as her plight: 'Just at present both Elsie & I have mild Influenzas or very bad colds, but we have to keep all on going because of Xtmas.' The Conrads were coming to visit for Christmas.[21]

Conrad was finding it hard to work alone, and both authors were despondent about the prospects for *Romance*, which Pinker had been unable to place as a serial, and suggested they should cut. They were now forced to recognize that they had not written a best-seller. None the less, during the three weeks the Conrads spent at Winchelsea that Christmas, Conrad again drew Ford into collaborative discussions of his work. Ford gave him the encouragement he needed to begin *Nostromo*; and on 2 January Conrad sent him the manuscript of *The Rescue*, which Ford suggested rearranging.[22]

In higher spirits in the New Year, Conrad arranged a joint party for Borys and Christina. 'Cara e Illustrissima Padrona!', he wrote to Elsie, suggesting arrangements with affectionate mock-formality: 'Xna to take the head, Borys the foot of the table each before a birthday cake bearing their joined names (But we won't look upon this as a definite engagement if you doubt the wisdom of the step owing to the youthfulness of the parties).' The party was planned for 16 January 1903, the day after Borys' fifth birthday. In his best mock-ceremonial manner, Conrad sent Ford a 'Protocol of the Celebration (official)', which testifies to the exuberant friendliness Conrad would display in his manic phases. Ford, out of loyalty to Conrad's memory, always played up this side of their relationship, whereas his detractors have played it down, taking Conrad's periodic denigrations of Ford as representative:

At 3.40 the Young Lady having had barely time to smooth her plumes shall proceed (attended by the Lady Regent [Elsie]—the Lord Regent [Ford] is at liberty to swoon

for fifty minutes) shall proceed—I say—to the Baronial Kitchen (where the feast is to
be engulphed) to receive the guests with the young Cavalier.

> Then she takes her arm-chair
> at the
> High End [. . .]
> Engulphing stops
> in the
> Natural course of things.
> Then
> The Young Lady
> Arises from her armchair

and proceeding up the table on *her* right pulls a cracker with every feaster on that
side. The Young Cavalier performs the same rite on *his* right side.

> Feasters don caps out of crackers.
> A Bell rings cheerfully!
> (It is then Five of the clock)[23]

For much of January and February Ford was in London, staying with the Garnetts
('no sleep last night after a slanging match with Edward'), breakfasting with
Galsworthy, negotiating about the publication of *Romance*, and trying to 'get
impressions' of London for a book to be illustrated by William Hyde (the illustrator
of *The Cinque Ports*). 'Romance settled', he finally wrote to Elsie on 11 February.
Pinker had first said they should get £400; then he thought £230. The publishers,
Smith, Elder, agreed to an advance of only £150. The first proofs arrived on 27
March. After about eight months away from the work, Conrad and Ford began
intensive corrections. The batches of proofs kept arriving until the end of August;
but the rewriting was so extensive that after a month the publishers sent the typescript
back so that the collaborators could do their revising before the type was set. The
proof corrections were finished in September. They went up to London to deliver
the final batch, and Conrad lay down on the floor of the jolting train to do some
last-minute correcting. 'To be suddenly disturbed is apt to cause a second's real
madness', wrote Ford, remembering his last experience of collaborating on *Romance*.
He touched Conrad on the shoulder, and Conrad sprang at his throat![24] Conrad was
beginning to sink into the abyss of depression from which he would produce his next
novel, *Nostromo*, a masterpiece of self-doubt in which (through the fate of the sceptical
Martin Decoud) he was to doubt even the scepticism in which he had put his trust.
The scene in the train brought to the surface Ford's suppressed doubts about what
Conrad really thought about him. It is a quintessentially Conradian moment, a jump
of blind animal impulse. The image of Conrad's 'suffused and madly vicious face',
however, is quintessentially Fordian in its hallucinatory vision of cruelty, torment,
and betrayal (compare Leonora's outburst during the 'Protest' scene in *The Good
Soldier*: 'Her eyes were enormously distended; her face was exactly that of a person
looking into the pit of hell and seeing horrors there', p. 55). It was episodes like this
that made Ford feel that you 'never know what, at the bottom of the heart, goes
on in your companion'.

Ford never lost his admiration for Conrad's genius nor his love for the man, but there are signs during 1903 that he sought relief from the burden of their interdependence. In March he joked to Olive Garnett, pastiching James and adding: 'observe the influence on my style of the Wings of the Dove!' But Conrad may have observed the influence of James's style on Ford's latest novel, *The Benefactor*, and realized that it was indeed James who had usurped him as Ford's exemplar. When Olive visited Winchelsea for a week in the spring she found both the Hueffers 'out of sorts'. Elsie was 'rather thinner & less active than formerly', and still wearing conventional mourning clothes (over a year after her father's suicide). She had rented her brother Leonard's cottage across the road, Olive was told, because she was 'bent on "writing" ', and needed somewhere to work in the mornings. Which was true, but it probably also screened the start of a more fundamental separation. Ford complained of 'indigestion & sleeplessness'. He may have feared that the strain over *Romance* heralded a recurrence of the previous year's depression. One luncheon he attacked Olive 'à propos of Joseph & his non-understanding of women, and about Tourguénieff who did understand them'. Despite the signs of enervation, Ford's criticism is just. And when his spirits picked up the next day, and they had 'a grand discussion à propos of the psychology of Edward's celebrated article about The Wings of the Dove', one senses again that Ford was turning from Conrad to James. Later in the year it became clear that—even before publication—Conrad had lost faith in *Romance*. In June 1902 he had told Edward Garnett that although he had 'lost utterly all faith' in himself, it was his share of *Romance* that filled him 'with the least dismay'. But when, the following year, Ford added the dates '1896–1903' to the manuscript, Conrad grew hysterical. He objected that to confess to six years of labour over the book would encourage reviewers to sneer that it hadn't been worth the effort. But, as Karl says, Ford could have read this 'as a veiled attack upon the whole idea of collaboration and time "wasted" on an effort which Conrad would have liked to renounce'. Three weeks after the publication he was renouncing the book explicitly (as he would later renounce *The Inheritors* and *The Nature of a Crime*): 'Je regarde *Romance* comme une chose sans aucune importance: j'ai collaboré pendant qu'il m'était impossible de faire autre chose.' Ford can't have been unaware of Conrad's contempt for the book, even if it wasn't expressed to his face. He would certainly have been aware of the irritation Conrad expressed in a letter to Elsie about her volume of Maupassant translations:

What does Ford mean in the preface about Maupassant being or even seeming a rhetorician in the *last sentences* of the chair-mender? It is either perverseness or carelessness—or I don't know what rhetoric is. To me its sheer narrative—sheer report—bare statement of facts about horse, dogs the relations of doctor to chemist and the tears in the Marquise's eyes. If its only one of his little jokes I am sorry that he let himself become folâtre before the high altar. Its the sort of thing that hardly pays.[25]

Romance was published on 20 October 1903. The reviews were mixed, reflecting not only the compromise of literary collaboration, but the compromise that was this project. Some reviewers who expected a Stevensonian romance of adventure were baffled by a work they recognized as 'admirably clever', but found 'positively chaotic' and contrived, where 'inspiration [was] drowned with elaboration'. Others were disappointed not to find the Conrad they expected. There was also some strong praise of the kind the collaborators needed: 'one of the best romances his [Conrad's] readers are likely to remember [. . .] Here is the real thing'; 'recalls Stevenson at his best [. . .] its literary and human force are unquestionable'. But the collaborators' disappointment at such comments gauges the measure of their expectations. It soon became clear that the book was not going to repay five years of effort, let alone fulfil their hopes of popular success. Furthermore, some of the doubts voiced about the book were telling. It is indeed, in the words of one review, 'a series of pictures [. . .] rather than a coherent and skilfully planned romance'. *Romance* is divided between Ford's psychological, reminiscential impressionism and the demands of rapid narrative. The result is a book at cross-purposes with itself: too contrived an adventure to allow psychological depth; too psychologically clogged for a gripping adventure of escape. The Hueffers and Conrads remained intimate for another six years, during which Ford and Conrad continued to be involved in each other's work. But, apart from one desultory attempt in 1906 on the unfinished story, *The Nature of a Crime*, they never engaged in full-scale collaboration again.[26]

Ford turned back to older projects, revising *The Benefactor*, and reconsidering what to do with his research into Henry VIII and Katharine Howard. Elsie had to go to London to nurse her mother, who was seriously ill, needing two painful operations. Both Ford and Elsie were shaken, thinking Mrs Martindale was dying. In November Elsie fell down ten feet of stone steps and broke an arm. Ford had to ask Robert Garnett to arrange a loan of £150 to cover the medical expenses. Elsie's worries were compounded by her fear Ford no longer loved her. He tried to cajole her out of her despair:

You are really very unthinking (I can't say it as a reproach) to imagine that I don't want you or don't love you, or find you a bore—or anything:
   I've told you so often that I do & why I do & why you do & always will attract me & hold me—so often that it would be no use repeating.—But I do—& if you would use your reason you'd see that I must.
   I mean, old thing, that having been thro' so much with you being without you is to have a sense of numbness—& I couldn't get on without you. You're charming & beautiful & nice—&, what's more to the point, you're just the right thing, in character, for me. Don't you see?—don't you *see?*—We've after all so much in common that we *couldn't* get on apart—&, as you know, it's always after we've been separated for a short time that we love each other the best.—And I *do* love you: do, do, *do* believe that.[27]

Yet there *is* a reproach under the banter; and the sense of futile reiteration expresses a numbness in his love rather than his loneliness. That isn't to say he was being insincere (on the contrary, it is, between the lines, probably more expressive than he meant it to be). He too was upset at the thought of their love numbing, and—as he said to her—didn't want to be the 'sort of a scoundrel' to desert her when she was down, or make her 'unhappiness a cause' for leaving her. But over the next few years her fears were proved right.

1904: LONDON

Despite, or perhaps because of, his financial difficulties, Ford decided to move to London. Oliver and Zoë were leaving their house in Campden Hill—10 Airlie Gardens—to go to Manchester; so Ford and Elsie rented it for the first quarter of 1904, and early in January they moved in. On 13 February Olive Garnett met W. H. Hudson, Conrad, Galsworthy, and Henry James there. She recorded James saying with gloomy relish: 'I am a crushed worm, I don't even revolve now, I have ceased to turn.' Olive, evidently depressed herself, then described an outburst of her own which perhaps puts into perspective Ford's occasional arguments with her. 'I told Ford that I was on the war-path against him, and Hudson that he was a philistine. Why do I do these absurd things?' The Conrads had followed the Hueffers to London on 17 January, taking rooms close by, at 17 Gordon Place. Ford took down six of the stories of *The Mirror of the Sea* from Conrad's dictation, occasionally prompting his reminiscences, and possibly collaborating on some of the stories. It is one of Conrad's most Fordian books, owing much to one of Ford's favourite works: as Conrad explained, it is 'a volume of Sea-sketches, something in the spirit of Turgeniev's Sportsman's Sketches'. Even Jessie Conrad, who came to hate Ford, said the book 'owes a great deal to his ready and patient assistance [. . .] That book would never have come into being if Joseph Conrad had had no intelligent person with whom to talk over these intimate reminiscences.' *Nostromo* was being serialized in *T.P.'s Weekly*, and, doubting his ability to meet the deadlines, and perhaps mistrusting his dependence on Ford for moral and creative support, he wrote to Galsworthy, 'It is a sort of desperate move in the game I am playing with the shadow of destruction'. Whether Conrad realized it or not, Ford too was under the same shadow. He later described 1904 as 'the most terrible period' of both Conrad's and his own life.[1]

In February the members of the household went down one by one with the influenza that was then sweeping through London. Ford had to get in a hospital nurse—'an added flail'—so that he and Conrad could go on working. Eventually even the German cook, Johanna, collapsed, 'face downwards on the kitchen table with her varnished scarlet cheeks in a great sieve of flour'. Conrad was coming round for meals and to work on *Nostromo*, so Ford silently took over the cooking, wanting to protect him from worry and disturbance. Then Ford too went down with the influenza. Jessie Conrad fell in the street, injuring both knees. She was then discovered to have a 'valvular defect of the heart'. As she recovered physically her nerves began 'giving way', Conrad told Meldrum: 'as I write to you in her bedroom she is lying lightheaded and groaning with neuralgia in all the limbs [. . .] Half the time I feel on the verge of insanity.' Conrad's bankers failed. He had to borrow nearly £200 from Pinker to pay off his overdraft to the receivers, which once again prevented him paying back the Hueffers any of the £200 he owed them. Conrad, said Ford, was 'taken with so violent an attack of gout and nervous depression that he was quite unable to continue his installments of NOSTROMO'. Conrad had counted on Ford being able to collaborate on the novel if necessary. Now Ford had to write most of the instalment published on 9 April.[2]

No sooner had he recovered enough to go out, than the next disaster struck: 'I opened my front door with my latchkey one day and met my eldest daughter coming downstairs with her hair and clothing on fire. I put the flames out and, as they had been streaming behind her, she was not hurt. She said that, as she had done nothing to hurt the fire-fairies, she could not see why the fire-fairies should hurt her.'[3] Recalling this incident in 1930–1, Ford moves immediately into a discussion of superstition and omens, saying that the sequence of 'every imaginable and unimaginable disaster' followed upon 'the presentation of an immense opal to a member of my household'. It was to Elsie that he had given that ring, and they both came to believe that the opal was responsible for the run of ill-luck. Moser shrewdly comments that 'their fixing upon the ring [. . .] surely suggests their own sense that, however their ill-luck had manifested itself, something was radically wrong with their union'.[4]

The Face of the Night, Ford's third book of verse, was published in the spring, and he had also been working on *The Soul of London*, despite not having found a publisher for it, and despite the domestic crises. But he began to suffer from 'fits of nervousness', which developed into a devastating nervous breakdown, charac-terized by agoraphobia and lasting throughout the rest of the year. It was while trying to get rid of the opal that Ford evidently had his first attack. According to the superstition, throwing the ring into running water would have neutralized its power, so he set out to throw it into the Thames: 'At once an indescribable lassitude fell on me. I was almost unable to drag my legs along and quite incapable of getting to the Thames. I thought of dropping the opal down a gutter grating. Sewer and flood water is disagreeable, but at least it runs. But near every grating that I passed in returning, a large policeman was stationed.'[5]

Ostensibly he cannot throw the ring away in front of a policeman for fear of being thought to have stolen it. But there is also a sense that figures of (paternal?) authority are stopping him from letting his marriage go down the drain—or even making it do so (a criminal act?). When he gets back he discovers a further disaster: a large hole has been burned in his dress suit, which he needs that evening. The next day he sees some nuns, the Little Sisters of the Poor, begging. This gives him the idea to offer the opal to their Mother Superior, explaining its history to her. She gladly accepts, but immediately after Ford has handed it in at the Post Office, agoraphobia strikes him again: 'I had no sooner turned the corner of the post office than I found myself almost completely unable to walk. Campden

Hill Road assumed an aspect as steep as the side of the Righi. I could hardly drag my feet along. There began the long illness.'[6] With hindsight the breakdown appears inevitable: a physical expression of the psychological impasse of his failing marriage, his floundering career, the mental strain imposed by Conrad's demands for his involvement, the stresses of moving house and of the ensuing series of deeply upsetting accidents. Yet neither could he go away from these things, for he was overpowered by guilt about Elsie, the child-bride he had spirited away from her family, only to betray in a squalid affair with her sister, and thus to precipitate (so it may have seemed to him) her father's suicide. Now that her mother appeared to be dying too, if he were to leave her he would be leaving her alone—apart from her children, whom he loved too much to want to leave. The agoraphobia thus immobilizes him, metaphorically as well as physically. He cannot go on, nor can he go. He can't keep all on going, like Meary Walker, so he can't walk. He is prevented from casting away the ring, a symbol of their marriage. Yet when he does manage to cast it off, he is still immobilized. He had inadvertently produced a crippling double-bind in his life.

One way his 'fits of nervousness' manifested themselves was in Ford's quickness to feel threatened or offended. As he was finishing *The Soul of London* he became anxious when he heard that James also planned to write a book of London impressions. 'Lord bless you, it is all right about your book,' James reassured him: 'My work is relegated to a dim futurity [. . .] Bring yours out & find all comfort, pride & profit in it: the sooner the better; then I shall be able to crib from you freely—yet shall [be] demurely acknowledging.' And when Galsworthy, whose own books Ford had criticized in friendly but searching detail, offered some comments on the manuscript of *The Soul of London*, Ford had been angrily defensive. Unfortunately neither Galsworthy's criticisms nor Ford's response have survived, but Galsworthy's patiently conciliatory reply is revealing. In seeking to clear it up, it makes reasonably clear what the misunderstanding had been about. But it also sheds light on Ford's state of mind, and on his developing views about art:

My dear Hueffer,

I feel like a pig and an impostor for having by a slipshod annotation opened the flood gates of your wrath and let out so much of your vital energy, especially as I agree with nearly every word you say. The fact is my note was meant to say (I can't remember what it did say) that: *talking of the third state which you mention* (man looking out of club window all which I took to mean an important quiescent enjoyment of things going on round you) non-artists would feel IT, i.e. third state when they were slightly drunk and artists at other times as well. You have turned my note topsy-turvy. I quite agree with you that non-artists feel, more deeply, more personally, and pathetically than artists, because they lack the impersonal, analytic, philosophic element; or at all events they feel more deeply for all practical purposes because they have nothing outside the personal to compare with their suffering and through which to fritter down the edge thereof.

You are evidently so sick for personal reasons of the word 'artist' that I regret to have employed it, and perhaps we do not mean the same thing by the word [. . .] I use the word 'artist' to include roughly people with more of the outside eye, habit of impersonal reflection, analytical spirit, and incidentally in some cases power of expression, than the rest of mankind. I don't exalt these people, I merely say that I think they form the one half of mankind—a smaller half than the other of course [. . .]

I'm so glad you're settled in comfortably, but I shall miss you very much—it was nice to feel one could 'drop-in'. If I ever do any more 'Forsytes' I will send it to you, in the meantime why not send me Chap V and risk some more slipshod annotations? You see I thought I was going to talk the thing over with you, rubbing out any remarks as I went along.[7]

Galsworthy writes in the same letter of Ford's 'natural indignation against all the snobbish cant that is talked by painters and men of letters—d——n their eyes', which suggests that Ford was sick of the literary and artistic establishment which had roused Madox Brown's indignation before him. But Ford's edginess, and Galsworthy's phrasing, indicate reasons more personal still. Ford had found it impossible to work with the temperamental Hyde, the artist who was to have illustrated *The Soul of London*. His association with Conrad had taken its toll. It is significant that his first major work after *Romance* was not a novel, but the impressionistic, though discursive, *The Soul of London*. What appears particularly to have annoyed him is what he misunderstood to be Galsworthy's exalting of the artist above the rest of mankind. His own recurrent division of humanity into artist and 'the stuff to fill graveyards' can sometimes sound like just such an exaltation. But Ford's ambivalence about the word 'artist' must be borne in mind, as must his periodic envy of the dead. One of the impulses behind the trilogy about *England and the English*, and *The Heart of the Country* in particular, was the desire to show how the stuff to fill graveyards includes people like Meary Walker: unhonoured and unremembered figures whose humanity seemed superior to the other people (mostly artists) Ford knew; the desire to proclaim the beauty of the humble and of the impotent, as Kropotkin had urged him a decade before.

The passage from *The Soul of London* that Galsworthy discusses is one which brings out a further ambivalence about art. It is a deeply personal passage; one which stands as a defence of impressionist narrative, and which brings out the connections between enervation and impressionism:

'It takes a good deal out of you,' this leisured life of display. You rush more or less feverishly, gathering scalps of one sort or another [. . .] But each of these things sinks back into the mere background of your you. You are, on the relentless current of your life, whirled past them as, in a train, you are whirled past a succession of beautiful landscapes [. . .]

You carry away from it a vague kaleidoscope picture—lights in clusters, the bare shoulders of women, white flannel on green turf in the sunlight, darkened drawing rooms with nasal voices chanting parodies of prayers, the up and down strokes of fiddle bows, the flicker of fifty couples whirling round before you as with a touch of headache you stood in a doorway, a vague recollection of a brilliant anecdote, the fag end of a conversation beneath the palms of a dimmed conservatory, and a fatigue and a feverish idea that if you had missed any one of these unimportant things you would have missed life [. . .] And, the breaks being less marked, the life itself is the more laborious and less of a life. For it is in the breaks, in the marking time, that the course of a life becomes visible and sensible. You realise it only in leisures within that laborious leisure; you realise it, in fact, best when, with your hands deep in your trouser pockets, or listless on your watch-chain, you stand, unthinking, speculating on nothing, looking down on the unceasing, hushed, and constantly changing defile of traffic below your club windows. The vaguest thoughts flit through your brain: the knot on a whip, the cockade on a coachman's hat, the sprawl of a large woman in a victoria, the windshield in front of an automobile. You live only with your eyes, and they lull you. So Time becomes manifest like a slow pulse, the world stands still; a four-wheeler takes as it were two years to crawl from one lamp-post to another, and the rustle of newspapers behind your back in the dark recesses of the room might be a tide chafing upon the pebbles. That is your deep and blessed leisure: the pause in the beat of the clock that comes now and then to make life seem worth going on with. Without that there would be an end of us.

For, whether we are of the leisured class, whether we are laundry-women, agricultural labourers, dock labourers, or bank clerks, it is that third state that makes us live. Brahmins would call it contemplation; the French might use the word *assoupissement*. It would be incorrect to call it reverie since it is merely a suspension of the intellectual faculties; it is a bathing in the visible world: it is a third state between work and amusement—perhaps it is the real Leisure.[8]

The clubman air might sound now like more of a pose than it was. Ford was a member of the National Liberal Club; and although he was not a member of the leisured class, he uses the club atmosphere to great effect in conjuring up a haven in the midst of the bustling city. 'Bathing in the visible world' is precisely what some critics of impressionism object to. Ezra Pound, for example, said it was too much of 'the eye'—and as a luxuriating in subjectivity it can also be too much of the 'I'. But this passage is the best explanation we have of *why* Ford tended to organize his narratives around series of scenes, moments of intense visual arrest. Though not explicitly about art, it has a deep affinity with his sense of how the arts 'do not instruct: they sensitize'. As he was to put it later: 'the immediate effect of the contemplation of matchless things is a marking time of the spirit, a deep oblivion of the material passions of the world surrounding you'. What is so curiously effective in the passage from *The Soul of London*, and a characteristic example of how Ford's works of art are creatively at odds with his critical pronouncements, is the way his writing about this 'suspension of the intellectual faculties' is alive with nuances of all the things which have been suspended. Those evocative images of the whip, the cockade, the sprawling woman, are fraught with hints of aggression, hurry, rank, and sex. The 'defile' of traffic is both the order of the city and its corruption. There is a lurking paranoid sense in that rustling 'behind your back in the dark recesses of the room': it is too close to 'whispering behind your back' for comfort. More importantly, there is a deeply paradoxical aspect to Ford's framing of this 'third state'. It is life appearing to stop which makes it worth going on with. This temporal paradox is central to impressionist art, which freezes time in order to suggest its processes; and it can be traced back to, say, Pater's celebration of the 'exquisite pauses in time' composed by the School of Giorgione: pauses in which, 'arrested thus, we seem to be spectators of all the fulness of existence, and which are like consummate extract or quintessence of life'. What Ford adds to this mode of response is the idea that any sense of the completeness of existence implies its completedness; that the timeless stasis of art connotes also the quintessence of death. The intimations of death and suicide are unmistakable. The life that such experiences make it seem worth going on with might be the frenetic social life that has been sketched; or it might be life *tout court*. For someone like Ford, who since his father's death had felt that he too might at any moment die of heart failure, the thought of a 'slow pulse', then a 'pause in the beat' would signal that life might be about to stop going on. A poignant poem written not long before, 'Sidera Cadentia', an oblique elegy for Queen Victoria's death, makes the same connection. The falling star, or the death for which it is an image, produces:

> A shock,
> A change in the beat of the clock;
> And the ultimate change that we fear feels a little less far.[9]

It is important to Ford, as to Galsworthy, that it is not only artists who attain this third state of abstractedness: something very close to a visionary trance or ecstasy. Yet it is equally (if paradoxically) important to him that such states can also characterize the experience of art—the 'insight' that he tentatively suggests unites his 'Nice People', enabling them to 'see beyond' the physical and the temporal.[10]

Part of Ford's anger towards Galsworthy comes from his doubts about himself as a man as well as an artist. As the financial pressures of family life grew unmanageable, his plans for commercial success with Conrad had foundered, and now his mental stability came under question, Ford was wondering whether he could be a 'nice' person as well as an artist. His involvement with Conrad had revealed to him the intolerable mental strain artists can exert on their companions. There is an awkwardness about the nursery term, which perhaps suggests the unvoiceable matters underlying the judgement: estrangement from Elsie, perhaps the affair with Mary, doubts about his ability to write well enough to make a living.

The description in the passage from *The Soul of London* of how 'you live only with your eyes' is thus at once a statement of a universal human tendency to moments of abstraction, and also an image of how a certain kind of artist—an impressionist—sees the world, and by extension how the viewer or reader experiences that artist's work. It could stand as a suggestive description of how we engross ourselves in reading, oblivious to our other senses, and not even aware of the words on the page as words, but something like a window one can see 'through' or 'beyond'. Similarly, the phrase 'time becomes manifest like a slow pulse' is evocative not only of a particular mode of perceiving the life around you, or your own life. It could also stand for the way in which fiction as time-conscious as that of Ford or Conrad makes one aware of the temporality of a character's life. It is pre-eminently in the time-shifts and temporal foreshortenings of fiction that 'a life becomes visible and sensible'. The description of 'the third state' is revealing about the time-shift—Ford's favourite technical device. The idea of a pause, or a change, in the beat of the clock is suggestive of how a novelist might change the rhythm or sequence of a narrative's ordering to give form to the course of a life. The very notion of a particular moment giving meaning to a whole life draws on the idea of death being the point that stamps the value on a life ('call no man happy until he is dead'). The Fordian time-shift characteristically reminds us of the death towards which the story is always leading, or which casts its shadow over the entire story. The first sentence about Meary Walker in 'Nice People' does this in miniature: 'I knew very intimately later an old country woman—she died last month.' Throughout the rest of the recollections we are aware of the proximity of this death. Ford's handling of time in narrative is thus intended to produce effects in the reader akin to the 'third state' of suspended fascination; and, as in the description of that state, the technical means serve to heighten the ironic, the pathetic, and the elegiac. Ford's nervous breakdown was the type of event that causes someone to re-evaluate the shape of their life. He felt it coming while he was writing *The Soul of London*—the very term 'soul', *psyche*, conveys a disconcertingly psychological approach to its subject. The states of mind it re-creates bear witness to his mental strain. It is a book of neurasthenia, enervation; but never an enervated book. On the edge of a severe mental collapse, Ford saw much about how his best writing worked. The insights of the trilogy *England and the English* (*The Soul of London*, *The Heart of the Country*, *The Spirit of the People*) are moving records of a fraught sensibility. But they are more far-reaching, revealing structures of feeling that are manifested in everything else he wrote.

In the spring of 1904 Ford wrote to W. H. Hudson, who was then in Wiltshire, to ask him to recommend a suitable farmhouse where he and his ailing entourage could recuperate. As soon as *The Soul of London* was complete he left Campden Hill for the New Forest, where he met Hudson and went walking with him. Twenty years later he recalled Hudson's talk about rooks, which was to be a model for what Ford hoped to achieve (specifically in the sequel to *The Soul of London*, *The Heart of the Country*; but generally in all his reminiscential impressionism):

This very tall man was voicing thus not his own reflections; he was following out the convolutions of the peasant intelligence, talking half humorously, and entirely at leisure. It was, indeed, this slow measure of his expressed thoughts that made him so charming a companion, since the thought expressed was just pure thought without any motive. It was neither thought to go into a book nor thought meant to impress a hearer . . .

Hudson suggested the village of Brockenhurst, saying it was 'the best country in England'. Once Ford was settled in Yew Tree Cottage, Setley (just outside Brockenhurst), Johanna and the children were dispatched to join him. The trip was an escape from the 'murderous house' on Campden Hill, not an escape from his family. By 8 April he appeared to be improving, writing to Elsie: 'I must have covered quite a mile & a half without getting dizzy'. Elsie joined them on the 12th. Conrad was quick to seize the lead in the competition of miseries, writing:

I am sorry for Your news—glad that you are better and I hope that Elsie and the chicks are flourishing.

Jessie has been carried downstairs yesterday—for the first time. She is so far a cripple. Massage, electricity and so on they say may restore her walking. I trust she will get all that but I don't *see* it. I have been bad all the time. 2nd part of *N[ostromo]* finished yesterday. It seems that I must give up but I suppose I won't.[11]

'I am awfully grieved to hear of your state', he wrote a month later: 'Mine though not identical is just as bad in its way and surely less excusable.' Moser argues that Conrad 'could not bear the notion of Ford's illness. While Ford was falling apart, Conrad was writing about the suicide of his own alter-ego, Decoud, and about Nostromo's bizarre, self-destructive passion for the sister of his betrothed'; though he doubts that Conrad knew that 'Ford was bearing the guilt of his secret affair with Mary Martindale'.

In May the Hueffers moved to Bridge House, Winterbourne Stoke, a village on Salisbury Plain only three miles from Stonehenge. Ford was dejected and perplexed enough by what had happened to him; but he was perhaps also assuming Conrad's tone when he wrote to his mother: 'This is rather a nice place, very hidden among the downs & extremely remote from civilisation. We have two cottages—in one of which I'm writing & in the other the daily life of the house proceeds. The children are in rude health: Elsie is well and I'm—umberufen [*sic*]—picking up slowly. I trust its surely, but in this vale of tears one never knows.'[12] *Unberufen*—literally 'unsummoned'—is said to placate Nemesis after a remark that might seem hubristic. It is an index to Ford's increasing tendency to think of his suffering as a matter of superstition that the phrase recurs continually in his letters. He was later to offer an explanation of superstition which relates it suggestively to hypochondria: 'As the power of the priest has waned and our thoughts are less and less fixed on the affairs of the next world, so the power of physical superstition has gained and gained.'[13] Escape from civilization didn't mean escaping from civilization's troubles. He was under increasing financial pressure. Robert Garnett had arranged a loan of a further £100 in March. His domestic troubles had simply been transplanted. The double cottages at Winterbourne Stoke reproduced the Hueffers' Winchelsea arrangements. Ford was seeking to pull himself out of his enervation by going back to his work on Henry VIII and Katharine Howard. But the daily life of the houses, the rudely healthy children, a suffering wife, and a failing marriage were evidently pressing in upon his concentration. It was beginning to seem as if they could not be happy in any home, or combination of them.[14]

By July the pattern of neurasthenia and accidents had returned. On 8 July Olive Garnett wrote that 'Elsie who has burnt her face with carbolic acid wishes me to go down to Salisbury at once'. She went on the 11th, and stayed for ten days. The publication of her nephew David Garnett's *The Golden Echo* nearly a half-century later prompted her to write a memorandum, expanding upon her diary entries. Together they form the best surviving record of Ford's state at the time:

Ford met me with trap & seemed pleased to see me. I think I had never heard of neurasthenia; & for a few days all went well; but it was a hot July, & on leaving Lake House (to which a College friend had given me a general invitation), to walk over the Plain to Amesbury [a walk of five or six miles], Ford had an attack of agoraphobia, & said if I didnt take his arm he would fall down. I held on in all the blaze for miles, it seemed to me, but the town reached, he walked off briskly to get tobacco and a shave; and when I pointed this out to Elsie she said 'nerves'. He can't cross wide open spaces. She said he had already consulted a local doctor. We explored further & went to Stonehenge, but he got worse. Elsie was usually silent while I argued & philosophised on our walks. But at last he burst out in a vitriolic attack on 'respectable' Garnetts & said '*I* would rather be notorious & hanged,' and was tearful: and next day on the plain as we lay about in the heat, we all wept. It seemed so hopeless. I was put up in a cottage across the road, & next morning Elsie came over & woke me & said I could catch the nine o'clock bus, with the market-women to Salisbury. Ford was asleep & wouldn't be up till mid-day. He had gone down stairs at 2 A.M. & afraid that he might commit suicide, she had crept after him, & found he was only putting the kettle on. Evidently I could do no good by staying longer & had better go.[15]

As Moser argues, Olive's diary also identifies the underlying causes of the couple's despair: Ford's failure to place *The Benefactor* or *The Soul of London*, and their doubts about the prospects for their marriage. Elsie and Ford returned to London on 30 July 1904, and Harri Martindale took Ford to see a specialist, Dr Tunnicliffe, who told him to leave England without Elsie. Olive recorded the verdict: ' "Nervous break-down; no work, diet, a sea voyage, *might* be well in two years, couldn't say" ', and added: 'Bromides & peppermint.' They asked her to send for another doctor for a second opinion, but he was away on holiday. Elsie wrote to her mother-in-law that Tunnicliffe's proposal would be 'hard to bear as we have never once been separated for so long since our marriage'.[16] She never wanted a separation, and never accepted his leaving her, even for years after he had unequivocally left; but she must have realized that, even in the doctor's view, their marriage was compounding Ford's distress; and that a further degree of separation only threatened an eventual parting.

They hadn't enough money for a sea voyage, so Olive Garnett suggested that Ford should visit his Hüffer relatives instead. Dr Tunnicliffe approved, so on 6 August, after going with Edward Garnett for a brief visit at the Cearne, Ford left for a five-month stay in Germany. 'I arrived safely in Rotterdam,' he wrote to

Elsie from a boat on the Rhine, 'Robert [Garnett] & M[rs.] H.[ueffer] supporting me on either side as far as Blackwall.' Elsie wrote to tell Henry James what had happened. 'What you tell me of your husband's condition, past and actual, excites my liveliest sympathy for both of you,' he replied,' 'and affects me as a very pathetic story indeed—even as an almost tragic one.'[17]

1904: GERMANY

I shall never utter the uttermost secrets aright
They lie so deep

('Night Piece')

Ford wrote regularly to Elsie and the children from Germany, not only because he missed them, but because he clearly needed to describe in writing his hypersensitive responses. His writing of 1904–5 contains harrowing passages which give a rare literary record of the phases of a nervous breakdown. This first letter is representative in its account of unsettling experiences, tempering self-pity with self-dramatizing humour; and in its rapid swings of mood, as his attempts to rouse his own spirits keep sinking back into depression:

I had a moderately nice crossing, not getting much sleep & being kicked out of my berth at 4—at least the steward delicately drew a curtain & left me, in my bed, exposed to the gaze of innumerable virgins in the other side of the saloon, so I thought it best to arise & dress after shrieking to the steward to pull the curtain again.—I *walked across Rotterdam*! to the Rhine steamer accompanied by a little German fellow passenger.—I have talked to everybody on board &, in that way keep up my spirits wh., naturally, sink when I'm alone.

I got on very well at the Cearne: Ed. talked of my writing a 'Holbein' wh. w$^{d.}$ almost pay these expenses if I went to Berlin and Basel to see the pictures there [. . .] I had a tremendous attack of dyspepsia this morning—but I had been rather upset because a Clayton boy stopping at the Cearne had an epileptic fit right on top of me just as I was leaving.[1]

He went to Boppard, a small town on the Rhine south of Coblenz, to visit one of his Hüffer aunts, Emma Goesen, and her daughter Mimi. One of his favourite uncles, Hermann Hüffer, a history professor at Bonn, was dying: 'it shocked me dreadfully to see him quite blind and impotent', wrote Ford, himself powerless to walk and troubled about his eyes. This shock, together with anxieties about money, his inability to write, and the state of his marriage all weighed on his mind, and he suffered relapses and collapses. Towards the end of August he was well enough to travel again, and moved north to Telgte, in Westphalia (near what is still the prime Hüffer haunt, Münster), where a second Hüffer aunt, Laura Schmedding, occupied 'a whole small hotel'. 'My cousins adore me—or behave as if they did', he wrote to Olive Garnett, adding: 'And, oh, it does one good to be adored sometimes!' 'I am treated here like a duke', he told her in a later postcard, 'because they have only just discovered the P.[re-] R.[aphaelite] B.[rotherhood] & the Great here fall down & worship when I produce my card.' After only three weeks in Germany he was beginning to feel a powerful affinity with his father's homeland that had never been his home, despite the locals' fears of growing tension in the towns: 'These things interest me & even agitate me', he wrote to Olive, discussing how the Prussian authorities were trying to discredit the Social Democrats by attributing all the violence to them. 'Germany all over is growing bitter & altering very much. I can notice it myself', he continued, perhaps because he could notice it in himself, '& Westfalen of course is my own country much more even than England—where I've no more any roots, as it were. Here I've a great many—besides the fact that I feel that I'm really liked & understood by everyone down to the smallest cötter [cottage-dweller].' He then breaks off in a characteristic recognition that he is sinking back towards self-pity: 'But probably all this stuff bores you. . . .' His feeling that he had found recognition and affection buoyed him up, even lent a manic edge to some of his experiences: 'I'm miles better', he told Olive, making 'miles' the measure of his temporarily restored mobility:

Except for sheer physical weakness I can walk like any other Xtian.—In Cologne the day before yesterday I positively walked about for three hours: attended mass at the Cathedral & so on.— You can't imagine the thrill of joy it gave me to be once more in the crowd of a large city. It's always been 'thrilling'—on that occasion it was one of those joys that one has only once or twice upon Earth.

Of course it meant a considerable reaction of nervous depression—naturally one has to pay for one's joys.—But that has—*unberufen*—begun to grow less.[2]

The musing and phrasing here perhaps has to do with the fact that Telgte, a kind of Westphalian Lourdes, attracted crowds of walking and riding Christians. The same letter contains a full description of the shrine ('a really wonderful statue of [the Blessed Virgin Mary]—13[th.] century—was discovered in 1650 in a hollow oak'), and describes the variety of the pilgrims, and the 'silver arms, legs, ships' hung around the statue in the hope of miraculous protections and cures. Ford's letters to Elsie from this time, doubting the wisdom of sending Christina to the convent school in Rye, La Sagesse, do not reveal him to be orthodoxly Roman Catholic. Nevertheless, his joy in the cathedral, and his preoccupation with the faith of Telgte's pilgrims, suggests that he too felt his mental illness religiously, perhaps as retribution visited upon him for sins (Freud thought that the anxiety felt in agoraphobia was the ego's fear of sexual temptation), but also as something that could be alleviated by faith, by miracle, turning him into a newly walking Christian. It was a good omen that he was taking a reanimated interest in his surroundings; but, as he appears to have sensed, the excitement was itself an omen of depression, a symptom of continuing nervous volatility.[3]

Still in this introspective and observant letter, Ford is stirred by thinking about his roots and his past into thinking about memory and narration. It is his earliest formulation to himself of the importance of reminiscence. So far he had written little reminiscence of his own, but it was to become one of his major modes of writing. Discussing the feeling of rootedness, he tells Olive:

You may ascribe it, however, to y^r mysterious land-attraction: I ascribe it simply to the material fact of knowing the same places & their association.—You meet people in hotels & naturally talk to them—naturally ab^t the places that you know or are going to, since you *can't* talk ab^t y^r self or y^r life.—Naturally, too, you are attracted to the people who know y^r places, for you can talk best with them [...] If [...] I meet a man who knows people that I know—in Westf.[alia] or Eng.[land], naturally I sit talking with him for a long time & we discover mutual sympathies—wh. aren't so good as differences for conversational purposes. It is not, believe me, anything telepathic: it is merely that man is a gregarious animal who delights to know his 'associations' by talking them over.

For, for that purpose, memory is given to us.

He wrote a cheerily miserable letter to Elsie touching on their relationship: 'But, after all, as to being dependent on one another, I suppose it's better to have someone really intimate with one than no one—& you can't, in this life have intimacy, without interdependence. . . .' The pained logic suggests that what you can have is what he had begun to feel he had had with Conrad, and was perhaps beginning to have with Elsie: interdependence without intimacy. Elsie, who given the social ethos of the time could not but be dependent on Ford for her identity as well as for her livelihood, was desperately worried. A later letter from Ford hints at what she might have been writing. He tells of an unsuccessful expedition with his cousin Mimi Goesen, and reports that she complained about it being Ford whom the hosts wanted to see, not her. 'Thus, you see', Ford tells Elsie, 'my Fate pursues me over land and rivers.'[4] The implication is that Elsie would say similar things, and that she had come to resent the fact that almost all their friends were Ford's friends, interested in him and his writing. She must have felt increasingly that she was left alone with the children while Ford went off to collaborate, or to gather impressions, or to take a continental 'cure'. And this perhaps suggests another motive behind her increasing literary activity, and attempt to get Conrad involved in her Maupassant translations and her own novel. She developed headaches, and started writing letters wringing Ford's heart about her state just as he was wringing hers about his. Because he felt guilty about having left her to cope with the children, debts, the move back to Winchelsea, and loneliness, while he was travelling, he tended to emphasize his illness; but this only made her more depressed. 'As for my letter having been strange in tone,' he wrote to her from Telgte, 'it was merely in answer to one of yours that seemed to me to be strange [...] It's obviously absurd to imagine that I think of you & the Kiddies as worries—I don't, I think of you very tenderly always.'[5] 'Of course I don't believe what you say as to having lost y^r looks', he reassured her in a later letter. But what must have been less than reassuring was his feeling at home in Germany just when she had ceased to feel so at Winchelsea. He wrote after she had moved back and written that she felt miserable in the Bungalow: 'I trust it was only a passing mood & that, when you get really settled you will have once

more a home-feeling [. . .] For, after all, if my roots are here, aren't y^rs. in W. . . .'
He even suggested, 'if I c^d. get a German connexion we might all, really, come
over to Germany for good'. That phrasing—'once more a home-feeling'—shows
how he was beginning to feel his language as well as his nationality as doubled.
He apologized to Elsie: 'I'm really getting to write an abominable mixture of
German-English.'[6]

'It's in a sense good to be here where one feels one has roots', he wrote to her
as he had to Olive; 'there isn't at least the tremendous feeling of loneliness & the
end of the world that I had latterly in England.—I feel sometimes when I'm rather
collapsible in the street, that here it would not matter—that people would
understand . . .' At this point he adds: 'However: this is rather egotistical.' It is
striking how, throughout all his very real suffering, made worse by his feeling that
it was 'purely imaginary', he is none the less observing and commenting on what
is happening to him. He suffers as both the victim and the novelist of the illness,
and the insights of his disabling state were later to enable his writing. As he
remarked to Elsie, 'I'm really having experiences wh. ought to provide good
"copy" sooner or later'. To distract Elsie from her own anxieties, he gave one
lively example, an account of meeting the poet and critic Levin Schücking:

I'm sure you'd have fallen in love with him. He's in face *exactly* like Stephen Crane,
only quite dark, 6 ft 6 high & dressed in brown corduroy.—He's naturally a poet. And
to sit before the great grate, with big logs on the dogs, burning in the great Georgian
drawing room with all the portraits of Schückings from centuries back, on the walls
& an ancient garden, all alleys, clipped hedges, old trees & moonlight & mist—& to
listen to Levin reading his own poems with tremendous force & verve in a sort of
suppressed baying voice—all that was most memorable really.

He read his own verses too, and the appreciative audience gave him a momentarily
renewed sense of his own powers. After 'a couple of days' violent discussion & long
walks' he said he felt none the worse. The excursion had been intellectually
stimulating: 'you've no idea how d——d intelligent these people are', he told Elsie.
'They take one's own points and interpret them—I mean the technical ones—before one does oneself.' But a relapse followed hard upon the exhilaration.[7]

Towards the middle of September Ford returned to Boppard, where he was
treated 'as a sort of demigod'. As with the intellectual ambience, the German
attitude towards mental illness made him feel at home. 'There's such a lot of
nervous breakdown in the land', he wrote to Elsie. 'They've a regular name for
lack of walking power here: Platz Angst.' It even appeared to be a Hüffer
trait—Mimi and three other cousins had the same trouble. For the first time in
months he was able to sleep without bromides, and he was able to say, 'except for
intervals, I can now walk anywhere, more particularly when I've some one with
me'. And yet any sense of recovery was precarious. He explained to Elsie why he
could not explain: 'As for my state of mind: it's impossible to explain except by
long & morbid self-analyses. These things are mostly part of the "disease" &, the
less said about them, the better.' What he did say about them expresses a sense

of impasse in which going on and not going on seem equally intolerable: 'when I can walk I'm depressed: when I'm cheerful I can't walk.' He *could* think of working, however—he needed money—and decided to return to his book on Holbein, despite the fact that Tante Laura had paid him the equivalent of a publisher's advance *not* to write it—a medical rather than a critical expedient. Perhaps because he was beginning to worry about work and money again, his condition did not improve, and the first of a series of dismal cures was administered: some of his teeth were pulled out. He was also worried about his eyesight.[8]

On 3 October 1904 he set off on what had originally been meant as a round trip, taking in Basel, Dresden, Darmstadt, Leipzig, and Berlin, to look at the Holbeins. He was still in a morbid state, and his work exacerbated rather than alleviated it. When he wrote a postcard to Olive Garnett he wrote over the picture of Basel: 'Here I am, hard at Holbein, whom I've been chasing all over Germany.' But the second sentence is drawn inexorably towards the painting that most affected him: 'Certainly, the "*Dead Man*" is a thing to impress a young lady—or anybody else' (any *body* else?) It was the same study of Christ in the tomb which transfixed Dostoevsky, who describes it in *The Idiot*.[9] What Ford wrote about the painting, possibly at this time, is clear about why the picture fascinated him:

The *Dead Man* is a frank piece of realism. The agonised, open mouth and the opened eyes add something to the horror of the visual conception, but they are all that Holbein added for the purpose of dramatisation, and one may doubt to what extent they serve that purpose. Otherwise it is just a dead man. Its 'literary' genesis and what it 'means' remain mysteries. No doubt Holbein meant that each beholder should interpret it for himself; each beholder must, at least, so interpret it. The inscription on the rock and the pierced side rudimentarily convert this dead man into a counterfeit presentment of that man who died that death might cease. Nevertheless it remains open to us to doubt whether these attributions were more than an after-thought.

The subject of Death was one that very much pre-occupied Holbein and his world. There were then, as it were, so many fewer half-way houses to the grave: prolonged illnesses, states of suspended animation, precarious existences in draught-proof environment or what one will, were then unknown. You were alive: or you were dead; you were very instinct with life: the arrow struck you, the scythe mowed you down. Thus Death and Life became abstractions that were omnipresent, and, the attributes of Death being the more palpable, Death rather than Life was the preoccupation of the living [. . .] It is the picture of the human entity at its last stage as an individual: the next step must inevitably be its resolution into those elements which can only again be brought together at the beginning of the next stage. It is the one step further—the painting of the inscription upon the rock and of the wound in the side—that identifies this man, dead, and trembling on the verge of dissolution, with that Man, dead, who died that mankind might go its one stage further towards an eternity of joy and praise. And, by thus turning a dead man into *the* Dead Man, Holbein performs, in the realm of literary ideas, a very tremendous fact with a very small exertion—for it is impossible to imagine a human being who will not be brought to a standstill and made to think *some* sort of thoughts before what is, after all, a masterpiece of pure art. It was that, perhaps, that Holbein had in his mind.[10]

This is the writing of someone who has felt himself near death, on the verge of dissolution; and who has felt that nervous breakdowns, or sanatoria, were half-way houses to death: prolonged illnesses, states of suspended animation, precarious existences indeed. As with the letter to Olive Garnett about feeling joy in Cologne Cathedral, it is the writing of a man whose mental distress and thoughts about his extinction made him think about religion. The repetitiousness enacts Ford's own preoccupation with death, and his own fascination before the painting: he has been brought to a standstill by the contemplation of the fact that brings us all to a standstill. There is the suggestion here of how the fear of death was involved in Ford's agoraphobia: a fear which stopped him making 'one step further', and which he could only allay through making *artistic* steps forward. Ford was later to perfect for himself the art which can produce tremendous effects with very small exertions (the way *Parade's End* will hint that *Chris*topher Tietjens will end up as another such a Dead Man is one example). But here what is striking is the way the picture takes hold of Ford's mind in its moment of morbid susceptibility, and shows him his own death and redemption. For if the painting ministers to his suicidal imaginings, it also shows how, as an artist, he can redeem others' (and his own) perplexities. It is, finally, an example of Ford's complex attitude to biography. Three pages earlier he parodies 'the German-hypothetic biographers', giving a fanciful impression of a possible dramatic situation behind a portrait. Here the analysis is doubly biographical: wondering at the identity of the dead man, and at the artist's intention. But Ford's final hypothesis is about Holbein as an artist: that what he had in mind was to grip his audience by the throat. What distinguishes the artist from the stuff to fill graveyards is his ability to bring others to a standstill.

Holbein was important to Ford in other ways. His monograph contains one of his earlier elaborations of a distinction between two kinds of art that was becoming one of the axes of his aesthetics. He compares Holbein with Dürer: 'Dürer could not refrain from commenting upon life, Holbein's comments were of little importance'; 'Dürer, then, had imagination where Holbein had only vision and invention'; 'we may *believe* in what Holbein painted, but in looking at Dürer's work we can never be quite assured that he is an unprejudiced transcriber'.[11] The terms are ones Ford uses about writing too, and reflect back upon the kind of writer he tried to be. The overall impression is that he finds Holbein's art the more congenial, for eschewing propaganda, for being believable. Yet Dürer's 'imagination', and the unreliability of his transcriptions, makes him sound the more Fordian. Ford's aesthetic sympathies are dually with both kinds, of course. His own best work combines vision and imagination; it creates a dual effect of belief and uncertainty.

After a week at Basel, viewing Holbeins and visiting Kaufmann cousins (the descendants of Francis Hueffer's mother, Julia *née* Kaufmann), Ford had his

worst breakdown. The Kaufmanns transferred him to the *Kuranstalt* (sanatorium)
at Mammern, on the Bodensee (Lake Constance). The first doctor he saw there
told him that his only trouble was that he had been starving himself to death; but
the proffered 'cure' only made him weaker. He described the routine on a
postcard to Katharine: 'Dearest Kid, Here is where pumpums is now: he has got
to get up at 6 o'clock & sit in a bath for an hour: at 11 o'clock he has an electric
bath & at 3 a cold footbath.'[12] In *Return to Yesterday*, written over a quarter of a
century later, Ford devoted a chapter to this period of his life, 'Some Cures'. As
with his book on Conrad, he presents this instalment of his 'volumes of memories'
as 'a novel' rather than an autobiography, saying: 'I have tried to keep myself out
of this work as much as I could—but try as hard as one may after self-effacement
the great "I," like cheerfulness will come creeping in' (as it does three times in
this comic sentence). The descriptions of his German nerve cures are like that:
they efface his psychological problems, foregrounding instead vivid, entertaining
impressions of the futile and demoralizing regimes at the sanatoria. The reminiscences can, taken at face value, be misleading, since in places he appears to be
denying that he had any mental illness:

As a matter of fact I was suffering from a slight fluttering of the heart which, after
periods of intense overwork and fatigue, caused—and indeed does still cause—me to
feel slightly faint for a second or two. This will naturally sometimes happen in the
street. The result therefore a little resembles agoraphobia which is, in effect, a disease
of the will-power and may be attributable to sexual disorders—but which equally well
may not.[13]

But as so often, what looks like denial or evasion or fiction in Ford's writing about
himself is only partly that. (Palpitations—like agoraphobia—can be brought on by
an anxiety neurosis.) When taken in the context of the work, it is only one voice
among two: a stiff-upper-lip suppression of feelings that none the less manage to
get expressed in the chapter as a whole—in, for example, the slippage between
the 'cheerfulness' that comes creeping in when he discusses his heart, and our
knowledge that heart defects were not cheerful subjects for him and his family;
or between his writing about having been depressed while seeming to deny that
too:

From 1903 to 1906 illness removed me from most activities. The illness was purely
imaginary; that made it none the better. It was enhanced by wickedly unskilful doctoring. In those days I wandered from nerve-cure to nerve-cure [...] I
suffered from what was diagnosed as agoraphobia and intense depression. I had
nothing specific to be depressed about. But the memory of those years is of one
uninterrupted mental agony and nothing marked them off one from the other. They
were lost years.[14]

When he says 'I had nothing specific to be depressed about' it sounds at first as
if he is rebutting the ('unskilful'?) diagnosis of 'intense depression'. And yet the
lost years could not have been 'uninterrupted mental agony' unless something was
seriously wrong, and not just with the doctors. Similarly, to call the illness 'purely

imaginary' could either be to call it non-existent, or to call it an illness of the imagination. Either way, it is once again a form of imitating his grandfather, who himself had a melancholic breakdown in 1853 and had left his wife and children for a month or so. Madox Brown had been 32 then; Ford was now 30. Brown later said he had suffered much from 'imaginary nervousness', adding that 'no man ever does any good in the world without passing through the phase some time between the ages of thirty and forty'—a comment Ford recorded in his biography of his grandfather. Ford later qualifies the notion that his agoraphobia was 'imaginary', saying it was 'in fact' due to heart palpitations. But the cheerlessness of his 1904 'I' comes creeping in, with the suspicion that even an apparently physical manifestation can have psychological causes, and that this is particularly true of heart conditions—which, as Ford knew so intimately when he wrote *The Good Soldier*, often get used as metaphors for emotional and psychological states. The impression that he conveys in *Return to Yesterday* by his complex handling of his years of breakdown is a characteristic dual effect: of someone both believing and not believing that he is really suffering. Saying he had 'nothing specific to be depressed about' may just mean that everything depressed him, or it may indicate that by 1930 he had needed to repress (in his own mind) the actual circumstances of the breakdown: the affair with Mary, the collapsing of his marriage, his agoraphobic hopelessness and helplessness, may all have been too painful to dwell upon even so long afterwards. Or it may have been a matter of literary—and social—tact to suppress them for his readers: Elsie was still alive, and anyway Ford was writing literary reminiscences, not self-analysis. Nevertheless, however specific were his guilt feelings, they contributed to his breakdown; and his breakdown only added to his feelings of guilt. After a few days at Mammern he was able to write to Elsie to explain what had been happening to him. But in trying to respond to her offer to visit him, and feeling guilt at not wanting her to come, the letter sinks into self-pitiful thoughts of suicide:

Of course I sh$^{d.}$ love to have you here: it seems a shame that I sh$^{d.}$ wander about in this lovely scenery & be so full of gloom that I cannot see its beauties, whilst you w$^{d.}$ enjoy it so immensely.—In fact, my dear child, the more I consider matters the more I think that I have in one way & another ruined y$^{r.}$ life.—Really, it w$^{d.}$ be best if I c$^{d.}$ just die & let you have a second instalment of life that w$^{d.}$ not be so filled with gloom by me.—(However, I shall make desperate attempts to pick up.) This is not a merely morbid view, but one that I have been carrying about with me for a long time—& it knocks me up as much as anything else: because I am really so very fond of you [. . .] Oh y$^{r.}$ wire has just come.—It's dear of you to think of coming: I wish you c$^{d.}$—but it is not absolutely necessary—we must Husband ourselves.[15]

The word 'Husband' demonstrates how the marital and financial worries had become interdependent: must they husband themselves because he was failing as a husband?

The diagnoses and treatments he was given would be comic had they been inflicted on those with senses of humour intact. The ocular specialist had told him he had 'gout in the brows'; the doctor at Mammern assured him, he told Elsie in this same letter, that 'except for the Great Nerve—whatever that may be—& Brain Fag there is nothing the matter'. When Uncle William suggested Ford might like to accompany him and his daughter Mary to Algeria, Ford replied thanking him, but saying:

Of course I would not think of burdening you with the company of an hypochondriac-lunatic—which is what I have become, I'm afraid. I get practically no better here—and have no hopes of doing so—though the Doctor here says there is nothing the matter, actually, with me except brain fag. That's more than enough, though—and I begin to think it's all up with me. . . . What a gloomy place this world seems to be!

Ford's mother decided to go out to visit him in the Kuranstalt, and she arrived on 25 October. On the 27th, when the baths were about to close, he was scarcely better:

I still remain incredibly stupid, a sort of weight pressing on my brain all the time [. . .] At any rate the Future begins to exist for me again, whereas until now I have lived in a state of hourly apprehension of going mad [. . .] I'm absolutely too stupid to work—even as I write now it seems as if someone else were writing, a long way away, thro' a sort of mist [. . .] I can't myself make up my mind whether [the doctor]'s a quack or a genius: I suppose the two are closely allied.[16]

That last comment reflects his own doubts about his own talent: whether he was the genius he had been trained up to be, or whether the illness that rendered him 'stupid' had shown him up as an impostor (the 'stupid donkey' of his father's remark). It also harks back to Madox Brown's perplexity about whether Oliver was a genius or a con-boy or mad. He follows this remark with a comment on Elsie's decision to take up the pen of the house: 'I'm glad you think of writing again—perhaps you'll have to keep me, a doddering idiot.'

The conjunction of ideas here—writing, madness, genius, imposture, the doubling of identity—began under the strain of collaboration, as can be seen in a curious story, 'The Baron', which Ford must have written at about the time *Romance* was completed. The narrator, a young Englishman, visits his German relatives, and falls in love with the daughter of a scientist. He is the 'baron', who is none the less obsessed by the conviction of his own illegitimacy. When invited to England to speak about his discoveries, he starts reciting his family history instead. The story exists for the *frisson* of its double-bind: scandal if the story is true; scandal if it's not, and the baron's mad. The baron's Fordian indifferentism about scandal could itself be either aristocratic *sang froid* or dementia. His renunciation of the title might correlate with Francis Hueffer's emigration from the fatherland (or possibly with Conrad's expatriation). But it is also the converse of Ford's (and Oliver's) humorous claims to ancestral titles. Though a slight magazine piece, its sense that 'free-thinking', love, and sexuality can lead to madness, and its preoccupation with the relationship between madness and telling fictional stories, between imposture and genius, are revealing about Ford's state of mind. And the way it brings these ideas together with ideas about a problematic

relationship to the German family suggest that it may not have been the best
'cure' for Ford to visit the Hüffers. In the title Ford gave the chapter of *Return
to Yesterday* describing this period—'Some Cures'—the 'Some' hovers between
catalogue and sarcastic exclamation.[17]

After leaving Mammern he had another relapse at Basel, and was transferred
to the Marienberg Heilanstalt (sanatorium) at Boppard. When he recounted this
phase in *Return to Yesterday* he made himself sound more resilient than he had
actually been; but the apparently disparate episodes and anecdotes—the bath
cures, breakfasting with Galsworthy, slaughterhouses, the death of rabbits, Zola's
superstitions, influenza, cooking—build up a subliminally coherent impression of
Ford's mental state. Though in retrospect he sounds buoyant, the morbidity
comes creeping back in through the felt pathos of the rendering, creating a dual
sense that he felt even worse than he is prepared to let on, and that his irony was
chastened by pain:

One single picture comes back to me. I had been trying a nerve cure on the Lake of
Constance. I had taken ninety cold baths and thirty tepid soda-water douches in thirty
days. I was so weak that, even if the so-called agoraphobia had not interfered with my
walking I should hardly have been able to get about. I had determined to pull myself
together and had gone to Bâle to write a life of Holbein.

I wrote the greater part of it in the house of a Swiss professor. He had lost his only
daughter and could not bear the silence of his immensely tall, gloomy, ancient and
crow-stepped house. He had filled it with clocks—every imaginable type of Swiss
clock. There was thus a continual ticking, striking, chiming and cuckooing whilst the
poor man continually wept. The noise of the clocks was not disagreeable but the
gloom of the house was profound. I worked in a room high in the gable. The upper
stories of the houses in that street jutted forward so as to come very close together.
Immediately opposite me lived a chimney sweep. He was jet black all over, wore a top
hat and carried behind his back a ladder and sacks of soot. His apartment, which I
could see into, contained a baby and a blonde pink and white young wife. Apartment,
baby and wife were all spotless. On the edge of the window sill was a little green and
white fence, on one side of the window hung a canary in a cage, on the other a
goldfinch. The chimney sweep never came home till dusk. By then the lights would
be lit behind a white blind. Then I would see the silhouette of the sweep, framed by
the window, in the black house-front that, itself a silhouette, stood out with crockets
and crow-steps against the dark sky and the immense stars.

He would stride joyously into the room. His shadow would catch the shadow of the
baby from the invisible cradle and, top hat, ladder, sacks all bobbing, he would throw
the baby up to the ceiling, again and again and again. I used to hang out over my
window sill and wonder with agony why God had made it impossible to transfuse
one's soul into another being. If only I could have made my soul enter that chimney
sweep's body whilst his was absent in sleep! His could no doubt have found a home.

I gave up Holbein and Bâle and went down the Rhine to a *Kaltwasser-Heilanstalt*
[he was there by 4 November] that seemed to me the most horrible of all the
monstrous institutions that had tortured me. They fed you there on pork and
ice-cream. On the Lake of Constance they had given me dried peas and grapes—one
grape every quarter of an hour for sixteen hours out of the day.[18]

The transitions of this passage suggest that his agonized watching of the happy family precipitated a crisis. The personal import of the scene is adumbrated by a letter to Elsie from Basel:

I'm sorry I wrote a depressing letter this morning.—The fact is that, like a fool, I've been working much too hard (but in the idea of making a little money)—& at times in the last two or three days I've been as bad as ever.

But I'll take more care & not be such a fool any more. And I do love you: from my window I can see into a lighted room where a chimney sweep is playing with his children!—I envy him immensely.

Goodnight, dearest.—Try to manage to get out here when I'm better.[19]

The story is meant to cheer up Elsie. The sweep's happy family makes Ford envy him, wishing he could be back with his family. The book version suggests another reason for envy: the sweep can work hard without destroying himself and those he loves. But whereas the wife is mentioned in the book, she is not in the letter. He envies the sweep's ability to play with his children, but not his wife. This makes the exhortation to Elsie to join him less than whole-hearted: she can come when he is better, but not yet (this is partly to protect her from his gloominess, but could also be to protect himself from the gloom her presence might provoke). The book version brings out another crucial ambiguity in the letter. He longs to transfuse his soul into the being of the chimney-sweep. But if this were possible Ford would not be reunited with Elsie, but would become part of another family. It is an example of how Ford's 'impressions' condense the complexities of his life. The description of the weeping professor's 'immensely tall' house, for example, clearly owes as much to Ford's own gloomy and weeping state as it does to the professor's. The conjunction of immense tallness (and 'the immense stars'), the foregrounding of the clock-ticking (as in *The Soul of London*), and the grief of a parent for his child, summons up the spectre of Francis Hueffer, and Ford's childhood grief for his larger-than-life parent, as well as his paralysing agoraphobic sense of smallness in the face of overshadowing largeness.

The emphasis on the blackness of the sweep and the spotlessness of his family generates significance (there are disconcertingly recurrent black-and-white contrasts throughout *The Good Soldier* too). The sweep's unmitigated blackness does not preclude his joyousness. Ford's rendering emphasizes the aspects that answer to his black moods and sense of shadowy guilt and gloom pressing down upon him. The shadow-picture of the family, 'framed' by the window, perhaps suggests that Ford felt he could only live with joy, reconciled to the guilt of the body, if he were transfused into another body, and if he had 'found a home' somewhere other than Winchelsea.

It is also highly characteristic that such a personally charged episode should also be presented in terms of art. Ford is trying to write a 'life' of a painter (in fact his *Holbein* is much more critical than biographical). But the life of the picture framed by the window opposite, which was 'very close' (close to his own desires?), makes him unable to write. The play of shadows—the silhouettes in the window within the silhouette of the house-front—form a shadow-play. Ford himself wrote a shadow-play before the First World War (during another dark period) and he used one for a climactic scene in the first part of *The Marsden Case*.²⁰ There, as here, the image of the white screen with the black figures upon it becomes a suggestive metaphor for writing and reading: for black figures on a white background which 'make you *see*' through, and beyond, the page; transfusing your being into the lives of others. As a novelist of 'sympathetic insight', Ford has a professional interest in transfusing his soul into the being of others.

There is an element of escapism here; even of a suicidal longing to end his life as himself (and note how he does not wish his predicament upon the dispossessed sweep's soul).²¹ The idea of a transfusion of self is important for all of Ford's writing, and particularly for those novels in which 'sympathetic identification' takes place between the characters: when Dowell tries to imagine being Ashburnham, or when Henry Martin actually exchanges roles with Hugh Monckton in *The Rash Act* and *Henry for Hugh*. It is a topic which will be discussed more fully later. Here it is necessary to show how Ford's escapist leanings are recognized as only that (he is literally hanging out over his window-sill); and how his rendering of his leanings knows escape is impossible. Not only has God 'made it impossible', but the passage is alive with all the factors that militate against such an escape (in the way it condenses grief, guilt, ambivalences about self and family, so that the expression of the desire to escape becomes simultaneously expressive of all the things from which escape is sought). One can see this in the ambiguity of the language. If you transfuse your soul into another being, how far have you escaped? It will still be your soul, and the body will be different. How much more does 'being' mean than 'body'? Which human 'being' would you then be? Yourself, the sweep, or a compound character? The very term 'transfuse' suggests a mixing and melding rather than a swapping around. The image is precisely suggestive of how novelists (or readers) do not actually believe they have become the characters they imagine, but instead, they imagine what it might be like to become them, nevertheless retaining their own vantage-point, their own 'personality', manifest in the style of the language in which characters are created. It is an image for the novelist's dual perspective, which is never simply escapist.

It is also suggestive in an autobiographical sense. That is, in writing *Return to Yesterday* Ford is exploring what effect his nervous breakdown had on his writing, how it made him a different kind of novelist from the one he might otherwise have been. Sympathy, pity and self-pity, identification, and the desire to escape became some of Ford's most effective themes. Stella Bowen, who lived with him after the war, wrote that: 'What he did not know about the depths and weaknesses of human nature was not worth knowing. The hidden places of the heart were his especial domain, and when he chose he could put the screw upon your sense of pity or of fear with devastating sureness.'²² As an example of the kind of psychologically insightful, convincing prose he was able to write because of what he had suffered in his early thirties, take the following passage from *A Little Less Than Gods* (1928). One of Ford's less compelling novels as a whole, this story of the renunciation of incestuous love not surprisingly draws upon Ford's experiences of guilt and agoraphobia (and also upon how these things recurred during the First World War). This description of Hélène de Frèjus' over-excited mental state probably gives a good impression of what Ford went through between 1903 and 1905, and again between 1908 and 1915, when his private 'affairs' became enervatingly public; and then again during the Battle of the Somme:

ever since the news of Waterloo she had lived under overpowering emotions of fear, passion and despair for public affairs. Now all these came to a head, and for a moment she no longer knew what happened. She saw vaguely Frèjus walking away beside the young general, the squad of soldiers marching at a decent interval behind them; the July sun beat down on her, but she was shivering, and she was aware of tottering, both her hands stretched out and downwards in order to balance herself . . . tottering and wavering towards a bench in the shade of the avenue. She must be in shade; she could not bear the light. Her heart beat rapidly like that of a linnet that she had once held in her hand; her lips were parted like that of the same linnet, the breath issuing from her parched mouth in little jets as fast as the beats of her heart. Her mind had stopped. She was aware that a woman's arms were about her [. . .] (pp. 164–5)

It is not only this mode of blindingly clear rendering of hallucinatory mental unclarity that Ford learned from his breakdown. His dual attitude as a novelist was also shaped by the experience: his characteristic transfusion of sympathy and aloofness, pity and irony, identification and objectivity.

'I *am* hideously weak & deadly stupid', Ford wrote to Elsie soon after his arrival at Marienberg (perhaps echoing his father's calling him a stupid donkey). 'What has become of my once mighty intellect I don't know & my memory has clean gone [. . .] I can walk & haven't the dreadful presentiments to anything near the same extent.' But once again the rituals of 'cure' there only seemed to intensify the illness:

I've grown so dreadfully lazy [he wrote to Elsie]: as if I had weights hung all over me—on my arms, on my legs, & above all my eyelids.—I go for four short crawls every day—&, for the rest of the time, lie on a sofa whilst M$^{rs.}$ H.[ueffer] reads rotten novels to me.

I have a cold douche at 7.a.m: eye-baths at 9: cold foot bath in iced water at 10.30: hot compress on the stomach after lunch: cold bath with massage at 3.30 and another hot compress after supper.—We walk in the park from 9.30–9.50 when I lie down: I walk alone into the town from 10.40–11, when I have oatmeal gruel and lie down. Dinner at 12.30.1.30: lie down from 1.30–3.30: walk down to the Goesens at 4: partake of milk & Zwieback [rusk] there & lie down till 5.30: walk back here & lie down till 7.30. Lie down from 8–9: walk from 9–9.30 & then bed & eye-baths, after wh. M$^{rs.}$ H. reads me to sleep.[23]

Depressed after two further bouts of tooth-pulling, Ford began to despair of the cures, telling Elsie, 'if I don't feel materially better soon I shall give it up & come back to Tunnicliffe's arms'. The image is evocative: Ford's agoraphobia receded when he could hold someone's arm, feel some human support or someone's arms about him; so his mental attempts to pick himself up relied upon a doctor's protective attention. Given the German treatments, one can sympathize with Ford's comment that: 'Those were the early days of that mania that has since beset the entire habitable globe.'[24] He had more cause than most to fall back on the defensive half-truism that it is the mad-doctors who are the mad. When he rejected the diagnosis of agoraphobia, he was rejecting the entire institution of spa nerve-cures. The experiences of this year left him woundedly cynical about mental specialists, and liable to equate the dismaying physiological treatment he endured with the radically different ideas of psychoanalysis. (There is no evidence that he read Freud.) But his impression that his case had been misunderstood was surely right; and at Marienberg he was beginning to understand why their routines could not help him. 'I've the feeling that if I c$^{d.}$ be back with you my troubles w$^{d.}$ vanish', he wrote to Elsie; but then realizing that he was deceiving both of them, he added: 'But, alas, they probably w$^{d.}$ not, being deep within my nature.'[25]

Moser is right to support the diagnosis of agoraphobia; right, too, to argue that the sources lay back in childhood. However, Ford writes little about his experiences of childhood; though one motif that recurs is his sense of being overshadowed by immense and superior beings: the Victorian Great Figures. His agoraphobia appears as a metaphorical repetition of such a scene. Many of its elements return him to a childlike dependence—upon the arms of grown-ups to support his walking; upon sweets (he took lozenges or peppermints to allay the attacks when he went out), which are often themselves reminders of earlier oral gratifications; upon the authority of doctors and the foster-care of nurses. It is striking how the Marienberg routine takes the regulation of convalescence to the point where it reduces its patients to helpless children. Everything Ford relates about his typical day has this childish aspect: prescribed times for getting up, having baths, and going to bed; minute attention to the digestion; supervised walks or 'crawls' in the park; being given milk and rusks (or ice-cream); even having teeth pulled; and above all, being read to sleep by your mother. One way to understand Ford's breakdown is to see it as a demand for support, love, and attention of a parental kind—a kind which had been denied by his father's death and his mother's subsequent separation from her sons; and which he had perhaps felt denied at an even earlier age, when a pretty sister and an expert attention-getting brother became rivals for parental love. Stella Bowen noted this quality of his personality and mode of expression: 'when Ford wanted anything, he filled the sky with an immense ache that had the awful simplicity of a child's grief, and appeared to hold the same possibilities of assuagement.' It can be heard in his letter to Elsie of 12 November 1904, telling her he had had yet another relapse, and urging: 'love me a little too, for I need it.' He wrote regular, touching postcards to his daughters from Germany. They are underscored with a self-reproach for not being with them, not being a better father. His loving, responsive tone with them, amusing them with fairy-tale snippets, being amused by their letters and drawings, can be felt struggling against the self-pity into which his depression dragged him. Their subtext is of a man trying to be the kind of father that he never had, and feeling (but *not* saying) 'love me a little too, for I need it'. Agoraphobia metaphorically reduces adults to helpless children. When Ford comments that his dyspepsia tended to 'paralyse' him, his choice of words suggests that his two worst complaints, agoraphobia and indigestion, had something in common.[26] Certainly the pain of severe indigestion can make it difficult to move. But 'paralysis' makes it sound more psychologically loaded: a need to become immobilized, helpless, a victim. One reason why Ford was not getting better was that no one, apart from himself in his darkest moments, was attempting to look deep within his nature: rather than being analysed, the problem was being obscured in the neurological jargon of the day. But another possible reason is that, rather than weaning him away from the circumstances of his agoraphobia, the sanatoria prolonged them, providing the nearest thing to a regression to childhood with full adult attention that a 31-year-old is likely to find. To speculate about possible unconscious motivation, his loss of memory sounds like it might be an attempt to deny the intervening years. This level of care would only continue while he remained abroad, and without dependants of his own to worry about. Relapsing was the only sure way to stay where he was.

At moments like these Ford sounds emotionally manipulative (in unconscious ways). Although the correspondence of this time has survived lopsidedly, with almost nothing of Elsie's, it is clear from Ford's responses to her queries and worries that she too needed to coerce sympathy and evoke guilt. But the partiality of the evidence makes an impartial judgement about who was manipulating whom elusive. The added difficulty in Ford's case (and to a lesser extent with Elsie's too) is that, being a writer, his medium is language and his materials are human situations and feelings. His letters to Elsie have the strange dual quality of being documents in a particular relationship, yet also attempts to express his psychology for and to himself. The point here is not to engage in special pleading that the artist should be exempt from normal human responsibilities. Rather, it is to suggest that an artist has a professional interest in manipulating responses. He or she needs to be expert at it to be able to 'get effects' in art. Our acts of self-understanding all have their 'dialogic' aspect: that is, we need to express convincingly to others what we feel ourselves to be before we can wholly be; we must internalize others' perceptions of ourselves. For an artist of Ford's kind this is particularly true. In order to alleviate his own feeling of guilt, he must make others feel pity for his guilty state. There is a logical paradox here: their pity confirms rather than assuages his suffering; and yet by making others feel for him, he is able to externalize and objectify, and thus master feelings which would otherwise paralyse him. He said he thought this period of breakdown was the only time he had 'failed to show composure in the face of adversity or the treachery of friends'. Writing helped him compose himself. There is a close connection between his agoraphobic dependence upon the supporting response of his companions and his artistic dependence upon the emotional response of his audience. All his writing is characterized by its imagining of the other: the other beings the writing creates, and the other beings who participate as readers in that creation. It is more than just a technical self-consciousness, a knowledge of which techniques can produce which effects. Beyond this, Ford's writing constantly imagines—implicitly or explicitly—a listener or reader.[27]

In Ford's reminiscences it is Conrad who is the type of this sympathetic audience. And it was a role Conrad showed himself willing to play when he wrote to encourage Ford: 'Don't imagine I have not been thinking of you in all the concern of the sympathy and affection which exist between us [. . .] I've been struck by your letter. Why not correspond in that tone? And even correspond with me—if you like; if You think that the idea of a concrete recipient of your prose may help you in the least.'[28] It was in effect another offer of collaboration, designed to help Ford write (and therefore earn a living). If Ford could write sketches of Germany, Conrad would get them typed, edit them, and get them to Pinker—for whom, said Conrad, Ford was 'the man who can write anything at any time—and write it well'. Conrad couldn't help undermining the sympathy his letter so elaborately constructs by adding, 'he means in a not ordinary way', which casts its doubts on Ford's art as much as on Pinker's taste. And he concluded with an expression of his exhaustion after completing *Nostromo*: 'There's no elation. No relief even. Nothing [. . .] The miserable rubbish is to be shot out on the muck-heap before this month is out [. . .] My mind runs on disconnected like the free wheel of a bicycle. I feel going down hill as it were. Love from us all'.

Return to Yesterday not only combines chapters on the collaboration and on nervous breakdown, but within the chapter 'Some Cures' it moves from Ford's travels in Germany back to the preceding experiences with Conrad at Airlie Gardens. Thus the form of the book connects agoraphobia with collaboration; and the link is more than a mere chronological closeness. It shows Ford aware that the strains of collaborating with Conrad had eventually overwhelmed him. But more than that, it suggests an understanding of how not only his own best subjects but his own best techniques as well had come out of his experience of breakdown. Ford describes one of his books, *A Mirror to France*, as 'the purest, the most will-less impressionism' (p. 18). Even as he is rebutting the diagnosis of agoraphobia ('which is, in effect, a disease of the will-power'), he understood that his literary methods had a curious proximity to the condition of agoraphobia. Impressionism is not a disease of the will; but it is a form of believing suspension of will, a subduing of the will, to impose one's own interpretations, propagandas, moralizings, meanings, upon things seen and rendered. As he explained: 'to get an impression—a true impression of the tenuous thing that Life is, you must make your record a thing of exact enough renderings; but they must be renderings of things that force themselves on your attention almost more than of the things that you really observe of your own will.' Ford's art is profoundly unmanipulative, eschewing the possibility of using his material to serve ends other than effective recording. Pound's obituary criticism that Ford 'felt until it paralysed his efficient action' gets hold of the wrong end of the right stick.[29] Fordian impressionism does have something in common with the paralysis of agoraphobia, but it is not itself a paralysis: rather, it is a contemplative state, a passive receptivity. Ford's critical language reflects the connection: the 'March' of Literature culminates in 'will-less impressionism', the reader held at a rapt standstill. Efficient *action* does not come out of such a state: not, at any rate, the sort of action that would count as efficient to such a master propagandist and 'factive personality' as Pound. But Pound's earlier comment more accurately gauged the issue, when he wrote: 'I find him significant and revolutionary because of his insistence upon clarity and precision, upon the prose tradition; in brief, upon efficient writing—even in verse.' Ford's writing about mental breakdown deserves its place amongst the best English examples: Coleridge, Mill, Conrad, Eliot, Waugh. It could hardly be further from the truth to say, as Mizener did, 'Ford liked to think about the psychological complications of other men's lives as little as he liked to think about his own'. Though his affinity for narrative rather than analysis makes him want to recount psychological complications rather than to theorize about them, he is (with Lawrence) one of the great English novelists of psychological complexity (more so than Conrad, or even than James). Mizener was discussing Ford's refusal to 'enter into the pathological details' in his monograph on Rossetti, as Garnett had suggested. His argument was not that it derogated from the dignity of man, but that it distracted from the criticism of art: 'how *can* I distinguish between the symptoms, on canvas, of chloral, uraemia, gout in the wrist and incipient blindness, all of wh. (not to mention chronic delusions) had a share?' He didn't want to discuss these things in a book on Rossetti's technique; but he was able to mention them exhaustively in a letter to Garnett.[30]

13

1905: LONDON

You see, I am not dead.

(*Return to Yesterday*)

In December 1904 Elsie began writing to encourage Ford to return. His response was a strange mixture of saying he wanted to rejoin her, and that in spirit he already had as far as he was able: 'living here in so much solitude, I seem to exist much more with you in W.[inchelsea] than here: in fact, for the last few days I've hardly known where I have been [. . .] I long for you so dreadfully.' William Rossetti lent his house at 3 St Edmund's Terrace for the winter. By 20 December Ford was back in London, and Conrad was assuring Pinker he was getting better, though Olive Garnett was less sanguine when she called at St Edmund's Terrace and found Ford lying on the dining-room sofa: 'Chatted with him till Elsie & tea came in. Ford was smiling and limp. Elsie energetic and worried.' It was while he was staying there that he saw Dr Albert Tebb, recommended to him by Conrad. Tebb, who had treated Jessie Conrad's knee, was an admirer of Ford Madox Brown and a friend of William Rossetti:

He was the most mournful looking man I have ever imagined. He was thinner than seemed possible—thinner than myself [Ford was down to about nine stone at the time]! He wore extremely powerful glasses that dilated his eyes to extravagant dimensions. He could cure all his patients, but he had at home a child he could not cure. It was a most tragic story.

He came into the room where I lay [. . .] I was lying on the sofa on which Shelley had passed the last night of his life. The room was a museum of Shelleyan and pre-Raphaelite relics. Tebb with his stethoscope in his top hat was like a ghost.

He sat beside me for more than two hours. He hardly spoke at all. Now and then he asked a question. It was as if his voice came from a tomb. My mind was full of finishing my life of Holbein that had been interrupted at Bâle [. . .]

After Tebb had been silent for an hour and a half, I said:

'Doctor, I know I am going to die. Mayn't I finish a book I have begun?'

'What book?' he asked cavernously. I said it was a life of Holbein.

Half an hour afterwards he said:

'Yes, you may as well finish your life of Holbein if you have time. You will be dead in a month.' He said it with a hollow and mournful vindictiveness that still rings in my ears. He told me to go to Winchelsea to do that work. If I was alive at the end of a month I could come and see him again. He went away, leaving no prescription.

As soon as he was gone I jumped up, dressed myself and all alone took a hansom to Piccadilly Circus. You are to remember that my chief trouble was that I imagined that I could not walk. Well, I walked backwards and forwards across the Circus for an hour and a half. I kept on saying: 'Damn that brute, I will not be dead in a month.' And walking across the Circus through the traffic was no joke.[1]

Ford took Tebb's advice, travelling down to Winchelsea with his friend Walter Jerrold, who kept him company while he 'plugged away stalwartly at Holbein': 'I was determined to justify my existence', Ford wrote later—revealing in the comment what is surely a prime motive for his creativity: the need to stamp his own life as that of an artist rather than of the stuff to fill graveyards; to alleviate a sense of unworthiness by transmuting 'personality' into 'genius'.

At the end of the month, I saw Tebb again. I said triumphantly:
  'You see, I am not dead.'
  He answered as mournfully and hollowly as if he were in despair at the falsification of his prophecy:
  'If I hadn't told you you would be dead, you would have been dead.' He was no doubt right.

Mizener calls this 'an unlikely story'. Certainly it has been worked up by Ford's imagination *into* a 'story': the outrageous precision of the lapses of time; the notion of Ford braving death by risking suicide in Piccadilly Circus; even Tebb's very appearance as a messenger or prophet of Death, are highly 'written'. And yet when Ford told the story three years earlier most of the details were identical. These details may or may not be factual (I think most of them are: what Ford particularly strives for is an effect of nightmarish unreality created out of a montage of the most ordinary objects: a top hat, a stethoscope, pebble-glasses. As he said of Trollope: 'the whole effect is extraordinary—because it is such an exact rendering of the very ordinary'). The important question is, what truths of insight and feeling does the story express? Ford presents it as the moment of cure. What can the story tell us about how this could be (and how Ford thought it could be) possible?[2]

The earlier version sheds light on what Ford meant by calling his mental illness 'purely imaginary': it treats his breakdown as caused by hypochondria. This comes in an essay, 'O Hygeia', on health and diet. He is explaining his 'conversion' from a puritan attitude that 'salvation lies only in negation of joy', and that therefore things you enjoy are bad for you, to his belief in the importance of *joie de vivre* (for which we significantly smuggle in a continental term), a belief that 'nothing will do you any harm if you like it'. He uses his own case as an illustration to support this change, so he emphasizes the hypochondria rather than attempting a full self-analysis. 'My own life was completely ruined and myself for six years reduced to a condition of hypochondriacal lunacy', he comments almost as an aside, 'by the chance remark to myself of a doctor who had been called in to see a member of my family':

that gentleman so efficiently auto-suggested me with the ideas that I suffered from a chronic disease one of whose sequelæ is epilepsy—so efficiently that for six years I expected at every minute—at *every* minute of the day—to drop under the dread malady which is alleged to have afflicted Napoleon and most other great men. I have not yet done so.

It would seem that destiny has decreed that mankind shall live in a dark forest of fears—of nightmares! (p. 769)

Near the end of the essay he gives a graphic account of this nightmare world:

my mother was the most careful of parents, and her injunctions made me the most careful of sons. I was impressed with the fact that I had a weak heart, an enlarged liver, a tendency towards tuberculosis, hereditary gout, and throat troubles—these last suggested by the eminent throat specialist who killed my father by telling him to get up and go about his business because there was nothing the matter with his throat. Actually he was suffering from a heart rendered temporarily weak by erysipelas and dropped dead at his bedside immediately after the specialist had left the room. That gentleman operated on my own throat six times—for tonsils and adenoids—that in itself being pretty bad for an already nervous child of eight. Thus, in short, from my tenderest infancy I was taught to watch my health at every minute of the day and night. I did so—and no human being can have had a much more miserable inner life than myself. Not *much* more! Then, when I was twenty-three or so I had the epilepsy-dread which, after I was thirty or so induced a nervous breakdown that lasted a year and a half during which I was unable to walk, forbidden to work, and reduced in weight to one hundred and twenty-eight pounds. I was taken to visit at least seven of the most eminent nerve-specialists in Europe—including Vienna!—and those gentlemen doing nothing to mend me, I came home to die. (p. 775)

Then Ford tells of Tebb's sombre visit, which helped him to recover from his breakdown, and of his subsequent visit to New York (in 1906) when his hypochondria was finally cured by a doctor who told him to abandon his punishing diet of rice, warm water, and pepsin tablets, and to eat whatever he liked. *Return to Yesterday* tells a comparable story: 'Miss Hurlbird and her sister, in the immense, shadowed drawing-room of the Heilanstalt promised me that if I would visit them at Stamford and eat their peaches and frozen cream for breakfast I should be restored to complete health. I eventually did so and the promise came true' (p. 270).

It is clear from the way Ford describes his fears and their obsessional quality that there was more wrong with him than palpitations of the heart, and that he knew it. Tebb did not need to prescribe because he saw that the illness was not organic but psychological, and what he managed to do (or what his visit came to symbolize, for Ford, his having done) was to invert the ground-rules of the illness, telling him he will certainly die, rather than offering him comfort or ministering to him. The effect was to change Ford's attitude to his own life. Tebb was not the sole cause; his visit caught Ford at a time when he was ready to have his self-confidence restored. But as far as Ford was concerned, before Tebb's visit he intended to die (the 'intention' was unconscious, but is visible in his *expectation* that he was about to die). Afterwards he is determined to live. By bringing Ford's fears out of their dark forest into the light of a social situation—a doctor's visit in what is effectively a literary salon—Tebb enables Ford to master and allay them. By personifying death for him, he enables Ford to exorcize the obsession with death. Ford never lost his fear of death, or his preoccupation with it; but though he occasionally complained of agoraphobic feelings, he never experienced the reprise he dreaded of a complete agoraphobic breakdown.

'It was as if his voice came from a tomb. My mind was full of finishing my life[. . .].' His own life?—Well, no, his life of Holbein which had been interrupted at Basle; but the transition subtly but surely raises the spectre of suicide before exorcizing it—through writing, through *not* letting the sentence be interrupted. As so often in Ford's autobiographical prose, there is always an oblique meditation taking place about what it is to write, and why one should write, and what makes Ford the kind of writer he is and not quite another kind. The unobtrusive cutting from one angle to another between 'my mind was full of finishing my life' and 'of Holbein' establishes the justification for a writer's life: you don't need to end it all if you can finish your books. Tebb's reply, as Ford remembers it, repeats the ambiguity: 'Yes, you may as well finish your life.' By not saying just this, he does not ostensibly say it at all (he actually says 'you may as well finish your life of Holbein'). And yet the possibility which his phrasing utters but which the rest of the sentence suppresses—that Ford might as well die, and will die, if he wants to—is precisely the sub-text of the interview.

A further detail of phrasing suggests that Ford perfectly realized the importance both of the breakdown and this faith-cure (cure by faith in himself, though, not by faith in God or superstition or doctors or physical therapies). It is not at first sight strange to say 'I imagined that I could not walk'. He *actually* could not, though the cause was mental rather than physical: all in the mind, 'imaginary'. But it *is* strange to say 'he was the most mournful looking man I have ever imagined', instead of 'ever seen'. It is not strange enough for us to stop and worry about it while reading, but it sows a subliminal doubt—one not enough in the foreground of consciousness for us to address it directly. But if we do just that, we find it touches on the crux of Fordian impressionism (which is appropriate in a passage in which he worries about the justification for his writing). Did Tebb *actually* have such a mournful look, or did Ford imagine he did? For the impressionist, the answer will be the same as to the question 'could he *really* not walk, or did he only imagine he couldn't?'. If he imagined it, if he had that impression, then it was true for him. It was true for Violet Hunt, too, that Tebb looked mournful: she called him a 'weedy man who stooped so for despair, not laziness. Himself he could not save.'[3] It becomes true for us too through Ford's vivid, macabre-comic rendering of the scene, which is explicitly a token of Ford's gratitude to Tebb, an advertisement for his skills. It was the change of attitude Tebb helped to effect which made Ford able to draw upon his imaginary illness in his imaginative renderings. ' "What book?" he asked cavernously.' Much of the humanity of *Return to Yesterday* comes from the *joie de vivre*—the gusto—in Ford's reimagining of the deathliness and despair of these dark years.

Ford read voraciously towards the end of his breakdown: Johnson, Boswell's *Life*, Hardy, and above all Turgenev. Turgenev's mastery of pathos, and his tendency to get attacked from all (political) sides, would have been congenial to Ford. But the affinity lay deeper. 'I think that the indispensable characteristic of the books that one offers one's friend in exchange for his', he wrote in a poignant description of the consolatory power of reading, is:

that it should grasp one, that it should hold one, at just those times when the mind most needs to be held: at just those times when, through distractions, illnesses, weaknesses or troubles, the mind seems to slip off from the pages of a book as you may see a newly fledged sparrow slide awkwardly down the slope of a roof.—It is just then that the mind most needs the solace of books—& it is just then, as a rule, that books most find us. Then indeed one's book for exchange is most precious—& it is then that I turn to the *Sportsman's Sketches* of Tourguénieff.[4]

It is a passage which says much about the significance of reading and writing in Ford's life and his work, as well as much about why his best work issues from periods of greatest mental disturbance.

'Johnson meant for me a return to interest in the facts of life', he said later. The passage he particularly remembered and often alluded to was the episode in Boswell of 'the fellow who said that he tried hard to be a philosopher but cheerfulness would come creeping in'. The phrase becomes a token for the way cheerfulness began to creep back into Ford's life in 1905, as his interest in 'the facts of life' returned: the facts of his own life, but also of the life of Holbein (he told Walter Jerrold in April he was writing it 'at the rate of twenty words a day'), the life of the English countryside (written up into *The Heart of the Country*, completed by July 1905), and the semi-fictionalized life of Katharine Howard to which he returned. He returned to Winchelsea, too, after staying in Sandgate for a week and visiting H. G. Wells, Mrs Bland (E. Nesbit), and the short-story writer W. W. Jacobs. On 13 January 1905 he saw the Conrads off to Capri. Pinker had managed to place both *The Benefactor* (though without getting an advance for Ford) and *The Soul of London*. Even literary success was beginning to creep back in, finally lifting Ford out of his breakdown. On 15 January Olive Garnett wrote: 'Ford and Elsie, radiant to supper. Not only "London" but "George" [*The Benefactor*] is accepted through Pinker. . . . Ford looks very much better.' It is, as Moser says, the last time she describes them as a happy couple.[5]

But now Elsie fell ill. First she developed an abscess under her tongue, from which, as Ford wrote to Wells on 1 February, 'issued a stone the size of a pigeon's egg.—It sounds mediaeval, but it's modern enough to have pulled her down very much & to make picking up a sort of hard labour.' Then she became more seriously ill, with the tubercular kidney that was persistently mis-diagnosed until 1908. The whole family moved to Mrs Martindale's House, 93 Broadhurst Gardens (now in NW 6). By March she had recovered enough to travel to France until May to convalesce. Once again separation was decided to be beneficial. It was possibly during this year that she discovered about Ford's relationship with

Mary. While she was away Ford stayed with Tebb, at 226 Finchley Road. Uncle William Rossetti, wanting to help Ford to earn some money, asked him in April to help him revise his articles for the eleventh edition of the *Encyclopaedia Britannica*, mainly on Italian painters. He agreed, working on them on and off until July. It was probably thus that his love–hate relationship with the *Encyclopaedia* was established, a relationship issuing most memorably in Tietjens' memorization of *Britannica* after his shell-shock amnesia in *Some Do Not . . .*[6]

The encyclopaedia of Hueffer catastrophes was not yet closed. At the end of April Ford told Olive Garnett that 'his children have caught ringworm. Elsie "raving mad"'. She added the comment: 'Exaggeration!', but it wasn't, even though, as Ford told Olive of their conversation that evening, it sounded like *Alice in Wonderland*. Throughout the year the ringworm persisted: it is a contagious, fungal disease (mainly of the scalp), for which the treatments were primitive and distressing, mostly involving the pulling out of hair.[7]

Ford's luck began to change when *The Soul of London* was published on 2 May 1905. René Byles, the managing director of the book's publishers, Alston Rivers, was a shrewd publicist. Ford, trying to re-create the euphoria of being 'boomed' in the press, told the story in *Return to Yesterday* of how Byles buttonholed Lord Northcliffe and read him extracts of the book, so conveying his enthusiasm that Northcliffe promised to review the book himself. Byles then persuaded Northcliffe's rivals that they should also carry reviews. Like many of Ford's stories about his own life, this one has been contested. It was not Northcliffe himself but one of his staff who reviewed the book in the *Daily Mail*. However, that only proves that Northcliffe did not write the review, not that he didn't say he would, nor that Byles didn't tell Ford he had said it. Otherwise the essential details of Ford's version are true: the book was reviewed on the day of publication by the three newspapers he mentions, and the reviews gave him the strongest praise he had yet received. The *Daily Mail* gave *The Soul of London* a full column, calling it 'the latest and truest image of London, built up out of a series of negations, that together are more hauntingly near to a composite picture of the city than anything we have seen before'. The *Daily News* said, 'no one has achieved or attempted what in this book Mr. Hueffer has done with power and fine insight'.[8]

The praise is just. Ford's English trilogy is his most perfect example of the paradox with which he defined 'impressionism': 'the Impressionist author is sedulous to avoid letting his personality appear in the course of his book. On the other hand, his whole book, his whole poem is merely an expression of his personality.'[9] The impressions of London, of the countryside, of the people, are from Ford's own experience and his own reading. But the books are not explicitly autobiographical. Nor do they have propagandistic designs. Unlike so much of the Edwardian writing about the 'Condition of England', they don't foment hysteria about foreign invasions, the degeneration of the race, and the 'Woman Question'. They contemplate social conditions, but render them with a poignant, tragic stoicism that everywhere expresses the morbidity it fends off. One particularly fine passage recalls visiting a woman who made matchboxes. One of the early Fabian successes had been the campaign led by Annie Besant to organize strikes by the young women who made matches for Bryant and May. Ford begins in radical and even feminist terms, saying that the poor female workers tend to be denied even the small solaces of hobbies and sports that entertain the men. He describes the scene, in which the matchboxes seem to define every aspect of her life:

She had four children under nine. She was a dark, untidy-haired woman with a face much pitted by small pox, and she had a horribly foul tongue. The room looked out upon a boxlike square of livid brick yards, a table was under a window, a sugar box held coals. Another, nailed above the mantel, held bits of bread, a screw of tea in white paper, a screw of sugar in blue, and a gobbet of margarine in a saucer [. . .] There was nothing else in the room except a mattress and, on a damp and discoloured wall, a coloured mezzotint of Perdita, the mistress of George IV. I do not know how she had come to be pasted up there.

Till the school bell rang the children worked at her side. I don't think they were ever either dressed for school or given breakfasts by her. She made matchboxes at 2¾d. THE 144, and it was wonderful to watch her working—engrossed, expressionless, without a word, her fingers moved deftly and unerringly, the light very dim, the air full of the faint sickly smell of paste and of the slight crackling of thin wood, and the slight slop-slopping of the pastebrush. Sometimes she would sigh, not sorrowfully, but to draw a deeper breath.

What was appalling to Ford was not the poverty: 'It was not the wretchedness, because, on the whole, neither the man or the woman were anything other than contented. But it was the dire speed at which she worked. It was like watching all the time some feat of desperate and breathless skill. It made one hold one's own breath.' Implicit here is an admiration for the technique of a fellow-craftsman. Ford then turns the episode to suggest that Fabian-style attempts to 'reform' such a life would be impertinent or patronizing, losing the person in the statistic:

In the face of it any idea of 'problems,' of solutions, of raising the submerged, or of the glorious destinies of humanity, vanished. The mode of life became, as it were, august and settled. You could not pity her because she was so obviously and wonderfully equipped for her particular struggle: you could not wish to 'raise' her, for what could she do in any other light, in any other air? Here at least she was strong, heroic, settled and beyond any condemnation.

He describes how, 'if you gave her 2¾d., the price of a gross of boxes—if you gave her time literally, she would utter long bursts of language that was a mixture of meaningless obscenities and of an old fashioned and formal English'. The point is not to condemn her prejudices (against the Irish, against her husband's friends, against meddling philanthropists), but to argue that if you translate her ideals 'into terms of greater material prosperity you find them identical with anyone else's'. To be in her presence was 'like interviewing the bedrock of human existence in a cavern deep in the earth'.[10]

The books are quests for such essences (the 'Soul' of London; the 'Heart' of the Country; the 'Spirit' of the People) in a world whose complexity baffles generalization. The danger of such impressionism is that what is offered as the 'personality' of an impersonal thing such as a city or a country might sound too much like the author's personality aggrandizing itself. But when it works, as here (and it is the effect Ford particularly admired in naturalists like Hudson), it can persuade us that something is being said about accumulated human lives and suffering. He ends the book with a Conradian image of a 'brooding and enigmatic glow'—('That is London writing its name upon the clouds')—which images just that cumulative significance: 'And in the hearts of children it will still be something like a cloud—a cloud of little experiences, of little personal impressions, of small, futile things that, seen in moments of stress and anguish, have significances so tremendous and meanings so poignant. A cloud—as it were of the dust of men's lives.'[11] Life, he says, is 'no more than a bundle of memories'. The same could be said of his impressionist prose, which renders justice to the life of the city by contemplating the human projects, dreams, and memories that have populated it. The last chapter, on 'Rest in London', sounds like it will continue the previous topic, 'London at Leisure', but in fact imagines resting in the peace of death: 'and what is London but a vast graveyard of stilled hopes in which the thin gnat-swarm of the present population dances its short day above the daily growing, indisturbable detritus of all the past at rest?' The essence of the city, its human significance for Ford, is the transience of human personality to which it everywhere testifies. The book is an impassioned elegy, saying to the city, as it were, 'Du bist die Ruh'. It is thus that Ford writes his name on the cloud of his impressions.[12]

'It *is* very good', Edward Garnett told Galsworthy, 'the best thing he's done; you will be interested to hear that Hueffer has at last been boomed, boomed furiously! and has come into his own. I am so very, very glad. I think that this success may go a long way to putting him definitely on his feet [. . .] for if ever a man wanted recognition, poor Ford does.' It is a telling comment: Ford 'wanted' recognition in both senses. His response once he had finally begun to get recognized thanks to Byles shows the extent of his dependency upon the approval of others: 'But for him [Byles] it is almost certain that I should have given up writing. But his enthusiasm for my work was extraordinary and infectious. He almost made me believe in myself. He certainly made the newspapers believe in me.' This follows on almost immediately after Ford has said, 'most of what I wrote was produced with the idea of reading it aloud to Conrad'. Without recognition, and without the destructive solace of collaboration, Ford's self-doubt had become overwhelming, suicidal. 'This is SUCCESS at last', he told his mother. The success of *The Soul of London*—it was a *succès d'estime* rather than a best-seller—restored something of that sense of his worth and gifts that he desperately needed. It also caused a slight reprise of his depression, since he was still in a state of nervous volatility. He wrote to Walter Jerrold: 'The rather overpowering reception of the work over excited me a little & has knocked me

over a little.' This experience of the press's power to confer an ephemeral and
spurious credibility was to go into *Mr Apollo*.[13]

Conrad, too, was still missing their collaboration. He had taken Jessie to Capri
to recuperate after a knee operation, and Ford sent him a copy of his new book.
'Hurrah for the Soul of London!', Conrad replied, adding: 'Brute as I am by
nature and training I was touched by the sight of these pages so familiar in a way
and so strange now, when far away from You. I went on following your thought
over-leaf from page to page.' Despite the characteristic double edge (telling Ford
his writing seems 'strange' from an objective distance?), Conrad's personal need
was as great as ever: 'Vous m'avez manqué affreusement' (I've missed you
terribly), he added. After Conrad's return the two men went back to an earlier
collaboration, 'One Day More'—a dramatization of Conrad's story 'Tomorrow',
with which Ford had helped early in 1904, but which was performed (in Conrad's
name alone) on 25–7 June 1905 at the Royal Theatre.[14]

Elsie was back in England in May. In July she and Ford visited Olive Garnett
together, and Ford was in better spirits. However, beneath the placid social
surface a crisis was approaching. Ford was still staying with Tebb. Early in July
Elsie suggested she should go abroad again—partly for her health, but probably
also as a mode of separation. In a deposition Ford wrote later, when he was trying
to divorce her, he said that: 'For a number of years previous to 1908 Mrs Elsie
Hueffer had been asking me, intermittently, to let her divorce me. I was at no
time anxious for a divorce, and headed her off the subject as well as I could.' This
was written at another of Ford's most desperate periods, and the melodramatic
nature of the rest of the deposition makes it more than usually difficult to
distinguish invention from recollection. But if it is true, it would confirm that
Elsie had recently found out about Ford and Mary. And it is supported by his
reply to Elsie's decision to travel, which suggests that she was talking in terms of
separation, if not divorce:

Of course, if you really want to go away: if you feel that it's the sort of liberty—the
sort of solution towards which we ought to go—it must be managed. The baby, I
suppose, could go into the convent & we could let the house, I remaining in London.
Perhaps in that case I could get on with work: but I don't, Heaven knows, desire a
separation—if you think that you can sustain the glooms that appear inevitably to
come over me, for no reason really adequate.

But think about it well & I will suggest it to Tebb.—I am so dreadfully sorry for
you—you couldn't say more on your own side than my conscience—& still more, my
heart—say for you. Do believe all that.

And do believe that I care for you very tenderly, old thing—[15]

Those obscure comments about his conscience could well refer to Mary; or they
could refer to his guilt at inflicting his gloom, his feeling that his depressions were
destroying their marriage. Either way, the couple had drifted into a tortuous habit
of self-deception, Elsie manœuvring Ford into giving her reassurances about
which he could not himself be sure (he cannot bring himself to say he *loves* her;

the kisses he sends are for 'the baby', the name he used to call her by, but which now only means Katharine, aged 5); and he explaining to her why the very thing *she* doesn't want (but has perhaps suggested to call his bluff)—a parting—is what *he* doesn't want, but she does, and why it would be for her own good (sparing her his glooms). One of the dominant features of his depression is a fear of the future, an inability to face it. At Mammern he felt that the future had begun to exist for him again. Now, feeling that he was beginning to emerge from his breakdown, he could at least imagine what it would be like to imagine a future: 'I think a course of [Tebb's] tranquil society is restoring me to a state of mind that ought to help me to face the future reasonably.' His only fictional imagining of the future, *The Inheritors*, had ended with despair and defeat, a solipsistic and agoraphobic withdrawal from society. Unlike H. G. Wells, he never again attempted to use fiction to look into the future. Yet his best work comes out of this dual attitude to the future: a need to attempt to face it reasonably, together with a fear that it didn't exist for him, that to face his future was to imagine his own death. His conviction that novels should render rather than prophesy was perhaps founded on a strong personal inclination to look backwards (into history, or historical romance) rather than forwards. It was at this time that he first conceived of the idea of *Ladies Whose Bright Eyes* (1911). Pinker, he told Elsie, was anxious that he should write 'the story of the man who went back to the XIII cent.'. After confronting modern England in *The Soul of London*, *The Benefactor*, and *The Heart of the Country*, which he was finishing in July, Ford's imagination was itself going back in time, to the sixteenth century of Henry VIII and Katharine Howard.[16]

Elsie left for the continent with Christina and Ford's mother in July, and Ford was as good as his words about being able to work. By 22 July he had finished *Holbein*; by 14 August *The Benefactor* was also finished, while Ford was nursing Katharine through ringworm. When Elsie suspected a coldness in the tone of his letters, he explained: 'since my illness, life has lost all its savour & I'm cold to *every* thing. You don't know what a grey world mine is.' He joined Elsie briefly at Étaples at the end of August, but she stayed on until the middle of September—by which time he was able to send Alston Rivers half of *The Fifth Queen*. After 'a positively *appalling* passage' Ford was back by 4 September, when he told Elsie that a rest with the H. G. Wellses 'revived me a little'. 'My dear child', he tried to reassure her:

I've been thinking a great deal about you. I *do* wish I could make you more happy. I suppose I *am* a selfish brute, but I can't, really, really, believe that I'm as bad as you think me. Because I *do* care for you—very much—& it makes me terribly miserable to think of your unhappiness.—*Do*, my dear child, try to believe that I care for you. It is as much your duty to try to believe it (since it is the truth) as it is mine to try to believe that I can walk. If you *don't* try you never will—& you will always be seeing these signs that I don't care for you. I do: I do: I do. *Do* try to believe it.[17]

His perplexity at his intimates thinking him worse than he could believe, his desire that they should believe better of him, and his frightening insight that

people's understanding of each other, even their psychological states, depend
upon beliefs or efforts of belief, loom large in his subsequent writings.

The Benefactor was published in October 1905. The faint praise it attracted in the
press must have been damningly dismaying to Ford, who had been writing and
revising the book for over four years—even though he feared 'it's really too
harrowing to be good'. The reviewers acknowledged its strange and strangely
compelling qualities: like all Ford's prose it is thoroughly readable, even where it
becomes transparently self-justifying. The *Academy* noted that it was 'at least not
like other people's novels', and judiciously (if datedly) assessed the qualities that
made it interesting, finding it 'bitter', but 'at the same time a manly and
clear-sighted novel, the sadness of which is very difficult to shake off', concluding
that it was 'much better written than most novels'.[18] That effect of sadness is more
effectively sustained than in *The Inheritors*, and the technical sophistication of the
book demonstrates how much Ford had learned about writing from the collaborative experiment. But it also shows how much he was beginning to emerge from
under the Conradian shadow; for the dominant influence on subject, style, and
form is not Conrad but Henry James.

   The subject matter tells much about how Ford was using fictional form to shake
off his own sadnesses. The sadness of adulterous passion—George Moffat is
separated from his wife and in love with Clara Brede, whom he ultimately
renounces. (As Thomas Moser says, it is Ford's first novel explicitly to treat
adultery.) The sadness of unrecognized talent—George is a good poet and
novelist, who deprecates his gifts and achieves only belated success. The sadness
of mental illness and suicidal depression, as manifested by Clara's father. The
sadness of personal betrayals—this is a more emphatic note in *The Benefactor* than
in the earlier novels. With the exception of Conrad, there is no evidence that Ford
thought his literary friends had betrayed him as George is betrayed by his
protégés in the novel. This feeling reflects a persecutory anxiety during Ford's
breakdown; but it also duplicates the example of Madox Brown, as does George's
role as artist-patron.[19] As Madox Brown had exhorted the young Ford to do (and
as Ford had done for Conrad), George beggars himself rather than refuse
assistance to others—emotionally and artistically as well as financially. Mizener
wrote well about how 'the disastrous consequences of George's altruism accumu-
late with nightmarish plausibility'; but his judgement on the book is representative
of a misunderstanding of what Ford is attempting: 'it is as if Ford could achieve
enough psychic distance from George to describe him accurately but not enough
to judge him [. . .] George never recognizes that this altruism is the product of
an unconscious and perhaps self-protective arrogance; and it is not clear that
George's creator recognized it either, though he provides the evidence for it.' This
is the perennial unclarity of Ford's fiction, the precise aim of which is to render
its subjects without authorial commentary. Providing the evidence is all one can
hope for from a novelist who eschews explicit judgement on principle. The form
and matter of such fictions can themselves intimate Ford's sympathies. He clearly

approves of George too much to consider that his altruism is *only* the product of arrogance, though he is too scrupulous not to permit the possibility that arrogance has a role to play. He wants us to be able to see George as genuinely moral, and at the same time someone whose morality becomes an alibi for fear and pride. Not long before beginning the book Ford had written to Olive Garnett: 'And so you are growing proud—well, well. How does it manifest itself & what is the cause? I have long needed to be taken down a peg or two—I never quite knew why. Some are born proud, others have pride thrust upon them.' The Ford who had written that knew about the arrogance that conceals uncertainties and doubts. And if he could see it in himself, how could he not see it in his creations? What he could see, but what critics and biographers cannot always see (in their determination to establish their critical distance from their subject), is the complexities of human motive. One of the main interests in the book is the way even an ostensible virtue like altruism can become inextricable from self-deception and destruction: the altruist can ruin his own life and the lives of those he tries to help. George is presented as a problem—even to himself—but a problem to be appreciated and experienced rather than a problem to be solved. The problem of Ford's art in the book is how to present his central character without prejudging him. It is a technical challenge which elicits much formal and tonal subtlety from a still relatively inexperienced novelist.[20]

One important way in which Ford shows his grasp of the moral complexities is in his using the idea of altruism as a means of exploring the nature of his own art. For George is one of his earliest characters whose activities have much in common with the novelist's. It is not just that George is himself a writer—a desultory poet whose work can none the less inspire a political movement (he is visited by Moldavians, whose revolutionaries adopted a song George had written to encourage Greeks fighting for independence); and, like Ford, a poet recently turned novelist. It is also that Ford perceives similarities between what George does with people and what he does with characters:

With him it was like drink—and he knew it. He came across men, vivid, real, with strong outlines, with intense hopes, and he entered into their desires and hopes, and made them more than his own. He went casting about, really taking unheard of troubles, and racking his brains. He did not want to do something for them so much as to set them in the position of their ideal as they represented it, or as he figured it. (p. 50)

George's altruism is a drug ('it was like drink') and an arrogance (he is like a god, fulfilling other people's wishes). The men he comes across already sound like fictional characters ('vivid, real, with strong outlines'). His task, like that of the Fordian non-propagandist novelist, is not to impose his desires on them, but to provide them with a context in which they can fulfil their own desires, and become fully themselves. The 'unheard of troubles' taken by George might represent the brain-rackings of Ford and Conrad for the *mot juste*, the effective word which, by virtue of its unobtrusive rightness, is 'unheard', not noticed.

George enters into the desires and hopes of others, making them 'more than his own', because he feels he has none of his own: 'Seeing always, clearly enough, the ends and aims of others; never having had any very conscious goal of his own, he had always been content to step out of the way, and to supply the immense incentive of applause. It was as if, recognising very fully the futility of human strivings, he were content himself to strive not at all (p. 214).' And yet this passage comes just as he is being forced to recognize that he does have desires—that, as Ford very clearly knows, his aloofness is a denial of desire. 'For the very first time in his life George found himself full of a personal envy'—for Carew, Clara's South American cousin and George's rival for her love. George, the detached altruist, 'very certainly desired this man's failure'. It is once again Carew who prompts the book's crux: George's full recognition of his passion for Clara, in terms which anticipate *The Good Soldier*:

And, afterwards, George had to listen to the thoughts of his own mind. All the barriers of altruism were levelled before a passion not to be held off. He wanted Clara Brede. He wanted her love; he wanted her to be enthralled; cut off—smiles, glances, tears and thoughts—from the rest of the world. Rationally or irrationally, for better or very much for worse, she had for him a charm that was, that could be, in no other person in the world [. . .]

He saw the words 'Not to be' scrawled across the prospect. But it is at once the solace and the curse of mankind that one must for ever picture the just impossible as the supremely desirable—that one must always imagine the place where such things might be, the place beyond the horizon, at the back of beyond. (pp. 278–9)

The phrase 'the barriers of altruism' knows precisely how altruism has become a self-protective screen, a defence against a destructive passion. And yet, as the next paragraph knows, it is precisely the barriers to passion, the taboos with which society seeks to hold it off, that make the 'not to be' the supremely desirable. It was when the Martindales tried to make his love for Elsie 'not to be' that he became all the more determined to have her. The intimation here is that it was precisely the incest taboo that made him desire Mary. This would be the centre of his best books too. *The Good Soldier* and *Parade's End* both turn on questions of adultery and intimations of incest. And in both, as in *The Benefactor*, such ideas are bound up with the desire to transgress another taboo, the religious injunction against suicide. Christopher Tietjens too recalls Hamlet, as he imagines his own death, and wonders whether the war will permit him to be, or 'not to be'.

Not only is Ford aware of the motives of altruism, but he is aware that his own stance as a novelist might be an expression of similar motives: his god-like aloofness from his characters is uncomfortably close to arrogance—his sympathy for individual human fates at odds with the almost contemptuous superiority in his attitude to 'the futility of human strivings'. When George gets Clara's sister Dora to marry the would-be author Hailes, he acts like a novelist gone wrong. His voyeuristic meddling is a perversion of the sympathetic identification the novelist needs. (So, in *A Call*, Robert Grimshaw marries off Pauline, the woman he loves, to his best friend. And so, in *The Good Soldier*, Leonora Ashburnham manages her husband's mistresses whenever she can.) Ford is aware, that is, that a pose of novelistic aloofness might itself be a denial of his emotional involvement with the material being reworked into fiction. Or perhaps one should say that it is a corrective injunction against self-indulgent involvement, since Ford's critical principles combine the need for objectivity with the need for subjectivity, artistic impersonality with art's expression of the artist's personality. When George says 'one can't get away from one's own personality', he sounds like Ford arguing with Conrad about whether a writer can so escape: 'This was the one subject upon which we never came to any agreement. It was the writer's view that everyone has a natural cadence of his own from which in the end he cannot escape. Conrad held that a habit of good cadence could be acquired by the study of models.'[21] Through *The Benefactor* Ford asks whether art can escape from or transcend the artist's personality and how private life can get confused with public art. The novel touches on the private life of George's brother Gregory and his wife in such a way as to usher in these questions. 'When he came in from business,' writes Ford, Gregory 'brushed against groups of ladies'—all quite proper so far: the ladies are debating on the landings:

Hardly more than two or three of them were even hazily aware of his identity. Half their number would have disputed the assertion that a certain Mr. Frewer Hoey was not Mr. Moffat—was not, in fact, *the* Mr. Moffat, 'who, don't you remember, wrote that delightful . . .' and then a pause of doubt as to what it was he *had* written.

Mr. Frewer Hoey was seen with her everywhere, a dark person with an extremely rigid spine, acting as her private secretary in her political activities. He was a quite good composer of ballads in his leisure moments. The confusion of identities, inextricable as it was, was excusable. (pp. 13–14)

There is a double confusion of identities here. *The* Mr Moffat is George, with whom his self-effacing brother is confused. But there is also the confusion about whether Mr Frewer Hoey, always seen with Mrs Moffat, is her husband. One implication is that Mr Frewer Hoey is acting as too private a secretary; and that the Mrs Gregorys of the world have no trouble with the scruples that cause George to feel he must renounce Clara rather than commit adultery. Another implication is that the identity of Mr Frewer Hoey, 'a quite good composer of ballads', could be excusably confused with that of Mr Ford Hueffer, also a quite good composer of ballads, who might in turn be confused with that writer, George. Frewer Hoey does not figure much in the rest of the novel. His appearance in this passage has a dual effect. It is at once a signature—an acknowledgement *within* the book that the person and personality of 'F.H.' is to be found in the novel; and at the same time a challenge: don't, like the imperceptive socialites, confuse F.H. with George, just because you notice contingent similarities! When Olive Garnett wrote, presumably suggesting that her brother Edward had been used as a model for one of the characters, Ford's excitedly defensive reply displays a similar dual attitude. He rejects particular attributions, and sends up the notion of being able to unlock the novel as if it were a *roman à clef*. And yet he does not deny the possibility of seeing real people in the characters; rather, the inventiveness of his response leaves the impression that he considers his fiction as inextricably bound up with the people around him, though not a simple transcription of them:

Dear Olive:

God help us all: do you think that I—even I—would wear my heart upon my sleeve for—well, say Hampstead—to peck at? [Olive lived in Tanza Road, on the edge of Hampstead Heath.]

And then Edward! Where, oh my Gawd!, does Edward come in? You just wait till I do *you*!

The failure of the book is of course in the presentation of Ford Edward & (shall we say) M$^{rs.}$ Patrick Campbell-Olive-Connie-Henriette Corkran-Mary-Rossetti Brede.

And the triumph of the book is . . . Ah well, it lay in that glorious gift of youth that made it go thro'—that will never, any more—not ever—make anything more go thro', for

y$^{r.}$ aff^{te}

Ford M. H.

You remind me, you know, of M$^{rs.}$ What was her name? who searched Shakespeare so minutely for bi-lingual[?] cyphers. But of course I love you for taking so much trouble. Did you identify the allusions p. 47 l[l.] 20–6 & p. 264 ll.1–17? If not, take a microscope![22]

Olive was convinced that Ford already had done her—as Clara. Certainly he meant to keep her wondering: his mock-threatening denial, 'just wait', is at odds with his adding of her name to the list of acquaintances making up the compound female character. It may have been this exchange that gave Ford the idea for the unequivocal satire of the Garnetts and the Limpsfield community in *The Simple Life Limited* five years later. In November 1905 she wrote in her diary: 'Ford came [. . .] We talked about "The Benefactor". He said he had Connie [Garnett] & [Henry] James in his mind in writing of Clara & George. I said I didn't believe it [. . .] He was in good spirits. "The Benefactor" represented me up to three months ago! He admitted it might be a little out of date.'[23] The fact that he is citing different 'originals' is partly to do with the good-spirited banter. Ford was seizing another opportunity to take the 'respectable Garnetts' down a peg or two. It can't have softened Edward Garnett's irritation with Ford to hear that his novel portrayed the Constance character as in love with the Ford-James character. But Ford's remarks could also be taken as an extension of the lists in his letter: the 'Ford Edward' character also has a touch of James. Rather than being portraits of particular individuals, Ford's characters are, in one of his favourite images, 'composite portraits', superimpositions of multiple photographs compounding a convincing personality from many particular sources, some observed and some imagined.

The relevance to Olive of the first of the 'allusions' cited in Ford's letter is not clear. But the second is yet another tease, referring to a moment when Clara catches herself thinking of flirting with her cousin in order to arouse George:

Above: 'The Last Likeness of Madox Brown'

Right: Catherine Hueffer, by Ford Madox Brown

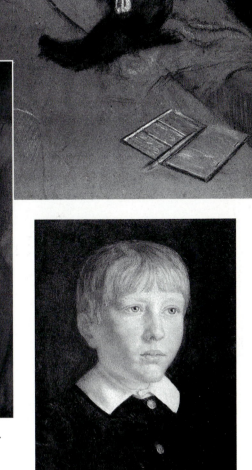

Above: Francis Hueffer, by Catherine Hueffer

Right: Ford, aged 8

Juliet Hueffer, aged 4, by Ford Madox Brown

Ford, aged 3, as 'Tell's Son', by
Madox Brown

Elsie Hueffer in 1895, by Catherine Hueffer

Mary Martindale

J. B. Pinker, *c.*1896

Pent Farm

Below: Joseph Conrad, 1896

Arthur Marwood, *c.*1903

Edward Garnett

Olive Garnett, 1893

Below: Lucy Masterman

C. F. G. Masterman

Supposing she put her hand on her cousin's arm [...] It struck her rather comfortingly that she was now a 'mere coquette.' She had always despised such women. She had fallen very low. She understood them now. It was a woman's right. She understood vividly that the fight between man and woman is according to no code of honour. Besides, she imagined that George himself admired a spice of coquetry in a woman. He had bantered her about her continual 'scruples.' (p. 264)

Ford certainly bantered Olive about her 'superiority', and they certainly had had at least one conversation (in July 1905) taking in these topics: 'Edward and Ford came [she wrote in her diary]; F. staying at Dr. Tebb's, saw H.J. on Sunday [...] Went for a walk with Ford through Golder's Hill (Calderon. James. The Heart of the Country. The reproductive instinct. Change in me) [...] Edward & Ford after dinner. The union of divine souls. The Mystic Rose. "You don't care." Flirtation.'[24] Ford's letter is as high-spirited as the earlier conversation appears to have been. But there is a more serious sub-text to Ford's riposte that Clara's contemplation of coquetry can be seen (microscopically) as an allusion to Olive. The new turn he gives to her humorously affectionate writing of herself into the book is to point out where such identification logically leads. If Clara is Olive to George's Ford, Olive is all but acknowledging an unspoken love; or at least she is noticing that Ford's story has obliquely spoken of it. The point to stress here is that the idea *is* a joke, if a flirtatious one. It is also revealing about the workings of Ford's imagination, and about the dangers of translating too literally from characters back to putative originals, as Olive was doing. Theirs was a very close friendship, uninterrupted until Ford's estrangement from Elsie was complete. She was his closest female friend, and while his marriage was collapsing he felt more at ease with her than with other women. While he had been in Germany Olive got fewer letters than Elsie; but whereas Elsie was burdened with Ford's day-to-day anxieties, the letters to Olive were chattier and more relaxed. None of this constitutes evidence of anything more than a close friendship, nor does *The Benefactor* represent such evidence. What it does demonstrate is Ford's habit of imaginative extrapolation. Rather than representing a suppressed affair with Olive, or even a desire for an affair, the book comes out of a creative wondering, an asking 'what if . . .' 'Free Love' and the 'New Woman' were the topics of the day, as Olive's records of their conversations show. *The Benefactor* is translating into fictional form the question that they might well have been debating: whether all friendships are affected by 'the reproductive instinct', or whether, in Dowell's deeply problematic words, 'the sex instinct [...] might be left out of the calculation'.[25] It is possible to see Ford's 'Tale of a Small Circle' as encompassing the small circle of Hueffers and Garnetts. One can even pose James as the circle's centre, to the extent that George draws on some of his mannerisms and Ford's style draws on his manner. Even the central theme of sexual renunciation is quintessentially Jamesian. It perhaps appealed to Ford because of his own tendency to disavow and displace his own sexuality. But Ford, who had been seeing and reading James avidly for several years, must also have been intrigued by the way someone so percipient about sexuality, and so evidently fascinated by its social manifestations, could lead a celibate life. Ford is explicit about how there are many possible ways of seeing real individuals in the characters. But as a novelist he has added the variable of passion, and thus transformed the biographical material into something quite other.

14

1906: POLITICS, MARWOOD,
THE FIFTH QUEEN

Do words make up the majesty
Of man . . . ?

('Geoffrey Hill, 'Three Baroque Meditations')

Elsie left for the continent again in February 1906, travelling first to Paris and
Rome, and later in the spring and summer to Florence and Milan. By now the
tension between her and Mary was evident. Ford wrote to Elsie: 'I think of you
very often—& always very lovingly'; 'I don't feel at all certain that Mary will
reach Rome: if she does I should think you had better go to see her'. He even
suggested (as Conrad had to him when he was ill in Germany) that she should
write up her 'impressions de voyage' and he would try to get them published.
Ford had asked Olive Garnett if she would accompany Elsie. 'I said I w$^{d.}$ if he
w$^{d.}$ come too!', she wrote in her diary. He also told her that he hadn't voted
in the General Election on 12 January (at which there was a Liberal land-
slide). He was staying in Hammersmith with his mother, and taking 'long
walks all over London every day—five miles at least'. 'I think it really agrees
with me better than the country', he told Elsie, 'because one sees little incidents
to keep one from brooding.' He worked as hard as he walked, finishing the
manuscript of *The Pre-Raphaelite Brotherhood*, his third monograph for Duckworth's Popular Library of Art (edited by Edward Garnett), correcting the revises
of *The Fifth Queen*, and beginning to write the third volume of the trilogy on
England and the English, The Spirit of the People. None the less he found time
to help Wells in his bid to hijack the Fabian Society. On 9 February
Wells delivered his paper on 'The Faults of the Fabian', in which he objected to
the way the meetings, dominated by the 'Old Gang' of Beatrice and Sidney Webb,
Shaw, and the Blands, had a social as much as a political tone—and a
selfdefeating middle-class tone at that. Ford joined in the same month, and in
March delivered a talk intended to divide the society to enable Wells to rule it.
'I've made my lecture violently insulting,' he wrote to Elsie just before delivering
it, 'so God knows how I shall get thro' it.' He did indeed receive the abuse he
knew he had provoked: 'My lecture was a great success in so far as it was meant
to incite discussion. It *did*. People fell on me & on each other; & I really think
that I have materially accelerated the split in the Fabian Society, wh. was what I

wanted to do.'¹ The only split he accentuated appears to have been the one
between Wells and the 'Old Gang', who 'wiped the floor', as Ford later realized.
His 'attack on Socialism' can only have damaged Wells's credibility as a potential
Fabian leader.

The next evening Ford drove down to Winchelsea with Oliver and Byles. His
description for Elsie of the journey is typical of the stories about Oliver, and
suggests how Oliver's histrionic 'presence' was a frustration to Ford, as well as an
incitement to perform:

Oliver took command as a person knowing every inch of the road. At 12.15 we pulled
up bang in the centre of a stockyard at the bottom of a valley seven miles from
Orpington. We all had to get out & shove in the manure &, in the middle of the
operations there appeared an infuriated ['farmer' deleted] lanthorn held by an invisible
farmer. So we learned that we had taken a private road. We ran backwards for ten
minutes because there was no room to turn. When we reached the highroad Oliver
once more took command. We performed a complete circle of five miles & arrived at
the Crays wh. we had left at 12.5: it was then 12.45.—Oliver then took command once
more. But the driver said Damn ...... & we reached Tunbridge by 1.30.—We then
pulled up in front of those old houses & ate sandwiches & drank whisky. I then took
command, because of course I know the road from Tunbridge via Frant, Roberts-
bridge & Brede. Oliver then talked.......... At 2.15 I was awakened by the chauffeur's
saying: 'Which way now, sir?'—We were at a road like this ——|——& it was
Mayfield. The turning off to Frant was 12 miles behind. The sign post said: To __
__ __ and Broad Oak. 8 Miles. I said: 'Oh well: Broad Oak is near Brede;' so we went
on till 2.45. & arrived by a sign-post at the end of the world. Road like this ——< the
North going to Cade Sᵗ the S. to Lewes 8 miles.—We were in Broad Oak, but not
Brede Broad Oak. Eventually we reached Hastings at five o'clock. Oliver talked the
whole way.... At H. Oliver & I had to get out & push the car, chauffeur & the
peacefully sleeping Byles up the hill to Ore.—I fell asleep carving the cold leg of
mutton which Mʳˢ· Field had left on the table. Byles fell asleep, the chauffeur fell
asleep. And Oliver, discovering that no one was listening to him, sang.²

Ford would take the children out at weekends from La Sagesse convent, taking
them to the sea, or to lunch with Wells or his new friend, Marwood.³ Arthur
Pierson Marwood was five years Ford's senior. He may have seemed to Ford as
Ashburnham seems to Dowell, 'like a large elder brother'. His father, George
Metcalfe Marwood, was a direct descendant of Edward III. The family had owned
the estate of Busby Hall, Stokesly, near Middlesbrough in Yorkshire, since the
fifteenth century. Arthur was the youngest of four sons, and had seven younger
sisters. He was a first cousin of Lewis Carroll, and was, like him, a gifted
mathematician. He was also an uncle of Margaret Kennedy, the author of the 1924
best-seller *The Constant Nymph*. After Clifton College he went to Trinity College,
Cambridge, in 1887 to read mathematics, but had to leave in his second year due
to ill-health. He had tuberculosis. His eldest brother died young; 'the second
became a distinguished civil servant in London, and the third was a battalion
commander in India. Thus', as Moser says, Arthur 'might have run the estate if

his health had permitted it.' Instead, he was in a Leeds private nursing home when he met Caroline Cranswick, a matron who nursed him there. They married in Leeds on 3 February 1903, and moved to Winchelsea, where one of his sisters lived in the 'Old Forge', in the hope that the milder climate would be good for his tuberculosis.[4]

Marwood seemed to Ford the type of the English gentleman, 'très grand seigneur': 'the heavy Yorkshire squire with his dark hair startlingly silver in places, his keen blue eyes, his florid complexion, his immense, expressive hands and his great shapelessness.' After Madox Brown, Conrad, and James, he was to become the most important man in Ford's life and in his writing. His traits can be glimpsed in characters from most of Ford's novels after 1905. Henry VIII in The *Fifth Queen* trilogy; the god in *Mr. Apollo*; Dudley Leicester in *A Call*; Mr Luscombe in *The Simple Life Limited*; Mr Sorrell in *Ladies Whose Bright Eyes*; both the Duke of Kintyre and Lord Aldington in *The New Humpty-Dumpty*; Mr Blood in *Mr. Fleight*; Ashburnham; George Heimann in T*he Marsden Case*; the English *milord* Assheton Smith in *A Little Less Than Gods*; and Hugh Monckton in *The Rash* Act and *Henry for Hugh*.[5]

Most discussions of Marwood's importance to Ford have concentrated on the ideal of the old-fashioned feudal Tory gentleman. He seemed to Ford an incarnation of 'The Last of England', and Ford's writing about him shrouds a personal elegy for his friend within a historical elegy: 'He possessed the clear, eighteenth century English mind which has disappeared from the earth, leaving the earth very much the poorer.' But, as here, it was Marwood's intellect, rather than his class or his politics, that most struck Ford. He valued 'the peculiar, scornful, acute quality of his mind [. . .]'. 'There was nothing under the sun that we did not discuss and no topic on which he could not in some minute particular at least correct my assertions. He would wait for a long time and then rather jestingly drop his correction into the middle of a quite unrelated topic.' 'He was a man of infinite benevolence, comprehensions and knowledges.' Conrad, whom Ford introduced to Marwood in 1905 or 1906, found him equally impressive. He described him as 'a great reader with a profound knowledge of literature, in whose judgement I have an absolute confidence'; he was 'the real Wise man of the Age'. According to Ford, Marwood said of himself 'beside Conrad's vibrating small figure: "We're the two ends of human creation: he's like a quivering ant and I'm an elephant built out of mealsacks!" .' Ford was to re-imagine the contrast as that between the wiry Macmaster and bulky Tietjens in the opening of *Some Do Not . . . .* Ford and Conrad were not alone in being impressed by Marwood's piercing intellect. 'He read voluminously, and seemed to have forgotten nothing of what he ever had read', wrote Archibald Marshall: 'He was the most remarkable instance of the encyclopaedic mind that I have ever come across. There seemed to be no subject upon which he did not possess a store of detailed information. He wrote with difficulty and wrote very little, but he had a clear and convinced appreciation of literary values.' All these traits are recognizable in the character Ford modelled most closely on Marwood (and, unusually, humbly acknowledged the resemblance): the 'meal-sack elephant', Christopher Tietjens of Groby.[6]

By a typical paradox, Ford liked to think of Marwood as his opposite—stable, a member of the 'county' establishment—as well as his double. Many of his descriptions hover between a sympathetic identification on the one hand, and on the other seeing himself and Marwood as being at opposite ends of human creation. Marwood was 'deliberate, slow in movement and extraordinarily omniscient'; Ford prided himself on his own impression of omniscience. Marwood's illness, the sense of suffering beneath the phlegmatic surface, seemed to reflect not only Ford's ideal of English self-suppression, but his sense of his own mental turbulence being overmastered. Marwood 'was, beneath the surface, extraordinarily passionate—with an abiding passion for the sort of truth that makes for intellectual accuracy in the public service'. In particular, as here, most of his comments about Marwood turn on the way he both was and wasn't like a writer. Ford, who had his own ambivalence about 'ambition' in himself as an artist, said Marwood 'was too unambitious to be a writer but, large, fair, clumsy, and gentle, he had the deepest and widest intelligence of all the men I have ever met'. He 'had the clear intelligence of a poet, but, rather than trespass on his own shyness and shamefacedness, he would spend days making corrections out of his head on the Margins of the Encyclopaedia Britannica'. About this latter feat (which Tietjens repeats), Ford explains in a way that is surely also autobiographical: 'he just wanted to bolster up his self-conceit to himself'. He was a visionary as well as a critic. 'He had his mysticisms', said Ford. 'When he talked of Higher Mathematics it was as if he were listening to the voice of angels. I suppose he saw the ocean round the throne when he considered the theory of waves, and that he saw resurrections when he thought of recurrent patterns in numbers.' One evening, while Ford was looking for something in his desk drawer, Marwood, who was sitting with him, saw a ghost, and suddenly said: 'There's a woman in lavender-coloured eighteenth-century dress looking over your shoulder into that drawer.' Like Ford, himself visionary and critic, Marwood incorporated both ends of human creativity.[7]

His style of utterance, too, let Ford see himself. What he most remembered about Marwood's conversation was the sweeping statement. 'I once discussed for a whole evening with him the characters of Shakespeare and of Our Redeemer. He said they both bored him—and he was perfectly serious.' Apropos his dictum that 'for any proper man there could only be four books in the English language that could be worth reading', Ford commented:

For myself I love sweeping dicta; they awaken trains of thought; and, the more obviously sweeping they are, the less they need to be taken *au pied de la lettre* and the more they may be refined down until the exact and balanced judgement is arrived at. If you wish to think, you must sketch in a rough design of the region that your thoughts may cover, so that you may proceed towards rendering it more exact and more precise.

His tribute to the stimulus of Marwood's friendship is at the same time his explanation of his own method of 'illuminative exaggerations'; a method which imagines Marwood as his perfect reader: the person who will proceed from Ford's impression to a 'more exact and precise' understanding.[8] The pleasure he found in pondering Marwood's thought-provoking paradoxes is the pleasure Ford's readers achieve when they read with sceptical humour, not *au pied de la lettre*.

Gerard Tetley, a nephew of Oliver's wife, acted as Ford's secretary for a while, and recalled his 'chronic dyspepsia when he dictated "The Heart of the Country" from his bed'; also his 'petulancy and his intolerance of stupidity'. He had written about London while he was living in Winchelsea; now that he was living in London, his mind characteristically brooded on the country. 'For the whole of life is really like that; we are almost always in one place with our minds somewhere quite other.' On Tuesdays or Wednesdays he would join the group of authors who met for lunch in the upper room at the Mont Blanc restaurant in Gerrard Street, Soho. Garnett (as 'London's literary—as if Nonconformist— Pope [. . .]', said Ford) sat at the top of the table, around which would be most of the major Edwardian literary figures: Belloc (who dominated the conversation, said R. H. Mottram, another habitué), Chesterton, Thomas Seccombe, Stephen Reynolds, Edward Thomas, W. H. Davies, R. A. Scott-James, Muirhead Bone, Perceval Gibbon, occasionally Galsworthy and W. H. Hudson, and less often, Conrad. *The Heart of the Country* begins with an atmospheric vignette about an unnamed naturalist (whom Ford later identified as Hudson) materializing at a 'dubious place of refection' (a literary lunch at the Mont Blanc). It becomes an allegory of the artist's visionary mental duality, as Hudson brings 'a touch of sweetness and magic' to the town from 'The Heart of the Country': 'So that, green and sinuous, a mirage seemed to dazzle and hang in air in the middle of the cigarette smoke, making a pattern of its own, vivid and thirst-inspiring, across the steely-blue of the restaurant mirrors.'[9]

Ford described the 'frantic rush' of his social life one weekend at the beginning of March: tea with James, followed by dinner with Wells on Saturday. On Sunday he picked up the girls from their convent and took them to the Bungalow, 'where H. G. had a fine argument with the great Marwood'. Then he went back to town, sitting up with Mottram, 'Galsworthy's protégé', until midnight. He was also seeing Conrad this year, and was beginning a new book, *The Nature of a Crime*, which would soon become a new collaboration. Ford described it to Elsie as 'a series of letters from a man about to commit suicide!—wh. Pinker wants me to publish anonymously. I think it will "go". It's awful piffle.' Signs of his depression were returning, so even a light-hearted reference to suicide was likely to alarm Elsie. He underwent a three-week 'Electrical cure' for renewed dyspepsia, explaining to Elsie that the 'Electrical Man [. . .] pumps electricity into me enough to send a tuppeny tube train from the Bank to Shepherds Bush & if he touches me a spark 5 inches long flashes across the room'; 'so if you like to pray for me do so. I daresay that will do more good than High Frequency.' 'As for enjoyment: God knows if I ever enjoy anything', he told Elsie: '& I'd probably effectively spoil all y^r enjoyment.—However: it's no use talking of that, is it?' The typescript of 'The Old Story'—a fragmentary draft of *The Nature of a Crime*—has a passage in which Ford was perhaps explaining to himself their unhappiness: 'If you have the nature of a seducer you will suffer, on this earth in special hell of your own creation.'[10]

He wrote a poem, 'Views', based on Elsie's visit to Rome, in which imagining being there and watching her gives way to a meditation on how the gap between impressions and reality troubles not only our knowledge of the world, but human relationships as well. It is, amongst other things, another expression of how he felt she did not know his world:

> Tho' you're in Rome you will not go, my You,
>   Up to that Hill. . . . but I forget the name,
> Aventine? Pincio? No, I never knew. . . .
>   I was there yesterday. You never came.
>
> I have that Rome; and you, you have a Me,
> You have a Rome and I, I have my You;
> My Rome is not your Rome: my you, not you
>   . . . For, if man knew woman
> I should have plumbed your heart; if woman, man
> Your me should be true I. . . .[11]

The woman is addressed as: 'You who have mingled with my soul in dreams, | You who have given my life an aim and purpose, | A heart, an imaged form.' But this romantic aspiration towards communion of souls is undercut by the idea that the soul mingling with his was his dream of her soul, not that soul itself; by the idea that he 'should have plumbed' her heart, but didn't; by the eerie sense that it is precisely his imaginative obsession with the woman, summoning her up as his companion 'In this unreal town of real things', that prevents a true rapport, only emphasizing the alienation between the self and its phantasms in the minds of others.

The Fifth Queen was published on 14 March. Alston Rivers had planned to bring it out on the 13th, but Ford felt superstitious about the date, and asked for a day's grace. Partly because of the acclaim of *The Soul of London*, and partly because the historical novel was enjoying an Edwardian vogue in the works of Baroness d'Orczy and Maurice Hewlett, Ford's novel of Henry VIII and Katharine Howard was enthusiastically received: reviewers said Ford had 'discovered his *métier*', and given 'the latest word upon method in the production of the historical novel'. The publicity cheered him up. When he went to dinner with Olive Garnett on 21 March, and took her to Hofmannsthal's *Electra* at the Court Theatre, they missed the train, so drove all the way in a cab, and returned with Dr Tebb. 'Ford's happiness and success', she wrote in her diary: 'His journalist admirers, speeches at clubs, portrait in Bystander, reviews & pecuniary satisfactions.' His synopsis for the history of Henry he had originally planned had begun with a paraphrase of a Holbein portrait:

A man stood, immense, imponderable; his heavy feet, set apart, making one feel that their pressure drew protests from the earth. From a great face, its first clear lines hidden by grey hair & blurred by opaque & slightly trembling flesh, looked out dull, threatening & authoritative eyes set in red & half masked by drooping lids. They would strike terror when the flesh of the face hardened & quickened under passions; but, when no hot rage, fierce greed, inscrutable cunning, or heavy joy inspired them, it was as if they were weighed down by passive disgust & perhaps with hidden fear of the supernatural.[12]

The novels have this dense pictoriality too: it is, after all, a highly novelistic tableau with which to open a history. This emphasis on the visual is not new in Ford's writing; it can be traced back to his admiration for Madox Brown's ability to make subjects known from 'the driest of testamentary or historic parchments' so picturesque that they appeared to 'palpitate with life'.[13] The visual emphasis, however, is more sustained in the Tudor trilogy. It is also better integrated with the action. Anchored in the illusion of historical reconstruction, and the recreation of the court world which comes down to us interpreted by Holbein, Ford's fascination with the optics of experience seemed less disturbing to the reviewers than had the more trance-like visual descriptions of *Romance* or *The Soul of London*.

The portrait of Henry in the synopsis is also highly suggestive of Ford's attraction to the subject. The conjunction of terror and authority, flesh and spirit, passion and indifference, efficacy and passivity, dullness and inspiration, connotes a powerful identification. As ever, the antinomies with which Ford identifies are not only those of a man, but an artist. He later explained how he had a more modern Henry in mind—Henry James: 'I may as well now confess that in drawing Henry VIII in one of my own novels I was rendering the Master in externals—and mighty life-like the Press of those days found the portrait to be.' Thinking of Henry VIII in terms of a second writer prevents the identification from sounding like romanticized self-glorification and self-justification: the poor, uninfluential, and problematically English artist, whose breakdown reduced him to impotent dependence, wishfully fantasizing about being the most powerful Englishman of his time. Alan Judd has praised Ford's 'eye for power, both in depiction of those who have it and in his sense of how it is used and how it affects'. As 'The Life and Times of Henry VIII' was reinvented as *The Fifth Queen*, Ford's allegiances became dual in another sense. His working title for the first novel indicates that he had come to think of the work as being as much about 'Katharine Howard' as about Henry. The novel is greater than a dual self-portrait of Ford, seen from inside and from outside, both as he is and as he would like to be. It is also a responsibly dual portrait of a doomed marriage. Moser says, 'No doubt his dismay at having betrayed Elsie, combined with his 'longings to be free, made the story of Katharine and Henry particularly vivid to him'; which is persuasive, apart from the slight anachronism of Ford's 'longings to be free': he certainly longed to be free from Elsie by 1908; before then he was deeply ambivalent. Henry represents a path Ford's Catholicism seems to debar, but that his Englishness makes him heir to.[14]

To understand the trilogy's relation to the facts of his marriage we need to understand its relation to the facts of the history it re-creates. Ford had written to Richard Garnett that he was 'engaged upon the amiable task of "whitewashing" Katharine Howard'. The whitewashing is principally of Katharine's sexuality; a denial of two charges: that she was ' "unchaste" with one, two, or three men and that she concealed this from her husband Henry VIII'; and that she was unfaithful to Henry after her marriage, receiving 'late at night in her bedchamber, her former suitor Thomas Culpepper'. By overturning most authorities on the subject, and denying both charges, Ford converts Katharine's death into a religious martyrdom: a matter of principle rather than prurience. It is here that, to modern sensibilities, the novel most appears to romanticize history; and it is a surprising measure of the shift in taste that some of the original reviewers complained that there was not enough of (what one called) 'the concentrating stimulus of true romance'. Ford immediately replied, assuring the reviewer in a letter to his editor, 'I have not had any intention or wish to keep that sacred and beautiful thing Romance out of my trilogy'. The question is, how much did he want to keep the received view of Katharine out of it? 'By whitewashing Katharine', says Moser, 'he could deny the unthinkable fact that he and Mary had been unchaste. By pitying Katharine, he could pity Elsie for the suffering he had caused.' He could perhaps also express the fear that he was endangering Elsie's life. Ford's language, however, suggests that what he intended was a dual view of purity and sexuality, like the dual moral view advocated by Throckmorton, Thomas Cromwell's spy: 'a man may act most evilly [. . .] and yet be the best man in the world.'[15] The polygamist need not be irredeemable; but then the idealist need not be impeccable. A whitewashing is not a vindication but a suppression, and to call the novel a whitewashing is to concede the felt presence of the problems being covered up. After all, *The Fifth Queen Crowned* ends—unusually for romance conventions—with the doomed heroine tormenting the hero by saying that he will never be certain about her fidelity to him. As with Ford's fictions about his own history, much of the trilogy's interest comes from the dual response it provokes precisely because of the way it is at odds with the received history. We cannot simply forget the received version. Mizener's comment that 'It is remarkable how cunningly he twists the best-known details of Katharine's story to his purposes' points up how Ford, by using the familiar material, keeps reminding us of the very interpretations he is denying (p. 475). This fabulatory vividness was becoming Ford's main mode of making his subjects (autobiographical as well as historical) come alive, giving them a moral and psychological three-dimensionality. And it doubled as a homage to his grandfather, by bringing back to life his manner of picturesque altering anecdote. The novels thus present Katharine as someone fundamentally honest, but about whom we cannot but have our doubts: a vivid problem, rather than the fairy-tale falsification she has been taken for. It is not only for these reasons that the trilogy is, in Mizener's words, 'a triumph of the historical imagination' (p. 475). It is because Ford's attraction to the subject is as much historical as personal; or rather, because—like all his best work—the trilogy is an attempt to frame his personal perplexities in a historical understanding. Henry VIII focuses Ford's concerns about polygamous desire, passion and omnipotence, and the obscure intimacy between altruism and sexuality. But the Tudor age is the cradle of modernity, with Thomas Cromwell as the figure who, as Ford put it in *The Critical Attitude*, 'gave us Modern England [. . .] not only the blessings it enjoys, but also its chief problem' (p. 16). At the turn of the century Ford had argued in *The Cinque Ports* that the chief need of his time was 'a just appreciation of the lessons of tradition—a possibility of being able to mould the future with some eye to the institutions of the old times before us' (p. 270). In the *Fifth Queen* trilogy he casts his eye back to the old times which shaped the present he was simultaneously analysing in his other English trilogy. The historical novels are thus a further, if oblique, instalment of Ford's analysis of Englishness. His own unhappiness is set in the broader context of the 'chief problem' of modern life: the widespread feeling that social structures and traditions were fragmenting, and that Edwardian England was becoming degenerate and dehumanized.[16]

The modern democratic state, Cromwell's legacy, is seen as the cause of such problems. Ford's unease with 'the levelling tendency of the unpleasant times we live in' can make him sound Pre-Raphaelite, beset by nostalgic romanticizations of a medieval feudalism. However, what the discussion of Cromwell in *The Critical Attitude* shows is that what Ford is attacking is not true democracy, and not socialism—even in his jeremiad to the Fabians—but the Liberal compromise: the 'discord [we would now say "contradictions"] that we have never muddled through into any harmonious resolution' (p. 17). One critic has commented on his hypothetical advocacy of views which anticipate Fascism. But the point is that Ford is not even hypothesizing about holding views such as this himself:

At present, not only does the State suffer degenerate persons to multiply, but by every means in its power it keeps alive the degenerate products of such unions, and in innumerable ways supports colonies of unnumbered creatures, maimed by mental and physical diseases

For all of these in the modern State the only logical remedies would be starvation, the axe, or the lethal chamber.[17]

Such Marwoodian 'sweeping dicta' are dangerous because so easily misunderstood. To some extent they are even intended to be misunderstood, or at least to provoke abuse: it is because the critic points out society's mental muddles that 'the critical attitude is so detested' (p. 22). But what Ford is advocating is not a murderous programme of racial hygiene, but 'the critical attitude', which will point out to citizens the 'logical' implications of their society's ethos. He is not attacking creatures 'maimed by mental and physical diseases'. The pity in the tone perhaps reveals a sense that under such a regime he would himself not last very long, regardless of whether his ailments were mental or physical. He is attacking the remorseless application of test of 'efficiency'. It is this that most disturbed him about Fabian socialism too. But the state towards which Ford was directing his critical attitude was not a socialist one, but Liberal England, then in the throes of the strange death chronicled by George Dangerfield. Ford's critique, though he seems only intermittently to realize it, is actually directed at Liberal capitalism, and the social imperialism of the Asquith cabinet. Whereas the medieval 'Christian Commonwealth' Ford opposes to the modern state is much closer to a socialist ideal:

The Church took the poor under its protection. It attempted to wrest from temporal powers as great a portion of their resources as it could. It administered more or less wastefully these resources, using them primarily in the interests of the cult, and secondarily in those of the poor, who are God's brothers. Thus after a fashion they left for Cæsar as little as they could of the thing that was Cæsar's, and rendered all the rest to God. (p. 17)

This opposition between past and present is central to *The Fifth Queen* too, as it is to most of Ford's work. Henry VIII represented to Ford 'the modern world being born out of the medieval'. As Mizener says, in the trilogy 'we are meant to see the life of our times reflected in the life of Henry VIII's'. Rather than an exercise in 'the politics of nostalgia', Ford's historical fiction takes a dual attitude to both present and past, trying to imagine each from within, as well as from outside, from the perspective of the other. The relationship is more diagrammatic in his purely fictional romance, *Ladies Whose Bright Eyes*, which literally transports a modern man into medieval times, in order to understand the benefits and the absurdities of both periods. The dual attitude is well-expressed in Moser's phrase about Ford's 'characteristic longing to leap out of the present so that he can look back at it'. The effect is not of escapism, but of making us see. Part of what we see is the temporal displacement. Ford later said that all his books before *The Good Soldier* had been 'in the nature of *pastiches*, of pieces of rather precious writing, or of *tours de force*'. This was an exaggeration, but it points up how a historical fiction such as *The Fifth Queen* is necessarily pastiche. This is true in two senses. First, a temporal sense: however compelling the historical reconstruction, we retain a dual attitude to it: it is a fake. We can go and see what Hampton Court looks like now, but we can't know exactly how everything looked in the sixteenth century, or whether the representation of speech is exact. Secondly, a veridical sense: we know the historical characters were real, and that some of the represented actions actually happened; but we also know that other actions, and most of the dialogue, is fabricated. This second sense, of course, shades off into the way *all* fiction is pastiche: ultimately fabulatory, however plausible. It is these dual attitudes to time and to reality that most engage Ford in his historical fiction as in his autobiographies.[18]

The Fifth Queen was Ford's first fully achieved fiction, and together with the English trilogy inaugurated the period which was the making of him as a writer, the decade between his breakdown and the writing of his first masterpiece, *The Good Soldier*; the decade which saw the *English Review*, 'Women & Men', *A Call*, *Ancient Lights*, and *Ladies Whose Bright Eyes*. When Conrad read the proofs of the concluding volume, *The Fifth Queen Crowned*, he wrote Ford a lyrical letter, explaining how he had just been trying to persuade a friend that 'of all the men that write to day it is only Hueffer who writes for love—for the sheer love of this world of vain appearances and mortal men [. . .] that sort of impartial love is a rare and distinguished motive of expression'. In *The Fifth Queen Crowned*, he continued:

There is not a single false note, not a jar, hardly ever a pause. It is a great harmony. How fine—how very fine! It is in fact—the whole cycle—a most noble conception. Last night when I closed the proofs for the last time I asked myself whether this was not the Swan song of Historical Romance.

Well nigh a hundred years is a long time for any form of artistic expression to endure. It is well that it should end with this pathetic and marvellous dignity—and for my part I can only say that I am glad *d'avoir vu cela*—the last gesture of historical romance: the hat cast upon the paving. Simply tremendous!¹⁹

1906–1907

Ford's brother-in-law David Soskice wanted to revisit Russia after the amnesty of 1905, and early in 1906 he and Juliet planned a trip. Ford thought he might be able to turn his knowledge garnered from Russian émigrés to effect if he went too. He sent an outline to Pinker:

What I propose to do in Russia is briefly this:
   To go to Petersburg with my brother-in-law David Soskice, who is a revolutionist of some considerable position—if that's the right word: to see as much as is practicable there of the revolution which is coming on (It has really only begun)—& to write, for as early publication as the posts will allow, a series of articles, forming a book of say 75,000 words—a book rather of impressions than statistics, of course.

He explained: 'Father Gapon, who organized the great movement which led to the January massacres, was actually hidden in my mother's house [in London] for a considerable time, &, since he is at present organizing the general strikes in Russia, he would be able to give me a great deal of help.' He had contacts in Moscow, Odessa, and Poland too. 'I should, I suppose, run a good deal of risk—but I don't fancy that I should shirk that, as far as I know myself.' Again there is the characteristic hint of noble suicide: would he not shirk risk because he sought it? Evidently Pinker couldn't interest a publisher, and wasn't prepared to finance the trip himself, so Ford never saw Russia, and unfortunately the improbable volume of revolutionary impressions remains unwritten. Soskice was arrested in Petersburg after Count Witte suppressed the Petersburg soviet, though his credentials as a British journalist got him released. Father Gapon was murdered by socialist revolutionaries in the spring of 1906.[1]
   When Levin Schücking arrived in England for a visit on 6 April Ford was pleased with the companionship, and took his friend to visit Swinburne and Watts-Dunton, and on various lunch calls at which they met celebrities including Beatrice Webb and Winston Churchill. But after five days (and the prospect of another two weeks) of 'Running about with Schücking', Ford wrote to Elsie that it was 'slowly destroying' him.[2]
   '[A] child is a most ingenious being,' he wrote to Elsie in a pose of naïve discovery: 'You tell it not to do every imaginable thing & in the next minute it immediately discovers six other things you have not thought of.' Christina and Katharine had seemed to Ford to have grown 'rather rough[?] and [. . .] unreasonably Papist' at La Sagesse, so he made arrangements to transfer them to

a convent near Brook Green, the Sacred Heart, where they could be day-pupils. Spending more time with these ingenious beings had given him opportunities to exercise his own ingenuity, and invent fairy-tales for them. At the end of the year Alston Rivers published a volume of them, *Christina's Fairy Book*. Ford's description of the series he had devised is representative of his knack of transposing adult facts into childlike fancies, and attaining a delicate humour of the *faux-sophistiqué*: 'I have pretty well settled the Fairy Tale series for Rivers. It will open with my short fairy tales & include a child's Baedeker to Fairy Land, a Fairy Biographical Dictionary, a series of Fairy plays for children & a fifth volume of some sort: the whole to be sold in a little wooden book-case.' It was also a therapeutic exercise. He explained in a preface that he was telling his children the stories in order to save them from his own childhood terrors: 'As a child I used to see wolves and demons. I can feel still some of the agonies I felt then. I wished to spare my children some of these fears by peopling their shadows with little and friendly beings.' His breakdown had brought home the fact that such terrors had never completely left him, though writing had become a means of keeping them at bay.[3]

He met the press baron Sir Alfred Harmsworth at the end of the month, in order to pursue the idea he had conceived of controlling a literary paper of his own. Harmsworth wanted to take over the *Academy* and install Ford as its editor. But Ford did not want his time consumed by the magazine's daily business, which would also necessitate his living in London all the time—something he told Elsie he did not want. He wanted to be able to control the policy while the day-to-day editing was delegated to someone else. He met Harmsworth several times between April and June, but his plans did not materialize yet. Harmsworth eventually hired Edmund Gosse to start the *Daily Mail* Literary Supplement. When he dismissed Gosse after six months and replaced him with Archibald Marshall, Ford became involved, writing his first series of 'Literary Portraits' between 20 April and 20 July 1907, and getting Max Beerbohm to provide some illustrations. Marshall thought Ford's column was 'perhaps the best regular feature in the paper'. It was the beginning of a period of intense literary criticism and editing, and of Ford's prominence in the literary life of London. He proposed a book on 'WRITING' to Methuen, who turned it down as unprofitable. And he took up another critical activity which he was to continue until he died: that of reading young novelists' manuscripts and advising them. He probably persuaded Methuen to publish Jessie Conrad's cookery book; Conrad described him as its 'Onlie begetter'. 'We regard him as an exceptionally gifted critic, both of style and technique', explained René Byles of Alston Rivers to a young author who took Ford's 'friendly criticism' in an unfriendly way. He had also persuaded Alston Rivers to let him edit a poetry series of twenty volumes. 'It will be a bit of a fag, but quite worthwhile', he told Elsie. They included two volumes of William Rossetti's *Democratic Sonnetts*, and five volumes by Nora Chesson, who had died that April. Her widower, W. H. Chesson, was a friend of Edward Garnett's, and worked with him at Fisher Unwin's. It was Chesson who had first recognized the talent in the manuscript of *Almayer's Folly*, and had passed it on to Garnett. Ford hoped the volumes would help provide for the Chessons' children. But Chesson became angry at a press announcement and, said Ford, sent 'a circular letter to the press abusing me, Rivers and everyone concerned'. In June Chesson was writing him 'an abusive letter by every post', he told Elsie.[4]

The Heart of the Country was published on 9 May 1906 after being serialized in the *Tribune*. Conrad told Galsworthy it was 'a very charming piece of writing'. There was an Edwardian preoccupation with a folk-culture that was perceived to be rapidly disappearing. Ford's 'English Trilogy'—*The Soul of London, The Heart of the Country, The Spirit of the People*—falls half-way between the novels of George Eliot and Thomas Hardy, on the one hand, showing rural life being transformed by the spread of the Industrial Revolution; and, on the other, the pre-war preoccupation with 'The Condition of England'. (For example, in *The Soul of London* Ford recounts with grim personal humour a modern doctor's ridiculing of 'the question of Physical Deterioration' as 'That Neurasthenia joke'.) Like the writings of W. H. Davies on tramps, of Edward Thomas on the life of the countryside (his *The Heart of England* appeared in the same year as *The Heart of the Country*), or the music of Vaughan Williams (who began collecting folk-songs in 1902), *The Heart of the Country* represents an attempt to put the culture back in touch with the land, and to allow a middle-class urban audience a vicarious contact with rural life. The genre is founded upon a contradiction: the writers about the land were not usually themselves of the land, but had been cultivated in literature. But Ford's writing about Meary Walker, Meary Spratt, and Ragged Ass Wilson neither patronizes nor condescends, because he genuinely admires them. In this sense the book (and its companions) need to be read as oblique autobiography impressions which express Ford's sensibility. 'For what I offer is not a statement of facts,' he said, in what was becoming a habitual gambit, 'it is precisely a set of analyses of feelings.' Although it was not 'boomed' as loudly as *The Soul of London*, *The Heart of the Country* received warm reviews, amongst them ones by Robert Lynd, Edward Garnett, Edward Thomas, and C. F. G. Masterman. Reviews and publicity upset him, however. 'It isn't, really, beer & skittles being boomed by the excellent Byles', he had told Elsie when *The Fifth Queen* was doing well. 'It makes me positively sick at times—his methods, & I feel as if other people must be despising me. However, I suppose they also envy me.' This time his success produced occasional feelings of depersonalization, as if he could not accept himself as worthy of the attention for which he had striven. He wrote to Elsie: 'Sitting here in the Library of the N.[ational] L.[iberal] C.[lub] I can see two men of whom one is reading the V Queen & the other the Heart of the Country. . . . But I feel very stupid & slack, so that I am lost in wonder to think of the brilliant creature who produced these fascinating works. I wonder under what layers of mortal fat [?] he hides himself away.' Jessie Conrad said Ford was 'rewarded by the Railway Company with a first-class pass to and from Winchelsea' for *The Heart of the Country*.[5] Certainly he was continually telling Elsie how much he was rushing about; and he wrote often and fully enough for this to be more than an excuse for not corresponding. He had not yet recovered enough to be able to cope with such a pace. Elsie was feeling worse, and Ford found her suffering intensely depressing. But in addition, the echoing of his father's condemnation of the 'stupid donkey' can scarcely be accidental, especially after a double proof that he had disobeyed the father's command never to write a book.

The Conrads came to stay for twelve days at the Bungalow on 11 May, during which time Ford helped Conrad with *The Secret Agent*, and Conrad probably reciprocated over *The Nature of a Crime*. 'A little of *The Secret Agent* was written by me,' wrote Ford, 'sentences here and there, mostly about the topography of Western London—which Conrad did not know at all—and details about police-men and anarchists.' Jessie Conrad, in an advanced state of pregnancy, and recovering from a nervous breakdown at the end of 1905, was more than usually exasperated with Ford: 'The two long week-ends that F.M.H. had stipulated he should come down were the longest I have ever known', she wrote, 'and a fit punishment for any sins I might have ever committed, or even contemplated.' The sins Ford committed included washing his greasy Panama hat and trying to dry it in the oven above the Sunday joint, and getting Conrad's 'robes of ceremony'—his frock coat and striped grey trousers—crumpled by using them as a substitute for blankets. When he noticed a cut in the breakfast tablecloth and said Elsie would be upset by it, Jessie angrily pointed out that she had brought her own linen with her and would take it away with her. When she rounded on him with an aggressive 'Are you satisfied?', he 'uttered a short vexed laugh' and began to stalk out of the house. She complained of his 'complete disregard' for her—which was presumably his way of coping (or not coping) with her aggression. These weekends too left Ford feeling exhausted.[6]

The Heart of the Country had been dedicated to James, and Ford sent him a copy inscribed 'Henry James, Esq. affectionately from Ford Madox Hueffer 9th May MCMVI'. On one of the Sundays the Conrads were at Winchelsea with Ford, 'the Great Man' came over to tea, bringing with him 'a Mr. Owen Wister—a mild U.S.A. author' who wrote *The Virginian*. Ford went back with them to Lamb House to catch the Rye post for his letter to Elsie (he was writing almost daily). He wrote from James's desk: 'It's curious to sit at this desk [. . .] near the window in the little room on the L. of the hall door [. . .] James himself has gone to see someone to the station. So I am the sole lord of the demesne.' The following month James and Claude Phillips, the keeper of the Wallace Collection, took Ford to Lamb House for dinner, and entertained him with what he called 'anecdotes not at all fitted for my youth & innocence until a very late hour'. When he wrote about this evening thirty years later, he remembered it as an example of James's duality. The master of scruple and euphemism could make 'his conversation heroically Rabelaisian, or, for me, really horrific, on the topics of esoteric sin or sexual indulgence'. 'I am in these things rather squeamish', said Ford. The conversations between James and Phillips ('a queer tiny being who lay as if crumpled up on the stately sofa in James's magnificent panelled room') 'made the tall wax candles appear to me to waver in their sockets and the skin of my forehead and hands prickle with sweat'. An ironic exaggeration, certainly: but Ford had been complaining of fits of giddiness in April. The intimated vertigo here, like those of his neurasthenic heroes, is precipitated by thoughts of sexuality.[7]

He planned a working holiday. Pinker lent £350 more (against the deeds of Elsie's Hurst-Cottage at Aldington), and on 2 July Ford took the girls, with the Martindale's retired maid to look after them, out to meet Elsie, who had travelled from Florence to Venice, and then to Germany. She visited Munich, and then went to Heidelberg, where she met Ford. It was probably this summer that a young American, Lawrence Marsden Price, spending his first day in Europe on the deck of the steamship from Rotterdam to Mannheim, heard the voice of an Englishman 'who took exception to the way the Dutch sat on the top deck playing cards in night-caps and "pyjahmas" '. It was Ford, who warmed to Price when he found him an enthusiast of the Pre-Raphaelites. Price had to sleep on deck—he had no cabin reservation—so Ford lent him a pillow and blanket. It was only years later that Price discovered the chief fact about the man who invited him to call on him in Heidelberg:

I spent several pleasant evenings with him and his family at the Molkenkur looking down on Heidelberg castle and on the Neckar valley far below. I do not know what we talked about, but I know it was not art and poetry, for it was not until many years later that I learned I had been entertained by a poet unawares [. . .] I got the impression all the time that I was conversing with an easy-going, rather fastidious gentleman of leisure.[8]

They met often over several weeks in Heidelberg, and Price was struck by how much more approachable Ford was than he sounded from the personae of his writings.

At the end of the month they visited the Hüffers living at Haus Markfort, near Münster, and Ford—demonstrating his prodigiousness to his relations—wrote a lyric in German, with a parallel English translation, in the visitor's book:

The Seasons rise & take their course: we travel on from Land to Land
Yet ancient, in its broad still fields, the house doth stand:
And little children, grown to men, do play & toil & dance their last,
Burying, weeping past & done, the seedtime & the harvest past
A voice from out the shadows cries: 'Oh human race, how short your day!'
And shadowlike all mortal things pass on their way.
Yet here above the ancient fields the ancient roof [tower's?] traceries
Nestle half hid in trees & great new suns that rise.
And 'neath the shadow and the shine we travel on from land to land
Till we return no more: yet the house doth stand.[9]

The girls were received into the Catholic Church while in Germany: after Ford's comment earlier that spring about 'unreasonable Papists', it is more likely that the Catholic Hüffers were applying pressure than that, as Mizener asserts, Ford had already made the decision in the spring. Tante Emma Goesen found them a new Catholic governess, Edmée Van der Noot, who was sent back with them and the maid to England. On 3 August 1906 Ford and Elsie set sail from Hamburg to New York on board the *Kaiserin Augusta Victoria*, for their first visit to America. In the deposition he wrote in 1913, when he was trying to get a divorce from Elsie, he claimed that: 'In 1906 she accompanied me to the United States with the avowed intention of procuring a divorce from me in that country, but the change of scene and my representations induced her to alter her mind.' He also said he regarded Elsie 'as neurotic and hysterical, and as of an exceedingly violent temperament'. Given the context of anger and legal mud-slinging after the *Throne* trial of 1913, these remarks should be taken warily. But it is not impossible that this was part of the reason for the trip, to protect the family—and particularly the children at their convent—from the scandal of a divorce.[10]

Pinker had encouraged Ford, telling him that the visit would help him get American contracts for the English trilogy and *The Fifth Queen*. In New York Ford met S. S. McClure (who had published *The Inheritors* and *Romance*), and began negotiating. Conrad wrote to the Galsworthys: 'Ford I guess is being now entertained in the skyscraping wigwams of the unpainted savages of the grrreat continent. I hope he'll find the war dances soothing to his nerves.' He did not, finding instead that America was 'hot, dusty, dull, and uninspiring, and the expenses are *appalling!*' 'May ruin and desolation wait upon the day when you inspired me to come to this land', he cursed Pinker. 'In revenge you will have to finance me.' He sent Pinker another instalment of *Privy Seal* (the second volume of the *Fifth Queen* trilogy) to secure a further £50 loan. Most of the people he wanted to meet had gone 'away in hills & woods where it seems impossible to follow'. But he did meet Willa Cather, who had begun to work for McClure's that year; and William Bradley, also then with McClure's, but who was to become Ford's friend and literary agent in Paris after the war.[11]

After two weeks in New York they left for Boston and Rhode Island at the end of August. In Boston Ford met Ferris Greenslet, then the editor of the *Atlantic Monthly*, who would later become one of his—numerous—publishers. Ford hoped to call on William James at Cambridge, but he too was away for the summer. On their way back to New York they visited the Misses Hurlbird in Connecticut, two elderly sisters Ford had met at the Marienberg Kaltwasser Heilanstalt 1904. They were 'not so much nervous in the restless way that distinguishes the neurotic Englishman or American—but so intolerably sad. They were like people of whom one reads in books, who have seen some dreadful supernatural phenomenon and remain for ever blighted.' One reads of them in the book Ford put them into, *The Good Soldier*, where as Florence Dowell's anxious maiden aunts they contribute to the intolerable sadness of Ford's 'saddest story'.[12]

In September Ford and Elsie visited Philadelphia, where he began to have what he called 'a gayish time'. McClure wanted to publish the English trilogy in one volume. It was originally to be called *The Anglo Saxons*, but he brought it out as *England and the English* in 1907, with a new introduction by Ford. He also expressed an interest in the first two volumes of *The Fifth Queen* trilogy, but none of the three novels were published in America during Ford's lifetime. Two dinners were given in Ford's honour in Philadelphia, he told Pinker, adding that he was meeting 'a world of people & publishers who w$^{d.}$ be glad enough to publish me', but that Elsie was 'quite ill & that makes things clouded & awkward'.[13]

Ford wrote that in a bar in Philadelphia he met a man he had known in England who said he had a small farm but could find no hired labour for the harvest, so Ford offered to help. Mizener casts doubt on this as one of Ford's 'improved stories', and it is true that he implies, in the reiterative descriptions of the fatigue of hacking corn with inappropriate machetes in the scorching sun, that the work went on for much longer than the time he actually spent in Pennsylvania, which must have been less than three weeks. On the other hand, in an unpublished version of the story which Mizener doesn't mention, Ford makes precisely the point that memory lengthens such agonizing times: 'I don't know how long it lasted. In my mind it remains a sun-aching Sahara of time; but as we never got that corn-cutting finished while I was there it was not perhaps a matter of so many years as it certainly seems.' (That combination of hyperbole and precision is characteristically vivid.) The five versions tally so closely that there is sure to be a basis in fact; probably that Ford couldn't resist the appeal to his farming expertise, and helped for a few days. He tells the story to point up the force of convention—the farmer won't mend his fences before a pre-ordained date, even though his sheep keep escaping; and (in the later versions) to relate the absurd comedy of the labourer he eventually hires, who jumps off the roof and breaks a leg while Ford was bringing the ladder: 'Why didn't you wait?', asked Ford; 'Well! I thaoght I'd see!'[14]

What Mizener doesn't notice is that the story also has an (oblique) aspect of literary autobiography. Ford's friend—he calls him 'Peter Dundee' in *Return to Yesterday*, but adds disavowingly: 'That is not his name but he is still living'—is in important ways a model for the narrator of *The Good Soldier*, John Dowell. His *story* is not Dowell's. 'Dundee' had met a con-man from Cincinnati in a London museum, and had been cheated out of most of his fortune. He lived in dread of the scandal that would be caused by his appearance in a London courtroom. He returned to the farm, and was working desperately to keep it going until Philadelphia should 'approach and swallow up his fields in an immense property boom'. He was apparently unmarried, though Ford tells of how the members of his church had decided he should marry 'the Widow——' who owned some adjoining property. 'He had made no advances to the lady.' After the clergyman explained the plan to him he came out 'with a face more meagre, grey and woebegone than before'. Yet his origin, reputation, and characteristics are all Dowell's. He was known as the 'laziest man in——', as Dowell is called 'the laziest man in Philadelphia'. Ford says of 'Dundee' 's farm: 'The title deeds were of wampum, the place having been in my poor friend[']s family ever since the days of let us say William Penn.' Dowell always carries about with him 'the title deeds of my farm, which once covered several blocks between Chestnut and Walnut

Streets. These title deeds are of wampum, the grant of an Indian chief to the first Dowell, who left Farnham in Surrey in company with William Penn.' Dowell too has been cheated, by his mercenary and adulterous wife. When Ford met him, 'Dundee' was making the kind of 'Grand Tour of Europe that used to be obligatory on men of culture', and that becomes obligatory for Dowell in another way when his wife's feigned heart-condition prevents their return to America. When he does eventually return after Florence's suicide, his amazement at Philadelphian gossip is comparable to 'Dundee' 's paranoiac tendency when he returns 'to find himself famous as the stupidest' man in the town, as well as the laziest: 'He detected covert titters everywhere and where he did not detect them he imagined them.' Dowell's credulity and reliability are of course themselves central issues. As always with such biographical 'sourcery', the transformations Ford effected on his memories of his stay in Pennsylvania are more surprising than the autobiographical tracks they cover. Ford's later stories about this trip—all of which were written *after The Good Soldier*—are not travel-journals but ruminations on the sources of his creative work, and testimonies to his belief that the significance of episodes is inexhaustible, however often or differently they are retold.[15]

When he told Pinker 'I have got a good many ideas for "copy" of one kind & another', it is unlikely either man realized that it would be a decade before these impressions would find their perfect context in a novel. But Ford was already contemplating subjects more suited to American readers than were his constata-tions of Englishness. While sailing up the Hudson River, Bradley had suggested that Ford should write about the navigator Henry Hudson. It was to be the first of a trilogy called 'The Three Ships': he always found trilogies a congenial grouping. The second was to have been 'The Mayflower', though only *The 'Half Moon'* got written. Ford later said he wrote part of it on the trains in Pennsylvania. Yet even as he was contemplating this novel, and collecting impressions that would go into *An English Girl* (in which Eleanor Greville accompanies her American millionaire fiancé on a visit to America), he had doubts, joking grimly to Pinker: 'I don't feel certain that the game is worth the candle. I mean that the U.S.A. will never appreciate *my* particular merits.—vast tho' they be.'[16]

They returned to New York for the last week of September. Ford reached an agreement with McClure's, but got much less than he had asked for: only an advance of $200 on *The 'Half Moon'* (which McClure eventually rejected) and a loan of $150. It wasn't enough. Ford had to send a cable to Pinker: 'Impossible return unless you wire sixty.' Pinker was as reliable as ever, and the Hueffers sailed home on a cattle-boat, the SS *Minnetonka*. Ford said he played poker with the impresario Fred Karno on the boat, lost, and had to give him an unpatented invention: a collar stud with a bayonet attachment.[17]

After they arrived back in London on 8 October Ford and Elsie took a furnished flat in Holbein House, Sloane Square, living there during the week and week-ending at Winchelsea. In the 1913 deposition Ford says that Elsie 'decided her health required distraction and town life'. But given her later dislike of town life, this is more likely to have been true of Ford himself, who referred to his years with Elsie in the country as a time in which he had 'buried' himself, and who was now thriving on the literary social life of the capital. He was working hard to finish *Privy Seal* and *An English Girl*, his latest novel, which he subsequently described as one of his 'pastiches in the manner of Mr. Henry James, written [. . .] as a variation on a book of essays to give the effect of a tour in the United States—an international affair'. The book is Jamesian in its emphasis on renunciation: 'the best thing' the altruist hero, the would-be reformer Don Kelleg, could do, 'is to have the self-restraint to abstain from muddling'. But it is also something Fordian protagonists have to learn: especially Henry VIII and Robert Grimshaw; and something the aloof novelist, the follower of Flaubert and Turgenev, must learn. Essentially, Don is a Fordian impressionist, complete with 'indifference to fact', 'insight enough to be uncertain', a susceptibility to 'Moral nervous dyspepsia', and a commitment to 'passionate inaccuracy' which is contrasted with the Marwoodian Tory precision of Eleanor's father—whose 'just'-ness is also reminiscent of Francis Hueffer. Don's own father dies, leaving a will designed to frustrate his son's philanthropic ambitions. When Eleanor's cousin repeats that old Mr Kelleg has left his son 'absolutely impotent', Don collapses. Anxieties of impotence permeate the book. Like Granger in *The Inheritors*, or Dowell, Don's sexuality is frustrated too. When he holds Eleanor in his arms and kisses her, it is on the forehead, and he 'whispered that he thought of her as a Papist thinks of his saints . . .' 'I only want a lover who'll know what he wants', she says. The novel attempts to combine in a melancholy mode Ford's William-Morris-Limpsfield self with his Tory scepticism—a combination that was to prove much more effective in the satirical *The Simple Life Limited*. We are told that 'in a sense, there couldn't be the least doubt that Don was a sort of a genius'; but the book tells us this without showing the genius, or specifying the sort. The attitude is dual; Ford wants to ironize aesthetic ambition, including his own; yet there cannot be the least doubt that he also wants to be thought a genius. Don's Conradian stepbrother Canzano writes a letter to Eleanor eloquently reproving her for renouncing Don, which brings together the ideas of filial impotence and artistic potential:

'Can't you see it! *Can't* you see it! The children of great men—and his father was a great man—are frequently weak: but generally they have qualities that only need a wise nursing to render them very sweet and very fine. Don was weak, if you will. He mightn't have fitted very well into your English life. But hadn't he a strength? Wasn't his craving to get at the best in life an action—wasn't it heroic?'

Both Elsie and Ford were the children of powerful fathers, and both were in need of 'a wise nursing' to bring out their best qualities. Though Don's temperament is close to Ford's, the correspondences between *An English Girl*'s plot and Ford's life are superficial. Yet Eleanor's renunciation of Don, which the novel too reproves, lends credence to Ford's claim in the 1913 deposition that it was Elsie who wanted to renounce Ford. The *Times Literary Supplement*'s reviewer shrewdly grasped Ford's attempt to render 'the tragedy of the fluid temperament—a temperament in this case, impulsive but shrinking, always noble but always ineffectual', finding that the book partook of the qualities of its protagonist, as 'both clever and disappointing'; like Don's courtship, 'the author never seems to be getting to the point'. Most of the other known reviews agree, though Ford's friend C. F. G. Masterman said he had 'arrived' in this romance, that he 'digs deep into elemental things. Yet he makes no attempt at preaching.' Edward Garnett told Conrad that the book 'had a real sound success'. And *An English Girl* elicited from Conrad his most elaborate appreciation of a book Ford had written without collaboration:

Dearest Ford.

It is as I thought. In many respects—and from an absolute point of judgement—the book is simply magnificent. There's no doubt of it: for the feeling one has is that this sort of thing could not have been done otherwise.

And it is a big thing. The more one thinks of it the better is seen the really amazing magnitude of intention and the measure of success. The psychology of two great nations one European the other extra European absolutely contained in the scheme of a novel—carried out with a delicacy of insight and breadth of view which simply makes me gasp! I say nothing of the ingenuity of the means. I admire in silence.

In the way of criticism I would say that the conversations (when Don is being talked about) are inspired by such delicate alert thinking that sometimes (for an ordinary reader) an effect of mysteriousness is produced. I think you will understand what I mean. The girl is superlative. The father most interesting and amusing (and by the bye he's a genial invention for concreting the inner meaning of many things) Canzano most delicately picturesque and sympathetic [. . .] Don himself suffers from being the peg—but that could not be avoided. A peg there had to be and at any rate hes *not* a wooden peg [. . .] the book in a curious indefinable way has a delicate distinction, something ingeniously individual and exceptional, even, I mean, amongst your own other work. I need not tell you that I am profoundly in sympathy with its feeling.[18]

From Ford's reminiscences of Conrad groaning over his earlier books perhaps he understood only too well the characteristic feline ambivalence underlying the hyperbole here. Certainly he (wisely) never used this letter as a testimony of Conrad's valuation of him. But for all its suggestion that Conrad might be gasping in horror at the ambition of Ford's intention and the failure of its realization, his particular criticisms are germane and constructive. (It may be significant that, when Ford needed a narratorial 'peg' upon which to articulate his next novel of transatlantic intrigue, he gave him a name that connotes the very idea of peg or linkage: Dowell.) Conrad's letters to Ford from Montpellier earlier in the year had been as intimate as ever. Describing the beauty of the scenery, he wrote: 'I am drunk with colour and would like dearly to have you to lean upon. I am certain that with no other man could I share my rapture.'[19]

In the spring of 1907 Ford took the next step in his and Elsie's tortuous separation. He moved to a three-floor unfurnished maisonette above a poulterer's and fishmonger's shop at 84 Holland Park Avenue. Douglas Goldring had the impression of 'almost pushing [his] way through the suspended carcases of rabbits, fowls and game-birds to get to the door, and of standing on a mixture of blood and sawdust' while ringing the bell. But Ford was 'fond of the view from his window looking over the avenue, especially at night when the horse omnibuses and hansom cabs pouring down this great artery of traffic presented a procession of twinkling lights to the tune of rumbling wheels and hooves'. Elsie and the children visited him here only rarely. She found London exhausting, and felt ill at ease with those of Ford's literary friends who were 'trying in fact to appear superior'. Goldring remembered her as 'a dark, tall, "formidable" woman, stern, implacable, of rigid principles'. Their marriage was becoming more like the Ashburnhams': a social 'form' to be preserved for others (the children, 'society', for each other's sake . . .), but rapidly losing its private content. Scott-James noted the contrast between the intermittent social performance of family life and the imminent disruption:

Elsie Hueffer was a striking, good-looking woman. It would be difficult to imagine a more happy-looking party than that of Ford playing merrily with the children on the floor and his wife contentedly looking on or lending a hand. The romantic elopement with which it had all started some thirteen years earlier seemed abundantly justified by this chivalrous husband and affectionate father, and the so obviously devoted wife. However . . .[20]

In a curious poem, 'Two Making Music', which was published this year (though Ford dropped it for his *Collected Poems*), he makes a meditation on art suggestive of the *angst* and fragility of domestic harmony:

> These are her songs: tho' his voice lifted be,
> And his hand wrote the words and set the key,
> She, listening, is voiced in what she hears:
> Here are her very form and melody
> Now rendered back to her beloved ears.
>
> She plays on him as on an instrument,
> And all his notes, resounding to her touch,
> Do give her forth into the twilight room.
> Here is her voice: it soundeth but of her;
> Here are her words: they tell of her alone;
> And here her penmanship: she guides his hand;
> Here are her face and presence: he sees naught
> But her in all the world, and he is naught
> But, as it were, a harp set quivering
> By memories of her that pass and pass
> Like little winds fretting the sounding string
> Stretched in dim arbours o'er the twilight grass.
>
> These are her songs: it is not he doth sing,
> But she herself hymning herself. Alas!

Here we have perfect beauty mirroring
Itself in a cracked glass.[21]

It is not known exactly when this was written, but that last line either anticipates the fracture of Ford's mind and his marriage—or looks back on it, as the poem looks back over the Hueffers' music-making at Bonnington and Winchelsea, where Ford composed and played. Katharine described Ford's 'love of music, composing, improvising, & the two of them playing & singing together—He had a beautiful touch on the piano & Mum had a lovely mezzo-soprano voice—I have never heard anyone with just her timbre', and added: 'All my knowledge of lieder came from lying in bed hearing them when I was going to sleep.' The poem turns on Ford's favourite aesthetic paradox, whereby the artist expresses himself best through self-effacement. Narcissism is at once invoked and escaped. But the ending seeks the effect of suppressed disturbance, suggesting the mental cost of becoming the instrument of someone else's will (or vanity?). As in Conrad's letters, there is an overlaying of the erotic and the literary. Art is presented as collaboration ('*Two* Making Music'); yet—as perhaps Ford was beginning to feel once again as a third collaboration was in the making—the one who wrote most of the words was in danger of being submerged in the emotionally more forceful other.[22]

His sister Juliet had written in the spring that Ford had 'grown so nice, so kind and serious' that she was sure David Soskice 'would not know him. He has quite lost the habit of boasting and talking big which was so unpleasant'. But he had not quite lost it. We catch a glimpse of him improvising a mischievous little historical romance to impress Ferris Greenslet, who weekended with the Hueffers at Winchelsea in the early summer of 1907, and solemnly recorded that Ford was a 'freeholder of the Cinque Ports, who could wear his hat in the presence of the King'. He was living out the world of The 'Half Moon', which he finished that June. But his social high spirits were camouflaging his private worries. Elsie's mother had died on 18 February 1907. Just as it must have seemed to Elsie that her life with Ford was nearly all she had left, she was feeling alienated from his London world. Both she and Conrad must have been provoked by the remark in The Spirit of the People: 'I know perhaps one Englishman and perhaps two Englishwomen that are absolutely and to the end sympathetic to me' (Conrad would have known that the Englishman was Marwood; Elsie might have read this as a public acknowledgement that she had a rival). She became iller, and as Ford said, her 'case was very badly mishandled by the doctors [. . .] all of them diagnosing it differently and wrongly'. (C. Pirquet introduced his new method of diagnosis this year.) Her brother Harri produced yet another mis-diagnosis, as a result of which she had another unnecessary but expensive operation for 'ulcer of the bladder and kidney stones'. Ford was sympathetic and supportive during her convalescence. But he had become increasingly anxious about money. In the summer he had told Pinker (to whom he then owed about £650) that if he raced to finish The Fifth Queen Crowned in two months, though he might clear his debt, he might 'also be useless for some time to come'. Now he wrote to him: 'Death & despair dog me', and asked for a further loan of £10 towards the operation. He probably asked Conrad, who was 'worrying' him to complete *The Rescue*, and who had received a government grant in 1905, if he could repay some of his debt, since there is a grim letter from Conrad to Galsworthy which suggests that Ford thought that Pinker might be made to increase his loan to Conrad if Ford were to make a 'legal attack' on him. Conrad said he'd written to Ford telling him 'to go ahead without compunction', but his imagining of the futility of the move— 'All he may do is to knock me over completely and utterly and even knock me out of house and home'—shows why Ford probably did no such thing: there is no evidence that he did, nor that Conrad repaid the debt (he was still stalling over a repayment of £140 in 1913). Ford wrote that Elsie's own brother Harri Martindale 'assured me most solemnly that no traces of tuberculosis were discoverable in her system, and directed me to treat her as if she were a hysterical subject'. Ford later thought that Harri 'was extremely anxious not to have it thought that there was tuberculosis in his family, and that this probably predisposed him not to discover the traces'. On 3 September Elsie was moved to Dr Tebb's house. Ford came over to read James's *The American Scene* to her while she recuperated. She had to be moved again—to a house in Maida Vale—when there was 'an increase in Dr. Tebb's family', but he continued to treat her. She appeared to recover, and returned to Holland Park Avenue, but didn't enjoy the social life there, and was still suffering. Ford wrote to Walter Jerrold that if Mrs Jerrold would call 'it w^d. delight E. who lies upon her back & groans thro' the heavy hours'.[23]

Ford now owed Pinker over £800, and wrote to him in desperation about how the last of that had disappeared 'into the pockets of doctors, nurses, chemists & specialists [. . .] My wife gets steadily worse & worse & I'm pretty much at the end of my tether.' In another letter he spelled out his minimum requirements and simultaneously expressed his dismay at his worsening predicament:

I do quite seriously need the sum I mentioned & can't get on without it. I thought it was of the essence of the contract I signed with you that you would let me have an advance against manuscript to the tune of about £2 per 1000 words [. . .] I *must* have money at about this rate &, altho' I haven't the least wish to appear unfriendly—or even to complain—I shall be simply forced by necessity to find someone who will make some such arrangement. I mean that I must pay off what I owe you & start afresh.

I don't at all want to do this, because I've always—& do—harbour the best of feelings towards you—but there's a proverb that whilst the grass is growing the steed is starving & that's quite literally my position [. . .]

I repeat that I feel a good deal of gratitude to you for having quite certainly 'made' me & it makes me feel really mean to worry you—but I really am so hard pushed that I *must*.[24]

As Mizener says, 'This is a cry of despair, but it sounds like a threat'. None the less, his treatment of the episode makes Pinker's piqued reaction sound reasonable, and Ford's provocation of it unreasonable. Yet there is reason on both sides. Ford makes it clear he knows how hard Pinker has worked for him, and how much of his own money he has risked on Ford's talent. He also knows Pinker is the last person he should be complaining to, or presenting with an ultimatum. Yet he had been writing so much at such high pressure, and getting well reviewed; so his frustration at nevertheless getting into increasing debt is entirely understandable. The frustration was directed towards Pinker because there simply wasn't anyone else Ford could complain to with effect. Though he wrote Pinker a placating letter, and did not leave to seek another agent, he quickly got into a similar fracas with Alston Rivers, who resented the similar suggestion that if they could not sell his works more effectively he would have to find another publisher. Bathurst, the chairman of Alston Rivers, wrote to Pinker:

we thank you for putting the matter so plainly before us. We quite recognise that in view of the failure of our strenuous and lavish attempts in the past to make Mr. Hueffer's works popular, you have every right to await the result of 'The Spirit of the People'. Still, when we feel that an author has not perfect confidence in us we should prefer that our relations with him should cease, and therefore beg to withdraw from the offer made by us on the 30th. of August for the publication of the volume in question. We need hardly say that we take this step with extreme regret.[25]

The difficulties with Pinker and the rupture with Alston Rivers are typical of the situations Ford tended to precipitate with his patrons, especially when the nervous exhaustion of writing was overlaid with anxieties about unsuccess. Yet both cases are also typical of the way Ford has been given the disadvantage of the doubt in such controversies. Mizener argued that 'it seemed to Bathurst reasonable to think [the books'] lack of success at least as much the fault of their writer as of their publisher' (p. 132). But by calling Bathurst 'sensible', he gives the impression that he too thinks it reasonable to talk as if publishers owned writers, and as if lack of popularity was a matter for blame. Mizener tended to patronize Ford by contrasting his optimistic hopes for success (which most artists live by) with the biographer's 'reasonable' hindsight. But in this case Ford wasn't being unreasonable. Bathurst's pique is all too evident behind his disingenuous 'regret'. He may have had good reason to feel piqued, since Ford could sound high-handed with publishers and agents. Yet Bathurst's sanctimoniousness betrays exactly the feelings that Ford had been concerned about. Alston Rivers were already thinking of their attempts to sell Ford's books as a 'failure'. Worse still, Bathurst's tone is characteristic of what can make artists resent their dealers and publishers. It is not just a matter of being patronizing. The life of an artist often stands as a reproach or a challenge to the businessman in its negation of the sacred values of power and manipulation. The businessman's response is to claim that business is true creativity, and that rather than business being parasitic upon art, art is parasitic upon the economy. These matters have become more pressing for us as the ideology of art has shifted from the former to the latter position in the last twenty years. Bathurst expects the writer to have 'perfect confidence' in the publisher; a statement which is as blind to the psychology of creation as it is deceitful about the business of publishing. Not all commercial publishers publish books they know to be bad. But where profit is the prime motive, few will risk money advertising books they doubt will sell. Bathurst makes the decision to drop Ford appear to turn on Ford's lack of confidence in the firm. Yet it is clear that Bathurst has less than perfect confidence in Ford, whose works need to be *made* popular. His is a world in which the publisher does the significant work—makes the 'strenuous and lavish' efforts—whereas the writer is guilty of the unforgivable crime of producing the unmarketable commodity. It is this double standard which is most patronizing, and which causes the artist most resentment against the art-merchants. Mizener makes the letter sound much more 'reasonable' than it is. Bathurst is not saying that the commercial failure of Ford's books is 'at least as much the fault of their writer as of their publisher'. He is saying that Alston Rivers's efforts are above reproach, and that their writer is solely responsible for his lack of popularity. The writer is at the publisher's mercy, and must approach, cap in hand, demonstrating the appropriate gratitude; whereas the publisher is free to regard the writer as 'never one of our best sellers' (Bathurst goes on to say: 'We perceive that a book like "The Spirit of the People" could not possibly be rushed into popularity in a few weeks') and to publicize the book accordingly. Ford wrote to Pinker in dismay: 'If Bathurst calls what he's doing with The Spirit of the People publishing he has weird ideas. He's not had a single advertisement of it in the London papers.' The crucial point here is that it was not an impulsive letter from Ford that brought about his rupture with Alston Rivers. Bathurst was replying to a letter from the reasonable Pinker, who must also have felt that the firm was not trying as hard with *The Spirit of the People*—another instalment of Ford's best ruminative, elegiac impressionism—as they had with his earlier books.[26]

The year 1907 was none the less one of Ford's most productive. He published an astonishing six books: *Privy Seal* (15 February), *England and the English* (18 May), *From Inland* (a volume of poems: 11 July?), *An English Girl* (probably 6 September), *The Spirit of the People* (probably 25 October), and *The Pre-Raphaelite Brotherhood: A Critical Monograph* (28 October). In this last he first articulated the crucial distinction between the Pre-Raphaelites, who 'gave to material phases of Nature a relative permanency, a comparative immortal life', and the Impressionists with whom he would increasingly identify himself, who sought 'that delicious sense of swift change, that poetry of varying moods, of varying lights, of varying shadows that gives to certain moods and certain aspects of the earth a rare and tender pathos'. He was also writing weekly 'Literary Portraits' between April and January, first for the *Daily Mail* Supplement, then when that folded towards the end of July, for the *Tribune*. The 'Half Moon' was written between February and June. *The Fifth Queen Crowned* was also finished that summer. He was due to have spoken at a demonstration on 1 November 1907 to protest against the censorship of Granville-Barker's play *Waste*, and the attempt by the examiner of plays, G. A. Redford, to censor Edward Garnett's *The*

Breaking Point. The programme was that 'The Dramatic Authors of England are to assemble in Trafalgar Square' on their way to hand a petition to the Liberal prime minister, Campbell-Bannerman:

Barrie will address them from the base of the Nelson column, and the Savoy orchestra will play 'Britons never will be slaves'. The procession will then form, and will be headed by Pinero and Shaw walking arm in arm. Immediately behind them will come Garnett and Galsworthy, each bearing the pole of a red banner with the inscription 'Down with the Censor!' An effigy of Redford, which is being prepared by the Savoy property-man, will be carried by Frederick Harrison and W. B. Yeats, and over its head will wave a banner, carried by Gilbert Murray, with the inscription 'Ecrasez L'Infâme!'. Arrived in Downing Street, Swinburne will declaim an 'Ode to C.B.', and the speakers will be Ford Madox Hueffer, Desmond MacCarthy, Maarten Maartens and Ernest Rhys—dramatists who cannot be suspected of interested motives, as they have never written any plays![27]

Unfortunately for what Richard Garnett calls 'this fanciful apotheosis of the liberty of the stage', Campbell-Bannerman fell ill, and a smaller deputation had to see the home secretary, Herbert Gladstone, instead. None the less, the plan testifies to Ford's status as an author and critic. Yet his financial position was so dire that at the end of 1907 he had to apply to the Royal Literary Fund for assistance. Conrad wrote a supporting letter, blustering about Ford's 'rare talent and unimpeachable industry'; the order in which he catalogued Ford's 'noteworthy achievement'—'verse, essays, fiction and criticism'— gives an idea of his opinion of what Ford had written most of: fiction and criticism. The fund turned him down, on the not entirely logical grounds that 'both his debts and his income were considerably higher than the average applicant [*sic.*]'.[28]

As in Conrad's case, Ford should not be judged by his letters alone, and especially not by his letters to agents and publishers. In haste and in need he sometimes struck the wrong note with his patrons, sounding provocative out of exasperation or wounded pride. He believed that publishers should commission works by established authors on trust, and when they insisted on seeing the manuscript before agreeing terms, he would generally refuse high-handedly. Yet he had shrewd reason. As he was to explain later: 'it is only beginners who are asked such a thing—& it w$^{d.}$ be a serious step backwards. Besides, it w$^{d.}$ injure me very much if [the publisher] read it & refused it & then told others that he had.' However, it is in his imaginative work that his deepest understanding of these things is manifested. His experiences first of being launched, and then of being left to flounder, went into the novel he began writing that winter, *Mr. Apollo: A Just Possible Story* (published on 20 August 1908). It is a wistfully satirical fantasy in which the pagan god descends—literally—upon Edwardian London. Much has been made of the parallels with Wells's romances about supernatural visitors. But while it is possible that Ford was influenced by *The Wonderful Visit* (1895) and *The Sea Lady* (1902), he turns the machinery of the plot to his own purposes, making of it something quite his own. One can see why the plot appealed to him.

It provided a variation upon a situation that recurs through his entire *œuvre*: that of an unusual, alien figure, moving amongst people of another dimension (*The Inheritors*), another time (*Ladies Whose Bright Eyes*), another nation (*The Good Soldier*), or simply of other values (*The Benefactor* and *Parade's End*).[29] The novel confronts with a true god the false gods of conventional religion, Fabian socialism, scientific rationalism, and journalism. In the last case, the satire is double-edged. For the newspaper magnate, Lord Aldington, is not only a pseudo-deity himself, seen to possess the god-like powers of a Harmsworth for making and breaking reputations; he is also drawn towards sensational stories of the pseudo-supernatural. The plot hinges on his decision to publicize a charlatan mind-reading act rather than printing Mr Apollo's articles asserting his own real divinity. Mizener argues that 'the result is that the book falls apart into a series of disconnected satiric scenes and the essential idea of *Mr. Apollo*, the divine dimension of experience that only gods and poets grasp, is largely ignored' (p. 140). Ford's method is as scenic as ever, certainly; but the essential continuity of the book is provided by the way he suggests a rapport between gods and poets. That is, he makes the book into an exploration of the nature of art. Alfred Milne, one of the few characters who maintains a genuinely open mind about whether or not Apollo is who he claims to be, says: 'Certain things must be put figuratively; you could not let a child know all the facts of life' (p. 296). Ford is recalling James's *What Maisie Knew*, its child-heroine perplexed by adult figures for the adult facts she cannot yet quite understand. The allusion is much more than a piece of self-conscious knowingness. The point of bringing literature into the argument is to suggest that literature is for, precisely, figurative expression of the things which it is hard to put in other ways. Mr Apollo is thus a figure for art and the artist. Ford later referred to Apollo as 'the very god of stylists'.[30]

The fake mind-readers, the Krakoffs, are contrasted with the people of true sympathetic imagination, the Milnes, and Mr Apollo himself. The profusion of the paranormal in *Mr. Apollo* does more than reflect the Edwardian preoccupation with psychical research and spiritualism. It is a figure for the way art brings the mind into contact with unfamiliar people and circumstances; for the way novelists and readers must to some extent 'read' the minds of others. Seen in this way, it is a much more coherent and effective novel than has been allowed. It could, however, be seen as a kind of omnipotence fantasy, Ford's revenge on those who had power over him (or whom he thought wanted it, like the Fabians), by confronting the demigods of commerce, politics, and publishing with the artist-like god of art. It is possible that Conrad thought of the book like this. He praised it with characteristic ironic hyperbole:

It comes off magnificently. What delights me most is this: that there you have *expressed yourself*. You have indeed done it. And it is perhaps the feeling that you were doing so which has given to the book that extraordinary serenity of diction and tone. It may indeed have been written by Mr Apollo himself; for one has a queer sensation of reading something impeccable and absolutely above criticism [. . .] And if you experience perchance that feeling of intimate secret gratification which visits sometimes an artist, then you may take it from me that in this case the moment of 'ivresse divine' is sufficiently justified.[31]

There's an insinuation here that Ford thought the book *was* written by Mr Apollo himself, and that what he has actually done is given himself away, in his self-intoxication and self-elevation to a point 'absolutely above criticism'. Like many of Ford's friends, Conrad was getting angry with him: partly for the increasingly evident strains of the Hueffer marriage; but partly because of Ford's new confidence of his own powers and his new status in the literary world. He was no longer Conrad's apprentice, and Conrad was unhappy with the shift in the balance of powers. A reading of the novel itself ought soon to correct such an interpretation. Though Ford does mean to re-establish the status and power of art in a world seduced by meretricious sensationalism and what we would now call 'hype', he has enough novelistic aloofness to portray even characters such as Aldington with sympathy, and with insight into the business of publicity, and how publicity generates glamour and awe. His purpose is not oblique self-aggrandize-ment, but the rendering of human situations. The figurative fable of Mr Apollo brings out the range of human possibilities. In so far as a Fordian novel can be said to have a moral, that of *Mr. Apollo* might be that 'it takes all sorts to make a world' (p. 289). And although Ford clinches the cliché with the aesthetic sense of how it takes an artist to make the world of a novel, this novel is alive with a feeling for ordinary people like the Milnes.

What isn't registered in the novel—not, at least, in any direct way—is the increasing domestic strain between Ford and Elsie, which exacerbated his volatility with Pinker and with publishers. On 16 December 1907 Elsie left for Sandgate, to take the sea air in a bath-chair. In Kent 'she was treated by a Folkestone doctor, who appeared to complete her cure by giving what were practically bread pills—this still pointing to the idea that her malady and the attendant pain were purely hysterical'. With the hindsight that Elsie's pains were only too real, this reads cruelly. Yet hysterical suffering is no less acute for being psychical, as Ford himself knew when he called his own mental breakdown of 1904 'purely imaginary'. What's more, the idea only seemed confirmed when Elsie 'discovered the doctor's stratagem', and 'the pains immediately returned'. In December 1907 she decided to leave the Bungalow. Mizener said she thought Winchelsea was becoming 'artificially fashionable'. But it is more likely that she wanted to leave the scene of her protracted misery. Ford said she 'never liked the place & was always more or less ill there'. The Conrads had left the Pent that September, and moved to Someries, a farmhouse on the Luton Hoo estate in Bedfordshire. Elsie asked them to find somewhere nearby for her, but they didn't. 'You have no idea of the soul corroding bleakness of earth and sky here when the east wind blows', Conrad told her, explaining that he had been 'too dismal and morally unwholesome to come near' her. So she decided to furnish her own house at Aldington, Hurst Cottage, which was renamed 'Kitcat' when she moved there at the beginning of March 1908.[32]

Douglas Goldring, who met Ford later that year, says that she 'began hostilities by dismantling their home at Winchelsea and removing herself and her children to the cottage at Aldington'. The hostilities were already well-entrenched by then; but otherwise this squares with Ford's self-justifying account in the 1913 deposition:

this lady, without my knowledge, and very much against my wishes, removed the greater part of my furniture from the house at Winchelsea, and began to furnish a house of her own [. . .] The rest of my furniture she warehoused. When I discovered this, she was too ill for me to remonstrate, and I had to let the matter pass. She established herself at Aldington in the early part of 1908, definitely giving me to understand that the establishment was her's and not mine, and that my position in it was that of a visitor. During all this period I remained in town, where I was engaged on work for various newspapers—the Daily Mail, the Tribune, the Daily News etc—but I visited her, both at Sandgate and Aldington, with the greatest regularity every Saturday to Tuesday, or Friday to Monday, never missing a week-end in the whole period. She also entertained rather freely at Sandgate, giving a fancy dress ball to the officers of the garrison, and so on.

She continued however, in great pain from the time of her removal to Aldington, and this pain made her very violent and ungovernable; she certainly had delusions at this date, and the directions that I had from various doctors and her brother to try to get her to regard the pain as imaginary, caused her to regard me with such aversion that at that date she began again to request me to let her divorce me.[33]

It was not to be the last time that Ford, like Tietjens, lost his furniture. When he explained the move to his mother, he made it sound like a joint decision: 'We have definitely unfurnished the Bungalow & stored the furniture—so there's an end of Winchelsea'; and he said that the cottage would be their joint 'country abode'. It is impossible to say whether he was exaggerating their differences in 1913, or playing them down in 1908, when he still hoped that at least an appearance of harmony could be maintained. Yet even in his letter to his mother—who was now staying in St Petersburg—his regret is evident: 'I'm sorry myself', he said, making it clear that the decision was really Elsie's.[34]

As he became increasingly estranged from Elsie, Ford lost the four friendships that meant most to him. The ruptures with Marwood, Conrad, and James were to come in 1909. In 1908 it was Olive Garnett who was put out. There had been signs of a cooling-off in 1906, when, after he asked if she would accompany Elsie to Rome: 'We had a Free Trade discourse: and a moment of hate? distrust? something peeped out.' The antagonism may have been over Ford's and Elsie's separation. The Garnetts were close friends of both Hueffers, and had been so involved with their courtship and marriage that it is as if Olive still wanted to try to bring them together. She may have been signalling in 1908 that she wasn't prepared to go on seeing Ford on the old basis as long as he was living separately from Elsie. We don't know exactly what the signals were, but Ford's response suggests that he felt disapproval from the 'respectable' Garnetts about the way his private life was becoming public: 'Have I *really* given O.G. cause for offence? If it's anything personal, pray make it up. If it's—as it were—public I guess it will pass over. But I'm having a remarkably rough time of it—tho' may be you don't believe it—& I don't like the idea of having done anything to hurt O.G. So—in vulgar parlance, *very* vulgar parlance—spit it out.' He inscribed a pre-publication copy of *The Fifth Queen Crowned* to her on 4 March—'affectionately from F.M.H.'—as a sign of goodwill. But she was to remain a close friend to Elsie from now on; as Elsie became further estranged from Ford, so did she.[35]

In May 1908 Ford found 'the most distinguished specialist in London', Dr Harry Fenwick, who at once diagnosed Elsie's tubercular kidney—without seeing the patient, but on the strength of Ford's descriptions—said Ford. Elsie's doctors had given up her case as hopeless. Fenwick was 'appalled' that the disease had not been treated properly, but he thought he could save her if the kidney and infected part of the bladder were removed immediately. Ford said Harri Martindale, whom he called, with irony, 'the most distinguished analyst in London', made yet another examination, and 'although he had ten times before examined the necessary matter without making any discovery, upon this occasion he immediately discovered plentiful traces of tuberculosis'. Fenwick operated on 30 May, at Aldington, 'where the patient would have a much greater chance of recovery than if it had been done in Town'. Ford was deeply involved, writing to Pinker that the operation obsessed him, and was the only thing he could think about. He also had to think about how to pay for it—two trained nurses had to be brought in—and he borrowed £440 from Marwood. In the 1913 deposition he claimed—reasonably enough—to have treated her with 'consideration' at this time. Yet, he added: 'She retained, nevertheless, her dislike of myself, and continued to entreat me to allow her to divorce me. I, however, disregarded these requests, and continued to visit her.' They were to go on meeting for another year or so. But the failure of communication, and the reluctance to let go, however painful the marriage, is typical of their relationship since Ford's breakdown. Mizener kept that note of Elsie's bitterness out of his book. (He befriended her daugher Katharine, and his account of the marriage relied heavily on Katharine's belief in her mother's innocence.) But Ford's deposition is plausible in its picture of her anger. It was to prove the saddest fact of both their lives that when Ford wanted to divorce, she then refused, and was intransigent for the rest of his life.[36]

While Elsie was convalescing in the country, lying in a thatched hut which (like Mark Tietjens) she had had built with adjustable sailcloth sides to keep out the wind and rain, Ford was throwing himself back into literary society. He lunched most days at the Mont Blanc; and he also went to meetings of the Square Club in Fleet Street, where writers such as Galsworthy, Masefield, and E. C. Bentley met under Chesterton's presidency.[37]

16

1908–1909: VIOLET HUNT AND
THE *ENGLISH REVIEW*

The revolution of the word began so far as it affected the men who were
of my age in London in 1908, with the LONE whimper of Ford Madox
Hueffer.

(Ezra Pound, *Polite Essays*)

During the latter half of 1908 Ford got to know Violet Hunt, and by June 1909
their friendship had developed into an affair which was to last a decade, with
disastrous consequences for both of them. Her father, Alfred Hunt, was a
well-known watercolorist, on the fringes of the Pre-Raphaelite circle; Ford and
Violet remembered meeting each other as children, though Violet, born in 1862,
was eleven years older. Their shared reminiscences made her all the more
appealing to Ford—whose love of Elsie had also had its basis in their childhood.
Her mother was a popular novelist, Margaret Raine Hunt, who had been a friend
of Tennyson, Browning, and Ruskin. Violet met Ford again on 21 March 1907,
at dinner with the Galsworthys, after which they 'walked home together along the
Kensington Road, talking of Pre-Raphaelitism and the price of copper'—she lived
at South Lodge, a semi-detached Victorian villa on Campden Hill Road, only a
few minutes from Holland Park Avenue. She mentions Ford occasionally in her
diary—as an interesting acquaintance rather than a potential lover; and she notes
that he came alone to her annual garden party on 2 May. But she described herself
as a 'sensualist of the emotions', and it is likely that Ford felt the attraction of her
sexuality. Goldring described her at a party seventeen years later, when she was
over 60: 'anyone who saw her for the first time and noted how the young men
crowd round her and laughed at her sallies would have supposed her to be at least
twenty years younger. She was the centre of attraction, a regular "honey pot",
sparkling, flirtatious and lavishly endowed with sex appeal.'[1]

Her editor at Heinemann suggested that she should get Ford to 'boom' her
latest novel, *The White Rose of Weary Leaf*, in one of his 'Literary Portraits'.
When she left Heinemann's office she met Ford coming around the corner. It was
to be five years before he did actually write the piece, which included a heightened
reminiscence of the scene: 'I was walking up Bedford Street when our author
suddenly jumped out at me from the door of No. 32, and exclaimed: "I say: Mr.
H. . . . n, the publisher, says that you have made the fortune of So-and-So by

writing a Literary Portrait of him. Why don't you do one of me?" This, you will observe, is the direct method.' He was, she said, 'awfully amused at my brass'. 'He looked very red and golden against that dark grey wall', she noted. 'I always do ask for what I want—of a man and especially of a man with reddish hair'; and she added: 'I'm a jelly wellstayed with a North country corset of grim whale-bone.'[2]

Like Ford's, Hunt's manner displayed a curious mixture of flirtatiousness and reserve. She trod a fine line between social respectability and bohemian out-rageousness, cultivating upper-class society at the same time as its enemies, the radical artists such as Ezra Pound, D. H. Lawrence, and Wyndham Lewis. The relationships between Edward Ashburnham and Florence Dowell in *The Good Soldier*, and between Christopher and Sylvia Tietjens in *Parade's End*, both draw upon their affair. What Sylvia says of her husband—that 'he's so formal he can't do without all the conventions there are and so truthful he can't use half of them'—is true of her own impeccably decorous violations of decorum too; and something like this is true of both Ford and Violet. Like Ford, she wrote novels in which the outlines of her own life were recognizable yet also recognizably transformed; she shared his attraction to literary innuendo, the need at once to reveal and to disguise her personal life. In 1908 'she still seemed quite young', said R. A. Scott-James—a friend of Ford's from the Mont Blanc, who met her at Galsworthy's that year:

She had a way of knowing everyone in London belonging to the worlds of literature, art and the theatre and gathering mixed assortments of celebrities at her 'At Homes'. She had the reputation of being very beautiful, but in fact her face just missed real beauty through its lack of gravity and significant expression, and its incapacity for repose. She was restless, inconsequent, impulsive, and always had the air of a spoilt child [. . .] Everyone knew and liked her, regarding her as something pretty, elfin, irresponsible, rather touching with her appealing eyes, to be humoured and made much of. And if she talked a little too freely—if she could not help gossiping—that was part of her make-up. She meant no harm.[3]

When Brigit Patmore met her several years later she was struck by 'the startling beauty of her eyes, for it was almost painful; their clear, curious green colour and the perfect leaf-shape of the lids around them were lovely, but the surprise of pain lay in the fact that, although she looked straight at one, she seemed to be seeing something else as well—something past or to come': Ford was always intrigued by that transcendent glance which characterized his 'Nice People'. 'Her pointed chin and sparrow-brown hair, plummy and softly drifting as her head moved, added to the impression of feyness', said Patmore; though it was 'quite contra-dicted' by her way of talking about herself as down-to-earth. With her self-pos-sessed 'superb grey Persian cat', she struck people (including, eventually, Ford) as having a witch-like aspect.[4]

Oscar Wilde had thought of marrying her, and proposed around 1880 when she was 17 or 18. She evidently refused him, but it was an inauspicious start to her love-life. In 1884 she began an affair with a painter, George Boughton. Yet in July 1887 Boughton married another woman, though the affair with Hunt dragged on for a further two years. Then, in 1892, she had a second affair with a man at least twice her age. Oswald Crawfurd was a diplomat—he had been the British consul at Oporto—and an amateur man of letters; he too was married. But when his invalid wife died in 1899 he married one of Violet's friends, Lita Brown. She wrote in her diary about Boughton: '[he] initiated me into the secret of what I *could* feel and has now left me—*inassouvie*'. Crawfurd had left her with syphilis, as she discovered in 1905. When her old friend Marguerite Radclyffe Hall fell in love with her, although Hunt couldn't reciprocate the passion, she carried on visiting, saying that she gave herself 'the airs of a Sultana', and noting 'how easily one is corrupted by adoration'. She had a reputation among her friends for her sexual candour. She recorded how her friend Ethel Clifford, Lady Dilke, 'pumped me about Lesbians': 'I tried to lighten just a little of her astounding innocence, but she stopped her pretty ears; "Do you know, dear Violet—I don't think I'll hear any more".' She had a brief affair with Somerset Maugham, and a year-long affair with H. G. Wells from the summer of 1906. When she was staying with the Wellses in 1907 she recorded: 'I hardly see H. G. alone. He sometimes wiles me into a tool shed which he calls his study.' Dorothy Richardson was also staying, and Hunt said that outside the shed Wells was 'in continual terror of Dorothy's sharp eyes'. But, she added: 'I am such a devil that I am only *nice* to him *outside*', becoming 'demure the moment I get into the hovel': 'He is getting very cross with me. . . .' Arnold Bennett was a friend, but was attracted more to Hunt's beautiful niece, Rosamond Fogg Elliot (even though he thought Rosamond was 'mad'): Bennett, she noted, 'finds *me* just clever and modern without much knowledge or interest in any traditional matters—my walk in life being too purely sexual for him'. 'Life is a succession of affairs,' she said in the first sentence of her memoir *The Flurried Years*, 'but there is always one affair for which the years, from birth, are a preparation, a hardening, a tempering, and a more or less serious erosion, possibly, of the sword of the fighter.' (We shall see how Ford too was fond of the pun on 'affair' as also a term of fictional technique—the human situation that the novel renders.) *The Flurried Years* gives her impressionistic rendering of her affair with Ford, which was '*the* affair' of her life.[5]

When she was seeing more of Ford in 1908 he was 34; she was 45, still unmarried, and alert to potential suitors. She had herself seen the folly of her involvement with Crawfurd: 'there would be something very ridiculous in my being engaged for a second time in an intrigue with a married man.' Her self-destructive streak is undeniable, as is her tendency to re-enact 'the cycle of daring flirtation, affair with a man unsuitable by age and marital status, prolonged recrimination, and rejection of respectability'.[6] Yet putting her trust in Ford was less absurd, despite the difference in age and the fact that he was another married man. He almost certainly would have married her if he had been able to.

She was regarded as 'an English Colette'; 'one of the leading women novelists of her time', though her prose has a precious obliqueness and ornateness that makes it sound self-congratulatory. Pinker was her agent too. She painted. She was an active suffragette, joining the Pankhursts' Women's Social and Political Union. In February 1908 her photograph appeared in *Black and White* collecting money for the suffragettes in Kensington High Street. She gave a dinner for Christabel Pankhurst in June 1909, and she and Ford arranged a meeting for her the following year. Ford's mother and sister had joined a suffrage procession ('in a small motor') in February 1907, and Ford became a supporter. Hunt's sense of Edwardian upper-middle-class propriety is illustrated by a diary entry of November 1907, when she sat next to Asquith—then chancellor of the exchequer, and prime minister the following year: 'When I got up to go [b]ehold some wag had tied our two chairs together with a napkin[.] Asquith allowed himself to be disengaged with weary patience—I suppose he thought I was accessory to the deed but I was not, although a mad suffragist. I don't think politics should ever be introduced into drawing rooms.' 'I happen to be the New Woman', she wrote in 1926—'Not the Newest Woman of all, but [. . .] the New Woman that people wrote about in the nineties.' This was the woman she wrote about, for example, in *Sooner or Later* (1904), the fictionalized version of the Crawfurd affair. 'The reason why she and Maugham so thrilled the young Edwardians, and so shocked their elders, was because they had both of them, in their different ways, introduced a note of Nastiness into English fiction [. . .] The possibilities represented by Nastiness were infinite and intoxicating.' Ford helped her with her writing, of course. He was taken with what he called her 'powers of observation, together with an unusually macabre seriousness and a hobgoblin power of making jokes'; and his work was influenced by her 'very real genius'. His fiction had always been romantic, but euphemistically so. Goldring said Hunt's best books had 'a quality of smouldering passion' absent from Ford's early work. Her outspokenness (in fiction and in life) helped him to write books like *A Call, The New Humpty-Dumpty, Mr. Fleight*, and *The Good Soldier*. Henry James—whom she had known since 1882, been friendly with since 1898, and whom she seemed to get a curious pleasure from failing to seduce—called her his 'Purple Patch' when she visited him in Rye in a 'purple get-up'. 'He "skoots" from passion as if he had been once bitten by it and yet I am sure that in *my* sense of the word he never has—he is incapable', she wrote, and complained that when he listened to her about the latest society gossip, 'he always wants my news but never more than half of it, always getting bored or delicately' [the completion of the sentence is missing from her diary]. She asked James if she could dedicate *Sooner or Later* to him. He sent a 'fervid telegram' agreeing, but was 'taken aback' when a friend wrote to him: 'Violet Hunt has gone and written a novel weltering with sex, and dedicated it to you!' Belloc's sister Marie Lowndes thought it her 'most important book': 'the first modern novel which dealt, in a serious sense, with the problem of illicit love.'[7]

Scott-James was staying at Holland Park Avenue as a paying guest over the summer of 1908, when he was invited to Hunt's annual garden party. He asked if he could bring Ford with him, and ('since it had become one of her principal pleasures to collect celebrities') she replied that he should. Scott-James regretted having thus 'been the unwitting instrument in bringing them together'—though they had already met several times during the previous sixteen months.[8]

Ford's other major involvement of 1908 and 1909 was the founding and editing of the monthly *English Review*. The story he sometimes told about starting the magazine in order to print a poem by Thomas Hardy that had been refused publication by one of 'the then orthodox periodicals' has more than merely an impressionistic truth. Hardy had sent 'A Sunday Morning Tragedy' to only one editor, who had returned it, saying that he could not print it because 'his review circulated amongst young people'. 'Of course,' Hardy wrote to Ford, 'with a larger morality, the guardians of young people would see that it is the very thing they ought to read, for nobody can say that the treatment is other than moral'; and he added: 'I could let you have a short poem of an ordinary and quite safe kind, if you do not like this.' Ford had of course wanted to edit a literary periodical before, and had a much broader purpose: namely, 'the definite design of giving imaginative literature a chance in England'.[9]

In part this meant giving the imagination a chance to consider topics frowned upon by 'Mrs Grundy', or suppressed by what Hardy, in the same letter to Ford, described as 'the hypocrisy of the age'. The *English Review* aimed to expose the sentimental stereotypes of popular fiction and morality to the mordancies of the 'Critical Attitude'. When the first issue appeared in December 1908, with 'A Sunday Morning Tragedy' as its vanguard, it was proclaiming the coming of age of Edwardian literature. Like *Tess of the d'Urbervilles*, Hardy's poem asserts the innocence of a young woman who is made pregnant by her lover (who at first refuses to marry her), and is then poisoned by her mother, who gives her a herbal medicine supposed to produce an abortion. The tragedy is clinched when the lover arrives to say he has changed his mind just as the woman dies. For this type of uncompromising look at this type of subject English readers would normally have had to turn to French novels. At the moment in *The Good Soldier* when the affair between Edward and Florence first becomes visible, the narrator writes: 'It was as if we were going to run and cry out [. . .] averting our heads' (p. 53); the *English Review* intended to get the English to view things from which they conventionally averted their heads. E. V. Lucas (a contributor to *Punch*) told Conrad the *Review* was 'too foreign for its title'.[10] Ford's advocacy of French writers—especially Flaubert and Maupassant—has too often been understood only as a crusade for literary technique. It is that; but it is also a crusade for the chance to write about sexuality without the distortions of bourgeois sentimentality. The year 1908 was a watershed in Ford's life: his affair with Violet Hunt slowly put him at the centre of a public scandal; the *English Review* quickly put him at the centre of literary London. It was also a watershed in his work. As he faced his own sexual needs, and his need to leave Elsie, sexuality and attitudes towards it became his great subject. These things had always been at the centre of his work, as in most fiction. But his treatment became more critically searching, and his writing much more powerful. The *English Review* was a crucial stage in Ford's maturing as a critic and as a creative writer.

The *Review* would give imaginative literature a chance in another way. Ford was determined to be quite unlike other publishers. He paid good prices, did not make a profit on his writers, and displayed a rare magnanimity as an editor, not requiring particular political, aesthetic, or moral positions from his authors; merely that their work should be well written. Ford explained to Edward Garnett, who, together with Marwood and Conrad, had been involved in the planning of the magazine, the scheme he had hit upon whereby the contributors should have the option of sharing in any profit that might be made:

I quite realize what you say as to the awkwardness of the profit-sharing idea, but the only people who come into it are very intimate friends of mine and I have put the matter perfectly plainly to every contributor—'Will you take £2 a 1000 words or will you take a sporting risk which might be estimated as a two to one chance against you, as a shareholder?'—and in order to avoid their incurring any liability I have added in a form of words to please Galsworthy 'I do not undertake legally to pay you anything at all, but this is my private intention.'

I know that inevitably there will be quarrels and recriminations, but in some things I am an idealist and my ideal is to run the 'English Review' as far as possible as a socialistic undertaking. The kicks I shall get will be the price I shall pay for indulging my idealism and these I trust to bear with equanimity.[11]

Since the only people Ford expects to quarrel over the arrangements are his intimates—Wells, Galsworthy, Conrad, Hunt, and Marwood—there is a disconcerting sense that he expects his closest friends to betray him; even that he is contriving their treachery. Yet the insight of *The Benefactor* is there too: that altruism can be an alibi for egotism—something that is 'indulged'. As so often, Ford's paranoid intimations about other artists recall Madox Brown's: here Ford is creating around him the brotherhood of internecine geniuses whose presence will guarantee his role as the embattled altruist, the poor lion in a den of savage Daniels, even as they demoralize him. And yet one should also recognize the true nobility of his ideal for the *English Review*. Conrad recognized its dignity and its doom when he advised Ford against a 'coalition' with McClure, when the *Review*'s finances were already in difficulty in the spring of 1909: 'Even the rumour of such a thing, in London, would be like a hint of failure', he wrote to Ford. 'The E.R. may have to stop, but it mustn't fail.'[12]

Conrad had reached an impasse in the writing of *Under Western Eyes*. He felt he had made a 'fatal move' to Someries, and wanted to get back to Kent. On 29 August 1908 he and Jessie rented rooms in Hogben House, a farmhouse at Aldington. He told Edward Garnett it would be for 'a week or so', while he took 'a long spell of heavy pulling at the novel without a name'. It has been suggested that he hoped to enlist Ford's help again; he certainly felt that Ford's proximity and encouragement would spur his creativity. They stayed for over three weeks. Ford wanted something of Conrad's for the *Review* and, thinking back to the autobiographical sketches in *The Mirror of the Sea* he had persuaded Conrad to dictate to him, he suggested another series of reminiscences. Seven instalments were published in the *Review* as 'Some Reminiscences'; in 1912 Conrad added 'A Familiar Preface', and published them as a book (also *Some Reminiscences*, though the title was later changed to *A Personal Record*). He wanted to 'make Polish life enter English literature'. As with all Ford's involvements with Conrad's work, there has been confusion and controversy about what exactly that involvement was. 'Hueffer suggested them to me and offered to take me down from dictation', Conrad told Pinker when he had written the first one and a half of the reminiscences; and he added: 'These are things which I could not dictate to anyone but a friend—and such a friend is Hueffer who consents to hold the pen for me—a proof of friendship and an act of great kindness.' Since this was written after nearly three weeks at Aldington, it probably means that Ford wrote down at least those one and a half papers. We know he took down some of the second instalment when he visited Conrad at Someries on the last weekend in September or the first in October, because Conrad wrote to him that the second instalment was complete 'without the few words which you were good enough to let me dictate to you when last here'. But it isn't known which words these were, or whether they were included in the magazine or book versions. Conrad told Pinker the reminiscences wouldn't have 'come into being' without 'the insistence together with actual help from Hueffer'.[13]

Part of that help was psychological. Conrad was already descending into his remembered past to write *Under Western Eyes*. Now the reminiscences that were to galvanize him back into creativity were also threatening his mental balance. He tried to pre-empt Wells's criticism of the serial by telling him: 'I fear it is a silly enterprise besides (what with the stirring up of all these dead) being a somewhat ghoulish one. I explain to you so that you should not suspect me of incipient softening of the brain.' He already suspected himself of mental trouble: 'I do long to see you. I am losing my grip on everything', he wrote to Ford. The 'Familiar Preface' to *A Personal Record* suggests the way that to write autobiographically was to engage in a struggle to maintain his grip on himself: 'I have a positive horror of losing even for one moving moment that full possession of myself which is the first condition of good service' (and of good memoirs). In a passage which may be a veiled rebuke to Ford, he explains: 'the danger lies in the writer becoming the victim of his own exaggeration, losing the exact notion of sincerity, and in the end coming to despise truth itself as something too cold, too blunt for his purpose—as, in fact, not good enough for his insistent emotion.' This was written in 1912, after they had quarrelled, and after Ford had advertised his 'profound contempt' for facts in the Dedication of *Ancient Lights*. In 1908, when, as even a scholar as hostile to Ford as Najder says, Conrad 'generally spoke of him in the most affectionate terms' ('my *intimé*', 'a brave fellow and a man of talent'), it was Ford who could stop Conrad losing his grip on his own self-mythologizing imagination. In the first of the reminiscences Conrad recalled the tag of Novalis that he had used as the epigraph to *Lord Jim*: ' "It is certain my conviction gains infinitely the moment another soul will believe in it." And what is a novel if not a conviction of our fellow-men's existence strong enough to take upon itself a form of imagined life clearer than reality and whose accumulated verisimilitude of selected episodes puts to shame the pride of documentary history.' Ford shared that conviction about the novel, as Conrad knew, and probably dictated to him knowingly. Sharing it, Ford made it his own, rephrasing it: 'It is certain that my conviction gains immensely as soon as another soul can be found to share it.' Like his narrator John Dowell, Ford too wants to convince himself of the reality of his own imagination by moving others to share it, or by being a reader who can share the author's convictions. He could be Conrad's Secret Sharer, able, as Frederick Karl says, 'to touch Conrad at the right moment and tap the resources that lay so deep within him'; also able to keep Conrad sane while he was becoming possessed by his past selves. Years later Conrad remembered Ford's role with fondness: 'The early E.[nglish] R.[eview] is the only literary business that, in Bacon's phraseology, "came home to my bosom." The mere fact that it was the occasion of you putting on me that gentle but persistent pressure which extracted from my then despondency the stuff of the *Personal Record* would be enough to make its memory dear.'[14]

Ford had now acquired a 'retinue' consisting of a sub-editor, the young Douglas Goldring, who was to call on Ford in the evening after his work for *Country Life*, and a secretary, Olive Thomas—'a remarkably competent lady', said Goldring. Olive Thomas later became Lloyd George's secretary. She and Ford may have had a brief affair. Goldring's first job was to spend a summer weekend at Aldington, where Ford dictated to him a letter, 'couched in terms of almost obsequious respect', to Hardy, asking for permission to publish 'A Sunday Morning Tragedy'. In the autumn the editorial team visited Conrad at Someries to discuss the magazine's policy and to plan the first number. Conrad later recalled: 'You arrived one evening with your amiable myrmidons and parcels of copy.' Goldring was overwhelmed by the talk that evening, as Ford and Conrad started, 'in a mixture of French and English, to discuss what the Review must Stand For', and then went on to contrast the disciplined French and casual English attitudes to 'the technique of the novel and the short story'. Conrad said he would never forget 'the desperate stillness of that house, where women and children were innocently sleeping, when you sought me out at 2 AM. in my dismal study to make me concentrate suddenly on a two-page notice of the "*Ile des Pingouins*." A marvellously successful instance of the editorial tyranny! [. . .] I have forgiven long ago.' Goldring was also impressed by Ford's 'baronial' manner during this visit. 'As Conrad was descended, or said he was, from a family of Polish or Ukrainian landowners in which titles were plentiful, it was natural that Ford should keep his end up by stressing an equally aristocratic background.' Goldring also remembered 'eating a frugal dinner of cold ham and brie, washed down with white wine', during which Ford told him he was a baron 'five times over':

He was Baron von Aschendrof, several other sorts of baron and finally *baron of the Cinque Ports!* I gazed at him with astonishment mingled with awe. His German barony gave him, it appeared, the entrée to the Kaiser's Court, and as he wished to interest

Wilhelm in *The English Review*, he proposed (so he said) to attend, and take me with him. I was thunderstruck. The project was abandoned because, as Ford remarked in his drawling, olympian tones, 'your uniform alone, my dear Goldring, would cost eight or nine hundred pounds!'.

Goldring cites this story as an example of Ford's self-presentation being a way of hiding himself under 'romantic disguises'. But his recollection of being 'thunder-struck', and of his own awe and astonishment, tells another story. Ford wasn't hiding (such a performance expresses much more about his desires than would a more banal literalism); he was teasing; and he was practising his power of spellbinding on a fresh audience.[15]

Back at Holland Park Avenue the front-door was left open, and would-be contributors came and went. When D. H. Lawrence took a copy of the first issue back to Jessie Chambers, her family were so impressed they decided to subscribe: 'The coming of the *English Review* into our lives was an event, one of the few really first-rate things that happen now and again in a lifetime.' When she sent in some of Lawrence's poems, the author was summoned to meet Ford in the autumn of 1909, and found him 'fairish, fat, about forty, and the kindest man on earth'. The three poems, 'Discipline', 'Dreams Old and Nascent', and 'Baby Movements' were published in the November issue. When in 1936 he recalled that meeting Ford gave Lawrence's first words on seeing him 'sprawling at his mercy, reading a manuscript before him' as: 'This isn't my idea, Sir, of an editor's office.' He said he reproached Lawrence later for calling him 'Sir', to be told: 'But you are, aren't you, everybody's blessed Uncle and Headmaster?' He was. He was also, Lawrence was later to say, 'the first man I ever met who had a real and true feeling for literature. He introduced me to Edward Garnett who, somehow, introduced me to the world.' Lawrence told Blanche Jennings that Ford was 'a really fine man, in that he is so generous, so understanding, and in that he keeps the doors of his soul open, and you may walk in'. Wyndham Lewis (according to Goldring) found that he left his other doors unlocked:

Getting no answer to his ring, he walked up to the editorial sanctum and found it deserted. Undeterred, he climbed another flight of stairs and, hearing at last sounds of human life, knocked at the door through which they came and marched in. It happened to be the bathroom, and there, reclining on his back in the bath, in two feet of hot water, with a large sponge in one hand, and a cake of soap in the other, was the missing editor. Disregarding any unconventionality in his surroundings, the 'Enemy' at once proceeded to business. After announcing in the most matter-of-fact way that he was a man of genius and that he had a manuscript for publication, he asked if he might read it. 'Go ahead', Ford murmured, continuing to use his sponge. Lewis then unbuttoned his coat, produced 'The Pole' and read it through. At the end, Ford observed 'Well, that's all right. If you'll leave it behind, we'll certainly print it.'[16]

Goldring, who retailed this story, said of it: 'I cannot vouch for the accuracy of this, or indeed of any of Ford's anecdotes, but if it didn't happen it ought to have done. Events of this description occurred daily, almost hourly, during the twelve months of Ford's editorship of the Review.' The two versions Ford published are more decorous—whether from modesty or accuracy is impossible to say—and though seventeen years apart, are remarkably close in essentials. Marwood and Ford agree that the number of the *Review* they were then assembling is 'rotten'. Ford gets Miss Thomas to say a prayer before the image of St Anthony ('the saint who still confronts us as we search our minds for the words that so difficultly come') in the hope that something better can be found. As if in answer, a shriek from Miss Thomas portends the arrival of Lewis, whom Ford said he assumed to be another Russian exile trying to sell him Tsar's diaries or 'accounts of the methods of the secret police'. 'Slowly and with an air of doom the stranger began to draw out manuscripts—from his coat-pockets, from his trouser-pockets, from his breast-pockets, from the lining of his conspirator's hat.' Ford remembered quailing before Lewis's silence: 'I have never known anyone else whose silence was a positive rather than a negative quality.' Lewis saw how deeply astonished was Ford: 'which lemonish pink giant', he added with pictorial sharpness, 'in his quilted dressing-gown, with his mouth hanging open like a big silly fish, surprised *me*.' (If Ford ever did tell the story as Goldring has it, the point of the transformation would have been to heighten the impression of his own vulnerability before Lewis's relentlessness.)[17]

Most of the stories about Ford's editing are studies in insouciance as well as of the exactitude of his judgement. He is the complete editor, his mind on matters of style and form even while he is ostensibly giving himself a bath or, as Goldring recalled, sitting in a box or the stalls of the local music-hall—his habitual sanctuary from the incessant visitors: 'After dinner I went out and stopped a hansom and editor and 'sub' drove down to Shepherd's Bush with the MSS which had accumulated during the day. During the performance, or rather during the duller turns, Ford made his decisions and I duly recorded them.' Violet Hunt visited Ford on 16 October 1908—at Wells's suggestion—to offer him some stories for the *Review*:

The editor, wearing a brown velvet coat that had belonged to Rossetti, came forward, and a lovely golden-haired girl whom he introduced [...] She was going to be secretary to the Review, and was making tea. I was shy; I always am of editors, because they are so powerful. I noticed some beautiful furniture, but very little of it. A large Broadwood piano filled up one corner, and there was a Chippendale bureau on which, the editor said, Christina Rossetti had written her poems. There was a cabinet that he said had belonged to the Duke of Medina-Sidonia, that he had picked up for a song. It was crammed with manuscripts, rammed in anyhow, bulging, sagging, sprouting out of the beautiful incrusted doors, and was in a shocking state. After tea, and not till then, the editor took my manuscripts all together between his two hands, and, opening and shutting them, flirted the pages ... There were three long-short stories. ...

He said suddenly, pausing at the middle one: 'I'll take this.'

I said, 'But you haven't read it!'[18]

But he had read enough to convince himself that she could write and, as Mizener says, had chosen 'The Coach', the best of her *Tales of the Uneasy*. They saw each other three days later, and Hunt asked him to luncheon at South Lodge the following week. After she was 'taken on a walk and inspected by Marwood', she was 'more or less incorporated into *The English Review* gang'. Ford's own recollection of reading another of the manuscripts submitted by Lawrence— 'Odour of Chrysanthemums'—shows a similar rhythm of working. It was late, and his eyes were tired. He gives a sentence-by-sentence commentary—one of his finest—on the first paragraph, then adds: 'And if you are an editor and that is what you are after, you know that you have got what you want and you can pitch the story straight away into your wicker tray with the few accepted manuscripts.' Immediately afterwards he went to a 'Trench dinner'—'a Dutch Treat presided over by Herbert Trench, the poet' at the Pall Mall Restaurant. He told Wells about Lawrence, whereupon Wells exclaimed: 'Hurray, Fordie's discovered another genius! Called D. H. Lawrence!' Lawrence himself was wry about having what Ford called 'that terrible word genius' applied to him. He remembered how, when he had heard Lawrence had written a novel, Ford had asked to see the manuscript of *The White Peacock*. 'He read it immediately, with the greatest cheery sort of kindness and bluff', said Lawrence. 'And in his queer voice, when we were in an omnibus in London, he shouted in my ear: "It's got every fault that the English novel can have [...] But," shouted Hueffer in the 'bus, "you've got GENIUS." [...] I always thought he had a bit of genius himself.' Ford 'could measure the quality of an unknown writer almost at a glance without personal or social prejudice'.[19]

They were high-spirited days. Goldring told another story about another member of what he called 'Ford's entourage', Perceval Gibbon, 'a pallid, dark-haired Welshman with a great command of the technique of the magazine short story and an equally great addiction to hard liquor'. He was also a 'merciless practical joker':

He arrived at the flat, late one snowy night, in a state of well-simulated consternation. 'Ford, what do you think has happened?' he gasped. 'I drove here in a four-wheeler, and just as we got near Holland Park Tube station the cab suddenly stopped. I got out to see what was up, and found the poor old cabby apparently *dead on his box*. We must go out and do something about it.' A wave of humanitarian emotion swept over Ford and his companion who, if I remember right, was Marwood. Murmuring 'doctor ... brandy ... cold and exposure ... poor old fellow' they hurried into their coats and rushed forth into the icy street followed by the chuckling Gibbon.[20]

Though the kind of joke seems old-fashioned now, it gives an insight into this group of writers' love of tall stories; their preoccupation with trying to trick people into believing the improbable. The proximity of their fictional experiments and their desire to entertain has been too easily forgotten when Ford's own tall stories have been reproved by the more moralistic.

The *Review* signalled the presence of English modernism. Given the literary sectarianism of the remaining pre-war years, Ford's clear-sighted eclecticism and sane tolerance is unequalled. He prided himself on his ability to discover geniuses;

and although he mocked his optimism that all his geese would become swans, it is remarkable how few of the contributors to the *English Review* time proved to be geese. Apart from the geniuses that Ford did effectively discover—Lawrence, Lewis, Pound, Norman Douglas, and R. H. Mottram were all virtually unpublished at that time—the *Review*'s more established writers still dominate our sense of their period. The first issue followed Hardy's 'A Sunday Morning Tragedy' with Henry James's 'The Jolly Corner', Conrad's 'Some Reminiscences', and Galsworthy's 'A Fisher of Men'. W. H. Hudson's 'Stonehenge' is followed by the first part of Constance Garnett's translation of Tolstoy's 'The Raid' and the first instalment of Wells's *Tono-Bungay*. The section headed 'The Month' included Ford's editorial on 'The Function of the Arts in the Republic', which is followed by his piece on 'The Unemployed', incorporating a review of Stephen Reynolds's *A Poor Man's House*. Conrad reviewed Anatole France's *L'Ile des pingouins*. Levin Schücking reviewed Swinburne's *The Age of Shakespeare*. Cunninghame Graham, W. H. Davies, and Henry Nevinson are also represented. All these writers figured in later issues as well, as did Vernon Lee, Yeats, Chesterton, Belloc, George Moore, Goldsworthy Lowes Dickinson, E. M. Forster, H. M. Tomlinson, Sturge Moore, Stephen Reynolds, Walter de la Mare, Frederic Manning, Gilbert Murray, Rupert Brooke, C. E. Montague, President Howard Taft, and Arnold Bennett. Ford thrived on the company of outstanding artists, and collected them as he collected outstanding pieces of furniture (preferably with a literary pedigree). But it would be wrong to imagine (as Conradians and Jamesians in particular have imagined) that he was parasitic upon the reputations of others. He was honoured to have been an intimate of writers such as James, Conrad, Wells, Galsworthy, Hudson, Lawrence, and the rest. No doubt it bolstered his sense—never secure—of his worth to be in the company of the Modern Great, who perhaps alone could exorcize those spectres of the overwhelming Victorian Great of his childhood. But he was not a literary hanger-on; his reminiscences are exercises in definition and self-definition, not in name-dropping. He was, anyway, an important literary figure in his own right after the publication of his English Trilogy and the *Fifth Queen* novels. He was writing his best criticism, and entering his most important phase as a novelist. As Malcolm Bradbury has written: 'he should serve as a model for editors of literary periodicals; his respect for the artist, the creative being, and his determination to nourish genius made him an invaluable figure in those opening years.'[21]

Ford's influence as the *Review*'s editor was much more profound than is apparent from the brevity of his tenure or the small circulation. He not only gathered together all the great talents of early English modernism; by constellating them he created a coherent impression not of a movement so much as of a literary moment—and of the qualities of writing to be prized at that moment. It was between the blue wrappers of the *English Review* that the young F. R. Leavis first read Lawrence, published alongside James and Conrad. Though the moral crusade he fought over what he called the 'Great Tradition' was entirely his own, his perception of what should constitute that tradition was sharpened by Ford's review. He thought Ford's 'claim to be remembered' was as 'the brilliant editor'.

The distinction of Ford's *English Review* was that its very intelligently active defence and promotion of the finer creativity was adapted to the irreversible new conditions: it accepted as one of them the restriction of concern for the higher cultural values to a small minority, while conceding nothing to the precociousness, fatuity or spirit of Aestheticism. Under Ford it was decidedly a literary review, and he gave proof of his critical perception, and of the courage of it, in his editorial policy.

'The *English Review* as by us established differed from the existing reviews in that our chief interest was with imaginative literature', wrote Ford. The early numbers began with verse, followed by 'imaginative prose' (stories, reminiscences, and essays):

Then we jammed in an enormous slice of serial, not because we believed that anyone ever wanted to read a serial, but because we believed that the publicity might be useful to the novelist [. . .] Into the remaining cracks in the structure we dropped the dreary imbecilities that pass for seriousness. We gave, that is to say, very infinitesimal space to Dardanelles problems, Chinese egg problems, Alaskan boundaries, Turkish debts and all the lugubrious pomposities which stuffed, like highly desiccated wadding, the brain of the unfortunate English reader of reviews.

It was, as Eric Homberger says, 'a brave assertion of the centrality of imaginative literature'. The *English Review* reversed the form of the 'serious' Edwardian quarterlies and monthlies, showing the way for successors: not only the host of modernist 'small magazines'—Pound too found Ford's editing exemplary, and tried to make the *Little Review* 'be what the English Review was during the first 18 months when F.M.H. ran it'—but also today's *London Magazine* or *Granta*. Ford's editorials, some of which were collected in the book *The Critical Attitude* in 1911, 'do not quite make up a sacred book of modernism, but they brilliantly define the doctrines upon which a modernism could be erected'.[22]

In Ford's political contributions too it is the unorthodox open-mindedness, the coexistence of usually opposed views that is striking. In 'A Declaration of Faith', written pseudonymously by Ford, he sets the political tone of the *Review*: 'In common with the great bulk of my fellow-countrymen I am by temperament an obstinate, sentimental and old-fashioned Tory.' He says he is 'for Mr. Balfour right or wrong', but continues: 'But I mistrust Mr. Balfour's party even more than I mistrust the mixed majority which supports Mr. Asquith.'[23] Ford's political 'temperament' is nevertheless at odds with the policies he supports, for he writes in the same article: 'I desire Home Rule for Ireland with as much fervour as I desire to see the vote given to women' (p. 548). On at least two of the three most controversial issues of the day, he takes up positions which were anathema to the Tory party: on the third, the growing industrial unrest and strikes, he is equally far from the Tory party line, open-mindedly weighing up his ambivalent feelings about Lloyd George's budget, despite its 'Socialistic lines':

inasmuch as I belong personally and by temperament to the 'haves', I object to being pillaged by Mr. Lloyd George for the benefit of anybody. At the same time I recognise that my votes are given me for the purpose, not of bolstering up myself or my class but in order that I may consider what is best for the nation and so vote as to help in bringing that best about. Now even as to this I am in two frames of mind. It is open to me to say *noblesse oblige* and to let myself be pillaged from the comparatively sentimental standpoint that the poor man has for so long had a bad time of it that the time has come when it is the duty of myself and of that class that for so long has had a comparatively good time of it to stand aside and to give the poor man what in the popular language is called 'a show.' I do not know that I should strongly object to doing this, and I very heartily wish that some breath of some such sentiment had made its appearance in the Conservative party utterances.

But on the other hand I am by no means certain that such legislation would be for the country's good. (pp. 544–5)

This is Toryism of Ford Madox Brown's or Marwood's kind, which aspires to a form of paternalistic socialism rather than *laissez-faire* capitalism. Marwood wrote an article, published in the first number of the *Review*, outlining 'A Complete Actuarial Scheme for Insuring John Doe against all the Vicissitudes of Life', which (despite the title, which makes it sound like Swiftian satire) advocates a state system of old-age pensions and pensions for widows and dependants, as well as sickness and unemployment benefits. In a similar socialistic vein, Ford wrote, 'I should like to see all men swept away who make a profit out of other men's labour'. If this is Toryism, it has become so extreme as to be indistinguishable from socialism. One can see why Ford said: 'I could always get on with the Extreme Right or the Extreme Left; moderates of any type I have always found insupportable.'[24]

His politics never interfered with his love of good writing. Thus he wanted to publish George Bernard Shaw, though Shaw's fee was too high. Ford parried good-humouredly: 'My charges for receiving post-cards containing defamatory words are £2,700 per post-card. You will thus see that when I have printed "Getting Married" you will owe me £12,000, cheque for which will oblige.' Shaw told him: 'The Review is certainly very good. You know where to look for your men.' Both were involved in the committee to found a National Theatre (it took nearly seventy more years before the South Bank theatres were opened). Ford had protested earlier in 1908 that money was to be spent on a memorial to Shakespeare, while 'at no playhouse at present open in London is there any play which any thinking man or any healthy-minded navvy could feel more than a languid desire to see'. When he proposed raising money from continental newspapers (which probably meant from his Hüffer relatives) for a theatre to which 'the players of Molière, of Goethe, of Calderon, and even of Gogol' should be invited, 'an institution in tone with the spirit of the age; democratic [...] international', Shaw rebuked him handsomely:

it would be an intolerable act of national pauperism to ask other countries to help us to build a theatre for ourselves. You do not appreciate this because a sort of international anarchism is part of your family program [. . .] It is one of your qualities as an artist that you have not got a British conscience; but you should, like me, get a nice little artificial one and keep it about you for use on great British occasions.[25]

In its imaginative literature, as in its political articles, *English Review* made a significant contribution to the crucial debates of the day: censorship and funding of the drama, the regulation of sexuality, the organization of society, the condition of England. When Ford's close friend C. F. G. Masterman, a Liberal MP, wrote his influential study *The Condition of England*, he had been greatly impressed by *Tono-Bungay*, which he began reading in the *Review*. His views, as well as his literary style and aspirations, had also been shaped by Ford's analyses of the English.

The *English Review* did not fail. It did not stop, exactly, either. But it lost money quickly. Ford's later estimate that he had spent £2,800 (most of it Hunt's, but £150 of it Elsie's) to Marwood's £2,500 seems probable, given that the original print-run of 5,000 copies soon appeared optimistic, and contributors, fearing that there would be no profits to share, began to withdraw from that scheme and demand outright payment instead. Ford originally had enough capital for four issues. When that ran out there was a crisis. He began looking for someone who would buy the *Review*, but leave him in control as its editor. Eventually his brother-in-law, David Soskice, came up with a scheme of forming a group of what Mizener calls 'men with similar political interests who would take over the *Review*, keeping Ford as the editor but controlling the political content'. The problem was that Ford did not share the political interests of the Soskice group, whom he felt were 'revolutionary extremists', ones of a Russian and anarchistic kind rather than sentimental Tories. An interim compromise was set up in the middle of May 1909. The Soskice group tried to find backers while Ford tried to mediate between their and Marwood's politics. He then approached Hunt's friend, Alfred Mond (later Lord Melchett), who did buy the *Review*. Ford had saved it from the Soskice faction, but had not saved it for himself. Mond was a Liberal MP, exactly the kind of moderate who would not be prepared to tolerate Ford's editorials. Mond fired Ford, replacing him by Austin Harrison (the son of Frederic Harrison and a journalist for the *Daily Mail*), and replacing Goldring by Norman Douglas. The last issue that Ford put together was the one for February 1910, the fourteenth, though under Harrison it continued to carry pieces that Ford had selected. The *Review* was a *succès d'estime*, though it provoked the *Academy*, which had incorporated a previous 'English Review', to threaten legal action. 'It's simply blackmailing, they are beasts', complained Constance Garnett, as she realized she might not get paid for her Chekhov sketches: 'And poor Ford has no money.'[26]

1909: THE WRECKS OF FRIENDSHIPS

But I would not have thy night thoughts
[. . . . .]
And I hear thee turn and mutter
As thy dawn-wards candles gutter—
For thou fear'st the dark . . . Hark. 'Judas!'
Says the dawn wind from the sea.
Round the house it whispers 'Judas!'
Friend of mine, my enemy.

('The Feather', *High Germany*)

As the *English Review* slipped out of Ford's hands, he approached the edge of a second breakdown. The first half of 1909 was his most fraught period since 1904. Entangling himself further and further into the role of literature's betrayed altruist, he rapidly alienated some of his best friends and contacts. In January he irritated Frank Harris by telling him over lunch at the Savoy that Marwood thought his story 'The Miracle of the Stigmata' 'a piece of blasphemous profanity which no right thinking man would publish anywhere'. When Ford said he didn't like the treatment of Rossetti in Harris's 'The Magic Glasses', Harris wrote to Bennett: 'The man's an ass!' Yet 'The Miracle of the Stigmata' duly appeared in the April 1910 issue of the *Review*. Next Ford got into a row with Bennett over the price of 'A Matador of the Five Towns'. He told Bennett that he would pay 'a good price'. The standard rate he was offering—a guinea per page—was generous enough to become notorious. Ford's friend Thomas Seccombe wrote a puff describing rumours 'as to the volume of rare and expensive utterance by which the first number of the *English Review* is to be introduced to an astonished world'. Ford said he would pay his contributors exactly what they asked: a gesture which was sure to produce the scenario of the betrayed altruist. Writers like Cunninghame Graham and Galsworthy, who did not need to live on their writing, could afford to meet Ford's self-sacrificial generosity, and 'suggested modestly the derisive sum of a couple of guineas for a forty-pound story'. But the harder-headed and more businesslike could be relied upon to disappoint Ford by being visibly self-interested. Bennett insisted on his idea of a good price—the full forty pounds—even though Ford's standard rate valued the story at about £25. However, when Bennett used Pinker to finalize the sale of the story, and Pinker agreed a price with Ford of 'six guineas or so' less than Bennett had asked,

Bennett felt he had been 'swindled'. He was not yet the successful and prosperous cynic that Ezra Pound portrayed him as in the poem 'Mr Nixon' from 'Hugh Selwyn Mauberley': his own debt to Pinker exceeded Ford's—it was £1,003 at the end of 1909—and he needed the money. What angered him was that Ford had given Pinker to understand that 'the original overtures' had come from Bennett rather than Ford, and that Bennett had offered a serial which Ford had declined, magnanimously offering to take a short story instead. Bennett wrote curtly to Pinker:

What Hueffer says is an absolute lie. He wrote me *Twice* asking for a story, before I suggested to him at all that perhaps later he might like a book which I was contemplating [. . . .] I have all his letters at home, and they can be produced to him, to prove beyond any possible question that the overtures came from him, that he was urgent and insistent, and that he offered the inducement of a good price.[1]

True that Ford approached Bennett. True that he asked for 'a Five Towns story'. Less true that he wrote twice before Bennett mentioned the serial. His two next letters to Bennett both express a willingness to see the serial, but remind him that Ford wants a story to appear first. Less true still is Bennett's 'guarantee' that one of these letters contains the phrase 'I will pay you a good [or high] price for it'. What Ford wrote was: 'please remember that I want a short story—of any length as long as it is long, and that I will pay a pretty good price for it'. Ford thought his two guineas per thousand words *was* a 'pretty good price', whether or not he knew that Bennett usually asked three guineas (though he told Ford his usual serial price was 'at least four'). Ford's joshing, studiedly anti-commercial letters were easily misunderstood. When Bennett had evidently hesitated, or demurred, after an early letter inviting a contribution, Ford was humorously high-handed: 'My dear Bennett, What the devil more did you expect me to write you after I had already written crawling on my belly in the dust before you to tell you that anything you sent would be published?'[2] Bennett was baffled, and sent the letter to Pinker for advice, adding a note: 'I may say I have never met Hueffer.' But he wrote the story, 'A Matador of the Five Towns', which Ford was proud to publish in the April 1909 number. 'I don't know a better piece of work in the English language, or a job better executed', he said of it later. But when he asked Bennett to come and see him, Bennett replied: 'The fact is, my dear Hueffer, that I should like to come and see you and have a chat, but the feeling that I have something against you would impair the naturalness of my demeanour.' 'Oh hang!', replied Ford, in a letter bristling with intimations of betrayal and self-destruction, curiously mingling with humorous bravado:

If you negotiate thro' Pinker what can you expect? If *you* had yourself stated a price I sh^d. just have paid it. I am running a philanthropic institution for the benefit of the better letters: I am perfectly resigned to bankruptcy & the sooner you bankrupt me the sooner my troubles with the Review will be over. I stand here to be shot at: shoot!—But not thro' Pinker [. . .] If the Review were a business concern it w^d. be different. But it isn't, it is a device by which I am losing £300 a month: I have not many £300's to lose: when they are gone: Finis. And *all* you chaps: *all*, do you understand are clamouring for this dissolution. Very well . . . . I won't fight you: I pay any price *any* author asks: no more: no less.[3]

If this shows Ford protesting his own martyrdom too loudly, the letter goes on to show not only his refusal to nurse a grievance, but also his frank understanding of his tendency to provoke such misunderstandings: 'I apologise if I misrepresented you to Pinker', he said. 'It was how the facts presented themselves to my mind.' Acknowledging that he had grown 'vindictive', he urged Bennett: 'Let it go [at] that and prove yourself the first generously-minded Author that ever existed. Do come in to dinner with Violet Hunt on Monday.' 'It's very good of you to have let me know how you felt', he added as a postscript.

The argument that Bennett should not have used Pinker to negotiate the price is one that has been taken for snobbery. Mizener suggests that Ford was offended that Bennett was taking a 'commercial attitude rather than dealing with him as a gentleman' (p. 157). But if it is, it is the superiority of the embattled brotherhood of artists against the bourgeoisie rather than the snobbery of the *haut bourgeois* against the person in trade. As he was at pains to explain to Bennett, Ford had nothing against Pinker, whom he liked and to whom he felt properly grateful. 'Thank God you consent to bury the hatchet', Ford wrote to Bennett soon afterwards. 'I didn't really deserve it because my letter to Pinker was silly.' But then he continues arguing about the means of negotiating: 'But I don't agree that the Pinker argument was illogical—not from my standpoint—& [. . .] it is one's standpoint that counts. I am not commercial: I can't be commercial & I'm not going to try to be. But when a commercial gent comes to me I simply feel it sporting to beat him at his own game.' As a gesture of peace and sincerity Ford sent Bennett a cheque for the amount of which he felt he had been cheated. Bennett went to dinner with him. 'It was honestly worth ten pounds', wrote Ford later. 'I took peculiar pleasure in Bennett's company and conversation.' Bennett told Hunt, 'I got on excellently with Hueffer'. 'We have been excellent friends ever since', he wrote in the *Outlook*—correcting Ford's version, and saying that he never 'quarrelled' with him over the price of the story. When his play *What the Public Wants* was premiered in London in May 1909, Bennett told Ford he would *give* it to him to publish—whether because of the prestige of the *English Review* or because he wanted to avoid another misunderstanding. This time he dealt with Ford directly, reporting incredulously to Pinker: 'but he said if it increased the sale he would pay me a royalty!!! I like him! I think he can't help being devious.' Yet deviousness implies an ulterior motive. Ford neither wanted to cheat nor alienate Bennett, as Bennett realized. Rather, Ford's sense of an effective *story* kept getting the better of his sense of fact—as he knew, and admitted. The play was published as a special supplement to the July issue. The following year Bennett was praising his editing highly: 'In fifteen months Mr. Hueffer has managed to publish more genuine literature than was ever, I think, got into fifteen numbers of a monthly review before.'

Ford got into similar tangles with Edward Garnett and with Wells. Garnett had added to the injury of a mixed review of *Mr Apollo* what Ford took as the insult of more criticism, this time delivered in front of 'capitalists and semi-strangers' Ford was trying to interest in the *Review*. 'I think I ought to tell you that I resent—and resent intensely—yr. telling people that I can't write', he wrote to Garnett. 'After all I am a writer as serious, as conscientious, & as earnest as yourself &, if our views of the functions of literature do not tally, that is not a reason for the denial of one's right to express one's views.' In another letter about the same difference, he tried his habitual way of seeking to end quarrels by extending hospitality:

Elsie says: won't you come down here for a day or two this week whilst I am here. Do! And pray be irritated and jump on me to any extent. I can't help my Olympian manner: it is due to a consciousness of high aims defended by a defiance concerning a conviction of miserable achievements tempered by resignation to the inevitability of failure and yr. (is it?) Race, wh. won't believe in high aims, observes smallness of achievement and hates resignation of any kind, yr. Race, naturally will be irritated [. . .] However, as you see, I don't bear resentment, or a shadow of it.[5]

It is a revealing passage in its tortuous frankness. It suggests why it was that Ford became nervously and offensively defensive when he felt others were not living up to his ideals: because he was conscious of failing to live up to them himself. In this case his anger and hurt would be anger with himself; and there is certainly a self-laceration in his obsession with betrayal.

In Wells's case Ford saw betrayal writ larger. For all his enthusiasm and work for the *Review*, Wells had been extricating himself by stages: getting out of contributing first to its funding, then to its editing. He tried to withdraw the serial of *Tono-Bungay*, then relented, but later worried that the selling-off of remaindered copies of the *Review* would interfere with the sales of his novel in book form. As it became apparent that there would be remaindered copies to sell off, Wells saw the *Review*'s potential profit disappearing: the profit, his share of which was to be his payment for the serial. When Wells wrote to tell Ford that the book version was going to come out a fortnight earlier than he had thought, Ford was furious—ostensibly about the damage this would do to the *Review*'s sales, but more woundedly about Wells's treatment of him (despite Ford's habitual over-protestation of personal indifference). He wrote to Wells's wife, Jane, partly because she acted as her husband's agent, but also to convey to Wells the message that he would convey no messages to Wells himself:

In the course of the transaction Wells has broken his word innumerable times whereas as you know I am giving him more than he originally stipulated for, for whereas he only stipulated for a fifth share of the profits of the Review I have since stated to you personally that it was my intention to give him a share of the Goodwill proportionate to the length of his contribution. The reason why I have not put this into writing or made it the basis of a form of agreement with Wells is simply this: if the consideration that Wells received for Tono-Bungay was a share of the Goodwill, Wells would become responsible for the liabilities of the Review along with myself. As the liabilities of the firm are enormous—quite big enough to ruin both myself & Wells I have simply told you that it is my private intention to give Wells a share of the Goodwill, thus imposing no legal liability upon him at all. This is an arrangement for Wells of an entirely 'Heads, I win. Tails, you lose,' as he has every chance of becoming a part owner of valuable property with no risks of any kind, his only contribution being a piece of work which he himself declared to be unmarketable & his immediate & certain profit a much wider publicity than he has ever had in his life before. My own profits in the matter have been and will be nothing. I have most studiously avoided in any way advertising myself in connection with the Review.[6]

There is much truth in this, though Wells had had plenty of publicity for his earlier scientific romances, and *Tono-Bungay* was not unmarketable. Ford's own name did not appear in the *Review* as editor or contributor before August 1909, when the serialization of *A Call* began. There was, at this early stage, still a chance that the *Review* might become a valuable property, though even Ford is aware that its liabilities are overwhelming. If Wells cannot lose from the arrangement, Ford cannot win. It is at moments like this, even while agitated and feeling maltreated, that he seems able to recognize how he has brought his destiny down upon himself. It is an example of what Graham Greene called Ford's 'Quixotism'—his theatrical gestures of self-destruction for the sake of unworkable ideals.[7] The letter to 'Jane' Wells continues with a characteristically unconvincing protestation of personal indifference:

Wells, as you must know, has behaved again & again most treacherously to me. I have always ignored the treacheries on account of his art which I admire sincerely & which I have continuously and always praised & tried to help forward. It is a great pity that Wells should give way to these panics and commit actions so questionable under their sway, but I am quite aware that these are the inevitable consequences of having anything to do with men of letters & regard them as being all in the day's journey. I would not write to Wells in any circumstances at all. His opinion of myself is of no consequence whatever, to me. Yours is however, & I think that my view of the matter ought to be put into black & white.

That desire for self-justification, putting his views of complexly grey areas into the black and white of writing, is a motive for Ford's fiction too; though in expressing himself he transforms 'the matter' into forms which do much more than justify himself.

There might have been a more personal cause for Ford's hysterical tone with Wells. Even as he recognized the skill of *Tono-Bungay*, he may have suspected that the character of Edward Ponderevo was based on him. Edward is the only uncle of the gifted young Wellsean narrator George. Edward's commercial project, the way he draws George in, his grandiose schemes, his loss of touch with moral and factual reality, are all consonant with how Wells was beginning to view Ford. But it would have been Edward's adulterous affair with a lady journalist that would have been most likely to make Ford feel he had been betrayed.[8]

Wells was too good a friend to bear a grudge over Ford's volatility, and he didn't take seriously Ford's threat that the *Review* would have to take legal action against him for damages—combined with the absurd altruist martyr's promise that if damages were awarded Ford would pay them himself. But the dispute simmered for several months, often conducted in the spirit of the raillery that was the medium of their friendship. When Wells told him he 'never based any extravagant hopes on your enterprise', he said he was prepared to 'waive any golden anticipation' he might have formed about what his share would be if the *Review* were sold. When such questions were settled, wrote Wells 'you will be relieved from such quaint, but I should think, irksome, necessities as you impose upon yourself at present, of pretending not to be yourself when speaking through the telephone to me, and of corresponding in strange and oblique manners'. Ford replied—obliquely, in a letter obviously dictated to and signed by Olive Thomas— that he 'was not aware of having spoken to [Wells] over the telephone in any voice, either feigned or unfeigned'. When he apologized to Wells for his other obliquity—writing business letters to Wells's wife, he said: 'I never quarrelled with any of my friends however much they defamed me & I never will'—which, though it ignores the way provoking friends to defame one is a form of quarrelling, is true enough about his self-abasing superiority in forgiving them anything for the sake of their art. 'As one's motives are known only to oneself, so one cannot quarrel with one's friends for misinterpreting them.' Betrayal and the inscrutability of motive were always his best subjects. Here they begin to take the form that dominate the rest of his fiction: the idea that (as the epigraph to *The New Humpty-Dumpty* has it) 'the heart of another is a dark forest'—even the hearts of one's partners and close friends.[9]

When Ethel Dilke asked Hunt if she could ask Ford to dinner with her, Violet said 'Yes Id like it', to which Lady Dilke replied 'lots of people wouldnt'. He also rowed with Stephen Reynolds—whom he had put up in the flat above his own, and given work as editorial assistant on the *Review* for a month—over the payment for *Holy Mountain* (though Goldring recalled them squabbling 'affectionately, by the hour together' and that they were really fond of each other). He even rowed with his solicitor, Robert Garnett, who had, Ford felt, betrayed his confidence by telling Pinker he had no private means. Mizener says that 'this alludes to Ford's assertions to Pinker that he does not wish to disturb his investments', which makes it sound like a lie that he had any investments to disturb. Ford was certainly not living on invested capital, but he and Elsie did own property other than Hurst Cottage and the Bungalow. As Mizener himself states: 'Ford's investments consisted of two properties [actually five houses] in London that had been purchased in 1896 for £779.17.6, the Hurst Cottage, which had been purchased in 1901 for £150, and £500 invested at 5 percent. The income from these assets was £75.17.0 a year' though most of this interest was offset by the interest the Hueffers owed on loans totalling £425 from Ford's mother, from Martha Garnett (Robert's wife), from Pinker, and from a Miss Wanostrocht—a cousin of the Garnetts. Ford had also lent Conrad £200, which he was loath to press Conrad to repay: he may have had this too in mind as an investment—in literature—he did not want to disturb.[10]

Ford went to see F. Norreys Connell's dramatization of *The Fifth Queen Crowned* at the Kingsway Theatre on 19 March. The single matinee performance was put on by Ada Potter, who (said Hunt) adored Ford. She played Katharine. Ford thought there were too many long scene-changes, and the *Athenaeum* agreed, complaining that the 'scrappy episodes' showed the authors 'lack the sense of the theatre'. Ford told Elsie it was 'very amusing', and that the actor Hearn was '*wonderful*' as Henry VIII. But his later reminiscences have him hiding under the bar of 'the pit refreshment saloon' out of shyness. He may well have found the production embarrassing enough to wish to avoid seeing acquaintances after it.[11]

His private life was putting him under increasing strain. There was a painful row with Elsie. She had taken up her writing again—her only published novel, *Margaret Hever*, was accepted by Duckworth and came out in 1909. Her feeling of neglect was compounded by the suspicion that Ford did not value her work. 'The more I think about matters,' he wrote to her afterwards, 'the more I see that you ought to divorce me. Don't think that there is any other woman in the case: there isn't. And do not think that it is due to jealousy: it is not. But the fact of the matter is that I am unbearable to you & my effect on you reacts upon me [. . .] such a scene as that about your work [. . .] is more than I can stand.' If Elsie's dating of this letter as 'Oct or Nov./ 08' is correct, then this is not as disingenuous as it might sound: Violet Hunt may have been on the scene, but she was not yet 'in the case'. Ford met her several times in the last three months of 1908, usually in the company of others. Violet was invited to Ford's Christmas party at Holland Park Avenue, where she witnessed Ford and Elsie quarrelling. Ford's 1913 deposition says that when Elsie came up to town for the Christmas season, instead of staying at Holland Park Avenue she took rooms of her own in Bloomsbury, where she stayed with Edmée Van der Noot. Also that she only visited Ford twice: once for tea, and once for a party he gave for her. 'She insisted that the invitations should be printed "Mr. Hueffer 'At Home', to Meet Mrs. Hueffer," and insisted too, on not receiving the guests, informing them that that was not her residence or her party. She did this, in order plainly to indicate that she lived apart from me, and to make it manifest to as many people as possible.'[12] But it was not until the summer of 1909 that Ford proposed to marry Hunt if he could get a divorce. She may have been at the back of his mind that December, and he may have wanted to ensure that she was not at the back of Elsie's, but he was probably sincere in saying at that stage that he did not want to divorce Elsie in order to marry someone else.

At the end of her visit to London, said Ford, Elsie asked him not to visit her for two months, because his 'society damaged her health', and 'she desired to feel free'. He also said she wrote him a letter containing the phrases: 'I shall never feel free until the divorce is completed . . . I know that I am not fit to be your wife, and perhaps not the wife of any man.' If she ever wrote such a letter it hasn't survived. Yet there was a separation in the New Year. Elsie annotated a letter from Ford which she dated about 20 March 1909, saying that it had been written 'after 2 months separation'. And a passage from his 1912 novel *The New Humpty-Dumpty* suggests that the separation was Elsie's idea: the Fordian Macdonald dares his wife to deny that she suggested they should separate. Since they had effectively been living separately for most of the previous four years, and since separation alone (without adultery or desertion) was not at that time considered legal grounds for divorce, the impression Ford gives of Elsie asking for a separation out of anger and frustration seems quite probable.[13]

Ford's 1913 deposition gives a lurid account of what happened when he resumed his visits to Hurst Cottage:

a violent quarrel arose as to whether the lady should publish a book that she had written, under her maiden name, or her married name, I suggesting that she should [. . .] use the name of Hueffer, because it already carried some weight in the literary world. This she regarded as an insult, and in the course of the discussion she struck me with a log of wood, and threatened my life with the gun that she habitually carried. After this scene she insisted that we should part for good and all, and, as I went in genuine fear of my life, I consented.[14]

Some discussion! If Ford's rendering of it seems over-written, too calculated to make a case for divorce after the humiliating scandal of the *Throne* case of 1913, one must remember that domestic violence is all too common. Ford's letters trying to reassure Elsie there was no other woman show she was jealous. There was most probably a gun at Hurst Cottage, as there had been at the Pent (though that was a rifle, which Elsie could scarcely have 'habitually carried'), and perhaps Elsie did threaten Ford with it. He was certainly to be in fear of his life by the summer, though by his own hand rather than Elsie's. It is the dialogues between Count and Countess Macdonald in *The New Humpty-Dumpty* that probably reflect the kinds of rows the Hueffers were having.

'What does it all mean?' she asked. 'I don't understand it! When I first knew you I could influence you [. . .] It's terrible, all this! It's killing me.'
    Touched by a pathetic—a nearly tragic note in her voice, Macdonald hesitated for a moment.
    'I don't know,' he said. 'It's a mystery. Or it isn't. But it's no good talking about it.'
    'You *ought* to think as I do,' she said. 'You did so once. Now you don't. Your whole mind is taken up with vanities . . . with frivolities.'

'You have Conservative ideas, and you live with the smart set now,' the Countess said coldly [. . .] And you want to get rid of me now in order to plunge into a whirl of dissipation. Do you suppose I don't know enough of the world to know what your having a room at your office means?' [. . .]
    'Of course, if it was only a trap,' he said, 'if you did not really want us to separate, there's an end of the matter [. . .]'

'You think,' his wife's voice droned on, 'that you have deceived me about this woman. Do you suppose that I have not any eyes in my head? Do you suppose that if it had not been for her you would ever have had the courage to tell me that you wanted to

separate? Do you suppose that I do not know the shilly-shallying creature that you
are?"[15]

He was in the worst possible state of mind to receive the news from Elsie,
probably in the middle of March 1909, that Marwood had been taking advantage
of his absence in London to make improper advances to her. Mizener said that
she 'asserted that he kept reminding her he had saved her life by paying for her
operation the year before and that she had incriminating letters from him'.[16] The
letters have not survived, and one can only speculate about Marwood's words and
actions. Something of the sort certainly happened. The letters existed. Elsie
showed them to Robert Garnett, who wrote to Ford:

I have read those letters: they tell me nothing I had not divined. E[lsie] forgot that
not only M[arwood] was flesh and blood but a highly impressionable & *unhappy*
person upon whom her confidences were certain to make the greatest mark. You & E
both make the same mistake: in your troubles you become self-concentrated and
oblivious of how you affect others. Your letters to me shewed this.[17]

Garnett's diagnosis of Ford's self-concentration under duress is accurate—Ford's
claim that Garnett had betrayed his confidence in telling Pinker about his finances
was still fresh in his mind. Mizener's comment that 'Elsie made as much of this
affair as she could, in the hope that it would persuade Ford to return to her',
suggests that her confiding in Marwood might have been more deliberate than
Garnett tactfully implies. Because she found Ford difficult to live with, and
because her grievances and her suffering are undeniable, she has been presented
as the innocent party. But complete innocence is a fiction in most such cases.
David Garnett (the son of Edward and Constance), Ford's friend but never his
partisan, said that she later became 'an embittered shrew'. Behind the sexist label
one glimpses an aggressiveness, possibly even a self-destructiveness, in her
suffering, which is borne out by what can be gathered of her letters to Ford. Ford
was increasingly presenting himself as the victimized altruist, his ideals betrayed
by others. Elsie may have wanted to remind him that she too felt victimized, by
being left, and by now being sacrificed to the *Review*. She may even have felt
jealous of his partnership with Marwood. Marwood was a sympathetic presence
there when Elsie needed sympathy, when she felt she was being valued neither
sexually nor intellectually. Did his 'flesh and blood' manifest itself in a demonstration of passion? Or is Dowell's comment on Ashburnham's advances towards
the servant-girl on a train the true picture: 'I think that, when he had kissed her,
he had desired rather to comfort her.' This is less than convincing in *The Good
Soldier*, though it is not impossible. Whatever actually happened, the effects on
Ford were devastating; and it is precisely his uncertainty—about sexuality, about
whose story to believe, about whether blissful ignorance is preferable to bitter
knowledge—that resounds through his novels which deal with tangles of sexual
betrayal: *The Fifth Queen*, *A Call*, *The New Humpty-Dumpty*, and above all *The
Good Soldier* and *Parade's End*. It is of course the relationship between Ashburnham and Dowell's wife, Florence, that draws most heavily upon this incident

between Marwood and Ford's wife. But what Ford's unprecedentedly unstable tone expresses in that book is his feeling that he is at once complicit and betrayed. For, like Dowell, he has—consciously or unconsciously—brought together his wife and his best friend, and created the circumstances for their betrayal of him. 'You would have said that he was just exactly the sort of chap that you could have trusted your wife with. And I trusted mine—and it was madness.' Since he was trying to divorce Elsie he might seem unlikely to have felt jealousy; though unconscious feelings do not behave logically (and anyway he might have been as jealous of Marwood as of Elsie). Mizener says that Ford 'eventually came to believe Elsie's story about Marwood'. But the example he gives in a footnote implies the opposite: 'in the analogous episode in *The New Humpty-Dumpty*, Pett spitefully spreads the lie that Kintyre is trying to make Countess Macdonald his mistress. At first Macdonald believes the story, but finally, like Ford, he is convinced of its falseness.' Ford's subsequent fiction suggests that he could *not* so convince himself: *The Good Soldier* and *Parade's End* both contain Marwood-like figures who do commit adultery. But the 1913 deposition unequivocally blames Elsie, in mentioning 'a quarrel which Mrs. Elsie Hueffer caused to arise between myself and Mr. Marwood'.[18]

Ford wrote a short story in 1909, 'A Silence', which, together with a one-act dramatization of the same situation, 'The Escape', expresses his bitter feelings about his predicament.[19] Henry Penred is a hypochondriacal squire of about 40, married but no longer speaking to a fiery South American. He had fallen in love with Brenda, the wife of his best friend George. But Brenda has died a month before—because she couldn't live without him, Penred thinks. Mrs Penred has got hold of Penred's love-letters to Brenda, and comes to taunt him about them; but he has just written his suicide note to George, asking for forgiveness, and poured himself a stiff prussic acid, which he drinks in sardonic silence, escaping his wife's fury. In the story she says she regrets not shooting him on their wedding night, and later springs at his throat; in the dramatization she threatens him with his revolver. But his suicide is triumphantly unanswerable. It's a feebly self-indulgent story, and an unperformable play; but both are significant for the way they express what Ford's own hatred of discussing his personal difficulties made it impossible for him to express any other way, and for how they anticipate the structures of feeling in his best fiction. As he was to do in *The Good Soldier*, Ford combines himself and Marwood into Penred, while spreading himself between the two main male characters. Like Tietjens in *Parade's End*, Ford in 1909 felt at once guilty of and the victim of sexual betrayal. Penred's suicide expresses Ford's sense of not wanting to live without Violet Hunt, and of death offering the only feasible escape from Elsie's rage. But it also expresses what he probably felt Marwood should have done under the circumstances—commit suicide and ask Ford's forgiveness. (According to this reading, Brenda would be the Elsie character, so the story kills her off too.)

What Ford dreaded was what happened. Marwood's behaviour with Elsie made it difficult for Ford to continue as his partner. The allegation struck at Ford's public as well as his private life. He wrote to Elsie, 'I think I have, without any offensiveness, let M. understand that I don't want to see him'. But without his backing Ford could not maintain control of the *Review*. He approached the German Hüffers for assistance. 'Fritz & Antonius are sending me over £500', he told Elsie. But at the rate he estimated the magazine was losing money that would not be enough for two issues. Garnett's letter (about the Marwood letters) includes the following cryptic antitheses: 'To decline to see M[arwood] would be a very great mistake for you to commit [. . .] I perfectly well appreciate the value of V[iolet] to you but M[arwood] is your partner. V means absolutely well by you but so does M.' What is strange is how Garnett writes as if the main obstacle to Ford's relation with Marwood were not Elsie's allegations, but Violet's involvement. The radical Tory Marwood would have been appalled at Hunt's plan to get Mond to take over the *Review*. Garnett's comment about the value of Violet to Ford might simply be a reference to her value as a possible finder of capital to back the magazine. But it sounds more as if Garnett knows, or suspects, Violet's sentimental value to Ford. Elsie had seen how much damage her revelations were doing, and both she and Garnett were trying to persuade Ford to see Marwood and effect a reconciliation. But Ford could not bear to meet him. Early in May he went to Garnett's office, only to be told that Marwood was also there in another room:

Robert tried very hard to get me to see him but I refused. He said however that Marwood spoke of me with the greatest 'affection & regret.' I pointed out to Robert that to accept his and Marwood's version of the matter must mean estrangement from you, but he did not seem to see it.

Such is mankind: my head is in a whirl about it. Certainly, I think we must never discuss these things again.[20]

One way he tried not to discuss them and to preserve his composure was by discussing Elsie's writing instead. She had sent him some essays sketching her invalid and reclusive life. 'I always did admire y^r style', he told her; 'now I like it better than ever.' But the terms in which he praised it suggest his unease with her style of talking to him: 'The essay form certainly seems to suit you: it is one of course that calls for *less* compromise than any other & leaves you free to say what you "want" to say.' Elsie wanted to publicize how the editor had abandoned her; the essay on 'The Art of Manners' is effectively an attack on the Kensington 'smart set', satirizing the chilly 'gush or boredom' of the manner displayed by one lady visitor (a friend of Violet's, sizing Elsie up perhaps?) The English have made a fetish of 'good form', she argues, at the expense of true good manners. Ford published four of her essays in the *Review*. He must have noticed their barbs. But by rising above personal antipathy to criticism of her style, he could use the *Review* to let her attack him in public.[21]

By insisting that the moral issue with Marwood was black and white, Ford made it blacker than it needed to be. Garnett had shown how peace could be made. After all, Ford himself had been prepared to settle rows with Elsie by coming to an understanding about there having been a misunderstanding. Why could he not accept that Elsie had simply misunderstood Marwood's motives, as Garnett was indicating; that she had been miserable, Marwood had tried to comfort her, had perhaps told her how fond of her he had always been, and how he would do anything he could to help now, as he had over the operation? One reason is that Ford wanted estrangement from Elsie, though he found it hard to face the fact that he wanted it; and in telling her that she is forcing him into a position of estrangement he is saying as much. The whirling head is to do with this repression, and the associated guilt over abandoning her; and it heralded a recurrence of agoraphobia, which struck for three days at the end of May. Goldring wrote that at the time divorce was 'hardly thinkable' 'in the most respectable families, particularly Catholic families'—it was 'something you read about in the papers'; Ford would not have wanted to alienate his wealthy German relatives.[22] But this does not account for the force, the excess, of his reaction. Betrayal always evinced that surge of anguish in him; and this spectacular tangle, in which everyone might have been betrayed by almost everyone else, was fraught with the possibilities of passion and paranoia. Ford's hyper-reaction to Marwood's 'advances' might be a projection of his guilt at betraying Elsie, a way of saying 'I am not the betrayer, but the betrayed'. But to say that is of course not to explain why he needs to betray and be betrayed.

One of his next actions illustrates his tendency to provoke rejection. He picked up a young German woman, Gertrud (or Hedwig) Schablowsky, in the lounge of the Shepherd's Bush Empire, and took her back to live at 84 Holland Park Avenue. According to Hunt, Ford 'always said that she was the thirteenth to whom he had made this proposition'. He then told Elsie about her:

I feel very much the not having the children with me. In a sort of way Miss Schablowski [*sic*] takes their place: she is quite as much a child as Baby & quite as ignorant & very much as innocent in mind (tho' that, I daresay, you will not believe) but you must believe that my relations with her are quite as innocent as with any child of my own. I take her, when I have a minute to spare to places like the Tate Gallery & Westminster Abbey & the Zoo & she is a great deal less 'fast' than, let us say, Hester Radford. I write about this—tho' I know, it must be painful to you & tho' I know you will think I am lying—because you want me to be perfectly open with you. Well: I am perfectly open. If you consider what I am, you will see that a poor little person—like this Hedwig, is just the sort of thing that I sh^{d.} pick up & try to be kind to. And, just because I sh^{d.} want to be kind to her I sh^{d.} let her alone in the other capacity. Indeed, she w^{d.} not accept any other position than that of a sort of adopted child because—tho' this too you may not believe—she w^{d.} scruple to come between a man & wife.

Do not be violently angry about this—don't regard me as contemptible. I know I am not that, & you know it too. It is not that I prefer her to you, or that she in any way takes y^{r.} place, for she is certainly not beautiful or alluring or capable of arousing passion as you are: & she is certainly not mentally active. But she satisfies the necessity I have to treat someone as a baby, to laugh at & to mock gently & to 'boss' [. . .] You know quite well that I do care for you & care for you very deeply & that, if it were at all possible, I w^d. live the sort of life you wish me to lead—the sort of life you lead yourself [. . .] But perhaps you will not wish me to come down at all after these 'revelations'.

I hope you will not take that attitude as, in sober truth, I have not been unfaithful to you in deed or mind & it w^d. grieve me very much—& I have griefs enough at present—to have you once more think me a liar. But perhaps that is inevitable. I hope not as I think that, lately, we have been working towards a greater comprehension of one another, which has been a real relief to me.[23]

Gertrud's presence has been seen as Ford's device to protect Violet's name, while giving Elsie the evidence of adultery which the divorce law of the time required before a divorce could be granted. It was common practice to hire an 'official' co-respondent and to fabricate the necessary evidence. As Goldring says: 'Had he consulted a lawyer experienced in Divorce Court procedure he would doubtless have been put in touch with a respectable clergyman's widow who, for a suitable fee, would undertake to share a room with him in an hotel and to spend the night playing double-dummy bridge, repairing to bed only a few moments before the arrival of the chamber-maid.'[24]

This was certainly part of Ford's motive, as he later presented it:

At about this time, in order to give Mrs. Elsie Hueffer grounds for a charge of adultery I took into my house a person called Miss von Schablowsky, the daughter of a Pole of some position whom I had met at Bonn, where my uncle was Chancellor of the University. Finding this girl upon the streets—I had been very much schocked [sic.]—she was about 17—and I had already made her a small allowance on condition that she would lead a respectable life, and I had tried to find her employment. Mrs. Elsie Hueffer was aware of these circumstances. At this time I still entertained doubts as to the genuineness of Mrs. Elsie Hueffer's desire for a divorce, but I had already, in order to spare her feelings, if that were the case, very carefully informed her that my relations with Miss von Schablowsky were absolutely innocent. I had, that is to say, written her a most explicit letter upon the subject, to which she returned no reply.

I accordingly took Miss von Schablowsky into my flat, the motive for this being partly charity [. . .] I treated Miss von Schablowsky exactly as if she were my daughter, she occupying her own rooms and so on, besides being as it were chaperoned by an elderly German woman whom I employed as housekeeper.

But his letter to Elsie bristles with the possibilities of other motives. It does not read like a letter written simply to furnish Elsie with the grounds of a divorce: it insists too much on the propriety and parental nature of the arrangement, and on his fidelity, for that. Ford expects Elsie to be jealous, but he is explicit about how her jealousy will malign him. It seems more to do with his need to upset Elsie (as he knows his letter will) to the point at which she will turn on him, than with legal manœuvrings. Like everyone else, he was most hurtful when most hurt—and vice versa. What is more, far from being part of a plan hatched with Violet, Gertrud's presence made Violet feel ill at ease. All this was done under the guise of altruism. Ford and Hunt both say he wanted her to come and be 'respectable'. If she hadn't been living by prostitution, a poem Ford wrote about her makes it sound as if she had, saying to her: 'You sell caresses.' (Edward Ashburnham, in *The Good Soldier*, 'was always trying to put prostitutes into respectable places'.) Under the guise of altruism—undeserved thoughtfulness about Elsie's feelings; charity to a fellow-German—he could provide grounds for divorce while protesting his innocence.[25]

Ford appears to have been testing Hunt's love too, by seeing how she would react to such an equivocal situation. It is a pattern which he repeated for most of his life. As he would patronize his protégés to the extent that most of them felt smothered, and later rejected him, so he would provoke jealousy in his lovers, with the apparent (and apparently unconscious) aim of causing them to reject him. He would invariably provoke his partners, whether they were partners in business (Pinker, publishers, Marwood) or in passion. David Soskice recognized an aspect of this when he wrote to Ford after the struggles to save the *Review*: 'it has been clear for some weeks that by sending me offensive letters you were simply seeking a pretext to resign.' In his private life it took the form of involving himself with two (or more) women at once. Provoking the rage of the partners to whom he was committed was a way of testing their feeling for him. Producing the very response he dreaded may have been a way of mastering the fear of that rage; a way of proving that he could survive its destructiveness. Or it may have been a way of projecting his own emotional voraciousness on to others; trying to feel that they were the ones to stop loving, not him. He had lived out the scenario of dual passions at least since the affair with Mary Martindale. It had been latent in much of Ford's fiction (*The Shifting of the Fire*, *The Benefactor*, *An English Girl*) and explicit in *The Fifth Queen*. Now, as he began to re-create it calamitously in his life, it was becoming his central fictional subject—perhaps in part due to the influence of Hunt's novels of adultery. First in *The 'Half Moon'*, published in March 1909, in which Edward Colman is killed when he reaches the shores of America by the witchcraft of Anne Jeal, the woman he has spurned in favour of Magdalena Koop—rather as Ford felt Elsie was driving him to suicide just as he was creating for himself a new world with Hunt and the *English Review*. And secondly in the novel that was serialized in the *Review* from August to November 1909, *A Call*, in which Robert Grimshaw is caught between his involvement with Katya Lascarides and his passion for Pauline Leicester. The book version was subtitled: 'The Tale of Two Passions', which could be read dually: as about Grimshaw's two passions, or about the two passions (in the Fordian and Christian sense of 'agonies') suffered by Grimshaw and his friend Dudley Leicester, to whom he married off Pauline. For Dudley doubles the scenario of two passions, being himself caught between his loyalty to Pauline and his apparent seduction by Etta Hudson. Polygamous passions are of course the central subjects of *The Good Soldier* and *Parade's End* too.[26]

In his fiction, as in his private life, the idea of victimization by women looms large. It is a feeling which curiously—in a characteristically dual manner—reinforces his commitment to the suffragette cause. In two of his public statements supporting votes for women he says, 'I have been persistently nagged, swindled, worried out of my life, and distracted during the course of my existence by some five or six women'. The argument is as subtle as it is perverse and histrionic: he later explains that he is putting 'the point of view of the true Briton', which he is not, being 'a sort of foreigner'; he is arguing against the stereotype of women as inferior beings, saying that it is only by granting full civic responsibility that you can expect women to be morally equal: 'personally, I want to get hold of a woman that I can trust better than any man. I want to change it. I want to be rid of this monstrous regiment of women [. . .] I am sick of women as they are. I want them changed; that is why I want women to have the vote.'[27]

It was necessary to Ford not only to see himself as, but also to some measure to make himself the victim of women. Such a need almost certainly originates in feelings about his mother, though speculations here are by nature vague and unproveable. One can only point to the three places in his reminiscences dealing substantially with his mother. In two cases Oliver is involved as well. One is the scene in which she gets Ford to hand his pet rabbit over to his brother. There is also the episode in which she receives a War Office telegram saying that Oliver was in hospital, wounded for the second time, but alive and safe: 'I have never seen greater contentment', writes Ford. Thoughts of Oliver's mortality lead Ford on to pondering the way his brother seemed a kind of *doppelgänger*. He adds: 'The same sort of, I suppose telepathic, *rapport* existed between my mother and myself, but not nearly in so marked a degree.' When Cathy Hueffer gets the telegram she is reading *Wuthering Heights*. The other significant sketch of her shows her reading *Lorna Doone* during an air raid.[28] It is entirely characteristic of Ford's literary autobiography that these recollections of his family feelings should be so bound up with feelings about fiction. This is not just because the Hueffers were such a literary family. It is because Ford is obliquely pondering the sources of his creativity. There is a suggestion here that it is the enviable rapport between mother and son—though between Cathy and Oliver, whose safety can produce in her a greater feeling of contentment than anything he has seen produced for himself—which Ford tries to recapture in the rapport between writer and reader. This is not to say, exactly, that Ford only wrote to gain the rapt attention that he lacked from his mother—as it were to kill off his brother. But it is to say that he recognized a structural similarity between the quasi-telepathy of literary sympathy and the intimacies of family life. It is, moreover, possible that in his later relationships with more than one woman at a time Ford was re-creating the circumstances of infantile 'betrayal' (the rabbit episode is doubly primal in this respect: the mother betrays Ford with the father and with the brother), confirming his doubts about not being loved, or loveable.

Violet Hunt was getting more involved 'in the case' during the spring of 1909, and though they were not yet lovers Ford had almost certainly made more explicit advances towards her than had Marwood to Elsie. Elsie was soon hearing gossip, and her attempt to make peace between Ford and Marwood became tangled with her anxiety about the nascent affair:

Dearest E:

I must confess that y^r. letter—as far as it affects Marwood—rather astonishes me. If it be true that he has attacked y^r. virtue and my honour (which is what it amounts to) I cannot for the sake of business have any friendly relations with him. Besides it's obvious that if I see him he will try to persuade me that your accusations are untrue—so that to have to do with him must mean breaking with you.

With regard to your sending his letters to Robert [Garnett]: I think [. . .] you ought to do it, for he is certainly inclined at present to consider that yr views are hallucinations. No doubt that is part of his professional line & desire to make everything smooth for all parties [. . .] It is a horrible & very ticklish matter for me. On the one hand I do not like you to be misjudged: on the other certain very ticklish negotiations are just being consummated, involving Marwood, Soskice, Robert and myself. R. is very anxious that I sh^d. attend a meeting on Monday & make it up with M.—This I do not intend to do [. . .] such a nightmare as all this is!

You are well out of it in y^r. solitudes. Here every prospect pleases (for the young green everywhere is lively) but I really believe that only man is vile.

However: I plug along. 'I think I ought to tell you' (as the friend of y$^{rs.}$ puts it) that Violet Hunt is coming to dinner. She's really doing her best to get the Monds to take up the Review. If they wd, there wd be an end of all these worries.

And, so far I cannot observe in the lady any signs of desiring more of a quid pro quo than the material desire to keep going a magazine with which she hopes to 'appear.'

Well goodbye old thing—Preserve Y^r. tranquillity

Y^r. Ford M H[29]

There are signs here that Ford was having trouble preserving his tranquillity too.

When he finally did consent to a meeting with Marwood he wrote to her to tell her that he had told her so: 'I have seen Marwood who absolutely swears that he had no disloyal intentions. It is all a weary mystery to me—& I am worn out with striving to keep the Review going.'[30] He was in an *impasse* with Marwood, feeling that, morally or emotionally, he could not deal with him, but that financially he could not do without him. He felt betrayed by either Marwood or Elsie. If her story was true, Marwood had devastated their friendship and jeopardized the *Review*; if untrue, Elsie had none the less damaged relations with Marwood, as well as destroyed Ford's trust in her. Ford could not challenge Elsie's veracity when—if the story were true—she most needed his trust. But he could not denounce Marwood if he was not convinced about Elsie's story. Instead, he emphasized self-destructively how destructive the episode had been, trying to master his own double-bind by putting Elsie in it with him, telling her she had either destroyed the marriage or the *Review*. 'No doubt when the world grows less complex we shall win through to peace', he wrote to her. The complex uncertainty of the affair was not something new to him; but the ever-increasing tangles of his relationship with Violet Hunt extended his sense of the distressing complexity of life. It is one of the major themes not only of his best fiction, but of his criticism and reminiscences.[31]

As Marwood had become a close friend of Conrad's, it was inevitable that Ford's other closest intimate would be entangled in the affair—especially since the Conrads had returned to Aldington in February. Elsie and Marwood independently both confided in Conrad, who was disturbed and irritated, and wrote Ford a long letter combining praise for the May issue of the *English Review* with prickly warnings about tactlessness and querulousness:

Last Monday on her way from the station your wife called here. She informed me that all your differences were happily settled and warned me against the plots and intrigues (vulgo, lies) of certain people. I confess I was literally shocked by the nature of her communication the more so that she implied that these dark untruth[s] had, in your opinion, already affected my attitude towards you. Against that I oppose an unqualified denial: and as this denial expresses the exact truth I warn you that I demand to be believed without any reservations or doubts whatever [. . .] I told Elsie with every consideration which is due to her in my house that I could not believe these people were as black as they appeared to her [. . .] Later on she proposed that you should come down and stay *with us* for a week. You know that no one is made more welcome under our roof. Let ten years of perfect confidence and intimacy be witnesses to it. But I said at once, No—that cannot be. If you are reconciled so completely, Ford's place, when he is in Aldington, is in the cottage.

What is the end of such a proposal, what object, what purpose can be served by recreating an equivocal situation? By such juggling with the realities of life, an atmosphere of plots and accusations and suspicions is created. I can't breathe in situations that are not clear. I abhor them. They are neither in my nature nor in my tradition, nor in my experience. I am not fine enough for them. We are a pair of silly innocents.

I need not tell you that we parted with Elsie on perfectly friendly terms and there is no earthly reason why they should not continue. That I am upset is beside the mark. I haven't eaten or slept properly nor yet written a line ever since. This evening the people in question have called. The man, when we were alone, said he felt bound to inform me that he had just dispatched a letter to you, breaking off your intimate relations. He told me he was very unhappy and in truth he looked ill. As he is of good birth and upbringing and has always seemed to me a gallant *homme* I can't give him up for a ruffian as long as he remains in the neighbourhood, which I imagine won't be long. He was your friend, not mine, and I have never sought his acquaintance. His devotion to you was notorious—a matter of public knowledge[.] What advantage he sought, what ends he had in view when he trotted about after you like a faithful dog, God only knows? You too, perhaps. In this case, if it is any satisfaction to you, you have done some crushing. I won't believe it[']s altogether without cause, but it strikes me, my dear Ford that of late you have been visiting faults of tact, or even grave failures of discretion in men who *were* your admiring friends, with an Olympian severity. A man who not often takes liberties, ventures to ask you now whether it is worth while. Unless words are wind, facts are mist, the confidence you've given me a mere caprice of fancy, and unless an absolute loyalty of thought and act on my part contra mundum gives no privilege I have the right to warn you that you will find yourself at forty with only the wrecks of friendships at your feet. You have always sought to do good to people—that I believe—but don't fail in the other kind of generosity. I've had four most unhappy days, but I am afraid you will dismiss it all with a wave of the hand. And indeed I don't know why I should be so wretched except from sheer affection.

Yours always

J. Conrad.[32]

For all Conrad's protestations of friendliness, the letter marks a sea-change in his attitude to Ford. His apprentice had become his impresario, and Conrad resented being patronized by his protégé. What he calls Ford's 'Olympian' dealings he was soon describing less flatteringly to others. 'He's a megalomaniac who imagines that he is managing the Universe and that everybody treats him with the blackest ingratitude', wrote Conrad to Pinker:

A fierce and exasperating vanity is hidden under his calm manner which misleads people. Writing to you *in confidence* I do not hesitate to say that there are cases, not quite as bad, under medical treatment. This is not a joke. I have suffered too much mental worry and moral discomfort to joke upon the matter [. . .] he has quarrelled with every decent friend he had; has nearly made mischief between me and some of my best friends, and is, from all accounts, having a most miserable time himself—because he has his lucid intervals. Generally he is behaving like a spoilt kid—and not a nice kid either.[33]

It is almost as if, while denouncing Ford's actions, Conrad recognizes their necessity to his art. 'The fact is that H. loves to manage people', he warned Norman Douglas. 'No doubt he helps too but his assistance has an obverse side.' But it was not just that Conrad had often failed to write without that assistance. Like Ford, he articulates personal conduct in aesthetic terms. The creation of equivocal situations, juggling with the realities of life, creating atmospheres of plots and accusations and suspicions, could, after all, stand as a fine definition of the Fordian or Conradian novel of intrigue and uncertainty. As Karl and Davies say, Ford's and Elsie's intrigue had 'brought to Aldington a whiff of "Razumov" '. And perhaps vice versa the intrigue and betrayal contributing to the atmosphere of *Under Western Eyes*.[34]

Conrad was anxious enough for his own sanity, his own grasp on reality, to be disturbed by Ford's disturbance at this time. What he deplored in Ford were precisely the tendencies he feared in himself. 'Megalomania' was a word he used twice in the second half of 1908 in connection with autobiography; the second time about the reminiscences he was writing for Ford, himself a compulsive reminiscer, who influenced both Conrad's volumes of memories: 'A megalomaniac's stuff but easy to spin out comparatively speaking.' He had hated the quest to the heart of the past, conducted dually in the reminiscences and the novel; and he may have blamed Ford for his anxiety. He held off his breakdown until he had written 'The Secret Sharer' and the manuscript of *Under Western Eyes* was complete; then he collapsed for three months at the beginning of 1910, speaking in Polish apart from the occasional 'fierce sentences against poor J. B. Pinker'. He wouldn't correct the manuscript or let Jessie touch it. 'It lays on a table at the foot of his bed and he lives mixed up in the scenes and holds converse with the characters', she wrote. He accused her and his doctor of trying to put him into an asylum.[35]

Conrad's attitude towards Ford had changed, and the ensuing hostilities ensured that the change was irrevocable. Ford's affair with Hunt evidently disturbed him. 'I am told that Violet Hunt is mothering him just now [. . .]', he wrote to Pinker. He became angry that the affair couldn't be kept at a distance, and wrote to Galsworthy:

We have fallen here into a most abominable upset: the execution of Marwood by Ford and Elsie [. . .] For weeks poor Marwood looked as if after a severe operation. My view of *M* is that he is [. . .] absolutely incapable of any black treachery. We couldn't keep the horrid affair off us anyhow—what with E coming with horrid details and revelations (I told her plainly I could not believe what she said—and she only smiled) which it was impossible to silence and the poor M's whom we *had* to listen to out of common humanity.[36]

In April relations deteriorated further. On Easter Sunday Ford turned up in a car to tell Conrad that he had unilaterally changed the arrangements for the following weekend, when their friend (and Conrad's doctor) Robert Mackintosh was due to visit. Ford 'uttered an unlucky phrase' which so angered Conrad that he told Ford he 'could take no account' of what Ford had told him until he consulted Mackintosh—to whom he duly complained of Ford's 'mania for managing the universe'. In May, Willa Cather was the inadvertent fuse of an already explosive situation. Elsie wrote to Conrad to ask if he would see Cather, who was then managing editor for *McClure's Magazine* and wanted a story from Conrad. Ford still hoped that McClure could be brought in to finance the *Review*; Conrad disliked and distrusted McClure, and thought that an association with him 'could only mean the debasing of the ideals' which were to have guided the *Review*. Conrad, who later claimed that he did not realize that Ford especially wanted him to see Cather, wrote a curt note back saying that he had no story for her, and 'that this is not the way to do serious business—that the thing looks like an intrusion'. Ford was offended, and wrote what Conrad calls an 'angry' letter (which has not survived). In Conrad's angry reproof, 'My Dear Ford' has cooled to 'Dear Hueffer', and is treated as the irresponsible child Conrad was now taking him to be: 'Stop this nonsense with me Ford. It's ugly. I won't have it.'[37]

It was perhaps in reply to this rebuke of Conrad's that Ford wrote the letter Conrad told Pinker about three months later, by which time he had heard a rumour 'that F[ord] H[ueffer] was going about saying he has "called Conrad out"' [to a duel]. According to Conrad, this letter contained '1° An apology which I did not demand. 2° a sort of hint of a challenge being possible. Why? God only knows. 3° A statement that he was on the eve of com[m]itting suicide. 4° An invitation in the most pressing terms to come and stay with him at his flat that very night.' Conrad abruptly terminated his serial of *Some Reminiscences* for the *English Review* after the instalment that appeared in the June number. Apart from his anger, and the loss of Ford's 'gentle but persistent pressure' and encouragement with the serial, Conrad had another reason for wanting to disengage himself from the *Review*: the involvement of Soskice, whom Conrad described as 'a Russian Jew refugee' and 'that horrible Jew'. Conrad's anti-Semitism, says Frederick Karl, 'was never of the virulent kind, but rather a not very deeply held feeling that came with his birth and class. He took the alleged coarseness and vulgarity of Jews for granted, and he also, to some extent, saw them as part of that radical or revolutionary world he detested.' His prejudice against Russians ran at least as deep, particularly while he was trying to keep a protective distance from '*his* Russians in "Razumov" by means of the old language teacher', the persona who narrates *Under Western Eyes*. Ford put a notice in the July issue of the *Review*: 'We regret that owing to the serious illness of Mr. Joseph Conrad we are compelled to postpone the publication of the next instalment of his Reminiscences.' Conrad was 'vexed by that silly editorial note', he told Edward Garnett, saying that though he had had 'a most damnable go of gout' which prevented him 'getting the 8ᵗʰ instᵗ of Rems ready in time', it was 'neither more nor less serious than other attacks of the kind for the last 15 years'. He added: 'I suppose one of them will finally do for me.' Although Conrad eventually published the Reminiscences as *A Personal Record* without continuing them, he was uncertain about their completeness. When Ford remonstrated with him that to abandon the serial in a 'ragged condition' would be to discredit the *Review*, Conrad wrote angrily back: 'If you think I have discredited you and the *Review*, why then it must be even so'; but he continued, 'in the book (if the book ever appears) the *whole* of the contribution to the E. R. as it stands now without the addition of a single word shall form the Part First'. As Mizener says, this is disingenuous. It is also transparently hurtful, rebutting the charge of incompleteness only to assert that he thought of continuing the Reminiscences with a Part Second. Though there was never to be a Part Second, Ford knew what the letter to Garnett makes clear: he was intending to write more than the seven instalments published in the *Review*.³⁸

There are no letters to Ford in Conrad's *Collected Letters* during the following twenty months, and after that Conrad only wrote in response to what Ford wrote to (or about) him. He had decided to keep Ford—and his women—at bay. Describing a visit of Elsie's, during which she had eaten some of the strawberries Perceval Gibbon had sent, Conrad told Gibbon: 'There are evils for which there is no remedy.' When she came again a week or two later, she told Conrad she and Ford were 'on the eve of starting a squabble over their girls'. (In fact this was not to happen for another four years.) She was back at the beginning of August, when Conrad complained: 'She upset my wife and spoiled my day for me completely.' Around the end of 1909 she summoned Conrad to Kitcat to deliver a 'tirade against the habits and manners of all literary people', and threatened 'to show up the whole literary world'. Conrad was particularly angered that she cast aspersions on Galsworthy. Conrad's comments about Ford towards the end of 1909 are unmitigatedly spiteful. 'Is that inf[ernal] Ford still going about raving?' he asked Stephen Reynolds. 'Hueffer goes about lying exuberantly about everything and everybody', he told Norman Douglas. 'His wife is apparently going to sue him for restitution of conjᵃˡ rights and then proceed further. But there is some plot under that and at any time they may get reconciled and turn together upon some one or other [as Conrad felt they had on Marwood]. However we are out of all that and see very little of her.' Only when taking stock of the year on New Year's

Eve did he allow himself to acknowledge their former friendship, as he wrote to David Meldrum that he was not likely to see anything of Ford in the future: 'Still after eleven years of intimacy one feels the breach.' Yet even here he is cryptic, not naming Ford but referring to him as an 'intimate'. He seemed not to understand the force of his reaction, saying self-deceptively: 'He's aggrieved—not I.' They were to meet only rarely from now until Conrad's death fifteen years later. Ford would send Conrad his new books, and write to him from time to time. Conrad was never more than frostily courteous, and never sought Ford out again. His attitude was soon 'widely known and damaged Ford's reputation considerably'.[39]

There were other reasons why the breach was so deep and irreparable. Lacking Ford's support, and struggling desperately to end *Under Western Eyes*, Conrad rounded on Ford's facility—the skill and versatility that had made him so useful: 'I am not like *FMH* who can dash off 4000 words in 2 hours or there abouts.' He blamed Ford for the loss of one of the two typescripts of *The Rescue*—the book over which Conrad had sought his help in 1903, and perhaps again in 1907, when he thought he had entrusted it to Ford again. 'What they have done with it God only knows', he told Pinker. 'Of course Ford says he never had it—but he is mistaken. It is somewhere in his drawers but as they broke up one or two homes since it has got mislaid.' Whether Conrad (who had himself broken up the Pent, and was in the process of breaking up Someries) was right or not, he clearly felt that Ford's unstable domestic life was threatening his own writing. The fact that Ford had quarrelled with many of their mutual friends upset him. Edward Garnett was now added to the list that included Wells, Reynolds, Robert Garnett, Pinker, and Marwood. David Garnett said that Edward never spoke to Ford again after the incident between Marwood and Elsie because he thought Ford was trying to 'frame' Marwood as a co-respondent in order to claim damages. Like many of David Garnett's interpretations, it bears little relation to the evidence. But it does testify to the breach between Edward and Ford. Conrad's comment about Marwood trotting about after Ford like a faithful dog bespeaks a jealous feeling that Marwood had ousted him as Ford's confidant. The result of the breach with Ford was that Marwood now ousted Ford as Conrad's closest friend, as Jessie Conrad triumphantly reported. Indeed, her anger at Ford must have been one powerful factor turning Conrad against him. There appears to have been one last reason. Conrad wrote to Ford at the end of 1908: 'I can't somehow get rid of the idea that I have been in some way indiscreet—I can hardly say offensive—vis à vis de Vous. I have said something to that effect in a letter to you which has remained unanswered.' As his editors speculate, this may refer to his hope that his 'remarks as to the No. [of the *Review*] did not offend'. But the letter goes on to suggest another kind of indiscretion:

Perhaps you thought it was not worth answering, the supposition being too silly. If so—good. And indeed it is incredible that you should suspect me of an offensive intention on the ground of some remarks which are not and could not have been of any consequence. And considering our friendship and the confidence You gave me in that particular matter even the charge of mere impertinence could not stand. It was an expression of very great interest which was *not* critical in its intention. But enough of that. I dare say you think I am mad—and truly sometimes I think so myself.

The confidence Ford gave Conrad could have been something Ford confided to him—perhaps about the possibility of a divorce (it can scarcely have been about Violet Hunt at this early stage). But it may have been something Conrad confided to Ford. 'I knew that J.C. did confide in him about a certain delicate matter', wrote Garnett, 'and afterwards he deeply regretted it.' What this 'delicate matter' was has eluded even Conrad's most sensational biographer, and seems unlikely ever to be known. Since the two men's finances and publishing arrangements had been so intertwined for a decade, it is unlikely that they would have treated information about Pinker or the *Review* so coyly. Whereas if it were a delicate matter of sex, Conrad may not only have feared for Ford's confidentiality (though if it *was* such a revelation, he needn't have worried, since Ford never revealed it) but may also have been further disturbed at Ford's adultery, once again seeing his own problems magnified in Ford.[40]

Something of the tortuous distress this period engendered in Ford can be seen in a letter to Elsie written the day before the compromise was agreed with Soskice's group, which left Ford feeling that 'practically the Review is dead', and that he too was on the verge of dissolution:

If [. . .] the Review shuts down I shall have to face bankruptcy—if I can face it. At present I am more resigned than I was because I am fairly satisfied that people are friendly towards me. At any rate I can lull myself with the false belief—if it be a false belief. In case I can continue to live I have determined to take a small cottage near Oxford & to set to work on my life of James I, working at the Bodleian, & also on a novel and some reviewing. But, in any case, I must have mental peace for a time and, for that reason, I think we had better not meet just yet.

As for the Marwood business I simply *cannot* go into it again: it w$^{d.}$ drive me mad—& I hardly think that we c$^{d.}$ start without touching on it.—Mind: I am not at all impeaching or doubting y^r. veracity: only, I cannot stand the doubt of all my friends that I know w$^{d.}$ arise again if we *did* meet M, after all, it is better to live in a fool's paradise than in Hell.

I am afraid this is a very sad letter & one that will sadden you: but I think it best that you sh$^{d.}$ know the limits[?] of the truth. (I write with pencil because it is easier to hold: I seem to have lost altogether the power to hold a pen.)[41]

Despite the suicidal enervation, Ford was emerging from the series of proliferating quarrels. 'I wonder if it is true that I am troublesome and quarrelsome to such a degree. I daresay it is', he wrote to Scott-James after another potential row had been defused. 'But you see, I am a troublesomely solitary nature without the least desire for the companionship of my kind. . . . However, this is egotism, so I will not go on refining.' Out of the estrangement from Marwood, Conrad, and Edward Garnett, and also out of his uncertain, aggrieved animosity towards Elsie, came the satirical novels, written under the pseudonym of 'Daniel Chaucer': *The Simple Life Limited* (1911) and *The New Humpty-Dumpty* (1912). Although relations with Conrad were probably already irreparable, Ford's satires completed the destruction of his other closest friendships: with Olive Garnett, who found *The Simple Life* 'scandalous'; with Marwood; and probably also with Elsie. After her realization that there now was another woman in the case, the bitter portrait of her as the Countess Macdonald in *The New Humpty-Dumpty* hardened her heart against Ford. His sad letter is also an early voicing of the tone and predicament of his greatest novel, which he had originally called 'The Saddest Story'. That tangle of doubt and belief, unbearable truth and foolish delusion, sexual betrayal, impotence, suicide, and madness is at the heart of *The Good Soldier*.[42]

18

1909: SUICIDAL PASSION: *A CALL*

Let us accept the true word
throbbing in our hearts.
So that our anguish is over,
so that our hearts are mended.

(Faiz Ahmad Faiz, from 'Prayer')

Despite the emotional stress he was under, and perhaps because of it, Ford was leading a frenzied social life, and spending much time in the companionship of his kind. He sent Elsie a list of the people he had seen in one week, probably to allay her fears about Hunt:

Saturday:
(Boat Race)
Norman Douglas, The Gibbons [Perceval Gibbon was a writer and journalist]
Mrs Radford: [Dollie and Ernest Radford were poets]
Margaret d° [ditto]
Ernest d°
Maitland d°
Scott[-]James's (tea)
Galsworthy's (dinner)
Sunday:
Mrs Radford, Margaret, Hester, Maitland, Ernest: G. K. Chesterton: Hilaire Belloc: Gerald Gould: [Sir] Oliver Lodge [Physicist; president of the Society for Psychical Research]: Connie & David [Garnett]: M^r & Mrs Ernest Rhys: Juliet: Soskice: Oliver: M^{rs} H[ueffer—his mother]: Mary: Ezra Pound (an American Poet) M^r & Mrs Sauter [Galsworthy's sister Lilian, and her painter husband Géorg]: Violet Hunt: [Henry] Baerlein [journalist and novelist]: May Sinclair: Gibbons: Wyndham Lewis.
Monday: Gerald Gould: Gibbon: [Herbert] Trench [director of the Haymarket Theatre]. Wyndham Lewis (the new Polish genius.) [. . .] & Mrs Alfred Mond.
Tuesday: Wyndham Lewis: [. . .] met Watt at station—[possibly A. P. Watt, the first English literary agent].
Wednesday: Gerald Gould: Mrs Beechington Greig: to dinner: M^r & Mrs Arnold Bennett: M^r & Mrs John Galsworthy: afterwards: Goldring, Norman Douglas: Wyndham Lewis {called at Scottie's [Scott-James] in afternoon Mrs Scottie has been operated on for appendicitis
Thursday: Dined with the Galsworthy's. Very busy all day with 'settling the form' of No VI [the May 1909 issue of the *Review*].

To-day [. . .] very busy writing editorial, Goldring & Miss T.[homas] having gone till Tuesday.[1]

Elsie had evidently been objecting to Ford's socializing with what in *The New Humpty-Dumpty* he calls 'the dissolute and idle Smart Set', for Ford adds: 'so that if you look thro' this list you will observe that only three names, those of Violet Hunt, M^rs. Mond & Baerlein, c^d. by any possibility be included as of that disastrous smart set—whereas Preraphaelite poets have taken up nearly all my time, sitting at my feet & listening to furious lectures on "technique." '[2] At least one of these 'Pre-Raphaelite poets' must have been Ezra Pound, who had recently arrived in London.

After James and Conrad, Pound was Ford's most significant literary friend. For the rest of Ford's life he was to be his fellow-conspirator in the revolution of literary modernism. He would also be his close confidant, taking the place of Conrad and Marwood. Pound arrived in London late in 1908. During March 1909 Pound wrote what he called 'a most blood-curdling sestina, which I think I have divested of the air of artificiality supposed to haunt that form'. 'Sestina: Altaforte', a Browningesque monologue spoken by the Provençal troubadour Bertran de Born, whom, said Pound, Dante put in hell 'for that he was a stirrer-up of strife', begins:

> Damn it all! this our South stinks peace.
> You whoreson dog, Papiols, come! Let's to music!
> I have no life save when the swords clash.

Hunt's friend May Sinclair thought he should submit it to the *English Review*, and took Pound to Holland Park Avenue to meet Ford. In *Return to Yesterday* Ford wrote that Sinclair had said 'she wanted to introduce the greatest poet to the greatest editor in the world. She could invent these courtesies when she wanted to.' He thought she must have forgiven him for another episode. There had been a party to launch her book *The Divine Fire*, at which 'you had to wear about you some attribute suggesting its title'. Ford had the idea of wearing a fireman's helmet. 'But she afterwards wrote a book whose villain was a striking likeness of myself, so perhaps she really had not' been so forgiving. Pound's 'Philadelphian accent was comprehensible if disconcerting' when Ford met him, he said; it became a running joke that Ford thought it became less comprehensible the better he knew him. He recalled the young Pound as 'astonishingly meagre and agile. He threw himself alarmingly into frail chairs, devoured enormous quantities of your pastry, fixed his pince-nez firmly on his nose, drew out a manuscript from his pocket, threw his head back, closed his eyes to the point of invisibility and looking down his nose would chuckle like Mephistopheles and read you a translation from Arnaut Daniel.'[3]

'Sestina: Altaforte' was published in the June number of the *Review*. It was Pound's first appearance in an English magazine. (He had had two poems published in the *Evening Standard and St James Gazette*.) Ford always thought of him as having a touch of Bertran de Born himself, an indefatigable stirrer-up of literary strife in his campaign to 'Make It New', a kindred spirit. The meeting shows Ford able to make new friendships even while the old ones were breaking up. It also signifies the realignment of his literary tastes. Just as he saw himself as a mediator between the Pre-Raphaelite past of his childhood and the Edwardian present, between Conrad's exoticism and Englishness or between Marwood's Toryism and Soskice's socialism; so he was becoming a mediator between the writers he always called impressionists—James, Conrad, Crane—and the modern-ists. This act of mediation—itself a brave and somewhat suicidal effort when literary politics was becoming so factional—was the mark of the *English Review*, with its extraordinary synthesis of established talent and the unknown young. He would increasingly spend his time with *les jeunes*, but always in the role of their *maître*. His best writing is a comparable act of mediation: between the remem-bered past and the style of the present in his memoirs; or between the world and the fiction of Edwardian England, and the modernist techniques of the writers he would increasingly associate with: Pound, Lawrence, Hemingway, Stein, Joyce.

'For about a year or two Ford was to become an outstanding figure of literary London', said David Garnett of the *English Review* days: 'he was arrayed in a magnificent fur coat;—wore a glossy topper; drove about in hired carriages; and his fresh features, the colour of raw veal, his prominent blue eyes and rabbit teeth smiled benevolently and patronisingly upon all gatherings of literary lions.' The gathering on Sunday 4 April that Ford told Elsie about was a *bouts-rimés* party he gave at Holland Park Avenue. Hunt said Ford loved to get his friends to play children's games ('Clumps, Honey-pots, not stopping short at Hunt-the-slipper'). *Bouts-rimés* was his favourite party-game for poets. The competitors would be provided with the rhyme-words of a poem, which they would have to complete against the clock. He sent Hunt a rhyming invitation, addressed 'To Violet Hunt. Poet.' David Garnett, proud to be the youngest person there, remembered some of the 'celebrated figures present [. . .] they certainly included Ezra Pound, who had just appeared in literary London, wearing one ear-ring, which was considered very scandalous by certain ladies. Dollie Radford won the first prize and looked very much like an Italian painting in the crown of bay leaves; Hilaire Belloc won the second prize.' 'I enjoyed the competition immensely, though I did do so badly', wrote May Sinclair: 'In fact, I don't know when I've enjoyed a party more, as you might tell by my squeals of happy laughter.'[4]

Other friends who called at Holland Park Avenue were R. B. Cunninghame Graham, 'who looked like a Spanish hidalgo', Hudson, Bennett, Edward Thomas, and Edgar Jepson. Ford said he remembered only one dull moment there, a party when 'nothing would go'. 'Thomas Hardy remained for the whole afternoon [. . .] talking in low tones to the wife of the Bishop of Edinburgh.' Pound had toothache. The silent Gilbert Cannan was next to Hugh Walpole, who 'was suffering agonies of fear lest his charming mother who was the wife of the Bishop of Edinburgh [. . .] might hear something that should shock her'. Goldring too remembered how 'suddenly there came the usual inexplicable hush' in the literary talk that day. It was broken by Hardy who, 'turning to an elderly lady by his side, remarked, with shattering effect, "And how is Johnny's whooping-cough?" '[5]

Though by the middle of 1909 Ford's nerves were fraught, and he dreaded publicity—especially about his private quarrels—other glimpses of him at this time reveal his remarkable ability to preserve his social composure (and live up to his ideal of English *sang froid*, personified in his characters Ashburnham and Tietjens). Scott-James went with Ford to an immense party given by 'the wonderfully learned man whom we all loved', Thomas Seccombe. Wells and Bennett were there too. As Bennett, Ford, and Scott-James were leaving at the same time, they caught a bus. 'We had not gone far when the bus drew in to the side of the road to pick up a passenger,' said Scott-James:

and the top, leaning towards the pavement, collided with a standard lamp, and brought glass crashing down on to the front top seats. A young girl seated there collapsed [. . .]

The conductor, Ford and myself got the girl down the steep steps of the bus and on to the pavement. She was shaken and trembling. We made enquiries about doctors, and learnt that there was one not far down the road on the opposite side. The bus went on, and it fell to Ford and me to get the girl across the road, each taking an arm, and bring her to the doctor's house. The doctor was in bed and not very willing to come down, and we were both rather shocked when he demanded the assurance of being paid before he would deal with the case. We fished out the necessary shillings; the doctor patched the girl up—she was not very bad. We hailed a passing hansom, handed the girl in, paid the fare, and sent her home.

Then we resumed our journey. The street was empty. The last bus had gone. We had several miles to walk and we stepped out briskly through the bleak solitudes of the Uxbridge Road. After we had gone some distance we saw a figure ahead of us trudging doggedly along. We overtook it, and found it was Arnold Bennett.

'Where did you get to?' we asked.

'I went on,' he replied in a matter-of-fact tone. 'I can't stand that sort of thing. A disturbance of that kind is upsetting to my nerves, and bad for my work.'

He did not ask what had happened to the girl [. . .] He seemed to imply that the first duty of a novelist is to guard his nervous system against friction.

A comparison with what Ford does with this episode gives an unusual insight into the working of his imagination. The version he tells in *Return to Yesterday*, written over twenty years later, preserves the essential situation: he is on a bus with Bennett on his way back from Seccombe's when the bus hits a street lamp; a girl is injured; Ford acts, Bennett doesn't. But the circumstantial details have been changed to an extent that would scandalize an anti-Fordian. He says he thinks Seccombe lived in Ealing (whereas Scott-James placed him correctly in Acton). He says Bennett went to Seccombe's with him, whereas he went with Scott-James, and met Bennett there. Scott-James doesn't figure in Ford's account: a Fordian would say because the story is focused on Bennett; another person would blur it; an anti-Fordian might argue that Scott-James's involvement would detract from the image Ford wants to project of himself as single-handed altruist.

Ford says the crash happened while the bus was passing a trolley car (rather than pulling over to pick up a passenger). The young woman gets two fractured ribs. The nub of Ford's story is his exchange with one of two policeman (who don't appear in Scott-James's version). Ford imperiously tells the policemen to take the woman to the doctor; the policeman answers: 'You don't know the lower classes, sir. Sharp as weasels they are to get damages out of the great companies.' Ford says he guaranteed the doctor's fee if the woman wasn't hurt (and thus had no claim on the bus company); Scott-James has the doctor insisting on his fee before examining her; and has himself and Ford paying the fee. In Ford's version the police behave 'like angels of kindness' to her when she is found to be seriously injured, and they pay for her transport home (whereas Scott-James says he and Ford paid). Ford says when he got back to the bus Bennett was standing on the top deck of it (rather than having walked on ahead). Bennett is aghast at Ford's behaviour: 'You dare to talk to the police like that?' Ford's point is about how different classes treat the police (and are treated by them) differently. Again, the anti-Fordian would say that Ford wants to present himself as socially superior to Bennett, and to congratulate himself on his stiff upper lip and feudal sense of social responsibility.[6]

It would be rash simply to assume that Scott-James's version is necessarily factually more accurate than Ford's. The essay for which it was written (though he cut it from the published text) was published nearly fifty years after the event, and doubtless his memory altered some details too. Yet the fact of his presence, which Ford wrote out of his reminiscence, shows at least one significant way in which Ford was transforming the past. On the other hand, Scott-James's presence isn't incompatible with Ford's version: he just doesn't mention it.

The anti-Fordian arguments are more persuasive in the case of Ford's other recasting of the episode, this time fictionally in *The New Humpty-Dumpty*. In this version, written less than two years after the event, the Fordian Macdonald 'walked down those bus steps smiling that smile of his, and he put his hand into his breast pocket and took out his card-case and gave a card to a policeman. He was actually humming. Yes! humming!' The story is told by the 'thinker' Pett, who is normally taken to be a portrait of H. G. Wells. He says that he and Macdonald were on their way back from a Fabian meeting at Ealing (which recalls Wells's involvement of Ford in his attempted Fabian coup). But Pett plays Bennett's part in this story, cowed by the police, and standing amazed on top of the bus. 'I shouldn't have thought it was possible', he recalls:

But when Macdonald came back he was rolling a cigarette and still humming. He couldn't see that he'd done anything at all, while as for me, it struck me as the bravest action I'd ever witnessed. And as for producing the half-sovereign—why, I dare say it was Macdonald's last coin. I know it was. And I was fairly well off, because I was beginning to make money then, owing very much to the way Macdonald had helped me to make a start.[7]

The question here is not one of fidelity to historical fact. *The New Humpty-Dumpty* is patently a fictional romance, and the novelist has every right to re-imagine his experiences. But, as with Ford's re-invented reminiscences, the question is, what is achieved by the transformation? As with most of this bitter novel, the story is a hysterical attempt to glorify Macdonald. One could argue that the hysteria is to some extent Pett's, who is already 'almost exasperated' before he begins telling the story, which he is doing as a way of coming to terms with a conception of 'duty' that he thinks is alien to his class. But behind his frustration Ford's desire to present Macdonald as the misunderstood and persecuted altruist that Ford wanted to be is only too evident. If Pett's tortuous account of how he owed his success to Macdonald sounds like a lecture, it's not enough to say that that is because Ford thought Wells was always lecturing people. It is also too transparently an image of the way Ford felt the victim of the very writers—such as Wells and Bennett—whose careers he had helped with the *English Review*. It is curiously hard to account for the difference between Ford's aesthetic failures and his successes: Ashburnham and Tietjens both perform similar acts of 'ruling class' humanitarianism, Ashburnham being generous with his tenants, Tietjens rescuing the suffragette from the police on the golf course. In both cases Ford's identification with his protagonists is fiercely evident. It isn't that he has failed to objectify Macdonald, since the use of Pett as narrator for this episode has its counterpart in the use of Dowell to narrate Ashburnham's story, and, as there (and as in *Parade's End*), the emphasis is precisely on the *other*ness—and indeed the insouciant self-destructiveness—of the glamorized protagonist. I think the note of falseness in *The New Humpty-Dumpty* comes from the caricature of the phlegmatic milord in the exaggerated details of him *smiling* as he moves into action, *humming* while presenting his card to the policeman, and recklessly giving away his *last* coin. Also from the exaggerated claim Pett makes: 'it struck me as the bravest action I'd ever witnessed.' Ford acquitted himself honourably in Scott-James's account, and must have felt that to maintain such composure under such emotional strain was an achievement to be proud of. Some of the greatest moments in his fiction celebrate comparable achievements: Ashburnham's apparently nonchalant parting from Nancy; Tietjens's struggle to retain self-control under bombardment. But Macdonald's emotional strain has not been adequately realized for us, so Pett has to tell us what the greater novels show us. And behind his voice we hear Ford's wanting to tell us of his qualities—precisely the English codes of self-suppression that forbid direct self-praise. It is in this feeling that he *has* performed an impressive action that Ford most differs from a Macdonald or an Ashburnham (Tietjens is altogether more self-knowing). As in most of his fiction, he wants to see himself from outside. But unlike Ashburnham and Tietjens, Count Macdonald is not much more than a fantasy of self.

When he returns the incident to autobiography in *Return to Yesterday*, he avoids these problems much more successfully. Writing in the first person lends a frankness to the presentation of class, which enables him to achieve the rare feat of writing about someone of a lower class without condescension. Though it suits prime ministers to pretend that class-differences are disappearing, class is still a reality. But now we are more easily embarrassed when talking about it, partly because we are more conscious of the way that acknowledging the differences can be an insidious way of endorsing and perpetuating them. Ford, as 'the historian of his own time', was fascinated by presenting class at work. *Return to Yesterday* frankly presents Bennett as Ford's social inferior, as he was. But the passage is as much an analysis of Ford's 'Olympian manner' as a celebration of it. His most surprising transformation of the incident is in not using it to present Bennett as humanly inferior—which is precisely the implication of Scott-James's version, where he comes across as cowardly, selfish, and callous. Though Scott-James doesn't say so, Bennett's excuse—invoking the élitism of the artist, whose calling privileges him to stand aloof from human contingencies—is shown up by the conduct of a better artist, Ford. Though his nerves probably needed more protecting at the time, he doesn't let that stop him from doing what he felt was his duty. There is no self-congratulation about the sanctity of art in Ford's versions. His interest in the story is less to glorify himself, and more to account for Bennett's conduct. Again, what is striking is how he puts it in its best light, explaining Bennett's detachment in terms of his socially-conditioned fear of the police (whom he may have interpolated into the story). Even the detail of having Bennett staying on the bus (transfixed by Ford's temerity) puts him in a better light than the figure slinking off down the road in Scott-James's version. I shudder to think what uses would have been made of the story if it had been pragmatic Arnold Bennett who took charge while Ford neurotically disappeared.

There are three points to be made here about Ford's impressionism in relation to fiction and autobiography. First, that he had an expert eye for dramatic episodes that could be the germs of more complex situations (so the biographer's task is not just to trace the fiction to its germ, but to show how it exfoliated). Secondly, despite the differences of detail, the central impression of the contrast between Ford's and Bennett's conduct is much the same. Though Ford stresses Bennett's surprise at his tone with the police, and Scott-James stresses Bennett's concern with his nerves, these emphases are not incompatible. Even if there were no police there, Ford's impression of Bennett transfixed may still be accurate; and his explanation of it in class terms is still plausible. Responses are to some extent class-governed: some give orders and organize rescues, some do not. Thirdly, Ford's versions are surprisingly close to each other, given the two decades between them, and their differences from Scott-James's. If we simply had Scott-James's reminiscence and the *Return to Yesterday* version (and if, as seems probable, Scott-James was the more factually accurate), then we would probably explain the difference either by saying that Ford's memory had failed him, or by accepting Mizener's view of him as someone who habitually 'improved' his experiences to suit himself. Yet the fact that after twenty years he could retell his version fairly exactly, when he is very unlikely to have had access to a copy of the rare novel, invalidates the first view. The fact that his transformations mostly work to 'improve' the presentation of the Bennett-figure militates against the second. What the existence of the *New Humpty-Dumpty* version, in between the event and the autobiography, suggests, is that Ford worked up a memory into a consciously fictional transformation of it in the novel. But he had so thoroughly lived out the fictional version in his imagination that when he came to recall the original episode twenty years later, what he remembered was the version he wrote, rather than the version he first experienced. This provides a model for the working of his autobiographical impressionism. Fiction rewrites memory, then replaces it. (We know from folk-legend or family memories how narrative transforms chronicle; myth usurps fact.)

In Ford's case the rewriting of memory can result not only from writing his own fiction, but from reading the imaginative work of others. He read with such close engagement that he sometimes felt he had actually lived the experiences he had merely read about. He was aware of it happening, and, as we shall see later, his memoirs often present a characteristic dual sense of the seductive power of imagined memories on the one hand, and on the other a teasing doubt that they can't have happened, or can't have happened to him. Yet sometimes the irony is so faintly signalled as to be imperceptible to all but those readers predisposed to find it. In *Return to Yesterday*, for example, Ford describes a visit to Lawrence 'in Nottingham', when he was 'astonished at the atmosphere in which he lived':

I have never anywhere found so educated a society. Those young people *knew* the things that my generation in the great English schools hardly even chattered about. Lawrence, the father, came in from down the mine of a Saturday evening. He threw a great number of coins on the kitchen table and counted them out to his waiting mates. All the while the young people were talking about Nietzsche and Wagner and Leopardi and Flaubert and Karl Marx and Darwin and occasionally the father would interrupt his counting to contradict them. And they would discuss the French Impressionists and the primitive Italians and play Chopin or Debussy on the piano.
I went with them on the Sunday to a Nonconformist place of worship. It was the only time I was ever in one except that I once heard the Rev. Stopford Brooke who was a Unitarian preach a sermon on Tennyson. The Nottingham chapel—it was I think Wesleyan—made me of course feel uncomfortable at first. But the sermon renewed my astonishment. It was almost entirely about—Nietzsche, Wagner, Leopardi, Karl Marx, Darwin, the French Impressionists and the primitive Italians. I asked one of Lawrence's friends if that was not an unusual sort of sermon. He looked at me with a sort of grim incredulity.

At first this description was treated as documentary evidence for Lawrence's biography. Then it was noticed that several of the details of Ford's reminiscence come from Lawrence's play, *A Collier's Friday Night*, which Ford read in manuscript. Lawrence's biographer John Worthen calls the story 'a finely-crafted imaginative account of the group's behaviour'. He may be right to assume the visit never took place; not least because the most likely time for it would have been between February and April 1912 (because Ford places it after Lawrence had to leave his Croydon school for health reasons; and Lawrence was back in Eastwood in the spring before leaving for Europe). But Lawrence saw Ford in London before he left; during those months Ford was staying by the Channel coast, prostrate with anxiety, and had lost the manuscripts of two of Lawrence's plays. Hunt wrote to Lawrence when they were found. There is no mention of a visit in these letters, nor any other evidence of it, and it is hard to believe that such a visit would not have left other traces: Lawrence, for example, often wrote to Edward Garnett about Ford; surely he would have sketched the Olympian editor in the mining town?[8]

The absence of other evidence does not, of course, prove the falsehood of the story. The visit just *might* have taken place during one of the school holidays—or even during a weekend—that Lawrence spent at Eastwood during 1910 or 1911. Or it may be that, having read the play while on the verge of a breakdown, twenty years later Ford could not remember whether he actually visited Lawrence or just read the play. It is possible he did both, and, as with his rewriting of the bus-crash episode in terms of his previous fictionalization of it, reimagined the actual visit in terms of the play he had read. The sermon doesn't appear in the play. If Ford didn't actually attend it, perhaps he could have heard about it from Lawrence. But, as with so much of Ford's work, there are tell-tale signs that factual verification is not what we should seek in it. 'Lawrence I think went home. At any rate I visited him in Nottingham.' The 'At any rate' sits oddly with the 'I think': if Lawrence *didn't* go home, how can Ford have visited him? The second sentence raises the very doubt it seemed designed to quell. Or take: 'He looked at me with a sort of grim incredulity.' This is at once the characteristic response Ford portrays himself receiving in life, and the response his prose provokes—as here, with the amusing excess of symmetry in the way the sermon covers the same topics as the group discussion. The story is about Ford's astonishment at Lawrence's culture, and anticipates that his readers will be as astonished by the story as Lawrence's friend was astonished by his astonishment. Though, as Worthen shows, it is not implausible. 'Our set is a bit astonishing', said Lawrence. They would have heard sermons like lectures on the philosophical and moral issues of the day. Furthermore, it is a true impression of Lawrence in a more significant literary-biographical sense. As John Beer has written, it 'helps to illuminate a particular stage of Lawrence's development from the more devout Congregationalism of his earlier youth to the personally defined vitalism of his maturity'. Ford tells us that he was 'less astonished by then as to the great sense of culture in his work'. Which gives a clue that it is precisely 'in his work' that he could visit Lawrence in Nottinghamshire even if he was not at home. The story is about the literariness of Lawrence's friends, and the way that literariness has impressed itself upon his literature. Ford's 'impression' of visiting Lawrence is thus a tribute to that literariness: a visit to him in literature, if not in fact, which scintillates with the power of literature to create illusion, while it is told with a glint in the eye.

Ford's alienation from Elsie, Marwood, and Conrad, and his fears for the *English Review*, made him feel suicidal. They also had the effect of throwing him into the arms of Violet Hunt, with whom he could imagine living a new life. She wrote in her diary for 8 May: 'Did F.M. drive back with me. Had I a pink cloth dress. Did he say "You[']ve made me abominably in love with you?" I don't wonder.' After the meeting on 16 May, when the compromise was arranged for the *Review*, Ford went straight to Elsie. Mizener (who gives no source) says he arrived at Smeeth station 'in a downpour, in his evening clothes, not very sober', and had to walk the mile or so to Aldington in the rain, arriving 'soaked to the skin and in a rage'. He says it was on the Smeeth platform the next morning, on his way back to London, that he asked Elsie for a divorce. This was probably the last time they spoke to each other privately.[9]

At the end of the month he followed Hunt to Selsey on the West Sussex coast, where she rented a cottage, 'The Knap', from her friend Edward Heron Allen. On the train back to London, while she was looking out of the window, Hunt suddenly screamed: 'I see blood on the buttercups!' For days after she was haunted by her gruesome vision, which she took to be an omen of danger. 'To the editor it suggested a poem', she said; an odd work called 'Modern Love', contrasting the combat of medieval knights with 'all the long, long fight | That lies before us, you of the dear eyes'—a subject that heralds the next novel he was to write, the medieval romance *Ladies Whose Bright Eyes*.[10]

She was still dazed by the vision when, back in London, he made what she called his 'astounding, romantic, nonsensical proposition, over the luncheon table among crumbled bread and smoking Irish stew, speaking in a dead level tone, as if he had simply been saying, "Have some more!" "Will you marry me if ever I am a divorced man?" ' ' "It was too sudden," as Victorian ladies used to say.' She didn't really think he was serious. She had also just heard of 'the death, far away in Switzerland, of such a one as we women [. . .] call "the only man we have ever loved" '—Oswald Crawfurd. So she 'put the question by', and got cross when he returned to it.[11]

She recalled how one evening 'he talked of suicide in the intervals of reading' his latest novel, *A Call*. 'I was actually on the point of committing suicide by means of prussic acid, when Miss Hunt came into my office', he wrote in the 1913 deposition: his state of mind was 'obviously disordered'. 'I had indeed had nothing to eat for some days.' Hunt's critical eye found him 'no longer so dreadfully thin, since the cough had gone, but he was white like a stick of asparagus grown in a cellar; at any rate, rather pasty. He smoked incessantly, and it made his teeth black. His cuffs wanted "trimming".' He told her he would throw himself under one of the 'great 'buses rolling down the hill from Notting Hill Gate'—she could hear them outside as he spoke—'and no one would think of having an autopsy of the mangled corpse . . . and so on'. Feeling she had to comfort him, she put one hand on the lapel of his coat, and said something like 'Don't look so unhappy!':

The other hand, by the will of Providence, stole to the loose, open pocket of the brown velvet jacket that Rossetti had once worn. It fished out a dark, fluted bottle, inscribed in the Futurist colours of danger, POISON. The blunt letters were like the head of a cobra suddenly reared. I took it to the light, and he waited like a condemned criminal.

'Were you?' I said; and he answered, 'I was.'[12]

For all the melodrama and staginess of the scene—it is hard not to believe that it was Ford's will, not Providence, that guided Violet's eye and hand to the lurid bottle—his desperation was sincere. As at other times when he was at the end of his tether, he needed to imagine himself as about to die, or as having almost died. Yet 'concealing a handy bottle labelled POISON about your person in such a way that the woman you hope to make your mistress will find it is not something anyone does without an eye to effect', as Alan Judd says. 'It is difficult not to feel he was a bit of an old rogue on this occasion, and Violet a willing (and older) dupe. It must have made everything more heady and intense.' On the other hand, that is to assume that Ford was consciously manipulating the situation. His own recollection stresses his unconsciousness even of his desire for Hunt at this time. 'I will not say that no desire to marry Miss Hunt was then in my mind, but, if it was, I was certainly unconscious of it', he wrote in the 1913 deposition. 'I regarded her with the deepest gratitude as having saved my life and my reason, but I was not aware of any deeper feeling.' This doesn't square with Hunt's memoir, which places this period *after* Ford's conditional proposal. (Presumably in the deposition he wanted to avoid giving evidence that would prove Violet an adulteress.) However, that idea of an honourable man conceiving a passion for another woman before he is quite aware of it—and in particular of a man being accused of loving another woman before he realizes it—is one that was to become central to all his best fiction. It appears in *A Call*, when Dudley Leicester is enticed back to Etta's house without intending to betray his wife. It anticipates Ashburnham's declaration to Nancy Rufford, which is the first he knows of his passion for her, and which is doubled by Dowell's surprise when he becomes conscious that he too wanted to marry Nancy. It is Christopher Tietjens's predicament in *Parade's End*, who is struggling not to realize that he has fallen in love with Valentine, long after his tormenting wife Sylvia understands. It figures too in the novel that is most closely based on this phase of Ford's life, *The New Humpty-Dumpty*. As the Countess berates Macdonald for talking of their separation, even though it had been her suggestion, she suddenly exclaims:

'This woman . . .' and then she stopped again.
    'There isn't any woman,' Macdonald said in a tone of intense weariness. 'What has put it into your head that there is a woman?'
    'It's your idea, then'—she evaded his question—'it's your idea that at Charing Cross we drive off in separate cabs? '[. . .]
    'I haven't any idea at all,' he replied. 'All I have said is that if you're still of the opinion that we can't live together any more . . .'
    'No, I can't stand you,' she answered; 'you are maddening to me. Everything you say. Everything you think.'[13]

'This woman' is Lady Aldington, whom Macdonald has met too recently to realize he loves. To the extent that Macdonald represents Ford, Emily Aldington represents Hunt. Yet, as her name suggests, she also represents the lady at Aldington, Elsie Hueffer, to whom Marwood-Macdonald is attracted. Lady Aldington's brutal, dissolute husband is Ford's portrait of how he feared Elsie saw him, and shows him characteristically seeing both sides of their situation even as he writes what has been taken (too simplistically) as being a self-justifying book. Macdonald's conduct is typical of Ford's heroes when beset by sexual desire: he suffers for it even as he denies it to himself. The recurrence of this scenario indicates that either Elsie had in fact accused him of having a lover (and perhaps named Hunt) before Ford had himself realized he had fallen in love (or, as he put it in another trope of denial, before Hunt had made him abominably in love with her); or, by 1913, he had imagined the scenario thus (in *A Call* and *The New Humpty-Dumpty*, and perhaps even in *The Good Soldier*, which he may have been planning) with such vividness that he could no longer imagine his own life having been any different. Whenever he became conscious of his love for Hunt, he doubtless experienced it as he rendered passion in his fiction: as passive suffering, as something deeply disturbing to his integrity and sanity; something acting on him, rather than enacted by him.

They probably became lovers on 10 June 1909. The next day Violet had to go to Oxford—she had arranged to go with her niece, Rosamond, to stay with the literary critic W. P. Ker. When she arrived she wrote to Ford: 'What happened last night made me know that I loved you. Never regret it, and always believe in me, and I won't fail you'; and she enclosed a poem she had written on the train:

> There's a witch upon the hill
> *Give me a kiss*
> There's a dragon I must kill
> *And there's this*
>
> The danger signal's up
> *Give me another kiss*
> There's poison in the cup
> *But there's this*
>
> There's the night comes long and deep
> *Give me another kiss*
> When you and I must sleep
> *But first there's this*
>
> Ah me there's sin and shame
> *Give me another kiss*
> Joy by another name.
> *This! This! This!*[14]

Hunt's niece, Rosamond Fogg Elliott, called simply 'the Beauty' in Hunt's memoirs, had also become infatuated with Ford; she was soon as anxious as Violet to get back to London—for similar reasons, as Violet gathered:

We leave tomorrow on the 10 train [she wrote to Ford] and I believe that Rosamond is unfortunately nearly as glad as I. She murmurs breathlessly, at intervals, 'Monday!' I haven't told her anything except that you are *not for her*—in a severe way, every now and then. And she tosses her head and says she knows that! The beautiful young man Lionel Smith, rather forced her thoughts away from you last night—she was impressed by his beauty in spite of herself but remarked that he 'had not *your expression!*' His eyes are brown and sad; yours blue and dancing. We must, I suppose cure her.[15]

Ford had sent her some poems, and her letter switches into literary criticism, testifying to the mental agility and literary sharpness that Ford found so attractive:

Dear, I am not a jealous woman but those poems make me jealous. I don't feel that you wrote them to E[lsie] somehow—and yet?—if you did, it was her due, for you *did* love her and had happy, sublime hours with her. Or are they the thoughts that drift away off a man's mind, like the thistledown off the fields when the little winds of life blow? Just what *has* to come away! *A l'addresse de personne?* They are all of them beautiful, most of them meaning, I think, that if anything you have too much facility. You *won't* make the thought tight and packed. . . . Because then it would be Browningesque and not Impressionist? But sometimes you hit it *just*. A woman brought up on Browning like me could never quite see art as you do.

Oh why aren't they written to me?

Ford kept up the literariness of this correspondence, writing novelistically about his sentimental re-education; combining an acute self-consciousness about how heightened feelings draw them both into using emotional clichés of which, as writers, they would be more wary:

Dear,

Your letters cause me the most extraordinary (or are they the most ordinary?) emotions. I want to 'do' things—oh, mystical, and wonderful things—and I end by kissing them in odd places. I kissed them for a long time in a taxi [. . .] the cab was halted at the tail of a bus [. . .] and then I perceived that the bus conductor was grinning indulgently [. . .]

These seem to be imbecile details (I wonder how they would look read out in Court and printed in the Times report?) but isn't it the imbecile details that give the colour to an affair?

[. . .] And your little poem! What a wonderful—what a wonderful creature you are! And how you get it into everything you do—that wonderfulness. I have read it again and again, just because it does express you—the fierceness that one adores, the tenderness that has saved one's reason and one's life [. . .]

Aren't you trying, dear, to persuade yourself that you do care? I daresay you want to care—because you would like to.

But you have so many claims on your attention—so many memories. I come in so late.

Don't think that I'm jealous of your memories: I am not or not very, or not at all. Somehow I feel that you are now mine and dearer than you ever were—more in tune to me, having suffered more. . . . But I feel that I shall never really get round you, never really encompass you. You will always remain a little baffling to me because I shall never really share all your associations. . . .

Ah but we do make a goodly couple, you know. If it isn't already too late mightn't we knock the world!—in the Old Kent Road! Because—tho' H.[enry] J.[ames] once called me '*le jeune homme modeste*', I am not really modest when I measure my possibilities against the wits of my fellows. My dear, all of the Shaws, Galsworthys Grahames and fine noble creatures, slow witted fools when it comes to real brain work beside you and me—and you—well, Helen of Troy and Semiramis The Blessed Damozel and Becky Sharp, St Catherine and Christina of Milan could not, all together extract from me the emotion and devotion that are yours. . . .[16]

Ford felt invigorated by the affair; he was also approaching the height of his powers as a writer. In the following two decades he would produce novels which do demonstrate his superiority as an artist to Galsworthy and Cunninghame Graham, and even to Shaw. Ford's critics might object here that even if such a thing were true, Ford ought not to be predicting it. Yet despite his protestation of immodesty, he is not so immodest as to include James and Conrad in the list of authors he and Hunt should be able to outdo. Violet was flattered by Ford's eulogy: 'I never thought there was anybody in the world like you, for me', she told him in August. But she later came to feel that she 'should have left the salvation of F.M.H. alone', recognizing what is implicit here: that Ford's driving need was to write, and that his relationships were ultimately governed by that primary devotion: 'the octopus tentacle of the extreme need of the artist-egotist for an Egeria—any number of Egerias—won', she said. 'He got his way. I am cynical, and I do think there was something of the literary octopus in the drawing, insinuating pressure of his desire, flung greedily in my direction.'[17]

Ford, certainly, had realized that he could only save himself from self-destruction by being explicitly egotistical—by facing and acting upon his desires, rather than indulging in the more insidious egotism of sustaining a pose of altruistic self-denial. What he wrote to Elsie at this time about the *English Review* also has a bearing upon his other involvement—his love for Violet, and his decision to commit himself to her:

I am having a rather anxious time owing to the quarrelsomeness of everybody connected with the Review—Soskice, Marwood, Robert & Duckworth are all fighting each other & I have to hold the balance [. . .] I am becoming, in fact, hard & determined on getting my own way: and perhaps that is just as well: I feel I have been too pliable all round in the past: now I mean to make myself felt.[18]

As Ford later put it (in icy legalese, for the 1913 deposition): 'having returned to some pleasure in existence, I remembered that the problem of Mrs. Elsie Hueffer was still to be solved.' (It was one he was never quite to solve.) At the end of the month Violet took Ford to her solicitor, C. O. Humphreys—who had, inauspiciously, been one of Wilde's lawyers—to find out about whether Ford would be able to get a divorce.[19] Somehow amidst all the manœuvrings he managed to get the *Review* edited.

Hunt took Rosamond to Aldeburgh early in July to stay with the rationalist and anthropologist Edward Clodd. They travelled with Thomas Hardy and Mrs Belloc Lowndes; and—though Hunt claimed she 'knew it not' till the train arrived at Aldeburgh—Ford, who had followed, bringing Gertrud with him as his 'secretary'. 'There was quite a tiny scandal', said Hunt (nevertheless, Ford plus 'secretary' were asked to dinner to meet the classicist Gilbert Murray: 'He came alone, of course'). Mizener thought it was part of Ford's and Hunt's plan to furnish Elsie with grounds for divorce. In July Ford met Edmée Van der Noot at Tonbridge—half-way between London and Aldington. Ford said (in the 1913 deposition) that Elsie had written to him requesting the meeting, and that he 'had no idea' of its object, until Van der Noot told him 'again that Mrs. Hueffer wished to divorce'. 'Edmee, I cannot believe that Mrs. Hueffer wishes to divorce me', he said he told her. 'I believe that it is only a passing craze.' He recorded Van der Noot as replying that she knew Elsie's mind 'very much better' than he did. Ford said he told her something to the effect that he wouldn't oppose the divorce if Elsie was determined it should go ahead. But the deposition is demonstrably unreliable here. It claims Ford thought 'at that time that the eventuality [of divorce] would never arise':

I was in fact, at that time, firmly determined to commit suicide. I was absolutely ruined; I had not succeeded in disposing of the English Review and its liabilities; owing to its obvious non-success I had lost nearly all my friends of the world of letters, who are mostly gentry looking out for what they can get. On the other hand, my life was very heavily insured, and in the case of my death, there would still be enough remaining after my debts were paid, to bring up and educate my children.

He was feeling like this in the spring, *before* the July meeting with Edmée; not afterwards. By July he was in love and exhilarated; and he had already approached Elsie about a divorce and must have guessed that the proposed meeting was her response. Yet in the deposition he placed the meeting with Edmée 'about a fortnight' before Hunt saved him from suicide (presumably to give the impression that Elsie's request for divorce had made him suicidal). Douglas Goldring thought Ford had been approached twice in 1909 by 'a third party' (in other words Edmée); and he places the second meeting in August. There may thus have been two meetings (which his memory later conflated into one): the first requested by Elsie (its purpose a mystery to Ford) at which Edmée relayed Elsie's proposal for divorce; the second, at Tonbridge on 18 July, at which Ford handed over a letter giving Elsie grounds to divorce. His daughter Katharine told Mizener (in the 1960s) that Ford handed Van der Noot this letter for Elsie, containing a description of how Gertrud had been living with him and travelling about with him. She said the letter was lost by Elsie's new solicitor, Sturges, in the Second World War, but that Elsie was anxious to retrieve it, because it proved that Violet Hunt had misrepresented her in *The Flurried Years*. Ford said he wrote to Van der Noot (though he said this was in the autumn) and said that he was 'ready to give Mrs. Elsie Hueffer the facilities for divorcing' him. According to Katherine, the letter Ford handed to Edmée in the summer—in a boat on the Medway—implied that Gertrud Schablowsky was the 'guilty party', in order to protect Hunt's name. Katharine said (nearly sixty years after the event) that when Elsie read it she determined to begin divorce proceedings 'in a fit of anger' at Ford's 'meanness' at citing Gertrud: 'The Schublowski [*sic*.] girl was *never* the issue.' But this is a transparent alibi for jealousy. Elsie knew that Gertrud was being used to shield another person; though she had her suspicions, she had no proof who the other person was. She may even have feared that it was Mary once again, who was now living in Hammersmith with Ford's mother, and had by this time become a friend of Violet. Whatever else Ford's letter said, he told her that he didn't want to live with her or even see her again, and that in the circumstances 'it was fair that she should have the custody of the children'.[20]

Ford and Hunt used a 'hideaway' in John Street—perhaps the flat that Ford used to share with Harrison Cowlishaw. At the end of July Ford was dispatched with her mother to stay with Hunt's sister Silvia, the mother of the 'Beauty' (and called 'Goneril' in Hunt's memoir). From a letter Ford wrote on the train to Bedburn, Margaret Hunt's incipient senility, as well as her unease with Ford, are already apparent:

Dear:

Composition is difficult in the circumstances. I feel the responsibility of your mother—but she won't let me write—so I am standing in the corridor, keeping an eye on her in the carriage looking-glass. The window commands a view only of the *lines of rails*. And there is about them something steely and remorseless . . . they go straight on . . . why do they not curve round?—to the SSW? Oh, these material objects! My mind is filled with purely *cliché* thoughts. I envy, for instance, this sheet of paper. You have said it will lie where I so desperately want to lie. How many times has this idea been used by happy and unhappy lovers!

I was interrupted by an R.C. Priest who came to tell me that your mother had lost her ticket. At first she thought I was a swindler and refused to proceed with me!

However, we are approaching Darlington—it is John Street, John Street, John Street all the way. Do you remember last night? Do you? Do you? Do you?

I adore you.[21]

Hunt doubtless wanted to get her family to accept Ford, though Silvia strongly disapproved of Violet's involvement with a still-married man. Rosamond had gone back to her parents, 'having refused Count A., who owned half Sicily', said Hunt. There was also apparently an idea that Ford's presence would cheer her up. But Ford wrote that 'Rosamond really is, I'm afraid, very unhappy and very nervous. She writes from my dictation and I notice that her hands tremble like an old man's, which I take it is not a good sign. However, it is obvious to me that I can do no good. I fancy the father stands for more in it than one thinks.' The father, Walton Fogg Elliot, was 'a simple sportsman and fisherman and local J.P., who had got himself on to the board on purpose to deal with poachers!' 'I think it was really a mistake my coming here,' he said, 'and I fancy I have made your sister dislike me. She is a terror.' 'I don't wonder, seeing the character of the country and its inmates that *Wuthering Heights* was written', Ford wrote to Hunt—populating the landscape with literature, as ever. The Fogg Elliots weren't used to Ford's Olympian manner; but nor were they completely wrong to feel that Ford despised them. He was 'dictating hard' to Rosamond, and told Hunt, 'the novel goes on by bounds'. Before the war he always wrote best when dictating to attractive women—his 'Egerias', as Hunt called them. Rosamond's 'hero-worship' of him only made her parents more irritated with him. 'It was so very plain', Silvia complained to Violet. 'She sat on a stool at his feet—as it were—and adored him—I confess I like him better in his own milieu.' Hunt persisted in trying to win her sister round, urging Ford to tell her that he wanted to marry, but Violet was 'a little half-hearted about it all, because of [. . .] being nearly eleven years older!' She hoped to persuade Silvia to ask them to stay together. Ford wrote a reply which is not only eloquent about her particular attractiveness, but also about his ideal of love as a form of conversation: 'Eleven years older! What nonsense, when you are the only live creature in the world! And you are mind. Don't you see all it means to me to be certain [. . .], only, of knowing one can talk to you for the rest of one's life! That, above all, would be Heaven. And then there's you in addition!' And he picked up the refrain of the Italian popular song they had associated with their affair—'You shall have all you wa-ant and a little bit mo-re', telling her: 'It's Heaven *and* the "little bit more"!'[22]

Towards the end of the summer Elsie sent Ford a letter 'obviously dictated by lawyer', to begin the process of petitioning for the restitution of conjugal rights: it ended: 'Come back and be the loving husband you always have been.' Hunt remembered being with him on a visit to Aubrey Beardsley's sister, Mabel Wright, at Sheringham, playing croquet on the lawn, when the letter was handed to him. 'He shoved it in his pocket and went on playing', she said, impressed by his *sang froid*. Edward Heron Allen advised her that Elsie would be within her rights to seize the furniture from Holland Park Avenue. They had to get it inventoried so that Hunt could buy it from Ford if Elsie took any steps to remove it. Meanwhile the Catholic Hüffer relations and Edmée Van der Noot were putting Elsie under increasing pressure not to divorce, lest the children, also Catholic, should be 'morally harmed'. Harri Martindale decided to step into his father's shoes, and tried to prevent Ford and Elsie dissolving the union that Dr Martindale had fought so hard to prevent. He visited Ford, who recalled sardonically: 'He greeted me with effusive friendliness, although I was not particularly pleased to see him, and at once began to ask me to give up any proceedings that I might be taking.' Ford pointed out that it was Elsie who was taking the proceedings. 'Oh dear,' she said much later, 'if people had not stepped in'; 'I *know* it would have been better for *me* if I had divorced him.'[23] It is true that she was inexperienced about such things, and would have been swayed by the family's advice. Katharine said that she was 'so simple minded' about questions of sex and law; that she was 'the victim of circumstances'; and that Ford's biographers, and his books like *The New Humpty-Dumpty* had created 'a completely erroneous picture of her'. Yet Elsie remained deeply ambivalent about

Ford. Until his death she and the children nursed the fond hope that he would return to them; and yet she told Katharine 'that she could never have him to live with her again', and 'conveyed the sense of her physical horror at such a suggestion'. She was not the passive victim of other people's actions that her memory remade her, and, proving Ford's point that she was a much stronger personality than she thought herself to be, she did some stepping in herself. Just before Violet's birthday on 28 September she and Ford took a fortnight's trip to Normandy to stay with her old friend Agnes Farley and her American dentist husband. Violet and Agnes had together translated Casanova's memoirs. In the mornings Ford dictated his Regency historical romance, *The Portrait*, to the two women. In the afternoons they walked, or visited cathedrals and chateaux. 'I have always regarded it as the happiest birthday of my life,' wrote Hunt, 'although we did have our first quarrel about the fly to the station.' When they arrived back, Elsie, who by chance had gone up to 84 Holland Park Avenue that day with her lawyer, had found out when they were due to return and ambushed them at Charing Cross station. 'It's all up, old girl! You will see,' said Ford, wearily omniscient in his moment of dismay: 'There'll be no divorce.'[24]

David Soskice was finding his compromise arrangement for the *English Review* troublesome to work, and had become irritated with Ford. Feeling that Ford's 'offensive letters' to him were trying to provoke a conflict, when Ford talked of resigning Soskice took the opportunity of his absence in France to look for a new editor. He threatened to find one unless Ford would reassure him that he intended to edit the November number. Ford, however, had not meant to resign; but he said he came back to find that Soskice had installed Galsworthy in the editorial chair.[25] Ford was furious, and wrote what Hunt described as 'a mad letter', 'declining the honour of J.G.'s future acquaintance on the score that J.G. was humanitarian, stole F.M.H.'s thunder, etc.'. Mad to think Galsworthy would have been knowingly complicit in the plot to eject him, certainly; but not mad to be maddened by the manœuvre. This was not the first outraged letter Galsworthy had had from Ford; none the less, he wrote a dignified and humanely conciliatory reply:

My dear Hueffer,

Well, well! I'm loth to think it's the last of our walks and talks, and I've no bad blood, and a lot of good feeling about it—but you may be right, if you feel as you seem to feel.

We should be more or less than human if we didn't each of us back his own temperament to outlive the other's, and our work is only our temperament sublimated. But I hope when we're both in the [E]wigkeit [eternity], and can watch that friendly little struggle, we shall be big enough to clasp hands on our own defects as warmly as now I clasp your hand and wish you good luck.

Always yours,

J.G.[26]

Ford tried to outmanœuvre the Soskice group by finding his own buyer for the *Review*—Alfred Mond. 'I do wish you would buy "The English Review",' he wrote with disarming frankness:

I have given such enormous labour to it that it would really break my heart to see it go to ruin, as it will if it passes into the hands of Mr. Grayson's backers. Of course I can see no valid reason why you should desire to keep my heart or other organs intact, but it is really a rather grave public matter that anything so intellectually established should pass into the hands of revolutionary extremists.

Liberal Mond did buy the magazine, but didn't want it edited by an anarchical Tory. Just when Ford thought he had saved his brain-child, he lost it altogether. 'For a week of mornings he did not address more than three words to me', wrote Violet.[27]

Hunt saw herself as 'one to whom sensation is the breath of life, and irregular situations are meat and drink'. After the scene at Charing Cross, people began to talk about her 'irregular situation' with Ford. Her friends expressed their disapproval that she was getting involved with another married man. Ford always hated having his private life discussed publicly. When H. G. Wells wrote to Hunt, 'much distracted by something "the veracious Pinker" had told him', and hoped that she 'wasn't going to get into another mess—any mess—a particular mess he had heard of ', Ford wrote Pinker a touchy, angry letter:

Wouldn't it be better, don't you think, to tell my overt enemies, rather than people like Wells, silly and untrue stories about my private life? [. . .] I have, though I now very bitterly repent it, allowed him the run of my house in the past. The result is that he now pretends to a past intimacy which he never possessed and spreads ingenious inventions which amuse him and tickle his vanity. This would be all right and I am so entirely indifferent to people's opinion that I would not think of protesting. But if you [. . .] start his fertile mind upon a new track with regard to a third party [Hunt] it seems to be a distinct hardship to that third party [. . .]

In the future tell these stories—and limit them please to those which damage me—to an avowed enemy [. . .] But if you would really like to know who the lady is—and I make no secrets—why not dine with me here [84 Holland Park Avenue] and go over the house. You could then tell everybody everything.

You will observe that I do not mount any high horse of rage, you are so much too off the mark and I know how inveterate a gossip you are. But don't bring me—and still more don't bring third parties—up against little animals like Wells. I don't know him; I don't want to know him and I try to forget that I ever made the mistake of knowing him. When he seemed to be in a bad way I and the third party whom you have libelled did our bests to get respectable people to call on his wife. That was the decent thing to do but I don't want, now [. . .] to have to think of him.[28]

The attempt to crush by means of class superiority would have been hard to forgive if Wells had ever got wind of this letter. But these quarrels with Galsworthy and Wells (as with Bennett) never lasted long. Wells remained Ford's loyal friend, as well as his affectionate satirist and critic, until his death.

The most hurtful act of social censoriousness came from Henry James. He had asked Hunt to visit him in November. But after the scene at Charing Cross, she and Ford thought they should put him in the picture about the anticipated divorce. However, it was a picture into which James did not want to be put. He immediately withdrew his invitation, saying that he had now to regard 'all agreeable or unembarrassed communication' between them as impossible, and regretting what he thought the 'lamentable position' in which she had been placed 'in respect to divorce proceedings about to be taken by Mrs. Hueffer'. Hunt replied that she was not in a lamentable position, arguing disingenuously that her connection with Ford was 'so far chiefly editorial', and that if her name were dragged into the divorce case she would have to 'speak the truth and defend' herself. But James got delicate at her explanation, which only made him more anxious to shy away from the whole affair:

Dear Violet Hunt.

I am obliged to you for your letter of Wednesday last, but, with all due consideration for it, I do not see, I am bound to tell you, that it at all invalidates my previous basis of expression to you on my receipt of F. M. Hueffer's letter. It appeared from that that the person best qualified to measure the danger feared your name might be made to figure in divorce proceedings instituted by his wife—I really don't see how an old friend of yours could feel or pronounce your being in a position to permit of this anything but 'lamentable', lamentable—oh lamentable! What sort of friend is it that would say less? I wasn't for a moment pretending to characterize the nature of the relations that may conduce to that possibility—relations, on your part, I mean, with the man to be divorced, which in themselves are none of my business at all. But your *position*, as a result of those relations—if I had it to speak of again I am afraid I could only speak of it so. That is not the point, however: the ground of my writing to you as I did was another matter, as to which your letter again makes me feel how right I was. I could see you, after so hearing from Mr. Hueffer only on a basis of impossibly avoiding or of still more impossible hearing of his or his wife's private affairs, of which I wish to hear nothing whatever; and you immediately illustrate this by saying 'as you know' they have been separated for years. I neither knew, nor know, anything whatever of the matter; and it was exactly because I didn't wish to that I found conversing with you at all to be in prospect impossible. That was the light in which I didn't—your term is harsh! forbid you my house; but deprecated the idea of what would otherwise have been so interesting and welcome a tête à tête with you. I am very sorry to have had to lose it, and am yours in this regret,
Henry James[29]

This episode has been misunderstood. Mizener says Ford and Hunt confided in James about the divorce 'perhaps with some ill-judged hope of enlisting his sympathy'. They did not always act with James's immaculate judgement; but in this case they judged well that James would not want to be drawn into a public scandal. If they had continued to see James without warning him, they would have been guilty of using him to try to confer respectability on their affair. Ford may also have feared that Elsie, in her anger, might descend upon James as she had upon Conrad the year before, exposing him to her side of the case. James's response has been taken to indicate priggishness or prudishness. Hunt evidently thought this herself, and could not accept James's desire to remain aloof. She was upset enough for Ford to write to James objecting to his judging of Violet; to which James replied that he had not 'for a moment pretended to judge, qualify or deal with any act or conduct of V.H.'s'. Though his tone with Ford is firm as he reiterates his distinction between private guilt (which does not concern him) and public litigation (which threatens to), it is a patient letter, which modulates from unwillingness even to write about other people's affairs, into a civil blessing: 'I wish for you very heartily that your complications may work out for you into some eventual "peace with honour".'[30] James's principled stand has also been used as evidence of 'distaste' for Ford. But there is little other evidence that James felt so antipathetic: just two stories from the embittered Archibald Marshall (one of which expresses unease that Ford had written a study of him, while wishing Ford well personally); and an anecdote that James made his secretary jump over a ditch to avoid meeting Ford in the road. This last story is, however, characteristic of James's husbanding of his writing-time—his dread of what he called 'time-murderers'—rather than of any particular animosity. Ford recalls James whisking him into a fruiterer's shop to avoid an American he had just seen; and Hunt records him making a sudden detour during a walk—to avoid his own secretary.[31] James was despondent and anxious over the apparent failure of his attempt to consolidate his reputation with the New York edition of his works. He had recently been harrowed by Edith Wharton's difficulties of marriage and adultery, and Morton Fullerton's blackmailing mistress; so he would have wanted to keep his distance from what promised to be a comparable tangle. Brita Lindberg-Seyersted suggests that his conduct *vis à vis* Ford and Hunt was motivated by 'an abnormal fear of unsavory publicity for *himself*', and that their 'affair may have been a catalyst for his (panicky?) burning of heaps of letters in the late fall of 1909'—including, presumably his letters from Hunt and Ford. But he had one further motive that has been neglected. He had been friendly with Elsie Hueffer for over a decade. He had written warmly to her in July 1908, congratulating her on her recovery after the operation, and proposing to visit Hurst Cottage; and on 12 October 1908—only three weeks before hearing about the imminent legal proceedings—he had written to thank her for sending a copy of her novel *Margaret Hever* (while tactfully warning her that he probably wouldn't read it, due to 'the uncanniest feature of my accumulated age and disillusionment—my almost insurmountable inability to persist in the perusal of any wanton Fable at all'). His loyalties were divided, and he was properly wary of aligning himself with either party.[32]

Hunt later told Ford that James had said to her friend Mrs Prothero: 'I kept out of it, I am too old to be mixed up in such awful messes!', and that he had added: 'The one bright spot in the whole business was that they both wrote and warned me, & V. would not come & stay without it! It was awfully decent of them!' He certainly didn't remain cool for long. He had a long illness in the new year, but on St Valentine's Day he wrote to Hunt as 'My dear Violet', thanking her for news of her 'roaring London world'. 'And I rejoice in your brave account of your own heroisms', he said: 'They come to me like vague confused strains and boom-booms of a Wagner Opera—that there are women of confirmed genius who take ravenous nieces to London balls.' He had heard that she had just published 'something very strange and fine and fierce', and asked if it would 'overtax the shaken nerves of your enfeebled yet unconquered and all faithful old Henry James'.[33]

Janice Biala recalls Ford's *joie de vivre* in the 1930s: 'With passion and a wry gaiety he could be happy, and was, at the drop of a hat.' Even in his darker moments he could find within himself resources of humour and enjoyment. Despite his dismay and frustration over the *English Review*, his apprehension about the looming publicity surrounding the divorce, and the clouding of yet more friendships, there are glimpses of him in momentary high spirits, which show how the record left by letters—written, as letters more often are, out of unhappiness rather than pleasure—represents only a part of his protean psychology. D. H. Lawrence found him and Hunt 'delightful' when he went up to Sunday lunch with them on 14 November 1909. Afterwards Ford took him to tea with Ernest Rhys, the editor of the Everyman Library, then on to call on H. G. Wells at Hampstead. Lawrence found Wells 'a funny little chap', he told Louie Burrows: 'his conversation is a continual squirting of thin little jets of weak acid: amusing, but not expansive.' Lawrence also went to Hunt's 'at home' at the Reform Club on the following Tuesday, which he found 'very jolly'. This is surprising, given that he lists 'Elizabeth Martindale' as one of the guests. But it is inconceivable that Elsie would have been socializing with Violet a mere month after the Charing Cross ambush. Lawrence must have meant Mary Martindale, and confused her with Elsie, whose essay he must have seen in the October number of the *Review*. Besides the variety actress Ellaline Terriss and the novelist Mary Cholmondley, Lawrence also met Pound there. 'He is jolly nice: took me to supper at Pagani's, and afterwards we went down to his room at Kensington,' he told Burrows, 'but his god is beauty, mine, life.' 'Aren't the folks kind to me', he mused. 'Hueffer is splendid. I have met a gentleman indeed in him, and an artist.'[34]

When Jessie Chambers visited Lawrence in London at the end of November 1909 she was dismayed to find that Ford had insisted he should take her to Holland Park Avenue, and then on to South Lodge for lunch. She noticed copies of the *Review* piled up on the black polished floor and on the window-seat. The photograph of Hunt on the mantelpiece was a sign—their joint entertaining was another—that they were now living together with a candour remarkable for the time. Jessie Chambers was struck by his 'penetrating gaze'. 'I suppose never before nor since has anyone talked to me with quite such charm,' she said, 'making me feel in the most delicate way that what I said was of interest.' Byles joined them on the way to South Lodge. When they arrived, she noticed Ford's 'pleasant manner in addressing the maid-servant who opened the door'. She was introduced to Pound: 'A young American poet who startled me by springing to his feet and bowing from the waist with the stiff precision of a mechanical toy.' When Carlyle and Ruskin were mentioned, Ford told Lawrence: 'You're the only man I've ever met [. . . .] who has read all those people.' And when Lawrence later remarked that he and Jessie had been brought up as Congregationalists—as had Byles—Ford 'smiled and said that all the nice young people he knew

nowadays seemed to be Congregationalists'. Hunt told of how suffragettes were
treated in prison ('A favourite form of torture was to hold a lighted match inside
the hand'). Later on, Pound started winding Ford up, asking him a question that
Chambers said 'electrified' her: 'How would *you* speak to a working man?' Ford
hesitated a moment (Chambers thought that perhaps he found her breathless gaze
embarrassing), and said: 'I should speak to a working man in exactly the same
way that I should speak to any other man, because I don't think there is any
difference.' Ford walked with Lawrence and Chambers in the afternoon, 'with
Lawrence almost skipping to accommodate his impatient steps to our slow ones'.
After Ford left them, Lawrence 'exclaimed in a sort of nervous exasperation:
"Isn't he fat, and doesn't he walk *slow*! He says he walks about London two hours
every day to keep his fat down. But he won't keep much down if he always walks
at that pace".' He was perhaps uneasy at the interest Ford had shown in Jessie
and her writing, and at her enjoyment of what she called 'the genial warmth of
Hueffer's personality'.[35]

Ford had read Lawrence's 'great mass of manuscript'—over 700 pages of
'Nethermere' (the working title of *The White Peacock*)—'with the greatest cheery
sort of kindness and bluff'. He didn't want to publish it in the *Review*, mainly
because of its length. But he wrote a 'crucial' letter to introduce Lawrence to
Heinemann:

Dear Mr Lawrence,
    I have now read your novel, and have read it with a great deal of interest, which,
in the case of a person who has to read so many MSS as I do, is in itself a remarkable
testimonial [. . .] Properly handled, I think it might have a very considerable success,
and I don't think that in these matters I am at all a bad judge; but a great deal depends
on its being properly handled, and if you are sending the MSS to a publisher, I should
advise you to try one of the most active—that is to say one who already has the ear
of the public. As you must probably be aware, the book, with its enormous prolixity
of detail, sins against almost every canon of art as I conceive it. It is, that is to say, of
the school of Mr William de Morgan—or perhaps still more of the school of Lorna
Doone. But I am not so limited as to fail to appreciate other schools than my own,
and I can very fully admire your very remarkable and poetic gifts. I certainly think
you have in you the makings of a very considerable novelist, and I should not have
the least hesitation in prophesying for you a great future, did I not know how much
a matter of sheer luck one's career always is.[36]

Heinemann was De Morgan's publisher. Lawrence was summoned on the
strength of Ford's recommendation, and Heinemann published Lawrence's first
novel in 1911.

Ernest Rhys, trying to recapture the spirit of the Rhymers' Club nights at the
Cheshire Cheese, used to host gatherings for poets to read their work. When Ford
came to one in December 1909, he was still proudly (and paternally) escorting his
discovery around literary London:

When the two entered the room together, they made a curious contrast, for Ford
always had the air of a man-about-town, well used to town occasions, while Lawrence

looked shy and countrified; perhaps a little overwhelmed by the fanfaron of fellow poets heard in the room, with W. B. Yeats and Ezra Pound dominating the scene [. . .] Willie Yeats was a capital opener of the feast [. . .] Ford read us a witty burlesque, after which we persuaded D. H. Lawrence, who had been sitting silent in a corner, to read us some of his verse [. . .]

Lawrence's reading went on and on [. . .] and the other poets became restive, and chattered *sotto voce*.

Rhys told him he must want a rest, at which Lawrence got up 'with an awkward little bow' and went back to his corner. Later on they tried to get Lawrence to read another lyric: 'but Madox Ford took him under his arm and marched him off murmuring wickedly, "Nunc, nunc dimittis".'[37]

Ford's emotional volatility at the end of 1908 and the beginning of 1909 was both a cause and an effect of a furious burst of creative as well as editorial activity. In the midst of establishing the review, editing it, writing articles for it, and entertaining its contributors, he wrote his best novel yet, *A Call*. It was produced under intense emotional pressure, and at great speed even by his own astounding standards of fluency and rapidity. He felt compelled to keep reworking the idea: it began as a short story, '4692 Padd', was re-imagined as a novel, and serialized in the *English Review* between August and November 1909. Ford then extensively revised it for book publication. Even then he was not satisfied that he had achieved the 'exhaustion of aspects' that he required of a novel—the full working-out of its narrative potential—and he added an 'Epistolary Epilogue' which has the curious effect of reinterpreting much of the novel for us.[38]

As Frederick Karl writes: 'It is both dangerous and futile to read fiction as autobiography; but it is very fruitful to read fiction for the psychological preoccupations of an author at the time of composition.'[39] The basic plot common to all three versions is one which touches upon Ford's most intimate preoccupations at the time. Yet it is remarkable for two features which illustrate both the complexities of the relationship between a writer's work and life, and the limits we should recognize in trying to map one on to the other. First, it is perhaps the most striking example of Ford's tendency to write fiction which anticipates the form of his life; or rather, to realize in his writing the forces which were at the same time shaping the course of his life. And secondly, for all the thematic connections with his own life, *A Call* is more striking for the way Ford has transformed the material to produce a fully realized dramatic situation that bears little relation to his actual experience.

Robert Grimshaw, the central consciousness, has married off Pauline, the woman he loves, to his best friend, Dudley Leicester. While Pauline is away, nursing her mother, Dudley meets his ex-fiancée, Etta Hudson, at a dinner. He walks her home, rather as Ford had walked Hunt home after dinner at the Galsworthys, while Etta reminisces flirtatiously about their mutual past: 'She had a way of thrilling out her "Don't you remembers——?" and then dropping into innocent laughter. . . . Well, if she wanted to lead poor Dudley Leicester on—I don't say she did—I merely state the exact facts—she couldn't have done so better.' She invites him in, ostensibly to look out one of his old letters to her, in order to settle a quibble about his pet-name for her. But while he is there the telephone rings (the telephone number of 84 Holland Park Avenue was '4267 Padd'); Etta shouts down to Dudley to answer it, and as he does so she turns off the light: 'That's the sort of woman Etta is, utterly reckless or utterly innocent, I don't know which.' The darkness into which Dudley is plunged is one of moral and psychological confusion, because the caller, who does not identify himself, recognizes Dudley's voice. Dudley lapses into a catatonic state, overcome by guilt at how hurt Pauline will be if she thinks him unfaithful, and perhaps at how close he came to being unfaithful; and obsessed by the identity of the sharer of his dark secret, the mysterious caller. The only time he speaks is to ask people if they made the call. The caller, of course, is Grimshaw, whose passion for Pauline drives him to continue interfering in her life. He had seen Dudley and Etta walking home together, and rang up 'out of a desire to know what sort of a man Pauline's husband was, and in that way to have some power to shield her if it were ever needed'.[40]

Thomas Moser has written well of the echoes of Ford's life in the book. Dudley is the first of a series of major characters fusing Fordian and Marwoodian characteristics. He is tall, blond, phlegmatic. His breakdown draws upon Ford's sense of doom in 1904, and his fear that he might be on the verge of another catastrophic collapse as his private affairs become public knowledge. The danger-ous excitement Dudley feels when with *Et*ta *Hu*dson probably reflects Ford's feelings while with Viole*t Hu*nt. But the marriage between Dudley and Pauline, and the emotional turbulence it causes Grimshaw, suggests the episode of Marwood's advances, either reckless or innocent, towards Elsie Hueffer; as does the possibility of an affair between Dudley and Etta. In the novel version Ford adds a telling complication. Grimshaw has been engaged to his cousin and childhood sweetheart, Katya Lascarides. She wants to live with Grimshaw as his mistress, but refuses to marry him—due, Moser says, to a 'neurotic (and fictionally unconvincing) fear of the ceremony', though in fact it is partly out of strange piety (her parents lived together unmarried), and partly out of a desire for power: to make him submit to her on her terms, as he eventually does. Katya has a sister, Ellida. The sisters Grimshaw has known since childhood thus reflect Ford's relationship with the Martindale sisters, and indicate that Dudley's guilt about the (possible) rekindling of his affair with Etta reflects Ford's guilt and breakdown over his affair with Mary (revealed due to a telegram, as opposed to a telephone call). Katya's jealousy over Robert's interest in Dudley has been taken to correspond to Elsie's feelings about Ford's involvement with first Conrad then Marwood. And Ford's inscription in a copy for Marwood on 9 February 1910 suggests that he meant the story to be connected with their story. He quoted Grimshaw's: 'Do what you want and take what you get for it' (suggesting that both men did what they wanted and are now taking what they get for it), and then the priest's addition: 'And God in His mercy pardon the ill we do' (suggesting that the ill done by both should be forgiven; and perhaps that the offering of the book was itself a token of Ford's forgiveness). But there are fundamental differences. Katya, one of the first psychotherapist-characters in English fiction, is an independent professional woman, who starts working to cure Dudley, massaging his temples. Any suspicion of a resemblance to Hunt here, who Ford felt had saved his life and his reason, is confirmed by two points. First, as a child Ford had known Hunt as well as the Martindales. More decisively: Robert, himself at the end of his tether from trying to suppress his love for Pauline, and from guilt at having blighted all their lives, finally acquiesces to Katya, agrees to her terms, at the time when Ford had determined to try to divorce Elsie, and to commit himself to Violet. Although this cannot prove that Ford thought of Katya as based on Violet, the relationship is consolidated by two highly ambiguous gestures of dedication. The 'Epistolary Epilogue' is addressed to an unnamed but representative critic of the *English Review* serial version who missed the point of the book. It begins with a pastiche ending portraying all the characters living happily ever after, concluding with the writer's farewell to the 'dear reader'. Ford then comments: 'Thus, my dear——, you would have me end this book, after I have taken an infinite trouble to end it otherwise' (p. 297). In the copy he gave to Hunt Ford filled in the blank line with the name 'Violet'. Ford is in effect dedicating the novel to her secretly—in February 1910 they were still trying to keep Violet's name out of the legal proceedings. But against the intimacy of the gesture one must set the curious tone of the epilogue, which, though jocular is also impatient and outspoken. Hunt had evidently continued teasing Ford about his impressionism which left essential details ambiguous or vague:

It is perfectly true you complain of me that I have not made it plain with whom Mr. Robert Grimshaw was really in love, or that when he resigned himself to the clutches of Katya Lascarides, whom personally I extremely dislike, an amiable but meddlesome and inwardly conceited fool was, pathetically or even tragically, reaping the harvest of his folly. I omitted to add these comments, because I think that for a writer to intrude himself between his characters and his reader is to destroy to that extent all the illusion of his work. But when I found that yourself and all the moderately quick-minded, moderately sane persons who had read the book in its original form failed entirely to appreciate what to me has appeared as plain as a pikestaff—namely, that Mr. Grimshaw was extremely in love with Pauline Leicester, and that, in the first place, by marrying her to Dudley Leicester, and, in the second place, by succumbing to a disagreeable personality, he was committing the final folly of this particular affair—when I realized that these things were not plain, I hastened to add those passages of explicit conversation, those droppings of the eyelids and tragic motions of the hands, that you have since been good enough to say have made the book.

If it is an affectionate joke it is one which relies on a knife-edge precision of tone, lest it be taken as an insult to the very readers to whom Ford is succumbing with his concessionary (but contemptible?) revisions. Only *moderately* quick-minded and sane? Ford also inscribed Violet's copy with the closing words of the novel: ' "Every way and altogether," she answered. To Violet Hunt.' After Grimshaw finally capitulates, and agrees to Katya's proposal that they should live together unmarried, she then fulfils Ellida's prophecy by saying that they should marry after all; to which Grimshaw says: 'So that you get me both ways.' As an impasse of desolation and bitter knowledge the ending imitates the ending of James's *The Wings of the Dove*, though Ford rewrites James's magnificent presentation of the mistrust and disabusal which makes a marriage impossible as something more appalling still: Grimshaw's enervated succumbing to a loveless and manipulative marriage. Etta Hudson, *née* Stackpole, bears the same name as James's very audacious and independent character Henrietta Stackpole (and thus, as with Henry Hudson in *The 'Half Moon'*, Ford conjoins elements of James and of W. H. Hudson). There is also a 'Madame de Mauvesine', alluding to James's story 'Madame de Mauves'. Grimshaw himself, 'like a seal', usually carrying about his dachshund Peter, is modelled on James, accompanied by his dachshund named after another emperor, Maximilian. Ford thus combines himself and his 'Master' in one portrait, repaying James for (as Ford was convinced) basing Merton Densher upon him.[41]

Hunt had written to Ford: 'I love Robert Grimshaw—he is a little like yourself?'[42] Ford's double dedication may have been an acerbic rejoinder: well, if I'm Grimshaw, you're Katya. Once again, though Violet might have been flattered to be told that she now had Ford 'every way and altogether', the accompanying suggestion that he disliked her must have been horrifying. Three months after the scene with Elsie at Charing Cross, it was becoming clear that there would indeed be no divorce. Grimshaw's desperation perhaps reflects Ford's growing sense of the folly of his own particular affair with Hunt. As in his exchange with Olive Garnett over the biographical bases of *The Benefactor*, a note of slight defensive hysteria creeps into his voice as he both entertains and fends off the possibilities of particular identifications.

Hunt's criticism was a just one, though Ford refused to concede that he had not made it clear with whom Grimshaw was in love. One reason why it is not clear is that he appears to have changed his mind during the course of revising the novel. In all the versions it is clear (or it should have been) that he is in love with Pauline—though there is ambiguity about whether he realized the fact before organizing her marriage to Dudley. What does change is his feeling for Katya. In the serial version he is, even quite near the end, a man torn between two equally undeniable passions: 'His passion for Katya Lascarides! He hadn't any doubt about it, but his longing to be perpetually with Pauline Leicester—as he had told Ellida Langham—to catch her going through all her life with her perpetual tender smile, dancing as it were a gentle and infantile measure, this too he couldn't doubt.' In one of the most significant revisions for the book version, this was rewritten to show Grimshaw now having doubts about his feelings for Katya:

His passion for Katya Lascarides! He hadn't *till that moment* any doubt about it. *But by then he knew it was gone; it was dead, and in place of a passion he felt only remorse; and* his longing to be perpetually with Pauline Leicester—as he had told Ellida

Langham—to catch her going through all her life with her perpetual tender smile, dancing, as it were, a gentle and infantile measure; this too he couldn't doubt.[43]

Ford's change of mind about Grimshaw may reflect his reappraisal of his own position. When he first expanded the story into the novel, he had not fully realized how his feelings for Elsie had changed. To recognize that he no longer loved her was to rewrite his idea of himself as a husband and a father. That Ford linked Katya with Violet in the 1910 'Epilogue' does not mean that he had her firmly in mind when he began the novel at the end of 1908. Biographers arguing (as Mizener does) that the affair with Hunt began at the turn of the year, and not after the spring fiasco with Marwood and Conrad, would want to use *A Call* as evidence that Ford had—mentally—committed himself to Violet by at least January 1909. He had certainly met Violet occasionally towards the end of 1908, and the novel may reflect his wondering what it would be like to have an affair with her. But it is a stage in his making up of his mind, rather than evidence that he had already made it up. A year later, when he was revising the serial into the book, there was enough bitterness on both sides for the truth to be undeniable: by then he knew that his love for Elsie was gone; it was dead, and in place of a passion he felt only remorse. But more ominously, he was also beginning to doubt his passion for Violet Hunt. This is to say that Grimshaw's feelings for Katya combine elements of Ford's feelings for Elsie and Violet. As the dominant woman he no longer loves but who won't let go of their relationship, she stands for Elsie; as the other dominant woman he is about to bind himself to, she represents Violet. That pattern of feeling bound to one woman and infatuated with another was one he re-enacted through his life.

However, the most pathological element in *A Call* is the one which (as far as we know . . .) has no evident relation to Ford's own experience: Grimshaw's renunciatory arranging of the marriage between the woman he loves and his best friend. Ford was prone to infatuations with unattainable women: he was quite capable of conceiving a passion for those he knew he would have to renounce, while at the same time realizing that he was behaving like a romantic cliché, thinking himself 'an amiable but meddlesome and inwardly conceited fool' who would soon be, 'pathetically or even tragically, reaping the harvest of his folly'. *The Good Soldier* refines the most pathos-or-tragedy out of this scenario, with Ashburnham's impossible passion for Nancy Rufford. Ford himself acted it out, first with Mary then with Rosamond (neither of whom were married by 1909); he was later to go through similar agonies over Brigit Patmore and then Jean Rhys (though in the first and last cases renunciation took place after consummation). But in none of these cases is there anything like the way Grimshaw perversely marries Pauline to Dudley when he himself (unlike Ford) is not bound by any formal ties to Katya. Nor is there any precedent in Ford's own life for that conjunction of loved woman and best male friend. In his shell-shocked state in 1917 he told Hunt he could have her 'through another woman'; it may be that he had justified his feelings for Mary and for Rosamond in the same way, and that

Grimshaw's attempt to have Pauline through another man was based on his own attempts to understand what he would later call 'polygamous desire'. Loving one person 'through' another could also describe what a novelist might do, imagining relationships between real people through the medium of fictional characters (as '4692 Padd' anticipated his affair with Hunt, and its consequences, through the characters of Grimshaw and Etta). As Moser says, one of the most fascinating things about *A Call: The Tale of Two Passions* is 'the way it foreshadows Ford's masterly *Good Soldier: A Tale of Passion*'. Yet the only comparable situations in that novel are Dowell's virtual complicity in his wife's affair with his best friend, Ashburnham (which reflects Ford's ambivalences about the episode between Elsie and Marwood); and Ashburnham's later passion for, and renunciation of, his ward Nancy (which reflects, amongst other things, Ford's feelings for Hunt's niece). *A Call* is instructive about the limits of criticism which seeks parallels between an author's novels and his life, since in it Ford could be imagining an entirely fictional liaison between Marwood and Violet, or Marwood and Rosamond.[44]

Lawrence said of *A Call* what he would continue to say of the formalist novel that Ford championed: 'I think it has more art than life.' Arnold Bennett agreed, describing it as 'profoundly and hopelessly untrue to life', but adding: 'regard "A Call" as an original kind of fairy tale, and it is about perfect.' He noted in his journal after reading it: 'slick work but not, I fear, really interesting. He doesn't get down to the real stuff.' 'Nor I think, does he in life', added Violet, after inserting this comment into her copy of the book.[45] As always, Ford's problem is plot. But rather than his more usual difficulty of giving narrative impulse to a series of visually charged scenes, here the plot is too evident. Its Maupassant-style twist revealing that Grimshaw, seeking to 'protect' Pauline, has all but destroyed her husband, his best friend, works better in the short story. In the novel, Dudley's breakdown (so unlike Ford's in its mechanical simplicity) and the Lascarides family history need to be contrived to 'justify' this plot. But although *A Call* does not render a fully convincing human situation, and represents only a step towards *The Good Soldier*, it remains a fine example of the imaginative fertility with which Ford transposed and transformed his experience. Its achievement of a resigned tone of tragic irony is considerable. Robert Green writes that 'Ford was entranced by the power of the "stiff upper lip" somehow to restrain and hide a man's acutest emotional conflicts'. But what Ford brings off more successfully in *A Call* than in his previous fiction is the Jamesian manner of making such acts of restraint themselves expressive of the conflicts they are designed to hide. At times the Jamesian manner becomes mannerism, as the conversations become catechisms of 'Oh's and 'Ah's. Nevertheless, it is one of Ford's most personal novels. Its study of dual passion and its destructiveness explores that volatility of desire which had become his prime subject.[46]

1910: PRISON, *LADIES WHOSE BRIGHT EYES*, GERMANY

There were already signs of Ford's sensitivity to comment about his affair with Violet Hunt. He was estranged from his mother, telling David Soskice that her 'behaviour' had kept him away from Brook Green. Then on 11 January 1910 Violet Hunt was walking down Kensington when a sandwich-board caught her eye:

MR. HUEFFER TO GO BACK IN FOURTEEN DAYS

The divorce court had made a decree of restitution of conjugal rights. Ford did not return to Elsie, of course; he merely waited for the granting of the decree nisi. But Elsie was not going to make it so easy. She abandoned the divorce proceedings, and steadfastly refused to divorce him for the rest of his life. However, the court had made the customary order that Ford should pay Elsie maintenance of £3 a week. He resented the implication that he was not supporting his family, since he had already been paying Elsie £3. 10s. 0d. a week since 8 December 1909, and had made over to her the 'considerable profits' from his Constable contract in March; so he refused to obey. Instead, he arranged to make the payments through Byles.[1]

He was summoned to Marylebone Police Court, said Hunt, where he was sentenced to ten days imprisonment in Brixton Gaol. This was perhaps the court appearance that Olive Garnett witnessed on 13 July 1910, saying of Elsie, who was also there: 'I never saw her look so pale before. She met Ford face to face in court this morning & obtained an order against him. Byles supported him & his counsel said Mr. Hueffer did not come there to plead poverty.' Katharine said that the last time Elsie heard Ford speak was to say—in court, or in the judge's chamber—'Of course I would not take the children from their mother.' Hunt thought Ford 'longed for the experience' of prison; also that he hoped it would bring Elsie around. He had become a paying guest at Violet's house, South Lodge, paying £3 a week to her mother; and while he was in prison Violet and Mary Martindale sold most of his library to raise him some money, and moved his furniture to South Lodge. At this point Harri Martindale arrived at 84 Holland Park Avenue, and was shocked to find Mary there. He dreaded the scandal that might have erupted should Ford and Mary start living openly together. He reported back to Elsie, added his voice to those advising her not to divorce, and supplied her with another reason—one which can only have brought back the bitterness of the earlier affair. Ford's feelings about Mary at this date aren't known. But Hunt wrote to him (the following year) about Mary's feelings for him: 'Byles thinks she depresses me. Her love for you does, rather, I admit'; and she added pragmatically: 'I wish she would marry.' Mary had become a friend of Violet's, who thought her 'a cheerful girl', and was captivated by her 'ringing laugh'. Mary and Ford's mother were later persuaded to come and live in South Lodge as well—'In order to make things even more respectable in the eyes of the world', said David Garnett, since they would become more active chaperones than Hunt's senile mother.[2]

Ford's friends took his prison sentence as a joke. Ezra Pound wrote from Italy calling him 'the Apostle in Bonds', said Hunt, and 'perpetrated shocking parodies on the comic event in the style of "The Ballad of Reading Gaol" '. There was only one book of fiction in the prison library—a girls' story by the prolific children's writer Mrs L. T. Meade—so to alleviate the boredom while he was not sewing post-bags, he sewed three pairs of his socks into tight balls and tried juggling 'practising the Cinquevalli "touch", endeavouring to keep the three woollen billiard balls going off his back and arms at the same time'. In one of his 'Daniel Chaucer' series in the *transatlantic review* Ford wrote, in doubly displaced autobiography, of 'a friend, not unpractised in letters who spent some weeks in one of His Majesty's Prisons—for the sake of conscience or because of obstinacy according to the point of view [. . .] It was perhaps Brixton or it may have been Wandsworth.' He recounts a fine argument with the prison chaplain about the moral effect of fiction: 'I had told him that I thought that *any* novel would be more improving, would give, as you would say, a greater sense of the values of life—which it was surely the job of a Prison to convey—than *any* work of devotion [. . .] he considered it an instance of depravity.' He says the novel was *Pickwick Papers*, which he read three times. If Hunt named the actual book, then Ford's later change would be an impressionist liberty, finding an equivalent which would convey to (mainly American) readers who might not have heard of Mrs Meade a similar impression of what Ford called a 'nuvvle'—the antithesis of the Flaubertian or Jamesian formal design. But anyway, Ford was not writing autobiography, as the 'Daniel Chaucer' pseudonym indicates; he wanted to give an impression of the prevailing British attitude to literature which considered morality to be primarily a matter of content.[3] Two days of his sentence were commuted because they fell on a weekend, according to Hunt. She thought he was 'a little hysterical' while in prison—speaking 'in a voice strangely unlike the editor's own'. Once he was out, she told him the bad news from Germany as soon as she thought he could bear it. His rich aunt, Laura Schmedding, had died while he had been in prison. She had altered her will—an hour before her death, said Hunt—to make the legacy on which Ford had been counting contingent upon his good behaviour until January 1911. Ford became obsessed with the idea that Tante Laura had been killed by the news that he was 'doing time'; that, because of his conscience or obstinacy, he had inadvertently disinherited himself.[4]

According to the 1913 deposition Ford still thought Elsie might go ahead with the divorce. But then around Easter his solicitor told him she wouldn't. 'I simply laughed at him incredulously', wrote Ford:

A little later I met another gentleman—Mr. Marwood—who informed me that Mrs. Hueffer was circulating the most abominable charges against me. There was literally no failing or vice, mentionable or unmentionable, that she did not attribute to me. She accused [me], for instance, of having communicated to her a disease. I am quite aware that this lady, being of an unbridled tongue, and having only an uncertain sense of the meanings of the meanings of words, meant no more than that my attempting to convince her that her pains during the illness from which she suffered were hysterical, had affected her health for the worse; but it is obvious that such a statement would be taken by any other person for an accusation of having caused her to suffer from syphilis. By a similar sort of malapropism she made the statement that I had a friend of Conservative principles—she herself being a Socialist—appear as if I were guilty of sodomy—the exact phrase that she used broadcast being that I and this gentleman were of unmentionable principles and practices. Here again I am quite ready to believe that she was not aware of the sense commonly applied to these words; indeed I should say that she was unaware of the existence of the vice itself [.] But it will readily be understood that the broadcast flinging of such accusations could only result in professional and social ruin for myself and everyone connected with me.

I therefore did all that I could to force her to formulate these charges in a court of law so that I could meet and disprove them. It was practically life and death to me, and so it continues to be.[5]

Jessie Conrad's account of Elsie's 'tirade' makes this accusation about her accusations more plausible than it might otherwise seem—for all its transparent pretence of taking her spite for innocent 'malapropism'. Katharine was 'horrified' that Ford could think Elsie wanted revenge, and could express the idea in *The New Humpty-Dumpty*: 'It just was not in her make up ever', she said. Her idolizing of the parent who brought her up is understandable; but Mizener was seriously misled into taking her long-censored view of Elsie on trust. The testimony of Joseph and Jessie Conrad, of Goldring, of Hunt, of Ford himself, and the way she used Marwood, show that Ford's portrait of her jealous rage was essentially true. His response was to write satire, the first of his pseudonymous novels, *The Simple Life Limited*, which Ford sent to Pinker as 'by a young author called Daniel Chaucer in whose work I am exceedingly interested. I may say that I have not the slightest doubt that it is just as good or better than anything I could do myself.'[6]

At the beginning of May Hunt took Ford, together with her mother and Gertrud (who was about to leave England), to Fordingbridge in Hampshire, not far south from Salisbury, where he had gone while trying to recover in 1904. Ford bought a camera, and took snapshots of Violet, their dog-cart, and the local sights. Fordingbridge was where Ford was to situate the Ashburnhams' house in *The Good Soldier*. Salisbury Plain was the setting for the novel he had thought of while recuperating in 1905, and was now writing—and for which Violet said she provided the Miltonic title—*Ladies Whose Bright Eyes*. She also found, on a tablet in Salisbury Cathedral, a name for the heroine, the Lady Dionissia de Egerton de

Tamworth. It was one of Ford's most popular novels, reprinted several times, then revised by him for a new American edition in 1935.[7] It brings together in an original way the popular forms of historical romance and tales of time travel, but is a far more compelling and stimulating work than the pot-boiler this might make it sound. The idea was suggested by Twain's *A Connecticut Yankee at the Court of King Arthur*. The bringing into relationship of different ages, different cultures, different characters always appealed to Ford. But he wanted to provide a corrective to the travesty of feudalism in Twain's comedy, where 'dummy knights in armour are discomfited by electrified barbed-wire fencing, and a modern American perturbs King Arthur by preaching down chivalric ideals to the tune of nineteenth century morality'. 'It occurred to me to wonder', wrote Ford, 'what would really happen to a modern man thrown back in the Middle ages...' In *Ladies Whose Bright Eyes*, William Sorrell, an Edwardian averagely philistine publisher and millionaire, is concussed in a train crash near Salisbury. When he comes round he gradually realizes that he has been thrown back to the year 1327. The main action occurs in this medieval setting, which is managed with great skill and encyclopaedic detail. One critic called the book 'about the best mediæval novel that has yet been written'. It was probably *Ladies Whose Bright Eyes* that the young T. S. Eliot gave to Alain-Fournier, who found in it 'tant de fièvre et tant de pathétique beauté'. Eliot himself later called it 'an admirable unappreciated novel'.[8]

Historical romance tends to minister to escapism and nostalgia, and Ford in 1910 had every reason to wish himself out of an increasingly tangled present and back in a romanticized and ordered past, in which he could recuperate from 'the extraordinary rush of modern life'. But Ford's is not the medievalism of Pre-Raphaelite sentimentality: he is unillusioned about the squalor and violence of daily fourteenth-century life. Furthermore, the framing of the medieval action by the contemporary beginning and ending means that we can never quite forget that Sorrell is not *of* the times *in* which he finds himself. The effect of this is a true juxtaposition of past and present, rather than an abandonment of the real present in favour of an imaginary past. It is a temporal doubling rather than an escapist displacement: the past gives a critical perspective on the present—Ford's emotional present as well as England's cultural present. For it is a historical fantasy on what was becoming his foremost theme, the doubling of passions. Sorrell becomes involved with not one but two married ladies: Lady Blanche de Coucy and Lady Dionissia. Blanche is usually read as a portrait of Elsie, conceived at least by Ford to be jealously and vindictively trying to keep him from his true love, Violet. The climax of the novel draws on his feelings of passive suffering due to the sexual aggression he has incited: the two ladies do not just 'Rain influence and judge the prize'; they get on their horses and joust over Sorrell—one of Ford's working titles had been 'The Tournament of Women'. The Charing Cross confrontation probably had a lot to do with Ford's conception of the book, as did the unachieved divorce: the train is heading towards London; Sorrell, who has managed to keep out of the divorce courts 'only by the most extraordinary exertions', has a mildly flirtatious conversation with Mrs Lee Egerton, who gives him the historic Tamworth–Egerton cross moments before the crash.[9]

Yet if we take seriously Hunt's claim that Dionissia is based on Rosamond, and take it to mean more than that there is a physical resemblance, then the biographical significance becomes obscure. Has Ford fused Violet and Rosamond into one character? Or does Blanche reflect Violet's attitude to Ford, as well as Elsie's; in other words, have Violet and Elsie been merged into one portrait of possessiveness (as in the character of Katya in *A Call*)? Such questions are impertinent, because novels do more than merely transcribe personal experience. Yet they suggest that Ford was using fiction to provide a new perspective on his own predicament, and was probing his tendency to reduplicate situations. For one implication of the plot's curious interfusing of characters is that the Ford–Elsie–Violet triangle had been transposed into the Ford–Violet–Rosamond one; that as soon as Hunt became his consort, he became infatuated with another woman, and again established a scenario of two passions.[10]

Ford's genius in this surprising book is to reinvent the form of historical romance, finding an ending which turns the book from an instance of the genre to a searching criticism of it: an intriguing exploration of the relationship between fiction and fact, fantasy and reality, as well as a subtle pondering about why we need art, especially literature—and about the elusive yet inescapable relationship between fiction and biography. Sorrell regains consciousness for a second time, which is disconcerting, since we weren't conscious that he had lost it again. Yet it soon becomes clear that his medieval experiences have been a dream vision, the after-effects of his crash. He never really escaped from his present. This could be a bad romancer's cop-out, rounding off the form with an apology for its hollowness. But for Sorrell it is the present which seems insubstantial. The chivalric values by which he has been dream-living, and his love for Dionissia, are what seem real. He wakes up in great pain. He is an early instance of the Fordian protagonist whose desire appears at once precipitated and frustrated by a head-injury. Whereas Dudley Leicester in *A Call* suffered catatonia due to his sexual guilt, Sorrell's coma is more benign; a dream-like state allowing the play of romantic fantasy. But the physical pain is doubled by overwhelming nostalgia. He wants to return to yesterday: 'his own voice said: "Let me go back! Ah, God, let me go back!" ' With a lesser writer we might then be in for self-congratulatory banalities about visionaries being the ones who see the real truth, about dreams being reality and reality merely a dream, and so on. Instead, it is exactly while delivering the ultimate romance stock-in-trade—the uniting of the lovers—that Ford makes the form most challenging. Like many of Ford's other protagonists (the Young Lovell, most of the characters in *The Good Soldier*, Christopher and Sylvia Tietjens), Sorrell is 'on the verge of madness', touched by visions he cannot forget. Moser has shown how the novel draws on Ford's experiences during his 1904 breakdown—a violent wrenching away from his familiar life—as *Parade's End* draws on his experience of shell-concussion in 1916. Sorrell is even a little ridiculous in his sorrow, as Ford summons the terrors of his own near-madness, in order to laugh them away now: ' "I can't face it,", he said. "I can't go there; I can't go back. Don't you understand? It's like being in hell. To love a woman who has been dead four hundred and fifty years. I am done. Used up. It's all over with me." ' In a desperate attempt to recapture the world he has lost he returns to Salisbury and rides around the area, trying at least to see the locations of his dream-past. He reaches Fordingbridge, accompanied by Mrs Lee-Egerton's son:

'My God!' Sir William said suddenly. 'Did you see? Who was that? In God's name who was that?'
    'Why?' young Lee-Egerton said. 'That was Nurse Morane! The one who nursed you till the first time they trepanned you. She broke down the day before they trepanned you the second time. My mother says she couldn't stand the excitement, because she was in love with you. My mother's always got her head full of ideas like that.'[11]

Nurse Morane is Dionissia Morane: the Lady Dionissia of his dream. 'What does it all mean?', he asks her, with the recurrent question of the baffled Fordian hero. He still cannot doubt the reality of his impressions. Once again, where a lesser writer might want to leave us awestruck at the quasi-mysticism of coexisting times, time travel, or the paranormal (as in Priestley's 'Time Plays', for example), Ford leaves Sorrell joyfully and slightly incoherently puzzled, but at least considering the most likely possibility: ' "Either I went back to the fourteenth century because you wanted me to. Either the fourteenth century is still here behind a curtain. Or else it was you, sitting beside my bed and reading old chronicles, that just put the thoughts into my head" ' (p. 359). The paradox becomes more subtle. Throughout the 'Envoi' we are shown glimpses of how, behind Sorrell's dream, were the realities of his injury: the high headgear of the medieval ladies was how he saw the white linen caps of the nurses; the two fights in which he is involved (against Hugh Fitzgreville, Dionissia's enemy, and against her husband, the knight of Egerton) correspond to the two operations on his head. The facts of the present are visible in the fictional imagining of the past: the Lady Dionissia *is* Dionissia Morane. This relationship between actual nurse and imagined lover presents, within the book, an allegory of the way writers (and their readers) see actual people in fictional characters, and fictional characters in actual people. But this does not—quite—enable us to say that Dionissia *is* Rosamond, or Violet, or even a composite portrait of both. For the other side of the paradox is that, if the vision was drawn from Sorrell's unconscious, or semi-conscious, sights and experiences, it was drawn by art: conjured up by Dionissia's reading of literature about the past. The vision is inescapably double, the product of fact and imagination. Where *Mr. Apollo* had realized one classical god of dream and vision, *Ladies Whose Bright Eyes* invokes his *alter ego*, Dionysus—whose ladies have bright eyes not because they weep and smile passively for their champions, but because they have attained the terrible frenzy of a Maenadic trance, and witness spiritual realities beyond the curtain of the visible. Like Apollo, Dionysus is associated with visionary rapture and with metamorphosis. *Ladies Whose Bright Eyes* also allegorizes the way artists metamorphose realities into compelling visions. Before his accident, Mr Sorrell published encyclopaedias and bio-graphies—two of the least imaginative and most factually based literary forms. *Ladies Whose Bright Eyes* tells the story of his transformation into a man of imagination, through the sympathetic presence of the woman who combines the roles of reader and lover. If we can recognize Rosamond and Violet in the portrayal of Dionissia, it does not mean that Dionissia is a 'portrait' of them—how, after all, can a painting be a portrait of two dissimilar individuals? She is a transformation; the actual women envisioned as something quite other. As Moser says, the notion that Dionissia's presence made Sorrell dream 'conforms to Ford's esthetic of fictional narration, which requires the presence of a silent, inspiring auditor, usually feminine, for the artist to create, whether he be John Kemp in the dock pleading for his like or John Dowell telling his saddest story to an imaginary listener' (p. 84). It does more than 'conform' to an aesthetic, however: it exemplifies and criticizes it. Ford was able to bring to bear on the writing of his historical and fantastical romance the insights developed during his phase of intense critical activity since 1907. 'I suppose I shall have to stick to historical novels for the Constable Contract,' said Ford, 'though I hate writing them.' In *Ladies Whose Bright Eyes* he found an exquisitely dual form—which accounts for its critical and popular success. It can be read both as an earnest historical novel, and as a psychological study of the historical imagination and of the processes of art.[12]

Ford and Hunt braved society. She gave 'a series of "afternoons"'. Henry James came to one. He sat 'talking animatedly to the Beauty, who could not talk but *looked*'. They gave garden parties in a big garden rented opposite South Lodge. At one, Violet 'had the felicity of introducing Miss Christabel Pankhurst to Mrs. Humphry Ward, the darling Die-hard of the opposition'. When D. H. Lawrence called on Ford in the middle of June he found Pound there, just back from Sirmione, and now dressed 'like a latest edition of jongleur', and talking of writing 'an account of the mystic cult of love—the dionysian rites'. In July Lawrence was 'bidden' to tea with Ford, and arrived dismayed to find a waiter announcing the guests:

I was so astonished I could neither find him a card nor tell him my name. At last he bawled my announcement, and I found myself in what seemed like a bargain sale. The room was packed. Breathless, I shook hands with Hueffer and Violet Hunt. She was tremendous in a lace gown and a hat writhed with blue feathers as if with some python. Indeed she looked very handsome. She had on her best society manners. She is very dexterous: flips a bright question, lifts her eyebrows in deep concern, glances from the man on her right to the lady on her left, smiles, bows, and suddenly,—quick curtain—she is gone, and is utterly somebody else's, she who was altogether ours a brief second before.

I knew not a soul. I talked a little while to a weird great uncle of Hueffers [probably William Michael Rossetti], then to a pretty and more-intimidated-than-I-was new secretary of Ford Madox, and then to the large, fair round cheeked sister of our host, who was married to a Russian. In the intervals I stared at the folk [...] I liked

Hueffer's sister: she was straight, frank, jolly—I liked her. But I wish Hueffer wouldn't introduce me as a genius. When a fellow hasn't enough money to buy a decent pair of boots, and not enough sense to borrow or steal a pair, he's ticketed 'genius' as a last resource: just as they call things 'very desirable' when nobody on earth wants them.[13]

Ford ticketed Lawrence in an even more uncomfortable way after reading the manuscript of *The Trespasser* (then called 'The Saga of Siegmund'). As Lawrence explained to Edward Garnett, Ford called it 'a rotten work of genius. It has no construction or form—it is execrably bad art, being all variations on a theme. Also it is erotic—not that I personally mind that, but an erotic work *must* be good art, which this is not.' He advised him that it might damage his reputation to publish it in that form; Lawrence worked on it for a further two years before publishing it. Though they remained friends, and Ford continued to help Lawrence with publishers, both men realized the irreconcilability of their views of art. When Ford left for Germany later that summer Lawrence felt abandoned, and began transferring his loyalty to Edward Garnett. Ford, he said, 'left me to paddle my own canoe. I *very* nearly wrecked it and did for myself. Edward Garnett, like a good angel, fished me out.'[14]

When Ford heard that Constance Garnett was worrying about her son David's education, he wrote (according to David): 'Send him to me for a few years, Connie, and I will teach him to write like Flaubert.' 'This offer was not considered seriously,' wrote Garnett, 'and I missed the opportunity of becoming a feather in Ford's cap.' But then Ford invited him to South Lodge, promising to take him to call on the zoologist Professor Adam Sedgwick. They left 'in a hired open carriage to leave cards and make formal calls [. . .] Ford with his top hat upon his knee, Violet Hunt, all veils and tocque and parasol beside him'. In retrospect Garnett thought their behaviour 'peculiar, as it positively invited gossip and scandal among the censorious'. But he said Hunt 'had something of the Elizabethan pirate in her'. She was 'a thin viperish-looking beauty with a long pointed chin and deep-set, burning brown eyes under hooded lids. There was a driving force within her,' Garnett wrote, 'which I afterwards recognised as insatiable ambition.' While he and Ford waited for Hunt to leave a card Ford said to him: 'You feel shy, David, but when I was your age, I was so shy that I would crawl through the hedge rather than pass a labourer on the road and have to reply, if he said it was a fine day, when he passed me. It's terrible feeling shy, but you get over it in time.' 'I don't think Ford had completely got over it that afternoon,' said Garnett, 'but Violet had made up her mind to drag him around Kensington and he could not stop her.' In June he inscribed a copy of *The Portrait* to her with a quotation from the novel's ending, including the speech: 'you have played with me as if I were a fish upon a hair line, & here I am!'[15]

Later in the summer of 1910 Hunt suggested a trip to Germany, partly to reinstate Ford with his relations, partly to escape from the claustrophobia and gossip of London society. To preserve the appearance of respectability for the German family she took a chaperone, Lita Brown, the woman who had married Oswald Crawfurd. They took a boat up the Rhine, eating, sleeping, and writing on board, and going ashore at Cologne to dine. A room had been booked at Assmanshäusen, where they stayed, visiting Tante Emma and cousin Mimi in nearby Boppard. David Garnett visited Boppard, where he was invited to meet Frau Goesen:

An ancient dame lay in a bath-chair and Ford was standing beside her. According to Violet Hunt, Ford and she had left London because of his debts. No doubt a good proportion were to his tailor, for he was exquisitely turned out in a summery tweed suit, with a mourning band on his arm, thoroughly well brushed and shaved, with grey spats and a scented handkerchief; infinitely better dressed than any German in Boppard and he was genially making agreeable conversation, with a tea-cup in his hand and showing the rabbit teeth in his shark's mouth.[16]

They invited Garnett to visit them at Assmanshäusen, where Ford and David had their photograph taken in front of the Germania monument, then strolled along the banks of the river from Rüdesheim. 'Ford, in the most excellent spirits, began to tell me stories', wrote Garnett, fondly recalling the outrageous magic of Ford's humorous, fantastical romances upon history:

'My family has lived hereabouts, *you know*, for very many centuries, probably from the time of Charlemagne. When I was a small boy I used to go and stay with my grandmother, who lived in a house on the end of the bridge, by the fortress of Ehrenbreitstein. They used to send me upstairs to play by myself in the attics. And those attics were full of *hats*. There were hats there of every size and shape and of all periods in German history—from the slashed cockscombs of the Minnesängers, right down to the eighteenth-century three-cornered hats and top hats and panamas.
  '*You see* my family had the hereditary right to stop anyone who crossed the bridge and ask for his hat. Bismarck put an end to it when they asked him for his. But, of course, most of the hats were military. *You see*, the *Grande Armée* crossed that bridge in 1812 on the way to Russia: no wonder the attics were full of shakos!'

It is typical of the way Ford cocooned himself in elaborate and mystifying narrative. Ford's German grandmother had died three years before he was born (though Garnett may have misremembered 'grandmother' for great aunt). Yet he was visiting his German relatives when he was 5, and may well have been elaborating on a true memory.[17] Either way, the story is as delightful for its sheer implausibility as for its precise detail: the imagination of the historical novelist is idling, spinning tales to entertain a sympathetic listener, to make him *see* a vivid impression of childhood wonder.

Mrs Crawfurd was 'anxious to get back to the hectic joys of her cure', so by at least the end of August she, Ford, and Hunt moved on to Nauheim, the spa town Ford was to use as the main setting for *The Good Soldier*. Hunt described some of the characters they met there, indicating that they became *The Good Soldier*'s characters: Count Lelöffel, one of the 'favourite officers of the Kaiser'; or the regnant grand duke of Hesse-Darmstadt, who resembled Edward VII, and appears in the novel as the grand duke of Nassau Schwerin. Tsar Nicholas II was staying at Friedberg, and would bring his family the three miles to Nauheim every day. Bomb outrages were feared: 'He went in danger of his life so obvious', wrote Hunt, 'that the craven and unbusinesslike municipality of Friedberg had insisted on his insuring the public monuments of that place at his own expense.'[18]

Early in the year Ford had written two essays for *Harper's* reminiscing about the Pre-Raphaelites. He was in a train near Nauheim when he read in a newspaper of the death of Holman Hunt on 7 September. He wrote an obituary essay immediately for the *Fortnightly*, beginning with a description of how the dazzling colours of the landscape composed a Pre-Raphaelite scene, in which Ford read about the death of 'the father of English Pre-Raphaelism'. 'I do not know whether there was something telepathic about Nature that she gave this brave Pre-Raphaelite show in Hesse-Nassau to frame for me an announcement that called up images so distant and so dim of a painter—of a set of painters who in their own day decided to do the thing well.' That 'set of painters' of course included his grandfather and his mother. The mention of 'telepathy' hints at a communication from the ghost of Madox Brown, that other 'father of English Pre-Raphaelism'. The German announcement (which Ford prints and translates) about this dead 'father' also hints at Ford's own father. The stirring of these familiar spirits stirred Ford to write more essays on his Pre-Raphaelite ancestry, which were incorporated into the volume *Ancient Lights*. As always, his reminiscences sprang from an elegiac impulse.[19]

Ford and Hunt took a fortnight's holiday at his favourite German hotel, the Hotel Zum Ritter at Marburg. There Ford became enthusiastic about the 'cinematograph', and they sat in the most popular cafe, Marchesi's, with a view down over the River Lahn. Then Hunt fell ill, and felt she was 'bleeding to death'; but she postponed the operation she needed because she had to return to London to attend to her mother's affairs—while she had been sailing up the Rhine her sisters had had Mrs Hunt certified as senile, and had taken legal action against Violet over her handling of her mother's finances. So she got the German doctor to 'mend' her up; and Ford dictated the end of *Ancient Lights* to her as she recuperated in bed. But she 'fell foul' of the phrase in the last chapter in which he imagines himself happy in London, and says, 'I will have upon my arm some one that I like very much'. It's not clear whether Violet detected and resented a suggestion that this person might not be her, or whether it was the word 'like' rather than 'love' that infuriated her.[20]

Ford had decided to stay in Germany. Tante Emma, now the head of the family, had suggested that he might acquire German nationality, in which case he might have been able to divorce Elsie under German law. Emma refused to receive Hunt until she was Ford's wife, though Cousin Mimi was prepared to meet her on neutral territory as a token of her affection for Ford. Lita Crawfurd knew a 'clever' lawyer at Giessen, called Ludwig Leun. 'The dear conceited Germans', wrote Violet to René Byles:

do not allow a whimsical father by one rash act to deprive his children of the inestimable advantage of German citizenship, and the Government makes it as easy as possible for them to resume it. They have only to *se donner la peine* of acquiring domicile and getting the burgomasters of some particular German town to accept them as persons likely to be good townsfellows and rich enough to pay their rates regularly.[21]

This was the plan they followed—disastrously. More than a year later Ford had not been able to resume German nationality, so he assumed it. Tired of seemingly interminable legal complications, he returned to England and claimed that he had divorced Elsie and married Violet. In retrospect the entire scheme appears ill-conceived and ill-conducted. But given the prevailing morality of the day, the pressure to seek a divorce was irresistible. Neither wanted to flout convention enough to damage Ford's children, or to jeopardize Violet's chances of keeping her mother living at South Lodge. But Elsie's determination not to divorce meant that if they lived together openly in London they would be flouting convention and alienating their society friends. They could not live together openly in Germany either. Besides the surveillance of burgomasters, there was the watchful eye of the wealthy family they did not want to risk alienating for a second time. The plan to establish Ford's German nationality at least gave them the opportunity to act, and the possibility of a solution to an intractable problem. And there were precedents. Holman Hunt had married his sister-in-law in Switzerland (it was forbidden under English law) after his wife's death. A closer analogy was the case of Sir Hubert Herkomer, portrait painter, Slade Professor at Oxford, and RA, who also wanted to marry his sister-in-law, so resumed the German nationality he had relinquished when he became a British naturalized subject.[22]

Even if Ford had been able to get a German divorce, he would still have been married to Elsie under English law. There was also the problem that, as Hunt explained to him, 'a German marriage would not be *socially* admitted here—none of the kind of people I liked would know me—and my old friends themselves, though sticking to the German Mrs. H. would have to be careful whom they asked to meet her'. She was getting contradictory advice. One friend urged her: 'Go it! & tell no one, justify yourselves to no one—let them rave! and expect about half your friends to stick to you.' Whereas their friend the novelist Mrs W. K. Clifford warned her that by the next spring 'not a single house would be open' to them. 'Well, I can bear it', she told Ford. But Hunt's copies of some of her letters to Ford in Germany (if that is what they are, and not the kind of retrospective reworkings she sometimes added to her diaries) explain how they hoped they could avoid having to bear ostracism or exile. They knew it would no longer be possible to keep Hunt's name out of any divorce proceedings. 'No dear, I won't defend a case if E. brings one', she told him: 'I can't. It would make it get into the papers and she is bound to have enough evidence by now.' Her trepidation suggests what a formidable opponent Elsie must have been: 'It would be a nightmare to me if I thought I had to stand up to her!' Nevertheless, they hoped that if Ford could establish German nationality he could then stop alimony payments as a way of pressuring Elsie into an agreement: if she would then grant him a divorce, he would promise her an allowance. 'I had thought of something like your plan, and I think it good,' Hunt told him, 'but it all hangs surely on whether Elsie continues to have a *legal* claim on you for alimony. If she has, surely it will be no good offering her the same sum as a bribe to let the divorce go cheap. As long as she can keep you out of England, make you spend £150 in costs, and get the £150 as well as soon as you care to come back here—she will.'[23] Since Ford never did serve her with legal papers demonstrating German nationality or divorce, that is exactly what she did. When Hunt heard she had been ' "raising" it' against Ford, and conducting a 'campaign of lies' about Ford treating her 'shamefully', she told him: 'Elsie will, I think, succeed in ruining us *socially*. No matter—we can both write.' 'I think Mrs. H. prefers injury to redress—that she can get rid of you & get her allowance in a moment if she chooses but prefers to be a martyr and ruin you.' Hunt did have the imaginative sympathy, however, to think that Elsie wouldn't release her hold on Ford because she still loved him. 'Only Elsie can injure where she loves, and I couldn't, she added, showing herself a better romantic novelist than a prophet.[24]

At the end of September Ford saw Hunt as far as Cologne, where they had a loving parting at the station, then went back to Giessen, where he took lodgings at 29 Nordanlage: two rooms, cluttered with 'about two hundred and fifty ornaments, ranging from bits of coral like human brains, to gilded busts of Lohengrin'. The landlady 'appeared to be a deaf mute, and had bad teeth'. 'Mrs. Braun was no cook', wrote Hunt. 'When there was fish it was so bad that, not to hurt her pride, the author would put it in a drawer and forget it. His mother found these proofs of good-feeling among his shirts when she came to stay there.' Ford threw himself into the project with gusto. He saw his lawyer, Leun, regularly, and was soon directing some of his novelistic energies towards the complexities of the law:

Just playing at law was a relaxation from the stern professional necessity of finding [. . .] *les mots justes*, and plenty of them. The wild-cat schemes, absurd solutions of the insoluble, incredible lapses, quick changes, like the permutations of a shilling shocker, that this artist liked to put up! He was determined to get—he could not help getting—the fierce ancestral colours—Brunonian madder red and vandyke brown—always into his plots, schemes, and books.[25]

After the plotting and scheming surrounding the *English Review*, Giessen soon became intolerably dull for Ford. Staying in Germany had at first felt like an escape; now it was like being marooned. Hunt too was 'appalled' when he told her Leun had said the naturalization might take eighteen months. 'I know it's ruinous to love me—it's tragic,' she replied, 'and you suffer so for it. It is awful—this exile—this Giessen—this dreary life you lead. Won't it spoil your writing?' It didn't. He was writing hard: *Ladies Whose Bright Eyes* was sent to Pinker on 13 November. Hunt called it 'superlative', and wrote: 'I think you are more than ever a genius—What a wonderful creature I have got to love me.' *Ancient Lights* was also completed this year (and Hunt said she gave it too its title), then Ford began writing *Women & Men*. But he was seeking pretexts to leave stolid Giessen as often as possible. The 'petty oppressions of a German principality' were becoming as infuriating as they had been to the playwright Georg Büchner, who was maddened by Giessen as a medical student there in 1833. Children would let off percussion caps outside Ford's window, or would climb on the railings, grinning in at him to shout '*Tag! Engländer!*' There were visits to see Schücking at Marburg, and to lecture to his students at Jena.[26]

When Violet had her operation in England, Mary Martindale sent Ford a telegram, and he made a brief trip, incognito, to be with her in the nursing home when she came round from the anaesthetic. The operation was probably a 'D and C', either due to the onset of menopause or to complications from syphilis. Ford must have known about the latter by this time, since when she had to have a tooth extracted because of an abscess she wrote to him: 'Can it be true what he [the dentist] hints at, that it may be because of the spots, and the lip, and the sore throat I always wake with?' 'I am all right,' she tried to reassure him, 'a toothless old crone. (2 gaps).' That note of anxiety over physical degeneration became insistent. 'What a disgusting piecemeal decaying thing a body is!—all while you live it goes on', she wrote: 'I die daily.' 'Dear darling, do you like my letters?', she asked. 'Aren't they like myself, patchy and scrappy, and altogether wild and disconcerting?' Lawrence (whose mother had just died) wrote to her to commiserate when he heard that she had 'had a break-down': 'I really am sorry that you should be played all out of tune, like a cruelly handled violin.' She had appreciated the play he had sent her to read, *The Widowing of Mrs. Holroyd*, but Ford had 'accused' him of 'Dostoieffskyism—it is an accusation, for all the dear cranky Russian's stuff is as insane as it can be'. Hunt recovered slowly, and her haemorrhages recurred. 'I am afraid it will happen again just about when I go to you', she wrote to Ford. 'Then you'll have a wife and not a wife.' On one of the ten days he was in England he went to St Leonards-on-Sea, next to Hastings, to visit his daughters in their latest school, the Convent of the Holy Child. It was the last time he was to see them until 1916, when he was preparing to go to fight in France.[27]

Back at Giessen he was missing his English literary contacts. When his friend Edgar Jepson wrote to him to keep him abreast of the latest literary gossip—about H. G. Wells, who had been ostracized by conservative society after the previous year's scandals of his novel *Ann Veronica* and his affair with Amber Reeves; and about Ford himself—Ford wrote one of his funniest letters for Jepson to read out at a Square Club dinner; a virtuoso self-dramatization in a scintillating multiplicity of roles:

Your letter made me glad, glad, glad! [. . .] I am glad that H.G. is troubling so many dovecotes; but I do not agree with you that his end will be blood. I think it will either be a country-house with a Tory Seat attached to it. Or else it will be the chains and straw of Bedlam [. . .] Good Lord, I remember years ago advising H.G. not to be afraid of using personalities in his work—to sacrifice all the scruples to the desire to be vivid. What a dangerous animal I begin to think myself. Mr. Jepson, sir, I am a high minded Idealist, sans peur et sans reproche. You are on the other hand an unprincipled villain. I have never, that is to say, been able to discover in your writings or in your conversation one word that showed you to be possessed of any principles whatever. I do not believe that if the Daily News knew what you really are that they would permit the pure-souled Scottie [Scott-James] to put his knees for one moment under the same table with you. Under, I mean, the bounties and the sparkling wit that adorn the round mahogany of the Square Club (This sentence has gone slightly astray because my secretary being unacquainted with the real deep mysteries of the English tongue has introduced some words that I did not intend and that I will not cross out because I hate the sight of erasures upon a page. But you will understand, who search all hearts).

I am glad your Non-Conformist friends so loved me. When you—the unscrupulous villain, and I, the pure-souled Idealist join forces how *that* dovecote will flutter! And I see no reason why you should desire to cut my throat, blast my reputation, reveal what you think to be my secrets or throw vitriol upon me. I never discovered your first work, offered you shelter, food, clothing or encouragement when you were starving. I never lent you money, wrote in praise of your writing or committed against you any of the twenty-seven Nonconformist Deadly Sins.

I am glad too that May Sinclair has put me into a book. The last person who did it was the brother of William James [. . .] Sir, it is my intention to deliver that paper. I should be glad to take the chances of vitriol. It cannot be delivered from any instrument of precision and the fun would be huge. Please thank Mrs. Jepson: Yes I will soon be supping with you again. I am, thank you, well, prosperous and occupied. With my right hand I am writing a history of cholera in Ireland; with my left an historical novel dealing with the divorce of Anne Boleyn, using it as a peg on which to hang many disquisitions on Divorce in general. My feet are dealing with the treadles of a type-writing machine that pours out the history of literature in England during the last two years, whilst my eyes are engaged in perusing the material for my gigantic life of Sejanus. Good bye; may you occupy the blind spot in the eyes of God. Then you will prosper.[28]

Mizener oddly cites the passage about betrayal by disciples as illustrating Ford's state of mind seven or eight months earlier, just before going to prison. Out of context it sounds like the paranoid diatribe Mizener makes of it, calling it an example of 'Lear-like irony'. But the context is that Ford is responding to an invitation to deliver a paper. It was evidently Jepson who mentioned the possibility that Ford might provoke even him into a vitriolic attack. What is remarkable about Ford's letter is how it certainly draws upon some of his rawest feelings of isolation, betrayal, frantic activity, doubts about his own scrupulous-ness as an artist and as a sexual being, about using the personalities of others as characters in his own books, and about being so used himself in others' books, about social and artistic conformity (the letter contrasts the avant-garde coterie of the Square Club with the 'Royal British Academy of Letters'). But it masters those feelings by dramatizing them *ad absurdam*, purging them, and turning them into unnervingly sharp comedy. It is characteristic of the way energies of paranoia and pathos charge rather than exhaust his creativity—as his loyal artist-friends like Wells, Pound, and Galsworthy understood.[29]

When Hunt was well enough in December she travelled to Spa, in Belgium, where Ford joined her. On New Year's Day they heard mass, kneeling over the tomb of Charlemagne in the cathedral of Aix-la-Chapelle. In Liége they 'nearly bought a lion's cub out of a travelling booth'.[30] At Giessen the legal delays multiplied. Hunt took Ford to Paris to try to reinstate him with cousin Hermann Hüffer. The rich banker approved of *her*, she thought, but he still did not approve of Ford's attempts to get divorced, for which he never forgave him. He was sceptical about Ford's attempt to become a German citizen 'without having fulfilled the military or other duties' required. He was pompous enough to rebuke Ford's style: 'Be more correct in your expressions', he told him. When Elsie had panicked after Ford wrote to her lawyer, Sturges, explaining his intentions, Hermann advised Elsie to 'wait quietly' until he could actually prove he had succeeded by serving a writ on her. He added shrewdly: 'I do not see how Ford should desire to become a German, and thus possibly ruin his career as an English author.' (This turned out to be prophetic, not of this attempt to achieve German nationality, but of the second time Ford left England—for good—in the 1920s.) Hunt told the story of how, while Ford was looking for lodgings in Giessen he had seen a deer penned up in the hotel yard, being fattened for the table. He bought the deer alive (for £2. 10s., Violet was probably piqued to note), 'hired a cart, took him to the Hunnen Grabe beyond the town, and let him bound away to the forest'. She felt the deer to be as apt a symbol for her life as Ford meant it as one for his: 'I lived like that deer, vulnerable, prodded at, shot at. . . .' Ford was feeling the loss of his children: 'Fate was very hard on him,' wrote Hunt, 'first the Review, then the children. After that January of 1911 I do not think he ever smiled much again.' He was to smile with other partners and friends; but his relationship with Hunt was to become increasingly fraught.[31]

1911: 'ART IS VERY BITTER'

One's literary life must turn frequently for sustenance to memories and
seek discourse with the shades.

(Conrad, 'A Familiar Preface' to *A Personal Record*)

Early 1911 saw the publication of two books which, taken together, bring out
Ford's duality: *The Simple Life Limited* and *Ancient Lights*. The former, which has
been described as 'a hilarious *roman à clef*', might seem to have little to do with
the latter, Ford's first volume of reminiscences, a poignant and spirited testimony
to, and elegy for, the nineteenth century. Yet both bear witness to Ford's need,
and his ability, to rise from the ashes of his past life, and to salvage his new life
from the wrecks of friendships.

The Simple Life Limited is Ford's farewell to Limpsfield and the Romney
Marsh, to his days with Elsie and amongst the Garnett circle of Fabians and
anarchists, and to his life in the country. The denouement—in which the émigré
Cyril Brandetski goes berserk, tries to shoot the impresario Everard, and then sets
fire to the Simple Lifers' colony—sounds fantastical, but seems less so given the
history of the Garnetts' circle, as so vividly recounted in Richard Garnett's
biography of his grandmother. In 1893 Constance's brother, Arthur Black, killed
his wife, his son, and then himself with a combination of a knife, revolver, coal-
hammer, and chloroform. In 1895 the Stepniaks moved to a cottage near the
Chart Woods, to be near the Garnetts. They were 'encumbered with some
Russian Armenians' who had escaped from the Turkish massacres, a poet, Avetis
Nazarbek, and his family, who arrived speaking no English. David Garnett said
that 'various humanitarian ladies of Limpsfield [. . .] were eager to hear these
terrible tales at first hand', and wanted to raise a subscription for them, until his
wife started accusing them of 'offering her husband money in order to enjoy
carnal intercourse with him'. Stepniak's mysterious death occurred that autumn.
Two years later Constance and Edward stayed with the Nazarbeks. But the
Armenians' 'uncouth bodyguards, who casually helped themselves to their
neighbours' fences for firewood, made themselves so unpopular,' wrote David
Garnett, that if their landlord-farmer had not turned them out, 'there might have
been a massacre of Armenians in the weald of Kent, at a time when Mr Gladstone
was still thundering against the unspeakable Turk'. Then, in 1901, the Garnetts'
hired man Bill Hedgecock 'went mad at the Cearne and had to be taken to the
infirmary as a criminal lunatic'. It's not clear what actually happened, but

Constance and David had to escape to Fanny Stepniak's house, and in the novel David wrote about it, *Beany-Eye*, the labourer besieges the house, battering on the doors with an axe, and throwing the dogs into the air. None of these particular events went into *The Simple Life Limited*, but their cosmopolitan atmosphere of volatility, frenzy, and absurdity did.[1]

The 'Daniel Chaucer' pseudonym is a further example of Ford's tendency to provoke reprisals through his joking. ' "Daniel Chaucer" is, we suspect, not so much a name as a *nom de guerre*,' wrote one reviewer, 'veiling the personality of an accomplished satirist who is probably by no means unknown to literary fame.' Ford's intimates would have had little difficulty in recognizing traits of themselves and of their satirist: the book is as much an act of self-revelation as of disguise. Moser suggests that Olive Garnett thought it was 'scandalous' because she saw the hysterical Cyril Brandetski as Ford's portrait of her adored Stepniak, and the 'tactless, strident, puritanical, outraged' Miss Stobhall as herself. Of course Ford may have used the pseudonym because he feared that one of his targets would sue for libel. He may have wanted to evade his contract with Constable. Or he may simply have wanted to disguise his productivity, lest people thought he was publishing too much. He also enjoyed the sheer fictionality of the enterprise, writing a 'Daniel Chaucer' letter to Hunt, but for the publisher, John Lane, setting forth the autobiography of 'a quiet country gentleman of ancient but impoverished lineage'.[2]

In the novel, Simon Brandson, *né* Simeon Brandetski, the author of *Clotted Vapours*, ineluctably calls Conrad to mind; Parmont, the weary critic who discovered him, is based on Edward Garnett. Moser rightly says the book 'fulfils a need beyond revenge'; but instead of expressing the 'profound self-loathing' he diagnoses, it uses the form of satire, including self-satire, to try to understand the rupture with Conrad. Moser is also right to say that the most Fordian character, Horatio Gubb, Brandson's disciple, is one of the least sympathetic of the characters. But what makes the book truly novelistic, rather than a satirical critique of the corrupt utopianism of the Simple Lifers, is the way it makes the eventual row between Brandson and Gubb fully dramatic, revealing both the strengths and weaknesses, the insights and the blindnesses of each. It is neither self-exculpation nor self-condemnation, but an attempt to portray both sides of an irresolvable conflict. Gubb's vanity is exposed: 'a vanity so great that he looks upon the truth as something to be manipulated, and people as objects to be exploited.'[3]

Yet these criticisms are made most forcefully by Brandson, who is presented as himself manipulative and exploitative. Neither are immune from the charge of parasitism: Gubb gives Brandson money, but is himself exploiting the Simple Life Colony for profit. Brandson is lazy and mentally unstable, and Gubb believes that 'Men whose brains have once been touched never escape again' (p. 240). In part, that is a prescient sketch of the fate looming for Conrad, struggling with *Under Western Eyes* to the verge of breakdown when he rowed with Ford. But of course it is also Ford's voicing of a fear that he too is entering another phase of breakdown, and that he will never be free from the danger of insanity. It is at this point that it becomes futile to think of the book as only, or even as significantly, a *roman à clef*, its complex drawings upon the characters and situations of his intimates serve quite other purposes than satire, purposes of psychological investigation and presentation—trying to make real and to make interesting a human configuration. As in most of Ford's fictions, it becomes impossible to produce a 'key' that will unlock the book and release its biographical secrets, because of the sheer multiplicity of biographical clues. None of the major characters 'represents' a single real person: they each display traits of several people. If Brandson is Conrad, he is also Ford; yet his prose poetry is Ford's splendid parody of the Pre-Raphaelite archaisms, the mouthing of long 'o's and 'a's, of Rossetti and William Morris—the writers of the very milieu he was remembering with nostalgia and affection in *Ancient Lights*:

> Oh, Ulalume lost! . . . Girl of the grey
> eyes and the milk-white feet: no more beside
> the love rath nor upon the lorn hillside shall
> thy silver hand beckon me to pursuit—

It is perhaps also a further dig at Garnett (from another angle than his parody as Parmont) whose prose-poems Ford called 'a Celtic protest against the tautological dullness of his decasyllabic predecessors'.[4] Similarly, Gubb in his role as Brandson's benefactor and apprentice looks like Ford; he is saturated with Brandson's phrases, as Ford may have felt anxious about the influence of Conrad's literary personality. But Horatio Gubb, with his Don Juan tendencies, 'his resemblance to a "Sunfish in outline" ', his illegitimate child, his lack of a classical education, and his persistent, if hypocritical, socialist politics recalls Wells—H. G. to his friends.[5]

The most sympathetic character, Gerald Luscombe, is a Marwoodian Tory squire, good-humouredly aloof from the frenetic propagandizing and self-deception of the Simple Lifers. When he had felt obliged to believe Elsie's allegations against Marwood, Ford had not been able to face his friend, yet once he had become finally estranged from her he sought to repair the breach with Marwood, calling on him early in 1912 with Violet Hunt. *The Simple Life Limited* could itself be read as an attempt to restore the friendship. Ford's way of doing this is not simply to present a sympathetic portrait of Marwood; for Luscombe is also highly Fordian—the Dr Jekyll to Gubb's Hyde. Thus, the novel is something much more intricate than an expression of self-loathing; it is an attempt to reconcile the contradictory elements of character; to bring together the unstable charlatan, the vain manipulator, and the magnanimous gentleman. This interfusing of real characters to form the novel's characters again provokes but resists biographical speculations. It also expresses Ford's views on character and imaginative sympathy. Mizener pays little attention to *The Simple Life Limited*, devoting much more space to *The New Humpty-Dumpty*, the more vitriolic of the 'Daniel Chaucer' satires, and more visibly a work of self-justification. The combination of favourable and unfavourable self-portraits would not suit his view of Ford as someone who is most concerned to present 'improved', flattering versions of himself. *The Simple Life Limited* shows that this is a travesty of Ford's creative processes. Like most novelists, he has something in common with all his characters—how else would he be able to create them? Instead of reading the novel as Ford's 'saying' that he is 'really' like Luscombe-Marwood (as the Mizenerian view might have it), or that he is 'really' like Gubb (and thus an expression of self-hate, as the Moserian view has it), we should note the moral complexity that the fusion of identities produces. This fusion suggests that 'character' is not always the separate entity we need to assume. The novelist who specializes in analysing character-types knows how traits reproduce themselves from person to person, whether by imitation or by chance. A novelist such as Ford has, in addition, a professional interest in being able to recognize the similarities between himself and others: to see the Marwood in himself, the Conrad in himself, even the Wells and the Morris. This recognition of the other in the self is, as we shall see later, the ground of Ford's aesthetic of imaginative sympathy. Conversely, he saw the self in the other: the portrait of Brandson is something far more searching than a spiteful rejection of Conrad. It is the apprehension that what he now mistrusted in Conrad was also the danger for himself: a degeneration into his own mannerisms. Conrad had reproved Ford for letting lesser activities like editing the *English Review* or dramatizing *The Fifth Queen Crowned* displace his creative work. These things were 'the reckless wasting of your substance'. But Ford was also doubting whether his novels were adequately substantial.

The most distinctive feature of *The Simple Life Limited* is its equanimity of tone—a surprising achievement given that it was being written at the time of Elsie's restitution order and the ensuing publicity. As Ann Snitow writes, the clashes between Luscombe and the egotistical Lifers 'are mediated by a third voice':

Ford's voice as author, a voice that narrates the backgrounds and the real but hidden motives of the characters with the most unambivalent irony in all Ford's *oeuvre*. Here was a case in which, for once, Ford knew quite clearly where his sympathies lay—with the gentle, confused, but essentially sound Gerald Luscombes of this world—while at the same time he was distant enough from the cranks and monomaniacs of the Simple Life to feel a certain detached affection for them, too. His tone in the novel is a consistent and lighthearted irony that indicates tolerance, calm, and the confidence and settled conscience he so rarely felt in relation to his more upsetting subject matter elsewhere.[6]

But how is such poise possible in a novel which reimagines the highly upsetting subject-matter of Ford's break with Marwood and Conrad? The new-found tonal assurance is not the literary equivalent of deciding never to discuss these things again. But it is, as Snitow says, a matter of distance: a distance achieved through a therapeutic writing-out. The novel is characteristically Fordian because, despite the magnanimity of its mutuality—of Ford's feeling about most of the characters: 'There but for the grace of God go I'—it is none the less satire. It is hard to imagine Conrad forgiving Ford for putting so much of him into Brandson. To that extent the book continues their quarrel by other means. But it is also a truce with the past, an attempt to set the antagonisms of the last three years behind him. This is one reason why he was surprised when offence was taken at his provocations. By the time he had finished articulating them, he had calmed the animosities and anguishes that evinced them: *he* was equable now; what was the other fellow complaining about?

There are significant continuities between his impressions of the Pre-Raphaelites in *Ancient Lights* and the novel he had been writing at the same time, *Ladies Whose Bright Eyes*. In his dream-vision of living in the Middle Ages, Mr Sorrell *lives* the primacy of 'impression' over fact that *Ancient Lights* cherishes in the artists it celebrates, and announces in its own impressionism. The vivid hyper-reality of Sorrell's impression is itself a Pre-Raphaelite pastiche, an attempt to reimagine in words the medieval past Madox Brown and Rossetti painted, as well as a penetrating exploration of the status of the 'impression'. *Ancient Lights* was more than Ford's elegy for the Great Dead of the nineteenth century. It is also one of his elegies for himself. He dedicated it to his children as 'the best Christmas present I can give you'—he couldn't afford to give them much by way of material things at the time, though they also had necklaces Hunt made from the amber beads she had bought in a Marburg pawnshop. But, as he explains in the dedication, there is also 'the spiritual gift of heredity'. The book is such a gift to them ('Shock number two out of that book!', said Hunt, when she discovered it wasn't dedicated to her). The gift of heredity is also its subject: what Ford had inherited from his Pre-Raphaelite background, and what gifts he hoped to pass on to his children. He wanted to write his impressions because they were 'beginning to grow a little dim'. Anxiety that he would himself grow dim in their memory fused with anxiety about his eventual mortal disappearance. Imagining himself punished by death was perhaps a way of absolving his guilt. The book's own end extends the elegy, imagining his own death as representative of the death of the kind of literature he valued in an age that could not support a publication like the *English Review*. The last chapter, 'Where We Stand', contrasts the Pre-Raphaelite past with the present:

Life is very good nowadays; but art is very bitter. That is why, though the light whirls and blazes still over Piccadilly, this book has become a jeremiad. For upon the one side I love life. On the other hand, Hokusai in his later years was accustomed to subscribe himself: *The old man mad about Painting*. So I may humbly write myself down a man getting on for forty, a little mad about good letters. For the world is a good place, but the letters that I try to stand up for are about to die. Will any take their place? Who knows? But as for anything else, let me put down the words of the Ritter Olaf, who was also about to die. He had married the king's daughter and was to be beheaded for it when he came out of church. But he begged for his life until midnight so that he might dance amidst the torches of his bridal banquet.

There is a personal implication too. Identifying with Heine's Ritter Olaf, Ford suggests that he expects to be punished for his 'marriage' to Hunt ('Oh, violet eyes of my fair bride, | I die for you willingly!', runs the last stanza).[7] The fantasy that he was about to die became stronger over the next five years; and though, as here, it claims a specious pathos (as though *Ancient Lights* had been written under sentence of death), it also drove him to write *The Good Soldier*.

When *The White Peacock* came out early in 1911, Violet Hunt wrote to congratulate Lawrence, and tell him she had reviewed it in the *Daily Chronicle* (where she called it a 'political document developed along the lines of passionate romance'). Lawrence told her he had had a long letter from Ford, 'full of sage advice and ironical cynicism'. His response is marvellously revealing about the two authors' contrasting modes of exorcising their frustrations:

Mr Hueffer is really such a lot better fellow tha[n] he thinks he ought to be, to belong to this shabby frame of things. So he daubs his dove-grey kindliness with a villainous selfish tar, and hops forth a very rook among rooks: but his eyes, after all, remain, like the Shulamites, doves eyes. He makes me jolly mad. I think the ironic attitude, consistently adopted, is about as tiresome as the infant's bib which he says I wear for my mewling and puking—in other words, he says it, mind. Some things are jolly bad, and while we're afflicted, the best thing to do is to howl to the ever-attentive heavens—if we feel like it.[8]

Ford had told him that he too had reviewed the book. Lawrence joked that if it was the piece in the *Standard*, in what he called Ford's 'Jove-abdicated-in-disgust' tone, he'd never forgive him. Certainly the reviewer took Ford's view of Lawrence: 'There is nothing whatever about novel writing as an art that Mr Lawrence has not still to learn. At the same time there are an infinite number of things in this book that no rules or advice or lecture could ever teach him; it is a book of quite extraordinary promise and of no performance whatever.' Lawrence later told Walter de la Mare, 'you see I suffered badly from Hueffer re Flaubert and perfection'. Ford knew he couldn't recast Lawrence in his own image (that wasn't, as a critic or an editor, what he ever tried to do). 'I don't—and I didn't then—think that my influence was any good to him.' And it was largely because Lawrence made it clear that he didn't think he could learn anything more from him that they soon lost touch with each other. Yet Ford's influence was probably more significant than he acknowledged. As Lawrence's biographer John Worthen explains, it was probably because Ford had suggested that he should write from his knowledge of the mining community that he wrote his first play, *A Collier's Friday Night*, and the story 'Odour of Chrysanthemums'. Their subject-matter and use of dialect are almost unprecedented in his *œuvre*, but characterize his major subsequent work.[9]

By February Ford had also drafted most of *The New Humpty-Dumpty* (published on 9 July 1912). The working title was 'The Dark Forest', alluding to the tag Count Macdonald repeats throughout the book: 'The heart of another is a dark forest.'¹⁰ What he chiefly refers to by the phrase is the sinister reserve of bitterness, envy, hatred, treachery, and violence within apparently civilized conduct.

The fantastical plot follows Macdonald's key role in a counter-revolution in the imaginary state of Galizia—whose Spanish language and culture give it some affinity with the former kingdom of Galicia in the north-west of Spain, though Ford associated himself with the other, Polish-Austrian, district of the same name, when he claimed descent from barons who were 'Ruthenian Galicians'. The book is (as Mizener said) 'often entertaining in its *Prisoner of Zenda* way'. But Ford wasn't interested enough in the adventure story to make it more than a frame for the portrait of Macdonald. The fictional dedicatory letter, from the fictional author 'Daniel Chaucer' Ford was using once more, offers the book as the 'life of old Mac', written by a friend. In his dedicatory letter to *The Good Soldier* Ford was similarly to offer that story of Ashburnham's life, narrated by his friend Dowell, as Ford's novel about a (possibly fictional) friend of his. *The New Humpty-Dumpty* is significant for its anticipations of that better novel; and—due to what Ann Barr Snitow calls 'the psychologically interesting sort of badness that characterizes most of this novel'—because it is biographically perhaps the most revealing novel Ford wrote. Mizener called it 'a disguised account of the cultural counterrevolution he had attempted as editor of *The English Review* and of his personal experience as the lover of Violet Hunt'. It also gives us the closest insights in Ford's fiction into his relationship with Elsie. It is a painfully self-justifying book, whose heart 'is its representation of Elsie Martindale as the Countess Macdonald and of Ford himself as Count Macdonald, a noble, long-suffering, selfless man tormented by his wife's uncomprehending accusations'.¹¹

Count Sergius Mihailovitch Macdonald's physical appearance, his neurasthenic depressions at the 'many basenesses' of others, his 'unusually high sense of personal honour', are all primarily Ford's impressions of himself. But his Russian anarchist background recalls Soskice, or more probably Kropotkin. And his ancestor who claimed to be the legitimate king of Scotland shows that Ford was also thinking of Cunninghame Graham, who spoke alongside Kropotkin and Stepniak at open-air demonstrations in London during Ford's own anarchist youth, and whom Ford said he heard reply sardonically to a lady in Scotland, who thought he should be 'the first president of the British Republic': 'I ought, madam, if I had my rights [. . .] to be the king of this country. And what a three weeks that would be!'¹²

Knowing Macdonald's Fordian hatred of 'scenes', the Countess tries to make as many as possible. Hearing that Lady Aldington, with whom Macdonald has been inevitably but subliminally falling in love, is one of the backers of the plot to restore the deposed king, she spreads a rumour that he is living off his mistress's money. She entertains the Marwoodian Duke of Kintyre, also a backer, and then spreads another rumour that Macdonald was taking his friend's money as the price for letting him make love to his wife. As Ford felt he couldn't let

Marwood continue to finance the *English Review* after he had made advances to Elsie, so Macdonald tells Kintyre sadly that he can have nothing more to do with him: 'Never in this world'. ' "I don't bear you any ill will," he said. "I dare say you thought she was free." ' It is after this poignant parting (which would have been more so had the men's friendship been fully presented) that Lady Aldington comes running out in terror. Like Hunt, 'she thought he might have poisoned himself'. Kintyre later tells the Countess that he philandered with her to help Macdonald: 'But I see that it was a sort of suspect—an unpleasant position.' Marwood can't have had Ford's consent in making love to Elsie. But could he possibly have made his advances out of some such misguided motive of getting her interested in other men than Ford? Or was it just what Ford wanted to believe, or how he wanted to show Marwood he bore him no ill will?[13]

The Countess is a devastating portrait of Elsie, and it must have hurt her, and only hardened her resolve against Ford and Violet still further. Macdonald made her into a simple-life anarchic socialist; but whereas his views have developed into a Marwoodian paternalistic Toryism, hers have not. (She even still wears the green dress Elsie made, together with regulation Pre-Raphaelite amber beads.) She wants her husband back, but threatens to ruin him if he won't return. She suggests a legal separation in order to prevent him from remarrying. 'I shall bring a divorce action against him so as to show to the whole world what an abominable, dissolute creature he is', she says. 'And then when I've got the decree I shall never apply to have it made absolute. He'll never be free.' This was what Elsie had in fact done; though whether Ford actually thought she had out of this vituperative malice, or whether he was trying to show her how she would appear, isn't clear. His response is to get a Russian dissolution of their marriage (as Ford tried to get a German divorce). Macdonald is appalled at the way the Countess uses the naïve young American, Mamie Dexter, who is also infatuated with Macdonald, as an intermediary in their rows. Perhaps Ford felt this about Elsie's use of Edmée van der Noot as go-between; and perhaps Edmée was similarly susceptible to Ford. (This re-imagining of James's *What Maisie Knew* was to be re-imagined in turn as the way Leonora Ashburnham urges her young ward to offer herself to her husband.) It is an example of the human viciousness that 'troubled him beyond all reason':

He was perfectly ready to avow that his fellow-beings were wolves [. . .] But always at the bottom of his heart there was the feeling—it may have been part of his Russian blood or it may have been part of his English public-school training—the feeling that all humanity, if you could understand them, if you could get at them the right way, were at least as chivalrous as himself. That a Russian Czar or a royal bureaucracy should execute a hundred and fifty thousand political prisoners a year did not disturb this serene philosophy. For that was part of their game—of their particular political game, and as you would expect nothing else, it was neither dishonest nor disappointing [. . .]

And even from his Countess there was literally nothing that he didn't in the end expect. The trouble was that he just simply couldn't discover what her code of morals was. He never had been able to. He had at first taken her to be honourable, truthful, patient, with some sort of comprehension for humanity and particularly for himself. But one by one all these things went by the board. And, though he let it go at that, he couldn't arrive at any fixed standard whatever. She seemed perpetually to be breaking out in a new place. He couldn't have imagined that she would have been capable of sending Miss Dexter to him as she had done, and he couldn't have imagined that she could have been capable of leaving the girl in the lurch as she did. That sort of thing gave him such severe shocks as to render him really ill. His mind was too sensitive to stand it, and for the time being he would be deprived almost of his senses and of the power to control himself.[14]

This isn't very persuasive. The sentence about having taken her to be honourable, truthful, patient, and comprehending cries out to be taken autobiographically. But people fall out of love and patience and tolerance for each other, without necessarily being guilty of lacking ethical consistency. The desire to blame Elsie for his mental difficulties comes across overwhelmingly, and is similarly unrealistic. Of course, *The New Humpty-Dumpty* is a novel, not an autobiography. But Elsie and their mutual friends and acquaintances could not have failed to notice the parallels. The sheer cruelty of the implication that Ford now thought her dishonourable, dishonest, and uncomprehending indicates that he was also losing control of himself, and beginning to lapse from the very 'English public-school training' he so valued in Macdonald, whereby gentlemen don't talk about their private affairs in public, and don't defame others, especially women. (The defence here is the sexist one that she is unfeminine.) The failure of objectivity shows that he was still too much in the grip of his anger, frustration, and depression; that he had been 'deprived almost of his senses' of words and style. Which is not to say that he didn't suffer as Macdonald does.

There are, however, four main points to be set against this failure. First, that the portrait is vindictive doesn't prove it unjust. It was taken as 'viciously unjust' by Mizener in his pioneering reading of the book, influenced by Katharine's insistence that it didn't match the mother she remembered. Doubtless Elsie did not get vitriol to throw in her husband's face, as the Countess pursues hers to Galizia in order to do—she is only foiled because Macdonald has already been shot in the back by one of his own counter-revolutionists—though Ford claimed she did threaten him with a revolver, which the Countess wields and considers using on Macdonald. But otherwise, her determination to make life as difficult as possible for her husband corresponds to the Elsie seen by Olive Garnett and the Conrads, and even the determined girl who defied her equally determined parents to elope with Ford. It was Mizener himself who provided some of the most striking evidence for the accuracy of Ford's rendering of the Countess's destructive pride. When Elsie read Galsworthy's novel *Fraternity* (1909), she became convinced it was based on her marriage. Galsworthy's heroine, Bianca, deliberately destroys her marriage to Hilary because of his diffident attentions to a model. 'Her pride had kept her back from Hilary [. . .] she had led the way to utter estrangement', wrote Galsworthy: 'this tragedy of a woman, who wanted to be loved, slowly killing the power of loving her in the man, had gone on year after year.' Though, as Mizener says, Elsie had more provocation than Bianca, the fact that she behaved 'something like that', and that she recognized Bianca's feelings in herself, shows how much more of the Countess there was in Elsie than Katharine or Mizener would allow. Galsworthy wrote to her as soon as he heard, to deny the suggestion, saying that Ford had never said a word to him or to his wife about their domestic affairs.[15]

Secondly, though it's a bitter portrait, it is not uncomprehending or unsympathetic. There is something attractive about the sheer panache of the Countess's self-dramatization. But Ford is too good a novelist (and too understanding a human being) not to see the lonely suffering beneath the vengeful fury—as when she breaks down in front of Kintyre at the thought of her husband in love with another woman: 'her voice shook with painful sobs. "Wasn't it enough that I've lost all I had in the world? Wasn't it enough that they should meet?" ' Thirdly, it is intended as a warning to Elsie of the monomaniac Ford feared she would become if she wouldn't divorce him, sacrificing her own life and others' to her desire for revenge. The menace comes across in Kintyre's prophecy: 'No one will ever think of you [. . .] You're nothing. You're nobody. And yet you might be rather a lot.' Sadly, she did damage all their lives in fulfilling Ford's prophecy.[16]

Fourthly, in rendering the Macdonalds Ford is trying to understand himself. And struggling against the pressure of self-justification is an attempt to analyse the causes of his breakdowns or collapses; an expression of the fear that the sensitivity that is necessary to his art makes him incapable of acting as he feels he ought. Macdonald is his most subtle presentation yet of the altruist. There is a clearer grasp of the contradiction at the heart of Fordian altruism: the high ideals for humanity, set against the disdain for, and rage at, those particular humans who fall short of them. Macdonald's problem of not being 'able to arrive at any fixed standard' is also Ford's new crisis of fundamental, ontological scepticism. When (as Ford said happened to him) Macdonald's lawyer tells him he has to stop payments to his wife, he finds the legal interference in decent conduct 'obscene'. He is even more horrified when he thinks the Countess believes him capable of wanting to leave her to starve. He's not certain she does believe it, but he is also forbidden by the lawyer from writing to explain his motives, so that, 'in a Russian phrase, all his soul shivered on the brink of uncertainty'. When he hears the rumours about himself, he becomes feverish: 'He couldn't get away from the feeling that if the whole world considered that he was a *souteneur*, that he had taken money from Kintyre and from Lady Aldington, that he had left his wife to starve—that if the whole world said these things of him they must be true. So for several days he felt that he couldn't lift up his head, that he couldn't look anyone in the face.'[17] Ford felt like this over the restitution proceedings, and he was to feel it more during the *Throne* scandal. But it's not just that shame is in the cheek of the accused. There is also an anxiety about impressionist psychology: an artist who invests everything in the power of the word to make you believe, is also at the mercy of words, and thus unusually sensitive to criticism. The contradiction

Ford felt between his own sense of honour and the names the world was calling him had become intolerable. *The New Humpty-Dumpty* is split in two by Ford's uncertainty about whether he is upholding altruism or satirizing it. In *The Good Soldier* he was to make uncertainty the narrative mode, magnificently bringing out the complex contradictoriness of the central characters.

The novel exists to assert that the world has maligned Macdonald (and therefore Ford too). One by one, most of the characters except the Countess acknowledge that he is fundamentally a good man. Lady Aldington says he 'never thought an unworthy thought and never did an unworthy action. He is what you and I aren't, and what almost no one is to-day—he is chivalrous!' Snitow gives an ingenious reading of the book in terms of Ford's fairy-tale 'Bingel and Bengel', in which two boys are sent by their mother to gather wood, and each meet the same wood-dwarf with his beard caught in a cleft in the tree, crying for help. Bengel only helps him after he has made the dwarf promise him the pot of gold at the end of the rainbow. But Bingel helps him at once, for which the dwarf rewards him by tapping his chest, and telling him that now: 'Your heart is in the right place, and you will find that very useful.' He is the altruist to Bengel's materialist. Bengel is beaten by his mother for his mistakes, whereas Bingel is forgiven, because his heart's in the right place. 'I don't know that this story has a very good moral', writes Ford: 'but that is the way of the world. Some people cannot do anything at all without being most severely punished. But you can do anything whatever that you like, so long as people will say that about your heart. It's as well to make sure beforehand, though.' Snitow calls it 'a real spiritual autobiography telling the sort of truth about how Ford felt about himself', and saying that Ford 'is both Bingel and Bengel; he feels sorry for himself as Bengel and self-satisfied as Bingel'. Macdonald, she says, is a Bingel in a world of Bengels. What she says of the story is true of the novel too: that it expresses 'Ford's longing to be above reproach, to be seen by everyone as essentially honorable and good'. But both are more complex than she suggests by saying 'the world is often unkind and takes a stick to him unfairly, mistaking him for Bengel, but he is really Bingel'; for as she has said, he is really both, and recognizes the Bengel in himself, however much he would rather be true to Bingel's ideals. *The New Humpty-Dumpty* doesn't acknowledge the Bengel in Macdonald. It goes through the motions of judging him by the standard of a critical attitude, acknowledging that he is not 'in any way rational or coherent in his idealism', and that he can't 'go on being like a Jesus Christ' all his life. He even recognizes in himself, and tries to check, the 'mania for managing the universe' that irritated Conrad about Ford, when he says: 'It's not my business to keep the world in order.' But though these may be judged failings by the world's standards, Ford ultimately admires them as heroic. Most of his writing—especially *The Fifth Queen, The Good Soldier*, and *Parade's End*—springs from this anxiety about the noble protagonist maligned by the world. But in those works the uncertainty is a real one; and our eventual faith in the goodness of Katharine Howard and Henry VIII, Edward Ashburnham, and Christopher Tietjens is earned by the way Ford confronts rather than sentimentalizes 'the dark forest' of motive, by the way he doesn't shrink from rendering the Bengel qualities that provoke the world's abuse, but strips away both that abuse and the desire for self-exculpation, leaving an essential sympathy for human contradictoriness. The ambiguity comes across when Macdonald asks: 'what have I done to get mixed up in this sort of loathsome business?' His cry from the heart hovers between the childish implication that he hasn't done *anything* to deserve such punishment, and a realization that, though his motives were honourable, they have made him responsible for dishonour and suffering.[18]

The New Humpty-Dumpty does acknowledge the Bengel in Ford, though, in oblique ways that show the novel to be much more complex and honest than a mere satirical swipe at those he felt had betrayed him, as it is according to Mizener's reading of Ford's psychology. As Mizener wrote to Rebecca West, in a more direct expression of his attitude than one finds in his book:

Ford habitually dreamed up a vision of a brilliant success (as for example with *The English Review*) in which he modestly played with astonishing insouciance a brilliant role and everyone else played parts that supported him in this role. Then, when the reality differed from his dream, he looked about for Judases, revising in his imagination the perfectly ordinary conduct of others until half a dozen of them fitted that part.[19]

Well, yes, an obviously fictional book like *The New Humpty-Dumpty* indeed revises in his imagination the conduct of real people. But Ford was not the naïve fantasist this implies, not least because, more Marwoodianly cynical than Macdonald, he expected failure; indeed, at an unconscious level he needed it as much as success. *The New Humpty-Dumpty* is itself an example of this need: an extraordinarily self-destructive book to publish, since it could only intensify the animosities it lamented. But then, self-destructiveness is one of the dangers in the dark forest the book explores.

The New Humpty-Dumpty's exploration of Ford's own 'dark forest' comes out in two ways. First, he divides himself between characters. It isn't only the Macdonalds' unhappy marriage that reflects the Hueffers'; the Aldingtons are also divorcing. And in Lord Aldington Ford portrays all the characteristics people most mistrusted, and that he most feared in himself. He married his wife for her fortune, forges her cheques, is a philanderer, keeps mistresses, is a cruel cynic. Everyone calls him a brute. He manages to summon up the decency to free his wife when she wants to marry Macdonald. But otherwise he is a savage self-indictment, which shows how affected Ford was by the things people said about him.[20]

Secondly, there is some justification for Hunt's claim that the characters are 'composite' in this book that she said she helped with, rather than portraits of particular individuals. Aldington is one example, since, as Moser shows, Ford gave him Marwood's appearance and background, and it was probably Marwood's resentment of this portrait that made him so angry over the novel. Marwood was simply too ill to be a philanderer on Aldington's scale; but the character suggests Ford still resented Marwood's advances to Elsie, even while he was forgiving him in his aspects of the loyal Duke of Kintyre or of Macdonald himself. Ford multiplies his divided *self*-portraits in a similar way, projecting aspects of himself not only into Aldington and Macdonald, but even where one might least expect it. This is even true of his bitterest portrait, that of Herbert Pett, a savage caricature of Herbert George Wells. Pett is an egotistical cockney, an authority on chemistry (which Wells studied), a 'thinker' who believes in the machine. As Ford predicted of Wells when Wells began to introduce his notion of a 'Samurai'-style élite into his Fabian socialism, Pett has reneged on his political beliefs to become what Rebecca West called a 'Nietzschean Tory' (but then, of course, so has Macdonald). Worse still, he has betrayed Macdonald, who made over his fortune to him (as Ford had felt Wells's benefactor when serializing him in the *Review*). Pett has an even worse mania than Macdonald's to manage everything. Only, having claimed the credit for others' ideas, he then backs out of his commitments, as Ford felt Wells had done over the *Review* (whereupon Macdonald has to deal with Mrs Pett, as Ford did with 'Jane' Wells). He is a philanderer who has an outburst of shrieking hysterics when he realizes that Lady Aldington thinks Macdonald the better man, and who spreads the Countess's rumours about him (as Ford felt Wells was jealous of his success with Wells's former mistress, Violet Hunt, and felt Wells had 'gossiped maliciously to Pinker and others' about them. While Ford was in Germany, Hunt fuelled his bitterness towards Wells, telling him Wells had implied he was still claiming money for *Tono-Bungay*, and adding: 'He is a worm that lies.'). Pett becomes so enraged that he irresponsibly persuades his fellow conspirators that Macdonald must be killed, even though he doesn't mean it, retracts his argument, and later joins the chorus of Macdonald's eulogists, telling the Countess he's 'the noblest and finest soul I ever came across, and you aren't fit to breathe the air on the same globe with him'. But it is too late: his words have done their work, and Macdonald is shot in the back—presumably by the rather Conradian Dom Carrasco, who is, however, a fanatical admirer of Dumas—at his moment of triumph, just as his plot has been successful and he has married Lady Aldington. Ford's final twist of the knife is to have Mrs Pett saying 'drearily', on hearing of his noble manner of dying: 'I loved Sergius Mihailovitch; when I used to see him playing with children, I wished he'd been the father of mine.'[21]

If Wells read the book (and since it was reviewed by Rebecca West in the *English Review*, he is unlikely not to have heard of it) his gentle mockery of Ford in *Boon* in 1914 is amazingly forgiving. The bitter assassination of Wells's character as Pett may not seem promising ground on which to claim that Ford is being honest about himself. Macdonald's superiority is articulated in terms of 'breeding'. The book's analysis of class has its Nietzschean aspect too. Mizener found it shocking ('when one remembers that he is more or less describing his own wife') that Ford expresses contempt for the Countess as representative of the shopkeeping classes. Pett tells the Countess: 'the difference between both you and

'The Bungalow', Winchelsea

Ford, by 'Jane' Wells

Elsie Hueffer

Below: Katharine and Christina
Hueffer, *c.*1908

Oliver Madox Hueffer, *c*.1895

Left: Ford, *c*.1904

Left: Juliet Soskice

Below: David Soskice

Above: Violet Hunt
Above right: South Lodge
Below: Rosamond Fogg Elliot
Below right: Brigit Patmore

Ford, *c.*1915

Ford and Violet Hunt

Left: Ford as an officer in the Welch Regiment

Below: Oliver Madox Hueffer

me and him is that we haven't got a spark of generosity in us. We've both conspired to injure that fine gentleman mortally. I'm ready to say that I'm Judas [. . .] We aren't either of us fit to loosen the shoe latchets of Sergius Mihailovitch. That's how the world has always been.' In so far as Macdonald is Ford, and Pett Wells, the objection that Ford is using the book as a transparent act of self-justification stands. But Pett is also Ford to Macdonald's Marwood. Pett, we are told, though he has disgraced himself in his conduct towards Macdonald, 'had been making experiences for himself'. That is, he is learning how to behave like Macdonald: 'and in any emotional experience of that sort in the future he was perfectly certain that he would act not like a blackguard and little cockney cur, but like an English gentleman. That was the only way one could rise from the ranks—by learning how to act well.' By learning good actions, or good acting? Either way, the meanness of this as applied to Wells is mitigated by the candour of it as applied to himself. Ford realized how, since knowing Marwood, he had modelled himself upon him, largely out of his own insecurity about Englishness and class. At the heart of his criticism of others, then, is his criticism of himself. Moser argues that Ford tried to assume Marwood's identity after his death in 1916. But *The New Humpty-Dumpty* shows that he began modelling himself on Marwood earlier—from at least the days of his editorship in 1908–9—and he knew it. Mizener said that what kept Ford from 'fulfilling his great promise, except on rare occasions', was 'his inability to work "down" past self-exculpation and self-aggrandizement to the depths of his imagination'. This is splendidly on the right track, though the spatial metaphor of depth misleadingly implies that the 'depths of his imagination' were somehow transcendentally 'beyond' or 'under' self-exculpation and self-aggrandizement. Rather, in his best work they became Ford's subject instead of his symptom. And even in a book as bad as *The New Humpty-Dumpty*, one can see him beginning to approach the problems from different, creatively enabling positions. That is why he could write his master-pieces out of the same emotions of baffled altruism, betrayal, breakdown, and uncertainty.[22]

These kinds of self-criticism in the characterization are not only analyses of moral problems; they are investigations into the sources of his art, and into whether there are necessary connections between his strengths as an artist and his anxieties about moral weakness. When Macdonald says 'it's my business to know men', one might hear Ford justifying paternalism by saying it's also the novelist's business to know men. Macdonald's impressionist memory is like Ford's (and like Dowell's): 'if I look back on the times we have had,' he tells Lady Aldington rather unflatteringly, 'I just remember spots of things here and there.' And he relates this to his feverish depressions, so as to suggest that they too are connoted by the phrase 'the dark forest': 'When I remember what we have been through, it just seems like a dark forest that I have come out of into this starlight. I don't see the interviews plainly; I don't see the people plainly. It's just a darkness.' (Compare Dowell: 'it is all a darkness.') Impressionist dicta are slipped into the conversations and the narrative. Lady Aldington says 'no properly conducted

English person understands even what an image is'. Macdonald knows that the point about similes is 'how far they come near expressing the necessary truth'. But then he 'had never really learnt that the truth is a dangerous thing'. His rendering of English history for the young king's benefit, 'contrived to let him see historical figures, like the princes and princesses of fairy tales'; as Ford's historical novels had, or as, conversely, this fairy-tale romance contrives to let us see its counts and countesses as historical figures.[23]

Pett's response to his own disgraceful conduct under stress is described in terms to suggest the artist's relation to his life: 'he didn't care very much. He remembered that in the end he was really a philosophic writer, and it affected him rather more as a scientific fact than as a personal detail. He would be able to describe in a future book exactly how a man of genius behaved when it came to action.' (This was to become the nub of Wells's much later counterblast, *The Bulpington of Blup*, in which the Fordian Bulpington displays cowardice in the Great War, but fantasizes it into heroic stories afterwards.) The terrible word 'genius' there indicates that Ford was thinking of his own powers too, and how they were increasingly drawing on the storms he was making of his life. Pett's way of 'making experiences for himself' is also the novelist's dual habit of living himself into interesting situations, in order to be able to transform them into fictional experiences. Pett is like the Fordian impressionist, who looks to the future, from the vantage-point of which the turbulent present will be a tranquil recollection. Like Ford, re-imagining his recent battles as past history, he wants to have 'remembrance now'. The 'dark forest' comes in here too. Macdonald's tribulations seem like a neurasthenic martyrdom as he undergoes them. But as he emerges from them into the 'starlight' of Emily Aldington's love, they begin to seem the trials which have tested his resilience, and the resilience of their love. (The motor-car company he works for as a front for his activities is called 'Resiliens'.) The dark forest is where you find the dragons and damsels of chivalric romance. In his dying words, the dark forest has become 'the dear dark forest'; not just love's foil, but the pain of love itself. That is, he and Emily have travelled through the darkness, to its heart. They have managed to win love out of their surrounding squalor and bitterness. The novel shows that though Ford (like Macdonald) abhorred talking about his private life explicitly, he could sometimes do so with an oblique vengeance in fiction. Certainly *The New Humpty-Dumpty* says everything about Elsie and Wells that Ford felt he couldn't or shouldn't say to their faces, or in court. But the vengefulness of its portraits has been emphasized at the expense of the story's main autobiographical affirmation: that Ford and Violet felt they had been able to transform bitterness into love—as a Flaubertian novelist, working through satire and sentiment, must also do. Though characteristically Ford imagines that sexual happiness will be the death of him. (Of course, if he had known about Hunt's syphilis this would not have been an unreasonable fantasy.)[24]

The dedication says that the publisher, John Lane, insisted on changing the book's title. He may have found 'The Dark Forest' too depressing, as he was said to have found 'The Saddest Story' too depressing a title in wartime, and insisted that that also be changed (to *The Good Soldier*). *The New Humpty-Dumpty* is more intriguing, poses the question of resilience and the cost of being involved with the king's men, and confesses the story's reimagining of fairy-tale. But Lane may also have wanted to deflect attention away from the sexual connotations of 'the dark forest'—connotations which were to become the essence of *The Good Soldier*— since, just before Macdonald dies: 'He turned his head into Lady Aldington's lap and he said: "The dark forest! The dear dark Forest". '[25]

Ford was also starting *Women & Men* that spring in Giessen: another work, though a very different one, turning on ideas of the relations between the sexes and sexual difference.[26] He wrote to Pinker describing the project: it was to be 'a sort of philosophical discussion on the relations and the differences between the sexes—something in the note on my Soul of London'. 'The relations and the differences between the sexes' had been becoming his central preoccupation. But as he is acknowledging this, and also planning to repeat the method of sociological impressionism that was so close to the methods of his novels, he was also realizing how the projected book drew not only on his interest in the suffragette cause (he was later to write to Pinker with characteristic ironic self-aggrandizement that the book would 'be bought in large quantities by my large following of suffragettes'), but also on the activity of reminiscing that has just produced *Ancient Lights*. *Women & Men* was conceived as an antidote to the oppressive, patriarchal Victorian Great looming over that book:

the book would be really Reminiscences of undistinguished people I have met in the course of my varied career, always keeping in mind the main thread of the differences between the sexes. Thus as undistinguished people are odder and more amusing than distinguished people, you would get a more amusing book than the Reminiscences actually are. I don't suppose you will see anything in the idea but you may trust the cavernous recesses of my brain do contain something worthwhile.[27]

The reminiscences of the uncelebrated do not come until the last two of the six instalments. Ford's 'Average People' are 'Mr. T.', a barrister who inherited a fortune when he was 25, and 'from that day to this he has never done anything. Nothing.' He and Ford like each other—'for some reason or other'—and they meet from time to time at their club (presumably the National Liberal Club; though Ford writes from Germany as if he were still in England, still regularly meeting this unidentifiable friend). His life is as regimentedly vacuous as the routines of the 'heart' patients in *The Good Soldier*, or Mark Tietjens in *Parade's End*, but lacking even the sexual excitements or the activity of public service of those characters. To this 'average man' of leisure, Ford contrasts the peasants he had known at Bonnington: Meary Spratt and her husband, Mr Sprattford, and Meary Walker.[28] The preceding sections had been discursive and speculative, querying whether there really *are* any gender differences which are not con-structed by social convention and literary stereotype; whether there really are 'essential' differences. The argument draws on the earlier 'Critical Attitude' editorials for the *English Review*, although there the emphasis was on the sexual ignorance and isolation of urban civilization: the problem which haunts *A Call* and *The Good Soldier*, of how men can 'know' anything about women other than through literature—a literature, however, which constructs an ideological fantasy of woman, 'The Woman of the Novelists'. In *Women & Men* there is less emphasis on the theory of how sexuality gets represented—though there is a spirited refutation of the misogynistic work by Otto Weininger, *Geschlecht und Charakter* (1903: *Sex and Character*). Instead, Ford tests his idea—radical for the times—of the unreality of the stereotypes against real acquaintances. As in the English Trilogy, the writing is a *tour de force* of literary as well as social criticism, besides being the brilliant impressionism for which Pound prized it. Ford presents, vividly and with pathos, but without sentimentality, exactly the lives that do not get into fiction, and scarcely into the middle-class consciousness, the lives of those on whom bourgeois conventions of respectability do not impinge. Meary Walker had lived with her gypsy lover for years, only marrying years later when a parson insisted upon it, though 'it did not trouble her much either way'.[29] Since what was troubling Ford most was people's insisting that he should be married to the woman he wanted to live with, it is not surprising that in Giessen, while he was impersonating a German *burger*, his memory should be drawn back to the peasants of the Romney Marsh as touchstones of unpretentious, tolerant humanity. Absence always made his imagination grow stronger: nostalgia always elicited his most powerful impressions. In Germany, as so often in his writing, his mind is 'somewhere quite other'. He recounts the stories he had told before, which revealed 'traces of great benevolence and of considerable heroism' in Meary Walker. Ford asks whether she is not 'the average woman', since 'there are more peasants in the world than there are anything else'. He finds a positive value in her very mundanity, saying in a deeply characteristic phrase that she was 'just a peasant woman'; later he says she was 'just a woman' (p. 59). That 'just' is far from being dismissive: it is a sign of authenticity and harmoniousness, as when he writes of a quintessential, unspectacular landscape as 'just country'; or when he titles some other reminiscences 'Just People': not the posturing 'Great Figures' who are generally the stuffing of reminiscence, but just people. The sympathetic impressionist should do justice to such people in *mots justes*—just words.[30]

In an argument about literary stereotypes, Ford might sound in danger of having succumbed to the most insidious stereotype of all, the 'natural': the authentic individual human essence which can be apprehended directly, by contrast with the over-sophistication and fragmentation of the urban, the cosmo-politan. There is a touch of Ford's radical Toryism in the suggestion that the peasants are more real—because more rooted in the actualities of earth and growth—than the middle classes. But Ford's argument is too subtle to set his Bonnington friends so crudely against the literary middle-class stereotypes of women and men. Meary Spratt, for example, 'was much more like the average woman of fiction. She was decidedly emotional, she was certainly not truthful' (p. 57). But is the 'woman of fiction' here the woman *in* fiction or is she the woman who *produces* fiction? Violet Hunt, like Ford, was 'decidedly emotional', and both were certainly not always factually 'truthful'. In the slightly disorientating excess of Ford's impressionistic description of Meary Spratt's begging, one senses that what is being described is not only a mode of conduct, but a mode of expression: a style of verbalization that has its relevance to Ford's persistent self-questioning about the effectiveness of literary modes: 'she would scream and howl and yell in the highest of keys, pulling her gnarled, rheumatic fingers into repulsive shapes and screaming like a locomotive to show how much they pained her, or sobbing with the most dramatic emphasis when she related how Meary Walker had saved her six little children from starvation' (p. 57). Mr Spratford 'died raving on the mud floor of his hut', wrote Ford, anxious that he too was getting dangerously close to madness once again. As in 1904, leaving Elsie and going to Germany had seemed his best hope for sanity. Would the consequences be as devastating this time? Meary Spratt's husband 'tore his bald head to ribbons with his nails and Mrs. Spratt for years afterwards could make anybody sick with her dramatic rehearsals of how he died. When she was really worked up over this narration she would even scratch her own forehead until it bled' (p. 59).

The 'dramatic rehearsals' and 'narration' suggest that what Ford values in Meary Walker is her freedom from Meary Spratt's histrionics and emotional manipulation; and that these are the things he eschewed in literature: melodramatic contrivance and narratorial intrusion. Meary Walker is not, however, devoid of literariness. She attracted 'no particular notice from her fellows' not because she did not narrate, could not express herself; rather, because her narrations were themselves unobtrusive. Like all the writers Ford admired most, she effaced herself in her stories—even when they were autobiographical, her own reminiscences: 'And even twenty years afterwards when she rehearsed these scenes and these words there would remain in the repetition a whole world of passionate wistfulness. But indeed, she translated her passion into words' (pp. 57, 55). That slight double-take—rehearsing a scene *after* its performance—is itself wistfully suggestive. Ford's language intimates that even a self-effacing narrator is presenting a performance of the self: that personality, whether in literature or in life, is dramatic even where it manages not to be histrionic. Even eight years after her death, Ford's rehearsals of Meary's narrations translate her passions into his words, quite other words. Her reminiscences have become his reminiscences, part of the on-going performance of his own self, which is itself characterized by the expressive virtues he admired in her. It is in this way that the writing is as profoundly suggestive of Ford's critical engagement with his materials and techniques, as it is expressive of the passionate wistfulness of Meary herself.

1911: GIESSEN

But one is English.
('On Heaven')

Ford was giving English lessons to the Giessen judge who (Hunt said) was to decide his case. But he was growing restless in the 'horrid town'. Suspecting that the legal delays might have been due to the authorities doubting his substance, he moved to a grander flat at 15 Friedrichstrasse. 'It looked so bad for the Judge to call on him and find him living in a pigstye, with a passage smelling of drains, and having to go through the bedroom to get to the sitting-room.' This fuelled a long-running argument about money with Hunt, who had now been granted the receivership of her mother's estate, but was still under the scrutiny of her sisters and their lawyers. She wanted him to take a furnished flat, but he insisted it should be unfurnished, so that he could 'exhibit some possessions of his own, not the landlady's', because 'the police here enquire into every stick of furniture in the house, and all is registered in the central office for the authorities to consult when they want to'. When she acquiesced, so did he, writing: 'Of course, since it upsets you, I must give up the idea of unfurnished rooms. You don't appreciate how important it is!' She also didn't appreciate how 'this astonishing man' was beginning to manœuvre himself into the position of her economic martyr. 'Of course you shall have your way about everything. You always do, you know', he told her. But his demands became more provocative as his guilt over his daughters made him angry with Hunt. She said the 'last straw' was his 'cool request for a pony and trap for the children to go to church in the holidays'. As with his relationship with Pinker, financial dependency brought out the Madox Brown in him. When she said he couldn't afford it, he replied with a 'deluge of words [. . .] cruel felicities of speech, apt verbal lunges'. She told him that the 'idea of debt' stood at her bedside 'like a spectre', whereas he seemed 'able to bear the sense of debt': 'the place in which the shoe pinches you is where it curbs your public generosity.' Ford would transform these exchanges into Leonora Ashburnham's management of her husband's estate in *The Good Soldier*.[1]

In the early spring Ford took a holiday in England. He went with Hunt to stay with Lady De La Warr, 'where he played bridge all night till ten with my lady and her daughter and a nice Catholic priest'. Hunt calls the priest 'Father Consett', implying that Ford used this visit as the basis for the episode at Lobscheid in *Some Do Not . . .* , when Sylvia Tietjens and her mother, Mrs

Satterthwaite, play with the priest. Ezra Pound, just back from New York, spent 'three splendid days' in London before leaving for Paris. 'Have seen Yeats, Plarr, Hueffer, May Sinclair, Lady Low, etc.', he reported to his mother: 'All of whom are revivifying.' Ford took his mother back to Germany, to visit the Münster Hüffers, and to stay with him at Giessen to give his flat 'the semblance of a general home'. About a month later Hunt was invited over. Ford told her to bring her 'harem skirt': 'the whole town is agog about this new fashion, I find, and I will ask some local swells in to tea to see you in it', he wrote. His new flat was 'imposing'; and he had acquired a couple who cooked and valeted for him. Cathy Hueffer took 'her priestly task of impressing the authorities' seriously, and was a stern chaperone: 'I don't think that Easter I was alone with Joseph Leopold for more than ten minutes', said Hunt. While she was there they visited the castle at Marburg to see Luther's Protest, and Ford spoke about how Protestantism 'all began with the signing of that bit of paper', ending with what Hunt seems to have felt was an (unjust) accusation that she was a Protestant. The scene appears (as we shall see), amazingly transformed, as one of the climaxes in *The Good Soldier*.[2]

Hunt said the German papers had been 'full of a book called *Ancient Lights*. Mimi had sent him the Coblentzer one, hailing him as the Prodigal Son who is about to re-enter the Fatherland.' But in England the book had had a mixed and muffled reception. The loyal Scott-James's *Daily News* called it 'the book which Mr. Hueffer, by nature, upbringing, and acquired experience, was designed by Providence to write', celebrating him—rightly—as 'first and foremost a story-teller'. Ford feigned a comic outrage at the possible suggestion that his stories were tall, joking about his persecutory sensitivity. 'Your notice of "Ancient Lights" was very touching', he wrote: 'I called at your office on the day it appeared and was told that you had left for the centre of Africa or some such improbable place. But you need not have been so alarmed. The large pistol that was sticking out of my pocket was not really loaded [. . .] you are the first man who has called me a liar in print and lived to tell the tale.'[3] It is a fine example of how so much of Ford's apparently paranoid behaviour draws on a form of frenetic bantering. The gusto is typical, as in the flourish with which ostensible history ('you are the first man to call me a liar in print') turns into yet another tall story ('and lived to tell the tale'). However, some of those who had known the ancients Ford was illuminating felt they had more earnestly to correct his impressions with their impressions of the facts. Uncle William, while announcing that he bore Ford no ill-will, wrote to the *Outlook* a litany of 'errors' on eighteen different pages. As Mizener, who was himself quick to reprove Ford for 'improving' his stories, says, Ford

uses his personal experience [. . .] without obtrusive vanity and, apart from a few quite deliberate exaggerations for comic effect, with little romancing. William Michael Rossetti, who knew the circumstances Ford was describing and was a comically literal stickler for accuracy, could find nothing more significant wrong [. . .] than Ford's ascription to Brown of some colourful language.[4]

When Hunt had to return to England, Ford came with her, bringing the lawyer, Leun, and another German friend to see the Coronation of George V on 22 June 1911. At the ceremony Hunt said she stood 'cheek by jowl with my old friend Mr. Lloyd George, who talked to me pleasantly, though I verily believe he thought I was someone else'. The *Sheffield Daily Telegraph* had commissioned Ford to report his impressions of the occasion. The article suggests his need to dramatize his sense of his own Englishness at precisely the moment when he hoped legally to lose his English nationality. He says about waiting in Westminster Abbey:

For this is the very heart of England; this is the very heart of Britain; this is the heart of hearts of the Empire [. . .] Must not, then, we, who are here to witness the crowning of a King, of an upholder of the law, of a high priest—must not we, then, witness too, and be waiting for the sanction of a high ideal of a great tradition? For even if England foundered to-morrow, these words could be written proudly enough [. . .]

One is accustomed to think beforehand, with a necessary remainder of cynicism that a king is just a man. But, dropping for a moment the feeling of corporate entity that I had, and that was so very real that it has made me all this while write 'we' with a genuine feeling instead of 'I', which might have seemed more natural, I do very solemnly affirm that I have never seen, and that I have never imagined, anything more immensely moving, more overwhelming than this sight. It was very much more than man; it was very much more even than a symbol. It was like a great moving island of red—the immense robe spread out, the scarlet pages seeming to be drawn along by a strong force [. . .]

No, I have never felt such an emotion, and I don't think that I shall ever again feel such a one. . . .[5]

Trying to become a naturalized German sharpened Ford's sense of his English patriotism, which he seeks to understand by rendering his responses. If he didn't feel exactly the same emotion again, he felt something similar on two important occasions: when he visited the Vatican the following year, and when he witnessed the Battle of the Somme. That feeling of awe at the apprehension of a power driving and unifying a vast body of 'millions and millions' of individuals (the empire, the Catholic Church, the army) is in each case related to the authority of a demigod-father figure (the king, the pope, Arthur Marwood), in a way that suggests a source for these emotions in his feelings for his dead father—whose process of emigration Ford was at the time trying to reverse.

While he was in England Ford took the German visitors to meet Marwood—who spoke 'any language', said Hunt—while she and Mary Martindale went to visit Conrad. The aim was to impress the Germans with Ford's importance. Ford even arranged a dinner on the stage of the Court theatre to help raise funds for the Irish players after their performance of *The Playboy of the Western World*, asking old friends like Ellen Terry, writers like Hardy, and probably politicians and aristocrats as well, to meet the cast and dine on the stage afterwards.[6]

But just as the naturalization plans were going smoothly, Ford's brother got involved in a divorce scandal of his own, and was named as the co-respondent in the case of Wightman vs. Wightman. He had committed adultery with Charlotte Wightman (whose stage name was Elaine Inescort) in December, and had evidently got himself blackmailed. Worried that the Giessen authorities might confuse the two Madox Hueffers, Ford had to write to the *Times*, who added a note to their report: 'Mr. Ford Madox Hueffer, of 15, Friedrichstrasse, Giessen, and temporarily of the Authors' Club, Whitehall, asks us to state that he is not the co-respondent in this case'.[7]

Punch spoofed Ford as 'Mr. Roland Pougher' ('puffer', to rhyme with 'huffer'? Or 'pouf-er'?—a 'pouf' meaning a 'would-be actor: theatrical' at the time). His 'new mediaeval romance will be published next Thursday', they announced a week after *Ladies Whose Bright Eyes* had been out, adding that it was 'confidently expected to stagger the meticulous pedants'. *Ladies* staggered most of its reviewers, and was more widely fêted than anything he had written since *The Fifth Queen* trilogy. It was described as 'extraordinarily engrossing', 'greatly superior' to the book by Mark Twain it reinvented, and as showing 'real imagination, insight, and a restrained and delicate sense of satire'; the 'most brilliant book of the season'. It rapidly established itself as one of his most popular and enduring works, a book for all seasons.[8]

By 1 August Ford was back in Giessen. His rows with Hunt over money had escalated over the summer. She tried not writing to him—'for a space at least', but said his 'pathetic reminders of exile' vanquished her 'pert and absurd resistance'. One of his letters in particular she said overwhelmed her: 'What ever you do or don't say or keep silent about, don't, *don't* Not Write. For there are cruelties and refinements of cruelties, but, however cruel you are to me in words, I would rather have it than silence. For you must remember, you must believe, that whatever you are or you aren't, you are the only link I have with the visible world.' Their affair had meant that she had lost touch with her favourite relation, Rosamond. Now she didn't want to be estranged from Ford too. She wrote. He had 'the voice of the charmer', she said, adding that when he wasn't able to practise the 'cunning use of inflections when the subject to be influenced is at hand', his 'useful trick of style' did as well: 'the perfectly balanced sentence, the due pathos, the almost biblical English, the note well-struck, with leisurely pauses suggesting deep-lying, sub-penetrative emotion.' That is an excellent description of Ford's strategies for affecting his readers, for telling them 'you must believe'. It is a letter which intimates much, not just about his love for Hunt and his need for verbal intercourse with her, but also about his need to write at all to convince himself he is not alone, to have what Dowell calls a 'sympathetic soul' to talk to, who will make him *see* the visible world. ('We are all so afraid, we are all so alone, we all so need from the outside the assurance of our own worthiness to exist.')[9]

He soon had another link with the visible world of literary London in the figure of Ezra Pound, who stayed with him for the first three weeks of August.[10] Pound's immediate response to the renewed friendship was irritation: 'Hueffer dragged me about to Neuheim, which is a springs and baths hell, and to several castles in the hope of broadening my mind', he wrote to his mother, unaware that Ford was broadening his own mind too, refreshing his memory of the setting for the fluid inferno of *The Good Soldier*, and even memorizing novelistic notes about his companion. The absurd Philadelphian Dowell owes something to the exaggerated Philadelphian Ford always teased Pound for being, even if it is sometimes the debt of being his diametric opposite. Hunt describes the scene when Pound was taken to see the church on the high Schiffenberg, near Giessen. He climbed up on to the old and rotten 'stage on which miracle plays had been enacted': 'Presently we saw him pottering about on top and declaiming his own verse in a sort of medieval chant which would not, perhaps, have disgraced one of the original performers. And then, with a small insidious crash, he disappeared and made his descent into hell, covered with the powder off heaven's floor.'[11]

Pound acted as Ford's secretary, as Richard Aldington, H.D (Hilda Doolittle), Caroline Gordon, and Robert Lowell would after him (and as Pound would also act for Yeats in the winter of 1913–14). 'Not that there was much work done', he complained to his mother: 'we disagree diametrically on art, religion, politics and all therein implied.' His irritation was partly defensive. Around 7 August 1911 Ford enacted some—literally—revolutionary criticism of Pound's verse. Pound never forgot the scene: Ford 'felt the errors of contemporary style'—meaning Pound's early style, which was then still archaistic rather than modern—

to the point of rolling (physically, and if you look at it as mere superficial snob, ridiculously) on the floor [. . .] when my third volume displayed me trapped, fly-papered, gummed and strapped down in a jejune provincial effort to learn, *mehercule*, the stilted language that then passed for 'good English' in the arthritic milieu that held control of the respected British critical circles [. . .]

And that roll saved me at least two years, perhaps more. It sent me back to my own proper effort, namely, toward using the living tongue (with younger men after me), though none of us has found a more natural language than Ford did.[12]

Pound came to regard it as one of the most decisive moments of his career, and remained unswervingly grateful that Ford had offered exactly the criticism he needed, though it may have been too humiliating for him fully to realize it or appreciate it at the time. He probably went through the superficially snobbish reaction he describes, before realizing the seriousness of Ford's response. It is alert testimony to Ford's ability to seem so preposterous while being so right. Two years later Pound wrote to Dorothy Shakespear: 'Verily [some archaisms still proved recalcitrant] the more people I meet the more respect I have for F.M.H.—When I think of how he struggled with me in germany!!' A quarter-of-a-century later he considered that: 'The revolution of the word began' (not as we might have thought, with *Blast*, but) 'so far as it affected the men who were of my age in London in 1908, with the LONE whimper of Ford Madox Hueffer'.[13]

Pound recognized how Ford was doing something more than trying to convert him to his own doctrines, but was trying to return him to his 'own proper efforts': to show him how to be true to himself as well as to his time and to the living language of his time. It was a lesson Ford had had to learn for himself, though one way he learned it was to remember his father's criticism of Rossetti's style, 'which a poet of Dante's age might have used if he had been able to read Shakespeare'. He told Stella Bowen he disliked his own 'early Pre Raph. poems. But one has to go thro' it'. It is characteristic of Pound, for all his savage and self-lacerating criticism of the dialect of the literary establishment, and for all the implied self-assurance that he would have found his own voice eventually, to remain self-abasingly modest before a true master. When Charles Olson visited him in St Elizabeth's Hospital for the Criminally Insane, where he was effectively imprisoned after his trial for treason (for making pro-Fascist radio broadcasts during the Second World War), Olson recorded Pound saying Ford had 'saved' his literary career at Giessen: 'F rolled on the floor, with his hands over his head trying to teach me how to speak for myself'; 'Ford knew, when I was still sucking at Swinburne'; 'Ford was the one contemporary & he was ignored'. Donald Davie has written that Ford's 'critical act' of modernizing Pound is 'the most important of the first half of this century, and that it is, moreover, irreversible'. He suspects that Ford's ideas lie behind Eliot's declaration in 1930 that 'we may say positively with Mr. Ezra Pound, that poetry must be at least as well written as prose'; which is precisely what Pound attributed to Ford fifteen years earlier: 'Ford Hueffer, a sense of the *mot juste*. The belief that poetry should be at least as well written as prose, and that "good prose is just your conversation".' As Ford said in 1921 (in a book Eliot knew, but did not speak positively about): 'I had to make for myself the discovery that verse must be at least as well written as prose if it is to be poetry.'[14]

Ford's act of criticism testifies to the rapid development of his own poetic tastes, as well as the development he was encouraging in Pound. Pound's *Canzoni* contains poems that now sound embarrassingly archaistic and vapidly imitative:

> Koré my heart is, let it stand sans gloze!
> Love's pain is long, and lo, love's joy is brief!
> My heart erst alway sweet is bitter grown.

Yet this is from 'Canzon: The Yearly Slain', one of the poems Ford had published in the *English Review* in January 1910. Pound's verse becomes more conversational, less stiltedly chivalric, in his subsequent volumes. But he rarely uses the colloquial to strive for the 'natural language' he admired in Ford. Rather than just being colloquial, Pound's modern verse comments upon the colloquial. The jejune exclamation marks are replaced by quotation marks, often invisible ones. His 'own proper effort' was to be his own Propertius—the poet of his 'Homage to Sextus Propertius', translated so as to bring out the verbal wit he thought other translators missed, and which he formulated in his fine definition of 'logopœia': 'the dance of the intellect amongst words.' In his later verse the 'tertiary archaisms' become something quite other: pastiche, parody, impersonation, irony. But he had to go through the phase of imitation first. Even in *Canzoni* he was beginning to find his ironic tones, as in the 'Song in the Manner of Houseman':

O woe, woe,
People are born and die,
We also shall be dead pretty soon
Therefore let us act as if we were
dead already.[15]

It is a manner almost entirely absent from Ford's verse; a diametrically opposed
mode of trying to put life into language. But he could value it in Pound; and he
could get it in prose—as in Dowell's dead-pan ironic pathos.

Both writers valued 'constructive criticism', and one effect of Ford's criticism of
Pound was that he in turn became one of Ford's most merciless as well as most
admiring critics. As Pound became more stringently diagnostic of what he called
'siphylization'—began, precisely, to see European liberalism as a disease in need of
a drastic regime of totalitarian hygiene—he suspected that Ford, despite being a
'flail of pomposities', was more of a symptom of the English malaise than its cure.
In the second of his two laudatory reviews of Ford's 1913 *Collected Poems* he called
Ford 'the best critic in England, one might say the only critic of any importance'.
Between the two reviews, he directed 'An Essay in Constructive Criticism' at Ford,
with the transparent subtitle: 'With Apologies to Mr. F—d M-d-x H—ff-r in the
"Stoutlook" —the last being a dig not only in Ford's substantial ribs, but at the
magazine he was then writing weekly essays for, the *Outlook*. He impersonates Ford
trying to write a sporting page. Though his spirited satire identifies its targets, its
travesty of Ford's digressiveness and discursiveness—his unbuttoned buttonholing
of his journalistic audience—does not so much convincingly represent Ford's
manner as it playfully misrepresents it:

golf is golf and as I have noticed—for I look about a bit and see a lot of things that
you and your likes would never think of seeing—I have noticed, I was about to say,
and will say in the run of a page or so that golfers get jolly narrow-minded and get
into clubs and pay no attention to the great mass of people who don't know a cleek
from a bunker, and I think it is a perfect shame so I am going with a certain
nonchalance to be sure, I am going to start some free and constructive criticism to
broaden the golfing mind [. . .] any way there are a lot of silly golfing prejudices to
be got rid of before we can chat comfortably together [. . .] that reminds me of a
prejudice of my own about a chap who used to use pink clubs. Always hated that chap
for using pink clubs but now by jingo after all these years, and I think it is a crying
shame that even I had to wait ten years to get over that prejudice and find out what
a fine game he plays . . . just my sort of game. He don't play golf, he just gives the
impression of it. . . . Beautiful form, of course not much direction—THANK GOD! not
much direction . . . doesn't get his ball into the holes but that is a rather silly thing to
do with a golf-ball anyhow [. . .] the only thing that matters is the impression. So
in following numbers I'm going to instruct the reader in constructive criticism of
golf by giving my impression of such noted golfers as Rachel Annand Taylor,
R. A. Scott-James, Joseph Conrad, and Christina Rosetti [*sic*].
HERMANN KARL GEORG JESUS MARIA[16]

Rather than being as hypersensitive to criticism as Mizener portrayed him, Ford took this kind of joke well, relishing real debates about literature (rather than character assassinations). After the war he described Pound as 'the kindest-hearted man who ever cut a throat'. He never resented the criticisms and parodies of fellow-artists like Conrad, Wells, Richard Aldington, or Dreiser. If anything, they heightened his creative excitement, and nurtured a sense of a common cause, 'the Republic of Letters'. Pound had Ford in mind when he wrote (in 1913): 'And the London life of letters? In my five years of residence I have found exactly one man who is really happy when someone else writes a good book; one man with a passion for good writing!'[17]

Groaning about the 'bloody distortion and misrepresentation of London LIFE 1908 to 1914', Pound exclaimed: 'Hell, Yeats for symbolism Hueffer for CLARITY [. . .] The main injustice is to Ford.' Pound made regular, loyal efforts to do him justice. But his propaganda campaign on Ford's behalf effected its own distortions, which have perpetrated another kind of injustice. Pound's Ford is a fiction, necessary to his own literary self-definition, but misleading about Ford's real achievements.[18] He celebrated the Ford who had helped make modernist verse possible: 'we would not be far wrong in calling Mr. Hueffer the best lyrist in England', he wrote in 1913. But his preoccupation with Ford's poetry and his ideas about poetry made him impatient about Ford's achievements in prose. ('I did not in those days care about prose', he said later.) For Pound, who thought he could condense the hundreds of pages of a Henry James novel into the fifteen or so pages of 'Hugh Selwyn Mauberley', Fordian impressionism was too spacious. Ford the novelist hardly existed for Pound. His opinion was formed before Ford wrote his best novels, and became an *idée fixe*. His sharp charges that Ford's work was uneven, that impressionism was excessively ocular and ineffectual, and that Ford was mesmerized by the idea of the English gentleman were sustainable before the war. But Pound kept reiterating them long after Ford had overmastered his unevenness in *The Good Soldier*, and had (in that novel and in *Parade's End*) triumphantly demonstrated the aesthetic potential of his preoccupations with class, vision, and will. Nevertheless, the way Pound makes his criticism is a challenge to the received version of modernist literary history. 'You prob can't ADmire Fordie's damNuvvls but PARTS of 'em', he told Brigit Patmore after the Second World War, 'and that he had all his faults, like his moustache, out in front where everyone cd see Yum. au fond a serious character as J.[ames] J.[oyce] the Reverend Eliot and even ole Unc Wm the yeAT were NOT.'[19]

1911: PERPETRATING BIGAMY?

> 'Then, indeed,' Robert Grimshaw said, 'we—I mean you and I—are to
> be creatures of two natures. We shall follow our passions—if they be
> passions of well-doing—till they lead us, as always they must, into evil'.
>
> (*A Call*)

In August 1911 Ford went to France, with Pound, who was on his way back to
London. Ford 'had an awful week of dentistry in Paris & was awfully cross & ill',
Hunt told Cathy Hueffer, after he came, 'toothless and feckless', to meet her at
the Gare du Nord. 'He had four teeth cut one morning without gas! The dentist
said he must have a week or ten days rest before beginning the lower jaw.' They
both needed to recuperate, so they found a big, cheap hotel on the Channel coast
at Fort-Mahon. Ford bathed, and played poker with Mrs Farley on the hotel
veranda, while Violet explained to his mother: 'He has his new front row (4 false
porcelain ones) in, and they look so nice. I believe the German business is all
right, but the naturalisation did not come in time for the divorce to be
pronounced before the courts rose for six weeks holiday. So that would make it
deferred till they sit again in October. Anyhow, no-one will see me or Ford again
till we are married.'¹ 'Unless,' she added, 'I run over from here next week to get
some clothes & do some business while Ford goes back to Paris and has his lower
jaw attended to. In that case you will see me—for I'll let *you* know.'

Even if the plan for a German divorce had succeeded, under English law Ford
would still have been married to Elsie. But Ford was not able to show Hunt any
naturalization papers. In her memoir, she has Ford claiming that the lawyer had
the papers, but then evading her attempts to see them. There may be some
justification for her feeling of having been deceived, though the originals have not
survived of the letters of his she quotes assuring her that Leun 'seems to think it
is all right now about the naturalisation', and that he said 'it is absolutely certain
now'. Yet Leun, who was being well paid, may have been misleadingly encouraging; and at this stage both Ford and Hunt had enough invested in the scheme
to be all too ready to deceive themselves. However, Hunt's letter to Ford's mother
sounds evasive, saying only that she *believes* the naturalization will be all right,
and hinting with that word 'anyhow' that even by then they had decided to return
saying they were married even if it wasn't. Her letter to Ford suggesting that he
might 'spirit' the children off to Germany, and adding 'but then, you couldn't sue
for reduction of alimony', indicates that Ford was not in a position to divorce

Elsie under German law, but still needed to apply pressure to get her to divorce him. He almost certainly didn't become a German citizen. When Elsie took legal action to stop Violet being called 'Mrs Hueffer', he failed to produce any evidence of German nationality, a German divorce, or a second marriage; and no evidence of any of these has been discovered since. And yet there is evidence that Ford and Hunt thought they had got married. In an arch note inserted between Parts I and II of *The Flurried Years* Hunt writes: 'There is a lacuna here and I may not fill it lest it should be said that I am representing myself to be what I then considered I was in law—his wife. I have been taught since that it was not so—that I never did become his legal wife.' This might be self-justification after the event; a desperate attempt, perhaps, like their conduct during the *Throne* case, to lend credibility to their 'marriage' by acting as if it were true. They may even have felt in the *avant-garde* of sexual morality. In Giessen Ford had told Hunt that 'marriage was a matter of behaviour', explaining how in Germany a husband could divorce a wife for nothing but disobedience. They certainly behaved as if marriage was a matter of behaving as if they were married. Ford had even contemplated this possibility in *A Call*, written two years earlier, in which Katya's sister Ellida suggests that Robert should take Katya (who refuses to go through the marriage ceremony) abroad, and then they should return *saying* they have got married. In *The Desirable Alien*, the book they wrote together about their time in Germany trying to impress the authorities with their desirability (how else would two authors express their desire for citizenship?), Ford wrote an impressionist preface concentrating on the unreliability of 'facts': 'countries, cities, and the hearts of men, are regions so wide, or, as it were, streams so profound, that it would appear that there is no man fitted to write a book of a factual kind about any city, any country, or, for the matter of that, about any single human being.' It was his great Conradian theme of the dark forest of the heart of man—and woman; and during these years he explored the depths in *The New Humpty-Dumpty* and *The Good Soldier*. Perhaps he and Hunt hoped that the legal questions of nationality and international divorce—the 'facts' of which, after all, depended on the caprice of the German authorities and the interpretations of lawyers—would be treated by society in a similarly impressionist light. Ford's indifference to 'facts' was less a denial that they existed, more a scepticism about their adequacy, and about our ability to select them. 'For, as far as facts go, we have nothing but them to go upon; and facts are selected for us either by blind Destiny that will have forced us into certain paths, or by our own inborn predilections that set us wandering about a country, directed to certain regions by who knows what?'[2]

D. H. Lawrence, who only knew Ford during his liaison with Hunt, said, 'Hueffer lives in a constant haze'. 'He has talent, all kinds of it, but has everlastingly been a damned fool about his life. He's fine in half a dozen lines of writing but won't stick to any one of them, and the critics can't stand that in a writer.' As far as Lawrence was concerned, part of Ford's haze was his desire to marry Hunt at all: 'she's too devilishly clever for a man ever to want to marry.' Hunt's memoir confirms the haze theory, writing ostensibly about Ford but perhaps also obliquely about herself: 'Wheedlers—people who can, by the lure of the literary tongue, "kid" the intelligence of others—do invariably possess inordinate powers of self-deception. It takes deep conviction to convince: neat and fine technique to be plausible.' Perhaps they were prepared to let the legal position appear hazy, the more easily to persuade themselves that they had in fact married. There is even a biographical haze around the date at which they might have thought a marriage occurred. Ford wrote to Pinker in October from Trier, saying: 'We were married on Sept. 5th.' On 9 October Lawrence got a letter from Ford telling him they were married. On 14 October the *London Opinion* announced the gossip that the marriage had taken place 'a few weeks ago'—in other words, in August or September. In 1919, after they had separated, Hunt wrote in a letter to Ford which she never sent: 'I have lived with you as your supposed wife for eight years, counting from the fifth of September 1911.'[3]

If the German divorce could not be arranged before October, then Ford's comment to Pinker about being married in September (it is *unlikely* to be a slip of the pen) suggests that he and Hunt had abandoned the plan of waiting for the divorce. On the other hand, Ford is asking Pinker to address Hunt as 'Mrs. Hueffer—We were married on Sept. 5th—and it is rather awkward in hotels if you address her by her literary name'. The date, given merely as a parenthesis in a postscript, might be a white lie to Pinker, forward-dating the event they expected to happen in order to make travelling easier. However, neither the possibility that they may have decided not to wait for the divorce, nor the haze over the precise date, proves that they did not go through some form of ceremony—perhaps like the mock wedding in Hunt's 1904 novel *Sooner or Later*. As Robert and Marie Secor write, in the best analysis of this mystery: 'Hunt and Ford assured Byles that one had taken place in Hanover [*sic*]. However, Dame Rebecca West, who was a close friend and confidante of Hunt's at the time, asserted in a private interview that Hunt and Ford did indeed undergo a marriage ceremony, not in Germany, but in a hotel room in France.'[4]

On 5 September they were in France, probably in Paris. This version is corroborated by a letter Ford wrote to Hunt during the war, when his commanding officer was questioning him about his nationality: 'I take it that these questions do not affect our marriage as that took place in France.' In *Some Do Not . . .*, Sylvia 'had led Tietjens on and married him in Paris to be out of the way'—in the English Church on the Avenue Hoche, where Ford had become a Catholic. Ford and Hunt certainly told Pound they were going to get married in Paris: 'Ford was going to be married in Paris yesterday & go to the dentists, or the same, in inverse order, I forget which,' wrote Pound to Margaret Cravens on 22 August. Presumably they didn't marry in August, for if they had there would have been little point in telling Pinker that it had happened in September. But there would have been little point in Pound's telling Cravens, an American living in France, or his mother, in Philadelphia, if he had known that the marriage was fictitious.[5]

If there was a ceremony in France, then it may have been conducted by a German (which is not impossible, given the amount of time they were spending in towns near the German border like Trier and Spa). So, at least, Hunt told Amy Dawson Scott (the founder of PEN), who wrote in her diary:

Dined with Violet Hunt [. . .] she said she had been thro' a ceremony with Ford and when she asked for her 'lines' he said the lawyer had them. As he was a German, tho' born in England, he had only to establish a domicile in Germany and she does not know whether he had done this. She had supposed that the German who married them and told her to say certain things in Latin was the Mayor. . . .[6]

Dawson Scott asked why it was necessary to *marry* Ford. Not many of her society friends and few of her literary ones would have objected if she and Ford had lived together without trying to marry.[7] Hunt's answer suggests another motive besides the desire for respectability: 'Because my sisters would not let me have my mother to live with us if I had not been married to him.'

The story of the mayor performing the ceremony is not inherently plausible, and Hunt raises doubts about it even as she retails it ('she does not know'; 'She had supposed'). It is unlikely that they would have been married by a priest, even though elsewhere Hunt said they had been. (Ford's third daughter, Julie, later said she had had it from her mother, Stella Bowen, that Hunt was 'one hell of a liar'): divorced or not, Ford could not have made a very Catholic marriage. Yet if there was a civil ceremony there should have been papers to document it. The Secors quote Hunt's foreword to the American edition of her memoir, *I Have This to Say*, which was 'significantly omitted from the English edition', saying that 'the whole truth' of the marriage lies 'at the bottom of the Well at Selsey'.[8] Given the way she hoarded her papers, this might not sound very likely either; but it might explain why her diaries for 1910–16 are not extant. Yet the Secors suggest why she and Ford may have decided not to contest Elsie's libel action against *The Throne*. Hunt's friends Ethel Colburn Mayne and Dollie Radford consulted R. Ellis Roberts on her behalf. Roberts—who may have remembered Ford when he later translated *Peer Gynt*—'warned them that it might open Ford to a charge of bigamy and that by English law Hunt would remain Ford's mistress, not his wife'. Roberts told Hunt, who dismissed the objection at the time. But it is plausible that later on she and Ford realized that their scheme of marriage had not only proved technically impossible, but that it could get them into trouble worse than disrepute. In the 1920s she wrote to her friend Ethel Mayne: 'if I could demonstrate my *bona fides* Ford would only be decried for having committed a bigamous attempt for love of me!' The *London Opinion* piece drew attention to the question of bigamy, while giving the earliest warning that their bid for respectability was about to bring them notoriety instead:

A piquant sensation is fluttering the literary world. Some time ago, a distinguished novelist bearing a foreign-looking patronymic, became separated from his wife. His wife did not divorce him. A few weeks ago he married a well-known lady novelist. The marriage took place on the Continent. It is alleged to be valid there, but not in England! [. . .]

The question is whether either of the parties is guilty of bigamy. It is a delicate problem. As both the parties are domiciled in England, it is possible that there may be exciting complications. According to British law, the first wife is still married to her husband. According to the law of the husband's native country, the second wife is married to him. The result is that the happy man has two legal wives.[9]

Certainly, by the time of the *Throne* case Ford and Hunt were convinced that bigamy had become the central issue. She wrote to his mother to explain why she could do nothing to defend Ford: 'I only know what your son tells me of the German business. I mean the divorce—that is his affair. Of course the marriage is mine & no one contested that, for of course Elsie wants to try and get Ford for bigamy. That is why I did not insist on going into court—for I might have been made to give date & place & witnesses. Now—nobody, not even you knows them.' But of course this might have been a ploy to make an embarrassing inability to produce documents look like a clever self-defence.[10] Ingenious special-pleading, turning the very absence of exonerating evidence into a tactical virtue? Or the truth? An attempt to save a marriage which they believed binding because they had been through a ceremony, however spurious? The evidence can't tell us conclusively what happened but it does say much about what Ford, Hunt, and their friends and acquaintances *thought* about it. It is all an impressionist haze.

Whatever their friends might have thought, it mattered to them to be married. Knowing that the plan failed, it is easy to dismiss it with hindsight as fantastical and doomed. But there was an excitement, too, in what Hunt called 'the romance of our wild marriage'. And it had seemed feasible enough for Ford to be continuously consulting Leun: Hunt said they spent nearly £500 on the scheme. Ellis Roberts thought Ford had become 'enchanted by the elaborate machinery of his own make-believe'. But besides Leun he also enlisted Tebb's support, asking him to find out about the procedure and rules of evidence in German courts. The loyal Tebb saw the Austrian vice-consul, ransacked libraries, went to Gray's Inn, asked a solicitor, and remained baffled.[11] But the legal elaborations were unlikely to have been entirely of Ford's own making. The lawyer must at least have colluded in the fantasy. Anyway, the international laws of divorce and domicile are not without their own degree of fictionality and haze.

The naturalization took longer than they thought, and they gave up waiting for it. Goldring imagined Ford, 'in a fit of exasperation', exclaiming: 'Hang it all. What does it matter? Let's go home and *say* we've been married. No one will ever find out.'[12] Most of the received accounts follow Hunt's lead in suggesting that Ford misled her about the naturalization, possibly even about the divorce—though she also suggests that he had himself been misled by the Goesens. (With hindsight that the plan had failed, and after their bitter separation, it suited her to seem the victim. Yet to witnesses like Lawrence and David Garnett she seemed the more dominant personality.) But they overlook the cardinal point: even if they had been through some form of marriage ceremony, and whether or not Hunt believed it valid by German law, she, like Ford, knew that it would not be recognized by English law. Ellis Roberts had warned her bluntly; her father's friend, John Westlake, warned her obliquely: 'when I contemplated an international marriage,' she wrote in a note left in Westlake's memoirs, 'complicated by a divorce—the man divorcing the wife for causes valid in Germany but not in this country—I asked [Westlake] if it were possible. He said it was but he wished I wouldn't.'[13] If she knew that the causes for divorce would not be valid in England, she must have realized that the divorce itself would not be valid either. The naturalization only affects the validity of the proposed marriage in Germany. Yet they never planned not to return to England. Violet wouldn't have wanted to abandon her mother. 'And he was worried to death about his children', said Goldring. While he was trying to establish his domicile, he was always in temporary lodgings: there was no plan to find a permanent house for both of them in Germany—which is perhaps why the German authorities were not persuaded that the 'desirable aliens' wanted to become desirable burghers. The real mystery is what good they thought a marriage would be to them back in England, and how they ever thought their claim to be married could possibly stand up in a British court. None the less, they wanted to be married. They may have hoped that they could persuade Elsie that a German divorce was imminent, so that she would grant Ford the British divorce he wanted in order to secure her allowance and to render their situation less ambiguous for the sake of the children. But they realized that she was not going to oblige. So, when the naturalization proved interminable, they may have thought that it wasn't worth waiting for since it would not validate the marriage in England. They were missing London literary life, and Hunt had her mother to look after, as well as herself. They may have followed the precedent of Stephen Crane and Cora, who simply 'came from the continent as if married'. But a marriage ceremony would have been a formal affirmation of their commitment to each other, as well as a defiance of Elsie. Did Ford feel a little like his Henry VIII, making a protestation of human desire in the face of a recalcitrant constraint? They may have thought, tortuously but not incomprehensibly, that since the marriage wouldn't be valid in England anyway, the German technicality about naturalization was irrelevant. If they did go through a ceremony, it was probably either in Paris in September, or in October, perhaps in Trier. And if they did, the irony would be that what has been considered their biggest lie would be in a sense true, and motivated by the desire *not* to lie. Either way, they both enjoyed taking risks, and were both well aware of the risks they were running. It would have been a fictional exercise, produced by private desires but published for an international readership. But Ford never denied their marriage.[14]

In 1912 Violet Hunt wrote a preface to a reprint of her mother's novel of 1873, *Thornicroft's Model*. In it she refers twice to Ford as 'my husband', and offers a gloss on the plot that could stand as her verdict on her own and Ford's position: 'Thornicroft was bound to err with the other sex, so my mother provided him with a respectable and quite Anglo-Saxon jealousy, and made him commit the quite respectable ecclesiastical crime—it is scarcely a sin—of bigamy.'[15] This ethical hauteur echoes the attitude Ford took in a review of five German novels in the summer of 1911. In each of them, he wrote:

if adultery be not the principal theme, it lurks in the background. And this particular form of breach of the Seventh Commandment is oddly enough not in the least connected with any propaganda of doctrinaire free love. Not in the least. Each of these books is written in a high romantic, moralising strain. But the moral simply seems to be that, if you are a serious, Overman of a hero, and you come across a mysterious, glamourous [sic], inscrutably virtuous, overwoman of a heroine, you and she must unite your destinies. And then you will find that you will be perfectly happy and sentimentally tranquil for the remainder of your lives. You won't be socially ostracised [. . .] It is as if a tremendous democracy, unable to take into its hands the reins of temporal power, had determined to revise, along the lines of its own common-sense, or of its own desires, all social and personal moral rules of ethics.

This doubtless expresses his hopes for his and Hunt's uniting of their destinies. But he also expressed a darker heart, singling out one of the novels (Georg von Omptela's *Maria da Caza*) in a way that foreshadowed his own best novels to come: 'in this book a real passion is treated, and one feels that the author wrote the book because he wished to express passion and the pain of passion.'[16]

Hunt's frustration over the difficulty of marrying Ford can only have been heightened by hearing, while in Paris, that Rosamond had got married without telling her aunt. (The Fogg Elliots had forbidden her to visit Violet or write to her because of the scandal, and because of the family feud over Mrs Hunt.) Ford and Violet tried distracting themselves with Parisian night-life. But an episode she recounted reveals Ford's morbidity at the time. He went by himself to see a show at *Les Ambassadeurs*, then came home and wrote the poem 'To All the Dead', 'about a vision he had had on the Hunnen Grabe, the Champs Elysées of Giessen, . . . the Germanic warriors rising, clasping to their iron breastplates the German maidens that have lain buried with them for the last thousands and thousands of years'. 'He had just seen a Senegalese actress in an open-air kiosk in the Champs Elysées who had suggested the "rice-pale queen" in his poem', commented Hunt, adding that she was herself 'nearly as pale through worry and waiting'. This haunting poem is another example of how thinking about death elicited Ford's best and most characteristic writing. It is also deeply typical of the mental and spatial dualities of his impressionism, which he was beginning to formulate more clearly ('we are almost always in one place with our minds somewhere quite other').[17] Opening with a vision of a long-dead Chinese queen, the poem moves into a more conversational manner, overlaid with complex Fordian visionariness. The narrator is watching two Chinese chiropodists across the street, and not-quite-listening to an American friend 'lecturing' him. The American's monologue none the less summons up a vision of America, a memory of seeing Indian burial mounds from a river-steamer. Then, via Trier—where Ford and Hunt went next—the poem moves to its climax: another vision of the dead, this time of a pair of lovers risen from their ancient graves in the Hunnen Gräber. The vision's status is uncertain. At first it appears to be the product of exhaustion, or an illusion of the dark and misty landscape. Afterwards, there is a suggestion that it may have been a dream-vision. It ends with a powerful image conjoining death and desire: the dead embracing, and crying 'Your lips!'

Ford understood his art's preoccupation with absence. 'That, you see, is *l'art moderne*', he explained years later: 'you paint New York from Provence & the shores of the Mediterranean from New York . . . Indeed it is the way I write.'[18] Thinking of the 'soul of London', Ford imagined the souls of those who died there. Writing of 'the heart of the country', his heart went out to those whose hearts had stopped there. In the story 'Riesenberg', published earlier in 1911, he had written of a landscape whose tremors are the movements of slumbering giants. Fordian landscape is generally at once an evocation and a suppression of the dead. In 'To All the Dead' the connection is explicit. But that poem, with its narrator who speaks of lying down in a graveyard and hearing the dead speak, is suggestive of another connection. Here, imagining yourself somewhere quite other shades off into imagining yourself quite otherwise: imagining your own death:

> For it's nothing but dead and dead and dying
> Dead faiths, dead loves, lost friends and the flying
> Fleet minutes that change and ruin our shows [. . .]
> And time flows on, and flows and flows.

The bleeding, the distress, and the distortion of his speech caused by his gruelling dentistry may well have exacerbated his sense of mortality and physical decay. Ford gave his humiliation at appearing toothless to Mr Fleight, who is beaten up—for being Jewish—and feels 'he couldn't let anybody in the world see him'. 'Along with his morbid vanity went a morbid fear that it should be known he considered himself handsome.'[19]

According to Hunt, from Trier they returned to Paris, staying in a hotel in the suburb of Bellevue and taking the boat past the Eiffel Tower into the city each morning; she made another quick visit to England; then back to Germany via Luxembourg. 'Three years of constant agitation had done their work', said Hunt. She fell ill, and they moved to Spa, where she had a second operation. It was probably during this visit that she drafted a plan for a novel which draws heavily on her growing ambivalence towards Ford, and her self-pity about her illness, both of which incited her to a—Fordian—imagining of her own death:

The story told autobiographically by a husband, alone in the magnificent house of a rich & crusty uncle from whom he has expectations. He is rather a spendthrift—a genius, who needs money to bring out his qualities. This is his wifes opinion and his wife has sent him to pay his respects & to win[?] over the uncle who is on his deathbed and who is surrounded by *respectable & dull* potential heirs. whom she being a very *business-like* person wishes to frustrate. She has only persuaded George to endure this couple of months purgatory, on the understanding that she herself will go and rest at Spa—and is going to have a child. She writes to him every day—and her letters are given *in extenso*. They treat of the place of her health of a little child she has taken a fancy to—of the people she meets of her doctor etc. They are essay letters. They go on for 2 months, and in that time he makes 'good'—giving all his mind & attention to the old gentleman ousts the relations & is left his heir—. The last letter from his wife is written in reply to his—telling her the good news saying Now come! He goes, sees the doctor who shows him her grave. she has been dead a month. He produces her last letter dated the day before. The problem is to find who wrote it, who posted it. She has left no word . . . except a recommendation, as they have no child (she has died of dropsy) to adopt little Fifine. He finds little Fifine with difficulty & it is the child of eight who has received an antedated packet of letters with orders to post one every day—He gets the information out of the child with difficulty—the people were mostly invented[?], and show considerably literary talent in a woman who has been heretofore regarded by her clever husband as a mere hard-managing, materialistic woman. The wife has gauged him thoroughly he is a genius & *il se consolise*[?]—Try & show the stages of the illness in the letters. After the *first month* the letters are of course 'fake'[.] The wife all along knew she was dying and wanted to secure for her easy going husband *la vie dor*[é]*e* which depended on his absence from her for these two crucial months, his heart free of care & anxiety for her. They had nearly had a quarrel to get him to go in the first instance in which he reproached her for money grubbing [. . .]

The woman he cuts out shall be the woman he flirts with & who is glad to lose if to him & who does the rooting out at Spa & marries him for pity learns to respect the dead wife he has a little denigré to her

The wife after a time never *answers* his remarks which is odd—('I don't like cutting her out') Also he notices[?] all letters numbered, & in order (does she want to print them?)[20]

A *Daily Mirror* reporter found Ford at Spa, playing his nightly game of billiards at Houtermans. Ford seized the opportunity to publicize *The Critical Attitude* (his fourth book published that year) as well as a book of Hunt's, *The Doll*, dedicated to Ford's mother. He went public with the story about his new marriage, which he interwove with other autobiographical romancing:

AUTHOR WEDS.
Mr. Ford Madox Hueffer Married Abroad
to Well-known Lady Novelist.

The Daily Mirror is able to announce that Mr. Ford Madox Hueffer, the famous novelist, has been married on the Continent to Miss Violet Hunt, the well-known authoress [. . .]

Mr. Hueffer was seen at the Red House, Spa, Belgium, yesterday, before starting for his daily motor-car ride with the second Mrs. Hueffer.

'I don't want to advertise myself,' he told *The Daily Mirror*, 'but it happens that both my wife and myself have books appearing to-day [. . .] I married her in Germany after divorcing my former wife on a technical ground, desertion, as I had a perfect right to do, being domiciled in Germany.

'I am heir to large entailed estates in Prussia, and have therefore retained my German nationality [. . .] I offered myself for service with the German army, but was not required to serve, and I attended Bonn University.

'My former wife brought an action against me for restitution of conjugal rights. Then we agreed upon a separation order, she having the custody of our two daughters, now fifteen and sixteen [. . .]'[21]

Ford may have wanted to stop the gossip about bigamy by making such a detailed public statement. Or he may have wanted to see, from a safe distance, what the reaction would be from England, and from Elsie. By 1926 Hunt was saying that she had advised against using the marriage to publicize their books: 'It is simply an odious literary "wheeze" unworthy of either of us.' But the following week her old friend Clement Shorter announced the marriage in the *Sphere* and the *Sketch*, which probably indicates that she was as eager as Ford to claim publicly that they were now legally married. Olive Garnett called the *Mirror* interview 'the bolt from the blue'. Elsie's solicitor told her she should deny Ford's statement as a libel and claim damages. She said there was 'a lot of fiction in F.M.H.'s statement' (presumably the ages of his daughters—Christina was now 14, Katharine 11—and the Prussian estates). By 8 November Ford had written to Elsie's solicitor 'regretting the publishing given his re-marriage by the press, as he had wished to spare his client "mortification" '. But though the paper backed down too, Elsie went ahead with her libel case.[22]

By Fordian chance, soon after he and Hunt returned to London in November Ford was commissioned by *Collier's*, only a month after he was announcing himself divorced and remarried, to go to Rome to report on the Investiture of American Cardinals. Arriving in late November, this improbable church reporter met with a secular welcome:

So, at the mercy of continental trains, I arrived in that Capital towards six in the morning, an ungodly time. I drifted, then, unhappily to the chief hotel of the city [. . .] It was a large place but I perceived no soul. Suddenly, however, a large, handsome lady was round my neck. She was exclaiming with joy:

'Traditore rinvenuto!'

'It was of course a mistake: I must at one time have had a flagitious double in that city. Nevertheless, during the period of my stay I remained unable to persuade the lady that I was not that returned traitor. I was offered free rooms in that giant caravanserai: I was mothered [. . .]

This story comes from an unpublished essay, 'Just People', written after the war, about acquaintances who had made lasting impressions on his memory. Besides its explosive farce, it ministers to Ford's preoccupation with doubles and mistaken identities. Might it not also, though written a decade later, betray a sense of guilt at leaving Elsie and the children?—Perhaps combined with a self-exculpation: 'women may accuse me of treachery, but they won't see who I am'.[23]

The report of the investiture was telegraphed to *Collier's* to catch the Christmas number. Ford prided himself on being 'the first man to send a Marconi message direct from the shores of the Mediterranean to New York':

I was so innocent that when the card of the Cavaliere Marconi was handed to me in the hotel I hesitated to receive him, the thought flashing through my mind that this was probably some three-card-trick man or poker sharp. The lady of the Bar [. . .] saved me from that disaster: indeed, she explained to me what Wireless was and I believe that it was she who had suggested to the Cavaliere that I, rather than the representative of any other of the great American journals, should be given the offer of flashing by invisible means, my prose across the Atlantic.[24]

Like most of Ford's occasional pieces, the article rises above its occasion. It is at once a news report and an intimate communion, offering his most sustained account of his feelings about religion, as well as providing a vivid testimony to his stressed mental state. 'I may confess myself an impressionable person, open to emotions of beauty', he writes, appearing to deflect a moral 'confession' into an aesthetic one. But what he is moved by is ethical and spiritual, not just a matter of visual satisfaction: 'I will confess that again and again I was deeply moved during this period of waiting [for the conferring of the red birettas to the cardinals elect], and I confess that the sight of a long row of Sisters of Mercy in light blue gowns, with the immense white coifs, brought me to real tears. I don't know why.'[25] The Sisters of Mercy evoked 'the feeling of great goodness and tenderness of those good women', their headgear and benevolence perhaps reminding him of Dionissia in *Ladies Whose Bright Eyes*—an idealized alternative to the actual demands and wilfulnesses of his two wives. The break with Elsie was now irrevocable, and he was unlikely to see much of his daughters again. He had entered the Catholic Church under the influence of his Hüffer family; but they were taking Elsie's side in the divorce attempts. Undesirably alienated from his German family, he had also failed, probably, to be received into that family's nationality. It is hardly surprising, then, that he perceived the Vatican ceremonies in terms of the familial. Not only does he write of 'the comparative family life' of the Colleges, but when the pope (whom he calls 'the Holy Father') speaks, he gives Ford a shock of familial recognition:

It is easy to see that the Holy Father is moved. He has little gestures, quaint movements of hand—the movements not of an orator or of a preacher but those of a kindly earnest parent. Then I understood something that I had never understood before. For this man there speaking seemed to me no more to be a sovereign Pontiff, no more to be high or distant [. . .] No. He was the kind and dear head of my family—of my own family. I was listening. I have never felt so at home. We are a great family, we Catholics, and I was in the private room of the head of us all, and I had the right to be there, and we all had the right to the blessing of the good and kindly head of our family, who will surely not refuse it to them that be of good will. (p. 11)

This scenario of radical belonging helps to explain why Ford found his time in Rome to be 'days of the very strongest emotions' (p. 12). Yet if these emotions were stronger than usual, they were continuous with the emotions which animate and structure his prose. His audience with the pope transposes the radical scenario of his art: the benevolent voice captivating and consoling its silent listener. Ford shows himself as the silent listener his prose perpetually calls into being. He often spoke of literature as a 'Republic'; yet his metaphors speak of families: calling writers 'confrères' approximates them to 'frères'; his genealogies of literary movements involve descent and inheritance. Old men mad about writing initiate *les jeunes* into the passion of art.

The speaking voice familiarizes the void, transcending silence by establishing a rapport with the absent father. Ford feels homeless until he hears this paternal voice. But, as so often when he imagines a father, he imagines a death; and, as so often, it is here his own death. One of the American cardinals elect is 'a dear, kindly looking old man—and I wish his hands might be extended over me in benediction when I come to die'. The voice that rises to meet the fear of death ends by speaking of death.

Ford's religion has been seen as a pose. Jean Rhys's character of H. J. Heidler in *Postures*—allegedly her 'portrait' of Ford during their affair in the mid-1920s—has been used to cast doubt on his sincerity: 'Marya turned to watch Heidler go down on one knee and cross himself as he passed the altar. He glanced quickly sideways at her as he did it, and she thought: "I'll never be able to pray again now that I've seen him do that. Never! However sad I am." And she felt very desolate.'[26] If this *is* based on a gesture of Ford's, what does it signify? Marya's childlike feeling of disappointment demands that he has done something despicable, which has blighted her equally childlike religious motivation (praying to alleviate 'sadness'). Does the sideways glance betray hypocrisy, a preoccupation with convincing the audience of one's sincerity rather than *being* sincere? It is a naïve view that equates integrity with solipsism in that way, and one which forgets that Marya has 'turned to watch Heidler'. Wouldn't any sensitive observer—even if concentrating elsewhere—be aware of that movement and that glance, from someone so close? Should Heidler be reproved for answering his lover's look?

In another sense, however, the juxtaposition of religion and sexuality is to the point (as it was in *The Fifth Queen*, and would be again in all his more powerful books). Janice Biala, his partner during the 1930s, clarified his attitudes to Catholicism then: 'I don't remember any talk about religion', she told Sondra Stang:

It didn't play any role in our life. I am an unreconstructed Jew. Ford was certainly no practising Catholic. He brought up his children as Catholics because he thought all children should be brought up in some religion, and he preferred Catholicism because he said if you wanted to break away from it you could make a clean break [. . .] He did say he admired the organization of the church. . . . When we entered a church Ford would make a half-hearted bow in the direction of the Virgin—but perhaps more because she was a woman than because she was the Virgin. And I imagine he believed in Catholicism philosophically.[27]

Though charged with morbidity and sentiment, it is a strength of Ford's style to resist self-indulgent morbidity and sentimentality, while recognizing and giving rein to the driving forces of his art. The *Collier's* essay is no exception both in taking the risk of confronting the abyss of self-abandonment to the point of self-absorption, and in characteristically discovering the resources within the self (within the style) to pull back from the abyss, and organize aesthetically the passions that have been given apparently free play. The published article does not mention the woman in the hotel, but it does return to the hotel, and to its American bar, in which he was apprehended. He finds another way of distancing himself from the emotional intensities of the Vatican ceremonies, through an ambiguous yet ironic vignette:

And now I am back in the hall of the Quirinal Hotel. The luggage of new travelers is coming in, the hall is full of loungers, and suddenly there is a great flash of scarlet. It is Cardinal O'Connell getting out alone from his carriage. He holds out his hand to one man and another in the hall. They genuflect and kiss his ring. Then, all blazing, he passes on to the lift and is jerked upward—a flash of scarlet—to his rooms. It is the Church and the world in an odd juxtaposition, for I never expected to see a cardinal in a lift.

But he disappears and I am left with the odd sensation that I am the only man in the hall to whom he did not offer his hand. I am conscious of a pang of jealousy that no doubt is the devil, and I pass toward the American bar, for I had no breakfast this morning.

So the world we live in gets under way for me again after these days of the very strongest emotions. (p. 12)

The world Ford lived mentally in was literary England, and he needed to feel it getting under way for him again. One way was to keep up the astonishing current of work, and to write about the kind of sexual intrigues that seemed destined to get him maligned as his own flagitious double. He finished *The Panel* 'in about a month', he told Pinker.[28] Subtitled 'A Sheer Comedy'; it is a curious example of Ford's mercurial tonality, in the way it draws on troubling material to produce amusing drawing-room comedy, and brings together questions of the literary market, social morality, and psychological difficulties to produce an engaging romance. Like most of Ford's fiction, this novel wants to make us see that (to adapt Lawrence's insight about Ford), though its protagonist has been blackened with a villainous selfish tar, his 'dove-grey kindliness' has survived intact: he is fundamentally a good man. Yet this doesn't quite make him, as Mizener claims, 'Ford's image of himself'. Edward Foster certainly reflects aspects of Ford; but he is not an artist. He is, rather, Ford's parody of himself—as the *jeune homme modeste* that Henry James (mis)took him for. The novel is another of Ford's satires on reformers: there are Societies for the Suppression of Sin, the Abolition of Conventional Marriage, for Theatre Reform, for the Abolition of Vice. At the start Foster is engaged to a fierce reformer, Olympia Peabody. But there is a farcical entanglement with a Violet-Hunt-like (but married) Lady Novelist, Mrs Kerr Howe, who says 'polygamous things' to him (p. 127). Then he falls in love with a younger Lady Mary Savylle, who spends much of the novel disguised as her own maid. Miss Peabody, outraged by the comings and goings in the country house (some of them through the secret panel of the title), eventually breaks off the engagement, denouncing the house as 'Sodom and Gomorrah', and making way for the romance ending. If the novel transposes and imagines a release from Ford's own marital tangle, it also sheds light on what he thought of his attempted German naturalization and marriage. The line between tact and fabrication is not always as easy to discern as Mizener rather censoriously implies: the well-meant white lie is a fundamental of *politesse*—as even a lesser reader of James than Foster would know. The German 'marriage' may have been just such a tactfully hazy fabrication, which Ford hoped would enable Elsie to remain un-divorced, without forcing Violet to remain unmarried as far as society would be concerned. That is, the plan may have been diplomatic rather than mendacious, and may have failed because Ford failed to imagine the tenacity of Elsie's bitterness, rather than because he couldn't tell the difference between fact and his own fabrication.

The dedication of *The Panel* to Ada Potter, who had produced the stage-version of *The Fifth Queen*, was prescient about the results of Ford's fabulations, however:

Why it should have come into your head to inspire me to a task so obviously frivolous and one which will draw down upon my head the reprehensions of the great and serious and the stern disapproval of eminent and various critics, is a matter that lies between yourself and your conscience. But I suppose, in this odd, frequently unpleasant and almost always much too serious world, even a person so earnest as yourself feels the desire to be made to laugh by an historian so obviously earnest as I am.

Ford wasn't only risking the censure of the actual reformers, such as the members of the National Social Purity Crusade and the National Vigilance Association. He was also satirizing the highbrow readers of James on the one hand, and on the other, the lowbrow tendencies of the circulating libraries, one of which had surreally censored James's *Italian Hours*, fearing the book 'would be detrimental to the good name our library holds for the circulation of thoroughly wholesome literature'.[29] As so often, he is provoking attacks upon himself from all sides, while presenting himself as the innocent, injured party. This dedication is one of his earliest posings of the problem of his 'earnestness'. The term was of course given prominence by Wilde, but Ford's aim is to create a more delicate tonal nuance. It becomes his predominant tonal quality, and can be seen emerging in the satirical works written between 1908 (*Mr Apollo*) and 1913 (*Mr Fleight*). It is the mode of *The Good Soldier* and also of the reminiscences: a fine poise between bitter earnest and exhilarating irony.

The other way Ford sought to get his literary world under way once more was by writing a highly personal appreciation of Conrad for the December issue of the *English Review*, attempting to salvage their wrecked friendship. It is deeply characteristic that Ford gets his present life under way by returning to yesterday: the yesterday of their collaboration and closest intimacy. 'A certain touch of nostalgia is an almost essential element for the imaginative writer.' It is back to *Romance* that Ford's mind turns, both as the main product of that intimacy, and as a statement of nostalgia: 'To yesterday and to-day I say my polite "vaya usted con Dios." What are those days to me? But that far-off day of my romance [. . .] that day I am not likely to forget.' Partly out of modesty, Ford distances himself from the collaboration: 'I knew at one time very well a writer who collaborated with Conrad in one or two books, and has very kindly presented me with the manuscript of these works.' He then quotes that opening of *Romance*, underlining Conrad's contributions. It was a technique he was to return to (notably in the Appendix to the book publication of *The Nature of a Crime*, 'A Note on

Romance'): a minute dwelling on the collaborative work that risks boasting of the association in order to abase his own contributions before Conrad's genius. The sheer tonal difficulty of this exercise might of itself account for that strange self-distancing. And yet, readers of Ford's own erstwhile journal, the *English Review*, and particularly those readers who would likely be interested by an article on Conrad unequivocally signed 'Ford Madox Hueffer', would be unlikely not to know that Ford is talking about himself in the third person here. The point is that Ford *is* the writer whom he knew at one time very well. Rereading *Romance*, his past self is conjured up by the prose, and revealed as something utterly changed, recoverable only in memory and in reading. This provides a tragic undertow to the gesture of friendly rapprochement: a recognition that today cannot be made to re-create the cherished past friendship. Once again, putting it like this makes the essay sound self-absorbed in a way it is not. Ford's achievement here is to turn idiosyncratic commentary (such as the preposterous romance about Conrad being essentially 'an Elizabethan') and egoistic concentration into a criticism which is truly revealing of its object, not just its author:

But when it comes to *Lord Jim*—why, it is a part of me. Yes, it is a part of my soul, of my life. It has entered into me like the blood in my veins; it has given me the English outlook, though I am a foreigner and have every kind of intellectual contempt for the countrymen of Tuan Jim. But it has made me understand the English-English with such a perfect comprehension—and what one perfectly comprehends one loves!

  Now that is a great achievement—for it is a great achievement to have overwhelmed any one soul, and there are few men's souls that can resist *Lord Jim* once they have found him out. The egotism of this personal confession is not meant to display myself. It is the best way of showing what this author's work can do [. . .]

It is in this spirit that Ford's reminiscential criticism deserves to be taken. He praises Conrad's constatation of Destiny in a passage that is both great criticism of Conrad and of Ford's own best books, and which hints at a neurasthenic *angst* at the form his own life was falling into once again, as circumstance 'conspired' to undo him:

that is the great faculty of this author—that he can make an end seem inevitable, in every instance the only possible end. He does this by every means—by the explanations of heredity, of temperament, of the nature of sea and sky, by the sound of a song, by the straws in the street. His sense of Destiny differs in its means of expression from that of the Greeks, its intensity is always as great as theirs [. . .] The Greek Destiny was embodied, commented on, chorussed. It was an all-overwhelming cloud. The Destiny of Conrad's books is hymned by no Chorus of Captive Women, and by no Bacchantes. That is not the temper of his time or ours. When all sorts of things, all sorts of little coincidences, nowadays force us to a course of action we do not any longer say that Atropos compelled us—we say that it seemed as if every blessed thing conspired to make us do it. And what Conrad does for us is to express for us the Three Sisters in the terms of every blessed thing.

As in his discussion of 'facts' in the preface to *The Desirable Alien*, he is obliquely wondering here what forces had led to his increasingly complex marital tangle, while outlining one of the central aims of the impressionist novel: here, that events should be prepared for so as to seem inevitable, or 'justified'.[30]

The essay effected a brief rapprochement with Conrad, who wrote to thank Ford: 'I am infinitely touched by what you say and by the accent you have found to express what may be critically just and true but to a certainty is the speech of a friend. What touches me most is to see that you do not discard our common past.' Conrad had tried to discard it after their quarrel, saying to E. V. Lucas, for example: 'I have been in no sense associated with the *E[nglish] R[eview]* except that I wished Hueffer well in his venture.' Now he was more nostalgic: 'These old days may not have been such very "good old days" as they should have been—but to me my dear Ford they are a very precious possession. In fact I have nothing else that I can call my own.' Back in England, Ford and Violet made an early appearance as Mr and Mrs Hueffer at a party for H. G. Wells given by the journalist Eliza Aria. Hunt's friend Lucy Byron (later 'Lady Houston of the millions') had lent them her house at Littlestone-on-Sea, and they hired a car, driving to Orlestone to pick up the Conrads and bring them back for lunch.[31] While Ford and Conrad sat inside discussing literature, Jessie Conrad was being more archaically tragic, hinting to Violet 'at some shadowy horror, some "catastrophe" or other which was preparing for me'. Hunt discounted the premonition at the time, but adds: 'I little knew.'

Ford knew. He had foreseen the catastrophe at the fateful scene at Charing Cross in October 1909. A story published in late 1911 is obliquely premonitory. 'What Happened at Eleven Forty-five' tells of another unforeseen meeting: a fatal coincidence. Probably in the autumn of 1903, he was accosted by a German tramp on the road from Rye to Winchelsea: an ill-paid court actor to a grand-duke, who had saved enough to pay his passage to the United States, where he hoped to improve his lot by becoming a waiter. He was robbed at Liverpool and had started walking back towards Germany. Ford gives him money—because he was a good impressionist as well as a deserving case: 'He made quite a distinct impression on me, being a little battered, cheerful fellow, who had really entertained me with his adventures.' He also may have felt sympathy for the German alienated in England (the tramp spoke no English). Eight years later, after visiting the Opera in Frankfurt, Ford orders a cup of coffee at the station restaurant. When he asks what it will cost, the waiter replies: 'I owe you three marks eighty, sir', and lays down that amount on the table. 'I asked him what the deuce he meant—but there he was, my friend of the Rye road', writes Ford. But that 'isn't the end of the story':

Two days afterwards I opened the Frankfurt paper and chanced to notice that there had been a particularly horrible murder in that city. A man had cut the throats of his wife, of his two children and of himself. And this man had been a waiter at Frankfurt chief railway station, and this waiter had been my waiter. He had told me his name. He had even asked me to come and see him at home if I had time. And not half an hour after he had been talking to me, this cheerful, battered, uncomplaining little person had murdered his wife, and his two children and had committed suicide without leaving the trace of a reason for his action.

Ford ends by pondering on the enigmatic motive; though the pathos of the waiter's madness and suicide evidently matter as much to him as their enigma. It was one of the episodes that haunted him, and about which he would continue to write.[32] After a grim joke about how the mere sight of his face may have been enough to cause the outburst, Ford finds deeper sympathies. First, he is sure 'from the acuteness of his memory' and his amusing manner that the man 'had a touch of imagination'; and that given the combination of memory, imagination, and lack of success, 'what despair may he not have known?' Then, probing deeper, Ford imagines all the memories that the chance encounter must have brought back to the waiter: not just his destitution, but the self-contempt that Ford in retrospect reads into the tramp's nonchalant manner of begging—'without a doubt, self-contempt is the greatest of all horrors. For one may be despised of all men and yet survive, but no man can stand the contempt of the final judge:— himself.' This sounds heartfelt, as if the encounter in Frankfurt had brought back Ford's own dark memories of the onset of his earlier breakdown; of his possible responsibility for Dr Martindale's sudden suicide; and, reaching back earlier still, his memory of the German teacher he felt his invective had helped to kill—a story which itself rekindled his anxiety over the sudden death of his German father. In addition, the story draws upon his feelings (both in 1904 and in 1911) that by his actions he was injuring the lives of his wife and children.

When he returned to the story after the war Ford was more confident in his diagnosis:

You know how, suddenly, in the midst of the brightest of days, a sudden recollection of past troubles or embarrassments will come over you and for a second or so you will feel inexpressibly troubled. Then it will pass. In the case of the poor little waiter it did not pass. The sight of me must have brought back to his mind the intolerable sufferings that he had undergone during his interminable tramp, his intolerable hoppings and shufflings, from the extreme north to the south of England. They must have come back to him with such unbearable vividness that he had gone suddenly mad.[33]

The waiter's breakdown may, similarly, have brought back to mind Ford's own breakdown, just when the tangle and haze of his affair with Hunt seemed set to produce another. His characteristic mode of treating such material is to fend off the anxiety by confronting it ('and for a second or so you will feel inexpressibly troubled'), and wondering what it all means; posing it as a perplexity, another instance of the dark forest that is the heart of another. Yet his mention of the waiter in *Ancient Lights* shows that there was more to his story. Never, since the day of his invective against the teacher, says Ford, 'can I remember having addressed a cutting speech to any living soul except once to a German waiter in the refreshment-room of Frankfort Hauptbahnhof'. This makes it much clearer why Ford should feel responsible for the man's suicide; and it makes it clear that the other versions repress precisely that responsibility—and that it is the repression that induces the feeling of uncanniness. In one sense the story is Ford's attempt at once to repress and to atone for whatever he said to him, and to come to terms with his potential for cruelty—something which his image of himself as altruist must have made it unusually hard to accept. In another sense, it is an allegory for the human cost of art; for the havoc that his artistry in expression was wreaking around him, and for the suicidal tendencies of the artist-figure himself. Finally, the different versions of the story show how the power of Ford's method of perplexity comes from his way of both suggesting and repressing unbearable thoughts, especially the paranoid thought that 'what it all means' is you, your omnipotence, your responsibility, your guilt. All these anxieties were to go into *The Good Soldier*, in which Ashburnham's unthinking speech (of passion) to Nancy leads to the destruction of his lover, of his ward's sanity, to his wife's breakdown, and to his cutting his own throat; and in which Dowell's dumb complicity is inextricable from a repressed sexual rivalry.[34]

Ford's and Hunt's catastrophe began to materialize when her maid went up to London to deliver a letter about Ford's daughters 'to their uncle'. The uncle was presumably Harri Martindale rather than Oliver, since the maid returned 'with the story of an Implacable Face . . . seen at the station. . . . She had felt awful all the way in the train coming back . . . seeing those Eyes'. She told the story, 'with details added and worked up', over dinner. Whether Ford imagined that Face as Elsie's, or as Destiny's, or an omniscient, punishing, paternal God's, the maid's story certainly started him imagining it. While Hunt was lying in bed, 'Joseph Leopold came up with a white, scared face'. He thought he had heard the doorbell, and spent much of the night barricading the house with dog-leads, string and a bicycle. 'And all this for fear that the Eyes had meant mischief', said Hunt. 'It was the beginning of a fresh attack of neurasthenia that lasted three whole years, and was responsible for many things, and much private and particular misery.'[35] They both suffered, and for more than three years. Ford did not fully recover his poise (though he sustained a passable impression of composure in public) until he finally broke with Hunt in 1918. She never recovered: by the time her bitterness over Ford's leaving had burnt itself out, her syphilis had burnt out much of her reason.

1912–1913: THE DARK FOREST

...it could pertain to the fundamental nature of existence that a complete knowledge of it would destroy one—so that the strength of a spirit could be measured by how much 'truth' it could take, more clearly, to what degree it *needed* it attenuated, veiled, sweetened, blunted, and falsified.

(Nietzsche, *Beyond Good and Evil*)

Hunt had completed an unfinished novel of her mother's, *The Governess*. But the publishers objected to Violet calling herself 'Mrs Hueffer' on the title page, arguing that it was 'very important that her maiden name shall appear'.[1] Another warning sign came when the *Daily Mirror* published a 'Withdrawal and Apology' after Elsie had threatened to sue them over the Spa interview in which Ford announced his marriage to Violet. The *Mirror* also had to pay Elsie £350 damages. 'A great day', noted Olive Garnett, who was seeing her regularly. Byles had been trying to negotiate a separation agreement, but now the attempt broke down.[2] Otherwise, for the first few months of the year Ford and Hunt seemed to have got away with their plan. Publicly at least, Ford appeared to be preserving his tranquillity, and they resumed their active social and literary life. Violet's society friends and their literary friends were still receiving them. Ford went to official dinners in London: at the Trocadero for the *Bystander*, a society magazine for which he had been writing weekly 'Causeries' since the autumn; then to the Saddler's Company.[3] He introduced Pound to W. H. Hudson, and also to Henry James. They only 'glared at one another across the same carpet' at this first meeting, though after meeting him again at a luncheon Pound was soon telling his parents that James was 'quite delightful'. Ford and Hunt also saw René Byles, and even Marwood and the Conrads. At first Conrad tried to put them off with his habitual apocalyptic hypochondria: 'My dear Ford I don't know if I ought to encourage you to come into a house full of 'flu. I too may be down by to-morrow. But as to coming to lunch on Sunday with you I really cannot manage it [. . .] If I get it too the bottom will be out of everything again. No luck. I know you like what I write, but you have an ever fresh and encouraging way of saying it to me—Thanks. It cheered a man who has no longer the consciousness of doing good work.' Like Florence in *The Good Soldier*, Hunt had some 'delicious oranges' sent to them, and Conrad wrote to her as 'Mrs Hueffer' to thank her. He was struggling to finish *Chance* ('I feel also done up with the worry of the novel'), the

book Ford had seen the beginning of in 1905, and thought 'something magnificent'. When Conrad had finished the novel he told Galsworthy that 'the great
F.M.H.' had visited him 'shortly after New Year with the somewhat less great
V[iolet] H[unt]'. Moser argues that 'the Great de Barral' in *Chance* 'looks, talks,
and acts like Ford; and his situation at the time of his greatness surely owes
something to Ford's in his *English Review* days'. 'Ford must have been much on
Conrad's mind while creating that cold, vain, self-deluded charlatan.' He also
shows how the plot—featuring a father, his daughter, and her lover on a
sea-voyage—rewrites (in a more compelling way) Ford's *An English Girl*.[4]

Ford wrote a review in which he characteristically appears to be commenting
obliquely on his private life; determining to brave scandal, or to convince himself that
he could: 'as is to be expected in a German novel, the book contains a complicated
tangle of prosperous love affairs; and there are mixed marriages between German
artists and members of the English upper classes; and it all goes very well—as indeed
it does in real life.'[5] Hunt herself gave a touching impression of how well their
relationship could go. Her account of her *Flurried Years* with Ford is not without
malice, but it is not a vengeful book: she was excited as well as enervated by the flurry,
and valued the intimacy with a man whose genius she admired:

He himself was abundantly psychic. It helped him, like any art that one practises
efficiently. While taking a deep interest in me, he took none in my life-history or that
of anyone else. But, did he so much as give himself the trouble to think about it, he
would find that he knew everything, past, present, and to come [. . .] I have known
this heavy man repeat to me, word for word, parts of a conversation held between
myself and a soldier friend of his in a cottage parlour in England while he himself was
in France [. . .] One explanation would be that, the author in the seër knew precisely
what this so ordinary soldier-man was likely to say to this so ordinary, jealous woman.
That would merely be the exercise of his trade. Any author should be able to
reconstruct the scene.

But it is uncanny to be linked in some sort to a supernatural being—as it were, the
changeling of a nursery tale.

Lawrence saw them together in London, and Ford took him to a matinée
performance by the Morality Play Society on 9 February 1912:

I found Hueffer getting very fat [. . .] But he's rather nicer than he was. He seems to
have had a crisis, when, dear Lord, he fizzed and bubbled all over the place. Now, don't
you know, he seems quite considerate, even thoughtful for other folk. But he *is* fat.

It's Violet's good influence. Do you know, I rather like her—she's such a real
assassin [. . .]

She looked old, yet she was gay—she was gay, she laughed, she bent and fluttered
in the wind of joy. She coquetted and played beautifully with Hueffer: she loves him
distractedly—she was charming, and I loved her. But my God, she looked old.

Perhaps because she wore—she was going to some afternoon affair of swell
suffragettes—a gaudy witch-cap stitched with beads of scarlet and a delicate ravel of
green and blue [. . .] and she peeped coquettishly under the brim—but she looked
damned old. It rather hurt me [. . .]

I think Fordy liked it—but was rather scared. He feels, poor fish, the hooks are through his gills this time—and they *are*. Yet he's lucky to be so well caught—she'll handle him with marvellous skill.

They sport a carriage now—have one on contract, I believe. Hueffer drove me in great state to the Court Theatre, where we heard some Morality Players—Yeats and Rev Something [J. G.] Adderley. It wasn't any *very* great shakes—but rather nice. Hueffer is really rather decent:—he likes to sark (verb to be sarcastic unto) me because I am 'a serious person at grips with life'.

But the honeymoon (if that's what it was) was over. Marwood advised Hunt to take Ford back to the continent, 'where writs didn't run', though he saw that she was tied to her mother, now in her eighties.[6]

Hunt's sisters tried to stop the publication of *The Governess*—they had already been suing her because they felt she was profiting unfairly from their mother's estate. Then, on 3 April, the *Throne*, a society magazine managed by Byles, announced the book. Ford, perhaps emboldened by Elsie's silence, called Violet 'Mrs Hueffer' in his preface—Chatto's appeared not to mind, or not to notice, as long as it didn't happen on the title-page. The *Throne* publicity picked this up, printing photographs of Mrs Hunt and Violet, and referring in the caption to 'Miss Violet Hunt (Mrs. Ford Madox Hueffer)'. Perhaps Ford and Hunt thought they could get away with it. But Elsie had already threatened to sue the *Lady* (for reporting their attendance at the Women Writers' League). It is hard not to feel that these continued announcements of being married were their most egregious acts of self-destructive provocation. (David Garnett thought they positively invited scandal.) Publication of *The Governess* went ahead on 18 April, but Elsie brought a libel suit against the *Throne* 'to assert her right to the title of being the lawful wife of her husband'. In the same year she sold the Bungalow, their marital home, for £641, using the money to add a tower and to make other improvements to Kitcat cottage at Aldington. Under the practical measure was a gesture of defiance: from now on she was committed to living in her own house, and did not hope to live again with the husband whose name she was fighting to keep. Edmée van der Noot, who with the Catholic Hüffers had persuaded Elsie that a divorce would morally harm the daughters, had to return to Belgium in 1912. Without her only close Catholic friend, Elsie must have felt more isolated than ever.[7]

Ford broke down while they were staying at Sandgate. Mizener said it was while waiting for the case to come to trial; but it had already happened by 5 April, when Lawrence got a letter from Hunt saying that her 'poor Ford' had had a breakdown, and 'mustn't even dictate a letter "if he can help it" '. In June Ford complained to Pinker about Constable's delay in publishing *The Panel*, the rapid writing of which had, he said, 'induced a very severe nervous breakdown from which I am still suffering'.[8] But the evidence points to a bout of depression rather than a complete collapse. The analysis of Count Macdonald in *The New Humpty-Dumpty* is perhaps Ford's diagnosis of his own state, as Mizener asserts, after the loss of the *English Review*, and the threat of still more litigation and scandal: 'his depressions came from that essential dark forest which is the heart of another. He had come across so many basenesses, little and big, and so many mere selfishnesses, big or little, and whether these affected himself or merely other people, they troubled him beyond all reason. It was the one thing that really affected him [. . .] His mind was too sensitive to stand it.'[9] Both he and Hunt were prescribed Adalin by Tebb, which 'made one something of a philosopher', 'living in a dream'. Ford's productivity didn't cease, it merely slowed down: in the next year he wrote another novel, *Mr Fleight*; a fine suffragette pamphlet called *This Monstrous Regiment of Women* for the Women's Freedom League; and three short stories.[10]

Outwardly the social and literary life continued. Douglas Goldring described how 'as host and hostess, Violet and Ford had few equals in literary London during the brief interval before the outbreak of war'. Their society friends kept aloof because of the scandal; which meant that their parties became more bohemian:

The place of the late Victorian celebrities and socially distinguished figures was taken by 'les jeunes' of the *English Review* circle, among whom Ezra Pound, P. Wyndham Lewis, Rebecca West, the Compton Mackenzies and W. L. George were prominent. Of Violet's older literary friends, May Sinclair, Ethel Colburn Mayne and H. G. Wells [who was of course an old friend of Ford's, from his Romney Marsh days] remained loyal, while Ford never lacked friends and admirers even if he did not always keep them. A distinction must be drawn between Ford's relations with the people with whom he associated, and his 'life of the mind'. His personal affairs might be in an agonizing muddle but his intellectual detachment and devotion to the arts he practised or appreciated, never faltered.[11]

Ford was (in Malcolm Bradbury's words) 'a crucial energizer and instigator of this lively pre-war scene'. Lawrence was taken to teas at South Lodge by Grace Crawford (a dancer whom Pound had introduced): 'He was attached to Ford but rather intimidated by Violet, and usually preferred seeing Ford in his own quarters.' In the summer the tea parties became tennis parties. Ford, Pound, Crawford, and Mary Martindale would play mixed doubles; Lawrence didn't play, but 'he liked to watch it and to keep score; he was a fast and agile ball-boy'. Ford said Pound played tennis 'like a galvanized agile gibbon'.[12] Old Mrs Hunt was becoming more eccentric. According to Crawford, she disliked Ford and Pound, and would hide their tennis gear every week. Lawrence said that she disliked him even more, and that it was a good thing he didn't play, or she would have burnt his things.

Mrs Hunt would come out with 'the most surprising and irrelevant remarks which Violet always received with complete calm':

Once, on being handed a cup of tea, the old lady sniffed it suspiciously and then in a deep and tragic voice said: 'What is this, poison? Well, never mind, I'll drink it if you like', downing it all in a single hearty gulp [. . .]
On one occasion she was more than usually difficult and asked each man in turn who he was and what he did, including Ford whom she saw nearly every day! A rather embarrassed silence ensued which was finally broken by Violet rather tartly saying,

'You know quite well who they are, Mother, and that they are all poets.' Mrs Hunt's only answer was a loud snort; for the rest of tea she fixed poor Lawrence with a basilisk stare, occasionally muttering under her breath: 'All poets indeed. Ha! All poets, indeed. Ha!'

Ford began going to the philosopher T. E. Hulme's Tuesday evenings, where he met Jacob Epstein, who found him 'a very pontifical person'.[13]

The New Humpty-Dumpty was published on 9 July. Some of the reviewers recognized Ford, praising 'the hall-mark of the best writer of historical novels we possess', and the 'genius that is struggling from a youth spent in the subtlest impressionism to the most literal realism of treatment; from *The Fifth Queen* to *The Panel*, in fact'. Others praised 'the author's humour and immense faculty for detail', and found the book 'irresistibly amusing'.[14] The 20-year-old Rebecca West wrote an incisive anonymous review for the *English Review*, praising Ford's 'fine mastery over events in the story', the 'new power in the gnome-like figure of the wretched little Mr. Pett, the Socialist turned Nietzschean Tory':

Of course, Daniel Chaucer is always very childlike; and one of the habits of childhood is to chuckle over jokes that it cannot explain. So the savage satire with which he cudgels Countess Macdonald, a horrible picture of what a wicked Fabian would be like, is sometimes incomprehensible. The same combination of wit and obscurity, that made one feel the force of the satire one was not permitted to understand, was observable in *High Germany* [the volume of verse Ford had published around February].

Violet Hunt wrote (about this novel) that 'when a literature-picture of a total personality is put together it is non-libellous in effect, being a mere blend—an action of A's, a speech of D's, a look of C, the hair or eyes of F. Surely such a preparation or composite of aliens cannot possibly be dubbed a description of Z.'[15] But when Marwood and Elsie recognized themselves in *The New Humpty-Dumpty*, it cannot have felt like they were reading a 'mere blend', concocted for purely novelistic purposes. Elsie was not a Fabian, but the savage satire of the Countess would have been much more comprehensible to her as the result of Ford's bitterness over her refusal to divorce, than it was to Rebecca West. Marwood fell out with Ford again as a result of the novel; and despite Ford's lasting affection for him, and continuing use of ever-more sympathetic Marwoodian heroes, the breach was now irreparable.

Rebecca West was invited to tea: they expected a 'dangerous woman', but found someone 'quite superiorly, ostentatiously, young—the ineffable schoolgirl'—who nevertheless, thought Hunt, 'already ruled Fleet Street'. Her 'incredibly wicked observations in a soft musical voice were hair-raising', thought another of the guests, Brigit Patmore. West made just such a wicked observation about being embraced by Ford, which she said was 'like being the toast under a poached egg'. She thought Hunt had a good line in musical wickednesses too: 'She was so *kind*. She said sharp things about people, but it was like a bird chirping. She never failed to bring a bit of good luck the way of a friend, even if it meant she had to put herself to quite considerable trouble.' Hunt held a garden party on 2 July; then she recalled that she and Ford spent a 'languid airless summer, rife with Law and Cubism' at her cottage in Selsey. However, as so often in *The Flurried Years*, she takes liberties with dates and details—her reminiscences are as 'impressionist' as Ford's—and has fused, or confused, the years 1912 and 1914.[16]

Ford was also seeing a lot of C. F. G. Masterman, who had been literary editor of the *Daily News* from 1903 (before Scott-James), and a Liberal MP since 1906, and who was to follow in the footsteps of Conrad and Marwood as Ford's chief male confidant until the end of the war. He was spending time with Masterman at Selsey. 'Ford is out in the *pouring* rain playing golf with Masterman & improving his views (M's views) on the political situation', Hunt wrote to Cathy Hueffer, and told her Ford was talking of returning '*alone* to this cottage for a fresh bout of golf with Masterman but I don't know if that will come off. One never knows anything with a raging fiend like Elsie hanging about. I am getting a mixture of desperate & philosophical.' Ford took Masterman to visit Katherine Mansfield and John Middleton Murry, who were staying in a cottage at Runcton, near Chichester. Back in London, he sent Pound to buy tennis balls for the afternoon games, which were now supplemented by criticism of the prose style of Pound's essay on the troubadours, 'Gironde'. 'F.M.H. finds my prose as bad as Stevenson,' Pound told Dorothy Shakespear, 'so I've made some alterations and inserted a soliloquy on fat middle-aged gentlemen in armchairs. F. has just returned from instructing the [. . .] personnel of your respected cabinet, so he is a little out of hand.' He found Ford's comments 'very helpful', and decided not to publish the essay; and he was pleased that Ford was 'pleased with the Ripostes', his latest volume of verse. Wyndham Lewis was also a frequent guest at South Lodge. 'These intellectual hosts were of that valuable kind of human, who shuns solitude as the dread symbol of unsuccess, is happiest when his rooms are jammed with people (for preference of note)', wrote Lewis, continuing with brilliant malice:

Hueffer was a flabby lemon and pink giant, who hung his mouth open as though he were an animal at the Zoo inviting buns—especially when ladies were present. Over the gaping mouth damply depended the ragged ends of a pale lemon moustache. This ex-collaborator with Joseph Conrad was himself, it always occurred to me, a typical figure out of a Conrad book—a caterer, or corn-factor, coming on board—blowing like a porpoise with the exertion—at some Eastern port.

What he *thought* he was, was one of those military *sahibs* who used to sit on the balcony of a club in Hindustan with two or three other *sahibs, stingahs* at their sides, and who, between meditative puffs at a cheroot, begins to tell one of Conrad's tales. He possessed a vivid and theatrical imagination: he jacked himself up, character as he was in a nautical story, from one of the white business gents in the small tropic port into—I am not quite sure it was not into a *Maugham* story—among the more swagger representatives of white empire in Asia.

At the end of September Ford and Hunt travelled to the North of England and to Scotland. Violet 'bounced in upon Goneril', as she calls her sister Silvia in *The*

Flurried Years (her other sister, Venice Benson, becomes 'Regan'; which presumably leaves Violet as an implausible Cordelia). If she expected reconciliation, she was disabused with a peevish dismissal, Silvia saying: 'Let the lawyers thrash it out!' When they got back to South Lodge, Mrs Hunt was seriously ill. Venice came, but refused Violet's offer of a reconciliation while their mother was dying, on 1 November.[17]

Early in December Ford wrote to Lawrence, who was now at Lake Garda with Frieda Weekley. His letter hasn't survived, but the thrust of his 'full opinions on the *Trespasser*' can be gathered from Lawrence's reply. 'I agree with you heartily', he wrote. 'I rather hate the book. It seems a bit messy to me'; and he asked Ford: 'Did you have a sudden flicker of affection for me that made you write this letter? I'm sure I wish it were so. And no doubt I am a lax and immoral young man—but ought not that rather to endear me to you than otherwise?' Later in the month Pound went with Ford and Hunt to the theatre: 'F. & V. had a box for [Stanley Houghton's] 'The Younger Generation' & it was very diverting, with a curtain raiser 'Aristide Pujol' [by William Locke] and a sentimental [J. M.] Barrie one act to finish. F. & I groaned so as to be heard all through the theatre.'[18]

Ford and Violet borrowed a cottage at Farnham Common, near Burnham Beeches, and invited Pound, Ford's nephew Frank Soskice, Mary Martindale, and the Compton Mackenzies for what Faith Mackenzie called 'a really notable Christmas':

My contribution to the household was a Sudbury ham, which was fallen upon with greedy enthusiasm by the other guest, Ezra Pound, who talked without ceasing throughout the festival. On Christmas Day Ford could only be approached through the keyhole of his bedroom, in which he was firmly locked against all comers. The cause of this retirement was not made known, but it gave a spice to the party, since Violet was continually running upstairs to entreat him, speculating loudly as to why he was up there at all [. . .] Ford, releasing himself from bondage on St. Stephen's Day, descended upon us with his store of intellectual energy unimpaired by festive excesses, full of benevolence, good cheer and lively conversation; in short, he was himself again. And Violet, her great eyes blazing, carved the turkey [. . .] her cheeks flushed at the excitement of his restoration.[19]

'Impossible to get any writing done here', wrote Pound to his mother on Christmas Eve. 'Atmosphere too literary. 3 "Kreators" all in one ancient cottage *is* a bit thick.' He told her he was staying 'for a week with the Hueffers in a dingy old cottage that belonged to Milton. F.M.H. and I being the only two people who couldn't be in the least impressed by the fact, makes it a bit more ironical.' What makes it more ironical still is that Milton lived six or seven miles away at Chalfont St Giles: someone, possibly Ford, had been having Pound on.[20]

Ford was evidently fighting back his depressions. Even Mizener, who says meanly that such performances were Ford's 'way of trying to avoid the knowledge of what was likely to happen at that trial that was gradually working its way to the top of the court calendar', has to acknowledge his 'remarkable self-control'.[21] One can hear him registering the pressure he was under, as well as some surprise that he was able to withstand it, when he wrote one of his finest letters—only a fortnight before the trial—a long, thoughtful response to Lucy Masterman's *Poems*. He begins by apologizing for taking so long to thank her: 'I have been very busy and fussed with one thing and another and moreover my doctor forbade me to read or write at all. Still, here I am.' He describes reading the first half of her book with pleasure: 'I felt really in contact with a poetic temperament, aloof, pleasant, and not common.' And he then modulates into tactful and constructive criticism: 'To jump quickly to what I want to say—to what I am always wanting to say—the note is too refined, too remote, too LITERARY.' It is the same lesson he delivered to Pound in Giessen, with patient argument taking the place of gesture. The central canons of early modernism are being originated: the stress on contemporary urban life, the imaginative significance of the machine, the struggle to escape from received ideas and styles, the primacy of technique, surprise, analysis, language. Though he urged other writers to remember Flaubert, Turgenev, Maupassant, James, and Conrad, his awareness of literary tradition was less obtrusive than in the work of the high modernists, Pound, Eliot, and Joyce, and it was always subordinated to his belief in the importance of a contemporary idiom. He was committed to an expressionist notion of 'personality' as what literature ultimately expressed; a notion which Eliot in particular was influentially to reject (even while writing the poetry that best expressed his own personality). Otherwise, Ford was as much the first modernist as 'the last Pre-Raphaelite':

That is what is the matter with all the verse of to-day; it is too much practised in temples and too little in motorbuses—LITERARY! LITERARY! Now that is the last thing that verse should ever be, for the moment a medium becomes literary it is remote from the life of the people, it is dulled, languishing, moribund and at last dead [. . .] You will, I hope, understand what I mean—it is that roughly, your work—like most work of to-day—suffers a little from the want of the quality of surprise, which in the end is the supreme quality and necessity of art. You ought to search your mind and your vocabulary much more thoroughly [. . .] sit down to write, metaphorically speaking, in a railway waiting room, or in a wet street, or in your own kitchen (not in your nursery, that would be too idyllic) or in the lobby of the House of Commons, I was going to say, but the jobs that are perpetrated there are too artificial. But go where something real is doing and let your language be that of the more serious witnesses in Blue Books [. . .] what the poet ought to do is to write his own mind in the language of his day.

Forget about Piers Plowman, forget about Shakespeare, Keats, Yeats, Morris, the English Bible and remember only that you live in our terrific, untidy, indifferent empirical age, where not one single problem is solved and not one single Accepted Idea from the past has any more any magic. Our Lord and his teachings are dead; and the late [Samuel] Smiles and his, and the late William Morris and John Ruskin and Newman and Froude—only that Newman was a very beautiful, unadjectival writer. It is for us to get at the new truths or to give new life to such of the old as will appeal hominibus bonae voluntatis [to men of goodwill]. Only to do that we must do it in the clear pure language of our own day and with what is clear and new in our own individualities.[22]

Ford realizes he has written 'a terrific sermon': terrific in both senses. Frightening in its morbidity, yet also full of intelligent gusto. It shows how writing was a therapy for Ford, that what kept him writing was (amongst other things) the way the activity of it could pull him through his depressions. These depressions invariably made him imagine death, but writing could give him 'new life'. Although he never loses his sense of his audience, his letters, like his other writings, confront mortality in order to console himself for it with the pleasures of the mind, human intimacy, and the timelessness of writing. The sages, moralists, and reformers have died. The teachings of Newman are dead; but his writing is beautiful.

Like all Ford's important friendships, this with the Mastermans was a highly literary one. But then, what most mattered to Ford, whether in literature or in love, was intimate communication. If his friendships seem conducted for the sake of literature, that literature is not an abstract, impersonal thing: it is a social activity: a matter for collaboration, endless discussion, mutual criticism; to be read aloud, inscribed to friends, treasured because of the artist's personality it expresses, as much as because of its objective technical achievement. It is something aloof, but with which it is important to feel 'in contact'. He could also be ironic about his need for such communication. 'Tell your husband to come and play golf with me at Le Touquet where I am going shortly', he told Lucy towards the end of this long letter. 'I will then sermonise him too with the utmost ferocity about the nature of things and he can listen with that splendid air of attention and respect which always does me as much good as attending at a first-rate farce. In fact, it must be good practice for him too, to listen to such huge dogmatism with an air of attention.'

Ford was with Hunt in Boulogne at the beginning of February, staying at the Hôtel Dervaux. Tebb wrote him a letter explaining that he had been attending him professionally 'for neurasthenia during the last six months', and giving his opinion that it would be injurious to Ford to appear in court. Hunt told Goldring that Ford had begun 'to punish the whisky bottle'. Ford stayed in Amiens this winter, where, he later recalled, he 'lounged about for a fortnight, going to picture-shows and talking to commis-voyageurs', and where, he said, 'very late at night, I saw in the most wonderful of all Gothic cathedrals the most wonderful thing I ever saw in my life. The immense nave was in pitch gloom; there was just one single candle alight in the whole bulding, and that was stuck in the gilt crown of an immense golden statue of Our Lady that some religious were wheeling from the north door towards the high altar . . .'[23]

Hunt returned to London for the trial, though she did not attend it either. Although the trial implicated her and Ford, they were frustratingly unable to participate. It was between Elsie and Illustrated Journals Ltd., the owners of the *Throne*. The case was tried in the King's Bench Division before Mr Justice Avory. Elsie's counsel outlined the collapse of the Hueffers' marriage. The part that really upset Ford when he heard about it later was the imputation that he had left Elsie to bring up the two children on only £3 a week, and then stopped even these alimony payments in 1912; whereas in fact she had her own income of £80 a year, and Ford and Hunt had been paying over £200 a year to keep the girls at what

Goldring called their 'aristocratic' convent school. The nub of Elsie's case was that she had been exposed to 'ridicule, hatred and contempt' by Violet's use of the name 'Hueffer', which either implied that Elsie 'was not his wife at all or that she was divorced'—this in the days when divorce was still considered scandalous. Her counsel said he thought Ford had not divorced Elsie, since 'no papers were ever served on the plaintiff, and inquiries had elicited no particulars of any divorce proceedings in Germany'.[24]

But the counsel for the defence had no intention of embroiling himself in arguments about whether Violet was actually 'Mrs Hueffer'. Presumably he had not seen any divorce papers either. Instead, he asked 'what people were to do when a woman passed as a man's wife and was widely reputed to be such', arguing that the action should never have been brought against the newspapers: 'It was a fight between two women and Mrs. Hueffer had succeeded in stamping Miss Hunt, in fact, if not directly, as an adulteress.'[25] The *Throne*, that is, had said nothing directly about Elsie, and, as the judge summed up, had simply described Violet by the name she was widely known by. The writer of the puff in the *Throne*, Frank Mumby, even explained in the witness-box that he had based it on the wording of Ford's preface. The jury found for Elsie, assessing the damages at £300. At this point Mr Storry Deans, Violet's lawyer, said:

I am instructed by a lady whose name has been mentioned with great frequency—Miss Violet Hunt—to state that she wishes it to be known that she believes herself to be Mrs. Ford Maddox [*sic*.] Hueffer, and intends so to call herself.
  MR. JUSTICE AVORY: I have nothing to do with this belief or any of her beliefs.
  MR. STORRY DEANS: Statements have been directed against—
  MR. JUSTICE AVORY: I cannot hear you any further [. . .] I decline to allow this Court to be made a medium of advertisement.[26]

Hunt wrote that only after hearing the verdict did she realize that she had never thought the *Throne* might lose. But it is hard to see how she thought it could win if she couldn't, or wouldn't, prove her marriage. The *Throne* also had to pay costs; altogether the newspaper lost £1,000, and went out of business. Hunt later claimed that she had lunched with the paper's editor, Comyns Beaumont, begging him not to defend the case, but to print an apology: 'I thought I was strong enough to stand it', she said. But Beaumont wrote that both Ford and Hunt had promised Byles that they were married, and that they would testify to it in court: 'our defence was vitiated by the disappearance of Hueffer and his lady friend.' If this were true, Ford's treatment of Byles, whom he said was one of his 'most intimate friends', would have been as shabby as Mizener implies. Yet Byles bore them no grudge. He was eager to publish Ford's next novel, and was still a friend of them both years later. Since Byles had supported Ford in court in July 1910, and since he must have known that the *Daily Mirror* had had to pay Elsie damages for reporting Ford and Hunt as married, he must have had a shrewd idea of Elsie's determination and of the likely outcome.[27]

Some of Hunt's friends called to support her after the trial: W. L. George and Brigit Patmore, who had testified in court that Ford and Violet were widely known as Mr and Mrs Hueffer; also Mary Martindale, who had come to stay at South Lodge for a while, and accompanied her to Charing Cross, but became 'hysterical', and 'nearly collapsed at the station when she saw our portraits, very large, on the placards'. Hunt told her to 'buy them all'. Long after Hunt had recounted all these details to him, Ford was to draw on them in *The Marsden Case*, in which George Heimann is harassed by the publicity for his libel case, and the hysteria of his sister and her friend Miss Jeaffreason. The reports of the case even followed Hunt across the Channel. They were sent to Coventry by the other English guests at their hotel. Ford had become ill—first a cold, then pains in the chest. He had lost his voice. They left as soon as the doctor allowed, travelling to Montpellier, Carcassonne, and to some of the Provençal towns mentioned in *The Good Soldier*—Beaucaire, Las Tours, Tarascon. It snowed; there were icy gales. 'We hardly spoke to each other that month', wrote Hunt, though Ford sent regular postcards to his daughters. They stayed at the Hôtel de la Cité in Carcassonne, and a French lieutenant shared their table, discussing the probability of war with Ford, and countering his arguments in favour of the Church of Rome with his own agnostic positivism. (Ford was to meet him by chance during the war, while his men were playing cricket behind the lines.) A hotel bathroom was offered as a study, and Ford began writing *The Young Lovell*, using the lid of the bath as a desk.[28]

The *Throne* case was a considerable scandal. Goldring likened it to the one caused by the affair between Georges Sand and Alfred de Musset. Both Ford and Hunt were well-known literary figures, at a time when intellectuals were pressing for divorce reform. Hunt was also a society suffragette. The *Throne* case put them at the centre of the Edwardian debates about sexuality, divorce, morality, and censorship, debates which the *English Review* had helped to air, and which were sharpened by other high-profile cases, such as that of Arthur Balfour, who lived with a woman he wasn't married to, and Edward VII himself, who not only had mistresses, but was involved in scandals and testified in divorce cases. Hunt evidently saw their case as a *cause célèbre* comparable to what she called 'the Holman Hunt imbroglio', or Lord Russell's trial for bigamy.[29]

The trial also meant the end of their striving for social 'respectability'. It publicized the fact that they were living together as man and wife without having proved that they were married. Hunt wrote to Ford's mother that she thought it had been worse for Ford. But ultimately the verdict was more damaging to Violet. Not only had she forfeited her social 'position'—Ford was her last potential husband. She was doubly humiliated.

Ford was devastated at the time. Hunt describes him as 'tremendously agitated, oft weeping as only a German can', after Marwood wrote to demand repayment of the money he had lent Ford for Elsie's operation. Conrad (who still owed Ford money) later wrote to tell him that Marwood had nearly died that winter, and wanted 'to put his affairs in order'. To Ford, it seemed at the time as if even his most respected friend believed the story about him leaving his children to starve.[30] He was often suicidally depressed between 1912 and the end of the war. Yet the mental strain and anguish of this period charged some of his best writing: *The Young Lovell*; the brilliant series of 'Literary Portraits' he wrote for the *Outlook* from September 1913 to August 1915; the milestone essay 'On Impressionism' and the Preface for his 1913 *Collected Poems*; the influential poem 'On Heaven'; and, above all, *The Good Soldier*. As he wrote to Pinker from St Rémy on Good Friday, 'after all, for my sins, I am a stylist!' The social codes mattered to Ford—and not just as a subject for novelistic investigation. But although he deeply wanted to be acceptable to the 'decent people', and to be accepted, his closest, literary, friends were not scandalized by the case, and stood by him and Violet. Recalling his friend Galsworthy's feeling that he should ostracize himself after being cited as co-respondent in 1905 by his cousin Arthur, with whose wife Ada he had been having an affair for a decade, Ford wrote years later:

Times of course have changed, but I think that even then the ordinary man would have taken the matter less tragically. Galsworthy, however, insisted on considering that his social career and more particularly that of his future wife was at an end, and that for the rest of their lives they would be cut off at least from the public society of decent people. He was, of course, quite wrong. Even at that date London society took the view that, for a decent man and woman, passing through the divorce courts was a sufficient ordeal to atone for most irregularities.[31]

Ford, however, at first took his own case just as tragically, like the extraordinary man he was. Because his case was not a simple divorce case, London society would be less likely to consider the trial its own punishment. Even a third of a century later, his language is still wondering whether the 'irregularities' of his own case had been atoned for in the eyes of London society. For the scandal of the case was not only to do with adultery and divorce. The notion that Ford and Hunt had lied unforgivably—had not behaved like 'decent people'—has been remarkably persistent, and persistently damaging to Ford's literary as well as moral reputation in England.

Ford's writing had always been concerned with fears that the protagonist might not be as he represented himself to be; or that he might be as he was misrepresented: notably George Moffat in *The Benefactor*, and Henry in *The Fifth Queen*. From *The Simple Life Limited* onwards, however, this fear takes on a specific form that has little to do with Ford's own circumstances (though it may reflect his fears for his estranged children, or any future children now that divorce from Elsie was definitively denied): that of illegitimacy, anxiety about which haunts the heroes of *The Young Lovell*, *The Marsden Case*, and *Parade's End*. Before the *Throne* case Ford's protagonists are misunderstood and betrayed idealists; the motives of their idealism is questioned, and they undergo their neurasthenic episodes, but they are fundamentally sound. Afterwards this soundness is itself called into question; Ashburnham, Dowell, Tietjens, Henry Martin, are all more problematic figures, living a lie, deceiving their friends, and often deceiving themselves. Ford spent the rest of his life grappling with the doubts raised by the *Throne* case.

Mrs W. K. Clifford, the novelist on whom Ford is thought to have based the character of Mrs Wannop in *Parade's End* (with traits added from Mrs Hunt), gave the couple a clear idea of what they could expect:

> Your old friends love you and will stand by you—*some* of them, but I don't think you know *how strong* the feeling about you is, and it would be *impossible* for you to go about and be received without first asking what sort of reception you would get or whether you would get any at all. I would do a good deal for you but I simply should quake if you came here on Sundays, and I believe other people would walk out.—*Go away for three years! and* trust to your old friends to smoothe things as far as they can for you. In these days everything is forgotten; you know I would help you all I can—so would a few others—but this is how we feel—and I beg you to be prudent.[32]

Hunt felt that to stay abroad would be to accept disgrace, and replied that she expected her friends to 'treat the attack with contempt' rather than to make it more difficult for them to live in England. Friends such as Henry James and Lucy Masterman had written supportively. She explained to Clifford:

> All my husband's relations expect me back as usual, not to speak of those . . . who entertained me and backed me up in my rescue of Ford from a state far worse than death, which indeed he did contemplate. . . . And that is why I am so surprised at your advice. Of course, I should not have thought of entering your drawing-room on Sundays without a very pressing invitation from you. I can't help saying that I should have expected it. I should expect all my real friends to accept my version of the affair naturally and easily—and if other friends walked out, let them![33]

Unfortunately it wasn't quite true that Ford's relations were all supportive. Though Hunt said Juliet Soskice wrote her 'a nice letter', Ford's mother was 'sad & depressed' by the case, and wrote to Violet 'severely'. Hunt's claim that she had had 'heaps of nice letters—making light of it & invitations' wasn't much truer; though doubtless she and Ford hoped that such talk would encourage the waverers. 'The only thing for Ford & me to do is to wipe the unjustifiable mud Elsie has thrown off our faces,' she told Cathy Hueffer, 'make ourselves presentable & go on as if nothing had happened.'[34] But this attitude was never going to work with their society friends. Mrs Clifford replied bluntly, saying she thought it 'foolish not to have courage to tell you what it is people *do* say', namely, that Ford's and Violet's story was 'impossible to believe'. She urged them to put an end to the doubts by getting her solicitor to state when and where Ford divorced Elsie; where the divorce decree was procured and before which judge; when the decree became absolute; and when and where she and Ford went through a marriage ceremony. She advised them either to advertise this information, or to send it to all her acquaintances.

Even their more bohemian friends felt the force of the scandal. May Sinclair wrote a kindly letter accepting Violet's resignation from the Committee of Women Writers (which included Mrs Clifford). 'Personally', wrote Sinclair, 'I don't care two straws whether your marriage holds good in this country or not. (and should *not* care if it had never taken place).' But it was felt that 'some foolish persons might object if you remained on the Committee and that they might make a fuss which would cause injury to the dinner—the sacred dinner!' She also advised staying abroad 'till all this has blown over and been forgotten'; though she estimated the memory of the 'decent people' at a mere six months. Ford's version of the double standards of *The Good Soldier*'s 'good people' has struck some readers as caricatured, just as his presentation of society's codes in *Parade's End* has been criticized as a fantastic, paranoiac, outsider's view.[35] Yet the *Throne* case shows how pervasive and punitive the moral codes were. Critics like Mizener, arguing that 'Ford's novels are never reliable representations of reality', are merely accusing them of not being *realist* novels, something that Ford the impressionist never intended them to be. His impressionism uses what Tietjens calls 'illuminative exaggerations'. On the other hand, the historian of a mannered milieu cannot always be confident in distinguishing verisimilitude from exaggeration. What now seems to us exaggerated is often accurate rendering of conventions and forms that themselves seem excessive by today's standards. Even in the 1920s Ezra Pound could write that appreciation of Ford was 'difficult for those not in eng. at least from 1908–20'. Commenting on the 'amusement' of the social satires *The Simple Life Limited*, and *Mr. Fleight*, he noted that they were: 'both in surface technique, presumably brilliant, and but for levity, wd. be recognized as hist. docs. are so recog. by those who know how close their apparent fantasia was to the utter imbecilities of milieu they portray. Unbelieved because the sober foreigner has no mean of knowing how far they corresponded to an external reality.'[36] With the possible exception of the older members of the Royal Family, we are all now sober foreigners to the stringent world of Edwardian drawing-room morality.

Ford wanted to compensate Byles for the *Throne* fiasco by letting him publish his next novel, *Mr. Fleight*, 'for nothing, that is to say without an advance'. Byles had set up a new publishing firm, Howard Latimer, with two young associates. Though it suited Ford's altruism to say 'it is really rather more in the nature of a present to him than anything else', he also had hopes that Byles would be as successful with this book as with *The Soul of London*, and would be able to publish his future novels too: 'Byles [. . .] is enthusiastic and will spend a great deal of money on advertising them', he assured Pinker. Ford recalled later that Byles

hit on the diabolical idea of hiring a carriage and pair with cockaded footmen and a passenger got up to resemble my principal character. This monstrosity drove all over the more aristocratic region of London leaving cards on which was engraved:
Mr. Fleight
 Palatial Hall
  Hampstead N.W.

Ford claimed Byles hadn't forewarned him, and that he was embarrassed when G. W. Prothero, the editor of the *Quarterly*, reprimanded him over tea that his 'passion for publicity' carried him too far. ('I did not explain the mistake and I never went to the Protheros' again', said Ford. 'I took the view that they ought to have known me better. Or perhaps they did not ask me. I suppose it doesn't matter'—even though he recalled their house as the one he best liked to visit after Dr Garnett's death.) The publicizing of *Mr. Fleight* suggests one explanation of why Byles had been prepared to risk the *Throne* being prosecuted. He had supported Ford during the case over the *Mirror*'s report, so he knew what was likely to happen. But he may have hoped that the case would provide good publicity for Ford's book (as the Martindale case had done for *The Queen Who Flew*). But, said Ford, Byles's partners had less capital than they had led him to believe, and 'the book was seized by the Sheriff's Office because Byles's firm could not pay its printer's bills'. Ford said that because of this the book was 'never actually published'. Certainly copies of it are very scarce, and his best novel between *The Fifth Queen* and *The Good Soldier* earned virtually nothing.[37]

Despite being written at what must have been his emotionally lowest point since 1904, *Mr. Fleight* is remarkable for its crispness and sureness of tone. It invokes much of the same material as *The New Humpty-Dumpty*—passion, suicide, madness, violence, corruption, divorce, the failure of the *English Review*. But instead of displacing them to the fairy-tale world of Galizian politics, it confronts them in the world Ford knew well: English political and literary life. Aaron Fleight is a wealthy Jew who—as Ford was to do six years later—has changed his name. He is fascinated by the Marwoodian Mr Blood, a 'last mastodon' Tory, a god-like, omniscient, detached observer, who is another of Ford's attempts to work through the paradox of the cynical altruist. Blood amuses himself by persuading Fleight to stand for parliament, predicting that a meteoric career can be guaranteed simply by his wealth. It will show the corruption of democratic liberalism, which to the revolutionary Tory seems merely the alibi for the rich to exploit the poor; and it will confirm Blood's conviction that 'it's a pretty beastly world'. He wants to reduce social climbing to absurdity: 'I'm trying to crush it all up into a short period so as to make the affair all the more an object lesson—or, rather, all the more of a joke, because I don't care whether anybody learns anything from it or not. I'm not a social reformer.' The plot draws on fairy-tale in charting Fleight's path from unprepossessing outsider to ruler. It is another version of the Bingel and Bengel story too. Blood can get away with murder (he has strangled his groom who betrayed him), whereas Fleight is beaten up without just cause. But though Fleight himself tries to believe that what matters is 'whether your heart is in the right place', the plot says that what matters is whether your blood is from the right place, from the right class. 'It still sounds like a silly fairy tale', says Augusta MacPhail, the German-bred editor who has been thought a portrait of Hunt (though she also recalls Gertrud Schablowsky). But she tells Blood: 'The way you say it makes it seem a nasty dirty business. I don't really like your cynicism.' That duality best describes the book: it is a fairy-tale told cynically.[38]

Mr. Fleight is dense with intimations of Ford's own experiences. Augusta's father went mad teaching English in Germany. Fleight finances a new review, which enables Ford to satirize the writers and readers who had failed to support his ideals. Blood's comparably omniscient brother has suffered a humiliating and hilarious divorce case, in which he hid in a laundry basket to avoid discovery by the husband, but was arrested when taken out of the basket for trying to avoid paying his train fare. As a result he was described as Falstaffian (a comparison that would be used increasingly); and he had become 'a hopelessly morbid monomaniac', with a paranoid fear that he kept hearing allusions to his case.[39]

There is much of Ford in Mr Blood too (that part of himself that enabled him to identify with Marwood). But it is with Fleight that he identifies most closely, which makes this an unusually sympathetic portrait of a Jew, scarcely touched by the prevalent Edwardian anti-Semitism (to which Ford was not always himself immune). Ford said, 'I am usually taken for a Jew'. Fleight is 'an artistic, nervous sort of chap', like Ford. He is described as a 'weary donkey'. He has a 'polygamous, Eastern heart' (like Ford and Ashburnham), having fallen in love with Augusta despite having a mistress installed in his mansion, Palatial Hall. Yet when the naïve young shop-girl he had befriended, Gilda Leroy, commits suicide on his steps for unrequited love of him, he becomes the object of undeserved calumny. He is thus one of Ford's many characters, like Macdonald, who is essentially good, though discredited in the eyes of the world. 'I haven't really got a bad record about women', Fleight protests. 'I know you haven't', answers Blood: 'but you'll never shake free of it—never in your life. And it'll do you good in the end—after the first year or so—because it will add a touch of romance to your figure.' That was Ford's fear—and his hope—in 1912–13, and the prediction was fulfilled to the letter. Like Macdonald, Fleight is depressed by the scandal. Blood assures him, 'you're the most creditable person I've ever come across'—for Fleight is an uncynical altruist. But Ford's language sustains the doubts Blood seeks to allay. Is a 'creditable' person someone who is in fact honourable, or merely someone *believed* to be so?[40]

Fleight shares Ford's blankness about his intentions. When questioned about them by Mrs Leroy (who hopes he intends to marry her daughter), he doesn't even realize what she means, but says instead that: 'What Mr. Blood intends me to do I shall do'—rather as Ford said he used to set his mind by Marwood. He is beaten up by the local youths, who resent an outsider paying attention to a local girl; so he thus becomes another of Ford's characters for whom sexual associations issue in physical violence. When Fleight speaks at a meeting: 'Because he was in genuine tribulation, he imparted into it a note of the highest passion.' Ford thus obliquely accounts for the force of his writing here, and in his next two novels, *The Young Lovell* and *The Good Soldier*. Like Ashburnham, Fleight 'loves with a wild, mad, helpless, impossible passion'—such as Ford may even then have been feeling for Brigit Patmore (of whom, more later). Unfortunately the novel is marred by its ending. Blood eventually persuades Augusta to marry Fleight, but she is frightened that he seems doomed to ill luck, so she agrees on condition that he wins the election. It seems a lost cause; but then, as if by fairy-tale, the opposing candidate, who was already on the edge of lunacy, drops dead. Though the plot is weak here, the reaction it produces in Fleight is extraordinarily effective, and suggestive about Ford's personality. His mind suddenly goes back to his jaded prophecy to Gilda Leroy about what his life would become. Now that Augusta is his, he seems unable to enjoy her. As Mrs Leroy had said: 'Folks is like that [. . .] Most of them can't stand what they want when they get it, and them as can, want something else.' (Compare Dowell: 'Why can't people have what they want?') Fleight's reaction is hard to understand in terms of the story, though it is true to the tone of the book, in which (as one politician thinks about the demagogic chancellor) one has 'a slight sense of seeing something dangerous and sinister lurking behind the hitherto flabby jocularity'. Biographically, however, it might perhaps be explained by the compacting of Hunt, Schablowsky, and Patmore into the figure of Augusta, expressing Ford's ambivalence about Hunt; his realization that by the time they were saying they were married, his polygamous heart longed for someone quite other.[41]

Hunt said Ford became 'what is called in society "a bear" '. When a rabid dog rushed past them, pursued by a cycling gendarme with levelled gun, and bit her skirt, neither of them said anything. Even when she 'nearly got lost down the old mine that the Romans used to build Les Baux with,' she said ruefully, 'it moved him not'. From Provence they went to Corsica for a week. 'He hated it.' It was there, she said, 'on the Sommet de la Paille, the highest peak of the Vizza-Vona, he opened the letter he had been carrying around in his pocket for days, and found no apology—a demand for more money': for Elsie's support of £3. 10s. a week. Olive Garnett noted that there was a 'summons proceedings' on 28 March about his failure to pay. 'F. sent excuse from Tebb', wrote Olive. He was still in Corsica, whence he sent postcards to both his daughters on that day. But Olive noted, 'V.H. present'. When Ford got back (via Paris, and a visit to the Farleys) he wrote the fifteen-page deposition in May outlining the stages of his separation from Elsie. Its version of him as systematically misled, insulted, and defamed by her was presumably an attempt to make a case for getting a divorce in England without her consent. In *The New Humpty-Dumpty*, Macdonald, who wants to offer the Countess the whole of his income from the Russian government, is horrified when his lawyer explains to him that he must stop her allowance until she files her petition. When he objects, the lawyer says, 'you've either got to hit her or stop her money for form's sake', and goes on to explain how Macdonald must seem to want to make things as difficult as possible for the Countess (as she is doing for him). He should 'fight all the points in order to concede them gracefully afterwards'. Which was presumably why Ford at some time after 1912 'formally claimed the custody of the children on the grounds that he was a German subject'. Elsie had to make an affidavit about their and Ford's English nationality; and, as with Ford's deposition, nothing came of these proceedings. But they show how the marriage was smouldering as it had begun, in the bitter ash of litigation.[42]

Hunt called the summer of 1913 a 'gorgeous season': 'Dinners in the House. *Fêtes champêtres* at the Monds' in Lowndes Square, Henley with the Harmsworths

[. . .].' She held her annual garden party on 1 July. But though she wrote that it was 'never so well attended', some of her older friends (who had perhaps been friends of her mother's) refused to come. One, while claiming she was 'not strait-laced', wrote: 'I cannot visit you until you have vindicated your position publicly.' Masterman was generously unconcerned that his career might suffer: he and Lucy saw a lot of Ford and Violet. But then, they were both writers, and from the *Throne* case onwards, it was the avant-garde that mainly frequented South Lodge. Edgar Jepson wrote that 'at Violet Hunt's parties you met not only the Vorticists themselves, but every intelligent person in Edwardian London worth meeting'.[43] Other guests included Yeats, Lady Gregory, Cunninghame Graham, F. S. Flint and his wife, Epstein, and Gaudier-Brzeska. When Ford heard that Scott-James was founding the *New Weekly* he wrote to encourage him, urging: 'I do hope you will not forget les jeunes—the quite young and extravagant; it is only on them that you can put your trust.' As he looked back over his own editing, it was his young discoveries that gave him most pride. He was to put his trust increasingly in *les jeunes* in aesthetic terms, aligning himself rather with the modernists than the Edwardians. But it was also partly that they put their trust in him, socializing with him and Hunt undeterred by the scandal that shocked the established literary figures. Pound introduced Richard Aldington and H.D. to Ford; and he also brought along another of his discoveries, the young American poet Skipwith Cannell, and his wife Kathleen.[44]

Kathleen Cannell was surprised by Ford's appearance: 'His almost huge, pink roundness, his silky straight canary-colored hair and moustache and very pale blue eyes gave him the air of an English country squire rather than the intensely sensitive and temperamental man of letters he was.' 'In a milieu bulging with balloon egos Ford's kindness and selflessness (like Ezra Pound's) in encouraging young talents were proverbial.' At the lavish South Lodge teas young writers would eat what was 'possibly their only meal of the day', and they 'learned about style from Ford, whose perception of their submerged word blocks was positively un-canny'. He would tell them: 'Observe, listen, cut, polish, place.' The tea-time con-versation was 'marvelous when one could follow it': Hunt 'favored unexpectedly dry non sequiturs. Ford's silky breathy tones often diminished to a mere rustle, Ezra either whispered or roared.' Pound would periodically fall off the sturdy chair 'specially provided for him among spindly heirlooms', and would be belaboured with oaths by Hunt's parrot, which the others had taught to squawk 'Ezra! Ezra!'[45]

'Ford was rather versatile about his insults and legpulls', wrote Cannell:

Ford's 'tests' were, I believe, another reason he has left such an unpopular image. He tried on me a test joke he used to see whether Americans had a sense of humor. The only word that stood out from his confidential rustle was spinach. But I was watching Ford's eyes and when they flickered I laughed falsely, looking into them with what I hoped was an appreciative gleam in mine. I was in.

She treated Ford with respect, 'not dreaming'—despite the significant looks—'in my naivete that his interest in any young female could be other than paternal, especially since he had lately taken a second wife'. He told her years later in Paris that this innocence had 'piqued his amour propre'. But she must have known already that he was susceptible to other young women, for both Ford and Violet made her their confidante. Violet was 'always smouldering', and would pour grievances into her ear 'in low intense tones'. Ford did much the same: 'His Egeria of the moment was often part of the tennis foursome and she too made me some confidences.'[46]

This Egeria of the moment was the fragile beauty Brigit Patmore. The saddest fact about the *Throne* case and its aftermath was that, just when Ford had publicly to demonstrate his commitment to Hunt, he fell in love with Brigit. Goldring noted that: 'Although Ford and Violet continued to keep up appearances by giving parties at South Lodge until 1915, when Ford left to join his regiment, it had become apparent, long before the war, that relations between them were getting strained and that a split was inevitable.' Ford's passion for Brigit was either a symptom of his increasing unhappiness with Violet or one of the causes. In 1907 Brigit had married Coventry Patmore's grandson, Deighton. Hunt knew the family, and called on them, quickly making friends with her. Later they moved to Kensington with two young children. Hunt asked her to South Lodge, invited her to come regularly to her Tuesday afternoon 'At Homes', offering as an enticement the chance to hear Mrs Pankhurst speaking.[47]

Ford 'was always kind to me', she wrote later, 'and sometimes he would come to my house and read his poems to me'. What else happened is unclear. Patmore wrote in her memoirs, half a century later: 'People have said that Ford was slightly in love with me, but he never attracted me. I admired his intellect, but that was all.' But Ford was more than slightly in love with her from 1913 to 1917. And though she may not have found him attractive, there is some evidence (and more speculation) that she wasn't entirely unresponsive. The evidence comes in Hunt's 1917 diary, when she is recording a day spent with both the Patmores at Byles's house:

She is as sweet as ever. Young looking hair dyed, weak & ill, no personality. That is her charm for F. She says he must always pose—never real—histrionic to his fingertips . . . Dreaming—*not* dreaming true—false to himself. Deighton is a worm. B doesn't care a pin for F. She succumbed from the flattery of his suit—his plausibility . . . and her motto is O Wilde's 'For each man kills the thing he loves.'[48]

Brigit had given Ford a ruby cross to wear around his neck. He would wear it even under his tennis shirt: 'it occasionally showed, making Violet, from her smoldering, burst into flames.' 'If Violet was jealous of Bridget [*sic*.] P., well V. *was* jealous & presumably often with reason & Bridget *was* terribly attractive,' said Iris Barry, adding that Ford behaved like an old philanderer.[49]

Ford's most interesting novels of these years, *The Young Lovell* and *The Good Soldier*, both draw upon Ford's infatuation with Patmore. Both are studies of the power of desire to enrapture and to endanger and of the conflicts between sexuality and society, passion and morality, pagan worship of desire and renunciation. *The*

Young Lovell is set in Northumberland in 1486. The knight Paris Lovell is entranced for several months by a vision of a 'White Lady', the goddess Venus. As Moser says, she 'must reflect Ford's newest love, the beautiful young Irish woman Brigit Patmore'. Lovell was engaged to marry the Lady Margaret, but after his visions 'The sight of this lady had been to him a sudden weariness, like the sound of a story heard over and over again. And hot anger and hatred had risen violently in his heart when she spoke. But then he perceived her anguished face, the corners of the proud lips drawn down and the features pale like alabaster.' And he resolves to marry her because 'he knew she was a loyal and dutiful friend to him', even though she was 'wearisome beyond endurance to him'. This clearly echoes Ford's feelings for Hunt. The setting even recalls their trip to Northumberland in the autumn of 1912; Lovell's body ends there, immured as a hermit, but his spirit is shown at the end of the book sporting with Gods 'in a very high valley of Corsica'—where Ford had been with Hunt in March.[50]

Ford told Pinker about *The Young Lovell*: 'if it is anything at all, it is really literature and I have spread myself enormously over it.' But he didn't mean that he had written a historical *roman à clef*. The novel explores aspects of his mind and his art with an astonishing explicitness and candour. While the plot charts Lovell's escape from warfare, litigation, family conflicts, an unwelcome engagement, and spiritual *Angst*, into a pagan heaven, the novel is far from the escapist fantasy that Moser claims. The presentation of Lovell's and Margaret's feelings must have made Hunt wince: 'Ever he sighed deeply and yet talked of the joy they would have in pleasaunces'; but she hears the heaviness of his heart, and 'with the bitter tears on her lids' changes the subject to the problem of regaining his control of his castle from his usurping bastard half-brother, the son of a witch. Margaret 'knew him so well she read his heart'.[51] Ford realized that Hunt realized as early as 1913—merely months after the *Throne* case—that he was staying with her out of a sense of duty rather than love. As with Elsie a decade or so before, he felt guilty about deserting her after causing such havoc in her life.

The book begins with a broken vow. Lovell has vowed to keep vigil in a chapel until dawn but he is beset by visions of monsters, demons, witches, and Satan himself. He resists, until he becomes aware of a mysterious presence watching him: 'Kind eyes; eyes unmoved. His heart beat enormously....' Hunt said the book Ford was writing in 1913 would be a very good one, 'for it was going to contain something quite unusual for him; there would be "heart" in it'. This might mean *The Good Soldier*—Ford's book that is most explicit about 'heart'. Or it might mean *The Young Lovell*—in its own, very different, archaic, intense, static way, also one of Ford's most beautiful novels.[52] Both are powerfully impassioned works, and—like the long poem 'On Heaven', written between them—both come from the same emotional predicament. Yet by describing Lovell's desire for an immortal woman, Ford is generalizing from particular situations; using mythology and fantasy to explore the forces that cause *any* vows to be broken. He might as well have been recalling his vows to Elsie, and the weary depressions when the love between them died, at the time when it was Violet who represented the ideal lover. The force of the novel comes from precisely this timeless quality from its presentation of how the power of sexuality de-realizes and disturbs all commitments and stabilities. Its transitions from the intensely visual presentation of 'real' fifteenth-century life in castles by the sea in the north of England to the visionary reality of Lovell's passion are extraordinarily effective.

The apparitions of Venus vary according to the eyes of the beholder. As the Bishop explains to the monk in the book, 'All those women were one woman': 'This apparition that you have seen and I, appeareth with many faces and bodies, being the spirit that most snareth men to carnal desires. So doth she show herself to each man in the image that should snare him to sin, with a face, kind, virtuous and alluring after each man's tastes.' Moser says that 'the Bishop's word "image" appropriately defines the apparition's other important aspect, its resemblance to art rather than life. For Lovell, she duplicates the Botticelli Venus. For Margaret, she takes a pose [. . .] recalling Rossetti's study of Guinevere that so enchanted Ford.' Yet it is not a question of 'art rather than life'. Henry James wrote a magnificent letter to H. G. Wells after Wells had satirized his aestheticism in *Boon*. For Ford, as for James: 'It is art that *makes* life, makes interest, makes importance, for our consideration and applications of these things, and I know of no substitute whatever for the force and beauty of its process.'[53]

The Young Lovell is imaging love. It is not that Ford cannot tell the difference between the real and the imaginary: he explores how love transforms our sense of reality: 'ever since you saw that lady's face this world has seemed as a mirror and an unreality to you.' The novel is one of Ford's most sustained fantasias on the theme of the creative imagination, and how art strives to embody its visions. Ford 'spread himself enormously over it' in this sense: *The Young Lovell* is an analysis of his art and his mind, rather than a veiled commentary on his love-life. As Moser suggests, 'no Fordian character before Henry Martin of *The Rash Act* is more explicitly a double man than he'. Lovell is divided between action and vision, 'caught between a dying social ideal, perfect feudalism, and an undying perfection, *la belle dame sans merci*, who finally seduces him away from all worldly struggle'. But if this doubled hero stands for Ford, it is not because he is the 'desperate neurotic' Moser says. It is because in his duality of acting in the world, and achieving a visionary aloofness from the world, he stands as an image for Ford's ambivalence about sexuality (Lovell becomes a holy hermit outwardly, while in imagination he is in a valley with the White Lady: in both cases a visionary); an image for 'an author unfortunately doubled with a man'; and finally, an image for the duality of the artist, who must combine the rapt visionary with the effective stylist. Ford said that for him 'the historical novel was always and almost of necessity a *tour de force*'. It is in the sustaining of a strange and compelling style of the past that his force makes itself felt in his historical fiction.[54]

The Young Lovell's emphasis on the visionary shows Ford following Conrad's credo (which echoes everywhere through Ford's prose): 'My task which I am trying to achieve is, by the power of the written word to make you hear, to make you feel—it is, before all, to make you *see*. That—and no more—and it is everything.'[55] An account of Ford's aesthetics needs to investigate the pheno-menology of literary experience—what might be called the metaphysics of writing and reading: how literature can 'make you *see*'; how it affects the mind, and how it can therefore have an effect on the world. Ford's critical thought is more coherent and more powerful than has been recognized. What it coheres around is the experience of seeing and reading; and these concepts inform his fiction and reminiscence as well as his criticism.

Seeing this changes the way we see Ford. For the question of what he *saw* (in imagination, in fact, in writing), and of what the power of the word made *him* see, has always been central to his biography. In his obituary Ezra Pound wrote: 'That Ford was almost an *halluciné* few of his intimates can doubt [. . .] he saw quite distinctly the Venus immortal crossing the tram tracks', which makes Ford sound like the kind of poetic visionary Pound was, in trying to re-create classical epiphanies and metamorphoses in the *Cantos*. Pound told Denis Goacher: 'There was the matter of "visions." There is no doubt whatever that Ford, from time to time, used to have visions without any effort at all: this was a little humiliating to dear Yeats, who spent a lifetime trying to have visions: he did have some, I think, but he would keep trying to have more than nature allowed him.'[56] Pound probably had *The Young Lovell* in mind. Caroline Gordon was another who felt that this book was quintessential Ford. She read it in terms of the 'Belle Dame Sans Merci', or of Robert Graves's 'White Goddess' theme as an allegory of creative inspiration, in which the visionary is rapt by a sexualized apparition—a muse. Edward Dahlberg put Ford into his category of 'sex visionaries'. Writers as disparate as Ford, Pound, Graves and Gordon all created myths of the imagination. Ford's White Goddess is more, however, than an image for how passion inspires art. It is, dually, an image for how art inspires passion (both are modes of visionary 'rapture'). For the white lady was probably inspired by the White Lady of Avenel in Scott's *The Monastery*, who brings Sir Piercie Shafton back to life after he is mortally wounded. Such allusions can reanimate dead authors; an allusion in a historical novel to the exemplary historical novelist suggests how the historical novel is itself a bringing back to life of the dead past. 'Visions' in Ford's writing tend to function in this way as suggestive allegories of writing and reading. But before examining the allegorical function, we need to consider the psychological implications.[57]

The kind of vivid apparition that appears to Lovell—as to many of his other characters—was a familiar occurrence for Ford, and the foundation of his aesthetics. It is not just that many of his fictional characters are subject to visions. He wrote in 1915:

I see myself visions, every day of my life—this morning I had a vision of a huge crab burrowing into a sandbank; yesterday of a buxom, dark lady in blue satin with a large blue hat, with a dog beside her, carrying a huge bunch of wild flowers and walking down my drive. I put them down to ocular fatigue and leave the matter at that, for I do not regard them as matters of legitimate art, though I suppose it is not illegitimate, now and then, to depict a character haunted by visions and to weave some sort of story into a series of apparitions.[58]

Most of Ford's writing is concerned to some degree with heightened visual or visionary sensitivity. All his reminiscences, for example, are characterized by uncannily arresting visual scenes. One of his favourite adjectives is 'vivid', indicating not so much a Pre-Raphaelite lurid clarity, as a psychological suscept-ibility to visual transport. Ford describes experiences which affected him deeply—whether remembering, reading, or simply seeing—as themselves visionary. Amongst his less directly autobiographic works, many are crucially involved with 'visions'; such as: *The Soul of London, Mr. Apollo, The 'Half Moon', 'Riesenberg', Ladies Whose Bright Eyes, The Young Lovell, 'A Day of Battle', No Enemy, Parade's End*, and *A Little Less Than Gods*. One of his highest critical tributes is to picture a vision of a writer's personality materializing through the page, smiling. It is the smile of the rapt artist (as in 'Nice People'), of the holy man in meditation, or of the day-dreamer. Reviewing Wells's *The Passionate Friends* soon after finishing *The Young Lovell*, Ford praised it by saying it 'is a piece of imagination—is, if you like, a piece of dreaming'.[59]

'Visions' are profoundly ambivalent, heralding inspiration or insanity. Fordian impressionism is founded on that ambivalence: his impressions are always poised between illumination and illusion (or sometimes delusion). His insistence on the truth of his impressions regardless of their factual accuracy inevitably makes us sceptical of their status. His art can 'make us see' things, but part of its process is to make us wonder whether we aren't 'seeing things'. He was fascinated by the way art appears able to strike to the heart of a person's being, through disturbing the sense of sanity or normality. But rather than the systematized delusions of paranoia, seeing the world as organized by principles of hostility, Ford's 'visions' were probably what could be called 'eidetic images': powerfully visual imaginings, such as occur at the intensest moments throughout his writings—possibly the kind of 'visions in mentally normal subjects' that Freud understood as regressions to childhood memories that had remained unconscious or been repressed.[60] They represent a glimpse of a world beyond: an apprehension of the abyss, or the promise of passion. Like the recurrent moments of divine apparition which energize Pound's *Cantos*, they are manifestations of hidden powers, at once disturbing and exhilarating.

Visions mark out a person as a 'seer', someone outside the bounds of normal social experience, of conventional definitions of sanity. By making us see, making us share its vision, art disturbs the community in order to re-establish it along different lines. By making us see his and his characters' visions, Ford is able to confirm a common humanity and to convince himself—and us—of his sanity in a deranged world. His 'visions' need to be seen (to be believed) alongside Proust's re-experiencings of the past, Pound's visions of pagan metamorphoses, Joyce's 'epiphanies', and Woolf's 'moments of being'; like all of these, they are attempts to find correlatives for otherwise inexpressible personal experiences.[61]

Since *The Fifth Queen* and *Ladies Whose Bright Eyes* had been his most successful books, Ford was perhaps hoping to achieve another popular success with a new historical romance dealing with the intervening century. He also wrote a new series of 'Historical Vignettes', this time for the *Outlook*, each dealing with a different period of European history. There are imaginatively apocryphal tales about Shakespeare getting his first job composing new speeches for old plays; St Mark beginning to write his gospel; the death of Napoleon; the burning of Joan of Arc; the death of the navigator Henry Hudson.[62] In the summer Ford wrote his study of Henry James.[63] One reviewer, Dixon Scott, who felt that the book was disappointing—'garrulous, slap-dash, untidy—worthy of neither of the eminent names its cover bears'—none the less observed that it was 'absolutely the first full-length official effort that has yet been made by English criticism to pay adequate homage to our greatest living man of letters'. Ford was not trying to write an 'official', academic estimate, of course. As always, his criticism is intimate, digressive, delicately astute. What was impertinent discursiveness to one reader was pertinent self-revelation to another, who found the book 'as nearly flawless as anything in the nature of literary criticism can possibly be', saying that 'this book has a double value: it tells us almost as much about Mr. Hueffer as it does about Mr. James.'[64] Wanton subjectivity or invigorating personality? Vanity or candour? Ford's writing about other writers invariably provoked such debates. Take, for example, his opening tribute, perhaps an example of the *obiter dicta* that the *Outlook* reviewer hoped would 'vex the souls of innumerable dunces':

Let me say at once that I regard the works of Mr. Henry James as those most worthy of attention by the critics—most worthy of attention of all the work that is to-day pouring from the groaning presses of continents. In saying this I conceal for the moment my private opinion—which doesn't in the least matter to anyone, though it is an opinion that can hardly be called anything but mature—that Mr. James is the greatest of living writers and in consequence, for me, the greatest of living men.

The paradoxical tone, revealing what it claims to be concealing, offering as a 'mature' opinion what it knows will be called hero-worship, blending playfulness with pathos (the 'groaning presses') and earnestness (the declaration of his admiration, that might have been embarrassing without the agile preamble), sounds provocatively out of place in a 'critical monograph'. Yet it turns out to be in key with what Ford is best at here: catching James's tones, his frissons of wonder as the private becomes public: 'for Mr. James English life is a matter of smoothnesses, civilisations, and that very avoidance of publicity which Mrs. Gereth felt to be her strongest weapon' (p. 33). After the *Throne* case, Ford knew all about the uses of publicity as weaponry. His sympathy with James is at once an attunement to his tones and methods, and to his views of civilized life. In fact this was what Dixon Scott was really objecting to, the way Ford's book 'claims its subject's support for a certain point of view, a certain sinister conception of humanity, which is so unutterably desolating and disquieting that one wants to denounce instantly and noisily'. Not a bad analysis of either James or Ford. That is why Ford is the greatest exponent of the Jamesian novel in English, and it is also why many reviewers wanted instantly to denounce some of his best books. *The Good Soldier*, in particular—the novel Ford was about to begin—was simply too 'desolating and disquieting' for much of its contemporary readership. In *Henry James* Ford sketches a scene that might well have come from his life during the *Throne* affair:

But alas, there is nothing to write! I do not mean to say that nothing could have been written—but it has all been done. Mr. James has done it himself. In the matchless— and certainly bewildering series of Prefaces to the collected edition, there is no single story that has not been annotated, critically written about and (again critically) sucked as dry as any orange. There is nothing left for the poor critic but the merest of quotations.

I desired to say that the supreme discovery in the literary art of our day is that of Impressionism, that the supreme function of Impressionism is selection, and that Mr. James has carried the power of selection so far that he can create an impression with nothing at all. And, indeed, that had been what for many years I have been desiring to say about our master! He can convey an impression, an atmosphere of what you will with literally nothing. Embarrassment, chastened happiness—for his happiness is always tinged with regret—greed, horror, social vacuity—he can give you it all with a purely blank page. His characters will talk about rain, about the opera, about the moral aspects of the selling of Old Masters to the New Republic, and those conversations will convey to your mind that the quiet talkers are living in an atmosphere of horror, of bankruptcy, of passion hopeless as the Dies Irae! That is the supreme trick of art to-day, since that is how we really talk about the musical glasses whilst our lives crumble to pieces around us. Shakespeare did that once or twice—as when Desdemona gossips about her mother's maid called Barbara [*sic.*] whilst she is under the very shadow of death; but there is hardly any other novelist that has done it. Our subject does it, however, all the time, and that is one reason for the impression that his books give us of vibrating reality. I think the word 'vibrating' exactly expresses it; the sensation is due to the fact that the mind passes, as it does in real life, perpetually backwards and forwards between the apparent aspects of things and the essentials of life. If you have ever, I mean, been ruined, it will have been a succession of pictures like the following. Things have been going to the devil with you for some time; you have been worried and worn and badgered and beaten. The thing will be at its climax tomorrow. You cannot stand the strain in town and you ask your best friend—who won't be a friend any more to-morrow, human nature being what it is!—to take a day off at golf with you. In the afternoon, whilst the Courts or the Stock Exchange or some woman up in town are sending you to the devil, you play a foursome, with two other friends. The sky is blue; you joke about the hardness of the greens; your partner makes an extraordinary stroke at the ninth hole; you put in some gossip about a woman in a green jersey who is playing at the fourteenth. From what one of the other men replies you become aware that all those three men know that to-morrow there will be an end of you; the sense of that immense catastrophe broods all over the green and sunlit landscape. You take your mashie and make the approach shot of your life whilst you are joking about the other fellow's necktie, and he says that if you play like that on the second of next month you will certainly take the club medal, though he knows, and you know, and they all know you know, that by the second of next month not a soul there will talk to you or play with you. So you finish the match three up and you walk into the club house and pick up an illustrated paper. . . .

That, you know, is what life really is—a series of such meaningless episodes beneath the shadow of doom—or of impending bliss, if you prefer it. And that is what Henry James gives you—an immense body of work all dominated with that vibration—with that balancing of the mind between the great outlines and the petty details. And, at times, as I have said, he does this so consummately that all mention of the major motive is left out altogether.[65]

It is a magnificent example of Ford's critical method: an illuminative anecdote, apparently digressive, which appears not to be able to say anything, but none the less manages to say one of the most important things about both James's and Ford's own writing. For the idea of the expressive effect somehow exceeding the visible means of its achievement is Ford's most prized feat. *Henry James* is not a novel (as Ford said his *Joseph Conrad* was), but its novella length is paced just as Ford said a novella should be, and as James had mastered it. It is not 'the economically worded, carefully progressing set of apparently discursive episodes, all resolved, as it were, in the *coup de cannon* of the last sentence, that are found in one of the *contes* of Maupassant'; but its own carefully progressing set of apparently discursive episodes and aperçus make it 'rather no more and no less than the consideration of an "affair" '—the affair being, in this case, Ford's reading of James (pp. 129–30). Ford's critical method—and this is what stops him sounding academic, and has alienated some of the more academically minded critics—is fundamentally novelistic. A powerful mind is at work, analysing techniques, considering effects. But he does not present his insights analytically. Instead, he tells a story, one which brings out circuitously the notion of a psychological sub-text—the way writing can intimate repressed anxieties and passions. The music critic Hans Keller developed a means of writing musical examples that would demonstrate techniques used in other pieces of music, on the grounds that a non-musical, verbal language, could never account for musical effects. He called this 'functional analysis', which would be a suitable bad name for Ford's method of illustrating aspects of fiction with improvised fictive examples.[66] Substitute polo for golf, and this vibrating sense of ordered, civilized life shadowed by imminent catastrophe foreshadows the world and tone of *The Good Soldier*.

Life had seemed really like that when Ford witnessed Galsworthy's anxiety about his imminent social trauma. But one reason why Ford's memory was so alert to that episode was that his own life became like that too in 1913. Not only was a woman (in the country) sending him to the devil and a court-case threatening (and partly causing) ostracism, but he was also subjected to the kind of financial humiliation mentioned in this passage. On 22 July there was a bankruptcy hearing.

'Elsie attended before the registrars & her counsel got further adjournment to examine F's accounts', wrote Olive Garnett. 'F & V.H. appeared.' If they were in court at the same time it must have been the last time Ford and Elsie saw each other.[67]

1913: QUIET TALKING

One is not a writer for having chosen to say certain things, but for having chosen to say them in a certain way. And, to be sure, the style makes the value of the prose. But it should pass unnoticed. Since words are transparent and since the gaze looks through them, it would be absurd to slip in among them some panes of rough glass. Beauty is in this case only a gentle and imperceptible force. In a painting it shines forth at the very first sight; in a book it hides itself; it acts by persuasion like the charm of a voice or a face. It does not coerce; it inclines a person without his suspecting it, and he thinks that he is yielding to arguments when he is really being solicited by a charm that he does not see.

(Sartre, *What is Literature?*)

An 'Imagist poem will produce little effect upon [a] man who is going through the bankruptcy court', said Ford not long afterwards. Nevertheless, he was soon meditating on literary technique once more. The interest in creating an impression with nothing at all is one that particularly preoccupied him at this time. He later wrote that he was 'trying to attain to quietude', and that he realized that he had formulated all he desired of literature when he said to someone he was 'very fond of ': 'I should like to write a poem—I should like to write all my poems—so that they would be like the quiet talking of some one walking along a path behind someone he loved very much—quiet, rather desultory talking, going on, stopping, with long pauses, as the quiet mind works. . . .'[1] He said it took him twenty-five years to realize this about his poetry-writing; his first poems were published in the early 1890s, so that would place this scene around 1913–14—the time when Douglas Goldring persuaded the firm of publishers he had become involved with, Max Goschen, to publish Ford's *Collected Poems*, for which Ford wrote a long, exploratory preface. The setting might be Selsey, and the companion might be Hunt or, more probably, Patmore. The *method* is the one he describes in James, whose 'quiet talkers', like their author's subdued, oblique manner, mean much more than they say. It is the method of such different works as *The Young Lovell*, 'On Heaven', and *The Good Soldier*, all of whose 'quiet talkers are living in an atmosphere of horror, of bankruptcy, of passion hopeless as the Dies Irae'. We have seen how Ford attributed this temperament to having been 'hammered by the Pre-Raphaelites' until he 'took refuge in an almost passionate desire for self-effacement'. Paradoxically this 'self-effacement', in literary terms, appeared a matter of effacing rhetorical falsifications of the self, as a means of true self-expression: 'the task appeared to me to be simply an affair of getting down to one's least rhetorical form of mind, and expressing that. In the end, that seemed to me to be a matter of self-forgetfulness'—perhaps because he had been so surrounded by the Pre-Raphaelite great that he had unconsciously absorbed their rhetorical manner: he remained an expert mimic. This is the view of Ford's contribution to modern writing that was propagated by Ezra Pound: 'It is he who has insisted, in the face of a still Victorian press, upon the importance of good writing as opposed to the opalescent word, the rhetorical tradition.'[2] But it is an entirely negative view, subduing, effacing, abandoning rhetorical excess. It gives no sense of what the noise and verbiage is being abandoned *for*. Talking quietly, in a desultory way, with long pauses, may be mercifully different to D. G. Rossetti and Swinburne, and it may claim fidelity to the way 'the quiet mind works'. But it doesn't sound a very promising manifesto for a poet. Lovers' whisperings are not necessarily suited to larger audiences. What makes it interesting? Ford's imagined (or real?) dramatic scenario gives the answer. The quiet talk is important not so much for itself, but for its relation to its context: it is while he is walking with someone he is very fond of, that he says he wants his verse to sound like he is talking quietly to someone he loves. The quiet tone, that is, should express its context as well as its content. The slow-motion, dream-like quality of *The Young Lovell* aims to convey the intensity of his rapture, and the pathos of his dual life. The intimate banter of 'On Heaven' seeks to capture both the anxieties of the lovers' torment (which causes them to dream of release), as well as the exhilaration of their relief. The stiff-upper-lip ironies of *The Good Soldier* work to express the agonies and passions the characters are suppressing. In *Thus to Revisit*, Ford explicitly connects the kind of scene that Dowell imagines for his narration to a 'sympathetic soul' with his verse-ideal of quiet intimacy: 'I arrived at the definite theory that what I was trying to attain to was verse that was like one's intimate conversation with someone one loved very much. One would try to render what one was like when, on a long winter's night before the fire, one talked, and just talked.' Ford generally expressed his aesthetics of duality through paradox. One paradox here is that the conscious artist strives for the effacement of conscious art, for the impression of a natural, un(self)conscious expression. This could scarcely be further from the Poundian attempt to escape the prosaic altogether by re-inventing art-speech. But a further paradox of Fordian impressionism is that the artist can transfigure ordinary language, making it into something quite other: something at once intensely expressive of the passions of its speakers, and expressive of the personality and skill of the artist who can so transfigure the commonplace. Here Ford participates in the high modernist project of escaping from outworn rhetorical modes.[3]

Quiet intimacy was something he cultivated in life too. Harold Loeb, a post-war friend of Ford's and Hemingway's in Paris, described him, in a way that also describes his style well, as a 'sensitive, emotionally tumultuous spirit hiding behind an impassive gentle face and an imperturbable manner'. Morley Callaghan, who, later in Montparnasse, would occasionally meet the man he thought of as 'Ford of many models', 'taking the night air all by himself, his hands linked behind his back', noticed how his breathless whisper compelled his listeners to lean towards him. His desire for a sympathetic listener doubles the spell of seduction with the craving for a forgiving soul to whom one can whisper a confession. Fordian listeners can be of either sex: Dowell is Ashburnham's, as the reader (substituting for Nancy, who can no longer understand?) is his. And Ford himself could be a bigger listener than talker, according to Janice Biala, as great a reader as he was a writer. He could both write in order to read aloud to Conrad, and be Conrad's listener, taking down his words from dictation. By writing as if he were talking quietly, he was both fulfilling and resisting that haunting paternal injunction to 'Speak up, Fordie!' The quiet talker and listener is the 'literary personality' that Ford's verse and prose aspires to express. His criticism speaks often of 'cadence': the trajectories of sentences that most intimately characterize a speaker, abstracted from the contingencies of voice which writing can't reproduce exactly, such as pitch or tone of voice.[4] 'Cadence' (from the Latin *cadere*, 'to fall') perfectly describes the dying falls of Ford's own delivery, which intimates the passing of language, of art too, felt against the pattern its motion brings to life.

In September 1913 Ford began writing his best series of literary *causeries*, which appeared weekly in the *Outlook* until August 1915, when he was in the army. It was yet another form over which this versatile writer had a complete mastery. Until the outbreak of the war they took the form of 'Literary Portraits': an incisive review, preceded by an anecdotal, biographical sketch of the author. They form a remarkably intelligent diary of Edwardian literary life, and deserve to be collected. He wrote to Compton Mackenzie from the Selsey Hotel: 'I am going to write for the Outlook of which I am "assuming the literary editorship".' The inverted commas may mean that he is 'assuming' it rather than having been given it. But it is perfectly possible that he *was* literary editor. His suggestion of printing his 'Literary Portrait' side by side with an article by the subject of that portrait was certainly one the magazine often followed. Mackenzie was flattered by Ford's telling him that, 'by the bye', his *Sinister Street* was 'all right', and replied: 'It's no good my telling you that you stand at the head of English criticism. You know that as well as I do.'[5]

Ford and Hunt went to visit Brigit Patmore in a nursing home: 'She had had a terrible operation.' They spent twenty-four hours in London, while with Pound's help Ford 'rearranged his poems, & mucked about the preface of his "Henry James"'. Then Ford and Hunt left for a boat-trip down the Rhine with Charles and Lucy Masterman. Ford always found Masterman good company. Frank Swinnerton remembered the quickness of his mind, and the 'most exquisite quiet malice' of his talk. 'Brigit Patmore has given delight to many by saying that "Masterman looked like a bandaged weasel"', reported Pound to Dorothy Shakespear. 'That pillar of your government together with their respective wives or concubines are now enjoying (or otherwise, probably otherwise in the case of

V.) the Rhine.' The Germans were less friendly than they had been two years earlier: Hunt called them 'sulky'. They got off the boat at Rüdesheim, and Masterman (who had helped Lloyd George with the Insurance Act, and was supposed to be studying the German equivalent) persuaded them to visit the battlefields of the Franco-Prussian War. But the visit became ominous of future hostilities. When, using Ford as interpreter, Masterman asked a waiter at Metz 'what nationality he considered himself to be', he replied: 'Muss-Preussen'—'Obligatory Prussian'. 'After that Masterman was saying on every available occasion: *"Muss-Preussen."*—We're all going to be *Muss-Preussens* before long, Ford old dear.' A plain-clothes policeman was following them. Their books mysteriously disappeared: Ford was reading the latest Arnold Bennett, Hunt had a copy of their recently published book, *The Desirable Alien*, with her. Ford was pessimistic, worried that they would be arrested at least until the police had read 'the two seditious volumes'. Hunt wanted to visit Ford's relations in Boppard and Giessen, but Ford was anxious about being stuck in Germany if war should break out: 'Do you want me to be shot or forced to fight against France?' he asked her. She says they then discovered from a Dutch newspaper that the Germans had mistaken Masterman for Winston Churchill.[6] The four of them signed a card to Wells, saying 'see "The Passionate Friends" (Macmillan & C)': Wells's novel of that title had just come out, and Ford was reviewing it for the *Outlook* on 27 September. Is there any significance in the joke? Does the experience of this trip figure in the 'Tale of Passion' about the 'foursquare coterie' Ford was to write next?[7]

After they got back to London in early October, Pound became so irritated with Harriet Monroe, the editor of the Chicago magazine *Poetry*, that he threatened to resign as its foreign correspondent. 'Dear Ford,' he wrote: 'Will you please take over the foreign correspondence of "Poetry" & communicate with them to the effect that I have turned it over to you.' Ford did no such thing, but wrote a tactful and witty peace-making letter to Monroe, suggesting she should 'make it up with him or reinstate him—or whatever is the correct phrase to apply to the solution of the situation whatever that may be'. Mocking Pound's inscrutability, he said: 'I don't know whether he has the literary advisership of your organ to dispose of, but I am perfectly certain that I could not do his job half so well as he has done.' And he continued, showing how he could be humorous even about his strong sense of victimization:

Besides, if I tried to help you that energetic poet would sit on my head and hammer me till I did exactly what he wanted and the result would be exactly the same except that I should be like the green baize office door that every one kicks in going in or out. I should not seriously mind the inconvenience if it would do any good, but I think it would really be much better for you to go on with Ezra and put up with his artistic irritations; because he was really sending you jolly good stuff.

Pound was soon explaining to Amy Lowell: 'I've resigned from *Poetry* in Hueffer's favour, but I believe he has resigned in mine and I don't yet know whether I'm shed of the bloomin' paper or not.'[8]

Ford wrote to Pinker about his career:

Yes, it is not a gay report. But, if you will remember, years ago I prophesied that the
bottom of my vogue, such as it was, as a novelist would fall out. You, on the other
hand, took all the heavy responsibility of saying that it would not. You, in fact, took
all the heavy burden of my fate on your shoulders. I might, but for that, by now have
been a be-diamonded stockbroker selling Marconi's to Cabinet Ministers. (I write this
more in sorrow than in anger.) Of course you will reply that 'Mr. Fleight' is my own
fault—and so it is. But the slump has been going on for years. For years and aching
years as the poets say, witness my hollow flanks and gaunt eyes of famine![9]

Ford was nearly 40. The two new novels he had published this year, *Mr. Fleight*
and *The Young Lovell*, were his seventeenth and eighteenth respectively, and
amongst the best he had written. Yet he was still unable to find a steady publisher,
who would give him reasonable advances and publicize his books adequately. No
wonder he could sound bitter and self-pitying when writing to his agent! The fact
that he needs to signal the tone ('more in sorrow than anger') reflects the conflict
of wanting to blame someone else, but none the less trying to face up to his own
responsibilities for his fate—as about his decision to give Byles's failing firm *Mr.
Fleight*. But it would be wrong to ignore the characteristic ironies and glints of
self-mockery of which he was capable even in his despairs. There is humour in
that image of himself as a 'be-diamonded stockbroker', as well as sorrow and
anger. And there is a curious histrionic distance in the image of his 'hollow flanks
and gaunt eyes of famine', as the photographs of the time make clear. It is as if,
by exaggerating and dramatizing his anxieties about failure, by turning them into
literature ('as the poets say'), he can overcome them. His friends saw a quite
different Ford. R. A. Scott-James, who saw him constantly 'In the year or two
before the war', said: 'Often, even at that time, Ford could be extremely pompous.
He was certainly vain. But more often he was gay, witty, and ready for fun of any
kind.' 'We chaffed him a lot in those days,' recalled Richard Aldington, 'and he
never stood on his dignity.'[10] Even in his darker moments, he never lost his
essential creative exuberance, his delight in the power of words.

Hunt's next move was unusually self-destructive even by her own standards.
Knowing Ford's feelings for Patmore, she none the less asked her to stay in the
cottage at Selsey as 'sole guest'. She realized she was losing Ford's love; perhaps
she thought, like Leonora in *The Good Soldier*, that she could manage him better
if she managed his love affairs as well as his money. And she may have felt sure
that her friend Brigit would faithfully resist Ford's advances. Hunt felt secure
enough to let her act as Ford's 'play secretary'.[11]

Ford wrote the poem 'On Heaven' while Patmore was staying at the Knap
Cottage.[12] He had written to Lucy Masterman that 'in a Papist sort of way I am
a tempestuously religious person and I do not think that any clearness of thought
is possible unless one either is or has been intensely religious'.[13] Hunt put his
beliefs to the test. 'You say you believe in a heaven', she said: 'I wish you'd write
one for me. I want no beauty; I want no damned optimism; I want just a plain,

workaday heaven that I can go to some day and enjoy it when I'm there.' But
Ford had no more use than she did for fatuous, sentimental theology. He later
told Basil Bunting a story about how young Rudyard Kipling was appointed to
repeat to young Ford the Sunday School teachings he had missed one day:

'If you are *good*, Fordie,' began Rudyard, 'you will go to a place on the clouds; and
there will be harps. You will sit on a cloud and sing praises unto the Lord, and that
is what you will do for ever and ever. You will wear a kind of white dress. And there
will be creatures like mama but with great wings. . . .' And Ford's face grew longer
and longer. 'But, continued young Kipling the realist, 'if you are *bad* . . . you will go
to a *much worse place.*'[14]

'Which may have been one reason for "On Heaven" ', says Hugh Kenner. Soon
after the poem was published Ford praised Heine's poem 'Die Mutter Gottes zu
Kevlaar' for its consoling 'idea of a divine person taking trouble and getting really
busy about one's poor affairs'—like 'On Heaven' 's God; though he imagined that
'a large number of worthy people will dislike those lines because they are
sentimental lines, or because they themselves are too sentimental to like the idea
of a human divinity, or because they like only rotund and balanced phrases'. This
captures both the combination of sentiment and irony he valued in Heine, and
his own genius for seeing how the denial of sentiment can become another form
of sentimentality (which is why he preferred poems familiarizing the spiritual to
the Pre-Raphaelite attempts to etherealize familiar passions).[15]

When Ford had finished 'On Heaven' he read it to the two women 'many
times', as Hunt recalled:

the effect, intensely personal, vaguely metaphysical, was hypnotic. One came to regard
the soft, effortless reading of it as if it were the solemn unwrapping of a cocoon, the
close, gluey sheath being slowly unwound from a new-born soul in religion! The
personalities of us three, all in sympathy, good Lord! perfect or imperfect—were
merged. We criticised the poem, actually. We were all artists for the nonce, a man
and two women in the strange, occasional solidarity that mutual pursuit of art for the
sake of art can give and maintain.

Yet she was dissatisfied by the text: 'Love without breadth, depth, or thickness,
without dimension', she complained. 'For the object—set up like an ikon to be
worshipped [. . .]—any sort of fetish, glittering, shining, compelling, will do.'
This may seem unfair, since she had asked for a poem about heaven, not about
Ford's love for her. But Ford's 'workaday heaven' is an essentially secular one:
its God realizes each person's conception of heaven for him, so for the narrator
and his lover heaven is 'a little town near Lyons' in which they can at last be
together, free from the cares and complications of an illicit affair. The poem is,
as Derek Stanford says, 'a narrative love idyll'.[16]

One explanation of Hunt's resentment is that by the time she was writing her
memoirs the poem had taken on another significance: what in 1914 had pictured
the lovers—her and Ford—escaping from the complications of lawyers and
families to a Provençal paradise, had by 1926 come to stand for Ford's longing to

escape from her—as he had done after the war with a new lover, Stella Bowen. But the poem must have hurt from the first, since the 'fetish' that Ford had 'set up like an ikon to be worshipped' sounds more like Brigit than like Violet. She is 'my young love', 'very tall and quaint | And golden, like a *quattrocento* saint'. Hunt's diary gives a less high-mindedly aesthetic picture of the *menage à trois*: 'To see his happy face when she came down to breakfast next morning ought to have told me.' She already knew, of course. She was as gifted as Ford at provoking disaster, and now she saw it coming: 'I confess I had thought of the ultimate cataclysm as, alone in the mornings while the dictation was going on, I wandered round one or other of the three beaches of Selsey.' 'I would come in late sometimes for lunch,' she wrote, 'and I would meet the poet rushing, hatless, down the village street, wanting to know if I had committed suicide.' The next paragraph begins: 'Not yet', but goes on to describe her 'poison ring' in which she could have put 'a mere pinch of nitrate of amyl', a poison which had been suggested to her for her 1897 novel *Unkist, Unkind!* Hunt kept medicine in her poison ring, 'in order to unnerve the man who took me in to dinner'; Florence Dowell keeps amyl nitrate in her medicine flask. A passage from the 1914 *Poetry* version of 'On Heaven' which Ford suppressed in the 1918 book version probably also touched a nerve: the Virgin Mary appears, says to the woman 'It is sad that you have no child', and then promises her a son if she make a pilgrimage to Lourdes.[17]

There are striking similarities between 'On Heaven' and *The Young Lovell*, which ends with the protagonist's death, and new life in paradise—unsurprisingly, since the two works were written out of the same emotional triangle. The similarities go deeper. In the novel there are really two heavens, the one Lovell tells Margaret about, in his dutiful but doomed attempt to persuade himself that he could be happy with her, and his transforming epiphany of Venus. In the poem, we have the heaven the narrator talks about, and the one he really desires. The poem tries to blur the two together. It is dedicated 'To V.H., who asked for a working Heaven', and can be read as a public declaration of his love for her, even as a proclamation that they have achieved marital bliss, regardless of whether society recognizes the marriage. Yet the poem to Violet is undermined by the one to Brigit—not just because the narrator's lover might sound like her, but because the logic of the poem implies that, if Ford is not going to achieve happiness with his lover until he is dead, then he has not achieved it with Hunt, and the lover is someone else. 'A poem', he wrote later, 'is a quiet monologue during a summer walk in which one seeks to render oneself beloved to someone one loves.'[18] Hunt must have been chagrined to realize that Ford was using 'On Heaven' to make himself beloved to Patmore. This dual address of the poem also accounts for its tonal confusion, hovering purgatorially between ecstasy and despair. 'On Heaven' is usually read as if Ford's technical quest for 'quiet, rather desultory talking' in verse were an end in itself. But here the tone is expressive of an emotional predicament—of trying to reassure someone while feeling desperate oneself. What makes it unconvincing as a vision of eternity is what makes it honestly expressive of Ford's state of mind—its precisely rendered half-heartedness.

Like most of Ford's work, 'On Heaven' doesn't appear particularly modern now. About the same length as 'The Waste Land', it marks the end of a literary era, as Eliot's early verse marks the beginning of the next. It is sentimental and relaxed. The verse-form that Ford used increasingly, almost *vers libre*, with lines of greatly varying length and metre, yet bounded by rhymes at unpredictable intervals, sometimes even approaching the stanzaic, is curiously poised between natural speech, effective musical form and the cadences of song, and ironic doggerel. The subject-matter is inimitably Fordian in its concern with English-ness, passion, and vivid impression:

> But one is English
> Though one be never so much of a ghost;
> And if most of your life have been spent in the craze to relinquish
> What you want most,
> You will go on relinquishing,
> You will go on vanquishing
> Human longings, even
> In Heaven.
>
> God! You will have forgotten what the rest of the world is on fire for—
> The madness of desire for the long and quiet embrace,
> The coming nearer of a tear-wet face; (p. 84)

It is the theme of *The Good Soldier*; what it lacks is that novel's feeling of intense passion *in the writing*. 'But one is English' sounds more like a pose than a diagnosis. The jaunty rhyming on 'relinquishing' and 'vanquishing' make the words jingle rather than jar with registered suffering. Ford said that: 'During the late war it was circulated by H.M. Department of Propaganda as being likely to make soldiers take a cheerful view of Death'; and perhaps that is what's wrong. The imagining of his own death summons up all its characteristic anguish and pathos, which the poem's form only serves to evade.[19]

Nevertheless, 'On Heaven' is important, both for its explicitness about desire, and for its attempt to break loose from etiolated Georgian lyricism. Ford later felt that it failed his test of quiet talking. He wrote: 'I find creeping upon me the suspicion that it is only melodrama'; but its rhythms of conversational intimacy are fresh and unobtrusively compelling. Mizener calls it 'that modernized "Blessed Damozel" '[20] The comparison is shrewd, though the attempt to modern-ize predominates over any attempt at imitating Rossetti: Ford's poem concerns adulterous love, unmediated by Pre-Raphaelite stereotypes of female purity and rhetorical lyricism.

Pound reassured Harriet Monroe (who published it in *Poetry*): 'The Hueffer good? Rather! It is the most important poem in the modern manner. The most important single poem that is'; and in his essay on Ford's *Collected Poems* in the same issue of *Poetry* he called 'On Heaven' 'the best poem yet written in the "twentieth-century fashion" '.[21] That 'yet' was prophetic, and reminds us that the poem was written before the works that have defined modernist verse for us: Eliot's 'The Love Song of J. Alfred Prufrock' (1917) and 'The Waste Land' (1922); Pound's 'Homage to Sextus Propertius' (1917) and 'Hugh Selwyn Mauberley' (1920). (*The Good Soldier* was being written when Joyce's *Dubliners* and *A Portrait of the Artist as a Young Man* first appeared.[22]) The influence of Ford's verse on the other modernists has not been recognized. When Richard Aldington read 'On Heaven' he responded with the parody, 'Vates, the Social Reformer'. 'I still remember how he chuckled when Ezra and I showed him my parody and how quickly and wittily he hit back', parodying Aldington's classicist imagism with 'Fragments Addressed by Clearchus H. to Aldi', an English poem written in classical Greek characters.[23] But (as with Pound) the impulse to parody was combined with a respect for Ford's significance. As with Ford's prose or his critical writing, one should not confuse it with the high modernism of Pound, Eliot, or Joyce. But Mizener's comment that the poems from *High Germany* are 'Victorian—Browningesque—rather than contemporary' misses the point that everybody else's verse—even Pound's—looked even more old-fashioned in 1911. Modernism would have looked very different without Ford. Aldington said that Ford 'sponsored the 1912 modernist verse (then modernist) which for some odd reason got attributed to Eliot'. When Harriet Monroe showed 'Prufrock' to John Gould Fletcher, he thought it 'very, very Huefferish'. The tenets of Poundian imagism, and Eliot's doctrine of the 'objective correlative' were both influenced by Ford, who joined the Imagist campaign, arguing that: 'Poetry consists in so rendering concrete objects that the emotions produced by the objects shall arise in the reader'—a formula that Eliot quoted in his pamphlet, *Ezra Pound: His Metric and Poetry* (1917), two years before his classic description of the 'objective correlative' in the essay on *Hamlet*.[24] Which meant that Ford was also amongst the first to recognize the talents of both Pound and Eliot. His championing of Pound has never been questioned, but Hugh Kenner decided some time ago that Ford could not appreciate Eliot. He could.

[I]n 1914 or 1915 'Prufrock' was accessible on any terms to very few readers. Pound's account of reactions to the poem in London after its *Poetry* publication suggests that no one could make anything of it except Ford Madox Hueffer: 'Hueffer having seen "Prufrock" came in the other day to find out if Eliot had published a book, as he wanted to write about him. WHICH shows that you can't do a good thing without its being took note of. F.M.H. was just as quick as I to see that Eliot mattered.'[25]

In July 1915 (after the publication of 'Prufrock' in *Poetry* that June, but two years before its appearance in volume-form) Ford wrote: 'and Mr. Lewis has discovered a new poet who shows signs of being very much after my own heart in Mr. T. S. Eliot.' Which is hardly surprising, given that Eliot's purgatorial townscapes had developed Ford's perception about the human expressiveness of the concrete objects of urban detritus: 'the ash-bucket at dawn is a symbol of poor humanity, of its aspirations, its romance, its ageing and its death.'[26]

While Patmore was staying Ford also dictated the beginning of *The Good Soldier* to her. When we read that Dowell imagines a 'sympathetic soul' listening silently to him telling the story across 'the fireplace of a country cottage', it makes a difference to know that this is how Ford created his novel.[27] But this isn't quite to say that he was trying to use the act of narration as a seduction—to elicit Brigit's love through the power of his art. Rather, because he was in love with her, and found the proximity exciting, he was able to imagine how effective could be an intimate narration to an unnamed listener.

Ford said that he sat down to write *The Good Soldier* on his fortieth birthday, 17 December 1913. Like Florence in the novel, he was superstitious about dates, and may well have felt it a propitious time to begin what (he later said) he felt would be his last book. He knew it was better than any of the forty-five he had already published, and later he felt it superior even to *Parade's End*, his only other work of comparable greatness. The symbolism of his story about the story is clear—it is perhaps because it is too clear that the date has been doubted: the novel is a product of a *crise de quarantaine*, a taking stock of his life and career.[28] The story also seeks a parallel with Conrad, whose first novel was published when he was 37, and about whom Ford had written a decade earlier: 'A man who does not write his first book—who has never thought of writing at all—until he is forty has that immense pull over all the rest of writers: he has felt his emotions single-heartedly. He has not desiccated them in note-books or stored incidents that he thinks will make good copy. He has not posed, he has lived.' Even as early as 1904 he knew how his literary posing cramped his writing. In 1913 he wasn't in the Conradian position of taking up writing after another career. Yet he did feel that he was making a new start in art, and was at last able to write the first novel that really expressed his talents: 'When he sits down to write—such a man—his memories, the things that really appealed to him, come back to him, plastic, tender, adaptable, ready for use [. . .] his conviction of the reality of the things he has seen is so strong that even when his memory plays him tricks he convinces his reader. He recreates in fact; he never records.'[29]

The date on which Ford dictated the novel's first words is of interest to biographers, who like to set verifiable limits to numinous intellectual processes. But Ford said he had finished the book before the writing began, that he had it 'hatching' within himself 'for fully another decade', and that he had carried it about all that time, 'thinking about it from time to time' ('Dedicatory Letter', p. 3). He told Allen Tate in 1929 that 'he had had the entire novel—every sentence—in his head before he began to write it in 1913', a claim which did not surprise Tate, who commented: 'He had the most prodigious memory I have encountered in any man. And *The Good Soldier* is not only his masterpiece, but in my view the masterpiece of British fiction in this century.'[30] In August Pound had ordered Alice Corbin Henderson, the associate editor of *Poetry*: 'For Gorrds sake dont compare the infant Richard [Aldington], dilectus filus etc. in the year one of his age to F.M.H. an artist mature, accomplished, perhaps the most accomplished writer in England. Almost a Great man', and he wondered why he couldn't quite apply that word 'Great' to Ford even though he thought of him as 'the most intelligent of ones friends'. At the end of the same letter he returns with an explanation, and a prophecy: 'About Hueffer, he is still playing about, but he has it in him to be the most important prose author in England, before he shuffles off, after James and Hardy have departed etc.'[31] With *The Good Soldier*, Ford began to show what he had in him.

THE GOOD SOLDIER: DESIRING, DESIGNING, DESCRIBING

> To be a biographer you must tie yourself up in lies, concealments, hypocrisies, false colourings, and even in hiding a lack of understanding, for biographical truth is not to be had, and if it were to be had, we could not use it.
>
> (Freud, letter to Arnold Zweig, 31 May 1936)

Desiring

Sexuality

Graham Greene wrote of *The Good Soldier*: 'the impression which will be left most strongly on the reader is the sense of Ford's involvement. A novelist is not a vegetable absorbing nourishment mechanically from soil and air: material is not easily or painlessly gained, and one cannot help wondering what agonies of frustration and error lay behind *The Saddest Story*.'[1] Technically the book is Ford's most sustained virtuoso performance. His later novels and reminiscences sophisticate some of the technical devices such as the 'time shift' or the rendering of 'duplicate cerebration', but often at the risk of indulging in technique for its own sake. *Parade's End* and the later novels have a breadth of human sympathy, a tender magnanimity, that sets them apart from the claustrophobic bitterness of *The Good Soldier*. But none of his other works has the same pitch of technical intensity and tortuous inevitability. Ford's description of its 'intricate tangle of references and cross-references' cannot be bettered for its tangling together of terms of technique and psychological bafflement. The phrase is itself a cross-reference to his grandfather's technique. When Ford reread *The Good Soldier* in 1927 he was 'astounded at the work' he had put into its construction. In thinking of 'work' he was also thinking of *Work*, Madox Brown's massive, intricate construction that Ford described (together with the painting of *Cromwell*) as a 'maze of references and cross-references'.[2] What is perhaps most compelling about the novel is the way its technical complexity and innovation is the entirely necessary articulation of its emotional intricacy. Greene's comment identifies this inter-animation of technique and felt experience, and tactfully acknowledges the point at which wondering *which* original people and events lie behind fictional ones turns to wondering *at* the novelist's involvement.

Ford's own few comments on the book he felt to be his best offer ways of discussing it which acknowledge his 'involvement' without letting the 'agonies of frustration and error' obscure the triumph of artistry as the novel masters and expresses its material. A 'gentleman' from Liverpool—presumably a circulating librarian—had no difficulty in recognizing that the main impulse behind Ford's 'Tale of Passion' was, precisely, passion: the problem of sexuality. Ford wrote an agilely ironic reply to his publisher, John Lane, who had told him about the Liverpudlian's objection:

Alas, it does indeed seem a monstrous thing, but after all, what is chaste in Constantinople may have the aspect of lewdness in Liverpool, and what in Liverpool may pass for virtue in Constantinople is frequently regarded as vice. Let us hope that when the Allies have entered the Dardanelles 'The Good Soldier' may come into his own, in several senses. You see, that work is as serious an analysis of the polygamous desires that underlie all men—except perhaps the members of the Publishers' Association—as 'When Blood is Their Argument' is an analysis of Prussian Culture.[3]

'The polygamous desires that underlie all men—except...' Even as Ford identifies his driving theme he invokes the techniques with which he investigates it. (The tone too, combining serious analysis with an irony that calls every protestation of innocence into doubt, is also close to the novel's.) The book is founded upon that hesitation: 'all men—except...' Do polygamous desires underlie *all* men? Which men in the novel, for example? Is male sexuality uniform? Is female sexuality comparable? Is Liverpudlian prudishness a hypocritical disavowal of lewdness? From how many perspectives can sexuality be analysed? The novel confronts sexual plurality—the duplexity and duplicity of desire—with aesthetic pluralism: narrating a tangle of characters from a multiplicity of times and viewpoints. Ford's preferred term for the proper subject of a novel—an 'affair'—puns promiscuously between textual design and sexual desire. It adulterates art and sex. As in the novel, the letter's clarity of presentation brings out the moral darkness: the balance of the sentences makes chastity and wantonness seem interchangeable, simply a matter of point of view. Opposites begin to appear as secret doubles. The letter shows how rash it is to read Dowell's views on sex (such as that he knows 'very little' of 'the sex-instinct'), as if they were simply Ford's. Conversely, the novel shows how warily we need to treat the letter. Do 'polygamous desires [. . .] underlie' Dowell himself, for example? The word 'underlie' intimates a world of uncertainty. Do the desires give the lie to the repressive surfaces they lie under? Or do they lie so far under the conscious self as to be imperceptible? Lawrence was properly wary of making moral generalizations from novels, as when he wrote, 'if a character in a novel wants two wives—or three—or thirty: well, that is true of that man, at that time, in that circumstance. It may be true of other men, elsewhere and elsewhen. But to infer that all men at all times want two, three, or thirty wives; or that the novelist himself is advocating furious polygamy; is just imbecility.' Like all the greatest tragic art,

The Good Soldier is interrogative rather than advocative. It brings desire into question.[4]

Ford was outraged when the American publisher Walter Page (of Doubleday Page, and later US ambassador to Britain) had objected to a sentence from *The Fifth Queen* which ran: 'You will find a chaste whore as soon as that.' Assuming 'whore' to be the offending word, Ford said he offered to replace it with a dash. Page replied: 'We certainly could not print the word "chaste." It is too suggestive.'[5] *The Good Soldier* is fascinated by the way the apparently pure and good can be (in the phrase Dowell echoes from Shylock) 'a goodly apple that is rotten at the core' (p. 11). The epigraph promises that the pure are blessed, '*Beati Immaculati*'; but all the characters are damned by this standard, with the possible exception of the adolescent Nancy Rufford, who, though emotionally she succumbs to and reciprocates Ashburnham's passion, gains her faith, and possibly her salvation, at the expense of her sanity. Dowell describes Leonora as the flower of chaste and immaculate womanhood, but in a narrative so perturbed by repressed sexuality, even mere description becomes fraught with intimations of the covert and the illicit. Dowell's disavowal of 'passion' for Leonora cannot but make us (even if only momentarily) suspicious:

I loved Leonora always and, today, I would very cheerfully lay down my life, what is left of it, in her service. But I am sure I never had the beginnings of a trace of what is called the sex instinct towards her. And I suppose—no I am certain that she never had it towards me. As far as I am concerned I think it was those white shoulders that did it. I seemed to feel when I looked at them that, if ever I should press my lips upon them that they would be slightly cold—not icily, not without a touch of human heat, but, as they say of baths, with the chill off. I seemed to feel chilled at the end of my lips when I looked at her . . . (p. 39)

How in the novel's world of doubts and suppressions can Dowell be *certain* about Leonora's sexual feelings? Doesn't his language, sensuously pressing and withdrawing the possibility of kissing Leonora, belie his categorical denial that he might ever have wanted to kiss her? If not, then why did the sight of her shoulders make him think of kissing them, and suddenly arouse sensation in his lips?

Leonora's confession of attempted adultery shocks and perplexes Dowell, opening an abyss of suggestion and hypocrisy beneath the impeccable surfaces of respectability:

Once I tried to have a lover but I was so sick at the heart, so utterly worn out that I had to send him away [. . .] just imagine me making a fool of the poor dear chap like that. It certainly wasn't playing the game, was it now?' [. . .]
   I don't know; I don't know; was that last remark of hers the remark of a harlot, or is it what every decent woman, county family or not county family, thinks at the bottom of her heart? Or thinks all the time for the matter of that? Who knows? (p. 16)

As in Henry James's novels, mysteries can suggest sexual concealments. The same uncertainty about sex bedevils Dowell's (or his reader's) judgements about all the main characters of Ford's 'Tale of Passion'. Is Florence's sexuality shared by 'every decent woman', or does it make her 'a common flirt' (p. 215). Dowell worries about male sexuality too: 'Am I no better than a eunuch or is the proper man—the man with the right to existence—a raging stallion forever neighing after his neighbour's womenkind?' (p. 16). Note how Ford's language charges the commonplace with the sexual: making us hear the stallion's 'neigh' at the heart of the social ties in which we place our trust: *neigh*bours. It is, of course, Ashburnham who is the main focus for this anxiety about sexuality. If Dowell is the eunuch, is Ashburnham the stallion?

'It may be said that the appeal of Madame Bovary is largely sexual', wrote Ford while he was still working on *The Good Soldier*. 'So it is, but it is only in countries like England and the United States that the abominable tortures of sex—or, if you will, the abominable interests of sex—are not supposed to take rank alongside the horrors of lost honour, commercial ruin, or death itself.'[6] *The Good Soldier* is written against precisely this convention. It tells a story in which the interests and torments of sex—for both English and American characters—are intricately tangled up with the horrors of lost honour, financial ruin, and death itself.

After Ashburnham's suicide, Leonora marries again. The innuendo of Dowell's repeated image for her second husband again unmasks the book's pervasive sexual motive: the insidiousness of polygamous and polyandrous desire. 'Leonora survives, the perfectly normal type, married to a man who is rather like a rabbit. For Rodney Bayham is rather like a rabbit, and I hear that Leonora is expected to have a baby in three months' time' (p. 214). *The Good Soldier* characteristically poses alternatives—polygamy and chastity, or fidelity and adultery—but then probes them in such a way as to confuse them, and reveal their hidden intimacies. Dowell contrasts the passionate with the conventional; and the first surprise is that, whereas throughout the book he has tended to contrast himself and Ashburnham in sexual terms, portraying himself as a 'woman or a solicitor' (p. 287), or a 'eunuch' beside Edward as a 'stallion' (p. 16), here he allies himself with Edward:

Mind, I am not preaching anything contrary to accepted morality. I am not advocating free love in this or any other case. Society must go on, I suppose, and society can only exist if the normal, if the virtuous, and the slightly deceitful flourish, and if the passionate, the headstrong, and the too-truthful are condemned to suicide and to madness. But I guess that I myself, in my fainter way, come into the category of the passionate, of the headstrong, and the too-truthful. For I can't conceal from myself the fact that I loved Edward Ashburnham—and that I love him because he was just myself [. . .]

Yes, society must go on; it must breed, like rabbits. That is what we are here for. (p. 291)

However hard Dowell tries to hold 'passion' aloof from sexuality, sex will come creeping back in (as it does here in the form of breeding rabbits). It would be merely glib to argue that Dowell's protestation of concealed love for Ashburnham reveals a homosexual impulse. But it would be slightly deceitful to deny that the thought crosses the reader's mind as Dowell makes his revelation. Ford's Tennysonian preoccupation with whether the sensitive artist can be a 'proper man' or not indicates how for him 'passion' is a concept which conjoins sexuality, love, sympathy, suffering, and art.[7]

Dual Perspectives

The Good Soldier is Ford's most complex and profound exploration of the dual perspective he found so intriguing. When, in 1924, he recalled the exhaustive discussions about technique with Conrad, he gives one of the fictive illustrations at which his criticism excels. Whatever else this sketch is remembering, it suggests precisely the moral, psychological, and interpretative centre of The Good Soldier.

it became very early evident to us that what was the matter with the Novel, and the British novel in particular, was that it went straight forward, whereas in your gradual making acquaintance with your fellows you never do go straight forward. You meet an English gentleman at your golf club. He is beefy, full of health, the moral [sic] of the boy from an English Public School of the finest type. You discover, gradually, that he is hopelessly neurasthenic, dishonest in matters of small change, but unexpectedly self-sacrificing, a dreadful liar but a most painfully careful student of lepidoptera and, finally, from the public prints, a bigamist who was once, under another name, hammered on the Stock Exchange.... Still, there he is, the beefy, full-fed fellow, moral of an English Public School product. To get such a man in fiction you could not begin at his beginning and work his life chronologically to the end. You must first get him in with a strong impression, and then work backwards and forwards over his past.... That theory at least we gradually evolved.[8]

It is this anguished double vision that gives his fiction its hallucinatory, holographic clarity of focus. We see both 'the moral of an English Public School product' and the neurasthenic liar and bigamist. He may look 'straight forward', but his life doesn't go straightforwardly. Ashburnham's character and history are different. He is hopelessly sentimental, financially reckless, a student of cavalry accoutrements, and a polygamist. But our first visual impression of him is exactly that of the stereotyped English gentleman—he is too good to be true:

I never came across such a perfect expression before and I never shall again. It was insolence and not insolence; it was modesty and not modesty. His hair was fair, extraordinarily ordered in a wave, running from the left temple to the right; his face was a light brick-red, perfectly uniform in tint up to the roots of the hair itself; his yellow moustache was as stiff as a toothbrush and I verily believe that he had his black smoking jacket thickened a little over the shoulder-blades so as to give himself the air of the slightest possible stoop.[9]

The structural principle of the novel is to superimpose all the subsequent information about Edward's long sequence of adulteries, with the resulting moral squalor and human wreckage, making up a composite portrait of him, without effacing the first impression (which is itself vibrantly self-contradictory: 'modesty and not modesty' . . .). It is crucial to the book's effect that we take its title both literally and ironically. He is 'the good soldier' both martially and maritally; both an honourable, admirable—even loveable—romance hero, and also a philanderer. Every aspect of the book is implicated in such doubleness, which is what has made it at once so inviting and also so dangerous for critics, since evidence can be found to support opposing interpretations. Dowell says he loves Leonora, but then he says he dislikes her (p. 226). He veers from being obtuse—expecting us to believe that he did not realize that his wife, Florence, was having an affair with Ashburnham, or that she committed suicide—to sounding knowing about passion and deceit, or even presenting scenes such as the 'Protest' incident at 'M——' when he can be seen repressing the obvious import of Leonora's frantic reaction as Florence touches Ashburnham.

The critics have generally tried to flatten out the novel's folds and disturbances, arguing that Dowell is either obtuse or percipient, Ashburnham is either viewed sympathetically and forgivingly as someone in the grip of overmastering sentimentality, or viewed ironically as a cynical libertine. The novel, however, insists on the complexity of human character, its contradictoriness and instability. It presents all these aspects as equally true, equally inescapable. The book foregrounds the difficulty of knowing and understanding. It articulates difficulty by chronological fragmentation, narrative and semantic intricacy. But its challenge involves more than just this. Its contradictory dual perspectives mean more to Ford than their purely technical exhilaration. What biographical explanation can account for the fascination Ford communicates?

The fictional novel-synopsis from *Joseph Conrad* is significant here too. For, if one were to make substitutions, saying that the man was a most painfully careful student of 'literature' instead of 'lepidoptera', and that he had been hammered in the divorce and bankruptcy courts (instead of on the Stock Exchange), the passage would be uncannily close to autobiography. One other thing it appears to be recalling is Ford's earlier life. A regular golfer in his 'Hueffer' days, he was at the time of his German 'nerve cures' 'hopelessly neurasthenic'. By 1924 he knew that Violet Hunt and her friends were saying that he was dishonest in matters of large change: that he had been living on Violet's money. He was a perpetual advocate of self-sacrifice in literary as well as personal matters. He was frequently denounced as a dreadful liar; particularly so just before the writing of *The Good Soldier*, and when, still 'under another name', he had appeared in the 'public prints' at the time of his alleged marriage to Violet Hunt, the legal suit brought by his original wife Elsie Hueffer, and the possible implication of bigamy in the affair.

What is particularly curious is the way Ford positions himself in relation to his own experience. His fictional bigamist is seen from outside, by an observer who only gradually discovers the different aspects of the story. But Ford knows these aspects from the inside too, in so far as they are aspects of *his* story. There is obviously a certain amount of protective camouflage in presenting the bigamist as an acquaintance. It is a story that suits his purpose as an example of the type of narrative evolved with Conrad, as it had served his purpose in his most Conradian novel. One need not search for special reasons why he would not have wanted to advertise the fact that it was also his own story. What is as important is his involvement with this particular technique. For within *The Good Soldier* itself, Dowell too tells his story at once from the inside and the outside. Ford translates his sense of his own national duality into the novel's dual national perspective on Ashburnham: Dowell, the American narrator, is an outsider to the world of upper-middle-class English society, but he tries to understand Ashburnham from the inside.

He too only gradually discovers the essentials of the story in which he has been involved. The method of dual perspectives is primarily a means of registering an observer's accumulative and contradictory discovery of another person—as with Dowell's gradual realizations and reconsiderations about Florence, Edward, and Leonora. But it is particularly significant for Ford because it can also correspond to a character's gradual *self*-realization—such as the process whereby Dowell earns the right to say 'I loved Edward Ashburnham [. . .] because he was just myself'. Ford's involvement with 'The Saddest Story'—the sense in which it can truly be said to be autobiographical—lies here. Dowell's identification with Ashburnham is in part the novelist's, as he tries to make us *see* his character, get an all-round impression: 'It is very difficult to give an all-round impression of any man.'[10] The questions he asks of his characters, the depths he sounds (of humanity as well as squalor), and the very manner in which these aspects become apparent to narrators and characters, all correspond to the devastating visions, doubts, and fears of his own nature—his nature as a *writer* as well as his nature as a man.

In the passage from *Joseph Conrad* he starts talking of 'us': he and Conrad, theorizing about writing. Then the pronoun shifts to 'you'. The pronoun is itself the focus for a subtle Fordian dual perspective. It could be the general pronoun (interchangeable with 'one'): everyone. The argument runs that 'you' can all assent to your knowledge of people being this gradual, time-shifted, and dual process; so why can't you see that novels should be written in the same way? As Ford puts it later in *Joseph Conrad*: 'We agreed that the general effect of a novel must be the general effect that life makes on mankind' (p. 180). But as the example of 'your gradual making acquaintanceship with your fellows' gets under way, the 'you' becomes more intimate. The gradual intimacy being charted in the example is doubled by the intimacy in the pronouns, as the narrator begins chatting in detail about a part of 'your' personal experience, your intimacies. At first the 'you' includes Ford; it then becomes his addressee' the 'you' who meets an English gentleman at your golf club. At this point the perspective is reversed as we realize that it is the English gentleman who is Fordian. He moves between imagining meeting someone, and imagining someone meeting him. This curious series of unobtrusive narrative 'cuts' is in a sense taking Ford outside himself, so that he can gradually make acquaintanceship with himself; see how he must appear to others who meet him at their golf club, hear gossip about him, or read reviews of his books or court reports about his marital affairs.

This autobiographical movement is characteristic of his writing in every genre. *The Good Soldier* is as serious an analysis of polygamous desire, of destructive, insatiable sexuality, as *When Blood is Their Argument* is 'An Analysis of Prussian Culture'. But what Ford writes about Prussian culture is drawn from his own experiences of living in Germany, and thus reflects his autobiography. It is inconceivable that a man who devotes his life's imaginative energies to analysing and understanding the motives of other characters would not ponder his own; and that such self-scrutiny would not be reflected in his imaginative writing. But this is not to say that his prose is solipsistically entrapped—that he can see only himself wherever he looks.[11] Ford's autobiographical self-reflection is unobtrusive, and never the only thing happening at any one time in his writing. It is a delicately reciprocal process (as in the play of pronouns): Ford's characters are not merely himself writ smaller, and critics should beware trying to read un-ironically back from the novels to the author. If the characters share some of Ford's traits, then it is because he is peculiarly alert to the ways in which one personality can double another. His imagining is a form of the Keatsian 'negative capability': a willingness to let his own identity be inhabited by other minds and personalities, instead of willing to colonize the other. When he finds reflections of himself, it is because human sympathies are capable of mirroring the experience of others. This is what it means to 'identify' with fictional figures. As so often, his terms to discuss how books should be written are simultaneously terms appropriate to the experience of reading them; the gradual acquaintanceship with imaginary persons and predicaments; the sacrifice of 'self' to the minds of the other. The autobiographical movement closes the circuit of response: by making his readers see someone quite other, Ford is simultaneously able to see and hear himself. Which is not to say that he is recognizable as a character in the book, as Dowell, or as Ashburnham; or even as a divided mind split between the two (which was how Hunt read the book, calling Ashburnham and Dowell Ford's 'Jekyll and Hyde—or say two Mr. Jekylls for neither is really wicked and Joseph Leopold [Ford] holds no brief for either. He simply doesn't know').[12]

The double perspective of *The Good Soldier*—its superimposing of altruism and appetite, its setting of the altruistic self-sacrifice *in* passion against the insidious egotism that can corrupt such altruism—this all derives from Ford's questioning of his own nature. Primarily this is a questioning of sexuality, but other perceptions flow from it: in analysing the 'polygamous desires' underlying himself, he was also grappling with the questions of his own fidelity—as Elsie's husband, but also as a Catholic; of his reliability and honesty—as he and Elsie became irreparably estranged. In *Henry James* he could write of 'the essential dirtiness of human nature', as if seeing it from outside, from the perspective of a god. *The Good Soldier* sees Ashburnham's nature from within as well. 'There is no priest that has the right to tell me that I must not ask pity for him,' says Dowell, 'from you, silent listener beyond the hearthstone, from the world, or from the God who created in him those desires, those madnesses . . .' Ford was perhaps also seeing with new force exactly why he had been drawn towards Henry VIII and his six wives. Ford had perhaps, like H. G. Wells, been flustered at the question he would have had to answer on the US Immigration form during his 1906 visit: 'Are you a polygamist?' His affair with Hunt had necessitated a certain amount of deception and concealment (from himself as well as from Elsie). So when he writes that 'in your gradual making acquaintance with your fellows you never do go straight forward', 'straight forward' puns between moral as well as narrative directness. There is a sense in which social intercourse, especially when it is entangled with the sexual, is not 'straightforward', but can be complex; that the gradual making acquaintance of your *bed*fellows might be a surreptitious or even a devious affair.[13] The *Throne* case forced these private self-doubts into the public glare. What might have remained a repressed anxiety about 'the disclosure of hidden basenesses in himself' was forced into consciousness by being publicized.[14]

From *The Shifting of the Fire* onwards, Ford's fiction is charged with polygamy, whether incipient (as in that novel) or explicit (as in *The Fifth Queen*). *The Good Soldier* certainly draws upon his fears about polygamy: what it might reveal about him, what the consequences might be. When Dowell tells the story of the troubadour Peire Vidal's suicidal passion for La Louve—or when he remembers Florence's guide-book chatter, as she 'started to tell us how Ludwig the Courageous wanted to have three wives at once—in which he differed from Henry VIII, who wanted them one after the other, and this caused a good deal of trouble'—Ford is, amongst other things, trying to set his apprehensions about his own desires into a historical perspective; showing how literature and religion are themselves intricately tangled up with the novel's history of desire.[15] But even—or perhaps especially—in cases such as this in which he was so emotionally involved, and which were the cause of such great anxiety, the energy with which his technical imagination transforms his experiences is astonishing. Violet Hunt furnishes a decisive instance, when she recounts a scene with striking resemblances to the climactic scene in *The Good Soldier*, in which Florence touches Edward's wrist while lecturing the others over the original Protest document at 'M—' (Marburg):

[Ford] was walking about in a state of ecstasy becoming rather to his calling of historical novelist than to his severe religious views.

'There,' he was saying to his mother—'there, that is what I have brought you to see. The Protest of Zwingli, Luther, and Bucer. That bit of paper *is* Protestantism. It all began with the signing of that bit of paper.' And turning to me: 'That is what you mean when you say you are a Protestant!'

'But I don't say it,' I remarked helplessly, as so many times before. 'I even deny it.'

Useless! A 'Prot' I am, and seemingly must remain so in the eyes of this black Papist.[16]

It would be rash to treat Hunt's impression as a reliable transcription of the 'original' scene. It is deftly and self-justifyingly stage-managed, indeterminably fictionalized. But the essentials are probably reliable. In the novel Ford has turned the scene around (and adapted it to other ends), giving his speech not to one of the men but to Florence:

'And there,' she exclaimed with an accent of gaiety, of triumph, and of audacity [. . .] 'There it is—the Protest.' And then, as we all properly stage-managed our bewilderment, she continued: 'Don't you know that is why we were all called Protestants? That is the pencil draft of the Protest they drew up. You can see the signatures of Martin Luther, and Martin Bucer, and Zwingli, and Ludwig the Courageous . . .' (pp. 52–3)

The transposition makes nonsense out of any psycho-biographic attempt to translate Florence back into Violet (rather as the transposition of Ford's own Catholicism to Ashburnham's *wife* frustrates any attempt to identify him with Edward, and Elsie with Leonora). The presence of Ford's mother at Marburg makes the reimagining of the scene all the stranger, since the original was evidently much less like the outburst amongst the adulterous foursome than the verbal parallels might lead one to think. It is possible that Cathy Hueffer's presence gave the visit—particularly to Ford's mind, preoccupied with ideas of Catholicism and polygamy—a connotation of sexuality and guilt. One could speculate that Ford felt his mother disapproved of his affair with Hunt, and that Dowell's presentiment of 'something treacherous, something frightful, something evil in the day' expresses Ford's feeling of filial and social, as well as religious, disgrace (p. 46). But it is a speculation that cannot be proved, and it does not account for the most effective elements in the reinvented scene: Florence's chilling 'accent of gaiety, of triumph, and of audacity'. That might be Ford's impression of Hunt's accent; but it is also the note she hears in his: that note of triumphant denunciation that won't brook her helpless and reiterated denials. Some of Ford's triumph comes from the writer's fascination with the power of the written word: with the way a scrap of paper can rewrite human history. (In Florence's words: 'It's because of that piece of paper that you're honest, sober, industrious, provident, and clean-lived'; p. 46.) But it also has to do with his excitement at the dramatic potential and complex irony of the scene. This is the moment before Florence touches Edward's wrist, making visible their dishonest and unclean-living relationship. (If anything comparable happened between Ford, Violet, and Elsie—or between Ford, Elsie, and Mary, or Ford, Violet, and Brigit, come to that—it would have been in London, not Marburg.) In the construction of *The Good Soldier* Ford found the perfect context for the scene. But his transformation of it suggests that, rather than writing novels in order to disguise and 'improve' his own experiences, the experiences themselves are those of a novelistic imagination. In this case he is not merely fictionalizing Hunt's character in *The Good Soldier*; instead, in acting out the scene she describes he was seizing upon a theatrical moment of emotional intensity to play a role, and thus to imagine what someone quite other—a character like Florence, say—would do in a comparable situation. Furthermore, he had *read* Hunt's account of the visit to Marburg in proof (when he added theatrically Germanic corrective footnotes to many of her 'impressions')—before he began to write the novel; so her text may have helped him to see himself from outside, as his novelistic imagination began to play over what could really be made out of a scene like that.[17]

The Good Soldier is a masterpiece not merely because of Ford's involvement with its material, but because of his mastery over both the material and his own involvement with it. He achieves a rare objectivity by immersing himself in nebulous, distorting subjectivity, and thus dramatizes the *problem* of objectivity. When he has Dowell write of Edward that he 'seems about that time to have conceived the naïve idea that he might become a polygamist. I daresay it was Florence who put it into his head. Anyhow, I am not responsible for the oddities of human psychology' (p. 224), it would be impertinent to take this as evidence that Ford had at some stage conceived the same naïve idea for himself. Yet in so psychological a novel, Dowell's disclaimer cannot but claim our attention. He may not be responsible for Ashburnham's psychology, but is he responsible for his own? Has he faced his real desires and motivations? He may not be responsible for what Ashburnham's psychology was like, but he is responsible for the way he has presented Ashburnham to us. It is characteristic of Ford, so often judged as irresponsible, to introduce scruples about responsibility into his fiction, and to understand a novel's intricate tangle of responsibilities, in which the moral responsibilities of characters are bound up with the aesthetic responsibilities of the artist. A hostile critic might feel that Ford is ventriloquizing Dowell in order to shuffle off his own responsibilities: 'I can't help it if my characters are incomprehensible, incoherent or immoral.' But his humane responsiveness to character is precisely a matter of not turning his creations into his creatures in order to manipulate them according to prearranged moral purposes. He is not 'responsible' for human desires, weaknesses, and enigmas; but his responsibility to his material makes him want to let these things reveal themselves. This is what he meant by saying that an artist should render, or be a mirror to, the times, rather than impressing himself or herself upon those times. His vision of the novelist's responsibility is to let his creations *be*.

One of Dowell's oddities is his combination of involvement and detachment. He tells us: 'I am so near to all these people that I cannot think any of them wicked' (p. 133). Yet his very familiarity, his feeling of the inadequacy of conventional moral labelling, is what leads him to describe them so minutely and from every angle, to the point where dispassionate sympathy begins to sound like passionlessness. He is so involved that he becomes alienated, detached from even his own story, so that it seems to him as a story he has 'heard', rather than as the one he has lived. Ford is perhaps using Dowell's detachment here to investigate his own detachment from his feelings: his habitual 'indifferentism'. In this sense, Dowell's detachment is Ford's involvement. Ford's relation to the fiction is similar to Dowell's, since he too is presenting elements of his own experience, however transformed, and making them sound like someone else's story; and he does this not only by writing the novel, but then, twelve years later, by doing it again in the 1927 dedication to Stella Bowen, when he says, 'the story is a true story and [. . .] I had it from Edward Ashburnham himself' (p. 3).

Instead of reading Ford's lips behind Dowell's words, what needs asking is what effects Ford produces with a sequence of remarks like the one about Ashburnham's naïve idea that he might become a polygamist. What is the purpose of the effects? What is being expressed? Certainly the theme of polygamy reflects the fraught period of the affair with Violet Hunt, and the *Throne* case. But the presentation of Ashburnham's case (and that of Dowell presenting it) also conveys attitudes towards the idea, and emotions arising from it. Ford is not 'betraying' his desires, for in the articulation of Edward's he can scarcely have avoided recognizing the relation to his own experiences. In objectifying his own response to polygamous desire he is seeing himself through Ashburnham— and Dowell—rather than seeing himself *in* either of them. But although self-recognition is a particularly important stage in the development of Ford's fiction, each novel is not merely a new phase of self-analysis—another instalment of autobiography, thinly veiled. Ford is always as concerned with rendering his times as he is with expressing himself. What, above all, the novel renders so plangently is the sadness and waste of passion; the depression that Michael Ignatieff has described as 'rooted in the primal insatiability of all human desiring, in the inability of any actual objects to satisfy our initial desire to regain a oneness with the world'.[18] It is the greatest tragedy of sexuality in English prose.

The portrait of the Ashburnhams, who appear a perfect, harmonious couple in public, but do not speak in private, draws upon the Hueffer marriage. The conflict between Edward's charity and Leonora's parsimony reflects similar ones between the Hueffers and also between Ford and Hunt.[19] But again, Ford has transposed some of the essential components: not only is Leonora made the Catholic (instead of himself); her husband's family is made the wealthier (instead of the Martindales). Florence seems the manipulative partner in the Dowells' marriage, making Dowell nurse her through an imaginary illness. (This reflects Ford's resentment against Elsie before her illness was properly diagnosed.) But Dowell has himself seemed manipulative to some readers: manipulative of people, as when he intimidates Florence by his display of violence against his black servant, or his curt refusal to let her visit the Ashburnhams; manipulative of words, of stories, of the sympathies of his imagined listener.[20] Ford may thus be obliquely understanding his own manipulations of Elsie at the time of his breakdown. And once again, it is the dramatic and emotive potential of such a bizarrely dual marriage that appealed to his fictional imagination, and which excited him to elaborate purely fictional details, such as the axe with which Florence entrusts her husband so that he can break down her locked door if her heart fails: which is her ploy to enable her to lock her bedroom door and ensure that Dowell will not disturb her adulteries.

Social and Sexual Politics

The Good Soldier, then, reflects Ford's marital predicament, and his attitudes about sexuality, in complex ways. But his case has a larger context, and one which has been largely overlooked by his critics. The 'Woman Question', the campaigns for female suffrage and for reform of the divorce laws, the relation of sexuality to morality and religion, were not simply Fordian idiosyncrasies: they were everybody's problems at the time, and perceived as problems which were intricately tangled. Part of the novel's fascination is that it reads as a compendium of most of the anxieties and disturbances afflicting Edwardian England; the changes that Ford observed 'coming about through the entry of women into social consciousness'. *The Good Soldier* is Ford's contemporary registering of these social changes: an attempt to capture a moment of social history, as he admired Madox Brown for doing.[21] It testifies to how Ford's emotional difficulties tended to make him an even more responsive, more astute recorder of his day. Samuel Hynes's excellent survey of all these issues, *The Edwardian Turn of Mind*, explains how the mere contemplation of liberalizing moves seemed to threaten every aspect of society:

The trouble with women during the Edwardian period was simply that their troubles could not be kept separate and distinct, but kept getting mixed up with each other and with other social issues: contraception threatened the family and the birth rate, divorce threatened the Church and the stability of society, suffrage threatened political balances, and so even the most moderate move toward liberation seemed a rush toward chaos.

Dowell is careful not to sound as if he were advocating 'free love': 'Society must go on, I suppose', he grudgingly concedes (in Ford's echo of Meary Walker's motto). His expression is dual: the way he says society must go on conveys that he wouldn't mind very much if it didn't, and that he doesn't much want to save himself. The phrase has a further vital ambiguity. He mixes up the sense of maintaining the *status quo* with that of reproducing itself ('it must breed, like rabbits'). But his concession itself reintroduces the polygamous desire which threatens social stability, the illicit form of 'goings on' with which the novel has occupied itself. The anonymous attack on H. G. Wells's *Ann Veronica* in the *Spectator* exemplifies the contemporary controversies Ford is responding to:

His is a community of scuffling stoats and ferrets, unenlightened by a ray of duty or abnegation [. . .] What we want to do [. . .] is to ask even those whose ears are deaf to [an appeal to the principles of Christianity] whether they think that it is possible to build up a self-sustained and permanent State upon the basis which underlies not only Mr. Wells's latest novel, but so considerable a section of the thinking and writing which are described as modern [. . .] Unless the citizens of a State put before themselves the principles of duty, self-sacrifice, self-control, and continence, not merely in the matter of national defence, national preservation, and national well-being, but also of the sex relationship, the life of the State must be short and precarious. Unless the institution of the family is firmly founded and assured, the State will not continue.[22]

We now take for granted a degree of mismatching between monogamy and desire, and do not regard divorce as criminal.[23] But the conservative defence of the family has not changed very much in the last eighty years, and these arguments have been familiar responses to the feminism of the 1970s and 1980s. What is harder to recapture is the hysteria and paranoia with which the feelings of fundamental threat were voiced. Now such responses tend to be made only to the liberalization of homosexuality, and claim their justification in the appalling menace of AIDS. *The Good Soldier* has one of the most sympathetic descriptions of the ontological disturbance following adultery and divorce. It comes when Nancy finally asks Leonora about the 'good read' she has had about the Brand divorce case in the papers:

'Then . . .' Nancy began. Her blue eyes were full of horror: her brows were tight above them; the lines of pain about her mouth were very distinct. In her eyes the whole of that familiar, great hall had a changed aspect. The andirons with the brass flowers at the ends appeared unreal; the burning logs were just logs that were burning and not the comfortable symbols of an indestructible mode of life. The flame fluttered before the high fireback; the St Bernard sighed in his sleep. Outside the winter rain fell and fell. And suddenly she thought that Edward might marry some one else; and she nearly screamed. (pp. 251, 254)

The vertigo of defamiliarization is heard in the rain, which 'fell and fell', while Nancy recognizes for the first time the possibility of adultery with Edward. That reading has begun her fall, her downfall into madness. The fire takes on a Fordian duality: domestic hearth providing warmth and security, or the shifting fire of passion presaging fires of hell? The Brands have ignited a conflagration. Representations seem unreal; what had seemed indestructible now appears as 'fluttering'. The St Bernard's sigh is a Flaubertian touch, enigmatically expressive. (But of what? Domestic claustrophobia, wishful dreaming, lost innocence?) The dog of the saint combines the bestial and the blest—like Edward and Nancy.

Robert Green, who has made the most thorough survey of Ford's political concerns, has argued that 'Ford's preoccupation with the limits of omniscient narrative [. . .] precludes the possibility of *The Good Soldier* being employed as a revolutionary, or even a reformist vehicle':

Ford has created a world whose only certainty is its lack of a moral architecture. Implicit in such nihilism is the futility of attempting to change a world which cannot even be understood.

The 'drive to neutrality' that characterises *The Good Soldier*, by means of which a limited criticism of conventional social arrangements is subsumed by a formal structure antipathetic to change, was patently useful to a novelist publicly critical of some bourgeois values but unable to discover a viable alternative.[24]

Ford certainly did not see himself as 'reformist'. *He* is not advocating 'free love' any more than Dowell; and not as much as Wells or Lawrence. His Browning-esque poem 'Süssmund's Address to an Unknown God' (1912) asks:

> Did I, dear God, ever attempt to shine
> As such a friend of Progress?[25]

Like 'On Heaven'—and like *The Good Soldier* itself, with its own plangent vision
of Heaven as a Provence of the soul (p. 213)—'Süssmund's Address' imagines a
heaven. It can accommodate almost anything but reformers:

> Oh, you sleeping God,
> I hope you sit amongst the coloured tents
> Of any other rotten age than this
> [. . .] in such a heaven
> Where there's no feeling of the moral pulse,
> I think I'd find some peace—with treachery
> Of the sword and dagger kind to keep it sweet
> —Adultery, foul murder, pleasant things,
> A touch of incest, theft, but no Reformers.[26]

Ford's satire on 'Reformers' continues with different degrees of bitterness until
after the war (when his advocacy of the small producer and self-sufficiency begins
to turn him into his own reformer). *An English Girl* (1907) was originally going
to be called 'The Reformers'; the title would have done as well for *The Simple
Life Limited*, *The Panel*, or *The New Humpty-Dumpty*.

In terms of party politics, Ford was inconsistent and contradictory: a Tory
advocate of female suffrage. He appears opposed to reforms which would include
divorce-law reform, at the same time that he, ostensibly a Catholic, was trying to
get a German divorce because under English law his wife can obstruct a divorce.
To berate these inconsistencies is to fail to see that the bitterness comes from
more than the questions of law and party-politics. It is bitterness for the inevitable
suffering caused by polygamous desire, and contempt for reformers who blandly
assume that such suffering can be eradicated by changing the law. In *Henry James*
he said that it was 'the profound moral purpose of the 90's, that really frightened
me out of my life'. It was, he said, 'a curious thing made up of socialism, free
thought, the profession of free love going hand in hand with an intense sexual
continence that to all intents and purposes ended in emasculation'.[27] In part the
fear is of the implicit converse: that opposition to free love may go hand in glove
with sexual incontinence. Or at least that the contradictions within the reformers
bring everyone else's sexual complications to light.

It is not so much that *The Good Soldier* makes 'a limited criticism of
conventional social arrangements [which] is subsumed by a formal structure
antipathetic to change'. The elaborately time-shifted narrative is a highly unconventional arrangement. It could only be said to be 'antipathetic' to change in the
sense that Dowell laments the changes which have already happened. It could be
argued that its intensely retrospective, elegiac mode seeks a sense of inevitability,
and that to do so is tantamount to a political quiescence. But this would be an
objection to all tragic forms, which represent characters crushed by fates (or
systems) which they cannot overmaster. Green's utopian Marxist clichés obscure

the point of the book's tragic vision of a desire which cannot be fulfilled or restrained by any conceivable social conventions; a vision of how some dilemmas are insoluble, and leave no alternative to helpless grief at irreparable loss.[28] There is a whiff of whiggish condescension in implying that Ford—who must be one of the least bourgeois English writers of his time—did not look hard enough for his viable alternative, which our hindsight shows us to be a more searching criticism of conventional society. Such an argument forgets the constraints on a writer entangled in that society. Dowell cannot discover a viable alternative because it is too late. There is no redemption of the devastation and waste he recounts. Ford is not concerned to change the society he has been diagnosing, because Dowell's world 'vanished in four crashing days at the end of nine years and six weeks' rather as European civilization vanished during the first four crashing days of August 1914 (p. 10). The war changes the political context, since the codes of suppression and repression have given way to overt enmities.

The Good Soldier provoked extreme responses. *The Morning Post* made a prediction which still holds: 'It will have no indifferent readers.' Both its subject-matter and its narrative manner were controversial. Those like Rebecca West, with a taste for the advanced, at once welcomed it on both counts: 'It is impossible for anyone, with any kind of sense about writing to miss some sort of distant apprehension of the magnificence of his work.' May Sinclair wrote to Ford to congratulate him, saying she thought the book 'extraordinarily fine', and its method 'simply triumphant'. Sidney Dark in the *Daily Express* called it 'An Amazing Book'; 'one of the cleverest novels' he had ever read: 'It may be one of the few works of fiction to be written down as "great" ', he suspected—and proposed to try to decide at once: 'I am going to read it again.' Theodore Dreiser trusted the tale more than the telling, complaining that he could scarcely read it once: 'The interlacings, the cross references, the re-re-references to all sorts of things which subsequently are told somewhere in full, irritate one to the point of one's laying down the book.'[29] The relentless rigour which disconcerted him in the novel's narration impressed him in its psychology. He found the story 'a splendid one from the psychological point of view', praising it because 'there is no blinking of the commonplaces of our existence which so many find immoral'. This sounds myopic to an age which is tirelessly explicit and knowing about the 'sex-instinct' which Dowell either turns blind eyes to, or wants 'taken for granted'. But Dreiser's honest relish for disabusal registers the novel's potential to shock. Many of its reviewers found immoral not just 'the commonplaces of our existence', but also the unblinkingness of Ford's look at them.

Most reviews discussed it as a psychological novel; and most thought they knew what they thought about that. The dominant note is of outrage with the subject, even when the quality of the writing was apprehended. *The Daily Telegraph* praised 'the excellent writing', but thought that 'only a reader with a considerable experience of the fiction of irregular amours could read this novel to the end without being more than a little nauseated'; it seemed 'a frankly and uncompromisingly unpleasant treatment of a tragic subject'. The *Saturday Review* responded with an unusual mixture of pettiness and magnanimity: it 'amounts in the end to no more than a chronicle of sordid treachery and vice [. . .] It is all very cleverly done, and it is clever of the author to contrive that we shall actually picture the miserable widower taking us into his confidence [. . .] Many novelists [. . .] would like to have the skill which went to [*sic*] writing 'The Good Soldier,' and most, we believe, would make better use of it.'[30] While one journal sneered that it could 'well imagine that the work will prove of some value to the specialist in pathology', others decried what they found to be 'most unsavoury': a 'sordid theme'; a 'distorted, sex-morbid atmosphere'; 'sordidly antipathetic'.[31] The point here is not to make condescending fun of a more repressively patrolled public morality, but to recover a sense of the risks Ford was taking, and of the complex responses he was provoking. The tone of the reactions proves that neither his choice of subject, nor his treatment of it, should be described as neutral. *The Good Soldier* gets to the heart of contemporary contradictions and uneasiness. What is more, Ford shared the perception that the regulation of sexuality was a thoroughly political issue. His novel should be seen as a contribution to that controversy.

Calling a book of this type 'The Good Soldier', when it was published in 1915, made it more controversial.[32] The following year the book Ford wrote with Violet Hunt, *Zeppelin Nights*, precipitated another storm: because Ford wrote explicitly about the fear of Zeppelins he was attacked as a coward in a vicious pseudonymous review. As the controversy intensified, an unidentified correspondent, 'M.F.', reverted to attacking *The Good Soldier*.

The title of his book cannot be so lightly condoned. Charming women, to whose refined minds the exploits of a vigorous stallion have no interest, are buying the book, in the belief [. . .] that it is a grateful tribute, from the pen of an able and delightful writer, to their men. Men whom they have born and trained to be 'Good Soldiers' in the truest and finest sense of the word. 'The Perfect Stallion' would have been an appropriate title for a book which none of Hueffer's admirers can have read without wondering what necessity he saw, in this hour when men have so gloriously fought for and entered into their Kingdom, to portray them in such a despicable light.[33]

Wells wrote a loyal and energetic defence to the editor's brother, G. K. Chesterton. But he was being wilfully—or tactically—blind in saying that 'M.F.' 'just lies about it—I guess he's a dirty-minded priest or some such unclean thing—when he says it is a story of a stallion and so forth'.[34]

Both of them are picking a single thread from the book's intricate tangle, and denying the existence of the others. The fact that they were incited to do so refutes Robert Green's anachronistic assurance that Dowell's summary of the sexual question 'could hardly be expected to disturb any male complacencies' (p. 98). *The Good Soldier*, as he suggests, may not have been so overtly disturbing because it was not as radical as *Ann Veronica* or *The Rainbow*. But it is none the less one of the foremost of what David Trotter has called 'Edwardian Sex Novels';

and it was certainly capable of disturbing such male complacencies as the one about what the refined minds of charming women are interested in.[35]

It came out in March 1915, several months before Ford got his commission. But his later account of how the title was changed improves the story by having him in the army before publication, in order to point up the contrast between his own soldiering and Ashburnham's: 'One day, when I was on parade, I received a final wire of appeal from Mr Lane, and the telegraph being reply-paid I seized the reply-form and wrote in hasty irony: "Dear Lane, Why not *The Good Soldier?*" . . . To my horror six months later the book appeared under that title.' No such telegrams have survived. But there is a letter—from South Lodge— which corroborates the gist of the story; though it suggests that the irony was less hasty:

My Dear Lane, I should have thought that you publishers had had eye-openers enough about monkeying with authors' titles, at the request of travellers. 'The Saddest Story'—I say it in all humility—is about the best book you ever published and the title is about the best title. Still, I make it a principle never to interfere with my publisher, but to take it out in calling him names. Why not call the book 'The Roaring Joke'? Or call it anything you like, or perhaps it would be better to call it 'A Good Soldier'—that might do. At any rate it is all I can think of.[36]

Written on his birthday, exactly a year after the day he said he had begun, this letter has a deliberateness about its flippancy. Its inimitable mixture of wounded pride feigning haughty indifference, and true humility (he had surprised himself with his best book) wrapping itself in exaggerated arrogance, is just what made it so hard for people—and especially publishers—to deal with him. What needs observing is that even in a letter he writes in the dual mode. It is not just a haughty letter from a gentleman to a person in business, but it becomes, disconcertingly, a parody of such a letter, as the gentleman makes threats of name-calling. The agile shift from what to call the blind monkey of a publisher to what to call the book suggests that the whole letter is a 'Roaring Joke'—a good-humoured shout to regain authority over his creation. If we take the roaring to be more anguished, then the irony here becomes truly double edged. The letter, like an excerpt from the novel, turns high ironic comedy out of despair. Ford's studiedly offhand 'that might do' sounds too like Ashburnham saying 'Might just be done!' before attempting a heroic feat at polo (pp. 36, 137)—or contemplating adultery.

The exquisite irony of 'The Good Soldier' as a title is that Edward both is and is not a good soldier (as a soldier): he has seen little military action, but has shown a heroic protectiveness in rescuing his men who had fallen overboard. Here too the Fordian duality sows a doubt. Is his heroism a suicidal impulse, an instance of self-deluded egotism rather than altruism? ('Leonora had got it into her head that Edward was trying to commit suicide', p. 200.) A further irony comes from the probable allusion to Heine's remark: 'You may lay a sword on my coffin, I was a good soldier in the warfare for humanity', in which the soldiering is metaphorical. According to this implication, the fight that sets the seal on Ashburnham's character is his struggle against his passion for Nancy, rather than his military exploits. And yet he both is and is not a good 'soldier' in the sense Beatrice gives it in *Much Ado About Nothing*:

MESSENGER: And [Benedick is] a good soldier too, lady.
BEATRICE: And a good soldier to a lady, but what is he to a lord?[37]

If he is a philanderer, he is one who dies from the effort at self-restraint.

Ford's ironic title invokes the long-serving connection between the military and the amatory. He dramatizes the connection in his later writing about the war, as when Sylvia Tietjens thinks: 'This whole war was an agapemone. . . . You went to war when you desired to rape innumerable women. . . . It was what war was for. . . . All these men, crowded in this narrower space . . .'.[38] However, readers who objected to their inference that by calling Ashburnham a good soldier Ford was calling all British soldiery licentious were probably responding to a contradictory connection. The 1904 'Report of the Inter-Departmental Committee on Physical Deterioration' had, as Hynes notes, aroused the very hysteria it was intended to allay, namely that the Imperial race was entering a phase of decadence and decline. One main stimulus for the investigation was 'the large percentage of rejections for physical causes of recruits for the Army'. 'The very fact that a report on "Physical Deterioration" existed was enough to make the idea current; and deterioration quickly became interchangeable with degeneracy or decadence, thus adding an implication of moral decline to the idea of physical worsening which the report was in fact intended to refute.' Deterioration was attributed to sexual indulgence—or 'impurity', as it was called in James Marchant's influential 1909 book *Aids to Purity*.[39] The army, deterioration, degeneracy, sexuality. *The Good Soldier* invokes this nexus of anxieties with its diagnosis of the adulteries, hypochondria, neurasthenia, madness, pining away, and suicides that revolve around its representative officer and gentleman. It is not surprising that Ford spoke defensively about his audacious title.

'A Touch of Incest'

He may have had even better reasons for being wary. Dowell's most familiar turn is a cry of uncertainty; an abdication of judgement: 'I don't know. I leave it to you' (p. 282). The evidence about 'the queer, shifty thing that is human nature' (p. 285) is presented by the time-shifty narrative as itself something perilously dual, contradictory, duplicitous. 'And yet again you have me', says Dowell. Have him to consider, or have him implicated by his own investigations? He continues: 'If poor Edward was dangerous because of the chastity of his expressions—and they say that is always the hall-mark of a libertine—what about myself?' But what about the prurience of those who find prurience even in chastity?

For I solemnly avow that not only have I never so much as hinted at an impropriety in my conversation in the whole of my days; and more than that, I will vouch for the cleanness of my thoughts and the absolute chastity of my life. At what, then, does it all work out? Is the whole thing a folly and a mockery? Am I no better than a eunuch or is the proper man—the man with the right to existence—a raging stallion forever neighing after his neighbour's womenkind?

I don't know. And there is nothing to guide us. And if everything is so nebulous about a matter so elementary as the morals of sex, what is there to guide us in the more subtle morality of all other personal contacts, associations, and activities? Or are we meant to act on impulse alone? It is all a darkness. (p. 16)

A darkness of uncertainty, or moral horror? Ford's novel will not 'guide us' either; even the facts, let alone what they all work out at, remain shrouded in mystery and suppression. Counting the women Ashburnham becomes entangled with—Leonora, the Kilsyte girl, La Dolciquita, Mrs Basil, Maisie Maidan, Florence, and finally Nancy Rufford—he could be more polygamously inclined than even Henry VIII. Yet there is little hard evidence that Edward actually committed adultery with more than two of these, La Dolciquita and Florence. Ford's manuscript revisions carefully excise some of the hard evidence. One revised passage originally read in the manuscript:

Yes, they quarrelled bitterly. That seems rather extravagant; you might have thought that Leonora would be just calmly loathing and he lachrymosely contrite. But that was not it a bit. For along with Edward's passions and his shame for them went the violent conviction that he must behave like a gentleman. Yes, every one of the girls that he ruined must be provided for as if she were at least the wife, say, of a bank manager, and every one of his illegitimate offspring must be sent to Eton or to the convent at Roehampton. It could not be done of course.

And Leonora saw to it that it was not done. Her idea was that about fifty pounds a piece was enough for the minxes and the children she put generally under the guardianship of her solicitor, providing about fifty pounds a year for each of them, or a little more in special cases. Yes, to the children she was quite generous. You see, she was childless herself.[40]

The revised text is ironically double: 'he was always trying to put prostitutes into respectable places—and he was a perfect maniac about children' (p. 69). Is it because they are *his* children and his mistresses that he is motivated towards such philanthropy? Or is it pure altruism? It is a triumph of the book that our inability to answer these (or Dowell's) questions does not diminish the force of the presentation; indeed, Ashburnham seems all the more bafflingly alive *because* there is so much we cannot gauge about him.[41]

One motive for Ford's removal of details about Edward's bastards might have been to sustain him as an object of at least potential sympathy for a readership of 1915. But there is another possible motive; one which leads to the darkest heart of the novel's passion. Removing explicit references to Edward's children stops us from thinking explicitly about who they might be; and this enables Ford to place unobtrusively at the centre of his story a suggestion of a relationship so disturbing that few critics have even commented upon it. The girl with whom

Ashburnham has become infatuated might be his own illegitimate daughter. I had known the novel for nine years before the thought occurred to me, but then immediately details began to fall into place. 'There was the complication caused by the girl's entire innocence; there was the further complication that both Edward and Leonora really regarded the girl as their daughter', says Dowell; but he then immediately half-retracts: 'Or it might be more precise to say that they regarded her as being Leonora's daughter', thus repressing the horrendous possibility that she might be 'really regarded' as Edward's daughter (p. 145). There is Nancy's mother's apparently unmotivated tirade of a letter to her daughter, which Dowell has not seen, but has deduced that it said something like: 'How do you know that you are even Colonel Rufford's daughter?' (p. 260). The fact that Edward has kept in touch with Nancy's mother, even though Nancy has been told she was dead, now assumes a sinister appearance. Nancy is Leonora's 'only friend's only child' (p. 110); so when Leonora comes to Nancy's convent to tell the girl that her mother is dead (which she isn't), it may be that Major and Mrs Rufford have come to some arrangement with the Ashburnhams, who might want to adopt her because of Leonora's childlessness (pp. 148–9). But like so many of the book's main elements, the action seems in excess of the given explanations, which anyway produce as much mystery as they dispel. Nancy's childhood terrors, her memories of violent scenes between her parents, *may* be to do simply with Mrs Rufford's infidelities; but there is at least the suggestion that they may be to do with Major Rufford believing that Nancy is not his daughter.[42] Dowell says Leonora is Nancy's 'guardian, if that is the correct term' (p. 110). Does his scruple imply that the relationship is not what it seems? Dowell (or Ford) might be hinting that Leonora did a poor job of guarding her ward; but there might be the much more sinister hint that she was acting as a pimp, bringing Nancy up specifically to be Edward's mistress, as a replacement for Maisie Maidan, and this time someone who would be a fellow-Catholic, obedient to Leonora, and would thus keep Edward's philandering under her control and 'in the family'.

Dowell explains Leonora's agony over Edward's passion for Nancy as her final despair over his infidelity. 'It's saddening that a man can't be quite true, even when he adores you,' says Pauline Leicester in *A Call*, 'but he can't. That's all.' A saddening story, but not the saddest? In 1927, when he was planning his novel explicitly about incestuous love, *A Little Less Than Gods*, Ford said that Conrad had desired to write about incest: not 'the consummation of forbidden desires', but 'the emotions of a shared passion that by its nature must be most hopeless of all'. There is little doubt that the saddest part of *The Good Soldier*'s story for Ford was the hopelessness of Edward's passion for his ward. Leonora's agony might thus spring from a horror of a worse sin than adultery. Why does she get 'one of her headaches' when Major Rufford visits? It is this Oedipal tangle of innuendo and suppression that makes the book so much more effectively disturbing than the idealization of the English Gentleman it has too often been mistaken for.[43]

Whether or not Edward is the actual father is to some extent a technicality: 'he had regarded her exactly as he would have regarded a daughter' (p. 131). So that when Dowell says that 'it had not even come into [Edward's] head that the tabu which extended around her was not inviolable', he could equally be talking of biological incest between father and daughter, or the psychological quasi-incest of guardian and ward (p. 132). Even a quasi-incestuous relationship between them is enough to tap powerful feelings of taboo-violation, as expressed in Dowell's melodramatic terms:

He certainly loved her, but with a very deep, very tender and very tranquil love. He had missed her when she went away to her convent-school; he had been glad when she had returned. But of more than that he had been totally unconscious. Had he been conscious of it, he assured me, he would have fled from it as from a thing accursed. He realized that it was the last outrage upon Leonora. But the real point was his entire unconsciousness. (p. 131)

Is Dowell protesting too much? Should we believe in Edward's unconsciousness that his love is more than platonic or paternal? Dowell cites the fact that even Florence wasn't jealous of Nancy to prove 'the obviously innocent nature of the regard of those two' (p. 152; though even here his language is equivocal: does 'regard' mean the way they appeared to others, or the way they regarded each other?) The novel suggests that more is happening than the characters or their narrator know of, pressing and repressing the idea of incest; such as when Edward felt 'the immense temptation to do the unthinkable thing' (p. 278). The book's climaxes—the protest scene, Maisie's death—present overwhelming emotions which cannot be thought, cannot become conscious, and yet cannot be escaped. It treats the point at which forbidden desires come into being. It conveys temptation and repression, and presents the struggle between the two as tragically destructive. When Leonora exclaims: 'Edward's dying—because of you. He's dying. He's worth more than either of us. . . .', Nancy 'looked past her at the panels of the half-closed door' (the perfect image for a repressed perception?), and says, twice: 'My poor father' (pp. 247–8). Because she cannot bring herself to think the unthinkable, and is thus thinking of something else—Major Rufford? Or because she can see all too clearly the implications of her temptation? Censorious reviewers were perhaps fleeing from Ford's novel as from a thing accursed because of its daring to speak about the unspeakable. The word 'incest' does not appear in the book. Ford's achievement is to hold pity for Edward's and Nancy's hopeless love in exacting tension with the terror aroused by the feelings aroused by the thought of transgressing the incest taboo (or something like it). In a review written soon after he had begun *The Good Soldier*, Ford said: 'I am not sure that there is not something after all in the English-German idea that if one saw the whole truth of things—being English-German oneself—one would go mad.'[44] The novel's tangle of adultery and betrayal is bad, but not bad enough for it to be 'the whole truth' that devastates the lives of the two couples, Maisie, and Nancy. It is only once one realizes that the truth verges on incest that the plot doesn't seem like romantic melodrama. Leonora is fighting to suppress that maddening vision of the truth. Towards the end of the novel her devastating headaches suggest that her hysterical urging of Nancy to become Edward's mistress has brought her again to the brink of insanity. When inexperienced Nancy sees what is happening, she does go mad. In the same essay Ford says that prose 'is a matter of looking things in the face'; in *The Good Soldier* he looks his characters in the face as they struggle not to look things in the face. Then, when they can no longer avoid knowledge, Ford shows how they finally do look things in the face, and face their resulting disabusal or destruction. The tragic, destructive double-bind for the characters is worked, for author and reader, into the affective double-bind of ironic tragedy.

The Good Soldier is not an isolated example of Ford's fictional interest in 'a touch of incest'. It is invoked in two cases which do not involve actual incest: *The Inheritors*, as we have seen; and in *A Call*, in which it makes a difference that Robert Grimshaw and Katya Lascarides are cousins. In *Parade's End* Valentine Wannop is rumoured to be an illegitimate daughter of Tietjens's father, which if true would leave Tietjens living with his half-sister.[45] Whereas in *Parade's End* we assume the rumour to be false (because it probably originates from Tietjens's malicious wife Sylvia), in *A Little Less Than Gods* (1928) Ford returned to the theme, this time making the lovers true half-siblings. This fact is hinted at throughout, but the lovers do not (or will not) consciously face their relation for a long time; though when they do, they decide to renounce their love.

Ford's feelings for his sister-in-law could be a source or a symptom of this interest. But his feelings for Hunt's niece, Rosamond, probably suggested to him the possibility of an affair between guardian and ward. Ford's daughter Katharine was convinced that Ford had based Nancy Rufford upon her. She wrote to Mizener: ' "the tortured & agonised eyes and quite extraordinary sense of fun". the "beastly bore of truthfulness." of Nancy. "the miracle of patience who could be miraculously impatient"—Do I need to explain to you what that is?' The hopeless love of a father who feared he would never see his daughters again flowed easily in his imagination into the hopeless love between guardian and ward. When, like Ashburnham putting prostitutes in respectable places, Ford brought Gertrud Schablowsky back to 84 Holland Park Avenue, he told Hunt that he had been drawn to her by the thought that 'the soul of his first-born who had died' had gone into Gertrud's body.[46] This may have been intended to reassure Violet that his feelings towards Gertrud were paternal rather than amorous. Gertrud used to call Ford 'Papa'. But then, as if her presence were not potentially scandalous enough, he wrote a poem to her and published it under a transparent pseudonym ('Francis M. Hurd') in the *English Review*. Goldring describes 'To Gertrude' as 'definite about the "purity" of the relations between the poet and his protégée, which are those of a father and a substitute daughter, united by suffering'.[47] But although it ends with an assertion of propriety—'Run off to bed. Good-night! It's very late'—it feels more like a renunciation of a sexuality that the preceding poem has been at pains to evoke:

It's very late: it's very cold:
And you're too young and I'm too old
You've your small cares and I've small ease.
Come nestle down across my knees.

Stir up the fire: draw out the chair,
Kick off your shoes: let down the hair:
Your white kimono now!—Disclose

(One has to work very hard to sustain the reading of a 'pure' relationship at this point—)

> Disclose
> The little budget of your woes.
> You shall have both my hands to hold:
> It's very late: it's very cold.

> [. . .] we two
> Have each of us such ancient work to do:
> You sell caresses: I, a song or so:
> And so we please each other . . .

As Goldring says, it is not one of Ford's best poems. It is too derivative of Rossetti's 'Jenny', in which the poet muses, with the girl's head in his lap, on the paradox of her basic innocence despite her fallen state. But, like *The Good Soldier*, it is effective in creating a dual attitude towards the sexual. It is doubly provocative: provoking the very desire it disavows; and provoking its readers, some of whom would have been wondering what Hueffer was up to with what Goldring calls 'a little German girl of the "unfortunate" class', into identifying 'Francis M. Hurd' with Ford M. Hueffer.

The Good Soldier blurs the parental and sexual relationships in exactly the same way: not only with the love between Edward and Nancy, but also with Edward's feeling for the women he kissed on the train (precipitating the 'Kilsyte case'). Dowell assures us: 'he assured me that he felt at least quite half-fatherly when he put his arm around her waist and kissed her.'[48] Ford himself may have felt at least quite half-filial in his relationship with Hunt. Besides Conrad, at least one other observer thought of her as maternal towards him.[49] Nancy nearly screams when she learns about adultery; not just because of the shock to her religious view of marriage as a sacrament, but because her love for Edward loses its innocence. The 'familiar' great hall seems utterly changed. Her suppressed scream is a protest against the defamiliarization that is incest.

Apart from a passing reference to having known about—and disapproved of—*The Interpretation of Dreams* before the war, there is no record of Ford's having read Freud. Nevertheless, the influence of Freud's ideas about the Oedipus complex is probable.[50] The 'purity' not only of parental but of religious love too is caught up in the novel's tangle of desire, confirming Hynes's point that a

challenge to sexual conventions is also a challenge to the structure of the family
and the institutionalization of morality. In a scene that must have been profoundly
disturbing to a culture that had not yet assimilated the later Freud's analysis of
religion, Dowell describes how Leonora finds Edward 'kneeling beside his bed
with his head hidden in the counterpane': 'His arms, outstretched, held out before
him a little image of the Blessed Virgin—a tawdry, scarlet and Prussian blue affair
that the girl had given him on her first return from the convent. His shoulders
heaved convulsively three times, and heavy sobs came from him before she could
close the door. He was not a Catholic; but that was the way it took him' (p. 125).
But how does it take him? Dowell comes from Quaker stock, so the word 'tawdry'
might represent the puritan's mistrust of ornament. Even to say that is to conjure
up puritan denunciations of Rome as the whore of Babylon: something that
placing the word 'scarlet' next to words like 'tawdry' and 'affair' does nothing to
dispel. Ashburnham's gesture could indeed be the innocent sentimentality Dowell
is only too eager to take it for, an expression of love for the virgin who gave him
the image. *Beati Immaculati*: blessed are the pure who can see someone clutching
the image of a virgin on their bed and *not* suspect a sexual aspect to their passion.
Ford seizes on the way religion itself blurs the categories of parent and child in
the image of the virgin mother, in order to redeem the guilt of sexuality. Of
course in the world of this novel, rejecting the cult of the virgin is no guide either,
since 'the basis upon which Protestantism rests' in England is Henry VIII's desire
for polygamy (p. 254). And Florence claims (though Dowell denies it) that the
room in which the Protest was signed was 'Luther's bedroom' (p. 52).

D. H. Lawrence, also engaged in sexualizing the Edwardian novel, divorces
sexuality from irony, seeking to confer upon it a mystical solemnity. Ford, by
contrast, ironizes the sexual, by revealing the extent to which the sexual touches
with irony the apparently non-sexual. (In the post-Freudian world no innocence
can be free of sexuality, though in the transitional world of *The Good Soldier* this
does not liberate the possibility of an uncorrupting sexuality.) The closest
equivalent to Ford's dual vision in *The Good Soldier* is to be found in its model,
Henry James's *What Maisie Knew*, where adult misdemeanours are seen simultaneously with the child's naïve wonder and the narrator's knowing irony. *The Good
Soldier* rewrites James's novel as tragedy, by removing James's comic proviso that
the young observer Maisie should not be corrupted by the circumambient adult
squalor and emotional abuse, and by doubling the obtuse observer and knowing
narrator in the single figure of Dowell. (It may have been Sir Claude's flirtatious
chivalry towards his stepdaughter that got Ford thinking about how a real passion
between guardian and daughter might end.) *The Good Soldier* is quite unlike
anything else in its sustained tragic irony, holding characters and readers in
suspense perpetually on the brink of the abyss of sexuality. It is a sustained
innuendo, inciting suspicions of the sexual, implicating its readers as well as its
characters and narrator for entertaining them.

The Good Soldier is thus more ambiguous in its sexual politics than has been
recognized. Provocative in its dispassionate emphasis on passion—its trick of

suggesting or insinuating that passion entangles everything, leaves nothing innocent—it aligns itself with the 'modern' in literature. Although it does not advocate change, the fact of its relentless interrogation of moral orthodoxies was felt to be subversive. Its 'analysis of the polygamous desires that underlie all men' allies it with the radical, controversial work of writers such as Edward Carpenter and Havelock Ellis on the psychology and sociology of sex.[51] On the other hand, confined to the Jamesian milieu of the upper-middle classes, the book's view of Tory England often feels like a Tory view—however uneasy with what it sees. Ford's nostalgic admiration for the paternal landowner is unmistakable, even as he reminds us that the *droit de seigneur* involves not only being a father to your tenants, but fathering their children.

Tone and Sexuality

Writing about *The English Review*, which was intended to accommodate subjects generally blinked at, Ford said: 'The trouble is that, at any rate in Anglo-Saxondom, the moment a man of distinction gets hold of an unorthodox idea—be it connected with politics or religion or sex—straight-way he loses most of his sense of proportion and nearly all his power of putting things.'[52] They order these matters better in France, of course. Ford shared James's and Conrad's conviction of the superiority of French over English fiction. At just about the time he began writing the novel he recalled how reading Lord Morley's *Life of Diderot* influenced him so profoundly: 'I became therein acquainted with Diderot's fictions [. . .] Those works caused in me a sort of awakening to the technical possibilities of fiction only equal to the mental fields that seemed to open before me when I first mastered the fifth proposition of Euclid.' He had an ambition 'to do for the English novel what in *Fort Comme La Mort*, Maupassant had done for the French', and reimagined Maupassant's plot of an old man doomed by his passion ('strong as death') for a much younger woman. Ford called Maupassant's novel 'that really greatest of all renderings of atrocious love—of atrociously painful love'; and he admired its 'peculiar feeling of passionate stress'. He wanted to write about desire without succumbing to the sentimentalities of English romance conventions. 'Romance, for me, is ethically wicked,' he wrote soon before beginning *The Good Soldier*, 'a cause of national deterioration of character, of selfishness, of cowardice.' 'Literature', he once observed, 'enters with an unparalleled intimacy into French life' (because the French take literature seriously, because French literature takes life seriously). May Sinclair thought she recognized in Ashburnham a reworking of Balzac's libertine Baron Hulot in *La Cousine Bette*. But the most important influence is Flaubert. Soon after *The Good Soldier* was published, Ford wrote about the difficulty of translating the first sentence of Flaubert's story 'Un Cœur Simple' into English.[53] *The Good Soldier* is profoundly Flaubertian in its transformation of the banal repetitions of Ashburnham's affairs into a narrative pattern of complex significance; in its disturbingly surreal juxtapositions; and in its ambivalence about whether a simple heart conduces to nobility or simple-mindedness (like Flaubert's Félicité, Edward is at once saintly and imbecilic). *The Good Soldier* owes much to *Madame Bovary* too (as if England were only ready in 1915 for its classic novel of adultery). Edward is a male Emma Bovary, naïvely romanticizing himself to self-destruction; and the novel repeats the Flaubertian double-bind of terror at the banality of the prosperously conventional, and pity for the victims of conventional morality. Ford was justifiably proud when his friend John Rodker called *The Good Soldier* 'the finest French novel in the English language' (p. 3). It is, precisely, an attempt to 'get hold of unorthodox—that is to say in this case repressed—notions about religion and sex (Protestantism, polygamy, adultery, divorce) without losing a 'sense of proportion'. Even the normally eloquent Dowell loses some of 'his power of putting things' while describing the Protest scene ('I can't define it and can't find a simile for it'). But the formal rigour of the novel lets Ford keep his sense of proportion over the vexed notion of sexuality, while letting him express his fascination with disproportion: excess, outrage, outbursts, scandal, chaos. Writing of Catholicism and divorce, Dowell apologizes: '(Forgive my writing of these monstrous things in this frivolous manner. If I did not I should break down and cry.)' (p. 60). The novel's dual tone keeps us perpetually uncertain about the proportions of what we are witnessing: 'Some one has said that the death of a mouse from cancer is the whole sack of Rome by the Goths, and I swear to you that the breaking up of our little four-square coterie was such another unthinkable event' (p. 9). Dowell characteristically doesn't say which unthinkable event the breaking up was like, leaving us unsure whether the public cataclysm magnifies or diminishes the private grief. Irony turns the monstrous into the ridiculous; repression turns the trivial into the overwhelming. This tonal duality is the perfect expression of Ford's dual attitude to 'the abominable tortures of sex—or, if you will, the abominable interests of sex'. That double bind of repulsion and attraction fixes Ford's bizarre review of Dreiser's *The Titan*:

This is the most revolting book I have ever read—the most horrible, the most demoralising, the most, perhaps, immoral. I say in the first place horrible, because, though no book, being a work of art, can be horrible which depicts tragedy, a book is horrible when it can reveal to a reader, not vastly squeamish, depths of cynical ill-doing such as that reader had never before conceived to lie in human nature. I say demoralising, because, although no work of art can be demoralising which passionlessly depicts immorality, that book can do unfathomed harm to the community which renders vice so attractive and engrossing that it may well damage for ever its reader's sense of proportion. I put 'perhaps' before the word immoral because I am uncertain of Mr. Dreiser's purpose in writing the book. He appears to approve of the hero wholeheartedly and without reserve. But perhaps he does not; perhaps he is merely giving us the adventures of a filthy beast in order to teach us to shun filth and beastliness.[54]

Dreiser may well have read this: it appeared three weeks before his own review of *The Good Soldier*, and so may help to explain his tone about Ford's novel. Ford's review tells us more about his own book than it does about Dreiser's. It came out eleven days before *The Good Soldier*, and shows Ford imagining possible reactions. It almost reads as a parody of the reviews he expected; but is also eloquent about the responses the book deserved. *The Good Soldier* 'passionlessly depicts immorality', but in a strangely dual way which 'depicts tragedy' even as it reveals 'depths of cynical ill-doing'. Ford wanted us to feel the challenge to our 'sense of proportion' in his own tale of atrocious love. His chief resource for doing this is to leave us uncertain about his judgements, the extent of his 'reserve'.

Ford's irony about passion does not mean that he didn't suffer from it, of course. He saw it (as he saw Englishness, or religion, or bohemianism, or the army) from inside as well as outside. Samuel Hynes's reading of the story as about a conflict between passion and convention gives one side of the story: it is perhaps itself the conventional view, the one that the participants themselves might have taken of their affairs. It tries to assimilate the book to the principles of Racinian tragedy. Ford's more Flaubertian view reveals how this tragedy is itself utterly conventional; how Edward and Nancy are acting out the ultimate romantic clichés: dying or going mad for love. (Ford and Hunt can't have been unaware of the conventionality of his talk of suicide, or of love saving his reason.) When Wyndham Lewis describes Bertha writing a letter to Tarr with facility, his comment that: 'She was so sure in the convention of her passion' is supposed to render her a risible automaton. Ford can find Edward absurd as 'a great reader' getting 'lost [ominous word] in novels of a sentimental type': 'I have seen his eyes filled with tears at reading of a hopeless parting.' But the irony doubles with tragedy when Edward and Nancy live out precisely such a hopeless parting without a flicker of visible emotion. As with Emma Bovary, the fact that the characters have nothing but cliché with which to express their agony only heightens the pathos. Though Dowell's tone is unconventional, too odd for cliché, none the less his mind too is made up from scraps of received ideas, books, sayings (Florence's guidebook talk; Provençal troubadours; 'Someone has said [. . .]').[55]

Designing

Form, Angst, Uncertainty

Dreiser's objection to the formal intricacy of *The Good Soldier* sheds an interesting light on the relation of its form to these subjects of sexual and social politics. He writes: 'The whole book is indeed fairly representative of that encrusting formalism which, barnaclewise, is apparently overtaking and destroying all that is best in English life.' The formal presentation of the narrative does in some way mime the claustrophobic formalism of Edwardian society, but to assent to the observation need not be to subscribe to the adverse criticism Dreiser makes out of it. Barnacles encrust, but an individual barnacle's shell is a necessary protection and support. 'The fact is that society is a club with certain rules', wrote Ford as he was working on the end of the novel (with Dowell's comment that 'society can only exist if the normal, if the virtuous, and the slightly-deceitful flourish, and if the passionate, the headstrong, and the too-truthful are condemned to suicide and to madness', p. 291). 'In England the rules require a man to be clean, out of debt, fit to be trusted alone with your wife, unemotional, uneccentric, and so on.' 'I like abiding by them when they do not get in my way,' he added, 'because if I follow them, I shall pass unnoticed in a crowd. And I want to pass unnoticed in the crowd that life is, because to be noticed interferes with my train of thought.'[56] After the *Throne* case, being able to pass unnoticed must have seemed particularly desirable.

The literary-critical argument here is about the necessity of form, and the relationship between form and expression. Most critics of *The Good Soldier* react to its pressing formal concentration, and many find it a moving book. But there has been no adequate account of how and why its very formalism enables its expressive power. All art involves some notion of form, but two attitudes towards it can be generalized from the history of the novel.[57] What could be called the 'vitalist' attitude finds form always in danger of constricting, stifling, or even killing life. In Lawrence, for example, shells and husks are what the ever-growing organism must burst out of and discard. The argument about fate and design is germane here too. For the type of novelist exemplified by Turgenev, it is crucial that the form of a book should follow the life and development of its characters; that no tendentious design or ideology should be imposed upon the plot. So far Ford would agree. His admiration for Turgenev ('The Beautiful Genius') and W. H. Hudson are couched in similar terms. He used to recall Conrad's praise of Hudson: 'You may try for ever to learn how Hudson got his effects and you will never know. He writes down his words as the good God makes the green grass to grow, and that is all you will ever find to say about it if you try for ever.' None the less, one must remember that Ford's humility before Hudson is the humility of the persuasive advocate of 'conscious art'—of knowing exactly how to get effects—acknowledging a quality which lies beyond the grasp of analysis, 'beyond the vicissitudes of conscious Art'.[58] Ford's attitude to form is characteristically dual. There is a strong 'formalist' element (visible, for example, in his criticism of Lawrence): a Flaubertian insistence that only through minute attention to every word and cadence can one hope to get the effect of artlessness; that a novel is animated *by* its formal mastery, not despite it; that it is precisely the form which expresses life. This formalism, the celebrated guiding technical principle of the modernist movement, trusts in the expressive power of design, shape, concrete objects. *The Good Soldier* is certainly no Imagist poem. But Ford wrote interestingly, while he was planning the novel, about how a novel's general effect could be compared to the same objects and abstractions that were being invoked by the Imagists: 'What we need, what we should strive to produce, is a novel uniform in key, in tone, in progression, as hard in texture as a mosaic, as flawless in surface as a polished steel helmet of the fifteenth century.'[59]

Dowell uses a comparably artistic simile which offers an insight into the need for form. What he says about travel is true of all his experiences: 'the world is full of places to which I want to return [. . .] Not one of them did we see more than once, so that the whole world for me is like spots of colour in an immense canvas. Perhaps if it weren't so I should have something to catch hold of now.'[60] His past, too, is composed of spots of time to which he compulsively returns. But their meaning, sometimes even their content, keeps eluding him. Even something as fundamentally definitive as Ashburnham's last words elude Dowell: 'He just looked up to the roof of the stable, as if he were looking to Heaven, and whispered something that I did not catch.'[61] As we trace Dowell's disorientating course, shuttling backwards and forwards in both space and time, we too feel the need of something to catch hold of. The formal symmetries of cross-reference and connection offer to provide this, by establishing a structure underpinning the book. But in the experience of reading the effect is dual, since a cross-reference makes us want to be in two places at once, loosening rather than tightening our grasp on the here-and-now.

Form is thus something that Dowell *needs* to secure his sense of his own existence. The book's formal disruption makes us feel this, miming Dowell's vertiginous dislocations. As the novel's form makes us feel the need of form, it becomes expressive of that need: of the moral chaos that it is adopted to stave off. Ford later described the psychological aftermath of the war in just such terms: 'it had been revealed to you that beneath Ordered Life itself was stretched, the merest film with, beneath it, the abysses of Chaos.'[62] *The Good Soldier* makes it clear that this sense of how little stands between high civilization and barbarism, insanity and squalor is, curiously, a perception which pre-dates the war or which could be said to anticipate it. Historians of pre-war society have brought out the increasing tension and hysteria of the time, manifested in the massive strikes of 1910–12, suffragette agitation, the panic about the possibility of a German invasion.[63] Rather than trying to categorize *The Good Soldier* as a pre-war book or a wartime book, we should recognize how it comes out of many of the same tensions and forces which produced the war. Dowell has an unforgettable image for the abysses of Chaos lurking under the facade of European culture:

Permanence? Stability? I can't believe it's gone. I can't believe that that long, tranquil life, which was just stepping a minuet, vanished in four crashing days at the end of nine years and six weeks. Upon my word, yes, our intimacy was like a minuet, simply because on every possible occasion and in every possible circumstance we knew where to go, where to sit, which table we unanimously should choose [. . .]

No, by God, it is false! It wasn't a minuet that we stepped; it was a prison—a prison full of screaming hysterics, tied down so that they might not outsound the rolling of our carriage wheels as we went along the shaded avenues of the Taunus Wald. (pp. 10–11)

As Dowell shifts dizzyingly from one view to another, Ford creates the dual sense of a formality striving to restrain destructive impulses. At the same time he gives a marvellous practical example of how something as abstract as music and dance—something 'uniform in key, in tone, in progression'—can be expressive of mental turmoil and *Angst*. The formal edifice of civilized ritual is revealed as the prison house of hysteria.

The rending of the veil that keeps Ordered Life safe from Chaos is exactly what is rendered at the moment when Nancy reads about the divorce case, and her stable world becomes unreal. The other crucial moment which reveals the frailty of order and convention comes with the 'Protest' scene. The devastation of the civilized round of spa-town tourism is initiated by the slightest touch: when Florence lays 'one finger upon Captain Ashburnham's wrist', the queer gesture reveals to Leonora that Florence intends to have an affair with Edward. For Leonora this means the crashing down of all her plans to reform him. Dowell, whether from obtuseness, repression, or simply because he does not yet know enough of Edward's history to grasp the significance of the personal contact (or because he is still too awed by his first impressions of Edward to think ill of him), fails to understand what exactly is going on:

I was aware of something treacherous, something frightful, something evil in the day. I can't define it and can't find a simile for it. It wasn't as if a snake had looked out of a hole. No, it was as if my heart had missed a beat. It was as if we were going to run and cry out; all four of us in separate directions, averting our heads. In Ashburnham's face I know that there was absolute panic. I was horribly frightened and then I discovered that the pain in my left wrist was caused by Leonora's clutching it. (pp. 53–4)

Like Nancy's shock of recognizing in the Brand case the possibility that Edward desires her, this is a moment when intimations of polygamous desire threaten a radical disruption. It is an illustration of how a threat to only one aspect of formal Edwardian society might be perceived as a threat to all.

For a fraught moment of terror the Ordered Life of the quartet hangs in the balance. For a moment Dowell glimpses that Leonora might be jealous of Florence. In a supreme instance of Fordian duality Dowell describes Leonora's despair, and her mastery and suppression of it as she finds something to catch hold of—Dowell's wrist:

She ran her hand with a singular clawing motion upwards over her forehead. Her eyes were enormously distended; her face was exactly that of a person looking into the pit of hell and seeing horrors there. And then suddenly she stopped. She was, most amazingly, just Mrs Ashburnham again. Her face was perfectly clear, sharp and defined; her hair was glorious in its golden coils.[64]

This description offers another example of the way a novelist's characters tend to be composites of disparate persons, gestures, and expressions. Two decades earlier, Ford had witnessed a peasant girl having an epileptic fit during a church sermon: 'I can still see that girl's face—the agonised eyes and the distorted mouth, as if she were looking into the pit of hell. It still, when I think of it, horrifies me more than many more ostensibly horrible things that I have since seen.' He was seeing it again when he wrote *The Good Soldier*, and was still needing to exorcize its horror while writing *Return to Yesterday* in 1931.[65]

What Leonora also finds to catch hold of is another explanation of her outburst—her own 'protest'—when she says 'don't you know I'm an Irish Catholic?' Dowell is only too pleased to be able to catch hold of this self-deceiving account: 'Those words gave me the greatest relief that I have ever had in my life.' But he misses the doubleness of Leonora's protestation. Certainly Florence has insulted her and her religion. But not just by her tactless and hypocritical remarks about the Protest (or does she mean them as irony? By this time she knows—or at least suspects—about Edward's affair with Maisie): 'If it weren't for that piece of paper you'd be like the Irish or the Italians or the Poles, but particularly the Irish . . .' (pp. 53–6). Florence's fingering of Ashburnham is another kind of insult to Leonora and her religion. Carol Jacobs, in an ingenious article on the novel, argues that the original Protestants spent most time arguing over the interpretation of Christ's Eucharistic sentence 'This is my body'. The debate about transubstantiation or consubstantiation is over the way in which communion bread can be said to be the body of Christ. Florence, laying a finger on Edward, is saying 'This is my body' in another sense.[66] Leonora, in professing her Catholicism, is reminding Florence that Ashburnham's body is hers, and indissolubly so. It might be objected that even though Ford would have known the sentence the Protestants found so problematic, it doesn't figure in the novel so is unlikely to be relevant to it. Yet the book frequently juxtaposes Protestantism and polygamy, and makes significant what's absent or concealed—especially the concealed body. Florence touching Edward's body in that room could stand as an example of the book's power of innuendo: its tendency to raise unsettling doubts where they're least expected.

The Good Soldier is ambivalent in the politics of its form too. The formalist position, seeing form as bastion against anxiety and chaos, tends to be a deeply conservative one. T. E. Hulme's political distinction between romanticism and classicism brings this out. The French Revolutionaries, he argued,

had been taught by Rousseau that man was by nature good, that it was only bad laws and customs that suppressed him [. . .] Here is the root of all romanticism: that man, the individual, is an infinite reservoir of possibilities; and if you can so rearrange society by the destruction of oppressive order then these possibilities will have a chance and you will get Progress.

One can define the classical quite clearly as the exact opposite to this. Man is an extraordinarily fixed and limited animal whose nature is absolutely constant. It is only by tradition and organisation that anything decent can be got out of him.[67]

When Hulme identifies the Church with the classical, and introduces the notion of original sin, it becomes clear that his aesthetic, like Ford's, was substantially a Catholic one. Formal regulation can be a defence against fear, a consolation for a feeling of corruption. Form can arouse desire, but it can also strive to hold desire and panic in check. It expresses the sense of temptation and chaos it simultaneously tries to allay. It offers something to hold on to, but also enacts the *difficulty* of holding on. The critic Percy Lubbock began his influential technical study *The Craft of Fiction* (1921) by stressing how books melt and shift in the memory: 'To grasp the shadowy and fantasmal form of a book, to hold it fast, to turn it over and survey it at leisure—that is the effort of a critic of books, and it is perpetually defeated.' It could be Dowell, trying to hold fast to his shifting feelings about his characters. Another essay of Hulme's confirms (in a different vocabulary) this connection between aesthetic preference and a state of mind. He is discussing a feeling of alienation attributed to 'primitive people':

One may perhaps get a better description of what must be their state of mind by comparing it to the fear which makes certain people unable to cross open spaces [. . .] They are dominated by what Worringer calls a kind of spiritual 'space-shyness' in face of the varied confusion and arbitrariness of existence. In art this state of mind results in a desire to create a certain abstract geometrical shape, which, being durable and permanent shall be a refuge from the flux and impermanence of outside nature.[68]

For all its anthropological naïvety or condescension, this is suggestive about the relations between abstract formalism, alienation, agoraphobia, mental distress, and sin. Dowell's 'terrible' vision of God's judgement upon Edward, Florence, and Maisie unites all these questions:

upon an immense plain, suspended in mid-air, I seem to see three figures, two of them clasped close in an intense embrace, and one intolerably solitary. It is in black and white, my picture of that judgement, an etching, perhaps [. . .] And the immense plain is the hand of God, stretching out for miles and miles, with great spaces above it and below it. And they are in the sight of God, and it is Florence that is alone. . . .

Dowell's radical uncertainty about the meaning of such an emotionally significant image ('The Just? The Unjust? God knows!') is a salutary reminder that one must be very wary of confining Ford to any one political label. Though his tragic account of sexual suffering and his use of form as restraint may sound conservative, this does not make him antipathetic to revolutions in that form. Not only do his views develop, but even at any one time he can encompass contradictory opinions. His humane contempt for politicians was too thoroughgoing—and his friendships with politicians were too diverse—for him to subscribe to only one party or category. His political persona of 'Tory revolutionary' corresponds with the exhilaratingly embattled combination in *The Good Soldier* of classicism and innovation, of elegy and manifesto.[69]

It has been a hard book for the literary historians to classify, its modernity of subject and technique restrained by impeccably Edwardian decorum and cadence. Its achievement is precisely what Ford always said he sought: to render his own times in terms of his own times. What makes it so much more than a piece of social history or the archaeology of style is that in using the manners of its society to penetrate that society, at the same time as it makes those manners seem outmoded, useless, it makes them deeply expressive of the anguish and desire they are meant to restrain. Thus its attitude to the society is truly dual, wanting to expose its hypocrisy, but recognizing its true integrity in the very process of its disintegration.

War and Fate

As suggested, *The Good Soldier* also has a powerfully dual relationship to the First World War. For a book largely written before the outbreak of war on 4 August 1914, its anxiety about human destructiveness and the decay of social structures makes it uncannily prescient about the devastation and change that would follow.[70] Whereas for a book published in March 1915, it stands out for its complete silence about the war. The familiar mode of elegiac retrospection makes *The Good Soldier* an Edwardian epitaph; a remembrance of the pre-war world. The main events of the book take place in 1904 (when the Dowells and Ashburnhams meet, and Maisie Maidan dies), and 1913 (when Florence and Edward both commit suicide). 'The Saddest Story' is a domestic tragedy, but Dowell's images of the deceptive apple, 'the falling to pieces of a people' (p. 9), God's judgement, give it overtones of national, cultural, global, even eschatological disaster.

In his study of Henry James, published in early 1914, soon after he had begun *The Good Soldier*, Ford explains why it is that a private affair such as the Ashburnham case should take on such public reverberations, and why a novel begun in 1913 should appear to prophesy the war. Given that James 'has given us a truthful picture of the leisured life that is founded upon the labours of all this stuff that fills graveyards', the problem we are presented with is this: 'if this life, which is the best that our civilisation has to show, is not worth the living; if it is not pleasant, cultivated, civilised, cleanly and instinct with reasonably high ideals, then, indeed, Western civilisation is not worth going on with, and we had better scrap the whole of it so as to begin again' (pp. 62–3).[71] James's own response, the day after England declared war on Germany, was that the war gave the lie to Western civilization and its complacencies about progress and enlightenment:

How can what is going on not be to one as a huge horror of blackness? [. . .] The plunge of civilization into this abyss of blood and darkness by the wanton feat of those two infamous autocrats is a thing that so gives away the whole long age during which we have supposed the world to be, with whatever abatement, gradually bettering, that to have to take it all now for what the treacherous years were all the while really making for and *meaning* is too tragic for any words.[72]

The war was widely felt to be an inevitable apocalypse. C. F. G. Masterman, then the junior member of Asquith's cabinet (as chancellor of the Duchy of Lancaster), recalled the meetings over the Bank Holiday weekend with which August 1914 began. His language, perhaps influenced by Ford's novel, is remarkably close to Dowell's in its nostalgic melodrama and its trouble with metaphor. Yet it is closest to the first pages of the novel, which we know Ford had written before the outbreak of war:

It was a company of tired men who for twelve hot summer nights, without rest or relaxation, had devoted their energies to avert this thing which had now come inevitably to pass. No one who has been through the experience of those twelve days will ever be quite the same again. It is difficult to find a right simile for that experience. It was like a company of observers watching a little cloud in the east, appearing out of a blue sky, seeing it grow, day by day, until all the brightness had vanished and the sun itself had become obscured. It was like the victim of the old mediaeval torture enclosed in a chamber in which the walls, moved by some unseen mechanism, steadily closed in on him day by day, until at the end he was crushed to death. It was most like perhaps those persons who have walked on the solid ground and seen slight cracks and fissures appear, and these enlarge and run together and swell in size hour by hour until yawning apertures revealed the boiling up beneath them of the earth's central fires, destined to sweep away the forest and vineyards of its surface and all the kindly habitations of man.[73]

Two chronological features make the novel more than a pre-war book that the war caught up with. First, its time-scheme takes Dowell's writing of his experiences as far as May 1916—which must have been disconcerting to those who read the book upon publication in March 1915. Secondly, there is the crucial date, 4 August, which reverberates through the novel, rendering its silence about the war eloquent:

She had been born on the 4th of August; she had started to go round the world on the 4th of August; she had become a low fellow's mistress on the 4th of August. On the same day of the year she had married me and on that 4th she had lost Edward's love and Bagshawe had appeared like a sinister omen—like a grin on the face of fate.[74]

The critical argument has been about whether this is a true coincidence—did Ford decide before the war to pivot the novel's structure on that particular date, only to find that the declaration of war added to the book's significance; or is the coincidence of dates contrived—put in retrospectively to use the historical cataclysm to validate the fictional one? Both cases have been argued, but the evidence is not conclusive because the precise dates of composition and correction of each section are not known.[75]

For example, this passage on the sinister coincidence of dates is written in as an addition to the manuscript, suggesting that Ford decided to emphasize Florence's (and Dowell's) obsessive fascination with the date *after* 4 August 1914. However, not only does the date 'August 1904' appear in the excerpt which appeared in *Blast* in June 1914; but the date '4th August' also appears, uncorrected, on the same page of the manuscript as the added passage, from Part III. Although it is possible that Ford wrote the last two chapters of the novel after 4 August, it is inconceivable that Part III was not drafted by then. Less than a month after sending the manuscript to the publisher, Ford said that he had written 'two chapters of a novel' since the war began. The last two chapters make up about 7,000 words, which Ford could certainly have written in one or two weeks. In the same article he sounds very much like the Dowell of the last two chapters of *The Good Soldier*, who claims to be writing 'a full eighteen months after the words that end my last chapter' (p. 210). Ford writes, 'I imagine myself to be ageing, intellectually petering out'—compare Dowell: 'it is just a record of fatigue' (p. 210): 'I am only an ageing American with very little knowledge of life' (p. 219); 'I am very tired' (p. 220); 'So life peters out' (p. 227). Ford appears to have chosen the '4th August' date *before* the declaration of war. Even a less superstitious writer would have seen what could be made of such an omen. Ford's genius seized the possibility coincidence had offered, since he appears to have rapidly gone back over the manuscript, making the chronological coincidences even more emphatic: turning a true coincidence to aesthetic effect.[76] There is a continuity between the superstitious fascination with dates within the novel, and the double coincidence of its composition: not only did Ford say he began writing it on his fortieth birthday, but it was also his birthday when he christened it in the letter to John Lane.

The insistence on the dates produces the familiar dual response: it demands acquiescence, while also arousing the reader's incredulity. Even for an analysis of superstitious minds, the novel treads on the brink of contrivance. Florence's superstition about her birthday might influence her choice of dates to begin a journey, an affair, or a marriage; but even her unconscious could not be responsible for the appearance of Bagshawe, the one man who can reveal to her husband her affair with Jimmy (the 'low fellow'), on that same day; nor for the fact that his appearance also coincides with her discovery that Edward now loves Nancy.

Readers object to contrivance in a novel when the shape of a plot, instead of appearing the inevitable conclusion of the fictional premises, registers the pressure of the artist's theory of the world upon its material. 'Never trust the artist. Trust the tale' says D. H. Lawrence. But what if the table already seems a contrivance? Champions of Turgenev and Lawrence as opposed to Tolstoy and Hardy might argue that it is a greater achievement to make a story seem inevitable than to make it seem merely coincidental. (As Ford told Galsworthy: 'one wants to feel after reading a book: this happened because it was absolutely impossible for it to have happened otherwise.') But no one who has studied the construction of *The Good Soldier* will accuse Ford of evading technical challenges. It is Jamesian in its exhilaration of difficulty. Nor does it eschew inevitability. Ashburnham's eventual tiring of Florence, his suicide, Dowell's ultimate dis-abusal: none of these could be staved off indefinitely. Rather, the book presents the inevitable coincidence of inevitability and coincidence in the working out of such an embroilment. Ford wants to catch Dowell's frisson of perplexity in the face of the incredible—and we should remember that it is not just the chronology that challenges his credulity, but also what he has discovered to have been happening on those dates. His baffled amazement (which largely pre-dated the war) may have been doubled by Ford's astonishment that the outbreak of war coincided with the pivotal date of his novel. His courage to risk his readers' incredulity, and his uncanny aesthetics of amazement, were perhaps enabled by a feeling that fate was grinning at him. Usually when he writes of 'Destiny' he precedes it by the adjective 'august'. The 'August' coincidence is likely to have appeared one of its manifestations. 'Coincidence is so continually creeping into my own life,' wrote Ford in defence of coincidence in his fiction, 'that if I left it out of my projections of the life of others I should be untrue to my art. . . .'[77]

Ford's treatment of fate succeeds in *The Good Soldier* partly because of the way the question is foregrounded. Just as the novel is superior to the aim he often avowed of making the author or narrator disappear (because it investigates and dramatizes the involvement of the narrator, his relativity and uncertainty), so it gains effect from the way it confronts the question of whether characters and acts might not be predestined. 'Madness? Predestination?', asks Dowell: 'Who the devil knows?' (p. 37). One anonymous critic commented on Ford's interest in how a man can 'see his own actions as at once free and moral'. The achieved tragedy of *The Good Soldier* rests on its perfect duality of vision, seeing each action as at once free and foredoomed; as (to use two of Ford's favourite terms of art) at once 'inevitable' and a 'surprise'.[78]

What makes the novel's patterns of coincidence compellingly bizarre is that they are not there simply to point a moral. Pattern implies design, significance. *The Good Soldier* is pre-eminently a work of design, but it has no palpable design upon us (Keats: 'We hate poetry that has a palpable design upon us.'). On the contrary, whether fate is responsible or not for the way Florence's life turns on 4ths of August, the meaning of the pattern is left unexplained. The very insistence on the coincidences, rather than foreclosing interpretation, only opens up further vistas of uncertainty. Boris Tomashevsky argued that the less writers emphasize causality, the more they emphasize time. Ford's novels bear this out. Dowell makes a fetish of chronology to console for the perplexity of meaning.[79] *The Good Soldier*'s formal 'perfection' has long been recognized. Whereas for James the pattern of history revealed the abyss as the meaning towards which it had been working, Ford registers a more fundamental disorientation. *The Good Soldier* sets pattern creatively at odds with its meaning, giving it the suggestive power of enigma.

'A Picture Without a Meaning'

Two paradoxes energize the book (and have generated much of the criticism about it). First, the paradox of its narration. Dowell admits that he is telling the story 'in a very rambling way so that it may be difficult for anyone to find their path through what may be a sort of maze' (p. 213). Yet Dowell's uncertainty coexists with the book's artistic certainty, its fierce clarity of visual detail and emerging formal structure. Hugh Kenner has written well on how 'we wait and wait for something to happen', reaching the end of Part I without discovering what happened during those 'four crashing days' in August 1913; yet 'those pages are never boring'.[80] As in a maze, a ramble through it reveals the definiteness of its pattern (though it may not reveal the way to its heart, or the way to escape). The most striking example comes at the end. Dowell claims he is trying to cheer us up with a description of Leonora's second marriage, to Rodney Bayham, whom he has already described as 'rather like a rabbit' (p. 274); 'that is the end of my story', he says sardonically (p. 292). But it isn't. He adds: 'It suddenly occurs to me that I have forgotten to say how Edward met his death' (pp. 292–3), and goes on to tell of his suicide after reading Nancy's telegram. Dowell's offhand manner is his defence against breaking down with grief. Ford combines his apparent inconsequence with the inevitable consequence of his story: the death towards which the whole work has been inexorably progressing. If we consent to that feeling of fatality, it is partly because of the way the ending has been prepared with a patterning that Ashburnham's death enables us to see in retrospect: each of the novel's four parts ends either with a death (Maisie Maidan's in Part I; Florence's in Part II; now Ashburnham's in Part IV), or with a macabrely ironic image of something like a death (the death, at the end of Part III, of Leonora's hopes of saving her marriage: 'Florence knocked all that on the head . . .').

The second paradox is that of meaning, and it follows from this problem of whether Dowell's intelligence or integrity should be trusted. The more Dowell explains, the harder it becomes (for us, as for him) to say what it all means: 'At what, then, does it all work out?' (p. 16). The story is an 'intricate tangle' for the interpreter as well. It is not just that the story tells of an 'intricate tangle'—a pattern of deceptions, betrayals, and suppressions, as the polished upper-middle class social world is shattered by adultery, suicide, and madness. It is also that the *telling* is an intricate tangle: wound up with care and delicacy, but impossible to unravel into a linear narrative. When James wrote of the 'baffled relation between the subject-matter and its emergence' in Conrad's *Chance* (1914), he could equally have been describing the great novel Ford was writing, in which there is bafflement about the subject-matter itself (what actually happened, and when), its emergence (the telling and the reading), and the relation between them (is the narrator telling, or understanding, the truth?).[81]

Ford presents the novel's intricate tangle as a problem to be experienced rather than to be solved. His technical certainty about what he is *doing* only focuses the uncertainty about what he is *meaning*. But then, that baffled sense of the problematic, the uncertain, was what, for him, represented 'life'. Ford felt the intricate tangle of his own life was representative of the complexity and confusion of the time.

By experiencing these things as a reader, we come to understand what Dowell's bafflement feels like. His closing vision of Nancy points the story's moral pointlessness, and the novel's characteristic disjunction of significance from meaning:

Enigmatic, silent, utterly well-behaved as far as her knife and fork go, Nancy will stare in front of her with the blue eyes that have over them strained, stretched brows. Once, or perhaps twice, during the meal her knife and fork will be suspended in mid-air as if she were trying to think of something that she had forgotten. Then she will say that she believes in an Omnipotent Deity or she will utter the one word 'shuttlecocks', perhaps. It is very extraordinary to see the perfect flush of health on her cheeks, to see the lustre of her coiled black hair, the poise of the head upon the neck, the grace of the white hands—and to think that it all means nothing—that it is a picture without a meaning. (p. 292)

What does it mean to say that Nancy's appearance is a picture without a meaning? One sense we could make of it would be that in her madness Nancy has been dispossessed of her personality; that like the house in which they sit, dispossessed of its original inhabitants, the Ashburnhams, Nancy is now opaque, perhaps an empty form, her content 'something that she had forgotten'. There is still something disconcerting about saying that someone is meaningless. What is the 'meaning' of even a sane person? To Dowell, who is by now himself in love with Nancy, the physical details he renders with such care might 'mean' passion. In the central rhapsodic passage about how Edward realized his love for Nancy, Dowell had written—in a way that (characteristically) cross-refers to the image of Nancy insane:

A turn of the eyebrow, a tone of the voice, a queer characteristic gesture—all these things, and it is these things that cause to arise the passion of love—all these things are like so many objects on the horizon of the landscape that tempt a man to walk beyond the horizon, to explore. He wants to get, as it were, behind those eyebrows with the peculiar turn, as if he desired to see the world with the eyes that they overshadow. (pp. 134–5)

Dowell's lingering on precisely those attributes—Nancy's 'strained, stretched brows', her strange speech and enigmatic gesture—does indeed suggest that it is as signs of sexuality that they have lost their meaning. That is, that they arouse in him a passion which can never now be fulfilled. Or have they lost their meaning? To say that she is 'utterly well-behaved as far as her knife and fork go' is itself enigmatic in its suggestive combination of silence and hyperbole ('*utterly* well-behaved'?). The qualification insinuates that she might be less than well-behaved in matters beyond table-manners (that she is only *outerly* well-behaved). Of course she is too mad to be polite: she enunciates her creed over dinner. But the cause of her insanity—her sinful passion for Ashburnham, a married man as well as her guardian—initiates her into the novel's world of tempting, goodly apples rotten at the core: impeccable surfaces concealing corrupt hearts. So besides representing the form of sexuality without its content, she simultaneously stands for the opposite. She is the picture of innocence without its meaning: she has 'English good form' as far as one can *see*, but the social fabric conceals repressed passion. Is she 'without a meaning' because susceptible of contradictory meanings: like Edward, at once a saint and a sinner? This perplexity in relation to meaning is at the heart of Fordian impressionism. Writing (a month after he had sent the novel to the printers) about his inability to write 'war poems', Ford echoed Dowell's account of how passion is created: 'I want something to stir my emotions and something sharply visual to symbolise them. I want a gesture, a tone of the voice, a turn of the eye.'[82]

The main critical focus has been on What Dowell Knows. Clearly this is crucial in considering the novel's awareness of sexuality. Arthur Mizener argues forcefully that 'the only recourse for criticism confronted by disagreement so radical as this [about whether Ford treats Dowell with irony or sympathy] is to such evidence of the author's intention as can be discovered outside the novel'. Finding that Ford's *propria persona* often sounds like Dowell on the subject of passion, he continues: 'everything he did in his life and everything he said shows that what Dowell says about passion is not intended as ironic exposure of Dowell's neurotic personality but is what Ford thought true'. But there is another recourse, which is to recognize the two-edgedness of the argument about irony. Instead of denying that the book is ironic because it chimes with its author, one might hear irony in Ford's own pronouncements—not least because 'everything he did' in his relationships with women make him sound much more like Ashburnham than Dowell. Or, more elusively, one might hear the author confronting with irony in his fiction what may or may not be ironic in his life. It is primarily because of this problem of irony that discussions of an artist's 'intention' can—though they need not—succumb to the 'intentional fallacy'. The fallacy in Mizener's argument can be seen where he has to suppress precisely those words (they are restored here in italics) which arouse suspicion of an irony:

Of the question of the sex-instinct I know very little and I do not think that it counts for very much in a really great passion. *It can be aroused by such nothings—by an untied shoe-lace, by a glance of the eye in passing—that I think it might be left out of the calculation.* I don't mean to say that any great passion can exist without a desire for consummation. *That seems to me to be a commonplace and to be therefore a matter needing no comment at all. It is a thing, with all its accidents,* that must be taken for granted, as, in a novel, or a biography, you take it for granted that the characters have their meals with some regularity.[83]

'Counts'; 'calculation'? There are obviously more things in heaven and earth than are dreamt of in Dowell's economics of the soul, and surely Ford means to cast a suspicion of doubt on his qualifications to pontficate on this of all subjects. The nothings that arouse the 'sex-instinct' are not after all so different from the things that aroused the passions for Nancy ('a turn of the eyebrow, a tone of the voice, a queer characteristic gesture'). What Dowell is saying here is oddly contradictory: is there no difference between leaving something out of a calculation, and not commenting on it? Why does he need to comment that it needs *no comment at all* ? Ford's placing together of the question of tact—of knowing when not to comment— and the question of what novels should contain, reminds us of his dictum that the novelist should never comment. One of the fascinations of *The Good Soldier* is exactly in the way it arouses the imagination of sexuality in subliminal and unspoken ways. It is the greatest example of Ford's mastery of the unspeakable.

Though meaningless in their autism and apparent inconsequence, Nancy's utterances pose the contradictory meanings attributable to fate. Can we believe that events are preordained by a beneficent deity, or are we shuttlecocks of indifferent chance? These questions matter to Dowell, but they also matter to his beneficent creator, Ford.[84] Coming so near the book's end, the comment that 'it all means nothing' means more than just that the description of Nancy is meaningless. 'It all' is the whole affair: Nancy's fate is emblematic of the entire story, since her madness is Dowell's despair, and was caused by Edward's death. But Dowell's bafflement in the face of his story's meaning is doubled by Ford's principled refusal to moralize. *The Good Soldier*, too, is 'a picture without a meaning'; a rendering without comment. Multifariously significant, a masterpiece of formal grasp and a triumph of the moral imagination, it cannot be reduced to a moral message. Instead, the book leaves the impression of a dual personality, both Dowell and his author; of purged emotions; of controlled picturing. It is the expression of Ford's feeling in *Henry James* that 'what life really is' is 'a series of such meaningless episodes beneath the shadow of doom—or of impending bliss, if you prefer it'—'*Beati Immaculati?*' (p. 155).

But the danger of accounts of the novel which come to rest on the ultimate undecidability of its meaning is that they neglect the impulse that drives through the whole book to try to find its meaning. An unsigned notice in the *English Review*, probably written by Ford, provides the requisite duality of the quest for knowledge and its bafflement: 'It is much more when we read him as if we were taking a walk with a man so self-concentrated and so strong that we are forced to take no notice of our environment. Rather we participate actively in the mental distraction of a personality that is always baffled in its attempts to read a meaning into things, but one that never desists from the attempt.'[85] Like *The Good Soldier*, this is dual in another sense: it refracts through the criticism of fiction an autobiographical sense of frustration at trying to understand one's own life and times. Recalling Ford's classes at Olivet College in the last years of his life, Robie Macauley described the thoroughly narrative nature of his mind: 'Almost any question could be answered or any idea presented in the form of a story and he was ill at ease in any more abstract conversation. I think that every subject he knew or cared anything about—and they were a great many, from garden farming to world politics—he conceived in terms of character and action, finally working into a plot.'[86] His narrative impulse often comes, like Dowell's, out of a bafflement over meaning. Being asked, or asking himself, a question, he tells an involved story. It is in this way that *The Good Soldier* is most relevantly autobiographical, for it is, above all, an exploration of what it is that makes someone want to talk, to bear witness, to tell their story, become a writer.

Describing

Impressionism, Memory, Personality

The tense opposition in *The Good Soldier* between felt significance and apprehended meaning is characteristic of the kind of writer Ford became. He is always preoccupied with experiences which command attention, which feel as if they must 'mean', but which elude analysis of what that meaning might be. This is one of the bases of his 'impressionism', which records those moments which by definition 'make an impression' on the consciousness, but which refrains from commenting upon their meaning. (In this sense the technique also recognizes the limits of conscious artistry, the business of which is to render the impression, but not to explain it.)

Impressionism is the technique which best answers to his sense of the significance of his own life. It is both a repertoire of consciously selected devices and at the same time an expression of the author's personality. He was particularly impressionable; he had a greater than average store of moving memories, experiences which he felt as profoundly significant. The question about this personal history which he returned to was how the discrete impressions cohered into a unified story: what was the meaning of a life of significances? This question translates directly into the terms of the prose. What gives artistic coherence to a series of rendered impressions? His autobiographical writing subtly but pervasively brings these two questions together, investigating ways in which the form of a book can, without diffusing, do justice to a life of elusive coherence.[87]

We can only speculate *where* Ford's conviction of significance comes from. Madox Brown's stress on 'genius' imparted the wish that his life should be extraordinary. This is to emphasize the value of individuality, of personality, and leads easily to discovering a significance and value in one's experience. We have seen that, as with many artists, death is the spur. Ford was always imagining his own death, and never with such chagrin and pathos as in Ashburnham's suicide. Later Ford could joke about his morbidity, turning Death into the ultimate impressionist: 'I occupy myself from time to time nowadays with preparing to meet the Recording Angel and hoping that his impressions will square with my own.' Such feelings are not uncommon, although they are not usually so individually or memorably expressed. Ford is peculiarly sensitive to the power of death to elicit beauty, writing: 'if we have consciences, we must seek to perceive order in this disorder, beauty in what shocks us, and premonitions of immortality in that which sweeps us into forgotten graves.'[88]

This feeling that art can come out of danger and death is matched by the reciprocal sense that danger can come from art. In part it is literature that is fatal for Ashburnham, 'whose mind was compounded of indifferent poems and novels', who 'talked like quite a good book', and who kills himself after reading a telegram (pp. 293, 34). *The Good Soldier* is instinct with a sense of the danger of language; of the power of words to deceive or to destroy; to utter the unthinkable or the unspeakable, and thus to transform our lives; to express to ourselves what it is that we are, and what we have been doing without realizing it. Ashburnham surprises himself by speaking to Leonora about Maisie Maidan (p. 202); later, he tells Dowell, without meaning to, of his love for Nancy (p. 287). When he declares this love to Nancy: 'It was as if his passion for her hadn't existed; as if the very words that he spoke, without knowing that he spoke them, created the passion as they went along. Before he spoke, there was nothing; afterwards, it was the integral fact of his life' (p. 137). Like Robert Grimshaw hearing his conscience muttering, Ashburnham 'was revealed to himself for the first time by words over which he had no control'. It is as if the 'meaning', the implicit, is, precisely, the repressed. More like Ashburnham than he realizes at the time, Dowell's first words after hearing of the death of Florence are: 'Now I can marry the girl.' Both men are like Freud's young patient who was in love with her brother-in-law: 'Standing beside her sister's death-bed, she was horrified at having the thought: "Now he is free and can marry me." ' Though they don't suffer from the hysterical pains that beset her once she repressed the thought (neither of them do repress it), they do both suffer from the cardinal Fordian affliction that Freud's paper is discussing: 'The Loss of Reality in Neurosis and Psychosis' (1924).[89] It is the odd duality of unconscious behaviour that disturbs the sense of reality. Ashburnham's compulsion to repeat the pattern of infatuation and adultery without knowing what he is doing makes his passion seem at once unreal and terrible. Dowell's desire to repeat Ashburnham's pattern is equally strange, pathetic. Both partake of the central Fordian moral duality: feeling oneself at the same time innocent-but-maligned, and also repressedly guilty. The novel's ultimate title calls Ashburnham 'good'. And much of Ford's fiction is damaged by a sentimental and evidently autobiographical urge to prove the protagonists 'good' men, misunderstood by the world that persecutes and calumniates them. But *The Good Soldier* opens up the question of goodness into an ironic abyss, leaving a sane and intelligent doubt (so that the title too gets disturbed by the doubt: is he a good soldier but *not* a good man?). Ashburnham deserves *sympathy*, but the novel shows that judgements of good and bad are too black and white for such a complex, grey world.

Communication in Ford is both the ideal and its devastation. Dowell imagines his sympathetic 'silent listener' to whom he can properly express himself. And yet even this relationship is fraught with danger, since the very silence of the listener can seduce the speaker into extreme intimacies of self-disclosure and self-betrayal. As Leonora tells Dowell, 'I said a great deal more to him than I wanted to, just because he was so silent' (p. 245). Dowell cannot forgive her 'for giving way to what was in the end a desire for communicativeness' in talking to Florence, about Edward (p. 223); and later to Nancy, because (like Dowell, craving for his listener—and Ford, craving his readers) 'She craved madly for communication with some other human soul' (p. 235).

Edward's declaration, in which the words 'created the passion as they went along', is thus both an instance of the unconscious coming into consciousness, and an allegory for the way the impressionist novelist gets his effects. Here Ford's practice is more intelligent than his critical pronouncements, for it recognizes that it is the flow of the language, the sustained pressure of voice, that is at least as important in creating the book's passions for us as is any rendering of concrete objects. Ford's thinking here also has important implications for literary biography. It reverses the conventional assumption that a writer has a feeling, and then expresses it in words, giving the words an uncanny priority over what they are supposed to express. The point here is not just to convey the surprising nature of the unconscious, but to suggest that it is only in the activity of expression that the artist discovers what it was he or she was expressing. *The Good Soldier* is haunted by the uncertainty and instability of desire; by Dowell's, as well as Ashburnham's, uncertainty about what he really wants. ('Why can't people have what they want?', he asks; but his claim that what he mostly wanted 'was to cease being a nurse-attendant' is singularly unconvincing—or at least one hopes so.)[90] It is in this sense that writing the novel helped Ford to come to terms with his own desires; to see himself from outside. His understanding of how desire and expression exist in a dialectical rather than a hierarchical relationship perhaps accounts for the curious way in which his fiction sometimes seems to anticipate and shape his life rather than reflect it.

Ford's characters often reflect his quest for meaning as they reflect explicitly upon the meanings of their predicaments. It is not only Nancy, reading about the Brand divorce case, who 'asked what, exactly, it all meant' (p. 253). Dowell is persistently trying 'to figure out what it all means' (p. 78).[91] Perplexity about the meanings of his experience is central to Ford's autobiographic prose too. The early, anonymous essay, 'Nice People', is a crucial document in the genesis of his impressionism, and its concern with how to juxtapose apparently disjointed vivid scenes. It shows Ford, even aged 30, going elegiacally over his past, puzzling over its patterns and meanings. If his reminiscing does not have Dowell's anguish and obsessiveness, it is because what he is considering is not 'passion' but 'personal magnetism'—the mysterious emotional significance to him of those acquaintances the essay simply and untendentiously assembles together.[92] They include a Dutchman: 'a novice of a certain Order with whom I was thrown at different times and in different places into strong contact'. He's not mentioned anywhere else in Ford's reminiscences, so it isn't possible to identify him (though there were Dutch Hüffers he certainly would have met on his European visits):

the process by which one enters his Order is terribly soul-breaking. It is a matter of seven years passed in scrubbing floors, in mechanical hard work to break the novice of his love for his family and his friends; and then of more years spent in mystical exercises at the bidding of a superior—to break in the soul to aloofness from the material world, to resignation and utter obedience. At the end of all the novice must, in a dark room, actually see a vision prescribed for him. (p. 571)

As Ford turns from the novice to the vision of Madox Brown's face 'in repose at the end of his life', the reason for bringing these reminiscences together begins to appear: 'The artist, too, looks past this world into another, and perhaps the lover; perhaps all "nice people" ' (p. 571). As Ford looks past the world of the present to the other world of his past, he recognizes himself as a denizen of both. And he connects his dual existence, between two worlds, with various forms of idealism: religion, Utopian politics, art. His envisioning of the novice training for his vision looks forward to his novel of 1913, *The Young Lovell*, which begins with Lovell having just such a vision after a long vigil. It also glances at that other mode of getting people to see visions which have been prescribed: literary impressionism. The solitary and mechanical hard work, the dedication to a sphere beyond family, friends and the material world, the striving for aloofness and resignation, all sound like the displaced autobiography of a literary novice—perhaps one who had only recently concluded the stylistic exercises undertaken at the bidding of his superior collaborator, Conrad.

Ford's reminiscential visions, dominated by artist figures, are dually *of* art, and *instances of* art: their author, too, 'looks past this world [back] into another'. It is a question of technique as well as subject. Ford's *mode* of associating incongruous figures and speculating about the other-worldly quality of 'personal magnetism' which they share, marks him out as one of them. He too is someone whose concentration penetrates beyond the circumstantial, the factual. In asking what his series of memories means, he joins the group of those who look beyond experience, asking what it all means.

One can see this duality, paradoxically, in the most incongruous of these portraits, that of the old country woman Mary Walker (he was not yet using the more phonetic spelling 'Meary'); the portrait that at first appears to have least to do with these questions of art, thought, and meaning. But as Ford characteristically writes her elegy—'she died last month'—it becomes clear not only that her memory means a great deal to him, but also that what she represents for him has been a profound influence on his ideas about humanity and about art. Her reappearances in Ford's books show that she has herself become the kind of touchstone which Ford remembers her using: 'She had, as it were, an unfailing touchstone that was like the insight into the secret of all lives. She reckoned we'd be all much alike if we could see into each other's minds' (p. 577). Seeing into each other's minds is exactly the business of novelist—especially of an impressionist novelist of consciousness. Mary Walker's insight is a version of Ford's doctrine of 'sympathetic insight', whereby the novelist provides the secret insight into a life which forges a bond of community between author, reader, and character, exemplifying a shared humanity. Mary Walker's presence in this essay shows Ford seeking—and finding—fundamental ways in which multifarious characters can be 'much alike', without forfeiting the individuality of character on which the life of the novel depends. She shares Madox Brown's 'gift of sympathy', for which Ford says he deserves to be remembered as a man. This essay is at once an exercise in sympathetic generalizing, and also an enquiry (of a ruminative rather than a rigorous kind) into 'the basis of all the arts' (p. 574).

One trait, common to humanity, but shared to a marked degree by Ford and Mary Walker, is an existence sustained by a tissue of memories. She is a source of entertaining impressions and anecdotes: a natural artist in narrative; the kind of 'peasant tale-teller' which Ford opposes to the 'conscious artist'.[93] Even her habit of talking to herself acquires a significance to Ford: 'Long solitudes beneath the sky had given her a trick of talking to herself, working out such problems as presented themselves to her in a leisurely monologue in undertone' (p. 575). In it Ford can recognize his own long solitudes spent perfecting a trick of writing; in particular, of writing the form of leisurely monologue that this essay presents, as it works out the problems of art's relation to humanity. It also shows Ford recognizing the extent to which his reminiscential writing is a form of talking to himself, at the same time that he is writing for an audience. He is, in this respect too, reproducing that dual predicament of the artist-figures he discusses here: people engaged in communication, but achieving this while abstracted, their minds 'somewhere quite other'. They are all visionaries, exemplars of sympathetic insight.

The essay's problems are of course not 'worked out' in the sense of 'solved' or resolved. But the narrative frame of the opening offers another way of thinking about resolution: namely, in musical terms.

I was stumbling through a fugue, the fourth of the Wohltemperierter Klavier. It is a little difficult for a person with stiff fingers but there are certain chords following on other chords, certain discords suspended for a long time and then resolving themselves so suddenly and so swiftly that when I am very much alone I sometimes sit playing it again and again, for an hour perhaps, in the hope of hearing mere fragments of it. I began to think of the nice people I had known; they suddenly rose up before me, one after the other, a great number of faces. I forgot that I was playing, and thought about them all, people who had, in one way and another, for me at least, 'personal magnetism.' Suddenly I found myself at the end of my fugue. I must obviously have played it without a stumble; but I had not heard a note. (p. 564)

Music is a paradigm for 'significance' liberated from meaning, its effects the result of technique, but resistant to paraphrase. If it can be said to express 'passion', 'longing', 'unrest', 'melancholy', or 'transcendence', it makes little sense to say that a particular piece 'means' any of these. Much later, Ford wrote in *Provence*: 'The—literally and only literally—meaningless contrapuntal passages of Bach are infinitely more emotional and the cause of emotion—and they are much more mystically so than the most realistic programme-music.' Ford aims to work his memories, and the problems arising from them, up into the literary equivalent to a fugue. His 'subjects' are introduced, suspended, repeated, counterpointed, and 'resolved' into a series of insights about the art and artists. It is important that he becomes oblivious of his playing as the memories are summoned up, because that oblivion places him amongst those whose art or their humanity is grounded on just such an obliviousness of their surroundings. It is however far from being a self-regarding trope, since it also describes the complete effacement of the artist. Bach's music has impelled the series of visions, but has itself been effaced by them. This is another version of Ford's recurrent image of art's mental duality: the way it answers to the duality of the imagination—its ability to transcend the here-and-now, superimposing other places and times upon it—with its own duality. For art's presentation of 'significance' both attracts our attention to its materiality—the words of the book or the chords and discords of the fugue—and it perpetually leads *through* these things to other quantities: emotions, expressions of personality, intimations of human solidarity. As with most of the instances in the essay, art works for Ford by this process of 'transfiguration', as the material and the circumstantial become abstract, expressions of something beyond themselves. As Caroline Gordon wrote of *The Good Soldier*: 'Every remark that Ford's narrator makes carries its own conviction; the tone is perfectly suited to the action. His way of achieving this effect is to keep reminding us of the human condition, for almost every sentence is a little world in itself, in which man's ineptitude, feebleness, blindness, are constantly measured against the infinite.'[94]

R. A. Scott-James gave a fine description of Ford's impulse to objectify his experiences by reinventing them:

Extraordinarily sensitive as he was, he had an endless capacity for shaking off his troubles and, while not forgetting them, refusing to let them take possession of him [. . . .] the central necessity of his being really was to go on trying to shape his experience into patterns, to use words to convey his fancy, his passing impressions, his vision, as beautifully as possible, whether they were light as feathers or more significant and poignant. You might have thought that he was all Epicurean, intent upon the moment flying or upon depicting it. There was that element in him, but it was not all. Much as he scoffed at excessive purposefulness, obtrusive moralism, and Pharisaism in all its forms, there still lingered on in him something almost akin to Puritanism which showed itself not only in his dislike of lewd talk and obscenity, but also in his sensitiveness to the idea that this or that in him might be considered immoral; he was annoyed with his own conscience for pricking him at the very time when he liked to assure himself that he had the *right* to be completely free from self-reproach.

It seemed that a great deal of his life was make-believe.[95]

Ford's presentation of 'significance', and his reliance on narrative frames as its adequate interpretation or resolution, are techniques integral to his impressionism. He advocated them on the grounds of their realism: they should produce the same effect on a reader as life produces on an observer (or, more strictly speaking, an illusion of that effect). As with most theories of realism, the individuality of the effects which the method produces gets effaced by the pressure of the general term 'life'. Biographical criticism needs to ask 'whose life?', and 'what kind of life?' Just as his particular emphases on the duality of 'impression' and 'meaning' come from a personal predisposition—one which feels incidents to be pressingly important, before it understands what their import is—so other literary techniques can be related to individual attitudes.

The Fordian use of the time-shift follows from his reminiscential impressionism. Playing a fugue transports you back to various spots of past time. The narrative of this agile mental process inevitably shifts backwards and forwards, juxtaposing a range of different times; building up a composite picture of a past. Each particular impression carries the mind back to a former impression; that memory can in turn evoke its predecessors, right back to a 'first impression'. Subsequent impressions can reinterpret former ones. Ford is pre-eminently a writer of recall and reinterpretation. This is equally true of his novels, his reminiscences, and his life. Moser argues rightly that *The Good Soldier* is especially animated by two periods of Ford's life: the time of his 1904 breakdown and foreign travel intended to recuperate him; and the time of his attempt to change his nationality, divorce Elsie Hueffer, and marry Violet Hunt—the time of the *Throne* case in 1913. But the novel does more than testify to the effects on the author of breakdown and scandal. As Moser himself candidly acknowledges, 'explaining the greatness of the novel is another matter'. (Freud said that psycho-biographic investigations 'are not intended to explain an author's genius, but they show what motive forces aroused it and what material was offered to him by destiny. There is a particular fascination in studying the laws of the human mind as exemplified in outstanding individuals.') One aspect of *The Good Soldier*'s greatness is its extraordinary recapturing of the mental processes of recalling and reinterpreting the past. Dowell's view of himself changes radically during the novel, from seeing himself as a 'sedulous, strained nurse', or as comparable to a 'eunuch', at the start, to his identification with Ashburnham ('he was just myself') right at the end (though he is even then having to nurse Nancy in her madness). His events of 1913 cause him to rethink, re-imagine, and retell the whole of his story, in particular the events of 1904, including his first impression of the Ashburnhams, the climactic Protest scene at Marburg, and Maisie's death. Something very similar was happening in Ford's own mind. The *Throne* case, with the complication that it brought into focus—namely that Ford might be guilty of bigamy—must have summoned up the series of related events in the past: his telling Elsie she should not expect him to remain faithful to her; the 'affair' with Mary Martindale; the affair with Violet Hunt, and Elsie's earlier court suit of 1910 petitioning for the restitution of conjugal rights; his infatuations first for Rosamond and then for Brigit Patmore while he was still living with Violet. As in all Ford's writing, make-believe is inseparable from reminiscence. In *The Good Soldier* he found a curious way of achieving an objective—albeit insecurely objective—perspective on the breakdown of his marriage to Elsie. Here, with a process of dual self-doubling, he draws on his adultery with Hunt for the relationship between Ashburnham and Florence Dowell. And he draws on his feelings of betrayal by Marwood by doubling himself with Dowell: a move which casts Ashburnham as a Marwood figure. Thus again it is the doubling of himself and Marwood in a character that makes him see his own predicament. For, while the novel presents Ashburnham as, doubly, the sentimentalist victim of passion, as well as the libertine opportunist, it recognizes unflinchingly both the devastation of the couples' world, and also the extent to which the destruction is the result of Ashburnham's actions. By contrast with the portrait of Elsie as the Countess Macdonald, Leonora is drawn with astonishing sympathy, which comes across especially during the mental stress of her realization that she has lost her husband to Nancy Rufford 'for good'. (As Conrad said, the women in the novel are indeed 'extraordinary'.) And this even when Dowell is discovering, as Ford was presumably discovering about Elsie, that he no longer found her likeable—the 'sympathetic soul' that Dowell craves as his ideal listener, and that Valentine represents for Tietjens in his ideal of marriage as an extended intimate conversation.[96]

The publicity surrounding the 1913 case affected Ford's public image; but it also changed the way he seemed to himself, as Dowell's experiences change his understanding of his past. It is characteristic of him that his life should be altered by what he read about himself, and by the stories circulated about him. It is also characteristic of the way his life is circumscribed by literature that his reconsidering of his past life takes place in part through a remembering and reinterpreting of his former writing. *The Good Soldier* not only reflects Ford's own mental life among his memories; it also recalls his earlier writing. In particular some of the crucial moments and many of the dominant themes return to his books which were being conceived and written around 1904: especially the English trilogy and *The Fifth Queen*. Whereas Dowell's manner and instabilities of tone come out of Ford's experiments in the *English Review*.[97]

The significance of the 'heart' recalls *The Heart of the Country*, with its rendering of the landscape in terms of passion, restless longing, the quest for fulfilment. Even what he described as 'the emotion of railway travel', which features expressively in the trilogy, is carried forward into Dowell's preoccupation with trains; his restless desire to return to past scenes; his anxieties about the need for heart patients to run in order to make their rail connections. His comment on passion being aroused by 'a glance of the eye in passing' recalls the emotion aroused in Ford by glancing out of train windows at passing landscapes in *The Soul of London* (pp. 58–62), and also the description in *The Heart of the Country* of how the town-dweller, 'as he sinks deeper into the life of the country', 'begins to note differences between the songs of birds' and begins to observe their individualities. Even as he becomes the naturalist, alluding to W. H. Hudson's *A Traveller in Little Things*, Ford's attention to what makes one bird different from another sounds very like Dowell trying to anatomize what makes one passion different from another: 'The differences lie in minute things, in the poise of the head, the way of setting down the foot, the glance of the eye in passing' (p. 46).[98] Whereas the English trilogy expresses emotions about the land by summoning up sexuality through metaphors of passion and corporeality, Dowell proposes a geographical psychology of passion. The only image he can find to express Ashburnham's inscrutable expressions when Leonora enters the room is one of property-ownership: 'At any rate, the expression was that of pride, of satisfaction, of the possessor. I saw him once afterwards, for a moment, gaze upon the sunny fields of Branshaw and say: "All this is my land!" ' (p. 36). *The Heart of the Country* contains a vignette which turns this tangle of sex and class into comedy. It is in effect the comic version of an encounter such as Ashburnham's with the Kilsyte woman on the train:

I remember, too, walking along a dark road from the station with a youngish girl of the scullery-maid type. She chatted amiably as long as I was invisible, but when the light of a carriage fell upon me she looked at me with startled eyes, uttered, 'Why, you're a *gentleman!*' and took to her heels. For in the eyes of the cottage mothers there is only one reason why a gentleman should wish to talk to a cottage girl. (p. 139)

The Spirit of the People also includes a scenario which provided the dramatic 'germ' of *The Good Soldier*.

I stayed, too, at the house of a married couple one summer. Husband and wife were both extremely nice people—'good people,' as the English phrase is. There was also living in the house a young girl, the ward of the husband, and between him and her—in another of those singularly expressive phrases—an attachment had grown up. P——— had not only never 'spoken to' his ward; his ward, I fancy, had spoken to Mrs. P———. At any rate the situation had grown impossible, and it was arranged that Miss W—— would take a trip round the world [. . .] The only suspicion that things were not of their ordinary train was that the night before the parting P——— had said to me: 'I wish you'd drive to the station with us to-morrow morning.' He was, in short, afraid of a 'scene.' [. . .] the parting at the station was too surprising, too really superhuman not to give one, as the saying is, the jumps. For P—— never even shook her by the hand; touching the flap of his cloth cap sufficed for leave-taking. Probably he was choking too badly to say even 'Good-bye' [. . .] as the train drew out of the station P—— turned suddenly on his heels, went through the booking-office to pick up a parcel of fish that was needed for lunch, got into his trap and drove off. He had forgotten me—but he had kept his end up [. . .] Miss W—— died at Brindisi on the voyage out, and P—— spent the next three years at various places on the Continent where nerve cures are attempted.

Ford varied some of the details for Nancy's leave-taking in *The Good Soldier*: Edward does not forget Dowell, though he 'swung round on his heel' and walks heavily and silently away. Nancy is being sent to her father in India rather than taking a trip round the world. Rather than the man having a breakdown, it is she who goes mad (in the Red Sea). Whereas Miss W—— died at Brindisi, it is from Brindisi that she sends the telegram which causes Edward to kill himself. Edward's suicide is the most significant transformation. Otherwise the basic situation is very similar; and P——'s words to Ford are almost identical to Ashburnham's to Dowell: 'Look here, old man, I wish you would drive with Nancy and me to the station tomorrow.'[99]

Ford later said he had had the story 'hatching' within himself 'for fully another decade' (which would again place the episode with P—— and Miss W—— at around the time of his breakdown); and that: 'the story is a true story' which Ford had 'from Edward Ashburnham himself', but that he could not write it 'till all the others were dead'. Biographers naturally want to know who P—— was, thinking it would solve the mystery of Ashburnham. But, as Moser reluctantly concedes: 'We shall probably never know. Elsie being in Rome, Ford was seeing a lot of the Marwoods while writing *The Spirit of the People*. Yet it is unlikely that he would use his new friends so blatantly and then give them a copy of the book.' Nor is there any record of Marwood having a ward. Janice Biala says that Ford once told her the names of the people, but she could no longer remember them. Where the novel seems based on reminiscence rather than 'make-believe', we can't even be sure to what extent Ford was recalling his own experiences, and to what extent transforming the experiences of others he had observed.[100] Ford argued that not knowing biographical details enhances our appreciation of art, and this is a case in point. For if we knew the name of a real person who had really fallen in love with his ward, our attention would be deflected from *The Good Soldier*. Furthermore, it would be assumed that the P——s were peculiarly important to Ford: that he was closely involved with them. Whereas this cannot be the case: the description fits none of the people who mattered emotionally to Ford before 1907. It is much more likely that they were not particularly close friends; as Ford says in *The Spirit of the People*, 'I won't say that I felt very emotional myself, for what of the spectacle I could see from my back seat was too interesting'.

What the transmutation of the episode shows is how Ford's art makes patterns not only out of his own experiences, but out of the experiences of others, whether witnessed, heard about, or read about. It is possible that there is no 'original' for

Ashburnham, even for 'P——', and that the scene in *The Spirit of the People* is itself fictitious, or at least partly fictionalized. There is a suggestion of this in the detail about nerve cures, which, as Moser notes, might draw on Ford's own breakdown. Ford himself of course had no ward: the only person in his life in anything like that position was Rosamond, whom he had not yet met when writing of 'Miss W——' (though he appears to have lived out comparable scenarios with her after writing *The Spirit of the People*, and with Brigit Patmore during and after the writing of *The Good Soldier*). To argue that the episode is a transformation of the affair with Mary Martindale would be to concede that the situation has been almost entirely rewritten. The instance shows the limits of biographical criticism, proving how the greatest art comes not necessarily out of the biography of the artist, but out of an imaginative involvement with a human predicament. Ford's tendency to get himself into muddles by violating taboos—whether of factuality, sexuality, society, or legality—would enable him to sympathize with P——'s situation, certainly. But that is only the beginning; and the reason why we might be interested in the 'who' of fiction is less a matter of the interest in the 'germ' in itself, but of the evolved novel into which it was metamorphosed. In *The Spirit of the People* the scene is offered as an example of the English adherence to social rules of 'good conduct'. But, as in the versions in the two novels, no moral judgement is being made. Another writer (such as Wells) might have wanted to see it as a parable of the folly of renunciation. But what matters in Ford's versions is the power with which the pathos comes across: the sadness of hopeless love, the courage and the absurdity in trying to 'go on' as if nothing had happened, when all one wants is to end.

Voice and Fictionality

From the very beginning of the novel we scarcely have a chance to ponder such questions about the author's own history. Rather than a fictionalized reminiscence, or the period-piece recreation of a vanishing gentry, it is, above all, the sustained presentation of a scintillating, problematic tone which makes the strongest impression: the sense of someone talking, and talking with complex and contradictory motives. This arresting sense of personality is Ford's greatest achievement in the novel, and it was what Conrad mainly commented on when he wrote to him about the book. He had declined when Ford asked him to review one of his wartime propaganda books, and his letter struggles to be polite yet distanced. 'The women are extraordinary—in the laudatory sense', said Conrad, drawing attention to the other sense: 'and the whole vision of the subject perfectly amazing. And talking of cadences one hears all through them a tone of fretful melancholy, extremely effective. Something new, this, in your work, my dear Ford—c'est très, très curieux. Et c'est très bien, très juste. You may take my word for that.'[101] Conrad said he was 'very jumpy, unsettled, and unable to work with any sort of continuity', so Ford's power may well have made him feel double-edgy. His comment on the effect of the book is a small masterpiece of ambivalence. He had delayed writing to Ford until he had finished the 'few pages' he was working on, he explained: 'With a writer like you (and a couple of others) it's merely a matter of prudence. Your cadences get into my head till I can't hear anything of mine, and become paralysed for days.'

Ford's new tonal mastery is audible in the first paragraph of the novel, bristling with intimation and suppression. It was the only passage in his writing that satisfied him, he told Herbert Read.[102] This characteristic mix of humility and pride is extraordinary, as one of his greatest books shrinks to one paragraph. But it should not blind us to the way *The Good Soldier* sustains its achievement. From that first startlingly low-key sentence: 'This is the saddest story I have ever heard', the novel involves all but the most resistant readers. Is it an extortion of our sympathy, or a simple statement of his own? Is it exaggeration or understatement? Is it even true (since Dowell was a participant, can he be said to have 'heard' the story)? From the measured reminiscences of the opening, through the catalogue of Edward Ashburnham's passions, and Dowell's revelation that his own wife Florence had been one of Ashburnham's conquests, to the frenzied torments of Ashburnham's final passion for his ward Nancy, the narrative pace accelerates and the tension increases: a dazzling example of the *progression d'effet* Ford always advocated.

Dowell's fictional scenario in which he imagines talking to the reader sitting opposite him poses the novel as an extended 'dramatic monologue'. The latent dubiety of the first-person blurs questions of truth and distance in order to focus questions about the integrity of the self, and about how a self is perceived. Is it an exercise of verbal power? If so, to what ends? Is it a confession or a seduction; a rendering of the self, or an attempt to manipulate the sympathies of the imagined 'sympathetic listener'? It is remarkable that Ford begins to investigate these formal possibilities of the first-person narrator at exactly the same time that he is advocating an 'impressionism' which should seem not to narrate at all.[103]

Dowell begins with a provocation: 'This is the saddest story I have ever heard.' Even as he takes us into his confidence, he immediately arouses our mistrust, and introduces the possibility of irony. He seems even to have provoked himself, for the second sentence shows him qualifying his own masterly exaggerations as he makes them:

We had known the Ashburnhams for nine seasons of the town of Nauheim with an extreme intimacy—or rather with an acquaintanceship as loose and easy and yet as close as a good glove's with your hand. My wife and I knew Captain and Mrs Ashburnham as well as it was possible to know anybody, and yet, in another sense, we knew nothing at all about them. This is, I believe, a state of things only possible with English people of whom, till today, when I sit down to puzzle out what I know of this sad affair, I knew nothing whatever.

How different is that first sentence from the information it imparts! How different from saying 'We had known the Ashburnhams well for nine seasons of the town of Nauheim'! What exactly is 'an extreme intimacy'? It sounds too extreme: on a first reading we might realize that something is wrong, but we cannot possibly know what; in retrospect, as Carol Jacobs suggests, an 'extreme intimacy' is an adultery. Mizener gives a fine description of one way of reading this basic tonal duality throughout the novel:

the most pervasive form of irony Dowell the narrator uses is to speak in such a way that we can take what he says as he would have meant it at the time the event occurred and also as he means it now that he understands what really happened. That is how he is speaking when he says Florence was never out of his sight 'except when she was safely tucked up in bed.' This kind of irony is pervasive because it is Dowell's means of keeping before us the double perspective of the novel, the simultaneous awareness of what the experience was like for a participant as it was actually occurring and of what the full knowledge of hindsight shows it to have been.[104]

This is the book many have tried to make out of *The Good Soldier*: a clear-cut moral tale of innocence and experience, in which Dowell thought he knew where he was, found out how wrong he was, and now knows where he is. Why, then, does he keep asking us all those questions, leaving all the answers to us? Those with a professional interest in providing morals and commentaries for fictions which leave them out tend to be unwilling to allow the book to remain morally undecidable. But, as some of the better recent criticism has begun to investigate, Dowell's combined tone of innocence and experience means that we can never know where we are, because we can never be sure where he is. The dual form of the first-person narration—Dowell's words, but Ford's book—blurs the distinctions between subjectivity and objectivity, between author's and narrator's perspective. *The Good Soldier* was possibly influenced by Wells's bravura performance in a similarly problematic first-person mode in *Tono-Bungay* (part of which Ford had serialized in the *English Review*). Thus it becomes impossible to tell whether Ford's art makes Dowell's narration artlessly revealing, or whether Dowell himself artfully enlists our sympathies for his side of the story. Again, Ford's manuscript revisions show him excising some of the comments that made Dowell sound *too* like a novelist—though he left in enough to raise our doubts about the narrator's manipulation of his story, making us wonder in turn whether he hasn't been less of a victim and more complicit in the deaths and madness of the affair.[105]

The book baffles critical attempts to disentangle knowledge from illusion. Indeed, in one sense that problem of epistemology—of what can be known—itself becomes superficial. In trying to define the extent to which the Dowells had 'known' the Ashburnhams, Dowell performs his characteristically vertiginous oscillation from one extreme ('intimacy') to another (loose acquaintanceship). The missing middle, the term the narrative represses, is 'friend': because he still is not sure whether either of the Ashburnhams should be called his friend. We cannot be sure of that, any more than we can be sure of how well he and his wife knew the Ashburnhams, until we know exactly what their relationships were. But as the innuendos start flying, it becomes clear that we cannot be sure of that either. Take, for example, 'an acquaintanceship as loose and easy and yet as close as a good glove's with your hand'. Is a loose and easy acquaintanceship any better than an extreme intimacy? Or very different? 'Loose' and 'easy' suggest comfort; but also laxity, as applied to women or virtue. 'As close as a good glove's with your hand' might simply be a warm friendship; but the 'hand in glove' co-operation also connotes the more sinister way of being 'close': secretive, conspiratorial.

Dowell's tendency to close cadences by leaving them open with a rhetorical question offers Ford another way of producing a dual response. By asking: 'At what, then, does it all work out?' (p. 16), or 'Good God, what did they all see in him?' (p. 33), Dowell expresses the desperate desire to know the answers, together with the feeling that it is futile to ask, because none of the possible answers are adequate, because the characters are all too complexly tangled and bristling with contradictory impulses and motives for any reductive labels or generalizations to be illuminating.

There is some truth in saying that Dowell's ambivalence towards Ashburnham draws upon Ford's feelings for Marwood, whom he still loved despite feeling that Marwood had betrayed him—even though (like Dowell) he could not be sure what had really happened between his best friend and his estranged wife. But the tonal duality goes much further, expressing ambivalent feelings about all the major characters. Even as he hates Florence, Dowell's vision of her, alone and judged, makes him want to comfort her (p. 69). He decides he dislikes Leonora; he begins to think of Nancy as cruel. Ambivalence becomes for him, as for Ford, a habit of sensibility: a mode of thinking about society, history, and morality. Above all, Dowell's tone embodies, and elicits, ambivalence about the very story he is telling. Fascinated by telling stories which were at once plausible and improbable, both compelling and outrageous, in *The Good Soldier* Ford invented a character, Ashburnham, at once sympathetic and outrageous, whose story is told by a narrator who is both convincing and ridiculous. 'Technically, the achievement is hair-raising in its virtuosity', said Edward Crankshaw, who went on to argue that what the book expresses is 'the flaw in the heart which makes human effort vain'; 'the lie in the soul'. 'Was Henry James the first to build a plot on a lie? Ford soon followed him.'[106] Conrad and Ford were both intrigued by the idea of living by selling untrue statements. It is in its textures of deceits and fabulation, its tones and forms, that the novel most profoundly reflects and expresses Ford's sense of himself.

For the Fordian impressionist, fictional form is the only answer; the only adequate interpretation of experience. *The Good Soldier* is 'a picture without a meaning' in the sense that Dowell cannot say what the meaning of his experience is. But this is not to say that, for its readers, the novel is meaningless. Instead, the meaning *is* the picture: the sense it leaves us with of having witnessed an affair in all its confused complexity. Discussing 'surprise' in *Joseph Conrad*, Ford explains that 'the indirect, interrupted method of handling interviews is invaluable for giving a sense of the complexity, the tantalisation, the shimmering, the haze, that life is'. Both writers sometimes made it sound as if it were merely a matter of transcription But in their best work they knew that it was a matter of finding a narrative method that could create a 'sense of the complexity, the tantalisation'. Conrad tells us in *Heart of Darkness* that to Marlow 'the meaning of an episode was not inside like a kernel but outside, enveloping the tale which brought it out as a glow brings out a haze'. His story seems to offer a 'kernel'—the possibility of finding a heart within the darkness: a destination in Africa; an explanation of Kurtz's activities that will allow a moral judgement. But 'heart' becomes a tantalizing mirage. Instead of finding a heart in the darkness that is Kurtz, Marlow finds that his heart is—darkness. Similarly, *The Good Soldier: A Tale of Passion*, another story in which hearts turn out not to be what they seem, appears to offer an illustration of an abstract noun, 'passion'. By the end of the novel we expect to have seen a representative instance of passion, which will enable us to understand it better (as, say, 'the polygamous desires that underlie all men'). Yet during the course of the story, the emphasis shifts from 'passion' to 'tale'. It is not just a tale *about* passion, but a tale told *out* of passion, told *with* passion. It is as if the heart of passion turns out to be story; not least because if Ashburnham hadn't read all those sentimental novels he might never have become the sentimental philanderer; and his taciturnity means that if Dowell didn't tell his story for him no one else (apart from Dowell and Leonora) would have even known that he was in love with Nancy.[107]

'*A Real Story*'

In Ford's own account of his involvement with the book the craft matters as much as the biography and autobiography. 'I had never really tried to put into any novel of mine *all* that I knew about writing,' he said, but with *The Good Soldier* 'I sat down to show what I could do.' Working with Conrad he had 'made exhaustive studies into how words should be handled and novels constructed'. His lesser fiction draws upon much of the same personal history that is visible in *The Good Soldier*: what sets this novel apart is its technical command. It is the masterpiece which emancipated him from his apprenticeship to Conrad and James.

   Until now Ford had only used fictional first-person narrators in the collaborations with Conrad. In *The Good Soldier*'s mode of narration he found a dual way of dramatizing his own infatuation with Englishness which *The Spirit of the People* and its companion volumes had expressed. First, the use of the American narrator enables him to see England from the outside. The related, but more important, difference between the 'germ' or the scene in *A Call* and *The Good Soldier* is the way the latter novel foregrounds the problematics of its telling. We can never completely forget the fact of narration. The immediacy of the I-witness account is always in tension with our doubts about his point of view, what he understands, what he might be concealing.

   One of the ways Ford makes the novel so effective is by using this first-person narration to dramatize the problem of trust between Dowell and Ashburnham in the relationships between Dowell and his imagined listener (the 'sympathetic soul'; p. 17), and between Ford and his readers. If we can come to trust Dowell—despite our uncertainties about him and his story—then we can begin to see how he could trust Ashburnham. (It is another moving feature of the novel that Dowell's love for Edward survives the corrosive knowledge that his friend had been cuckolding him: but is this sympathetic identification, true Christian magnanimity, or the pathetic emotional inadequacy of someone who can't even feel jealousy?) What remains opaque to us about Dowell, even as he addresses his reader, is analogous to what remains opaque about Ashburnham to Dowell's gaze. In the essay 'On Impressionism', written while he was getting towards the end of *The Good Soldier*, Ford discussed his interest in a verbal control that could inspire a trust which would in turn suggest a penumbra of doubt. He is describing an editor-friend (who may have been himself) and an 'ideal critic'; but it is also true of Dowell that he is a 'person who can so handle words that from the first three phrases any intelligent person [. . .] will know at once the sort of chap that he is dealing with':

I don't mean to say that he would necessarily trust his purse, his wife, or his mistress to the Impressionist critic's care. But that is not absolutely necessary. The ambition, however, of my friend the editor was to let his journal give the impression of being written by those who could be trusted with the wives and purses—not, of course, the mistresses, for there would be none—of his readers (p. 169)

Dowell certainly gives the impression that he could be trusted with other people's wives, such as Leonora. (Ashburnham can confidently entrust his mistress to Dowell, even though it is Dowell's own wife.) And Ashburnham gave him the same impression: 'You would have said that he was just exactly the sort of chap that you could have trusted your wife with. And I trusted mine—and it was madness' (p. 16). His language here might imply an exclusively male readership; but we need to set against such suggestions the seductive power of his narration to an imagined listener who might well be female. Either way, Ford sexualizes the act of narration itself.[108]

This emphasis on 'story' and narration makes the book at once the most and least impressionist of Ford's books. On the one hand, it is his most thorough application of the principle that the story should go 'backwards and forwards', as the impressions recur to the narrator. Furthermore, whatever our doubts about him, Dowell gives quite a good *impression*, at least, of being trustworthy. On the other hand, the novel appears to violate the impressionist canon that the author should 'not narrate but render . . . impressions': 'the object of the novelist is to keep the reader entirely oblivious of the fact that the author exists—even of the fact that he is reading a book. This is of course not possible to the bitter end, but a reader *can* be engrossed, and the nearer you can come to making him entirely insensitive to his surroundings, the more you will have succeeded.'[109] Yet of course—as Ford's qualification acknowledges—it is an ideal that is impossible to realize. However, by making us unusually aware that the *narrator* is telling the story, has written the book we are reading, Ford uses the first-person form to efface himself behind the narrator's persona. Indeed, with a brilliant audacity, he chooses as his explicator the most deceived and least suspicious character—the one who will have the most trouble in piecing together a seamless narrative and understanding it; and whose very difficulty in sustaining an engrossing illusion is precisely what becomes engrossing.

When Ford said he put all he knew about writing into *The Good Soldier*, then, he was not just talking about all the techniques he had used. He was also indicating that the book can be read as 'about writing'. Though he didn't want to make it too obvious an allegory of the artist (which is why he removed some of Dowell's explicit comments on writing novels), he used Dowell's act of narration to focus his own concerns about narrative fiction. The novel is a profound investigation, not only into why, and how, people deceive each other sexually and socially, but also into why people tell stories, and listen to them, or read them. 'On Impressionism' wonders about these questions too, in a Dowellian vein: 'one writes for money, for fame, to excite the passion of love, to make an impression upon one's time. Well, God knows what one writes for' (p. 327). Dowell says: 'You may well ask why I write. And yet my reasons are quite many. For it is not unusual in human beings who have witnessed the sack of a city or the falling to pieces of a people to desire to set down what they have witnessed for the benefit of unknown heirs or of generations infinitely remote; or, if you please, just to get the sight out of their heads' (p. 9). The way the impressionist writer gets the sight out of his head is to get it into his reader's. Freud, who found that hysterical patients were generally 'visual' types, and often described vivid visual memories while denying that they were meaningful, noted how the act of describing tended to disperse the memory: '*The patient is, as it were, getting rid of it by turning it into words*', he wrote.[110] Ford uses Dowell as a new way of living up to the task Conrad had articulated for him: using 'the power of the written word' 'to make you *see*'. One way to exorcize anguish and bafflement is to transfer it on to another person (which is why victims so often become abusers in their turn); or on to another relationship—rather as, in psychoanalysis, the patient's unconscious conflicts are projected on to his or her relationship with the analyst, in the powerful emotions produced by what Freud called 'transference'; or to express it in a work of art. Ford's art in *The Good Soldier* is pre-eminently an art of transference, as Dowell's feelings about Ashburnham get taken up into his relationship with his silent listener, and into Ford's rapport with his reader. That rapport provides the missing middle term between the 'acquaintanceship' and 'extreme intimacy' of the Ashburnhams and Dowells. The power of our responses to art comes in part from a similar transference, in which we project our unconscious selves into the art-object. The site of the narration does not simply replicate the conflicts of the past, however. As Dowell gets the sight out of his head, keeping his tears back by sharing his burden of grief and perplexity, he is also able to alleviate the solitude he has been left in, with Edward dead, and Nancy unreachable. His narration is his talking cure. Dowell's description of passion (Edward's passion for Nancy) could itself be a manifesto for the 'impressionist' author or reader, needing the solitude of writing or reading in order to express the desire for identification:

He wants to get, as it were, behind those eye-brows with the peculiar turn, as if he desired to see the world with the eyes that they overshadow. He wants to hear that voice applying itself to every possible background [. . .] the real fierceness of desire [. . .] is the craving for identity with the woman that he loves. He desires to see with the same eyes, to touch with the same sense of touch, to hear with the same ears, to lose his identity, to be enveloped, to be supported [. . .] We are all so afraid, we are all so alone, we all so need from the outside the assurance of our own worthiness to exist. (pp. 135–6)

Nancy's madness frustrates Dowell's desire to identify with her, to hear her telling him what it is like to be her. His story is told, as the novel is written, *out of* this kind of bafflement, rather than simply being 'about' it. Writing desires this identity, but speaks its perpetual frustration.

Yet the final paradox—it is one which enables art, particularly impressionist writing—is that though we cannot know, or be, another, literature can give us an 'all round impression' of them. It is ultimately at this level that the novel can be read as autobiographical: not because Dowell and Ashburnham represent Ford himself, but because the novel is an expression of Ford's fiercest desire, which was to write—in particular, to write fiction. He wrote vivid, compelling books of reminiscence too, but even these are highly fictionalized, and are as obliquely revealing as are Dowell's approaches to Ashburnham, or to himself. *The Good Soldier* is a fictional version of Ford's own autobiographical mode: Dowell is an impressionist reminiscer. And by Ford's definition, impressionism is necessarily reminiscential, 'the record of the impression of a moment': 'it is not a sort of rounded, annotated record of a set of circumstances—it is the record of the recollection in your mind of a set of circumstances that happened ten years ago—or ten minutes.' Ford was working on *The Good Soldier* when he said this, and of all his fiction it best fits the definition. Not only because Dowell is recollecting the circumstances of the previous decade, but because Ford said he had the novel 'hatching' within himself for a decade before he wrote it down. Only fiction answered to Ford's sense of experience, and its uncertainties of order, morality, and knowledge. 'We work in the dark—we do what we can—we give what we have. Our doubt is our passion and our passion is our task. The rest is the madness of art': these words from the dying writer in James's story 'The Middle Years' show how Ford was not alone in seeing questions of delusion, doubt, passion, and madness, as tangled up with questions of art.[111] Only fiction could express Ford's vision of human alienation, and his understanding of the human desire to overcome solitude by sharing others' visions, even as we remain sceptical of them. *The Good Soldier* presents what Ford knew best: someone telling a story, reshaping it and wanting his listeners to *see*, and to be moved by it. It tells this 'true story' too, in which the story-ness matters as much as its truth. Ford consoles himself for the perplexity of meaning by telling stories: 'I console myself with thinking that this is a real story and that, after all, real stories are probably best told in the way a person telling a story would tell them. Then they will seem most real' (p. 213). But is a 'real story' a rendering of what really happened, or a thorough fable? As Stella Bowen said: 'He was a writer—a complete writer—and nothing but a writer.'[112]

When he dedicated *The Good Soldier* to Bowen in the second edition of 1927, Ford wrote that he had always regarded it as his best book. When he wrote it he thought of it as his last book. (Imagining his own death as Ashburnham, he imagined his death as a novelist.) And years after he had written his other novelistic masterpiece, *Parade's End*, he alluded to *The Good Soldier* by calling it simply—and with a modesty for which he has received scant credit—his 'one novel'. For all his ambivalences and self-doubts about his life and art, even Ford could not really doubt the magnificence of *The Good Soldier*. A decade later he said that 'at a given point' in his life—presumably when he took his 'farewell of Literature' after writing the book, and went to the war—'I forgot, literally, all the books I have ever written'. This may have been literally true when he suffered shell-shock, and complete amnesia for three weeks. Forgetting his books was a frightening idea for a writer who set so much store by his ability to plan out and store prose in his head. 'I always think over the general plan of a novel for six months before beginning it,' he wrote, 'and generally have at least the first and last chapters in my head before putting pencil to paper.' But when he began *The Good Soldier*, he said: 'I had almost every word of it ready in my head, and I dictated it very quickly in consequence, I should think in six weeks.' After the war he said he was translating *The Good Soldier* from memory, 'by simply rewriting the book in French without looking at the English'. It was his 'one novel' in the sense of being the one that was too personal ever to forget.[113]

26

1914–1915: HOSTILITIES

> It is the original curse of Anglo-Saxondom that her civilization forever
> wavers between the Teutonic and the Latin that are the opposed currents
> of her two-fold soul.
>
> (Ford, 'The Real France, That Goes to Bed at Nine',
> *New York Herald Tribune Books*, 31 March 1935)

Ford wrote about the season of 1914 in *Return to Yesterday*, his volume of
reminiscences which ends with the start of the First World War. He was finishing
the book in 1930, and recalled finding his engagement book for 1914 two years
before. It is a characteristic act of complex historical imagination, which reaches
back from the Depression, beyond the Wall Street Crash (of October 1929), to
the prosperous 1920s, when he had hoped to make his fortune in America, and
had decided to move his 'headquarters' to New York. This remembrance of the
time before one catastrophe reminds him of the earlier catastrophe, the war, and
of the contrast with the 'extraordinary rush' of the frenetic social life of the last
months of peace:

From the middle of May to the end of June, except for the week-ends which I had
spent either at Selsey where I lived next to Masterman and the editor of the *Outlook*
or at other people's country houses—there were only six days on which I did not have
at least three dinner and after-dinner dates. There would be a dinner, a theatre or a
party, a dance. Usually a breakfast at four after that. Or Ezra and his gang carried me
off to their night club which was kept by Mme. Strindberg, decorated by Epstein and
situate[d] underground.[1]

Frida Strindberg had been the second wife of the playwright, whom she had
divorced in 1897. Hunt said she 'had a letch' for Ford (or perhaps for Hunt
herself) and called her a 'charming sorceress'. She deserves a biography to herself.
Her Cabaret Club was the Cave of the Golden Calf, at 9 Heddon Street, complete
with a golden calf by Eric Gill, two white plaster caryatids by Epstein, and murals
by Wyndham Lewis and Spencer Gore. There were 'obsolete Vorticist dances,
the Turkey Trot and the Bunny Hug', and cabaret acts—Edgar Jepson called
them 'violent, Vorticist assaults on the drama'. Ford wrote a 'shadow play' for
Mme Strindberg, who used to give him and Hunt supper, but had to act it himself
'in place of the lovely actress who should have done it'. Mme Strindberg told
Pound that it was her need for money that drove her to take up 'prostitution' 'in
this particular form'. Nevertheless, she used to invite impoverished artists to her

table to eat for free. Pound also reported that once she waved a customer away from this table, saying that 'sleep with him she would, but talk to him, never': 'One must draw the line *somewhere*.' She drew it the other side of Augustus John and Wyndham Lewis. The latter referred to her as 'the Strindberg', and called her a 'very adventurous woman'. Ford's best evocation of the period comes in his novel *The Marsden Case*—whose narrator also writes a shadow play for a subterranean night-club. In that book, too, Ford presents a powerfully expressive diptych: pre-war excitement, verging on hysteria, contrasted with post-war loss and grief—the war itself an eloquent absence, a fracture across the social memory.[2]

Sometimes there would be a party after the night-club. Ford wrote later: 'The gayest season that this writer can remember was that of London in the summer before the war'; 'the memories which most consecrate that forever-vanished halcyon mood and time are those of the chafing-dish parties, that, always at dawn or toward it, finished the day—on a flat roof, on a stoop, or in a garden, and in peace, to the great sound of the orchestra of London's awakening birds.'[3]

Ford was becoming more closely allied with the avant-garde. 'It was like an opening world', he wrote of the pre-war literary scene. 'For, if you have worried your poor dear old brain for at least a quarter of a century over the hopelessness of finding, in Anglo-Saxondom, any traces of the operation of a conscious art—it was amazing to find these young creatures'—Pound, Lawrence, Norman Douglas, H.D. (Hilda Doolittle), Aldington, Flint, Frost, Eliot, Gaudier-Brzeska, and Epstein—'evolving theories of writing and the plastic arts', and creating a public for their work. 'Fat Ford has come back & the days are mercifully shorter', Pound wrote to Dorothy Shakespear. He gave a big dinner for Pound, at which: 'The Faun [Richard Aldington] told Ford *all* about Elizabethan drama last night—just like Gosse, & he has just been in with the Dryad [H.D.] to tell me *all* about it again—*electric*.' When Pound and Shakespear decided to get married in April 1914, Ford promised them 'six High Wycombe chairs', and took the occasion to lecture *les jeunes* on furniture: 'He says it gives tone', Pound told Dorothy, and added: 'He says V.[iolet] has got to give us something else & she says they are both going to give us something together—Unanimism again!' That week Pound gave an interview to publicize his anthology, *Des Imagistes*, and he took the opportunity to correct the misconception that Ford was one of his disciples, and to boom Ford as 'one of our strongest forces to-day'. Lecturing, reviewing, discussing, finding a new form for the novel—Ford was in the vanguard. Yet he also portrays himself as under attack from the avant-garde—or, to be more specific, Lewis. The two men respected each other, but were not close. Ford retells the story of how Lewis denounced Ford's art to him, while force-marching him down Holland Street, telling him he was 'Finished! Exploded! Done for! Blasted in fact! Your generation has gone. What is the sense of you and Conrad and Impressionism? [. . .] This is the day of Cubism, Futurism, Vorticism. What people want is me, not you. They want to see me. A Vortex. To liven them up. You and Conrad had the idea of concealing yourself when you wrote. I display myself all over the page. In every word. I . . . I . . . I . . . .' Ford had prophesied his demise at the hands of the remorseless young back in 1901 (the year that saw *The Inheritors*, on much the same theme) in 'To Christina at Nightfall':

> When I am weak and old,
> And lose my grip, and crave my small reward
> Of tolerance and tenderness and ruth,
> The children of your dawning day shall hold
> The reins we drop and wield the judge's sword
> And your swift feet shall tread upon my heels,
> And I be Ancient Error, you New Truth,
> And I be crushed by your advancing wheels . . .

Nevertheless, Ford and Hunt hired Lewis to display himself all over the wall above the mantelpiece in Hunt's study at South Lodge. Contact with *les jeunes* led Ford to exaggerate his outmodedness. In early May he dined at an old haunt of his days with Conrad and James, the Mermaid Inn, Rye, with Aldington, H.D., and Aldington's parents. Ford 'sensed the virgin sucker at once', said Aldington, recalling his scholarly father's responses to Ford's literary anecdotes. 'My father was swimming in bliss, although once or twice he looked a little puzzled. And then Ford began telling how he met Byron. I saw my father stiffen.' It was perhaps Ford's humorous revenge for Aldington's lectures on Elizabethan drama. Even though Aldington thought Ford 'himself seemed to realise that his character more nearly resembled fiction than fact, and lavished on his legend all the imaginative resources a novelist would devote to a favourite character', he had the generosity to concede that there was 'probably a substratum of fact' in all Ford's stories, and that 'even the Byron story may have been an authentic tradition which Ford over-dramatised in his devotion to artistic form'. He said he had known few men 'so fundamentally innocent of real harm' as Ford.[4]

Wyndham Lewis and Kate Lechmere opened their Rebel Art Centre in Great Ormond Street in the spring of 1914, showing works by Vorticists such as Gaudier-Brzeska, Bomberg, and William Roberts, as well as Lewis himself. Pound contributed a sign for the wall reading 'End of the Christian Era'. Ford gave a lecture there, dressed in rebellious tails. While he was talking, Lewis's art rebelled. One of his largest paintings, *Plan of War*, suddenly fell off the wall and right on top of 'this dignified literary figure'. 'Luckily, however, no harm was done,' Lechmere recalled, 'since the frame broke loose from the picture and crashed to the floor, leaving the canvas perched harmlessly on Ford's head.'[5]

The Vorticist magazine *Blast* appeared on 20 June, with the first three-and-a-half chapters of *The Good Soldier*, under its original title, 'The Saddest Story', looking slightly out-of-place, its intense Conradian attention to the Edwardian social surface at odds with the Vorticist dismissal of the British Empire—its sardonic 'Blast'ing of the establishment, and 'Bless'ing of the machine and energy. Is Ford's epigraph for his novel, '*Beati Immaculati* an ironic riposte to *les jeunes*? The phrase from Psalm 119, 'Blessed are the undefiled', is precisely the kind of piety the Vorticists were noisily rejecting. There was a dinner at the Dieudonné restaurant in Ryder Street on 15 July to celebrate. The American poet Amy Lowell had been invited—she wanted to start a new magazine, and was thinking of using Ford and Pound to run the London end. But Ford became irritated by Lowell's apparent anxiety to leave England in case of war. He recalled her as 'a disagreeably obese Neutral', a 'disagreeably intelligent being', and they 'disagreed flatly about literary principles'.[6] Lowell held a return match two nights later, in the same restaurant: this time it was to be an *imagiste* dinner. Ford was invited, and Lowell even asked him to give a speech. John Gould Fletcher was there, and wondered whether Ford was 'embarrassed at these honours thrust upon him', but said that he was 'equal to the occasion':

He began by informing us that he did not know in the least what an imagist poet was. Ezra had assured him that he was an imagist poet, but if so, he had been one long before the world had ever heard of imagism. His poems, which Ezra had insisted should be printed in *Poetry* as examples of imagistic poetry, were all derived from Heine and Browning. He personally doubted whether Miss Lowell was an imagist poet, or for that matter, whether Ezra himself was, though he knew him to be interested in imagist poetry. The only imagists he saw present at that table were Aldington and H.D., whose imagism seemed to him entirely devoid of foreign admixture. He sat down, amidst an embarrassed silence.[7]

It was one of the more dignified performances of the evening. Allen Upward, Pound, and others made fun of Lowell's figure. Her poem 'In a Garden', which had appeared in the anthology *Des Imagistes*, had a line: 'Night and the water, and you in your whiteness, bathing!' 'Pound carried in from an adjoining salon, where it had been placed under a leak, a circular tub, clearly large enough for Miss Lowell to bathe in. He set it down in front of her and announced that *Les Imagistes* were about to be succeeded by a new school, *Les Nagistes*.' The battle for the leadership of 'Imagism' had begun—Lowell was trying to organize her own, redefining, anthology.[8] It is the factional, scholastic aspect of literary coteries that Ford was presciently satirizing in his speech. He had characteristically presented his incisive satire in such a way as to provoke hostility from all sides, by doubting *anyone's* claim to the title of *imagiste*. As when he denounced Fabianism to the Fabians, it was a gesture that cast himself as the pariah.

When Lowell wrote to Harriet Monroe that 'Violent jealousy has broken out' amongst the poets, she was still smarting from her guests' mockery; but she offers some telling remarks about Ford: 'My impression is that Hueffer is also in a gloomy way. I went to a lecture which he gave at which there were just nine people present, counting out his wife, the man who introduced him, and myself (who had to go because I dined with them). He is on the verge of nervous prostration, poor fellow—'[9] which is hardly surprising, given the fact that he was also finding the time and energy to write *The Good Soldier*. Ernest Jessop, the narrator of *The Marsden Case*, found the underground night-club 'extraordinarily soothing' after the conflicts of the surface world, and says: 'I was not on the verge of a nervous breakdown—or perhaps I was' (p. 90). There is a suicidal strain

running through his *Outlook* pieces during the summer. Punctuating the penetrating essays on May Sinclair, the Imagists, Yeats, Robert Frost, Lewis, and
Marinetti (whom Ford had heard lecture at the Doré Gallery) among others, are
remarks like: 'I who am, relatively speaking, about to die, prophesy that these
young men will smash up several elderly persons—and amuse a great many
others.' This came in a review of Lewis and *Blast*, and is a characteristically dual
response: Ford expects to be smashed up by *les jeunes* because they think him
'Finished!'; yet he can remain amused by the spectacle. When Britain declared
war on Germany on 4 August, the public cataclysm appeared to validate Ford's
feeling of personal crisis. He mistrusted the jingoistic rhetoric asserting that the
war would be over by Christmas, predicting that it could last eight years.
Imagining what the post-war world and literature of 1922 might be like, he wrote:
'it is my ambition to be dead by that date'. Such feelings cast another light on
the aesthetic of poetry as quiet talk:

inasmuch as the personality of the writer is still the chief thing in a work of art, any
form that will lead to the more perfect expression of personality is a form of the
utmost value. I suppose that what I have been aiming at all my life is a literary form
that will produce the effect of a quiet voice going on talking and talking, without much
ejaculation, without the employment of any verbal strangeness—just quietly saying
things. Of course I do not lay that down as a canon for the whole world. The universe
is very large and in it there is room for an infinite number of gods. There is room
even for Mr. Marinetti's declamations of battle-pieces. But one is very tired; writing
is a hopeless sort of job, words are very hard to find, and one frequently wishes that
one were dead, and so on. It is at such times that one welcomes the quiet voice that
will just go on talking to one about nothing in particular, just to keep one from
thinking.[10]

Ford's own subdued verse has just this duality: it expresses his depression
precisely by intimating the attempt to suppress it. Although the review is
ostensibly talking about verse, Ford knew that he had just found the form he
craved in prose. That 'effect of a quiet voice going on talking and talking' captures
the peculiar quality, at once disturbing and soothing, enervating and consoling,
of the narrator of *The Good Soldier*.

Ford said he 'took a formal farewell of Literature'. He remembered it as being
in the *Thrush*; but though he had written for this magazine of Goldring's (in
1909), it had expired four years before, in 1910. It has been assumed that he was
thinking of the essay 'On Impressionism', published in Harold Monro's *Poetry
and Drama* in 1914, in which he wrote: 'for my part I am determined to drop
creative writing for good.' But the fact is that he was making repeated farewells
that summer, more or less formal, to literature and to life. He even 'wrote to Xtina
that he was dying', as Olive Garnett recorded in May. It was as if, having
imagined Ashburnham's suicide, he was trying to live it out as his own.[11]

He and Hunt gave a party for the Vorticists at South Lodge, selling copies of
Blast at half-price. Several of the guests were blasted or blessed. ' "Some of my
family in it?", Mr. Thesiger said. "Oh, I must have one." Lady Aberconway,

finding herself blest, was no longer eager.' Then, towards the end of July they travelled to Scotland. They had been invited to a country-house party given by the American novelist 'Mary Borden' (who had married 'an extraordinarily humorous looking red-headed Scotsman' called Turner, but later became Lady Spears) in a manor house she had rented at Duns, near Berwick-upon-Tweed. Other writers were invited: Wyndham Lewis, and also E. M. Forster, who noted: 'Hueffer, rather a fly blown man of letters, was in the house, and kept exclaiming how bored he was'. 'We sat on the lawns in the sunlight,' recalled Ford, 'and people read aloud—which I like very much.' He read from the proofs of 'The Saddest Story' in *Blast*; Mrs Turner read from Joyce's *Portrait of the Artist as a Young Man*, which was being serialized in the *Egoist*.[12] Otherwise they were preoccupied by the inexorable slide towards war. Hunt said they had asked Richard Aldington to send them a daily news telegram. 'Russia mobilising, France mobilising, England mobilising. It was like a rattle of sharp musketry every morning', she said. Lewis recorded a conversation at breakfast:

Mrs Turner was emphatic [. . .]
'There won't be any war, Ford. Not here. England won't go into a war.'
Ford thrust his mouth out, fish-fashion, as if about to gasp for breath. He goggled his eyes and waggled one eyelid about. He just moved his lips a little and we heard him say, in a breathless sotto voce—
'England will.' He had said that already. He passed his large protruding blue eyes impassively over the faces of these children—absorbed in their self-satisfied eras of sheltered peace.
'England will! But Ford,' said Mrs. Turner, 'England has a Liberal Government. A Liberal Government cannot declare war.'
'Of course it can't,' I said, frowning at Ford. 'Liberal Governments can't go to war. That would not be liberal. That would be conservative.'
Ford sneered very faintly and inoffensively: he was sneering at the British Government, rather than at us. He was being omniscient, bored, sleepy Ford, sunk in his tank of sloth. From his prolonged sleep he was staring out at us with his fish-blue eyes—kind, wise, but bored. Or some such idea. His mask was only just touched with derision at our childishness.
'Well, Ford,' said Mrs. Turner, bantering the wise old elephant. 'You don't agree!'
'I don't agree,' Ford answered, in his faintest voice, with consummate indifference, 'because it has always been the Liberals who have gone to war. It is *because* it is a Liberal Government that it *will* declare war.'[13]

Ford's political pronouncements, especially those made at this time, have often been taken as evidence of an anachronistic form of fantasy-feudalism. His first *Outlook* article after Britain's declaration of war was 'an indictment of the Parliamentary system and of democracy'. He explained this by saying that:

the present war, as I see it, is simply a product of the indefinite, mysterious, and subterranean forces of groups of shady and inscrutable financiers working their wills upon the ignorant, the credulous, the easily swayed electorate [. . .] England will probably come out of it all right; I pray God that England may come out of it all right! But I pray God, too, that, when it is all over there may be a revaluing of democracy, of Rousseauism, and that the Rights of Man may be put for ever into a dishonoured dustbin, along with the groups of financiers to whom they have given power. For men have no rights—they have only duties.[14]

Ford's politics are always paradoxical and elusive—he wrote of 'the true Toryism which is Socialism', and argued that: 'The Tory sees life as a corporate state in which we should all do our best for the whole, but we should have the greatest possible liberty in and scope for individual freedom—for criticism, in fact. The Whig sees life as a matter of efficient Individualists caught up in a party machine that allows of not the slightest cavil or carping'.[15] What is wrong with liberal democracy, according to Ford, is not that it offers too much freedom, but that what it offers are false freedoms. It is an ideology of 'rights' and 'equality', but in practice democracy always means plutocracy; and wars are held over commercial interests rather than the ostensible issues of human rights and liberties. After fascism and Stalinism, and now the collapse of communism, it is fashionable to say that, whatever the faults of liberal capitalism, we haven't yet found anything preferable. But at a time when power and money are more closely allied than they have been since 1914, it is well to remember Ford's scepticism. The feudalism is really a red herring: an emotional predisposition and a historical 'impression' rather than an earnestly advocated position. It needs to be judged by what it defines itself against. It is for the workers at least as much as for the landowners. In *A History of Our Own Times*, written during the last decade of his life, as the prospect of a second world war became visible, he wrote: 'this Writer's own predilections and sentiments sway him towards the Right, towards the Past, towards handicrafts as against mass production, towards feudalism as against rule by demagogues. . . .' (p. 7). Yet even such a candid credo is immediately qualified by Fordian ironic disavowal. He considers that 'the Feudal System was the most satisfactory form of government that humanity has yet evolved', not on the grounds of justice, or stability, or even any recognizable claim of pragmatism, but, unexpectedly, 'simply because it provided responsible heads to lop off if the state failed to prosper' (p. 8). Furthermore, he recognizes the fictionality of a twentieth-century feudalist position: 'it would today be the merest waste of time to adopt Feudalism as the underlying inspiration of a history of modern developments' (p. 8). And then his mind takes a literary turn, to consider how the vogue for *Prisoner of Zenda*-type romances set in 'imaginary principalities' proves that 'humanity has a certain love for the antique-picturesque in the way of governments' (p. 8). Ford's feudalism is thus a literary notion, an insight which he then pursues by explaining the continuing need for romance heroics in 'an age when the hero has practically ceased to exist' as a proof that people desire 'vicariously to enjoy the delights of feudalism'; and he adds shrewdly: 'For what is the hero of a book but the feudal overlord of the other characters.' It's not only a penetrating criticism; it's also illuminating about the conflict at the heart of all Ford's novels—but especially *The Good Soldier, Parade's End*, and *A Little Less*

Than Gods—between idealization and remorseless criticism; between altruism and cynicism; between romance and realism.

The discussion of feudal ideas in the *Outlook* essays has its literary context too. First, *The Good Soldier*. The most remarkable feature of Ford's journalism of late 1914 is that its voice is Dowell's, and many of its views are Ashburnham's. Ford has imagined himself so fully into his characters that he inhabits the personae beyond the novel; tries them out in his own person. He develops his self by inhabiting his fictions, and in doing so he becomes one of the writers who best reveals for us the problematics of modernist selfhood. He also has the presence and power of mind in his wartime journalism to imagine the effect of the war upon the world, and upon literature. This is remarkably creative thinking for a first response, written between 4 and 8 August:

And what is the good of writing about literature—the 'edler Beruf,' the noble calling? There will not be a soul that will want to read about literature for years and years. We go out. We writers go out. And, when the world again has leisure to think about letters, the whole world will have changed. It will have changed in morality, in manners, in all human relationships, in all views of life, possibly even in language, certainly in its estimates of literature. What then is the good of it all. I don't know.

It is extraordinary to think of the usually good and kindly Germans, the sinister Russians, the detestable Servians, those queer people the French, the highly civilized Austrians, and ourselves, all at each other's throat. And about what? God knows. But perhaps God does not know . . .'[16]

The book he is discussing, Charles-Louis Philippe's *Le Père Perdrix*, is a story of poverty, bereavement, blindness, illness, and suicide. Ford might equally have been thinking of his own 'Saddest Story' of madness and suicides when he wrote: 'It is not a very cheerful story; but if you want to know about life you do not address yourself to cheerful stories for information on what is always a sad affair.'

If his feudalism is a fictional construct, this essay helps one to understand its motives and dynamics. He feels that 'what is senseless, what is imbecile, are the ideas for which people are dying—the ideas for which the "noble callings" are to be strangled for a decade'. This is because the ideas are ideological propaganda masking the financial interests: 'the only reason for France's backing up Russia is that groups of financiers have sunk their money in Russian enterprises, or in the bolstering up of the Russian autocracy, and that is a very horrible reason for a war that may well destroy for ever all the gracious fairnesses of life in the Western World.' Ford's August articles have a hysterical note, but it is not the note of the national hysteria. He felt personally implicated to a disturbing degree: 'I like the French so much; I like so much the South Germans and the Austrians. Whichever side wins in the end—my own heart is certain to be mangled in either case.' He decried 'the want of chivalry in expressions of nationality', and argued at the end of August that the war should be 'fought in terms of "the gallant enemy" ', rather than of 'mad dog', 'brute', or 'tyrant'.[17] Even here, in the most disturbed of his responses to the outbreak of the war, Ford discusses the language of war, and the difficulties of writing poetry, which 'needs crystallisation, needs reflection', under the strain of war.

Far from causing him to retreat into a fantasy of the feudal English Tory gentleman (as his novels, too, have been taken to indicate he did), the war made him redefine himself as a European, and a writer: 'because for my sins I am a cosmopolitan, and also, I suppose, a poet so apt to identify myself with anyone's sufferings as to be unable to take sides very violently, I have probably thought more about these things, and certainly suffer more over them, than most people.' 'Sympathetic identification' with the minds of others was always his strength as a novelist. Henry James wrote about Turgenev: 'He felt and understood the opposite sides of life; he was imaginative, speculative, anything but literal.'[18] As a literary descendant of both Turgenev and James, Ford too could comprehend the opposing sides, whether of Henry VIII, Ashburnham, feudalism, or the world war. His advocacy of a chivalric attitude was more than a romantic anachronism: it was a way of maintaining imaginative sympathy with his various national intellectual traditions. It was also a way of provoking attacks, of course. He saw that the stories about 'German atrocities' were mainly propaganda, and when he wrote expressing his scepticism, and arguing that to fight for such ideas was to demean the notion of chivalry, Mr Hueffer was assumed to be pro-German. He was setting up once again the situation his fictive imagination revelled in: that of the altruist attacked by an uncomprehending world.

According to Edgar Jepson, Ford was back in London by 2 August:

He told me that he had had a hard morning, and I gathered that both Asquith and Grey had spent a couple of hours with him, laying the facts of the situation before him, and reiterating the question: 'Shall we fight, Hueffer, or shall we not fight?'

I had gathered from little things he had let slip earlier that his opinion was highly esteemed by Leading Politicians [. . .] but I had not known that it was esteemed as highly as that, and I have always wished that he could have seen his way to forbid them to fight.

Impression or transcript? He had visited Masterman on 3 August at the Foreign Office, where they discussed Britain's ultimatum threatening to declare war if the Germans crossed the Belgian frontier. Ford was an expert on Germany, as his contributions to *The Desirable Alien* and his subsequent wartime propaganda books show. Masterman would certainly have asked his opinion. Ford knew other cabinet ministers through Masterman, and probably knew Asquith and Lloyd George through Hunt. The story is not essentially implausible, though the phrasing provokes doubt. However, before condemning Ford's wartime exaggeration (as Mizener does), one must remember that it is *Jepson*'s story. He 'gathered' that Asquith and Grey asked Ford's advice; Ford may not have said as much. In *Return to Yesterday* he played down both his role and his prescience. There is no mention of Asquith and Grey; he tells Masterman that: 'The German troops will never cross the Belgian frontier . . . . Never . . . . Never . . . .' Jepson always enjoyed Ford's stories, and may have added some impressionistic lustre to this one himself.[19]

When he had reviewed Gerhart Hauptmann's *Atlantis* in January 1914 Ford, feeling his way through *The Good Soldier*'s intricate tangle, had reflected on his nationality, its bearing on neurasthenia, truth and fantasy, writing, and the position of the artist. In *The New Humpty-Dumpty*, the hearts of others was the dark forest which induced Macdonald's neurasthenia. In Hauptmann's story, says Ford, 'the dark forest is the hero's neurasthenia'. Hauptmann's hero has Ford's trick of imagining things that seem more real than reality: he 'in fact indulges much more in the stuff of dreams than in any observation of the life which surrounds him, and so vividly are the dreams rendered [. . .] that one can hardly tell at any given moment whether one is reading of the surgeon's hallucinations or of his adventures.' The same could be said of *Ladies Whose Bright Eyes*, or *The Young Lovell*. After the war, Ford would explore the borderline of fantasy and reality in novels of contemporary life. What dissatisfies him about the Hauptmann, however, is that it is 'quite artless', 'a German fairy-tale'. Also, Hauptmann's social status, as 'a very great figure', works against him: 'I fancy in order to write really good prose you have got to be something of a pariah.' This is more than a restatement of Ford's mistrust of the moralizing Victorian Great:

Because humanity doesn't like you, you may very well conceive what Flaubert called une fière idée de l'homme. Indeed, Flaubert himself, who was the greatest of all prose writers, had to invent for himself the idea that he was something of a pariah—that all artists are regarded as pariahs. That put more power into his elbow. And indeed it is an immensely sustaining thought for anybody.[20]

He was realizing that he had himself been inventing just such a sustaining conception of himself as a pariah. It animates most of the rest of his writing, most visibly in the unpublished novels 'True Love & a G.C.M.' and 'Mr. Croyd', in *Thus to Revisit* and the later reminiscences, and in *The Marsden Case* and the figure of Tietjens in *Parade's End*.[21] In the same essay he even explains this dual attitude, whereby one can be sustained by one's own inventions, by nationality. 'The German writers adore truth, but cannot stomach it; the Latins have no philosophic respect for the quality, but they can't exist without it.' Here too, Ford is 'English-German'. His impressionism is founded on a philosophic disrespect for truth, without which it can't exist (because the authenticity of the impressions must be absolute, however fictional). Yet even his most Flaubertian novel, *The Good Soldier*, is driven by a quest for truth, whatever the cost; truth which none of the characters can stomach. Is fiction (to borrow Dowell's terms) 'slightly-deceitful' or 'too-truthful'? Or can we only stomach its 'true truth' because of its slight deceit?

Ford became worried that his writing as a cosmopolitan, a European expert, was dangerous. Readers might miss the ironies of his protean identifications when he wrote sentences like: 'I am writing for the moment as a good German.' Could you write *as* a good German while remaining a loyal Englishman? Masterman was able to assure him about his civil status, and took the opportunity to use his expertise. The government had put Masterman in charge of a secret department to counter German propaganda in America. He summoned a group of 'eminent authors' to Wellington House, where he ran the National Health Insurance Commission. At that time newly appointed cabinet ministers were expected to resign their seats in the House of Commons, and run for re-election before they could take up their posts. When Masterman did this in 1914, after being appointed chancellor of the Duchy of Lancaster, he narrowly lost his seat and thus had to resign from the government in February 1915. Arnold Bennett went to the Wellington House meeting on 2 September 1914, as did Hardy, Wells, Galsworthy, Chesterton, J. M. Barrie, Hall Caine, Sir Arthur Conan Doyle, Maurice Hewlett, John Masefield, Israel Zangwill, and Gilbert Murray among others. Kipling and Arthur Quiller Couch couldn't attend, but sent messages of support. Surprisingly, given his friendship with Masterman, Ford was not there, though he was soon writing for 'Wellington House', as the War Propaganda Bureau's operations became known.[22] That month Ford began the first of his two propaganda books, *When Blood is Their Argument: An Analysis of Prussian Culture*. 'For how can they charitably dispose of anything, when blood is their argument?' (*Henry V*, IV. i.). Are 'they' the bloodthirsty Germans, or all the warring nations? It depends who 'one' is. Ford's arguments are unusually charitable, for propaganda, crediting Southern Germany with its cultural splendour, but lamenting its disappearance with the triumph of Prussian *Kultur*, which he characterizes as materialist, egoistic, philological, and militarist. The book is levelled against 'the professorial hypocrisy of impersonalism', 'the refuge of an empty and non-constructive mind that is afraid of setting down its own conclusions as its own conclusions' (p. xi). In analysing the Prussian mentality, Ford was clarifying and articulating a philosophy of education which informs all his discursive prose, whether propagandistic, historical, critical, or autobiographical:

the purpose of education in any sensible scheme of the universe is not to turn our sons into efficient creatures, grabbing money from some other unfortunate or perfecting already too perfect machines. That is the province of instruction. And Prussia is the enemy because Prussia taught the world, for the first time, to value instruction more highly than the evolution in the young of a sense of values, the mysteries, and the joys of life. (p. 294)

We are in a new phase when education is in danger of becoming valued less than instruction (or 'training'); when creativity and thought are becoming subservient to efficiency and wealth. Ford's prose is a timely reminder of the value—the necessity—of a liberal, humane education. The propaganda books exemplify his thesis, managing to be learned and detailed, yet principledly personal. To read them, as with all his prose, is to come into contact with a personality—impassioned and opinionated, but stimulating thought and provoking scepticism rather than seeking to repress by indoctrination. He charts German 'Civil and Financial History' up to 1880, then gives some illustrative sketches of individual German personalities: Frau Rath (a 'fierce and energetic' lady with whom he had discussed literature while staying in Germany), Bismarck, Wagner, and Nietzsche. The third part offers 'a condemnation of German materialism and Prussian education, and an exposure of the Prussian government's perversion of the Goethe myth'.[23]

He had a new secretary now to help with this extra work. Sections of Part III of *The Good Soldier* had been dictated to H.D.—Hilda Doolittle, the Imagist poet, who had taken over after Brigit Patmore had had to return to her husband. Ford later re-created the scene:

worst of all, there is the almost irresistible temptation to write at the secretary [. . .] You have the silent back or the emotionless face of the doomful creature presented to you. You dictate for a little while and nothing happens. And nothing and nothing. It gets to be like being in the presence of a marble block. At last you say: 'Damn it all, I *will* make that creature smile. Or have a tear in its eye!' Then you are lost. . . . When I was dictating the most tragic portion of my most tragic book to an American poetess she fainted several times. One morning she fainted three times. So I had to call in her husband to finish the last pages of the book. He did not faint. But he has never forgiven me.[24]

The story about the dictation's effect could stand as an allegory for the intimate effect Ford wants his fiction to have on its readers. The attitude of the husband suggests an element of sexuality, of seductiveness, in the act of speaking (as Ashburnham's words create the passion out of nothings as they go along). H.D.'s husband was Richard Aldington, who was now taking Ford's dictation. Despite Aldington's unflattering portrait of Ford as Herr Shobbe in *Death of a Hero* in 1929, and a dismissive review of *No More Parades*, he wrote about Ford with a respect and an affection that suggested he had forgiven him: 'I wouldn't have missed him for anything.' In fact, even the portrait of Shobbe shows an intelligent understanding of Ford's character, and why it provoked people:

Shobbe was an excellent example of the artist's amazing selfishness and vanity. After the comfort of his own person he really cared for nothing but his prose style and literary reputation. He was also an amazing and very amusing liar—a sort of literary Falstaff. As for his affairs with women—my God! Yet, after all, were they really so lurid? Probably they were grossly exaggerated because Shobbe had talent, and everybody was jealous of it . . .

But his familiarity with Ford had by late 1914 bred the contemptuous illusion that he had no more illusions about him:

I still think him a good critic—when not blinded by prejudice or *interest*—a good poet in a few of his poems—and a very bad novelist. But he is incurable (*sic*) vain and self-satisfied. He repeatedly tells me that he is 'the only poet there has been during the last three hundred years' and 'the greatest intellect in England'! And about a fortnight ago he said that he was after all the only real Imagiste!

'We worked every morning', recalled Aldington:

I took down from his dictation in long hand. Ford claimed that writer's cramp made it impossible for him to write himself, and he certainly wrote a detestable hand. But

I think he enjoyed dictation. He was a great worker. He did a long literary article every week and at the same time was engaged on a novel, *The Good Soldier*, and his propaganda book [. . .] During the months I worked with him I believe he turned out 6000 to 8000 words a week. Which didn't prevent his writing poetry. I well remember his reading us the first draft of his best poem, *On Heaven*, and later on, the poem about Antwerp and some shorter poems inspired by the delicate intense work of H. D.[25]

Antwerp was written after the city surrendered to the Germans on 9 October. Ford was moved by the pathos of the Belgian refugees he saw at Charing Cross and by the altruism of the Belgian dead, wondering 'how could they do it?', and finding in 'that clutter of sodden corpses' 'a strange new beauty' (perhaps suggesting to Yeats the refrain from 'Easter 1916', 'A terrible beauty is born'). He also described feeling for them what he called 'the most real, historic emotion of my whole life' (though characteristically he felt it obliquely, while watching a play that was about Belgium but not about the war). T. S. Eliot called *Antwerp* 'the only good poem I have met with on the subject of the war'.[26]

To raise money for Belgian refugees, Ford gave a reading of 'On Heaven' and *Antwerp* to a full room at Harold Monro's Poetry Bookshop on 15 December. Monro, observed one of the audience, 'was very obsequious to him [. . .] he plainly regarded the visit as a high favour; and Hueffer, one felt, took unto himself the air of a wise uncle encouraging the efforts of his green and inexperienced nephew'. When he read 'On Heaven': 'He went through it in a hurried panting manner, starting each tirade high in the voice, pouncing heavily on the irregular and unexpected rimes, and finishing fairly low down. After he had done this a few times, he asked, as if in parenthesis, if he were not reading too fast. He was answered he was not (by Monro from the stairhead).'[27]

Aldington also remembered Ford doing impressions of Hunt's telephone manner: 'Yes, this is Violet Hunt. Who is it speaking? Oh, Lady de Lammermoor—how *are* you? What! What? I said you had a baby before you were married? Oh, nonsense, I said that about Lady Bridlington.' His relish for caricature and parody was a sign that the writing of *The Good Soldier* had pulled him through the period of neurasthenia brought on by his marital difficulties. In November Ford published a story called 'The Scaremonger', satirizing Hunt's old friend and Selsey neighbour Edward Heron Allen, and his paranoia about submarine invasions. 'Allen *did* go frightening girls about a German invasion', said Hunt. But it was characteristically provocative, not least because Allen rented The Knap cottage to Hunt. He had shown 'signs of amorousness' towards her in 1907, and, as he became violently anti-German, increasingly resented her affair with Ford. Allen was furious about the story, and wrote to Hunt: 'I did not believe that even a German Journalist would sit at one's table, make one's house a sort of Inn for the entertainment of his friends and use one's time money & brains in his service for years & then perpetrate an outrage of the kind.' He was a successful lawyer, with government contacts (having previously been Edward Fairfield's secretary at the Colonial Office). Ford suspected that it was at Allen's suggestion that, on 2

January 1915, he was ordered by the chief constable of West Sussex to leave the county. He had provoked the attack—whether consciously or unconsciously; but it vindicated his earlier anxiety about his civic status. The order was withdrawn four days later. But Ford had none the less returned to South Lodge, and was still anxious enough to consult Masterman about the withdrawal: 'Does that strike you as being sufficient to frank me through the perils of Selsey, or is the junior subaltern of the Hants Cyclists' Corps at liberty to arrest me at any moment? We are going down to Selsey to-morrow in any case, till Tuesday when there will be Dinner and Auction as usual, supposing of course that the Hants Cyclists have not already shot me.'[28] Ford told Masterman he could not receive payment for *When Blood is Their Argument*. Lucy Masterman explained that 'in certain circles there was a kind of *chic* in a civilian refusal to benefit by the war'. In Ford's case it was a matter of scruple; of putting into practice the noble standards he had been preaching. Despite being hard up, he felt the book was 'so very largely a product of German hospitalities that it would be the very basest return to use those experiences as a means for making money'. But when Masterman encouraged him to write a second propaganda book answering the arguments of pacifists and pro-Germans, and dealing with the origins of the war, the same objection didn't apply. He felt 'as good as mad' thanks to the combined strain of overwork, and Hunt worrying him about his finances; and he asked Masterman if 'Wellington House' could pay him a salary of £15 or £20 per week. He probably didn't get it, but he did write the book.[29]

Between St. Dennis and St. George also takes its title from *Henry V*: 'Shall not thou and I, between St. Denis and St. George, compound a boy, half-French half-English, that shall go to Constantinople and take the Turk by the beard?' In *When Blood is Their Argument* Ford had written as the half-English, half-German his genealogy made him. In its sequel, he wrote as the half-English, half-French *writer* that he had made himself. The book is 'A Sketch of Three Civilisations' (Ford is more than just 'homo duplex'). It has been criticized for looseness. Ford himself worried, in a preface addressed to Lucy Masterman, that it might 'present the aspect of a number of essays thrown together' (p. v). It certainly isn't written in the *form* of the polemics it was opposing—works by writers like Shaw, Bertrand Russell, and H. N. Brailsford. Ford said he wanted to confront them 'with various facts and with various figures'. 'But I dislike denouncing my fellow-beings,' he explains, 'and it seemed to me only fair to present these gentlemen with my own constructive view of the state of Europe before the outbreak of the present war. Thus it has come about that the constructive part has overshadowed the controversial' (p. v). That is, the facts and figures are relegated to appendices, one criticizing 'apologists for Prussia', and the second taking issue with Shaw's *Common Sense about the War*. Rebecca West reviewed *Between St. Dennis and St. George*, saying: 'One is surprised when one reads this masterly appendix that an artist can make so fine a controversialist; but as one reads the book of which that is only the sting in the tail one wonders how any but an artist can ever be a controversialist.' Goldring thought it 'perhaps the finest exposition of the value and significance of French culture which has yet been written by an Englishman'.[30] Like Maupassant in 1870, Ford wanted to champion the French against the invading Prussians. But the body of the book, 'the constructive part', is that odd thing, a propaganda book directed not so much against particular propaganda, but against propaganda itself. In its form as well as its content it champions art over instruction, personality over statistics. Ford had already waged a long campaign against what he called propaganda in art, as he found it in the Victorians, or in Wells and Galsworthy; and he deploys the familiar argument here. Shaw, Russell, and the others, are 'intellectual fictionists' (p. 9):

The methods, in short, of this whole school of controversialists are those of the artist—and of the irresponsible artist at that. Just as the novelist of a certain school will make all landowners appear to be oppressive and unimaginative, or just as novelists of another school will make all Socialists appear in the guise of wife-beaters or usurers, or all Christians fornicators and dipsomaniacs, so these writers treat of secret diplomacy. (p. 18)

Ford wants to see what people really *are*, not what the argument requires them to be: 'I am attempting to reconstruct from my own consciousness the psychologies of the three Western Powers chiefly engaged in the present contest' (p. 29). The method he offers is impressionism, which is why the form of these books is so similar to that of his English Trilogy—personal impressions and anecdotes combined with generalizations into expressive patterns; and also why he uses the same image for the result:

In arriving at such impressions as these the writer or the observer makes use of a method that, in photography, used to be popular in the nineties of the last century. This was called making a composite photograph. Supposing that the photographer desired to get at a rendering of A Poet rather than of any one poet, he took upon the same plate photographs of profile portraits of Dante, Shakespeare, Milton, Burns, Goethe, Wordsworth, and Tennyson. The result was a queer, blurred image, but the result was none the less striking, and the individual arrived at by this composite process had an odd but quite strong individuality. (p. 80)

The aim is to describe 'truthfully and as carefully as possible the frame of mind of the average Englishman of July 1914', and the average Frenchman and German as well. Though it is a fundamentally novelistic approach—as L. L. Farrar says, 'he is a novelist creating three characters'—Ford intends it to be 'a method of controversy', and one which is superior to the standard exploitation of national-character stereotypes. The composite-photograph image helps to explain the advantages: 'There are, of course, extremes, but the resultant is the mean.' In composite photography you can see the extremes *in* the picture, whereas the stereotype selects out only the mean. It is an image for how art can comprehend opposing sides (rather as the novelist compounds characters from contrasting individuals).

The method here is the same for all Ford's history writing, from his early book on the Cinque Ports to his later study of Provence, or the composite photograph of world civilization that gives the queer, blurred, but none the less striking image of the 'Great Trade Route'. The idiosyncrasies of these books, their inclusion of autobiographical sketches within their composite pictures, has often caused them to be treated cavalierly, dismissed as too subjective and unreliable. Ford has not been given credit for the way his approach to history anticipated one of the major movements of historiography this century, the study of *mentalités* represented by the French school associated with the journal *Annales*, founded in 1929. Ford is not attempting their analytic rigour; as always his primary aim is an imaginative writer's—to make you *see*. But he was ahead of his time in seeing the need to move beyond the wartime obsession with military and diplomatic history, and to understand such things in their social and psychological contexts.

Early in March 1915 'Jane' Wells drove Ford and Hunt down to visit Lawrence, who had been lent the poet Alice Meynell's house at Greatham in Sussex. Ford said Masterman was concerned that Lawrence was being persecuted for being a 'pro-German', so asked Ford to go and 'see what could be done for him'. It is no easier than usual to be sure about what really happened, since the visit was written about by Ford and Hunt, and also by Lawrence's wife Frieda, born Baroness von Richthofen (and cousin to the 'Red Baron', Manfred von Richthofen). She gave at least four different versions of her side of the story, none of which quite tallies with Ford's or Hunt's. The visit probably took place on 6 or 7 March 1915, since both Hunt and Frieda agree that Lawrence was away visiting Bertrand Russell in Cambridge. But in 1936 Ford thought this was the last time he had seen Lawrence, though he says he wasn't able to talk to him. What undeniably did happen was that Frieda got into a heated row with one of the visitors. It was either with Catherine Wells or with Hunt, and probably about the fate of Belgium. Violet said that Frieda, discussing Ford's *Antwerp* (the pamphlet of which, illustrated by Wyndham Lewis, had appeared in January), had said: 'Dirty Belgians! Who cares for them!' Ford simply said they 'fell into a discussion as to the merits of the Belgians', but that as Frieda made 'unfavourable remarks as to the uniform' he said he was wearing, he had to 'retire to an outhouse and await the close of the discussion', because he was supposed to be reporting back to Masterman and didn't want to have to make matters worse for the Lawrences— probably also because it was the sort of scene he hated. Frieda denied that there was an outhouse, but her versions don't tally with each other or with Violet's, which agrees that Ford left the room (which she says he did with Catherine Wells). Violet said Frieda was arguing with her. Ford thought the argument was between Frieda and Catherine—as perhaps the part he saw was, before he and Catherine left, after which Frieda and Violet may have taken up the argument. When his reminiscence of the episode was published in *The American Mercury* in 1936, Frieda wrote to the editor insisting that Lawrence wasn't there at the time of their visit; that Ford had not been in uniform; and that Violet had denied Ford was German, but had claimed 'Russian descent' for him. Though in 1925 she had said to Lawrence, while they were being interviewed by Kyle Crichton: 'Do you remember the time he came with Garnett at the first of the war and Mrs. Wells was there? [. . .] I mentioned something about Germany and he puffed up right away and started talking about his Dutch relatives.' *The American Mercury* didn't publish her letter, nor Ford's splendid reply, balancing indignation and irony:

I can't help it if I am descended from barons. I am. So is Mrs. Lawrence. My barons were, however, not Rhinelanders but Ruthenian Galicians. I can't believe that Miss Hunt whom Mrs. Lawrence doesn't like said 'Russian descent.' I have been called in my time French, English, German, Polish, Welsh, Scotch, and Galician Ruthenian, and more often than anything, American, but never, no never, Russian. Mrs. Lawrence is incorrect in saying that I prefer to be an Englishman. That also I could not help. I was born in England. One does not preside at the destiny of one's birth.[31]

However, she was probably right about Lawrence's absence. Ford's prose does an odd double-take over the question, which indicates a doubt that his memory might be playing him false. Talking of the day Lawrence brought him part of the manuscript of *The Trespasser*, he says: 'I never saw him again . . . to talk to'; and then later explains: 'But I was not talking without the book when I said that I never saw him again to talk to. The Gods saw otherwise.' The hint of an oath of accuracy to his impressions should remind us that these need not be factually true, and that he too may have seen 'otherwise'. He offers a vision of his 'last image' of Lawrence during the argument at Greatham, 'standing there, a little impotent, his hands hanging at his side, as if he were present at a dog fight [. . .] He was smiling slightly, his head slightly bent. But his *panache*, his plume of hair with the sunlight always in it—and his red beard—were as disturbingly bright as ever.' It's a wonderfully evocative sketch of Lawrence's quizzical observant personality, and that slight smile suggests that Ford has the image as much from the literary personality manifesting itself in Lawrence's work as from an actual sight of him. The argument between the women disturbed him enough for him to need to leave the room; by his own account, he wouldn't have been there long enough to see much of Lawrence; and his disturbance and embarrassment probably confused his later memory about whether Lawrence was there or not.

In his 1990 biography of Lawrence, Jeffrey Meyers makes an astounding claim that Ford provided a 'secret, semi-official report on the Lawrences' opposition to the war and supposedly suspicious behavior in Greatham'; and he asserts that, together with Lawrence's anti-war story 'England, My England', and his association with Bertrand Russell's pacifist activities, Ford's alleged report contributed to the suppression of *The Rainbow* in 1915 and Lawrence's expulsion from Cornwall in 1917. The gravity of Meyers's charge, which would imply a kind of treachery on Ford's part that he was particularly outspoken against, demands investigation. But there is no hard evidence that Ford did any such thing. The accusation is based on a letter in which an earlier biographer of Lawrence, Harry Moore, told Richard Aldington in 1960 that David Garnett 'believes that Ford warned the government in 1915 that the Lawrences were pro-German, and that all their troubles during the rest of the war stemmed from Ford's report'. David Garnett was very liberal with unsubstantiated malicious gossip about Ford. Himself a notable fantasist, he was perfectly capable of reimagining hearsay and retailing it as fact, as when he garbled the episode of Ford's break with Conrad and Marwood, saying unscrupulously that Ford made love to Marwood's wife, rather than Marwood to Ford's wife. Aldington relayed the slur to Lawrence Durrell, calling Ford a liar as he did so. Meyers takes this, and another letter (in which Aldington says 'I'd hate to think that fat Fordie had been so goddam mean as to put in an unfavourable official report on the civisme of Lorenzo and Frieda. If he did, what a bastard') as 'Aldington's confirmation of Garnett's testimony'. This is no more 'confirmation' than Garnett's opinion is 'testimony'. Meyers claims Ford 'invented evidence ("Dirty Belgians!") to incriminate Lawrence by association with Frieda'. If his next sentence is true, claiming that Frieda had been suspected by the locals of flashing signals to zeppelins, then no report from Ford would have been needed for the Lawrences to have been put under surveillance. The phrase 'Dirty Belgians!' was not put into Frieda's mouth by Ford, but by Hunt years after Ford had left her; so it is scandalous that it should be offered as evidence that Ford 'invented evidence'. Terms like 'testimony', 'confirmation', and 'evidence', try to give the illusion of the biographer as impartial judge. But when, on this flimsy basis, Meyers writes as if his wild allegation was fact, saying that later 'Ford justified his treachery by claiming he had gone to Greatham to help Lawrence instead of to betray him', it is the biographer who is inventing the evidence (the 'secret, semi-official report'), and being opportunistically and cavalierly indifferent to the obligation to find proof before libelling the dead. But then the distinction between factual and invented evidence cannot matter much to someone who can quote, as examples of Ford's conversation, the speeches from Aldington's novel, *Death of a Hero*, by the Fordian character Shobbe. *The Rainbow* was suppressed on the grounds of obscenity, not Lawrence's anti-war feelings. And—as Meyers even says—his real persecution didn't begin until 1917. If there had been any connection to be made between either of these, and Ford's visit to Greatham, surely it would have been made by the Lawrences—neither of whom ever accused Ford of betraying them; or by Aldington, who was working with Ford at the time, and rowed with him, but to whom the idea didn't occur until he heard of Garnett's opinion.[32]

27

1915–1916: ARMY

One is never glad that someone is alive, one is only afraid that they may die, since life in one's companions seems to be what one has the right to expect. And one thinks suddenly that anyone may be dead at a distance. Anyone. . . . Anyone in the created world. Oh, God. . . .

(Ford, 'In Memoriam. Helen George', *New Weekly*, 2 May 1914)

The imaginative artist like every other proper man owes a twofold duty—to his art, his craft, his vocation, and then to his State.

(Ford, 'Hands Off the Arts', *American Mercury*, April 1935)

Ford's propaganda work kept him busy through the first half of 1915. At the end of July he enlisted in the army—a brave decision for a not particularly fit 41-year-old, who could easily have had a safe war by arguing that his propaganda would be more valuable to the war effort than his military service. Yet he clearly felt, like the romantic George Heimann, that propaganda work wasn't enough: 'It had for him to be enlistment or nothing.' He wrote at once to Lucy Masterman: 'You may like to know that I went round to the W[ar] O[ffice] after seeing you and got thrown into a commission in under a minute—the quickest process I have ever known [. . .] I can assure you, for what it is worth, that it is as if the peace of God had descended on me—that sounds absurd—but there it is! Man is a curious animal.'[1]

That feeling of peace was partly due to feeling he had fulfilled a social obligation. He had been arguing that men have duties, not rights; now he was doing his duty, as he explained to his mother: 'Dear M[rs] H; 'You ask me why I have gone into the army: Simply because I cannot imagine taking any other course. If one has enjoyed the privileges of the ruling classes of a country all one's life, there seems to be no alternative to fighting for that country if necessary. And indeed I have never felt such an entire peace of mind as I have felt since I wore the King's uniform.'[2] That peace of mind owed something to the way enlistment would silence those who misconstrued his writing as pro-German. (Misconstruction of his motives always upset Ford, particularly since he felt he should not defend himself in public.) Patriotism was another motive; but it was not the patriotism of chauvinistic hysteria, or of the lust for glory. Wyndham Lewis saw Ford's cynical percipience about that:

there were the tales of how a certain famous artist, of military age and militant bearing, would sit in the Café Royal and addressing an admiring group back from the Front, would exclaim: '*We* are the civilization for which you are fighting!'

But Ford Madox Hueffer looked at me with his watery-wise old elephant eyes—a little too crystal-gazing and claptrap, but he knew his stuff—and instructed me upon the very temporary nature of this hysteria. I was too credulous! I *believe* that he tipped me the wink. He was imparting to me I believe a counsel of commonsense.

'When this war's over,' he said, 'nobody is going to worry, six months afterwards, what you did or didn't do in the course of it. One month after it's ended, it will be forgotten. Everybody will want to forget it—it will be bad form to mention it. Within a year disbanded "heroes" will be selling matches in the gutter. No one likes the ex-soldier—if you've lost a leg, more fool you!'

'Do you think that?' I said, for he almost made my leg feel sorry for itself.

'Of course,' he answered. 'It's always been the same. After all the wars that's what's happened.'

This worldly forecast was verified to the letter.[3]

Nevertheless, Ford was intensely patriotic, and expressed his feelings in the prevalent Georgian mode which identified 'England' with the English landscape. Alan Judd says the poem Ford wrote between Christmas 1917 and New Year's Day 1918, 'Footsloggers', 'gives as good an account of his and others' motivation as anything else written':

> But, in the 1.10 train,
> Running between the green and the grain,
> Something like the peace of God
> Descended over the hum and the drone
> Of the wheels and the wine and the buzz of the talk,
> And one thought:
> 'In two days' time we enter the Unknown,
> And this is what we die for!'
> And thro' the square
> Of glass
> At my elbow, as limpid as air,
> I watched our England pass . . .
> The great downs moving slowly,
> Far away,
> The farmsteads quiet and lowly,
> Passing away;
> The fields newly mown
> With the swathes of hay,
> And the wheat just beginning to brown,
> Whirling away. . . .
> [. . . . . .]
> What is love of one's land?
>   Ah, we know very well
> It is something that sleeps for a year, for a day,
> For a month, something that keeps

Very hidden and quiet and still,
And then takes
The quiet heart like a wave,
The quiet brain like a spell,
The quiet will
Like a tornado, and that shakes
The whole being and soul . . .[4]

Travel becomes an impression of transience here. The dots after 'pass' intimate as much, as we realize when the suppressed idea is expressed later, in the line 'Passing away'.[5] Motion often stirs Ford's emotion. 'The great downs moving slowly' puns between the visual effect as the spectator moves through the landscape, and the emotional effect produced by the scene. 'Moving' becomes a crucial word in Ford's descriptions of the war, in which the massive and fraught movements of troops amidst an impassive landscape moves him to wonder and terror. Here the wonder comes from the slight suggestion that the human feelings expressed towards the land have humanized it: animated the great downs into a heaving breast, shaken by reciprocal emotions.

But there were other motivations. The army was also an escape—from financial anxiety, and from the strain of writing and getting scant recognition. He wrote: 'If not to-day, then tomorrow, I hope to be up and away to regions where I shall be precluded from uttering injunctions to find le mot juste.' Which 'regions'? The fields of Flanders, or the Elysian fields? One reason why Ford thought of the English fields as 'passing away' was that he felt he was about to die to achieve an honourable form of suicide, or at least escape. He was perhaps remembering this decision made in his forty-second year when he wrote later about the abdication of Edward VIII:

you have to remember that the King today is aged just 42 . . . and that is the dangerous age for men who have had overworked and repressed youths and desperately overworked and unbelievably repressed manhoods. Such a man comes one day to the conclusion that almost everything connected with careers, duties, routines, achievements, is a weariness . . . And irresistible impulse urges him, at whatever cost to shake off his chains; he will betake himself to the forests, the hillsides, the harsh seas . . . Or he will exclaim as so many have exclaimed: All for love or the world well lost. . . . And I do not know who can blame him.

He also wanted to escape from Hunt. She said he sprang his decision on her when he got back to Selsey, sheltering 'behind the presence of a third person', telling her in front of his secretary. If Ford minded that her 1913 novel, *The Celebrity's Daughter*, published just before the *Throne* case, based its plot on Elsie's restitution proceedings and his spell in prison, he isn't known to have complained. But *The House of Many Mirrors*, published in June 1915, had a much less sympathetic portrait of Ford as Alfy Pleydell. It was the story she had thought out while ill at Spa. Pleydell is a 'genius' (an architect in the novel) who needs

money to exercise his talent for collecting *objets d'art*, and marries Rosamond, a
wealthy widow years older than himself. His rich relatives disapprove of the match,
so when Rosamond is dying of cancer she tells Alfy she is going to have a child,
and persuades him to spend time with his uncle while she goes to Spa. The plan
works, and is Hunt's fantasy about how her self-sacrifice (in staying away while he
was at Giessen) saved Ford while she felt it was killing her. It would have been
hard for their acquaintances not to see Alfy, who 'could always talk to any woman,
however stupid', and who lives off his wife's income while being 'wickedly
interesting' to other women, and Rosamond, whom the *Outlook*'s reviewer (almost
certainly a friend) described as 'a devouringly vivid feminine personality obsessed
to the point of madness by its passion for a profoundly selfish male', as portraits
of Ford and the author. Two years later, in a Red Cross hospital where he was
feeling smashed by a shell-concussion, Ford told Hunt: 'You achieved Alfy of The
H[o]use of Many Mirrors whilst I still shared your bed and board—an[d] I often
think it was really Alfy who smashed me socially.' Joining the army was his way
of asserting economic independence. But Hunt continued to vent her feelings about
him in print. In a review of Pinero's *The Big Drum* she wrote of how 'heroics' came
more easily to artists in wartime, in a transparent allusion to the way Ford had put
himself into the hands of the army instead of his partner: 'The author has only to
throw down his pen, shoulder a rifle, and putting himself into the hands of his
colonel instead of his publisher, address himself to the Front.' This piece also
contained some bitter observations on the artistic nature: 'What is the matter with
authors that they cannot easily be human?' she asked, in a way which would again
have been taken by their acquaintances to be her verdict on Ford, and answered:
'it is the careful recording machine within that is antipathetic to the outsider.' 'In
a man this waiting, watching power of fruitful observation suggests to his fellow
men and women a selfish opportunism, a cynical habit, cruelty even.' And she used
one of Ford's favourite biblical quotations to describe such artistic 'indifference':
'His is presumably the peace that passeth understanding.' It is a sympathetic
account of how an artist's psychology can be misrepresented by those who don't
understand the merciless obsession of art; and she was writing as much of herself
as of Ford. But his horror of having his private life made public would have made
such candour seem threatening. So too would have been the passage which alludes
to his neurasthenic period before the writing of *The Good Soldier*, and offers a
brilliant description of Ford's ability to create, and make creative use of, the
suffering he desired:

I have known persons who, having courageously invited and purveyed for themselves
what is known as a 'bad time,' who having conscientiously weltered in painful but
picturesque circumstances for a year or more, have emerged from these circumstances
safe and sound, with the light of fresh battle shining in their eye and the tale of their
vital struggle safely encysted for all time between two boards of a novel. But the public
feels unable to sentimentalise over a mentality whose throes have been so ably set forth
by the one that endured them.

What happened to Ford in the war was what happens in his best novels: what he 'escaped' to shocked him into a more direct perception of what it was he was trying to escape from. In the Ypres salient he wrote: 'I used to think that being out in France would be like being in a magic ring that would cut me off from all private troubles'; 'but', he added, with the wisdom of grim experience: 'nothing is further from the truth'.[6]

Ford himself gave another explanation for his decision, when he was recalling Gaudier-Brzeska: 'Gaudier will remain for me something supernatural. He was for me a "message" at a difficult time of life. His death and the death at the same time of another boy—but quite a commonplace, nice boy—made a rather doubtful way quite plain to me.'[7] It was probably in the second number of *Blast* (which included Ford's poem 'The Old Houses of Flanders') that he read of Gaudier's death: '*Mort pour la patrie.*' 'All my life I have been very much influenced by a Chinese proverb,' writes Ford, 'to the effect that it would be hypocrisy to seek for the person of the Sacred Emperor in a low teahouse. It is a bad proverb, because it is so wise and so enervating. It has "ruined my career".' As he explains, it enshrines a stoic attitude: a shrugging-off of the world's disappointments and betrayals: 'It meant that it would be hypocrisy to expect a taste for the finer letters in a large public; discernment in critics; honesty in aesthetes or literati; public spirit in lawgivers; accuracy in pundits; gratitude in those one has saved from beggary, and so on.' Lewis noted Ford's resigned cynicism about Gaudier's death: 'It was absurd, Ford agreed. But there it was, he seemed to think. He seemed to think *fate* was absurd.' Ford reads his impressions of Gaudier dually in terms of the proverb. First, in a general sense, he is asking 'what do you expect?'—of course the world will destroy one of its most promising artistic geniuses! Lewis goes on to say—unjustly: 'I am not sure he did not think Gaudier was absurd.' Ford did not. For, secondly, he takes Gaudier as something of a supernatural manifestation precisely because he is the exception to the wise proverb. At Amy Lowell's *Imagiste* dinner in 'an underground restaurant', when Ford had first become aware of Gaudier, he was so impressed by the sculptor's aloofness—'It was like the appearance of Apollo at a creditors' meeting. It was supernatural'— it seemed as if he had found a Sacred Emperor in a low tea-shop. 'Alas, when it was too late, I had learned that, to this low tea-shop that the world is, from time to time the Sacred Emperor may pay visits.' Gaudier is another of Ford's 'nice people': 'he seemed so entirely inspired by inward visions [. . .] he spoke as if his eyes were fixed on a point within himself; and yet, with such humor and such good-humor—as if he found the whole thing so comic!' Ford's own eyes are fixed on a point within himself as he writes these words, which are also the best description of his own speciality of visionary irony. Not only was the appearance of the visionary Gaudier *like* a visionary apparition; it *gave* Ford visions, as he read of the sculptor's death, and then again as he later recalled the effect of that reading.[8]

Reading of Gaudier's death, the French phrase probably adding to his feeling of patriotism and pathos, Ford said he 'began to want to kill certain people'. 'I still do—for the sake of Gaudier and those few who are like him.' He had identified Prussia with the commercialism which threatened to swamp art with journalism and kitsch. Fighting in the war was his only means left to express his rage at a largely indifferent public, and against hostile critics and publishers:

For the effect of reading that announcement was to make me remember with extraordinary vividness a whole crowd of the outlines of pieces of marble, of drawings, of tense and delicate lines [. . .] He seemed, at last, to be an extraordinarily real figure—as real as one of the other sculptor's [Epstein's] brutal chunks of granite. Only, because of the crowd one hadn't seen him—the crowd of blackmailers, sneak-thieves, suborners, pimps, reviewers, and the commonplace and the indifferent—the Huns of London. Well, it became—and it still remains! one's duty to try to kill them.

Ford had always said that humanity for him divided into artists and 'the stuff to fill graveyards'. His notorious unhappiness at this time had driven him to put his precept into practice. Though his feelings about the 'commonplace, nice boy'—presumably the 'Teddy Jewell' mentioned earlier, again with Gaudier, as another casualty, though nothing else is known of him—show, if any proof were needed, that he didn't only care about the lives of artists. By 1929, when he finally published *No Enemy*, he felt uncomfortable enough with the paranoid tone to insert a distancing footnote after the phrase 'crowd of blackmailers', explaining that 'Gringoire is too fond of this word', and means by it anyone who dislikes the works he likes. Yet he let the passage stand as an impression of his state of mind when reading of Gaudier's death. Though it sounds callous and bloodthirsty—more like Lewis or Hemingway than like Ford's usual generous tolerance—we should remember that it *is* only an impression. Not long after he had enlisted, he wrote to his mother: 'I don't *relish* the idea of fighting, tho' I hope to behave all right if it comes to that.'[9] It is also characteristic of him that even in the context of such an outburst he can write delicately about art: he is interested in how a piece of prose produced a response, 'the effect of reading that announcement'. The prose produces a vision of Gaudier's art and of his person. The example of Gaudier's patriotism stirred Ford's, and made the 'doubtful way' of what he should do in the war quite plain to him: he should follow Gaudier's example—an ambiguous example, of course, since any desire to avenge his friend's death is offset by his desire to make the same sacrifice: to die for Gaudier's sake, as much as to kill for it.

The book Ford published with Hunt on 18 November 1915, *Zeppelin Nights*, ends with a discussion amongst the literary group who have been gathering, *Decameron*-style, to hear the latest historical vignettes by 'Serapion Hunter', a fictionalized Ford having an affair with 'Candour', a non-shrinking Violet. The stories are all Ford's, mostly written for his 1908 and 1913 series in the *Daily News* and the *Outlook*. Hunt's contribution is usually thought to be the linking commentary, given that the book was being prepared while Ford was in the army and too busy to write; though he spent some of his leaves at Selsey. The project was perhaps their way of reaffirming their union publicly just as Hunt must have been fearing she was going to lose Ford. The concluding conversation seems to capture his voice, and his preoccupations at the time, better than Hunt normally manages elsewhere. It is probable that Ford was at least collaborating:

'I don't know,' the gentleman who had originally asked where we all stood, said. 'I sometimes think that, if one has too much power to resist great waves of popular emotion, one cannot be much of a poet—much of a writer at all [. . .] Poetry, in the end, is the voicing of emotions of humanity, and, if the emotion embraces enough of us, it has got to be voiced or the art is wronged. So it is with one. The emotion goes on. It is cried in the streets; it calls to you from the walls [. . .] it gets hold of your heart; it writes itself for you with those moving fingers'—and the speaker pointed to the searchlights—'with those. And then—when you're sure; when you can't but be sure—you, if you're any sort of a poet, do something. You get naturalised on the side you adhere to [. . .] you . . . you . . . enlist . . . you . . .'
'No . . . no . . . no!' Candour called out. 'It isn't right. Serapion is too good. The country needs his writings. Isn't he a great artist? Do you want to extinguish that power of words by using it to stop a bullet? . . .'
Serapion looked at her with that superior air, that air of masterfulness that made us all wonder how she could do anything but detest the fellow . . .
'My dear,' he said heavily, 'no man ever knows whether he is an artist or no—no artist who is ever worth his salt. What is there to show me that I'm an artist? Popular support? I don't get it. My inner convictions? I have not got them; or I haven't got them half as much as the worst writer in the halfpenny press or the last literary knight. And our amiable friends here? If you asked them they'd say that I was a very valuable person, too good for cannon fodder. But they would not believe it, because every one of them thinks that he alone is good enough to be the exception. Then here I stand. If I had the conviction, I might stand out. Or no, I could not. For that would be an argument for every man to stand out. There is no man—no shoeblack, no baker who does not feel the conviction that he has an intimate and precious gift that should exempt him from the embraces of death. And the pressure of which our friend and master has spoken is too strong. It has spoken to me from the streets; it has delivered its messages from the walls [. . .] Damn it all, haven't I been for forty years or so in the ruling classes of this country; haven't I enjoyed their fat privileges, and shan't I, then, pay the price?'[10]

The Masterman-like 'contemplative politician' teases Serapion, asking whether he isn't just saying this because he's 'going to spend six months in room 2981 at the War Office'—doing something like Ford's propaganda work, perhaps. 'Damn it all, we all of us wish that we could enlist', he says. The book ends with Candour crying out: 'Oh, don't you understand? [. . .] Serapion enlisted this morning. He put his age down at thirty-three and they jumped at him'; then she exits, crying. It is a powerful example of Ford's histrionic panache: Serapion's stiff upper lip prevents him boasting about his sacrifice, yet enables him to marshal all the arguments in its favour, and provoke all the scepticism and mockery of the other men, while holding back the trump card which reveals him at last to be the misunderstood altruist.

Ford wrote a bitter, wry letter to John Lane, which conveys both his torn wartime loyalties, and also his disappointment about the reception of the novel over which he said he 'sweated real drops of sweat and shed real drops of tears':

I should be obliged if you could pay me the fifty pounds that became due to me on the delivery of the ms. of the 'Saddest Story.' These are, I know, hard up times but I guess I am harder up than you as I have had to give up literature and offer myself for service to George Five; so shortly you may expect to see me pantingly popping cartridges into garrison guns directed against my uncles, cousins and aunts advancing in pickelhaubes. And presumably if the said uncles cousins and aunts penetrate behind said garrison guns they will suspend me on high. Whereas, though I daresay you deserve it quite as much, I do not believe they would hang you. So you will perceive the equity of my request.[11]

It was typical of Ford's luck that he should publish one of his two greatest fictions when what the public wanted was newsworthy books. Though *The Good Soldier* went into a second impression in 1915, it only earned Ford £67. 11s. 11d.[12]

Ford was 'true to his fantastic temperament', said one friend: 'this least Celtic of men' got a commission in a Welsh regiment. He was gazetted on 13 August 1915 as a second lieutenant in the Welch Regiment (Special Reserve). He had been eager to get into uniform, and had probably taken an introductory course at the Chelsea Barracks:

I was on parade again, being examined in drill, on the Guards' Square at Chelsea. And, since I was petrified with nervousness, having to do it before a half-dozen elderly gentlemen with red hatbands, I got my men about as hopelessly boxed as it is possible to do with the gentlemen privates of H.M. Coldstream Guards. Whilst I stood stiffly at attention one of the elderly red hatbands walked close behind my back and said distinctly in my ear, 'Did you say *The* Good *Soldier?*'[13]

He enjoyed wearing the uniform, and would wear it to civilian parties throughout the war.

On 30 July Ford changed his name by deed poll. He changed the middle name on his baptismal certificate, 'Hermann', to the 'Madox' he had been using since his twenties. It was an official gesture of allegiance to his British grandfather. As another gesture defying anyone who doubted his loyalty, he had his British nationality confirmed on 23 August.[14]

He wrote that he last saw Henry James on 14 August, accidentally, in St James's Park, and that James said to him: 'Tu vas te battre pour le sol sacré de Mme. de Stael!' and added, 'putting one hand on his chest and just bowing', that 'he loved and had loved France as he had never loved a woman!'[15]

Hunt asked close friends to South Lodge 'to bid him good-bye' on 16 August, before Ford left to report to Tenby, on Carmarthen Bay in Wales. Goldring found the evening 'a hectic one—Violet was always lavish with her drinks—but the departing guests did not take Ford with them, as seemed to be anticipated'. He stayed on for a last drink; her secretary said Ford was eventually thrown out, drunk, after a violent quarrel. Goldring was sure that 'this was probably the last time that they would entertain their friends as "Mr. and Mrs. Hueffer" '. In fact it wasn't, since Hunt asked Ford to attend her parties, as official host and husband, even after the war when he was living in Sussex with Stella Bowen, and, out of his feeling of responsibility for Violet's unenviable social position, he agreed. But they both must have known that their relationship was essentially doomed by 1915—which is partly how Ford could write with such chilling brilliance about the fictional marriages enacted by the Ashburnhams and Dowells.[16]

Ford remembered Conrad's old binoculars, and must have asked if he could take them out to France. Conrad replied that the pair in question had, 'in the process of time (and by some help from [his younger son] John's hands) dissolved into its primitive elements'. And he took up this instance of disintegration as an emblem of his latest depression—about the war (his elder son, Borys, was to enlist the following month); about his own sense of failing powers as he struggled with *The Shadow Line*, touched, perhaps, with a sense that Ford had just shown that his powers were at their height; about the wreckage of their shared past; and over what would survive of them:

You won't be surprised to hear that you have been much in my thoughts of late. It must have been an enormous change in your mental habits; but I know your wonderful intellectual adaptability and your letter, most welcome, is very much what I expected it to be.
Yes! *mon cher!* our world of 15 years ago is gone to pieces: what will come in its place, God knows, but I imagine doesn't care.
Still what I always said was the only immortal line in *Romance*: 'Excellency, a few goats,' survives,—esoteric, symbolic, profound and comic,—it survives.
Love from us all here.[17]

Life with the 3rd Battalion of the Welch Regiment at Tenby was 'just a matter of plainsailingly doing one's duty, without any responsibilities except to one's superiors & one's men', he wrote to his mother. That the responsibilities to both his superiors and his men seemed negligible shows how heavily his domestic responsibilities had been weighing upon him. 'Of course it is a pretty hard life,' he continued, 'but I am really enjoying every minute of it'—even the examinations which he found 'very tiring & exciting'. 'Here I am and hard at it—6 a.m. to 7 p.m. everyday, like any V form boy & about the same sort of stuff', he wrote to Masterman: 'Literature seems to have died out of a world that is mostly interesting from its contours. (A contour is an imaginary line etc.) But I am really quite happy except for an absolute lack of social life. I suppose you or Lucy don't know anyone hereabouts to whom you cd. give me an introduction?' It was the first time he had had a job—other than the *métier de chien* that he and Conrad agreed was writing. When Pound saw him on leave in London on 24 September he found him 'looking twenty years younger and enjoying his work'.[18]

Ford's brother Oliver also got his commission, in the East Surrey Regiment, that autumn. According to Pound he had had his expenses paid to America 'on the condition that he should not return to england', and while abroad had got himself mistaken for Ford once again. Pound thought him 'quite capable of taking advantage of the fact that he is occasionally taken for Ford', and advised Alice Corbin Henderson: 'No, Most emphatically, NO. "Ford" was NOT in America last winter, but if "Oliver" has robbed a bank, or borrowed money or committed a rape it may be as well to print a definite statement in the notes at the end of *Poetry*' denying that Ford was there, and saying: 'Mr O. M. Hueffer is likewise an author but the two men are by no means identical.'[19]

At the end of the year Ford was moved to Cardiff, where his battalion was stationed at the castle. 'I go down to Porthcawl every Sunday to play golf with an old major who is a soothing person', he told Lucy Masterman in February, and continued flirtatiously: 'I wish you w^d. come down there. Couldn't you? & we c^d. have a day or two together. Some of these places are *wonderfully* beautiful just now: if I ever wrote poems now they w^d. be full of Celtic twilight—with your beautiful hair to give them colour.'[20]

As in the literary world, it was *les jeunes* he felt most at ease with—the younger officers, to whom he was 'most kind and helpful, like an elder brother or senior boy at school'. As Alan Judd says, Ford as a junior subaltern (second lieutenant) was 'more than twice the age of the great majority of subalterns and older than most commanding officers'. They all liked him in the mess, one fellow officer recalled: 'The thing that struck me most perhaps, was the "softness" of his voice.' He was kept busy with paperwork, which left him feeling 'hopelessly stupid till bedtime'.[21] But he relished some of the absurdities of army life. One night one of the men brought a young woman named Violet Heyman into the 'tumble-down skating rink [. . .] laid out in stalls like a cattle market' where the men were quartered. She was 'chased round and round by sergeants, over the men's beds and the like', Ford explained to Lucy Masterman; and when they had caught her, she was handed over to the police. Ford had to write a memorandum to try to keep the affair (and his men) out of the civilian courts. Ford used to amuse his fellow officers and himself with pastiches of literary language—after the mess they would urge him: 'Speak like a book, H. . . . Do speak like a book for a minute or two', and he would perform with clichés like: 'After mature consideration I have arrived at the conclusion [. . .]'. He wrote the memorandum in his best solicitorese, and could even recall the gist of it twenty years later:

And moreover the charge against the defendant Violet Heyman—of '*being on enclosed premises the property of H.M. the King for the purpose of committing prostitution*' will not lie because she did not enter the premises *proprio motu* but at the instance of the prisoner Lance Corporal Plant of the 7th Welch Regt so that the offence of prostitution could not have taken place, the essence of prostitution being soliciting . . . which she had found unnecessary.

He was amused by the irony that his 'forcible document' was sent back by the garrison commander, as being illegible and illiterate, and Ford was told to rewrite it neatly, like a schoolboy. 'And so everybody strafes everybody else in this microcosm,' he wrote, '& without doubt discipline is maintained.'

Ford became the centre of another controversy in January 1916, when the *New Witness* published a virulent attack on him which, under the guise of reviewing *Zeppelin Nights*, commented that 'it is generally supposed that Mr. Hueffer is not exactly of pure European extraction', and insinuated that the book's exploration of fear proved him a coward. The reviewer, writing under the pseudonym 'J. K. Prothero', was Ada Elizabeth Jones, who later married the editor of the *New Witness*, Cecil Chesterton. J. M. Barrie wrote to defend Ford, pointing out that he was not a Jew but a Catholic, and that he had taken the far from cowardly step of enlisting. 'Prothero' replied with an astounding outburst, dismissing the 'facts' about Ford's age and army service as 'hardly being of European importance': 'I am content to be labelled "ignorant" concerning them, as I am of the "fact" that because a man adopts the Catholic religion he ceases to be a Jew. One might as reasonably say that if a black-a-moor adopts Calvanism [*sic*] he immediately turns white.' Such anti-Semitism and racism was more common then amongst the English upper-middle classes than it is now; what is remarkable about this squalid affair is the way Ford's German name, cosmopolitanism, his self-definition as rather un-English—an outsider—in his dedication to the arts, and perhaps his portrayal of Jewish characters (like Aaron Fleight) were enough to cause some people to attack him as Jewish. 'Prothero' also dragged *The Good Soldier* into the row, denigrating it as 'centring round a particularly brutal type of sensualist'. Ford's friend E. S. P. Haynes wrote to challenge this, wanting to record his conviction 'that *The Good Soldier* is one of the ten greatest novels so far published in the twentieth century'. After two more attacks on Ford, the editor declared the correspondence closed. But H. G. Wells wrote privately to G. K. Chesterton, the editor's brother:

This business of the Hueffer book in the *New Witness* makes me sick. Some disgusting little greaser named [Prothero] has been allowed to insult old F. M. H. in a series of letters which make me ashamed of my species. Hueffer has many faults no doubt, but first he's poor, secondly he's notoriously unhappy and in a most miserable position, thirdly he's a better writer than any of your little crowd and fourthly, instead of pleading his age and his fat and taking refuge from service in a greasy obesity as your brother has done, he is serving his country. His book [*The Good Soldier*] is a great book [. . .] The whole outbreak is so envious, so base, so cat-in-the-gutter-spitting-at-the-passer-by, that I will never let the *New Witness* into the house again.[22]

If the noise of the fracas reached Cardiff Castle, Ford didn't complain. He usually avoided entering controversies or justifying himself publicly, as he made clear to Wells, who was soon writing to him at Hunt's prompting. 'I am much touched by your letter,' Ford replied to him, 'tho' I do not really know what to make of it. I hadn't the least idea that there was any difference between Violet & myself—or at least anything to make her face the necessity of talking about it.' But one can hear between the lines his knowledge that there was a difference, and that it was by now irreparable: 'I, at any rate, haven't any grievance against her & want nothing better than to live with her the life of a peaceable regimental officer with a peaceable wife. Of course that is not very exciting for her & her enjoyment of life depends so much on excitement. But one's preoccupations can't, now, be what they were in the 90's—or even three or two years ago. That, I suppose, is the tragedy—.'[23]

Despite his adding that it is the tragedy of 'the whole of Europe', it is also the tragedy of individual passion: the fact that Ford no longer felt for her what he had 'three or two years ago'. When Hunt wrote to ask if she could stay with Rosamond, now a vicar's wife at Fingleton, near Barnard Castle, her niece explained that there had been 'a great deal of talk and objection' to the suggestion. 'The idea is that being a vicarage, in George's absence I should have no one whose doings the Church cannot sanction and that it might do him great harm.' Hunt added a note to Ford:

This is what you have brought on me, dear Ford, and you are happy in Cardiff and leaving me to bear it alone. It is this sort of thing all the time—and loneliness—and I wish now I was out of this world you have made for me, or that you'll say we made, so that we could live together. That's the joke! And this is the last straw, more than I can bear. Don't write to Rosamond on any account. You have done me enough harm already. V.

It's not clear whether she sent this to him. Goldring found a copy of Rosamond's letter, with Hunt's note appended, in a copy of *The Good Soldier*. He said that, like Lizzie Siddall (the subject of her last book, *The Wife of Rossetti*), she 'deliberately collected scraps of evidence about her own woes and planted them where she hoped they would be found'. Perhaps she hid the letters in which she told him what she really felt, fantasizing that Ford would only read them when she was dead (so that, like Alfy Pleydell, he would only then realize what she had suffered for him, and how nobly she had suppressed her own feelings).[24]

In March Ford was assuring her (via Wells) that 'there isn't anyone else (but I don't know what she has got into her always romantic head)'. She may have got his poem 'What the Orderly Dog Saw' into her head. When it was published in his 1918 volume *On Heaven and Poems Written on Active Service*, he dated it 'Cardiff Castle, 12/12/15'. It is a routine performance of Ford's *homo duplex* visionariness: 'The seven white peacocks against the castle wall' remind him of a courtly tapestry, which reminds him of his distant lover; he imagines how, when he goes in to do his battalion paperwork, he will still be envisioning her. Ford had begun writing poems again, and they were full of Celtic twilight. But they weren't addressed to Lucy Masterman. When this one was first published (in *Poetry* in March 1917) it was dedicated 'To Mrs Percy Jackson'—Hunt's friend, Eleanor Jackson. Since Hunt dedicated her 1916 novel, *Their Lives*, to Eleanor, it's unlikely that she suspected her of having an affair with Ford. There's no evidence that he did; not even any other evidence that he was thinking of her when he wrote the poem; only that he dedicated it to her some fifteen months later (while suffering from shell-shock), and also gave her the manuscript of one of his poems—probably this one. Even if he did write it for her, it may simply have been offered in the spirit of his compliment to Lucy Masterman about her hair. Or, as Alan Judd observes, 'he was quite capable of writing nostalgic pieces to an imaginary female presence'.[25]

However, two remarks in Hunt's 1917 diary suggest there might have been more to it. On 26 February she notes 'Eleanor Jackson to lunch at Kardomah Café': 'I was very sad. She was sad & preoccupied, trying to disillusion me about F telling me of all his inclinations to all my female friends (well favoured) attempted kissings & so on! She had to spend the afternoon at S Lodge to put me back in my *assiette* again. Ford is certainly a *crétin* of genius. Not one single gentleman's impulse, only savage, secret furtive animal ones.' The syntax is ambiguous: was Jackson disabusing Hunt of things Ford had been saying (but which by implication weren't true), or disabusing her *by* telling her of advances Ford had in fact been making? The latter seems more probable. Hunt's entry for 15 April suggests that Jackson had in fact been one of the female friends in question. A Mrs Tarbutt has rented The Knap cottage for 'Nell & Percy'. But 'Percy won't now let Nell come down—The Knap is contaminated for him by the tenancy of Ford. How maddening they are!' Again, this doesn't prove anything about 1915–16, only that Ford had at least provoked jealousy by 1917, when he was struggling to regain sanity after being shell-shocked.[26]

By the later spring or summer of 1916 Ford appears to have got someone else into *his* always romantic head. He was anxious to get out to France, and it was the second half of May before he was told to hold himself in readiness to go to the Front. He expected to be sent out in the middle of June, but had to wait another aggravating month. Hunt was told he had a girl in Wales called Miss Ross, and when Ford was recovering from shell-shock at Cap Martin he wrote her a love letter, which Hunt somehow managed to get hold of. Nothing is known of Miss Ross, except that according to Hunt she was 'a clerk at 25/- a week'. Ford appears not to have denied a liaison with her, though his replies to Hunt's accusations (which she recorded in her 1917 diary) are evasive: he claimed that 'if he wrote a love letter to Miss Ross it was in delirium & intended for Brigit with whom he is still infatuated, and who wrote to him at Cap Martin'. Hunt then accused him of using Brigit Patmore to cover his retreat 'from the flirtation with a second rate garrison hack like Miss Ross', adding: 'It sounded better—an undying passion for a married woman with 2 boys & half her inside cut away.' Ford, who never believed in kissing and telling, simply said: 'My dear, you're too clever by half, that's the matter with you', not specifying whether she was too clever because she had discovered the truth, or because she hadn't. He later denied having written the letter to Miss Ross at all, even though Hunt claimed she had it. But he didn't deny the flirtation; and two poems he wrote only ten days before leaving for the Front may well confirm it. 'The Silver Music' describes a visit to the Wye near Tintern, and begins: 'In Chepstow stands a castle; | My love and I went there.' The second, 'After the War', describes the road from Cardiff to Penarth, 'With, at its end, a pleasant hearth', and a 'she who sits beside the hearth'. Miss Ross lived with a 'Mrs Braine of Cardiff' (and as

Penarth is adjacent to Cardiff, she could well have lived on the road between them). The poem suggests nothing more erotic than Ford's ideal of intimate, sentimental communication. Characteristically, he imagines himself into the future, when the two will be able to reminisce, and 'Talk of these days as memories'. A third poem, 'Claire de Lune', written from 'Nieppe, near Plugstreet, 17/9/16', asks:

> Do you remember, my dear,
> Long ago, on the cliffs, in the moonlight,
> Looking over to Flatholme
> We sat. . . . Long ago! . . .
> And the things that you told me . . .
> Little things in the clear of the moon,
> The little, sad things of a life. . . .
> We shall do it again
> Full surely,
> Sitting still, looking over at Flatholme.

Flat Holm is a small island in the Bristol Channel, visible from the cliffs at Penarth.[27]

'After the War' was one of a group of poems Ford said were written 'in moments of leisure in the O[rderly]. R[oom]. of No. 1 Garrison Coy., Welch Regiment. These were poems written to *bouts rhimés*', he explained, 'supplied to me by my friend and old O.C. Coy [Officer Commanding Company] H. C. James. When in a minute or two I had filled in the lines in English, in a few seconds he would supply the Latin version. Of course they are rough products: they were written whilst attending to the needs of 890 returned Expeditionary Force men.' The 'Memorandum' reproduced along with the poems in an Appendix to *On Heaven* explains how the game was constructed as a military joke. Captain James listed the rhyme-words as if they were privates requiring disciplinary action ('49522 Pte. Eyes 49642 Pte. Skies', and so on). The date is given as 3 July 1916, two days after the bloodiest battle in English military history. If they had any sense then of the scale of the Battle of the Somme, and yet could divert themselves so light-heartedly, it was perhaps because they knew they would themselves soon be fighting on the Somme. One could read it as a mad denial of war's insanity, or as a typically Fordian fascination with how expressive a stiff-upper-lip expressionlessness could be. Readers of *Parade's End* will recognize how, after that experience, Ford was to re-imagine the inventing of these 'rough products' in the coruscatingly produced, surreally insane scene in *No More Parades* in which Tietjens tries to distract the enervated Captain McKechnie and himself with *bouts rimés* just after a bombardment, and McKechnie offers to turn his sonnets into Latin hexameters in three minutes.[28]

The nerve-wracking period of waiting continued. He made his farewells. He recalled being 'motored to Dunmow station' in Essex the day Kitchener died—15 June. Perhaps he was visiting the H. G. Wellses at nearby Easton Glebe, where

Hunt recalled them joining 'the famous hockey parties there': 'I would watch a Cabinet Minister "taking tosses" and Joseph Leopold [as she calls Ford] landing Miss Violette Selfridge, as she was then, one on the chest with his hockey stick. He prostrated himself with apologies, of course, and wrote to enquire and his letter was answered fully from Berlin, where this young lady and her mother were spending the week-end.' Ford said he had a 'valedictory interview' with Conrad in June. Conrad had been unable to refuse Ford's request the previous summer that he should become Ford's joint literary executor together with Hunt—though he hoped he would 'never have to exercise' the trust (did he foresee himself in an unhappy triangular battle with Violet and Elsie?), and said he thought that 'your wife by herself would be eminently fit to do the job (Hunt amended this in her memoirs to 'Violet by herself', suppressing Conrad's equivocation about *which* wife). Ford's later claims about this 'valedictory interview' proved highly contentious: that they 'settled about the Ney collaboration' (his attempt to link Conrad's unfinished *Suspense* with his own novel about Maréchal Ney, *A Little Less Than Gods*); and that Conrad asked him to write a memoir of him if he survived. Conrad in 1915 or 1916 would have dreaded both ideas. It's just possible that he might have assented to Ford's suggestions to avoid further discussions or arguments, as he was to do in 1924 when he reluctantly let Ford republish *The Nature of a Crime*. Mizener imagined Conrad merely nodding as Ford sketched his idea of literary biography. But it's equally likely that, having written his memoir, Ford decided to claim Conrad's sanction to pre-empt the criticisms he rightly anticipated (in which case it would be a characteristically provocative move: telling a lie from honourable motives, but then getting angry when the people who have been provoked to doubt his word are thereby doubting his honour—as probably happened with his continental 'marriage'). But if Ford's account of this meeting is impressionistic, it is so out of his desire to recapture the romance of their former friendship, and to project it into the present and future: to have remembrance now. And there is an impressionistic kernel of truth to both claims, even if they are not literally true. Conrad had relied on Ford before as the man who would be able to finish a book were Conrad to die leaving it unfinished. Conrad had talked of a 'Mediterranean novel' as early as 1902, during the collaboration on *Romance*. A Napoleonic book may well have been one of the many projects they considered and put aside. As for the memoir, Ford may have remembered Conrad's letter to him responding to a tribute he had written. Conrad's teasing of the *jeune homme modeste* all but asks him to write about him after his death:

What your modesty and tenderness prompt You to say of myself I reject utterly in its literal sense. It is a delusion of your affection—and as a delusion I accept it with a melancholy eagerness; for it is a delusion which, for me, is of infinite 'douceur'. And precisely after reading it once more I shall burn Youre letter. If you wish to repeat that thing after I am dead I shall not come out of my grave to protest.

If they did meet in the summer of 1916, thoughts about their own deaths must have been sharpened by the death of Marwood, on 13 May, aged 47. Together

with the death of Henry James, on 28 February of the same year, it can only have
confirmed the sense that their world of fifteen years ago had gone to pieces. Ford
also asked his daughters to come to London, where he took them to lunch at a
Lyons café. Katharine, then 15, was mute with shyness. Christina, who was 17,
wanted to become a nun. Ford asked her to postpone her decision until he
returned from France, but she became distressed, told him that waiting would
make no difference, and refused. It was the last time he ever saw either of them.
Christina had a letter from him a few days later, saying: 'I took the communion
and prayed for you both.' Eventually, on 13 July 1916, he left Cardiff, and on the
17th, departed for France from Waterloo station. He had rung Juliet to ask her
to 'buy him a catholic medal of St. Michael and get it blessed by a priest for him'.
She took Violet with her to see him off. 'V. wept very copiously', she told David
Soskice, but added that one 'never knows with her what her real feelings are'.
Masterman, whose brother turned out to be Ford's colonel, arrived at the last
minute with a copy of the French translation of *Between St. Dennis and St. George*.
'He took it with him to read on the journey.' Ford 'seemed very popular with the
other officers', said Juliet. 'They all thumped him on the back and shouted "Hullo
Hueffer" when he came along.'[29]

ABBREVIATIONS

Editions of Ford's books used

Published in London unless otherwise indicated. {Abbreviations used in notes given in curly brackets}

Ancient Lights and Certain New Reflections (Chapman and Hall, 1911)
Antwerp (The Poetry Bookshop, 1915)
The Benefactor (Brown, Langham, 1905)
Between St. Dennis and St. George: A Sketch of Three Civilisations (Hodder and Stoughton, 1915)
The Brown Owl (T. Fisher Unwin, 1891)
A Call (Chatto & Windus, 1910)
Christina's Fairy Book (Alston Rivers, 1906)
The Cinque Ports (Edinburgh and London: William Blackwood and Sons, 1900)
Collected Poems (Max Goschen, [1913, though dated '1914'])
Collected Poems (New York: Oxford University Press, 1936)
The Critical Attitude (Duckworth, 1911)
England and the English (collecting Ford's trilogy on Englishness—*The Soul of London*; *The Heart of the Country*; *The Spirit of the People*—into one volume; New York: McClure, Phillips, 1907)
An English Girl (Methuen, 1907)
The English Novel: From the Earliest Days to the Death of Joseph Conrad (Constable, 1930)
The Face of the Night (John Macqueen, 1904)
The Feather (T. Fisher Unwin, 1892)
The Fifth Queen (Alston Rivers, 1906)
The Fifth Queen Crowned (Eveleigh Nash, 1908)
Ford Madox Brown (Longmans, Green, 1896)
From Inland and Other Poems (Alston Rivers, 1907)
The Good Soldier (John Lane, 1915)
Great Trade Route (George Allen & Unwin, 1937)
The 'Half Moon' (Eveleigh Nash, 1909)
Hans Holbein (Duckworth, 1905)
The Heart of the Country (Alston Rivers, 1906)
Henry for Hugh (Philadelphia: J. B. Lippincott, 1934)
Henry James (Martin Secker, [1914, though dated '1913'])
High Germany (Duckworth, 1912)
{*History*} *A History of Our Own Times*, ed. Solon Beinfeld and Sondra J. Stang (Manchester: Carcanet Press; Bloomington and Indianapolis: Indiana University Press, 1988)
A House (The Poetry Bookshop, 1921)
The Inheritors (William Heinemann, 1901)
It Was the Nightingale (William Heinemann, 1934)
Joseph Conrad: A Personal Remembrance (Duckworth, 1924)

Ladies Whose Bright Eyes (Constable, 1911)

Last Post (Duckworth, 1928)

{*Letters*} *Letters of Ford Madox Ford*, ed. Richard M. Ludwig (Princeton, NJ: Princeton University Press, 1965)

A Little Less Than Gods (Duckworth, 1928)

A Man Could Stand Up— (Duckworth, 1926)

The March of Literature (George Allen and Unwin, 1939)

The Marsden Case (Duckworth, 1923)

Mightier Than the Sword (George Allen & Unwin, 1938; published in USA as *Portraits from Life* (Boston: Houghton Mifflin, 1937)

A Mirror to France (Duckworth, 1926)

Mister Bosphorus and the Muses (Duckworth, 1923)

Mr. Apollo (Methuen, 1908)

Mr. Fleight (Howard Latimer, 1913)

The Nature of a Crime, with Joseph Conrad (Duckworth, 1924)

The New Humpty-Dumpty, pseud. 'Daniel Chaucer' (John Lane, 1912)

New Poems (New York: William Edwin Rudge, 1927)

New York Essays (New York: William Edwin Rudge, 1927)

New York is Not America (Duckworth, 1927)

No Enemy (New York: Macaulay, 1929)

No More Parades (Duckworth, 1925)

On Heaven and Poems Written on Active Service (John Lane, 1918)

The Panel (Constable, 1912; published in USA as *Ring for Nancy*, Indianapolis: Bobbs-Merrill, 1913)

Poems for Pictures (John MacQueen, 1900)

The Portrait (Methuen, 1910)

The Pre-Raphaelite Brotherhood (Duckworth, 1907)

Privy Seal (Alston Rivers, 1907)

Provence (George Allen & Unwin, 1938)

The Queen Who Flew (Bliss, Sands & Foster, 1894)

The Questions at the Well, pseud. 'Fenil Haig' (Digby, Long, 1893)

The Rash Act (Jonathan Cape, 1933)

{*Reader*} *The Ford Madox Ford Reader*, ed. Sondra J. Stang (Manchester: Carcanet, 1986)

Return to Yesterday (Victor Gollancz, 1931)

Romance, with Joseph Conrad (Smith Elder, 1903)

Rossetti (Duckworth, 1902)

The Shifting of the Fire (T. Fisher Unwin, 1892)

The Simple Life Limited, pseud. 'Daniel Chaucer' (John Lane, 1911)

Some Do Not . . . (Duckworth, 1924)

Songs from London (Elkin Mathews, 1910)

The Soul of London (Alston Rivers, 1905)

The Spirit of the People (Alston Rivers, 1907)

This Monstrous Regiment of Women (suffragette pamphlet, publisher not given, 1913)

Thus to Revisit (Chapman & Hall, 1921)

Vive Le Roy (George Allen and Unwin, 1937)

When Blood is Their Argument: An Analysis of Prussian Culture (Hodder and Stoughton, 1915)

When the Wicked Man (Jonathan Cape, 1932)
Women & Men (Paris: Three Mountains Press, 1923)
The Young Lovell (Chatto & Windus, 1913)
Zeppelin Nights, with Violet Hunt (John Lane, 1915)

Abbreviations used of others' works

Belford, *Violet*	Barbara Belford, *Violet: The Story of the Irrepressible Violet Hunt and Her Circle of Lovers and Friends—Ford Madox Ford, H. G. Wells, Somerset Maugham, and Henry James* (New York: Simon and Schuster, 1990)
Bennett, *Journals*	*The Journals of Arnold Bennett*, ed. Newman Flower, 3 vols. (London: Cassell and Company, 1932)
Bowen, *Drawn from Life*	Stella Bowen, *Drawn from Life* (London: Collins, 1941; repr. London: Virago, 1984)
Brebach	Raymond Brebach, *Joseph Conrad, Ford Madox Ford and the Making of 'Romance'* (Ann Arbor, Mich.: UMI Press, 1986)
Conrad, *Collected Letters*	*The Collected Letters of Joseph Conrad*, ed. Frederick R. Karl and Laurence Davies 8 vols. projected (Cambridge: Cambridge University Press, 1983–)
Conrad, *A Personal Record*	Joseph Conrad, *A Personal Record* (London: Dent, 1923)
Jessie Conrad, *Joseph Conrad and His Circle*	Jessie Conrad, *Joseph Conrad and His Circle* (London: Jarrolds Publishers, 1935)
Ezra Pound and Dorothy Shakespear	*Ezra Pound and Dorothy Shakespear: Their Letters: 1909–1914*, ed. Omar Pound and A. Walton Litz (London: Faber and Faber, 1985)
Ford Madox Ford: The Critical Heritage	Frank MacShane (ed.), *Ford Madox Ford: The Critical Heritage* (London: Routledge and Kegan Paul, 1972)
Garnett, 'A Bloomsbury Girlhood'	A typescript selection from Olive Garnett's diaries, ed. Anne Lee-Michell. Unreliable, but contains material excluded from *Tea and Anarchy!* and *Olive & Stepniak* (qq.v)
R. Garnett, *Constance Garnett*	Richard Garnett, *Constance Garnett* (London: Sinclair-Stevenson, 1991)
D. Garnett, *The Golden Echo*	David Garnett, *The Golden Echo* (London: Chatto & Windus, 1953)
Goldring, *The Last Pre-Raphaelite*	Douglas Goldring, *The Last Pre-Raphaelite: A Record of the Life and Writings of Ford Madox Ford* (London: Macdonald, 1948)
Goldring, *South Lodge*	Douglas Goldring, *South Lodge: Reminiscences of Violet Hunt, Ford Madox Ford and the English Review Circle* (London: Constable, 1943)

Green, *Ford Madox Ford: Prose and Politics*   Robert Green, *Ford Madox Ford: Prose and Politics* (Cambridge: Cambridge University Press, 1981)

Hardwick, *An Immodest Violet*   Joan Hardwick, *An Immodest Violet: The Life of Violet Hunt* (London: André Deutsch, 1990)

Harvey   David Dow Harvey, *Ford Madox Ford: 1873–1939: A Bibliography of Works and Criticism* (Princeton, NJ: Princeton University Press, 1962)

Hunt, *The Flurried Years*   Violet Hunt, *The Flurried Years* (London: Hurst & Blackett, [1926])

Hunt, *I Have This to Say*   Violet Hunt, *I Have This to Say: The Story of My Flurried Years* (New York: Boni and Liveright, 1926); the American edition of the above, but containing extra material

Hunt and Ford, *The Desirable Alien*   *The Desirable Alien: At Home in Germany*, by Violet Hunt. With Preface and Two Additional Chapters by Ford Madox Hueffer (London: Chatto and Windus, 1913)

Hynes, *The Edwardian Turn of Mind*   Samuel Hynes, *The Edwardian Turn of Mind* (Princeton, NJ: Princeton University Press, 1968)

Jefferson, *Edward Garnett*   George Jefferson, *Edward Garnett: A Life in Literature* (London: Jonathan Cape, 1982)

Jepson, *Memories of an Edwardian*   Edgar Jepson, *Memories of an Edwardian* (London: Martin Secker, 1938)

Judd, *Ford Madox Ford*   Alan Judd, *Ford Madox Ford* (London: Collins, 1990)

Karl   Karl, *Joseph Conrad: The Three Lives* (London: Faber and Faber, 1979)

Lawrence, *Letters*   *The Letters of D. H. Lawrence*, general editor James T. Boulton, 7 vols. (Cambridge: Cambridge University Press, 1979–93)

Lindberg-Seyersted   Brita Lindberg-Seyersted, *Ford Madox Ford and His Relationship to Stephen Crane and Henry James* (Atlantic Highlands, NJ: Humanities Press International, Inc. | Solum Forlag, Norway, 1987)

Marshall, *Out and About*   Archibald Marshall, *Out and About: Random Reminiscences* (London: John Murray, 1933)

Mizener   Arthur Mizener, *The Saddest Story: A Biography of Ford Madox Ford* (London: The Bodley Head, 1972)

Morey   John Morey, 'Joseph Conrad and Ford Madox Ford: A Study in Collaboration' (Cornell University: unpublished dissertation, 1960)

Moser   Thomas C. Moser, *The Life in the Fiction of Ford Madox Ford* (Princeton, NJ: Princeton University Press, 1980)

Najder   Zdzisław Najder, *Joseph Conrad: A Chronicle* (Cambridge: Cambridge University Press, 1983)

Olive & Stepniak   Olive & Stepniak: The Bloomsbury Diary of Olive Garnett: 1893–1895, ed. Barry Johnson (London: Bartletts Press, 1993)

Patmore, My Friends When Young   My Friends When Young: The Memoirs of Brigit Patmore, ed. Derek Patmore (London: Heinemann, 1968)

Pound/Ford   Pound/Ford: The Story of a Literary Friendship, ed. Brita Lindberg-Seyersted (London: Faber and Faber [1983])

Presence of Ford Madox Ford, The   The Presence of Ford Madox Ford, ed. Sondra J. Stang (Philadelphia: University of Pennsylvania Press, 1981)

Rossetti, Selected Letters   Selected Letters of William Michael Rossetti, ed. Roger W. Peattie (University Park and London: Pennsylvania State University Press, 1990)

Secor and Secor, The Return of the Good Soldier   Robert Secor and Marie Secor, The Return of the Good Soldier, English Literary Studies Monograph no. 30 (University of Victoria, BC, 1983)

Snitow   Ann Barr Snitow, Ford Madox Ford and the Voice of Uncertainty (Baton Rouge, La.: Louisiana State University Press, 1984)

Soskice, Chapters from Childhood   Juliet M. Soskice, Chapters from Childhood: Reminiscences of an Artist's Granddaughter (London: Selwyn & Blount, 1921)

Stang   Sondra J. Stang, Ford Madox Ford (New York: Frederick Ungar, 1977)

Stang and Smith, 'Music for a While'   Sondra J. Stang and Carl Smith, ' "Music for a While": Ford's Compositions for Voice and Piano', Contemporary Literature, 30:2 (Summer 1989), 183–223

Tea and Anarchy!   Tea and Anarchy!: The Bloomsbury Diary of Olive Garnett: 1890–1893, ed. Barry Johnson (London: Bartletts Press, 1989)

NOTES

To avoid cluttering the text with index numbers, I have normally gathered together the references to form one or two footnotes per paragraph. Letters and manuscript material are at Cornell University (Department of Rare Books, Olin Library) unless otherwise indicated. Items preceded by an asterisk in the notes were missing from David Dow Harvey's bibliography, or from the supplementary bibliographies in the Ford issue of *Antæus*, no. 56 (Spring 1986).

Preface

1 *'Unlucky Eccentric's Private World', *Sunday Telegraph* (17 June 1962), 6.
2 Burgess, *You've Had Your Time* (London: Heinemann, 1990), 130. Letter to Michael Roberts, July 1937: *Ezra Pound: Selected Letters: 1907–1941*, ed. D. D. Paige (New York: New Directions, 1971), 296. Donald Davie, *Studies in Ezra Pound* (Manchester: Carcanet, 1991), 38. *Pound/Ford*, 180.
3 *Return to Yesterday*, 29. Samuel Hynes, 'The Genre of *No Enemy*', *Antæus*, 56 (Spring 1986), 140.
4 The descriptions of Ford are from: Lloyd Morris, *A Threshold in the Sun* (London: George Allen and Unwin, 1943), 216–18; Herbert Gorman, 'Ford Madox Ford: The Personal Side', *Princeton University Library Chronicle*, 9 (Apr. 1948), 121; Samuel Putnam, *Paris Was Our Mistress* (New York: Viking, 1947), 123; Norman Douglas, *Late Harvest* (London: Lindsay Drummond, 1946), 45; Harold Loeb, *The Way It Was* (New York: Criterion Books, 1959), 188–9. Max Alan Webb has written astutely on how Fordian role-playing 'distances his opinions, frames them as coming from a source held just a hairbreadth away from the real person'. 'Ford Madox Ford's Nonfiction' (unpublished dissertation: Princeton, 1972), 325. See also ibid. 281.
5 Harvey, *Ford Madox Ford: 1873–1939: A Bibliography of Works and Criticism*. Mizener, *The Saddest Story: A Biography of Ford Madox Ford*. I have indicated any significant departures from Mizener, at the risk of sounding more combative than grateful that the preliminary, often necessarily tentative work had already been done. The bibliographies in the Ford special issue of *Antæus*, no. 56 (Spring 1986), 219–44, list the secondary material up to 1985. The publication of other letters by Pound (to Lewis, Dorothy Shakespear, and Margaret Cravens) has rescued more useful material about Ford. Two volumes of Garnett's diaries have now been published: *Tea and Anarchy!: The Bloomsbury Diary of Olive Garnett: 1890–1893*, and *Olive & Stepniak: The Bloomsbury Diary of Olive Garnett: 1893–1895*, both meticulously edited by Barry Johnson. If a page reference to these volumes is not given, the reference is to the original diary in the possession of Olive's great niece, Mrs Caroline White.

Introduction

1 'The Other House', *New York Herald Tribune Books* (2 Oct. 1927), 2.
2 *Return to Yesterday*, 128–9.
3 For examples, see *Letters*, 98, 155, 165, 168. For the 1927 'Avignon Edition' of *The Good Soldier* Ford added a 'Dedicatory Letter to Stella Ford'. Janice Biala was later called 'Mrs Ford', even in print. An 'Editor's Note' to an article of Ford's

which she illustrated refers to her as 'Biala, in private life Mrs Ford': 'Take Me Back to Tennessee', *Vogue* (New York) (1 Oct. 1937).

4 *It Was the Nightingale*, 119–20, connects his father's and his own changes of name. Here Ford says that Gerald Duckworth (his publisher during the 1920s) said: 'If only you'd sign your books "Ford" I might be able to sell the beastly things.'

5 Frederick Karl compares Ford's change of name with Conrad's: *Joseph Conrad: The Three Lives*, 432 n. Violet Hunt refers to Ford as 'Joseph Leopold' (his Catholic baptismal names) throughout *The Flurried Years*—thus making him the double of the other Joseph, Conrad. Ford told Arnold Bennett the Pseudonym Library story on 16 Jan. 1911: *The Journals of Arnold Bennett*, ed. Newman Flower, 3 vols. (London: Cassell and Company, 1932), ii. 1. He elaborated upon the story in *Joseph Conrad*, 90, almost suggesting that Conrad almost suggested it was one of Ford's own books, *The Shifting of the Fire*, published in a similar series of Garnett's, the Independent Novel Series (though under the names 'H. Ford Hueffer' on the title page, and 'Ford H. Hueffer' on the cover). Richard Garnett's biography of *Constance Garnett*, 140, confirms that Conrad submitted *Almayer's Folly* for the Pseudonym Library on 5 July 1894.

6 *Ancient Lights*, 154, 235. Ford told J. B. Pinker that he changed his name 'partly to oblige a relative & partly because a Teutonic name is in these days disagreeable': 5 June 1919: *Letters*, 93. Similarly, he told Herbert Read on 2 Sept. 1919 that he had made the change 'to please a relative from whom I have expectations' (as well as for camouflage): ibid. 98. He kept to this story for several years, changing it only slightly. Harriet Monroe was told he had changed names 'to fulfil the terms of a small legacy': 10 Feb. 1921: *Reader*, 481. But I have found no proof of any such legacy. The likeliest Hüffer relations to have left him money were his uncle Hermann and his aunt Emma Goesen, but they had died in 1905 and 1917 respectively. He told Anthony Bertram that he changed names 'for testamentary reasons', 'on the 28/6/19—or whatever was the date of the signature of the peace treaty' (23 June 1922: *Letters*, 139–40), which shows how much the association with the peace treaty mattered. It is most likely that the story of the 'relative' he wanted to oblige was an oblique way of referring to his common-law wife, Stella Bowen, whose money he wanted to protect against possible legal action by his wife Elsie Martindale or alleged wife Violet Hunt.

7 See the 1927 'Dedicatory Letter to Stella Ford', prefaced to *The Good Soldier* (Oxford: Oxford University Press, 1990), 2. Also *Thus to Revisit*, 25.

8 *Thus to Revisit*, 25. Shakespeare, *Hamlet*, I. iv. 32–4. Ford felt ghostly before the war had ended. Back in England after two spells in France he wrote to Lucy Masterman on 8 Sept. 1917, 'I haven't had any news of you for a long time—or indeed from anybody: it is like being a ghost, rather': *Letters*, 84.

9 For examples see: Ford's preface, signed 'Miles Ignotus', to Violet Hunt's *Their Lives* (London: Stanley Paul, 1916), 4; the manuscript *'Epilogue', 13 (Princeton); *The Marsden Case*, 144; prospectus for the *transatlantic review*, Nov. 1923, reproduced by Goldring, *South Lodge*, 143–6; 'Emma', *New York Herald Tribune Books* (10 June 1928), 1, 6; and *No Enemy*, 9.

10 *It Was the Nightingale*, 3. Ford's demobilization is discussed in vol. 2, Chs. 5 and 6 Cassirer, *Language and Myth*, trans. Susanne K. Langer (New York: Harper & Brothers, 1946), 51.

11 'Preparedness', *New York Herald Tribune Magazine* (6 Nov. 1927), 7, 18. *It Was the Nightingale*, 118.

12 Goldring, *The Last Pre-Raphaelite*, 35–7.

13 The *typescript at Cornell dates from 1903–4: *published, ed. Sondra J. Stang and Richard Stang, *Yale Review*, 78/4 (Summer 1989), 511–24.

14 *Mightier Than the Sword*, 264.

15 Ibid. 139. The version in *Return to Yesterday*, 296, has a similar emphasis.

16 'Literary Portraits—IX: Mr. Thomas Hardy and "A Changed Man" ', *Outlook*, 32 (8 Nov. 1913), 641–2.

17 'Thomas Hardy, O.M.: Obiit: 11 January, 1928', *New York Herald Tribune Books* (22 Jan. 1928), 1–3. That this is the first version that mentions the confession of Anglicanism may suggest that Ford's tact prevented him from revealing it while Hardy was still alive. Violet Hunt also heard Hardy telling ghost stories: *The Flurried Years*, 68.

18 Marshall, *Out and About: Random Reminiscences* (London: John Murray, 1933), 152.

19 Ibid. 149. The complaint about Ford's influence is on p. 139. Marshall was also an admirer of Violet Hunt's, and may have been influenced by her animosity after Ford left her: see Louis Golding to Hunt, 9 Feb. 1924, saying that Marshall speaks of her with delight: Cornell.

20 Shanks, 'Ford Madox Ford: The Man and his Work', *World Review* (June 1948), 59–60. West, *'Unlucky Eccentric's Private World', *Sunday Telegraph* (17 June 1962), 6.

21 *Return to Yesterday*, 251.

22 Mizener, 317–18. 'On Impressionism: I', *Poetry and Drama*, 2 (June 1914), 167.

23 Moser, p. xi.

24 See e.g. *Thus to Revisit*, 94–5. *No Enemy*, 109. Letter to the editor of the *American Mercury* [Nov. 1936]: *Letters*, 267. The five biographies are those already cited by Goldring, Mizener, and Moser; Frank MacShane, *The Life and Work of Ford Madox Ford* (London: Routledge & Kegan Paul, 1965); and Alan Judd, *Ford Madox Ford*. The half is Goldring, *South Lodge: Reminiscences of Violet Hunt, Ford Madox Ford and the English Review Circle* (London: Constable, 1943).

25 Robie Macauley, 'The Good Ford', *Kenyon Review*, 11 (Spring 1949), 278. *It Was the Nightingale*, 25.

26 *The Rash Act*, 159. *Mightier Than the Sword* [published in the USA as *Portraits from Life*], 139, 160.

27 *'Men and Books', *Time and Tide*, 17/21 (23 May 1936), 761–2. Ford was often drawn to Galton's photographic experiments in 'composite portraiture': see Francis Galton, *Memories of My Life* (London: Methuen & Co., 1908).

28 Ford to Galsworthy [Oct. 1900]: *Letters*, 10. 'Men and Books', 761. *South Lodge*, 37.

29 Quoted by Richard Ludwig, 'The Reputation of Ford Madox Ford', *PMLA*, 76 (Dec. 1961), 549. T. S. Eliot, 'Tradition and the Individual Talent', *Selected Essays*, third enlarged edn. (London: Faber and Faber, 1951), 18.

30 Hunt, *The Flurried Years*, 123.

31 See Conrad's 'A Familiar Preface' to *A Personal Record*, p. xxi.

32 William Empson, *Some Versions of Pastoral* (London: Chatto & Windus, 1935), 102. Moser, for example, sees a 'characteristic tendency to shift about, in similar but ever-changing patterns, a group of familiar fictive counters closely connected to a few human beings': p. xi. T. S. Eliot, *The Use of Poetry and the Use of Criticism* (London: Faber and Faber, 1964), 30.

33 Douglas Goldring's two books on him celebrate his art, but give little space to discussing it. 'Men and Books'. *Provence*, 169.

34 Preface to *The Nigger of the 'Narcissus'*: first printed as an 'Author's Note' after the serialization of the novel in the *New Review*, 17 (Dec. 1897), 628–31. *Provence*, 166.

35 'Jean Rhys and Ford Madox Ford: What "Really" Happened?', *Mosaic*, 16/4 (Fall 1983), 15–24. He begins with Rhys's paradox, relevant to Ford's fabrications: 'How could I explain now what really happened? If I did he'd think me a liar.' Critics who have begun to discuss Ford's *avant la lettre* deconstruction are: Carol Jacobs, 'The (Too) Good Soldier: "A Real Story"', *Glyph*, 3 (1978), 32–51; Cornelia Cook, 'Going Beyond Modernism', *English*, 33 (Summer 1984), 159–67; and (implicitly) Michael Levenson, *A Genealogy of Modernism* (Cambridge: Cambridge University Press, 1984), 118–19. Ford's essay 'The Woman of the Novelists' (*The Critical Attitude*, 147–69) is the classic example, pioneering an argument about how literature colludes in sexual ideology: 'You see—poor, honest, muddled man with the glamour of the novelist's woman on him—he is always looking about somewhere in the odd and bewildering fragments of this woman who has the power to bedevil, to irritate, to plague and to madden him. He looks about in this mist of personal contacts for the Cordelia that he still believes must be there' (p. 164). He also said: 'The Englishman's mind is of course made up entirely of quotations'; and he described the Englishman as 'A person entirely without intellect himself': 'Women & Men: II', *Little Review*, 4 (Mar. 1918), 38.

36 Sanders, 'Polishing the Bright Stars: Ford's Drama of Narration', *Agenda*, 27/4–28/1 (Winter 1989–Spring 1990), 89.

37 Oliver Madox Hueffer, *A Vagabond in New York* (London: The Bodley Head, 1913), 9.

Chapter 1

1 Goldring, *The Last Pre-Raphaelite*, 27. *It Was the Nightingale*, 121–2. Francis Hueffer's passion for Provence led him to write his book on *The Troubadours* (London: Chatto and Windus, 1878).

2 W. M. Rossetti, *Some Reminiscences* (London: Brown, Langham, 1906), 332–3. Cathy Madox Brown to Franz Hüffer, 28 Sept. 1870: Cornell. See e.g. Flaubert to Louise Colet [9 Dec. 1852]: 'An author in his book must be like God in the universe, present everywhere and visible nowhere': *The Letters of Gustave Flaubert: 1830–1857*, selected, edited and translated by Francis Steegmuller (London: Faber and Faber, 1981), 173–4. See *The English Novel*, 123. *It Was the Nightingale*, 120.

3 'Die Hüffer', from Wilhelm Schulte, *Westfälische Köpfe* (Münster: Verlag Aschendorff, 1963). I am indebted to Dr Anton Wilhelm Hüffer for sending me this genealogical essay, and for providing further information. Franz Hüffer studied Modern Languages at Münster, Munich, Leipzig, and Berlin, taking a degree from Göttingen in 1869 for his work on the history of the troubadours. His diploma from Münster is at Cornell. Aldington, *Life for Life's Sake* (London: Cassell, 1968), 145. *The Last Pre-Raphaelite*, 19, 22, 25–6. Moser, 6.

4 *Ancient Lights*, 156–7.

5 *Ancient Lights*, 42–3, 17, 192. *Ford Madox Brown*, 10, 13. 'Die Hüffer'. Rossetti, *Some Reminiscences*, 332–3. Mizener, 4. *Ancient Lights*, 41. W. M. Rossetti to Swinburne, 5 Apr. [1876]: *Selected Letters*, 341.

6 Franz Hüffer to Cathy Madox Brown, n.d. *Ancient Lights*, pp. ix. 41–2. Cf. *It Was the Nightingale*, 249. *A Mirror to France*, 172.

7 Catherine Hueffer's portraits of her husband and daughter-in-law are reproduced in this volume. *It Was the Nightingale*, 121, 249–50, 255. Soskice, *Chapters from Childhood* (London: George Prior, 1973), 202–4. See Moser, 15, on Ford's recurrent involvements with two women; though he is misleading in saying that Ford needed 'another admiring woman in addition to the beloved'. More often, the other woman *was* the beloved, whereas he would provoke his partner's animus by falling out of love with her.

8 *Ancient Lights*, pp. viii–ix. Cf. *Mightier Than the Sword*, 192–3. In *Provence*, 201, Ford says his second memory was of seeing Ellen Terry offering him a lily between his bouts of delirium due to diphtheria. As Mizener says, Ford certainly had scarlatina in 1881, and had his throat scraped by Sir Morell Mackenzie, who had treated Frederick III: 526–7, n. 19. *History*, 200–1. In another passage of the *History* (written nearly half-a-century after the event(s), Ford recalled 'peeping into a cage of doves' in Madox Brown's studio, while Turgenev was standing behind him: 15–16. If this refers to the same episode (though it need not, since he probably often looked in the cage), it occurred in 1881, when Ford was almost 8.

9 Moser, 134–5.

10 *It Was the Nightingale*, 250, 254–5.

11 Rossetti to Madox Brown: Berg Collection, New York Public Library; quoted by Robert and Marie Secor, *The Return of the Good Soldier*, English Literary Studies Monograph no. 30 (University of Victoria, BC, 1983), 20, 40. *Ford Madox Brown*, 292–3. William Rossetti to Swinburne, 5 Jan. [1875]: *Selected Letters*, 320–1; Nolly died on 5 Nov. 1874; see ibid. 319.

12 Mizener, 3. 5 Fair Lawn Villas is now 245 Kingston Road. *Ford Madox Brown*, 267. Madox Brown to Cathy Hueffer, 30 Dec. 1875. *Ancient Lights*, 51–2.

13 Mizener, 3, says Oliver was born four years after Ford, and Juliet eight. But in fact Oliver was just over two years and Juliet just under seven years younger: see Moser, 8 (though he gives Juliet's birthday wrongly as 4 Nov.). Elizabeth Longford, in her Introduction to *Chapters from Childhood* (London: George Prior, 1973), gives Juliet's date of birth erroneously as 1879. Francis Hueffer to Cathy, 16 July 1879: Cornell (she's in Bonn with the boys, and he is about to join them). *It Was the Nightingale*, 345. Ford remembered himself as 'rising seven' on his first European trip, whereas this letter shows him rising 6. He told Elizabeth Cheatham he spent a long time at Arles as a boy, and remembered the Roman tombs at Les Alyscamps: postcard, 25 Oct. [1928].

14 *Ancient Lights*, 13. Rossetti, 'In Memoriam': MS at Cornell. Soskice, *Chapters from Childhood*, p. 71. *'Nice People', 573.

15 Brown's other daughter, Lucy Rossetti, named her eldest child after Oliver too: Olive Madox Rossetti. *It Was the Nightingale*, 250–2. Cf. *Ancient Lights*, 13, and *Ford Madox Brown*, 238. Ford's memory of forty years ago is corroborated by Olive Garnett's diary. On 12 Mar. 1893 she recorded Robert Garnett's conversation with Madox Brown: 'He cannot come to any conclusion about Oliver,

sometimes he thinks he is a genius, & at other times that he is fooling him. His conduct is extraordinary'; Ford's story about seeing him getting out of a carriage of the duke of Westminster's is corroborated by her entry for 5 July 1893: *Tea and Anarchy!*, 161, 210. *It Was the Nightingale*, 250. Though Oliver's career makes him sound like one of Ford's more flamboyant characters, his own writing is much flatter.

16 *Ancient Lights*, 101.

17 *'Pure Literature', *Agenda*, 27/4–28/1 (Winter 1989–Spring 1990), 7. *Ancient Lights*, 104 (on p. 103 Ford says Oliver 'was always very much the sharper of the two'). *It Was the Nightingale*, 249. *The Shifting of the Fire*, 295. *Ancient Lights*, 197–8. Cf. *Ford Madox Brown*, 392–3, 400–1; on p. 124 Ford quotes Brown's diary discussing Rossetti's altruism and lack of professional rivalry.

18 One of the few times Ford discussed nascent feelings of creative envy was in a piece on A. E. Coppard, discussed in vol. 2, Ch. 12. The importance of 'sympathetic insight is discussed *passim*, esp. vol. 2, Ch. 21. Klein, 'Infantile Anxiety-Situations Reflected in a Work of Art and in the Creative Impulse', in *Love, Guilt and Reparation* (London: The Hogarth Press and the Institute of Psycho-Analysis, 1985), 210–18; esp. 214, 217.

19 Freud, 'Family Romances' (1909), *Standard Edition of the Complete Psychological Works of Sigmund Freud*, vol. 9 (London: The Hogarth Press, 1959), 235–41. 'Notes for a Lecture on *Vers Libre'*, *Critical Writings of Ford Madox Ford*, ed. Frank MacShane (Lincoln: University of Nebraska Press, 1964), 156; cf. *Ancient Lights*, 222–3. *Ford Madox Brown*, 54. *'Nice People', 572. Moser, 37. *The Brown Owl*, 19. *Ancient Lights*, 1–2. Thackeray, *The Newcomes*, chs. 16 and 19 describe 120 Fitzroy Square. *Thus to Revisit*, 18.

20 *Ford Madox Brown*, 1–7. Ford's comment about Frederick is supported by an undated letter from Brown to the editor of the *Dictionary of National Biography*. *'Nice People', 572–4. *The Pre-Raphaelite Brotherhood*, 12, 23 (where Ford distances himself from the view of Brown as 'father' of the movement, while effectively according him at least a claim to the title by discussing him at the start of his monograph). *Ford Madox Brown*, 356; see Mizener, 14. Gerard Tetley to Elsie Hueffer, 11 Dec. 1945. Ford wrote to Harry Quilter towards the end of 1896: 'An exhibition of Madox Brown's work without "Work" wd. be the play of Hamlet without Hamlet. This picture is so important—plays so large a part in Madox Brown's life-work that it would be really tragic if it should not appear in the first complete exhibition of his pictures': [n.d.]. *Ford Madox Brown*, 189–95 and *passim*. Brown's ten-hour painting day is described on p. 354. *Ancient Lights*, 238.

21 *Return to Yesterday*, 334. *'Nice People', 572–4. *Ancient Lights*, 222–3, 117. *Ford Madox Brown*, 394–5, 400 (cf. 175 and 336 on Brown's anger at being patronized). *'F. H.', 'The Town Hall Frescoes', *Manchester Guardian* (24 May 1892), 12. The attribution is confirmed by Olive Garnett's diary entry for 9 June 1892: *Tea and Anarchy!*, 86. Ford's only periodical publication that might precede the letter is the publication of the poem 'The Wind's Quest' in the *Torch*, which he said occurred in 1891; but like Harvey (p. 139) I have been unable to verify this. See *Ancient Lights*, 162 on Brown's contempt for non-artists, and especially tradespeople; and see *Ford Madox Brown*, 86, 96, 176, 249, and 251 for examples of Brown's paranoid feelings about the art establishment; p. 273 shows how, like Ford after him, he could recognize this tendency in others—in this case Rossetti.

22 Ford has Brown using the expression at least five times. See *Ancient Lights*, 8, 139, 225; *It Was the Nightingale*, 251. 'Pre-Raphaelite Epitaph', *Saturday Review of Literature*, 10 (20 Jan. 1934), 419. W. M. Rossetti, 'Mr. Madox Hueffer's Inaccuracies' (Letter to the Editor), *Outlook*, 27 (22 Apr. 1911), 507–8. *Tea and Anarchy!*, 65: entry for 3 Mar. 1892. *Ancient Lights*, 120–1. David Garnett recalled Ford wearing the Morris-type smock frocks in the late 1890s—which Ford later satirized in *The Simple Life Limited*, published in the same year (1911) as *Ancient Lights*. Garnett to George Jefferson, 21 Mar. 1980, quoted in George Jefferson, *Edward Garnett* (London: Jonathan Cape, 1982), 299–300.

23 *Ancient Lights*, 3. Ruskin, *Unto this Last: And Other Writings*, ed. Clive Wilmer (Harmondsworth: Penguin Books, 1985), 23–4, 294.

24 Garnett, diary entry for 20 Nov. 1895; quoted by Moser, 35. *Ford Madox Brown*, 391; p. 36 quotes from Brown's lecture 'Style in Art'. *The Flurried Years*, 121. *TLS* (1 July 1939), 384. See vol. 2 on Ford's radio broadcasts.

25 *Chapters from Childhood*, 32. Cf. *Ford Madox Brown*, 392. See p. 238 on Brown's gout. Ibid. p. 54. *Ancient Lights*, 222–3, 45. 'Towards a History of English Literature': Part II 'Great Writers', 40: typescript at Cornell. Ford discusses Waterton, whom he says he read at the age of 8, in 'From China to Peru', *Outlook*, 35 (19 June 1915), 800–1. Ford to Edward Garnett [n.d.: 1901?]: *Letters*, 15–16.

26 Jean-Paul Sartre, *Les Mots* (Paris: Gallimard, 1964), 19.

Chapter 2

1 Soskice, *Chapters from Childhood*, p. xv. *Great Trade Route*, 19, describes Ford's imaginary voyaging with his playmate Walter Atterbury, the nurse's son. *Return to Yesterday*, 72–3; cf. *Ancient Lights*, 95. *Ancient Lights*, 99, 31, 12. *Mightier Than the Sword*, 242–4.

2 *Mightier Than the Sword*, 245–7. *Ancient Lights*, pp. x–xi, 5. *Thus to Revisit*, 202. Ford's picture of the intrigues is borne out by—for example—Diana Holman-Hunt's book, *My Grandfather, His Wives and Loves* (London: Hamish Hamilton, 1969), esp. 286–91; though on p. 287 she suggests that Brown's outspokenness could exacerbate the gossip. *No Enemy*, 64. Helen Rossetti Angeli, quoted by Mizener, 526, n. 8. Ford wrote that he was 'very severely disciplined' as a child, though he conceded that 'for a man of his date' his father 'must have been quite mild in his treatment of his children': *Ancient Lights*, pp. viii–ix.

3 Brown to Ford, 21 Apr. 1880.

4 *Mightier Than the Sword*, 191–3, 241. Turgenev had met Brown ten years earlier, when he had visited Fitzroy Square and was introduced to Morris, Gosse, and Swinburne. Patrick Waddington, *Turgenev and England* (London and Basingstoke: Macmillan, 1980), 189, 195, 283–5. *Ancient Lights*, 186–8; Ford says he would also read Hudson when dispirited; he recalled Turgenev talking about birds in Madox Brown's studio, so perhaps Hudson's naturalist writing reminded Ford of the author of *A Sportsman's Sketches*.

5 Mizener, 10. Goldring, *The Last Pre-Raphaelite*, 31–2. *Provence*, 214–15. 'Literary Portraits: XXVII. Mr. Charles Doughty', *Tribune* (25 Jan. 1908), 2. Robert T. Skinner, *The Schoolmaster Looks Back* (Edinburgh: privately printed by T. & A. Constable, 1947), 22–3; quoted by Harvey, 591. In *When Blood is Their Argument*, p. viii, Ford wrote, 'For as long as I can remember, I have been accustomed to

think indifferently in French, in German, or in English'. *'Nice People', *Temple Bar*, 128 (Nov. 1903), 571–2.

6 *The March of Literature*, 717. *Provence*, 214–15.

7 Mizener (527, n. 22) cites *A History of Our Own Times* (without giving a page reference); but I think he must have meant 'Towards a History of English Literature', where Ford discusses Rossetti's present on pp. 41–3 of an unpublished essay, 'Great Writers': Cornell. Ford was probably recalling *The Romancist, and Novelist's Library*, published in weekly instalments, 4 vols. (London: J. Clements, 1839–40). *Captain Singleton* does indeed appear here, in vol. 1. There is no Sue in it, however, and *Udolpho* doesn't appear. But there are other pieces by Radcliffe, and many other Gothic and picaresque works. 'Stocktaking: Towards a Re-Valuation of English Literature' (published pseudonymously as by 'Daniel Chaucer'), X.: The Reader', *transatlantic review*, 2/5 (Nov. 1924), 503–4. *Ancient Lights*, 180, also mentions his familiarity with *Lorna Doone*. 'Great Writers', 42–3. 'True Love & a G.C.M'. (typescript at Cornell: discussed in vol. 2), 27–9.

8 'Stocktaking [. . .]: X', 503. In 'Literary Portraits—XXIII.: Fydor Dostoievsky and "The Idiot" ', *Outlook*, 33 (14 Feb. 1914), 206–7, Ford recalled reading 'as one used to do as a child, pressed against a tall window-pane for hours and hours, utterly oblivious of oneself, in the twilight'. 'Jack Harkaway' was probably *Harkaway Dick*, recalled in *Ancient Lights*, 41, 103, 228–9. Cf. *Return to Yesterday*, 78. *Provence*, 52.

9 'Stocktaking [. . .] X', 504; the influence of Smiles's book is examined in Volume 2. Ford to Madox Brown, 'Thursday 5' [July?] 1883.

10 *Ancient Lights*, 101–3. Ford to Edward Garnett [n. d., but 1894]: *Letters*, 7–8. See Moser, 6.

11 *Ancient Lights*, 103–4. Mark Samuels Lasner, [and Margaret Diane Stetz, eds], 'A BBC Interview with Helen Rossetti Angeli', *Journal of Pre-Raphaelite Studies*, 2/2 (May 1982), 11. Watts-Dunton to Brown, 3 Jan. 1889.

12 Ford was 12 at the time of Liszt's Jubilee—a little old for sitting on the knees of someone so old? Which may be why he placed the episode earlier in successive versions: *'Nice People' places the episode when Ford was 'perhaps ten'; i.e. about 1883–4, but *Ancient Lights*, 70–2, says he was 'a very small boy indeed'. *Mightier Than the Sword*, 199, 241, places it firmly in 1881 (when he was 7). Another version is told in the *Daily News* (13 Feb. 1912), 3.

13 *'Nice People', 565. *Ancient Lights*, 70.

14 Robert Skinner, quoted in Goldring, *The Last Pre-Raphaelite*, 32–3. Skinner, 'A Notable Family: Oliver Madox Hueffer', *Scotsman* (27 June 1931), 18. Skinner, quoted by Martin Ray, 'Ford Madox Ford at Folkestone: Some New Biographical Information', *Notes and Queries*, 231 (June 1986), 178–9. John Dixon Hunt, *The Wider Sea: A Life of John Ruskin* (New York: Viking, 1982), 400. Mizener, 24, says that Elsie had been bedridden for nearly two years when she was 3 or 4 because of a tubercular vertebra in the neck. When, aged 10, she injured her knee, that too became tubercular, and an iron wire was inserted. Moser, 298, n. 9, says she had a tubercular gland removed from her neck in her teens, and was confined to bed for a year. These details got exaggerated by Olive Rossetti, as reported in Olive Garnett's diary for 24 Mar. 1893: 'an iron kneecap & a hole in her breast. Diseased bones show consumption, her family is consumptive & so is she.' In the

Scotsman obituary, and his letter to Goldring, Skinner says Ford saw him off at Limehouse; but in a letter to J. M. Bullock, quoted by Ray, he said it was Tilbury. A former Irish nationalist MP sued *The Times* for publishing letters from Charles Stuart Parnell; the Commission proved they were forgeries in February 1890.

15 William to Lucy Rossetti, 1 Jan. 1889; quoted in *Selected Letters*, 524, n. 2. 'O Hygeia', *Harper's*, 156 (May 1928), 768–76: Ford says an eminent throat specialist had killed his father 'by telling him to get up and go about his business because there was nothing the matter with his throat', and that his father 'dropped dead at his bedside immediately after the specialist had left the room'. He also writes there that the same specialist responsible for killing his father 'operated on my own throat six times—for tonsils and adenoids—that in itself being pretty bad for an already nervous child of eight. Thus, in short, from my tenderest infancy I was taught to watch my health at every minute of the day and night. I did so—and no human being can have had a much more miserable inner life than myself' (p. 775). W. M. Rossetti, *Some Reminiscences*, vol. 2, 322–33, quoted by Goldring, *The Last Pre-Raphaelite*, 21. Soskice, *Chapters from Childhood*, 34, p. xiii, 1. W. M. Rossetti to Cathy Hueffer, 25 Jan. 1889 (Berg Collection, New York Public Library), discussed by Moser, 8. Rossetti to Lucy, 20, 22, and 24 Jan. 1889: *Selected Letters*, 523–7; 535, n.1 quotes Rossetti's diary from 29 May 1889, which supports Juliet's story about the pension.

16 Rossetti to Cathy Hueffer, 24 Jan. 1889; to Lucy Rossetti, 6 Feb. 1889, and diary for 4 Mar. 1889: *Selected Letters*, 528–32. Moser, 8.

17 Rossetti, diary for 4 Feb. and 4 Mar. 1889: *Selected Letters*, 529, n. 2. 'Stocktaking [. . .]: VII', *transatlantic review*, 2/1 (July 1924), 66, mentions the texts set for 'the preliminary Civil Service Examinations of a higher class which were open to young men of my day'. *Ancient Lights*, 157. One of Ford's fictional clerks is discussed below, p. 105. *Some Do Not . . .*, 9. Mizener, 12 and Moser, 7, follow Goldring (*The Last Pre-Raphaelite*, 33) in saying that the boys left Pretoria House immediately after their father's death. In 1931 their schoolmaster, Robert Skinner, remembered them as still there when he left the school in July 1889: Ray, 'Ford Madox Ford at Folkestone'. But William Rossetti's diary for 10 May 1889 says Ford 'is now attending University College School: Oliver is about to attend there also': *Selected Letters*, 527, n. 2. Presumably Skinner had forgotten that Ford had left before July, though Oliver may still have been at Folkestone.

18 *Ancient Lights*, 35. *Provence*, 215–16. Kinross, quoted in Goldring, *The Last Pre-Raphaelite*, 34; Kinross later owned Ford's Winchelsea 'Bungalow'.

19 *Ancient Lights*, 76–8.

20 Mizener, 16, 528, n. 12. *Ancient Lights*, 79, 223. (The slightly incoherent syntax, omitting the essential negative, also appears in the version in *Harper's*, 122 (Mar. 1911), 617–26.)

Chapter 3

1 Madox Brown told Herbert Gilchrist Ford had left school by 1 December 1890: see Harvey, 3. *Ancient Lights*, 79–81. 'The Old Conflict', *Macmillan's*, 89 (Dec. 1903), 120–31 (see esp. 124). Mizener, 528, n. 12, says Ford 'made a slight effort to enter the Royal College of Music', but he only cites this passage from *Ancient Lights*, which doesn't specify the institution. It is more likely to have been the

Royal College than the Royal Academy, since the principal of the Academy from 1888 to 1924 was Alexander Mackenzie, for two of whose operas Francis Hueffer had written the libretti: *Colomba* (1883); *The Troubador* (1886). Mackenzie was knighted in 1895. Ford only gives the principal's name as 'Sir C—— D——'. This is more likely to have been Sir George Grove, who was the director of the Royal College of Music from 1883 to 1894, and had been knighted in 1883. Violet Hunt had a painting by Ford called 'Pier and Seapiece' (see Mizener, 564, n. 11). Gerard Tetley, 'The Frailties of Ford Madox Ford', *Footnote*, 1 (June 1949), 9–13, mentions his painting. Stang and Smith, ' "Music for a While": Ford's Compositions for Voice and Piano', *Contemporary Literature*, 30/2 (Summer 1989), 212–13; an abridged version appeared in *Agenda*, 27/4–28/1 (Winter 1989–Spring 1990), 120–38, as 'Ford's Musical Compositions'. 'The Music of the Future'.

2 *Mightier Than the Sword*, 126–8. The unpublished MS of *'Princess Goldenhair' is at Cornell. Mizener, 17.

3 *Tea and Anarchy!*, 1, 11. Richard Garnett, *Constance Garnett: A Heroic Life* (London: Sinclair-Stevenson, 1991), 88. Brown told Herbert Gilchrist on 1 Dec. 1890: 'Mrs. Hueffer and her children are now living with me': quoted by Harvey, 3. *Provence*, 249–50.

4 *Return to Yesterday*, 11, 173. *Tea and Anarchy!*, 58 (2 Dec. 1891). Richard Garnett, *Constance Garnett*, 73–4, 81–6; pp. 112–14 describe how the Garnetts heard of the assassination at the end of 1893, and decided to regard 'the whole affair as one past, and removed from the sphere of our comprehension'. Donald Senese, *S. M. Stepniak-Kravchinskii: The London Years* (Newtonville, Mass. 1987), 37. *Return to Yesterday*, 130.

5 Soskice, *Chapters from Childhood*, 1, 4–5. *Return to Yesterday*, 78, 109–11. After four decades he had misremembered the chronology, saying that his poem was published in 1891, after the press was moved to Goodge Street following the death of Lucy Rossetti. But in fact Mrs Rossetti died in 1894, and the move was to Ossulston Street. There was, however, a newsagent on Goodge Street who distributed the paper. (I am grateful to Barry Johnson for information about the Torch Press.) Olive Garnett's diary for 17 Nov. 1894 says: 'Ford gave me a copy of the "Wind's Quest" which the Rossettis printed at the Torch Press, when they were benevolently inclined': *Olive & Stepniak*, 133. This may mean that the poem was published not in the magazine, but as a piece of jobbing printing. Garnett's diary for 23 Oct. 1892 records Olive Rossetti saying: 'Our cousin [Ford] has given us some poems to print.' *Collected Poems* [1913], 227. Ford's anecdote may be conflating two titles: that of the lecture on 'The Foolishness of Anarchism' he told Elsie he had heard: [26 Feb. 1894]; and Shaw's 1893 Fabian Society pamphlet *The Impossibilities of Anarchism*. See Dan H. Laurence, *Bernard Shaw: A Bibliography*, 2 vols. (Oxford: Clarendon Press, 1983), i. 24. The bibliography doesn't list *Why I am an Anarchist*. If Ford 'improved' the title, he may have had in mind a pamphlet such as Shaw's *Anarchism Versus State Socialism* (London: Henry Seymour, 1889), which Shaw had felt some embarrassment about; or an article such as 'Why I am a Social Democrat', *Liberty*, 1 (Jan. 1894), 5.

6 Richard Garnett, *Constance Garnett*, esp. 81–8. *Provence*, 250. Ford to Edward Garnett, 5 May 1928. The novel was *The Benefactor*, discussed above, pp . 200–4. *Return to Yesterday*, 129, 111, 106. *Provence*, 250. *History*, 85–6 (where he also says

he knew François-Claudius Ravachol, executed in 1892 for murders and bomb outrages in Paris), 239, n. 17. Ford is the friend with the 'characteristically casual and omniscient manner' Conrad credits with the germ of *The Secret Agent* in his 'Author's Note'; but he unfairly doubts whether he had ever seen more than 'the back of an anarchist'.

7 Ford to Olive Garnett, 13 Feb. 1892: Northwestern. *Tea and Anarchy!*, 62 (24 Feb. 1892), 63 (26 Feb. 1892), 64 (29 Feb. 1892), 107 (19 Oct. 1892), and 67 (6 Mar. 1892); the passage about the anarchist messiah (6 Mar.) was omitted from *Tea and Anarchy!*. *Ford Madox Brown*, 394. Stang and Smith say that at least four of Ford's song-manuscripts look as if they were prepared to be sent out for publication: 'Music for a While', 197. Goldring said Ford asked Walter Jerrold to place four of them, but they are not known to have been published: *The Last Pre-Raphaelite*, 62. In *South Lodge* he described arriving at Ford's flat in Holland Park Avenue to find him playing a published song at the grand piano. ' "One of my few popular successes, my dear Goldring" Ford remarked [. . .] "I didn't put my name to it, out of respect for my father's reputation, but it was sung everywhere for a couple of seasons" ': 39. Another Huefferism, perhaps, but not impossible. Goldring (who was well used to, and enjoyed, Ford's fabulations) doubted that ' "L'honneur" would have allowed him to claim the authorship of something that was not his'.

8 Rossetti, diary for 3 Jan. 1892: *Selected Letters*, 552-3, n. 1. *Provence*, 138. See Mizener, 20.

9 *Tea and Anarchy!*, 69-71: entries for 25 and 26 Mar. 1892. Garnett's diary for [17] Mar. 1894: *Olive & Stepniak*, 59. Mizener, (who did not know about Olive Garnett's diary) says (p. 18) that Ford began courting Elsie seriously in the summer of 1892, regularly visiting the Martindales who summered at Winchelsea, near Rye. Ford's memory of going courting near Rye just after the publication of his first book could support an earlier date: *Return to Yesterday*, 3. Moser, 216, says he took his first *novel* to Elsie in 1892 to launch his courtship. But the courtship was well launched by Oct. 1892 when *The Shifting of the Fire* was probably published. In *Return to Yesterday* Ford says his first *book* had just been published (i.e. *The Brown Owl*, published *c*. Oct. 1891). So the passage in *Return to Yesterday* could refer to the March visit recorded by Garnett. The manuscript at Cornell, 'As a wounded hart . . .', includes a poem: 'On Taplow lock the sun shines down'. Moser, 14, assumes that Olive Garnett's reference to a 'conquest'; and her question: 'what becomes of the young lady at Hampstead in whose beauty and virtues I so firmly believe?' (diary for *c*. 29 Oct. 1892) refers to Ford's 'conquest' of Elsie, and takes it as evidence of a previous involvement. It is tempting to think this may be the 'young Hampstead lady' Ford said 'came near to being my first—and who knows whether she would not have been my only—love'. One day he saw her home from Madox Brown's, discussing Olive Schreiner's *Dreams*, the seriousness of which, 'when Miss Schreiner took to arguing with God', Ford found comic. He said as much to the young lady (her name isn't recorded), and she 'ended up by saying that I was as vulgar as I was stupid. So there, that romance came to an end!': *Ancient Lights*, 228. However, the diary passage almost certainly refers not to Ford but to Oliver.

10 Soskice, *Chapters from Childhood*, 235. *Tea and Anarchy!*, 85-6 (9 June 1892). The '3 volume novel' was perhaps 'The Wooing in the Wind', discussed above, pp.

78–9 [1894]. Rossetti to Lucy Rossetti, 20 May 1892: *Selected Letters*, 554. In *Return to Yesterday*, 13, Ford said: 'I am now conscious that I acted and spoke to others as if my birth permitted me to meet them as equals'.

11 Mizener, 19, 528, n. 21. *'An Epicure Dines in Lent', *New York Herald Tribune Magazine* (1 Apr. 1928), 20. *Return to Yesterday*, 112–17. *When Blood is Their Argument*, 157–61.

12 *When Blood is Their Argument*, 158–9. Cf. *Return to Yesterday*, 117–28, and *History*, 187, where the details are slightly different. Mizener, 528, n. 21, says Schabrowsky is the same woman as the 'emancipierte' mentioned in the *History* (p. 187), who 'wore a Russian, almost Nihilist, fur toque, smoked cigarettes and when bicycling appeared in knickerbockers'; but this is more likely to be the young woman Ford said 'disquieted' him by talking about 'the Weltanschauung of a writer called Ibsen'; she wore an astrakhan cap, but was the sister of a professor from Hamburg: *When Blood is Their Argument*, 161. Since Ford makes the point that the hat was *de rigueur* for a self-respecting revolutionist, similarity of hat doesn't prove identity of persons.

13 Ford to Mrs Martindale [3 Oct. 1892]. Olive Garnett's diary for 18 Oct. 1892.

14 Alison Lurie, 'Ford Madox Ford's Fairy Tales for Children', *The Presence of Ford Madox Ford*, 134. *The Feather*, 181–2, 37. *The Feather* was reviewed unfavourably: see Harvey, 275–6.

15 Conrad to Ford, [12] Nov. 1898: *Collected Letters*, ii. 118–19.

16 *The Shifting of the Fire*, 321. Moser, 28–9; p. 30 gives an intriguing account of how details of the novel foreshadowed subsequent events: in particular, the Martindales' forbidding of the marriage; Ford's threats of suicide; Ford and Elsie going to live in Kent; and Dr Martindale's own suicide, by poison. Ford later told Olive Garnett he had written it when he was 16 (which may indeed be when he began it), and found it 'one of the most vulgar books' he had ever read: Garnett's diary for 23 Nov. 1895: *Olive & Stepniak*, 222. In *Provence*, 200–1, Ford told of a young cousin 'who had come to London from Richmond, Virginia, by way of Paris'. She had come to see Ellen Terry, who invited them both to lunch, and the cousin died in Paris soon after her return. In an unpublished 1928 typescript, 'Auto-Plagiarism', Ford remembered being on a cross-channel ship 'in very early life' with 'a little American connection [. . .] to whom, as I long since discovered, it was the wish of my family that I should become engaged—and to whom I certainly should have become engaged if she hadn't, poor little Hattina, died almost immediately afterwards of meningitis. So that, had that real tragedy not happened it is odds but I should now be engaged planting tobacco near Richmond in Virginia. I wish I were' (pp. 4, 7). If these refer to the same cousin, Olive Garnett's fragmentary diary entry between 28 Nov. and 7 Dec. 1892 suggests a possible date. She noted: 'Ford told Mamma that Ellen Terry had fallen in love with him & he didn't like it.' *The Shifting of the Fire* had already been published by then; but Ford may have met 'Hattina' in Paris during the previous year. She is also mentioned in *Henry James*, 90, and is probably the girl mentioned in *It Was the Nightingale*, 64. *Great Trade Route*, 140, implies that it was Uncle Leopold who lived in Richmond. Garnett's diary for 23 Oct. 1892.

17 Moser, 29. *The Shifting of the Fire*, 289.

18 *The copy was owned by Eric Quayle, who kindly supplied the information (which does not appear in Harvey's bibliography). After Brown's death Oliver got

hold of it, since he re-inscribed it to 'Miss Olive Garnett with the author's brother's kindest regards. June 94'. There are two manuscripts of the obituary at Cornell: *'Tennyson', and *'In the Autumn the Fall of the Leaf'. It was intended for the *Speaker*, but apparently not published.

19 Mizener, 21, 529, n. 23: an official copy of Ford's baptismal record is at Cornell. *Return to Yesterday*, 102-4. In *A Mirror to France*, 24, he mentions 'succeeding winters spent in a tranquilly luxurious, gilded *appartement* of a very rich Paris-American relative'. Mizener, 20, ever eager to convict Ford of exaggeration, complained that he claimed 'my boyhood . . . was passed very largely in Paris'; what Ford actually wrote (in *Henry James*, 90) is 'I first read *The American* during a period of my boyhood that was passed very largely in Paris'. *Between St. Dennis and St. George*, p. 75. The story about the opera comes from an untitled typescript at Cornell, beginning 'When that I was a little, little boy', 4. *'Nice People', 566-8. *Provence*, 135, 140.

He said he studied kitchen-gardening 'at the Sorbonne under the great professor Gressent'. *Return to Yesterday*, 112. Cf. *No Enemy*, 171, *Joseph Conrad*, 15-16, and *It Was the Nightingale*, 106. It is one of the stories Mizener doubts, saying Ford 'remembered himself as having studied' there—as if it were simply fantasy: 529, n. 23. But most of Ford's fantasies originated in fact. Olive Garnett's diary, and indeed Ford's extensive, if impressionistic, erudition, show him to have been a formidable and highly motivated autodidact. It is very probable that his cousins or their friends were studying at the Sorbonne, and that he attended lectures there, even if he was not formally enrolled. Gressent would have been in his seventies then, but did lecture in Paris.

He also stayed 'in the most opulent of hotels' on the Riviera with Uncle Leopold at about this time. Ford said his uncle gave him a sovereign a day to gamble with provided he didn't get into debt. 'I did not play much', said Ford laconically. The daily loss of the sovereign cured him of any urge to gamble. He went to bed early to read Eugène Sue while the orchestra of the Café de Paris played 'Tararaboomde-ay' and 'The Man who Broke the Bank at Monte Carlo'. What he most remembered was another brush with mortality, this time involving a father-figure's violent (though saving) outburst. He and his uncle were dozing off, when Leopold suddenly smashed a window to stop them being suffocated by the stove's fumes. 'Zola and his wife had just died in that way in Paris', Ford explained, and added that had the firemen not arrived, 'I should not be writing here now'. *Provence*, 265-6; p. 36 n. says he ate bouillabaisse at the 'Grand Hotel du Louvre et de la Paix at Marseilles in 1891' but p. 265 says he supposes he was 'seventeen or eighteen'. If 18, the year would have been 1892. Mizener, 19, has Ford on the Riviera some time in August or September; but Ford remembered visiting 'rather chilly winter resorts'—hence his story about the stove. 'I Revisit the Riviera', *Harper's*, 166 (Dec. 1932), 65-6. He told Stella Bowen he had visited Perugia, Siena, Assisi, and Florence when he was about 18: 10 Mar. 1923.

Chapter 4

1 Mizener, 20, says he was back by the beginning of 1893. But he appears to have been in London by some time between 28 Nov. and 6 Dec. 1892, when Olive Garnett reported the comment he made to her mother about Ellen Terry. He was certainly back before 22 Dec., when Lucy Rossetti told Olive that 'M^r [Madox]

Brown took all his seven grandchildren to see *King Lear* the other night': *Tea and Anarchy!*, 139. Henry Irving had got him two boxes at the Lyceum. 'The anarchists didn't seem to mind sitting in the royal box', their mother noted tartly. Ford was staying with Madox Brown at St Edmund's Terrace in March 1892 (see *Tea and Anarchy!*, 69; his letter to Mrs Martindale about the ring for Elsie was written on Brook Green stationery on 3 Oct., so he may have moved back by then. *Tea and Anarchy!*, 146 (10 Jan. 1893).

2 Ford to Elsie Martindale, 25, 27 Feb. 1893. Did Ford really not know that his father was the son of Johann Hermann, the son of Christoph? *Tea and Anarchy!*, 159 (9 Mar. 1893). Garnett added: 'This news makes me realise how very dear they are to me, those two'; but she didn't say whether it was the news of them being away from London, or the news of Ford's engagement. Garnett's diary for 12 and 15 Mar. 1893: both passages omitted from *Tea and Anarchy!*, 161, 162. *The Shifting of the Fire*, 193. Soskice, *Chapters from Childhood*, 202.

3 *Tea and Anarchy!*, 162 (16 Mar. 1893).

4 Garnett's diary for 15 Mar. 1893. Mizener, 23–4, 27. Ford to Elsie, [2 May; 1 May; 2 June; 19 July; 27 May; 2? June 1893]. Mizener, 23.

5 *Tea and Anarchy!*, 182 (23 Apr. 1893).

6 Ford to Elsie [12 May; 5 June; 17 July; 22 July 1893]. *The Questions at the Well*, 11, 42. *Poems for Pictures*, 44. Mizener, p. xv. *The Shifting of the Fire*, 62. Ford to Edward Garnett [n.d., but before Aug. 1893]: Texas. Ford to Walter Jerrold [27 May 1893]. Ford to Olive Garnett, 9 Aug. 1893: Northwestern.

7 *Tea and Anarchy!*, 202–3 (20 June 1893); 79–80 (19 May 1892); 210 (5 July 1893); and 165 (23 Mar. 1893). Mizener, 24–5. Ford to Elsie [n.d., but identified as 'June 15/93/July?' in another hand]; and [n.d.: catalogued as Oct.–Dec. 1893, but [2 Oct. 1893] sounds as if it were written soon after by way of explanation of the depression Ford has mentioned; so it probably precedes Madox Brown's death on 6 Oct.

8 Garnett's diary for 29 July 1893 shows that he had just left England. Ford, postcard to Elsie [dated 8 Aug. in pencil but postmarked 10 Aug. 1893 at Paderborn]. Ford to Elsie, 'Wednesday Night' [postmarked 10 Aug. 1893], also from Paderborn, says he leaves for Driberg on Saturday, and for England the following Saturday (19 Aug. 1893). Ford to Elsie [2 Oct. 1893]; [19 July 1893] and [20 July 1893]. [Yeats], *Speaker*, 8 (26 Aug. 1893), 220–1. The attribution is not made by Harvey, but the piece is collected in *Uncollected Prose by W. B. Yeats*, ed. John Frayne, vol. 1 (London: Macmillan, 1970), 288–91.

9 *'Nice People', 574. Brown died on 6 Oct. 1893.

10 William to Lucy Rossetti, 6 Oct. 1893: *Selected Letters*, 568–9. *Ford Madox Brown*, 63, 397–8, 402. Soskice *Chapters from Childhood*, 68–73. *The Good Soldier*, 71. *Ancient Lights*, 128. On p. 212 Ford describes being sent to Holman Hunt to ask him to attend Brown's funeral. '[Memoir on the death of his grandfather, Ford Madox Brown]'. *'Nice People', 571.

11 Ford to Elsie [26 Oct.; 3, 9, and 10 Nov. 1893]. In *Mightier Than the Sword*, 129, Ford said he had gone on a Wessex walking tour and had dropped in on Thomas Hardy six months after the publication of *The Brown Owl* (i.e. in 1892). He was in Sussex in the spring of 1892, but near Salisbury in the following spring. But he was near Dorchester again this winter of 1893. Mizener, 27, 529, n. 12.

12 Ford to Elsie [8 Jan. 1894].

13 Ford to Elsie [7 Dec. 1893]. *The Queen Who Flew*, 75, 84.

14 Ford told this story in at least four places. The details remain remarkably consistent, with one exception: the date. The earliest and most personal version, *'Nice People', 568–70, written in 1903, places it 'about the time of the Trafalgar Square riots'—1886 and 1887. *Ancient Lights*, 284–5, places it 'at the time of the great Dock Strike'—1889. The version in *A History of Our Own Times*, 168, was cut from that book by Ford (though restored by his editors) because he used it verbatim in *Return to Yesterday*, 106–8. In this version it is placed 'during the great coal strike of 1893'. However, in the *Return to Yesterday* version Ford was about to publish a fairy-tale, which in 'Nice People' he identifies as his second. This would place it in 1892. *History*, 243–4, n. 15.

15 From the typescript of 'Poems in Two Keys': House of Lords Record Office. Harvey, 123, cites three other drafts, now at Cornell.

16 *Ancient Lights*, 119–21: 'There used to be terrific rows between Socialists and Anarchists in those days [. . .] They were always holding meetings at which the subject for debate would be, "The Foolishness of Anarchism." ' Ford to Elsie [26 Feb. 1894].

17 Mizener, 26. *Ancient Lights*, 121.

18 *Ancient Lights*, 284. *Return to Yesterday*, 108. *'Nice People', 569. The unpublished story might be *'The Last Sowing': discussed above, pp. 105–6. Ford later met Kropotkin at Limpsfield, where Constance and Edward Garnett lived. See *Return to Yesterday*, 69. Juliet remembered Ford taking her to tea with Kropotkin, whom she found 'almost holy': Soskice, *Chapters from Childhood*, 236.

19 Ford to Elsie [7 Dec.; 6 Jan.; n.d.; 14 Dec. 1893]; all also quoted in Dr Martindale's Affidavit, dated 1 June 1894.

20 Ford to Elsie [n.d., but from Brook Green, therefore written before their marriage in May 1894].

21 *Ford Madox Brown*, 354, 296, 394. Emma Madox Brown died on 11 Oct. 1890. Ford wrote the poem 'In Memoriam: E.M.B.' for her: *The Questions at the Well*, 60. Soskice, *Chapters from Childhood*, 71. *Ancient Lights*, 2. 'Literary Portraits—XLV.: Mme. Yoi Pawlowska and "A Child Went Forth." ', *Outlook*, 34 (18 July 1914), 79–80.

22 'Not Idle', *New York Herald Tribune Books* (1 July 1928), 1, 6; see also *It Was the Nightingale*, 59, 69. For the importance of reverie, see *'Nice People', and *'The Idealist' (unpublished MS, House of Lords Record Office). For 'the stuff to fill graveyards', see p. 166. *The Inheritors*, 304. *Ford Madox Brown*, 278.

23 *Thus to Revisit*, 193. *Ancient Lights*, pp. xv, 223, 191.

24 Samuel Hynes's fine study, *The Edwardian Turn of Mind*, charts these themes. *Ancient Lights*, pp. vii–x. In *A History of Our Own Times*, 13, Ford describes his project as an attempt to 're-memorize' the past he has been astonished to find himself having forgotten.

25 'On Impressionism', *Poetry and Drama*, 2 (June and Dec. 1914), 167–75, 323–34.

26 *Ancient Lights*, 223, 289.

27 Moser, 49.

28 *Ancient Lights*, p. xv. Cf. *A Call*, 299: 'You go to books to be taken out of yourself, I to be shown where I stand.'

Chapter 5

1 *Tea and Anarchy!*, 237 (21 Dec. 1893). Garnett's diary for 12, 14, and 28 Jan. 1894. She also noted them as attending a lecture by Hubert Crackanthorpe on 11 Feb. *Olive & Stepniak*, 30, 33, 35.

2 Ford to Elsie [7 Jan.; 14 and 21 Feb. 1894]; [3 Nov. 1893]; [3 Mar. 1894]. Martindale Affidavit.

3 Martindale Affidavit. Mizener, 27–8, interpreted the sequence differently here, saying that Martindale called on Mrs Hueffer *because* 'the poor doctor was so shaken by this revelation of his daughter's views that he swallowed his pride' (which is unfortunately characteristic of his tendency to give more sympathy to others than he does to Ford). However, Martindale dated this remonstrating with Elsie as occurring on 3 Mar.—the same day on which he visited Mrs Hueffer. If the argument with Elsie had taken place before that visit, surely he would have forbidden Ford the house when he saw Mrs Hueffer. But his doing that the following day suggests that he first went to Mrs Hueffer, argued with Elsie that evening on his return, and then resolved to banish Ford. Ford to Dr Martindale [12 Mar. 1894] ('you have told her she has no right to think'); Ford to Elsie [dated 5 Mar. 1894 in the Martindale Affidavit and the Cornell catalogue; but presumably written on the night of the 4th or the early hours of the 5th].

4 Dr Martindale's undated note. Elsie to Dr Martindale, 5 Mar. 1894; with his annotations on the letter and envelope. Ford to Elsie [n.d., but dated 'About 5th March' in the Martindale Affidavit. Shaen Roscoe was the firm Robert Garnett worked for.

5 W. M. Rossetti to Martindale, 8 Mar. 1894. Mizener again casts Martindale as the peacemaker, saying he decided to consult Rossetti. Yet Ford's letter to Elsie saying he will 'rouse W.M.R. and a few more great guns' shows he initiated the move. Martindale wrote to Ford on 10 Mar. saying: 'As you had consulted Mr Rossetti & given him your view of matters & I had done the same [. . .]'

6 Mizener, 29, says Ford 'refused' to do what Rossetti suggested. But the evidence he cites—saying he was 'in effect countering by suggesting to Elsie that [. . .] Mrs Hueffer would be glad to have Elsie come to live in Brook Green'—comes from the letter written 'About 5th March', several days *before* he had received Rossetti's terms. Martindale to Ford, 10 Mar. 1894. The letter from Ford to Martindale dated 'Saturday Mch 10/93' (in a hand other than Ford's) might be Ford's reply [and thus be misdated for 10 Mar. 1894: the 10 Mar. was a Friday in 1893, but a Saturday in 1894]. This says: 'Elsie has just come over here in the usual distress—I am unable to understand quite the whole business—I have just received a letter from you, which does not explain it.—Hereupon follows Harri to take Elsie back & she goes. The question that I should be glad to have answered at your convenience is, whether the letter remains as an offer or no. If so, may I call on you at Cavendish Street—& when?' Ford to Martindale [12 Mar. 1894]. Martindale to Ford, 12 Mar. 1894, repeated the charge that Mrs Hueffer had deceived him, 'intentionally', though he disputed that he had used the phrase 'infamous liar'. Cathy Hueffer wrote to Martindale after the scene on the 5th saying that he had no right 'to break the promise you made Fords grandfather to whom you gave your solemn word that you had no thought of breaking the engagement between Ford and Elsie'. Mizener, 28 n, says Cathy Hueffer's letter 'appears to have been composed by Ford. It is in his style rather than in Mrs Hueffer's faintly illiterate one'. But it *is* faintly illiterate (no apostrophe; the awkward repetition of Ford's name). Believing Ford did write it, Mizener says he was exaggerating because there was no engagement when Martindale talked to Brown. But Olive Garnett said Ford had told Madox Brown, who was telling everyone else, about it by 9

Mar. 1893—well before Brown went to see Martindale in May: *Tea and Anarchy!*, 159. W. M. Rossetti told Martindale in his letter of 8 Mar.: 'As a man of honour & character, you wd. certainly not wish to recede from the sort of qualified sanction (even allowing that it was not a definite sanction) wh. you gave some while ago to the engagement.' So Ford and Elsie considered they were engaged, as did Madox Brown; the Martindale didn't regard it as a formal engagement, but they probably gave qualified assent along the lines that they would have to wait until Elsie was old or well enough (as Olive Garnett said), or until Ford was well enough off. Martindale to Ford, 12 Mar. 1894. Ford to Elsie ['About 8th March'; quoted on Martindale Affidavit].

7 Ford to Elsie [12 and 13 Mar. 1894]. See Moser, 19. Ford wrote 'A Romance of the Times Before Us' between two and four years later: unpublished MS at Cornell (see Harvey, 117).

8 Mizener, 29–30. He says the Garnett relative lived in Bath, but Garnett, 'A Bloomsbury Girlhood', 247 says Mrs Garnett lived at Clifton. Rossetti to Martindale, 16 Mar. 1894. Olive Garnett, diary for 16 May 1894: *Olive & Stepniak*, 75.

9 Olive Garnett's diary, Saturday [17, misdated 16] Mar. 1894: *Olive & Stepniak*, 58–60. David Garnett, *The Golden Echo* (London: Chatto & Windus, 1953), 36.

10 Garnett's diary for [17] and 18 Mar. 1894: *Olive & Stepniak*, 58–61. The barrister was Job Bradford: see *Tea and Anarchy!*, 27; and 110, n. 20 on the Belchers. Garnett's diary shows that it was because of this story about Arthur's explosives that W. M. Rossetti 'had destroyed all the *Torch* type etc'. Ford later said it was done when Rossetti's wife, who had sanctioned the printing, died (*Return to Yesterday*, 108–9). This is borne out by Olive Garnett's diary for 2 May 1894, commenting on how 'Mr Rossetti made a clean sweep' of the press and other anarchist paraphernalia less than three weeks after his wife's death: *Olive & Stepniak*, 71. Norman Sherry, *Conrad's Western World* (Cambridge: Cambridge University Press, 1971), 228–52; and Ian Watt, 'The Political and Social Background of *The Secret Agent*', in *Conrad: The Secret Agent*, ed. Ian Watt, Casebook Series (London and Basingstoke: Macmillan, 1973), 229–51. Moser, 17. When William Rossetti had been to see Dr Martindale on 8 Mar. he had asked if the *Torch* 'had not been the cause of dissensions'; but Martindale said he did not even know of its existence: Martindale's notes on the meeting.

11 Garnett's diary for 18, 19, 22, 23, and 20 Mar. 1894: *Olive & Stepniak*, 60–3. George Jefferson, *Edward Garnett: A Life in Literature* (London: Jonathan Cape, 1982), 28. Lucy Rossetti died on 12 Apr. 1894.

12 Garnett, diary for 28 Mar. 1894. The 'new novel' might be *'The Last Sowing', discussed above, pp. 105–6.

13 Mizener, 30. [Wilson & Son] to Shaen Roscoe [Massey] & Co., 20 Mar. 1894. Shaen Roscoe Massey & Co. to Martindale's solicitors [Wilson & Son], 21 Mar. 1894; Elsie to Martindale, 20 Mar. 1894: Martindale Affidavit.

14 Mizener, 30. Martindale Affidavit. An undated draft letter Martindale wrote to William Rossetti says: 'He has for ever forfeited my regard for him, as I find even before the past week's unpleasantness he had deceived me.' This presumably refers to his reading of Ford's letters after Elsie had eloped.

15 Garnett's diary for 26 Mar. (*Olive & Stepniak*, 63) and Tuesday [10, misdated 9] Apr. 1894. *Tea and Anarchy!*, 23.

16 Mizener, 30–1. Garnett's diary for 30 Apr. 1894: *Olive & Stepniak*, 69. Elsie to Martindale, 5 May 1894.

17 Mizener, 31, 530, n. 18. The fullest account of the case is the law report in *The Times* (10 Aug. 1894), 14–15: *'High Court of Justice: Chancery Division: (Before Mr. Justice North.): In re Martindale'. Garnett's diary, entry made on 14 June about 6 June 1894: *Olive & Stepniak*, 87–8.

18 Garnett's diary for 20 and 26 May, and 5 June 1894: *Olive & Stepniak*, 76, 80, 86–7. Mizener, 33, dated the sale 29–31 May (and said it made £1,350: 530, n. 1); Garnett noted the proceeds on the title-page of vol. 28 of her diary. *Ancient Lights*, 137.

19 Garnett's diary, entry made on 14 June 1894, about the 6th. Alan Judd, *Ford Madox Ford*, p. 42, implies that the court order forbade sexual intercourse; the *Times* report on 10 Aug. makes it clear it was 'to forbid all communications' between the couple. Perris to Felix Volkhovsky [n.d., but *c.* 23 June 1894]: Hoover Institution. The paragraph appeared in the *Star* on the same afternoon as the hearing—6 June 1894. There was a similar paragraph in the *Morning* the following day, which was copied into the *Pall Mall Gazette* of that day, and the *People* of the 8th. See 'In re Martindale', *The Times* (25 June 1894), 3. Perris, eight years older than Ford, was also a friend of the Garnetts, and a writer on international affairs. He published *Leo Tolstoy, the Grand Mujik* in 1898 (with a preface by Volkhovsky), and *Russia in Revolution* in 1905, with chapters on Volkhovsky and Stepniak. He founded the Literary Agency of London in 1899, that was later taken over by Curtis Brown. See *Tea and Anarchy!*, 29, and Mizener, 530, n. 1.

20 Garnett's diary, entry written on 14 June 1894 for 6, 7, 8, and 9 June: *Olive & Stepniak*, 87–91. Moser, 20. Ford's setting of the Tennyson is amongst his musical MSS at Cornell. Longman had originally asked William Morris. He declined, but suggested William Rossetti, who in turn suggested his wife. But Lucy Rossetti died not long after beginning the book. William then suggested Ford. W. M. Rossetti, *Some Reminiscences*, 543–4.

21 *Pall Mall Gazette* reported the day's hearings on 15 June 1894 (p. 7): 'Mysterious Chancery Proceedings' (because heard in private). Garnett's diary for 22 and 23 June 1894: *Olive & Stepniak*, 92–3. *'The Courts and the Press', Star* (23 June 1894), p. 3.

22 Garnett's diary for 23 June, 2, 7 [18, misdated 17] July, and 9 Nov. 1894: *Olive & Stepniak*, 93, 95, 102–3, 128. Goldring, *The Last Pre-Raphaelite*, 58, 61. Mizener, 34. The house, which Mizener calls 'Bloomfield Villa', is now known as 'Fir Trees Villa', and is just off the B2067, on the road between Priory Wood and Park Wood: Mizener, 530, n. 2. Ford, 'Autobiographical entry . . . *Portraits and Self Portraits*' (typescript at Cornell). Garnett's diary for 1 Oct. 1894: *Olive & Stepniak*, 121. By 7 Apr. 1895 she was recording Oliver's 'contempt for Ford's Arcadian Shepherd mode of existence': *Olive & Stepniak*, 167. *Tea and Anarchy!*, 166, n. 14.

23 *The Times* (10 Aug. 1894), 14–15. Garnett's diary for 9 and 10 Aug. 1894. Ford to Perris (n.d., but 'Sunday' soon after Thursday 9 Aug. 1894]: original in possession of Mrs Helen Gomme, and quoted with her kind permission.

Chapter 6

1 *Return to Yesterday*, 139. *Ancient Lights*, 226, 241. Ford is slightly misquoting R. L. Stevensons's 'Requiem'.

2 Garnett's diary for 9 and 14 Nov. 1894: *Olive & Stepniak*, 128, 131–2. Richard Garnett's claim that Edward was commenting on Ford's 'impossibly woolly life of his grandfather' is itself impossible, since the book was not then written; the *conception* was what was vague: *Constance Garnett*, 101. Ford (signed 'Fraud. H') to Garnett [n.d., but second half of 1894]; *Letters*, 7–8.

3 Garnett's diary for 17 Nov. 1894: *Olive & Stepniak*, 133–4.

4 Garnett's diary for [19, misdated 20], 20, 21, and 25 Nov.; 14 Mar. 1894: *Olive & Stepniak*, 134–6. Her entries for 22 and 23 Nov. mention that Elsie was sending MSS to magazines such as the *Cornhill* and the *Yellow Book*.

5 Elsie to Martindale, 25 Dec. 1894 and 4 Jan. 1895; Martindale to Elsie [n.d., but *c*. Dec. 1894] and 30 Dec. 1894. Moser, 39. Garnett's diary for 7 May 1895.

6 Garnett's diary for 8, 21, and 23 Feb.; 5, 10, 18, and 30 Mar.; 1 Apr.; and 23 June 1895: *Olive & Stepniak*, 152–3, 159, 162, 164–5, 190; Mizener, 34. In *Return to Yesterday* Ford said '£400 a year was sufficient for the luxurious support for a man about town' in the 1890s: 14. Ford to Garnett [n.d., but between 8 Feb. (when Longman's took the book) and 20 Feb. (when Ford and Elsie dined with Olive in London)]: *Letters*, 8–9. Rossetti, *Selected Letters*, 585–6. Garnett's diary for 26 June says they 'bought the Morris sociable for £5. It was a good bargain' (a 'sociable' was a tricycle for two with seats side by side).

7 Garnett's diary for 29 Jan., 14, 10 Feb., 14 and 7 Apr. [13, 19], and 21–6 Sept. 1895: *Olive & Stepniak*, 148, 152, 151, 170, 167, 199–203.

8 Dated 22 July 1895: Stow Hill Papers. Stang and Smith, 'Music for a While', 187, n. 6, say Juliet sang professionally.

9 Ford to Garnett [n.d.]: Texas (quoted by Mizener, 35). Garnett's diary for 28 [Sept. 1895] and 17 Nov. 1894: *Olive & Stepniak*, 205, 133 (the remark about Edward's paradoxes is quoted in Jefferson, *Edward Garnett*, 21). R. Garnett, *Constance Garnett*, 101, 50, 79–80. Goldring, *The Last Pre-Raphaelite*, 64.

10 Garnett's diary for 16 and 18 Nov. 1895: *Olive & Stepniak*, 216–19. R. Garnett, *Constance Garnett*, 138, 145–52. The name signified that the house was 'encearned' or encircled by woods (Mizener, 37). Moser, 21. Mizener, 63. Ford's comment about fidelity was recorded by their daughter Katharine Lamb, in a letter to Mizener, 11 Dec. 1966.

11 Garnett's diary for 19, 20, 22 Nov. 1895: *Olive & Stepniak*, 219–21. Moser, 35–7. Vasily Vasil'evich Bervi was a philosopher who wrote under the name of N. Flerovsky: *Tea and Anarchy!*, 241, n. 6. But as Barry Johnson says, since Mme Bervi's autobiography was apparently not published, Fomin's story isn't known: *Olive & Stepniak*, 229, n. 25.

12 Garnett's diary for 23 and 24 Nov. 1895: *Olive & Stepniak*, 221–3.

13 Moser, 35–6. Garnett, *Constance Garnett*, 97–8. In 'From a Paris Quay (II), *New York Evening Post Literary Review* (3 Jan. 1925), 1–2, Ford wrote that Cervantes, gave us 'the death of altruism — of Christianity itself'. Stepniak was killed by a train on a level crossing on 23 Dec. 1895. 'Coming so soon after the confession, the accident was supposed by some to have been suicide; his friends however remembered his faculty of wrapping himself in his thoughts. The oblivion that enabled him to survive so many English dinner parties proved fatal; the engine driver saw him, blew frantically at the whistle, but Stepniak did not look up': Garnett, 'A Bloomsbury Girlhood', 373.

14 Garnett's diary for 10 Dec. 1895: *Olive & Stepniak*, 226. Martindale to Elsie, 10 Dec. 1895: Cornell.

15 *The Cinque Ports*, 127–8. *The Heart of the Country*, 152.

16 *The Heart of the Country*, 110. *'Nice People', 577. Meary Walker is also mentioned in a letter to Olive Garnett, written probably at the end of 1900: 'Elsie has gone to a sale with Mrs Walker': *Reader*, 466–7. Elsie was also moved to write about her: see Garnett's diary for 24 Nov. 1895: *Olive & Stepniak*, 223. A story about Mary Walker and Jane Sprattford (who sounds like Ford's 'Meary Spratt') called 'Going Home', *Speaker*, 12 (22 July 1905), 390, can be attributed to her (Ford to Elsie [n.d., but Summer 1905]. In it she elaborates upon the anecdote sketched in 'Nice People' of how Mary prevents the parson from burying another woman in the grave next to her husband's by sitting in it herself. She was probably the 'old woman' who told Ford the ghost stories retailed in *The Cinque Ports*, 72–3. He also wrote about her in 'Nice People'; *The Heart of the Country*, 109–31; the section about her in 'Women and Men' (*Little Review*, 4 (July 1918), 51–4 and (Sept. 1918), 54–9; 52–61 in the book version) was incorporated, with minor changes, into *Return to Yesterday*, 139–50. See p. 143 for another version of their meeting. There is also a brief reminiscence of her in 'Saint Christopher', *New York Herald Tribune Books* (3 June 1928), 1, 6. He frequently echoed her words: see e.g. 'Thomas Hardy, O. M. Obiit 11 January 1928', *New York Herald Tribune Books* (22 Jan. 1928), 1–3. In *The Heart of the Country* (1906) Ford said she had been 'dead for a year or so' (110), and that she had died very suddenly at the age of 74 (115); the Bonnington parish records give her age as 73 when she died on 11 Apr. 1903. *Return to Yesterday*, 143.

17 *Return to Yesterday*, 145–7, 139. *The Heart of the Country*, 156–7.

18 *Return to Yesterday*, 148–53, 140, 157–8. *The Heart of the Country*, 146–52, gives the ages of Meary Spratt and Spratford as 70 and 79, and the number of children as twenty-three. Garnett's diary for 22 Nov. 1895 mentions a visit from Meary Walker; on 25 Nov. Mrs Walker was back again, with Mrs Spratt: *Olive & Stepniak*, 219–20, 223. When Ragged Ass Wilson was doing some work for the Hueffers at their next house, the Pent, he began to open up an old ingle-nook that had been bricked up by a previous tenant. Ford went to bed, and when he came down the next morning there was Wilson 'asleep on an old coffin stool in the opened up ingle. His arms were above his head, one hand holding a great hammer, another a cold-chisel, his legs were extended before him': *Return to Yesterday*, 153.

19 Pound ['The Inquest'], and 'Ford Madox (Hueffer) Ford: Obit', *Pound/Ford*, 70; 174. *The Heart of the Country*, 213–14, 94–5. Compare the story 'Riesenberg', *English Review*, 8 (Apr. 1911), 25–45, in which a hill is imagined as a slumbering giant. 'The Small Farmer Soliloquizes', from 'Two Monologues', *The Face of the Night* (1904), repr. in *Collected Poems* [1913], 121–2. An early draft is part of *'The Union', a macabre discussion between the ghosts of the workhouse dead: House of Lords Record Office.

20 Mizener, 530, n. 7, 36. Elsie to Olive Garnett, 12 Dec. 1896; quoted in Goldring, *The Last Pre-Raphaelite*, 61. Olive journeyed to Russia between 5 Aug. 1896 and 24 May 1897, which is why she doesn't figure in the roll of visitors for late 1896; but this letter shows her still in touch with the Hueffers (see her diary entries for 11 Aug. 1896 and 24 May 1898). *Joseph Conrad*, 21–2. Mizener, 36. Ford to Jerrold [n.d.]; quoted in *The Last Pre-Raphaelite*, 62. Cf. *Ancient Lights*, 230 and 241, on

the idealizing of peasant life, and the fashion for young men 'to waste only too many good years of their lives in posing as romantic agriculturists'.

21 Mizener, 36. When Ford reviewed his own book anonymously a decade later his style verges on a parody of the Olympian 'grand manner': *'The Pre-Raphaelite Brotherhood', *Quarterly Review*, 204 (Apr. 1906), 352–74 (for the attribution see Garnett's diary for 2 Nov. 1905, and Ford to Elsie, 28 Apr. 1906. *The Times* (12 Nov. 1896), 12; *Dial*, 21 (16 Dec. 1896), 382; *Magazine of Art* (Jan. 1897), 158–9: Harvey, 277. Elsie to Olive Garnett, 12 Dec. 1896; quoted in Goldring, *The Last Pre-Raphaelite*, 61. Ford also wrote the catalogue: see Harvey, 91. Ford's claim in *Ancient Lights*, 13, that he was organizing this exhibition is borne out by a letter to Mr Fairfax Murray [n.d., but Oct.–Dec. 1896]: Texas. Ford to Jerrold [n.d.], quoted by Mizener, 37. Ford to Elsie, 14 July 1897.

22 Goldring, *The Last Pre-Raphaelite*, 64, says the uncle died in 1895. Elsie Hueffer told Katharine Lamb (19 May 1945) that she thought it was Wilhelm, 'Baron Hueffer' (*sic*) in Rome. Wilhelm, 'the Baron', died childless in that year, so would have been likely to leave his large fortune to his relatives. But Mizener, 35, says it was Leopold, who died on 18 Feb. 1897. This accords with Ford saying his '*oncle d'Amerique* had performed as American uncles should' (*Return to Yesterday*, 170). But he did not die childless, as Mizener said he did. Leopold died leaving three sons. Ford's and Oliver's legacies could have come from either uncle, or indeed from both. (*Return to Yesterday*, 51, says: 'I too had my *oncle d'Amerique*. Indeed, I had two.) See 'Die Hüffer', in Wilhelm Schulte, *Westfälische Köpfe* (Münster: Verlag Aschendorff, 1963). There is a receipt for Ford's subscription to the Hythe Golf Club at Cornell, dated 30 Oct. 1897. *Return to Yesterday*, 140–1, 175.

23 Mizener, 38, says they moved to Grace's Cottage on 20 Mar. R. Garnett, *Constance Garnett*, 168, gives the date as 4 Mar. (as does George Jefferson in *Edward Garnett*, 36). Goldring, *The Last Pre-Raphaelite*, 64. *Joseph Conrad*, 17. *Return to Yesterday*, 63–5, 28, 30, 47–8. It must have been disturbing to Ford to see the Cearne furnished with pieces bought at Madox Brown's sale: 'the Broadwood square piano, which neither of them played', and the William Morris 'heavy oak dining table with its ecclesiastical legs and impractical bevelled edges', plus chairs (*Constance Garnett*, 138, 154). *Constance Garnett*, 70, 90, 164, 168 (quoting Constance to Richard Garnett, 4 Mar. 1898), and 174. *Mightier Than the Sword*, 41–44, 50. In *Thus to Revisit*, 106, he gives Crane's words as: 'That's a bully ol' battlement.' See p. 110 for another version of his attack on Ford's poetry. 'Stevie', *New York Evening Post Literary Review* (12 July 1924), 881–2. Ford also wrote about Crane in: 'Literary Causeries: V. Revivals and Revivalists', *Chicago Tribune* (Paris), no. 5 (16 Mar. 1924), 3, 11; and 'Stevie & Co.', *New York Herald Tribune Books* (2 Jan. 1927), 1 (repr. as the third essay in *New York Essays*). See Lindberg-Seyersted, *Ford Madox Ford and His Relationship to Stephen Crane and Henry James*. Thomas Beer, *New York Evening Post Literary Review* (19 July 1924), 910, objected that Crane's handwriting wasn't minute. Ford's own was in the 1920s and 1930s.

24 R. Garnett, *Constance Garnett*, 146, 42. Norman and Jeanne MacKenzie, *The First Fabians* (London: Weidenfeld and Nicolson, 1977), 39–40, 99. *Return to Yesterday*, 33.

25 See *An English Girl*, 263–8, for an example of Fordian ambivalence towards
reformers. David Garnett, *The Golden Echo* (London: Chatto & Windus, 1953),
36–7. He called Ford's beard 'hay on his face'.

26 D. Garnett, *The Golden Echo*, p. 36.

27 R. Garnett, *Constance Garnett*, 170, 285. D. Garnett, *The Golden Echo*, 37–8.
Lawrence, interview with Kyle Crichton, in Edward Nehls, *D. H. Lawrence: A
Composite Biography*, 3 vols. (Madison: University of Wisconsin, 1957–9), vol. 2
(1958), 412. Lawrence confused Soskice with Stepniak; but *The Golden Echo*, 37–8,
retails the same two 'statistics'. Mizener, 531, n. 12. For further information on
Soskice see Barry Hollingsworth, 'David Soskice in Russia in 1917', *European
Studies*, 6 (1976), 73–97; Thomas Moser, 'Ford Madox Hueffer and *Under Western
Eyes*', *Conradiana*, 15/3 (1983), 163–80; and Conrad, *Collected Letters*, iv. 266 n.
The marriage took place on 20 Sept. 1902 (not in Oct. as Moser says). Secor and
Secor, *The Return of the Good Soldier*, 60, n. 71. Gerard Tetley, 'The Frailties of
Ford Madox Ford', *Footnote*, 1 (June 1949), 11.

28 Najder, 169–70. *Ancient Lights*, 226. R. Garnett, *Constance Garnett*, 168. *Return to
Yesterday*, 51. *Constance Garnett*, 167 and 379, n. 36, shows that Conrad had been
staying up to at least 7 Sept. The precise date of the meeting is shrouded in the
familiar cloud of error and controversy. Jessie Conrad thought in 1935 that it had
taken place during a visit to Stephen and Cora Crane in Feb. 1898, but her
recollections are no more reliable than those of Ford, Conrad, or Jean-Aubry,
whose second biography of Conrad, *The Sea-Dreamer* (Garden City, NY: Doubleday, 1957), 232, gives this earlier date, which might have suggested it to Jessie
Conrad (*Joseph Conrad and his Circle*, 58). Otherwise the case for a meeting before
Sept. was based on three of Conrad's letters written on Pent Farm stationery; but
all of these have now been re-dated by Frederick Karl and Laurence Davies as: 17
May 1899 to Hugh Clifford; 10/11 Aug. 1899 to David Meldrum; and 10? Oct.
1899 to Galsworthy (*Collected Letters* ii. 179–80, 190–2, and 202–3 respectively).
See Karl, *Joseph Conrad: The Three Lives*, 426–7, who originally inclined towards
a mid-May meeting, and Najder, *Joseph Conrad: A Chronicle*, 236, who disputes
it. Jocelyn Baines, *Joseph Conrad: A Critical Biography* (London, 1960), 214–15,
calls the collaboration 'the most important event in Conrad's literary career'.
Najder, 237, disagrees, arguing that Garnett had more influence on Conrad's
writing; though he stresses the 'psychological importance' of the relationship.

Chapter 7

1 *Return to Yesterday*, 52. R. Garnett, *Constance Garnett*, 169, confirms that Edward
Garnett brought Conrad to meet Ford. Conrad's letter to Ford, 15 Dec. 1921
(Yale), confirms Ford's scenario, and lends credence to his comment about Conrad
thinking he was the gardener: 'The first time I set eyes on you was in your
potato-patch.'

2 *Joseph Conrad*, 130, 11.

3 *Joseph Conrad*, 145.

4 Jessie Conrad's comments are discussed in vol. 2, Chs. 12 and 16. The cancelled
passage is quoted from John Morey, 'Joseph Conrad and Ford Madox Ford: A
Study in Collaboration', 212. 'On Conrad's Vocabulary', *Bookman* (New York), 67
(June 1928), 405.

NOTES TO PP. 103–47

5 All the MSS described in this section are at Cornell. This one is catalogued as *'[Bodurdoe and Gunter]', and dates from some time between 1891 and 1895. The story was not completed, possibly because the material was re-conceived into the *'Elspeth' story. One other MS fragment at Cornell, not otherwise discussed here, is *'[Lausanias & Glaucus]', which was to have been about 'the Levantine pirate who took Julius Caesar prisoner'. Ford said he put into it a portrait of his American relation Hattina (see p. 511, n. 16) as 'the gorgeous slave—or perhaps daughter—of the pirate Lausanias', and that he should 'certainly have made of her Caesar's first love' if he had finished the story. *'Auto-Plagiarism' (unpublished typescript), 4–5.

6 Garnett's diary for 24 Nov. 1894 records Ford giving her the MS of 'The Land of Song' to read. *Wagner and the Music of the Future* (London: Chapman and Hall, 1874); *Richard Wagner*, 'The Great Musicians' series (London: Sampson Low, Marston & Co. [1881]). The essay on Wagner is at Cornell, and is discussed by Stang and Smith in 'Music for a While', 186–7. *When Blood is Their Argument*, 66.

7 *Ford Madox Brown*, 59. *'The Last Sowing' is probably the same work as 'The Sowing of the Oats', the novel Olive Garnett mentions in her diary for 20 Nov. 1894, saying that Elsie told her she and Ford wrote it together. She certainly wrote down pp. 4–251 (pp. 252–342 are in Ford's hand). The first three pages are missing, as might be the former title-page. Edward Garnett tried to get Dent to take 'The Sowing of the Oats': Olive's diary for 14 Nov. 1894. But early in 1895 Ford spoke to Edward of 'the bloody novel that Dent wouldn't have': *Letters*, 8–9, dated '[1895?]' by Ludwig; the mention of 'the 1st two chapters' [of *Ford Madox Brown*], which Ford was enclosing with this letter, and which Olive Garnett records as having been typed by the entry for 24 Jan. 1895, allows a more precise dating of early-mid Jan. for the letter. Mizener, 35, cites this letter as evidence that 'Sometime in 1895 he completed a novel that was never published'; whereas in fact the novel was completed in 1894. In the summer of 1906 Ford submitted to Brown, Langham a novel called 'Love the Ploughman', which Mizener, 123, calls 'otherwise unknown'. Ford can't have had time to draft a new novel in the spring and summer of 1906. That title isn't recorded elsewhere, but is probably an alternative to 'The Sowing of the Oats'/'The Last Sowing'. Ford gave the manuscript of 'The Last Sowing' to Olive, who held it in trust for Katharine Hueffer Lamb (see Garnett to Lamb, 25 Feb. 1949: Cornell). 'The Last Sowing', 29, 69, 100, 104, 132–3, 171, 194, 192, 203, 204, 271, 241, 243, 250, 274–5, 280, 283, 315, 317.

8 The probable dates for this work are from Dec. 1896 to July 1898. Two of the three fragmentary drafts bear this title; the third is called 'Times Before Us: A Romance of Peasant Uprising'. See Harvey, 117. Quotations are from the longest (and presumably the final) version, written in Elsie's hand with Ford's corrections. We have seen Ford use the title-phrase in a letter: *The Cinque Ports*, 270, speaks of 'the unpleasant times we live in', and of a century (as the book was published in 1900 it's not clear which he means) 'whose chief need is a just appreciation for the lessons of tradition—a possibility of being able to mould the future with some eye to the institutions of the old times before us'. On invasion novels see Hynes, *The Edwardian Turn of Mind*, 34–53.

9 Quotation from the first (?), fifty-seven leaf, version, 'Times Before Us', 31.
10 *Great Trade Route*, 19.
11 *Mightier Than the Sword*, 29. 'Envoi' to the third[?] version.

12 'Times Before Us', 21.

13 Ford to Garnett [n.d. but Jan.–Mar. 1895]: *Letters*, 8. Mizener, 39. *'A Mother', 27. In Jan. 1903 Ford suggested to J. B. Pinker that 'the *Mother*' could be placed with *Macmillan's* magazine. The *Cornhill* had already rejected it, but it is not known when the story was finished: *Letters*, 17.

14 Mizener, 42–5. *Joseph Conrad*, 17–18. The story appears in *Thus to Revisit*, 27; *Joseph Conrad*, 37; and *Return to Yesterday*, 39–40, 66. Najder, 222. Conrad to Ford, [12] Nov. 1899, confirms that it was Conrad who proposed the collaboration: *Collected Letters*, ii. 219–20. Najder, 222; on 239 he agrees that Conrad needed Ford's fluency and awareness of connotations.

15 *Joseph Conrad*, 37–8. Cf. *Thus to Revisit*, 27 and *Return to Yesterday*, 46, 71. In fact Conrad never met Henley, so Ford was right to doubt Conrad's story. See Conrad to the chairman of the Provisional Committee of the Henley Memorial, 17 Feb. 1904: *Collected Letters*, iii. 115.

16 *Return to Yesterday*, 66. *Ancient Lights*, 196.

17 Conrad, *Collected Letters*, ii. 107–8. David Garnett said that Edward Garnett rejected 'Seraphina', but that 'It occurred to him that Ford and Conrad might collaborate in rewriting it': *Great Friends: Portraits of Seventeen Writers* (London: Macmillan, 1979), 14, 42. Najder, 240, echoes Conrad's belief that Ford would have less trouble finding a publisher if he could invoke Conrad's name. But the letters he cites (543, n. 14) show merely that in these cases it was Conrad who was negotiating. Although 'The Last Sowing' is known have been rejected by one publisher, there is no evidence that Ford had even submitted 'Seraphina' to publishers before meeting Conrad. He got eight books published before the first of the collaborations. *Romance*, the major collaboration, actually proved more difficult to publish than most of these.

18 Conrad to Henley, 18 Oct. 1898; to David Meldrum, 12 Oct. 1898; to Ford, 29 Sept. 1898 (discussing the tenancy); to Galsworthy, 28 Oct. 1898; to Ford, 17 Nov. [1898], telling Ford to come when he likes: 'I would be very, very pleased to *hear* Seraphina *read*. I would *afterwards* read it myself': *Collected Letters*, ii. 108, 101–2, 93–4, 112, 119. Jessie Conrad, *Joseph Conrad and His Circle*, 66.

19 The cancelled passage is quoted by Morey, 209. Conrad to Kazimierz Waliszewski, 8 Nov. 1903: *Collected Letters*, iii. 75–7. Moser, 41.

20 *All the Year Round*, 22 Jan. 1870. *Joseph Conrad*, 13, 21–2. Ford probably knew Heine's poem of love and the sea, 'Seraphine'.

21 *Joseph Conrad*, 23–4, 14, 28. 'L'envoi' to 'Seraphina', 11.

22 'On Conrad's Vocabulary', *Bookman* (New York), 67 (June 1928), 405. *Joseph Conrad*, 168–9. Conrad to Ford [13 June 1901]: *Collected Letters*, ii. 332.

23 *Joseph Conrad*, 28. Garnett, *Nation and Athenaeum*, 36 (6 Dec. 1924), 366, 368.

24 *Return to Yesterday*, 191–2.

25 Mizener, 44, 49. Conrad's comment to Elsie, 3 Dec. 1898, is taken from her daughter Katharine Lamb's transcription at Cornell. *Joseph Conrad*, 42. Conrad to Wells, 23 Dec. 1898 (*Collected Letters*, ii. 136) gives a less incredible, more mundane account: 'There was an Invisible Man (apparently of a jocose disposition) on your doorstep because when I rang (modestly) an invisible finger kept the button down (or in rather) and the bell jingling continuously to my extreme confusion.' Mizener, 534, is quick to note the Fordian 'improvement' upon fact, but not the way the story glamorizes Conrad, presenting him as a being of magical

experiences and explosive humour (rather than the confused, nervous impression made by his letter). Despite citing Conrad's letter, Mizener says: 'The date of the visit to Sandgate is approximately fixed by Conrad's letter to Galsworthy [now in the possession of *Forbes Magazine*], written early in November, 1898, in which Conrad says Ford is at the Pent with him.' But the letter of 23 Dec. 1898 to Wells fixes the date of the visit as 'yesterday'; whereas the letter to Galsworthy must be the one now dated as '[25 March 1899]' by Karl and Davies (*Collected Letters*, ii. 175). Galsworthy, *Castles in Spain* (New York, 1927), 117, 113, 123–4.

26 Olive Garnett, diary for [24 and 25 Mar.] and 27 Mar. 1899. Conrad to Galsworthy [25 Mar. 1899] and to Garnett [31 Mar. 1899]: *Collected Letters*, ii. 175–7. *Return to Yesterday*, 224. Wells had denied the earlier version of this story that Ford told in *Joseph Conrad*, 39, 51–2: *letter to the editor, *Manchester Guardian* (27 Nov. 1924), 5. But his claim that the story (which he appeared not to have read, but to have come across in Hugh I'A Fausset's review of the book in the *Manchester Guardian* of 19 Nov. 1924, p. 7) is 'a pure invention' is disingenuous, given that he himself recalled advising Ford against the collaboration in a letter to the editor of the *English Review*, 31 (Aug. 1920), 178–9. It was perhaps the idea that he had cycled over especially to warn Ford that he wanted to deny; though Ford (if he ever read this letter of Wells's) remained convinced about the episode.

27 Goldring, *The Last Pre-Raphaelite*, 243, said the collaboration actually harmed Ford's reputation. Conrad to Garnett [31 Mar. 1899]; and to Galsworthy [12 Mar.? 1899]: *Collected Letters*, ii. 174–7.

28 *Mightier Than the Sword*, 88. The chapter on Conrad was first published in the *American Mercury*, 35 (June 1935), 169–76. Ford says Conrad had come to stay with him at the Pent, but it must have been the other way around, since the Conrads had taken over the Pent before *Heart of Darkness* was completed. In a cancelled passage of *Joseph Conrad*, Ford recalled working 'minutely and with attention' over all of Conrad's books from *Heart of Darkness* to *Nostromo*: Morey, 213.

Chapter 8

1 '*The Inheritors*', *A Conrad Memorial Library: The Collection of George T. Keating* (New York: Doubleday, Doran, 1929), 76. Jessie Conrad remembered Ford as 'a very frequent visitor' at the Pent, staying 'sometimes for many days'; after the Hueffers moved to Winchelsea, the Conrads would drive over, staying in a hotel but spending their days with the Hueffers: *Joseph Conrad as I Knew Him*, 48. *The Good Soldier*, 136. Karl, *Joseph Conrad*, 537–8, 520.

2 It is surprising that no one has suggested that Jim's character might draw upon Conrad's knowledge of Ford. Although *Lord Jim* was probably started in Apr. 1898, and had established the basic character by the summer, the novel was completed throughout 1899 and 1900: see Najder, 229, 248–50, 321. Jim's romantic cast of mind, his patrician role-playing, even his physical type could all have gained their definition from Ford. In *Return to Yesterday*, 193, Ford said that he thought *Under Western Eyes* 'a long way the greatest' of Conrad's novels, and added: 'It is almost the only great one in which I had no finger at all.' But, as Moser has argued, Ford and Violet Hunt are *portrayed* in the book, as Peter Ivanovitch and Madame de S.; and the novel draws on Ford's knowledge of

Russian anarchists: 'Ford Madox Hueffer and *Under Western Eyes*', *Conradiana*, 15/3 (1983), 163–80. *Lord Jim* had been begun before 3 June 1898 (probably in April); but by Feb. 1899 Conrad had only written 20,000 words; as the novel grew, it postponed the collaboration; *Heart of Darkness* was begun around 15 Dec. 1898, after Conrad met Ford: Najder, 248–9, 259. On p. 289 Najder says Conrad's best work was written at the Pent.

3 Mizener, 50. *Mightier Than the Sword*, 45. Ford to Crane [n.d., but headed 'Aldington', thus between Apr. 1899 and 2 Jan. 1900 (when Ford saw Crane for the last time): Columbia University Library; Lindberg-Seyersted, 21, 23–4, 18.

4 Mizener, 56. *The Cinque Ports*, pp. v–vi. Ford to Garnett [Nov.? 1900]: Northwestern. Crane to Sanford Bennett (whose wife Ford had patronized while telling her about a French painter): Thomas Beer, *Stephen Crane* (London: Heinemann, 1924), 253. Ford reviewed this in July 1924, so it precedes *Joseph Conrad*. Berryman, *Stephen Crane* (London: Methuen, 1950), 251, gives a different version: 'You are wrong [. . .] about Hueffer. I admit he is patronizing. He patronized his family. He patronizes Conrad. He will end up by patronizing God who will have to get used to it and they will be friends.' See Lindberg-Seyersted, 18. Ford quoted Crane's comment from memory—not exactly, but with reasonable accuracy—in *Joseph Conrad*, 232; *New York Essays*, 25; *Return to Yesterday*, 32; and *Mightier Than the Sword*, 54.

5 See Mizener, 51, on how the Cromwell idea figures in *The Inheritors*, in which Churchill and Granger have written a *Life of Cromwell*. Najder, 234. C. T. Watts, 'Joseph Conrad, Dr. MacIntyre, and "The Inheritors" ', *Notes and Queries*, 212 (July 1967), 245–7. Conrad to Garnett, 29 Sept. 1898: *Collected Letters*, ii. 94–6.

6 Carl Heath was a friend of Edward's, 'who became a Quaker and devoted himself to the peace movement and so came to know Gandhi': R. Garnett, *Constance Garnett*, 58.

7 Elsie Hueffer's diary; quoted by Mizener, 51. See Conrad's letter to Ford of [12] Nov. 1899, quoted above, pp. 120–1. Conrad to Cunninghame Graham, 19 Jan. and 13 Feb. 1900: *Collected Letters*, ii. 242–3, 248–9. Najder, 262–3.

8 [12] Nov. 1899: *Collected Letters*, ii. 219–20.

9 Batchelor, *The Edwardian Novelists* (London: Duckworth, 1982), 98. Karl, 524.

10 Conrad to Garnett, 26 Mar. 1900: *Collected Letters*, ii. 256–7. Mizener, 51–4.

11 Mizener, 44. *Joseph Conrad*, 123.

12 Garnett, (ed.), *Letters from Joseph Conrad* (Indianapolis: Bobbs-Merrill, 1928), 168–9. Mizener, 54. Garnett's reviews of *Joseph Conrad* are discussed in vol. 2, Ch. 12

13 'The Other House', *New York Herald Tribune Books*, (2 Oct. 1927), 2.

14 'Thus to Revisit. V.: Biography and Criticism', *Piccadilly Review* (20 Nov. 1919), 6. *The Good Soldier*, 177. In the manuscript 'Great Writers' (an unpublished part of 'Towards a History of English Literature'), 49, Ford calls Butler's *The Way of All Flesh* 'the only really great English novel'.

15 19 July 1901; *Collected Letters*, ii. 342–3.

16 *Thus to Revisit*, 115; 'Stevie and Co.', *New York Essays*, 25. *Mightier Than the Sword*, 36. *Return to Yesterday*, 196, 199. 'The Other House'.

17 Juliet Hueffer to David Soskice, 17 Apr. 1900 (House of Lords Record Office). Jessie Conrad to Marguerite Poradowska, 10 May 1900; in John A. Gee

and Paul J. Sturm (eds.), *Letters of Joseph Conrad to Marguerite Poradowska: 1890–1920* (New Haven, Conn.: Yale University Press, 1940), 102 n. Quoted by Harvey, 507.

18 Mizener, 57. Lindberg-Seyersted, 23–6. Najder, 265. Ford to Olive Garnett, 12 July 1900 (Northwestern).

19 Conrad to Galsworthy [20 July 1900]: *Collected Letters*, ii. 284–5. Najder, 267. *Joseph Conrad*, 220–9, describes the Belgian trip (225, 226). *Ancient Lights*, 245. *Return to Yesterday*, 77–8.

20 Conrad to Galsworthy, 11 Aug. and 19 Sept. 1900: *Collected Letters*, ii. 287, 295. Jessie Conrad, *Joseph Conrad and his Circle* (New York: Dutton, 1935), 71. Karl, 503, suggests that Jessie was also jealous of Elsie. Conrad to David Meldrum, 31 Oct. 1900: *Collected Letters*, ii. 298. Mizener followed an earlier misdating of this letter, and thus conflated these two bouts of collaboration into one: 59.

21 Transcribed from Garnett, 'A Bloomsbury Girlhood', 413–17. Garnett, *Petersburg Tales* (London: W. Heinemann, 1900).

22 Ford's intimate and entertaining letters to Olive Garnett are held by Northwestern University Library. Four are included in the *Reader*, 465–8.

23 Ford's letters to Elsie while staying with the Conrads during 1901 and 1902 refer to 'Novel No. 1'. In Sept. 1902 Conrad returned the MS of her only published novel, *Margaret Hever*, by Elizabeth Martindale (London: Duckworth & Co, 1909), apologizing for having kept it for a long time. Thus she was certainly writing it during the spring and summer of 1902, but may have begun earlier. See Conrad to Elsie [late Sept. 1902], *Collected Letters*, ii. 443–5.

24 Ford to Garnett [n.d., but Nov.? 1900]: Northwestern. Ford to Elsie [n.d., but *c*.May 1902]. *The Benefactor* was subtitled 'A Tale of a Small Circle': Ford's comment to Olive about having 'a small, very small, circle of people to whom one concedes the right to do anything' glances at his fictional coteries as well as his coterie of fiction-writers.

25 See *Reader*, 465–7, and also the [Nov.? 1900] letter at Northwestern (discussed above and below) for Ford's earlier comments on the *Petersburg Tales*. J. J. Martin, 'Edward Garnett and Conrad's Reshaping of Time', *Conradiana*, 62 (1974), 89–105. Ford sent Olive a spoof sacred text entitled 'Codex Petro-quasi-Rubren-sis[?]' mocking the superior moral tone of the family: 'In the beginning *were* the Superior *Persons*. And wisdom *was* with the Superior *Persons*. And the Superior *Persons were* wisdom', etc.: Northwestern.

26 [Nov.? 1900]; Northwestern.

27 Ford to Edward Garnett, 5 May 1928: there is a photocopy of this letter at Cornell; the original is in the possession of Richard Garnett. Wells, *Boon, The Mind of the Race, The Wild Asses of the Devil, and The Last Trump* (London: T. Fisher Unwin, 1915), 91, 123–4. *H. G. Wells in Love: Postscript to an Experiment in Autobiography* (London: Faber and Faber, 1984), 25, 30–1. Ford to Wells, n.d., but misdated '1907' in a later hand; the address ('Aldington') establishes the date as before 10 Apr. 1901: Illinois. Conrad to Ford [Sept. 1903]: Yale. See Mizener, 537, n. 18.

Chapter 9

1 Olive Garnett's diary: 21 Jan. 1901. *Return to Yesterday*, 9, 16. Mizener, 61–2; Moser, 53. A cryptic diary entry of Violet Hunt's, who became a friend of Mary's

after Ford and Elsie had separated, might be evidence that Hunt knew of the affair: 'And Ford writes—coldly—a letter that he wld not have written even to Mary Martindale in the old days': Secor and Secor, *The Return of the Good Soldier*, 55; entry for 4 Apr. Mary is recorded as having been in Winchelsea in January 1903 (Conrad, *Collected Letters*, iii. 10). Ford told Olive Garnett on 20 Feb. 1903 (Northwestern) that Mary was to visit again from 21 to 27 Feb. These dates might support Katharine Lamb's recollection; though the affair may have been the reason for these visits rather than their outcome. Goldring said Mary was 'for a time almost one of the household': *The Last Pre-Raphaelite*, 92.

2 Moser, 28, 30, 47. *The Inheritors*, 323. *Poems for Pictures*, 56; repr. in *Collected Poems* [1913], 165. Ann Lee-Michell in her TS version of Garnett, 'A Bloomsbury Girlhood', 511.

3 *Return to Yesterday*, 11–14. Ford thought Mrs Clifford was worried about James's eyes; but it was in fact his rheumatic right hand. Lindberg-Seyersted, 29–32, 97, n. 1.

4 *Return to Yesterday*, 14–16, 217–18. Rossetti's rank was in fact senior assistant secretary from 1869.

5 James to Ford, Tuesday [Jan. 1897?]; 30 Dec. 1897; 9 July 1897; 23 May 1900. Lindberg-Seyersted, 32–6, 97, n. 7. James reviewed the Brown exhibition in *Harper's Weekly*, 61 (20 Feb. 1897), 183; part of which was reprinted as 'Lord Leighton and Ford Madox Brown' in *The Painter's Eye*, ed. John Sweeney (London: Rupert Hart-Davis, 1956), 247–50. Garnett's anonymous review, 'As Subtle as Life', appeared in *Outlook*, 3 (10 June 1899), 620. Olive Garnett, diary for 18 July 1899. David Garnett, *The Golden Echo*, 63–4. *The Inheritors* was sent to Heinemann on 16 Mar. 1900: Mizener, 51.

6 Leon Edel to Mizener, 1 Sept. 1966: 'I think HJ disliked Ford too much to ever consider putting him into a novel'; a curious notion—that novelists only write about people they like. Edel is doubting Ford's claim that James based Merton Densher upon him in *The Wings of the Dove*. See *Mightier Than the Sword*, 36–7. In another letter to Mizener he claims that Ford's claim is 'sheer fiction', and that Morton Fullerton is a more likely 'original' (20 June 1966). It sounds like a case of the biographer adopting the likes and dislikes he imputes to his subject, and then trying to sweep someone *he* dislikes out of the private life of his master. James to Ford, 16 May 1901: Lindberg-Seyersted, 36–7.

7 *The March of Literature*, 783 n. Mizener, 64.

8 *Joseph Conrad*, 136. Conrad inscribed a copy of the novel for George Keating, saying: 'There is little of my actual writing in this work. Discussion there has been in plenty. F.M.H. held the pen': reproduced in *Return to Yesterday*, 205.

9 *Joseph Conrad*, 135–6, 138. *The Inheritors*, 205. Moser, 46.

10 *The Times* (3 Sept. 1901), 9; see Harvey, 281. *New York Times Saturday Review* (13 July 1901), 499. Conrad's reply appeared in the issue for 24 Aug. See Najder, 275.

11 Jessie Conrad, *Joseph Conrad and his Circle*, 87. Conrad's defence is reprinted in full in *Ford Madox Ford: The Critical Heritage*, 20–2, and in Conrad, *Collected Letters*, ii. 346–9. It is discussed in Karl, 460–1. Conrad to the Abbé Joseph de Smet, February 1911: *Collected Letters*, iv. 410–11.

12 Ford to Garnett [n.d., but Nov.? 1900]: Northwestern. *Joseph Conrad*, 133–4. Mizener, 53. Conrad to Ford [23 July 1901], *Collected Letters*, ii. 343–5, recounts Pawling (Heinemann's partner) reading Crockett into the character of Callan.

Najder, 260, thinks Churchill might represent Salisbury. Jeffrey Meyers, *Joseph Conrad* (London: John Murray, 1991), 99, suggests that Soane is Roger Casement. There is a fine discussion of the political background to the novel in Green's *Ford Madox Ford: Prose and Politics* (Cambridge: Cambridge University Press, 1981), 23.

13 Transcribed from Garnett, 'A Bloomsbury Girlhood', 432-5. There is no date on the letter, but it is transcribed after the last entry for July 1901. The 'scrap of verse' is a variant draft of the epigraph to *Romance* (which was itself revised to become the fourth poem of 'A Sequence' in *The Face of the Night*: see *Collected Poems* [1913], 105.

14 Conrad to Blackwood, 24 May 1901: *Collected Letters*, ii. 327-8; see 332-4 for the details of the second visit (17-24 June). Mizener, 64-5; 69, 537, n. 18; though he confusingly includes a visit from the Conrads in Mar. 1902 in the account of the collaboration during 1901. Najder, 276-7. Conrad to Ford [25 July 1901]; to Pinker, 18 and 23 Jan. 1901: *Collected Letters*, ii. 346, 320-31. Pinker had become Conrad's agent in Sept. 1900: ibid. 194 n.

15 Mizener, 531, n. 14. Ford to Pinker [June 1901]: Princeton, shows that he was thinking of it by at least June. Conrad's letter, saying 'Don't let this interrupt your work on the dear old Harry', dated by Mizener as '*c.* July 4, 1901', has been dated by Karl and Davies as [23 July 1901], though their note—'Henry VIII; preliminary work on *The Fifth Queen* (1906)' is misleading. Ford certainly used this research for his Tudor trilogy, but it had been done with a biography in mind. See Charles G. Hoffmann, ' "The Life and Times of Henry VIII": An Original for Ford Madox Ford's Fifth Queen Trilogy', *Notes and Queries*, 14 (1967), 248-50, for a discussion of Ford's work on this project.

16 Meldrum to Blackwood, 5 Aug. 1901: quoted by Najder, 274. Conrad to Blackwood, 26 Aug. and 7 Nov. 1901: *Collected Letters*, ii. 354, 356-7.

17 Ford to Conrad [n.d.]: dated by Mizener, 73. Conrad to Ford [23 July 1901]: *Collected Letters*, ii. 343-4. Moser, 44. 'A Note on *Romance*', appended to *The Nature of a Crime* (London: Duckworth and Co., 1924), 106. There has been some confusion about the attributing of Parts; not least because Conrad changed his story. See Karl, 520. At the time the work was sent to Blackwood there were only four parts; it was the third that Conrad held back, rewrote, and expanded into Parts Third and Fourth of the published version. Thus as the book stands there are five Parts, and it is Part Fourth which is mainly Conrad's. See Raymond Brebach, *Joseph Conrad, Ford Madox Ford and the Making of 'Romance'* for a detailed analysis (see esp. 36-7, 52). Karl, for example, gets misled by the renumbering to introduce confusions about who wrote what when (*Joseph Conrad*, 516-19). See Mizener, 74, for an excellent discussion of the collaboration on this book.

18 Conrad to Pinker, 7 Nov. 1901 and 6 Jan. 1902: *Collected Letters*, ii. 357-8, 366. Mizener, 72; see also 65-9, and Karl, 524-7. By 1908/9 Conrad owed Pinker around £1,600.

19 Swinnerton, *An Autobiography* (London: Hutchinson, 1937), 242-3. Joyce, *Ulysses*, ed. Jeri Johnson (Oxford: Oxford University Press, 1993), 435. Mizener, 65-6. Swinnerton's description and the letter from an unknown author are quoted from *Letters of Arnold Bennett*, ed. James Hepburn, 3 vols.; vol. 1 (London, 1966), 22-8. *Return to Yesterday*, 58-60 (cf. Ford to Eric Pinker, 19 Mar. 1928: Cornell: 'I was

always having obscure rows with your father which distressed me, but which I
could never understand').

20 Olive Garnett's travel diary for 11 and 15 Nov. [1901, misdated 1902]. Garnett,
diary for 7 Apr. 1899. Ford to Elsie [7 July 1905].

21 Olive Garnett's travel diary for 23 and 21 Nov. [1901, misdated 1902]. Ford was
in London from 18 to 21 November, to discuss *Rossetti* with Garnett. See
Jefferson, *Edward Garnett*, 80. Kestner, 'Ford Madox Ford as a Critic of the
Pre-Raphaelites', *Contemporary Literature*, 30/2 (Summer 1989), 230. *Rossetti*, 4,
182, 2, 92, 110, 130, 136, 168, 24, 82–4, and 183. See 186, 189 on sympathetic
identification: the topic is discussed more fully in vol. 2. Ford to Garnett [1902]:
Reader, 470.

22 Ford to Cathy Hueffer, n.d. [17–24 Dec. 1902]: House of Lords Record Office.
Conrad to Cunninghame Graham, New Year's Eve 1901; to Pinker, 6 Jan. 1902:
Collected Letters, ii. 360–1, 365–7. Mizener, 73, says Conrad was back at the Pent
by 1 Jan.; but the letter he cited (to Meldrum, 7 January: ibid. 367–9) is explicit
about Conrad having intended to return then, but having been detained because
of Ford's health. Conrad's letter to Pinker from the Bungalow on 6 Jan. says 'I
have been here since Xmas, very hard at work'. 'A BBC Interview with Mrs.
Helen Rossetti Angeli', ed. Mark Samuels Lasner [and Margaret Diane Stetz],
Journal of Pre-Raphaelite Studies, 2/2 (May 1982), 11.

23 Conrad to Meldrum, 7 Jan. 1902 [n.d., but early 1902]: see Mizener, 73, 538,
n. 7. Conrad to Pinker, 24 Jan. 1902, records Ford as at the Pent: *Collected Letters*, ii. 374–5. *Joseph Conrad*, 41.

24 Diary for 2, 5, and 7 Feb.: quoted by Moser, 52.

25 The verses are not 'Ford's poem', as Mizener thought (76, 538, n. 13), but are
adapted from ll. 352–5 of Shelley's 'Adonais', which he had also used for his
grandfather's epitaph: *Ford Madox Brown*, 423 (quoted accurately). Shelley's lines
none the less speak to Ford's *Angst* about the torment of passion: 'He hath
outsoared the darkings of our night | Envy and heartache and all the grief and
pain | And that unrest which men miscall delight | Can touch him not and torture
not again.' Ford's version is at Cornell.

26 Mizener, 78; see also 84 for the 1903 revision.

27 *The Benefactor*, 346. Moser, 61.

28 Mizener, 77. Najder, 273; on 279–80, says they finished on 10 Mar.; but
Conrad told Ford on 9 Mar. 'I took the last of *Romance* to London on Friday', 7
Mar. Conrad to Ford, 9 Mar. and 15 Apr. 1902: *Collected Letters*, ii. 387–9, 408–9.
They had also thought the book finished in the previous June and again in Nov.:
Conrad to Pinker, 7 June and 7 Nov. 1901: 331, 357–8. Conrad to Galsworthy, 10
Mar. 1902; to Elsie, [17] Mar. 1902; to Ford, [23 Apr. 1902]: ibid. 390–1, 393, 409–10.
Conrad to Cathy Hueffer, 31 Dec. 1902 and 26 Dec. 1903: House of Lords.

Chapter 10

1 *The Works of Joseph Conrad, Volume 1: Almayer's Folly, Tales of Unrest* (London:
William Heinemann, 1921); Tales of Unrest, pp. viii–ix.

2 Conrad to Wells, 20 Oct. 1905: *Collected Letters*, iii. 287. See e.g. Karl, 673.

3 'On Conrad's Vocabulary', *Bookman* (New York), 67 (June 1928), 405. See Karl,
60, on the doubling of Conrad's heroes. Moser observes other parallels between

the writers' interests: fatigue (42); unjust trials of characters who are, or who feel, innately blameless (48). Conrad to Kazimierz Waliszewski, 5 Dec. 1903: *Collected Letters*, iii. 89. Ford, 'Literary Portraits—IV.: Mr. Arnold Bennett and "The Regent."', *Outlook*, 32 (4 Oct. 1913), 464. Najder, 241.

4 Conrad later wrote to Ford that *The Nature of a Crime* 'seemed to me somewhat amateurish': 10 Nov. 1923 (Yale). Tetley, 'The Frailties of Ford Madox Ford', *Footnote*, 1 (June 1949), 10. Karl, 527. The reactions to Ford's memoir, *Joseph Conrad*, are discussed in vol. 2. 'The Inheritors', from *A Conrad Memorial Library*, ed. George T. Keating (New York: Doubleday, Doran, 1929), 75–6, 80. See Mizener, 69–70 (on 'Amy Foster'); 88–9 (on the *Mirror*); 107–8 (on the dramatization). It is possible that the story of *Under Western Eyes* was suggested by Ford's knowledge of the police spy and ultimate dual agent Azev (though both men could have heard of Azev through the Garnetts, and would have read David Soskice's article on 'The Azeff Scandals in Russia' in the *English Review*, 1 (Mar. 1908), 816–32): see *Mightier Than the Sword*, 94. Karl, 668, 683–4, discusses how Conrad's breakdown while writing *Under Western Eyes* was precipitated by his feelings about Ford's affair with Violet Hunt. Also see Moser, 'Ford Madox Hueffer and Under Western Eyes', *Conradiana*, 15/3 (1983), 163–80; and Moser, 98 (on *Chance*). Norman Sherry, *Conrad's Western World* (Cambridge: Cambridge University Press, 1971), 205–323 on *The Secret Agent*; and 209 on the sketch of Ford in Conrad's story 'The Informer' as the collector of acquaintances ('he has met with and talked to every one worth knowing on any conceivable ground. He observes them, listens to them, penetrates them, measures them, and puts the memory away in the galleries of his mind': *A Set of Six* (London: Methuen 1908), 79. Jessie Conrad thought much the same of Ford: 'F.M.H. had an uncanny way of picking out people from the point of interest, and having found anyone to his mind was extremely tenacious of them': *Joseph Conrad and His Circle*, 116. Moser, 42.

Conrad mentioned two further ideas for collaborations that never materialized. One (Conrad told Meldrum confidentially) was to be 'a great novel about the Ana Baptists, of which sect Hueffer (who is of the great German publishing family of that name) has great masses of information': David Meldrum to William Blackwood, 2 Feb. 1899: quoted in Conrad, *Letters to William Blackwood and David S. Meldrum*, ed. William Blackburn (Durham, NC: Duke University Press, 1958), 44: Harvey, 508. The other was to be based on Ford Madox Brown, dealing 'with a picture of an old and famous painter and the low and perverse intrigues among the entourage of a great man who has been successful but who—precisely because he was a supreme artist—has remained unappreciated': Conrad to Kazimierz Waliszewski, 8 Nov. 1903, translated from the French by the editors: *Collected Letters*, ii. 75–7.

5 Martin, 'Edward Garnett and Conrad's Reshaping of Time', *Conradiana*, 6/2 (1974), 92–3. Garnett's essay was published as an introduction to Constance's translation of *A Lear of the Steppes and Other Stories* (London: William Heinemann, 1898), pp. v–xv.

6 R. Garnett, *Constance Garnett*, 183, shows Constance still working on the translation in the middle of January. The Hueffers arrived in March. Edward's 'Introduction' is dated Oct. 1898. The quotation is from p. ix. In 'Emma', *New York Herald Tribune Books* (10 June 1928), 1, 6, Ford unequivocally credits Conrad with the technique of the time-shift. Crankshaw, *Joseph Conrad: Some*

Aspects of the Art of the Novel (London: John Lane, 1936), 150–1. Conrad told Pinker, 9 Aug. 1911 (*Collected Letters*, iv. 470–1) that Garnett hadn't seen a line of his work before publication since *Lord Jim* (published in 1900). Ford took over this role once the collaboration began in earnest.

7 Karl, 435–6. Mizener, 47–8. *Return to Yesterday*, 185. *Joseph Conrad*, 48. 'The Younger Madox Browns', *Artist*, 19 (Feb. 1897), 52. Brebach, 101, 63, 38. *An English Girl*, 42. The expression of love for Conrad comes from a passage cancelled from p. 6 of his memoir *Joseph Conrad*, transcribed by Morey, 207; it follows on from another cancelled passage making explicit the connection between impressionism and 'indifference': 'the novelist, according to the Impressionist canon, must be indifferent to his characters'. The passage about Conrad as raconteur was cancelled from p. 85: Morey, 217. See Conrad, 'A Glance at Two Books', *Last Essays* (London: Dent, 1928), 132–7 (132): 'The national English novelist seldom regards his work—the exercise of his Art—as an achievement of active life by which he will produce certain definite effects upon the emotions of his readers.' *Return to Yesterday*, 203. Stang, *Ford Madox Ford*, 26. Goldring, *The Last Pre-Raphaelite*, 63.

8 Ford to Cathy Hueffer [*c.*17 Dec. 1902]: House of Lords. *Return to Yesterday*, 170–2. Here Ford says it was while he was 'slightly stunned' at hearing about Pollard that Richard Garnett suggested he should look up the trial of Aaron Smith as a subject for a novel. But (as Harvey says, p. 117), this can't be right, since the first page of the synopsis and sample chapter of 'The Life and Times of Henry VIII' is on Winchelsea stationery, and thus dates from after 1901 (whereas Ford began 'Seraphina' before 1898); and the chapter is written 'on the backs of a fragment of uncorrected *Romance* typescript'. Neither Harvey, nor Mizener (p. 39) explain Ford's 'improvement' of the sequence of events. The reason is perhaps that the reordering emphasizes Conrad's effect on Ford's writing. Placing the disappointment over the Henry VIII biography before the writing of 'Seraphina' makes it seem like another impasse from which the advent of Conrad saved him. *'Creative History & the Historic Sense', ed. Sondra J. Stang and Richard Stang, *Yale Review*, 78/4 (Summer 1989), 511–24. *Rossetti*, 30. There are three MSS, one a fragment, of a verse-play entitled 'Katharine Howard'. It was probably this that Olive Garnett heard read from in Nov. 1901: (travel diary for 12 Nov.), since the title-page of the typed (final?) version is headed 'The Bungalow', where Ford moved in Apr. 1901. This suggests that Ford had already decided to fictionalize Katharine's story (in verse) while he was working on the biography, and before he heard about Pollard's book. He didn't need external pressures to turn history to romance.

9 Mizener, 78, makes Ford's frustration over McClure sound unreasonable. Conrad to Pinker, 28 Feb. [1902]; to Ford, 15 Apr. 1902, [30 May 1902]: *Collected Letters*, ii. 385–6, 408–9, 414–15.

10 Ford to Cathy Hueffer [n.d., but June 1902]: House of Lords. Mizener, p. xviii, cites Ford's amusing story of James asking the advice of a housemaid at the Bungalow whether he should employ a 'Lady Help', taking it as evidence that Ford was trying to suggest he led a more affluent life than he did. But Ford's letters show that he was not exaggerating about employing servants. Ford sent Edward Garnett a complete draft of the novel he was then calling 'the Altruist' around May 1902, saying 'I'm sick of it': [n.d.]: Texas.

11 The marriage certificate is dated 2 Mar. 1897, and gives Oliver's 'Rank or Profession' as 'Gentleman'. Robert Garnett to Ford, 31 Dec. 1898, 1 and 12 Jan.

(two letters) 1899. Garnett tried to dissuade Ford from the loan, but his letters imply that Ford agreed to it. Garnett, 'A Bloomsbury Girlhood', 432. Ford to Wells [n.d. but May–Aug. 1902]: Illinois. Ford to Cathy Hueffer [June 1902] and [n.d. but *c.* 17 Dec. 1902]: House of Lords.

12 *Joseph Conrad*, 242–4. Conrad to Ford, 10, 19, and 24 June (two letters and a telegram) 1902: *Collected Letters*, ii. 423–4, 427, 428–30. Ford to Olive Garnett [11 July 1902]: *Reader*, 468. Mizener, 79, calls the holiday a 'walking trip through the New Forest'; but besides Ford's letter to Elsie from Ringwood, on the edge of the Forest (7 Aug.), there are also letters from Dorchester (8 Aug.) and Kingsbridge, Devon (12 Aug.). Ford to Cathy Hueffer [n.d., but June 1902]: House of Lords.

13 Ford to Elsie [7 Aug. 1902] from Ringwood, and [8 Aug. 1902] from Dorchester. Conrad to Ford, 19 June 1902; Conrad to Elsie, [late Sept. 1902]: *Collected Letters*, ii. 427 and 443.

14 Ford to Elsie [n.d., but August 1902, not 'ca. March 1902?' as provisionally dated at Cornell. Ford was using Winchelsea stationery, but was writing within view of boats 'going up from Plymouth'.]; and [n.d.]; quoted from Mizener, 79 ['endless business']. 'Dedicatory Letter to Stella Ford', written for the 1927 'Avignon Edition' of *The Good Soldier*, and repr. in the Oxford World's Classics edition, 1–4. Ford told an interviewer that after the war 'he wrote two novels in anger which were not published. He intended to write no more. He changed his mind, however': Review of *New York is Not America*, *Time*, 10/25 (19 Dec. 1927), 32. Bowen, *Drawn from Life*, 63, said Ford 'Revealed himself as a lonely and very tired person who wanted to dig potatoes and raise pigs and never wanted to write another book'.

15 *Return to Yesterday*, 143. Mizener, 55. Edward Shanks, 'Ford Madox Ford: The Man and His Work', *World Review* (June 1948), 61, identified an 'ecstasy of self-pity' as an important component of *Parade's End*. Lionel Stevenson's review of Richard Cassell's *Ford Madox Ford: A Study of His Novels in English Fiction in Transition*, 5/1 (1962), 63, argued that 'his heroes are always autobiographical, especially in their victimization by greedy, jealous wives, and that Ford's personal failure to find adjustment and satisfaction in life dictates the elusive note of self-pity that prevents his novels, as it prevents Gissing's, from achieving the full status of great fiction'.

16 *It Was the Nightingale*, 32–5.

17 e.g. *Ancient Lights*, 150; *Return to Yesterday*, 48. The lecture, delivered after the war, has been published as 'The Literary Life', ed. Joseph Wiesenfarth, *Contemporary Literature*, 30/2 (Summer 1989), 171–82.

18 Ford's fullest account of their fictional techniques is in *Joseph Conrad*, 167–215. See 204–8 on 'justification'. For *progression d'effet* see 210: *It Was the Nightingale*, p. vi; *The March of Literature*, 580. 'A Haughty and Proud Generation', *Yale Review*, 9 (July 1922), 704, speaks of 'progressive effect'. Several other passages which don't explicitly mention the term evidently describe it—often in relation to another of Ford's favourite terms, the *coup de canon* ending. Thus in 'Literary Portraits—XX.: Mr. Gilbert Cannan and "Old Mole" ', *Outlook*, 33 (24 Jan. 1914), 110–11, Ford says: 'Let me try to define what "form" means for myself [. . .] every word in a novel should help the story forward towards the taking of that last trick which is your final effect.' In *Return to Yesterday*, 209–10, Ford writes of his and Conrad's ideas: 'a Novel was the rendering of an Affair: of one embroilment, one set of embarrassments, one human coil, one psychological progression [. . .] the

whole novel was to be an exhaustion of aspects, was to proceed to one culmination, to reveal once and for all, in the last sentence, or the penultimate; in the last phrase, or the one before it—the psychological significance of the whole.' *Henry James*, 129–30, talks of 'the economically worded, carefully progressing set of apparently discursive episodes, all resolved, as it were, in the *coup de canon* of the last sentence, that are found in one of the *contes* of Maupassant'; and *Mightier Than the Sword*, 95, argues that detective fiction must 'progress from paragraph to paragraph until the final effect is got by the last word'.

19 *Return to Yesterday*, 40–1. Ford told the story again in 'Memories of Oscar Wilde', *Saturday Review of Literature*, 20/5 (27 May 1939), 3–4, 15–16; repr. in *Reader*, 138–45.

20 David Garnett, *The Golden Echo*, 127–8.

21 Ford to Cathy Hueffer [*c*.17 Dec. 1902]: House of Lords.

22 Mizener, 80–1. Conrad, *Collected Letters*, iii. 3–4. Two years later Conrad was still depending on the then-convalescent Ford as his secret sharer, telling Pinker (confidentially) he could get Ford to help him block out *The Rescue*: 21 Dec. 1904: ibid. 193–4. Ford evidently didn't do more than this for the book. Jessie Conrad said: 'I am thankful I persuaded Conrad not to allow Ford Madox Hueffer to assist in the finishing. It appeared a sacrilege to me': *Joseph Conrad as I Knew Him*, 149.

23 Conrad to Elsie Hueffer [8 Jan. 1903]; to Ford [11 Jan. 1903]: *Collected Letters*, iii. 7–10.

24 Mizener, 81–2. Ford read 'some chapters of his "London" ' to Olive Garnett in the first week of Apr. 1903: Garnett's travel diary for 4 Apr. 1903. Ford to Elsie, 11 Feb. 1903. Mizener, 75. Ford to Pinker, 28 Sept. 1902: *Letters*, 16. Ford recalled Galsworthy's breakfasts in *It Was the Nightingale*, 34. Brebach, 76–7, 83. *Joseph Conrad*, 156–7; discussed in vol. 2, Ch. 12. Mizener, 540, n. 27.

25 Ford to Garnett, 4 Mar. 1903: Northwestern. Garnett stayed from 30 Mar. to 6 Apr.: travel diary for 31, 30 Mar., 4 Apr. 1903. Conrad to Ford [early Sept.? 1903]: *Collected Letters*, iii. 58–60. Karl, 550. Conrad to Kazimierz Waliszewski, 8 Nov. 1903: *Collected Letters*, iii. 75–7; translated as: 'I look on *Romance* as something without any importance: I collaborated on it while it was impossible for me to do anything else.' Conrad to Elsie Hueffer, 1 Oct. 1903: ibid. 64–5.

26 Harvey suggests 16 Oct., but he found no reviews before 30 Oct. Conrad to Pinker, [7 or 14 Oct.? 1903], fixes the date: *Collected Letters*, iii. 67. *Academy*, 65 (31 Oct. 1903), 469; *Nation* (New York), 79 (11 Aug. 1904), 121; see Harvey, 282–3. *Spectator*, 92 (2 Jan. 1904), 21–2, for example, lamented a changed Conrad. *Outlook* (London), 12 (7 Nov. 1903), 402; *Outlook* (New York), 77 (18 June 1904), 424–5. Conrad was staying with the Hueffers from 27 Oct. to about 2 Nov. 1903: see *Collected Letters*, iii. 69, n. 2. Jessie Conrad, *Joseph Conrad as I Knew Him*, 152, describes finding some of *The Nature of a Crime* in Conrad's writing. It might be the fragment of three folio pages recorded (but wrongly titled as 'Marriage', and described as from an unpublished MS of Conrad's) in *A Conrad Memorial Library*, 448. Ford certainly supplied the idea, which was based on an anecdote of Madox Brown's (see *Return to Yesterday*, 194). The typescript 'The Old Story' at Cornell is almost certainly Ford's attempt at a first version, upon which the collaboration was based.

27 Mizener, 84. Ford to Edward Garnett, [n.d.] (Texas). In fact Mrs Martindale lived until 18 Feb. 1907: Conrad, *Collected Letters*, iii. 410 n. W. M. Rossetti to Ford, 10 Nov. 1903, quoted in Goldring, *The Last Pre-Raphaelite*, 115. Ford to Elsie [14 Dec. 1903].

Chapter 11

1 Mizener, 85. Ford discussed Campden Hill around 1903 in *It Was the Nightingale*, 33–4. Garnett, diary for 13 Feb. 1904. Ford, *Joseph Conrad*, 30, says Conrad dictated 'a great part' of *The Mirror* to him. Najder, 298, says Ford 'magnified' his involvement, but the six out of fifteen stories he says Ford helped with (as opposed to Mizener's figure of seven out of twenty-two: 88–9) do represent a substantial amount of dictation. Mizener, 88–9, argues convincingly that some of the stories may have been collaborations. *Return to Yesterday*, 194–5. Najder, 296–9. Conrad to George Harvey, 15 Apr. 1904: *Collected Letters*, iii. 132 (Conrad even thought of calling the book 'A Seaman's Sketches'). Jessie Conrad, *Joseph Conrad and His Circle*, 87. Conrad to Galsworthy [7 or 14? Jan. 1904]: *Collected Letters*, iii. 109. *Joseph Conrad*, 212. The ordeals of Airlie Gardens are also described in *Return to Yesterday*, 278–90. See Najder, 294–5, on Conrad's 1903/4 depression.

2 *Return to Yesterday*, 278–81. As Olive Garnett didn't hear of the flu outbreak until 6 Mar. (Moser, 53), it must have occurred between 13 and 25 Feb.—the latter being the date James wrote to Elsie to commiserate about both the flu and Christina's accident: Lindberg-Seyersted, 45. Conrad to Pinker, 29 Mar. 1904, says that he had flu the previous week: *Collected Letters*, iii. 126. Mizener, 89. Conrad to Meldrum, 5 Apr. 1904 (which also bears out Ford's memory of Conrad's gout): *Collected Letters*, iii. 128–9. Ford to George Keating, 27 July [1923 or 1925: date indistinct], quoted in Morey, 120–1. Conrad to Elsie Hueffer (who had had to ask Conrad for money while Ford was ill in Germany later in the year), 2 Sept. 1904: *Collected Letters*, iii. 160–1. For the suggestions that Ford could write parts of *Nostromo*, see Conrad to Pinker, [6] Feb.; to Galsworthy, 16 Feb.; to Pinker, 17 Mar. and 22 Aug. 1903: ibid. 16–18; 23–4; 55–6. Mizener, 89–90.

3 *Return to Yesterday*, 290. Mizener, who places this accident before the flu episode, says that Johanna threw a blanket around Christina, burning herself badly in the process; but he cites no evidence for deviating from Ford's account (p. 86). Olive Garnett's diary says 'Nurse burned', which might indicate that the flu preceded the fire (Moser, 53); but she thought the nurse was hired for Elsie, who was 'in bed with something internal' when Robert Garnett visited on 5 Mar. Of course neither version precludes Ford from also having acted himself to save his daughter.

4 It may have been bitterness against Elsie who, even a quarter of a century later had still refused to grant Ford a divorce, that made him suppress her name. Or it may have been his characteristic reticence about his marital relations. But Garnett, diary for 6 Mar. 1904, identifies it as 'the opal ring Ford gave Elsie'. Moser, 54.

5 Ford to Elsie [n.d., but from Brockenhurst, therefore Apr.–May 1904]: Cornell. *Return to Yesterday*, 293–4.

6 *Return to Yesterday*, 294–5. Garnett, diary for 6 Mar. 1904, confirms Ford's reminiscence, saying of the opal that 'Ford tried to lose it down drains, & at last, meeting a Little Sister of the Poor gave it her, asking her to sell it for charity.

Elsie now says it should have been put under running water to break the charm. Very sad!'.

7 James to Ford, 14 Apr. 1904: Lindberg-Seyersted, 47. Galsworthy to Ford, 14 Apr. 1904: printed in Goldring, *The Last Pre-Raphaelite*, 117–19. The Cornell manuscript entitled 'London' includes this chapter, but has no annotations. Galsworthy's letter shows that Ford had written at least as far as the penultimate chapter of *The Soul of London* by then. The book was finished in mid-May: Mizener, 88. See *Letters*, 10–15 for Ford's criticisms of *Villa Rubein* and *A Man of Devon*.

8 *The Soul of London*, 120–3 of the chapter 'London at Leisure'.

9 See *Pound/Ford*, 10, 68. 'Hands Off the Arts', *American Mercury*, 34 (Apr. 1935), 406–7. Pater, *The Renaissance* (London: Macmillan, 1913), 156–7: 'Sidera Cadentia'; first published in *The Face of the Night*; *Collected Poems* (1913), 109. Cf. *The Heart of the Country*, 102–3, on 'the things that keep us going nowadays through the between-beats of the clock'; and *No Enemy*, 34, on hearing of the death of Kitchener: 'It was just one of those situations in which one thinks nothing—a change in the beat of the clock.'

10 See pp. 445–7 above for a further discussion of this anonymous essay.

11 'Literary Causeries: XI: "Huddie . . ." ', *Chicago Tribune Sunday Magazine* (Paris) (27 Apr. 1924), 3, 11 (p. 3). Hudson to Ford, 2 Apr. [1904]: Goldring, *The Last Pre-Raphaelite*, 119–24, prints Hudson's letters to Ford from this time (119–21). Ford to Elsie [7 Apr. 1904] and [8 Apr. 1904]. *Return to Yesterday*, 278. Moser, 54 (based on Olive Garnett's diary entry for Saturday, 9 Apr., that Elsie would go 'on Tuesday'); which overturns Mizener's date of May: 91. Conrad to Ford [25? Apr. 1904]; *Collected Letters*, iii. 134–5.

12 Conrad to Ford, 29 May 1904: *Collected Letters*, iii. 142. Moser, 57. Ford to Cathy Hueffer [n.d.]: House of Lords. Quoted by Mizener, 91.

13 Ford wrote to Olive Garnett on 11 July 1902: 'We've just seen the new moon—that *always* means ill luck. My only, firmly rooted superstition. But it's inevitable and deadly': *Reader*, 468. 'O Hygeia!', *Harper's*, 156 (May 1928), 774.

14 Ford to Elsie [n.d., but between 2 and 7 Apr. 1904]. Mizener, 93, says Ford felt persecuted about *Romance*, and demanded that Conrad repay him £100. But he only cited Conrad's letter of 29 May, which expresses Conrad's desire to repay Ford (especially now that Ford's illness was preventing him from earning); there is no mention of a demand from Ford. Mizener, 84.

15 The memorandum is at Northwestern University; 1–3. See Moser, 53–6, to which I am greatly indebted.

16 The Northwestern Memorandum, 4; Moser, 56. Garnett, diary for 30 July 1904. Elsie to Cathy Hueffer [n.d., but 30 July–6 Aug. 1904]: House of Lords. See Mizener, 93–4.

17 Garnett, diary for 2, 6–10 Aug. 1904. Mizener, 93, dates the departure 'early in June', but Olive Garnett's diaries fix it as the Saturday after Wednesday, 3 Aug. Elsie to Cathy Hueffer [n.d.], says 'I wonder if you could go to see him off. He will start on Saturday' (House of Lords); he had lunch with Galsworthy and Edward Garnett on 3 Aug. (Moser, 56); on 8 Aug. he was on board ship, writing to Elsie from between Nijmegen and Emmerich-am-Rhein; so the Saturday must have been 6 Aug. James to Elsie, 11 Aug. 1904: Lindberg-Seyersted, 48–9.

Chapter 12

1 Ford to Elsie [8 Aug. 1904]. Edward Garnett first suggested the Holbein project to Ford in Nov. 1903: see Mizener, 84, 540, n. 3.

2 Ford to Olive Garnett [30 Aug. 1904] and [9 Oct. 1904]: Northwestern. Hunt, *The Flurried Years*, 126. Mizener misplaces Frau Schmedding in Boppard: 94.

3 Mizener, 97. Freud, 'Inhibitions, Symptoms and Anxiety' (1926), *The Standard Edition of the Complete Psychological Works of Sigmund Freud*, vol. 20 (London: The Hogarth Press and the Institute of Psycho-Analysis, 1959), 109.

4 Ford to Elsie [25 Aug. 1904] postmarked 'Rüdesheim'; and [15 Sept. 1904]: Cornell.

5 This and the quotations in the rest of the paragraph are taken (unless otherwise indicated) from two letters, both [n.d., but early Sept. 1904].

6 Ford to Elsie, [n.d. but *c*.10 Sept. 1904]; [25 Aug. 1904].

7 *Return to Yesterday*, 266. Ford to Elsie '[Early Sept. 1904]'. Mizener, 95, 541, n. 25.

8 Two letters to Elsie, both [15 Sept. 1904]; and Ford to Elsie, 28 Sept. 1904: Cornell. Mizener, 95, 97, 99. Ford wrote to William Rossetti expressing anxiety about a £40 debt. 'Pray think no more about that tin', replied the kindly uncle: 3 Oct. 1904: Rossetti, *Selected Letters*, 641.

9 Ford to Elsie [30 Aug. 1904] and [15 Sept. 1904]. He had second thoughts about Dresden and Berlin because of the expense: Mizener, 99. Ford to Garnett [9 Oct. 1904]: Northwestern. *The Idiot*, trans. and introduced by David Margarshack (Harmondsworth: Penguin Books, 1955), 7, 90.

10 *Holbein*, 62–4. The catalogue of the sale of Madox Brown's effects (Cornell) lists as item 126: 'Portrait of a Man, by F. Madox Brown, after Holbein.'

11 *Holbein*, 146, 148.

12 [15 Oct. 1904], quoted by Mizener, 99. The feeling of weakness is described in *Return to Yesterday*, 266.

13 *Return to Yesterday*, pp. viii–ix, 268–9.

14 See Freud, 'On the Grounds for Detaching a Particular Syndrome from Neurasthenia under the Descriptions "Anxiety Neurosis" ' (1895), *Standard Edition*, vol. 3 (London: The Hogarth Press and the Institute of Psycho-Analysis, 1962), 94–6. *Return to Yesterday*, 266.

15 *Ford Madox Brown*, 95, 315. Moser, 33. See Elliot Jaques, 'Death and the Mid-Life Crisis', in *Work, Creativity, and Social Justice* (London: Heinemann, 1970), 38–63. Ford to Elsie [17 Oct. 1904].

16 Mizener, 97. Ford to Rossetti, quoted in Rossetti, *Selected Letters*, 643, n. 1. Ford to Elsie [27 Oct. 1904].

17 'The Baron', *Macmillan's*, 87 (Feb. 1903), 304–20. In a second story published in 1903, 'The Old Conflict', Ford wrote about 'the eternal conflict between the creator and the man who, standing on the platform, seems to be eternally twisting the thing created into a means of displaying himself'. Ostensibly about the relationship between composer and performer, the story also suggests Ford's own inner conflicts: 'Writer and critic? Self and anti-self?' Author and collaborator? Or the relationship between creativity and personality? In this story it is clearer that Ford's concern with his self-division is primarily an investigation into the nature of his art. Fordian man, like the artist, is 'homo duplex'. *Macmillan's*, 89 (Dec. 1903), 120. Stang and Smith, 'Music for a While', 217 n.

18 See Elaine Lees, 'Novels of Impressions: Ford Madox Ford's Autobiographies' (unpublished dissertation: University of Pittsburgh, 1976), 74. *Return to Yesterday* (New York: Liveright, 1932), 261–2; the English edition, 267 omits the words 'with agony' from the sentence beginning 'I used to hang out'. Ford to Elsie [4 Nov. 1904]. Mizener, 100.

19 Dated '[ca. end Oct., 1904]' at Cornell; but more likely to be the beginning of Nov. Ford was still at Mammern on 31 Oct. (Cornell has a postcard to Katharine postmarked with that date), and in Marienberg by 4 Nov.

20 See p. 461; also vol. 2, Ch. 8.

21 Such a longing to escape has been taken to be a prime motive for Ford's writing: by Mizener, for whom Ford's fictions are revised versions of a reality he could not face; and by Moser, for whom writing is an attempt to 'become' someone quite other. Moser, 269. My criticisms of his challenging book are elaborated in 'Poor Ford', *Essays in Criticism*, 33/2 (Apr. 1983), 163–73. Also see vol. 2, Ch. 21.

22 Bowen, *Drawn from Life*, 62.

23 Ford to Elsie [4 Nov. 1904] and '[? Nov., 1904]'. These experiences were to go into Dowell's obsessive memories of the regimentation of nerve-patients at Nauheim (which Ford also visited, though in 1910 with Violet Hunt: see Mizener, 201). Elsie was building a studio extension on to the Bungalow for Ford, designed by Cowlishaw, and in this letter he says the work has begun. Mizener, 96. Judd, *Ford Madox Ford*, 134, calls it a 'touching testimony to Elsie's attempt to help her husband and to save her marriage'.

24 Ford to Elsie [16 Nov. 1904], [20–2? Nov.], and '[ca. end Nov., 1904]'. *Return to Yesterday*, 269.

25 '[ca. end of Nov., 1904]'.

26 Ford to Elsie [25 Aug. 1904]: 'with the peppermints in my pocket I can do anything or go anywhere': Cornell. Olive Garnett recalled walking with Ford before he left England, 'sitting down on every seat & putting a lozenge into his mouth against agoraphobia': Northwestern Memorandum, quoted by Moser, 56. *Drawn from Life*, 63. Ford's cards to Christina and Katharine are at Cornell.

27 *It Was the Nightingale*, 89.

28 5 Sept. 1904; cf. Conrad to Elsie, 2 Sept.: *Collected Letters*, iii. 164–5, 160–1.

29 'Literary Causeries: VI. The Herb Oblivion', *Chicago Tribune* (Paris) (23 Mar. 1924), 3. Pound, 'Ford Madox (Hueffer) Ford; Obit', *Nineteenth Century and After*, 126 (Aug. 1939), 178–81; repr. in Pound, *Selected Prose: 1909–1965*, ed. William Cookson (London: Faber, 1973), 431.

30 Pound, 'Mr Hueffer and the Prose Tradition in Verse', *Poetry*, 4/3 (June 1914), 111–20; repr. as 'The Prose Tradition in Verse' by T. S. Eliot (whose excision of Ford's name from the title is characteristic of his attitude to Ford) in *Literary Essays of Ezra Pound* (London: Faber and Faber, 1954), 377. Pound, *Guide to Kulchur* (London: Faber, 1938), 194. Mizener, 76. Ford to Garnett [1902]: *Reader*, 469.

Chapter 13

1 Ford to Elsie [3 Dec. 1904]. Conrad to Pinker, 21 Dec. 1904; *Collected Letters*, iii. 194. Garnett's diary, 20 Dec. 1904: quoted by Moser, 58. Mizener, 97, 100–1. *Return to Yesterday*, 271–3.

2 *Return to Yesterday*, 268. Mizener, 101. 'O Hygeia!', *Harper's*, 156 (May 1928), 775. 'Phineas Re- read', *Daily News* (1 November 1911), 4.

3 Hunt, *The Flurried Years*, 33-4.

4 'Literary Portraits—IX. Mr. Thomas Hardy and "A Changed Man" ', *Outlook*, 32 (8 November 1913), 641-2. Mizener, 101. 'Literary Causeries: IV: Escape. . . . .', *Chicago Tribune Sunday Magazine* (Paris) (9 Mar. 1924), 3, 11, mentions his mother reading him Boswell through the insomniac nights of his breakdown, though he doesn't say whether that was while in Germany or after his return. Isaiah Berlin, introduction to Turgenev, *Fathers and Sons* (Harmondsworth: on Penguin Books, 1975), 42. *'Books for Exchange: II'. This manuscript at Cornell was almost certainly either an early draft for part of, or a probably unpublished continuation of *'A Literary Causerie: The Less-Known Flaubert', *Academy*, 69 (11 Nov. 1905), 1175-6, which begins with a discussion of men of letters exchanging the names of books, and mentions the Turgenev.

5 *Return to Yesterday*, 271. Ford alludes to Johnson's fellow collegian, Edwards, who said: 'You are a philosopher, Dr. Johnson. I have tried too in my time to be a philosopher; but I don't know how, cheerfulness was always breaking in.' Boswell, *Life of Johnson*, entry for 17 Apr. 1778. Garnett, quoted by Moser, 59. Mizener, 102.

6 Ford to Olive Garnett [5 Jan. 1905]: Northwestern. Mizener, 102. Ford to Wells, 1 Feb. 1905: Illinois. Moser, 59, suggests very plausibly that Elsie's unconscious attitudes towards Ford after finding out about the affair may have 'contributed to the return of tuberculosis'. Rossetti, *Selected Letters*, 341, n. 3.

7 Five months later Olive noted that the disease was still dominating their lives: diary for 1 May, 26 Sept. 1905.

8 See Harvey, 285. *Return to Yesterday*, 238-9. Archibald Marshall, who worked for Alston Rivers, wrote a bitter reproof of Ford's account in *Out and About*, 114-21. But Marshall's version is no more trustworthy: eager to indict Ford's inaccuracies, he confuses the order in which his firm published Ford's books (putting *The Fifth Queen* before *The Soul of London*). Mizener, 103. Edward Garnett told Galsworthy: 'H[armsworth] read the book for 10 minutes, and said "We'll give it a column" ': *Letters from John Galsworthy, 1900-1932*, ed. E. Garnett (London: Jonathan Cape, 1934), 59. This sounds more probable. Mizener suspected that Garnett was repeating what Ford had told him, but that is unlikely given Garnett's usual scepticism about Ford.

9 'On Impressionism', *Poetry and Drama*, 2 (June and Dec. 1914), 323.

10 Norman and Jean MacKenzie, *The First Fabians*, 91. Ford would probably have heard about the match-girls from the Garnetts: R. Garnett, *Constance Garnett*, 100-1. They also figure in *An English Girl*, 67. *The Soul of London*, 87-92. See Mizener, 105, and Judd, *Ford Madox Ford*, 122-8, for good discussions of the book.

11 'I personally regard the great city with horror,' wrote Ford (and before he met Conrad): 'it is for me a hideous shadow, continually brooding on the horizon': 'William Hyde: An Illustrator of London', *Artist*, 21 (Jan. 1898), 4.

12 *The Soul of London*, 76, 148.

13 Garnett to Galsworthy, 8 May 1905, in *Letters from John Galsworthy*. Galsworthy answered on 13 May: 'The news you give of Hueffer is really fine—may it be more than a passing boom, and cheer him into perfect health again': 59, 62. Mizener, 104. *Return to Yesterday*, 235-6. Ford to Catherine Hueffer [3 May 1905]: House of Lords. Ford to Jerrold [n.d.].

14 Conrad to Ford, 9 May 1905: *Collected Letters*, iii. 241–2. Mizener, 107–8. There is a partial dramatization (entitled 'Tomorrow') in Ford's hand. Najder, 315.

15 Garnett, diary for [18–19] July 1905. Mizener, 109, said Elsie moved from the Bungalow into Hurst Cottage at Aldington in July; but he may be confusing this with her definitive departure from the Bungalow in Dec. 1907. It's true she went there sometime between 3 July 1905 (when Ford wrote to her at Winchelsea) and 7 July (when he addressed her at Hurst Cottage); but the latter says 'When you go back, if it's soon, you might send up the m.s. of the Vth Queen', the tone of which suggests he thought she would return before leaving for the continent later that month. She was certainly back at the Bungalow when she returned to England; Ford wrote to her there on 21 Sept. 1905. The deposition (now at Cornell), headed *'Self ats Hueffer' (*sic*), was written from Violet Hunt's South Lodge, and is dated 27 May 1913, when Ford and Hunt were suffering from the scandal of Elsie's libel suit against the *Throne*: see above, Ch. 23. Ford to Elsie [3 July 1905]. Another letter to Elsie [13 July 1905], sheds ambiguous light on the question of when Elsie found out about Ford and Mary. While assuring her that he cares for her, and urging her not to 'think sudden & bitter thoughts', he tells her that he has just met Mary and been to supper at Broadhurst Gardens. Did Elsie still not know? Was Ford trying to allay her suspicions? Or was he suggesting that it was all now over and they should all behave like civilized people?

16 Ford to Elsie [3 July 1905]; and [7 July 1905].

17 Ford to Elsie [14 Aug.; 10, 21, and 4 Sept., 1905].

18 Ford to Elsie [4 Sept. 1905]. *Academy*, 69 (28 Oct. 1905), 1130–1.

19 Moser, 60.

20 Mizener, 466–7. Moser, 60, argues that Ford fails to achieve adequate detachment from George. Ford to Garnett [n.d., but 1899]: University of Kansas, Lawrence. Ann Barr Snitow gives the best discussion of the tonal complexities and problems of *The Benefactor* in *Ford Madox Ford and the Voice of Uncertainty*, 87–91.

21 See *The English Novel*, 123, on 'the novel of Aloofness'. He told Galsworthy: 'You too are miles above any of the characters you create; you must be or you could not create them': [Oct. 1900]: *Letters*, 12. In *'Creative History and the Historic Sense' Ford wrote about the proximity of pity and contempt from the Olympian perspective: 'the possession of the historic sense makes first of all for comprehension. It implies an immense tolerance, an immense understanding, possibly an immense pity or possibly an immense contempt for one's kind': *Yale Review*, 78/4 (Summer 1989), 522. *The Benefactor*, 190; *Joseph Conrad*, 200.

22 [30 Oct. 1905]: Northwestern. Henriette Corkran knew Henry James, and was mostly in Rye while writing *Oddities, Others, and I* (London, Hutchinson, 1904).

23 Garnett, diary for 2 Nov. 1905. See Moser, 60. In *Provence*, 243, Ford said of Constance: 'I will even confess that I popped her as heroine into the novel I was then writing.' Ford may well have been portraying Olive Garnett's earnestness about altruism over the previous decade or so. For example, after a disillusioning conversation with Madame Bervi she wrote: 'If there is no disinterestedness in those whose faith & profession is altruism, where then is it, & if it doesn't exist what's the use of my existing, for mine must be a delusion; & how can I ever again exhort those whose profession & faith is egoism': diary for 1 July 1895.

24 The first passage tells how George's disciple Hailes has become parasitic on his possessions (as well as his genius). Ford *might* have had Conrad, or Edward Garnett in mind. Garnett, diary for [18–25] July 1905.

25 See Moser, 59, for a discussion of how Olive had more sympathy for Elsie than Ford from about this time. *The Good Soldier*, 135.

Chapter 14

1 Ford to Elsie [23, 27 Feb.; 10 and 13 Mar. 1906]. Mizener, 106, garbles the letter of 27 Feb., and calls it very unfairly 'a transparent effort to appear depressed by her absence'. In fact he is saying he is *less* depressed in the city. Garnett, diary for 23 Jan. 1906. Wells, *Experiment in Autobiography*, ii. 661. Hynes, *The Edwardian Turn of Mind*, 110. Edward Garnett had also joined the Fabians to help Wells: R. Garnett, *Constance Garnett*, 230.

2 Mizener, 118. Ford to Elsie [14 Feb. 1906] and [13 Mar. 1906].

3 It isn't known exactly when Ford met Marwood. In *Return to Yesterday*, 372, he places the meeting 'a little later' than his first call to Wells's Spade House, which was being built in December 1900—though from the perspective of 1930 this could mean anything from weeks to years later. Douglas Goldring (who didn't meet Ford until 1908, when Marwood was helping him with the *English Review*) thought they met soon after Ford moved to Winchelsea in 1901: *The Last Pre-Raphaelite*, 92. But Marwood doesn't appear in the Winchelsea electoral register until 1905, in the register valid from 1 Jan.: East Sussex County Records Officer to Max Saunders, 23 Feb. 1989. So the Marwoods probably arrived there in 1904. This squares with the fact that they married in Leeds in Feb. 1903, and probably moved to Mill Road, Winchelsea, some time after this, as Moser says (65). It is also supported by Najder's belief that Conrad didn't meet Marwood until May 1905: *Joseph Conrad*, 322. (Though, as he notes, Jessie Conrad placed their first meeting in July 1906: Najder, 562, n. 119.) Ford unlikely to have known Marwood for very long before introducing him to Conrad. Moser, 65, says that 'a native of Winchelsea who worked for the Marwoods as a young girl puts the date early in 1905'. Certainly Ford knew him by Christmas, 1905, when he inscribed a copy of *Rossetti* for him. However, as Marwood chose Winchelsea because he had a sister living there, it is possible he met Ford on a previous visit: Moser, 65. Ford told Olive Garnett 'I called with my bosom friend Marwood as chaperone' in an undated letter that was assigned to 'c. 1901' by Sondra Stang: *Reader*, 467–8. But there is no internal evidence to support such an early date. On the contrary, the reference to Elsie's improved health makes it more likely to date from 1905–8. The paper on which the original (at Northwestern) is written is exactly the same as that of another letter to Olive dated 15 January 1908. Unusually for Ford, who generally used headed writing-paper, neither letter bears an address. The letter mentioning Marwood is thus probably from late 1907 or early 1908. The reference to having walked from Hampton Court might suggest the early date: Ford may have wanted to take another look at the palace before sending *The Fifth Queen Crowned* to the publishers (it came out on 26 Mar. 1908, and was dedicated to Marwood). Alternatively, the reference to Elsie's health might place it after her operation of 30 May 1908.

The Marwoods don't appear on the guest register the Hueffers kept inside their grandfather clock before March 1908. But then there are no entries between June

1903 and 3 Mar. 1908, when Elsie moved to Hurst Cottage, renamed 'Kitcat Cottages'. The Marwoods thus presumably got to know the Hueffers after June 1903, and before Christmas 1905.

4 Moser, 64–5, 303. *The Good Soldier*, 291. Najder, 322, 562, n. 120. Goldring, *The Last Pre-Raphaelite*, 97.

5 Ford to Herbert Read, 19 Sept. 1920: *Letters*, 126. *It Was the Nightingale*, 188.

6 *Return to Yesterday*, 371–3, 375. *It Was the Nightingale*, 203, 188. Ford had dedicated *Privy Seal* to his aunt Laura Schmedding, who, like Marwood, 'so often combated my prejudices, and corrected my assertions'. Conrad, quoted by F. L. Grant Watson, *But to What Purpose: The Autobiography of a Contemporary* (London: Cresset Press, 1946), 149. Conrad to Marwood, Apr. 1915, quoted by Jessie Conrad, *Joseph Conrad and His Circle*, 117. Archibald Marshall, *Out and About*, 275. His bitter book contains a long discussion of the implausibility of Ford's—consciously exaggerated—story about Marwood purposely introducing errors into his examination answers so as not to be encumbered with the title of 'Senior Wrangler': 275–9. The story (in *Return to Yesterday*, 374) is intended to bring out Marwood's dislike of ostentation.

7 *It Was the Nightingale*, 202–3. *Thus to Revisit*, 59. Ford to Read, 19 Sept. 1920: *Letters*, 126. *Mightier Than the Sword*, 106.

8 *Thus to Revisit*, 218. 'Thus to Revisit . . . : III.—The Serious Books', *Piccadilly Review* (6 Nov. 1919), 6. Ford explains that Marwood meant each man would create his own list of four, though it should include Clarendon's *History of the Great Rebellion* and Mayne's *Ancient Law*. *No More Parades*, 252.

9 Ford to Elsie [29 Mar. 1906]. Tetley to Elsie, 14 Mar. 1948. 'On Impressionism', 174. *Mightier Than the Sword*, 59. George Jefferson, *Edward Garnett*, 128. *The Heart of the Country*, 3–7. 'Literary Causeries: XI: "Huddie" ', *Chicago Tribune Sunday Magazine* (Paris) (27 Apr. 1924), 3, 11.

10 Ford to Elsie [6 Mar. 1906—misdated 10 Mar. by Mizener], [24 Mar. 1906], [23 Mar. 1906], and [27 Feb. 1906]. The Cornell MS 'The Old Story' is an early version of *The Nature of a Crime*. Its twenty-seven pages are perhaps as far as Ford got before involving Conrad. The quotation is from the first page of the main story, after the seven-page introduction by 'Daniel Chaucer'. Ford told Elsie that he and Conrad were doing 'a rather larky collaboration': quoted by Najder, 321, who dates the letter 17 May 1906, but I have been unable to find the quotation in either of the two letters of that date at Cornell.

11 *Collected Poems* [1913], 71–2. The poem was re-imagined as the opening of *The Nature of a Crime*.

12 Ford to Elsie [6 Mar. 1906]. Harvey, 288. *TLS* (16 Mar. 1906), 93; *Athenaeum* (7 Apr. 1906), 417; *'Fiction', Outlook*, 17 (17 Mar. 1906), 382–3. Garnett, diary for 21 Mar. 1906. 'Synopsis of a book to be called (provisionally) The Life & Times of Henry VIII'; quoted by Charles G. Hoffmann, ' "The Life and Times of Henry VIII": An Original for Ford Madox Ford's Fifth Queen Trilogy', *Notes and Queries*, 212 (July 1967), 248–50.

13 *Ford Madox Brown*, 372.

14 *Thus to Revisit*, 123. Katharine, too, is given qualities which Ford associates with artists. Like the 'Nice People' of his essay, she is a visionary. Her eyes tend to look beyond the actual, and she speaks abstractedly: see for e.g. *Privy Seal*, 208. Judd, *Ford Madox Ford*, 158. Moser, 62. As always with Ford's (or most writers')

novels, it is not only in the central figures that autobiographical material can be traced. Lascelles, 'smiling as he thought of new lies to tell' his sister in *The Fifth Queen Crowned*, is reminiscent of the raillery between Ford and his sister Juliet: 156.

15 Ford to Garnett [May or June 1904]: *Reader*, 471. Moser, 61, 64. *Tribune* (14 Mar. 1906), 2, and (15 Mar. 1906), 2. *The Fifth Queen*, 222.

16 See Ch. 25, on *The Good Soldier*.

17 Camilla B. Haase, 'Serious Artists: The Relationship between Ford Madox Ford and Ezra Pound' (dissertation: Harvard University, 1984), 118. *The Critical Attitude*, 20. Cf. 'A Declaration of Faith' [signed 'Didymus'], *English Review*, 4 (February 1910), 543–51; discussed on pp. 250–1; also see p. 467 for a fuller discussion of Ford's politics.

18 'Synopsis of a book to be called (provisionally) The Life & Times of Henry VIII'. Mizener, 470. Robert Green, *Ford Madox Ford*, ch. 2. Moser, 49. 'Dedicatory Letter to Stella Ford', *The Good Soldier* (Oxford: Oxford University Press, 1990), 1.

19 Conrad to Ford, 20 Feb. 1908: *Collected Letters*, iv. 46–7. For good discussions of *The Fifth Queen*, see: Mizener, 133–4 and 469–7; William Gass, 'The Neglect of *The Fifth Queen*', in *The Presence of Ford Madox Ford*, 25–43; and A. S. Byatt, 'Introduction' to the Twentieth Century Classics edn. (Oxford: Oxford University Press, 1984).

Chapter 15

1 R. Garnett, *Constance Garnett*, 298. Ford to Pinker [n.d. but February? 1906]: *Letters*, 23. Misdated '[November, 1905]' by Ludwig; and Mizener, 544, n. 10, says Ford didn't hear of the Soskices' plan until March. But his previous note cites a letter from 12 Feb. (actually dated 'Sat' [10th] by Ford, and postmarked the 12th [Monday]) in which Ford says: 'Juliet goes to Petersburg on Monday'. Mizener, 116. On 544, n. 10 he concedes that the story about Mrs Hueffer concealing Gapon 'seems to be true'. It is accepted by Barry Hollingsworth, 'David Soskice in Russia in 1917', *European Studies*, 6 (1976), 79. Juliet Soskice, 'Father Gapon', *New Leader* (1 Dec. 1922), 10; (8 Dec. 1922), 12–13. *Letters*, 23, n. 2.

2 Ford to Elsie [6 Apr. 1906] and [11 Apr. 1906]: Cornell. Mizener, 120, implies (misleadingly) that the visit took place after the publication of *The Heart of the Country* in May.

3 Ford to Elsie [? Apr. 1906], [28 Apr. 1906], [3 May 1906], and [29 Mar. 1906]. *Christina's Fairy Book*, 11.

4 Ford to Elsie [28 Apr. 1906]. Harmsworth became Lord Northcliffe in 1905. Mizener, 120–1, gives too much credence to Marshall's spiteful reminiscences, *Out and About*, 136–40; he also misconstrues Marshall's comment that 'Conrad finally cleared up my thoughts about it many years later': 'it' is not Ford's conduct over the *Mail* Supplement, but Marshall's self-confessed 'obsession of Hueffer'. Conrad may (as Mizener implies) have expressed to Marshall his hardened view of Ford as destructively monomaniacal; but Marshall presumably means that Conrad denounced Ford as a writer, as he was later to do in conversation with Hugh Walpole (see vol. 2, Ch. 7). Beerbohm's drawing of Hall Caine is at Harvard. A. M. S. Methuen to Pinker, 23 June 1906; Byles to Pinker (including a copy of Byles to 'Miss Campbell'), 8 Nov. 1906: Northwestern. Mizener, 112, implies that

Ford was deluding himself that he had 'an influence on the firm's policies'; but this is unfair. Ford did advise both the firm and its authors; Mizener himself thought Ford suggested the idea of Jessie Conrad's cookery book: 126. Conrad to Ford, 25 Jan. 1907: *Collected Letters*, iii. 410–1. Mizener, 113, was wrong to think that only one volume appeared. Rossetti, *Selected Letters*, 391 n. Robert Temple, *Catalogue 79* (London, 1992) lists all five of the Chesson volumes. See Conrad, *Collected Letters*, ii. 18–20 on W. H. Chesson; also R. Garnett, *Constance Garnett*, 140. Nora Chesson, née Hopper, was well reviewed by Yeats, and a prolific contributor to the press. Ford wrote an introduction to the first volume, in which he said he had known her for 'some years': *Dirge for Aoine and Other Poems*, p. xi. Ford and the Galsworthys helped R. H. Mottram select his poems for a volume, but it evidently never materialized: *For Some We Loved* (London, 1956), 76–7. Harvey, 91–2, says that other poets considered included W. H. Pollock, Barry Pain, and someone called Davis. Pollock's *Sealed Orders, and other poems* (London: Alston Rivers, 1907), was indeed in Ford's 'Contemporary Poets Series'. Ford to Elsie [23 Feb. 1906], [27 Feb. 1906], and [19 June 1906].

5 Conrad to Galsworthy, 11 May 1906: *Collected Letters*, iii. 330–1. See Hynes, *The Edwardian Turn of Mind*, 63. *The Soul of London*, 172. Ford, 'Author's Note', *England and the English*, p. xvii. Reviewers noted the disparity between Ford's urbanity and literary skill on the one hand, and his subject-matter on the other. See e.g. *Robert Lynd's particularly eulogistic full-page review, 'Our Book of the Week: An English Gentleman in the Country', *Sunday Sun* (London) (20 May 1906), 1. *The Good Soldier*, 291. Garnett, *Tribune* (9 May 1906), 2; Thomas, *Bookman* (London), 30 (June 1906), 111–12. Masterman, *Daily News* (9 May 1906), 4. Ford to Elsie [9 May 1906]; [21 Mar. 1906]; and [17 May 1906]. Jessie Conrad, *Joseph Conrad and His Circle*, 112.

6 Conrad to Galsworthy, 11 May 1906: *Collected Letters*, iii. 330–1. Karl, 609, argues that the collaboration took place between May and July. Mizener, 113–14. Najder, 318, 321–2; he suggests it was during this visit that Ford introduced Conrad and Marwood. *Return to Yesterday*, 194. Also see *Joseph Conrad*, 230–2, and *Mightier Than the Sword*, 94. Mizener, 113–14. Jessie Conrad, *Joseph Conrad and His Circle*, 113–16.

7 Ford to Elsie, Sunday [20 May 1906]. Ford to Elsie [24–5 June 1906] (Mizener, 544, n. 7 misdates this letter as 15 June). *Mightier Than the Sword*, 27. Mizener, 115. Ford to Elsie [28 Apr. 1906].

8 Mizener, 123. There are postcards (at Cornell) from Elsie to Ford from Venice [8 and 14 June 1906] and Heidelberg [22 June 1906]. Ford to Elsie [24–5 June 1906]. Price, 'Ford Madox Hueffer', *Poet Lore*, 31 (Autumn 1920), 432–4; 'Ford Madox Ford', *University of California Chronicle*, 27 (October 1925), 360.

9 29 July 1906. Dr Anton Wilhelm Hüffer to Max Saunders, 15 Jan. 1987.

10 Mizener, 123. Ford, *'Self ats [sic.] Hueffer', 1. *Return to Yesterday*, 348–51, tells an amusing story about his Russian companions on the voyage, who claimed to be smuggling the Imperial crown jewels to safety in New York in case of revolution.

11 Ford to Pinker [early Sept. 1906]: *Letters*, 23–4 (where it is misdated as Aug.; but Ford says they have been in America for three weeks, and must have arrived in the middle of Aug.). Conrad to Galsworthy, 14–15 Aug. 1906: *Collected Letters*, iii. 349–50. Mizener, 124. Ford to Pinker [n.d. but 15–19 Sept. 1906]: Huntington.

12 Elsie, postcard to Katharine from Boston, postmarked 25 Aug. 1906. Mizener, 127. William James to Ford, 22 Aug. 1906 (Cornell) was posted to Ford's New York address, the Hotel Earlington on W. 27th Street, from where it was forwarded to Newport, RI, the second postmark bearing the date 30 Aug. Elsie sent another postcard to Katharine ('Babs') from Rhode Island, postmarked 1 September; Elsie's postcard to Christina from Boston bears a Sept. postmark; the day is unclear, but probably the 4th. The Hurlbirds are mentioned (as 'the Misses H——') in *'The Passing of Toryism', *McNaught's Monthly*, 5/6 (June 1926), 174–6. In this version, as in *The Good Soldier*, 92–4 and *Return to Yesterday*, 270, Ford says they live in Stamford, Connecticut; whereas Mizener, 124, says Waterbury, confusing the aunts with Uncle John Hurlbird: *The Good Soldier*, 22. Ford sent postcards to his daughters from Waterbury as well during this trip.

13 Ford to Pinker [15–19 Sept. 1906]: Huntington [mis-catalogued as Aug.].

14 *'Just People' [1919–22], 13–20. Mizener, 123–4, 546. He is variously unfair here. None of the five versions talks of 'working whole summers' on the farm. The comment that Ford 'hints' in *Great Trade Route*, 140, that he 'spent some time on his Uncle Leopold's plantation in Virginia' is based solely on the sentence: 'My uncle Leopold's negroes, I said, used to haul their tobacco in two- and, sometimes, three-runnered sleds'—which Ford presumably heard from Leopold in France. (Anyway, as Mizener says, Ford explains that he never did get to Lexington; so whatever suggestion there is of an eyewitness account is candidly disavowed.) The dinner of the Gloucester, Massachusetts, fishing fleet, which Ford says in *A History of Our Own Time*, 213, he attended—and which gets 'improved' to 'dinners' in Mizener's account 123–4) may not be independently documented; but (as Mizener says in the following note, 546, n. 25) Ford *did* visit Gloucester while he was staying in Boston; and he did write about soon afterwards, in 'Literary Portraits: IV. Mr. W. W. Jacobs', *Daily Mail Books Supplement* (11 May 1907), 1; and 'Literary Portraits: XXI. The Town of Gloucester and her Annalist', *Tribune* (14 Dec. 1907), 2. It is not unimaginable that his agent or prospective publisher wouldn't arrange such an invitation for the author of *The Cinque Ports*, who was proposing to write the trilogy *Three Ships* (see n. 16 below). In short, there are more reasons for believing the gist of Ford's anecdotes than for reproving them. The published versions of the farming episode are in 'Literary Portraits—XLII. Mr. Robert Frost and "North of Boston" ', *Outlook*, 33 (27 June 1914), 879–80; *Return to Yesterday*, 161–3 (which follows the version in 'Just People' very closely); *Portraits and Self-Portraits* collected and illustrated by Georges Schreiber (Boston: Houghton Mifflin, 1936), 39–40; and *Great Trade Route*, 228–9, 237, which briefly alludes to the version in *Return to Yesterday*. Ford's letter to Pinker from Philadelphia doesn't mention the farming (he wouldn't have wanted Pinker to think his money was financing Ford's charity, rather than his career); but it at least corroborates that the weather was '*ferociously* hot'. Ford mentions working on this farm in two other probably unpublished essays. In *'Weather' (1934), he wrote: 'Climatically speaking [. . .] the most agreeable short period that I can remember I passed in the Blackstone Hotel in Chicago in mid-winter, 1925–26. The most appalling was a couple of days spent in a Philadelphia hotel that I won't name during a heat wave during the late fall of 1906' (p. 1), and recalled a ground-floor hotel room whose window he couldn't open for the 'screams from the trolley-car wheels' (p. 11). The other is an untitled piece, beginning: *'When that I was a

little, little boy—oh, a long time ago, I worked for a time on a farm near Philadelphia'. Though the details vary as the episode was retold at least five times over more than a decade, the basic consistency indicates that the central fact was true. The story of a Philadelphia city politics scandal in *Return to Yesterday*, 164–6, and in *Great Trade Route*, 239–41, is briefly referred to in a review written much closer to the event: 'A Literary Portrait: Chicago', *Outlook*, 35 (6 Mar. 1915), 302–3.

15 Quotations from *'Just People'. *The Good Soldier*, 19–20, 9, 179–80.

16 Ford to Pinker [early Sept. 1906]: *Letters*, 23–4. Mizener, 124. *Great Trade Route*, 221. Mizener, 127, says Ford began *The 'Half Moon'* in Feb. 1907, after finishing *An English Girl*. If so, he may have been confusing *The 'Half Moon'* with his previous historical series, *The Fifth Queen*, which he was certainly working on while in America. On the other hand, a letter from McClure, Phillips and Co. to Ford, 26 Sept. 1906, says that '*The 'Half Moon'* was originally to have been a part of a trilogy called *The Three Ships*...' (quoted by Harvey, 29), which suggests that Ford had at least begun planning the novel before returning to England. And the date of its 'Dedication' to Bradley means it was finished by 8 June 1907, so it must have been started between autumn 1906 and spring 1907. Mizener, 135. Besides the English and *Fifth Queen* trilogies, Ford wrote three long fairy-tales; three art monographs; *Parade's End* was written to stand as a trilogy before he decided to write *Last Post*; *The Rash Act* was originally planned as the first of three, though *Henry for Hugh* was its only sequel; and the travel books *Provence* and *Great Trade Route* were to have been supplemented with a third, *Portraits of Cities*.

17 Elsie, postcards to Christina and Katherine from New York [22 Sept. 1906]. Mizener, 124. *It Was the Nightingale*, 109.

18 Mizener, 546, n. 1. 'Self ats Hueffer', 1. Mizener, 126–7, contradicts himself about the date Ford finished *An English Girl*, saying first May 1907, then the beginning of Feb. This is because he wanted to portray as unrealistic Ford's comment to Pinker that he would finish the novel soon after returning to London in Oct. But as his p. 546, n. 1 explains, the novel was in proof by May, so the writing must have been finished much earlier: probably by the Feb. date—in which case Ford did indeed complete the novel rapidly. *Return to Yesterday*, 139. *Joseph Conrad*, 176. *An English Girl*, 270, 42, 118, 61, 57, 280, 189, 271, 276. Mizener, 128, said trenchantly that Don 'sees the truth that Ford had seen in *The Soul of London*, that the poor have a heroism of their own that is beyond the understanding of upper-class reformers'. *TLS* (20 Sep. 1907), 285–6. Conrad to Ford [16] Oct. 1907, and 1 Oct. 1907: *Collected Letters*, iii. 501–2, 485–6.

19 Conrad to Ford, 8 Jan., 1907: *Collected Letters*, iii. 403.

20 Mizener, 127, says they gave up the Sloane Square flat on the first of the year, and that Elsie returned to Winchelsea while Ford went to live with his mother at Brook Green. But the report of Elsie's restitution suit in the *Globe* (11 Jan. 1910), 11, says both Ford and Elsie came to live in London in 1907; whereas *'Self ats Hueffer', 13, says Elsie 'occupied rooms of her own constantly in London'. 'Self ats Hueffer', 1. Goldring, *South Lodge*, 16. R. A. Scott-James, 'Ford Madox Ford When he was Hueffer', *South Atlantic Quarterly*, 57 (spring 1958), 241, 240. Elizabeth Martindale, 'The Art of Manners', *English Review*, 3 (Oct. 1909), 431. *South Lodge*, 22. Ford was still publicly giving his address as 'Winchelsea', as in *The Spirit of the People*, p. xvi, and *The 'Half Moon'*, p. v.

21 Published only in *From Inland and Other Poems*, p. xiv. It is one of only two poems from this volume not known to have been published previously in a magazine. It is unlikely to date from before Aug. 1905—the earliest date of previous publication for the other previously uncollected poems here.

22 Katharine Hueffer Lamb to Moser, 2 Feb. 1978: quoted by Moser, 298-9, n. 12. Elsie played a prominent part in a Winchelsea Town Hall concert on 30 Dec. 1893, for which the programme is at Cornell.

23 Juliet Soskice to David Soskice, 21 Mar. 1907 (House of Lords Record Office). Greenslet, *Under the Bridge* (Boston: Houghton Mifflin, 1943), 104. Ford to Pinker [n.d., but *c.*June 1907]: Huntington; and [n.d., but late Aug.-early Sept. 1907]: Princeton. *The Spirit of the People*, 171. *'Self ats Hueffer', 1-2. Conrad to Galsworthy, 15 Sept. 1907: *Collected Letters*, iii. 474-5. Ford to Jerrold [n.d., but autumn 1907].

24 Ford to Pinker, both n.d.: Huntington. The first is quoted by Mizener, 131.

25 L. J. Bathurst to Pinker, 5 Oct. 1907: Northwestern.

26 Ford to Pinker, [n.d.]: Huntington; quoted by Mizener, 132. There was also a misunderstanding with Eveleigh Nash, the publisher of *The Fifth Queen Crowned*, which suggests that Pinker was being careless in his dealings at this time. Nash to Pinker, 30 Dec. 1907 (Northwestern) complains that when the firm commissioned 'a new historical novel by Mr Hueffer' it was not told to expect the third volume of a trilogy. As a result Ford got poorer terms. Mizener, 133.

27 Conrad, *Collected Letters*, iii. 410 n. Mizener, 130. Ford to Pinker [n.d., but late Aug.-early Sept. 1906]: Princeton. Mizener, 130, 127, 135. *The Pre-Raphaelite Brotherhood: A Critical Monograph*, 164-5. R. Garnett, *Constance Garnett*, 227-8.

28 Conrad to Arthur Llewelyn Roberts, 6 Jan. 1908: *Collected Letters*, iv. 13.

29 Ford to Stella Bowen, 3 May 1919. See Mizener, 139. Other examples would be *The Rash Act* and *Henry for Hugh*, in which the protagonist has to live within a new identity (and thus an unfamiliar world of family, lovers, and associates); and *Katharine Howard*, the idealist beleaguered in a world of men's intrigues and plotting.

30 *It Was the Nightingale*, 160. Wells described the angel of *The Wonderful Visit* as 'the Angel of Art' (London: J. M. Dent & Co., 1895), 35.

31 Friday Night [31 July or 7 Aug.? 1908]: *Collected Letters*, iv. 98. His letter to Pinker [11 Aug. 1908] praises the book apparently without irony: 'It's far and away the best thing he has ever done; and apart from being essentially a *good* piece of work with a peculiar originality in it, it is extremely readable. I prophesy a very fine reception for it—perhaps a fine sale too': ibid. 101-2. But since it was in Conrad's interest that Pinker should lend Ford more money, the praise should perhaps not be taken at face value.

32 See Elsie's essay on 'The Spirit of Melody', *English Review*, 4 (Jan. 1910), 250, on the horror of bath-chairs. *'Self ats Hueffer', 2. The details about the placebo pills are borne out by a letter from Ford to his mother written at the turn of the year (and postmarked 12 Jan. 1908 when it arrived in St Petersburg): 'I got a Dr. to pretend that he had discovered something the matter with her that no other Dr. had discovered—& to pretend to cure the evil & that really does seem to have proved effectual.' Mizener, 130-1, is unreliable here: he has Elsie coming to Holland Park Avenue for Christmas, and quarrelling with Ford at their Christmas tea party; but, as his note (p. 547, n. 13) explains, his sources are describing the

following Christmas, 1908. Conrad to Elsie, 1 Jan. 1908: *Collected Letters*, iv. 3, n. 3).

33 Goldring, *South Lodge*, 87. Goldring is, as often, muddled about the chronology. He places Elsie's move after her operation, which took place on 30 May. *'Self ats Hueffer', 2–3. Ford's dating is borne out by the guest register inside the Hueffer's clock, which reads: 'We came to Kitcat Cottages March 3rd 1908': photograph at Cornell.

34 Ford to Cathy Hueffer, n.d., but postmarked 12 Jan. 1908 on arrival in St Petersburg: House of Lords. Mizener, 547, n. 11.

35 Garnett, diary for 23 Jan. 1906. Ford to Garnett, 15 Jan. 1908: Northwestern. The inscription is recorded in R. A. Gekoski's Winter 1991 catalogue, *A Miscellany From Stock*, item 67; though the initials are misread as 'F.M.F.', and Olive is mis-identified as David Garnett's sister. Anne Lee Michell, letter to Max Saunders, 14 Nov. 1988, said that it was Ford's affair with Violet Hunt that completed his estrangement from Olive, as well as from Robert Garnett (who continued to act as Elsie's solicitor).

36 *'Self ats Hueffer', 4, 5. Mizener, 137. He says the operation was at the Bungalow, though it had been vacated and unfurnished three months earlier. Ford's deposition says Aldington, which is more likely. Ford to Pinker [n.d., but 29 May 1908]: Huntington.

37 Mizener, 107, 137–8. Ford to Pinker, 16 Oct. 1908: *Letters*, 26–7.

Chapter 16

1 Goldring, *South Lodge* is the best eyewitness account of Hunt, whose memoir of her life with Ford, *The Flurried Years*, was published in the USA as *I Have This to Say*. Mizener was the pioneer in trying to construct her biography. There are also two recent biographies: Joan Hardwick, *An Immodest Violet*; and Barbara Belford, *Violet. The Flurried Years*, 18. Hunt, diary for 1907, 16. *South Lodge*, 135.

2 'Literary Portraits—V.; Miss Violet Hunt and "The Desirable Alien" ', *Outlook*, 32 (11 Oct. 1913), 497–8. One version of Hunt's diary for 1907 places this meeting on 25 Apr. a month after the Galsworthy dinner. This is the dating followed by Mizener, 175–6. But an entry for 14 June reads as follows: 'Hueffer says that he is able to "boom" authors, and points to the succès *fulgurante* of William De Morgan's novel owing to his article in "The Mail". *I thought it was the Tribune and I think it was? When did he tell me all this? As I was leaving Heinemann's office H had told me to ask him to boom me. I did coming straight out of H's office and meeting him round the corner'*. Hunt's first book with Heinemann, *White Rose of Weary Leaf*, wasn't published until 1908. The entry for 14 June 1907 begins: 'John Galsworthy has, so F M Hueffer says, spent at least £1600 pounds on sending paupers to Canada.' This sounds like she did meet Ford in June 1907, but added later the reminiscence of the meeting outside Heinemann's, as her remark 'When did he tell me all this?' probably suggests. Ford's Portrait of De Morgan indeed appeared in the *Mail*, as Ford said, on 15 June 1907. He did not start his *Tribune* portraits until 27 July 1907. Mizener calls Ford's *Outlook* reminiscence 'a slightly improved version' (p. 553, n. 11). But it is probably less altered than Hunt's reworked diary entry (perhaps rethought as she typed it up later, as she did habitually). Ford says he was still writing the *Tribune* Portraits at the time, and that he would have done

NOTES TO PP. 239-42

one on Hunt 'if the *Tribune* had not stopped'. His last *Tribune* Portrait was 25 January 1908, which tallies with the period Heinemann would have been thinking about publicity for *White Rose*. Where Ford's account must be 'improved' is in saying that, apart from 'passages in a Pre-Raphaelite infancy', he had only previously met her once—'the day before'. The point of the improvement is to emphasize her chutzpah. (Otherwise the accounts tally in essentials.) Hunt wrote that she didn't meet him again 'for a year' after the Galsworthy dinner: *The Flurried Years*, 18. This again points to a spring 1908 date for the conversation about booming her novel. It's possible they met twice at Galsworthy's. Scott-James met her there in Mar. 1908, and that year he walked her home (and she broached the question of whether he would review *White Rose* too): typescript of his essay 'Ford Madox Ford when he was Hueffer' (passage cut for the *South Atlantic Quarterly*, 57 (Spring 1958), 236-53): Texas.

3 *Some Do Not . . .*, 44. Lloyd Morris (reviewing the American edition of *The Last Pre-Raphaelite*, entitled *Trained for Genius*), *New York Herald Tribune Books* (22 May 1949), 1, 18. Review of Goldring, *South Lodge*, *TLS* (9 Oct. 1943), 486. Typescript of 'Ford Madox Ford when he was Hueffer', 218-19.

4 Patmore, *My Friends When Young*, 50, 58.

5 Richard Ellmann, *Oscar Wilde* (London: Hamish Hamilton, 1987), 221. Mizener, 145-9, 151-2. Hunt, diary for 22 Sept. 1890; Aug. 1907; 1 and 4 Jan. 1907; 13 June 1907. Belford, *Violet*, 116-20. Ted Morgan, *Somerset Maugham* (London: Jonathan Cape, 1908), 94-9 (though he places the affair in 1903-4). Hardwick, *An Immodest Violet*, 52; on p. 54 she wrongly says that Hunt 'was one of the few women who did not succeed in becoming Wells's mistress'. *H. G. Wells in Love*, ed. G. P. Wells (London: Faber and Faber, 1984), 63, is explicit about their affair.

6 Diary for 1890: quoted by Mizener, 148. Secor and Secor, *The Return of the Good Soldier*, 34.

7 Goldring, *South Lodge*, 42. Hardwick, *An Immodest Violet*, 174. Mizener, 174, 49. Belford, *Violet*, 133-4. Hunt, diary for 15, 4, and 2 Nov. 1907; diary for 3 June 1909. Christabel Pankhurst to Ford, 4 June 1910. R. Garnett, *Constance Garnett*, 232. Hunt, *The Flurried Years*, 215, 243-4. Patmore, *My Friends When Young*, 53, said he would criticize Hunt's work severely. Ford, 'Literary Portraits—XXII.: Mrs Herbert and "Garden Oats"', *Outlook*, 33 (4 Feb. 1914), 173-4; 'Literary Portraits—V.: Miss Violet Hunt and "The Desirable Alien"', *Outlook*, 32 (11 Oct. 1913), 497-8. Goldring, *The Last Pre-Raphaelite*, 170. Hunt's friendship with James is charted by Robert Secor, 'Henry James and Violet Hunt, the "Improper Person of Babylon"', *Journal of Modern Literature*, 13/1 (Mar. 1986), 3-36. Lowndes, quoted by Belford, *Violet*, 118.

8 'Ford Madox Ford when he was Hueffer', *South Atlantic Quarterly*, 242. Hunt's diary dates the party as 2 July 1908. Her comments, 'Ford came alone. Mrs. Scott J. Kind' presumably mean that Ford came without Elsie, but with the Scott-Jameses.

9 *Thus to Revisit*, 58 n. In *Mightier Than the Sword*, 132, he identified the journal as the *Cornhill*. It is misleading of Mizener to call Ford's statements about starting the *Review* misleading. The passage he quotes from *Return to Yesterday*, p. 195, which says that printing Hardy's poem in the *Review* was primarily Marwood's idea, is corroborated by both the other versions. Hardy to Ford, 9 Sept. 1908 (in Hunt's transcription). Ford to Scott-James [n.d., but *c*. Jan. 1910]: *Letters*, 39-40.

10 Conrad, *Collected Letters*, iv. 246, n. 2. In 'Literary Portraits—XX.: Mr. Gilbert Cannan and "Old Mole" ', *Outlook*, 33 (24 Jan. 1914), 110–11, and *It Was the Nightingale*, 55–60, Ford tells a story about Lucas saying he was 'not really English'.

11 17 Oct. 1908: *Letters*, 27–8. The 'profit-sharing' arrangement was recorded by Wells as follows: 'The Publisher [Duckworth] was to bear all expenses of printing, publishing and everything except advertisement and was to receive in exchange one fifth of the gross receipts; a capitalist was to be found by Mr Hueffer to find money for advertisement and such contributors as took their payment in money. To him a share of one-fifth in the proceeds was also payable. The share of Mr Hueffer was to be one-fifth. The remaining two-fifths of the gross receipts was to be divided among the as yet unpaid contributors in the proportion of the space filled by them': Wells's memorandum, sent with a letter from Catherine Wells to Ford, 29 Jan. 1909: Cornell. Ford agreed it was 'substantially correct' except that it was the profits that were being shared, not the proceeds. Though this meant the contributors had less to gain, they would not be liable for any losses: Ford to Mrs Wells, 1 Feb. 1909: *Letters*, 34–5. Thus Mizener, 163, was wrong to say it was Ford's muddle that Wells talked of receipts, not profits. Ford's letter to Garnett is unambiguous about sharing the *profit*. £2 per thousand words was the rate at which Ford had told Pinker he had to have money: see above, p. 230.

12 Ford later wrote explicitly about his tendency to provoke attacks from his protégés: first in 'Literary Portraits—LIII.: The Muse of War', *Outlook*, 34 (12 Sept. 1914), 334–5 ('Of course there are the people whom I have helped or tried to help, and those, with a charming trueness to type, have kicked me in the eye or blackmailed or backbitten me. But that is only to teach one not to meddle; that is one's own fault'); and more fully in 'Literary Portraits—LXXI.: Enemies', *Outlook*, 35 (16 Jan. 1915), 79–80 ('I like a scrap, of course').
    Conrad to Ford [n.d.: see Ch. 17, n. 32]: *Collected Letters*, iv. 221.

13 Conrad to Garnett, 28 Aug. 1908; to Pinker, 18 Sept. [1908]; to Arthur Symons, 29 Aug. 1908: *Collected Letters*, iv. 111–13; 124; 113–14. Owen Knowles, *A Conrad Chronology* (London: Macmillan, 1989), 72. The date of the Conrads' return to Someries is fixed by Conrad to Galsworthy, 19 Sept. 1908: ibid. 127. Ford himself was responsible for some of the confusion, when, in a splendid letter to George Keating ([Dec. 1936]: *Letters*, 267–8) he recalled taking dictation, but conflated *The Mirror of the Sea* and *A Personal Record*. After almost thirty years he also thought Conrad was still at the Pent when coming to Aldington to dictate. However, his implication that, in coercing Conrad 'with friendly and at times quite angry violence', he took down all of the book from dictation is justified, since he was answering Keating's question about *Some Reminiscences* (New York: Paul R. Reynolds, 1908), which was a limited edition of the Dec. 1908 instalment to secure American copyright. See Conrad, *Collected Letters*, iv. 125, n. 3. James T. Babb, 'A Check List of Additions to *A Conrad Memorial Library* 1929–1938', *Yale University Library Gazette*, 13/1 (July 1938), 35–7, confirms Ford's account of the 1908 publication. See Mizener, 166 and Najder, 341, 566, n. 241. Najder even goes so far as to doubt both Conrad's and Ford's claims that Ford suggested the series, arguing that Conrad 'wanted to safeguard himself against suspicions of self-defense and egotism'. Conrad to Pinker, [7] Oct. 1908: 18 Sept. [1908]: *Collected Letters*, iv. 138; 125. Conrad told Galsworthy Ford had been for the weekend [29 Sept. or

6 Oct. 1908]: ibid. 132-3. Conrad to Ford [12 Oct. 1908]: ibid 144. Conrad's occasional secretary, Miss Hallowes, probably took down some of the reminiscences: see Conrad to Pinker, 13 Oct. 1908: ibid 145. Conrad to Pinker, 17 Dec. 1908: ibid 167.

14 Conrad to Wells, 3 Nov. 1908; to Ford, 10 Oct. 1908: *Collected Letters*, iv. 149; 142. Conrad, *A Personal Record*, pp. xvii, xviii, 15. Najder, 347. *Between St. Dennis and St. George*, p. vi. See also *Collected Poems* [1913], 13; Ford to Harriet Monroe, 7 Nov. 1921: *Letters*, 136-7. Ian Watt, *Conrad in the Nineteenth Century* (Berkeley: University of California Press, 1979), 40-1. Karl, 653. Conrad to Ford, 23 Oct. 1923: see vol. 2, Ch. 10 for a discussion of the variants of this letter.

15 Goldring, *The last Pre-Raphaelite*, 141. James Randall to Mizener, 19 Mar. 1966 (Cornell) mentions an unnamed lover who helped Ford with the *Review*. Mizener to Katharine Hueffer Lamb, 3 Apr. 1966 (Cornell) identifies her as probably Olive Thomas. He didn't use the information in his book because Randall's informant thought Thomas might still be alive. May Sinclair's story, 'Lena Wrace', discussed in vol. 2 might be evidence Ford had such an affair. Mizener, 155, 166. He follows Goldring in dating the editorial visit to Someries as 'Early in November' (see *South Lodge*, 23). But Conrad to Ford, 15 Oct. 1908 (*Collected Letters*, iv. 146) says: 'Do come and bring your secretary. Miss H[allowes]. is going away on Saturday [17th]', which implies Conrad expected Ford's party in Oct. Mizener says Ford employed Goldring 'In the fall'; *The Last Pre-Raphaelite*, 140, says 'early summer'. *South Lodge*, 24-5. Conrad to Ford, 23 Oct. 1923. *South Lodge*, 37-8.

16 *D. H. Lawrence: A Personal Record*, by E.T. (Jessie Chambers), 2nd edn., ed. J. D. Chambers (London: Frank Cass, 1965), 156, 163. Keith Sagar, *D. H. Lawrence: A Calendar of his Works* (Manchester: Manchester University Press, 1979), 12-13. Lawrence to Jessie Chambers [*c.* 11 Sept. 1909]; and to Blanche Jennings [and not to Jessie Chambers, as Mizener says, 171], 1 Nov. 1909: *The Letters of D. H. Lawrence*, ed. James T. Boulton, vol. 1 (Cambridge: Cambridge University Press, 1979), 138, 141. Introduction to *The Collected Poems of D. H. Lawrence*, published in *Phoenix: The Posthumous Papers of D. H. Lawrence*, ed. Edward D. McDonald (London: Heinemann, 1936), 253. *Mightier Than the Sword*, 107. Goldring, *South Lodge*, 40.

17 Ford actually edited the review for fourteen months. 'Literary Portraits—XLIII.: Mr. Wyndham Lewis and "Blast" ', *Outlook*, 34 (4 July 1914), 15-16. In *Return to Yesterday*, 406-8, Lewis is referred to as 'Mr. D.Z.'. Lewis's own version (which refers to Ford's without disagreement) adds the detail that he had left no address on the MSS. When he returned some weeks later he was pleasantly surprised to be given proofs of 'The Pole': *Rude Assignment* (Santa Barbara: Black Sparrow Press, 1984), 130, 161.

18 Goldring, *South Lodge*, 32. Mizener, 176. Hunt, diary for 16 Oct. 1908. Hunt, *The Flurried Years*, 21.

19 Mizener, 176. Lawrence to Louie Burrows, 11 Dec. 1909, says he sent two stories ['Odour of Chrysanthemums' and 'Goose Fair'] to Ford on 9 Dec.: *Letters*, i. 147. *Mightier Than the Sword*, 103; 99. Ford had in fact received the manuscript of *The White Peacock* five weeks before, and the poems before that; so he already had inklings of Lawrence's genius before seeing the stories: Lawrence to Blanche Jennings, 1 Nov. 1909: *Letters*, i. 141. John Worthen, *D. H. Lawrence: The Early Years* (Cambridge: Cambridge University Press, 1991), 216, says Ford's

reminiscence is misleading because 'based on the conviction' that he saw the story before the poems and novel. This is unfair. Ford moves from the letter from Jessie Chambers to the story by saying: 'In that way I came to read the first words of a new author.' It's true this gives the impression they were the first words Lawrence wrote, and the first of his that Ford read. But what is important is the impact these first words of the story made on Ford. The phrase 'in that way' simply elides the tentative stages of his recognition of Lawrence's gifts. Lawrence, 'Autobiographical Sketch', *Phoenix II*, ed. Warren Roberts and Harry T. Moore (London: Heinemann, 1968), 593–4. Lawrence later told Ernest Collings: Ford Madox Hueffer discovered I was a genius—don't be alarmed, Hueffer would discover *anything* if he wanted to: 14 Nov. 1912: *Letters*, i. 471. Mizener, 167; ibid. 552, n. 4 argues that Lawrence was misremembering Ford's similar comments about his second novel, *The Trespasser*. He cites Lawrence to Garnett, 18 Dec. 1911, relaying what Ford 'said' about that book. But Lawrence to Louie Burrows, 9 Sept. 1910, describes a *letter* Ford had written Lawrence calling *The Trespasser* a 'rotten work of genius'—the same phrase Lawrence recalled in the letter to Garnett: *Letters*, i. 339–40, 178. Lawrence is unlikely to have misremembered what Ford wrote in a letter as having been said in a bus.

20 Goldring, *South Lodge*, 35–6.

21 Juliet and David Soskice both had pieces published. 'Mamka', *English Review*, 4 (Jan. 1910), 235–48, was by Juliet. 'The Azeff Scandals in Russia', *English Review*, 1 (Mar. 1909), 816–32, is signed 'D.S.'. Ford also got Edward Garnett to review 'Mr. Doughty's Poems', *English Review*, 3 (September 1909), 369–76; and published a story by Olive Garnett: 'A Certainty', *English Review*, 2 (June 1909), 512–16. Bradbury, 'The English Review', *London Magazine*, 5 (Aug. 1958), 57. Levin Schücking wrote 'Some Notes on Present-Day German Literature' for the Apr. 1909 number, pp. 165–71.

22 E. Olive Thomas to H. G. Wells, 31 Mar. 1909 (Illinois) says that the circulation of the first two numbers was 2,000 copies. F. R. Leavis, *Thought, Words and Creativity* (London: Chatto & Windus, 1976), 37–8. Ford, 'Foreword', *The English Review Book of Short Stories*, compiled by Horace Shipp (London: Sampson Low, Marston, 1932), pp. vii–viii. Homberger, 'Ford's *English Review*. Englishness and its Discontents', *Agenda*, 27/4–28/1 (Winter 1989–Spring 1990), 61–6. Homberger's essay is also the best discussion of the politics of the review. Pound to Margaret Anderson [9 May 1917]: *Pound/The Little Review*, ed. Thomas Scott and Melvin Friedman (London: Faber and Faber, 1989), 41–3. Ford edited the review for fourteen months, not eighteen.

23 Signed 'Didymus', *English Review*, 4 (Feb. 1910), 544.

24 Marwood, *English Review*, 1 (Dec. 1908), 171–5 and (Jan. 1909), 363–69. 'A Declaration of Faith', 545–6. *Return to Yesterday*, 409; pp. 396–7 describe Ford meeting the (Unionist) Bonar Law at Lady St Helier's and trying to interest him in Marwood's ideas. James Boulton, editor of *The Letters of D. H. Lawrence*, i. 12, notes the left-wing bias of the review. Also see Worthen, *D. H. Lawrence*, 216.

25 Ford to Shaw, 25 Nov. 1908: *Reader*, 472–3. Shaw to Ford, 27 Nov. 1908. Ford, letter to the editor, *Daily News* (20 Mar. 1908), 4.

26 Ford to Wells, 2 Apr. 1910: *Letters*, 42. Mizener, 160–2, 187–8, 195. Olive Thomas to Wells, 31 Mar. 1909 (probably dictated by Ford: Illinois) calculates that the first

four numbers lost about £300 each. Mizener cites this letter (p. 160) as evidence of 'Ford's capacity for being unrealistic about money'. But if, by saying 'the circulation of the first two numbers has been 2,000 copies, or a little more, bringing in about £200. o. o.' Ford meant that the first two numbers had sold 2,000 copies *each* (which is surely what the word 'circulation' generally indicates), rather than 2,000 copies for *both* issues (as Mizener assumes) then his figures are perfectly realistic: £200 income from sales and £35 advertising revenue for each issue; offset by production costs of £200 and contributions costs of £300 per issue; amounting to a loss of £265 on average per issue. Conrad to Pinker, 18 Sept. [1908]; to Norman Douglas, 29 Sept. 1908: *Collected Letters*, iv. 126; 130–1. Ford to Soskice, 8 June 1909, arguing that 'to turn the Review into a purely Socialist Organ would be to lose immediately nearly all our present readers & absolutely all our present advertisers'. Goldring, *The Last Pre-Raphaelite*, 151–2. Hunt, *The Flurried Years*, 90–1. Constance to Edward Garnett [n.d.]: R. Garnett, *Constance Garnett*, 253.

Chapter 17

1 The lunch with Harris, which Ford described in *It Was the Nightingale*, 291–5, took place between 5 and 17 Jan. Harris, *Frank Harris to Arnold Bennett: Fifty Eight Letters 1908–1910* (Merion Station, Pa: American Autograph Shop, 1936), 17 (quoted by Harvey, 531). Mizener, 164. 'The English Review', *Reader's Review* (Nov. 1908) (quoted by Harvey, 295). Hunt, *The Flurried Years*, 29. Bennett to Pinker, postmarked 11 Jan. 1909: *Letters of Arnold Bennett*, ed. James Hepburn, vol. 1, *Letters to J. B. Pinker* (London: Oxford University Press, 1966), 119; 120 n.

2 Ford to Bennett, 6 Oct. 1908, 24 Nov. 1908, and [n.d., but either just before or just after 24 Nov. 1908]: Texas. Bennett to Pinker, 8 Jan. 1909; to Ford, 26 Mar. 1909: *Letters of Arnold Bennett*, i. 118–19, 250–1.

3 'Literary Portraits—IV.: Mr. Arnold Bennett and "The Regent" ', *Outlook*, 32 (4 Oct. 1913), 463–4. Bennett to Ford, 26 Mar. 1909: *Letters of Arnold Bennett*, vol. 2 (London: Oxford University Press, 1968), 250–1. Ford to Bennett [n.d., but Mar. 1909].

4 Ford's version of the incident in *Return to Yesterday*, 400–2, is characteristically impressionistic: the texts of the letters are of course reinvented. The detail that Ford mistook Bennett for the man from Lincoln and Bennett who was due to collect his top-hats for ironing is improbable, given that Ford claims that at this point Bennett demanded his cheque in person, whereas Bennett says Ford sent him the cheque. Yet the story is remarkably true to the stages of the disagreement and reconciliation. Bennett to Hunt, 23 Apr. 1909: Cornell. Bennett, letter to the editor, *Outlook*, 32 (11 Oct. 1913), 499. Bennett left Paris on 6 Mar. to return to England. His *Journals* record a dinner with Ford and Galsworthy on 7 Apr. (entry for 9 Apr.), so either met Ford that evening, or during the preceding month. *The Journals of Arnold Bennett*, ed. Newman Flower, 3 vols. (London: Cassell, 1932–3), i. 316. Mizener, 159, misleadingly omits the crucial fact that Bennett did eventually go to the dinner. Margaret Drabble, *Arnold Bennett* (London: Weidenfeld and Nicolson, 1974), 167. Bennett to Pinker, 11 May 1909: *Letters of Arnold Bennett*, i. 121. Bennett [pseudonym 'Jacob Tonson'], 'Books and Persons', *New Age*, 6/20 (17 Mar. 1910), 471.

5 Both letters are at Texas, undated, and printed in *Letters*, 29–31. Garnett's review, *'The Visit of "Mr. Apollo" '*, appeared in *Nation*, 3 (29 Aug. 1908), 779–80. As all the reviews found by Harvey are dated Aug. or Sept., the letter in which Ford says 'Apollo is being slated all round' should probably be dated Sept. 1908 instead of Ludwig's suggestion of Dec. The original is illustrated with sketches of the 'Greek vase' form on which Ford argues he modelled *Mr. Apollo*, and the 'Chinese dragon-pot' which he says Garnett criticizes it for not having become. The sketches make it a much more exuberant letter than is evident in the published version. The second of these letters in Ludwig's volume should presumably come first, since it expresses the resentment that the other elaborates after receiving a reply from Garnett; in which case this letter should also be re-dated [Sept.? 1908].

6 29 Jan. 1909: *Letters*, 31–3.

7 Greene marked this passage in his copy of Ford's *Letters*, and noted 'Quixote' against the page number in the index he compiled in the back of the book. In similar ways he also noted 'Quixote' against the long passage from Ford's letter to C. F. G. Masterman, 28 June 1919, explaining why he had left Hunt, from 'I have left South Lodge' to 'I take it to be a duty': 95–6 And he noted two further passages as examples of 'Quixotism'. One from an earlier letter in Ford's quarrel with Wells over the review (Ford to Mrs Wells, 23 Feb. 1909; 38: 'We intend, therefore, deliberately to proceed against Wells, though as I have told you it is my intention to pay whatever damages are proved, to the Review out of my own pocket. This seems to be the only honourable course to pursue'). The other from a letter to Gertude Stein, 18 Sept. 1924 (p. 162), in which Ford describes himself as 'a sort of green baize swing door that every one kicks both on entering and on leaving': 162. Greene's connection is a shrewd one. Cervantes is one of the very few classic authors Ford cannot write generously about. He felt Cervantes's parody had helped to destroy 'the gentle ideal of chivalry', and that this was an unforgivable disservice to the world. But he also called him 'the first modern novelist': *The March of Literature*, 680–1, 56. Ford's modern novels are precisely concerned with showing protagonists torn between chivalric ideals and a cynical society. It is as if he identifies dually with the novelist and with the Don, but finds the novelist's ridicule of the Don a personal affront. See Stang, *Ford Madox Ford*, 26, on Dowell as Sancho Panza to Ashburnham's Quixote.

8 Hunt said Wells told her he had modelled Beatrice on her: *The Flurried Years*, 43.

9 Ford to Mrs Wells, 23 Feb. 1909: *Letters*, 38. Wells to Ford, 2 Apr. 1909: Cornell. 'E. Olive Thomas' to Wells, 5 Apr. 1909: Illinois. Ford to Wells [Feb. 1909]: *Letters*, 37.

10 Hunt, diary for 27 January 1909: Cornell. David Garnett, *The Golden Echo*, 130. Harold Wright, ed., *Letters of Stephen Reynolds* (Richmond: Hogarth Press, 1923), 113–16. Goldring, *South Lodge*, 35. Mizener, 164–5, 96, 541–2, n. 26. He calls Miss Wanostrocht 'Miss Wanostrom': Robert Garnett to Elsie Hueffer, 2 Mar. 1905 gives the correct form, which matches the name Ford gives to the headmistress of the school Valentine Wannop is teaching at in *A Man Could Stand Up—*. The details of the Hueffers' investments comes from an undated memorandum (titled 'Description of Property') drawn up by Garnett for Elsie. Mizener argues that it dates from 1905.

11 Ford to Elsie [*c*.20 Mar. 1909]. Hunt, diary for 1909: entry for 19 March. Hunt, *The Flurried Years*, 49. Ford dedicated *The Panel* to Ada Potter. *Athenaeum* (27

Mar. 1909), 386. Conrad to Ford, 9 Mar. 1909: *Collected Letters*, iv. 201-2, says Marwood has told him 'horrid news' of the 'utter disorganization of the production'. 'The Learned Sock', *Outlook*, 36 (14 Aug. 1915), 206-7; and *'Literary Causeries: XIII: The Play's the Thing . . .', *Chicago Tribune Sunday Magazine* (Paris) (11 May 1924), 3, 10. Here Ford implies that Ada Potter was also involved in lifting the dialogue out of the novel as a basis for the play-text. Mizener, 184 n., doubts both Ford's assertion that he didn't collaborate on the dramatization, and that he hid during the performance. But the 'all but complete dramatization of *The Fifth Queen* in Ford's hand at Cornell' is a version of the verse drama 'Katharine Howard', presumably the work Olive Garnett heard read in 1901. In his recollections of the performance, Ford doesn't say he spent the whole performance hiding. In the *Outlook* he says Mrs Clifford dragged him out, but he returned 'as soon as she had her hands off me'. In the *Chicago Tribune* he says he ended up under the bar ('without a drop of drink taken') 'towards the end of the performance'.

12 Ford to Elsie [Oct. or Nov. 1908?]. Hunt, diary for 25 Dec. 1908. Mizener, 131, places this quarrel a year earlier; but his note makes it clear that 1908 is meant (547, n. 13). The party was on a Sunday after 17 Dec.: see Conrad to Ford, 17 Dec. 1908: *Collected Letters*, iv. 166—thus probably on Sunday, 27 Dec. Mizener, 176, quotes an invitation to Hunt to join him and McClure at the Empire, signed 'Yours until death and after'. Mizener dates this as the end of December 1908, but gives no evidence for such an early dating. (Presumably he is following Hunt, *The Flurried Years*, 36.) It is possible Hunt's diary entry for 22 Dec. 1908, which might read 'Empire party', establishes the date of this evening. But see n. 32 below for evidence that the evening might have been in Mar. McClure was in London in July 1909: Conrad, *Collected Letters*, iv. 261, n. 1; and possibly again in Dec. 1909, when he appears to have entertained Perceval Gibbon: Conrad to Gibbon, 19 Dec. [1909]: ibid. 301-2. Either of these later dates seems more probable. Both Hunt and Ford recall Gibbon as being present when they dined with McClure. *Return to Yesterday*, 318. Certainly, Hunt's diary for 1909 shows Ford being noticeably infatuated with her (her friend Marc-André Raffalovich noticed on 26 Apr., saying he was 'so sorry to hear he was married'), but not declaring his love before May: see above, p. 285. *'Self ats Hueffer', 5.

13 Ford to Elsie [*c*.20 March 1909]: Cornell. Mizener, 175, says Elsie offered Ford a temporary separation the preceding spring. But he gives no source. Instead, his note (553, n. 9) supports the 1909 date, citing Goldring, *South Lodge*, 88, where Goldring says Ford was approached by a third party (presumably Edmée Van der Noot) in 1909 to ask if he would let Elsie divorce him. *The New Humpty-Dumpty*, 91. The 1909 separation and offers of divorce are discussed above, p. 290. Even desertion was not by itself a ground for a wife to divorce her husband before 1923; he had also to have committed adultery. But desertion could justify a 'judicial separation', which Elsie might have desired if she truly didn't want to go on seeing Ford: it could have prevented his visits, without giving him the freedom to remarry.

14 '*Self ats Hueffer', 6. This may be the 'scene [. . .] about your work' that Ford referred to in the letter Elsie dated Oct. or Nov. 1908—in which case one of them must be wrong. If Elsie's date is wrong, then Ford's letter about there not being another woman in the case is more disingenuous, since he was seeing Hunt

regularly by Mar., and was obviously attracted to her. Alternatively, there may well have been two arguments about Elsie's publishing. *Margaret Hever* gave her name as 'Elizabeth Martindale', as did her essays in the *English Review* in Oct. 1909 and Jan. 1910.

15 *The New Humpty-Dumpty*, 86, 92, 93.

16 Mizener, 180. He cites no evidence for this paraphrase: presumably he heard it from Katharine Hueffer Lamb. It is impossible to date the incident with precision. Mizener, in his determination to brand Ford as irresponsible, says that he rowed with Marwood over the *Review* first, and then heard Elsie's revelations. There are, however, few unassailable dates amongst the evidence. Elsie's letters have not survived, Ford did not date his during this period, and Conrad did not date his crucial letter about 'the wrecks of friendships' (discussed below). In some cases Elsie tentatively added dates to Ford's letters; though the tentativeness suggests that she may have done this too much later for the approximations to be reliable. The envelopes for these letters of Ford's have survived: but there are difficulties here too. Not only does Elsie's attempts to date the letters indicate that they may not have always been kept with the respective envelopes, but in some cases the date Mizener gives does not correspond with the postmark on the envelope now filed with the letter at Cornell. In Ford's letter to Elsie, dated by her 'Mar 20th (about)', he tells her: 'I am determined not to have Marwood up here: either I shall pay him off & shut the Review down, or I shall, if I can raise capital enough, pay him off & keep it on: but, as far as I am concerned he is as dead as—let us say Reynolds. So that, unless he molests you, never mention him again to me. I hope it will not trouble you very much longer'. The interpretation of these distraught and oblique letters is no less problematic than their dating, but, like all the other signs of Ford's estrangement from Marwood, this sounds more like a response to sexual betrayal than a fantasy about Marwood getting too much credit for the *Review*. In the same letter Ford describes the performance of the dramatization of *The Fifth Queen Crowned* which took place on 19 Mar. It is thus probable that Ford had heard of Marwood's advances by the third week of Mar. Conrad to Galsworthy, 30 Apr. 1909, says Marwood looked ill 'For weeks' after his 'execution' by Ford and Elsie (*Collected Letters*, iv. 223–5; discussed below). That would place the 'execution' towards the beginning of Apr., which again would support a date of around the third week of Mar. for Marwood's advances, and Ford's hearing of them. Other problems of dating and interpretation are discussed in the notes

17 [n.d.]. Quoted by Mizener, 183, who dates it *c.* 28–30 Mar. 1909. But it must come after the letter, dated [8 May 1909] at Cornell (and discussed below, n. 29), in which Ford agrees that Elsie should show Garnett the letters.

18 Garnett, *Great Friends* (London: Macmillan, 1979), 45. *The Good Soldier*, 68, 16. Mizener, 182. *'Self ats Hueffer', 6.

19 'A Silence', *Bystander*, 24 (29 Dec. 1909), 681–4. *'The Escape', typescript at Cornell.

20 Ford to Elsie [24 Mar. 1909], [14 Apr. 1909], and [postmarked 5 May 1909, and written the same day as the visit to Garnett—either the 4th or the 5th].

21 Ford to Elsie [dated by her *c.*28 Mar. 1909]. Mizener quotes from this letter on 180, making it seem as if Ford's anger over Marwood getting credit for the review came before his advances to Elsie; whereas in fact the letter makes it clear Ford has already heard of those, and thus his anger with Marwood is due to his shock

of betrayal, not petty jealousy over the review. Elizabeth Martindale, 'Two Essays', *English Review*, 3 (Oct. 1909): '1. The Art of Manners', 426–31; '2. The Art of Contentment', 432–6. 'Two Essays', *English Review*, 4 (Jan. 1910); 'I. The Spirit of Melody', 249–54; 'II. The Art of Enjoyment', 254–6.

22 Ford to Elsie, dated 'Monday' by Ford, to which Elsie has prefixed 'Whit': therefore 30 May 1909. Goldring, *South Lodge*, 88.

23 Mizener, 175. Hunt, *The Flurried Years*, 50–1. Ford to Elsie, 14 Apr. 1909 [dated in Elsie's hand, and also by the envelope's postmark].

24 Goldring, *The Last Pre-Raphaelite*, 156. Mizener, 190, says that Ford and Violet planned together that 'Ford would write Elsie a description of the way Gertrud had been living at 84 Holland Park Avenue and traveling about with him'. This is surely the letter of 14 April, which makes his scenario of Ford handing it over to Edmée Van der Noot at Tonbridge on 18 July most implausible (he cites no evidence for it).

25 'Self ats Hueffer', 11–12. The comparable episode in *The New Humpty-Dumpty*, in which Macdonald 'befriends a naive girl from Hamburg adrift in London, and secure in his innocence, writes the Countess all about it' (Mizener, 227: though he calls it 'the novel's improved version'), implies Ford's relations with Gertrud *were* innocent. Jeffrey Meyers, *Joseph Conrad* (London: John Murray, 1991), 247, simply asserts that Ford had an affair with Gertrud. But then he is trying to substantiate his crassly reductive bracketing of Ford together with Wells as both 'extremely promiscuous' (p. 225). Hunt, *The Flurried Years*, 85. Although Hunt says she had become 'quasi-mistress' of the *English Review* office by 1909, she says she did not yet have Ford's 'confidence' in the spring of 1909, when Gertrud was installed. *The Flurried Years*, 45, 51. The poem is discussed on p. 425. *The Good Soldier*, 69.

26 Soskice to Ford, 4 Oct. 1909. *A Call* is discussed in greater detail above, pp. 299–304. In *Women & Men*, 17, Ford tells the story of his relation Tristram Madox's wife discovering with horror that her husband kept a mistress and his children by her at a separate establishment. It is the classic Fordian revelation that desolates a world without changing it materially.

27 Quotations are taken from Ford's contribution to *Women's Suffrage and Militancy*, ed. Huntly Carter (London: Frank Palmer, 1911), 25–8; repr. in *The Presence of Ford Madox Ford*, 165–9. This is an expanded version of his letter to the editor of *New Age*, 8 (9 Feb. 1911), 356–7. Ford's pamphlet, *This Monstrous Regiment of Women* [London: published for the Women's Freedom League by the Minerva Publishing Co. Ltd., 1913], is a more conventionally persuasive essay; reprinted in the *Reader*, 304–17.

28 *It Was the Nightingale*, 121–2, 253–5, and 80 respectively.

29 [8 May 1909]. Quoted by Mizener, 182, who does not give it a date, and implies that it comes five or six weeks earlier. He presents it as Ford's immediate response to Elsie's revelations. But Ford has already had time to talk to Garnett, and scarcely sounds as shocked as one would expect him to if he had just heard about Marwood's advances. It reads more like a response to Elsie's attempts to get him to see Marwood after Ford had broken off relations with him. The dating is taken from the envelope with which the letter is now filed. It is possible that this envelope was at one time exchanged with the similar one postmarked 7 April. But the 8 May envelope is written with a broader nib than the 7 Apr. envelope; as is the letter beginning 'I must confess'. The references to the negotiations over the

Review and to the Monds also point towards the May dating. Since Mizener misdates a letter from April as '8 May' (see below, n. 32), presumably these two letters were in each other's envelopes while he was working on them. If Elsie did not get to hear rumours about Ford and Hunt until May, the case for the affair having begun by the spring is weakened, and Mizener's charge that Ford was lying to Elsie about 'another woman' no longer sticks.

30 [n.d., catalogued as 'ca March 30 1909', but must be after Ford's refusal to see Marwood on 4 or 5 May].

31 [5 May 1909]. Because the subject was difficult to discuss, Ford's comments are oblique, which has fostered some misunderstanding. Mizener quotes a letter to Elsie in which Ford says he has written to Marwood 'saying that upon reflection my own position appeared so open to misrepresentation that I must put the matter upon a proper financial basis'. He takes this as an instance of Ford's rashness, arguing that Ford had quite arbitrarily decided that Marwood was getting too much of the credit for the *Review* (p. 180). He says the letter bears no date, which enables him to place it before Elsie's bombshell. But Elsie herself wrote on it the date 'Mar. 28th (about)', which (according to my chronology) places it afterwards; in which case Ford's comments about the *Review* are a part of his larger anxiety about Marwood and Elsie. Putting the matter upon a proper financial basis would then probably mean either getting Marwood disentangled from the *Review*, or at least formalizing their agreement, lest it should appear that Ford was prepared to countenance an affair between Marwood and Elsie as long as Marwood was providing money for the *Review*. That is certainly how Ford said he saw it in 'Self ats Hueffer': 'I was forced to refuse to continue in partnership with him or to accept from him more money for the carrying on of the Review, that position being forced upon me by considerations of honour': 6–7.

32 Conrad, *Collected Letters*, iv. 192 and n. Najder, 346, blames Ford for renting such dismal premises (above a butcher's shop, with a view of the slaughterhouse). But in fact Conrad had found the place himself during his previous stay: Conrad to Galsworthy, 19 Sept. 1908: *Collected Letters*, iv. 127. They stayed in Aldington until June 1910, when they moved to Capel House, also in Kent: ibid. 340.

Conrad to Ford [n.d.]: ibid. 220–3. The importance of this letter for both Conrad's and Ford's biography has guaranteed regular speculation as to its date. Mizener dates it 31 Mar. 1909 (p. 553, n. 27), without registering that the letter is undated, and without giving his reasons for his dating. Najder included it in 'Joseph Conrad: A Selection of Unknown Letters', *Polish Perspectives*, 13/2 (Feb. 1970), 37–40. He argues for a date of early May; in his *Joseph Conrad* he emends this to 28 Apr. or 5 May (p. 567, n. 274), on the grounds of the reference to the article on the Panama Canal written by President Taft for the May issue. But all Conrad says is: 'Any coalition with McC[lure] apart from an occasional buying of some Taft article—and by the by in that transaction the good man with characteristic levity nearly left you in a whole [*sic*.]—could only mean the debasing of the ideals which, on your own declaration, were to guide your Editorship.' This could be a reference to the announcement in the Apr. issue that 'We regret that owing to the exigencies of the American Copyright Act we are compelled at the last moment to hold back President Taft's article upon his election until the June number of THE ENGLISH REVIEW. To the May number, however, Mr. Taft will contribute an article on the subject of the Panama Canal.—ED.' (p. 134). As Karl and Davies say, 'the comments on the latest review are not specific enough to identify it as the Apr. issue, received in late March, or the May issue, received in late April'. They argue that four pieces of external evidence 'suggest' the later date; and on this basis they assign an unqueried date of '[28 April or 5 May 1909]'. However, none of these stands up to scrutiny.

(i) The 'account of what Conrad termed on 30 April "the execution of Marwood" '. In that letter to Galsworthy Conrad says: 'For weeks Marwood looked as if after a severe illness.' In the letter to Ford he says he has seen Marwood that evening, and 'in truth he looked ill'. This letter was begun two days after the Conrads first heard of the row with Marwood; they heard of it from Elsie who called 'Last Monday'. The letter was therefore probably written 'weeks' before the letter to Galsworthy of 30 Apr.

(ii) 'Ford's letter to Elsie of 8 May: "I have had a long letter from Conrad pointing out the evil of my ways" (Mizener, p. 184).' The problem here is that Mizener misdated Ford's letter, which should be dated [7 Apr. 1909]: see n. 29 above. Though Ford did not date this letter himself, it tells Elsie that Marwood replied to Ford saying that he was putting the matter in the hands of a solicitor, and 'The solicitor turned out to be Robert'. It thus immediately precedes Ford's letter to Elsie dated by her 'April 10th' (the Saturday before Easter), in which Ford reassures her that he doesn't think 'that M. has any sinister motives in applying to Robert'. (Elsie's dating is supported by Ford's promise to 'come down for baby's [i.e. Katharine's] birthday'—16 Apr. He also mentions the Boat Race the previous Saturday: it fell on 3 Apr. 1909.) If the letter from Conrad is the one in question (as I think it must be: though Conrad's previous letter to Ford calls him 'a prodigal of your toil and your talent' apropos *The Fifth Queen Crowned* dramatization, it is kindly meant, and the letter was written on 9 Mar.—before the 'execution' of Marwood: *Collected Letters*, iv. 201–2), then it must have been written in time to catch an early enough post to London to allow Ford time to tell Elsie about it on Wednesday 7 Apr. Conrad headed the letter 'Wednesday evening', but (as Najder argues in his *Polish Perspectives* article) it was continued the following day: hence the reference to Conrad's 'four most unhappy days' since Monday, rather than three. This rules out 7 Apr. itself. The earliest possible date is 24 Mar. (the first Wednesday after 19 Mar., the date of the disastrous performance of *The Fifth Queen Crowned* to which Conrad refers). This leaves two possible dates: 24 or 31 Mar.

(iii) An 'allusion in the letter of [4 August] to a half-crazed letter of apology from Ford "about the beginning of May" '. Too many assumptions must be made if this is to be accepted as evidence. First, that Conrad's confessedly approximate recollection is correct. Secondly, that Ford replied at once. Thirdly, that he was replying to this letter, and not Conrad's second letter of rebuke, 20 May 1909: *Collected Letters*, iv. 235–7. My own guess would be that it was this much more aggressive letter that elicited the hysterical reply Conrad describes; whereas Ford told Elsie in the letter of [7 April] that he had replied 'amiably' to Conrad's [first] letter pointing out the evil of his ways.

Finally, Conrad's anger at Ford's 'vapouring about making the *Spectator* crawl' also points to a Mar. date. Karl and Davies refer to the *Spectator*, 102 (20 and 27 Mar., 3 Apr. 1909), 451–2, 495, 537. But they miss the magazine's first of this sequence of comments on the *English Review*, that in the issue for 6 Mar.

(pp. 382–5), complaining of the sensationalism with which the *Review* advertised as censored Hilaire Belloc's article on censorship, saying that: 'It would seem as if the methods of advertising described in *Tony-Bungay* [*sic.*] had inspired those responsible for the conduct of the magazine.' It is more likely to have been this that angered Ford. Conrad hopes the 'phase of coalescing with McC[lure] and the phase of making the *Spectator* crawl' are now over, which would be consonant with a date of late March. (Though Ford's attempts to interest McClure were still not over by 20 May—the date of Conrad's angrier letter about Ford's attempt to get him to see Willa Cather, discussed on p. 271—they had begun much earlier.) Hunt says that McClure was in London at about the time of the first number of the *Review*—i.e. Dec. 1908; but she implies that this was also the time Ford dined with him and Perceval Gibbon at the Savoy and took him to the music-hall with Hunt; yet she also says this party is the one Conrad was scornful about, asking if McClure offered to 'buy up the ER including the Editor, lock stock and barrel including the shop downstairs and the tube station': *The Flurried Years*, 36–7.

Thus on the basis of Ford's letters, which the Conradian scholars have not generally studied first-hand, this letter of Conrad's should be re-dated. I would incline towards 31 Mar. This is partly because 24 Mar. sounds slightly too early for Conrad to have seen the Apr. issue of the *Review* (though the first issue—Dec. 1908—was ready by 25 Nov., I haven't found any evidence that other issues were produced more than three or four days before their cover date). And partly because Conrad's comment that he and Jessie have been 'aware for a week or so that there was some tension', taken together with the hypothesis that Ford heard about Marwood's advances around 20 Mar. (see n. 16 above) would support the date of 31 Mar.

33 Conrad wrote of 'our Olympian FMH' to Edward Garnett, 27 Jan. 1912: *Letters from Joseph Conrad*, edited by E. Garnett (Indianapolis: Bobbs-Merrill, 1928), 239. Conrad to Pinker [4 August 1909]: *Collected Letters*, iv. 265–6. He also wrote to Perceval Gibbon about Ford's 'general carryings on like a spoilt kid': [4 or 11 July 1909]: ibid. 253.

34 Conrad to Douglas [14 Mar. 1909]: *Collected Letters*, iv. 205. ibid. 222, n. 3.

35 Moser, 89. Conrad to Arthur Symons, 29 Aug. 1908; to H. G. Wells, 25 Sept. 1908: *Collected Letters*, iv. 113–14; 128–9. Karl, 680–1; see also 655.

36 Conrad to Pinker [4 Aug. 1909]. Karl, 663, 672, 277–80. Conrad to Galsworthy, 30 Apr. 1909: *Collected Letters*, iv. 223–5.

37 Conrad to Mackintosh [11 Apr.] 1909; to Ford 20 May 1909: *Collected Letters*, iv. 214–15; 235–7. Najder is characteristically harsh, saying 'Ford nonchalantly invited himself, his wife, and Conrad's physician [. . .] to dinner at the Conrads': *Joseph Conrad*, 347–8. He follows Jessie Conrad, *Joseph Conrad and his Circle*, 138–9; whereas Conrad's letter to Mackintosh makes it clear Conrad was expecting the Mackintoshes on the Sunday, Ford had irritatingly taken it upon himself to change the time to six, and to ask Mackintosh to stay the previous night with him. Jessie's version, published twenty-four years later, is palpably inaccurate despite her claim that it is 'absolutely true in every detail'; she has Ford arriving on Saturday to tell them his guests were coming that weekend. Whereas Conrad's letter shows he turned up on Easter Sunday, to suggest arrangements for the following weekend. Mizener, despite saying that her pompous put-down 'sounds as implausible as most of the speeches Jessie ascribes to herself in her books', none

the less chose to believe her story at Ford's expense. Conrad to Ford [31 Mar.? 1909—as re-dated in n. 32 above]: 220–1. Ford wrote to Elsie: 'The Miss Cather business upset me very much: so much hung upon it': [25 May 1909].

38 Conrad to Pinker [4 Aug. 1909]. Conrad says he received this hysterical letter 'about the beginning of May'; but [as I argue above in n. 32] it was more probably a reply to Conrad's letter of 20 May, which one would have to have an extremely low opinion of Conrad to think he would write after receiving the kind of letter he describes here. Conrad to Galsworthy [17 July 1909] and to Pinker [4 August 1909]: *Collected Letters*, iv. 255, 265–6. By 23 June Conrad had decided he would be unlikely to appear in the *Review*'s pages again: letter to E. V. Lucas: ibid. 247. Karl, 867; see also 659, 668 on Conrad's attitude to Soskice and Russians. Conrad to Garnett, 19 July 1909; to Ford, 31 July 1909: *Collected Letters*, iv. 258–9; 263–4. *English Review*, 2 (July 1909), 824. Mizener, 187.

39 Conrad to Pinker [13? May 1909] says he's sending Ford an agreement with Nelson (for the 7d. edition of *Romance*), but no covering letter has survived. Conrad to Gibbon [4 or 11 July 1909]; to Maisie Gibbon [18 July 1909]; to Pinker [4 Aug. 1909]; to Reynolds, 27 Nov. 1909; to Douglas, 23 Dec. 1909; to Meldrum, 31 Dec. 1909: *Collected Letters*, iv. 233, 253; 257–8; 265–6; 293; 308–9; 312–13. Jessie Conrad, *Joseph Conrad and his Circle*, 139–40. Mizener, 186. Conrad's remark in the 'Familiar Preface' to *A Personal Record* could be read as an oblique criticism of Ford: 'the danger lies in the writer becoming the victim of his own exaggeration, coming to despise truth itself as something too cold, too blunt for his purpose—as, in fact, not good enough for his insistent emotion': p. xvii.

40 Conrad to Pinker [11 Oct. 1909] and 21 Jan. 1909: *Collected Letters*, iv. 276–8, 189–90. Conrad to Ford, 2 January 1903: ibid. iii. 3–4. Najder, 347. Garnett, *Great Friends*, 48. Jessie Conrad, *Joseph Conrad and his Circle*, 116. Conrad to Ford, 17 Dec. 1908 and [7 Dec. 1908]: *Collected Letters*, iv. 165–7, 157–8. Karl assumes (very unsensationally) that Conrad's letter referred to the confidence Ford gave him in the matter of his reminiscences: *Joseph Conrad*, 664. Edward to Olive Garnett, 9 Dec. 1924: transcribed in Garnett, 'A Bloomsbury Girlhood', 542–3. Jeffrey Meyers, *Joseph Conrad*, 137, suggests that Brandson's seduction of his typist in *The Simple Life Limited* might imply that Conrad married Jessie because of 'his fear that Jessie might be pregnant'. It's not easy to imagine Conrad telling Ford this; but perhaps Ford intuited it from the sentence Meyers quotes from a manuscript: 'I can imagine that correct young man perfectly capable of setting himself deliberately to worry a distracted girl into surrender'. Meyers follows Keating in thinking this 'an unpublished fragment on marriage'; in fact it is part of a version of *The Nature of a Crime*, so is as likely to have been written by Ford as by Conrad (the quotation appears on p. 71 of the book). Other suggestions as to what Conrad may have confided to Ford include his suicide attempt, and his relationships with Emilie Briquel and his aunt Marguerite Poradowska. Finally, there is a passage Ford cut from the typescript of *Joseph Conrad* which may be relevant: 'There comes in here another rather curious—but actually real coincidence between the career of Conrad and the writer—a friendship with the same lady, now a celebrated costumière, but then in much more humble circumstances. She had been the mistress of the financier [who was keeping Conrad waiting in Rouen because he couldn't raise the necessary capital for Conrad's ship] and during the period of his eclipse fell before the charms of the handsome, passionate and

romantic sea captain. When his ship sailed away she set out for Paris and became the—let us say—cynosure of a group of students of whom the writer was one. The writer wishes he could swear that she ever mentioned Conrad whom she had known, but he can't [. . .] And she used to say of one of her former lovers—it may pass in French!—"Quand il avait fini de moi j'en avait pour trois jours sur ma chaise longue. . . ." But whether that was the financier or the mariner the writer cannot say.' Cut from p. 106 of the book: see Morey, 219. I am grateful to Robert Hampson for these suggestions. Conrad was in Rouen in late 1893–early 1894. But Ford's youthful visits to Paris occurred *before* this date. So if there is a germ of truth in the story, Ford must have known her first.

41 Ford to Elsie, postmarked both 15 and 16 May 1909. This is the only mention of the projected life of James I. Ford's handwriting deteriorated rapidly during this spring. Not since 1904 had it been so seismographically nervy.

42 Ford to Scott-James [January 1910]: *Letters*, 40–4. Olive Garnett, diary for 10 April 1911 (though this remark was added later): Moser, 91.

Chapter 18

1 Epigraph translated by Mahmood Jamal, *Penguin Book of Modern Urdu Poetry* (1986) [postmarked 10 Apr. 1909; written Friday 9 Apr.]. The Sunday gathering was the *bouts-rimés* party described below. Bennett's *Journals* entry for Friday 9 Apr. confirms that he had dinner at Ford's with the Galsworthys on the Wednesday: i. 316.

2 *The New Humpty-Dumpty*, 214.

3 The relationship is documented in *Pound/Ford*. Humphrey Carpenter, *A Serious Character: The Life of Ezra Pound* (London: Faber and Faber, 1988), 108–10. *Collected Early Poems of Ezra Pound*, ed. Michael John King (London: Faber and Faber, 1977), 108–9. *Pound/Ford*, 4. Goldring, *South Lodge*, 39. In 'Ezra', *New York Herald Tribune Books* (9 Jan. 1927), 1, 6 (reprinted in *Pound/Ford*, 82–7), Ford recalled Sinclair bringing Pound to the *Review* office, but recalled the poem as 'The Ballad of the Goodly Fere', which wasn't published in the *Review* until Oct. (whereas the 'Sestina' appeared in the June issue). It isn't known exactly when they met, but Ford's glossing of Pound as 'an American Poet' in his letter to Elsie of 9 Apr. suggests that he can't have known him long. If Carpenter is right about the poem being written in Mar., they must have met in Mar. or early Apr. *Return to Yesterday*, 371, 388, 326. 'Literary Portraits: VI. Miss May Sinclair', *Tribune* (31 Aug. 1907), 2.

4 D. Garnett, *The Golden Echo*, 129–30. Sinclair to Ford, 6 Apr. [1909]: Cornell. As Mizener says (p. 552, n. 7) Hunt may be describing the same party (though she implies it took place at Christmas 1908) since she also mentions 'Mrs. Garnett and her boy', 'the Radford girls', and Belloc: *The Flurried Years*, 44. Her diary mentions a *bouts-rimés* party on 4 Mar. 1909; but Ford's invitation to her ('We bid you to this pleasant joust of wit / In these too sober days most rare and fit': Cornell) says 4 Apr., which tallies with Sinclair's letter and Ford's letter to Elsie. (Of course there *may* have been two such parties . . . or Hunt may have misread her diary when she typed it up later from her scarcely legible handwriting.)

5 Goldring, *South Lodge*, 33. *Return to Yesterday*, 412–13.

6 This passage from pp. 223–5 of the typescript at Texas was cut for the publication of 'Ford Madox Ford When he was Hueffer', *South Atlantic Quarterly*, 57 (Spring

1958), 236–53. Scott-James dates the party 'a few months after' the period he has just been discussing, which is primarily the summer of 1908, but with a prolepsis to mid-1909. The party must have been after Ford met Bennett in the spring of 1909. Bennett returned to France in May, so the party was either between 6 Mar. and 12 May 1909, or during Bennett's next visit to England, from the end of Nov. 1909 to 18 Mar. 1910: *Journals. Return to Yesterday*, 402–3. Seccombe's address is given by a letter to Ford [n.d., but late 1908]:

7 *The New Humpty-Dumpty*, 72–3. The Cornell MS, 'The Dark Forest: Part II', is dated 17 Feb. 1911: this passage comes on pp. 177–8. See Harvey, 118 (though he doesn't make the connection with *The New Humpty-Dumpty*, and thus wrongly assumes the MS is unpublished. Mizener, 224, notes the connection between the novel and the episode in *Return to Yesterday*, but didn't know of Scott-James's version.

8 *Return to Yesterday*, 392. Nehls, *D. H. Lawrence: A Composite Biography*, 3 vols. (Madison: University of Wisconsin, 1957–9), i. 151–2. John Beer, 'Ford's Impression of the Lawrences', *TLS* (5 May 1972), 520. *Malcolm Elwin, 'Ford and Lawrence', letter to the editor, *TLS* (19 May 1972), 576. Worthen, *D. H. Lawrence: The Early Years* (Cambridge: Cambridge University Press, 1991), 171. Sagar, *D. H. Lawrence: A Calendar of his Works* (Manchester: Manchester University Press, 1979), 25–7.

9 Mizener, 188. *'To-Day's Courts', *Evening News* (11 Jan. 1910), 3, has a report on Elsie's restitution suit, 'Novelist and his wife', which says 'she had not seen him since last May'.

10 Hunt, diary for 30 May 1909. Ford to Elsie [Whit] Monday [30 May 1909] was written from Selsey. Hunt, *The Flurried Years*, 58–9. *Collected Poems* [1913], 76–7.

11 Hunt, *The Flurried Years*, 59, 54. Crawfurd died at Montreux on 31 Jan. 1909. Mizener, 149, 179. On 179–80 he is particularly unfair, reversing the chronology so that Elsie's telling Ford of Marwood's advances reads as if it were her response to Ford's involvement with Violet in June.

12 Hunt, *The Flurried Years*, 55–7. The chronology of these months is uncertain. *The Flurried Years* places the visit to Selsey and Ford's proposal *after* the scene with the poison bottle. Whereas her diary has Ford following her to Selsey on 30 May 1909; and the entry for 10 June says 'Dined FMH', followed by '& he threatened suicide', though this phrase has been deleted; it is followed by the (undeleted) word 'Final?'. It is not clear whether she had second thoughts about the dating, or simply wanted to remove the entry.

13 Judd, *Ford Madox Ford*, 178. *'Self ats Hueffer', 10. *The Good Soldier*, 137, 123. *The New Humpty-Dumpty*, 90–1; cf. 289.

14 Belford reduplicates Hunt's confusion, saying that 'for the first time after one of their dinners, Ford escorted her home' (as Hunt says about the poison-bottle evening, though her diary has Ford driving back with her on 8 May); and then saying she returned to Holland Park the following evening, when they became lovers. This is presumably based on the fact that Hunt's letter saying 'What happened last night [...]' is catalogued as '[12 June 1909]' at Cornell, whereas Hunt deleted her first dating of 'Saturday 12' and replaced it with 'Friday 11'. They can't have become lovers on the 11th (as Belford implies), because that evening Hunt was at Oxford: *Violet*, 149–50. Hardwick has them becoming lovers on 9 June; but she cites no evidence: *An Immodest Violet*, 71. Hunt to Ford, 11

June 1909. If 'What happened last night' happened the same evening as the poison-bottle scene, then according to *The Flurried Years*, 57, 'for the first time after one of our dinners, he walked home with me—and it was only half-past ten when all was said and done'. In other words, they are unlikely to have gone to bed together by this date; or if the cliché 'when all was said and done' is meant to imply that they did, she is unequivocal that they didn't spend the night together. This interpretation is supported by the poem, in which 'the night comes long and deep [. . .] When you and I must sleep'—though this suggests the consummation of death too.

15 Hunt to Ford, subsequently dated by her 13 June 1909; but, as Mizener shows (554–5, n. 38), the dating is unreliable—she dates Ford's answer to this letter 'June 12 1909'. Her diary has her in Oxford over the weekend of 11–13 June; the most probable sequence is Hunt to Ford (including the poem), 11 June [the date she ascribed after deleting 'Saturday 12'; Hunt to Ford 13 June [a Sunday: the letter implies that 'tomorrow' is Monday]; then Ford to Hunt [13 June, though dated the 12th by Hunt], in which he mentions both of her letters. These letters only survive in her transcription; it is impossible to say what editing, conscious or unconscious, has been performed on the originals. Like so much of the document-ary evidence of Ford's life, these texts come down to us already mediated by, and perhaps reshaped by, a powerful literary intelligence.

16 Dated 12 June 1909 by Hunt; but probably [13 June] (see previous note).

17 See e.g. Mizener, p. xviii. Hunt, *The Flurried Years*, 25. Hunt to Ford, 3 Aug. 1909]

18 Ford to Elsie [14 June 1909].

19 Hunt, dairy for 28 June 1909. Mizener, 177, 189.

20 Timothy Hands, *A Hardy Chronology* (Basingstoke: Macmillan, 1992), 128–9, has Hardy at Aldeburgh for a four-day visit from 2 July 1909. Hunt's diary for 2 July 1909 says 'FMH insisted on coming' to Aldeburgh, which casts doubt on her claim not to know he would come; the change would be typical of her attempts to present herself as the injured party. Goldring, *South Lodge*, p. 88. *'Self ats Hueffer', 9, dates the poison-scene 'About a fortnight after the date of my meeting with Miss Van der Noot', and dates that meeting 'About August' 1909. But Hunt's diary places the meeting with Edmée on 18 July (*The Flurried Years*, 70–1 also has it around July). If the deleted dating of 10 June for the suicide scene is correct (and if that refers to the evening with the poison-bottle) then she places it before the meeting with Edmée. The discrepancy may be explained by Ford's determina-tion to present himself in the 1913 deposition as suicidal because of Elsie's desire to divorce, to give the impression that she wanted it more than he did. He may (consciously or unconsciously) have rearranged the chronology to that effect. On the other hand, 'Self ats Hueffer', 10, says he remembered 'Miss Van der Noot and her proposals for divorce', the plural perhaps indicating more than one meeting. Katharine Hueffer Lamb to Mizener, 23 Apr. 1964 and 18 Jan. 1967: Cornell. She says 'Tunbridge Wells', but both *The Flurried Years* (71) and Hunt's diary (entry for 18 July) say 'Tonbridge', and the 1913 deposition agrees, though misspells it 'Tunbridge'. Mizener wrote patronizingly of Ford's description of his conduct to his mother that he has 'as usual, convinced himself of the purity of his motives and the dignity of his conduct' (192). But the undated letter he quotes as evidence, in which Ford says: 'Abso[l]utely the only thing that she [Elsie] could

allege against me with any shadow of proof and absolutely the only wrong I will admit having done her is having a housekeeper [Gertrud] younger than convention demands' also refers to his having failed to place his 'last book but one'. If, as Mizener plausibly suggests, this is *The 'Half Moon'*, then the letter could not have been written later than Jan. or Feb. 1909. The novel was published by 19 Mar., and so must have been placed with Eveleigh Nash around the beginning of the year. At this stage Ford's affair with Hunt cannot be said to have begun, and he is being much more truthful than Mizener implies by quoting the letter while discussing the events of Aug. and Sept. 1909.

'Self ats Hueffer' explains what else the divorce facilities involved: 'I was informed by my solicitor that in order to establish desertion, I must refrain from sending Mrs. Elsie Hueffer any more money. I strongly objected to this, but Mrs. Elsie Hueffer had already informed me that she had saved a considerable sum out of the £8 a week that I allowed her—certainly sufficient to keep her until the restitution proceedings should be completed. In addition I arranged with a third party to send her various sums without indicating their origin': p. 11.

Two reports of Elsie's 1910 restitution suit indicate what Ford communicated to her 'In July last': *'London Author and his Wife', *Globe and Traveller* (11 Jan. 1910), 11; 'Novelist and his wife', *Evening News* (11 Jan. 1910), 3.

21 Ford to Hunt [31 July 1909]. *Return to Yesterday*, 175. Mizener, 191.

22 Mizener, 190-1. Hunt, *The Flurried Years*, 72-3. Ford to Hunt; Hunt to Ford; Silvia Fogg Elliot to Hunt; all [5 Aug. 1909]; Silvia Fogg Elliot to Hunt [n.d.]. Ford wrote three years later, in a preface to *The Governess*, written by Silvia's and Violet's mother (and finished by Violet): 'I have suffered in my time a good deal at the hands of those queer, odd, unimaginative people—the populations of Yorkshire, Lancashire, Durham, Northumberland, and Cumberland': p. xiv. The novel he was dictating was probably *The Portrait*. Ford to Hunt [n.d., but Aug. 1909].

23 Hunt's letter to her maid, Annie Child, describing the lawyer's letter has been dated Aug. 1909. This date is supported by Hunt to Byles (about the furniture), 17 Aug. 1909. See Mizener, 556, n. 15 on the Oct. 1909 bill of sale for the furniture. Elsie's actual petition for restitution of conjugal rights is dated 16 Sept. 1909—after Ford had failed to comply with her letter. Hunt, *The Flurried Years*, 74, names Mabel Wright. But Hunt's typed copy of her letter [to Child] is headed: 'From West Runton, Cromer Ina[?] Mathias' and the carbon is annotated 'Lady Cromer'. Katharine Hueffer Lamb to Mizener, 18 Jan. 1967. The Hüffer clan also resented the fact that Elsie had begun legal proceedings before consulting the German elders. See Hermann Hüffer to Robert Garnett, 20 Oct. 1910. Mizener, 191. *'Self ats Hueffer', 12. Katharine Hueffer Lamb to Mizener, 18 Jan. 1967.

24 Katharine Hueffer Lamb to Mizener, 3 Nov. and 11 Dec. 1966. *The Flurried Years*, 75-80. When, in about 1946, Elsie wrote to her daughter Katharine, she was still unable to see her own part in the breaking of the marriage: 'People took P [Pumpums, i.e. Ford] from me just as someone kept you from him. I do not know of course who no doubt burnt those answers of yours, but I do know who parted him from me. In fact she has told me so': [n.d.]. Violet spoke to Elsie when she paid an impulsive visit to her house in 1920 (see Mizener, 312-13). Katharine Hueffer Lamb to Mizener, 3 Nov. 1966 and 18 Jan. 1967. Mizener, 194.

25 Soskice to Ford, 4 Oct. 1909: Cornell. Since Ford was in France then, he presumably didn't get the letter. *It Was the Nightingale*, 36.

26 14 Nov. 1909. Hunt's comments are on the envelope of the letter at Cornell.

27 Draft of a letter from Ford to Mond [n.d.]. Hunt, *The Flurried Years*, 91.

28 Hunt, 'Read, Mark . . .', *Saturday Review*, 134 (5 Aug. 1922), 222. Ford to Pinker [n.d.]: Princeton.

29 James to Hunt, 31 Oct. 1909 (Barrett Library, University of Virginia Library, quoted in Lindberg-Seyersted, 62) and 2 Nov. 1909: *Henry James: Letters*, ed. Leon Edel, vol. 4 (Cambridge, Mass.: Harvard University Press, 1984), 533–4. Hunt to James [n.d.]: Cornell; quoted by Secor, 'Henry James and Violet Hunt, the "Improper Person of Babylon" ', *Journal of Modern Literature*, 13/1 (Mar. 1986), 29. James to Hunt, 5 Nov. 1909: Barrett.

30 Mizener, 196. Leon Edel notes that 'HJ wanted to avoid any possibility of being mentioned in the attendant publicity': *Letters*, ed. Edel, iv. 534. See Goldring, *South Lodge*, 91, for example. James to Ford, 8 Nov. 1909: Lindberg-Seyersted, 63.

31 Marshall, *Out and About*, 272 (quoting James to Marshall, 18 Jan. 1914) and 282; James to Hunt, 20 Aug. 1907; Hunt, Diary for 4 Nov. 1907: all quoted in Secor, 'Henry James and Violet Hunt', 30, 19, and 20 respectively. Secor advances the 'distaste' theory, 29–30. *Return to Yesterday*, 213.

32 Leon Edel, *Henry James: The Master: 1901–1916* (Philadelphia and New York: J. B. Lippincott, 1972), 410–25, 436–7. Secor, 'Henry James and Violet Hunt', 28. James to Elsie Hueffer, 12 July 1908: Lindberg-Seyersted, 56–7. Lindberg-Seyersted is the only commentator to consider James's feelings for Elsie a factor in his conduct towards Ford and Hunt: see 56, 64–5. James to Elsie, 12 Oct. 1909: printed by Goldring, *The Last Pre-Raphaelite*, 112–13.

33 James to Hunt, 14 Feb. 1910: transcript at Cornell. Hunt to Ford [Dec. 1910]. Mrs Prothero had also met Elsie 'there'—presumably at James's house—which suggests how James was trying not to alienate any of the parties.

34 'Janice Biala', memoir in *The Presence of Ford Madox Ford*, 197–8. Lawrence to Louie Burrows, [Saturday] 20 Nov. 1909: *The Letters of D. H. Lawrence*, vol. 1, ed. James T. Boulton (Cambridge: Cambridge University Press, 1979), 144–5.

35 *D. H. Lawrence: A Personal Record*, by E.T. (Jessie Chambers), 2nd edn., ed. J. D. Chambers (London: Frank Cass, 1965), 164, 169–75.

36 Ford to Lawrence, 15 Dec. 1909: quoted from Worthen, *D. H. Lawrence*, 221–2, 594. This letter was not thought extant before Worthen's rediscovery of it. See *The Letters of D. H. Lawrence*, i. 149, n. 1.

37 Rhys, *Everyman Remembers* (New York: Cosmopolitan Book Corporation, 1931), 243–9. Lawrence's letters to Louie Burrows, 11 Dec., and Grace Crawford, 12 Dec. 1909, show that he was due to read for the Rhyses on or shortly after 18 December: *Letters*, i. 147–8.

38 It is not known exactly when he began the novel; but it was probably after writing the story, which was published in the *Bystander*, 20 (supplement to 9 Dec. 1908), 3–7. The novel was about half-finished in January 1909, and the completed MS had been sent to Methuen on 7 Mar. 1909. Methuen and Hutchinson both turned it down, finding it too short. This is one reason why Ford added the epilogue (though it is only ten pages). It was eventually published by Chatto and Windus on 3 Feb. 1910. See Mizener, 198–9. *Thus to Revisit*, 44.

39 Karl, 668.

40 '4692 Padd', 6, 7.

41 Moser, 78, 79; 308, n. 44. Mizener, 480. Compare Katya massaging Dudley with the scene in *Some Do Not* ..., 148–53, in which Mrs Wannop massages Tietjens' temples, as he has, or thinks he has, a syncope. *A Call*, 297, 302–3, 61, 60, 3. Harvey, 29. Lawrence M. Price, 'Ford Madox Ford', *University of California Chronicle*, 27 (Oct. 1925), 360, notes that Henry Hudson in *The 'Half Moon'* has James's physiognomy; which suggests that Ford thought of his character as a composite of two of his favourite authors: James and W. H. Hudson.

42 Hunt to Ford, 11 Aug. 1909. She had either read (or been read) the MS, or seen the first instalment in the *English Review*.

43 *English Review*, 3 (November 1909), 648. *A Call* (London: Chatto and Windus, 1910), 283 (italics added). There is evidence of haste in the revisions, as, for example in the slight incoherence produced here: 'this too he couldn't doubt' no longer makes sense once Grimshaw *has* doubted his passion for Katya.

44 Secor and Secor, *The Return of the Good Soldier*, 80; there is a comparable idea on p. 49, where Ford tells Hunt that 'if he wrote a love letter to Miss Ross it was in delirium & intended for Brigit with whom he is still infatuated [...]'. Moser, 80.

45 Lawrence to Blanche Jennings, 1 Nov. 1909: *Letters of D. H. Lawrence*, i. 141. Bennett, *Journals*, i. 362: entry for 6 Mar. 1910. Bennett [pseud. 'Jacob Tonson'], 'Books and Persons', *New Age*, 6 (17 Mar. 1910), 471.

46 Green, *Ford Madox Ford: Prose and Politics*, 81.

Chapter 19

1 Ford to Soskice, 1 Jan. 1910 (House of Lords Record Office). Hunt, *The Flurried Years*, 92–3. The Order was reported in the **Star*, 3, the **Globe*, 11, and the **Evening News* (11 Jan. 1910), 3 the **Standard* (12 January 1910), 12; and in the *Daily News* (12 Jan. 1910), 5, and other morning papers. Oddly, Elsie told the court she had not seen Ford since the previous May, though she had decidedly seen him (though not to speak to) with Hunt at Charing Cross. See Mizener, 555, n. 6. Goldring, *South Lodge*, 90; *The Last Pre-Raphaelite*, 157–8. Mizener, 197, n. 7. Katharine Hueffer Lamb to Mizener, 8 May 1966: Cornell. Olive Garnett's diary records a hearing on 16 May 1910: Moser, 99. But I have been unable to trace any records of it, or to verify Hunt's chronology here. The relevant court records are missing from the Greater London Record Office; Brixton Prison's records for 1910 have not been kept. Several of the London papers weren't published on 16 May; those that were were too devoted to the late king's lying in state and funeral arrangements to report any but the major legal news. *The Times* report of the *Throne* case (7 Feb. 1913), 3, says Ford was ordered in April 1910 to pay a lump sum of £25 and weekly payments of £3, and that he refused. Byles's involvement is recorded in the *Daily Express* (8 February 1913), 5. Mizener, 201, 556, n. 15.

2 Mizener, 198, 191. Garnett, quoted by Moser, 99. Katharine Hueffer Lamb to Mizener, 2 Mar. 1966: Cornell. Hunt to Ford, 1911. According to the reports of the Restitution decree, it was when Ford sent the message to Elsie saying that he no longer wished to see her that he added: 'In these circumstances [...] it was

fair that she should have the custody of the children': *Evening News* (11 Jan. 1910), 3. Hunt, *The Flurried Years*, 97–8. Katharine Hueffer Lamb to Mizener, 8 May 1966. The Mizener version, that Harri went to Holland Park Avenue while Ford was in prison, does not square with the Martindale version (as recalled over half-a-century later by Katharine) that Elsie stopped the proceedings after Harri had found Mary at Holland Park Avenue, and that it was then that Ford stopped paying maintenance and went to prison. Ford was still using Holland Park Avenue stationery into 1911: see Ford to Robert Ross, 27 Mar. 1911. Mizener, 191, also says that Mary also wanted to marry Ford; but she would have known that the law prohibited a woman from marrying her brother-in-law. *The Flurried Years*, 50. Garnett, *The Golden Echo*, 182.

3 Hunt says the book was *A Story for Girls*, but I have been unable to locate a book by Mrs Meade with this title. Hunt, *The Flurried Years*, 98, 100. 'Stocktaking: Towards a Re-Valuation of English Literature: I: Working Out a Standard', *transatlantic review*, 1/1 (January 1924), 72–3.

4 In fact Laura Schmedding left DM 15,000 (about £750) to Christina and Katharine; but Hermann Hüffer only explained this to Elsie in a letter of 22 Aug. 1912, and it isn't known whether Ford ever heard about their legacies. Anton Hüffer to Elsie, 6 January 1933, shows they still hadn't received it by that date.

5 *'Self ats Hueffer', 14–15. Ford to Cathy Hueffer [n.d.], shows that he had certainly considered 'an action for slander' against Elsie: House of Lords; quoted by Mizener, 192. There is no suggestion in *The New Humpty-Dumpty* that, when the Countess accuses Macdonald of 'dissolute' and 'disgusting' practices, she doesn't realize her implications (223, 426).

6 Katharine Hueffer Lamb to Mizener, 7 May 1968: Cornell. Elsie told Katharine some fairly mad things about Ford, such as that ' "Of course he *really* did it all for us", meaning the V. H. business': in other words that he only left Elsie for Violet so that he would be able to support his family: Katharine to Mizener, 8 May 1966: Cornell. *The Simple Life Limited* was being finished in Mar.: Ford to Pinker, 30 March 1910: *Letters*, 41–2.

7 Hunt, *The Flurried Years*, 100–2. Hunt evidently financed Gertrud's departure, sending her a cheque for £20 in Koenigsberg, Prussia, on 10 May 1910, and another for £25 in Freemantle, New South Wales, on 18 July 1910. Mizener, 541, n. 17. The revisions are discussed by John Meixner, *Ford Madox Ford's Novels* (London: Oxford University Press, 1962), 74–7; Richard Cassell, *Ford Madox Ford* (Baltimore: Johns Hopkins Press, 1962), 90–106; and Mizener, 484–5. The style was made sparer, and the contemporary references were brought up to date; so that, for example, lovers set off to start a new life in the Soviet Union, instead of living a more Pre-Raphaelite existence in restored medieval English buildings. The 1988 Carcanet reissue was based on the text of the 1935 Lippincott edition.

8 *Rossetti*, 93. Ford's inscription in Crosby Gaige's copy of the novel, quoted by Harvey, 34. *E. B. Osborn, 'Mediæval Novels', *Morning Post* (30 Sept. 1921), 8. *Alain-Fournier to Eliot, 25 July 1911: *The Letters of T. S. Eliot*, ed. Valerie Eliot, vol. 1 (London: Faber and Faber, 1988), 25–6 ('so much feverish emotion and heart-rending beauty'). *Eliot, 'Introduction' to Charlotte Eliot, *Savonarola* (London: R. Cobden-Sanderson [1926]), p. ix).

9 *Ladies Whose Bright Eyes*, 5. Ford to Pinker, 21 June 1910: *Letters*, 43.

10 Moser, 82, argues for the combination of Violet and Rosamond in Dionissia, but does not consider the possibility that Ford may have had ambivalent feelings about the former even at this early date.

11 Moser, 84. *Ladies Whose Bright Eyes*, 333, 347–8. Sorrell's arithmetic can't be right: the novel is set in 1327. Even if Dionissia had lived another seventy-three years to 1400, she would have been dead for 510 years.

12 Ford to Pinker, 21 June 1910: *Letters*, 43–4.

13 Hunt, *The Flurried Years*, 106–8. Lawrence to Grace Crawford, 24 June; 9 July; and 24 July 1910: *Letters*, i. 165; 168–71. The letter of [Saturday] 9 July says Ford had 'bidden' Lawrence for Sunday, thus the party he describes took place on 10, 17, or 24 July.

14 Ford to Lawrence [9 Sept. 1910]: Lawrence to Louie Burrows, 9 Sept. 1910, says Ford had written that morning, but the letter is not known to have survived. Lawrence to Grace Crawford, 12 Oct. 1910, said that Ford had abused him 'roundly' for the book; Lawrence to Garnett, 18 Dec. 1911: *Letters*, i. 178, 182–3, 339–40. Ford was interceding with Seckers on Lawrence's behalf in 1912: Lawrence to Edward Garnett, 13 Aug. 1912: ibid. 433–4. Lawrence to Ernest Collings, 14 Nov. 1912: ibid. 471.

15 D. Garnett, *The Golden Echo*, 182–4. Harvey, 31.

16 Goldring, *South Lodge*, 94, Mizener, 200. D. Garnett, *The Golden Echo*, 187–8.

17 D. Garnett, *The Golden Echo*, 192 (I have italicized the expressions that show Ford trying for effect). Despite the debts, Ford sent Garnett 100 marks when he ran out of money in Freiburg (p. 194). Franz Hüffer to Catherine, 16 July 1879: Cornell.

18 Hunt, *The Flurried Years*, 132–4. The name 'Lelöffel' is as likely to be taken from Ford's novel as from life, though Ford frequently used real names for characters and places (he is, besides, presumably also the 'Lieutenant L——' mentioned in *The Desirable Alien*, 98). *The Flurried Years* consistently changes names. Hunt later provided a 'Description of Characters' (now at Cornell), which unlocks this obliquely impassioned *autobiographie à clef*. 'Goneril' and 'Regan' are her sisters Silvia Fogg Elliot and Venetia Benson respectively. 'Hermosa' is Olive Thomas; 'Elizabeth Schultz' is Gertrud; 'Paul John' is Ludwig Leun; 'Maleine' is Brigit Patmore. *The Desirable Alien*, 89; 88–97 describes the Nauheim *Kur*.

19 See Harvey, 166–7. 'William Holman Hunt, O. M.', *Fortnightly*, 87 (Oct. 1910), 657–65; repr. in *Ancient Lights*, 210. The dedication also mentions Tolstoy, who died on 10 Nov. 1910 (p. xi).

20 Hunt to Ford [*c*. December 1910]. Mizener, 202–3. Hunt and Ford, *The Desirable Alien*, 141–51. Hunt, *The Flurried Years*, 142–3. *Ancient Lights*, 288.

21 Hermann Hüffer to Robert Garnett, 20 Oct. 1910. *The Flurried Years*, 138, 141. Mimi Goesen to Ford, 23 Aug. 1910.

22 Goldring, *South Lodge*, 93–4 (though he misplaces Holman Hunt's marriage in Holland). Diana Holman-Hunt, *My Grandfather, His Wives and Loves* (London: Hamish Hamilton, 1969), 284.

23 Hunt to Ford, five undated letters.

24 Hunt to Ford, five undated letters.

25 Hunt to Ford, 28 Sept. 1910, and 11 or 12 Oct. 1910. Hunt, *The Flurried Years*, 148. The *Personenstands-Ausnahme* (residence register) at Giessen says Ford was there from 3 Oct. 1910 to 1 May 1913. *The Flurried Years*, 155.

26 Hunt to Ford [*c*.November 1910] and [n.d.]. Ford to Pinker, 13 Nov. [1910]: Huntington. Mizener, 210, 557, n. 3. Though *Ancient Lights* was not published until 24 Mar. 1911, the 'Dedication' speaks of it as 'the best Christmas present' that he could give his daughters, suggesting that it was finished in 1910 (p. vii). Hunt, *The Flurried Years*, 142, 147. Georg Büchner, *Danton's Death, Leonce and Lena, Woyzeck*, ed. Victor Price (Oxford: Oxford University Press, 1971), p. ix. Mizener, 205. Ford, postcards to Christina from Marburg, 12 Nov. 1910, 13 Feb. 1911.

27 Hunt, *The Flurried Years*, 146, 150. Rebecca West thought that Ford found out about the syphilis when a doctor told Hunt he would have to examine her 'husband'. West thought that was 'the real cause of their breakup'. I think this is unlikely, since Ford knew of the syphilis before their attempted marriage. Mizener, 205. Hunt to Ford, transcript of a postcard, 15 Oct. 1910, and two undated letters. In another undated letter Hunt discusses her 'change of life', which a friend had attributed to 'sexual indulgence'. Lawrence to Hunt, 13 Dec. 1910: *Letters*, i. 199–200; 226–7, n. 2 prints Hunt to Lawrence, 3 Feb. [1911], saying she was ill from 17 Aug. to 1 Dec. 1910. Hunt to Ford [n.d., *c*. Nov. 1910]: Cornell; quoted by Belford, *Violet*, 175–6.

28 28 Oct. 1910: *Letters*, 44–6. As Ludwig says, Sinclair's novel is probably *The Creators: A Comedy*. Unfortunately Jepson's letter appears not to have survived.

29 Mizener, 198. He also gives a misleading emphasis to a dispute with Constable, the publishers of *Ladies Whose Bright Eyes*. Ford sent the MS to his old friend Thomas Seccombe (who had helped plan the *English Review*) asking for his comments. But he had not known that Seccombe was a reader for Constable, and was upset when he replied on the firm's stationery. Mizener says Ford was 'involved in his usual complicated quarrels with publishers', as if all the disputes were equally unreasonable (p. 210). This one, however, was entirely reasonable. Constable used Ford's approach to Seccombe as a reason for delaying the payment due when Ford submitted the completed MS. Ford welcomed the friendly criticism of one writer to another, but resented the idea that a publishing firm should tell him how to write. The incident certainly touched on his sensitivity about how men of commerce should defer to, rather than patronize, artists. But the main reason for his exasperation was that he badly needed the money, and thought Constable had reneged upon their contract. Hunt had been bickering with him over the expense of the German venture, and the presents he wanted to send to his children; but then wrote disarmingly to him around December: 'Dearest, it would be very bad manners for you to starve.' See Ford to Pinker, 15 Dec. 1910 (Huntington); Hunt, *The Flurried Years*, 155–8.

30 Hunt, *The Flurried Years*, 154. Mizener, 209. The New Year's Day mass is also mentioned in Hunt and Ford, *The Desirable Alien*, 321, and 'Literary Portraits—LIII.: The Muse of War', *Outlook*, 34 (12 Sept. 1914), 334–5.

31 Mizener, 204–5, 209. Hermann Hüffer to Elsie, 15 September 1910 and October 1910: Cornell. Elsie also enlisted the support of William Rossetti, who told her he thought Ford's father hadn't had the children registered as German: Rossetti to Elsie, 17 Sept. 1910: *Selected Letters*, 669–70. Hermann told Elsie in 1924 that he had cut Ford and Oliver on a street in Paris the previous year because he did not 'like to seem to approve their way of acting and thinking by approaching them in

a natural and unreservedly cousinly way': 20 July 1924; quoted by Mizener, 556, n. 24. Hunt, *The Flurried Years*, 156-9. Hunt also describes the altruistic menagerie at South Lodge: 'the young owl, Ann Veronica, bought in Covent Garden market [. . .] the bulldog, given to *me* sooner than shut him up because he worried sheep; nine Persian cats and two parrots—one that I went to Charing Cross and fetched on receipt of a telegram—"Will you have the parrot or shall I kill him?"—and another with only one eye that we bought from the public house next door to save him from ill-treatment' (p. 109). Ford gave Sylvia Tietjens a bulldog.

Chapter 20

1 R. Garnett, *Constance Garnett*, 91-3, 149-50, 153, 171, 189-90. D. Garnett, *The Golden Echo*, 39-40. The anarchist circle of the young Rossettis was comparably anarchic, and Ford may also have been remembering some of the episodes and characters fictionalized in *A Girl Among the Anarchists*, by 'Isabel Meredith' (pseudonym for Olive and Helen Rossetti) (London: Duckworth & Co., 1903).

2 Ford to Pinker, 3 June 1912: *Reader*, 474-5. MacShane, *The Life and Work of Ford Madox Ford*, 126, suggests that Ford wanted to conceal his earnings from creditors. Ford (as 'Chaucer') to Hunt, 9 Apr. 1911: *Letters*, 49-51. Moser, 91.

3 Moser, 91, 95. He gives a detailed account of possible biographical sources (91-8; also see 307, n. 31). Mizener, 212. **Saturday Westminster Gazette* (1 Apr. 1911), 12. The *Athenaeum*, for example (11 Mar. 1911), 273, thought it 'no difficult matter to make a shrewd surmise concerning the identity of "Daniel Chaucer," [. . .] whom we take to be a writer who has worked with some success in a widely different field of fiction'. Oddly, the *English Review*, 8 (Apr. 1911), 175-6, thought the author a woman. The **Morning Post* (27 Mar. 1911), 2, printed an enthusiastic review of the novel, without hazarding a guess as to the author's identity, on the same page that Wilde's friend Robert Ross wrote a carping review of *Ancient Lights* entitled **'Pre-Raphaelite Chestnuts'*. Ford's firmly generous reply was published in **Robert Ross: Friend of Friends*, ed. Margery Ross (London: Jonathan Cape, 1952), 211.

4 *The Simple Life Limited*, 144. It is another indication of Brandson's derivativeness that the name comes from Poe's 'Ulalume'. *Thus to Revisit*, 210.

5 *The Simple Life Limited*, 253, 53. Moser, 95. Gubb has also been claimed as a portrait of Pinker. Other suggested identifications are: George Everard (Frank Harris); Mr Major (Harrison Cowlishaw); Mr Hangbird (Stephen Crane); Ophelia Brandson (Juliet Soskice); Cyril Brandetski (David Soskice); Miss Stobhall (Constance Garnett—though Moser, 307, n. 31, identifies her with Mrs Lee): see *Letters*, 49-50 n., and Mizener, 558, n. 12. Mizener, 120.

6 Mizener, 199, says the novel was finished by 30 Mar. 1910. Snitow, *Ford Madox Ford and the Voice of Uncertainty*, 146-7.

7 *Ancient Lights*, pp. vii, x, 296-7. Mizener, 205. Hunt, *The Flurried Years*, 151. Heine's poem is number 10 of the sequence 'Abroad' from 'Sundry Women' in *New Poems*; translated as 'Sir Olaf' by Hal Draper, *The Complete Poems of Heinrich Heine* (Boston: Suhrkamp/Insel, 1982), 370-2.

8 Hunt to Lawrence, 3 February [1911]; Lawrence to Hunt, 9 February 1911: Lawrence, *Letters*, i. 226-8. *Chronicle* (10 Feb. 1911), quoted in ibid. 227, n. 5.

9 Ford's review is not in Harvey's bibliography. Boulton notes that no pre-1914 records have been kept to identify the *Standard*'s reviewers. That paper's review (3 Feb. 1911), 5, is certainly Olympian, and makes Ford's complaint that Lawrence has genius

without technique. Lawrence to de la Mare, 10 June 1912: *Letters*, i. 416–17. *Mightier Than the Sword*, 121. Worthen, *D. H. Lawrence: The Early Years*, 216–18.

10 The Cornell MS 'The Dark Forest' (173 leaves in large script), corresponding to Part II of the book, bears the date 17 Feb. 1911. See Harvey, 118; though he thought the MS was unpublished. The title-page of the book attributes the saying to 'Tambov', which, as Moser says (p. 105), is the name of the place the Russian in *Heart of Darkness* comes from. The quotation is in fact from Ralston's translation of Turgenev's 'Liza'. Ford also alludes to it in *Ancient Lights*, p. xi; and in 'Literary Portraits—XIX. Gerhart Hauptmann and "Atlantis" ', *Outlook*, 33 (17 Jan. 1914), 77–9.

11 Ford to the editor of the *American Mercury*, 19 Jan. 1937: *Letters*, 269–70. Mizener, 223, 226. Snitow, 149–54. There is also a lively reading of the book by Moser, 104–10, to which I am indebted. Mizener, 560, n. 8, suggests that the Galizian Da Pinta is Ford's version of Soskice; and that the rich American, Edward U. Dexter, 'plays the role S. S. McClure had in the affairs of *The English Review*'. However, Dexter is also based on the Colonel Harvey Ford identifies as J. P. Morgan's representative in *It Was the Nightingale*, 293. Morgan figures as the financier Mordaunt, whose name Ford took from another Edwardian divorce scandal: see Mizener, 233. Moser mentions a portrait of Robert Garnett (as one of the 'murderers' along with the Countess and Pett): 105. Perhaps he means the lawyer, Mr Lumsden.

12 *The New Humpty-Dumpty*, 28, 303, 372, 17, 70, 26. *Joseph Conrad's Letters to R. B. Cunninghame Graham*, ed. Cedric Watts (Cambridge: Cambridge University Press, 1969), 5. *Return to Yesterday*, 38.

13 *The New Humpty-Dumpty*, 331, 350–2, 333, 339, 356.

14 Ibid. 360, 44, 87, 284–5, 215–16, 366, 303–4.

15 Ibid. 424. Mizener, 180–1.

16 *The New Humpty-Dumpty*, 213, 361.

17 Ibid. 309–10, 367.

18 Ibid. 241, 319, 351, 366, 388, 170, 287. Snitow, 149–50, 153. The story was published in *Christina's Fairy Book* in 1906.

19 Mizener to West, 7 June 1968.

20 *The New Humpty-Dumpty*, 6–9, 15, 268, 30, 34–5, 69.

21 Hunt, *The Flurried Years*, 213. Pett, like Aldington, is the name of a village near Winchelsea. *The New Humpty-Dumpty*, 16, 69, 123, 186–7, 185, 313–18, 337, 341, 351, 428. Mizener, 225–6. West's unsigned review appeared in *English Review*, 12 (Sept. 1912), 332; repr. in *Ford Madox Ford: The Critical Heritage*, 40–1. See above, p. 368. Hunt to Ford [*c*. Oct. 1910]: Cornell. Similar feelings about sexual betrayal and pique get into a feeble story, 'The Fun of Genius', *English Review*, 13 (Dec. 1912), 52–63, in which the character 'Wert Best' is, approximately, [Her]Bert Wells. Ford expresses ambivalence about 'geniuses' as at once supermen and outcasts. In a weird scene, the hero reads his own book and begins to realize his own immorality according to his own views, and contemplates suicide.

22 *The New Humpty-Dumpty*, 40, 426–7, 422. Mizener, 181. Moser, 212. Mizener to West, 7 June 1968.

23 *The New Humpty-Dumpty*, 102, 257, 26, 178, 83, 175. *The Good Soldier*, 16.

24 *The New Humpty-Dumpty*, 420, 296.

25 See Moser, 108: 'He is, of course, quite right. Sexual passion is the major source of the dark forest.'

26 The first two chapters were sent to Pinker in March, and the MS was completed by Jan. 1912 (Mizener, 210; Harvey, 56). However, it was not published until 1918, when Pound persuaded Margaret Anderson to bring the series out in the *Little Review* (for which Pound was the London editor) between Jan. and Sept. 1918. They were then collected into booklet form when published by William Bird's 'Three Mountains Press' (Paris, 1923), in a series edited by Pound. Pound thought them some of Ford's best prose: see *Pound/Ford*, 69. Mizener, 210, says that 'for some reason no more of *Women & Men* was ever written'. However, a MS entitled **'Epilogue', recently donated to Princeton by Pound's son, Omar, is a draft of what was probably intended to be the concluding chapter. It was written after the battle at Vimy Ridge in Feb. 1917 (which it mentions), and while Ford was still in the army (i.e. before 7 Jan. 1919). It continues the 1911 observations to consider the relations between the sexes after the war, and it might well have been written for the *Little Review* serialization. There is no indication why the 'Epilogue' was not published; though it was perhaps for the same reason that Pound had to refuse Marianne Moore's poems, explaining to her: 'The confounded trouble is that I have come to the end of my funds, and can not pay for any more mss. for *The Little Review*' (16 Dec. 1918: *Selected Letters of Ezra Pound*, 133). The 'Epilogue' was later reworked into the 'Rosalie Prudent' chapter of *No Enemy*, which explains why it was not published in the booklet version of *Women & Men*. See James Longenbach, 'Ford Madox Ford: The Novelist as Historian', *Princeton University Library Chronicle*, 45 (Winter 1984), 150–66. The original of the carbon typescript pages of this manuscript have recently been added to the Cornell Ford collection.

27 Ford to Pinker, 31 January 1911: *Letters*, 46–7. Ford to Pinker, 9 Mar. 1911 (Northwestern): Mizener, 210.

28 'Women and Men: V. Average People', *Little Review*, 4 (July 1918), 49. The remembrances of the Bonnington women and men were repeated, with minor variations, in *Return to Yesterday*, 141–50.

29 'Women and Men: VI. Average People', *Little Review*, 4 (Sept. 1918), 54. See *The Critical Attitude*, ch. 7.

30 'Just Country' is Chapter 6 of *No Enemy*: see esp. 127. *'Just People' is an unpublished typescript at Cornell. Some of its anecdotes were retold for *Return to Yesterday*: the waiter (301–3); the violinist (300); and American farmer friend (159–61, 164–5). See Paul Skinner, 'Just Ford'; *Agenda* 27/4–28/1 (Winter 1989–Spring 1990), 103–9, on the importance of the term (and the pun) to Ford's aesthetic.

Chapter 21

1 Belford, *Violet*, 177–9. Hardwick, *An Immodest Violet*, 92. Hunt, *The Flurried Years*, 166–81.

2 Hunt, *The Flurried Years*, 171–5. Mizener, 211. Pound to Isabel Pound, quoted in *Ezra Pound and Margaret Cravens*, ed. Omar Pound and Robert Spoo (Durham and London: Duke University Press, 1988), 66–7. Pound was in England between 28 Feb. and 3 Mar. 1911. Hunt and Ford, *The Desirable Alien*, 157–60. See above, p. 339. Mizener, 203, places this visit to Marburg in the autumn of 1910. But the presence of Ford's mother makes the spring of 1911 the more likely date. Ford made frequent visits to Schücking at Marburg (15 miles or so from Giessen): see postcards to Christina, 12 and 23 Nov. 1910; to Katharine, 28 Nov. 1910; and to Christina, 13 Feb. and 15 Aug. 1911.

3 Hunt, *The Flurried Years*, 171. Harvey, 305–8. *Daily News* (24 Mar. 1911), 3. Ford to Scott-James, 11 May 1911: *Letters*, 51–2.

4 *Outlook*, 27 (22 Apr. 1911), 507–8. Mizener, 205–6.

5 Hunt, *The Flurried Years*, 175–7. Mizener, 210–12. *'The Ceremony in Westminster Abbey', *Sheffield Daily Telegraph* (23 June 1911), 1–2; reprinted in *Zeppelin Nights*, 285–303, although on 284–5 the Fordian narrator Serapion Hunter says of it: 'I don't mean to print it. It's altogether too bad'; and says that the Hunt-like Candour took it down from his dictation. Ford's press card for the Coronation is at Cornell. He also described the Coronation in his 1936 radio talk about the abdication, *'Last Words about Edward VIII'.

6 *The Flurried Years*, 202–4. Ford to Mrs Joseph Pennell, 16 June [1911]: Library of Congress. Hardy to Ford, 18 June 1911, in *The Collected Letters of Thomas Hardy*, ed. Richard Purdy and Michael Millgate, vol. 4 (Oxford: Clarendon Press, 1984), 160. Ellen Terry to Ford, 22 June [1911]: UCLA. Ford to Otto Kahn, 23 Dec. 1927, perhaps exaggerates the story to encourage Kahn to give the players financial help. He says in 1910 he 'took the whole theatre and invited everyone in London to be present as [his] guest and afterwards gave a sort of collation on the stage with the curtain up. It really succeeded admirably because all London attended, from Mr. Asquith and Mr. Balfour to the Duke and Duchess of Westminster and Ellen Terry, and of course the result was tremendous social publicity'. *Provence*, 199–200, mentions 'a rehearsal by the Abbey Theatre players at the Court—a rehearsal during the short period whilst, for my sins, I was responsible for that company'. Goldring quotes a letter from Ralph Cope, who recalled being introduced by Ford to Yeats and Lady Gregory. *The Last Pre-Raphaelite*, 164–5.

7 *Times* (12 July 1911), 4: Harvey, p. 307. Mimi Goesen to Ford, 10 Aug. 1911.

8 *'Book Chat', *Punch*, 141 (16 Aug. 1911), 122–3. *Penguin Dictionary of Historical Slang*. E. C. Bentley (author of *Trent's Last Case* and the inventor of the Clerihew), *Daily News* (9 Aug. 1911), 7; *Athenaeum* (19 Aug. 1911), 211; *Bookman* (London), 41 (Oct. 1911), 59–60.

9 Hunt, *The Flurried Years*, 181. *The Good Soldier*, 17, 136.

10 Pound wrote to Dorothy Shakespear on 16 July 1911: 'My address after Aug. 1st is c/o F. M. Hueffer, 15 Friedrichs Strasse': *Ezra Pound and Dorothy Shakespear*, 37–8. He was back in England by 20 Aug. (Pound to Cravens, 22 Aug. 1911: *Ezra Pound and Margaret Cravens*, 85).

11 Hunt's accounts of her own activities at the time are obscure and contradictory. She says she was with Ford and Pound on this Schiffenberg excursion in *The Desirable Alien*, 72–2 (followed by Mizener, 215–16). But *The Flurried Years*, 178–80, has her in England between (the Coronation in) June and (her reunion in Paris with Ford in) Aug., while Ford is 'rushing about the duchy that he desired to adopt him', taking 'his lightsome secretary Ezra' to Homberg and Nauheim.

12 Pound to Isabel Pound, 29 Aug. 1911 and [Aug.] 1911; quoted in *Pound/Ford*, 8, 59, 117. Camilla Haase, 'Serious Artists' (unpublished dissertation: Harvard University, 1984), 140–2, speculates about Dowell and Pound. Pound 'Ford Madox (Hueffer) Ford: Obit', *Selected Prose*, 431–2. The book was probably *Canzoni*, published in July, but actually Pound's fifth volume of verse. Mizener, 218.

13 Pound to Shakespear [9 May 1913]: *Ezra Pound and Dorothy Shakespear*, 226–7. Pound, *Polite Essays* (London: Faber and Faber, 1937), 50; quoted in *Pound/Ford*, 142.

14 Francis Hueffer, 'Memoir', in *Ballads & Sonnets by Dante G. Rossetti* (Leipzig: Bernhard Tauchnitz, 1882), 23. Ford paraphrased the remark to Lucy Masterman, 23 Jan. 1913: *Letters*, 55; and in 'The Literary Life: A Lecture', ed. Joseph Wiesenfarth, *Contemporary Literature*, 30/2 (Summer 1989), 176. Ford to Bowen [n.d., but mid-Mar. 1923]. Pound, 'Mr. Hueffer and the Prose Tradition in Verse', *Poetry*, 4 (June 1914), 111–20; repr. in *Literary Essays of Ezra Pound* as 'The Prose Tradition in Verse' (London: Faber and Faber, 1954), 371–7, and in *Pound/Ford*, 16. Donald Davie, *Studies in Ezra Pound* (Manchester: Carcanet, 1991), 246, 38. T. S. Eliot, 'Introductory Essay' to Samuel Johnson, *London: A Poem and The Vanity of Human Wishes* (London: Frederick Etchells & Hugh Macdonald, 1930), 11. Pound, 'Affirmations', *New Age*, 16/15 (11 Feb. 1915), 410. *Thus to Revisit*, 210: *Pound/Ford*, 53–4. Eliot may have been recalling Pound's advertisement for 'Mr Hueffer's realization that poetry should be written at least as well as prose' in the earlier essay 'Mr. Hueffer and the Prose Tradition': *Pound/Ford*, 17. Catherine Seelye, ed., *Charles Olson & Ezra Pound* (New York: Grossman Publishers, 1975): *Pound/Ford*, 177. Seelye includes a fine poem by Olson about Ford: **'Auctor', 135.

15 Peter Brooker, *A Student's Guide to the Selected Poems of Ezra Pound* (London: Faber and Faber, 1979), 152–3. *Collected Early Poems of Ezra Pound*, 163–4.

16 Pound described *Mr. Fleight* as 'that flail of pomposities' in his first review of *Collected Poems*: 'Ford Madox Hueffer', *New Freewoman*, 1 (15 Dec. 1913), 251. Pound to Ford, 17 Apr. [1933]: *Pound/Ford*, 122–3. 'Mr. Hueffer and the Prose Tradition in Verse'. **Egoist*, 1/4 (16 Feb. 1914), 76. Rachel Annand Taylor was a Scottish poet and biographer. Ford published 'Three Poems' of hers in the *English Review*, 3 (Oct. 1909), 378–9. See Lawrence, *Letters*, i. 141 n. Pound added a footnote, signed 'William Michael R-s-tti' complaining: 'My grand-nephew in law is at this, as at most points, wilfully mendacious.' Curtis Brown gave a better impression of Ford discussing golf. See vol. 2, Ch. 13.

17 *Thus to Revisit*, 167. Aldington's parody is discussed on p. 339. Possibly another weapon in this tournament of parodies is **'L'Indépendant', *transatlantic review*, 1/4 (Apr. 1924), 210–12. Signed 'Giovanni Scudo', it is probably either Ford's parody of Pound, or Pound's of Ford. Pound, 'The Approach to Paris, I', *New Age*, 13/19 (4 Sept. 1913), 551–2. See Haase, 'Serious Artists', 281–2.

18 Pound to William Carlos Williams, 24 Jan. 1937: *Pound/Ford*, 164. In his obituary of Ford Pound was more clear about Fordian 'CLARITY': 'For the ten years before I got to England there would seem to have been no one but Ford who held that French clarity and simplicity in the writing of English verse and prose were of immense importance as in contrast to the use of a stilted traditional dialect, a "language of verse" unused in the actual talk of the people, even of "the best people," for the expression of reality and emotion': *Pound/Ford*, 171.

19 'Ford Madox Hueffer', *New Freewoman*, 1/13 (15 Dec. 1913), 251: *Pound/Ford*, 15. 'Ford Madox (Hueffer) Ford; Obit': *Pound/Ford*, 173. Pound to Felix Schelling, 8–9 July 1922: *Selected Letters*, 180. Pound's misjudgement of Ford is discussed more fully in my 'Ford/Pound', *Agenda*, 27/4–28/1 (Winter 1989–Spring 1990), 93–102. Pound to Brigit Patmore [n.d.]: Texas; quoted by Mizener, 239.

Chapter 22

1 Hunt to Cathy Hueffer [n.d., but late Aug./early Sept. 1911]: House of Lords. Mizener's quotation (on 217) is inaccurately transcribed from Hunt's hand, which was generally even less legible than Ford's. Hunt, *The Flurried Years*, 185. *The Flurried Years* has Violet meeting Ford in Paris after his first bout of dentistry with Farley *after* the Coronation (22 June) and after Pound's visit to Giessen in August. On p. 212 Mizener wrongly places this episode in April, saying that Hunt reached Paris on the 20th, and they left on the 29th. The only source he cites which gives any date is *The Flurried Years*, 184. But Hunt only says that she left England on the 20th: she does not give the month, but in the preceding pages describes the Coronation, and says 'We were in for a hot July'. The date of the dentistry is firmly established as later summer rather than Easter by this letter from Hunt to Mrs Hueffer, which was written some time during the six weeks before the court was to sit again in Oct. Depending on the Oct. date, this places the letter between mid-Aug. and mid-Sept. If Hunt reached Paris on 20 Aug., it must have been written between then and the first week of Sept. (allowing for Ford to complete his first awful week of dentistry, and for them to take about ten days rest at Fort-Mahon). There are two postcards from Hunt to Child, dated '29–8' and 9 September. Neither bore the year, and Hunt later misdated them as belonging to 1913; but they confirm the Aug.–Sept. dating of Ford's dentistry and recuperation.

2 Hunt to Ford, 'Tuesday 25' [possibly Oct. 1910, but more probably July 1911]. Hunt, *The Flurried Years*, 191, 182, 187, 128. Mizener, 211, follows Hunt's implausible presentation of herself as Ford's dupe. *A Call*, 259. See Moser, 78. *The Desirable Alien: At Home in Germany*, by Violet Hunt, with Preface and Two Additional Chapters by Ford Madox Hueffer, p. vii. Ford's chapters were written by the autumn of 1911, and published in the *Saturday Review*, 112 (30 Sept. and 7 Oct. 1911), 421–2, 454–6, as "High Germany: I. How it feels to be members of subject races; II. Utopia'. Mizener, 202–3.

3 *D. H. Lawrence: A Composite Biography*, ii. 412. Hunt, *The Flurried Years*, 66. Ford to Pinker, quoted by Richard M. Ludwig, 'The Reputation of Ford Madox Ford', *PMLA*, 76 (December 1961), 547. Lawrence to Louie Burrows, 10 Oct. 1911: *Letters*, i. 309. *'Round the Town', *London Opinion*, 31 (14 Oct. 1911), 48. Hunt to Ford [n.d.]: Princeton. See Mizener, 218, 559, n. 20. Belford, *Violet*, 185. On 5 Nov. they could have been in Belgium (they were in Spa until at least 21 Oct.); France; or—more probably—Germany. Ford sent postcards to Christina from Trier (3 Nov.) and Coblenz (8 Nov.). Hunt's whereabouts are uncertain at this time; but she wrote to Lawrence from Brussels saying she would be back in England on 21 Oct. (though as the *Daily Mirror* article about the marriage appeared that day, she may have changed her plans): Lawrence to Louie Burrows, 16 Oct. 1911: *Letters*, i. 315. Lawrence told Ada Lawrence: 'Hueffer has married Violet Hunt in Germany. They'll be home soon, living in her house'; [16 Oct. 1911]: ibid., 316.

4 Belford, *Violet*, 117, 182. Secor and Secor, *The Return of the Good Soldier*, 20–1.

5 Ford to Hunt, 12 May 1918: quoted by Secor and Secor, *The Return of the Good Soldier*, 21. Ford's inference is perplexing. Would the marriage have been affected had one taken place in Germany? Surely what is put in question by Ford's allegiance to King George during wartime is his German nationality, upon which

the projected divorce from Elsie turned. A marriage in France would not, of itself, secure that. *Some Do Not . . .*, 187. *Ezra Pound and Margaret Cravens*, 85. Pound repeated the idea to his mother as soon as he was back in London, saying of Ford: 'he's being married this afternoon or else this A.M. and going to the dentists in the P.M.': [n.d., but 21 Aug. 1911]: quoted in *Pound/Ford*, 8.

6 Entry for 10 Dec. [1925?]: in Marjorie Watts, *P.E.N.: The Early Years: 1921–1926* (London: The Archive Press, 1971), 32.

7 R. Ellis Roberts told Hunt that 'in the society in which they moved very few people would bother whether their union was legal or not'. He was told—though he said he 'never pried into the exact details—there was a divorce in Baden; there was a marriage in Baden-Baden, under the august auspices, we were told, of the Grand Duke': *New Directions*, No. 7 (Norfolk, Conn., 1942), 484–5.

8 Hunt to Ford (the unsent draft shown to Jepson): Princeton; quoted by Mizener, 218. Julie Loewe to Mizener, 12 Apr. 1967. *The Return of the Good Soldier*, 220.

9 Of course Hunt may have destroyed any 1910–16 diaries after she had written her memoirs of the period, to conceal any liberties she had taken with the facts. Roberts recalled the consultation in *New Directions*, No. 7, pp. 483–6. Naumburg: quoted by the Secors, 21–2. *'Round the Town', 14 Oct. 1911. Ford knew of this piece. The tearsheet of it at Cornell (from Hunt's papers) was sent to him, possibly by his mother. The inscription is barely legible, but begins: 'Dearest Ford I enclose London Opinion—there [is?] an allusion to two wives.' The squiggle below this major part might be an 'M'; there follows a partially indecipherable note, 'I saw advertisement just now [. . .]', and the final word of this *might* be 'Mother'.

10 19 Feb. 19[13]: House of Lords. Quoted by Mizener, 232. In a later fragment Hunt stuck to her claim that there had been a marriage: 'I should never have let Ford live in the house, marry[ing] me so doubtfully', she wrote: 'But if I had not I should never have "seen Carcassonne" '. In another remark she added: 'And if I had not married him, he would not have stuck to me, especially if I had shut my purse strings.' These passages come from the autobiographical writings filed in box 13, folder 18 of the Wallis papers at Cornell. On the other hand, a passage from her 1917 diary suggests that there was no marriage, or at least that if there was both knew it was void: 'Eleanor Jackson came', she wrote on 19 Apr.: 'She says Nora H thinks F a "good man—a martyr to his pledged word, he says he is to stick to me whatever I do, since the circumstances in which we came together make it impossible for him to leave me." If I were married to him, he would do so without compunction as he did Elsie. So he gives it all away! my poor reputation for an ounce of flattery from Nora Haselden!': Secor and Secor, *The Return of the Good Soldier*, 57. This doesn't prove anything: it suggests that by 1917 Hunt didn't feel she was married to Ford in England. Ford may only have meant that he didn't want to leave her because people would then assume they had been lying about being married (in other words, *he* may still have felt they were married). Besides, she may have meant that he was 'giving away' the fact that they were no longer happy, rather than saying they never married.

11 Hunt to Ethel Colburn Mayne [n.d., but *c.*1925]: Princeton; quoted by Belford, *Violet*, 258. Hunt to Catherine Hueffer, 13 Feb. 1913: House of Lords. *New Directions*, No. 7, p. 485. Goldring, *South Lodge*, 96–7.

12 All the records of the Giessen Stadtarchiv and the town's marriage records were destroyed during World War II, so the proof of any putative naturalization is now

probably irrecoverable. (Professor Dr E. Knauss to Max Saunders, 28 Jan. 1989.) But there are several pieces of evidence weighing against Ford's having secured it. First, in 1915 he got his British nationality confirmed. There is a copy at Cornell, dated 12 June 1919, of a statement from the Public Records Office made on 23 Aug. 1915, reading: 'We certify that the above named Ford Madox Hueffer is a British born subject.' The original statement was made shortly after Ford received his commission, and was thus perhaps required either by the army or by Wellington House. The later copy might have been made in connection with his change of name to 'Ford Madox Ford' in June 1919. In 1918 he was confronted by his CO about the old *Daily Mirror* interview. Again, he said that his British nationality was not in question (Ford to Hunt, 12 May 1918: quoted by Secor and Secor, *The Return of the Good Soldier*, 21). Statements of allegiance while Britain is at war with Germany do not necessarily amount to a denial that he ever became a German national: he might have had dual nationality. Yet on 15 Feb. 1927 Ford wrote to the editor of the *New York Herald Tribune Books* unequivocally denying that he had become a German national: 'I never became a German for legal or illegal reasons or for any reason. I should be flattered to be included among your countrymen, but I always was and shall always be a British subject' (published in the issue of 20 Feb.: in *Letters*, 170–2). Hunt also later wrote a note saying that: 'The plan [for the divorce and remarriage] was defeated by the inertia—or malice—of the male protagonist' (Goldring, *South Lodge*, 130). But by July 1930 she was embittered by their separation: *The Flurried Years* (and Mizener's biography) depicts a Ford energetically romancing about the law rather than being inert or malicious. Other problems with this account are discussed below. *South Lodge*, 97.

13 Hunt, *The Flurried Years*, 128. Quoted in Goldring, *South Lodge*, 130. Goldring takes this as her 'final statement' about the 'marriage' (129). Hunt to Scott-James [n.d., but Mar.–Apr.? 1921], says that Westlake had advised that German domicility (though she presumably means nationality) would protect Ford from a charge of bigamy: Texas. Certainly by 28 Mar. 1917, when it came to a question of property she didn't consider she was legally married in England. She wrote in her diary that they argued and Ford said South Lodge 'was half his—he had a *right* to a room in it', statements she found 'Astounding', and wondered: 'Does he believe them?': Secor and Secor, *The Return of the Good Soldier*, 53. But it's unclear whether she was astounded that Ford considered they were married, or that he thought any rights based on their marriage could be upheld in England.

14 Ford sent postcards to Christina from Trier on 29 Sept. and 3 Oct. A cryptic passage about Hunt from a letter to Stella Bowen, 5 May 1919, may be hinting that there never was a marriage: 'And I have one thing up my sleeve that w^d. absolutely damn her to hell for ever with everyone that I w^d. use if she tried anything on against you, here.' Berryman, *Stephen Crane* (London: Methuen & Co. Ltd., 1950), 186.

15 pp. xi, ix, xiii, xi. Preface to *Thornicroft's Model* by Mrs Alfred Hunt (Margaret Raine Hunt) (London: Chatto and Windus, 1912). The proofs of the preface are at Cornell, with 'Ford's Pref' pencilled in by Violet Hunt. The attribution is doubtful. Both the proofs and Chatto's list of new books for 1912 attribute it to Violet Hunt. It does not sound much like Ford, though he may have helped with it. In her late dementia Violet Hunt may have confused this preface with the one

written by Ford to *The Governess*, an unfinished novel by Mrs Hunt which Ford and Violet Hunt completed and published also in 1912. I have been unable to find a copy of the published book of the 1912 *Thornicroft's Model*, although it received several reviews. It is possible that Chatto decided to suppress it because of the *Throne* case.

16 *Daily News* (12 July 1911), 3.

17 Hunt, *The Flurried Years*, 159, 144, 160, 185. Hunt thought she heard of the marriage when in Paris in 1910, but Rosamond married the following year. See Belford, *Violet*, 226. On Violet and Rosamond, see also Mizener, 200; Goldring, *South Lodge*, 93; and Hardwick, *An Immodest Violet*, 98. Violet implies Ford wrote '[To] All the Dead' while in Paris early in 1911, at about the time that they 'lunched with Arnold Bennett and his new wife' (160). Bennett's *Journals* note seeing Hunt twice on 16 Jan. 1911: for lunch with the author, Beryl de Zoete, then after dinner, when she called with Ford, and they stayed 'till 12.15'. However, 'To All the Dead' was first published in *High Germany* (London: Duckworth and Co., [1912]), which bears the dates of composition: '*Paris*, Sep. 6th–*Giessen*, Nov. 1st MCMXI.' The later date is borne out by the poem itself, which describes a train journey from Paris to Trêves (Trier) made after the first week in September. Hunt mentions having been in Trier at that time: *The Flurried Years*, 193, 198. *The Desirable Alien* has a chapter on Trier, pp. 269–93; but on p. 272 Hunt says Ford had been to Rome just before arriving at Trier; whereas Ford sent postcards to Christina from Trier on 29 Sept. and 3 Oct., but was in Rome from about 18 to 27 Nov. (see n. 23 below). Ford was probably alone in Paris, getting his teeth finished, while Hunt made her quick trip back to England. Also see Mizener, 218. 'On Impressionism', 174.

18 Ford to Julie Ford, 11 Sept. 1935: *Letters*, 238.

19 Mizener, 558, n. 7. *Mr. Fleight*, 152–3.

20 Hunt, *The Flurried Years*, 193–9. ['Plan of an Autobiographical Novel']: Cornell. The plot went into *The House of Many Mirrors* (London: Stanley Paul, 1915), though Hunt used an omniscient rather than a first-person narration. The plan is written on the stationery of the Grand Hotel de Laeken, Spa, which is presumably where they stayed during one of their visits. It is also where the novel's heroine, called Rosamond, stays: see 272.

21 Hunt, *The Flurried Years*, 198–9. Mizener, 218. *Daily Mirror* (21 Oct. 1911), 3. Mizener says Ford played into the paper's hands. One of its reporters had questioned Robert Garnett about Ford and Hunt in October: Garnett to Elsie, 16 Oct. 1911. He advised her to tell her solicitor Sturges to warn the papers that they would be calling Hunt 'Mrs Hueffer' at their own risk. Since it was the paper which faced damages when Elsie threatened to sue in January, Ford might have wanted to use them as a shield behind which to test Elsie's resolve.

22 Hunt, *The Flurried Years*, 199. Belford, *Violet*, 181. Garnett, diary entries for 23 and 26 Oct., 8 Nov., 7 and 11 Dec. 1911: quoted by Moser, 99–100. Did Ford really misremember his daughters' ages? Or was he deliberately introducing errors so that he could later say he had been misreported?

23 Mizener (who omits this Italian trip) says they returned to England 'early in December' (218). But the editorial preface to the *Collier's* article says Ford was 'sent from London to Rome'. If this is accurate, Ford must have returned from

Germany to London in Nov., since he was in Rome reporting on the ceremonies at the American College from Monday 20 to Thursday 23 Nov. and describes having been there from at least Saturday [the 18th]. He was still in Rome on 27 Nov. (when he sent postcards to Christina and Katharine: Cornell). Hunt gives an account of their rough channel-crossing back to England, with Ford stumbling to the steward's cabin, 'where he keeps his champagne. . . . "You can't be sick here, sir!" "I can! gravely, and was." ', claiming that 'the anecdote was in *Punch* next week': *The Flurried Years*, 200. But there is no mention of Ford in *Punch* from Oct. to Jan. He may have returned from *Rome* in early December. (*The Flurried Years*, 200, says he was crossing back for Mrs Aria's At Home, which Belford says was on 3 Dec. 1911: *Violet*, 185. But there is no evidence that Hunt accompanied him there. Indeed, in *The Desirable Alien*, she describes herself as 'a woman who has never seen Rome and never hopes to do so': 272. Ford wrote of being in Rome in *Return to Yesterday*, 330–3; though he remembered the visit as taking place in the summer. *'Just People': typescript at Cornell; 8–9. The 'justness' of the woman's accusation may have seemed sharper after the war, when Ford's life had doubled its own pattern with a bitter separation from Hunt. Could Ford have thought his brother Oliver was his 'flagitious double'?

24 *'Just People', 9. Marconi sent the first message across the Atlantic (from Cornwall) in 1901. In 'The Baron', *Macmillan's*, 87 (Feb. 1903), 304–20, Ford mentions 'the Marconi pole' and telegrams (317). Katya sends a marconigram in *A Call* (97–8); so Ford was not entirely innocent of the nature of wireless in 1911. But *Collier's* was certainly proud of the technology, mentioning it twice in the introduction to Ford's article.

25 'The Investiture of the American Cardinals', *Collier's*, 48 (16 Dec. 1911), 11.

26 Jean Rhys, *Quartet* (Harmondsworth: Penguin Books, 1973), 74.

27 'An Interview with Janice Biala (1979)', in *The Presence of Ford Madox Ford*, 225.

28 The two instalments went to Pinker on 22 and 27 Dec. See Mizener, 559–60, n. 26. The novel was published in June 1912 by Constable and Co., and revised for American publication as *Ring for Nancy* (Indianapolis: Bobbs-Merrill Company, 1913). Ford to Pinker, 3 June 1912: *Reader*, 474–5.

29 Ford may have hoped Potter would put on the more obviously stageable *Panel* too. A dramatization was prepared by E. Lyall Swete around 1912–13, but appears not to have been produced: Swete to Ford, 26 July 1912 and 6 Feb. 1919: Cornell. See Hynes, *The Edwardian Turn of Mind*, ch. 8, esp. pp. 282 (on the relation between the Crusade for Social Purity and the fear of war), 291 (on the circulating libraries and the policing of morals, and 301–2 (on the complaint against James). When Boots Libraries had refused to circulate Hunt's *White Rose of Weary Leaf*, 'on the score of impropriety', she wrote to protest, arguing that it was 'a serious attempt to trace out the result of moral deviation in the character and fate of certain persons with the greatest possible degree of reticence compatible with clearness and an avo[i]dance of all superficial glossing over of main issues of right and wrong'; and she enclosed her photograph, asking 'if you think it looks like the authoress of an improper novel': [n.d., but 1908–9].

30 'Joseph Conrad', *English Review*, 10 (Dec. 1911), 78, 82. 'Young American Abroad', *Saturday Review of Literature*, 1 (20 Sept. 1924), 121–2.

31 See Karl, 707. John Batchelor, *The Edwardian Novelists* (London: Duckworth, 1982), 116, takes *The Simple Life Limited* as evidence for his crude argument that

Ford hated Conrad by 1911. But the novel was finished in the spring of 1910. Whereas this exchange suggests that writing the novel had purged his bitterness over the 1909 quarrel, and that by 1911 he was already seeking a rapprochement. If Conrad knew of the book, he appeared able to forgive Ford. Mizener, 218 and 559, n. 22. Conrad to Ford, 21 Dec. 1911; to Lucas, 14 June 1909: *Collected Letters*, iv. 524–5; 243–4. Conrad to Ford, [26] December 1911, ibid., 528–9, asks Ford and Hunt to drive over to lunch on Saturday [30 Dec.]. Hunt, *The Flurried Years*, 202–4. Belford, *Violet*, 185–6. Hunt says the house was at Sandgate, but Conrad to Ford, 2 Feb. 1912 (Harvard) was sent to Sunnyside, Littlestone-on-Sea, Kent. Mizener, 559, n. 22, gets confused, not realizing that Lady Byron married the multi-millionaire shipowner Sir Robert Houston, MP, in 1924. He says Ford was in Sandgate in March. See Comyns Beaumont, *A Rebel in Fleet Street* (London: Hutchinson, 1944), 135.

32 *Throne*, 5 (25 Oct. 1911), 142–3. The Frankfurt waiter is also mentioned in *Ancient Lights*, 79, in a passage which first appeared in *Harper's* in Mar. 1911. Thus the encounter must have taken place between autumn 1910 and early 1911. Ford sent postcards to Christina and Katharine from Frankfurt on 30 Nov. 1910. He first described the tramp in *The Heart of the Country*, 45, which shows that the first meeting alone made the strong impression he recalled. The unpublished MS *'Just People' reworks the story (2–6). Another version is in *Return to Yesterday* (London, 1931), 308–11. The episode may be an oblique source for the climactic hotel scene in *The Marsden Case*, 323–37, in which the story of the waiter who is almost dismissed after upsetting a sauce-boat over George's boots suggests that Ford was still disturbed by the reminiscence in 1922.

33 *'Just People', 5; written between 1919 and 1922. The essay is explicitly written to work through Ford's feelings about fate, which (he explains) had been heightened by the war; he now had a further set of 'inexpressibly troubled' recollections to be affected by.

34 The story of the German teacher, from *Ancient Lights*, 79, is discussed on pp. 40–1 above. *Return to Yesterday*, 217–18.

35 Hunt, *The Flurried Years*, 201–2. Tebb certified (during the *Throne* case in 1913) that 'this bout of neurasthenia' was triggered by a 'nervous shock' around Christmas 1911: see Goldring, *South Lodge*, 104.

Chapter 23

1 Hunt, *The Flurried Years*, 206, says Ford helped with the novel, though this could mean that he helped by writing the preface. On the same page she says it was 'finished by me', and Ford's preface bears this out (p. xvii). Robert and Marie Secor say that Ford helped Violet to complete the book after her mother's death; but Mrs Hunt did not die until 1 Nov. 1912: Secor and Secor, *The Return of the Good Soldier*, 18. Chatto and Windus to Pinker, 1 Dec. 1911 (Northwestern). Mizener, 219, argues that the publishers wished to spare themselves a lawsuit. But they would also have felt that 'Violet Hunt' was a more familiar name to readers, and that using it would demonstrate that the mother's novel had been completed by the daughter. Chatto did not censor Ford's reference to Violet as 'Mrs Hueffer' in his preface to the book; which supports the idea that they were concerned more

with sales than with litigation (especially since this argument preceded the *Daily Mirror*'s 'Withdrawal and Apology'.

2 *Daily Mirror (8 Jan. 1912), 3. Moser, 99–100. Olive had had 'A grand Xmas Dinner' with Elsie the fortnight before. *Daily Express* (8 Feb. 1913), 5.

3 *Bystander, 32 (15 Nov. 1911)–33 (6 Mar. 1912): see Moser, 311, though he misdates the first article as 8 Nov. 1911. Mizener, 220. Ford to Harold Monro, 23 Jan. 1912 (British Library: I am grateful to Mrs Joy Grant for information about this letter).

4 Pound to Isabel Pound, 21 Oct. 1911; 21 February 1912; to Homer Pound, 14 Mar. 1912: Yale; see *Pound/Ford*, 9. *Ezra Pound and Margaret Cravens*, 108. James noted in his diary for Apr. 1912: 'Met Violet Hunt and F. M. Hueffer and went home with them for half an hour': Leon Edel, *Henry James: The Master 1901–1916* (London: Rubert Hart-Davis, 1972), 434. Conrad to Ford, 19 Feb. 1912: British Library [Ashley 2923*]. Conrad to Galsworthy [end of Mar., 1912]: Jean-Aubry, *Joseph Conrad: Life and Letters* (London: Heinemann, 1927), ii. 138–9. Moser, 98.

5 Review of Hedwig Sonntag, *Max von Bahring und Seine Freundinnen*, *Daily News* (13 Feb. 1912), 3.

6 Hunt, *The Flurried Years*, 61, 202. West, interview with Mizener: see his typescript 'Notes on an interview . . . Rebecca West': Cornell. Lawrence to Edward Garnett, 10 Feb. 1912: *Letters*, i. 363–5. Goldring, *South Lodge*, 92.

7 'Mrs. Hueffer Wins her Libel Suit', *Daily Mirror* (8 Feb. 1913), 4: reproduced by Mizener, illustrations following 296. Belford, *Violet*, 198. According to *The Times* (7 Feb. 1913), 3, the arrangement to pay Elsie through Byles ended around May (the *Express* report says June). Ford and Hunt presumably hoped the freeze would persuade Elsie to drop her suit against the *Throne*. D. Garnett, *The Golden Echo*, 183. Mizener, 547, n. 14, 131. Katharine Hueffer Lamb to Mizener, 18 Jan. 1967.

8 Mizener, 221. Lawrence to Edward Garnett, 5 April 1912: *Letters*, i. 381–2. Hunt was perhaps exaggerating the seriousness of Ford's condition to excuse the fact that he had only just returned the MSS of two of Lawrence's plays—*A Collier's Friday Night* and 'The Merry-go-Round'—that he had had since at least 6 Oct. 1911, and then lost: Lawrence to Garnett: ibid. 309. Ford to Pinker, 3 June 1912: *Reader*, 474–5.

9 *The New Humpty-Dumpty*, 303–4. Mizener, 228. The passage casts doubt on Hunt's suggestion that Ford was able to concentrate on his work by excluding her anxieties: *The Flurried Years*, 213.

10 *The Flurried Years*, 211. *This Monstrous Regiment of Women* is repr. in the *Reader*, 304–17. The stories are: 'The Fun of Genius', *English Review*, 13 (Dec. 1912), 52–63; and *'The Medium's End', *Bystander*, 33 (13 Mar. 1912), 551–2, 554. He also reviewed H. M. Tomlinson's *The Sea and the Jungle* in *Rhythm*, 2 (Dec. 1912), pp. iv–vii. Hunt says that he was writing poetry too (*The Flurried Years*, 215), but if he did none of it is known to have survived.

11 Goldring, *The Last Pre-Raphaelite*, 163.

12 Bradbury, 'Introduction', *Parade's End* (London: Everyman's Library, 1992), p. viii. *Grace Lovat Fraser (née Crawford), *In the Days of My Youth* (London: Cassell, 1970), 140–1. *Return to Yesterday*, 427.

13 Fraser, *In the Days of My Youth*, 128, 141. There is evidence that Mrs Hunt could be even more difficult when alone with Violet. In some notes for her lawyer, Humphreys, presumably written in connection with her sister's suit over the

management of their mother's estate she wrote: 'I have always regarded the gifts as bribes to me to stay on in the house with her, & as solaciums after a prolonged period of bullying & bad temper when I had been made rather ill by being waked [?] (waked up at night by her coming in to make recriminations) hitting me & throwing glasses of dirty water in my face': n.d. Of course she may have been exaggerating to strengthen her case. *Epstein: An Autobiography* (London: Hulton Press, 1955), 60.

14 *Outlook*, 30 (5 Oct. 1912), 460-1; ['Rebecca West'] *English Review*, 12 (September 1912), 332; *TLS* (8 May 1912), 199; *Bookman* (London), 42 (August 1912), 220.

15 [West], *English Review*, 12 (Sept. 1912), 332; repr. and attributed in *Ford Madox Ford: The Critical Heritage*, 40-1. Hunt, *The Flurried Years*, 213.

16 Patmore, *My Friends When Young*, 52. West to G. B. Stern, paraphrased by Victoria Glendinning, *Rebecca West* (London: Weidenfeld and Nicolson, 1987), 38. West to Mizener, 16 Apr. 1968: Cornell. Elizabeth Robins to Hunt, 8 June 1912 (Cornell), accepts the invitation for 2 July. Hunt, *The Flurried Years*, 214-15.

17 Hunt to Cathy Hueffer, 12 May [1912]: House of Lords. Mizener, 228. He says the meeting with Mansfield must have been in Aug., citing Anthony Alpers' first biography of her. However, from the chronology in Alpers' second, fuller, life it must have happened after 4 Sept.; Ford and Hunt left for the north at the end of Sept., so the meeting is more likely to have happened during that month: Alpers, *The Life of Katherine Mansfield* (New York: The Viking Press, 1980), 148-50, 407. Hunt and Ford called on Pound on 23 Sept. to summon him to tea the day before they left London. Pound to Shakespear [17 and 14 Sept. 1912]: *Ezra Pound and Dorothy Shakespear*, 158-9, 155, 161. Lewis, *Rude Assignment* (London: Hutchinson, [1950]), 121-2. Hunt, *The Flurried Years*, 219-20. There are postcards (at Cornell) from Ford to Christina and Katharine from Durham (27? and 30 Sept.); Alnwick (1 Oct.); Bamburgh (4 Oct.); Edinburgh (9 Oct.); and Durham again (11 Oct.).

18 Lawrence to Ford, 10 Dec. 1912: *Letters*, i. 485-6. Pound to Shakespear [22 Dec. 1912]: *Ezra Pound and Dorothy Shakespear*, 167.

19 Faith Compton Mackenzie, *As Much as I Dare* (London: Collins, 1938), 271-2. Mizener says Ford's state was due to the fact that Elsie wouldn't let him spend Christmas with Christina and Katharine: but he gives no source; 229.

20 Ezra Pound to Isabel Pound, 24 Dec. [1912]. D. D. Paige, in *The Letters of Ezra Pound* (New York: Harcourt Brace, 1950), 28 misdates this letter 1913. See *Ezra Pound and Dorothy Shakespear*, 166 (Pound [22 Dec. 1912] saying he's going for a week) and 171 (written from 'Casa di Jiovanni Miltoni, Burnham Beeches', according to Pound [28 Dec. 1912]).

21 Mizener, 229.

22 23 Jan. 1913: *Letters*, 53-6; though I have followed Frank MacShane's partial transcription in *Critical Writings of Ford Madox Ford* (Lincoln: University of Nebraska Press, 1964), 153-5, in reading 'condemnation' instead of Ludwig's 'combination'. The formal salutation, 'Dear Mrs Masterman', suggests Ford was writing a letter she could show to publishers, as he had for Lawrence. The Latin *hominibus bonae voluntatis* means 'to men of good will'—a favourite expression of Ford's, that connotes the sympathetic listener, reader, or correspondent.

23 Hunt, *The Flurried Years*, 226; 223 says that Hunt persuaded Ford to return to Germany in the New Year, in order to settle his naturalization. But, as Mizener

(561, n. 16) shows, Ford was in London on 23 Jan., and in Amiens on 6 Feb. Mizener says it is impossible he returned to Giessen; it's unlikely, but he was travelling a great deal between 1910 and 1914, and may have felt that another change of scene would reduce anxiety about the trial. However, if Hunt is right, and if Ford's German naturalization was not secure, then she is inadvertently casting doubt on their claim to have been married. The Giessen Stadtarchiv records Ford as being at Giessen from 3 Oct. 1910 to 1 May 1913. It's hard to see where they got the latter date from if Ford were not in fact there in Apr. (unless that were simply the date on which the authorities discovered, perhaps from his lawyer, that he had left). Mizener (233) says that Hunt rejoined Ford in Boulogne the day after the trial, and that their trip to the south of France lasted until their return to London in May. However, the only evidence he cites is a letter from May Sinclair to Hunt of 10 May 1913, printed in Goldring, *South Lodge*, 111. Yet Goldring gives no indication of where the letter was sent to. They—or Ford alone, though this is less likely—could have revisited Giessen in April. This would make more sense of Hunt's very definite statement that she insisted Ford returned to Giessen: she may just have misremembered in placing the trip before the trial. On the other hand, there is no other evidence than the archive entry that they were in Germany in Apr. 1913; though *The Flurried Years*, 237, says she was 'egging' Ford to go to Germany in the spring of 1913. *South Lodge*, 104–5, 114. The American edition of *The Flurried Years*, retitled *I Have This to Say* (New York: Boni and Liveright, 1926), 226–7, prints a different letter from Tebb. Mizener, 230. 'Literary Portraits—LIII.: The Muse of War', *Outlook*, 34 (12 Sept. 1914), 334–5.

24 Goldring, *South Lodge*, 103. Mizener, 561, n. 18. *The Times* (7 Feb. 1913), 3.

25 **The Times* (8 Feb. 1913), 3. Goldring, *South Lodge*, 102–3.

26 'Book Notice Libel: Novelist's Wife Gets £300 Damages: What a Lady Believes Her Position Is', *Daily Herald* (8 Feb. 1913), 3: Harvey, 313. Mizener, 230. **'Mrs Hueffer Wins her Libel Suit', *Daily Mirror* (8 Feb. 1913), 4.

27 When she published *The Flurried Years* in 1926 Hunt was still maintaining—as she did for the rest of her life—that she thought she was married to Ford. In 1924 she wrote to the *Weekly Westminster*, no. 12 (NS) (19 Jan. 1924), 388 to correct its error about Ford's poems. She referred to him as 'my husband', and signed the letter 'Violet Hunt Hueffer'. Mizener, 229–30. *The Flurried Years*, 224–5. Beaumont, *A Rebel in Fleet Street* (London: Hutchinson & Co. (Publishers) Ltd. [1944]), 75–6. *Return to Yesterday*, 235. Hunt was still dining with Byles in 1917: see *The Return of the Good Soldier*, 45, 57.

28 Hunt, *The Flurried Years*, 233. Cornell has Ford's postcards to his daughters from Amiens (6 Feb.), Beauvais (8 Feb.), Montpellier (10 Feb.), Carcassonne (14 Feb.) [where they had arrived by the 13th, and stayed until at least the 23rd: Hunt to Cathy Hueffer, 13 Feb. 1913 (House of Lords)], St Rémy de Provence (25 Feb.), Avignon (26 Feb.), Arles (28 Feb.), Tarascon (5 Mar.), St Rémy again (5, 6, 9, 13, 18, 19, 20, and 21 Mar.), Beaucaire (20 Mar.), Corsica (every day from 26 to 30 Mar.), Nice (31 Mar.). *The Flurried Years*, 237. When he revised *Ladies Whose Bright Eyes* for the 1935 edition, he gave the dates of composition as 'Carcassonne, Nov. 1910. New York, Dec. 1934'. C. H. Sisson rightly says that 'The published *Letters* make it unlikely that he set eyes on Carcassonne at this time' ('An Afterword' to *Ladies Whose Bright Eyes* (Manchester: Carcanet, 1988), 300). I have

found no other evidence that he was there in 1910—he was too busy shuttling between Giessen and England. Yet it seems unjust to say, as Sisson does, that 'the mention of Provence was a retrospective cover-up of the kind to which he was notoriously given'. What, over thirty years later, could he have been trying to cover up? His 'confused attempt to obtain German citizenship'? It's much more likely that, having only his distant memories to rely on, he confused his two historical and visionary novels of this period: he remembered writing one of them in Carcassonne, and mistook Oct. 1910 (when he was indeed writing *Ladies*) for Feb. 1913. Mizener, 231. *The Flurried Years*, 236-42. On 254 she calls the Frenchman 'Monsieur le Capitaine Taste'; she calls the hotel 'Jordy's': Jordy was the proprietor of the Hôtel de la Cité (see Hunt to Cathy Hueffer, 19 Feb. [1913]: House of Lords). *A Mirror to France*, 276-8. See *Henry James*, 104, on James's description of Carcassonne in *A Little Tour in France*.

29 Violet's undated 'Notes for autobiography' (Cornell), 8. This draft also describe Russell's trial (he was sentenced to three months in 1901), and also lists more recent cases. Russell was Bertrand's elder brother; his unsuccessful bill to liberalize divorce laws is discussed by Hynes, *The Edwardian Turn of Mind*, 186-92. Their friend E. S. P. Haynes wrote an essay on 'Divorce Law Reform', *English Review*, 3 (Nov. 1909), 724-9. Ford mentioned his work in *Some Do Not . . .*, 228. Mizener, 233.

30 Hunt, *The Flurried Years*, 240-1, 236-7. Conrad to Ford, 27 Mar. 1913 (Ashley 2923*, British Library). Hunt (probably exaggerating the extent to which she financed Ford) said the demand was for £440 (and Mizener, 232, repeats this figure), but Conrad's letter says Marwood has given Ford six months to repay £40. Moser, 110-11 and 308, n. 57, assumes Conrad either made a mistake, or was only talking of the interest on the original loan. But Conrad writes 'forty' later in the letter; he didn't omit a zero. And if Marwood felt he was dying, surely he would have asked for repayment of the entire debt, not just the interest. Mizener, 137 n., cites Goldring, and assumes his information came from Ford. But in fact the passage he cites, *The Last Pre-Raphaelite*, 166, quotes *The Flurried Years*; so there is no other evidence to confirm the scale of Marwood's demand in 1913. Mizener also says the Marwood family claimed the debt was never repaid.

31 Ford to Pinker [21 Mar. 1913]: Princeton. James Gindin, *John Galsworthy's Life and Art* (London: Macmillan, 1987), 81-2, 154-5. *Mightier Than the Sword*, 175. This essay, 'Galsworthy', was written between Dec. 1935 and Apr. 1936 (when it was first published in the *American Mercury*).

32 Mrs Clifford to Hunt, 11 Mar. 1913. Quoted in Goldring, *South Lodge*, 108.

33 Goldring, *South Lodge*, 108-9. Goldring transcribed this from an unsigned draft; but presumably something similar was sent, judging from Mrs Clifford's reply, quoted by him on 109.

34 Hunt to Cathy Hueffer, 13 and 19 Feb. 1913: House of Lords. Mizener, 232.

35 Goldring, *South Lodge*, 111-12. *Nation and Athenaeum*, 35 (24 May 1924), 258, quoted by Mizener, 257, says *Some Do Not . . .* presents 'an England that Englishmen generally will have some difficulty in recognizing'. John Carey, 'Soldier Blues', *Sunday Times* (3 June 1990), Section 8, 1. Melvin Seiden, 'Persecution and Paranoia in *Parade's End*', *Criticism*, 8/3 (Summer 1966), 246-62; repr. in *Ford Madox Ford: Modern Judgements*, ed. Richard Cassell (London: Macmillan, 1972), 153-68.

36 Mizener, 207. *No More Parades*, 252. Pound, '[The Inquest]' [1924?], *Pound/Ford*, 70.

37 Mizener, 232–35. *Return to Yesterday*, 240–2. Ford to Pinker, [Feb. 1913] and 4 Mar. 1913: *Reader*, 475–6. Mizener calls Ford's story 'exaggerated', arguing that the book was widely reviewed. But review copies would have been sent out before publication, whereas the remaining stock could still have been impounded soon afterwards. There was a later colonial edition (see Harvey, 38–9). Ford to Pinker, 21 Nov. 1913, lamenting his poor earnings, and saying: 'Of course you will reply that "Mr. Fleight" is my own fault—and so it is', confirms that Ford can't have made money on the book: *Letters*, 57–8.

38 See Mizener, 234–7 for a fine discussion of the book. Also Bryan Cheyette, *Constructions of 'The Jew' in English Literature and Society: Racial Representations, 1875–1945* (Cambridge: Cambridge University Press, 1993). *Mr. Fleight*, 14, 253, 91, 194, 193. Moser, 112.

39 *Mr. Fleight*, 117–18. In 'And on Earth Peace', *New York Herald Tribune Books* (26 Dec. 1926), 1, 6. Ford told a similar story about a man shamed by echoes of his divorce case. Both versions have striking similarities with the vignette of the golfer on the verge of ruin in *Henry James*, 154–5.

40 'Joseph Conrad', *English Review*, 10 (Dec. 1911), 68, contains the comment: 'Now I do not like Jews', then goes on to express admiration of the respect for literature shown to him by a Belgian Jew. Such a comment needs to be set alongside Ford's pro-Zionist campaigning in the 1930s, discussed in volume 2. *Ancient Lights*, 295. *Mr. Fleight*, 247, 138, 208, 234, 238.

41 *Mr. Fleight*, 166–7, 220, 172–3, 56. See n. 47 below for a discussion of when Ford met Patmore. *The Good Soldier*, 273.

42 Hunt, *The Flurried Years*, 242. Mizener, p. 233, says Hunt stayed in France until they came back together in May. Perhaps she rejoined him after the hearing on 28 Mar. Garnett, quoted by Moser, 100. If Ford's recollection is correct of being in London while Byles was publicizing *Mr. Fleight*, then he must have been back at the end of Apr. or the start of May. The novel was probably published on 30 Apr.: Harvey, 39. Conrad to Ford, 27 Mar. 1913, was re-directed from St Rémy to Corsica, and thence to the Farleys in Paris. 'Self ats Hueffer' (acquired by Cornell in 1991, and apparently not known by Mizener) is headed 'S[outh] L[odge] C[ampden] H[ill] R[oad]', and dated 27 May 1913. *The New Humpty-Dumpty*, 306–9. William Sturges to Katharine Hueffer Lamb, 28 Feb. 1945: Cornell. Sturges later wrote to Hamish Hamilton that his firm no longer had the relevant papers: 10 May 1966: Cornell.

43 Hunt, *The Flurried Years*, 243. Goldring, *South Lodge*, 112–13. Jepson, *Memories of an Edwardian* (London: Martin Secker, 1938), 154.

44 Aldington, in *New Directions: Number Seven* (Norfolk, Conn.: New Directions, 1942), 456–8. Mizener, 238. Patmore, *My Friends When Young*, 51–2. MacShane, *The Life and Work of Ford Madox Ford* (London: Routledge & Kegan Paul, 1965), 124. William Wees, *Vorticism and the English Avant-Garde* (Toronto and Buffalo: University of Toronto Press, 1972), 44. Ford to Scott-James [January 1914?]: *Letters*, 58–9. Kathleen Cannell, 'Portrait of a Kindly Eccentric', *Providence Sunday Journal* (20 Sept. 1964), W-20.

45 'Portrait of a Kind Eccentric'. Mizener, 238.

46 Kathleen Cannell to Mizener, 26 May 1964.

47 Goldring, *South Lodge*, 115. Patmore, *My Friends When Young*, 52. There is some confusion about exactly when they met. Derek Patmore's Introduction is firm about how he was 4 years old when Brigit met Ford (he is refuting Ford's playful suggestion that he might have been Derek's father!); 9. Since Derek was born in Jan. 1908 (p. 5) this would place their meeting in 1912. Yet some of Brigit's reminiscences suggest an earlier date: she recalls Hunt's 'pretty niece [Rosamond], whom she was taking out socially and she used to give luncheons for her at the Reform Club'; but this must have been before the middle of 1910, when Rosamond was summoned back home. She also says Ford had 'just started' the *English Review*, which suggests 1908–9 rather than 1912; and she says she 'soon realized that Violet Hunt had fallen in love' with Ford. This must be before the *Throne* case; even before Ford's announcement of their 'marriage' in 1911. Nevertheless, although Ford may have met her when Derek was younger than four, there is no evidence of Ford's feelings for her before 1913. Jepson, *Memories of an Edwardian*, 167, met Pankhurst at South Lodge around 1913. Hunt, *The Flurried Years*, 107, mentions her as a guest in 1910.

48 Patmore, *My Friends When Young*, 52–3. Mizener, 239 n., says she did not much like Ford; but her memoirs give an affectionate portrait. Hunt, entry for 20 Apr. 1917: *The Return of the Good Soldier*, 57. Rebecca West told Mizener that she thought Ford and Patmore were lovers (the notes for his interview are at Cornell).

49 Cannell to Mizener, 5 Dec. 1964. Mizener says Ford 'claimed' Brigit had given him the cross: she 'flatly denied' the story to Mizener in the 1960s; yet neither Cannell nor Hunt seemed to be in any doubt. Barry to Mizener, 31 Jan. 1967.

50 Moser, 116. Ford inscribed a copy of the novel to Patmore: Harvey, 40. *The Young Lovell*, 218.

51 Ford to Pinker, 17 Mar. [1913]: *Letters*, 56. *The Young Lovell*, 287.

52 *The Young Lovell*, p. 4. The opening of the novel is reprinted in the *Reader*, 61. Hunt, *The Flurried Years*, 243. She mentions the MS of *The Good Soldier* on the following page (claiming that she found it torn up and thrown into a dustbin at Selsey, and that she reassembled it. The MSS at Cornell bear no signs of this particular ordeal, which may be accounted for by the version she told Goldring: that she had the fragments retyped: *The Last Pre-Raphaelite*, 170. However, there are signs of slight scorching on the original MS at Cornell (Mizener, 566, n. 22). No damage has been done to the Cornell MS of *The Young Lovell* (the handwritten parts of which seem to be in Ford's hand). There *is* a typescript of some sombre love poetry written at the start of the war, and this has been torn up and pasted back together ('Tristia': Cornell). Hunt may have fused together the two works). But she has Ford working on his book with 'heart' before their Sept. trip to Germany with the Mastermans. *The Young Lovell* was probably published in Oct. Ford said he began *The Good Soldier* on his fortieth birthday, 17 Dec. 1913. Although the precise dates of its composition are impossible to establish, the novel wasn't published until Mar. 1915; Ford is unlikely to have begun it before the end of 1913. He dictated Part I to Patmore; this is most likely to have been while she was staying at Selsey in Jan. and Feb. 1914: Moser, 189, 315, n. 95 (his investigations of the MS corroborate Hunt's claim about Patmore taking dictation: Hunt, *I Have This to Say*, 210). Also see p. 369 above, and Ch. 24, nn. 12, 28 below, about Hunt's confusion of 1912 and 1914 in *The Flurried Years*.

53 *The Young Lovell*, 234, 238. Moser, 115. James to Wells, 10 July 1915: *Henry James and H. G. Wells*, ed. Leon Edel and Gordon N. Ray (London: Rupert Hart-Davis, 1959), 267.

54 *The Young Lovell*, 133. Moser, 114. Snitow, *Ford Madox Ford and the Voice of Uncertainty*, 115. Hunt, *The Flurried Years*, 123. *Return to Yesterday*, 290.

55 Preface to *The Nigger of the 'Narcissus'*; first printed as an 'Author's Note' after the serialization in the *New Review*, 17 (Dec. 1897), 628–31.

56 *Pound/Ford*, 172, 179. Goacher, 'Pictures of Ezra Pound', *Nimbus*, 3 (Winter 1956), 31–2.

57 Gordon, *A Good Soldier: A Key to the Novels of Ford Madox Ford* (University of California Library: Davis, 1963), Chapbook No. 1. Dahlberg, *Alms for Oblivion* (Minneapolis: University of Minnesota Press, 1964), 10.

58 'Sologub and Artzibashef, *Outlook*, 35 (26 June 1915), 830–1.

59 On 'vivid' see *Ancient Lights*, pp. viii, 2, 40; *Return to Yesterday*, 4, 61, 63, 106, 195, 249; and *Mightier Than the Sword*, 198. For the writer as smile (discussed vol. 2, Ch. 23) see *Henry James*, 10; *Mightier Than the Sword*, 191, 205; and *The March of Literature*, 467. 'Riesenberg' was first published in the *English Review*, 8 (Apr. 1911), 25–45. 'A Day of Battle', *Reader*, 456–61, is discussed in vol. 2. 'Literary Portraits—III.: Mr. H. G. Wells and the "Passionate Friends" ' *Outlook*, 32 (27 Sept. 1913), 414–15.

60 *The Interpretation of Dreams* (1900): *The Standard Edition of the Complete Psychological Works of Sigmund Freud*, volumes 4 and 5 (London: The Hogarth Press and the Institute of Psycho-Analysis, 1953), volume 4, p. 544.

61 See Hugh Witemeyer, *The Poetry of Ezra Pound: Forms and Renewal 1908–1920* (Berkeley and Los Angeles: University of California Press, 1969), 23–43.

62 Published between 19 Apr. and 5 July: see Harvey, 171–2. The first series appeared in the *Daily News* from 5 Sept. to 28 Nov. 1908, under the title 'A Pageant' (Harvey, 161). Both series were collected together (with the exception of the last of the *Outlook* vignettes) and incorporated into *Zeppelin Nights*, in collaboration with Hunt in 1915.

63 Mizener (241) follows Harvey (43) in assuming that *Henry James* was intended as a tribute for James's seventieth birthday. Yet the birthday fell on 15 Apr. Ford's study wasn't in proof until Sept. (Mizener, 562, n. 32); it wasn't published until 1 Jan. 1914 (Harvey, 43). Ford wrote to Macmillan on 29 May 1913 to ask to borrow (or buy at half-price) a set of James's New York Edition of 1907–9 (of which Macmillan was the English publisher) so that he could write his 'critical monograph'; on 3 June he wrote again to thank them for the loan, and ask if he could keep the books until the end of Aug. (British Library: Macmillan 55268). It is more likely that James's birthday alerted Ford to the need for such a book, which is more a tribute to James's New York Edition.

64 'In Defence of Henry James', *Bookman* (London), 45 (Mar. 1914), 302–7. *Outlook*, 33 (17 Jan. 1914), 76–7. The anonymous reviewer would have known Ford's contributions to that magazine since the spring, and probably knew Ford.

65 pp. 152–55. Cf. Hunt, *The Flurried Years*, 74, which recounts parallel episodes from 1909 and 1915. See Philip Davis's fine discussion of the significance of this passage in 'Ford's Anaesthetic', *Agenda*, 27/4–28/1 (Winter 1989–Spring 1990), 31–8.

66 Keller, 'Functional Analysis: its Pure Application', *Music Review*, 18 (1957), 202–6. Ford's use of this technique is widespread, but some of the most sustained

and effective examples of it are: the discussion of *A Call*'s ending, in the
'Epistolary Epilogue' to that novel; the discussion of how to begin stories, in
Collected Poems [1913], 10; Mr Jones's aversion to rabbit-pie, in the essay 'On
Impressionism', *Poetry and Drama*, 2 (June and December 1914), 167-75, 323-35;
the rewriting of 'The Lake Isle of Innisfree' in 'Literary Portraits—XXXIX.: Mr.
W. B. Yeats and his New Poems', *Outlook*, 33 (6 June 1914), 783-4; the poet trying
to write about the Pole Star in *Thus to Revisit*, 145-8; the skeletal novella about
Mr Slack within his 'novel' *Joseph Conrad*, 180-93; *The March of Literature*, 841,
rewriting a paragraph of Thackeray as impressionism.

67 Garnett, quoted by Moser, 100. Katharine Hueffer Lamb told Mizener 'the last time
Mum actually saw Pum must have been at Charing X Stn'—when she ambushed Ford
and Hunt in 1909 (11 Dec. 1966: Cornell). But they certainly faced each other in court
on 13 July 1910 (see Moser, 99); and probably at the bankruptcy court three years later.
Without the benefit of Garnett's diaries, Mizener (228) erroneously placed the
bankruptcy in 1912. Hunt, *The Flurried Years*, 209, talks of the 'spectre' of bankruptcy
after the summer of 1912, and says Hunt didn't think Ford 'minded the idea much'.
Ford's swerve from naming bankruptcy to 'the Courts or the Stock Exchange' in the
passage from *Henry James* (and to the Stock Exchange again in the comparable passage
from *Joseph Conrad*, 129) suggests another story.

Chapter 24

1 'On Impressionism', 330. 'Notes for a Lecture on Vers Libre', *Critical Writings of
Ford Madox Ford*, 155-6. Written in the 1920s.

2 Goldring, *People and Places* (Boston and New York: Houghton Mifflin, 1929), 284.
Ford's preface was a revised version of 'Impressionism—Some Speculations',
Poetry, 2 (Aug. and Sept. 1913), 177-87, 215-25. (See p. 32 on being 'hammered.')
Thus to Revisit, 202, 211. Pound, 'Mr. Hueffer and the Prose Tradition in Verse',
Poetry, 4 (June 1914), 111-20. It is the view still being offered by Hugh Kenner.
See e.g. his lively exploration of this aspect of Ford's prose in *A Sinking Island*
(London: Barrie and Jenkins, 1988), 86-97.

3 *Thus to Revisit*, 213. On 212 he elaborates his desire to avoid rhetorical inflation.
For other examples of the 'quiet talk' ideal see: 'Literary Portraits—XXIII.: Fydor
Dostoievsky and "The Idiot"', *Outlook*, 33 (14 Feb. 1914), 206-7; 'Literary
Portraits—XXXVI.: Les Jeunes and "Des Imagistes" (Second Notice)', *Outlook*,
33 (16 May 1914), 682-3; letter to Iris Barry, 4 July 1910: *Letters*, 87-8; *Mightier
Than the Sword*, 278.

4 Loeb, 'Ford Madox Ford's "The Good Soldier"', *London Magazine*, 3/9 (Dec.
1963), 68. *Callaghan, *That Summer in Paris* (New York: Coward-McCann Inc.,
1963), 119. Biala, in conversation with Max Saunders, 22 Sept. 1990. See Ford's
'Preface' to *The Nature of a Crime*, 11. *Ancient Lights*, 103. On 'cadence' see
'Literary Portraits—XIII.: Viscount Morley and "Politics and History"', *Outlook*,
32 (6 Dec. 1913), 790-1; 'Literary Portraits—XXXIII.: Mr. Sturge Moore and
"The Sea is Kind"', *Outlook*, 33 (25 Apr. 1914), 559-60; 'Literary Portraits—
XXXVI.: Les Jeunes and "Des Imagistes" (Second Notice)'; *Thus to Revisit*,
213-14; 'Stocktaking [. . .]: X.: The Reader', *transatlantic review*, 2/5 (Nov.
1924), 504. *Joseph Conrad*, 200-3; *No Enemy*, 132; and 'Those Were the Days',
Ford's preface to the *Imagist Anthology* (London: Chatto & Windus, 1930), p. xiii.

5 Ford to Mackenzie [3–8 Sept. 1913]: Texas; published in Mackenzie's *My Life and Times: Octave 4* (London: Chatto & Windus, 1965), 199. After the outbreak of the war the essays tended to deal with the political situation, albeit from a literary point of view. Many of these were incorporated into his two propaganda books of 1915. See Nora Tomlinson and Robert Green, 'Ford's Wartime Journalism', *Agenda*, 27/4–28/1 (Winter 1989–Spring 1990), 139–47. Richard Aldington wrote that he hoped for a collected edition of all Ford's work, 'including the best of his literary journalism': *New Directions: Number Seven*, 458. [Mackenzie] to Ford [3–8 September 1913].

6 Hunt, *The Flurried Years*, 245–58. *Swinnerton: An Autobiography*, 262. Pound to Shakespear [17 and 23 Sept. 1913]: *Ezra Pound and Dorothy Shakespear*, 256–7, 259–61. Hunt said they left on 15 [Sept.], after dining with the Mastermans on the 14th. This is probably accurate. By 18 Sept. they had got as far as Braubach (near Boppard): Ford, postcard to Katharine. *Return to Yesterday*, 420–1, gives the itinerary as from the source of the Rhine to Bingen (Hunt mentions stops at Dusseldorf, Cologne, and Assmanshäusen), then across the mountains to Trèves (Trier), Metz, and the battlefields (Hunt mentions Gravelotte, Mars-la-Tour, and Sedan). Lucy Masterman, *C. F. G. Masterman* (London: Nicholson and Watson, 1939), 259–61, doubts Hunt's Churchill story, and Ford's story about Lucy Masterman's kodak being tampered with because she was photographing militarily sensitive subjects. Goldring, *South Lodge*, 98. Hunt and Ford, *The Desirable Alien*, 322–3, shows Ford trying to convince himself and Hunt that there would be no war, yet realizing that the Germans were preparing for one.

7 Ford, Hunt, and the Mastermans to Wells, 20 Sept. 1913 (Illinois). I am grateful to Lawrence Iles for drawing it to my attention. The Mastermans' son Neville thought his parents later became estranged from Ford and Hunt after Hunt went about saying 'Poor Charlie'; implying 'either that my mother had fallen for Ford, or Ford for her, or perhaps both': letter to Max Saunders, 13 May 1986. Yet they continued on close terms throughout the war, and although Ford stopped seeing them afterwards (perhaps because they sided with Violet after Ford left her), Masterman was still quoting Ford's poetry admiringly in his *England After War* (London: Hodder and Stoughton [1922]): ch. 7 has twelve lines of 'Footsloggers' as an epigraph (144). Of course, there are two major qualifications to be made about this tenuous speculation. First, Ford may have *imagined* what the consequences would be were he to have an affair with Lucy; so if the book draws upon such imagining, it is not evidence of actual passion, let alone adultery. Secondly, this is only one of several scenarios from his own life that Ford may have drawn upon (the Hueffers' relationships with the Conrads and the Marwoods are more significant sources). Ultimately it makes little difference to a reading of the novel: what matters is the effect of the book, not where Ford's mind ranged in search of telling details.

8 Pound to Shakespear [11 Oct. 1913] says he 'Tried the Cabaret [i.e. the Cave of the Golden Calf: (see p. 461) on Tuesday [7 Oct.] with the F.M.H's [. . .]': *Ezra Pound to Dorothy Shakespear*, 270–1. Pound to Ford' [7–12] Nov. 1913; Ford to Monroe, 12 Nov. 1913: *Pound/Ford*, 21. Pound to Lowell, 26 Nov. 1913: *The Selected Letters of Ezra Pound*, 26–7.

9 Ford to Pinker, 21 Nov. 1913: Princeton. *Letters*, 57–8. I have followed Mizener's reading (244) of 'The slump has been going on', instead of 'had been'.

10 'Ford Madox Ford When he was Hueffer', *South Atlantic Quarterly*, 57 (Spring 1958), 249. Mizener, 243-5, was misled here as elsewhere by the fact that most of Ford's known surviving correspondence from this period concerns problems with publishing into taking Ford's high-handedness with businessmen as representative. Aldington, in *New Directions: Number Seven*, 457.

11 Hunt, *The Flurried Years*, 215.

12 In the 'Preface' to *On Heaven* (London and New York: John Lane, 1918), 5, Ford said: ' "On Heaven" was written, as far as I can remember, during the early months of 1914'. Goldring agrees that it 'dates from the spring of 1914 and was written at Selsey' (*The Last Pre-Raphaelite*, 175), despite Hunt's confused placing of it in 1912 in *The Flurried Years* (see n. 28 below for details of this, and further corroboration by Pound). Nevertheless, there is evidence pointing to the summer of 1913. Although she gets the year wrong, Hunt recalled Ford writing it in a 'languid airless summer'. For the acknowledgements in his 1936 *Collected Poems* Ford said the poem was 'written in 1913'. In *Return to Yesterday*, 420, he said Masterman 'had a good deal of it by heart', and drove Ford 'nearly crazy' during their German trip 'by quoting at the most inopportune moments [. . .] in his solemn and unctuous parliamentary voice'. (Though both here and in the *Collected Poems* acknowledgements Ford tells an improbable story about the *Fortnightly Review* planning to publish the poem in England, but deciding against publication after Masterman asked the advice of the Home Secretary, who said he would have to authorize a prosecution for blasphemy because 'it gave a materialist picture of heaven': *Return to Yesterday*, 420). In the preface to *On Heaven and Poems Written on Active Service*, 5-6, Ford says: 'If it is a materialist's Heaven I can't help it. I suppose I am a materialist', which sounds as if *someone* had made the charge. The home secretary's involvement might have been informal, so it is perhaps not surprising that there is no trace of the incident at the Public Records Office. But there is no trace in Pinker's files at Northwestern University, though there is correspondence from the *Fortnightly* from 1906 and from after the war. The story got taller with age, which might cast doubt on the memory of Masterman quoting 'On Heaven' in Sept. 1913.

Ezra Pound's testimony is perhaps the safest guide. He had seen Ford on 7 Oct. 1913. Yet his first known mention of 'On Heaven', sounding as if he has just heard about it, doesn't come until 7 Mar. 1914: 'Ford gave me a large dinner last evening. He has done a really fine long poem that will be in Poetry for June (bar messes)': *Ezra Pound and Dorothy Shakespear*, 315-16. This supports Ford's 1918 (but admittedly still shell-shocked) memory, that the poem was written in the first months of 1914.

13 23 Jan. 1913: *Letters*, 54. Cf. the parenthesis in *Henry James*, 103: '(I am aware that I write a little as a black Papist and, for what it is worth, a Tory mad about historic continuity.)' Mizener, 245, takes these comments to represent an invented 'conception of himself, as 'a medieval Catholic astray in the modern world'. This is certainly a persona Ford adopts; but not without irony—as in 'a *little* as a *black* Papist'.

14 Hunt, *The Flurried Years*, 216. Quoted from Hugh Kenner, *A Sinking Island* (London: Barrie & Jenkins, 1988), 93. Bunting told Kenner the story in 1980; Ford would have told Bunting when he was working for the *transatlantic review*, 1923-4 or later. Kenner says: 'I can vouch for nothing about the story save that I heard

it' (270). Though, in another version of the story told during a radio broadcast on 15 Feb. 1974, Bunting said: 'It cannot be true and yet it is so typical of Kipling that it is better tha[n] the true story might have been', it is not impossible ('The Only Uncle of the Gifted Young': transcript at Washington University, St Louis). As Kenner says, Kipling's uncle Burne-Jones knew Ford Madox Brown; and in *Something of Myself* Kipling recounts the holidays spent with the Burne-Joneses in London (Harmondsworth: Penguin Books, 1987), 39–40. Kipling was eight years older than Ford, and was being educated in England from 1871–82 (when Ford was 9).

15 'Literary Portraits—XLVI.: Professor Cowl and "The Theory of Poetry in England" ', *Outlook*, 34 (25 July 1914), 109–10. 'Stocktaking [. . .] II: Axioms and Internationalisms', *transatlantic review*, 1/2 (Feb. 1924), 58, on Heine. See e.g. Tietjens's scornful comment apropos Rossetti that: 'We're always, as it were, committing adultery [. . .] with the name of Heaven on our lips': *Some Do Not . . .*, 29.

16 Hunt, *The Flurried Years*, 217–18. 'On Heaven', 80; quotations are taken from the volume *On Heaven* unless otherwise stated. Stanford, 'The Best Poem Yet Written in the Twentieth-Century Fashion', *Agenda*, 27/4–28/1 (Winter 1989–Spring 1990), 110.

17 See Joseph Wiesenfarth, 'The Ash-Bucket at Dawn: Ford's Art of Poetry', *Contemporary Literature*, 30/2 (Summer 1989), 256. Hunt, *The Flurried Years*, 219. 'Diary of Jan. & Feb. 1914': entry for 3 Feb. *The Flurried Years*, 217. *The Good Soldier*, 126–7. The excised passages are quoted by Harvey, 191. In his preface to the volume *On Heaven* Ford said he 'determined to suppress the poem' after its American publication, because he felt it 'too sloppy', but that he was now reprinting it in the hope 'that it will bring comfort to the hearts of some of my comrades and some of the womenfolk of my comrades' (6). (This, incidentally, is a more probable explanation for the fact that it wasn't published in a magazine in England. Harold Monro asked Ford for it for the Poetry Bookshop after Ford had included it in a reading there on 15 Dec. 1914; but Ford replied that he was 'chary of publishing' it again: 16 Dec. 1914 (UCLA). It may be that in the 1930s Ford re-imagined his own desire to suppress the poem as the home secretary's desire to suppress it. Other people complained that Ford's own feelings got ascribed to them in his memoirs. See e.g. Lucy Masterman, *C. F. G. Masterman* (London: Nicholson and Watson, 1939), 402–6; quoted by Harvey, 560.

18 The poem ends with ambiguous candour on this point. The last page talks of 'lovers, married or never yet married', which, in a poem written by Ford and dedicated to Hunt, cannot but recall the doubt about whether they were married or not. Then it ends by imagining God coming over to his café table 'to welcome my dear, dear bride' (110). 'Bride' rather than 'wife', because these lovers can only marry in Heaven, not on earth; because 'in England | She had a husband' (88). In *The Nature of a Crime* the narrator is haunted by the *Liebestod* from *Tristan und Isolde*. Perhaps Ford conceived of the poem as presenting a comparable 'love in death' motif in the furthest possible register from the grand manner of Wagnerian song-drama. Ford to Iris Barry, 4 July 1918: *Letters*, 87–8.

19 'Acknowledgements' to 1936 *Collected Poems*, p. v.

20 Ford to Harold Monro, 16 Dec. 1914: UCLA. Mizener, 245.

21 23 May 1914: *The Selected Letters of Ezra Pound*, 37. Pound, 'Mr. Hueffer and the Prose Tradition in Verse', *Poetry*, 4 (June 1914), 111–20. Repr. as 'The Prose Tradition in Verse', *Literary Essays*, 373.

22 *Dubliners* (London: Grant Richards, 1914) was published in June; *A Portrait* was first serialized in the *Egoist* between 2 Feb. 1914 and 1 Sept. 1915. See Morris Beja (ed.), *James Joyce: Dubliners* and *A Portrait of the Artist as a Young Man: A Casebook* (London: Macmillan, 1973), 18–19.

23 Aldington, in *New Directions: Number Seven*, 457. Both parodies were printed in *Des Imagistes*, edited by Pound (London and New York: The Poetry Bookshop and Albert and Charles Boni, 1914), 59–62.

24 Mizener, 240. Aldington to John Atkins, 22 June 1957: Texas. Quoted in Fred Crawford, *Mixing Memory and Desire* (University Park and London: Pennsylvania State University Press, 1982), 7. Stanley Coffman, *Imagism* (Norman: University of Oklahoma Press, 1951), 42–3. 'From China to Peru', *Outlook*, 35 (19 June 1915), 800–1. The gist of this fine review is reprinted in *Pound/Ford*, 25–6. Wiesenfarth, 'The Ash-Bucket at Dawn'. 'Literary Portraits—XXXIII.: Mr. Sturge Moore and "The Sea is Kind" ' (25 Apr. 1914): 'the poetic frame of mind is induced solely by the rendering of concrete objects'; 'he renders such objects as shall induce a thrilling of the kind desired in the reader'. Ford restated the argument in the second notice of *Des Imagistes* in the *Outlook* (16 May 1914): 'any very clear and defined rendering of any material object has power to convey to the beholder or to the reader a sort of quivering of very definite emotions'. He returned to the idea in his preface to the *Imagist Anthology*: 'Those Were the Days', p. xiii. Pound had argued in 1911–12 that: 'Technique is the means of conveying an exact impression of exactly what one means in such a way as to exhilarate': 'I Gather the Limbs of Osiris', *Selected Prose*, 33. Eliot's pamphlet on Pound is reprinted in *To Criticize the Critic*; see 181. Eliot, 'Hamlet and his Problems', *Athenaeum* (26 Sept. 1919), 940–1; repr. as 'Hamlet', *Selected Essays*, 3rd edn. (London: Faber and Faber, 1951), 141–6.

25 Kenner, 'The Poetics of Speech', in *Ford Madox Ford: Modern Judgements*, ed. R. Cassell (London: Macmillan, 1972), 172. The argument is reworked in *A Sinking Island*, 92. Ellen Williams, *Harriet Monroe and the Poetry Renaissance* (Urbana: University of Illinois Press, 1972), 127, quoting Pound to Harriet Monroe, dated 'July 1915' by Monroe.

26 'On a Notice of "Blast" ', *Outlook*, 36 (31 July 1915), 143–4. Ford also wrote appreciatively about Eliot's verse in 'Literary Causeries: X. Mystifications', *Chicago Tribune* (Paris) (20 Apr. 1924), 3; *Thus to Revisit*, 136; *Return to Yesterday*, 180. Pound told Harriet Monroe: 'You can take Hueffer's commendation of Eliot to back up mine, if it's any use to you': 2 Oct. 1915: *Selected Letters*, 63–4. Preface to *Collected Poems* [1913], 17. Wiesenfarth, 'The Ash-Bucket at Dawn'.

27 p. 17.

28 'Dedicatory Letter to Stella Ford', dated 9 January 1927, and first published in the 1927 second American edition; repr. in the Oxford World's Classics text, pp. 1–4. In *Return to Yesterday* (1931), 429, he refers to *The Good Soldier* as 'my one novel'. Mizener, 245, doubts Ford's story about starting the book on his birthday, arguing that he probably started it in the summer as soon as he had finished *Henry James*. But the only evidence he cites is *The Flurried Years*, 215–16; but Hunt says (211) that she is describing the summer of 1912. She also ascribes the composition of 'On Heaven' to this period, whereas it was written in 1913 or 1914 (see n. 12 above). Pound wrote to Dorothy Shakespear on 7 Mar. 1914 that Ford's 'new

novel is—as far as it has gone—above his others': *Ezra Pound and Dorothy Shakespear*, 316. The editors gloss this as *The Young Lovell*, published in Oct. 1913. But it's more likely to have been *The Good Soldier*, 'as far as it has gone', if Ford read Pound the incomplete MS. The suggestion that the novel had not got very far by Mar. confirms a starting-date of Dec. rather than July–Sept. Ford has come back to London from Selsey, where he had been since at least the end of Dec. (Ford to A. G. Gardiner [n.d., but end of Dec. 1913: British Library of Political and Economic Science [at the London School of Economics]). The only other evidence that he might have begun *The Good Soldier* in the summer of 1913, which Mizener doesn't cite, is *The Flurried Years*, 243. There Hunt says that in the summer of 1913 Ford was writing a book that would have 'heart' in it. The next page mentions *The Good Soldier*, which has plenty of 'hearts' in it. Yet, as I have argued above, p. 383, this could equally refer to *The Young Lovell*. The publication of that book was planned for 6 Oct. 1913 (Chatto and Windus to Pinker, 29 Sept. 1913: Northwestern); so Ford would probably have been working on it until Aug. It is hard to see how he would have had time to start a new novel that summer. He is unlikely to have finished *Henry James* before the end of Aug. (Ford to Macmillan, 3 June 1913, asks to keep the James edition until the end of August: British Library; Macmillan 55268). He was writing 'Historical Vignettes' until 5 July. The first part of 'Impressionism—Some Speculations' came out in *Poetry*, 2, in Aug. (pp. 177–87: the essay was revised to form the preface to the 1914 *Collected Poems*). Ford *was* in Selsey in early Sept. (see the letter to Mackenzie written from the Selsey hotel [3–8 Sept. 1913], discussed above, p. 393). But he had the first of his *Outlook* 'Literary Portraits' to write; and then he left for the Rhine tour on 15 Sept. (according to *The Flurried Years*, 245). Brigit Patmore, to whom Ford dictated the opening of the novel, was in a nursing-home when Ford and Hunt visited her before they left for Germany. This makes it seem less likely that she could have taken dictation in Sept. But if Ford had begun dictation in July or Aug., then the book would have taken a year to write. For all the book's brilliance, this would seem slow for someone averaging three substantial books per year at the time. Ford himself said he 'wrote it with comparable rapidity' ('Dedicatory Letter', 3), and thought six months long enough (in *Return to Yesterday*, 417, he recalled it as finished by 28 June 1914; but see p. 601 below for a discussion of later dates). In short, there is no reliable evidence for disbelieving Ford's dating.

29 *'Joseph Conrad', *T.P.'s Weekly*, 3/63 (22 Jan. 1904), 113. Unsigned.
30 *Memories and Essays* (Manchester: Carcanet, 1976), 58. Cf. Mizener, 253, 565, n. 22, quoting a Boni and Liveright publicity release of 6 Apr. 1928 with another version of Ford's claim.
31 8–9 Aug. 1913: *The Letters of Ezra Pound to Alice Corbin Henderson*, ed. Ira B. Nadel (Austin: University of Texas Press, 1993), 52–4.

Chapter 25

1 'Introduction', *The Bodley Head Ford Madox Ford*, vol. 1 (London: The Bodley Head Ltd, 1962), 12.
2 *It Was the Nightingale*, 143. 'Dedicatory Letter to Stella Ford', first published in the 'Avignon edition' of the novel (New York: Albert and Charles Boni, 1927); repr. in the Oxford World's Classics edition, 3. *Ford Madox Brown*, 415.

3 28 Mar. 1915: *Reader*, 477–8.

4 *The Good Soldier*, 135. Mizener's equation of Ford's and Dowell's views on sex, 259, is discussed on p. 440 above. Paul Armstrong has a useful note on this question: *The Challenge of Bewilderment* (Ithaca and London: Cornell University Press, 1987), 217 n. 'The Novel' (1925), in *Phoenix II: Uncollected, Unpublished, and Other Prose Works by D. H. Lawrence*, ed. Warren Roberts and Harry T. Moore (London: William Heinemann, 1968), 422.

5 *Return to Yesterday*, 320–1. An earlier version appeared in ' "Ulysses" and the Handling of Indecencies', *English Review*, 35 (Dec. 1922), 543. A fictionalized variation occurs in *Some Do Not . . .*, when mad Revd Duchemin's outburst interrupts the opulent breakfast: ' "Chaste!" he shouted. "Chaste you observe! What a world of suggestion in the word . . ." ' (125).

6 'On Impressionism', *Poetry and Drama*, 2 (June and Dec. 1914), 167–75, 329.

7 See e.g. *Ancient Lights*, 241–2: 'It was Henley and his friends who introduced into the English writing mind the idea that a man of action was something fine and a man of letters a sort of castrato'. See Christopher Ricks, *Tennyson* (London and New York: Macmillan, 1972), 193, 218.

8 *Joseph Conrad*, 129–30. The similar, more autobiographical-sounding character-sketch in *Henry James*, 154, is discussed above, p. 389. Also see 'And on Earth Peace', *New York Herald Tribune Books* (26 Dec. 1926), 1, 6. Hunt, *The Flurried Years*, 74, says that when, during a croquet match, Ford was handed the letter from Elsie demanding his return: 'He shoved it in his pocket and went on playing—just as he did six years later on the golf links at Selsey when a police officer handed him an order to leave his house on the coast because he was supposed to be a German.'

9 *The Good Soldier*, 30. See Moser's fine discussion of this scene in his introduction to the Oxford World's Classics edition, pp. xvii–xviii.

10 *The Good Soldier*, 140. When he revised the MS Ford deleted several passages which made Dowell sound too transparently like a surrogate novelist. See Charles G. Hoffmann, 'Ford's Manuscript Revisions of *The Good Soldier*', *English Literature in Transition*, 9/3 (1966), 145–52.

11 Moser, for example, says of a later book: '*Mightier Than the Sword*, like every other impressionistic novel, only more so, will really be about the author [. . . It] needs to be read ultimately as Ford's last and, in many ways, best portrait of himself as artist and human being. Its eleven chapters on his eleven friends are like a circle of distorting mirrors in a fun house' (p. 287).

12 *I Have This to Say*, 202–3. She also claimed (rather disingenuously or obstructively, given Florence's resemblances to her, and given her argument that characters are compounded, not merely transcribed) that she had 'to support the character of Leonora'; and that Nancy was Brigit Patmore.

13 *Henry James*, 137. *The Good Soldier*, 59. The immigration question provides the disconcerting first words of Wells's *The Future in America* (London: Chapman & Hall, 1906), 3. Ford was fond of that pun on 'straight forward'. See *Some Do Not . . .*, 290.

14 *The Heart of the Country*, 15. The phrase comes from an obliquely autobiographical impression probably recalling his suicidal phase at Winterbourne Stoke: 'The inflictions that Fate can bestow upon a man are ingenious and endless; he may have, say, the temperament of a poet, a hopeless passion, a neglected genius, the

disclosure of hidden basenesses in himself, the consciousness of personal failure, the ingratitude of friends.'

15 *The Good Soldier*, 21–2, 47. Moser notes in his edition of the novel (301) that Dowell 'means' Philip the Magnanimous (who had a son and a grandson called Ludwig).

16 Hunt and Ford, *The Desirable Alien*, 160. Hunt is ironic about her own 'Mrs. Markham-bounded knowledge of German history' (290); Dowell says of Florence's attempts to 'educate' Edward: 'Did you ever read Mrs. Markham? Well, it was like that . . .' (49).

17 *The Desirable Alien* was probably published in Sept. 1913: Harvey, 39.

18 Michael Ignatieff, 'Paradigm Lost', *TLS* (4 Sept. 1987), 939–40.

19 Katharine Hueffer Lamb to Mizener, 8 May 1966: 'one disagreement between them was that she said "Charity begins at home" and he always thought a good deal more about outsiders than she did.'

20 *The Good Soldier*, 107, 104.

21 'Literary Portraits—XXVI.: Miss Amber Reeves and "A Lady and her Husband" ', *Outlook*, 33 (7 Mar. 1914), 310–11: written while Ford was working on *The Good Soldier*. *Ford Madox Brown*, 165.

22 Hynes, *The Edwardian Turn of Mind*, 211. *The Good Soldier*, 291. See e.g. 277: 'that wretched fellow knew [. . .] exactly what was going on'. 'A Poisonous Book', *Spectator* (20 Nov. 1909), 846–7; quoted in Hynes, 294.

23 Hynes, *The Edwardian Turn of Mind*, 188.

24 Robert Green, *Ford Madox Ford: Prose and Politics*, 102.

25 *Collected Poems* [1913], 65.

26 *Collected Poems* [1913], 213, 64.

27 *Henry James*, 45. He was presumably thinking of people like Edward Carpenter, Shaw, or the Garnetts, rather than H. G. Wells.

28 Samuel Hynes gives a fine reading of the novel's antinomy of passion and convention in his 'The Epistemology of *The Good Soldier*', in *Edwardian Occasions* (London: Routledge & Kegan Paul, 1972), 54–62.

29 *Morning Post* (5 Apr. 1915), 2; West, *Daily News* (2 Apr. 1915), 6; Sinclair to Ford, 3 Apr. 1915. *Dark, 'An Amazing Book', *Daily Express* (25 Mar. 1915), 2. The *Globe* agreed with him, calling it 'an amazingly clever psychological study' (10 Apr. 1915), 8. The *Illustrated London News* agreed with both, saying 'the psychological interest of the book is intense', and that the reviewer reread it at once: 146 (24 Apr. 1915), 542. Dreiser, 'The Saddest Story', *New Republic*, 3 (12 June 1915), 155–6.

30 *'Current Literature', *Daily Telegraph* (6 Apr. 1915), 4. *Saturday Review*, 119 (19 June 1915), p. iv.

31 *Bookman* (London), 48 (July 1915), 117. *Outlook* (London), 35 (17 Apr. 1915), 507–8. *Boston Evening Transcript* (T. S. Eliot would have been proud of them) (17 Mar. 1915), 24. *Truth*, 77 (5 May 1915), 722. Reviews besides those cited by Harvey, 321–5, also include: Henry Murray, 'Novels in Brief', *Sunday Times* (4 Apr. 1915), 5; *Evening Standard* (6 Apr. 1915), 7 and *Westminster Gazette* (17 Apr. 1915), 16.

32 Frank MacShane reprints some attacks on this novel and *Zeppelin Nights* in *Ford Madox Ford: The Critical Heritage*, 122–7.

33 *New Witness*, 7 (10 Feb. 1916), 449. See p. 489.

34 Printed in Maisie Ward, *Gilbert Keith Chesterton* (London: Sheed and Ward, 1944), 350–2.

35 Trotter, 'Edwardian Sex Novels', *Critical Quarterly*, 31/1 (Spring 1989), 92–106. Though the essay omits discussion of Ford, it gives a good indication of *The Good Soldier*'s intellectual and literary context.

36 Mizener, 251. 'Dedicatory Letter to Stella Ford', 3–4. Ford to John Lane, 17 Dec. 1914: *Reader*, 477. Curiously, the novel was still being referred to as 'The Saddest Story' in the advertisements bound into the first edition of the novel.

37 Heine, 'Journey from Munich to Genoa', *Reisebilder*, part III, ch. XXXI, last paragraph. See *Werke und Briefe*, 3 (Berlin: Aufbau Verlag, 1961), 265: 'Aber ein Schwert sollt ihr mir auf den Sarg legen; denn ich war ein braver Soldat in Befreiungskriege der Menschheit.' The translation is from the epigraph to Lucy Masterman's biography of her husband, *C. F. G. Masterman*—which suggests that Ford was probably familiar with the quotation. *Great Trade Route* says: 'let it be remembered that even amongst murderers there is honour and the definition of a good soldier is not merely that he is one who wins battles, or even one who wins battles at all. A good soldier is one who wins or loses battles with the least possible loss of the men entrusted to him': 366. If Ford had this definition in mind for the novel written over two decades earlier, there is a double irony in applying it to Ashburnham: not only does he lose his battles (against Leonora, against his own desires); but he loses the lives of Florence and himself, and devastates those of Nancy and Dowell. Richard Stang has suggested (in conversation) that the novel's title may allude to Socrates' description of the military duty the citizen owes to the *polis*: 'if it leads you out to war, to be wounded or killed, you must comply [. . .] you must not give way or retreat or abandon your position': *Crito*, in Plato, *The Last Days of Socrates*, trans. by Hugh Tredennick (Harmondsworth: Penguin Books, new edn., 1959), 91. Socrates is arguing that he ought to face execution rather than let his friends help him escape, so not abandoning his position represents an honourable form of suicide (though from another perspective the suicide is abandoning his position). Ford discusses the *Crito* and *Apology* in *The March of Literature*, 147. Shakespeare, *Much Ado About Nothing*, I. i. 51–3.

38 *No More Parades*, 167.

39 Hynes, *The Edwardian Turn of Mind*, 23–4, 169.

40 See Joseph Wiesenfarth, 'Criticism and the Semiosis of *The Good Soldier*', *Modern Fiction Studies*, 9/1 (Spring 1963), 39–49. 'The Saddest Story', 88, 88A, 88B: Cornell. This passage was revised into the one on pp. 68–70 of the published text (from 'Yes, they quarrelled bitterly' to 'You see, she was childless herself'). Dowell's comment in the revision—'I trust that I have not, in talking of his liabilities, given the impression that poor Edward was a promiscuous libertine'—could thus stand for Ford's feeling that he *had* given that impression.

41 Charles Hoffmann argues that 'Ford apparently rejected his original idea that Edward fathered innumerable children as being too grossly libertine for a sentimental philanderer': 'Ford's Manuscript Revisions of *The Good Soldier*', 148. But this is to deny the complexity of Ford's tone. He does not reject the idea of Edward's children, but leaves it as a suggestion, a repressed possibility. For example, Dowell tells us twice, once near the beginning, and once near the end of the book, that Edward spent £200 (and 'a great deal of time') to get the daughter of one of his tenants acquitted from a charge of having murdered her baby: 35, 226. Ostensibly it is an example of Edward's ability to act the *grand seigneur* even under great personal pressure. But the repetition might signify that

he had a vested interest in this girl: that he enjoyed that *droit de seigneur* as well as the duties.

42 Moser, in his introduction to the Oxford World's Classics *The Good Soldier*, p. xxii, says 'Readers have actually opined that Edward is Nancy's father'. Dowell says Nancy is 21 soon after Florence's suicide (in 1913). Therefore she was born in 1891/2, at least a year before Edward married Leonora. As Edward is unlikely to have met Mrs Rufford except through Leonora, this makes it unlikely that he could actually be Nancy's father. However, the novel's chronology is inconsistent on at least one other crucial point. Dowell places his meeting of the Ashburnhams on the evening of 4 Aug. 1904; yet that is the day that the two couples made the excursion to see the Protest documents. (See R. W. Lid, 'On the Time-Scheme of *The Good Soldier*', *English Fiction in Transition*, 4/2 (1961), 9-10.) That the arithmetic does not quite work out does not mean that Ford may not have intended the possibility of Edward's being Nancy's father.

43 *A Call*, 129. 'Tiger, Tiger: Being a Commentary on Conrad's *The Sisters*', *Bookman*, 66/5 (Jan. 1928), 497. Ford's thoughts about Conrad and the theme of incest are discussed further vol. 2, Ch. 17. *The Good Soldier*, 150.

44 Ruth C. Sabol and Todd K. Bender, *A Concordance to Ford Madox Ford's 'The Good Soldier'* (New York: Garland, 1981). 'Literary Portraits—XIX.: Gerhart Hauptmann and "Atlantis" ', *Outlook*, 33 (17 Jan. 1914), 77-9. Cf. *The New Humpty-Dumpty*, 83: 'He had never really learnt that the truth is a dangerous thing'.

45 *Last Post*, 154. *The Shifting of the Fire* also draws on feelings about incest. Moser (30) has shown how old Mr Kasker-Ryves draws upon William Martindale; so for Ford to describe his marriage to Edith (who draws upon Elsie) is—however obliquely—to contemplate father–daughter incest.

46 Ford may have come across the affair between guardian and ward in James's first novel, *Watch and Ward*, though the references to it in *Henry James* suggest he hadn't read it: 45, 108. There is also a possible influence from Rossetti's 'The Last Confession', though there the man ends by murdering the woman. Katharine Hueffer Lamb to Mizener, [n.d., but *c*.July 1966]. She adds, showing once again how much Ford changed his character-sources: 'but we *never* had to pay fines'. Katharine also recognized herself in Valentine Wannop: 'I really laughed at Valentine's "frown"—as I was always being told not to frown. & the turned up nose.' Katharine Lamb to Mizener, 11 Dec. 1966. Mizener, 175. Hunt, *The Flurried Years*, 50.

47 *'Two Poems', *English Review*, 4 (Feb. 1910), 383-4. Mizener was misled by the presence of a copy amongst Hunt's papers into thinking she had written the poem (175). Belford, *Violet*, 157, and Hardwick, *An Immodest Violet*, 69, repeat the error. Goldring salvaged a MS of the poem (signed 'G. Angel') from Ford's editorial waste-paper basket: *South Lodge*, 36; *The Last Pre-Raphaelite*, 156-7. Though he was wrong in thinking it unpublished, he can't have been mistaken that it was in Ford's handwriting. The fact that the other poem is Ford's 'The Exile' confirms the attribution. These is a letter from 'George Angel' to Ford, 9 Mar. 1909; but this was presumably a joke played on Goldring or Hunt.

48 p. 139. John Colmer, *Coleridge to Catch-22: Images of Society* (London: Macmillan, 1970), 141, argues that Ford based the episode of Tietjens seducing or being seduced by Sylvia on a train upon the case of Valentine Baker, an officer who was

accused of indecently assaulting a woman on a train in 1875. The Kilsyte case is more closely based on this incident.

49 The protagonist of Norah Hoult's novel, *There Were No Windows* (London: Heinemann, 1944), generally agreed to be based on Hunt and Ford, describes her feelings for her lover as 'more maternal, pity rather than love' (23). See Harvey, 533–4.

50 ' "Ulysses" and the Handling of Indecencies', *English Review*, 35 (Dec. 1922), 544.

51 See Hynes, *The Edwardian Turn of Mind*, ch. 5.

52 'Declined with Thanks', *New York Herald Tribune Books* (24 June 1928), 1, 6. Cf. *The Critical Attitude*, 33: 'what we so very much need to-day is a picture of the life we live. It is only the imaginative writer who can supply this, because no collection of facts, and no tabulation of figures, can give us any sense of proportion.'

53 'Literary Portraits—XIII.: Viscount Morley and "Politics and History" ', *Outlook*, 32 (6 Dec. 1913), 790–1. *The Good Soldier*, 3. *Thus to Revisit*, 97. 'Literary Causeries: X. Mystifications', *Chicago Tribune Sunday Magazine* (Paris) (20 Apr. 1924), 3. 'Literary Portraits—VIII.: Professor Saintsbury and the English "Nuvvle" ', *Outlook*, 32 (1 Nov. 1913), 605–6. Goldring, **The Nineteen Twenties* (London: Nicholson & Watson, 1945), 264. Sinclair to Ford, 3 Apr. 1915: Cornell. 'Un Coeur Simple', *Outlook*, 35 (5 June 1915), 738–9; this essay was incorporated into Ford's second book of propaganda, *Between St. Dennis and St. George* (London, 1915), 199–205.

54 *The Good Soldier*, 9. 'On Impressionism', p. 329. In 'Stocktaking [. . .] II', *transatlantic review*, 1/2 (Feb. 1924), 58, he wrote: 'not to know how Heine mixed, alternated or employed flippancies and sentiment is to have a blind spot in your knowledge of how a part of humanity may be appealed to.' Critics have been confused by this trick of dual tone into wanting to read the book too univocally as tragic or comic. See e.g. Mark Schorer, 'An Interpretation', printed as an introduction to the 1951 Vintage edition, pp. v–xv; Hynes, 'The Epistemology of *The Good Soldier*'; Moser, 120: 'The saddest story is that love dies, dies because man is mad. (Sane he would perhaps not love at all)'; Avrom Fleishmann, 'The Genre of *The Good Soldier*: Ford's Comic Mastery', *Studies in the Literary Imagination*, 13/1 (Spring 1980), 31–42. For a more balanced reading see: Snitow, *Ford Madox Ford and the Voice of Uncertainty*, 84–5. 'A Literary Portrait. Chicago', *Outlook*, 35 (6 Mar. 1915), 302–3.

55 Hynes, 'The Epistemology of *The Good Soldier*', 60. Flaubert said of *Madame Bovary*: 'The irony does not detract from the pathetic aspect, but rather intensifies it. In my third part, which will be full of farcical things, I want my readers to weep': letter to Louise Colet [9 Oct. 1852]: *The Letters of Gustave Flaubert: 1830–57*, ed. Steegmuller (London: Faber, 1981), 171–2. *Tarr (The 1918 Version)*, ed. Paul O'Keefe (Santa Rosa: Black Sparrow Press, 1990), 169. *The Good Soldier*, 34.

56 'Literary Portraits—XLVII.: Mr. W. R. Titterton and "Me as a Model" ', *Outlook*, 34 (1 Aug. 1914), 142–3.

57 My discussion of this distinction is indebted to Wilbur Sanders, who not only discussed the issue with me, but kindly lent me his notes for a lecture on Turgenev.

58 *Mightier Than the Sword*, 190, 73. 'Literary Portraits—IX.: Mr. Thomas Hardy and "A Changed Man" ', *Outlook*, 32 (8 Nov. 1913), 641–2.

59 'Literary Portraits—XX.: Mr. Gilbert Cannan and "Old Mole" ', *Outlook*, 33 (24 Jan. 1914), 110. See Green, *Ford Madox Ford: Prose and Politics*, 85.

60 *The Good Soldier*, 19. In *The Spirit of the People* Ford argued that the English 'feel very intimately as a set rule of conduct, whenever we meet a man, whenever we talk with a woman: "You will play the game." ', and that this means that the Englishman has 'in the world a place to which to return': 152–3; repr. in *Reader*, 297–8.

61 p. 293. In the MS Dowell originally did hear the words, which were: 'Girl, I will wait for you there.' See Hoffmann, 'Ford's Manuscript Revisions of *The Good Soldier*', 149.

62 *It Was the Nightingale*, 49. This passage is discussed in greater detail in vol. 2, Ch. 7.

63 See e.g. George Dangerfield's *The Strange Death of Liberal England* (London: Constable, 1936).

64 The cross-references are peculiarly suggestive here. Florence's touch on Edward's wrist is doubled by Leonora's clutching at Dowell's. Dowell discusses Leonora's wrist in that odd earlier passage raising the possibility of his having felt 'the beginnings of a trace of what is called the sex instinct towards her', only to deny that he felt it. Yet given the significance of the wrists in the Protest scene, his claim that Leonora's 'lines' 'seemed to conduct your gaze always to her wrist' might imply that he is not immune from the desire to lay a finger on hers. *The Good Soldier*, 55, 39.

65 *Return to Yesterday*, 122–3.

66 Carol Jacobs, 'The (Too) Good Soldier', *Glyph*, 3, *Johns Hopkins Textual Studies* (Baltimore: Johns Hopkins University Press, 1978), 32–51.

67 'Romanticism and Classicism', in *Speculations*, ed. Herbert Read (London: Kegan Paul, Trench, Trubner and Co., 1924), 116.

68 'Modern Art', *Speculations*, 86.

69 *The Good Soldier*, 82: there is a fuller discussion of this vision in vol. 2, Ch. 14 Green, *Ford Madox Ford: Prose and Politics*, 14.

70 According to this view, as Ford was to argue in his preface to Hunt's *Their Lives* (London: Stanley Paul, 1916), 4–5, the war could be seen as an expression of a *fin de siècle* sexual and social catastrophe.

71 The use of 'instinct' here to mean the opposite of 'instincts' is characteristic of the way Ford's thinking in 1913 also anticipates Freud's great essays *Beyond the Pleasure Principle* (1920) and *Civilisation and its Discontents* (1930). As Sondra Stang noted: 'The novel and the essays most startlingly illuminate each other': 'A Reading of *The Good Soldier*', *Modern Language Quarterly*, 30/4 (1969), 545.

72 James to Howard Sturgis, 4–5 Aug. 1914: Green, *Ford Madox Ford: Prose and Politics*, 95, compares James's letter to Ford's novel; on 200, n. 23, he cites *Letters of Henry James*, ed. Percy Lubbock, 2 vols. (New York: Charles Scriber's Sons, 1920), ii. 384, but misdates the letter as 14 Aug.

73 The beginning of *The Good Soldier* was published in the first issue of *Blast* in June 1914. Masterman's reminiscence was published in the *Daily Chronicle* a few months after the publication of *The Good Soldier*. It is quoted in Lucy

Masterman, *C. F. G. Masterman* (London: Nicholson and Watson, 1939), 266; and in Hynes, *The Edwardian Turn of Mind*, 356.

74 See Mizener, 268. *The Good Soldier*, 140–1.

75 Most of the novel was written before the declaration of war, and the complete MS probably went to the publisher later that Aug. The printers received their copy on 3 Oct. 1914. Hoffmann, 'Ford's Manuscript Revisions of *The Good Soldier*', 145–52, prefers the theory that Part II was begun after 4 Aug. 1914. See Mizener, 565 and Moser, 315 for cogent correctives.

76 'Literary Portraits—LII.: "Cedant togae . . ." ', *Outlook*, 34 (5 Sept. 1914), 303–4. Mizener, 565, n. 21; Moser, 315.

77 Lawrence, *Studies in Classic American Realism* (London: Martin Secker, 1924), 9. Ford to Galsworthy [Oct. 1900]: *Letters*, 11 (a passage marked by Graham Greene in his copy). *Great Trade Route*, 27.

78 *TLS* (15 June 1962), 437–9. *Joseph Conrad*, 189, 197, 204. See Moser, 149–50 (' "Surprise" almost sums up Ford's view of experience').

79 Letter to J. H. Reynolds, 3 Feb. 1818: *Letters of John Keats*, ed. Robert Gittings (London: Oxford University Press, 1970), 61.

80 Kenner, 'Introduction', Signet Classic edition of *The Good Soldier* (New York: Penguin Books USA Inc., 1991), pp. viii, xii. Malcolm Bradbury, 'Introduction', *Parade's End* (London: Everyman's Library, 1993), p. xi, calls *The Good Soldier* a 'work of brilliant indirection and complex irony'.

81 James, 'The New Novel', in *Selected Literary Criticism*, ed. Morris Shapira, 2nd edn. (Cambridge: Cambridge University Press, 1981), 338.

82 'Literary Portraits—LIII.: The Muse of War', *Outlook*, 34 (12 Sept. 1914), 335–6.

83 Mizener, 258–9. W. K. Wimsatt and Monroe C. Beardsley, 'The Intentional Fallacy', in Wimsatt, *The Verbal Icon* (Lexington, University of Kentucky, 1954). *The Good Soldier*, 135.

84 Not least because 'shuttlecocks' alludes to James's preface to *What Maisie Knew*: 'The wretched infant was thus to find itself practically disowned, rebounding from racquet to racquet like a tennis-ball or a shuttlecock': *The Art of the Novel*, ed. R. P. Blackmur (New York: Scribner, 1934), 140.

85 *Notice of Richard Jefferies, *The Hills and the Vale*, ed. Edward Thomas (London, Duckworth and Co., 1909), in 'Publications Received', *English Review*, 4 (Dec. 1909), 155.

86 'The Dean in Exile', *Shenandoah*, 4/1 (Spring 1953), 45.

87 See Max Saunders, 'A Life in Writing: Ford Madox Ford's Dispersed Autobiographies', *Antæus*, no. 56 (Spring 1986), 47–69.

88 'Preparedness', *New York Herald Tribune Magazine* (6 Nov. 1927), 7, 18. *The Critical Attitude*, 9.

89 *A Call*, 281. Sondra Stang wrote well of the power of language in 'A Reading of Ford's *The Good Soldier*'. *The Good Soldier*, 19. Freud, *Standard Edition*, vol. 19 (London: The Hogarth Press and the Institute of Psycho-Analysis, 1961), 184.

90 *The Good Soldier*, 273. Cf. *A Call*, 128, when Pauline says she has learned 'that we can't have what we want'. See Paul Armstrong, *The Challenge of Bewilderment* (Ithaca and London: Cornell University Press, 1987), 220.

91 The same question resounds throughout Ford's earlier fiction. See 'The Incorruptible', *Throne and Country*, 5 (13 Dec. 1911), 422–5; *Ladies Whose Bright Eyes*,

349; *The New Humpty-Dumpty*, 86; also the MSS of *'The Last Sowing' (331) and *'The Troubles of Tolputt' (26) at Cornell.

92 *Temple Bar*, 128 (Nov. 1903), 564–78.

93 'Literary Portraits—IX.: Mr. Thomas Hardy and "A Changed Man" ', *Outlook*, 32 (8 Nov. 1913), 641–2.

94 *Provence*, 240. Gordon, *How to Read a Novel* (New York: The Viking Press, 1958), 145–6.

95 'Ford Madox Ford When he was Hueffer', *South Atlantic Quarterly*, 57 (Spring 1958), 248.

96 Moser, 192. Freud, Preface to Marie Bonaparte's *The Life and Works of Edgar Allan Poe: A Psycho-Analytic Interpretation* (1933), *Standard Edition*, xxii. 254. See also 'Dostoevsky and Parricide', *Standard Edition*, xxi. 177: 'Before the problem of the creative writer, analysis must lay down its arms.' *The Good Soldier*, 12. Mizener, 63.

97 See *The Critical Attitude*, 164–5 on man's literary view of woman, for example; or 186 for an expression of solipsism.

98 See also *Ancient Lights*, 209–13, on looking out of a train window after reading about the death of Holman Hunt; and *The Spirit of the People*, 172, on Ford's desire, while at Mammern, to return to Romney Marsh, expressed in images to which he returned to express Dowell's longing to recapture past innocence: 'I was obsessed always with an intense longing to see once more the sails of ships above the sea wall, the wide stretch of land, the church spire of Lydd breaking the distant horizon—and I longed, ah! beyond bearing, to hear English spoken again'. See Mizener, 541, n. 24.

99 *The Spirit of the People*, 148–50; included in the excerpt repr. in the *Reader*, 293–8. *The Good Soldier*, 288, 287. Ford had also fictionalized this scene for one of *A Call*'s climactic moments, 27–8, when Ellida Langham watches the renunciatory parting—also at a railway station—of Robert Grimshaw and Pauline Leicester, who faints after throwing Grimshaw's violets back to him. Also see the scene between Ernest Jessop and Clarice Honeywill as he is leaving by train in *The Marsden Case*, 303–4.

100 *The Good Soldier*, 3. Moser, 143. Biala, conversation with Max Saunders, 10–11 Apr. 1987. She wrote to Mizener (25 June 1970) that Ford had told her the names, 'and that "Edward" died of drink'. In some 'Publicity Notes from Albert & Charles Boni', dated 6 Apr. 1926, Ford said: 'In the case of the GOOD SOLDIER, for personal reasons, I thought about the subject at intervals for ten years before beginning on it.' (Mizener, 565, n. 22, cites this, but mis-describes it as a 1928 Boni & Liveright handout.) *Edward* Ashburnham has been described as a composite picture of Arthur Marwood and King Edward VII. William Amos, *The Originals: Who's Really Who in Fiction* (London: Jonathan Cape, 1985), 22. Also see Geoffrey Wagner, 'Ford Madox Ford: the Honest Edwardian', *Essays in Criticism*, 17 (Jan. 1967), 75–88. Other partial models for Ashburnham include the Captain Campbell described in *Return to Yesterday*, 270–1, a retired lancer crusading to make more humane the slaughtering of cattle: 'His extraordinary passion burning through a heavy and slow body was something hardly to be believed in'; and the 'Waring' described in *It Was the Nightingale*, 200–1, on whom Ford based Tietjens in *Parade's End* as well as both Ashburnham and Dowell. Ford had written earlier about the historical Ashburnham, a 'body

servant' to Charles I, who later preserved the executed king's clothes as the 'blood-stained relics of a martyr': *The Cinque Ports*, 36, 57.

101 See Caroline Gordon's fine comments on the novel's tone in *How to Read a Novel* (New York: Viking, 1957), 145–6; cited by Harvey, 526. Ann Barr Snitow has written the fullest account of Fordian tone: *Ford Madox Ford and the Voice of Uncertainty*. Michael Levenson, 'Character in *The Good Soldier*', *Twentieth Century Literature*, 30/4 (Winter 1984), 373–87, argues that it is 'Ford's boldest stroke to imagine a personality virtually without attributes—subjectivity before it has assumed the articulations of character' (383)—which is a good explanation of why it is that doubts about him as an 'unreliable narrator' seem not to prevent many readers from sympathetic identification. Conrad to Ford, 'Sunday' [after 18 Mar. 1915, when Ford inscribed a copy of the novel for Conrad: Harvey, 44]: typed copy at Cornell; original in Berg collection, New York Public Library.

102 *Read, 'An Old Man Mad about Writing', *New English Weekly*, 16 (9 Nov. 1939), 57–8.

103 See 'On Impressionism'. Ford restated the opposition between impression and narration in *Joseph Conrad*, 194–5. See Paul B. Armstrong, 'The Epistemology of Ford's Impressionism', in *Critical Essays on Ford Madox Ford*, ed. R. Cassell (Boston: G. K. Hall & Co., 1987), 135–42.

104 Jacobs, 'The (Too) Good Soldier', 35, 49, n. 8. Mizener, 268.

105 Hoffmann, 'Ford's Manuscript Revisions of *The Good Soldier*', 147. Stang, 'A Reading of *The Good Soldier*', suggests that Dowell may have known more than he pretends to us. Wiesenfarth ('Criticism and the Semiosis of *The Good Soldier*') and Jacobs ('The (Too) Good Soldier') argue that the novel is sceptical of the possibility of finding 'truth', 'full knowledge' of 'what really happened'.

106 'The Black and Merciless Things', *Observer* (17 June 1962), 26.

107 *Joseph Conrad*, 191, 180. *Heart of Darkness*, 8.

108 'On Impressionism', 172, describes writing as 'the seductive occupation'. Here, where the 'silent listener' is figured as male, the artist has become female, and must 'employ all the devices of the prostitute' (333).

109 'On Impressionism', 169. *Joseph Conrad*, 182, 186.

110 Freud, 'The Psychotherapy of Hysteria', in *Studies on Hysteria, Standard Edition*, vol. 2 (London: The Hogarth Press and the Institute of Psycho-Analysis, 1955), 280.

111 'On Impressionism', 174. Hugh Kenner argues that *The Good Soldier* denies its readers the conventional securities offered by narratives that sound like history or like autobiography: 'Introduction', Signet Classic edition, p. v. The reason is perhaps that it manages to sound like both at the same time, each fused disconcertingly with the fictive. 'Dedicatory Letter to Stella Ford', 3. James, *The Aspern Papers and Other Stories*, ed. Adrian Poole (Oxford: Oxford University Press, 1983), 154.

112 *Drawn from Life* (London: Collins, 1941), 80.

113 *The Good Soldier*, 1. Stella Bowen confirms his reluctance to write another novel after the war in *Drawn from Life*, 109. *Return to Yesterday*, 417. *The Nature of a Crime*, 8. 'Publicity Notes from Albert & Charles Boni', 6 Apr. 1926. Allen Tate, *Memories & Essays: Old and New: 1926–1974* (Manchester: Carcanet, 1976), 58.

Chapter 26

1 *Thus to Revisit*, 181–2. *Return to Yesterday*, 429. Goldring, *South Lodge*, 71, described the 1914 season as 'a positive frenzy of gaiety'.

2 Hunt, 'Biog. of Eminent Friends', typed draft, 1. Hunt, *I Have This to Say*, 267. Mizener, 246, 563, n. 8. Jepson, *Memories of an Edwardian*, 155. *Return to Yesterday*, 430. Noel Stock, *The Life of Ezra Pound* (Harmondsworth: Penguin, 1974), 181. Margery Morgan, *August Strindberg* (Basingstoke and London: Macmillan, 1985), 171–2. Lewis also had some trouble over a shadow play there: see *The Letters of Wyndham Lewis*, ed. W. K. Rose (London: Methuen, 1963), 45–6. Lewis, *Rude Assignment*, ed. Toby Foshay (Santa Barbara: Black Sparrow Press, 1984), 134. *The Marsden Case*, 89–110, 127–8. The Cabaret Club ran out of money and closed on 13 Feb. 1914: *William Wees, *Vorticism and the English Avant-Garde* (Toronto and Buffalo: University of Toronto Press, 1972), 51. So Ford's reminiscence of going there in the summer of 1914 may be a conflation of 1913 and 1914. Richard Cork, 'The Cave of the Golden Calf', *Artforum*, 21/4 (Dec. 1982), 56–8. Cork, *Art Beyond the Gallery* (New Haven and London: Yale University Press, 1985), 61–115. Ford remembered winning a bet with Mme Strindberg that he could identify 'any wine from the Rheingau that she liked to give me': *New York Herald Tribune Books* (18 Aug. 1929), 3. The club also appears as the 'Silver Cow' in Hunt's novel *The House of Many Mirrors*, 50–2. See Hardwick, *An Immodest Violet*, 126, 135. Ford said he had seen the prince of Wales there: 'Last Words about Edward VIII' (typescript of radio broadcast); Mizener, 563, n. 8.

3 *'Four in the Morning Cookery', *Harper's Bazaar* (Oct. 1938), 107, 134–6. He gives nine chafing-dish recipes, from oysters to Welsh rarebit and *soupe à l'oignon*.

4 *Thus to Revisit*, 136. Pound to Shakespear, Saturday [7 Mar. 1914]; Tuesday (10 Mar. 1914): *Ezra Pound and Dorothy Shakespear*, 315–16; 322–6; the latter includes a reference to the interview with Pound, *' "The Imagistes", a Talk with Mr. Ezra Pound, Their Editor', *Daily News and Leader* (18 Mar. 1914), 4, which is repr. on 323–5. *Return to Yesterday*, 418. See vol. 2, Ch. 13 for other versions of Lewis's denunciation. *Rude Assignment*, 131. *Collected Poems* [1913], 127. Hunt, *I Have This to Say*, 214, 267–78. Aldington, *Life for Life's Sake* (London: Cassell, 1968), 137–8, 142.

5 Hunt and Patmore were in the audience: Hunt, *I Have This to Say*, 213 (the passage on Rebecca West and on Vorticism, 204–16, does not appear in *The Flurried Years*). Wees, *Vorticism and the English Avant-Garde*, 68–70. Lechmere, quoted by Richard Cork, *Vorticism and Abstract Art in the First Machine Age*. Vol. 1, *Origins and Developments* (London: Gordon Fraser, 1976), 158. The lecture took place between late Apr. (the prospectus at Cornell says the centre was to open on 26 Apr. 1914) and June. Mizener, 247.

6 *No Enemy*, 205. S. Foster Damon, *Amy Lowell* (Boston and New York: Houghton Mifflin, 1935), 232–3. Mizener confuses the date of the publication of the first *Blast* (20 June) with the date of the dinner (15 July). The second dinner was two days after this—17 July, not 22 June as he implies (248).

7 Fletcher, *Life is My Song* (New York: Farrar and Rinehart, 1937), 148–9. Ford had made a similar protestation of uncertainty in his 'Literary Portraits—XXXV.: Les Jeunes and "Des Imagistes" ', *Outlook*, 33 (9 May 1914), 636–7: 'I do not, for the purposes of this article, know what Imagisme is'.

8 Stock, *The Life of Ezra Pound*, 205–7; though he garbles Lowell's line. See Peter Jones (ed.), *Imagist Poetry* (Harmondsworth: Penguin Books, 1972), 87.

9 20 July 1914: quoted by Ellen Williams, *Harriet Monroe and the Poetry Renaissance* (Urbana, Ill.: University of Illinois Press, 1977), 130–1.

10 See Harvey, 188–98 for the summer *Outlook* portraits. Marinetti's lecturing is mentioned in portraits 36 (16 May), 44 (11 June), and 49 (15 Aug.). 'Literary Portraits—XLIII.: Mr. Wyndham Lewis and "Blast" ', *Outlook*, 34 (4 July 1914), 15–16. 'Literary Portraits—XLIX.: A Causerie', *Outlook*, 34 (15 Aug. 1914), 206–7. 'Literary Portraits—XXXVI.: Les Jeunes and "Des Imagistes" (Second Notice)', *Outlook*, 33 (16 May 1914), 682–3.

11 *Thus to Revisit*, 25. 'Dedicatory Letter to Stella Ford', *The Good Soldier*, 2. *Return to Yesterday*, 419. Harvey, 165, 192. Cf. *It Was the Nightingale*, 172, where he says he made his farewell in 1916 [though the events described must have happened in 1917] after seeing one of his own books 'under the shrouded lamps of the railway bookstall at Hazebrouck'. Garnett, quoted by Moser, 120. In 'Those Were the Days', *Imagist Anthology* (London: Chatto & Windus, 1930), p. xiii, Ford wrote of 1913–14, 'at that date I died: I determined to become [. . .] dead and silent.'

12 Hunt, *I Have This to Say*, 215. Wees, *Vorticism and the English Avant-Garde*, 197. *Return to Yesterday*, 433. Mizener, 248–9, 564, n. 13. It is impossible to date the visit to Berwick precisely. In *Return to Yesterday*, 417, 433–6, Ford remembers himself reading of the assassination of Archduke Franz Ferdinand (which happened on 28 June) while waiting on the Berwick platform for the connection to Duns (435). This is impossible, since we know Ford went to Duns after being at dinners in London on 15 and 17 July. Mizener, 564, n. 13, puts this down to a desire to 'dramatize his reading about the murder'. A slip of memory is more likely after a quarter of a century. Lewis's dating is too vague to corroborate either date: he placed the beginning of the visit 'some weeks or so before the War appeared on the horizon'. In *Between St. Dennis and St. George*, written in 1915, Ford gives one correct date for being in Berwick: 20 July 1914 (38–42); p. 46 says Ford read in the paper 'that Austria-Hungary was going to do something in regard to the crime of Sarajevo'. Austro-Hungary delivered an ultimatum to Serbia on 23 July, and declared war on the 28th; so it is quite possible that the papers were saying on the 20th that some action was imminent. (And if this account written the following year is accurate, it helps explain the distortion when Ford reminisced a decade-and-a-half later: he misremembered an announcement about the *response* to the assassinations in July as the *report* of the assassinations in June.) The date of the 20th is corroborated by Forster to Alice Clara Forster (22 July 1914): **Selected Letters of E. M. Forster*, ed. Mary Lago and P. N. Furbank (London: Collins, 1983), 210–11. The question of when he returned to London is more problematic. Hunt, *I Have This to Say*, 255–6, implies they were away for seven days, and back on the day war was declared (4 Aug.). But Edgar Jepson recalled seeing Ford in London on 2 August, and in *Return to Yesterday* he sees Masterman at the Foreign Office on the 3rd. (See p. 469 above.) In *Some Do Not . . .* , 236, Tietjens escorts Mrs Duchemin on the train from Berwick to London during 'the great rout of the 3–8–14'. These pieces of evidence point to Ford's having returned before war was declared. Yet his *Outlook* essay published on 8 Aug. begins: 'I am sitting up here in Scotland.' It was written after 'the ultimatum which Great Britain delivered to Germany on Tuesday'; that Tuesday was 4 Aug. The end of

Return to Yesterday implies that he was still in Scotland on the 4th, and read the northern papers there. Is it possible he came down to London by the 2nd, but returned to Duns by the 4th?

Jeffrey Meyers, *The Enemy: A Biography of Wyndham Lewis* (London: Routledge & Kegan Paul, 1980), 73, says the house was Charter Hall, not Duns Manor; but his chronology says 'Marchmount'; 334. Ford later said he had not heard of Joyce before hearing Mrs Turner reading out instalments. But, as Joseph Wiesenfarth shows, Ford had already spoken to Pound about *Portrait* in April: 'Fargobawlers: James Joyce and Ford Madox Ford', *biography*, 14/2 (Spring 1991), 95; Pound/Joyce, ed. Forrest Read (New York: New Directions, 1967), 25.

13 Hunt, *I Have This to Say*, 255. Lewis, *Blasting and Bombardiering*, rev. edn. (London: John Calder; and New York: Riverrun Press, 1982), 58–9. Lewis first fictionalized the episode as one of his 'Cantleman' stories, in which Ford appears as 'Leo Makepeace Leo': *'The Countryhouse Party, Scotland' was not published in Lewis's lifetime: *Unlucky for Pringle: Unpublished and Other Stories*, ed. C. J. Fox and Robert Chapman (London: Vision Press, 1973), 45–9. This was then revised and incorporated into *Blasting and Bombardiering*. As Mizener says (564, n. 13), Lewis's memory of Ford's political views is borne out by a similar argument in *A History of Our Own Times*, 112.

14 'Literary Portraits—XLVIII. M. Charles-Louis Philippe and "Le Père Perdrix" ', *Outlook*, 34 (8 Aug. 1914), 174–5.

15 See Mizener, 249, for one of the most influential accounts of Ford's alleged 'feudalism'. *The Spirit of the People*, 83. *'The Critical Attitude: Applied to the Affairs of the World at Large', *Bystander*, 32 (15 Nov. 1911), 345–6.

16 'Literary Portraits—XLVIII. M. Charles-Louis Philippe and "Le Père Perdrix" '.

17 'Literary Portraits—LI.: The Face of Janus', *Outlook*, 34 (29 Aug. 1914), 270–1.

18 'Literary Portraits—XLVIII'. James, 'Ivan Turgénieff', *Partial Portraits* (London: Macmillan and Co., 1888), 296.

19 Jepson, *Memories of an Edwardian*, 176. *The Flurried Years*, 43, 177. *Return to Yesterday*, 424. Robert Lowell's poem, 'Ford Madox Ford', recalls Ford's story about playing golf with Lloyd George, though he thought it one of his 'lies that made the great your equals': *Life Studies* (London: Faber and Faber, 1972), 63–4. Ford discusses conversations with John Burns (who was president of the Board of Trade, and the first working-class cabinet minister), on pp. 397 and 426 of *Return to Yesterday*. Ford was certainly friendly with Burns: there is an undated letter to him (from Holland Park Avenue, thus from 1907–11): British Library, Additional Mss 46302f.272. He described how Masterman consulted him in 1915 about possible peace terms with Germany: Ford to Malcolm MacDonald, 27 Feb. 1939: *Letters*, 311.

20 'Literary Portraits—XIX.: Gerhart Hauptmann and "Atlantis" ', *Outlook*, 33 (17 Jan. 1914), 77–9.

21 In 'Literary Portraits—LI.: The Face of Janus', *Outlook*, 34 (29 Aug. 1914), 270–1, he wrote: 'I am not a very distinguished writer; I am too much outside of things, and I believe I am too much disliked to have much right to speak from my fellow-authors.' In 'Literary Portraits—LXXI. Enemies', *Outlook*, 35 (16 Jan. 1915), 79–80, he discusses why he has 'had "enemies"—shoals and shoals of enemies'. See Camilla Haase, 'Serious Artists: The Relationship Between Ford Madox Ford and Ezra Pound' (unpublished dissertation: Harvard University, 1984), 289.

22 'Literary Portraits—XIX.' Lucy Masterman, *C. F. G. Masterman* (London: Nicholson and Watson, 1939), 267, 272. Bennett, *Journals*, ii 103–4 (entry for 3 Sept.). Peter Buitenhuis, *The Great War of Words: Literature as Propaganda 1914–18 and After* (London: Batsford, 1989), pp. xiv, 12–15.

23 In 'Literary Portraits—XLI.: Mr Richard Curle and "Joseph Conrad"', *Outlook*, 33 (20 June 1914), 848–9, Ford calls this speech from *Henry V* 'the finest passage of prose in the English language'. L. L. Farrar, Jr., 'The Artist as Propagandist', *The Presence of Ford Madox Ford*, 147.

24 *It Was the Nightingale*, 220–1. Moser, 315–16, n. 101, indicates how the holograph portions of the MS support the story. It is also corroborated by Aldington to F. S. Flint (4 July 1914): 'Hilda has not been well—nothing much, largely mental strain through working too hard with Hueffer on his novel': *Richard Aldington: An Autobiography in Letters*, ed. Norman T. Gates (University Park, Pennsylvania: Pennsylvania State University Press, 1992), 10.

25 William Amos, *The Originals* (London: Jonathan Cape, 1985), cites Ford as Shobbe's 'original'. *Death of a Hero*, 143. See also 118, 131–43, 370. Aldington, 'Notes on the War Novel', *This Quarter*, 2 (Jan., Feb., Mar. 1930), 542–3, describes *No More Parades* as 'poppycock, pure bunk, told with superb virtuosity'. Aldington, *Life for Life's Sake* (New York: Viking, 1941), 149–50. Aldington to Amy Lowell, 14 Nov. 1914, quoted by Charles Doyle, *Richard Aldington* (Basingstoke: Macmillan, 1989), 34. *New Directions Number Seven*, 457. Patmore wrote to Hunt about the 'little "hits" against Richard [Aldington] and Hilda [Doolittle] that used to appear in the Outlook articles', suggesting one way in which Ford had provoked Aldington's reprisals: Secors, *The Return of the Good Soldier*, 24. See Mizener, 251 and 565, n. 18.

26 'Literary Portraits—LXVIII.: "Et in Terra Pax"', *Outlook*, 34 (26 Dec. 1914), 822–3. Eliot, review of *The New Poetry*, ed. Harriet Monroe and Alice Henderson (New York: Macmillan, 1917), *Egoist*, 4 (Nov. 1917), 151. Ford's use of the hours of the clock may have influenced Eliot's 'Preludes' and 'Rhapsody on a Windy Night'. *I Have This to Say*, 259, describes Ford visiting Charing Cross to get 'copy' for his poem. It was first published anonymously as *'In October 1914'*, *Outlook*, 34 (25 Oct. 1914), 523–4, then as a booklet. As Mizener says: 'It is typical of Ford's generosity with young artists that he repaid Lewis's attacks by persuading Harold Monro to have Lewis do the designs for Ford's *Antwerp* when the Poetry Bookshop published it in January, 1915' (p. 247). The poem is discussed in vol. 2, Ch. 7

27 Ford to Monro, 28 Oct. 1914: Texas. Monro's records of the Poetry Bookshop are at the British Library. I am indebted to Joy Grant for this information. Grant, *Harold Monro and the Poetry Bookshop* (London: Routledge, 1967), 80–1, quoting the recollection of B. G. Brooks. Yeats and Rupert Brooke also gave readings at the Poetry Bookshop.

28 Aldington, *Life for Life's Sake* (London: Cassell, 1968), 138–9. *'The Scaremonger: A Tale of the War Times', *Bystander*, 44 (25 Nov. 1914), 273–4, 276. Allen to Hunt, 16 Dec. 1914. See Mizener, 250, 151. *The Return of the Good Soldier*, 79, n. 120. 46, n. 22. Ford to Masterman, 15 Jan. 1915.

29 Ford to C. F. G. Masterman, 15 Jan. 1915. Lucy Masterman, *C. F. G. Masterman*, 273. Ford told the adjutant, 9/Welch B.E.F., 7 Sept. 1916, that he had written the book and done other work 'without pay, for H.M. Government': *Reader*, 478.

30 Shakespeare, *Henry V*, v. ii. 204–7. Ford is at his most corrosive with Shaw: 'It is my purpose to comment upon or to answer, sentence by sentence, as much of Mr. Shaw's complete writings about the present war as I imagine a fairly patient reader can bring himself to contemplate' (233). I am indebted here to L. L. Farrar Jr.'s shrewd discussion of both propaganda books: 'The Artist as Propagandist', *The Presence of Ford Madox Ford*, 145–60. West, *Daily News* (11 Nov. 1915), 4; repr. in *Ford Madox Ford: The Critical Heritage*, 53. Goldring, *South Lodge*, 117.

31 Mizener, 281–2, 569, n. 10. 'D. H. Lawrence', *American Mercury*, 38 (June 1936), 167–79; repr. in *Mightier Than the Sword*, 121–2. Hunt, *I Have This to Say*, 259; though she misdates the visit as 'the autumn of 1914'. Crichton's memoir is in *D. H. Lawrence: A Composite Biography*, ed. Edward Nehls, ii. 412. For Frieda Lawrence's third and fourth versions of the story, see her letters to Mabel Luhan, 5 Apr. 1927, quoted in Luhan's *Lorenzo in Taos* (New York, Alfred A. Knopf, 1932), 324–5; and to Harry T. Moore, 14 Jan. 1955, **Frieda Lawrence: The Memoirs and Correspondence*, ed. E. W. Tedlock, Jr. (London: Heinemann, 1961), 351–3. Ford to the editor, *The American Mercury*, 19 Jan. 1937: *Letters*, 269–70. The Lawrences were at Greatham from 23 Jan. to 30 July 1915, so it is probable that the visit occurred before Ford got his commission (Keith Sagar, *D. H. Lawrence: A Calendar of his Works* (Manchester University Press, 1979), 63). Though, as Mizener explains, Ford quite possibly got his uniform immediately after getting the commission at the end of July, and before the appointment was gazetted on 13 Aug.

32 Meyers, *D. H. Lawrence* (London: Macmillan, 1990), 177–81. Garnett to Mizener, 2 Mar. 1966: Cornell. Aldington, *Death of A Hero* (London: Chatto & Windus, 1929), 143; quoted by Meyers, 178. Aldington's study of Lawrence, *Portrait of a Genius, But . . .* (London: William Heinemann, 1951), doesn't mention the incident; the suppression of *The Rainbow* is described on 171–3. F. S. Flint to Ford, 9 Jan. 1917, mentions the 'row' between Ford and Aldington: Texas. Aldington to Durrell, 20 Aug. 1960: *Literary Lifelines: The Richard Aldington–Lawrence Durrell Correspondence*, ed. Ian S. MacNiven and Harry T. Moore (London and Boston: Faber and Faber, 1981), 149. Harry T. Moore, in *Richard Aldington: An Intimate Portrait*, ed. Alister Kershaw and F.-J. Temple (Carbondale and Edwardsville: Southern Illinois University Press, 1965), 90–1. Paul Delany, *D. H. Lawrence's Nightmare* (New York: Basic Books, Inc., 1978), 100–3, discusses the episode, and suggests that Ford was spying for Masterman.

Chapter 27

1 *The Marsden Case*, 242. Mizener, 279–81. 31 July 1915: *Letters*, 60–1.
2 18 Sept. 1915: House of Lords. In an undated letter (written from the Cardiff area, where Ford was moved towards the end of 1915), he repeats the argument: 'I think this is my perfectly plain duty': House of Lords.
3 Lewis, *Blasting and Bombardiering*, 185. Lewis doesn't date the conversation, but he says they were talking about Gaudier-Brzeska's death. It therefore (probably) took place between 5 June 1915 and Mar. 1916, when Lewis volunteered.
4 Judd, *Ford Madox Ford*, 257. When Eleanor Farjeon asked Edward Thomas what he was fighting for: 'He stopped, and picked up a pinch of earth. "Literally, for

this." ': *Edward Thomas: The Last Four Years* (Oxford: Oxford University Press, 1958), 154. *On Heaven*, 72–6.

5 This line recalls the opening of the third of Christina Rossetti's *Old and New Year Ditties*: 'Passing away, saith the World, passing away.' Ford quotes the stanza in 'Pure Literature', *Agenda*, 27/4–28/1 (Winter 1989–Spring 1990), 13.

6 'A Jubilee', *Outlook*, 36 (10 July 1915), 46–8. *'Last Words about Edward VIII', 3. Mizener, 280–1. Hunt, *The Flurried Years*, 260. Hardwick, *An Immodest Violet*, 134–5. *The House of Many Mirrors* (London: Stanley Paul & Co, 1915), 54, 31. The novel's implication that Ford had abandoned Hunt while she was dying must have rankled, not least because the way Rosamond leaves Alfy to go to her death must have grated on Ford's sense that he was leaving Hunt to go to his own death. The novel abounds with echoes of their life together, and with parallels with *The Good Soldier*. Ford is recognizable as a model for Alfy in his 'perfect man of the world' mien, his 'altruism', his vanity about being able to influence people; his hypochondria, 'honorable mania', evasion of scenes; his 'polite sulkiness' when people don't play the game, or fail to live up to his expectations; his eagerness for renunciation, and his 'Quixotic' generosity: 54, 38, 185, 186, 232, 234, 235, 247, 404. Hunt's identification with Rosamond is even more thorough, and seen particularly in her paradoxical mix of 'kindliness' and 'sinister materialism'; her desire to bring round her husband's wealthy relations; her ease with younger men; and her self-destructiveness: 82, 38, 299, 314. Her 'own haughty, refined, if intense standard of passion, in which physical necessities played only a romantic part', means that the bond between her and her husband was 'of such passionate spirituality that though it included the physical relation it would have been possible to ignore or neglect the manifestations of sense': 103–4—which is remarkably similar to Dowell's notion that the sex instinct might be left out of the calculation. Belford, *Violet*, 222. 'Novels', *Outlook*, 35 (12 June 1915), 775–6. Ford to Hunt, 6 Jan. 1917: Princeton. Hunt, 'Not Even Half a Hero', *Outlook*, 36 (11 Sept. 1915), 332–3. Harvey, 326. 'A Day of Battle', *Reader*, 460.

7 *No Enemy*, 210–11, 216–17. It is Ford's persona, Gringoire, talking here. But we know that (as with most of the book) his experiences were also Ford's, since the entire section on Gaudier was first published, under Ford's own name, as 'Henri Gaudier: The Story of a Low Tea-Shop', *English Review*, 19 (Oct. 1919), 300, 303. It was repeated, with minor revisions, as 175–84 of *Thus to Revisit*.

8 *Blast*, 2 (July 1915), 34. *No Enemy*, 211–12, 206–7, 216. 'Henri Gaudier', 301: *No Enemy* garbles the sense by reading 'public's' for 'public': 211–12. Lewis, *Blasting and Bombardiering*, 184.

9 *No Enemy*, 216–17, 69. Ford to Cathy Hueffer [Sept.? 1915]: House of Lords.

10 *Zeppelin Nights*, 304–6. The 'friend and writer' who asked them where they all stood sounds like Henry James, whom Ford parodied elaborating on the expression 'so that here we all are' (see *Mightier Than the Sword*, 35), and who became a naturalized British subject on 26 July 1915. Ford got his own British nationality certified on 23 Aug. 1915: see above, p. 486.

11 *Letters*, 61. There is doubt about the dating of this letter. As Mizener says, 'the exact day appears to be the 10th, but the second digit is not unquestionably clear': 565, n. 21 (if not a zero, the second digit is probably '2'). Ford gave the year as 1914, which Mizener accepts, but Ludwig changes it (without any indication that he has done so) to 1915, and gives the day as 12 Aug. Aug. 1914 is nearer to the

date Ford finished the novel; he was hard up during both years. He was unlikely to wait a year before asking for the money; yet he may have been trying to set his finances in order before going into the army. He offered his services to 'George Five' in 1915, but, as Mizener explains, he may have considered doing so in 1914, just before Masterman asked him to work for Wellington House (though 'I have had to [. . .]' makes it sound more like a *fait accompli*). That Ford is still calling the novel 'The Saddest Story' might suggest that the letter was written before the book was published under its new title. But Ford might be being exact: the *manuscript* was called 'The Saddest Story'; or he may have been sustaining his pique that Lane had insisted on the change, and implying that as far as he was concerned that was what it was still called. The 'hard up times' are perhaps a little more likely to apply to publishing conditions after a year of war.

12 'Literary Portraits—LXXI.: Enemies', *Outlook*, 35 (16 Jan. 1915), 79–80. There are two pages of 'Press Opinions' of the novel at the end of *Zeppelin Nights*, several of them not in Harvey's bibliography. Lane to Pinker, 26 July 1920 (Northwestern), quoted by Harvey, 45. The figure for Ford's earnings perhaps does not include the advance.

13 R. Ellis Roberts, in *New Directions: Number Seven*, 485. Ford wrote to Stella Bowen on 1 Nov. 1918 of 'when I was with the Guards at Chelsea'. 'Dedicatory Letter to Stella Ford', *The Good Soldier*, 4. Mizener, 281, 569, n. 9. Judd, *Ford Madox Ford*, 267.

14 Mizener, 282, says he had already dropped 'the Joseph Leopold of his German days'; he may have used those names amongst the Hüffers, but even in Germany he had been signing himself 'Ford Madox Hueffer'—the name under which he had issued nearly all his books. It is only Hunt who refers to him as 'Joseph Leopold', partly to parody his attempts to become a German, partly to imply Ford's kinship with, or imitation of, 'Joseph Conrad'; and perhaps partly to protect herself against another libel suit. See Hunt, *The Flurried Years*, 32, 34. There is a certified copy of the nationality certificate at Cornell dated 12 June 1919 by the Public Record Office.

15 *Thus to Revisit*, 125 ('You're going to fight for the sacred soil of Mme. de Stael'). The story was reprinted in *Return to Yesterday*, 220. Ford has James give almost the same speech (though using 'vous') in 'Chroniques', *transatlantic review*, 14 (Apr. 1924), 199. Hunt tells a story in which James makes a similar remark after she read his propaganda essay for *The Book of France* and told him she didn't know he could be so passionate: 'Ah, madam,' she has him replying, 'you must not forget that in this article I am addressing—not a Woman, but a Nation!': *The Flurried Years*, 267.

16 Goldring, *South Lodge*, 118.

17 Hunt, *The Flurried Years*, 261, says Hunt wrote to ask for the binoculars, but Conrad's reply is addressed to Ford: 30 Aug. 1915: *Joseph Conrad: Life and Letters*, by G. Jean-Aubry, ii. 169 (the original letter is in the British Library, Ashley 2923*). Karl, 772–3. Jessie Conrad said the letter showed that Conrad 'had a really high opinion of the intelligence of his one-time collaborator, and also a great affection for the child of their joint fabrication, *Romance*': *Joseph Conrad and his Circle*, 198–9.

18 Ford to Cathy Hueffer, 18 Sept. 1915: House of Lords. Ford to Masterman, 28 Aug. 1915: *Letters*, 61. Judd, *Ford Madox Ford*, 272. Pound to Harriet Monroe, 25 Sept. 1915: *Selected Letters of Ezra Pound*, 63.

19 *The Letters of Ezra Pound to Alice Corbin Henderson*, ed. Ira B. Nadel (Austin: University of Texas Press, 1993), 104–5: 25 May 1915.

20 Ford to Oliver Hueffer, 5 Oct. 1915: House of Lords. Ford to Lucy Masterman, 15 Feb. 1916: *Letters*, 63.

21 Mizener, 283. Judd, *Ford Madox Ford*, 273. Frank MacShane, *The Life and Work of Ford Madox Ford*, (London: Routledge & Kegan Paul, 1965), 129. Ford to Catherine Hueffer, n.d.: House of Lords.

22 The review and consequent controversy can be found in *Ford Madox Ford: The Critical Heritage*, 122–7. Mizener, 278, mistakenly attributes the editorship to G. K. Chesterton. Harvey, 329, suggests that the passages from *Zeppelin Nights* that 'Prothero' quoted in order to condemn were probably written by Hunt.

23 22 Mar. 1916: *Letters*, 63–4.

24 Goldring, *South Lodge*, 118–19. Belford, *Violet*, 222, 226.

25 Ford to Wells, 22 Mar. 1916. *On Heaven*, 29–32. *Poetry*, 9 (Mar. 1917), 293–4. Ford to F. S. Flint, 19 Feb. 1917: *Letters*, 83–4. Mizener, 284, 570, n. 14. Judd, *Ford Madox Ford*, 275.

26 *The Return of the Good Soldier*, 44–5, 57.

27 Ibid. 47, 49, 52, 58, 60, 63, 67, 73, 77. The first mention of Miss Ross is on 4 Mar. 1917. But the entry for 2 June (p. 63) makes it clear he had known her before the previous Christmas. Since Ford was back in Wales in the autumn of 1916 (this time at Kinmel Park, near Rhyl on the north coast), whatever happened with Miss Ross may have happened after Ford's return from France. However, 'The Silver Music' is dated 3 July 1916; and its companion piece, 'The Iron Music', written from the Somme and dated 22 July 1916, says: 'For it's just nine weeks last Sunday | Since we took the Chepstow train.' As Mizener calculates, the visit would have taken place on Sunday 14 May (283–4, 570, n. 14). Mizener does not mention Miss Ross—Hunt's 1917 diary was not available to him. He implies that these poems too might have been addressed to Mrs Percy Jackson. 'After the War' is not individually dated in *On Heaven*, but is included in the group in the Appendix which Ford and Captain James wrote or translated on 3 July 1916 (see below). *On Heaven*, 33–6, 113, 118–20, 44–5.

28 *On Heaven*, 10, 113. Ford told Lucy Masterman: 'I have been writing silly little lyrics which no one will print': 11 July 1916: *Letters*, 65–6. *No More Parades*, 46–55 (McKechnie is there referred to as Mackenzie, since Tietjens hasn't yet heard his name correctly). The Cardiff memory is fused with another that Ford recounts in *No Enemy*, 102–3, of a bombardment: 'I was sitting on the side of my camp-bed talking to an extremely intoxicated and disheveled elderly officer who was nevertheless a man of no ordinary talent. That is to say that his harangues about everything under the sun were interspersed with a great number of classical quotations of singular aptness.' Moser, 323, n. 11, opines that McKechnie is based on Borys Conrad.

29 Ford to Pinker, 1 June 1916: Princeton [quoted by Mizener, 284–5]. Hunt, *I Have This to Say*, 264. *No Enemy*, 29. Anthony West, *H. G. Wells: Aspects of a Life* (Harmondsworth: Penguin Books, 1985), 10, 56–7. Mizener, 284–5, 570, n. 16. *Return to Yesterday*, 198–9. Conrad to Ford, 12 Aug. 1915: Cornell [in Hunt's transcription]. Hunt, *The Flurried Years*, 262. Hunt makes other distortions here, claiming that Conrad's letter to Ford of 21 Dec. 1911 (*Collected Letters*, iv. 524–5) was written to her, and in 1915 or 1916. *Joseph Conrad*, 5–6, also says Ford

appointed Conrad as literary executor (though there he is talking about making 'a hasty will' 'Nine years ago'—in 1915; and he says he has written the memoir 'that Joseph Conrad asked for'. Mizener, 54, 582, n. 6. See vol. 2, for details of the controversies. Owen Knowles, *A Conrad Chronology* (London: Macmillan, 1989), 96–9. Conrad to William Blackwood, 5 June 1902: *Collected Letters*, ii. 423. See Najder, 486. Conrad to Ford, 29 Mar. 1906: *Collected Letters*, iii. 324–5. Marwood did not die on 1 May, as Mizener said (156), but twelve days later, at his home, Water Farm, Stowting, in Kent. Moser (204) has the correct date, but follows Mizener in saying Marwood died of cancer. His death certificate gives two causes of death, both associated with his tuberculosis: 'Tubercular nephritis and cystitis left kidney removed seventeen years ago', and 'Araemia'. Juliet Soskice to David Soskice, 17 and 19 July [1916] (House of Lords Record Office).

INDEX